D0529507

The Adventures
in Literature Program

Adventures for Readers: Book One
Test Booklet
Steps to Better Reading: Book 1*
Teacher's Manual
Many Voices 7, a longplay record

Adventures for Readers: Book Two
Test Booklet
Steps to Better Reading: Book 2*
Teacher's Manual
Many Voices 8, a longplay record

Adventures in Reading
Test Booklet
Steps to Better Reading: Book 3*
Teacher's Manual
Many Voices 9, a two-record
   (longplay) album

Adventures in Appreciation
Test Booklet
Steps to Reading Literature: Book 1*
Teacher's Manual
Many Voices 10A, a longplay record
Many Voices 10B, a longplay record
   of *Julius Caesar*

Adventures in American Literature
Test Booklet
Steps to Reading Literature: Book 2*
Teacher's Manual
Many Voices 11, a two-record
   (longplay) album

Adventures in English Literature
Test Booklet
Steps to Reading Literature: Book 3*
Teacher's Manual
Many Voices 12A, a longplay record
Many Voices 12B, a longplay record
   of *Macbeth*

* Programed Instruction

ADVENTURES

IN ENGLISH

LITERATURE

LAUREATE EDITION

J. B. PRIESTLEY

JOSEPHINE SPEAR

Series Editor: MARY RIVES BOWMAN

Harcourt, Brace & World, Inc.

New York   Chicago   Atlanta   Dallas   Burlingame

J. B. PRIESTLEY, literary critic and historian as well as one of England's most renowned playwrights, essayists, and novelists, is a frequent visitor to these shores. Among the versatile Mr. Priestley's best-known works are the critical history *Literature and Western Man,* the essay collection *Midnight on the Desert,* the novel *The Good Companions,* and the recent *Charles Dickens: A Pictorial Biography.* He is also co-editor of two twelfth-grade books in the ADVENTURES IN GOOD BOOKS series: *Four English Novels* and *Four English Biographies.*

JOSEPHINE SPEAR, who is co-editor of the Olympic Edition of *Adventures in English Literature,* has been Chairman of the English Department at the University School of Indiana University since 1954. Dr. Spear received her A.B. degree in English from DePauw University. She did her graduate work in education (M.S., Ed.D.) at Indiana University and is a former president of the Indiana Council of Teachers of English.

The Series Editor, MARY RIVES BOWMAN, holds degrees in English from the University of Texas (B.A.) and the University of Chicago (M.A.) and has also done graduate work in English at the University of Colorado and at East Texas State College. She has been active in various professional organizations and has devoted much of her time to the training and supervision of high school English teachers. She is co-editor of three earlier editions of *Adventures in American Literature* and of two editions of *Adventures for Readers,* Books 1 and 2.

The sections entitled "Behind the Scenes in English Literature" are based on The Scholar Adventurers *by Richard D. Altick (Macmillan, 1950; paperback edition, 1960) by permission of the author and the publishers, The Macmillan Company.*

Artists who have contributed to the illustration of this book are: Seymour Chwast, Harold Faye, Eugene Karlin, Gil Miret, Tom O'Sullivan, Isadore Seltzer/Push Pin Studios, Robert Shore, and Earl Thollander.

FRONTISPIECE: *A view from Trafalgar Square in London (Photo Researchers, Inc.).*

© *1963, copyright 1958, 1952, 1949, 1946, 1941, 1938, 1931, by Harcourt, Brace & World, Inc.*

All rights reserved. No part of this book may be reproduced in any form, by mimeograph or any other means, without permission in writing from the publisher.

PRINTED IN THE UNITED STATES OF AMERICA

CONTENTS

THE ELIZABETHAN AGE

THE
SEVENTEENTH CENTURY

THE
EIGHTEENTH CENTURY

THE ROMANTIC AGE

THE VICTORIAN AGE

THE
TWENTIETH CENTURY

MODERN BIOGRAPHY

NOTE: The initials J. B. P. are used throughout as the signature of Mr. Priestley.

THE LAND AND ITS PEOPLE

by JACQUETTA HAWKES *and* J. B. PRIESTLEY

Allow me to introduce myself. I am an Englishman, born in the North of England in 1894. I have been a professional writer for forty years and have produced such a pile of novels, plays, and books of essays that people are now getting tired of me in many different countries. My wife writes under the name "Jacquetta Hawkes." She is a well-known archaeologist, and a poet and storyteller. Fifty years ago I often did without lunch so that I could buy books; I haven't to do that now, but if it came to a pinch I think I would still prefer books to lunch. Enjoying books and authors has meant so much to me that I want other people, especially those now growing up, to understand this enjoyment and to share in it. We hope that the following pages will help you to understand our country a little better and thus enjoy more fully the literature that its people have created.

The Land of Britain

FOR a vast stretch of time the area which became the British Isles was a mere bulge on the western coast of Europe. Then about 8,000 years ago, water from the melting ice sheets of the last glaciation made the sea level rise until the North Sea and the Atlantic Ocean flowed together, creating the English Channel and making Britain an island. It is quite a small island, the whole area of England, Wales, and Scotland being about equal to that of the combined areas of Utah and Connecticut (and Ireland, the neighboring island, is only about as big as Maine), yet it has greater variety of countryside than can be found across thousands of miles in some parts of the United States. This is due to Britain's geological history.

THE VARIETY OF BRITISH LAND FORMATIONS

Within Britain's small compass, nearly all the main geological epochs are represented: from that of nearly a billion years ago when life itself was still in its faintest, most shadowy beginnings, through the long ages when amphibians and reptiles roamed the world, down to the ice ages of relatively recent times. It so happens that the oldest land formations tend to be in north and west, the

BRITAIN: *A view of the Thames River north of London.* ▶

youngest in the east and south of Britain. Thus if someone enters the island from the European continent by any of the shorter routes — say at Tilbury or Harwich — and travels across the country either westward into Devon and Cornwall or Wales, or northward to Scotland, he will be journeying further and further back into the past so far as the antiquity of the land is concerned. Usually the older the formation is the more it will have been alternately hardened and buckled by the heat, pressure, and violent upheavals suffered during hundreds of millions of years. Thus the traveler journeying westward or northward will also be going from the gently undulating soft lands of southeast England, through the chalk and limestone hills of medium age, and into the jagged and picturesque mountain country of the most ancient parts of Britain.

THE INFLUENCE OF THE LAND ON HISTORICAL DEVELOPMENT

The land formations of the country have been of very great importance throughout British history: the island faces Europe with open arms, as it were, and welcomes invaders as well as traders and refugees into the gentle lowland country, so fertile, open, and easy either to conquer or traverse. So it is not surprising to find that the eastern coasts of England have always had contacts both friendly and hostile with the European countries just opposite — that is to say, with northern France, the Low Countries, and Denmark — while England's southern coasts have been open to the more westerly regions of France, particularly Brittany. The whole of lowland England, therefore, has been subject to continental influences, whether these were introduced by invaders or by friendly travel and trade. But as these influences reached further into the upland country, they naturally became weaker, more broken up, until finally they were lost altogether in the wild mountains of Wales and Scotland. Also, just as during frontier times in the United States the Indians were pushed further and further west until today they are to be found mainly in the Southwest, so in Britain older populations were often pushed into mountain country and there left undisturbed. That is why, as we shall see, old racial stocks, old languages, and old ways of life still survive in Wales and Scotland today.

Although the western and northern coasts where the mountain country fronts the Atlantic with cliffs and rocky promontories is wild and tempestuous, like all such coasts it has many coves and inlets offering good harborage to small ships. By referring to a map, you can see that these shores of Devon and Cornwall, Wales, Ireland, and Scotland can be reached without any very long voyages out of sight of land by seafarers feeling their way northward from Spain and Portugal and southward from Norway and Sweden. These Atlantic coast routes were used, though relatively rarely, by small groups of people coming to Britain to raid or settle, so that they provided a sort of backdoor entrance to Britain, the main entrance being southeast England.

Photo Researchers, Inc.

Throughout the centuries, the land of Britain has strongly affected the minds and hearts of its writers. ABOVE: *Gently rolling lowland country in southern England.*

Photo Researchers, Inc.

ABOVE: *Hill country in northern England and the old Roman wall.* BELOW: *Picturesque mountain country in northern Scotland.*

Edwin Smith

BRITAIN
Topography, areas, and cities of literary interest

NORTH

ENGLAND

Whitby
YORKSHIRE MOORS
YORK
SWALE
Jarrow
TYNE
DURHAM
PENNINE CHA
WESTMOR
LAND
CUMBERLAND
Keswick
DERWENT
Grasmere
Windermere
LAKE
DISTRICT
Lancaster
ISLE OF MAN

NORTHUMBERLAND
CHEVIOT HILLS
Berwick
Abbotsford
Selkirk
Peebles
Ecclefechan
DUMFRIES
SOLWAY FIRTH
KIRKCUD
BRIGHT
WIGTOWN

SCOTLAND
ABERDEEN
Aberdeen
KINCARDINE
BANFF
DEE
MORAY FIRTH
Forres
MORAY
SPEY
NAIRN
Inverness
LOCH NESS
ROSS AND CROMARTY
SCOTTISH HMTS.
INVERNESS
HIGHLANDS
ARGYLL
GRAMPIAN
ANGUS
Kirriemuir
Dunsinane
Dundee
Birnam Wood
Scone
PERTH
TROSSACHS
KINROSS
CLACKMANNAN
STIRLING
Bannockburn
DUMBARTON
RENFREW
Glasgow
CLYDE
LANARK
AYR
Auchinleck
AFTON
DOON
AYR
FIRTH OF CLYDE

FIFE
FIRTH OF FORTH
Dunfermline
Edinburgh
W LOTHIAN
MIDLOTHIAN
E LOTHIAN

MULL
SKYE
HEBRIDES
ISLAY

NORTH CHANNEL

NORTHERN IRELAND
GIANT'S CAUSEWAY
ANTRIM
Belfast
LOUGH NEAGH
BANN
LONDONDERRY
TYRONE
DONEGAL
DOWN
ARMAGH
MONAGHAN
CAVAN

NATURE AND LITERATURE

To what extent does Britain's varied scenery make itself felt in her literature? First of all, thinking of the country as a whole, it has of course a temperate climate, knowing no such extremes as does continental Europe. Britain gets more than its fair share of rain, and this gives it an atmosphere which is seldom hard and bright even in spring and summer, while autumn is a "season of mists," and winter is one of mist, fog, and heavy downpours. Many people believe that this accounts in part for the strong poetic element which has always underlain the matter-of-fact nature of the British and given them so many poets. Perhaps this is so. The British character possesses a misty, romantic tendency in great contrast to the sharp logic and more prosaic intellectual power of the Latin peoples living in the clear light of southern Europe. Certainly much English poetry and fiction reflects the greenness of the English countryside, the abundant streams, and great quantities of flowers — all of which result from the wet and temperate climate. From the opening of Chaucer's *Prologue* onwards, English literature abounds with buttercups and daisies, daffodils and cowslips, honeysuckle and violets, streams, and fertile valleys, and green meadows.

Fred Maroon

England has a mild and misty climate.

HIGHLANDS AND LOWLANDS

All this rejoicing in verdant nature is perhaps characteristic of English writing, and especially English poetry. But the literature also reflects the strong contrasts which were created by the island's geological history. Anyone who knows the country intimately can distinguish between the various scenery of the English lowlands. In poems or in the background of novels he will recognize the rich farmlands of East Anglia and also its harsh and lonely fens, marshes, and reedy lakes; he will distinguish between the pale, curving hills of the southern chalk country with its villages tucked into narrow valleys and the red-soiled dairy country of Devon and Somerset, broken by wild moors on its granite outcrops; and between all these and the Midlands of England, a region of heavy clay lands and slow, broad rivers which in prehistoric times was covered with impenetrable forests of oak, ash, and elm, and which is still considerably wooded.

But for those who cannot know Britain so well, the one great and most conspicuous distinction shows itself, as would be expected, between the whole of these English lowlands and the highlands of Cornwall, Wales, northwest England, and Scotland. Ireland, too, can be included in this highland zone. Here green fields, quiet rivers, and abundant vegetation are largely replaced by rocky mountains, dark, heather-covered moors, gushing mountain streams, lakes, and tarns. The birds and plants and trees of the highlands are different; so too is the quality of the light. While the moisture which always sweeps in from the Atlantic often veils mountains and moors in mist, in fine summer weather it creates the brilliance of coloring — blues and purples — which is so essentially a part of the beauty of this part of the world.

No poet could be more expressive of the lowland scene than Thomas Gray, whose country churchyard was in Buckinghamshire, or Robert Herrick, whose subjects, "To Blossoms," "To Daffodils," and the rest, speak of

Ace Williams from Shostal

Wordsworth's lake country in northwest England.

flowery Devonshire, where he lived for many years. Shakespeare grew up on the edge of the Midlands, near the Forest of Arden, a remnant of the primeval forests, and brought the freshness of that outdoor world to the London theater in many a descriptive passage. Among the many lowland novelists, none expresses the placid, prosperous life of the country houses, villages, and small market towns of the southern counties better than Jane Austen, who passed most of her days in Hampshire. Hardy owes much of his greatness to the poetic expression he gave in his novels to the countryside and country people of his native Dorset.

British Travel

Fred Maroon

ABOVE: *Haworth Moor and High Withens, the isolated moorland farmhouse of Emily Brontë's* Wuthering Heights.

LEFT: *Dylan Thomas' house in the village of Laugharne, Wales.*

"Under the new made clouds and happy
     as the heart was long,
   In the sun born over and over,
   I ran my heedless ways . . ."

from "Fern Hill" by Dylan Thomas

MOUNTAINS AND MOORLAND

Now, in contrast, let us look at some of the writers inspired by the ancient mountains and moorland. Inevitably there are far fewer, for, because of its very nature, this region is sparsely populated. To begin with early days, the Scottish ballads usually reflect the rough, tougher life of that country. Then Burns, though he did not live in the real highlands of Scotland, pictures the harder life of the north in many of his poems.

Emily Brontë (even more than her sisters) writes straight out of the purple heather and dark crags of the wild, remote Yorkshire moors where she lived and which she loved so passionately. But the great man who beyond all the rest speaks for this part of Britain is William Wordsworth. Born and passing by far the greater part of his long life in the beautiful lakeland scenery of northwest England, he put all the feeling it aroused in him into his poetry — to so great an extent that much of the spirit of the English Romantic movement seems to be identified with crags and waterfalls, caves and mountain tracks. More profoundly than anyone else, too, Wordsworth has told us of the way in which a writer (or any other artist) can be inspired by his childhood surroundings:

> . . . the sounding cataract
> Haunted me like a passion, the tall rock,
> The mountain, and the deep and gloomy wood,
> Their colors and their forms, were then to me
> An appetite; a feeling and a love . . .

It is certainly true to say that had Wordsworth been born and bred in some quiet county in the south of England both the man and his work would have been altogether different.

Also a great poet of the highlands is W. B. Yeats. Although he was not a nature poet, the old tales and beliefs which even today still linger on in Ireland play a big part in his early plays and poems. Fairies, ghosts, and legendary heroes fill his pages.

Another modern writer strongly influenced by his natural surroundings was Dylan Thomas, whose *Under Milkwood*, depicting life in a small Welsh village, has as its setting Thomas' home village of Laugharne on the estuary of the river Taf.

Thus, throughout the centuries, the land of Britain — highlands, lowlands, moors, fens, and mountains — has strongly affected the minds and hearts of its writers and colored English literature with its many-faceted variety. Through climate and natural surroundings, Britain's past lives in the present, its present in the past.

Photo Researchers, Inc.

The English Character and Language

The major influences on English literature are two in number. Just as the British land has greatly influenced English literature, so too has the literature of the English-speaking peoples been shaped by Britain's history.

It was at least a hundred and fifty years after the Norman Conquest that the odd mixture of people which invaded and settled in Britain after the departure of the Romans finally became a nation — no longer considering themselves Anglo-Saxons, Danes, and Normans, but *Englishmen*. It might be said of the English that once they were aware of themselves, they were immensely aware of themselves. Even before the Elizabethan Age, foreign observers noted that the English were very conscious of being English and — let us admit it — highly satisfied and pleased with themselves. This sense of identity owed much to the fact that the English were islanders, cut off by the sea from many European influences. They were well away from any menacing centers and personages of power. Developing largely on their own and turning from a continental point of view, they became what we might now call an "offbeat" people. Many of the early English characteristics have endured over the years, indeed lasting until our own time. Since these have played a very important part in molding and coloring English literature, we should take a look at some of them.

A FLEXIBLE SOCIAL SYSTEM

Almost from the first the English had a class system that was never a caste system. The distinction is very important. Unless it is understood, the difference between English life and that of most European countries cannot be grasped. In a caste system there is a great fixed gulf between various groups within a society. It is almost impossible for men and women to marry outside their particular castes. The structure of a caste society is rigid, inflexible. Birth decides everything. But the English class system, though it recognizes various social levels, was never from the first so rigid and inflexible. One class, so to speak, shaded into another. There were no impassable gulfs. Birth might be important, but it did not decide everything. Men of ability could raise themselves into a higher social class, and very frequently did so, often marrying into a higher class. And because the system was so flexible, because merit might send one family up the social scale while a continued lack of merit might send another family sliding down it, the English nobility and aristocracy never made the haughty claims to superiority that we find throughout history in most European countries, as for example in France almost to the end of the eighteenth century, when the French Revolution cast class pride into the dust. English aristocrats may always have had a good opinion of themselves and their class, but they also knew that no rigid caste system maintained them and gave them permanent superiority. Thus they were careful not to be too overbearing in their claims.

THE TRADITION OF INDEPENDENCE

Moreover, within the English class system the people in each class were aware of their particular rights and privileges and were always ready to defend them. Throughout many centuries, visitors from abroad were astonished by the air of independence, the "boldness and turbulence" of the English "common people." One reason for this is that the English monarchy, unlike rulers abroad, never maintained a large standing army of professional soldiers, but in time of danger had to depend upon raising an army from these same "common people." Also, the monarchy was dependent upon Parliament in that it was compelled to summon that body simply because Parliament alone had the power to find money for the government, and any king who tried to govern without Parliament soon found himself facing bankruptcy. Again, because both money and soldiers came from their subjects, the English monarchs and their great officers of state had to agree to respect the rights of these subjects. Over the years various safeguards, such as the famous *Habeas Corpus* Act (which protects a man from being kept in prison without being charged with a specific offence), were initiated and now form an essential part of the tradition of both British and American common law.

SENSE OF CHARACTER AND INDIVIDUALITY

Because, then, the English were islanders off on their own, because they could develop in their own way, because they had no rigid caste system but a flexible class system, and because they were not subject to a vast overbearing authority but had some independence on every social level, they soon began to develop all manner of odd characters, together with a taste for and relish of such people. From Chaucer onwards, all this is clearly reflected in English literature, enlivening and enriching the work of dramatists and novelists alike. The typical English creative writer delights in sheer variety and richness of character. He does not want to analyze a few prominent types, but aims at creating a rich gallery of odd, entertaining characters. This sense of character and delight in its variety can be seen influencing English literature down the centuries. This same feeling can be found in English public life, where a Winston Churchill is widely popular not only because he was a great war leader but also because he is obviously a tremendous character.

Not only are English fiction and drama filled with odd, original characters, but English literature itself, in the persons of its authors, is equally rich in such characters. It is crowded with authors determined to go their own way, to write exactly as they, as individuals, please. Where authors in other countries have acknowledged the discipline of an academy, have conformed to given standards, or have combined together to create a movement, English authors down the centuries have usually gone their own way.

ARTISTIC INDEPENDENCE

Where there is an authority to be obeyed, rules to be followed, traditions to be observed, as in France (except when the Romantics rebelled), authors will inevitably be concerned about the form and structure of their work. Every piece of writing must be given its proper shape, be written in the approved style. There will be one way of writing a tragedy, which will be tragic throughout, and another way of writing a comedy, which will be comic throughout. The accepted pattern must be followed, or, if the pattern is to be broken, a new form must be carefully planned. Now all this is alien to English literary genius, which has almost always been indifferent to conventional form and structure, to conscious planning and organization. What it prefers is a strong suggestion of likeness to life, to all the bustle and variety and changing tragicomedy of this world. When, for example, we compare a play by a famous seventeenth-century French writer such as Racine, a play in which every syllable has been weighed, with any play by Shakespeare, we feel at once that the Shakespearean play, with all manner of folk coming and going on the stage, is packed with roaring life; and that compared with the French dramatist, who gives a small amount of life an exact form and structure and creates something

English writers delight in the richness and variety of their own people. Here are a few of them: a farmer from the island of Sark, a gentleman in a London park, a Welsh miner, a young fisherman on the southern coast, and a lady in the waiting room of a London railway station.

NBC

Houston Rogers

obviously artificial, Shakespeare in his own poetic fashion is a kind of realist. Though in fact he has his own kind of inner structure, he seems at first simply to be offering us all the rich confusion that we find in real life. And this is true too of most of the major English novelists, who seem too busy telling us who was there and what happened to do much planning, organizing, and careful shaping. Of course a novel is none the worse for being planned, organized, carefully shaped — and many famous English novels suffer from the want of such attention — but the typical English writer, like the typical English reader, will risk defects of form and structure if the illusion of an energetic, varied, complex life is preserved. For there is no use giving a novel a perfect shape if in the end it seems lifeless. An untidy and badly constructed story crowded with characters who seem alive is better than a perfectly constructed story that appears to have in it nothing but ghosts.

"ARTLESSNESS" IN ENGLISH LITERATURE

It is true to say, however, that much of English literature is *artless*. If we think of art as the product of a highly conscious effort to achieve form, structure, style, to impose a pattern on the raw material of life, to create — however artificial the result may appear — perfection, then a great deal of English literature, perhaps most of it, is outside art. So we need not be surprised when we learn, for example, that French critics, in the eighteenth century and even early in the nineteenth century, regarded Shakespeare as a wild barbarian, incapable of writing civilized drama. That he might have been a great artist, which of course he was, never occurred to such critics, who thought of art in terms of form, structure, an accepted style, and various rules and conventions. The artist, in their view, always knows exactly what he is doing or trying to do, and plans, organizes, shapes, like a cabinetmaker producing an elaborate piece of furniture. This is much too narrow a view of art. But in order to widen our view and at the same time to deepen our understanding of

Among the many memorable characters created by English writers are these from some of Shakespeare's plays. Left to right: Ariel, Prospero, and Miranda from The Tempest; *Falstaff and Mistress Quickly from* Henry IV; *Laertes and Hamlet dueling, from* Hamlet.

Little Theater of the Rockies, Colorado State College

English literature, we must appreciate the difference between the conscious and the unconscious parts of our minds.

When we are asleep and no longer conscious, the unconscious part of our minds has free play to indulge in its own dramatic picture-language, and so we have dreams, sometimes beautiful, sometimes comic, sometimes terrifying. They are quite outside the control of our conscious minds, so that we cannot decide that we will have a beautiful dream instead of a terrifying one. Now genuinely poetic art arrives in the same way that dreams do, through the unconscious and not the conscious part of the mind, although the poet may consciously improve, refine, or change what the unconscious has offered him. However clever and strong-willed a writer may be, he cannot simply tell himself to go ahead and be deeply tragic, magically poetic, gloriously comic, as if he were making a box or a chair. The essential material does not come from the conscious part of the mind but from the unconscious. Great poetic creation is rare because only a few men, whom we call men of genius, are able to compel the apparently wild, ungovernable unconscious to serve the purposes of the conscious mind, supplying on demand, so to speak, all the wonderfully rich raw material. What we call creative imagination is really a man's ability to make use of his unconscious, to summon the wonderful dreams that he needs. Characters like Shakespeare's Hamlet, Cleopatra, Falstaff, though the scenes in which they appear may have been consciously planned, are created essentially in the magical depths of the unconscious. And writers like Shakespeare or Dickens, immensely rich and fertile and able to work at astonishing speed, could depend upon the wonderful resources of their unconscious minds, like characters in fairy tales who have a number of trolls or other magical creatures helping them. Moreover, what a writer's unconscious gives him has a powerful effect on us, his readers, just because its appeal goes down to our depths, is not superficial but deep and lasting. And this effect, even though it may be associated not only with lyrical or epic verse or tragedy but also with humor, is often described as being "poetic."

THE "POETIC" ELEMENT

Now this "poetic" element, coming from the unconscious, plays a very great part in English literature, just as the consciously "artistic" and formal element, as we have seen, plays a much smaller part and is indeed much weaker in English than it is in several other literatures. And this brings us to a special feature of English literature: it is uniquely rich, at all periods, in good poetry written by men who were not poets by profession but wrote occasionally, in their spare time, for their own pleasure. Age after age shows us scores of these fine amateur poets. Some of their poems, generally lyrics, are enduring little masterpieces. Now at first sight it seems odd that so many Englishmen, at all times, should have written so much poetry. For although Shakespeare excites the admiration of the world, this same world has never thought of us English as a very poetical people. We have always been considered a prosaic, practical, matter-of-fact people who pride ourselves on showing little or no emotion, on hiding any feelings we might have. Not for us the raised voices, the flashing eyes, the large gestures of the Latin races, or the misty-eyed sentimentality of the Germans! The typical Englishman of legend and caricature seems a cold fish of a fellow without a glimmer of poetry about him. Yet the fact remains — and is impossible to argue away — that this "nation of shopkeepers," as Napoleon called us, has continued producing, century after century, an astonishing wealth of poetry. What is the explanation?

First, it must be understood that the typical Englishman of legend and caricature, this cold fish, is not really typical of the whole nation but only of a small class, which was — and still is to some extent — a ruling class, trained from childhood to a high degree of self-control, itself part of the aristocratic tradition. But even so, let us agree that the English as a whole appear outwardly to be more prosaic and practical, far less romantic and poetical, than most other European peoples. They are in fact trying to appear *un*romantic and *un*poetical. But what is suppressed in ordinary conduct may have the greater need of an outlet somehow, somewhere. There may be all the more poetical feeling *inside* just because so little of it is expressed in ordinary life. In the same way, some men who consciously act a highly poetical part in their daily lives — perhaps a velvet-coated and shaggy-bearded French painter or a gesticulating, wild-eyed Italian tenor — may be, in their inner lives, hard and calculating and never really driven by their emotions. This is the reverse of the English pattern. The English write poetry so that they can take the lid off the unconscious. Their inner life is all the more poetical because their outer life is so unpoetical. And this explains not only all the treasure of verse in English literature but also the eccentricities and half-mad hobbies of so many Englishmen.

◀ *A depth of feeling often hidden by the average Englishman is revealed in his respect and affection for his monarch, here shown at a garden party.*

REGENT'S PARK

EUSTON ROAD

MARYLEBONE ROAD

BAKER STREET

WIMPOLE STREET

TOTTENHAM COURT RD.

University
of London

Russell
Square

Foundling
Hospital

British
Museum

Bloomsbury
Square

NEW OXFORD ST.

HIGH HOLBORN

Dickens's
Curiosity

DRURY LANE

OXFORD STREET

Marble Arch
Tyburn

NEW BOND ST.

REGENT ST.

Burlington
House

ST. MARTIN'S LANE

Covent
Garden
Theater

Drury
The

Covent Garden
Market

Bu
Coff

Turk's
Coffeeh

Berkeley
Square

STRAND

HYDE
PARK

Chesterfield House

Devonshire House

PICCADILLY

Shepherd's
Market

HAYMARKET

Royal
Opera House

St. James
Square

Trafalgar
Square

Charing Cross

Scotland
Yard

VICTOR

The Serpentine

GREEN
PARK

St. James
Palace

PALL MALL

THE MALL

WHITEHALL

KNIGHTSBRIDGE

Hyde Park
Corner

Buckingham
Palace

Westminster Hall

Westminster Abbey

WESTMINST

BRIDGE

Houses of
Parliament

THAMES

BUCKINGHAM PALACE RD.

VICTORIA STREET

LAMBETH

BRIDGE

Harold K. Faye

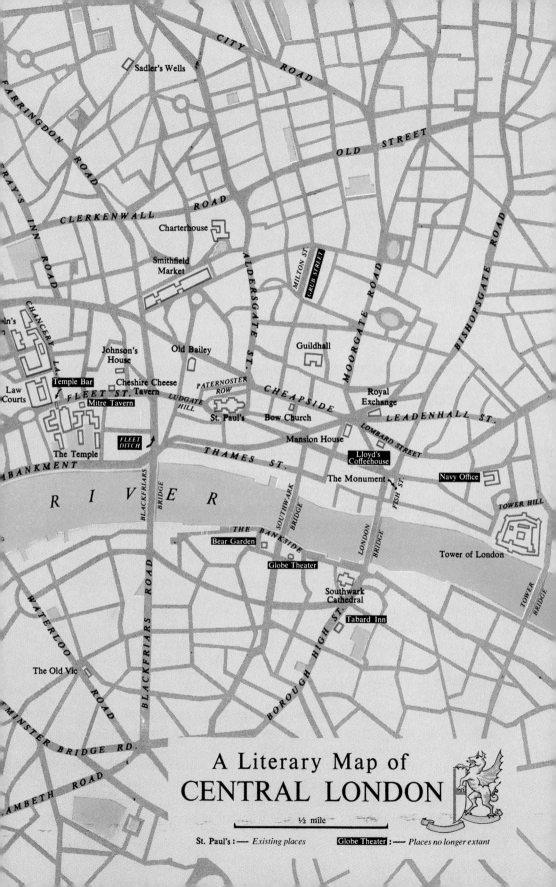

Sadler's Wells

CITY ROAD

OLD STREET

FARRINGDON ROAD

GRAY'S INN ROAD

CLERKENWALL ROAD

Charterhouse

Smithfield Market

ALDERSGATE ST.

MILTON ST.

GRUB STREET

MOORGATE ROAD

BISHOPSGATE ROAD

Johnson's House

Old Bailey

Guildhall

Temple Bar

Cheshire Cheese Tavern

PATERNOSTER ROW

CHEAPSIDE

Royal Exchange

LEADENHALL ST.

Law Courts

FLEET ST.

Mitre Tavern

LUDGATE HILL

St. Paul's

Bow Church

Mansion House

LOMBARD STREET

FLEET DITCH

The Temple

Lloyd's Coffeehouse

Navy Office

EMBANKMENT

THAMES ST.

The Monument

FISH ST.

TOWER HILL

R   I   V   E   R

BLACKFRIARS BRIDGE

SOUTHWARK BRIDGE

LONDON BRIDGE

THE BANKSIDE

Bear Garden

Tower of London

Globe Theater

Southwark Cathedral

TOWER BRIDGE

WATERLOO ROAD

BLACKFRIARS ROAD

Tabard Inn

BOROUGH HIGH ST.

The Old Vic

WESTMINSTER BRIDGE RD.

LAMBETH ROAD

A Literary Map of
CENTRAL LONDON

½ mile

St. Paul's : — *Existing places*   Globe Theater : — *Places no longer extant*

HUMOR IN ENGLISH LITERATURE

The strength and persistence of this unconscious element are responsible for other characteristics of English literature. For example, compared with other literatures, notably the French, it is on the whole deficient in the finest satirical wit, a highly conscious product. (Most of the best satirical wit in English literature has come from the Irish, from Swift to Bernard Shaw.) During the past fifty years there has been far more witty satirical writing of the better sort in America than in England. What we discover in English literature, from Chaucer onwards, is something very different from wit and satire — namely humor. Now genuine rich humor is never entirely a conscious product. It shares with poetry the unconscious element, those unforced contributions from the mind's depths. Great comic characters — and English literature has a wonderful gallery of them — cannot be coldly constructed, cannot be willed into life, but have to be created by the whole mind, conscious and unconscious. There is a kind of poetry in them. They are not merely funny, just as great clowns, like Chaplin in films or Grock (ah, you should have seen him!) in circus or vaudeville, are not merely funny, but seem to have an extra dimension, as close to tears as it is to laughter. Again, satire and wit are as hard as they are bright. They work outside sympathy and affection; whereas real humor is based partly on sympathy and has much affection in it. The notorious attachment of the English to old things is not simply a slavish attitude toward tradition; there is affection in it. In many countries the public is often merciless in rejecting aging actors and singers, and politicians who promised more than they could perform; but the English rarely display this cruelty, and, remembering old enthusiasms, will out of affection applaud incompetent and fading figures. All this is reflected in English literature.

A SMALL, LONG-SETTLED COUNTRY

England is a small and cozy sort of country, free from hurricanes, typhoons, terrible blizzards, vast floods, and earthquakes. Nature may often seem to display a surly unfriendliness, bringing too many gray and raw days, but it is not violently hostile, appallingly menacing, as it often is elsewhere, in many parts of America, for example. As soon as Americans, freed from the influence of English authors, really began writing as Americans, this difference in background in the literature of England became apparent at once. If we compare two famous semi-autobiographical novels, Dickens' *David Copperfield* and Mark Twain's *Huckleberry Finn,* we see that the English novel is written against the background of a small, long-settled, rather crowded country while the American story suggests a huge, semi-wild, vaguely menacing continent, whose people are seen against a vast darkness. Perhaps this explains why English fiction — though not the earlier work of the poetic dramatists — seems

Photo Researchers, Inc.

England is a small and long-settled country. Typical of many another small and cozy English community is the town of Albury, Sussex, on the old Canterbury road.

to lack mystery and tragic intensity, except here and there. It is the small, cozy and domestic, long-settled and rather crowded England that can be discovered in most of our novels.

THE CITY OF LONDON

London, England's capital city, may be regarded as the focal point of this rather crowded country of ours. Long one of the cultural centers of the world, it has literary associations dating back many hundreds of years, for London is the city of Chaucer, of Shakespeare and the Globe Theater, of Samuel Pepys, Addison and Steele, Johnson and Boswell, Charles Lamb, Thomas Carlyle, the Brownings, and in our own time, Somerset Maugham and T. S. Eliot, among many others. A study of the literary map of London on pages 18–19 and frequent reference to it as you proceed through this book will underline the importance of this city in English literature and give strong support to the pronouncement of the eighteenth century's most famous literary personage, Dr. Samuel Johnson, who stated flatly that a man tired of London is tired of life.

DEBITS AND CREDITS: AN ASSESSMENT

Two questions must be answered, however briefly. By way of examples and influences, what does English literature owe to other literatures? That is the first question. The second question is, what do other literatures owe to English literature? Let us look first at the debts, and then afterwards at the credits.

All the early influences on English literature proper, as distinct from Anglo-Saxon literature, came from the South. This was inevitable because, during the later Middle Ages and the Renaissance, the mainstream of European culture was making its way westward along the length of the Mediterranean Sea. In Chaucer's day, and for some time afterwards, the main influence was French. This was largely replaced during the Elizabethan Age by Italian influences. Italian verse forms were imitated, before Elizabeth's reign began, by Surrey and Wyatt; and then half a century later, Shakespeare and his fellow dramatists, in search of plots, made much use of Boccaccio and other Italian story-tellers. Indeed, Italy is the favorite background of Elizabethan and Jacobean plays. Spanish influences came later and were largely the result of the growing fame of Cervantes' masterpiece, *Don Quixote,* which was imitated everywhere well into the eighteenth century, more than a century after it had first appeared. But realistic prose fiction, especially the so-called *picaresque* tales about rogues and vagabonds, had been written in Spain throughout the sixteenth century. On the other hand, the "Golden Age" of Spanish drama had little influence on English drama. In the eighteenth century French influence was strong, especially in the theater, where French comedies were frequently translated or freely adapted, often without any acknowledgment of their original authors. The Romantic Age turned from France to Germany, where the Romantic movement first began. It was not until the last years of the nineteenth century that English fiction began to show the influence of the French realists and Russian novelists like Turgenev, Tolstoy, Dostoevski and Gorki, that some English playwrights began to study the work of the great Norwegian, Henrik Ibsen, and that a few English poets and critics came under the spell of the French Symbolist movement. French and Russian (pre-Revolution) influences on English writing continued into this century and were very strong in the years before World Wars I and II. A feature of the period since World War II, and one not to be found earlier, is the influence of American fiction on the younger English novelists. So much for the debts.

ENGLISH CONTRIBUTIONS

The credits are very impressive. The debt of world literature to the English is immense. Shakespeare alone brings it to a vast total. For a hundred and fifty years after his death, he meant little or nothing outside England, but then one country after another found in him a supreme dramatic-poetic genius. Mean-

Frank Monaco

The debt of world literature to the English is immense. Pictured above is one of England's outstanding libraries, that of Trinity College, Cambridge, founded in 1546.

while, the eighteenth-century English novelists, especially Samuel Richardson, began to be imitated by novelists everywhere. Then Byron in poetry and Scott in fiction were regarded as the two most influential masters of the Romantic Age. During the middle of the nineteenth century, the vast popularity of Dickens carried his influence far and wide. It was particularly strong in Russia, where, among others, Dostoevski was one of his most admiring and enthusiastic readers. One of the many ironies of literary history is that later English novelists and critics, who singled out Dostoevski for their special admiration, were also ready to declare their contempt for Dickens. In this century no English writers have captured the world's imagination as William Shakespeare and Charles Dickens did, though George Bernard Shaw has conquered the theater everywhere (except perhaps in France), H. G. Wells has been a force in world education, and a host of English novelists, playwrights, poets, and essayists have had their work reproduced throughout the civilized parts of this planet. Indeed, literature has long been one of England's best exports. What Englishmen, in their own unique island fashion, have thought and felt during these many centuries has found its way into innumerable libraries, theaters, homes — from Iceland to Patagonia, Cape Town to the Yukon. The political might and power of England may vanish from men's sight and even their memory. But so long as men can read, this nation created out of Celts and Anglo-Saxons and Normans, these poetic and humorous islanders behind their white cliffs, will be remembered with gratitude, admiration, and affection for the widely-scattered treasures of their great literature.

THE ANGLO-SAXON PERIOD

449 – 1066

First, why do we date the Anglo-Saxon period from 449 to 1066? It was in 449 that the first band of Germanic or Teuton people crossed the North Sea to England to settle in what is now the county of Kent. They were Jutes, from the peninsula of Jutland in Denmark, and they were the first of many such invaders. Following the Jutes came Angles and Saxons. Together these invaders created the Anglo-Saxon England ("Angle-land") that lasted until 1066, when the Norman-French, led by William, Duke of Normandy, successfully invaded and conquered the country. But from 449 to 1066 is a long time — over six centuries.

Most of these centuries come within a period frequently described as the "Dark Ages." This description, meant to suggest a time of barbarism, ignorance, confusion, and violence, is now generally considered by historians to be misleading. These ages in fact were not as dark as they were once thought to be. They were by no means without knowledge, communications, and trade, and had arts and crafts of a fairly high order. True, it was a time filled with violence, cruelty, and much confused fighting, but then our own world today can hardly be said to be free from such vices and follies.

A GLANCE BACK: BRITAIN UNDER ROMAN RULE

What seemed to plunge the western world into comparative darkness was the collapse of the vast Roman Empire, which for centuries had maintained order from Hadrian's Wall, in the north of England, to distant Arabia. (It

◀ The items in the frontispiece are identified on page 45.

25

was possible, at the height of the Roman Empire, to travel on post roads, and use the same currency, from what is now Northumberland to the Middle East, beyond the Red Sea. It has never been possible to do this since that time, for all our talk of the progress we have made.) For hundreds of years, far longer than the British ruled India, the southern half of Britain had been part of the Roman Empire. Once they had conquered the British inhabitants, a Celtic people, the Roman legions remained as defenders. It was when the Romans were finally withdrawn, when Rome itself was threatened, that the Jutes, Angles, and Saxons, during the fifth and sixth centuries, undertook their successful invasions.

A wonderful picture of later Roman Britain can be found in Kipling's *Puck of Pook's Hill* stories — "A Centurion of the Thirtieth" and "On The Great Wall." If ever you visit England you can easily find plenty of fascinating remains of this Roman Britain, such as the ruins of public baths or what is left of the tiled floors (which were ingeniously heated) of Roman villas. Many of the great highways of England have as their foundations the original military roads made by the Roman legions. And familiar place names ending in "caster" or "chester" owe their origin to the Roman occupation, for the Latin word for a camp was *castra*.

THE GERMANIC INVASIONS

Once the Roman legions, composed of highly trained professional soldiers, were taken away, the Romanized Britons were no match for the invaders from across the North Sea. The Britons, however, did not retreat to the mountains and moors without a struggle. Behind the half-legendary King Arthur, afterwards transformed into a hero of medieval romance, was the figure of a Celtic leader better able than the rest to organize some determined resistance. But the sturdy invaders from the North and the East arrived in wave after wave — Angles, Saxons, and Jutes — taking possession of the best land, creating tiny kingdoms of their own, until at last they too were compelled to organize themselves into larger units in order to resist further invasion. For it was not long before the men from farther North, the true Norsemen, the terrible Vikings, began their raiding, pillaging, and burning.

Finally, after the Viking pirates came Danish settlers, who occupied northern and eastern England, bringing with them their own customs, laws, and attitudes of mind that long outlasted the Norman Conquest. Indeed, to this day, the people of East Anglia and northern England exhibit certain traits of character not generally found among the people in southern and western England. (This is what makes history, when it is not a mere chronicle of

Among the present-day remains of Roman Britain are these public baths located in southwestern England in the city of Bath, called Aquae Sulis by the Romans.

Photo Researchers, Inc.

kings and battles, so fascinating. We are all *in* history.)

The political and military history of these times, roughly from the eighth century to the middle of the eleventh, is both confused and tedious. But a few important facts do stand out. Exceptional Anglo-Saxon kings like Alfred the Great and Athelstan were successful in their struggle against the Norse invaders. The Anglo-Saxons were converted to Christianity, partly through the efforts of Celtic missionaries from Ireland and Scotland, also by Rome itself. Augustine, sent by Gregory the Great of Rome, founded the see of Canterbury and did much toward promoting the spread of Christianity throughout England. When the kingdom was conquered by William of Normandy in 1066, it was Christian, and although so much of it even then was Danish in its laws, customs, and characteristics, we can call it Anglo-Saxon.

THE ANGLO-SAXONS

What kind of people were these Anglo-Saxons? Before we answer this question, we should remember that whenever and wherever a people are ruthlessly conquered, there will always be a pretense by their conquerors — or by chroniclers and historians writing from the point of view of the invaders — that such people have a much lower level of civilization than that of their conquerors, that they are mere barbarians whose defeat is inevitable and a sign of the world's progress. There can be no doubt that the Anglo-Saxons have been victims of this bad habit. Most people even today have a vague idea of them as a slow-witted, oafish, tribal folk, much given to drinking enormous quantities of ale and mead. One might imagine that the Anglo-Saxons were fit only to be the serfs of their Norman conquerors, but this idea is quite false. Indeed, the Normans were superior only in military organization and tactics and in architecture; in many other respects they were inferior to the Anglo-Saxon civilization that they conquered but did not entirely destroy.

Probably everybody knows that the Anglo-Saxons (and here we include all the kindred peoples) were hardy and brave, as stubborn in defense as the ordinary English soldiery has been ever since. And no doubt it is fairly common knowledge that while these people easily developed great loyalty to a chosen leader, they had a natural tendency toward what we should call now a democratic habit of mind — that is, they liked to hold meetings in which people could express openly what they thought and felt. (One kind of meeting was called a "moot," and to this day we talk about "a moot point," meaning something which can be settled only through deliberation by an assembly.)

ANGLO-SAXON CIVILIZATION

But what is not generally realized is that the Anglo-Saxons developed a common deep feeling for beauty. Thus they had a passion for fine ornament, and their craftsmen produced many beautiful pieces, such as brooches and

Gloucester City Museum, England

bracelets of exquisite design and workmanship. They were in fact a more artistic and poetic people than their Norman conquerors, who were essentially soldiers and administrators. Behind the glories of English literature, as it has come down to us, is a mixture of the Celtic and Anglo-Saxon temperaments, a combination of the misty mountains and moors, to which the Celts had retreated, and the bright meadows cultivated by the Anglo-Saxon peasants.

It is easy for an American student, living far away in time and space from these Anglo-Saxon people, to imagine that what was thought and felt

An Anglo-Saxon mirror.

so long ago, so far away, is completely unimportant today except to the historian and scholar. But this is wrong. We are all *in* the same history that contains these ancient people, part of a continuous living web. To take an obvious example, perhaps these words are being read on a Tuesday, Wednesday, or Thursday. The names of these days come from the names of old Anglo-Saxon gods: Tuesday from *Tiw,* the dark god; Wednesday from *Woden,* the chief Teutonic god of war; Thursday from *Thor,* god of thunder. Then too, Friday comes from *Frigga,* goddess of the home, so that we cannot live a week without being in touch with the Anglo-Saxons. And although nowadays the United States and Britain are quite different countries, many basic American traditions in law, conduct, outlook, language, and literature were originally a legacy from these same Anglo-Saxons.

ANGLO-SAXON LITERATURE

Long after they had been converted to Christianity and had developed a recognizable civilization, the Anglo-Saxons were fond of semi-communal feasting to celebrate successful battles or expeditions. In the great "mead hall," after the food had been attacked with hunting knives and fingers and the bones had been flung to the dogs, the scop (poet) or the gleeman with his harp would entertain the company. Songs, gay or melancholy (and more often melancholy, as they are to this day among English common soldiers), were sung; heroic tales were retold; or the poet, as an all-round entertainer, put elaborate riddles to those members of his audience who were still awake. To the Anglo-Saxon the riddle was an intellectual exercise. Can you guess the subject of this one?

I'm prized by men, in the meadows I'm found,
Gathered on hill-sides, and hunted in groves;
From dale and from down, by day I am brought.
Airy wings carry me, cunningly store me,
Hoarding me safe. Yet soon men take me;
Drained into vats, I'm dangerous grown.
I tie up my victim, and trip him, and throw him;
Often I floor a foolish old churl.
Who wrestles with me, and rashly would measure
His strength against mine, will straightway find himself
Flung to the ground, flat on his back,
Unless he leave his folly in time,
Put from his senses and power of speech,
Robbed of his might, bereft of his mind,
Of his hands and feet. Now find me my name,
Who can blind and enslave men so upon earth,
And bring fools low in broad daylight.

BRITAIN IN ALFRED'S TIME

Although with the coming of the church a written literature was evolved, the great tradition, which persisted for centuries and long after the Norman Conquest, was oral, not written down but committed to memory by generation after generation of poets, gleemen, and minstrels. The rhymes (or alliteration, which the Anglo-Saxons used) and emphatic rhythms of poetry awaken a strong emotional response, as we all know. But for the Anglo-Saxons these poetic devices also served another purpose, long before printed books arrived and indeed long before poets could read and write, and that was as aids to memory. When we find ourselves remembering a nursery rhyme, as we often do just because it has alliteration and a strongly marked rhythm, we might give a thought to the old Anglo-Saxon poets and gleemen standing in the firelit mead halls.

Although there must have been a great wealth of heroic narrative verse and, later on, of dramatic monologues of a somewhat lyrical nature, highly suitable for recitation, very little has survived. We have only the great epic, *Beowulf;* portions of other epics, together with later fragments of battle pieces; and a small group of dramatic poems, of which "The Seafarer" is an excellent example. There is a good reason why so little of this poetry has come down to us. To survive it had to be written down. From the seventh century, when Anglo-Saxon England was rapidly converted to Christianity, the only men who could have written it down were priests. They, however, were only too anxious to rid the country of all pagan influences and saw no reason why they should transcribe poetry which was essentially pagan in spirit. The churchmen who wrote verse generally wrote in Latin, though occasionally they included lines in the vernacular. It was from their imitation of church hymns in Latin that the gradual introduction of rhyme into English verse developed.

The earlier prose writers and chroniclers among the Anglo-Saxon churchmen also wrote in Latin. The greatest of these was known as the Venerable Bede (673–735), the most learned and industrious writer of the whole period, author of the *Ecclesiastical History* (731), an excellent historical authority of its time. As an historian Bede is rightly regarded as "the father of English

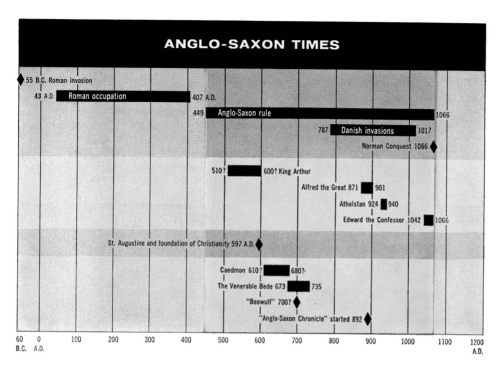

history." Nearly two centuries later, Alfred the Great (871–901), the ablest and most remarkable of all English kings, not only became the patron of scholars and educators but turned author and translator himself after delivering his kingdom from the Danes. Anglo-Saxon prose and history owe most to his influence and his example. Rather than use Latin as had been the custom, Alfred promoted written use of the vernacular and was responsible for the initiation of the *Anglo-Saxon Chronicle*, the first historical record to be kept in English. The briefest study of Alfred's reign makes nonsense of any idea of the Anglo-Saxons as drunken oafs existing in a "Dark Age." He maintained diplomatic relations with all neighboring kings and princes, sent frequent embassies to Rome, corresponded with the Patriarch of Jerusalem, and may even, as we are told, have sent a mission as far as India. Alfred also formulated a code of law and founded the first English "public schools." He was a truly great man, ruling and doing much to educate a society that, with its social organization and laws, its letters and arts and crafts, was far from being barbarous, but, indeed, made an enduring contribution to our civilization.

J. B. P.

Note: The dates given throughout after the names of kings and rulers are the dates of their reigns; those after the names of literary and other historical figures are birth and death dates.

The Seafarer

Translated by J. DUNCAN SPAETH

From earliest times to the present day, English literature reflects the
vital part played by the sea in English life. "The Seafarer" may be
called the ancestor of the many poems about the sea which appear
in this volume. This famous poem was written by an unknown author of the fifth or sixth century, but its powerful descriptions,
metrical charm, and flowing alliteration please a modern reader.
These qualities have been skillfully preserved by the translator. He
has, however, made one interesting change. The original poem was
not written as a dialogue, but Dr. Spaeth sensed in it two opposite
attitudes. His arrangement shows the enthusiasm of a youth for new
adventure, in spite of warnings from an old sailor of the hardships
to be faced on the sea.

THE OLD SAILOR

True is the tale that I tell of my travels,
Sing of my seafaring sorrows and woes;
Hunger and hardship's heaviest burdens,
Tempest and terrible toil of the deep,
Daily I've borne on the deck of my boat.   5
Fearful the welter of waves that encompassed me,
Watching at night on the narrow bow,
As she drove by the rocks, and drenched me with spray.
Fast to the deck my feet were frozen,
Gripped by the cold, while care's hot surges   10
My heart o'erwhelmed, and hunger's pangs
Sapped the strength of my sea-weary spirit.

Little he knows whose lot is happy,
Who lives at ease in the lap of the earth,
How, sick at heart, o'er icy seas,   15
Wretched I ranged the winter through,
Bare of joys, and banished from friends,
Hung with icicles, stung by hailstones.
Nought I heard but the hollow boom
Of wintry waves, or the wild swan's whoop.   20
For singing I had the solan's° scream;
For peals of laughter, the yelp of the seal;
The sea-mew's cry, for the mirth of the mead hall.
Shrill through the roar of the shrieking gale
Lashing along the sea-cliff's edge,   25
Pierces the ice-plumed petrel's° defiance,

21. *solan* (sō′lăn): a sea bird like a gull. (Throughout this book the small circle ° is used with poetry
to indicate a footnote. Each footnote is identified by the number of the line in which the footnoted
word appears.) 26. *petrel:* a sea bird.

"The Seafarer," from *Old English Poetry*, translated by J. Duncan Spaeth, published by Princeton University Press. Reprinted
by permission of the publisher.

And the wet-winged eagle's answering scream.
Little he dreams that drinks life's pleasure,
By danger untouched in the shelter of towns,
Insolent and wine-proud, how utterly weary 30
Oft I wintered on open seas.
Night fell black, from the north it snowed
Harvest of hail.

THE YOUTH

Oh, wildly my heart
Beats in my bosom and bids me to try 35
The tumble and surge of seas tumultuous,
Breeze and brine and the breakers' roar.
Daily, hourly, drives me my spirit
Outward to sail, far countries to see.
Liveth no man so large in his soul, 40
So gracious in giving, so gay in his youth,
In deeds so daring, so dear to his lord,
But frets his soul for his sea adventure,
Fain to try what fortune shall send.
Harping he needs not, nor hoarding of treasure; 45
Nor woman can win him, nor joys of the world.
Nothing does please but the plunging billows;
Ever he longs, who is lured by the sea.
Woods are abloom, the wide world awakens,
Gay are the mansions, the meadows most fair; 50
These are but warnings, that haste on his journey
Him whose heart is hungry to taste
The perils and pleasures of the pathless deep.

THE OLD SAILOR

Dost mind the cuckoo mournfully calling?
The summer's watchman sorrow forebodes. 55
What does the landsman that wantons in luxury,
What does he reck the rough sea's foe,
The cares of the exile, whose keel has explored
The uttermost parts of the ocean ways!

THE YOUTH

Sudden my soul starts from her prison house, 60
Soareth afar o'er the sounding main;
Hovers on high, o'er the home of the whale;
Back to me darts the bird sprite and beckons,
Winging her way o'er woodland and plain,
Hungry to roam, and bring me where glisten 65
Glorious tracts of glimmering foam.
This life on land is lingering death to me,
Give me the gladness of God's great sea.

AN ANCIENT SEA POEM

1. To what aspects of Anglo-Saxon life do the following phrases refer: line 23, "the mirth of the mead hall," line 42, "so dear to his lord," line 45, "harping he needs not"?

2. What different seasons of the year are described? Relate the contrast between the seasons to the conflict of opinion between the old sailor and the young man. Could these conflicts be within the mind of a single person? Discuss.

LITERATURE AND THE ARTS

The contemporary reconstruction of a Viking ship shown on page 33 is based on modern archaeological findings and gives us an excellent idea of the type of ship familiar to people of the Anglo-Saxon period, in whose lives the open sea played so great a role. Long and narrow, their high, pointed prows carved with a snake or dragon's head, these ships usually carried about twenty oars and sixty men.

BEHIND THE SCENES IN ENGLISH LITERATURE

Manuscript hunting, cryptography, literary scholarship — what do you think of when you hear these terms? And what does this sort of thing have to do with your study of literature?

To begin with, we might define the literary scholar as the historian of literature. As such, his chief business is to find all the discoverable facts about a literary work and its author in order that he and others may properly interpret and evaluate it. All sorts of facts are pertinent. To understand a writer as a human being as well as an artist, the scholar must read letters, memoirs, diaries, previous biographies (if any) not only of the author but of his friends and acquaintances. He should be familiar with the writer's social and political environment and be at home in the type of world in which he lived. To establish the details of his story, he may have to consult weather reports, legal documents, court proceedings, timetables, psychological and medical literature, mercantile records and accounts, church registers — even old menus and laundry bills. For the genesis and history of a given work, he may have to read a vast quantity of literature preceding or contemporary with it which the author also read — or might have read. He must study successive editions and revisions. He must learn about the writer's methods and the conditions he worked under. He may need to refer to printers', publishers', and copyright records, old theatrical programs, advertisements, and the like.

Sometimes he must be a linguist in order to compare, for example, earlier and later versions of a medieval poem or variant readings by different scribes. He may become involved in chemical analyses of paper and ink as a means of establishing dates or detecting forgery, or he may find himself deciphering codes, shorthand, or damaged or illegible manuscripts.

The literary researcher must be a patient searcher in musty archives, newspaper morgues, libraries, attics, and even barns. His work may take him on romantic journeys — or merely dull and unrewarding ones. But at the end, after unraveling a great tangle of obscure, misleading, or purposely distorted "facts," he may find exciting information that clears up a great mystery or totally revises an accepted theory. Through all of this he must combine the objectivity and detachment of the scientist with the imagination of the artist or critic who sees how apparently unconnected facts are related.

Throughout this book, we shall look at some examples of the work of the literary scholar, who, through his careful detective work, adds immeasurably to our knowledge and appreciation of literature.

Beowulf

Translated by J. DUNCAN SPAETH

Beowulf, the oldest known English epic poem, is the greatest piece of literature to come down to us from the Anglo-Saxons. Much that we would like to known about it is lost in the distant past and will probably never be discovered: who wrote it? When? Where? Scholars have found enough evidence in the poem itself to determine that it was probably composed by a single gifted poet sometime during the seventh or eighth century. The existing manuscript of a later date is no doubt a copy of an earlier one. The author was perhaps a Christianized West Saxon who drew his story from old pagan legends brought over from the continent; or perhaps monks substituted Christian references for pagan ones when they copied the manuscript. The character of Beowulf seems to be a blending of a historical figure with various mythical heroes of an earlier day.

The theme is universal — the age-old story of a great leader who saves or tries to save a people in grave danger. The action takes place in Sweden and Denmark. The characters are all people of noble birth. Though persons of low rank are introduced into the poem, their individual names are not given.

Beowulf is the hero of the story. Strong, fearless, an advocate of freedom and justice, he typifies the Anglo-Saxon ideals of personal conduct. The villains are the fire-drake or dragon from the dark caves and the cannibal-ogre Grendel [1] and his mother who live in the miasma of swamps in the land of mists and cold nights. The tone of the poem is dark, melancholy, and austere. In simple, direct, majestic verse, a literary legacy from the earliest writers of English poetry, an exciting story of adventure and heroism is told.

◁ ▷

The poem begins as a mysterious ship from an unknown country one day comes into harbor. It brings an infant called Scyld [2] to the homeland of the Spear-Danes. This child later becomes their king, and a good king he is, reigning long and successfully. When he dies, his subjects spare no pains in honoring him. As is the custom in Scandinavia, they clothe him in armor, surround him with treasure, place him on a ship, and send him back to the sea.

Years pass. Scyld's descendant, Hrothgar,[3] wins great fame and wealth in battles with enemies. He builds the greatest of mead halls, called Heorot,[4] where his loyal warriors may gather. Hrothgar feels that he has earned peace, rest, and enjoyment of the riches he has won. But fate has other things in store for him. There now appears on the scene a villain, a superhuman monster named Grendel.

---

[1] *Grendel* (grĕn′dĕl).   [2] *Scyld* (shĭld).   [3] *Hrothgar* (hrŏth′gàr).   [4] *Heorot* (hā′ō·rŏt): literally, Hart Hall, because the horns of a stag or hart adorned its gables. The site of Heorot may be identified with Leire in Seeland, Denmark.

Selections from *Beowulf* from *Old English Poetry*, translated by J. Duncan Spaeth, published by Princeton University Press. Reprinted by permission of the publisher.

In the darkness dwelt a demon-sprite,
Whose heart was filled with fury and hate,
When he heard each night the noise of revel
Loud in the hall, laughter and song.
To the sound of the harp the singer chanted   5
Lays he had learned, of long ago;
How the Almighty had made the earth,
Wonder-bright lands, washed by the ocean;

All is happiness How he set, triumphant, sun and moon
in the new home To lighten all men that live on the earth.   10
until the angry He brightened the land with leaves and branches;
fiend Grendel Life he created for every being,
comes from his Each in its kind, that moves upon earth.
lair. So, happy in hall, the heroes lived,
Wanting naught, till one began   15
To work them woe, a wicked fiend.

The demon grim was Grendel called,
Marsh stalker huge, the moors he roamed.
The joyless creature had kept long time
The lonely fen,° the lairs of monsters,   20
Cast out from men, an exile accurst.
The killing of Abel, brother of Cain°
Was justly avenged by the Judge Eternal.

When night had fallen, the fiend crept near
To the lofty hall, to learn how the Danes   25
In Heorot fared, when the feasting was done.
The athelings° all within he saw
Asleep after revel, not recking of danger,
And free from care. The fiend accurst,
Grim and greedy, his grip made ready;   30
Snatched in their sleep, with savage fury,
Grendel enters Thirty warriors; away he sprang
the main hall Proud of his prey, to repair to his home,
at night and His blood-dripping booty to bring to his lair.
carries off thirty At early dawn, when daybreak came,   35
warriors. The vengeance of Grendel was revealed to all;
Their wails after wassail° were widely heard,
Their morning woe. The mighty ruler,
The atheling brave, sat bowed with grief.

So Grendel wrongfully ruled the hall,   40
One against all till empty stood
That lordly mansion, and long remained so.
For the space of twelve winters the Scyldings' Friend°

---

20. *fen:* low marshland, a moor. 22. This is one of a number of passages which indicate that the author of the epic in its present form was a Christian. For the story of Cain and Abel, see Genesis 4. 27. *athelings:* nobles. 37. *after wassail* (wŏs″l): after the festive drinking of the night before. 43. *Scyldings' Friend:* Hrothgar.

*The murders
continue for twelve
years, and gleemen
spread the news
abroad.*

Bore in his breast the brunt of this sorrow,
Measureless woe. In mournful lays   45
The tale became known; 'twas told abroad
In gleemen's songs, how Grendel had warred
Long against Hrothgar, and wreaked his hate
With murderous fury through many a year.

The wise men take counsel together, erect altars to their heathen
gods, and pray for relief from the monster, all to no avail. At last,
from an unexpected source, Hrothgar and his people are given new
hope of deliverance.

THE COMING OF BEOWULF

Thus boiled with care the breast of Hrothgar;   50
Ceaselessly sorrowed the son of Healfdene,°
None of his chieftains might change his lot.
Too fell was the foe that afflicted the people
With wrongs unnumbered, and nightly horrors.
Then heard in his home King Hygelac's thane,°   55
The dauntless Jute, of the doings of Grendel.
In strength he outstripped the strongest of men
That dwell in the earth in the days of this life.
Gallant and bold, he gave command

*Beowulf makes
plans to go to the
aid of the Danes.*

To get him a boat, a good wave-skimmer.   60
O'er the swan-road,° he said, he would seek the king
Noble and famous, who needed men.
Though dear to his kin, they discouraged him not;
The prudent in counsel praised the adventure,
Whetted his valor, awaiting good omens.   65
He with fourteen followers hardy
Went to embark; he was wise in seamanship,
So Beowulf chose from the band of the Jutes
Heroes brave, the best he could find;
Showed them the landmarks, leading the way.   70
Soon they descried their craft in the water,
At the foot of the cliff. Then climbed aboard
The chosen troop; the tide was churning
Sea against sand; they stowed away
In the hold of the ship their shining armor,   75
War gear and weapons; the warriors launched
Their well-braced boat on her welcome voyage.
Swift o'er the waves with a wind that favored,
Foam on her breast, like a bird she flew;
A day and a night they drove to seaward,   80
Cut the waves with the curving prow,
Till the seamen that sailed her sighted the land,
Shining cliffs and coastwise hills,

---

51. *Healfdene* (hä′ălf·děn·nà): half-Dane; that is, his mother was a foreigner. 55. *Hygelac's*
(hĭg′ĕ·läks) *thane:* Beowulf. Hygelac is a historical character — king of the Jutes, a people who lived
in southern Sweden, according to most authorities, or in northern Denmark. 61. *swan-road:* sea.

Headlands bold. The harbor opened,
Their cruise was ended. Then quickly the sailors,   85
The crew of Weder folk,° clambered ashore,
Moored their craft with clank of chain mail,
And goodly war gear. God they thanked
That their way was smooth o'er the surging waves.

At the coast, Beowulf and his men are met by a guard, who, after
being convinced of their good intentions, conducts them toward the
palace. They enter the hall, and Beowulf introduces himself to
Hrothgar and his thanes. His last words voice a characteristic German attitude.

"Hail, King Hrothgar: Hygelac's thane   90
And kinsman am I. Known is the record
Of deeds of renown I have done in my youth.
Far in my home, I heard of this Grendel;
Seafarers tell the tale of the hall:
How bare of warriors, this best of buildings   95
Deserted stands, when the sun goes down
And twilight deepens to dark in the sky.
By comrades encouraged, I come on this journey.
The best of them bade me, the bravest and wisest,
To go to thy succor, O good King Hrothgar;   100
For well they approved my prowess in battle,
They saw me themselves come safe from the conflict
When five of my foes I defeated and bound,

Beowulf declares Beating in battle the brood of the monsters.
the prowess that At night on the sea with nickers° I wrestled,   105
makes him a fit Avenging the Weders, survived the sea peril,
opponent for And crushed in my grip the grim sea monsters
Grendel. That harried my neighbors. Now I am come
To cope with Grendel in combat single,
And match my might against the monster alone.   110
I pray thee therefore, prince of the Scyldings,
Not to refuse the favor I ask,
Having come so far, O friend of the Shield-Danes,
That I alone with my loyal comrades,
My hardy companions, may Heorot purge.   115

Moreover they say that the slaughterous fiend
In wanton mood all weapons despises.
Hence — as I hope that Hygelac may,
My lord and king, be kind to me —
Sword and buckler° I scorn to bear,   120
Gold-adorned shield, as I go to the conflict.
With my grip will I grapple the gruesome fiend,
Foe against foe, to fight for our life.
And he that shall fall his faith must put

---

86. *Weder* (wā′dẽr) *folk:* another name for the Jutes. 105. *nickers:* sea demons, probably walruses
or whales. 120. *buckler:* a kind of shield worn on one arm.

In the judgment of God. If Grendel wins,   125
He is minded to make his meal in the hall
Untroubled by fear, on the folk of the Jutes,
As often before he fed on the Danes.
No need for thee then to think of my burial.
If I lose my life, the lonely prowler   130
My blood-stained body will bear to his den,
Swallow me greedily, and splash with my gore
His lair in the marsh; no longer wilt then
Have need to find me food and sustenance.
To Hygelac send, if I sink in the battle,   135
This best of corselets that covers my breast,
Heirloom of Hrethel,° rarest of byrnies,°
The work of Weland.° So Wyrd° will be done."

Hrothgar replies with complimentary reference to Beowulf's father,
and then once more recounts the horrors of Grendel's visits to
Heorot. A banquet is prepared, with the usual eating and drinking
and minstrel's song. Unferth (ŭn'fârth), a jealous Danish courtier,
belittles Beowulf by sarcastic comment on his defeat in a swimming
match with Breca, a young prince of another tribe. Beowulf replies
by giving his version of this adventure, in which he had killed nine
sea demons. Then Beowulf goes on to accuse Unferth of murdering
his own brothers, a kenning (or metaphor) meaning that he fled
from a battlefield where they were killed.

    After this tilt the banquet proceeds. The queen, Wealhtheow
(wā'ĕl·thā·ō), passes the ale cup. The noisy revel continues until at
last Hrothgar and his followers leave Heorot to Beowulf and his
men. After once more asserting that he will meet Grendel unarmed,
Beowulf and his men lie down and go to sleep.

BEOWULF'S FIGHT WITH GRENDEL

Now Grendel came, from his crags of mist
Across the moor; he was curst of God.   140
The murderous prowler meant to surprise
In the high-built hall his human prey.
He stalked 'neath the clouds, till steep before him
The house of revelry rose in his path,
The gold-hall of heroes, the gaily adorned.   145
Hrothgar's home he had haunted full often,
But never before had he found to receive him
So hardy a hero, such hall guards there.
Close to the building crept the slayer,
Doomed to misery. The door gave way,   150
Though fastened with bolts, when his fist fell on it.
Maddened he broke through the breach he had made;
Swoln° with anger and eager to slay,

---

    137. *Hrethel:* father of King Hygelac; *byrnies:* coats of mail. 138. *Weland* (wā'lănd): the celestial blacksmith of the Northmen, corresponding to Vulcan of classical mythology; *Wyrd:* Fate. 153. *Swoln:* swollen.

The ravening fiend o'er the bright-paved floor
Furious ran, while flashed from his eyes   155
An ugly glare like embers aglow.
He saw in the hall, all huddled together,
The heroes asleep. Then laughed in his heart
The hideous fiend; he hoped ere dawn
To sunder body from soul of each;   160
He looked to appease his lust of blood,
Glut his maw° with the men he would slay.
But Wyrd had otherwise willed his doom;
Never again should he get a victim
After that night.

        Narrowly watched   165
Hygelac's thane how the horrible slayer
Forward should charge in fierce attack.
Nor was the monster minded to wait:
Sudden he sprang on a sleeping thane.
Ere he could stir, he slit him open;   170
Bit through the bone-joints, gulped the blood,
Greedily bolted the body piecemeal.

Grendel devours Soon he had swallowed the slain man wholly,
a sleeping man, Hands and feet. Then forward he hastened,
then attacks Sprang at the hero, and seized him at rest;   175
Beowulf. Fiercely clutched him with fiendish claw.
But quickly Beowulf caught his forearm,
And threw himself on it with all its weight.
Straight discovered that crafty plotter,
That never in all mid-earth had he met   180
In any man a mightier grip.
Gone was his courage, and craven fear
Sat in his heart, yet helped him no sooner.
Fain° would he hide in his hole in the fenland,
His devil's den. A different welcome   185
From former days he found that night!
Now Hygelac's thane, the hardy, remembered
His evening's boast, and bounding up,
Grendel he clenched, and cracked his fingers;
The monster tried flight, but the man pursued;   190
The ravager hoped to wrench himself free,
And gain the fen, for he felt his fingers
Helpless and limp in the hold of his foe.

'Twas a sorry visit the man-devourer
Made to the Hall of the Hart that night.   195
Dread was the din, the Danes were frighted
By the uproar wild of the ale-spilling fray.
The hardiest blenched as the hall foes wrestled
In terrible rage. The rafters groaned;

162. *maw:* stomach. 184. *Fain:* gladly.

'Twas wonder great that the wine hall stood 200
Firm 'gainst the fighters' furious onslaught,

*The mead hall is
almost wrecked
in the fury of the
battle.*

Nor fell to the ground, that glorious building.
With bands of iron 'twas braced and stiffened
Within and without. But off from the sill
Many a mead-bench mounted with gold 205
Was wrung where they wrestled in wrath together.
The Scylding nobles never imagined
That open attack, or treacherous cunning,
Could wreck or ruin their royal hall,
The lofty and antlered, unless the flames 210
Should someday swallow it up in smoke.
The din was renewed, the noise redoubled;
Each man of the Danes was mute with dread,
That heard from the wall the horrible wail,
The gruesome song of the godless foe, 215
His howl of defeat, as the fiend of hell
Bemoaned his hurt. The man held fast;
Greatest he was in grip of strength,
Of all that dwelt upon earth that day.

Loath in his heart was the hero-deliverer 220
To let escape his slaughterous guest.
Of little use that life he deemed
To human kind. The comrades of Beowulf
Unsheathed their weapons to ward their leader,
Eagerly brandished their ancient blades, 225
The life of their peerless lord to defend.
Little they deemed, those dauntless warriors,
As they leaped to the fray, those lusty fighters,
Laying on boldly to left and to right,
Eager to slay, that no sword upon earth, 230
No keenest weapon, could wound that monster:
Point would not pierce, he was proof against iron;
'Gainst victory blades the devourer was charmed.
But a woeful end awaited the wretch,
That very day he was doomed to depart, 235
And fare afar to the fiends' domain.

Now Grendel found, who in former days

*Beowulf tears
Grendel's arm
from its socket,
and the mortally
wounded Grendel
crawls to his lair.*

So many a warrior had wantonly slain,
In brutish lust, abandoned of God,
That the frame of his body was breaking at last. 240
Keen of courage, the kinsman of Hygelac
Held him grimly gripped in his hands.
Loath was each to the other alive.
The grisly monster got his death wound:
A huge split opened under his shoulder; 245
Crunched the socket, cracked the sinews,
Glory great was given to Beowulf.
But Grendel escaped with his gaping wound,

O'er the dreary moor his dark den sought,
Crawled to his lair. 'Twas clear to him then,   250
The count of his hours to end had come,
Done were his days. The Danes were glad,
The hard fight was over, they had their desire.
Cleared was the hall, 'twas cleansed by the hero
With keen heart and courage, who came from afar.   255

ANGLO–SAXON ADVENTURES

1. In what ways does the poem bring out the following Anglo-Saxon ideals of conduct: (*a*) love of personal freedom, (*b*) allegiance to lord or king, (*c*) repression of emotions, (*d*) love of glory as the ruling motive of every noble life? Which of these remain as ideals in America today? Which have been changed or modified?

2. Do you think that such monstrous creatures as Grendel or such supermen as Beowulf really existed? If not, how do you explain the frequent appearance of such beings in early literature? If possible, give examples of such exaggerated characters in modern literature. What purpose do they serve?

ANGLO–SAXON VERSE

Anglo-Saxon, or Old English, verse has three characteristics:

a. Each line has *four principal beats* but may have any number of syllables.

b. Some of the four beats *alliterate* — that is, begin with the same sound — at least one in each half of the line. (In original Old English verse the third beat *always* alliterates with the first, or second, or both. The translation by Dr. Spaeth is very close to the original in this respect.)

c. The verse is *not* rhymed.

Practice reading parts of the poem aloud in order to get the swing of the four-accent lines. This form is admirably suited for narrative poetry to be recited aloud. It is simple to understand, easy to listen to, easy to catch in its alliteration (which is its principal ornament), easy to compose. The jingle about Old King Cole might sound like this in the Anglo-Saxon verse form:

Cole was the king; he was keen and merry;
Mirthful he was, with minstrels in mead hall.
He called for his cup; he called for his pipe.

His fiddlers were three, and fine was their trilling.

The beat of the line is hypnotizing, yet its elasticity keeps it from becoming boring. It has been used a number of times by later poets. Coleridge, for example, was influenced by the Old English rhythms. The American poet Edna St. Vincent Millay wrote her operatic play, *The King's Henchman,* in this style. T. S. Eliot in his play *The Cocktail Party* returns to the native English principle of a four-beat loose line, though he has given up the alliteration. In *Beowulf* the line moves fast, and its hammer strokes make the battles and the boasting forceful. When chanting the poem, the gleeman probably struck a chord on his harp with each accented syllable.

LITERATURE AND THE ARTS

For the artistic reconstruction of an Anglo-Saxon mead hall (page 41), drawn by Seymour Chwast especially for this book, original manuscript sources were consulted, so that here, except for the design of the fabrics on the wall, about which we know few details, we have an authentic representation of a hall such as Heorot, where the story of Beowulf unfolded.

The typical mead hall, high-ceilinged and made of wood, its walls hung with shields or colorful hangings, was the center of Anglo-Saxon society. Here hospitality was dispensed; here the evening's entertainment took place. The company congregated around the fire laid in the center of the floor. After a simple meal, usually of vegetables and fish or salted meat, attendants removed the board and trestles which served as a table. Ale or wine was then served and, often led by minstrels or gleemen, the evening's merriment — singing, dancing, the recounting of exploits — then began.

BEHIND THE SCENES IN ENGLISH LITERATURE

The chances of survival for the rare or ancient literary document are amply illustrated by the perils that befell the sole surviving Anglo-Saxon manuscript of *Beowulf*.

The 140-page manuscript was copied by two scribes sometime in the tenth century. Later it was bound in a codex [1] with other manuscripts, but nothing else is known of its history for the next five hundred years. At the top of the first page is written "Lawrence Nowell, 1573," which seems to indicate that the manuscript was acquired by Lawrence Nowell, Dean of Lichfield, one of the earliest students of Anglo-Saxon literature. Its next known owner was the zealous antiquarian Sir Robert Cotton (1571–1631), whose library of Anglo-Saxon manuscripts was the finest in existence. In 1700 this collection was given to the English nation.

About thirty years later, Cotton's famous library was moved to what were thought to be safer quarters, which promptly burned down. About one hundred of the precious manuscript volumes were destroyed and half the rest seriously damaged. Amidst the ineffectual fire-fighting, library trustees and others managed to rescue almost half the collection, including the *Beowulf* codex, which was merely charred at the margins. The charring, however, was enough to make the already dry parchment begin to flake away.

Some fifty years later, an Icelandic scholar, G. J. Thorkelin, went to London in search of historical material about the Danes in England. Among other things, he examined the *Beowulf* manuscript and became so enthusiastic that he had two complete transcripts made. In 1807, when, after twenty years' work, Thorkelin was ready to publish a scholarly edition of the poem, Napoleon occupied Copenhagen, and the British Navy, in retaliation, bombarded the city. Thorkelin's home and manuscripts went up in flames. Fortunately, however, his two transcripts survived.

Forced to start all over again, Thorkelin then retraced his steps, re-edited the manuscript, and finally, in 1815, brought out the first printed edition of *Beowulf*.

[1] A collection of manuscripts bound into a book.

READING LIST FOR
THE ANGLO–SAXON PERIOD

Bryher, Winifred, *Roman Wall*
——, *Ruan*
Costain, Thomas B., *The Conquerors*
Durant, G. M., *Journey into Roman Britain*
Hosford, Dorothy, *By His Own Might: The Battles of Beowulf*
Kingsley, Charles, *Hereward, the Wake*
Kipling, Rudyard, *Puck of Pook's Hill* and *Rewards and Fairies* (sequel)
Longfellow, Henry W., "The Discoverer of the North Cape" (in his *Collected Poems*)
Muntz, Hope, *The Golden Warrior*
Tennyson, Alfred, "The Battle of Brunnanburh" (in his *Collected Poems*)
Trease, Geoffrey, *Escape to King Alfred*

FOR LISTENING

A selection from *Beowulf*, lines 90–138, has been recorded and is available on *Many Voices 6A*.

ANGLO–SAXON FRONTISPIECE: The illustrations opposite the unit openings in this book are designed to suggest, with facsimiles and original articles, the background of each literary period. Pictured on page 24 are (1) a manuscript page from the eighth-century *Book of Kells;* (2) a cloak, shield, and helmet which are part of a costume worn in the Norse fire festival held in the Shetland Islands each January; (3) a model of a Viking ship; and (4) three pieces of Anglo-Saxon jewelry.

THE GROWTH OF
THE ENGLISH LANGUAGE

The Old English Period

Ð A þæſ onbuһᵹum beopulf ſcyldınᵹa leo
leob cyninᵹ lonᵹe þнаᵹe рolcum ᵹeррсо
ᵹe рædeⱦ ellop hpɛaⱦ aldoⱦ oрɛaⱦ de
ob þ hım ɛⱦc onpoc hɛah hɛalⱦ dɛne hɛolb
þⱦⱥ dⱦ lⱦ dе ᵹamol 15uð pⱦoup ᵹlæde ſcyl
dınᵹaſ ðam рⱦeopⱦ beaⱦⱦ роⱦ ᵹɛumed ın
poⱦold pocⱦm peopⱦ ða ⱦlⱦ þa hɛopo ᵹaⱦ
hⱦoð ᵹaⱦ ⱦhalᵹa ⱦl hyⱦde ıc þelan cⱦe
hɛado ſulⱦⱦⱦⱦaſ hɛalſ ᵹebeðða þaⱦɛ hⱦoð
ᵹaⱦe hɛⱦe ſⱦed ᵹyⱦⱦ рⱦⱦ рⱦⱦ mynd þ

From the *Beowulf* manuscript

Today English is more widely spoken than any other language in the world; in the future, English may become the universal language. As you progress through the centuries in this book you will see how our language, which had its beginnings more than fifteen hundred years ago, has gradually changed. The language we use today no more resembles its original form than a grown man resembles the baby he once was.

A page of Old English in the early runic alphabet would be a complete mystery to you. Later forms of writing, like that in the sample from the *Beowulf* manuscript reproduced above, still look much like a foreign alphabet. Even printing it in our present alphabet would not clarify its meaning. But scholars, by long study of language forms and histories, have been able to translate the Old English writings so that we can recognize the roots of present-day English in those old manuscripts. Look, for example, at this passage from *Beowulf* describing Grendel's gloomy abode:

OLD ENGLISH

(*Printed in the modern alphabet.*)

Hie dygel lond
Warigeath, wulf-hleothu, windige naes-
sas,
Frecne fen-gelad, thaer fyrgen-stream
Under naessa genipu, nither gewiteth
Flod under foldan.

LITERAL TRANSLATION

(*Language similarities become evident.*)

They [a] darksome land
Ward, wolf-cliff, windy nesses.
Frightful fen-paths, where mountain-
stream
Under nesse's mists nether wanders,
A flood under earth.

FREE POETIC TRANSLATION

(*The lines take on meaning and present
a vivid picture.*)

Lonely and waste is the land they in-
habit,
Wolf-cliffs wild and windy headlands,
Ledges of mist, where mountain torrents
Downward plunge to dark abysses
And flow unseen.

While many other languages have contributed extensively to present-day English, the *basic* words are derived chiefly from the speech of the Anglo-Saxons.

It is not only in vocabulary that this kinship with Old English is shown, but also in the very structure of sentences. If you have studied the elaborate declension of nouns and conjugation of verbs in Latin, you realize how much simpler English word forms are. We have few changes within a word itself to express case, number, and tense, and show most relationships by little words such as *to, for, of, have, had, will,* and many others. Old English was originally more highly inflected than modern English is, for there was always a tendency in England to simplify grammar, to shorten words, and to drop forms that seemed unnecessary. Some dialects of Old English were more highly inflected than others. It was usually the plainer, easier dialect that survived in speech and consequently influenced the later development of the language. A good example of this long process of simplification is the changes in the verb *had.*

OLD ENGLISH	MIDDLE ENGLISH	MODERN ENGLISH
Singular	*Singular*	*Singular*
1. haefde	1. hadde	1. had
2. haefdes(t)	2. haddest	2. had
3. haefde	3. hadde	3. had
Plural 1, 2, 3	*Plural* 1, 2, 3	*Plural* 1, 2, 3
haefdon	hadde(n)	had

Some of the irregular forms of our present language, such as the plural *en* in *oxen* and *children,* are survivals from Old English inflections.

Contributions from other languages were few during the Anglo-Saxon period. They came chiefly from two sources. The Danes, who finally occupied the northeast half of England, supplied many words, especially sea terms and place names. The names of about six hundred towns in the east of England still end in *by,* Danish for *town,* and the same word is preserved in *bylaw.* Other common words from Danish are *fellow, skin, happy, ugly,* and *knife.* To the Danes we also owe the tendency to put a strong accent on the first syllable and slur over the vowels in following syllables. This characteristic of English speech is called "the law of recessive accent." Words later adopted from a tongue with quite a different accent system, like French, often became Angli-

cized by a shift in accent as well as by changes in sound. The French word *quantité,* equivalent to the English *quantity,* is a case in point.

The second foreign influence, that of Latin, accompanied Christianity to England, naturally introducing many church terms. In a few centers of learning, such as King Alfred's court, Latin also played a part, but the widespread adoption of Latin words into English came during later periods. Perhaps the most significant change in these early centuries was the gradual substitution of the Latin alphabet for the crude Germanic runes, which are still to be found in ancient inscriptions recently excavated.

For six hundred years the English language was as narrow and isolated as a river near its source. Later chapters will show how it gradually widened as it received new tributaries, until it eventually enriched the whole world.

The use of Latin in Anglo-Saxon times is evident from this detail of a map of the world dating from the tenth century. Latin was the only language used in the church schools and universities of this period. On the map north is to the left, and the British Isles are in the lower left-hand corner.

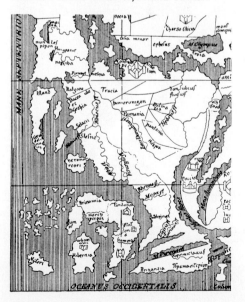

THE
MEDIEVAL
PERIOD

1066 – 1485

In 1066, at the Battle of Hastings, Harold, the Saxon king of England, was defeated by William "the Conqueror," Duke of Normandy, who invaded England to support his claim that he had been promised the English throne. An efficient and ruthless soldier, with a number of experienced soldiers of fortune among his followers, William was soon able to conquer the whole country. Once it was pacified he ordered that a complete description of the land be prepared for him. This became the famous Domesday Book, in which are mentioned many English towns and villages we know today.

NORMAN ENGLAND

William's Normans now became the great landowners. They built castles that were both their homes and their fortresses, and as is usual with successful conquerors, they became the new ruling class, the aristocracy. (So from this time on, "Norman descent" and "Norman blood" have suggested the highest English aristocracy.) The gulf between the Norman dukes, earls, and counts and the Saxon peasants who worked for them as serfs was all the greater because for a long time they did not speak the same language, the nobles speaking Norman-French and the peasants Anglo-Saxon.

Oddly enough, in England today we still recognize this difference between noble and peasant. We follow the Anglo-Saxon peasants in calling the animals they had to look after in the fields "sheep" and "pigs." We follow their

◀ The items in the frontispiece are identified on page 101.

Norman masters, who were interested in the animals chiefly in terms of the kitchen and dining hall, in referring to them not as living creatures but as something to be eaten: "mutton" and "pork." So as we speak English today, we are following both Norman and Saxon usage.

If you have ever read Scott's *Ivanhoe,* you will remember that even long after the reign of William the Conqueror, there were not only Anglo-Saxon-speaking peasants but even some Saxon nobles who still used the language of their ancestors. The fact that Norman-French and Anglo-Saxon existed so long together before finally blending into the English language is of great importance in the development of our literature. It made our language a literary instrument of unusual complexity and power. Even now, if we want to make a simple statement, we favor words which are Anglo-Saxon in origin. If, on the other hand, we want to suggest more dignity and pomp, we use words that first belonged to the Norman conquerors.

GROWTH OF THE ENGLISH NATION

It took about two hundred and fifty years for Normans and Saxons to merge their individual identities into one English nation. Unfortunately for both England and France, the English monarchy never voluntarily relinquished its hold on its French possessions. As a result there were endless stupid and costly wars in France. These wars, known collectively as The Hundred Years' War (1337–1453), were generally won, from the time of Edward I onward, by the terrible longbows of the English infantry. These six-foot bows, with yard-long arrows capable of penetrating armor, were the most formidable weapons known to Western Europe before gunpowder was used, and by that time the Middle Ages were at an end.

Because the English kings and barons, unlike those in other countries, depended upon their bowmen, who came from the common folk, these folk showed an independent spirit not to be found in peasants abroad. But before the triumph of the bowmen in the Hundred Years' War, the power of the king and his officers had been challenged and checked. As early as 1215, the barons compelled King John, a bad ruler and a vicious man, to sign the famous Magna Charta. This was a very elaborate charter of rights and privileges that concerned chiefly the barons themselves, although some of its many clauses did apply to other classes of men. The Magna Charta did not in fact include many supremely important legal rights — for example, trial by jury, or the principle of *habeas corpus,* which prevents men from being kept in prison without being charged and tried — that lawyers and historians later assumed it did include. Nevertheless, it was rightly regarded as the great symbolic document of English common law. The term common law refers to law which is common to the whole country and all its people, in contrast to kinds of law applying only to certain classes of persons. It developed as society itself developed, but always depended not so much on legal codes as on usages and precedents — that is, on what good judges had already decided and laid down as law. Common law was taken by the Pilgrim fathers to America, where it is now sound American law. When a great American lawyer, Justice Oliver Wendell Holmes, said "the life of the law is not logic but experience," he probably came as near to defining the old English common law as it is possible to do in a few words.

Living on an island, these increasingly independent Englishmen were conscious of themselves as a nation earlier than most European peoples. They thought of themselves as Englishmen. This sense of nationality was unusual in the Middle Ages, when nationalism, as we know it now, had not yet come into existence. To understand this, we have also to understand how and why this period differed from later times.

MEDIEVAL CIVILIZATION

Roughly from the eleventh to the fifteenth century, Western Europe achieved a complete civilization and a complete culture of its own. Simply because so many things we use now had not been invented then, we must not make the mistake of underrating this civilization. In some ways the medieval age was superior to our own. To begin with, medieval society had a secure foundation and framework of religion. It was not so much a number of different countries, made up of people believing very different things, as "Christendom," where all people were the sons and daughters of the Church and on their way to Hell, Purgatory, or Heaven. Fierce and powerful rulers could sometimes be seen walking barefoot to do penance for their sins. Everybody, from the high-

British Information

Famous Salisbury Cathedral was completed in the mid-thirteenth century.

Photo Researchers, Inc.

Religious dramas were a prominent feature of medieval civilization. Here is a modern re-enactment of a medieval miracle play at York, where a well-known cycle of religious plays was presented in the fifteenth and sixteenth centuries.

est to the lowest, was conscious of being on trial here on earth. Of course people misbehaved then just as they did before this time and have done since, but then they knew that they were misbehaving and that they were miserable sinners. This world to them was like a transparency through which gleamed the fire of Hell or the bright blue of Heaven.

We must not be deceived by medieval pictures, which seem to us either romantically picturesque or quaint and absurd. Actually, society in the Middle Ages was elaborately organized, left little to chance, and in many ways was far more logical, consistent, and soundly based, than our society is. The Church was responsible for the spiritual life of all Christendom. It linked together all the kingdoms, dukedoms, principalities, and free cities. In Latin it had a language common to all. Its chief scholars and philosophers (like the famous Thomas Aquinas) moved freely — far more freely than such men do now — from university to university and from country to country. Its abbeys and monasteries were not only the chief centers of learning and the arts in the period before the establishment of the universities of Oxford and Cambridge in the thirteenth century, but, as economically self-sufficient units, were also often immense farms, places where all manner of handicrafts were taught and practiced. In addition, monasteries also served as hotels for travelers; it was also part of their duty to feed the poor, and after Henry VIII closed the monasteries (1536–39), the poor suffered, and various measures had to be devised to help them. We must remember too that the great Gothic cathedrals, which are among the most impressive and noblest creations of men's minds and hands, were built during this period. England has some of the finest specimens of these astonishing buildings, which are poetry and music in stone.

BRITAIN
1066-1485

SCOTLAND

1 Bannockburn
Dunfermline
Glasgow Edinburgh
2 Lindisfarne
3 Hadrian's Wall
Jarrow
4
Whitby
5
Lancaster
6 York
Hull
IRELAND
ENGLAND
7 Chester
SHERWOOD FOREST
8 Ashby
Bosworth Field
Ely
Cambridge
WALES
Harwich
Oxford
9 Westminster
10 Eton
London
15 Bath
11 Windsor
Southwark
12 Runnymede
Canterbury
Stonehenge
London–Canterbury pilgrimage route
16
14 Winchester
13 Hastings
Tintagel 17 KING ARTHUR COUNTRY

1 Battle site where Robert the Bruce defeated the English (1314). 2 Site of well-known Anglo-Saxon monastery. 3 Built by Romans (123 A.D.) against raids by Picts and Scots. 4 Seventh-century monastery where the Venerable Bede lived. 5 The Anglo-Saxon poet Caedmon was a monk here. 6 A Celtic, Roman, Angle, Danish, and Norman settlement. 7 Settled successively by Romans, British, Saxons, Danes; Chester cycle of mystery plays, 13th–16th centuries. 8 Site of famous tournaments. 9 Caxton's press founded here (1477). 10 Eton College; founded 1440. 11 Chief residence of English kings since time of William the Conqueror. 12 Magna Charta signed here (1215). 13 Scene of last invasion of England (1066) when Normans under William the Conqueror defeated King Harold and Saxons. 14 Seat of government of Alfred the Great and early center of learning. 15 Roman settlement and hot springs. 16 Prehistoric circle of stones dating back to Bronze Age. 17 Picturesque ruins on the coast of Cornwall; the supposed birthplace of King Arthur.

53

MEDIEVAL SOCIETY

Existing alongside the Church was the complicated feudal system. Nobody owned land independently but only as a vassal of an overlord, who in turn owed allegiance either to some great noble or to the king himself. The system was really an elaborate chain of loyalties, with rent, so to speak, paid not only in money and products but also in military service. As the towns grew, the craftsmen and tradesmen organized themselves into guilds, which decided wages and prices, insisted upon a good standard of material and workmanship, and regulated the terms of apprenticeship for the particular craft or trade. Indeed not only apprenticeship but almost everything in medieval society, including the clothes a man wore, was regulated and carefully ordered.

Everybody knew what his place was in this society. Men of humble birth might be promoted to positions of great power and influence only in the Church. If we suddenly found ourselves members of such a society we should undoubtedly feel that much of our personal freedom had been taken away from us. Because it was essentially a society with a secure religious foundation, there were, however, some compensations. For example, as we see in Chaucer, people belonging to very different classes could quite happily go on a pilgrimage together, in a way that would have been impossible in later periods, including our own. Men had rights as well as particular obligations and responsibilities of their rank or class. There was less downright brutal tyranny than there was in the centuries that followed the Middle Ages, or indeed in some of the totalitarian systems our world has known during the past forty years. There were some tyrants, of course, but a Hitler or a Stalin would have been impossible, for he would have been successfully threatened with the wrath of God.

MEDIEVAL LIFE

Medieval life was austere in many ways: no modern comforts and conveniences; not much choice in dress; travel was difficult and often dangerous; and food (lacking sugar, potatoes, among many other things) even for the wealthy offered little variety. Most foodstuffs could not be preserved, sometimes a lot had to be eaten quickly — and this explains the special feast times — while at other times ordinary folk might find themselves on a very poor diet. (But there was so much salmon in England that the parents of apprentices, who were fed by their masters, stipulated that the boys should not be given salmon more than a certain number of times a week.) But again, there were other compensations.

Because there was no industry, no enormous factories pouring out smoke, no railroads, no vast dark cities, both in its towns and its countryside the Middle Ages were bright and full of color, a perpetual feast for the eye. A great noble would have a crowd of retainers dressed in gay livery. Costumes were often fantastically varied and rich, and a typical medieval throng would look to us like a splendid ballet. Religious festivals provided plenty of holidays, when the people enjoyed themselves, singing and dancing and playing games, watching the archers compete for prizes or the knights in their magnificent tournaments.

During the High Middle Ages, say from the twelfth to the middle of the fourteenth century, the English of all classes lived well on the whole. In 1348–49, however, came the Black Death, the terrible plague which cut the population almost in half, and after that the ruinous Wars of the Roses. These civil wars (1445–85) arose out of a dispute between the House of York, whose emblem was a white rose, and the House of Lancaster, represented by a red rose, over succession to the throne. After the death of Richard III at the Battle of Bosworth Field, the quarrel was finally resolved by the uniting of the two families through marriage and the founding of the Tudor line. By the middle of the fifteenth century, when the fanatical feud between the rival houses of York and Lancaster began, the social scene had changed for the worse. By 1485 when Henry VII, the first Tudor, came to the throne, the real Middle Ages had vanished.

THE CRUSADES

Something must be said about the Crusades. Their history makes mournful reading because each Crusade began in high hope, in a genuine desire to rescue Jerusalem from the Turks, and ended squalidly in raiding, looting, and a tangle of power politics. But in the end Western Europe gained much from these expeditions to the Near East, for during those years Arab culture (especially in mathematics and medicine) reached its highest level. Commercial and intellectual horizons were greatly broadened, and both knowledge and all manner of refinements in living were brought back from the East. It was the Crusades too, even though they ended so badly, that encouraged the ideal of true knightly behavior known as *chivalry*.

CHIVALRY AND THE MEDIEVAL ROMANCE

Today we use the term *chivalrous* to describe the conduct of well-mannered and sensitive men toward women, but the medieval ideal of chivalry, though it included the relations between the sexes, went far beyond this. It sought, with

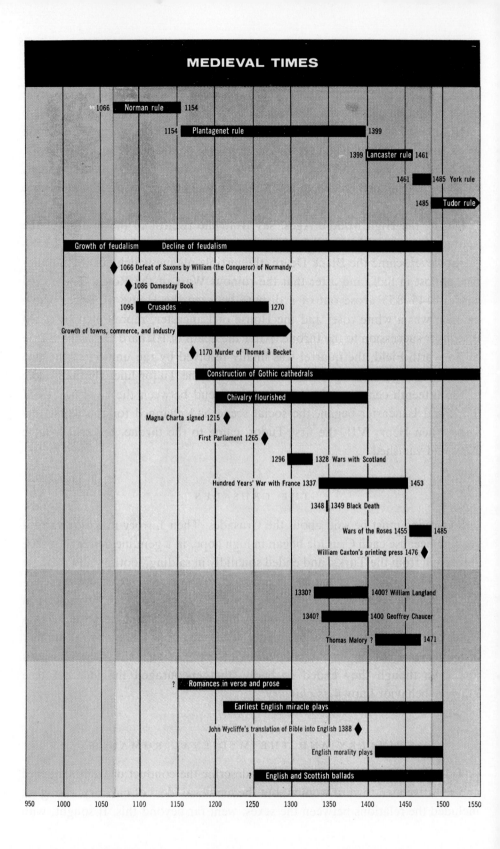

MEDIEVAL TIMES

1066 Norman rule 1154

1154 Plantagenet rule 1399

1399 Lancaster rule 1461

1461 1485 York rule

1485 Tudor rule

Growth of feudalism Decline of feudalism

◆ 1066 Defeat of Saxons by William (the Conqueror) of Normandy

◆ 1086 Domesday Book

1096 Crusades 1270

Growth of towns, commerce, and industry

◆ 1170 Murder of Thomas à Becket

Construction of Gothic cathedrals

Chivalry flourished

Magna Charta signed 1215 ◆

First Parliament 1265 ◆

1296 1328 Wars with Scotland

Hundred Years' War with France 1337 1453

1348 1349 Black Death

Wars of the Roses 1455 1485

William Caxton's printing press 1476 ◆

1330? 1400? William Langland

1340? 1400 Geoffrey Chaucer

Thomas Malory ? 1471

? Romances in verse and prose

Earliest English miracle plays

John Wycliffe's translation of Bible into English 1388 ◆

English morality plays

? English and Scottish ballads

950 1000 1050 1100 1150 1200 1250 1300 1350 1400 1450 1500 1550

Richard I (1189–99), who preferred military life to statecraft, left government affairs to his ministers and spent most of his ten-year reign outside of England. Because of his great valor and his military exploits during the third crusade, he was called Richard "the Lion-Hearted." This statue of him stands outside the Houses of Parliament on the banks of The Thames in London.

Photo Researchers, Inc.

the aid of the Church, to make the knightly warrior as devout and tenderhearted off the battlefield as he was bold and fearless on it. The bloodstained ferocious history of the Crusades suggests that chivalry was an ideal rather than an actual code of conduct. It was, however, of considerable importance in literature, where, as noble ladies insisted upon more and more songs and tales to please their taste, it was joined to the companion idea of *romance*. In the famous legends of King Arthur and his Knights of the Round Table, collected and retold by Malory in his *Morte d'Arthur, chivalry* and *romance* play equal parts.

Later in history, centuries further on, we shall come to a period in English literature known as the Romantic Age, but although, as we shall see, these later Romantics often dealt with medieval themes and settings, it is a mistake to suppose that the literature of the Romantic Age and the literature of *romance* belonging to the later Middle Ages are the same kind of thing. Medieval *romance* largely consisted of tales of chivalry to which were added a love interest (to please the ladies) and all sorts of wonders and marvels — faerie enchantments, giants, dragons, wizards, and sorceresses. The humbler folk of the Middle Ages were ready to believe anything of this kind; the aristocrats and the clergy, though better informed, still existed in a world largely unexplored and not mapped, a little world, poised between Heaven and Hell, in which the natural merged into the marvelous and the supernatural.

GEOFFREY CHAUCER

Nevertheless, a master poet and storyteller like Geoffrey Chaucer (1340?–1400), the first truly great name in English literature, might be ready to traffic in the fashionable romance while obviously being quite skeptical about it and as sharply realistic as a modern novelist in much of his work. Because Chaucer is so far removed from us and his manner and language, especially in the original Middle English, seem so quaint, we can easily underestimate this astonishing man. He was not only a great poet and a fine storyteller but also the first of the poker-faced humorists. There is just a twinkle in his eye as he gravely, often ironically, adds one descriptive stroke to another, never failing, if we are alert, to make his points. This demure little man, whether moving from one royal court to another as a diplomat or lounging about an innyard among people, missed nothing. And his greatest work belongs not to *romance* but to poetic and humorous realism.

WILLIAM LANGLAND

One of the people, their spokesman, was the rather mysterious William Langland (1330?–1400?), who wrote *The Vision of Piers the Plowman*. This is the first of the innumerable protests that English writers, through age after age, were to make on behalf of the common people. Langland belongs to the time when the true medieval system, the society completely contained by religion, was breaking down, allowing many abuses that this writer did not hesitate to denounce.

FOLK POETRY AND THE BALLAD

From the people, too, came ballads, not written down but recited and sung in innumerable alehouses and at thousands of firesides. This folk poetry, for that is exactly what these ballads were, existed for hundreds of years, and it was not until the middle of the eighteenth century that they were carefully collected and printed. Through the German poet Herder, who had a passion for folk poetry, these English and Scotch ballads came to influence the whole German Romantic movement and then, later, our own Romantic poets. But most of them originally belong, as their themes and settings suggest, to the later Middle Ages, to whose unknown wandering minstrels many future generations of poets were enormously indebted.

MIRACLE AND MORALITY PLAYS

The next age, the Elizabethan, shows us popular drama raised to a tremendous height, but the origins of this popular drama are to be found in these Middle Ages. During the frequent holiday times celebrating various religious festivals, the trade guilds entertained the crowd with what are called miracle plays, rough dramatizations of Biblical stories performed on large wagons or on platforms erected in market places or innyards. As a rule in these miracle plays, probably because they had to amuse a holiday crowd, the wicked characters, including the devil himself, were played as comic characters, thereby creating a tradition of popular comedy that the Elizabethan dramatists followed. It was all very rough-and-ready, but in these humble performances there was already stirring the glorious theater of Shakespeare.

Toward the end of the Middle Ages in England, during the fifteenth century, a dark troubled time when unbelief was challenged by a gloomy fanaticism, the miracle plays gave place to the morality plays. These plays, although presented in the same way as the miracle plays, tended to be more elaborate and sophisticated and were dramatic allegories in which characters representing various virtues and vices confronted one another. The most famous of the morality plays, and one still often performed in many countries, was *Everyman,* which was not English in origin, though a thoroughly English adaptation of it soon became very popular. Even during the present century this play has been performed in the English theater fairly often.

Though there was no printing until the second half of the fifteenth century, when the Middle Ages had come to an end, English literature owes a great deal to this period, in which so many forms had their origin. The High or Gothic Middle Ages, best represented now by their glorious cathedrals, have always haunted the imagination of the more poetic English writers. They have had a vision of it, so bright and gaily colored, with its cavalcades of knights and squires, its green troupes of archers, its minstrels and pages and fine ladies in their castles, its monks and friars, its guilds of craftsmen, its theologians and philosophers (known as "Schoolmen") disputing at the universities, its crusaders and pilgrims and troubadours. But the real secret of the appeal of this period at its best does not lie in its romantic picturesqueness, enchanting though that may be. It comes from the fact that during these years Western Man, that restless, inventive, aggressive, troubled creature, achieved an elaborately organized way of life completely contained within a common religion. The greatest single achievement of the Middle Ages was the idea of Christendom, a kind of spiritual and cultural empire uniting men of different nationalities, but speaking many different languages and enjoying many different regional ways of life. Since this time science and invention have given us things that would have seemed to the medieval mind like so many strange miracles and the marvels of sorcerers. However, we have not yet achieved our own equivalent of Christendom, a whole society, a civilization and a common culture, united under God.

J. B. P.

EARLY ENGLISH
AND SCOTTISH BALLADS

From the common people came the ballads of early England and Scotland. Generation after generation sang them before they were, after many centuries, recorded in written form. It is impossible, therefore, to date them or to identify their original authors. As they were told and retold, the ballads changed — listeners forgot lines or improvised their own. Gradually there came to be many versions of a single story.

Unlike the literary ballads of later times, such as those by Walter Scott and Samuel Coleridge, this early poetry of the people resembles modern "popular songs." It deals with the comedies and tragedies of everyday life: quarrels among members of a family or lovers or friends, death, war, fear of the unknown, and the adventures of outlaws. Wherever the English and Scottish people went, they carried with them their old ballads. Early settlers brought them to North America; some versions are still sung in the mountain sections of the South. They have crept into our folklore, influenced the work of our writers and musicians, and become a part of our heritage.

The old ballads use common devices in telling a story. Most often the ballad is simple and direct — it usually stresses a single incident and plunges into the narrative with little or no introduction of background. The narrative is often hinted at rather than told in detail. You must do considerable guessing as to what happens between stanzas or who is the speaker of certain stanzas. The story is developed largely through dialogue. Often standard speeches have a definite meaning, as if they were part of a code. For example, calling upon his mother to "make the bed soft and narrow" means that the speaker is dying.

As you read the ballads, you will easily recognize that they are meant to be sung. There is much use of refrains, as when the last line of a stanza is repeated. This suggests the way in which ballads were often sung or recited to a group, with a single voice carrying the main part of the stanza, and everyone chiming in on the chorus. Perhaps in old times the group danced to these rhythms, for the French word from which *ballad* comes once meant *to dance*.

Get Up and Bar the Door

Most medieval ballads are concerned with a tragic theme in which love and death play important roles. But there are a few that strike a lighter note. Usually these humorous poems tell of some amusing conflict between a husband and wife in which the man is the victor. In the following ballad the tables are turned, and the wife wins the argument.

It fell about the Martinmas time,°
　And a gay time it was then,
When our goodwife got puddings to make,
　She's boild them in the pan.

The wind sae cauld blew south and north,　5
　And blew into the floor;
Quoth our goodman to our goodwife,
　"Gae out and bar the door."

"My hand is in my hussyfskap,°
　Goodman, as ye may see;　10
An it shoud nae be barrd this hundred year,
　It's no be barrd for me."°

1. *Martinmas time:* November 11.

9. *hussyfskap:* household duties. 11–12. "The door will not be barred in a hundred years if I have to bar it."

60

They made a paction° tween them twa,
  They made it firm and sure,
That the first word whaeer° shoud
    speak,   15
  Shoud rise and bar the door.

Then by there came two gentlemen,
  At twelve o'clock at night,
And they could neither see house nor
    hall,
Nor coal nor candlelight.   20

"Now whether is this a rich man's house,
  Or whether it is a poor?"°
But neer a word wad ane o' them° speak,
  For barring of the door.

And first they° ate the white puddings,
  And then they ate the black;   26
Tho muckle° thought the goodwife to
    hersel,
  Yet neer a word she spake.

Then said the one unto the other,
  "Here, man, tak ye my knife;   30
Do ye tak aff the auld man's beard,
  And I'll kiss the goodwife."

"But there's nae water° in the house,
  And what shall we do than?"
"What ails ye at the pudding broo,° 35
  That boils into° the pan?"

O up then started our goodman,
  An angry man was he:
"Will ye kiss my wife before my een,
  And scad° me wi pudding bree?"°

Then up and started our goodwife, 41
  Gied three skips on the floor:
"Goodman, you've spoken the foremost
    word;
  Get up and bar the door."

13. *paction:* agreement. 15. *whaeer:* whoever.
21–22. The strangers ask this question.
23. *them:* the man and his wife. 25. *they:* the
strangers. 27. *muckle:* much. 33. *water:* probably to scald the beard in order to scrape it off.
35. "What's the matter with using the pudding
water?" 36. *into:* in. 40. *scad:* scald; *bree:* broth,
liquor.

Bonny Barbara Allan

There are many versions of this tragic love
ballad in England, Scotland, and America;
ninety-two different versions have been
discovered in Virginia alone. The selection
given here is one of the oldest versions, and
it is probably as near to the original Scottish story as any that can be found. One of
the interesting characteristics of these old
ballads is that their telling and retelling has
caused details to be changed. For instance,
in "Bonny Barbara Allan" the hero's name
has become in various versions Sir James
of the Grave, Jemmy Grove, and John
Green. Sometimes Barbara dies repentant
of her cruelty; sometimes she maintains
her hurt pride and scorn to the end. The
last two stanzas printed here originally belonged to another love ballad but were
grafted onto this one. This little tragedy
has many musical settings.

It was in and about the Martinmas time,
  When the green leaves were a-falling,
That Sir John Graeme, in the West
    Country,
  Fell in love with Barbara Allan.   4

He sent his men down through the town
  To the place where she was dwelling:
"O haste and come to my master dear,
  Gin° ye be Barbara Allan."

8. *Gin:* if.

O hooly, hooly° rose she up,
   To the place where he was lying,   10
And when she drew the curtain by,
   "Young man, I think you're dying."

"O it's I'm sick, and very, very sick,
   And it's a' for Barbara Allan";
"O the better for me ye's never be,   15
   Though your heart's blood were a-
      spilling.

"O dinna ye mind,° young man," said
   she,
"When the red wine ye were fillin',
That ye made the healths gae round and
   round,
   And slighted Barbara Allan?"   20

He turned his face unto the wall,
   And death was with him dealing;
"Adieu, adieu, my dear friends all,
   And be kind to Barbara Allan."

And slowly, slowly raise she up,   25
   And slowly, slowly left him,
And, sighing, said she could not stay,
   Since death of life had reft him.

She had not gane a mile but twa,°   29
   When she heard the dead-bell ringing,
And every jow° that the dead-bell geid,°
   It cried, "Woe to Barbara Allan!"

"O mother, mother, make my bed!
   O make it saft and narrow!
Since my love died for me today,   35
   I'll die for him tomorrow."

They buried her in the old churchyard,
   And Sir John's grave was nigh her.
And from his heart grew a red, red rose,
   And from her heart a brier.   40

They grew to the top o' the old church
   wall,
   Till they could grow no higher,
Until they tied a true love's knot —
   The red rose and the brier.

9. *hooly:* slowly. 17. *dinna ye mind:* don't you remember. 29. *not gane a mile but twa:* gone only two miles. 31. *jow:* stroke; *geid:* gave.

Sir Patrick Spens

Good old Sir Patrick Spens, who obeyed orders and braved the ocean at the stormiest, most dangerous time of year, was a man who would obviously appeal to the people of the rugged north.

It is not clear whether Sir Patrick is an actual historical figure, for he is not mentioned in any of the documents of the time. In some versions of this ballad, however, there are references to Norwegian lords; and it is known that in the thirteenth century a group of Norwegians did come to Scotland to escort home their king, Eric, and his bride, Margaret, daughter of Alexander III of Scotland. So there is perhaps some historical background for the ballad.

The king sits in Dumferling° toune,
   Drinking the blude-reid wine:
"O whar will I get a skilly° skipper,
   To sail this new schip of mine?"

O up and spak an eldern knicht,°   5
   Sat at the kings richt kne:
"Sir Patrick Spens is the best sailor,
   That ever sailed the se."

The king has written a braid° letter,
   And sealed it wi his hand,   10
And sent it to Sir Patrick Spens,
   Was walking on the strand.

The first line that Sir Patrick red,
   A loud lauch lauched he;
The next line that Sir Patrick red,   15
   The teir blinded his ee.°

"O wha is this has don this deid,
   And told the king o' me,
To send us out at this time o' the yeir,
   To sail upon the se!   20

"Mak ready, mak ready, my mirry men
   all,
   Our guid schip sails the morne."

1. *Dumferling* (dŭm·fĕr'lĭng): a town near Edinburgh, now Dunfermline. 3. *skilly:* skillful. 5. *eldern knicht:* older knight. 9. *braid:* on a broad sheet, or long. 16. *ee:* eye.

"Now, ever alake,° my master deir,
    I feir a deadlie storme.

"I saw the new moone late yestreen,
    Wi' the auld moone in hir arme,   26
And if we gang to se, master,
    I feir we'll cum to harme."

O laith,° laith wer our guid Scots lords
    To weet their cork-heild schoone;°
Bot lang owre° a' the play was playd,
    They wat their hats aboone.°   32

O lang, lang may their ladies sit,
    Wi their fans into their hand;
Before they se Sir Patrick Spens   35
    Cum sailing to the strand.

And lang, lang may their maidens sit,
    Wi their gold kems° in their hair,
All waiting for their ain deir loves,
    For thame they'll se na mair.   40

Haf owre,° haf owre to Aberdour,°
    'Tis fiftie fadom deip,
And thair lies guid Sir Patrick Spens,
    Wi the Scots lords at his feit.

23. *alake:* alack, alas. 29. *laith:* loath, unwilling. 30. To wet their cork-heeled shoes. 31. *owre:* ere, before. 32. Their hats floated above them.

38. *kems:* combs. 41. *Haf owre:* half over, halfway; *Aberdour:* a small town near Edinburgh.

Robin Hood Rescuing Three Squires

Old ballads are the chief source of the many legends clustering about the name of Robin Hood. What historical basis there is for such a person is only guesswork. Some think he was the last Saxon to take a stand against the Norman overlords, some that he was merely a symbol of the ideal yeoman. In him the Saxons could center their wishful thinking and could express their glee at the trouble he caused the upper classes.

Robin Hood is represented as a skilled archer, an outlaw who robbed the rich and strong to help the poor and weak. A brave leader who aroused the devoted loyalty of his followers, he was a true sportsman, recognizing worth and skill even when he was defeated. Later in Elizabethan times he was represented as the disguised Earl of Huntingdon, who had forfeited his estate to the Normans. One writer carefully prepared a family tree to prove Robin's title. Maid Marian was introduced where the feminine element was needed for the May Day dances based on old ballads. Through additions such as these it was easy to supply a happy ending to Robin's life, a feature the older tales never had. In the early versions Robin Hood bleeds to death when betrayed by a false cousin. One of the best-known later treatments of Robin Hood is in Scott's *Ivanhoe*, where the merry outlaw is disguised under the name Locksley. Light opera, motion pictures, and television have also made his story familiar in our own century.

Bold Robin Hood ranging the forest all round,
    The forest all round ranged he;
O there did he meet with a gay lady,°
    She came weeping along the highway.°

3. *gay lady:* Under the circumstances, she could hardly be gay in our common meaning of the word. Originally the word referred to great excitement from any cause. 4. *highway:* As the word is found in this and other ballads in a position to rhyme with *he* or some other *ee* sound, we may infer that the North Country pronunciation of *highway* gave it more of an *ee* sound. In line 8 *die* is pronounced *dee*. This is still common Scottish pronunciation. A familiar example is the last line of "Annie Laurie" — "I'd lay me doon and dee."

In a long conversation with this lady it comes out that she is sad because her three sons are condemned to die. Robin Hood then enumerates several possible crimes, asking whether any of these are the cause of the sentence. The lady denies all of them.

"What have they done then?" said jolly Robin, 5
 "Come tell me most speedily."
"Oh! it is for killing the king's fallow deer,
 And they all are condemned to die."

"Get you home, get you home," said jolly Robin,
 "Get you home most speedily, 10
And I will unto fair Nottingham go,
 For the sake of the squires all three."

Then bold Robin Hood for Nottingham goes,
 For Nottingham town goes he,
O there did he meet with a poor beggar-man, 15
 He came creeping along the highway.

"What news, what news, thou old beggar-man?
 What news, come tell unto me":
"O there is weeping and wailing in fair Nottingham,
 For the death of the squires all three." 20

This beggar-man had a coat on his back,
 'T was neither green, yellow, nor red;
Bold Robin Hood thought 't was no disgrace
 To be in a beggar-man's stead.

"Come, pull off thy coat, you old beggar-man, 25
 And you shall put on mine;
And forty good shillings I'll give thee to boot,
 Besides brandy, good beer, ale and wine."

Bold Robin Hood then unto Nottingham came,
 Unto Nottingham town came he; 30
O there did he meet with great master sheriff
 And likewise the squires all three.

"One boon, one boon," says jolly Robin,
 "One boon I beg on my knee;
That for the deaths of these three squires, 35
 Their hangman I may be."

"Soon granted, soon granted," says great master sheriff,
 "Soon granted unto thee;
And you shall have all their gay clothing,
 Aye, and all their white money." 40

"O I will have none of their gay clothing,
　Nor none of their white money,
But I'll have three blasts on my bugle-horn,
　That their souls to heaven may flee."

Then Robin Hood mounted the gallows so high,　　　45
　Where he blew loud and shrill,
Till an hundred and ten of Robin Hood's men,
　They came marching all down the green hill.

"Whose men are all these?" says great master sheriff,
　"Whose men are they? Tell unto me."　　　50
"O they are mine, but none of them thine,
　And they're come for the squires all three."

"O take them, O take them," says great master sheriff,
　"O take them along with thee;
For there's never a man in all Nottingham　　　55
　Can do the like of thee."

BALLADS GAY AND TRAGIC

1. What does "Get Up and Bar the Door" tell you about the lives of common folk in the England of long ago? In what way is this humorous situation applicable to family life today?

2. Why do you think "Bonny Barbara Allan" is such a popular ballad? Compare the version given here with others.

3. What superstitious belief in evil omens is brought out in "Sir Patrick Spens"? What other sea poems and stories have you read in which similar beliefs are revealed? At what place in the narrative do you first realize that the poem will end tragically?

4. What characteristic of Robin Hood is emphasized in the last ballad? Does he appear in a favorable or unfavorable light? How do you know that the sheriff had encountered Robin Hood and his men before this incident? What features of this ballad are characteristic of Robin Hood's exploits?

THE POWER OF WORDS

SCOTTISH DIALECT

With the limited communication of ancient days, many different dialects developed within the small area of the British Isles. A great deal of this variety of speech persists today. One of the commonest differences between dialects and standard English is the pronunciation of internal vowels: *o* is sometimes *a* as in *lang, au* as in *cauld,* or *ae* as in *gae, sae.* There are often also consonant changes: *knicht* and *richt* for *knight* and *right,* showing that these words were pronounced gutturally as in German. Over the years this sound became silent in standard English.

LITERATURE AND THE ARTS

Robin Hood, one of the best known English legendary characters, figured not only in the early ballads but also in a popular folk dance, the morris dance, which was part of the annual celebration of May Day. Still observed in some parts of rural England, May Day was a great public holiday especially in medieval and Tudor England. On this day spring was greeted with games and dancing around the Maypole.

The stained glass window reproduced on page 64 depicts the traditional characters of the morris dance. They are, from left to right, top to bottom: franklin or gentleman of fortune, Maypole, minstrel with pipe and tabor; yeoman, hobby horse with ladle in mouth to collect money from spectators, Robin Hood; Tom Fool, Maid Marian, Friar Tuck. The window itself, called the Betley window, dates from 1490–1520 and is located at Leigh Manor, Minsterley, Shropshire.

GEOFFREY CHAUCER

1340?–1400

Chaucer is often called "the father of English literature," and to him goes the honor of being the first great English humorist and realist. To appreciate Chaucer's achievement it is necessary to understand the interrelations between his development as a man of affairs and as a man of letters. He was born in London into the home of a successful wine importer who was able to place his young son as a page in a household associated with the court of King Edward III. As he grew up in this household, Chaucer mastered medieval bookkeeping, and, what was more important, he acquired a knowledge of Latin, French, and Italian. His knowledge of these languages fitted him for civil service and diplomatic positions and also prepared him to translate and adapt literary works in all three languages.

Chaucer's position as page brought him into close contact with the royal family and their distinguished guests from overseas. He soon became a court favorite and later married one of the ladies-in-waiting to the queen. In these surroundings Chaucer enjoyed the opportunity of meeting contemporary authors, collecting numerous pieces of literature, and listening to the critical appraisal of literary works. During the reigns of Edward III, Richard II, and Henry IV, he served his country loyally as soldier, courtier, diplomat, civil administrator, and translator of books into the English language — a language which he more than any other writer helped to create.

Some of Chaucer's experiences were as dramatic as the fictional stories he wrote. In 1359, while still in his teens, he went with the English army to France and participated in the siege of Rheims. He was captured, but released after the king contributed sixteen pounds toward his ransom. Chaucer evidently never felt any personal hatred toward the French as a result of this experience. He never speaks ill of them in his writing. In subsequent years, he made several trips to France and to Italy on government affairs. He found poetic inspiration in the French poets, and the influences of the three great Italian poets — Dante, Petrarch, and Boccaccio — are reflected in the works he wrote after his last visit to Italy in 1378.

Following his journeys abroad, Chaucer became Comptroller of Customs for the Port of London and later a Member of Parliament. On later occasions he served as Justice of the Peace; as Clerk of the Works, during which time he supervised surveying, in addition to construction and building repairs in Westminster Abbey, the Tower of London, and Windsor Castle; and finally as subforester of one of the king's forests. Throughout, he enjoyed the patronage of the influential John of Gaunt and received various annuities and pensions from the crown. At his death, Chaucer's renown was well established. He lies buried in the Poets' Corner of Westminster Abbey, the first of many great English writers to find a resting place in that famous shrine. Today in the annals of English literature Chaucer's name stands second only to that of Shakespeare.

Throughout his active public life, Chaucer was an indefatigable reader and a diligent scholar. He collected about sixty volumes which he kept hidden away in a chest, for, as you can well imagine, in the days before printing such a library was a highly prized treasure. Chaucer's own works were circulated widely during his lifetime, and after his death new copies continued to appear in England and abroad. Eighty-four different manuscripts of *The Canterbury Tales* have survived. His writings were among the first to be put into print by William Caxton, England's first printer, who saluted him as "the worshipful father and first founder and embellisher of ornate eloquence in our English" and as one who "ought eternally to be remembered."

Like an apprentice, Chaucer learned his craft by reading extensively, by imitating literary masters, and by evolving his own style from them. Chaucer was indebted to the Latin classics as well as to the writings of his Italian and French contemporaries and predecessors for hints as to style and plot, but his writing transcends any borrowing. Early in his career he achieved mastery of his craft by infusing a spontaneity and an individuality in his writing. He played down formality in an age of formalism, and in his later work withdrew from mechanical literary techniques.

In *The Book of the Duchess,* probably written for John of Gaunt upon the death of his first wife in 1369, Chaucer's style is colored by the French poetry with which he was familiar. In 1387 he began his most ambitious project, a creative endeavor marked by both originality and individuality. This was *The Canterbury Tales,* our first collection of short stories in English literature. In this masterpiece Chaucer drew on his own times as a setting for his stories and thereby helped to establish a realistic pattern of English writing that was to persist for centuries.

Chaucer ties together his collection of tales by having his storytellers travel together on the then familiar London-to-Canterbury route of pilgrimage to the shrine of Thomas à Becket. This shrine, erected in 1174 in memory of Archbishop Thomas à Becket, who was martyred four years earlier at the hands of Henry II, was magnificently decorated with donations of gold, silver, and jewels, making it the most spectacular in the cathedral. It was the custom throughout Europe in those days for members of all classes to travel to religious shrines to seek miraculous cures, to gain remission of their sins, or to satisfy the wanderlust in their hearts. In England the pilgrimage to Canterbury Cathedral, site of this splendid shrine, was the most popular.

The plan of setting a group of stories within such a narrative framework was not original with Chaucer. However, as you will see, though he used an already-established narrative device, he brought to

Harvard University

this work his own special gifts as a remarkably effective storyteller. John Dryden, a critic of the seventeenth century, has this to say about Chaucer's narrative technique: "As he knew what to say, so he knows also when to leave off — a continence which is practiced by few writers." Chaucer establishes the background of his stories with dramatic and picturesque details, an important element of his style. Once he develops the conflict, he quickly brings his story to an end. It is then that the reader realizes how cleverly the various parts of the story have been fitted together.

No writer has been more successful than Chaucer in achieving both universality and realism in his treatment of setting and character. Chaucer's characters, all brought vividly to life, represent a cross section of medieval society and include three important groups: feudal, ecclesiastical, and urban. The characters who are members of the feudal system are related to the land; these are the Knight, the Squire, the Yeoman, the Franklin, the Reeve, and the Plowman. Those in the ecclesiastical order represent individuals belonging to the medieval church: the Parson, the Summoner, the Monk, the Prioress, the Friar, the Pardoner, and the Clerk. The other pilgrims are professional and mercantile laymen, who reside in the ever-increasing English towns of Chaucer's day: the Physician, the Lawyer, the Manciple, the Merchant, the Shipman, the Tradesmen, the Cook, the Clothmaker (the Wife of Bath), and the Innkeeper. Although

Chaucer does not attempt to individualize all the characters in the *Prologue* to *The Canterbury Tales,* his pilgrims become real human beings seemingly on a real pilgrimage.

In *The Canterbury Tales* Chaucer is an interpreter of human actions, a commentator on life. He superimposes the comic upon the tragic. His tone is often serious; almost half of the narrators of the tales are sober-minded pilgrims. But Chaucer also has a keen sense of humor which appeals to the modern reader. As you will see, his writing suggests a wide range of comedy. At times he views his pilgrims with comic detachment; occasionally he converts comedy into irony and sometimes satire. You will note, however, that his customary tone is that of a genial person who has sympathy for his fellow man. "Pity runneth soon in gentle heart," Chaucer says. He smiles happily and uncritically at the Reeve's tale; he is amused by the ironies of life in the Nun's Priest's tale. Only occasionally, as in his description of the Summoner, does Chaucer reflect moral indignation. The dominant tone of the *Prologue* and of the work as a whole is one of amused tolerance, despite the fact that here the poet is dealing critically with some of the current problems of his day.

Though, as we have said, *The Canterbury Tales* is our first collection of short stories in English literature, these stories are written in poetry rather than in prose, like the modern short story. Chaucer experimented with a variety of rhyming combinations of the five-beat couplet, later known as the heroic couplet. He seems to be very much at ease with this verse form, and the simplicity which his poetry suggests often conceals the care with which he practiced his art.

Chaucer's plan for *The Canterbury Tales* was an ambitious one. Each pilgrim was to tell two stories en route to Canterbury and two on the way back. The poet died, however, before the work was completed and, instead of the proposed one hundred and twenty stories, only twenty-four were written. Parts of the *Prologue,* in which the pilgrims are identified, and one of the stories, *The Nun's Priest's Tale,* are given here.

Prologue to The Canterbury Tales

Turn back the clock of time to the year 1387. Approaching Tabard Inn in the town of Southwark [1] across the river from London is a band of pilgrims. Traveling on horseback, they will have a long, slow journey to Canterbury, about sixty-five miles to the southeast. Although it is only midafternoon, the air from the Thames River is chilly. The travelers, tired and hungry, are planning to spend the night at the inn and travel on the morrow.

Inside the inn the landlord bustles about preparing for the comfort of his approaching guests. As they come across London Bridge, he hears the shrieking bagpipe played by one of the pilgrims and the jingling bells on the bridle reins of the horses. He orders firewood, food, boards for the trestles in the main room, and wooden trenchers to be placed upon them.

[1] *Southwark* (sŭth'ẽrk).

Now all is tumult and confusion as the travelers come clattering into the innyard. Stable boys shout as they rub down the horses; serving men rush to and fro with bowls so that the travelers may wash their hands. Since forks are unknown and two people generally use a trencher, or platter, between them, clean hands are doubly necessary. The cooks bring in food and place it on the boards — fish and fowl and meats cooked in garlic, onions, mustard, vinegar, and spices; bacon and pea soup; puddings and pastries; wine and Southwark ale.

After eating, the company eagerly agrees to follow the landlord's suggestion of telling stories to and from Canterbury. The travelers then pay for their food and lodging and retire. Now let Chaucer continue with the *Prologue,* which follows in a modern English version by Ruth M. Stauffer.

WHEN April showers with sweetness pierce the root
Of droughts of March, and make the buds upshoot,
And bathe the veins in sap, wherefrom the flowers
Are born to blossom in these vernal showers;
When soft west winds have breathed upon the trees,   5
And tender sprouts appear on all the leas,
And when the youthful sun has run his course
Half through the Ram° — the sign of springtime's force —
When little birds — so stirred by nature's might
They seem with open eyes to sleep all night —   10
Make melody at dawn; then folk also
On pleasant pilgrimages long to go,
And palmers° want to seek some far-off strands
And distant shrines, well known in many lands;
Especially from every county's end   15
Of England down to Canterbury they wend;
The holy blessed martyr° there they seek,
That help will give if they are sick or weak.

Befell that in that season, on a day
In Southwark at the Tabard, as I lay   20
Ready upon my pilgrimage to start
To Canterbury with a pious heart,
At night there came into that hostelry
Full nine and twenty in a company
Of sundry folk, by chance together there   25
In fellowship; and pilgrims, too, they were
That on to Canterbury meant to ride.
The rooms were spacious, and the stables wide,
And comfortable indeed we all were made.
And shortly, ere the sun his head had laid   30
To rest, I spoke with all the fellowship,
And so they let me join them on their trip;
And we made compact then to rise betimes,
And take our way there, as I've told in rimes.
But now, while still I have the time and space,   35
Ere that I farther in this story pace,
I think it only reasonable and fair
To tell you what each one was like: his air,
His rank, his bearing, what he traveled in,
And at a knight then will I first begin.   40

THE KNIGHT

A *Knight* there was, and that a worthy man,
That from the very time he first began

---

8. *Ram:* the first of the twelve signs of the zodiac. The time indicated by the passage is about
April 11. The year is 1387. 13. *palmers* (päm'ẽrz): pilgrims who had visited the Holy Land and wore
two crossed palms to indicate this. 17. *martyr:* Thomas à Becket, Archbishop of Canterbury, murdered in 1170; canonized in 1172.

To ride abroad, had loved high chivalry,
Truth, and all honor, freedom, and courtesy;
And thus he rode out in his liege lord's war 45
In Christian lands and heathen — none so far.
In fifteen mortal battles had he been —
Crusades against the Turk and Saracen;
And fought in tournaments, and won the prize;
And yet, although most worthy, he was wise, 50
And in his bearing meek as is a maid.
He never had in all his lifetime said
An ill-bred word to serf or man of might:
He was a very perfect gentle knight.

THE SQUIRE

With him there was his son, a youthful *Squire;* 55
To be a knight was now his heart's desire.
He tried to train his hair to curliness!
Of twenty years of age, he was, I guess,
And singularly quick, and very strong.
In France and Flanders he had served full long, 60
And valiant been, considering his years:
He hoped his fame would reach his lady's ears.
He wore the latest clothes: the gown, indeed,
Quite short, and all embroidered like a mead°
Of springtime flowers; the sleeves hung down his side, 65
Extremely long and very, very wide.
He played the flute or sang the livelong day.
He was as fresh as is the month of May.
A well-trained squire, one skilled in horsemanship,
He sat a horse with just the expert's grip, 70
Could ride in jousts, and make his charger prance,
Compose love songs, and draw, and write, and dance.
This lad had fallen in love; by moonlight pale
He slept no more than does the nightingale!
Courteous he was, willing and meek; and able 75
To carve before his father at the table.°

THE YEOMAN

One servant had the knight — no retinue;
For straight from war he went to pay his due
Of thanks for safe return. This servingman
Had close-cropped hair, and face of swarthy tan; 80
And he was clad in coat and hood of green;
A sheaf of peacock arrows, bright and keen,
Under his belt he carried thriftily;
And in his hand a mighty bow had he;

---

64. *mead* (mēd): meadow. 76. This line refers to the custom of the time for the son to carve his father's meat and wait upon him.

A sword and buckler° by his side were hung,   85
A hunting horn across his shoulder slung;
The baldric° was of green; and on his breast
Saint Christopher° in silver kept him blest.
A *Yeoman* was he, and a forester,
And knew the ways of woodcraft, I aver.   90

THE NUN

There was a Nun, a pleasant *Prioress*.
This lady's smile was coy, I must confess.
And she was known as Madame Eglantine.
She liked to chant the services divine;
But then, in truth, she sang straight through her nose!   95
And as a court-bred dame she liked to pose:
She spoke fair French, but with an accent queer,
For Paris she had never come anear.
Her mien was stately, and her courtesy
So overnice it strained gentility.   100
Her table manners were indeed a treat:
With dainty grace she reached to take her meat;
Her upper lip she wiped so very clean
That never was the slightest fraction seen
Of grease within the rim upon her cup;   105
She never let a morsel she took up
Drop down upon her breast; nor did she wet
Her fingers in her sauce too deep. And yet,
In spite of all her social poise and art,
She had a very, very tender heart.   110
Upon my word, this Prioress would cry
To see a mouse caught in a trap and die!
Pet dogs she had, which she herself saw fed
Upon roast beef and milk and sweetened bread:
But if one died, she wept till she was sick;   115
Or if you struck them smartly with a stick,
When they got underfoot as pets will do.
Well built and tall she was, and handsome, too:
Her eyes as gray as glass; a noble head;
Her mouth was winsome — small and soft and red.   120
Her cloak was modish, and her wimple,° note,
Was pleated carefully about her throat.
Her rosary was coral; it was strung
With green; a golden locket from it hung,
Engraved in Latin: first, the letter *A;*   125
Then followed, *Amor vincit omnia.*°

---

85. *buckler* (bŭk′lēr): a shield. 87. *baldric* (bôl′drĭk): a belt, worn over one shoulder, to support a bugle or sword. 88. *Saint Christopher:* patron saint of travelers, whose figure on a brooch or medal is believed to shield the wearer from danger. 121. *wimple* (wĭm′p'l): a covering of silk or linen material for head, neck, and chin. It is still worn by nuns, but in medieval times it was worn by all women. 126. *Amor vincit omnia:* Love conquers all things.

She was an amiable and gentle dame.
Another Nun and three priests° with her came.

THE MONK

A *Monk* rode with us on a palfrey° brown.
He wore fine boots and fur bands on his gown;   130
A bowknot held his hood, a curious jewel.
He loved to hunt. What matter if the rule°
Said monks must stay at home and labor? Faugh!
He didn't give a plucked hen for that law.
He thought that text was not worth even an oyster   135
Which says that monks must not stray out of cloister!
For all such strict old forms he just passed by!
And right he was! The world needs men, say I.
Why should a man do nought but pore o'er books,
And study all the time until he looks   140
Just like a ghost? Or in a monastery
Stay all day long, and never find life merry?
A stable full of thoroughbreds he owned;
And coursing greyhounds, swift and silver-toned.
And when he rode, men might his bridle hear   145
Jingling in a whistling wind as clear
And just as loud as do the chapel bells
In the far abbey where this fat monk dwells.

THE FRIAR

One Hubert came along, a jolly *Friar*.
He knew the taverns well in every shire: 150
The barmaids and the landlords were his friends.
He said one never seemed to gain his ends
By helping sick and poor — such vulgar scum!
They never made it worth his while to come.
To have to deal with those who beg their bread   155
Would never get you anywhere, he said.
And so he kept in touch with richer folk
And prosperous country squires. His yoke
Of penance was not harsh to men of thrift:
The sign of *true* repentance was a gift   160
Of alms and dole to humble friars, you know!
So pleasant was his *"In principio"*°
That even a poor widow with no shoe
Would give a farthing° without more ado.
Of double worsted was his semicope,°   165

---

128. *three priests:* It is supposed that "and three priests" was added by some scribe to fill out
a line left incomplete by Chaucer. Only one priest is mentioned again, and the count of "nine
and twenty" allows for only one. 129. *palfrey* (pôl′frĭ): a saddle horse. 132. *the rule:* the regulations
of the Benedictine monastic order, to which the monk probably belonged. 162. *"In principio"*
(ĭn prĭn·sĭp′ĭ·ō): "In the beginning," the opening of the Gospel of John, a favorite passage used by
begging friars. 164. *farthing:* quarter of a cent. 165. *semicope* (sĕm′ĭ·cōp): a short cape.

Handsome enough for abbot or for pope.
No threadbare cope of poverty for him!
He played the fiddle well and sang with vim.
His eyes, like stars upon a frosty night,
Would twinkle as he trilled with all his might.   170
He lisped a little when he talked or sung,
To make his English sweet upon his tongue.

THE MERCHANT

There was a *Merchant,* rich, as you'd suppose,
With well-trimmed beard, and fine imported clothes.
He watched the market and a profit made   175
When he exchanged his gold in foreign trade.
And it was his opinion, spoken free,
That England ought to guard the Northern Sea
'Twixt Harwich° and The Netherlands, and rout
The pirates, when he sent his ventures out.   180
He was a self-made man, and talked you blue
With all the business deals that he'd put through.
So pompous was he, and so shrewd, I bet
That no one guessed he really was in debt.

THE OXFORD SCHOLAR

A *Clerk* — that is, an Oxford scholar — who   185
Looked hollow to his bones, and threadbare, too,
Rode with us on a nag lean as a rake.
The youth was poor, and starved for learning's sake.
He'd rather spend his gold on books than food,
Or on gay clothes or fun, as others would.   190
Of ethics and philosophy he read,
Kept Aristotle° right beside his bed.
He seldom spoke; but what he said was clear,
And full of sense, so that you wished to hear;
Of high ideals and virtue was his speech;   195
And gladly would he learn, and gladly teach.

THE LAWYER

A famous *Lawyer* on the trip did go —
A learned man, at least he sounded so;
In jurisprudence wise; knew all the laws;
And in the best-made wills could pick out flaws.   200
He knew by heart decisions and decrees
From William° down. Codes, statutes — these
Were play to him; in litigation, skilled;

179. *Harwich* (hăr′ĭj): an important seaport on the North Sea. 192. *Aristotle* (ăr′ĭs·tŏt″l): Greek philosopher (384–322 B.C.), regarded by medieval scholars as the highest authority on all matters of learning. 202. *William:* William the Conqueror (see page 49).

With presents and with fees his chests were filled.
A busier man than he you'd find nowhere, 205
Yet he seemed busier than he was, I'd swear.

THE FRANKLIN

He brought with him a hearty *Country Squire,*
Whose jovial face shone red as any fire
Through beard as white as is a daisy. He
Enjoyed good food, loved hospitality; 210
Kept open house back home — in fact, you'd say
It snowed both meat and drink there every day!
His greatest joy was eating all the while:
Good meats, good wines, and all in hearty style;
For Epicurus'° son he seemed to be, 215
So sure good meals meant true felicity!
He kept his table standing always set
Ready to entertain whome'er he met.
He bragged of having dishes out of season.
His cook was scolded far beyond a reason 220
If anything was wrong, or dinner late!
In his own shire° he was a man of weight:
Had sat in Parliament, been judge at court;
Had held all county offices, in short.

THE GUILDSMEN

There were five members of a city guild,° 225
Who rolled in wealth because they were so skilled.
They all were dressed alike, for their attire
Must match their guild: *Upholsterer* and *Dyer,*
A *Carpenter,* a *Hatter, Weaver* — these
Had silver-mounted daggers, if you please! 230
To be an alderman, each one seemed fit,
And how their wives would have rejoiced at it!
To have a mantle carried like a queen,
Be called *"ma dame!"*° and frequently be seen
At vigils° leading all the company, 235
Would flatter any woman's vanity.

THE COOK

They had a *Cook* along, whose skill was known
In boiling chicken with the marrow bone;
The king he was of culinary art:
He knew the use of flavorings, keen and tart; 240
Could roast and bake and broil and boil and fry;

215. *Epicurus* (ĕp'ĭ·kū'rŭs): Greek philosopher (342?–270 B.C.), who taught that happiness is the goal of life. 222. *shire* (shīr): county. 225. *guild:* See page 54. 234. *"ma dame"* (mà·dàm'): French for "my lady." 235. *vigils:* The eves of some church festivals often became social gatherings where women showed off their finery.

Could make good soup, and triumphed at a pie!
It seemed a pity that upon his shin
He had a running sore, for he could win
At making rich blancmange,° and never fail   245
To judge the different grades of London ale.

THE SHIPMAN

A *Shipman* rode his horse as best he could!
Bad gales and storms at sea he had withstood:
His weather-beaten face made this quite plain.
He knew the coast from Jutland° down to Spain,   250
Or Hull° to Carthage° — dangers and the tides,
The harbors and the pilotings besides;
With many a tempest had his beard been shaken.
Full many a draft of wine he'd deftly taken
While merchant slept, and many a mother's son   255
Had walked the plank in sea fights he had won.
Smuggler and pirate both he'd been, in fine,
This hardy skipper of the *Madeline.*

THE PHYSICIAN

And various others took this pilgrimage:
A skilled *Physician,* pompous, rich, and sage;   260
Astrology he knew, and by the spell
Of stars, his patients' ailments he could tell;
And his prescriptions gave the druggist trade —
For each, brisk business for the other made!
His fad was dieting and moderate fare;   265
He did not read his Bible much, I'd swear!°
Though fine his clothes, he hoarded well the pence
That he'd collected in the pestilence;°
For gold° is used in doses, I've heard tell:
That must be why he loved his gold so well.   270

THE WIFE OF BATH

A *Wife of Bath*° did much to keep us gay
With tales of love and love charms, on the way —
A lively soul, who knew the inmost art
Of how to win a spouse and hold his heart;
For she had had five husbands in her time,   275

---

245. *blancmange* (blá·mänzh′): French for "white food"; not a dessert as today, but a concoction of minced chicken, rice, milk, sugar, and almonds. 250. *Jutland* (jŭt′lănd): peninsula on the mainland of Denmark. 251. *Hull:* a seaport in northern England; *Carthage* (kär′thĭj): a port in North Africa. 266. In medieval times, doctors, and other men interested in science, were commonly thought to be skeptical of religion. 268. *pestilence:* the Black Death, which ravaged all Europe in the fourteenth century. 269. *gold:* It was an actual medieval belief that gold dissolved in medicine was a remedy for certain ailments. 271. *Wife of Bath:* A wife was a matron, or married woman. Bath is a town in the southwest of England known for its medicinal springs.

Not counting scores of lovers in her prime!
She'd grown a little deaf, but nought she cared:
Now forth to foreign lands each year she fared,
Since fate decreed she seek out every shrine.
(Her teeth grew far apart — a certain sign   280
That she should travel far!) She'd seen Boulogne,°
And Rome, and Palestine, Spain, and Cologne.°
Abundant gold she had, for she could weave
So well, that even in Flanders,° I believe,
You could not find her match. She liked fine gear,   285
And o'er the parish wives to domineer.
She took precedence on the relic days°
In offering alms to manifest her praise.
If any dame went first, so wroth was she
That in her heart she lost all charity!   290
The towering headdress worn upon her hair
On Sunday weighed a full ten pounds I'd swear!
But now she wore a wimple and a hat
As broad as any buckler, and as flat.
The mantle round her waist did not conceal   295
Red stockings, and a spur upon each heel.
She kept the other pilgrims all in gales
Of laughter, listening to her merry tales.

THE PARSON

A kindly *Parson* took the journey too.
He was a scholar, learned, wise, and true   300
And rich in holiness though poor in gold.
A gentle priest: whenever he was told
That poor folks could not meet their tithes° that year,
He paid them up himself; for priests, it's clear,
Could be content with little, in God's way.   305
He lived Christ's gospel truly every day,
And taught his flock, and preached what Christ had said.
And even though his parish was widespread,
With farms remote, and houses far asunder,
He never stopped for rain or even for thunder;   310
But visited each home where trouble came:
The rich or poor to him were all the same.
He always went on foot, with staff in hand;
For as their minister, he took this stand:
No wonder that iron rots if gold should rust!   315
That is, a priest in whom the people trust
Must not be base, or what could you expect

---

281. *Boulogne* (bōō′lōn′): a city in northern France on the English Channel. 282. *Cologne* (kō·lōn′):
a German city on the Rhine River. 284. *Flanders* (flăn′dĕrz): old name for Belgium, which was well
known for its fine weaving. 287. *relic days:* Certain Sundays were set apart for offering gifts to
religious relics, such as the bones of dead saints (see *The Pardoner*, page 79). 303. *tithes* (tīthz):
taxes for the Church, consisting of one-tenth of the individual's yearly income or production.

Of weaker folk? The Shepherd must perfect
His life in holiness that all his sheep
May follow him, although the way is steep,   320
And win at last to heaven. Indeed, I'm sure
You could not find a minister more pure.
He was a Christian both in deed and thought;
He lived himself the Golden Rule he taught.

THE PLOWMAN

The brother of the Parson came along: 325
A *Plowman* used to work, and very strong.
A kindly, simple laboring man was he,
Living in peace and perfect charity.
With all his heart he loved God best, and then
His neighbor as himself. For poorer men   330
He'd thresh and dig and plow — work all the day
In heavy toil without expecting pay:
It was enough if Christ approve his deed.
He rode a mare, the poor man's humble steed.

THE MILLER

The *Miller,* Robin, was a thickset lout,   335
So big of bone and brawn, so broad and stout
That he was champion wrestler at the matches.
He'd even break a door right off its latches
By running at it with his burly head!
His beard, broad as a spade, was fiery red;   340
His mouth, a yawning furnace you'd suppose!
A wart with bristly hairs stood on his nose.
A clever scamp he was, with "thumb of gold"
To test the flour he ground; for when he tolled
His share of grain, he sneaked the payment thrice!   345
The jokes and tales he told were not so nice.
A drunk and vulgar rogue he proved to be.
But yet he played the bagpipe cleverly,
And to its tune he led us out of town.
A blue hood wore he, and a short white gown.   350

THE MANCIPLE

There was a *Manciple*° among the band:
He bought provisions, as I understand,
For thirty lawyers at an Inn of Court.
This steward was a canny man; in short,
Shrewd as the lawyers were, he fooled them all,   355
Got rich on fat commissions — made a haul!

---

351. *Manciple* (măn'sĭ·p'l): a servant who bought provisions for a college or an Inn of Court.
The latter was a society of lawyers and law students.

THE REEVE

The *Reeve,*° or bailiff, rode a horse called Scot.
Tall, thin, clean-shaven, and his temper hot,
He was the despot of his lord's estate,
And hounded all the tenants into hate.   360
They feared him like the plague; but yet, you see,
Farming he understood from A to Z;
For he knew by the drought and by the rain
The yielding of his seed and of his grain;
His master's sheep, his stock, his horses too,   365
His poultry, swine, and cows, this bailiff knew.
He managed all so well that he himself
Was slowly gathering in the lord's own wealth —
Contrived to lend his master craftily
What was his own and rightful property!   370
A Norfolk° man, he came from Baldeswell.°
A carpenter he'd been, so I've heard tell.

THE SUMMONER

A *Summoner* whose duties are to search,
And bring to court, offenders 'gainst the Church —
A kind of church policeman — joined us there.   375
He had a fiery face — enough to scare
The children with its blotched and pimpled skin,
Its scurfy eyebrows, and its beardless chin.
His eyes were little, and were much too narrow;
His temper quick; he peered just like a sparrow.   380
Garlic and onions were his special taste;
And when with drafts of wine his wits were braced,
He shouted Latin phrases learned in court,
And "*Questio quid juris!*"° he'd exhort.
(For like a parrot he was really dense;   385
He'd learned the words, but could not grasp the sense.)
He'd set a garland on his round bald head,
And made a buckler out of cake and bread!

THE PARDONER

The *Pardoner,*° who came along with him,
Carried a wallet° filled up to the brim   390
With pardons hot from Rome, and relics old
(At least, he said they were), and these he sold
To poor believers back in lonely towns,
And priests as stupid as the country clowns:

---

357. *Reeve* (rēv): estate manager. 371. *Norfolk* (nôr′fŭk): a county in eastern England; *Baldeswell* (bôld′ĭs·wĕl): a town in Norfolk. 384. "*Questio quid juris!*": "The question is, what is the law?" 389. *Pardoner:* a preacher who raised money for religious works by soliciting offerings to which indulgences (pardons) were attached. The granting of pardons for offerings was often abused, however, and fake pardoners were not infrequent. 390. *wallet:* a sack.

A pillowcase he called Our Lady's veil;   395
He showed a fragment of the very sail
Of Peter's boat;° a cross weighed down with stones;
And in a glass he had pig's-knuckle bones!
And yet in church he read the lesson well,
And sang the offertory like a bell: 400
He knew that when that anthem had been sung,
He then must preach, and polish up his tongue
To make the silver tinkle in the plate.
A noble churchman this, the reprobate!
His hair hung down in stringy yellow locks: 405
His priest's hood he had trussed up in his box,
For he observed the new bare-headed style.
He and the Summoner did the way beguile
By brisk duets: they sang the latest hit,
"Come hither, love, to me!" Our ears were split!   410
The Pardoner's voice was shrill as any goat;
The other sang the bass deep in his throat.

Now that I've told you shortly, in a clause,
The rank, the dress, the number, and the cause
Why these were all assembled at the inn   415
Called Tabard — near the Bell — I must begin
And tell you what we did that selfsame night,
And later of the pilgrimage I'll write.
But first I pray you of your courtesy
If they appear ill-bred, do not blame me;   420
For anyone, you know, who tells a tale
He heard another speak, should never fail
To use the selfsame words and matter too,
Or else be found a liar and untrue:
Plato° himself has said — if Greek you read —   425
The words must be the cousin to the deed.
So even if the language be not fine,
But rude or coarse, the fault is theirs not mine;
And if some questions of their rank arise
Through my poor wit, I here apologize.°   430

THE HOST

Our *Host*° gave us good cheer. He served a meal
That gratified us all, and made us feel
(Especially when we had drunk his wine)
In high good humor, genial and benign.
A handsome man this host was, I declare;   435

---

397. *Peter's boat:* St. Peter was, of course, a fisherman before he became a disciple of Christ.
425. *Plato:* a Greek philosopher (427?–347 B.C.). Chaucer could not read Greek, but he knew
Plato through Latin translations. 430. Chaucer is here apologizing for the fact that the pilgrims
do not tell their tales in order of rank, as would have been considered proper in medieval society.
431. The Host has been almost certainly identified with a real innkeeper named Harry Bailly,
who had an inn at Southwark in Chaucer's time.

A fine official he'd be anywhere;
A portly, keen-eyed man, whose speech was bold,
But such as sound experience would uphold
In common sense; a merry fellow, too;
For when the feast was ended, and he knew   440
That each of us had settled our account,
His amiability began to mount,
And in a jovial mood, he had his say:
    "Well, gentlemen, I have enjoyed your stay.
To tell the truth, I have not seen this year   445
A group so jolly as you've gathered here.
In fact I'd like to conjure up some scheme
That would amuse, and win me your esteem.
Ha! of a plan I've just this moment thought:
A good pastime — and it shall cost you naught.   450
    "You go to Canterbury. Heaven speed you!
The blissful martyr's self reward and heed you!
You mean, I'm sure, unless my memory fails,
To liven up the way by telling tales;
For certainly to ride along alone   455
In utter dumbness, silent as a stone,
Is not a bit of fun in pilgrimages.
Now by my father's soul (he's dead, these ages),
In truth I've hit upon the very thing!
Don't be afraid; it hasn't any string.   460
Just take a vote and let me know your mind."
    We did not think it worth our while to find
Objections to his friendliness, and so
Declared we all desired his plan to know.
    "Well, this it is, my lords. Suppose we say   465
That each of you tell four tales by the way,
Two as you go, and two as you return;
And then the one whose tale is best will earn
A festive supper here at Tabard Inn,
Paid by the rest. Now that's a prize to win!"   470
    We heartily agreed, and took him up.
But first we set the price at which we'd sup
On our return; you see, we thought it wise
To fix beforehand, just how much the prize
Should cost us all. And it was understood   475
That he should manage all, for well he could.
    So then we went to bed. And next we knew
The dawn had come; and all our motley crew
The busy Host assembled, like a cock
That gathers all his hens and leads the flock.   480
    Then forth we ambled at a snail-like pace
Until we reached St. Thomas' watering place;°
And here our Host pulled up his horse, and said:
    "Well, here we are. Now you have made me head;

482. *St. Thomas' watering place:* less than two miles from the Tabard Inn.

If evensong and morning song agree,°   485
You must obey the orders given by me.
Whoever is a rebel to my will,
We'll cast accounts, and make him foot the bill.
Here are the lots: who gets the shortest straw
Must be the first to speak. Now let us draw.   490
"Sir Knight," he said, "my master and my lord,
Let's see how Lady Luck will you award.
Come near," quoth he, "my lady prioress;
And you, sir clerk, don't be so modest — yes,
We'll all take turns. Here, sir, the first is yours.   495
Now, mind, the shortest cut first tale ensures."
    We drew the lots; and, as was only right,
The shortest straw of all fell to the Knight.
It was good luck, indeed, a happy choice;
It made us all applaud and much rejoice.   500
When this good man perceived that it was true,
He did not "Hem!" and "Ha!" as lesser do,
But said: "Well, since I must begin the game,
Why, welcome be the lot, in God's good name!
Now let us ride, and hark to what I say."   505
And with that word we rode along the way;
And he began a pleasant tale in rhyme;
He told it thus: "Now, once upon a time . . ."

Heere endeth the prolog of this book; and
heere bigynneth the first tale which is the Knyghtes Tale.

485. If you feel this morning as you did last night.

Parts of the Prologue

IN THE ORIGINAL MIDDLE ENGLISH

Now that you have read the *Prologue* in a modern English version, you will be curious to see the language in which Chaucer wrote. It is Middle English, the language which emerged from the mixture of Anglo-Saxon dialects and Norman French and which became the foundation of the later English speech that we use. At first glance it looks almost like a foreign language, but you will soon recognize words here and there that resemble our modern English. The pronunciation, too, will seem strange the first time you hear it and speak it. But have a try! Read the words freely and openly, enjoying their poetic qualities — musical sounds and rhythmic combinations.

    Probably the best way to learn to read Chaucerian English is to hear and imitate an experienced reader. But you can work out the pronunciations yourself quite well by using the pronunciation table on page 84. Read a few passages first to get the "feel" of the language, and then turn to this table for specific help. Practice aloud until you can read smoothly, enjoying the sense of the lines as well as the sounds.

Whan that Aprille with his shourës sootë
The droghte of March hath percëd to the rootë,
And bathëd every veyne in swich licour,
Of which vertu° engendrëd is the flour;
Whan Zephirus eek with his swetë breeth 5
Inspirëd hath in every holt and heeth
The tendrë croppës, and the yongë sonnë
Hath in the Ram his halfë cours y-ronnë,
And smalë fowlës maken melodyë,
That slepen al the night with open yë, 10
(So priketh° hem nature in hir corages°):
Than longen folk to goon on pilgrimages,
And palmers for to seken straungë strondës,
To fernë halwës,° couthe° in sondry londës;
And specially, from every shirës endë 15
Of Engelond, to Caunterbury they wendë,
The holy blisful martir for to sekë,
That hem hath holpen, whan that they were sekë.
    Bifel that, in that sesoun on a day,
In Southwerk at the Tabard as I lay 20
Redy to wenden on my pilgrimagë
To Caunterbury with ful devout coragë,
At night was come in-to that hostelryë
Wel nyne and twenty in a compaignyë,
Of sondry folk, by aventure y-fallë 25
In felawshipe, and pilgrims were they allë,
That toward Caunterbury wolden rydë;
The chambrës and the stablës weren wydë,
And wel we weren esëd attë bestë.
And shortly, whan the sonnë was to restë, 30
So hadde I spoken with hem everichon,
That I was of hir felawshipe anon,
And madë forward erly for to rysë,
To take our wey, ther as I yow devysë.
    But natheles, whyl I have tyme and spacë, 35
Er that I ferther in this talë pacë,
Me thinketh it acordaunt to resoun,
To tellë yow al the condicioun
Of ech of hem, so as it semëd me,
And whiche they weren, and of what degree;° 40
And eek in what array that they were innë;
And at a knight than wol I first beginnë. . . .

THE SQUIRE

With him ther was his sone, a yong Squyer,
A lovyer, and a lusty bachelor,
With lokkës crulle, as they were leyd in pressë.

---

4. *vertu:* power, strength. 11. *priketh:* stirs, arouses; *corages:* hearts. 14. *fernë halwës:* distant shrines; *couthe:* known. 40. *degree:* rank.

Of twenty yeer of age he was, I gessë.
Of his stature he was of evenë lengthë.°   5
And wonderly delivere,° and greet of strengthë.
And he hadde been somtyme in chivachyë°
In Flaundrës, in Artoys, and Picardyë,°
And born him wel, as of so litel spacë,
In hopë to stonden in his lady gracë.   10
Embroudëd was he, as it were a medë
Al ful of fresshë flourës, whyte and redë.
Singinge he was, or floytinge,° al the day;
He was as fresh as is the month of May.
Short was his goune, with slevës longe and wydë.   15
Wel coude he sitte on hors, and fairë ryde.
He coudë songës make and wel endytë,°
Juste° and eek daunce, and well purtreye and wrytë
So hote he lovedë, that by nightertalë°
He sleep namore than doth a nightingalë.   20
Curteys he was, lowly, and servisablë,
And carf biforn his fader at the tablë.

5. *evenë lengthë:* moderate height. 6. *delivere:* agile. 7. *chivachyë:* military expeditions. 8. *Flaundrë:* . . . *Artoys . . . Picardyë:* place names, all concerned with Edward III's war with France. 13. *floytinge:* playing the flute. 17. *endytë:* write. 18. *Juste:* engage in a joust, or single combat. 19. *nightertalë:* nighttime.

PRONUNCIATION TABLE

The exact pronunciation of Chaucerian English is a difficult and uncertain matter. Nevertheless, if you follow these rules, you will produce something very close to what Chaucer himself must have said.

VOWELS

a — always the sound *ah*. It may be prolonged as in *bathëd* (bahth·ed), line 3, and *maken* (mahken), line 9; or shortened in *at, and*. Note that *a* is never pronounced as in modern *hate* or *hat*, but always with the *ah* sound.

ai, ay, ei, ey — as in *day. Veyne,* line 3; *array,* line 41.

au, aw — as in *house. Straungë,* line 13; *Caunterbury,* line 16; *felawshipe,* line 26.

oo — usually pronounced like modern *ō*. See *sootë,* line 1; *rootë,* line 2.

e, long — as in *hate, they. Swetë* (swā-ta), line 5. A vowel doubled is always long. *Eek* (āke), line 5; *breeth* (brāth), line 5.

e, short — as in *men. Hem,* line 11; second syllable of *slepen,* line 10, and *priketh,* line 11.

Note that the final *e* — printed as *ë* — which would usually be silent in modern English, is almost always pronounced in Middle English. Its sound is like the final *a* in modern words. Thus *sootë,* line 1, is like the last two syllables of *Minnesota.*

When the final *e* precedes a vowel or *h*, it is not pronounced, as in line 2, *droghte of March.* In this text the *e* which is to be pronounced as another syllable is indicated thus: *ë*.

CONSONANTS

Most of the consonants are as in modern English. A few show foreign influence.

g — as in *get,* except in French words before *e* and *i* where it is like *zh. Corages,* line 11; *pilgrimages,* line 12 (similar to modern *garages*).

gh, ch — never silent as in modern English. Pronounced like the German *ch* in *nicht. Droghte,* line 2; *night,* line 10. In *knight,* line 42, the *k* is also pronounced as in German (k·nicht). Before a vowel or at the end of a word *ch* is pronounced as in *church.*

c and **t** are never blended with a following *i* as in modern *condition,* or *special;* but the *i* is pronounced as a separate syllable. (*C* has the sound of *s* when it comes

before *i.*) *Specially* (four syllables), line 15; *condicioun* (four syllables), line 38.

CHAUCER AND HIS PILGRIMS

1. Chaucer is a great satirist, though he is almost never malicious, bitter, or savage when he pokes fun at the foibles and weaknesses of people. Point out examples of satire in the *Prologue* that particularly amused you, or struck you as a true appraisal of human character.

2. You can find in *The Canterbury Tales* a cross section of English society of medieval times as described on page 68. Place each pilgrim under the appropriate heading: feudal system, the church, town and trades. Which of the professions represented in the *Prologue* have survived to this day? Which have ceased to exist?

3. Not only do you learn about people in Chaucer's time from the *Prologue* but also about Chaucer himself. Find passages that reveal (*a*) his genial sense of humor, (*b*) his good-natured acceptance of people, even if they are not particularly distinguished, (*c*) his appreciation of loyalty and honesty in people. Which of the characters in the *Prologue* do you think Chaucer himself most resembles? Whom does he most admire? least admire?

4. Compare a passage of fifteen or twenty lines in the original Middle English with the same lines in the modernized version. How would you describe the differences you may find in (*a*) meaning and (*b*) poetic rhythm and rhyme?

VISUALIZING CHARACTERS

Chaucer is acclaimed for his realistic portrayal of people in his own times. Now that you have finished reading the *Prologue,* try to form a mental picture of each character and a clear impression of his personality. Review the *Prologue* and notice the ways in which Chaucer portrays his characters: (1) At times he uses purely pictorial details. From these you get neither a favorable nor an unfavorable impression of character traits, just a picture. (2) His descriptions often make you smile at some human foible or frailty that is not very serious. (3) On occasion he arouses your disapproval of a serious character fault or your distaste for someone's appearance. (4) Other descriptions make you admire worthy traits of character. Find passages which best illustrate these four ways of portraying the pilgrims.

THE POWER OF WORDS

METAPHOR AND SIMILE

The terms *metaphor, figure of speech, simile,* and *figurative language* all refer to the use of words to make *comparisons* between unlike things. Metaphor is used in everyday speech constantly (the "heart of the matter," the "seat of our troubles" are metaphors, and so is "make hay while the sun shines"). In poetry, metaphor allows the writer to express himself imaginatively and colorfully. Chaucer, for example, compares the young Squire to the month of May, his embroidered gown to a meadow of flowers, and his sleeplessness to that of a nightingale.

When the comparison is expressed with *like* or *as,* it is called a *simile.* The poverty of the Oxford scholar is impressed upon us by the description of his horse as "lean as a rake." What picture of the horse do you see? Find other examples of figurative language in which Chaucer pokes fun at the characters.

CLASS ACTIVITIES

1. Select a committee to write a short radio play based on the *Prologue,* and then stage it with members of the class taking the various roles. Use a public address system or a screen to separate the actors from the class audience.

2. Form groups to study and report on medieval life. Make comparisons between modern and medieval customs and conditions of (*a*) travel, (*b*) table manners, (*c*) the practice of medicine, (*d*) commerce and manufacturing, (*e*) religious observances.

3. Prepare a talk to give in class on (*a*) Thomas à Becket, (*b*) Canterbury Cathedral and the town of Canterbury, (*c*) the French influence on Chaucer's English. Students of French will want to try the last of these topics, using several passages of the original Middle English to point out French words.

SUGGESTIONS FOR WRITING

Write a prologue of your own, based upon some "pilgrimage" of modern life such as an athletic event, a speech tournament, a district or state meeting of some club. Chaucer's *Prologue* will furnish you with numerous ideas, and so will these similar but later works: Longfellow's *Tales of a Wayside Inn,* Whittier's *The Tent on the Beach,* and John Masefield's *Reynard the Fox.* Chaucer himself may have borrowed the idea for *The Canterbury Tales* from the *Decameron,* a collection of tales by the fourteenth-century Italian writer Boccaccio. In the *Decameron* a group of young people withdraw to a country place to avoid the plague raging in their city and, as a means of passing time, fall to telling tales.

LITERATURE AND THE ARTS

The wood-block print on page 85 was done by Richard Pynson for his illustrated edition of Chaucer's *Canterbury Tales,* issued in 1526. Like his contemporaries, the printers William Caxton and Wynkyn de Worde, Pynson designed portraits of all of Chaucer's Canterbury pilgrims. *The Canterbury Tales* was an immediate success on publication, but it was not until considerably after Chaucer's death that illustrated editions of this work began to appear.

The pilgrim shown here is the knight, who told the first of the Canterbury tales. The lettering on the trappings of his horse indicates that the knight was among the Crusaders who journeyed to the Holy Land.

The Nun's Priest's Tale

CHANTICLEER AND PERTELOTE

The first of the Canterbury pilgrims to relate a tale is the Knight. He tells of two noble young captives of war who fall madly in love with a beautiful young girl whom they watch as she walks to and fro in the garden beneath their prison window. It is a sad tale of broken friendship and unrequited love. After several of the other travelers tell their stories, the Monk relates no less than seventeen tales about tragedies that befell illustrious men. To offset the depressing effect of these, the Host asks the Nun's Priest, Sir John, to cheer the travelers with something bright and lively. And this, in a modern version by Rewey Belle Inglis, is the story he tells them.

Once on a time a widow old and frail
Lived in a tiny cottage in a dale.
Her life was simple and her income slight;
She and two daughters lived as best they might
By frugal planning and hard work. Three cows,   5
A sheep called Molly, chickens, and three sows
Formed all her fortune. She could not afford
To serve rare morsels at her humble board;
But all the dainties that she went without
Kept her from apoplexy and the gout.   10
She drank no wine — no, neither white nor red —
And never had she dizziness of head.
The color of her meals was white and black —
Milk and brown bread — of these she had no lack.

Sometimes an egg or two, or bacon slice,   15
Would give a special meal an added spice.
    A yard she had, protected all about
With sticks, and just beyond a ditch dug out.
Here lived her cock, a bird named Chanticleer.°
No other cock in crowing was his peer.   20
His merry voice outdid the organ's swell,
And every hour of day he knew so well
That the poor widow had no need of clock —
She timed her actions by her faithful cock.
His ruddy comb like coral was in hue;   25
His bill jet black, his legs and toes of blue.
His nails like whitest lilies; and like gold
His burnished body flashed in perfect mold.
This noble cock o'er seven hens was lord.
They followed at a distance and adored.   30
Of these the fairest was named Pertelote,°
On whom Lord Chanticleer did truly dote.
So courteous, discreet, and debonair,
Companionable was she, and so fair
That from the day when she was seven nights old   35
She truly had his heart within her hold.
What joy it was at sunrise in fair weather
To hear them sing "My Love's Away" together.
For in those days, I'd have you understand,
The birds and beasts could speak in every land.   40
    One day just as the sun was to appear,
The seven wives surrounding Chanticleer
Were startled by a groaning in his throat
As if from troubled dreams. Then Pertelote
Aghast cried out, "What ails you, my heart's dear,   45
That you should groan in sleep as if in fear?
You a fine sleeper!" quoth she. "Fie! For shame!"
Then Chanticleer awoke and answered, "Dame,
Think not amiss that I have suffered fright,
For such an evil dream I've had this night   50
That I pray God I may its meaning read,
To keep my body from foul prison freed.
Methought that in the yard I roamed around,
When suddenly I saw a fearful hound
That would have seized me and have left me dead.   55
His color was between yellow and red,
But both his ears and tail were tipped with black.
His piercing eyes would slay me. O alack!
This was the horrid sight that made me start."
    "Away!" quoth she. "Shame on you, faint of heart!   60
Have you a beard and call yourself a man?
I cannot love a coward; no woman can.
We want our husbands hardy, wise, and free.

---

19. *Chanticleer* (chăn'tĭ·klēr): from the French meaning "clear singer." 31. *Pertelote* (pĕr'tĭ·lōt).

What is a dream? Nothing but vanity.
It may arise from eating too rich food. 65
No doubt this came from choler of the blood,°
Which often makes men dream of arrows, fires,
Great beasts of prey, and hideous vampires.
Just so, if melancholia should attack,
You then would dream of bears and bulls of black. 70
Lo, Cato,° wise man, as the world must deem,
Has bid us take no notice of a dream.
Now when we leave the perch, I strongly urge
That you a laxative shall take to purge
Yourself of choler and of melancholy. 75
To fail to do so would be utter folly.
Although our town has no apothecary,
I can instruct you so you need not tarry.
Here in our own yard I am very sure
You'll find the herbs to bring about your cure. 80
But if you scorn my counsel — or forget —
A tertian fever° may develop yet.
Now for a day or two eat worms alone,
And this will give your system just the tone
To take the centaury° and hellebore,° 85
Or caper spurge,° or several doses more
Of fumitory,° then the gay-tree° berry,
And our ground ivy, sure to make you merry.
Just peck at these wherever they are found,
And you need fear no nightmares, I'll be bound. 90
Cheer up now, husband, and I'll say no more."
    "Madame," quoth he, "I thank you for your lore,
But this Lord Cato, though he may be wise
Opposes greater minds when he denies
The prophecy of dreams, for joys or woes 95
Are often forecast thus, experience shows.
One of the greatest authors° men may read
Tells of two friends, and both devout indeed,
Who on a pilgrimage came to a town
Where lodgings there were none, though up and down 100
They walked inquiring at each hostelry.
At last they found they must part company
If they would have a place to sleep at all.
Now one of them found quarters in a stall
Where he beside the oxen had to rest. 105

66. *choler* (kŏl′ẽr) *of the blood:* an excess of yellow bile in the blood. According to medieval medical theory, the individual's temperament and physical condition were determined by the predominance of one of the four "humors" (blood, phlegm, black bile, yellow bile), or fluids, which existed in the body. The dominance of blood made one cheerful (sanguine); phlegm, sluggish (phlegmatic); black bile, melancholy; yellow bile, choleric, or irritable. 71. *Cato:* In the fourth century some unknown author compiled four books of popular maxims in Latin. The work was attributed to Cato the Elder (234–149 B.C.). 82. *tertian* (tûr′shăn) *fever:* a fever recurring every other day. 85–87. *centaury* (sĕn′tô·rĭ), *hellebore* (hĕl′ē·bōr), *caper spurge* (kā′pẽr spûrj), *fumitory* (fū′mĭ·tō′rĭ): medicinal plants; *gay-tree:* dogwood. 97. *One of the greatest authors:* Cicero (106–43 B.C.), a Roman statesman, writer, and orator.

The other man was luckier in his quest,
And found a room where he could have a bed.
But in his dreams his friend appeared and said,
'Dear brother, in an ox's stall I lie,
And by a murderer's hand I soon must die   110
If you come not to save me from this fate.'
The man awoke, but then bethought him straight
That dreams are vanity, and slept once more;
But then he had the same dream as before.
Again he woke, and then he slept again.   115
This time the friend reproached, Now I am slain.
Behold my bloody wounds are deep and wide.
Now rise up early in the morningtide
And at the west gate stand until you see
A farmer's cart which has apparently   120
Nothing upon it but a load of dung.
Here underneath my murdered corpse is flung.
Now stop that cart and you will learn the truth.
It was my gold they killed me for, in sooth.'
Then rose the man and sought his comrade's inn.   125
'Your friend left just as daylight did begin,'
The landlord said. The man's suspicion grew.
He sought the west gate, and there soon came through
A farmer's cart exactly as foretold.
The man was now convinced and made so bold   130
As to cry justice for his murdered friend.
The folk rushed forth and tipped the cart on end.
There was the body cut with gashes new!
Murder will out, and dreams come surely true!"

Chanticleer offers several other examples to convince his wife, quoting the life of St. Kenelm, stories of the Old Testament, and legends of Greek mythology.

"Now let us speak of mirth and stop all this;   135
Dear Madam Pertelote, as I have bliss,
In one thing God has sent me wondrous grace,
For when I see the beauty of your face,
Your lovely eyes all rimmed with scarlet-red,
Then suddenly is scattered all my dread;   140
For certainly as *In principio*
Mulier est hominis confusio° —
Now the true meaning of this Latin is
'Woman is man's delight and all his bliss' —
And such a joy to me your bright eye's beam   145
That I defy the warning of the dream."
    Then down he flew and found a grain of corn,
Chucked at his hens and blithely hailed the morn.
No longer fearful, like a lion grim

141–142. *In principio*, etc.: "In the beginning, woman is man's destruction." Note the contrast to Chanticleer's interpretation.

He paced about the yard, his hens with him.   150
He strutted on his toes scarce touching ground,
And crowed with every grain of corn he found.
Thus see we Chanticleer a royal king,
But later there befalls a dreadful thing.
    A coal-black fox, full of iniquity,   155
That in the grove, for three years secretly
Had lived, now saw a chance to do his worst,
And through the hedge that very night he burst
Into the yard where Chanticleer the fair
Would with his wives be likely to repair.   160
Concealed among the herbs the villain lay
Until about eleven the next day,
Waiting to fall upon poor Chanticleer,
Just as a human murderer lingers near
His victim. O thou false Iscariot!°   165
Thou Sinon° who took Troy with subtle plot!
Poor Chanticleer! Accursèd be that hour
That brought thee from thy perch to this brute's power!
Venus, thy patron goddess, was away,
And it was Friday, that ill-fated day!   170
The warning dream he quite ignored, alas!
What God foreknows, however, comes to pass,
Although the scholars still have great dispute
Upon this point, and some would quite refute
The argument that God's foreknowledge still   175
Can make us act contrary to our will.°
In metaphysics° I take little stock,
So let's proceed. My tale is of a cock —
A cock who took his wife's ill-timed advice.
'Twas Eve drove Adam out of Paradise!   180
(But think not I would slander woman's wit;
'Tis but in jest I gave that little hit.
Some authors like to cast on woman a slur,
But I have never seen the harm in her.)

    Fair Pertelote was bathing in the sand   185
With all her sisters six; the air was bland,
And Chanticleer was singing lustily,
As merry as a mermaid in the sea.
It then befell that as his roving eye
Followed the flutter of a butterfly,   190
It saw the visage of the hidden fox,
Hereditary foe of all the cocks.
Then the poor bird no longer wished to crow.

---

165. *Iscariot* (ĭs·kăr'ĭ·ŏt): Judas Iscariot, who betrayed Christ. 166. *Sinon* (sī'nŏn): the designer of the wooden horse by which the Greeks captured Troy in the Trojan War. 176. Scholars of religion in Chaucer's day were deeply concerned with the relation of the individual's freedom of will to God's omnipotence and omniscience. 177. *metaphysics* (mĕt'à·fĭz'ĭks): the philosophy of first principles which asks such questions as "What exists?" "What is real?" and "How do we know?"

"Cok, cok," he cried in fright and turned to go.
But quickly said the fox, "O gentle sir,   195
I am your loyal friend. Why all this stir?
My presence here no harm to you can bring.
I simply came to hear your lordship sing.
How like an angel's voice from heaven each note
That flows melodious from your noble throat!   200
My lord your father (may God rest his name!)
Also your mother to my house once came,
And truly I would like to please their son.
But as to singing I have known no one
Save you, your father's equal. By my eyes,   205
How he could sing to help the sun arise!
He'd crane his neck and stretch upon his toes,
And singing from the heart, his eyes he'd close.
I'm sure his son to match him must aspire;
Let's see if you can imitate your sire."   210
    Poor Chanticleer, intrigued by flattery,
Began to flap his wings and shut his eye
And stand on tiptoe, but before a note
Was voiced, the fox had seized him by the throat
And dragged him to the wood without pursuit.   215
The lady hens, however, were not mute:
They raised such outcry as was made in vain
By Trojan women for King Priam° slain,
And Pertelote shrieked louder than the rest
Because among the seven she loved him best.   220
No louder shrieked the great Hasdrubal's° wife
When she at Carthage saw him lose his life
And threw herself into the deadly flames.
No greater wailing among Roman dames
When Nero° had the guiltless senators slain,   225
But to our story let's return again.
    When the poor widow and her daughters two
Heard the hens making such a great to-do,
They rushed outdoors, saw the fox disappear
Within the grove, bearing their Chanticleer.   230
They rushed pell-mell to save the frightened prey.
"Out! Out!" they shouted. "Harrow!° Weylaway!°
Ha, ha, the fox!" and after him they ran.
Out dashed with staves their neighbors to a man.
The dogs ran barking, Collie and Gerland;   235
Then Malkin° followed, distaff still in hand.
The cows and calves ran too, and even hogs
So frightened by the barking of the dogs
And shouts of men and women at their backs,

---

218. *King Priam* (prī′ăm): the last king of Troy, who was slain when the Greeks conquered the city. 221. *Hasdrubal* (hăz′drōō′băl): the defender of Carthage when the Romans destroyed the city in 146 B.C. 225. *Nero* (nē′rō): a Roman Emperor (A.D. 54–68), famous for his brutal tyrannies. 232. *Harrow* (hăr′ō): an ancient Norman cry to arouse pursuit of a thief; *Weylaway* (wăl′à·wā′): alas. 236. *Malkin* (măl′kĭn): one of the widow's daughters.

Scampered till due to fall right in their tracks.   240
They yelled like fiends in hell; the ducks quacked shrill,
Thinking the men with sticks were out to kill.
The geese went flapping up into the trees,
And from the hive out flew a swarm of bees.
Such sights and sounds, ah *benedicite!*°   245
I hope I ne'er again may hear and see.
Some came with horns of brass, and some of box,°
And some of bone, and blew to scare the fox.
They whooped and hollered, blew and bellowed all,
Until you'd think the very heavens would fall.   250
  Now listen while I tell to your amaze
How fortune may reverse her tricky plays.
The cock who helpless lay upon the back
Of Master Fox, though frightened, had no lack
Of ready wit, and said, "If in your place,   255
Safe by the entrance to the wood, I'd face
Around, and to these silly men and girls
I'd shout, 'Turn back, turn back, you haughty churls!
A plague upon you all! The cock is mine.
I'll eat him up. Just think how well I'll dine!'"   260
The fox, quite blind to methods he'd begun,
Replied at once, "In faith, it shall be done!"
And thus to speak, unthinking spread his jaws.
The cock, I can assure you, did not pause
For second thought, but flapped his wings in glee,   265
And presto! perched upon a lofty tree.
  Now when the fox discovered he'd been duped,
A second time to trickery he stooped.
"Alas, my friend," quoth he, "did I alarm
By holding you so tight? I meant no harm.   270
Surely you can't suspect some base intent.
Come down and let me tell you what I meant.
I'll speak the truth to you this time, I swear."
"Nay then," quoth Chanticleer, "you speak me fair,
But let me be accursed, both blood and bone,   275
If from experience I've no wiser grown.
You fooled me once, you shall not fool me twice.
If I came down you'd eat me in a trice.
Who shuts his eyes when he should watchful be
Need never hope from God prosperity."   280
"Nay," quoth the fox, "and God shall never cease
To plague the chattering tongue that should keep peace."
  Lo, thus it goes with carelesssness, you see,
And with too great a trust in flattery.
Now do not judge as folly, my good men,   285
This simple tale of fox and cock and hen.
It has a moral hidden in a laugh;
Be wise and take the grain, but leave the chaff.

---

245. *benedicite* (bĕn'ĕ·dĭs'ĭ·tĕ): bless you. 247. *box:* boxwood.

THE TALE OF CHANTICLEER AND PERTELOTE

1. Describe the difference in personality between Chanticleer and Pertelote. What amusing characteristics of husband and wife are given to the cock and hen?

2. What is the moral of the tale? Is the story told primarily to teach a moral or to poke fun at some typical family situations? Quote passages to support your argument.

3. The story of the cock and hen is one of the oldest and most popular in the arts. Read Aesop's fable on this theme and note similarities and differences, or look up the French writer La Fontaine's version for a comparison. You may also enjoy reading a modern drama based on the cock story, Edmond Rostand's *Chantecler*.

RECOGNIZING LITERARY DEVICES

1. Over and over again in the world's literature, writers have chosen to teach a moral — or make some statement of belief — by clothing it in the form of a story. We call such stories *fables, allegories,* and *parables.* Make sure you know the meaning of these terms. Someone in the class should read a book-length — and highly entertaining — fable that satirizes Communist dictatorship, George Orwell's *Animal Farm.* Report to the class on the comparison between Orwell's modern English and Chaucer's Middle English fables.

2. Chaucer uses a dream to present "a story within a story." Do you know of any current novels, plays, or short stories in which this device is used? How does Chanticleer's dream bear on the main story? How does Pertelote interpret it?

THE POWER OF WORDS

WORD FAMILIES

In the opening lines of the *Prologue* in the original Middle English (page 83), we find such forthright Anglo-Saxon words as *eek, holt,* and *heeth,* side by side with such graceful French terms as *licour, vertu,* and *melodye.* Pick out six other terms on this page that you judge to be Anglo-Saxon, and six you think are French. Verify your choices in a dictionary.

In the story of the cock, there are many illustrations of the social significance of the two parent languages. Since this is a farm story it is filled with Saxon nouns: *herb, hoard, stitch, cart, distaff, churls, chaff.* But part of the humor of the story lies in the portrayal of the cock and his favorite hen as nobility — like the Normans in England, as a matter of fact. The very names Chanticleer and Pertelote are French. The cock addresses the hen as *Madame,* and he is called *royal* and *debonair.*

In this story, find at least ten Saxon and ten French derivatives that are used in modern English, beyond those quoted here. You may be fooled by words like *lord* (Saxon) and *grain* (Latin), so use a dictionary to make sure.

BEHIND THE SCENES IN ENGLISH LITERATURE

In the work of the literary scholar, the scientist is often able to lend valuable assistance, as one astronomer did in the dating of Chaucer's second great masterpiece, *Troilus and Criseyde,* a long poem about the tragic love of two characters in the legend of the Trojan War. The date of this poem's composition is important to the tracing of Chaucer's poetical development, but scholars knew only that it was written sometime between 1373 and 1386.

Then, in 1923, Professor Robert Root of Princeton noticed a passage in which Criseyde is being entertained at a party by her uncle, Pandarus, who wants her to meet Troilus, whom he has temporarily concealed in a closet. The time comes for Criseyde to go home, but it is pouring; and Chaucer notes that "The bente moone with hire hornes pale, Saturn and Jove in Cancro joyned were." All the ladies at the party were much upset by the "smoky reyn."

What struck Professor Root was the unlikely conjunction of the moon and two planets in the zodiacal sign of Cancer. Chaucer frequently inserted contemporary allusions into his stories. Could this rare event possibly have happened when he was writing the poem?

Consulting a colleague in the Astronomy Department, Professor Root learned that this occurrence is indeed extremely rare, and that in April 1385, when Chaucer was active as a writer, Saturn and Jupiter met in Gemini and moved into Cancer for the first time in over 600 years. There the moon joined them in mid-May, the time of Pandarus' dinner party.

Such an unusual event could not have escaped the notice of so keen a writer and student of astrology as Chaucer, and he would have known what it portended — heavy rain and floods and, as people in those days believed, other misfortunes influencing the lives of men. But how could Chaucer (or Pandarus) have seen the moon or stars in a pouring rain? He didn't, of course. In a medieval chronicle Professor Root found that on July 14, 1385, two months after the dinner party, a thunderstorm broke over England such as had never before been seen. Chaucer, while writing of the meeting of Troilus and Criseyde, evidently combined the July thunderstorm and the unusual crossing of the stars in May into one, thereby symbolizing the unhappy fate awaiting his characters. The dinner party scene, it thus now seemed clear, could not have been written before the rare heavenly conjunction in the spring of 1385.

SIR THOMAS MALORY

?-1471

All of us know King Arthur and his Round Table through the countless stories that make him, of all the medieval heroes, the most familiar in English literature. The real Arthur is a shadowy figure in history. He was probably a Celtic chieftain of the sixth century, known for his bravery in war and his just rule of an ancient tribe of Britons. No contemporary records or accounts of him exist, yet in the centuries that followed his reign many writers celebrated him in song and story.

In the twelfth century the story of Arthur was told in Latin by Geoffrey of Monmouth and in French by Wace, who added the Round Table legend. The first version in English is the *Brut*, a poem by Layamon. But by far the most important of the early accounts is *Morte d'Arthur* ("Death of Arthur") by Sir Thomas Malory. Because it is a long story in prose, it has sometimes been called the forerunner of the novel, though it bears only a faint resemblance to novels as we know them today. *Morte d'Arthur* has served as the inspiration for many later writers. Tennyson's *The Idylls of the King* and the American poet E. A. Robinson's series of Arthurian legends are based on it, as are poems by John Masefield and others. A modern British writer, T. H. White, has retold the legend in four short novels that have been combined under the title *The Once and Future King*. The separate novels are *The Sword in the Stone, The Queen of Air and Darkness, The Ill-Made Knight,* and *The*

Candle in the Wind. The most recent appearance of the story of Arthur has been on the stage. Lerner and Loewe's "Camelot," based on the T. H. White novels, is now retelling the legend once more in the form of a Broadway musical.

Little is known of Sir Thomas Malory himself. He was a knight who fought in the Hundred Years' War in France. Recently, evidence has been discovered that he was several times arrested for robbing and assaulting his neighbors. Malory apparently undertook his great story while serving a twenty-year prison sentence. He died in 1471, one year after completing *Morte d'Arthur*. Fourteen years later it was published by William Caxton, who introduced printing into England.

Morte d'Arthur

The legends told by Malory begin with the birth of Arthur and end with his mysterious death. They relate the adventures of the Round Table, about which Arthur gathers a group of knights, among them Sir Launcelot, Sir Percivale, Sir Gawaine, and other familiar figures. Another of his constant companions is Merlin, the court magician. The knights go on dangerous missions, fight in tournaments, and pledge their honor to ladies of the court, all in the spirit of chivalry. Far and wide King Arthur becomes known as a brave, just, and wise ruler. But after a time the glory of the court declines. Queen Guinevere, who also loves Sir Launcelot, is faithless to her husband. One after another, the knights become discontented, selfish, or disillusioned. Finally, the court is threatened by attack from without. During King Arthur's absence on a conquest, Sir Mordred, his traitorous nephew, organizes a plot against him. In a final battle, Arthur's knights are defeated; Sir Gawaine, his faithful nephew, is killed, and Arthur himself is borne away on a barge to his last rest by three mysterious ladies.

In the following account, Arthur receives his famous sword Excalibur from the Lady of the Lake. According to an account given by Malory elsewhere in his book, Arthur received the sword as a boy when he one day pulled it from a block of stone, thus proving his right to rule England. He further establishes this right by subduing twelve rebellious princes and winning twelve great battles against Saxon invaders. Because these legends grew up at different times, there are many such contradictions throughout the Arthur stories.

The following selection is taken from an early part of Arthur's life, when he was winning his reputation as the flower of chivalry. Here you will find an excellent picture of the knight-errant, who roams the woods in search of wrongs to right, and you will get a sense of the mysticism of medieval days.

HOW ARTHUR FOUGHT WITH KING PELLINORE AND HOW MERLIN SAVED ARTHUR'S LIFE, AND ARTHUR BY THE MEAN OF MERLIN GAT HIS SWORD EXCALIBUR.

THEN ON the day there came in the court a squire on horseback, leading a knight before him wounded to the death, and told him how there was a knight in the forest had reared up a pavilion [1] by a well, and hath slain my master, a good knight, his name was Miles; wherefore I beseech you that my master may be buried, and that some knight may revenge my master's death. Then the noise was great of that knight's death in the court, and every man said his advice. Then came Griflet that was but a squire, and he was but young, of the age of the king Arthur, so he besought the king for all his service that he had done him to give the order of knighthood.

Thou art full young and tender of age,

---

[1] *pavilion* (pá·vĭl′yŭn): a tent.

said Arthur, for to take so high an order on thee.

Sir, said Griflet, I beseech you to make me knight.

Sir, said Merlin, it were great pity to lose Griflet, for he will be a passing [1] good man when he is of age, abiding with you the term of his life. And if he adventure his body with yonder knight at the fountain, it is in great peril if ever he come again, for he [2] is one of the best knights of the world, and the strongest man of arms.

Well,[3] said Arthur.

So at the desire of Griflet the king made him knight.

Now, said Arthur, unto Sir Griflet, sith [4] I have made you knight thou might give me a gift.

What ye will, said Griflet.

Thou shalt promise me by the faith of thy body, when thou hast jousted with the knight at the fountain, whether it fall [5] ye be on foot or on horseback, that right so ye shall come again unto me without making any more debate.

I will promise you, said Griflet, as you desire. Then took Griflet his horse in great haste, and dressed his shield [6] and took a spear in his hand, and so he rode a great wallop till he came to the fountain, and thereby he saw a rich pavilion, and thereby under a cloth stood a fair horse well saddled and bridled, and on a tree a shield of divers colors and a great spear. Then Griflet smote on the shield with the butt of his spear, that the shield fell down to the ground.

With that the knight came out of the pavilion, and said, Fair knight, why smote ye down my shield?

For [7] I will joust with you, said Griflet.

It is better ye do not, said the knight, for ye are but young, and late made knight, and your might is nothing to mine.

As for that, said Griflet, I will joust with you.

That is me loath, said the knight, but sith I must needs, I will dress me thereto.

Of whence be ye? said the knight.

Sir, I am of Arthur's court.

So the two knights ran together that Griflet's spear all to-shivered; and therewithal he smote Griflet through the shield and the left side, and brake the spear and the truncheon [8] stuck in his body, that horse and knight fell down.

When the knight saw him lie so on the ground, he alighted, and was passing heavy,[9] for he weened [10] he had slain him, and then he unlaced his helm and gat him wind, and so with the truncheon he set him on his horse, and so betook him to God,[11] and said he had a mighty heart, and if he might live he would prove a passing good knight. And so Sir Griflet rode to the court, where great dole [12] was made for him. But through good leeches [13] he was healed and saved.

Then King Arthur was passingly wroth for the hurt of Sir Griflet. And so he commanded a privy man of his chamber that ere it be day his best horse and armor, with all that longeth [14] unto his person, be without the city or tomorrow day.[15] Right so on tomorrow day he met with his man and his horse, and so mounted up and dressed his shield and took his spear, and bade his chamberlain tarry there till he came again. And so Arthur rode a soft pace till it was day, and then was he ware of three churls [16] chasing Merlin, and would have slain him. Then the king rode unto them, and bade them: Flee, churls! then were they afeard when they saw a knight, and fled. O Merlin, said Arthur, here hadst thou

---

[1] *passing:* exceedingly. [2] *he:* the knight at the fountain. [3] *Well:* It is well, or so be it. Arthur is replying to Griflet's request, not to Merlin. [4] *sith:* since. [5] *fall:* happen. [6] *dressed his shield:* took up his shield in position for combat. [7] *For:* because.

[8] *truncheon* (trŭn'chŭn): spear shaft. [9] *passing heavy:* exceedingly grieved; weighed down with sorrow. [10] *weened:* supposed. [11] *betook him to God:* left him to the care of God. [12] *dole:* grieving. [13] *leeches:* doctors. [14] *longeth:* belongs. [15] *without . . . day:* outside the city before daylight tomorrow. [16] *churls:* peasants.

been slain for all thy crafts [1] had I not been.

Nay, said Merlin, not so, for I could save myself an I would; and thou art more near thy death than I am, for thou goest to the deathward, an God be not thy friend.[2]

So as they went thus talking they came to the fountain, and the rich pavilion there by it. Then King Arthur was ware where sat a knight armed in a chair.

Sir knight, said Arthur, for what cause abidest thou here, that there may no knight ride this way but if he joust with thee? I rede thee leave [3] that custom, said Arthur.

This custom, said the knight, have I used and will use maugre [4] who saith nay, and who is grieved with my custom let him amend it that will.

I will amend it, said Arthur.

I shall defend [5] thee, said the knight. Anon [6] he took his horse and dressed his shield and took a spear, and they met so hard either in other's shields, that all to-shivered their spears. Therewith anon Arthur pulled out his sword.

Nay, not so, said the knight; it is fairer, said the knight, that we run more together with sharp spears.

I will well, said Arthur, an I had any more spears.

I have enow, said the knight; so there came a squire and brought two good spears, and Arthur chose one and he another; so they spurred their horses and came together with all their mights, that either brake their spears to their hands. Then Arthur set hand on his sword.

Nay, said the knight, ye shall do better, ye are a passing good jouster as ever I met withal, and for the love of the high order of knighthood let us joust once again.

I assent me, said Arthur.

Anon there were brought two great spears, and every knight gat a spear, and therewith they ran together that Arthur's spear all to-shivered. But the other knight hit him so hard in the midst of the shield, that horse and man fell to the earth, and therewith Arthur was eager, and pulled out his sword, and said, I will assay [7] thee, sir knight, on foot, for I have lost the honor on horseback. Then the knight alighted and dressed his shield unto Arthur. And there began a strong battle with many great strokes, and so hewed with their swords that the cantels [8] flew in the fields. So at the last they smote together that both their swords met even together. But the sword of the knight smote King Arthur's sword in two pieces, wherefore he was heavy.

Then said the knight unto Arthur, Thou art in my danger whether me list to save thee or slay thee, and but thou yield thee as overcome and recreant, thou shalt die.[9]

As for death, said King Arthur, welcome be it when it cometh, but to yield me unto thee as recreant I had liefer die than to be so shamed. And therewithal the king leapt unto Pellinore,[10] and took him by the middle and threw him down, and raced off [11] his helm. When the knight felt that, he was adread, and anon he brought Arthur unto him, for he was a passing big man of might, and raced off his helm and would have smitten off his head.

Then came Merlin and said, Knight, hold thy hand, for an thou slay that knight thou puttest this realm in the greatest damage that ever was realm: for this knight is a man of more worship than thou wotest of.[12]

---

[1] crafts: magic arts. [2] thou goest . . . friend: You are going to your death unless God favors you. [3] rede thee leave: advise you to give up. [4] maugre (mô′gẽr): in spite of. [5] defend: prohibit, prevent. [6] Anon: at once.

[7] assay (ă·sā′): test, try. [8] cantels (kăn′t′lz): pieces or fragments cut or sliced off, presumably from their shields. [9] Thou art . . . die: You are at my mercy whether I wish to save or slay you, and unless you admit that you are defeated and a coward (recreant: rĕk′rē·ănt) you shall die. [10] Pellinore: the knight of the fountain. [11] raced off: tore off. [12] more . . . wotest of: more importance than you know.

Why, who is he? said the knight.

It is King Arthur.

Then would he have slain him for dread of his wrath, and heaved up his sword, and therewith Merlin cast an enchantment to the knight, that he fell to the earth in a great sleep. Then Merlin took up King Arthur, and rode forth on the knight's horse.

Alas! said Arthur, what hast thou done, Merlin? Hast thou slain this good knight by thy crafts? There liveth not so worshipful a knight as he was; I had liefer than the stint of my land a year that he were alive.[1]

Care ye not, said Merlin, for he is wholer than ye; for he is but asleep, and will awake within three hours. I told you, said Merlin, what a knight he was; here had ye been slain had I not been.

Right so the king and he departed, and went unto an hermit that was a good man and a great leech. So the hermit searched all his wounds and gave him good salves; so the king was there three days, and then were his wounds well amended that he might ride and go, and so departed. And as they rode, Arthur said, I have no sword.

No force,[2] said Merlin, hereby is a sword that shall be yours, an I may.

So they rode till they came to a lake, the which was a fair water and broad, and in the midst of the lake Arthur was ware of an arm clothed in white samite,[3] that held a fair sword in that hand.

Lo! said Merlin, yonder is that sword that I spake of. With that they saw a damsel going upon the lake.

What damsel is that? said Arthur.

That is the Lady of the Lake, said Merlin; and within that lake is a rock, and therein is as fair a place as any on earth, and richly beseen;[4] and this damsel will come to you anon, and then speak ye fair to her that she will give you that sword. Anon withal came the damsel unto Arthur, and saluted him, and he her again.

Damsel, said Arthur, what sword is that, that yonder the arm holdeth above the water? I would it were mine, for I have no sword.

Sir Arthur, king, said the damsel, that sword is mine, and if ye will give me a gift when I ask it you, ye shall have it.

By my faith, said Arthur, I will give you what gift ye will ask.

Well! said the damsel, go ye into yonder barge, and row yourself to the sword, and take it and the scabbard with you, and I will ask my gift when I see my time. So Sir Arthur and Merlin alighted and tied their horses to two trees, and so they went into the ship, and when they came to the sword that the hand held, Sir Arthur took it up by the handles, and took it with him, and the arm and the hand went under the water. And so they came unto the land and rode forth.

Then Sir Arthur looked on the sword, and liked it passing well.

Whether[5] liketh you better, said Merlin, the sword or the scabbard?

Me liketh better the sword, said Arthur.

Ye are more unwise, said Merlin, for the scabbard is worth ten of the sword, for whiles ye have the scabbard upon you, ye shall never lose no blood, be ye never so sore wounded; therefore keep well the scabbard always with you. So they came unto Carlion,[6] whereof his knights were passing glad. And when they heard of his adventures, they marveled that he would jeopard[7] his person so, alone. But all men of worship said it was merry to be under such a chieftain, that would put his person in adventure as other poor knights did.

---

[1] *liefer . . . alive:* I had rather have him alive than have a year's income from my land. [2] *No force:* no matter. [3] *samite* (săm'īt): heavy silk, interwoven with gold and silver. [4] *beseen:* decorated.

[5] *Whether:* which. [6] *Carlion:* Arthur's residence; it has been identified with the modern town of Caerleon in southwest England. [7] *jeopard* (jĕp'ĕrd): risk.

British Museum

MEDIEVAL ROMANCE

1. Many of the traits that made Arthur an ideal leader in his day are shown in this selection. What are they? Compare him with Beowulf in this respect. Which of these traits make for good leadership even today?

2. What can you find in this legend that reveals medieval rather than sixth-century customs, material goods, and standards of conduct? How much do you learn about the "code of chivalry"?

3. As you did with Chaucer's tales, select words of Saxon and of French origin from Malory's writing. Which of the two languages seems to prevail in the conversations?

CLASS ACTIVITY

Students who have read Mark Twain's *A Connecticut Yankee in King Arthur's Court* may report to the class and relate incidents from this book which illustrate how Mark Twain satirizes medieval chivalry and magic.

LITERATURE AND THE ARTS

In the illustration above, Merlin (the figure at the right), friend and mentor of King Arthur, is building Stonehenge, the best known of the great stone circles erected in England by men of the Bronze Age. There are varying stories about Merlin and the other characters of the Arthurian legends; that Merlin helped to build Stonehenge is simply one of them. Though the facts are obscured, it is generally believed that the character of Merlin derives from a Welsh bard and soothsayer.

This drawing, probably the earliest attempt to depict Stonehenge, is from a manuscript of the mid-fourteenth century, an abridgment of Wace's chronicle of English history up to the year 1338. The drawing also represents an early example of manuscript illustration. The decoration of manuscripts which was done in the early Middle Ages was gradually broadened to include full-fledged drawings as well as the ornamentation found in the earliest illuminated manuscripts.

READING LIST FOR THE MEDIEVAL PERIOD

Chute, Marchette, *Geoffrey Chaucer of England*
Chaucer has come to mean more to the public at large since this very readable account appeared; it is both historically accurate and lively in style.

Converse, Florence, *Long Will*
The title refers to William Langland of *Piers the Plowman* fame. Chaucer, and Wat Tyler, who stirred up a revolt, are also characters in the story.

Costain, Thomas B., *Below the Salt*
An historical romance of Eleanor, the Lost Princess, who had a better claim to the throne of England than her wicked uncle, King John. A convincing picture of events leading to John's forced signing of the Magna Charta.

———, *The Magnificent Century*
The second volume of his history, *The Pageant of England,* covering the long reign of King Henry III, from 1216, just after the signing of the Magna Charta, to 1272.

Doyle, A. Conan, *Sir Nigel*
Edward III and the Black Prince are actors in this stirring tale, which includes the Battle of Poitiers in France and the tragic results of the Black Death. Doyle's *The White Company* is a sequel.

Eliot, T. S., *Murder in the Cathedral*
A poetic drama on the martyrdom of Thomas à Becket by an outstanding poet and dramatist of our day.

MacLeod, Mary, *King Arthur and His Noble Knights*
If you wish to read more about the Knights of the Round Table, you will find this modernization easier than the original Malory.

Noyes, Alfred, "Sherwood," in *Collected Poems*
Poetic drama romantically picturing Robin Hood's band in Sherwood forest.

Scott, Sir Walter, *Ivanhoe*
One of the best fictional pictures of the Middle Ages, featuring a tournament, the siege of a castle, Robin Hood (under the name of Locksley), and a witchcraft trial.

———, *Quentin Durward*
Medieval life on the Continent. A plain Scotsman becomes involved in French plots under Louis XI and finally wins the hand of an aristocratic lady.

Shaw, George Bernard, *Saint Joan*
A tense drama of the famous Joan of Arc's rise to power, her trial, and her martyrdom. The unusual theme of the last act: What would we do with Joan today?

Stevenson, Robert Louis, *The Black Arrow*
A message foretelling the death of others is attached to the arrow that kills one of the soldiers. This is just one incident in a long series of thrillers. The setting is the Wars of the Roses.

Tennyson, Alfred, *The Idylls of the King*
Classic tales in verse of the knights of King Arthur. If you have missed these during your high school career, now is the time to make up for it.

Twain, Mark, *A Connecticut Yankee in King Arthur's Court*
One ridiculous incident after another shows the superiority of modern common sense over the false glamour of chivalry.

White, Terence H., *The Once and Future King*
Four short novels which tell the complete story of the legendary characters of the Arthurian epic.

FOR LISTENING

The following selections have been recorded and are available on *Many Voices 6A:* ll. 1–42 from Chaucer's *Prologue* to *The Canterbury Tales,* in Middle English; "Sir Patrick Spens"; "Get Up and Bar the Door." Further selections from the *Prologue* to *The Canterbury Tales* are available on *Many Voices 12A.*

MEDIEVAL FRONTISPIECE: Pictured on page 48 are an illustration of a carved choir screen from Canterbury Cathedral with statues of Henry V, Richard II, and Ethelbert; a copy of a helmet from a suit of armor used 1440–60; a fifteenth-century crossbow; a copy of a thirteenth-century Italian lute; a replica of a bishop's mitre.

THE GROWTH OF
THE ENGLISH LANGUAGE

The Middle English Period

After the Norman Conquest in 1066, England became a land of three tongues. It took several centuries for these to fuse into what might be truly called the *English* language. The conquered English spoke Old English; the Norman overlords spoke French; the churchmen used Latin. Since the country was without a common national language, it is no wonder that chaos prevailed for many years.

What little writing was done was in the language of the class for which it was intended. The ballads, some of which you have recently read, were the literature of the common people. If they do not *look* like Old English, remember that these songs and tales were passed on largely by word of mouth. The versions that you see here were written down in later centuries after many language changes had taken place. The castle people were interested primarily in long tales of chivalry, composed at first in French and often celebrating a French hero, such as Roland or Charlemagne. In the monasteries, monks were writing in Latin about church doctrines, philosophy, and the lives of saints. But people of all classes had to communicate with one another, and so there developed a kind of common tongue, with an Old English basis enriched by French and Latin words. Gradually this hybrid language gained standing. In 1362, three centuries after the conquest, Parliament was for the first time opened by a speech in English instead of French.

In the fourteenth century a few individual authors emerged from the great mass of anonymous writing. The most important of these was Geoffrey Chau-cer. The short passage on page 83 gave you the first chance you have had in this volume to read English just as it was written six centuries ago.

At about the same time came Wyclif's translation of the Bible into the vernacular. Earlier the Bible had been available only in Latin and was therefore a closed book to all except the clergy. But now, even though a man could not read or write, he could listen to a reading of the life of Christ in language that he understood.

Both Chaucer and Wyclif used the Midland dialect, which was the speech of London and central England. The island was dotted with dialects. Men of the South and men of the North probably understood each other with difficulty, if at all. Which of these many forms of speech would win out in the end? Chaucer and Wyclif had much to do with the answer to this question. Later they were ably seconded by William Caxton, who brought to London in 1476 that amazing new invention from the Continent — the printing press. He produced hundreds of copies of the works of Chaucer and other writers. Until then it had often taken years of a scribe's life to write out a single manuscript, a treasure that few could afford. Since printing always gives stability, permanence, and wide circulation to any form of language, it is easy to see why the Midland dialect figured so heavily in what finally became accepted as standard.

It is also easy to see why certain spellings which were originally phonetic were retained long after their pronunciation had changed with the passing of time.

Many modern English surnames developed from the names of medieval guilds, members being referred to by their occupations. Above, left to right, are the coats of arms of the guilds to which the mercer, skinner, goldsmith, and cook belonged.

As English has always had a tendency to clip and shorten pronunciation, there remains in our spelling a great residue of silent letters which originally were pronounced. A most striking example is our final silent *e,* which you will find usually pronounced in Chaucer's writing as a separate syllable. Some of these final *e*'s have disappeared from modern English; others have been retained, chiefly to indicate that the preceding vowel is, or was originally, "long." Other familiar silent letters are in *often, knight, cough, drought,* etc.

With printing, language now crystallized so quickly that by the end of the fifteenth century a page of English prose seems almost modern, compared with a page of Chaucer. A quick glance at the selection from Malory on page 96 will convince you of this. *Morte d'Arthur* too is in the Midland dialect.

The other dialects never died out completely but became the backbone of dialects most noticeable today in southwestern, western, and northern England, and in Scotland. In fact, the Scottish and northern dialects produced a rich literature of their own. Examples of its use in modern times are the poems by Robert Burns (page 347) and the story of Yorkshiremen by Eric Knight (page 632).

Just how did the impact of French and Latin during the Middle Ages affect English? Not in sentence structure, for, unlike the French, we still put the adjective before the noun. Latin might have influenced us to retain the complex inflections of Old English, but it didn't. During the Middle Ages the gradual changes that took place in syntax seemed to grow out of native English tendencies. We still use the little linking words like *of, to, for* to glue our sentences together. We generally follow the subject-verb-object order in our sentences. It has been said that we could write natural and idiomatic sentences today using only words of Old English derivation, whereas we could not compose an acceptable sentence using only words from French or Latin.

Nouns alone can tell us a great deal about the social history of the Middle Ages. What conclusions can you draw from the following groups of words?

Of Anglo-Saxon derivation: *man, woman, child, house, home, horse, dog, cow, king, sheriff, outlaw, arrow.*

Of French derivation: *chivalry, armor, homage, government, nobility, madam, mansion, tournament, royalty, banquet.*

Of Latin derivation: *cathedral, chaplain, charity, miracle, paradise, apostle, saint, sacrament, salvation.*

The close contacts between England and France throughout the Middle Ages made French the most influential outside language. These early borrowings have become so intimately a part of our language that we are not immediately aware of their origin, but regard them as native English words. Some good examples are *place, large, change, pay, state.*

Our stream of English, which ran its narrow course during Anglo-Saxon times, has now been broadened by two great tributaries, Latin and French. Just as the Mississippi becomes a different kind of river after the great waters of the Missouri and the Ohio flow into it, so Middle English became a quite different language from Old English.

THE
ELIZABETHAN
AGE

1485–1625

ENGLAND's Elizabethan Age was created partly by a general European movement that we call the Renaissance. It is necessary therefore first to understand something about the Renaissance, which did not destroy the Middle Ages (though this is often suggested) so much as build out of the wreck and ruin of that period what we think of as a new age. Where the Middle Ages had related man to God, the Renaissance concentrated more upon man himself, creating a less strictly ordered, looser form of society, but with it an age of extraordinarily gifted and brilliant individuals, probably not to be matched, especially in their versatility, by men in any other age.

THE RENAISSANCE

Many important things happened almost simultaneously to bring about this Renaissance. First, the capture of Constantinople (1453) by the Turks of Eastern Europe drove many Greek scholars to take refuge in Italy, there to revive classical learning. Then there was the discovery of printing by movable metal types, which enormously increased the production and spread of books. The development of banking (the main idea was brought to Italy from the East by Marco Polo), capital investment, and letters of credit, made trading easier and more prosperous, creating a wealthy and influential merchant class in the growing cities. Finally, there were the great voyages of discovery, giving us America and the wonderful globe itself almost as we know it now. Indeed, the Ren-

◀ The items in the frontispiece are identified on page 209.

Henry VIII, by Hans Holbein

Baron Thyssen

aissance is the beginning of the modern world. All our minds are shaped and colored by it.

The common religious faith of medieval times disappeared with the Middle Ages. Not long after all the discoveries of the Renaissance had first excited men, the Reformation arrived to challenge the corruption and later even the doctrines of the Church. This religious movement, which began as a protest against various practices of the Roman Catholic Church, received its impetus from the European continent, where Martin Luther in Germany and John Calvin in Switzerland were the most notable proponents of the new religious thought. John Knox led the growing Protestant movement in Scotland.

There were now Protestants and Catholics, and many of them believed that it was impossible to live in peace alongside people who did not share their particular faith. This opinion led to ruinous wars in France and later in Germany. But others were more tolerant. These others formed a kind of center party, and when they also happened to be scholars, like the great Erasmus, we call them humanists. These men were not irreligious, but they disliked fanaticism and bigotry, considered individual human beings more important than institutions, and believed that men had the right to think and act for themselves. The influence of the humanists on literature, both in England and abroad, was great and far-reaching.

In England the ruinous Wars of the Roses ended, as we have seen, with the defeat of Richard III (whom many people believe to be a good king blackened by Tudor propaganda) by Henry Tudor, who became Henry VII. The country had had enough of civil war and of quarrelsome nobles with private armies, and Henry VII (1485–1509), a shrewd, hard man, made his throne secure by taking more and more power into his own capable hands. His son, Henry VIII (1509–47), seemed at first a handsome, jolly giant but later became suspicious, tyrannical, and cruel. He did not marry six wives because he was fond of girls (though he was) but because he needed a son to succeed him. Though the Pope's refusal to allow Henry to divorce his first wife, Catherine of Aragon, may have been the immediate cause of Henry's break with Rome and the subsequent establishment of the Protestant church in England, it was by no means the sole cause. There were political and ecclesiastical as well as personal reasons: the growth of English nationalism made the subjection of English affairs to an outside power increasingly unacceptable, and the strong Protestant movement on the continent had greatly influenced English thought.

THE REIGN OF QUEEN ELIZABETH

Elizabeth, daughter of Anne Boleyn, whom Henry married after breaking with Rome, succeeded her half-sister Mary (who had married Philip of Spain and tried to restore her kingdom to the Pope). Elizabeth (1558–1603) came to the throne when she was only twenty-five, and her position was very difficult indeed. A Protestant, she had still many Catholics among her subjects. And Philip of Spain, who had the best army in Europe, still coveted England for the Pope and was constantly enraged by the piratical raids on his treasure ships, coming from North and South America, by Elizabeth's daredevil sea captains. Though progressing fast under the firm government of the Tudor monarchs, England was not yet one of the great powers. What Elizabeth needed was time, and she played for that time with an astonishing mixture of masculine audacity and feminine wiliness. She was in fact — this thin red-haired woman who could not resist making favorites out of her most

handsome courtiers — by far the cleverest ruler of her age. She was unusually well-educated, at once brilliant and shrewd, capable of outwitting any diplomat sent to her. She was careful with public money to the point of meanness, yet was forever compelling her wealthier subjects to entertain her lavishly to keep both her and her people amused. She was cautious and crafty in her efforts to preserve peace but magnificently bold when danger threatened her and the country. By stimulating foreign commerce and exploration, she promoted English sea power and colonial expansion; by pursuing moderate religious policies, she prevented the danger of open conflict between Protes-

Elizabeth I, by School of Marc Gheeraerts

National Portrait Gallery

tant and Catholic; by respecting its privileges, she assured the loyalty of Parliament; she reduced taxes, broadened education, and encouraged scholarship and the arts. By the later years of her reign, England had achieved remarkable prosperity. Elizabeth, in short, was an astonishing woman, certainly one of the greatest in all English history, and she well deserves to have her name given to one of the most glorious epochs in that history.

Elizabeth had been reigning thirty years and was, for those days, an elderly woman when what she had always dreaded, and had schemed to avoid, came to pass. In 1588, the Spanish Grand Armada, a fleet of huge galleons crammed with the finest soldiers in Europe, sailed at last, after many delays, for the invasion of England. Unlike Philip of Spain, Elizabeth had no regular army of veterans, only bands of militia. The Spanish galleons had only to effect a landing and Elizabeth's kingdom was doomed. But David beat Goliath. The smaller and faster English vessels, superbly handled by the best seamen in the world, outmatched the unwieldy Spanish galleons, more like floating fortresses and barracks than ships, and then a great storm arose to scatter and then destroy the Armada. England was saved. The menacing shadow of Spain under which Elizabeth had lived ever since she took the crown suddenly vanished. The queen, the great "Gloriana" as she was called, and her cheering, bell-ringing subjects came out into the sunshine.

THE FLOWERING OF ELIZABETHAN LITERATURE

All the chief glories of the Elizabethan Age in literature — and many of them arrived during the reign of Elizabeth's successor, James I — came after the defeat of the Spanish Armada. It was as if the nation suddenly found itself,

National Portrait Gallery

discovering new sources of confidence, energy, and delight, all these finding expression in literature. Up to that time, in all but the last twelve years of the sixteenth century, England, though making rapid progress under the Tudors, had been far behind Italy, France, and Spain in literature and the arts and the whole new civilizing process of the Renaissance.

Sir Philip Sidney, soldier, scholar, poet, literary patron, courtier, and member of Parliament, is often referred to as the ideal Renaissance gentleman.

The English poets, such as they were, could only imitate foreign models. The most important of these was the sonnet form, originally Italian. The sonnet was always a poem of fourteen lines, but its elaborate rhyming pattern could be varied. The Earl of Surrey and Sir Thomas Wyatt, both of whom died at a comparatively early age, successfully used the sonnet form during the first half of the sixteenth century. Much later, Shakespeare, and much later still, Milton, raised this form to a great poetic height.

Photo Researchers, Inc.

Old Moreton Hall, a small country manor house in the typical Elizabethan black-and-white half timber style.

The prose in Elizabethan times was stiff and ungainly, creaking in its joints. Somehow the language, as an instrument, was not ready for great literature: there it was, like a vast organ, with nobody knowing yet how to handle the keyboard and work the stops. It was as if the queen's taut anxiety, her unsleeping watchfulness during these first thirty years of her reign, had influenced the whole mood of the nation, which wanted to sing but could only keep clearing its throat.

Once the Spanish menace was removed, the tremendous release that followed changed everything. The aging queen was by this time a fabulous figure, and the whole nation suddenly flowered. It is from this time on that we find the Elizabethans of legend, with all their extraordinary energy and self-confidence, beginning to flourish. And this transformation is perfectly reflected in the literature of the time. The English language, that great instrument which nobody had known how to play, suddenly came right. If this may seem an exaggeration, then we must remember that within ten years after the defeat of the Armada, Shakespeare was not only writing some of the greatest poetry the world has ever known but was also using a vocabulary unequaled in its size, variety, and richness even among the world's greatest poets. These later Elizabethans, of all classes, had a passion for magnificent language: they got drunk on words. And some of us, reading now what they wrote during those distant years, can still feel something of their intoxication.

When a whole society has an overwhelming passion, things begin to happen. Our society, with all its technological resources and ingenuity, has a craving for speed and rapid travel, with the result that one engineering marvel after another arrives to hurry us along the roads or through the air. So we have done more for quick transport in the last twenty-five years than men could do in the previous 250,000 years. Well, the Elizabethans had a similar general passion for poetry, both lyrical and dramatic, and out of it they too created one marvel after another, crowned by the immortal works of Shakespeare. There are now scores of cities in the United States and Britain larger than Elizabethan London, yet between 1595 and 1625 that London could produce more good poets and dramatists than the combined populations of the United States and Britain have been able to produce in the last hundred years. History shows us over and over again this direct and deep connection between what a society wants and what it creates. We should always keep this in mind. So, for example, if it is true, as we are told, that America is now spending more on symphonic music than it is on baseball, we might expect — and there are signs of it already — a rapid development here in musical composition.

ELIZABETHAN LONDON

The Elizabethan society which produced the great plays was itself essentially dramatic. Within its new national unity it was richly varied: there was the fabulous Queen Elizabeth herself and her splendid court (and many a young nobleman spent all he possessed just to make a fine appearance there). At the court there were magnificent court masques (both Elizabeth and James I were extremely fond of them) that were generally acted by amateurs but devised and written by professional dramatists, notably Ben Jonson. The staging of masques was often very elaborate, and a great architect like Inigo Jones did not think it beneath his dignity to design the decorations and stage machinery.

Then there was the growing middle class of merchants, many of them already tending toward Puritanism and providing a sturdy opposition (itself provocative of drama) to poets and players and all the swaggering roisterers; there were the sea captains and sailors from the ends of the earth, the crowds of lively young apprentices, and the hearty common folk who packed the theaters to listen for hours to poetic drama. Elizabethan London was like a gigantic fair, crammed and noisy with all manner of characters, some of them magnificent in costumes paid for by the sale of their estates, others in rags and tatters. In the noblemen's palaces off the Strand, running down to the river, musicians sang to lutes and poets brought copies of their verses; in the taverns of Eastcheap the wits exchanged rapid quips and the girls giggled; and not far away was the sinister bulk of the Tower with its thumbscrews and racks and executioners' axes. And in the oval-shaped roofless theaters nearby, packed almost every afternoon, the players were saying lines that are now immortal. What a place, what a people!

THE ELIZABETHAN THEATER

Great poetical drama is far rarer, far harder to achieve, than great lyrical or narrative poetry or prose fiction, just because so many things have to be right for it all at the same time. There must be not only exceptional dramatic poets but also exceptional players, theaters, and audiences. All these must be on a high level simultaneously. And here the Elizabethan dramatists were fortunate. All the evidence we possess suggests that English acting in Shakespeare's time was very good indeed, so that companies of English players were in demand abroad. It is true that women's parts were played by boys, but these boys were highly trained in movement, gesture, and the speaking of verse. What we would now call the "stars" among the men, players like Alleyn and Burbage, who had substantial shares in the playhouses (as Shakespeare finally had), must have been very fine performers indeed. And all these actors, while capable of making themselves heard from the pit to the uppermost gallery, were able to get through their scenes at what seems to us now an astonishing pace. We know this because very long plays like *Hamlet* could be performed in their entirety during an afternoon, within hours roughly known to us. In ordinary productions of Shakespeare's longer plays, it has been the practice ever since the eighteenth century to make many cuts, whole scenes often being omitted to enable modern actors, in their slower pace, to present the play in a reasonable length of time.

The Elizabethan stage which favored this rapid pace, just as it favored an intimate and imaginative relationship between poet, players, and audience, came into existence almost by accident. Before the London playhouses were built, the wealthier nobles had kept troupes of players among their retainers and had often sent these troupes touring the country, where Shakespeare as a boy must have seen them, for records show that towns no larger than Stratford might have visits from six troupes in a year. When playing in towns, these touring companies used innyards, where the crowd could surround the platform that was erected and the superior patrons could seat themselves in the galleries running outside the bedrooms of the inn. The London playhouses merely improved upon this setting. Their stages still had a platform coming out into the audience, but they also had proper entrances at each side, a small inner stage that could be curtained off, and, above, an upper stage or balcony.

All outdoor scenes were played on the platform or forestage, with the curtains of the inner stage drawn to hide it. These curtains were pulled back, to reveal a throne or whatever was needed, for any indoor scene. The balcony was used whenever two different levels were necessary, for sentries on battlements or girls like Juliet looking for their lovers. For swift, imaginative poetic drama, this type of stage was far superior to the "picture frame" stage, with its elaborate painted scenery, that succeeded it. The play could move quickly from one short scene to the next, more like our films than most of our contemporary plays. Not having a scene painter and lighting electrician to help him, the dramatist had to use words to describe his scene or to create an atmosphere: he was compelled to be imaginative and so was his audience. It is a great pity that the plays of Shakespeare and the other Elizabethan dramatists, all written for this kind of staging, are not still performed in this swift and imaginative fashion.

As we know from what the dramatists themselves tell us, the popular audiences liked to have in their plays some clowning, dancing, and sword combats. But they must have enjoyed the poetry too, whether comic or tragic; otherwise they would not have filled the playhouses. It is fortunate for English literature that the university scholars and wits, who wanted stiff and solemn drama in the style of the Roman dramatist Seneca, did not have their way. The professionals who ran the London playhouses refused to imitate the classics and made good use of the crude but valuable dramatic material, the wealth of popular entertainment, already in existence. For though the men who built and ran these theaters had to look to the court and the more important nobles both for the necessary licenses and official patronage, they knew that to keep their companies in employment and to fill their pits and galleries popular support was essential.

The rapid development of Elizabethan drama, from primitive comedy and tragedy to great masterpieces within twenty-five years, is astounding. It produced not only the incomparable Shakespeare but with him a large group of dramatists, all with talent and some touched with genius. In this group were Ben Jonson (1572–1637), Christopher Marlowe (1564–93), George Chapman (1559?–1634?), John Marston (1575?–1634), Thomas Dekker (1570–1632), and later, actually Jacobean not Elizabethan dramatists, there were Thomas Middleton (1570?–1627), Thomas Heywood (d. 1650?), John Webster (1580?–1625?), Francis Beaumont (1584–1616), John Fletcher (1579–1625), Philip Massinger (1583–1640), and John Ford (fl. 1639). Some of these dramatists, as the anthologies show us, could also write exquisite lyrical verse. The poet Spenser could achieve an ingenious epic form in his huge allegorical panorama, *The Faerie Queene,* and a generation later John Donne might be deeply introspective and metaphysical in his verse; but, outside the drama, this age is notable chiefly for its effortless, enchanting lyrics, the songs it lightly tossed into the air. No age that came afterwards ever quite captured this golden singing, ever returned to this May morning of English poetry.

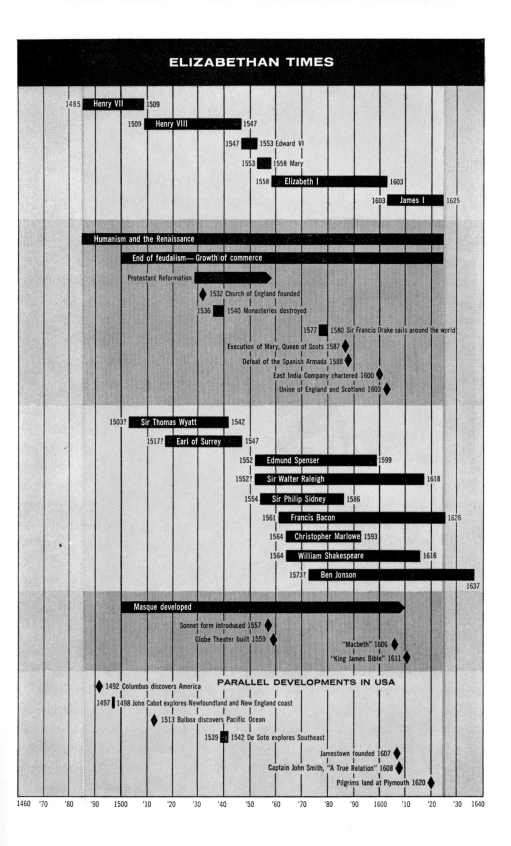

ELIZABETHAN TIMES

1485 Henry VII 1509
1509 Henry VIII 1547
1547 1553 Edward VI
1553 1558 Mary
1558 Elizabeth I 1603
1603 James I 1625

Humanism and the Renaissance
End of feudalism—Growth of commerce
Protestant Reformation
1532 Church of England founded
1536 1540 Monasteries destroyed
1577 1580 Sir Francis Drake sails around the world
Execution of Mary, Queen of Scots 1587
Defeat of the Spanish Armada 1588
East India Company chartered 1600
Union of England and Scotland 1603

1503? Sir Thomas Wyatt 1542
1517? Earl of Surrey 1547
1552 Edmund Spenser 1599
1552? Sir Walter Raleigh 1618
1554 Sir Philip Sidney 1586
1561 Francis Bacon 1626
1564 Christopher Marlowe 1593
1564 William Shakespeare 1616
1573? Ben Jonson 1637

Masque developed
Sonnet form introduced 1557
Globe Theater built 1559
"Macbeth" 1606
"King James Bible" 1611

1492 Columbus discovers America   PARALLEL DEVELOPMENTS IN USA
1497 1498 John Cabot explores Newfoundland and New England coast
1513 Balboa discovers Pacific Ocean
1539 1542 De Soto explores Southeast
Jamestown founded 1607
Captain John Smith, "A True Relation" 1608
Pilgrims land at Plymouth 1620

1460 '70 '80 '90 1500 '10 '20 '30 '40 '50 '60 '70 '80 '90 1600 '10 '20 '30 1640

ELIZABETHAN PROSE

James I, the son of Mary Queen of Scots, joined his kingdom of Scotland to the English throne, which he rightly inherited after the death of Queen Elizabeth in 1603. A pedantic, cowardly man who considered himself king by "divine right," he was soon unpopular with most of his English subjects, who disliked his Scots favorites and his pro-Spanish policy. But he must be credited with one great contribution to English literature, for in 1604 he set his bishops the task of making a new translation of the Bible, first published in 1611 and known from then on as the King James Version. Its fidelity as a translation has often been criticized by later scholars, but what cannot be questioned is the

National Portrait Gallery

James I

sheer beauty, the haunting magic, of its English. This is the Bible that centuries of writers have known from childhood onwards, and echoes of this noble old work can be heard in nearly all the finest English prose.

But although the chroniclers and pamphleteers, men like Greene and Dekker and Nashe (who also tried his hand at fiction), were busy during the later years of the century, although before the age ended it had given us the essays of Francis Bacon (1561–1626) and the stately

narratives of Sir Walter Raleigh, prose as a general instrument of expression was hardly yet completely mastered. It was still not sufficiently flexible. (Much of the prose dialogue in the drama, however, is superb.) Bacon and Raleigh in their very different ways — or an eccentric scholar like Robert Burton, whose *Anatomy of Melancholy* (1621) is one of the masterpieces of the age — might have been able to compel the prevailing prose style to serve their various purposes, but it was not until the following age that both the grand and the familiar prose styles came easily to authors.

The earlier years of Elizabeth's reign were anxious and difficult; the later years of James I were strangely corrupt, unhealthy, as if the sun had stopped shining. Between these years, let us say, roughly, from 1590 to 1610, was one of the miraculous golden times of literature, when the London streets were filled with richly gifted men, bursting with energy and zest for life. As we know, one of the greatest of these men, now loved and admired wherever books are read and plays performed, was William Shakespeare. It is our privilege to share the language in which he wrote, one of the marvels of all the ages.

J. B. P.

EDMUND SPENSER

1552–1599

Because he had an astonishing control of the poet's craft and great creative imagination, Edmund Spenser is often called "the poet's poet." Unlike Shakespeare, who was concerned with the problems and mixed emotions of real human beings, Spenser created a dream world in which his knights move as symbols of noble ideals.

Spenser, the son of a London cloth-maker, attended school on a scholarship set up for poor boys. While still a student, he became adept at translating and introducing classical meters into English poetry. Shortly after taking degrees from Cambridge University, he published *The Shepherd's Calendar,* which consists of twelve descriptive poems, one for each month, about the beauties of the countryside. This series won Spenser court recognition and began the vogue for pastoral poetry.

Encouraged by Sir Walter Raleigh, a court favorite, Spenser next wrote his greatest work, *The Faerie Queene.* The title so obviously referred to Queen Elizabeth that the flattered patron ordered a generous pension for the poet. Spenser did not receive all his money, however, from the unwilling treasurer; and, feeling out of favor, he returned to his home, a picturesque old castle, in Ireland. After a native rebellion broke out, the castle, together with his belongings and some manu-scripts, was burned. Broken and impoverished, Spenser returned to London and died not long after. He was buried in the Poet's Corner in Westminster Abbey, next to another great poet, Geoffrey Chaucer.

Spenser's masterpiece, *The Faerie Queene,* is the longest well-known poem in English literature. It is not as long as Spenser originally intended it to be, however. He set out to write twelve books, each recounting the story of a knight who personifies one of the virtues of a perfect gentleman. But only six of the adventures were completed — those of the knights representing Holiness, Temperance, Chastity, Friendship, Justice, and Courtesy.

The work is written in a stanza of the poet's own invention, ever since called the Spenserian stanza. It consists of eight lines in iambic pentameter and a ninth line containing two extra syllables. The rhyme scheme always follows the form given in the stanza below. This stanza was widely imitated by later poets whom you will be reading — Burns, Byron, Shelley, and Keats. To enable you to recognize it and remember its origin when you meet it again, a stanza from *The Faerie Queene* is quoted here. It is a famous description of the House of Morpheus (sleep), stanza 41 from Book I, Canto I. Notice the skillful handling of sound effects.

	Rhyme scheme
And more, to lulle him in his slumber soft,	a
A trickling streame from high rock tumbling downe,	b
And ever-drizzling raine upon the loft.°	a
Mixt with a murmuring winde, much like the sowne	b
Of swarming Bees, did cast him in a swowne:°	b
No other noyse, nor peoples troublous cryes,	c
As still are wont t'annoy the wallèd towne,	b
Might there be heard: but carelesse Quiet lyes,	c
Wrapt in eternall silence farre from enemyes.	c

3. *upon the loft:* upon the roof. 5. *swowne:* swoon, fainting spell.

Amoretti

As a young man Spenser was sent to Ireland, where he spent many years of his life. There he met and married Elizabeth Boyle, of whom little is known outside of the descriptions of her in Spenser's sonnet sequence *Amoretti* (little love poems).

After Sir Thomas Wyatt introduced the sonnet from Italy, it became the vogue in the English court to honor one's lady in this form of verse. Spenser, Sidney, and Shakespeare all wrote famous sonnet sequences. A sonnet is always fourteen lines long, each line in iambic pentameter, that is, ten syllables with stress on every other syllable. The rhyme scheme of a sonnet may vary according to the preference of the poet. The Elizabethans created their own order of rhymes, but later poets returned to the original Italian rhyme scheme, which became standard.

Sonnet 26

	Rhyme scheme	
Sweet is the rose, but grows upon a briar;	a	
Sweet is the juniper, but sharp his bough;°	b	
Sweet is the eglantine, but pricketh near;	a	
Sweet is the fir-bloom, but his branch is rough;	b	
Sweet is the cypress, but his rind is tough;	b	5
Sweet is the nut, but bitter is his pill;°	c	
Sweet is the broom-flower, but yet sour enough;	b	
And sweet is moly,° but his root is ill.	c	
So every sweet with sour is tempered still,	c	
That maketh it be coveted the more:	d	10
For easy things, that may be got at will,	c	
Most sorts of men do set but little store.	d	
Why then should I account of little pain,	e	
That endless pleasure shall unto me gain!	e	

2. *his bough:* In the sixteenth century *his* was still used where today we use *its*. "Bough" was probably pronounced to rhyme with "rough" in medieval times, to which Spenser likes to refer. 6. *pill:* center or core. 8. *moly:* an herb with white blossoms and a black root.

Sonnet 37

What guile is this, that those her golden tresses
    She doth attire under a net of gold;
    And with sly skill so cunningly them dresses,
    That which is gold, or hair, may scarce be told?
Is it that men's frail eyes, which gaze too bold,   5
She may entangle in that golden snare;
And, being caught, may craftily enfold
Their weaker hearts, which are not well aware?
Take heed, therefore, mine eyes, how ye do stare
Henceforth too rashly on that guileful net,   10
In which, if ever ye entrappèd are,
Out of her hands ye by no means shall get.
    Fondness° it were for any, being free,
    To covet fetters, though they golden be!

13. *Fondness:* foolishness.

CHRISTOPHER MARLOWE

1564–1593

and SIR WALTER RALEIGH

1552?–1618

Christopher Marlowe is one of the most romantic and tragic figures of Elizabethan England. He was killed in a tavern brawl at the age of twenty-nine, when he was at the height of his poetic powers. He had grown up in Canterbury and had studied at Cambridge, where it is said he engaged in secret governmental work, much to the displeasure of his tutors. "Kit" Marlowe was an impetuous young man, endowed with a genius that poured out, during six short years, into magnificent tragic dramas. *Tamburlaine* pictures a great Asiatic conqueror of the fourteenth century. *Dr. Faustus* tells the age-old legend of the man who sells his soul to the devil, a story used by the German poet Goethe in *Faust* and also in Gounod's opera *Faust*. In his plays Marlowe perfected blank verse, which Shakespeare later used. He was admired by many poets; Ben Jonson speaks of his ability to write a "mighty line" with sonorousness and power.

Sir Walter Raleigh is known chiefly as the English explorer who tried to start a colony in America. He called it Virginia in honor of Elizabeth, the Virgin Queen. He was one of the bright stars of a bright age, a friend of Spenser and Marlowe, and a favorite of the queen. Raleigh was handsome, ambitious, vigorous, hot-tempered, and sometimes unscrupulous, and he led an adventurous life — in and out of favor with the queen, in and out of prison. Finally he died under the executioner's ax. While imprisoned in the Tower of London for thirteen years, Raleigh wrote a lengthy

National Gallery of Ireland

Sir Walter Raleigh

History of the World; earlier he had written an account of his journey to the Americas. Like other courtiers of the time, he was also a poet and could write a pastoral lyric, like the following one, with grace and wit.

"The Passionate Shepherd to His Love" and "The Nymph's Reply to the Shepherd" are a famous pair of lyrics in English literature. In the first pastoral, Marlowe pictures a perfect, idyllic love and expresses the Elizabethan ideal of courtship. In the second, Raleigh replies in a way that shows that the Elizabethans were realistic as well as romantic. Notice how the passionate shepherd is suddenly brought down to earth by a very practical nymph.

117

The Passionate Shepherd
to His Love

CHRISTOPHER MARLOWE

The Nymph's Reply
to the Shepherd

SIR WALTER RALEIGH

Come live with me and be my love,
And we will all the pleasures prove
That hills and valleys, dales and fields,
Or woods or steepy mountain yields.

And we will sit upon the rocks,   5
Seeing the shepherds feed their flocks,
By shallow rivers, to whose falls
Melodious birds sing madrigals.

And I will make thee beds of roses,
And a thousand fragrant posies,   10
A cap of flowers, and a kirtle°
Embroidered all with leaves of myrtle;

A gown made of the finest wool,
Which from our pretty lambs we pull;
Fair linèd slippers for the cold,   15
With buckles of the purest gold;

A belt of straw and ivy buds
With coral clasps and amber studs;
And if these pleasures may thee move,
Come live with me and be my love.   20

Thy silver dishes for thy meat
As precious as the gods do eat,
Shall on an ivory table be
Prepared each day for thee and me.

The shepherd swains shall dance and
    sing   25
For thy delight each May morning;
If these delights thy mind may move,
Then live with me and be my love.

11. *kirtle* (kûr′t′l): a dress.

If all the world and love were young,
And truth in every shepherd's tongue,
These pretty pleasures might me move
To live with thee and be thy love.   4

Time drives the flocks from field to fold,
When rivers rage, and rocks grow cold;
And Philomel° becometh dumb;
The rest complains of cares to come.

The flowers do fade, and wanton fields
To wayward Winter reckoning yields;
A honey tongue, a heart of gall,   11
Is fancy's spring, but sorrow's fall.

Thy gowns, thy shoes, thy beds of roses,
Thy cap, thy kirtle, and thy posies,
Soon break, soon wither, soon forgot-
    ten,   15
In folly ripe, in reason rotten.

Thy belt of straw and ivy buds,
Thy coral clasps and amber studs,
All these in me no means can move
To come to thee and be thy love.   20

But could youth last, and love still
    breed,
Had joys no date,° nor age no need,
Then these delights my mind might
    move
To live with thee and be thy love.

7. *Philomel* (fĭl′ō·mĕl): the nightingale.
22. *no date:* no final date; no end.

118

ELIZABETHAN LOVE POEMS

1. What bit of wisdom does Spenser use as the principal thought in Sonnet 26? How does he apply this to his own life in the last two lines? What kind of troubles do you think he might have had in mind? Which of the plants mentioned are familiar to you? Which do not grow in your vicinity? You can probably find pictures of these plants in a good botany reference book.

2. In Sonnet 37 what do you learn of ladies' hairdressing styles of that day? In what double sense does the poet use the word *net* in line 10? At what stage in his love affair does he seem to be?

3. Review what was said about the Spenserian stanza on page 115, then study the stanza given on that page until you are familiar with its form — rhythm, line length, and rhyme scheme. Notice that the rhyme scheme of the Spenserian stanza is the same as that of the first nine lines of the Spenserian sonnet.

4. Why is Marlowe's "The Passionate Shepherd to His Love" called a pastoral lyric? Which of the promises of the shepherd are obviously far-fetched?

5. In Raleigh's poem show how the nymph answers each of the shepherd's statements. How would you describe her attitude, especially if you were to think of her as a modern woman?

BEHIND THE SCENES IN ENGLISH LITERATURE

In his short lifetime, the impetuous and free-thinking Christopher Marlowe, who had once been in jail for an unknown offense, acquired a fairly gaudy reputation for riotous living. And so his early and violent death by stabbing in a tavern brawl seemed eminently fitting to some of his pious and scandalized contemporaries who frequently commented upon Marlowe's end. But no two of their accounts agreed exactly — about the scene of the brawl, the cause of the quarrel, the assailant, or anything except the stabbing.

One early source identifies the assailant as "one named Ingram," and the burial records of St. Nicholas' Church in Deptford, where the brawl took place, show that Marlowe was "slain by Francis Frezer" or "Frizer." This was all anyone knew until 1924, when John Leslie Hotson, an American scholar, started work on another matter in the ill-organized Public Records Office in London, a huge depository of legal documents dating back to the Middle Ages. In one set of documents he ran across a reference to a certain "Ingram Frizer," and recollected that both names figured in the Marlowe story. He decided to investigate and searched for days in post mortem and criminal records without success. Then he remembered that many of the traditional reports gave Marlowe as the aggressor; if so, surely the murderer would have pleaded self-defense and requested pardon. Turning to the index of pardons, he found there, "The Queen 28th day of June [1593] granted pardon to Ingram Friser in self-defense." Next the pardon itself: this gave the details of the pardon and a summary of the inquest. Was there a full record of the inquest? A long search finally produced it; here, at last, was the real story.

Apparently Marlowe met with Frizer and three other men on the morning of the day of the murder and conferred secretly all day. After supper there was a quarrel over the reckoning; Marlowe attacked Frizer and Frizer, snatching the dagger from him, inflicted the fatal wound. But who were Marlowe's three companions? In spite of Hotson's careful searching, this is still something of a mystery. Marlowe and his companions, however, were evidently deeply involved in undercover political intrigue, and this probably explains Marlowe's earlier imprisonment as well as the true cause of the quarrel.

WILLIAM SHAKESPEARE

1564 – 1616

It is impossible to talk about Shakespeare without using superlatives. Critics never tire of saying that he is the greatest of English writers and perhaps the greatest poet in all world literature.

Yet for all this glory, and despite the efforts of several generations of scholars, the circumstances of Shakespeare's life are shrouded in mystery and may never be clarified. We do know that he was born in Stratford on Avon. The house assumed to be his birthplace still stands and has been converted into a museum filled with mementos and first editions of his works. Nearby stands the grammar school he probably attended as a boy and the guild hall where in all likelihood he enjoyed the plays presented by traveling actors during his boyhood. Shakespeare's mother was a member of the gentry; his father was prominent in Stratford: a high bailiff, alderman, and justice of the peace who with the passage of time became a squire and was granted a coat of arms.

At the village of Shottery near Stratford is the cottage of Anne Hathaway, who at twenty-six was married to Shakespeare, then only eighteen. After the birth of their three children, Shakespeare went up to London alone to seek his fortune. Whether he and his wife were estranged or whether he saw his family at intervals has been a subject of great conjecture, but there is no actual proof for either theory.

After about twenty years as an actor and playwright in London, Shakespeare returned to Stratford and apparently took up the life of a wealthy squire. Today it is possible to see the site of the handsome house he bought there, though the building itself no longer stands. At fifty-two he died, leaving provision in his will that he be buried in the chancel of Trinity Church in Stratford. Wishing to avert the practice of that day whereby the bones of those long interred were often removed from burial places, Shakespeare had this last poem placed on his tomb:

Good friend, for Jesus' sake forbeare
To dig the dust enclosèd heare;
Bleste be the man that spares these stones,
And curst be he that moves my bones.

With all this concrete evidence in Stratford, Shakespeare seems like a real person; but in London, where he spent most of his life and did his most important work, he seems almost like a myth. A few records show that he acted minor parts in the theaters across the Thames and owned a share in the old Globe Theater.

After his death, his friends and co-workers collected and published his plays in what is known as *The First Folio* (1623). This was a difficult task, for Shakespeare had taken no steps to preserve his writings. Fortunately most of them could be found in old theater records.

While there is no definite proof that the portrait above is that of Shakespeare, its pedigree goes back to within fifty years of his death, and it has stronger claims to authenticity than any other painting thought to be of Shakespeare. (Courtesy National Portrait Gallery)

120

Shakespeare is now credited with one hundred and fifty-four sonnets, four long poems, and thirty-seven plays of all types — farce, history, romantic comedy, and tragedy. Not all the writings attributed to him have been verified as his, but most of them bear his unmistakable mark: versatility, a power over words, and a wide and deep understanding of human nature such as no other English writer has equaled.

It is impossible to give exact dates for the writing of Shakespeare's plays, but they can be placed in four general groups that could conceivably represent periods in his life from youth to an approaching old age.

The plays of the first period are marked by youthful dreams and exuberant spirits. Paramount among them are *A Midsummer Night's Dream,* loveliest of poetic fantasies; *The Merchant of Venice,* with its dramatic trial scene; *The Taming of the Shrew,* his most popular farce; and *Romeo and Juliet,* a romantic tragedy of ageless beauty and world renown.

The second period is that of the great chronicles and romantic comedies. The fat, rollicking Falstaff rolls through the two plays of *King Henry IV* and recurs in *The Merry Wives of Windsor,* said to have been written at the queen's request to see Falstaff in love. By this time Shakespeare had a proprietary interest in the Globe Theater, for which he wrote three great comedies: *Much Ado about Nothing, As You Like It,* and *Twelfth Night.* They have certain elements in common, such as the profusion of choice lyrics, the plot turning on concealed identity, the witty, self-reliant heroines (in the last two disguised as boys), and the highly individualized comic characters.

Depression and tragedy mark the plays of the third period. What sorrow or disillusionment in Shakespeare's life may have darkened his spirit we can only guess, for there is no definite record. Among several plays laid in ancient Greece and Rome, the best known is *Julius Caesar,* analyzing man's relation to the state. Even greater are four tragedies which touch the depths of human experience in various stages of life. The young prince in *Hamlet* shows a sensitive and subtle intellect struggling against the adverse circumstances of life and against elements in his own nature.

Othello is a powerful study of love in middle life destroyed by overmastering jealousy and suspicion. *King Lear* gives an unforgettable picture of an aged and proud king driven mad by the ingratitude of his daughters. *Macbeth* analyzes the soul of the mature, grasping ruler who sacrifices everyone to gratify his personal ambition.

With the fourth period the storm and stress of Shakespeare's inner spirit seems to have passed away. *A Winter's Tale* and *The Tempest* are plays of warmth and reconciliation. Old wrongs are righted and forgiven in the end. He returns, especially in his last play, *The Tempest,* to the spirited fantasy and tender romance of the earlier comedies, which he now suffuses with a mellow philosophy.

Thus Shakespeare's genius completes its full circle with no lessening of poetic power and with an almost godlike return of poise.

Songs from the Plays

In Shakespeare's day, music was a familiar part of the theater. Shakespeare himself wrote 124 beautiful songs for his plays. These were all set to music in his lifetime; over the centuries many composers (notably Schubert) have given them new musical settings.

Hark, Hark, the Lark

In the play *Cymbeline* (Act II, Scene iii), musicians hired by her lover sing this song to Princess Imogen.

Hark, hark! the lark at heaven's gate
    sings,
  And Phoebus° 'gins arise,
His steeds to water at those springs
  On chaliced° flowers that lies;
And winking Marybuds° begin   5
  To ope their golden eyes.
With everything that pretty is,
  My lady sweet, arise!
  Arise, arise!

2. *Phoebus* (fē′bŭs): the sun, personified as the driver of a chariot. 4. *chaliced* (chăl′ĭst): cup-shaped. 5. *Marybuds:* marigolds.

Blow, Blow, Thou Winter Wind

This song from *As You Like It* (Act II, Scene vii) is sung by Amiens to the banished Duke in the Forest of Arden.

> Blow, blow, thou winter wind!
> Thou art not so unkind
>   As man's ingratitude;
> Thy tooth is not so keen,
> Because thou art not seen,   5
> Although thy breath be rude.
>
> Heigh ho! sing, heigh ho! unto the green
>   holly;
> Most friendship is feigning, most loving
>   mere folly.
>   Then, heigh ho, the holly!
>   This life is most jolly.   10
>
> Freeze, freeze, thou bitter sky!
> That dost not bite so nigh
>   As benefits forgot;
> Though thou the waters warp,
> Thy sting is not so sharp   15
>   As friend remembered not.°
>
> Heigh ho, sing, heigh ho! unto the green
>   holly;
> Most friendship is feigning, most loving
>   mere folly.
>   Then, heigh ho, the holly!
>   This life is most jolly.   20

16. As what a forgotten friend feels.

Who Is Silvia?

This serenade from *The Two Gentlemen of Verona* (Act IV, Scene ii) is better known than the play itself. Of the more than twenty musical settings for it, Schubert's is the most famous. By repeating the last line, he was especially successful in building up each stanza to a climax of melody.

> Who is Silvia? What is she,
>   That all our swains commend her?
> Holy, fair, and wise is she;
>   The heaven such grace did lend her,
> That she might admirèd be.   5
>
> Is she kind as she is fair?
>   For beauty lives with kindness.
> Love doth to her eyes repair,
>   To help him of his blindness,
> And, being helped, inhabits there.   10
>
> Then to Silvia let us sing,
>   That Silvia is excelling;
> She excels each mortal thing
>   Upon the dull earth dwelling:
> To her let us garlands bring.   15

O Mistress Mine

In *Twelfth Night* (Act II, Scene iii) we find this quaint love song. It is one of the few Shakespeare songs for which we still have sixteenth-century music.

> O Mistress mine, where are you roam-
>   ing?
> O stay and hear! your true love's coming
>   That can sing both high and low;
> Trip no further, pretty sweeting,
> Journeys end in lovers' meeting —   5
>   Every wise man's son doth know.
>
> What is love? 'tis not hereafter;
> Present mirth hath present laughter;
>   What's to come is still unsure;
> In delay there lies no plenty, —   10
> Then come kiss me, Sweet-and-twenty,
>   Youth's a stuff will not endure.

Three Songs
from *The Tempest*

Here are three songs from one of Shake-speare's finest plays, *The Tempest*. A party of Italian nobles is shipwrecked on a strange enchanted island. Over them hovers Ariel, a delicate invisible spirit, whose songs are a significant part of the play. By the first song the young Prince Ferdinand is convinced that his father is drowned (Act I, Scene ii). The second song expresses Ariel's happiness as he thinks of the freedom his master has promised him (Act V, Scene i). In the third song Ariel warns the honest counselor, Gonzalo, that a plot is brewing (Act II, Scene i).

I

Full fathom five thy father lies.
    Of his bones are coral made;
Those are pearls that were his eyes;
    Nothing of him that doth fade
But doth suffer a sea change   5
Into something rich and strange.
Sea nymphs hourly ring his knell:
                    Dingdong!
Hark! now I hear them — Dingdong,
    bell!

II

Where the bee sucks, there suck I;
In a cowslip's bell I lie;
There I couch when owls do cry.
On the bat's back I do fly
After summer merrily.   5
Merrily, merrily, shall I live now
Under the blossom that hangs on the
    bough.

III

While here you do snoring lie,
Open-eyed conspiracy
    His time doth take.
If of life you keep a care,
Shake off slumber, and beware.   5
    Awake, awake!

SHAKESPEARE'S LYRICS

1. What is the mood of each lyric? What does this show about the range of Shake-speare's powers?

2. As you would expect, the most effective way to approach these songs is to hear them in their musical settings. Try to obtain recordings of the songs. Listen carefully to the music and then reread the songs. Does the music enhance them in any way? Does it detract from them?

3. Because there is no set form for a song, great variety in rhythmical pattern may be found. Are any two of these alike in pattern? Note rhyme schemes and variations in length of line. Show examples of refrain and of alliteration.

SUGGESTION FOR WRITING

Try writing a short lyric of your own. Poets and musicians in the class might collaborate on original words and music.

Sonnets

Of all the sonnet sequences written by Elizabethan poets, none can equal the sonnets of Shakespeare in perfect form and depth of thought and feeling; nor have they been excelled in all English literature. No one knows whether Shakespeare's sonnets — one hundred and fifty-four in all — reflect the poet's own emotional experiences or imaginary situations. Many of them seem to be addressed to a young friend and others to a mysterious "dark lady" with whom Shakespeare apparently is deeply in love. The identity of these persons has been guessed at but never proved by Shakespearean scholars.

Shakespeare does not use the Italian rhyme scheme but a form preferred by many of the Elizabethan sonneteers. You will notice that there are three four-line stanzas with an alternate rhyme in each. Then the thought is summarized in a rhymed couplet at the end. In comparing the rhyme scheme with the one Spenser used (see page 116), you will see a slight difference, though in general they follow the same plan.

Sonnet 18

	Rhyme scheme	
Shall I compare thee to a summer's day?	*a*	
Thou art more lovely and more temperate:	*b*	
Rough winds do shake the darling buds of May,	*a*	
And summer's lease hath all too short a date;	*b*	
Sometimes too hot the eye of heaven shines,	*c*	5
And often is his gold complexion dimmed;	*d*	
And every fair from fair sometime declines,	*c*	
By chance, or nature's changing course, untrimmed.°	*d*	
But thy eternal summer shall not fade	*e*	
Nor lose possession of that fair thou owest;°	*f*	10
Nor shall Death brag thou wanderest in his shade,	*e*	
When in eternal lines to time thou growest —	*f*	
So long as men can breathe, or eyes can see,	*g*	
So long lives this, and this gives life to thee.	*g*	

8. *untrimmed:* deprived of its beauty. 10. *owest:* own.

Sonnet 29

When in disgrace with fortune and men's eyes
I all alone beweep my outcast state,
And trouble deaf heaven with my bootless° cries,
And look upon myself, and curse my fate;

Wishing me like to one more rich in hope,   5
Featured like him, like him with friends possessed,
Desiring this man's art, and that man's scope,
With what I most enjoy contented least;

Yet in these thoughts myself almost despising,
Haply I think on thee — and then my state,   10
Like to the lark at break of day arising
From sullen earth, sings hymns at heaven's gate;

For thy sweet love remembered such wealth brings
That then I scorn to change my state with kings.

3. *bootless:* useless.

Sonnet 55

Not marble, nor the gilded monuments
Of princes, shall outlive this powerful rime;
But you shall shine more bright in these contents°
Than unswept stone, besmeared with sluttish time.

When wasteful war shall statues overturn,   5
And broils° root out the work of masonry,
Nor Mars his sword° nor war's quick fire shall burn
The living record of your memory.

'Gainst death and all-oblivious enmity°
Shall you pace forth; your praise shall still find room   10
Even in the eyes of all posterity
That wear this world out to the ending doom.

So, till the judgment that yourself arise,°
You live in this, and dwell in lovers' eyes.

3. *these contents:* the contents of this poem. 6. *broils:* fights, brawls. 7. *Mars his sword:* Mars'
sword. 9. *all-oblivious enmity:* war which sends all to oblivion. 12–13. These lines refer to the belief
that the world will come to an end with a final day of judgment, when all the dead will arise; *that
yourself:* when you yourself.

Sonnet 73

That time of year thou may'st in me behold
When yellow leaves, or none, or few, do hang
Upon those boughs which shake against the cold,
Bare ruined choirs, where late the sweet birds sang.

In me thou see'st the twilight of such day   5
As after sunset fadeth in the west,
Which by and by black night doth take away,
Death's second self, that seals up all in rest.

In me thou see'st the glowing of such fire,
That on the ashes of his youth doth lie   10
As the deathbed whereon it must expire,
Consumed with that which it was nourished by.

— This thou perceiv'st, which makes thy love more strong,
To love that well which thou must leave ere long.

Sonnet 116

Let me not to the marriage of true minds
Admit impediments. Love is not love
Which alters when it alteration finds,
Or bends with the remover to remove —

O, no! it is an ever-fixèd mark   5
That looks on tempests, and is never shaken;
It is the star to every wandering bark,
Whose worth's unknown, although his height be taken.

Love's not Time's fool, though rosy lips and cheeks
Within his bending sickle's compass come;   10
Love alters not with his brief hours and weeks,
But bears it out ev'n to the edge of doom —

If this be error, and upon me proved,
I never writ, nor no man ever loved.

SHAKESPEARE'S SONNETS

1. Although these sonnets are as musical as many songs, they are densely packed with thought; each one presents what is almost an "argument" in verse. Write a brief statement in your own words of the central idea in each sonnet.

2. In Sonnet 29 (one of the most famous), what two moods are contrasted? What causes each mood? To what element in the world of nature does Shakespeare compare this change of mood? Look up information on the English skylark — you will run across this bird in many poems of later periods — to see why the lines here and in "Hark, Hark, the Lark," on page 121, are especially meaningful.

3. In Sonnet 55, why does the poet think that his poem is a more permanent tribute than a stone monument? Do you think the time that has elapsed since then proves or disproves his point?

4. What is the mood in Sonnet 73?

5. In Sonnet 116, what characteristics of love are emphasized? To what is love compared in the second quatrain? How is Time pictured in the third? How many words or phrases can you find that emphasize permanence? Contrast this with the emphasis on change in the three preceding sonnets.

UNDERSTANDING THE SONNET FORM

To appreciate the sonnet fully is to understand the pattern of this exacting form of lyric verse. You have read that Spenser and Shakespeare, both great Elizabethan sonneteers, developed their own form from the Italian sonnet (see page 116), which was established by the Italian poet Petrarch.

A sonnet always has fourteen iambic pentameter lines; that is, ten syllables with a stress on every other syllable. The Italian form is divided into two parts: the octave, or the first eight lines, rhymes *abba abba;* the sestet, or the last six lines, rhymes in various ways, but usually with two rhymes, *cd cd cd.*

In this book you will find many examples of these sonnet patterns, in both early and modern writings. If you are interested in comparing the Shakespearean with the Italian form, read the sonnets of Milton (pages 238–39), who excelled in the true Italian form.

You will notice that sonnets are concerned with serious subjects, subjects worthy of deep thought. The pattern for such themes, consequently, demands a strict form into which much thought can be compressed.

THE THEATER

IN SHAKESPEARE'S

TIME

From C. Walter Hodges, The Globe Restored, *courtesy Ernest Benn, Ltd.*

There was excitement in the theater in Shakespeare's time. Never before had drama flourished with such gusto in England; never had so many people flocked to the playhouses to enjoy such superb dramas. The Globe, where Shakespeare was part owner and actor as well as playwright, was built in 1599, in Southwark. The Rose and the Swan, two older theaters, were its neighbors. On fine days, flags flew from the roofs, announcing that a play would be performed that afternoon.

What kinds of people crowded the theaters? They were a motley collection of Londoners: ordinary citizens, town idlers, seafarers ashore, travelers out to see the sights, and a few bold women. They carried their lunches, or bought fruit from girls selling apples and oranges at the door. There were men of higher rank in the audience, too: noblemen and students, country squires, masked women with men escorts. Entrance to the theater cost a penny; another penny entitled one to a seat in one of the galleries. Young dandies sometimes sat on the stage.

In its structure, the Elizabethan theater was far different from the ones we know today. The Globe was an eight-sided building, open to the sky in the center. The sides, covered by a thatched roof, held three tiers of galleries. The acting platform, surrounded on three sides by standing spectators, projected into the pit, which was the open area in the center. An inner stage at the rear of this platform was hidden by a curtain which could be drawn aside when indoor scenes were portrayed. Below the platform stage were trapdoors used for spirits and ghosts. There was a balcony above the stage, used for the second story of a house in a street scene, or for the battlements of a castle, and for the musicians. At the sides of the inner stage, and behind it, were the actors' dressing rooms. No actresses appeared in the Elizabethan theater; women's roles were taken by boys, and the audience would have been shocked to see a woman on the stage. There were props and costumes but little scenery — the spectators used their imaginations.

Imagine, then, that you are at the Globe, waiting for the play to begin. There is no dimming of lights — for the light comes from the sun; no curtain going up — for there is no curtain. Actors appear on the stage, the audience grows quiet, and the first act of *Macbeth* unfolds.

127

Macbeth

William Shakespeare's *Macbeth* is a powerful drama of a man whose weakness first brought him power, then defeat. As a play for acting, it outdistances most because of its admirable construction and its many scenes that are theatrically powerful as well as inherently dramatic. The story is based on historical fact; Shakespeare adapted it from two episodes related in a contemporary history book, Holinshed's *Chronicles* (1577), a work frequently used by Shakespeare for his history plays. This play was probably written in 1606 as a tribute to James I, who traced his ancestry to the Scottish nobleman Banquo. Alive with the passions of eleventh-century Scotland, yet timeless in its impact, *Macbeth* is one of the most gripping of Shakespeare's tragedies.

Dramatis Personae

DUNCAN, *king of Scotland*
MALCOLM ⎫
DONALBAIN ⎬ *his sons*
MACBETH ⎫ *generals of the*
BANQUO ⎭ *king's army*
MACDUFF
LENNOX
ROSS *noblemen of*
MENTEITH *Scotland*
ANGUS
CAITHNESS
LADY MACBETH
LADY MACDUFF
Gentlewoman attending
   on Lady Macbeth
HECATE, *goddess of witchcraft*
Three Witches
FLEANCE, *son to Banquo*

SIWARD, *Earl of Northumberland,*
   general of the English forces
Young SIWARD, *his son*
SEYTON, *an officer attending*
   on Macbeth
BOY, *son to Macduff*
An English Doctor
A Scotch Doctor
A Sergeant
A Porter
An Old Man
Apparitions
Lords, Gentlemen, Officers,
   Soldiers, Murderers, Attendants,
   and Messengers

SCENE: *Scotland; England*
TIME: *The eleventh century*

◀ *"This castle hath a pleasant seat; the air nimbly and sweetly recommends itself unto our gentle senses."* — *Duncan arrives at Macbeth's castle.*

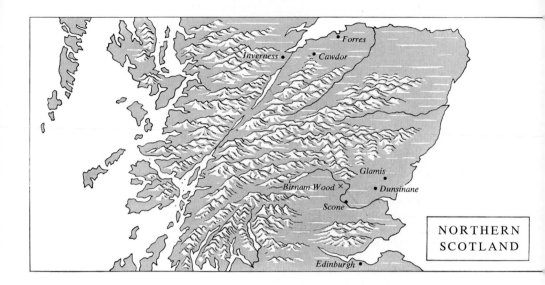

NORTHERN
SCOTLAND

ACT I

SCENE I. *A desert place.*

[*Thunder and lightning. Enter three* WITCHES.]

FIRST WITCH. When shall we three meet again
    In thunder, lightning, or in rain?
SECOND WITCH. When the hurly-burly's done,
    When the battle's lost and won.
THIRD WITCH. That will be ere the set of sun.   5
FIRST WITCH. Where the place?
SECOND WITCH.   Upon the heath.
THIRD WITCH. There to meet with Macbeth.
FIRST WITCH. I come, Graymalkin!°
SECOND WITCH. Paddock° calls.
THIRD WITCH. Anon.°   10
ALL. Fair is foul, and foul is fair:°
    Hover through the fog and filthy air.   [*Exeunt.*

SCENE II. *A camp near Forres.**

[*Alarum*† *within. Enter* DUNCAN, MALCOLM, DONALBAIN,‡ LENNOX,
with ATTENDANTS, *meeting a bleeding* SERGEANT.]

DUNCAN. What bloody man is that? He can report,

8. *Graymalkin:* cat. 9. *Paddock:* toad. According to the superstition of the times, the cat and the toad were animals which the witches used to obtain knowledge. 10. *Anon:* at once. 11. *Fair . . . fair:* To mix things up thus is a witch's delight. The line suggests that the witches completely reverse accepted standards.

* *Forres* (fôr′ĭs): a town in northeast Scotland. † *Alarum:* a trumpet call, sounded off stage.
‡ *Donalbain* (dŏn′ăl·bān).

As seemeth by his plight, of the revolt
The newest state.
MALCOLM.   This is the sergeant
Who like a good and hardy soldier fought
'Gainst my captivity. Hail, brave friend!   5
Say to the king the knowledge of the broil°
As thou didst leave it.
SERGEANT.   Doubtful it stood,
As two spent swimmers, that do cling together
And choke their art.° The merciless Macdonwald —
Worthy to be a rebel, for to that   10
The multiplying villainies of nature
Do swarm upon him — from the western isles
Of kerns and gallowglasses° is supplied;
And fortune, on his damnèd quarrel smiling,
Showed like a rebel's wench. But all's too weak;   15
For brave Macbeth — well he deserves that name —
Disdaining fortune, with his brandished steel,
Which smoked with bloody execution,
Like valor's minion° carvèd out his passage
Till he faced the slave;   20
Which ne'er shook hands, nor bade farewell to him,
Till he unseamed him from the nave to the chaps,
And fixed his head upon our battlements.
DUNCAN. O valiant cousin! worthy gentleman!
SERGEANT. As whence the sun 'gins his reflection   25
Shipwrecking storms and direful thunders break,
So from that spring whence comfort seemed to come
Discomfort swells.° Mark, king of Scotland, mark:
No sooner justice had with valor armed
Compelled these skipping kerns to trust their heels,   30
But the Norweyan° lord, surveying vantage,
With furbished arms and new supplies of men
Began a fresh assault.
DUNCAN.   Dismayed not this
Our captains, Macbeth and Banquo?
SERGEANT.   Yes;
As sparrows eagles, or the hare the lion.°   35
If I say sooth, I must report they were
As cannons overcharged with double cracks, so they
Doubly redoubled strokes upon the foe.
Except they meant to bathe in reeking wounds,
Or memorize another Golgotha,°   40
I cannot tell.

6. *broil:* battle. 9. *choke their art:* prevent each other from swimming. 13. *kerns and gallow-glasses:* light-armed and heavy-armed troops. 19. *minion:* favorite. 27–28. *So . . . swells:* On the heels of good news, comes bad news. 31. *Norweyan* (nôr·wā′yăn): old form of Norwegian. 35. *As sparrows . . . lion:* No more than eagles are dismayed by sparrows, or lions by hares, were Macbeth and Banquo upset by the Norwegian lord's new men. 40. *memorize another Golgotha* (gŏl′gŏ·thá): cause a slaughter of the enemies that would make the place as memorable as Golgotha, where Christ was crucified.

But I am faint, my gashes cry for help.
DUNCAN. So well thy words become thee as thy wounds;
    They smack of honor both. Go get him surgeons.

                    [*Exit* SERGEANT, *attended.*

    Who comes here?

              [*Enter* ROSS.]

MALCOLM.   The worthy thane° of Ross.   45
LENNOX. What a haste looks through his eyes! So should he look
    That seems to speak things strange.
ROSS.   God save the king!
DUNCAN. Whence camest thou, worthy thane?
ROSS.   From Fife, great king;
    Where the Norweyan banners flout the sky
    And fan our people cold. Norway himself,   50
    With terrible numbers,
    Assisted by that most disloyal traitor,
    The thane of Cawdor,° began a dismal conflict;
    Till that Bellona's bridegroom,° lapped in proof,°
    Confronted him with self-comparisons,   55
    Point against point rebellious, arm 'gainst arm,
    Curbing his lavish° spirit; and, to conclude,
    The victory fell on us.
DUNCAN.   Great happiness!
ROSS.   That now
    Sweno, the Norways' king, craves composition;°
    Nor would we deign him burial of his men   60
    Till he disbursèd at Saint Colme's inch°
    Ten thousand dollars to our general use.
DUNCAN. No more that thane of Cawdor shall deceive
    Our bosom interest.° Go pronounce his present° death,
    And with his former title greet Macbeth.   65
ROSS. I'll see it done.
DUNCAN. What he hath lost, noble Macbeth hath won.   [*Exeunt.*

SCENE III. *A heath near Forres.*

[*Thunder. Enter the three* WITCHES.]

FIRST WITCH. Where hast thou been, sister?
SECOND WITCH. Killing swine.°
THIRD WITCH. Sister, where thou?
FIRST WITCH. A sailor's wife had chestnuts in her lap.
    And munched, and munched, and munched. "Give me," quoth I.   5

---

    45. *thane:* a Scottish title of rank, similar to the English earl. 53. *Cawdor* (kô′dẽr). 54. *Bellona's* (bĕ·lō′näz) *bridegroom:* Bellona was the Roman goddess of war. Macbeth, as a great soldier, is called her bridegroom; *lapped in proof:* dressed in armor. 57. *lavish:* insolent. 59. *craves composition:* desires peace. 61. *Saint Colme's inch:* an island near Edinburgh, Scotland (now called Inchcolm). 64. *bosom interest:* most vital concerns; *present:* immediate.
    2. *killing swine:* a practice attributed to witches by superstition.

"Aroint thee,° witch!" the rump-fed ronyon° cries.
Her husband's to Aleppo° gone, master o' the *Tiger;*
But in a sieve I'll thither sail,
And, like a rat without a tail,
I'll do, I'll do, and I'll do.　　　　　　　　　　　　10
SECOND WITCH. I'll give thee a wind.
FIRST WITCH. Thou'rt kind.
THIRD WITCH. And I another.
FIRST WITCH. I myself have all the other,
　　And the very ports they blow,　　　　　　　　15
　　All the quarters that they know
　　I' the shipman's card.°
　　I will drain him dry as hay;
　　Sleep shall neither night nor day
　　Hang upon his penthouse lid;°　　　　　　　20
　　He shall live a man forbid.°
　　Weary se'nnights° nine times nine
　　Shall he dwindle, peak,° and pine;
　　Though his bark cannot be lost,
　　Yet it shall be tempest-tost.　　　　　　　25
　　Look what I have.
SECOND WITCH. Show me, show me.
FIRST WITCH. Here I have a pilot's thumb,
　　Wrecked as homeward he did come.　　　　　[*Drum within.*
THIRD WITCH. A drum, a drum!　　　　　　　30
　　Macbeth doth come.
ALL. The weird sisters, hand in hand,
　　Posters° of the sea and land,
　　Thus do go about, about;
　　Thrice to thine and thrice to mine　　　　　35
　　And thrice again, to make up nine.
　　Peace! the charm's wound up.

　　　　[*Enter* MACBETH *and* BANQUO.]

MACBETH. So foul and fair a day I have not seen.
BANQUO. How far is 't called to Forres? What are these
　　So withered and so wild in their attire,　　　40
　　That look not like the inhabitants o' the earth,
　　And yet are on 't? Live you? or are you aught
　　That man may question? You seem to understand me,
　　By each at once her choppy finger laying
　　Upon her skinny lips. You should be women,　　45
　　And yet your beards forbid me to interpret
　　That you are so.
MACBETH.　　　　　　Speak, if you can. What are you?
FIRST WITCH. All hail, Macbeth! hail to thee, thane of Glamis!°
SECOND WITCH. All hail, Macbeth! hail to thee, thane of Cawdor!

---

6. *Aroint thee:* begone; *ronyon:* mangy creature. 7. *Aleppo:* city in Syria. 17. *card:* compass.
20. *penthouse lid:* eyelid; literally, the roof of a shed. 21. *forbid:* accursed. 22. *se'nnights:* weeks.
23. *peak:* grow thin. 33. *Posters:* couriers. 48. *Glamis* (glämz).

THIRD WITCH. All hail, Macbeth, that shalt be king hereafter!   50
BANQUO. Good sir, why do you start, and seem to fear
   Things that do sound so fair? I' the name of truth,
   Are ye fantastical,° or that indeed
   Which outwardly ye show? My noble partner
   You greet with present grace and great prediction   55
   Of noble having and of royal hope,
   That he seems rapt° withal; to me you speak not.
   If you can look into the seeds of time,
   And say which grain will grow and which will not,
   Speak then to me, who neither beg nor fear   60
   Your favors nor your hate.
FIRST WITCH. Hail!
SECOND WITCH. Hail!
THIRD WITCH. Hail!
FIRST WITCH. Lesser than Macbeth, and greater.   65
SECOND WITCH. Not so happy, yet much happier.
THIRD WITCH. Thou shalt get kings, though thou be none;
   So all hail, Macbeth and Banquo!
FIRST WITCH. Banquo and Macbeth, all hail!
MACBETH. Stay, you imperfect speakers, tell me more.   70
   By Sinel's death° I know I am thane of Glamis;
   But how of Cawdor? The thane of Cawdor lives,
   A prosperous gentleman; and to be king
   Stands not within the prospect of belief,
   No more than to be Cawdor. Say from whence   75
   You owe this strange intelligence,° or why
   Upon this blasted heath you stop our way
   With such prophetic greeting? Speak, I charge you.   [WITCHES *vanish.*
BANQUO. The earth hath bubbles, as the water has,
   And these are of them. Whither are they vanished?   80
MACBETH. Into the air; and what seemed corporal° melted
   As breath into the wind. Would they had stayed!
BANQUO. Were such things here as we do speak about?
   Or have we eaten on the insane root
   That takes the reason prisoner?°   85
MACBETH. Your children shall be kings.
BANQUO.   You shall be king.
MACBETH. And thane of Cawdor too: went it not so?
BANQUO. To the selfsame tune and words. Who's here?

    [*Enter* ROSS *and* ANGUS.]

ROSS. The king hath happily received, Macbeth,
   The news of thy success; and when he reads   90
   Thy personal venture in the rebels' fight,
   His wonders and his praises do contend

---

53. *fantastical:* creation of the imagination. 57. *rapt:* absorbed, or lost in his own thoughts. 71. *Sinel's* (sī'nĕlz) *death:* Sinel was Macbeth's father. 76. *intelligence:* knowledge. 81. *corporal:* material, of bodily substance. 84–85. *Or have ... prisoner:* a common superstition of the times, that eating of a certain herb caused insanity.

Which should be thine or his.° Silenced with that,
In viewing o'er the rest o' the selfsame day,
He finds thee in the stout Norweyan ranks,   95
Nothing afeard of what thyself didst make,
Strange images of death.° As thick as hail
Came post with post; and every one did bear
Thy praises in his kingdom's great defense,
And poured them down before him.

ANGUS.   We are sent   100
To give thee from our royal master thanks;
Only to herald thee into his sight,
Not pay thee.

ROSS. And, for an earnest° of a greater honor,
He bade me, from him, call thee thane of Cawdor;   105
In which addition,° hail, most worthy thane!
For it is thine.

BANQUO. [*Aside*] What, can the devil speak true?

MACBETH. The thane of Cawdor lives; why do you dress me
In borrowed robes?

ANGUS.   Who was the thane lives yet;   110
But under heavy judgment bears that life
Which he deserves to lose. Whether he was combined
With those of Norway, or did line° the rebel
With hidden help and vantage, or that with both
He labored in his country's wreck, I know not;   115
But treasons capital,° confessed and proved,
Have overthrown him.

MACBETH. [*Aside*] Glamis, and thane of Cawdor!
The greatest is behind.° [*To* ROSS *and* ANGUS] Thanks for your pains.
[*To* BANQUO] Do you not hope your children shall be kings,   120
When those that gave the thane of Cawdor to me
Promised no less to them?

BANQUO.   That, trusted home,°
Might yet enkindle you unto the crown,
Besides the thane of Cawdor. But 'tis strange;
And oftentimes, to win us to our harm,   125
The instruments of darkness tell us truths,
Win us with honest trifles, to betray 's
In deepest consequence.
Cousins, a word, I pray you.

MACBETH.   [*Aside*] Two truths are told,
As happy prologues to the swelling act   130
Of the imperial theme.° — I thank you, gentlemen.
[*Aside*] This supernatural soliciting
Cannot be ill, cannot be good. If ill,

---

93. *Which . . . his:* whether he should praise you or wonder at you. 96–97. *Nothing . . . death:* Macbeth killed many of his enemies and saw them die, but he was not afraid of death for himself. 104. *earnest:* pledge, or assurance. 106. *addition:* title. 113. *line:* support. 116. *capital:* deserving death. 119. *behind:* yet to come. 122. *home:* fully. 131. *imperial theme:* that Macbeth would eventually be king.

Why hath it given me earnest of success,
Commencing in a truth? I am thane of Cawdor.   135
If good, why do I yield to that suggestion
Whose horrid image doth unfix my hair
And make my seated heart knock at my ribs,
Against the use of nature?° Present fears
Are less than horrible imaginings;   140
My thought, whose murder yet is but fantastical,
Shakes so my single state of man that function
Is smothered in surmise;° and nothing is
But what is not.

BANQUO.   Look, how our partner's rapt.

MACBETH. [*Aside*] If chance will have me king, why, chance may crown me,   145
Without my stir.

BANQUO.   New honors come upon him,
Like our strange garments, cleave not to their mold
But with the aid of use.°

MACBETH.   [*Aside*] Come what come may,
Time and the hour runs through the roughest day.

BANQUO. Worthy Macbeth, we stay upon your leisure.°   150

MACBETH. Give me your favor.° My dull brain was wrought
With things forgotten. Kind gentlemen, your pains
Are registered° where every day I turn
The leaf to read them. Let us toward the king.
[*To* BANQUO] Think upon what hath chanced, and, at more time,   155
The interim having weighed it, let us speak
Our free hearts each to other.

BANQUO.   Very gladly.

MACBETH. Till then, enough. Come, friends.   [*Exeunt.*

SCENE IV. *Forres. The Palace.*

[*Flourish.* * *Enter* DUNCAN, MALCOLM, DONALBAIN, LENNOX, *and* ATTENDANTS.]

DUNCAN. Is execution done on Cawdor? Are not
Those in commission yet returned?

MALCOLM.   My liege,
They are not yet come back. But I have spoke
With one that saw him die; who did report
That very frankly he confessed his treasons,   5
Implored your highness' pardon and set forth
A deep repentance. Nothing in his life
Became him like the leaving it; he died
As one that had been studied in his death

---

139. *Against ... nature:* in such an unnatural way. 141–43. *My thought ... surmise:* An act of murder is as yet only imagined by Macbeth, but the thought of it shakes him, so that he cannot act. 146–48. *New honors ... use:* Macbeth wears his new honors like a new suit of clothes; as yet, they don't seem to fit him. 150. *we stay upon your leisure:* we are waiting for you. 151. *Give me your favor:* Pardon me. 153. *registered:* recorded (in his heart).
* *Flourish:* a trumpet fanfare.

         To throw away the dearest thing he owed,   10
         As 'twere a careless trifle.
DUNCAN.   There's no art
         To find the mind's construction in the face;°
         He was a gentleman on whom I built
         An absolute trust.

            [*Enter* MACBETH, BANQUO, ROSS, *and* ANGUS.]

               O worthiest cousin!
         The sin of my ingratitude even now   15
         Was heavy on me. Thou art so far before°
         That swiftest wing of recompense is slow
         To overtake thee. Would thou hadst less deserved,
         That the proportion both of thanks and payment
         Might have been mine! Only I have left to say,   20
         More is thy due than more than all can pay.
MACBETH. The service and the loyalty I owe,
         In doing it, pays itself. Your highness' part
         Is to receive our duties; and our duties
         Are to your throne and state, children and servants,   25
         Which do but what they should, by doing everything
         Safe toward° your love and honor.
DUNCAN.   Welcome hither;
         I have begun to plant thee, and will labor
         To make thee full of growing. Noble Banquo,
         That hast no less deserved, nor must be known   30
         No less to have done so, let me infold thee
         And hold thee to my heart.
BANQUO.   There if I grow,
         The harvest is your own.
DUNCAN.   My plenteous joys,
         Wanton in fullness, seek to hide themselves
         In drops of sorrow.° Sons, kinsmen, thanes,   35
         And you whose places are the nearest, know
         We° will establish our estate upon
         Our eldest, Malcolm, whom we name hereafter
         The Prince of Cumberland; which honor must
         Not unaccompanied invest him only,   40
         But signs of nobleness, like stars, shall shine
         On all deservers.° From hence to Inverness,°
         And bind us further to you.
MACBETH. The rest is labor, which is not used for you.°

11–12. *There's . . . face:* There is no way to read a man's character from his face. 16. *before:* as used here, ahead. 27. *Safe toward:* with sure regard for. 33–35. *My . . . sorrow:* In other words, Duncan is so happy that he weeps for joy. 37. *We:* Duncan here, and elsewhere in the play, speaks of himself in the plural, as was the custom of kings. 35–42. In these lines Duncan establishes his son Malcom as his successor but indicates that the others will receive suitable rewards for their services. In this period of Scottish history, lines of succession to the throne were not hereditary. Macbeth might have succeeded Duncan legitimately, but Duncan's pronouncement now makes this impossible. 42. *Inverness:* Macbeth's castle, twenty-five miles away. 44. *The rest . . . for you:* Anything done for you is a pleasure; everything else is tedious (*labor*).

I'll be myself the harbinger and make joyful   45
The hearing of my wife with your approach;
So humbly take my leave.
DUNCAN.   My worthy Cawdor!
MACBETH. [*Aside*] The Prince of Cumberland! That is a step
On which I must fall down, or else o'erleap,
For in my way it lies. Stars, hide your fires;   50
Let not light see my black and deep desires;
The eye wink at the hand; yet let that be,
Which the eye fears, when it is done, to see.   [*Exit.*
DUNCAN. True, worthy Banquo; he is full so valiant,
And in his commendations I am fed;   55
It is a banquet to me. Let's after him,
Whose care is gone before to bid us welcome.
It is a peerless kinsman.   [*Flourish. Exeunt.*

SCENE V. *Inverness.* MACBETH'S *castle.*

[*Enter* LADY MACBETH, *reading a letter.*]

LADY MACBETH. "They met me in the day of success; and I have learned by the
perfectest report, they have more in them than mortal knowledge. When I
burned in desire to question them further, they made themselves air, into
which they vanished. Whiles I stood rapt in the wonder of it, came mis-
sives° from the king, who all-hailed me 'Thane of Cawdor'; by which   5
title, before, these weird sisters saluted me, and referred me to the coming
on of time, with 'Hail, king that shalt be!' This have I thought good to deliver thee, my dearest partner of greatness, that thou mightst not lose the
dues of rejoicing, by being ignorant of what greatness is promised thee.
Lay it to thy heart, and farewell."   10

Glamis thou art, and Cawdor; and shalt be
What thou art promised. Yet do I fear thy nature;
It is too full o' the milk of human kindness
To catch the nearest way. Thou wouldst be great;
Art not without ambition, but without   15
The illness° should attend it. What thou wouldst highly
That wouldst thou holily; wouldst not play false,
And yet wouldst wrongly win. Thou 'ldst have, great Glamis,
That which cries, "Thus thou must do, if thou have it";
And that which rather thou dost fear to do   20
Than wishest should be undone.° Hie thee hither,
That I may pour my spirits in thine ear,
And chastise with the valor of my tongue
All that impedes thee from the golden round,°

5. *missives:* messengers. 16. *illness:* as used here, wickedness. 18–21. *Thou 'ldst ... undone:* The
thing that you want, great Glamis, requires doing certain things to obtain it, things you are afraid
to do, but, once done, you will not want undone. 24. *golden round:* crown.

Which fate and metaphysical aid° doth seem   25
To have thee crowned withal.

[*Enter a* MESSENGER.]

                                   What is your tidings?
MESSENGER. The king comes here tonight.
LADY MACBETH.   Thou 'rt mad to say it!
   Is not thy master with him? who, were 't so,
   Would have informed for preparation.
MESSENGER. So please you, it is true; our thane is coming.   30
   One of my fellows had the speed of him,
   Who, almost dead for breath, had scarcely more
   Than would make up his message.
LADY MACBETH.   Give him tending;
   He brings great news.   [*Exit* MESSENGER.
                        The raven himself is hoarse
   That croaks the fatal entrance of Duncan   35
   Under my battlements. Come, you spirits
   That tend on mortal thoughts, unsex me here,
   And fill me from the crown to the toe top-full
   Of direst cruelty! make thick my blood;
   Stop up the access and passage to remorse,   40
   That no compunctious visitings of nature°
   Shake my fell purpose, nor keep peace between
   The effect and it! Come to my woman's breasts,
   And take my milk for gall, you murdering ministers,°
   Wherever in your sightless substances   45
   You wait on nature's mischief! Come, thick night,
   And pall thee in the dunnest smoke of hell,
   That my keen knife see not the wound it makes,
   Nor Heaven peep through the blanket of the dark,
   To cry "Hold, hold!"

[*Enter* MACBETH.]

                        Great Glamis! worthy Cawdor!   50
   Greater than both, by the all-hail hereafter!
   Thy letters have transported me beyond
   This ignorant present, and I feel now
   The future in the instant.
MACBETH.   My dearest love,
   Duncan comes here tonight.
LADY MACBETH.   And when goes hence?   55
MACBETH. Tomorrow, as he purposes.
LADY MACBETH.   O, never
   Shall sun that morrow see!
   Your face, my thane, is as a book where men
   May read strange matters. To beguile° the time,

25. *metaphysical aid:* the supernatural help implied by the witches' prophecy. 41. *compunctious . . . nature:* natural feelings of pity. 44. *milk . . . ministers:* turn my milk to bitterness (*gall*), you spirits of murder. 59. *beguile:* deceive.

Look like the time; bear welcome in your eye,   60
Your hand, your tongue; look like the innocent flower,
But be the serpent under 't. He that's coming
Must be provided for; and you shall put
This night's great business into my dispatch;
Which shall to all our nights and days to come   65
Give solely sovereign sway° and masterdom.
MACBETH. We will speak further.
LADY MACBETH.   Only look up clear;°
To alter favor° ever is to fear.
Leave all the rest to me.   [*Exeunt.*

SCENE VI. *Before* MACBETH'S *castle.*

[*Hautboys and torches.** *Enter* DUNCAN, MALCOLM, DONALBAIN, BANQUO,
LENNOX, MACDUFF, ROSS, ANGUS, *and* ATTENDANTS.]

DUNCAN. This castle hath a pleasant seat;° the air
Nimbly and sweetly recommends itself
Unto our gentle senses.
BANQUO.   This guest of summer,
The temple-haunting martlet, does approve,
By his loved mansionry,° that the heaven's breath   5
Smells wooingly here; no jutty, frieze,
Buttress, nor coign of vantage, but this bird
Hath made his pendent bed and procreant cradle.°
Where they most breed and haunt, I have observed,
The air is delicate.

[*Enter* LADY MACBETH.]

DUNCAN.   See, see, our honored hostess!   10
The love that follows us sometimes is our trouble,
Which still we thank as love. Herein I teach you
How you shall bid God 'ild° us for your pains,
And thank us for your trouble.
LADY MACBETH.   All our service
In every point twice done and then done double   15
Were poor and single business to contend
Against those honors deep and broad wherewith
Your majesty loads our house; for those of old,
And the late dignities heaped up to them,
We rest your hermits.°

---

66. *solely sovereign sway:* absolute royal power. 67. *look up clear:* show a look of innocence.
68. *alter favor:* change appearances; in other words, to look afraid.

   * *Hautboys* (hō′boiz): oboes, used to announce the entrance of royalty; *torches* indicate that it is
night. 1. *seat:* location. 5. *mansionry:* building. 6–8. *no jutty . . . cradle:* The martlet (a bird like a
swallow) has made his nest and cradle for the young (*procreant cradle*) everywhere about the castle,
in every advantageous corner (*coign of vantage*). 13. *God 'ild:* God reward (us). 20. *We rest your
hermits:* This means "We shall pray for you." Hermits were sometimes paid by a person or family
to pray for the employer's soul.

DUNCAN.　　　　　　　　　　Where's the thane of Cawdor?　　　20
　　　　We coursed° him at the heels, and had a purpose
　　　　To be his purveyor;° but he rides well;
　　　　And his great love, sharp as his spur, hath holp him
　　　　To his home before us. Fair and noble hostess,
　　　　We are your guest tonight.
LADY MACBETH.　　　　　　　　Your servants ever　　　25
　　　　Have theirs, themselves, and what is theirs in compt,°
　　　　To make their audit at your highness' pleasure,
　　　　Still° to return your own.
DUNCAN.　　　　　　　　　　Give me your hand;
　　　　Conduct me to mine host. We love him highly,
　　　　And shall continue our graces toward him.　　　30
　　　　By your leave, hostess.　　　　　　　　　[*Exeunt.*

SCENE VII. MACBETH'S *castle.*

[*Hautboys and torches. Enter a* SEWER,* *and divers* SERVANTS *with dishes
and service, and pass over the stage. Then enter* MACBETH.]

MACBETH. If it were done when 'tis done, then 'twere well
　　　　It were done quickly. If the assassination
　　　　Could trammel up the consequence, and catch
　　　　With his surcease success;° that but this blow
　　　　Might be the be-all and the end-all here,　　　5
　　　　But here, upon this bank and shoal of time,
　　　　We'ld jump° the life to come. But in these cases
　　　　We still have judgment here; that we but teach
　　　　Bloody instructions, which, being taught, return
　　　　To plague the inventor. This even-handed justice　　　10
　　　　Commends the ingredients of our poisoned chalice
　　　　To our own lips.° He's here in double trust;
　　　　First, as I am his kinsman and his subject,
　　　　Strong both against the deed; then, as his host,
　　　　Who should against his murderer shut the door,　　　15
　　　　Not bear the knife myself. Besides, this Duncan
　　　　Hath borne his faculties so meek, hath been
　　　　So clear in his great office, that his virtues
　　　　Will plead like angels, trumpet-tongued, against
　　　　The deep damnation of his taking-off;　　　20
　　　　And pity, like a naked newborn babe,
　　　　Striding the blast, or heaven's cherubin, horsed

21. *coursed:* chased. 22. *To be his purveyor:* to arrive ahead of him. 26. *compt:* readiness. 28. *Still:* always.
　* *Sewer:* a server, a servant whose duties are to arrange the table. 2–4. *If . . . success:* If only the murder would have no consequences, but be final and successful with Duncan's death (*surcease*). 7. *jump:* risk. Macbeth would risk the consequences of murder in afterlife if he could be sure there would be no bad consequences in this life (*this bank and shoal of time*). 8–12. *that we . . . own lips:* If we practice murder, we teach others to murder us. This impartial (*even-handed*) justice offers (*commends*) the same fate to us that we propose for others.

Upon the sightless couriers° of the air,
Shall blow the horrid deed in every eye,
That tears shall drown the wind. I have no spur   25
To prick the sides of my intent, but only
Vaulting ambition, which o'erleaps itself
And falls on the other.°

[*Enter* LADY MACBETH.]

                 How now! what news?
LADY MACBETH. He has almost supped. Why have you left the chamber?
MACBETH. Hath he asked for me?
LADY MACBETH.   Know you not he has?   30
MACBETH. We will proceed no further in this business.
    He hath honored me of late; and I have bought
    Golden opinions from all sorts of people,
    Which would be worn now in their newest gloss,
    Not cast aside so soon.
LADY MACBETH.   Was the hope drunk   35
    Wherein you dressed yourself? Hath it slept since?
    And wakes it now, to look so green and pale
    At what it did so freely? From this time
    Such I account thy love. Art thou afeard
    To be the same in thine own act and valor   40
    As thou art in desire? Wouldst thou have that
    Which thou esteem'st the ornament of life,°
    And live a coward in thine own esteem,
    Letting "I dare not" wait upon "I would,"
    Like the poor cat i' the adage?°
MACBETH.   Prithee, peace!   45
    I dare do all that may become a man;
    Who dares do more is none.
LADY MACBETH.   What beast was 't, then,
    That made you break this enterprise to me?°
    When you durst do it, then you were a man;
    And, to be more than what you were,° you would   50
    Be so much more the man. Nor time nor place
    Did then adhere,° and yet you would make both.
    They have made themselves, and that their° fitness now
    Does unmake you. I have given suck, and know
    How tender 'tis to love the babe that milks me;   55
    I would, while it was smiling in my face,
    Have plucked my nipple from his boneless gums,
    And dashed the brains out, had I so sworn as you
    Have done to this.

---

23. *sightless couriers:* the winds. 28. *other:* i.e., the other side. 42. *ornament of life:* the crown.
45. *the poor cat i' the adage:* This refers to an old adage or proverb which goes "The cat would eat
fish but would not wet her feet." 46–48. *I dare . . . to me:* Macbeth is defending himself. It isn't
cowardice (as his wife suggests) that made him change his mind about killing Duncan; he'd dare
anything that becomes a man. In that case, says Lady Macbeth, it must have been something other
than a man (a *beast*) who started the whole business. 50. *to be more than what you were:* that is, to
be king. 52. *Did then adhere:* was then appropriate. 53. *that their:* their very.

MACBETH.　　　　　　　If we should fail?
LADY MACBETH.　　　　　　　　　We fail!
　　But screw your courage to the sticking-place　　　　　　60
　　And we'll not fail. When Duncan is asleep —
　　Whereto the rather shall his day's hard journey
　　Soundly invite him — his two chamberlains
　　Will I with wine and wassail° so convince°
　　That memory, the warder of the brain,　　　　　　65
　　Shall be a fume, and the receipt of reason
　　A limbeck only.° When in swinish sleep
　　Their drenchèd natures lie as in a death,
　　What cannot you and I perform upon
　　The unguarded Duncan? what not put upon　　　　　　70
　　His spongy officers, who shall bear the guilt
　　Of our great quell?°
MACBETH.　　　　　　　Bring forth men children only;
　　For thy undaunted mettle should compose
　　Nothing but males. Will it not be received,
　　When we have marked with blood those sleepy two　　　　75
　　Of his own chamber and used their very daggers,
　　That they have done 't?
LADY MACBETH.　　　　　　　Who dares receive it other,
　　As we shall make our griefs and clamor roar
　　Upon his death?
MACBETH.　　　　　　I am settled, and bend up
　　Each corporal agent° to this terrible feat.　　　　　　80
　　Away, and mock the time with fairest show;
　　False face must hide what the false heart doth know.　　[*Exeunt.*

64. *wassail:* an intoxicating drink; *convince:* overcome. 66–67. *the receipt . . . only:* The mind (*receipt of reason*) would become like a still (*limbeck*) which will distill only confused thoughts. 72. *quell:* murder. 80. *corporal agent:* bodily power.

"THE INSTRUMENTS OF DARKNESS TELL US TRUTHS."

ACT I

1. Why is it important that Macbeth should *at first* be presented to us as a brave and honored soldier? How is he so presented?

2. In Scene iii, how did the witches' greeting affect Macbeth? What is the importance of Macbeth's sudden promotion to be thane of Cawdor?

3. The Elizabethan audience actually believed in witches; a modern audience does not. What difference would this make in the reaction of the two groups to the witches' prophecies?

4. Notice Banquo's speeches concerning the witches. Can the weird sisters *make* anything happen, or do they merely foresee the future? Are they put in the play as symbols of certain thoughts and emotions? Are they evil, mischievous, or neutral? Explain your answers by specific reference to the play.

5. In Scenes v–vii, how much evidence can you find that Macbeth is more frightened by the plan to kill Duncan than Lady Macbeth is? that they have previously considered doing so? Which of the two is the "brains" of the team? Analyze Macbeth's argument with himself at the beginning of Scene vii. What is he really afraid of? How does Lady Macbeth manage to stiffen his courage? Are her arguments logical? Are they just? What would Macbeth's future relations with his wife have been had he not followed her lead in their scheme?

ACT II

SCENE I. *Court of* MACBETH'S *castle.*

[Enter BANQUO, *and* FLEANCE* *bearing a torch before him.]*

BANQUO. How goes the night, boy?
FLEANCE. The moon is down; I have not heard the clock.
BANQUO. And she goes down at twelve.
FLEANCE.   I take 't, 'tis later, sir.
BANQUO. Hold, take my sword. There's husbandry° in heaven;
     Their candles are all out. Take thee that too.°   5
     A heavy summons° lies like lead upon me,
     And yet I would not sleep. Merciful powers,
     Restrain in me the cursèd thoughts that nature
     Gives way to in repose!

[Enter MACBETH, *and a* SERVANT *with a torch.]*

                 Give me my sword.
     Who's there?   10
MACBETH. A friend.
BANQUO. What, sir, not yet at rest? The king's abed.
     He hath been in unusual pleasure, and
     Sent forth great largess to your offices.°
     This diamond he greets your wife withal,   15
     By the name of most kind hostess; and shut up
     In measureless content.°
MACBETH.   Being unprepared,
     Our will became the servant to defect;
     Which else should free have wrought.°
BANQUO.   All's well.
     I dreamt last night of the three weird sisters: 20
     To you they have showed some truth.
MACBETH.   I think not of them;
     Yet, when we can entreat an hour to serve,
     We would spend it in some words upon that business,
     If you would grant the time.
BANQUO.   At your kind'st leisure.
MACBETH. If you shall cleave to my consent, when 'tis,   25
     It shall make honor for you.
BANQUO.   So I lose none
     In seeking to augment it, but still keep

---

    * *Fleance* (flē'ăns). 4. *husbandry:* economy. 5. *Take thee that too:* Apparently he gives Fleance his sword belt as well as his sword. 6. *heavy summons:* great weariness. 14. *largess to your offices:* gifts of money to the servant quarters. 16–17. *and shut up in measureless content:* The king has retired to his room, happy and well satisfied. 17–19. *Being . . . wrought:* Had Macbeth had more warning of the king's visit, his hospitality would have been more lavish.

My bosom franchised and allegiance clear,
I shall be counseled.°
MACBETH.　　　　　　　　Good repose the while!
BANQUO. Thanks, sir; the like to you!　　　　　　　30

　　　　　　　　　[*Exeunt* BANQUO *and* FLEANCE.

MACBETH. Go bid thy mistress, when my drink is ready,
She strike upon the bell. Get thee to bed.　　[*Exit* SERVANT.
Is this a dagger which I see before me,
The handle toward my hand? Come, let me clutch thee.
I have thee not, and yet I see thee still.　　　　35
Art thou not, fatal vision, sensible
To feeling as to sight?° or art thou but
A dagger of the mind, a false creation,
Proceeding from the heat-oppressèd brain?
I see thee yet, in form as palpable°　　　　　40
As this which now I draw.
Thou marshal'st me the way that I was going;
And such an instrument I was to use.
Mine eyes are made the fools o' the other senses,
Or else worth all the rest; I see thee still,　　　45
And on thy blade and dudgeon° gouts of blood,
Which was not so before. There's no such thing.
It is the bloody business which informs°
Thus to mine eyes. Now o'er the one half-world
Nature seems dead, and wicked dreams abuse　　50
The curtained sleep! witchcraft celebrates
Pale Hecate's offerings,° and withered murder,
Alarumed by his sentinel, the wolf,
Whose howl's his watch,° thus with his stealthy pace,
With Tarquin's ravishing strides, toward his design　　55
Moves like a ghost. Thou sure and firm-set earth,
Hear not my steps, which way they walk, for fear
Thy very stones prate of my whereabout,
And take the present horror° from the time,
Which now suits with° it. Whiles I threat, he lives;　　60
Words to the heat of deeds too cold breath gives.　　[*A bell rings.*
I go, and it is done; the bell invites me.
Hear it not, Duncan; for it is a knell
That summons thee to heaven or to hell.　　　　[*Exit.*

25–29. *If you . . . counseled:* Macbeth promises to reward Banquo (*It shall make honor for you*)
if he agrees to support Macbeth (*cleave to my consent*) when the time comes, and Banquo says
that he will listen to Macbeth (*be counseled*) if he loses no honor in seeking to increase (*augment*)
it and if he can keep his conscience free (*bosom franchised*) and retain his loyalty to the king
(*allegiance clear*). 36–37. *sensible to feeling as to sight:* capable of being felt as well as seen. 40. *pal-
pable:* real, in the sense of being capable of being touched or felt. 46. *dudgeon:* handle. 48. *informs:*
creates forms. 51–52. *witchcraft . . . offerings:* Witches pledged allegiance to Hecate (hĕk′ăt), goddess
of the underworld and of witchcraft. 54. *howl's his watch:* tells time by howling. 59. *present horror:*
the silence of midnight. 60. *suits with:* matches.

SCENE II. *The same.*

[*Enter* LADY MACBETH.]

LADY MACBETH. That which hath made them drunk hath made me bold;
　　　　　What hath quenched them hath given me fire. Hark! Peace!
　　　　　It was the owl that shrieked, the fatal bellman,°
　　　　　Which gives the stern'st good night. He is about it.
　　　　　The doors are open; and the surfeited grooms　　　　　5
　　　　　Do mock their charge with snores. I have drugged their possets,°
　　　　　That death and nature do contend about them,
　　　　　Whether they live or die.
MACBETH. [*Within*] Who's there? what, ho!
LADY MACBETH. Alack, I am afraid they have awaked,　　　　　10
　　　　　And 'tis not done. The attempt and not the deed
　　　　　Confounds° us. Hark! I laid their daggers ready;
　　　　　He could not miss 'em. Had he not resembled
　　　　　My father as he slept, I had done 't.

[*Enter* MACBETH.]

　　　　　　　　　　　　　My husband!
MACBETH. I have done the deed. Didst thou not hear a noise?　　　15
LADY MACBETH. I heard the owl scream and the crickets cry.
　　　　　Did not you speak?
MACBETH.　　　　　　　When?
LADY MACBETH.　　　　　　Now.
MACBETH.　　　　　　　　As I descended?
LADY MACBETH. Ay.
MACBETH. Hark!
　　　　　Who lies i' the second chamber?
LADY MACBETH.　　　Donalbain.　　　　　　　　　　　　　20
MACBETH. This is a sorry sight.　　　　　　　[*Looking on his hands.*
LADY MACBETH. A foolish thought, to say a sorry sight.
MACBETH. There's one did laugh in 's sleep, and one cried "Murder!"
　　　　　That they did wake each other. I stood and heard them;
　　　　　But they did say their prayers, and addressed them　　　25
　　　　　Again to sleep.
LADY MACBETH. There are two lodged together.
MACBETH. One cried "God bless us!" and "Amen" the other,
　　　　　As they had seen me with these hangman's hands.
　　　　　Listening their fear, I could not say "Amen,"　　　　　30
　　　　　When they did say "God bless us!"
LADY MACBETH.　　　　　　　　　Consider it not so deeply.
MACBETH. But wherefore could not I pronounce "Amen"?
　　　　　I had most need of blessing, and "Amen"
　　　　　Stuck in my throat.
LADY MACBETH.　　　　　These deeds must not be thought
　　　　　After these ways; so, it will make us mad.　　　　　35

---

　3. *fatal bellman:* On the night before an execution, a bellman rang a hand bell outside the cell
of the condemned, bidding him to repent his sins. 6. *possets:* bedtime drinks. 12. *Confounds:* ruins.

MACBETH. Methought I heard a voice cry "Sleep no more!
        Macbeth does murder sleep," the innocent sleep,
        Sleep that knits up the raveled sleave° of care,
        The death of each day's life, sore labor's bath,
        Balm of hurt minds, great nature's second course,   40
        Chief nourisher in life's feast —
LADY MACBETH.   What do you mean?
MACBETH. Still it cried "Sleep no more!" to all the house;
        "Glamis hath murdered sleep, and therefore Cawdor
        Shall sleep no more; Macbeth shall sleep no more."
LADY MACBETH. Who was it that thus cried? Why, worthy thane,   45
        You do unbend your noble strength, to think
        So brainsickly of things. Go get some water,
        And wash this filthy witness from your hand.
        Why did you bring these daggers from the place?
        They must lie there; go carry them; and smear   50
        The sleepy grooms with blood.
MACBETH.   I'll go no more.
        I am afraid to think what I have done;
        Look on 't again I dare not.
LADY MACBETH.   Infirm of purpose!
        Give me the daggers. The sleeping and the dead
        Are but as pictures; 'tis the eye of childhood   55
        That fears a painted devil. If he do bleed,
        I'll gild the faces of the grooms withal;
        For it must seem their guilt.   [*Exit. Knocking within.*
MACBETH.   Whence is that knocking?
        How is 't with me, when every noise appalls me?
        What hands are here? Ha! they pluck out mine eyes.   60
        Will all great Neptune's ocean wash this blood
        Clean from my hand? No, this my hand will rather
        The multitudinous seas incarnadine,°
        Making the green one red.

                  [*Re-enter* LADY MACBETH.]

LADY MACBETH. My hands are of your color; but I shame   65
        To wear a heart so white. [*Knocking within.*] I hear a knocking
        At the south entry. Retire we to our chamber;
        A little water clears us of this deed.
        How easy is it, then! Your constancy°
        Hath left you unattended. [*Knocking within.*] Hark! more knocking. 70
        Get on your nightgown, lest occasion call us,
        And show us to be watchers. Be not lost
        So poorly in your thoughts.
MACBETH. To know my deed, 'twere best not know myself.   [*Knocking within.*
        Wake Duncan with thy knocking! I would thou couldst!   [*Exeunt.* 75

---

38. *raveled sleave:* tangled skein. 63. *incarnadine* (ĭn-kär′nȧ-dĭn): make red. 69. *constancy:* firmness of purpose.

SCENE III. *The same.*

[*Knocking within. Enter a* PORTER.]

PORTER.° Here' a knocking indeed! If a man were porter of hell gate, he should
   have old turning the key. [*Knocking within.*] Knock, knock, knock! Who's
   there, i' the name of Beelzebub? Here's a farmer, that hanged himself on
   the expectation of plenty. Come in time; have napkins enow about you;
   here you'll sweat for 't. [*Knocking within.*] Knock, knock! Who's there,   5
   in the other devil's name? Faith, here's an equivocator, that could swear in
   both the scales against either scale; who committed treason enough for
   God's sake, yet could not equivocate to heaven. O, come in, equivocator.
   [*Knocking within.*] Knock, knock, knock! Who's there? Faith, here's an
   English tailor come hither, for stealing out of a French hose. Come in,   10
   tailor; here you may roast your goose. [*Knocking within.*] Knock, knock;
   never at quiet! What are you? But this place is too cold for hell. I'll devil-
   porter it no further; I had thought to have let in some of all professions
   that go the primrose way to the everlasting bonfire. [*Knocking within.*]
   Anon, anon! I pray you, remember the porter.   [*Opens the gate.*   15

[*Enter* MACDUFF *and* LENNOX.]

MACDUFF. Was it so late, friend, ere you went to bed,
   That you do lie so late?
PORTER. Faith, sir, we were carousing till the second cock;° and drink, sir, is a
   great provoker.
MACDUFF. I believe drink gave thee the lie last night.   20
PORTER. That it did, sir, i' the very throat on me. But I requited him for his lie;
   and, I think, being too strong for him, though he took up my legs some-
   time, yet I made a shift to cast him.
MACDUFF. Is thy master stirring?

[*Enter* MACBETH.]

   Our knocking has awaked him; here he comes.   25
LENNOX. Good morrow, noble sir.
MACBETH.   Good morrow, both.
MACDUFF. Is the king stirring, worthy thane?
MACBETH.   Not yet.
MACDUFF. He did command me to call timely on him.
   I have almost slipped the hour.
MACBETH.   I'll bring you to him.

---

1. The speech that follows is said by a drunken porter (man who tends the gate) and is full of
puns and jests that refer to current happenings of Shakespeare's day. The porter, talking to himself, says that if a man were porter at *hell's gate*, he would grow old from letting so many damned
souls in (lines 1–2). He invokes the name of *Beelzebub* (bĕ·ĕl′zĕ·bŭb), Satan's assistant (line 3);
speaks of a farmer who hanged himself in profiteering on prices, a favorite object of satire in England
at this time (lines 3–4), and advises the farmer to bring plenty of towels with him; speaks of an
equivocator (liar) who could not lie himself into heaven (lines 6–8); and pretends to admit to hell
an *English tailor* whose goose — this word meant a tailor's iron — is to be cooked, or roasted because he has stolen a French fashion. The English critic De Quincey praises this speech as an admirable way of relieving the great tension of the preceding scene. 18. *second cock:* 3 A.M.

MACDUFF. I know this is a joyful trouble to you;   30
     But yet 'tis one.°
MACBETH. The labor we delight in physics pain.°
     This is the door.
MACDUFF.   I'll make so bold to call,
     For 'tis my limited service.°   [*Exit.*
LENNOX. Goes the king hence today?
MACBETH.   He does — he did appoint so.   35
LENNOX. The night has been unruly: where we lay,
     Our chimneys were blown down; and, as they say,
     Lamentings heard i' the air; strange screams of death,
     And prophesying with accents terrible.
     Of dire combustion and confused events   40
     New hatched to the woeful time. The obscure bird°
     Clamored the livelong night; some say, the earth
     Was feverous and did shake.
MACBETH.   'Twas a rough night.
LENNOX. My young remembrance cannot parallel
     A fellow to it.   45

[*Re-enter* MACDUFF.]

MACDUFF. O horror, horror, horror! Tongue nor heart
     Cannot conceive nor name thee!
MACBETH. ⎫
LENNOX. ⎬   What's the matter?
MACDUFF. Confusion now hath made his masterpiece!
     Most sacrilegious murder hath broke ope
     The Lord's anointed temple,° and stole thence   50
     The life o' the building!
MACBETH.   What is 't you say? The life?
LENNOX. Mean you his majesty?
MACDUFF. Approach the chamber, and destroy your sight
     With a new Gorgon.° Do not bid me speak;
     See, and then speak yourselves.   [*Exeunt* MACBETH *and* LENNOX.
                             Awake, awake!   55
     Ring the alarum bell. Murder and treason!
     Banquo and Donalbain! Malcolm! awake!
     Shake off this downy sleep, death's counterfeit,
     And look on death itself! Up, up, and see
     The great doom's image!° Malcolm! Banquo!   60
     As from your graves rise up, and walk like sprites,°
     To countenance° this horror! Ring the bell.   [*Bell rings.*

[*Enter* LADY MACBETH.]

LADY MACBETH. What's the business,
     That such a hideous trumpet calls to parley

31. *one:* a trouble nevertheless. 32. *physics pain:* cures pain, or is pleasant. 34. *limited service:* assigned duty. 41. *obscure bird:* the owl. 50. *The Lord's anointed temple:* the body of the king. 54. *Gorgon:* a female monster (of Greek mythology) who turned to stone those who gazed upon her. 60. *The great doom's image:* Duncan's murder is compared to the end of the world. 61. *sprites:* ghosts. 62. *countenance:* be in keeping with.

The sleepers of the house? Speak, speak!

MACDUFF.   O gentle lady,   65
'Tis not for you to hear what I can speak;
The repetition, in a woman's ear,
Would murder as it fell.

[*Enter* BANQUO.]

                                        O Banquo, Banquo,
Our royal master's murdered!

LADY MACBETH.   Woe, alas!
What, in our house?

BANQUO.   Too cruel anywhere.   70
Dear Duff, I prithee, contradict thyself,
And say it is not so.

[*Re-enter* MACBETH *and* LENNOX, *with* ROSS.]

MACBETH. Had I but died an hour before this chance,°
I had lived a blessèd time; for, from this instant,
There's nothing serious in mortality.   75
All is but toys:° renown and grace is dead;
The wine of life is drawn, and the mere lees
Is left this vault° to brag of.

[*Enter* MALCOLM *and* DONALBAIN.]

DONALBAIN. What is amiss?

MACBETH.   You are, and do not know 't:
The spring, the head, the fountain of your blood   80
Is stopped; the very source of it is stopped.

MACDUFF. Your royal father's murdered.

MALCOLM.   O, by whom?

LENNOX. Those of his chamber, as it seemed, had done 't.
Their hands and faces were all badged with blood;
So were their daggers, which unwiped we found   85
Upon their pillows.
They stared, and were distracted; no man's life
Was to be trusted with them.

MACBETH. O, yet I do repent me of my fury,
That I did kill them.

MACDUFF.   Wherefore did you so?   90

MACBETH. Who can be wise, amazed, temperate and furious,
Loyal and neutral, in a moment? No man.
The expedition° of my violent love
Outrun the pauser, reason. Here lay Duncan,
His silver skin laced with his golden blood,   95
And his gashed stabs looked like a breach in nature
For ruin's wasteful entrance; there, the murderers,
Steeped in the colors of their trade, their daggers

---

73. *chance:* occurrence. 76. *toys:* trifles. 78. *vault:* as used here, world. Macbeth is echoing Macduff's feeling that Duncan's murder spelled the end of the world. 93. *expedition:* hasty action.

Unmannerly breeched° with gore. Who could refrain,
That had a heart to love, and in that heart   100
Courage to make 's love known?
LADY MACBETH.   Help me hence, ho!
MACDUFF. Look to the lady.
MALCOLM. [*Aside to* DONALBAIN] Why do we hold our tongues,
That most may claim this argument for ours?
DONALBAIN. [*Aside to* MALCOLM] What should be spoken here, where our fate,   105
Hid in an auger hole, may rush, and seize us?°
Let's away;
Our tears are not yet brewed.
MALCOLM.   [*Aside to* DONALBAIN] Nor our strong sorrow
Upon the foot of motion.°
BANQUO.   Look to the lady: [LADY MACBETH *is carried out.*
And when we have our naked frailties° hid,   110
That suffer in exposure, let us meet,
And question this most bloody piece of work,
To know it further. Fears and scruples shake us.
In the great hand of God I stand; and thence
Against the undivulged pretense I fight   115
Of treasonous malice.°
MACDUFF.   And so do I.
ALL.   So all.
MACBETH. Let's briefly put on manly readiness,
And meet i' the hall together.
ALL.   Well contented.

[*Exeunt all but* MALCOLM *and* DONALBAIN.

MALCOLM. What will you do? Let's not consort with them;
To show an unfelt sorrow is an office   120
Which the false man does easy. I'll to England.
DONALBAIN. To Ireland, I; our separated fortune
Shall keep us both the safer. Where we are,
There's daggers in men's smiles; the near in blood,
The nearer bloody.°
MALCOLM.   This murderous shaft that's shot   125
Hath not yet lighted,° and our safest way
Is to avoid the aim. Therefore, to horse;
And let us not be dainty of leave-taking,
But shift away. There's warrant in that theft.
Which steals itself, when there's no mercy left.   [*Exeunt.*   130

---

99. *breeched:* completely covered. 105–106. *where our fate . . . seize us:* Malcolm and Donalbain sense
there is danger for them in this murder; any small event (*auger hole*) may lead to their downfall.
109. *Upon the foot of motion:* is not yet moving. 110. *naked frailties:* The guests of Macbeth were
still in their nightclothes. 115–116. *Against . . . malice:* I fight against the as yet unrevealed treason
which has committed this crime. 124–125. *the near in blood, the nearer bloody:* the closer the relationship (to Duncan) the more likely the danger of being murdered. 125–126. *This . . . lighted:* More
murder may follow.

SCENE IV. *Outside* MACBETH'S *castle.*

[Enter ROSS *and an* OLD MAN.]

OLD MAN. Threescore and ten I can remember well;
    Within the volume of which time I have seen
    Hours dreadful and things strange; but this sore night
    Hath trifled former knowings.
ROSS.   Ah, good father,
    Thou seest, the heavens, as troubled with man's act,   5
    Threaten his bloody stage. By the clock, 'tis day,
    And yet dark night strangles the traveling lamp.°
    Is 't night's predominance, or the day's shame,
    That darkness does the face of earth entomb,
    When living light should kiss it?
OLD MAN.   'Tis unnatural,   10
    Even like the deed that's done. On Tuesday last,
    A falcon, towering in her pride of place,
    Was by a mousing owl hawked at and killed.
ROSS. And Duncan's horses — a thing most strange and certain —
    Beauteous and swift, the minions of their race,   15
    Turned wild in nature, broke their stalls, flung out,
    Contending 'gainst obedience, as they would make
    War with mankind.
OLD MAN.   'Tis said they eat each other.
ROSS. They did so, to the amazement of mine eyes
    That looked upon 't. Here comes the good Macduff.   20

[Enter MACDUFF.]

    How goes the world, sir, now?
MACDUFF.   Why, see you not?
ROSS. Is 't known who did this more than bloody deed?
MACDUFF. Those that Macbeth hath slain.
ROSS.   Alas, the day!
    What good could they pretend?
MACDUFF.   They were suborned;°
    Malcolm and Donalbain, the king's two sons,   25
    Are stolen away and fled; which puts upon them
    Suspicion of the deed.
ROSS.   'Gainst nature still!
    Thriftless ambition, that wilt ravin up°
    Thine own life's means! Then 'tis most like
    The sovereignty will fall upon Macbeth.   30
MACDUFF. He is already named, and gone to Scone°
    To be invested.
ROSS.   Where is Duncan's body?
MACDUFF. Carried to Colmekill,

---

7. *traveling lamp:* the sun. 24. *suborned* (sŭb·ôrnd′): bribed. 28. *ravin up:* gobble up. 31. *Scone* (skо̄о̄n): the ancient place of coronation of Scottish kings.

The sacred storehouse° of his predecessors,
And guardian of their bones.
ROSS.   Will you to Scone?   35
MACDUFF. No, cousin, I'll to Fife.°
ROSS.   Well, I will thither.
MACDUFF. Well, may you see things well done there. Adieu!
    Lest our old robes sit easier than our new!°
ROSS. Farewell, father.
OLD MAN. God's benison go with you; and with those   40
    That would make good of bad, and friends of foes!   [*Exeunt.*

34. *sacred storehouse:* tomb. 36. *Fife:* Macduff's castle. 38. *Lest . . . new:* Macduff here shows his misgivings about the future with Macbeth as king.

"I HAVE DONE THE DEED."

ACT II

1. In the brief dialogue between Banquo and Macbeth at the beginning of the act, what do you learn about their regard for each other?

2. Analyze the "dagger speech," lines 33–64. In how many different ways does Macbeth see the dagger? What does the speech show of his mental state? Is he becoming mentally stronger or weaker than he revealed himself in Act I?

3. How is the feeling of intense horror made impressive at the beginning of Scene ii? Do the knocking and the actions of the porter increase or destroy this horror? (A report by a student on De Quincey's essay "On the Knocking at the Gate in Macbeth" will throw some interesting light on its effect.)

4. Why did Macbeth kill the grooms? Was it a wise move? What reason did he give to the others?

ACT III

SCENE I. *Forres. The palace.*

[*Enter* BANQUO.]

BANQUO. Thou hast it now: king, Cawdor, Glamis, all,
    As the weird women promised, and, I fear,
    Thou play'dst most foully for 't; yet it was said
    It should not stand in thy posterity,
    But that myself should be the root and father   5
    Of many kings. If there come truth from them —
    As upon thee, Macbeth, their speeches shine —
    Why, by the verities° on thee made good,
    May they not be my oracles as well,
    And set me up in hope? But hush! no more.   10

[*Sennet* sounded. Enter* MACBETH, *as king,* LADY MACBETH, *as queen,*
    LENNOX, ROSS, LORDS, LADIES, *and* ATTENDANTS.]

8. *verities:* truths. **Sennet:* sound of trumpets announcing entrance of a person of importance.

MACBETH. Here's our chief guest.
LADY MACBETH.   If he had been forgotten,
    It had been as a gap in our great feast,
    And all-thing° unbecoming.
MACBETH. Tonight we hold a solemn supper,° sir,
    And I'll request your presence.
BANQUO.   Let your highness   15
    Command upon me; to the which my duties
    Are with a most indissoluble tie
    For ever knit.°
MACBETH. Ride you this afternoon?
BANQUO. Ay, my good lord.   20
MACBETH. We should have else desired your good advice,
    Which still hath been both grave and prosperous,
    In this day's council; but we'll take tomorrow.
    Is 't far you ride?
BANQUO. As far, my lord, as will fill up the time   25
    'Twixt this and supper. Go not my horse the better,
    I must become a borrower of the night
    For a dark hour or twain.°
MACBETH.   Fail not our feast.
BANQUO. My lord, I will not.
MACBETH. We hear, our bloody cousins are bestowed   30
    In England and in Ireland, not confessing
    Their cruel parricide,° filling their hearers
    With strange invention. But of that tomorrow,
    When therewithal we shall have cause of state
    Craving us jointly.° Hie you to horse; adieu,   35
    Till you return at night. Goes Fleance with you?
BANQUO. Ay, my good lord. Our time does call upon 's.
MACBETH. I wish your horses swift and sure of foot;
    And so I do commend you to their backs.
    Farewell.   [*Exit* BANQUO. 40
    Let every man be master of his time
    Till seven at night. To make society
    The sweeter welcome, we will keep ourself
    Till suppertime alone; while° then, God be with you!
               [*Exeunt all but* MACBETH *and an* ATTENDANT.
    Sirrah, a word with you: attend those men   45
    Our pleasure?
ATTENDANT. They are, my lord, without the palace gate.
MACBETH. Bring them before us.   [*Exit* ATTENDANT.
               To be thus is nothing;
    But to be safely thus.° — Our fears in Banquo
    Stick deep; and in his royalty of nature   50

---

    13. *all-thing:* altogether. 14. *solemn supper:* formal banquet. 16–18. *to the which . . . knit:* my duties are inseparably bound to your commands. 26–28. *Go not . . . twain:* In other words, unless his horse is swift he'll not be back before dark. 32. *parricide:* killing of a parent. 35. *Craving us jointly:* demanding the attention of both of us. 44. *while:* until. 49. *But . . . thus:* unless we are safely thus.

Reigns that which would be feared. 'Tis much he dares;
And, to that dauntless temper of his mind,
He hath a wisdom that doth guide his valor
To act in safety. There is none but he
Whose being I do fear; and, under him,   55
My Genius is rebuked,° as, it is said,
Mark Antony's was by Caesar. He chid the sisters
When first they put the name of king upon me,
And bade them speak to him; then prophetlike
They hailed him father to a line of kings.   60
Upon my head they placed a fruitless crown,
And put a barren scepter in my gripe,
Thence to be wrenched with an unlineal hand,
No son of mine succeeding. If 't be so,
For Banquo's issue have I filed° my mind;   65
For them the gracious Duncan have I murdered;
Put rancors in the vessel of my peace
Only for them; and mine eternal jewel
Given to the common enemy of man,
To make them kings, the seed of Banquo kings!°   70
Rather than so, come fate into the list,
And champion me to the utterance!° Who's there?

[*Re-enter* ATTENDANT, *with two* MURDERERS.]

Now go to the door, and stay there till we call.   [*Exit* ATTENDANT.
Was it not yesterday we spoke together?
FIRST MURDERER. It was, so please your highness.
MACBETH.   Well then, now   75
Have you considered of my speeches? Know
That it was he in the times past which held you
So under fortune, which you thought had been
Our innocent self. This I made good to you
In our last conference, passed in probation with you,°   80
How you were borne in hand,° how crossed, the instruments,
Who wrought with them, and all things else that might
To half a soul and to a notion crazed
Say "Thus did Banquo."
FIRST MURDERER.   You made it known to us.
MACBETH. I did so, and went further, which is now   85
Our point of second meeting. Do you find
Your patience so predominant in your nature
That you can let this go? Are you so gospeled
To pray for this good man and for his issue,
Whose heavy hand hath bowed you to the grave   90
And beggared yours for ever?

---

56. *My Genius is rebuked:* Banquo stands in the way of Macbeth's realizing his ambition. 65. *filed:* defiled. 68–70. *and mine eternal jewel . . . the seed of Banquo kings:* Macbeth has sold his soul to the devil to make Banquo's descendants (rather than his own) kings. 72. *champion me to the utterance:* challenge me to fight to the finish. 79–80. *This . . . with you:* I gave you proof at our last meeting that Banquo was your enemy. 81. *borne in hand:* deceived.

FIRST MURDERER.   We are men, my liege.
MACBETH. Ay, in the catalogue ye go for men;
    As hounds and greyhounds, mongrels, spaniels, curs,
    Shoughs, water rugs, and demiwolves, are clept°
    All by the name of dogs; the valued file°   95
    Distinguishes the swift, the slow, the subtle,
    The housekeeper, the hunter, every one
    According to the gift which bounteous nature
    Hath in him closed, whereby he does receive
    Particular addition, from the bill   100
    That writes them all alike;° and so of men.
    Now, if you have a station in the file,
    Not i' the worst rank of manhood, say 't;
    And I will put that business in your bosoms,
    Whose execution takes your enemy off,   105
    Grapples you to the heart and love of us,
    Who wear our health but sickly in his life,
    Which in his death were perfect.°
SECOND MURDERER.   I am one, my liege,
    Whom the vile blows and buffets of the world
    Have so incensed that I am reckless what   110
    I do to spite the world.
FIRST MURDERER.   And I another
    So weary with disasters, tugged with fortune,°
    That I would set my life on any chance,
    To mend it, or be rid on 't.
MACBETH.   Both of you
    Know Banquo was your enemy.
BOTH MURDERERS.   True, my lord.   115
MACBETH. So is he mine; and in such bloody distance,
    That every minute of his being thrusts
    Against my near'st of life; and though I could
    With barefaced power sweep him from my sight
    And bid my will avouch° it, yet I must not,   120
    For° certain friends that are both his and mine,
    Whose loves I may not drop, but wail his fall°
    Who I myself struck down; and thence it is,
    That I to your assistance do make love,
    Masking the business from the common eye   125
    For sundry weighty reasons.
SECOND MURDERER.   We shall, my lord,
    Perform what you command us.
FIRST MURDERER.   Though our lives —
MACBETH. Your spirits shine through you. Within this hour at most
    I will advise you where to plant yourselves;

---

94. *clept:* called. 95. *valued file:* list of those considered first class. 99–101. *whereby . . . alike:* i.e., every good dog has some special quality which makes him more than simply a "dog." 107–108. *Who wear . . . perfect:* In other words, Banquo's being alive is as an illness to Macbeth. 112. *tugged with fortune:* pulled about by bad luck. 120. *avouch:* justify. 121. *For:* because of. 122. *but wail his fall:* To cover up, Macbeth must seem to bewail Banquo's death.

Acquaint you with the perfect spy o' the time,°   130
The moment on 't; for 't must be done tonight,
And something from° the palace; always thought
That I require a clearness;° and with him —
To leave no rubs nor botches in the work —
Fleance his son, that keeps him company,   135
Whose absence is no less material to me
Than is his father's, must embrace the fate
Of that dark hour. Resolve yourselves apart;°
I'll come to you anon.
BOTH MURDERERS.   We are resolved, my lord.
MACBETH. I'll call upon you straight; abide within.   140

[*Exeunt* MURDERERS.

It is concluded. Banquo, thy soul's flight,
If it find heaven, must find it out tonight.   [*Exit.*

SCENE II. *The palace.*

[*Enter* LADY MACBETH *and a* SERVANT.]

LADY MACBETH. Is Banquo gone from court?
SERVANT. Ay, madam, but returns again tonight.
LADY MACBETH. Say to the king, I would attend his leisure
            For a few words.
SERVANT.   Madam, I will.   [*Exit.*
LADY MACBETH.   Naught's had, all's spent,
            Where our desire is got without content.   5
            'Tis safer to be that which we destroy
            Than by destruction dwell in doubtful joy.

[*Enter* MACBETH.]

How now, my lord! why do you keep alone,
Of sorriest fancies your companions making,
Using those thoughts which should indeed have died   10
With them they think on? Things without all remedy
Should be without regard; what's done is done.
MACBETH. We have scotched° the snake, not killed it;
            She'll close and be herself, whilst our poor malice
            Remains in danger of her former tooth.   15
            But let the frame of things disjoint, both the worlds suffer,
            Ere we will eat our meal in fear,° and sleep
            In the affliction of these terrible dreams
            That shake us nightly. Better be with the dead,
            Whom we, to gain our peace, have sent to peace,   20
            Than on the torture of the mind to lie

130. *the perfect spy o' the time:* the exact moment. 132. *something from:* some distance from. 132–133. *always . . . clearness:* It must always be remembered that I remain clear of this. 138. *Resolve yourselves apart:* Make your own decision.

13. *scotched:* wounded. 16–17. *But let . . . fear:* Let the universe fall apart and heaven and hell perish (*both the worlds suffer*) before we let this murder unnerve us.

In restless ecstasy.° Duncan is in his grave;
After life's fitful fever he sleeps well;
Treason has done his worst; nor steel, nor poison,
Malice domestic, foreign levy, nothing,   25
Can touch him further.
LADY MACBETH.   Come on;
Gentle my lord, sleek o'er your rugged looks;
Be bright and jovial among your guests tonight.
MACBETH. So shall I, love; and so, I pray, be you.
Let your remembrance apply to Banquo;   30
Present him eminence,° both with eye and tongue;
Unsafe the while, that we°
Must lave our honors in these flattering streams,
And make our faces vizards° to our hearts,
Disguising what they are.
LADY MACBETH.   You must leave this.   35
MACBETH. O, full of scorpions is my mind, dear wife!
Thou know'st that Banquo, and his Fleance, lives.
LADY MACBETH. But in them nature's copy 's not eterne.
MACBETH. There's comfort yet; they are assailable;
Then be thou jocund; ere the bat hath flown   40
His cloistered flight, ere to black Hecate's summons
The shard-borne beetle° with his drowsy hums
Hath rung night's yawning peal, there shall be done
A deed of dreadful note.
LADY MACBETH.   What's to be done?
MACBETH. Be innocent of the knowledge, dearest chuck,   45
Till thou applaud the deed. Come, seeling night,
Scarf up the tender eye of pitiful day;°
And with thy bloody and invisible hand
Cancel and tear to pieces that great bond°
Which keeps me pale! Light thickens, and the crow   50
Makes wing to the rooky° wood;
Good things of day begin to droop and drowse;
Whiles night's black agents to their preys do rouse.
Thou marvel'st at my words; but hold thee still;
Things bad begun make strong themselves by ill.   55
So, prithee, go with me.   [*Exeunt.*

SCENE III. *A park near the palace.*

[*Enter three* MURDERERS.]

FIRST MURDERER. But who did bid thee join with us?
THIRD MURDERER.   Macbeth.

---

22. *ecstasy:* madness, mental torment. 31. *Present him eminence:* Make much of him. 32. We
are not safe as long as we. . . . 34. *vizards:* masks. 42. *shard-borne beetle:* the beetle borne aloft by
its brittle wings. 46–47. *Come . . . day:* This figure is drawn from falconry. Young falcons were
trained by having their eyelids seeled (sewn shut). 49. *great bond:* that which binds me; i.e., Banquo's life. 51. *rooky:* full of rooks, or crows.

SECOND MURDERER. He needs not our mistrust, since he delivers
　　　Our offices° and what we have to do
　　　To the direction just.°
FIRST MURDERER.　　　　　　Then stand with us.
　　　The west yet glimmers with some streaks of day;　　　　　5
　　　Now spurs the lated traveler apace
　　　To gain the timely inn; and near approaches
　　　The subject of our watch.
THIRD MURDERER.　　　　　Hark! I hear horses.
BANQUO. [*Within*] Give us a light there, ho!
SECOND MURDERER.　　　　　　　Then 'tis he; the rest
　　　That are within the note of expectation°　　　　　　10
　　　Already are i' the court.
FIRST MURDERER.　　　　　　His horses go about.
THIRD MURDERER. Almost a mile; but he does usually,
　　So all men do, from hence to the palace gate
　　　Make it their walk.
SECOND MURDERER.　　　A light, a light!

　　　　　　[*Enter* BANQUO, *and* FLEANCE *with a torch.*]

THIRD MURDERER.　　　　　　　'Tis he.
FIRST MURDERER. Stand to 't.　　　　　　　　　　　　　　15
BANQUO. It will be rain tonight.
FIRST MURDERER.　　　　　Let it come down.

　　　　　　[*They set upon* BANQUO.]

BANQUO. O treachery! Fly, good Fleance, fly, fly, fly!
　　　Thou mayst revenge. O slave!

　　　　　　[*Dies.* FLEANCE *escapes.*]

THIRD MURDERER. Who did strike out the light?
FIRST MURDERER.　　　　　　　　Was 't not the way?
THIRD MURDERER. There's but one down; the son is fled.
SECOND MURDERER.　　　　　　　　We have lost　　　20
　　　Best half of our affair.
FIRST MURDERER. Well, let's away, and say how much is done.　　　[*Exeunt.*

SCENE IV. *The same. Hall in the palace.*

[*A banquet prepared. Enter* MACBETH, LADY MACBETH, ROSS,
　　　LENNOX, LORDS, *and* ATTENDANTS.]

MACBETH. You know your own degrees; sit down.° At first
　　　And last the hearty welcome.
LORDS.　　　　　　　　　Thanks to your majesty.

---

3. *offices:* duties. 4. *direction just:* exact detail. 10. *within . . . expectation:* among the invited guests.
1. *You . . . down:* The lords and ladies were seated according to rank (or *degree*).

MACBETH. Ourself will mingle with society,°
    And play the humble host.
    Our hostess keeps her state, but in best time   5
    We will require her welcome.
LADY MACBETH. Pronounce it for me, sir, to all our friends;
    For my heart speaks they are welcome.

                [*First* MURDERER *appears at the door.*]

MACBETH. See, they encounter thee with their hearts' thanks.
    Both sides are even; here I'll sit i' the midst;   10
    Be large in mirth; anon we'll drink a measure°
    The table round. [*Approaching the door.*] There's blood upon thy face.
MURDERER. 'Tis Banquo's then.
MACBETH. 'Tis better thee without than he within.°
    Is he dispatched?   15
MURDERER. My lord, his throat is cut; that I did for him.
MACBETH. Thou art the best o' the cutthroats: yet he's good
    That did the like for Fleance. If thou didst it,
    Thou art the nonpareil.°
MURDERER.   Most royal sir,
    Fleance is 'scaped.   20
MACBETH. Then comes my fit again. I had else been perfect,
    Whole as the marble, founded as the rock,
    As broad and general as the casing° air;
    But now I am cabined, cribbed, confined, bound in
    To saucy doubts and fears. But Banquo's safe?   25
MURDERER. Ay, my good lord; safe in a ditch he bides,
    With twenty trenchèd gashes on his head,
    The least a death to nature.
MACBETH.   Thanks for that;
    There the grown serpent lies; the worm° that's fled
    Hath nature that in time will venom breed,   30
    No teeth for the present. Get thee gone; tomorrow
    We'll hear ourselves again.°   [*Exit* MURDERER.
LADY MACBETH.   My royal lord,
    You do not give the cheer. The feast is sold
    That is not often vouched, while 'tis amaking,
    'Tis given with welcome.° To feed were best at home;   35
    From thence the sauce to meat is ceremony;°
    Meeting were bare without it.
MACBETH.   Sweet remembrancer!
    Now, good digestion wait on appetite,
    And health on both!

---

3. *Ourself will mingle with society:* Macbeth will come down from the special seat of honor accorded royalty and sit among his lords. 11. *measure:* toast. 14. *'Tis . . . within:* The blood is better outside you than inside him. 19. *the nonpareil* (nŏn′pá·rĕl′): something without equal. 23. *casing:* enclosing. 29. *worm:* little snake. 31–32. *tomorrow . . . again:* Tomorrow Macbeth will consider what's to be done about Fleance. 33–35. *The feast . . . welcome:* The feast in which the host does not continually assure his guests of their welcome is like a bought meal. 35–36. *To feed . . . ceremony:* Merely to eat, one had best stay home; when dining out, politeness or ceremony adds a pleasant flavor to the meal.

LENNOX.   May 't please your highness sit.

[*The* GHOST *of* BANQUO *enters, and sits in* MACBETH'S *place.*]

MACBETH. Here had we now our country's honor roofed,°   40
    Were the graced person of our Banquo present;
    Who may I rather challenge for unkindness
    Than pity for mischance!°
ROSS.   His absence, sir,
    Lays blame upon his promise. Please 't your highness
    To grace us with your royal company.   45
MACBETH. The table's full.
LENNOX.   Here is a place reserved, sir.
MACBETH. Where?
LENNOX. Here, my good lord. What is 't that moves your highness?
MACBETH. Which of you have done this?
LORDS.   What, my good lord?
MACBETH. Thou canst not say I did it; never shake   50
    Thy gory locks at me.
ROSS. Gentlemen, rise; his highness is not well.
LADY MACBETH. Sit, worthy friends; my lord is often thus,
    And hath been from his youth. Pray you, keep seat;
    The fit is momentary; upon a thought   55
    He will again be well. If much you note him,
    You shall offend him and extend his passion.
    Feed, and regard him not. Are you a man?°
MACBETH. Ay, and a bold one, that dare look on that
    Which might appall the devil.
LADY MACBETH.   O proper stuff!   60
    This is the very painting of your fear;
    This is the air-drawn dagger which, you said,
    Led you to Duncan. O, these flaws and starts,
    Impostors to true fear, would well become
    A woman's story at a winter's fire,   65
    Authorized° by her grandam. Shame itself!
    Why do you make such faces? When all's done,
    You look but on a stool.
MACBETH. Prithee, see there! behold! look! lo! how say you?
    Why, what care I? If you canst nod, speak too.   70
    If charnel houses° and our graves must send
    Those that we bury back, our monuments
    Shall be the maws of kites.°   [GHOST *vanishes.*
LADY MACBETH.   What, quite unmanned in folly?
MACBETH. If I stand here, I saw him.
LADY MACBETH.   Fie, for shame!

---

    40. *Here . . . roofed:* We would have all the most honored men in the country under our roof.
42–43. *Who . . . mischance:* Macbeth says he attributes Banquo's absence to discourtesy rather
than to accident. 58. *Are you a man?:* This is addressed to Macbeth, out of the hearing of the
guests. 66. *Authorized:* vouched for. 71. *charnel houses:* burial vaults. 73. *maws of kites:* stomachs
of vultures. In other words, it would be better to let vultures devour the dead if they are going to
break out from their tombs and come back to haunt the living.

MACBETH. Blood hath been shed ere now, i' the olden time,   75
     Ere humane statute purged the gentle weal;°
     Ay, and since too, murders have been performed
     Too terrible for the ear. The time has been,
     That, when the brains were out, the man would die,
     And there an end; but now they rise again,   80
     With twenty mortal murders on their crowns,
     And push us from our stools. This is more strange
     Than such a murder is.
LADY MACBETH.   My worthy lord,
     Your noble friends do lack you.
MACBETH.   I do forget.°
     Do not muse at me, my most worthy friends;   85
     I have a strange infirmity, which is nothing
     To those that know me. Come, love and health to all;
     Then I'll sit down. Give me some wine; fill full.
     I drink to the general joy o' the whole table,
     And to our dear friend Banquo, whom we miss;   90
     Would he were here! to all, and him, we thirst,
     And all to all.
LORDS.   Our duties, and the pledge.

             [*Re-enter* GHOST.]

MACBETH. Avaunt! and quit my sight! let the earth hide thee!
     Thy bones are marrowless, thy blood is cold;
     Thou has no speculation° in those eyes   95
     Which thou dost glare with!
LADY MACBETH.   Think of this, good peers,
     But as a thing of custom; 'tis no other;
     Only it spoils the pleasure of the time.
MACBETH. What man dare, I dare.
     Approach thou like the rugged Russian bear,   100
     The armed rhinoceros, or the Hyrcan° tiger;
     Take any shape but that, and my firm nerves
     Shall never tremble; or be alive again,
     And dare me to the desert° with my sword;
     If trembling I inhabit° then, protest me   105
     The baby of a girl. Hence, horrible shadow!
     Unreal mockery, hence!   [GHOST *vanishes.*
                 Why, so; being gone
     I am a man again. Pray you, sit still.
LADY MACBETH. You have displaced the mirth, broke the good meeting,
     With most admired disorder.°
MACBETH.   Can such things be,   110
     And overcome us like a summer's cloud,

---

76. *Ere . . . weal:* before humane laws made the state civilized. Before that time, lawless barbarism prevailed. 84. *I do forget:* At this point Macbeth turns back to address the company. 95. *speculation:* intelligent expression; that is, the ghost's eyes were glassy. 101. *Hyrcan* (hûr′kăn): from an ancient province of Asia, southeast of the Caspian Sea. 104. *desert:* a place from which neither could escape. 105. *inhabit:* remain indoors. 110. *admired disorder:* as used here, amazing disorder; distraction.

Without our special wonder? You make me strange
Even to the disposition that I owe,°
When now I think you can behold such sights,
And keep the natural ruby of your cheeks, 115
When mine is blanched with fear.
ROSS.   What sights, my lord?
LADY. MACBETH. I pray you, speak not; he grows worse and worse;
          Question enrages him. At once, good night.
          Stand not upon the order of your going,°
          But go at once.
LENNOX.   Good night; and better health 120
          Attend his majesty!
LADY MACBETH.   A kind good night to all!
                    [*Exeunt all but* MACBETH *and* LADY MACBETH.
MACBETH. It will have blood; they say, blood will have blood.
          Stones have been known to move and trees to speak;
          Augurs and understood relations have
          By maggot-pies and choughs and rooks brought forth 125
          The secret'st man of blood.° What is the night?
LADY MACBETH. Almost at odds with morning, which is which.
MACBETH. How say'st thou, that Macduff denies his person
          At our great bidding?
LADY MACBETH.   Did you send to him, sir?
MACBETH. I hear it by the way; but I will send. 130
          There's not a one of them but in his house
          I keep a servant fee'd.° I will tomorrow,
          And betimes I will, to the weird sisters.
          More shall they speak; for now I am bent to know,
          By the worst means, the worst. For mine own good, 135
          All causes shall give way. I am in blood
          Stepped in so far that, should I wade no more,
          Returning were as tedious as go o'er.
          Strange things I have in head, that will to hand;
          Which must be acted ere they may be scanned. 140
LADY MACBETH. You lack the season of all natures, sleep.
MACBETH. Come, we'll to sleep. My strange and self-abuse
          Is the initiate fear° that wants hard use;
          We are yet but young in deed.   [*Exeunt.*

SCENE V. *A heath.*

[*Thunder. Enter the three* WITCHES, *meeting* HECATE.]

FIRST WITCH. Why, how now, Hecate! you look angerly.
HECATE. Have I not reason, beldams° as you are,

112–113. *You . . . owe:* You make me seem to behave unnaturally. *Owe* means *own* here. 119. *the order of your going:* Just as the lords and ladies were seated according to rank, so they customarily departed according to rank. 124–126. *Augurs . . . blood:* Augurs, or fortunetellers, have been able by the flight of birds to discover even the most secret murders. 132. *fee'd:* in my pay as a spy. 143. *initiate fear:* fear of one who is just beginning.
    2. *beldams:* hags.

Saucy and overbold? How did you dare
To trade and traffic with Macbeth
In riddles and affairs of death;   5
And I, the mistress of your charms,
The close° contriver of all harms,
Was never called to bear my part,
Or show the glory of our art?
And, which is worse, all you have done   10
Hath been but for a wayward son,
Spiteful and wrathful, who, as others do,
Loves for his own ends, not for you.
But make amends now; get you gone,
And at the pit of Acheron°   15
Meet me i' the morning; thither he
Will come to know his destiny.
Your vessels and your spells provide,
Your charms and everything beside.
I am for the air; this night I'll spend   20
Unto a dismal and a fatal end;
Great business must be wrought ere noon.
Upon the corner of the moon
There hangs a vaporous drop profound;
I'll catch it ere it come to ground;   25
And that distilled by magic sleights
Shall raise such artificial sprites
As by the strength of their illusion
Shall draw him on to his confusion.
He shall spurn fate, scorn death, and bear   30
His hopes 'bove wisdom, grace, and fear;
And you all know, security°
Is mortals' chiefest enemy.
        [*Music and a song within:* "Come away, come away," etc.
Hark! I am called; my little spirit, see,
Sits in a foggy cloud, and stays for me.   [*Exit.* 35
FIRST WITCH. Come, let's make haste; she'll soon be back again.   [*Exeunt.*

SCENE VI. *Forres. The palace.*

[*Enter* LENNOX *and another* LORD.]

LENNOX. My former speeches have but hit your thoughts,
Which can interpret further;° only, I say,
Things have been strangely borne.° The gracious Duncan
Was pitied of Macbeth; marry, he was dead;
And the right-valiant Banquo walked too late;   5
Whom, you may say, if 't please you,° Fleance killed,

---

7. *close:* secret. 15. *the pit of Acheron* (ăk'ĕr·ŏn): hell. In Greek mythology, Acheron is the River of Woe leading to Hades. 32. *security:* false feeling of safety.

2. *Which...further:* from which you can draw your own conclusions. 3. *borne:* managed. 6. Notice that from here on Lennox is using sarcasm. He is opposed to Macbeth and suspects his treachery.

For Fleance fled; men must not walk too late.
Who cannot want° the thought how monstrous
It was for Malcolm and for Donalbain
To kill their gracious father? Damnèd fact!   10
How it did grieve Macbeth! Did he not straight
In pious rage the two delinquents tear,
That were the slaves of drink and thralls of sleep?
Was not that nobly done? Ay, and wisely too;
For 'twould have angered any heart alive   15
To hear the men deny 't. So that, I say,
He has borne all things well; and I do think
That had he Duncan's sons under his key —
As, an 't please Heaven, he shall not — they should find
What 'twere to kill a father; so should Fleance.   20
But, peace! for from broad words° and 'cause he failed
His presence at the tyrant's feast, I hear
Macduff lives in disgrace. Sir, can you tell
Where he bestows himself?
LORD.   The son of Duncan,
From whom this tyrant holds the due of birth,°   25
Lives in the English court, and is received
Of the most pious Edward with such grace
That the malevolence of fortune nothing
Takes from his high respect.° Thither Macduff
Is gone to pray the holy king, upon his aid   30
To wake Northumberland and warlike Siward;
That by the help of these — with Him above
To ratify the work — we may again
Give to our tables meat, sleep to our nights,°
Free from our feasts and banquets bloody knives,   35
Do faithful homage and receive free honors;
All which we pine for now; and this report
Hath so exasperate the king that he
Prepares for some attempt of war.
LENNOX.   Sent he to Macduff?
LORD. He did; and with an absolute "Sir, not I,"   40
The cloudy° messenger turns me his back,
And hums, as who should say, "You'll rue the time
That clogs me with this answer."°
LENNOX.   And that well might
Advise him to a caution, to hold what distance
His wisdom can provide. Some holy angel   45
Fly to the court of England and unfold
His message ere he come, that swift blessing
May soon return to this our suffering country
Under a hand accursed!
LORD.   I'll send my prayers with him.   [*Exeunt.*

8. *want:* be without. 21. *broad words:* unguarded expressions. 25. *From whom . . . due of birth:* Malcolm's claim to the throne is withheld by Macbeth. 28–29. *the malevolence . . . respect:* In spite of his misfortunes, his reputation is intact. 34. *Give . . . nights:* Normal life is impossible, in other words, under Macbeth's tyranny. 41. *cloudy:* surly. 43. *clogs . . . answer:* makes me return reluctantly.

"BLOOD WILL HAVE BLOOD."

ACT III

1. For what reason does Macbeth want Banquo murdered? What different reasons does he give the murderers? Why?

2. In this act how have Macbeth and his wife exchanged places since the murder of Duncan? Do Scenes i and ii suggest that Macbeth has risen or fallen in a moral sense? Give reasons for your answer.

3. Scene iv is considered the turning point of the play. On pages 190–91 refer to the discussion of plot, and then explain how this scene may be considered a climax.

4. Why is Macbeth so upset by the escape of Fleance? What speeches of Macbeth seem to call forth the appearance of Banquo's ghost? What is ironic about this timing?

5. Considering all the circumstances of the two scenes, why does the illusion of the ghost show a more serious state of nerves than that of the dagger in Act II?

6. In this act what hints are given of the gathering forces of opposition to Macbeth?

ACT IV

SCENE I. *A cavern. In the middle, a boiling caldron.*

[*Thunder. Enter the three* WITCHES.]

FIRST WITCH. Thrice the brinded° cat hath mewed.
SECOND WITCH. Thrice and once the hedge pig whined.
THIRD WITCH. Harpier° cries, " 'Tis time, 'tis time."
FIRST WITCH. Round about the caldron go;
    In the poisoned entrails throw.   5
    Toad, that under cold stone
    Days and nights has thirty-one
    Sweltered venom sleeping got,
    Boil thou first i' the charmèd pot.
ALL. Double, double toil and trouble;   10
    Fire burn, and caldron bubble.
SECOND WITCH. Fillet of a fenny snake,
    In the caldron boil and bake;
    Eye of newt and toe of frog,
    Wool of bat and tongue of dog,   15
    Adder's fork and blind worm's sting,
    Lizard's leg and howlet's wing,
    For a charm of powerful trouble,
    Like a hell broth boil and bubble.
ALL. Double, double toil and trouble;   20
    Fire burn, and caldron bubble.
THIRD WITCH. Scale of dragon, tooth of wolf,
    Witches' mummy, maw and gulf°
    Of the ravined salt-sea shark,
    Root of hemlock digged i' the dark,   25
    Liver of blaspheming Jew,

---

1. *brinded:* striped. 3. *Harpier:* one of the spirits attending the witches. 23. *maw and gulf:* stomach and throat.

        Gall of goat, and slips of yew
        Slivered in the moon's eclipse,
        Nose of Turk and Tartar's lips,
        Finger of birth-strangled babe   30
        Ditch-delivered by a drab,
        Make the gruel thick and slab;°
        Add thereto a tiger's chaudron,°
        For the ingredients of our caldron.
ALL. Double, double toil and trouble;   35
        Fire burn, and caldron bubble.
SECOND WITCH. Cool it with a baboon's blood,
        Then the charm is firm and good.

        [*Enter* HECATE *to the other three* WITCHES.]

HECATE. O, well done! I commend your pains;
        And every one shall share i' the gains;   40
        And now about the caldron sing,
        Like elves and fairies in a ring,
        Enchanting all that you put in.
                [*Music and a song:* "Black spirits," etc.
                          [HECATE *retires.*

SECOND WITCH. By the pricking of my thumbs,
        Something wicked this way comes.   45
          Open, locks,
        Whoever knocks!

              [*Enter* MACBETH.]

MACBETH. How now, you secret, black, and midnight hags!
    What is 't you do?
ALL.   A deed without a name.
MACBETH. I conjure you, by that which you profess,   50
        Howe'er you come to know it, answer me;
        Though you untie the winds and let them fight
        Against the churches; though the yesty° waves
        Confound and swallow navigation up;
        Though bladed corn be lodged° and trees blown down;   55
        Though castles topple on their warders' heads;
        Though palaces and pyramids do slope
        Their heads to their foundations; though the treasure
        Of nature's germens° tumble all together,
        Even till destruction sicken; answer me   60
        To what I ask you.
FIRST WITCH.   Speak.
SECOND WITCH.   Demand.
THIRD WITCH.   We'll answer.
FIRST WITCH. Say, if thou 'dst rather hear it from our mouths,
        Or from our masters'?
MACBETH.   Call 'em; let me see 'em.

---

  32. *slab:* like thick mud. 33. *chaudron:* entrails. 53. *yesty:* foaming. 55. *corn . . . lodged:* wheat laid flat by the wind before it can be harvested. 59. *nature's germens:* seeds of all living things.

FIRST WITCH. Pour in sow's blood, that hath eaten
    Her nine farrow; grease that's sweaten   65
    From the murderer's gibbet throw
    Into the flame.
ALL.   Come, high or low;
    Thyself and office° deftly show!

        [*Thunder.* First Apparition: *an armed* HEAD.*]

MACBETH. Tell me, thou unknown power —
FIRST WITCH.   He knows thy thought;
    Hear his speech, but say thou naught.   70
FIRST APPARITION. Macbeth! Macbeth! Macbeth! beware Macduff;
    Beware the thane of Fife. Dismiss me. Enough.   [*Descends.*
MACBETH. Whate'er thou art, for thy good caution, thanks;
    Thou hast harped° my fear aright: but one word more —
FIRST WITCH. He will not be commanded: here's another,   75
    More potent than the first.

        [*Thunder.* Second Apparition: *a bloody* CHILD.†]

SECOND APPARITION. Macbeth! Macbeth! Macbeth!
MACBETH. Had I three ears, I 'ld hear thee.
SECOND APPARITION. Be bloody, bold, and resolute; laugh to scorn
    The power of man, for none of woman born   80
    Shall harm Macbeth.   [*Descends.*
MACBETH. Then live, Macduff; what need I fear of thee?
    But yet I'll make assurance double sure,
    And take a bond of fate.° Thou shalt not live;
    That I may tell pale-hearted fear it lies,   85
    And sleep in spite of thunder.

    [*Thunder.* Third Apparition: *a* CHILD *crowned,*‡ *with a tree in his hand.*]

                      What is this
    That rises like the issue of a king,
    And wears upon his baby brow the round
    And top of sovereignty?
ALL.   Listen, but speak not to 't.
THIRD APPARITION. Be lion-mettled, proud; and take no care   90
    Who chafes, who frets, or where conspirers are.
    Macbeth shall never vanquished be until
    Great Birnam wood to high Dunsinane hill
    Shall come against him.   [*Descends.*
MACBETH.   That will never be.
    Who can impress the forest, bid the tree   95
    Unfixed his earth-bound root? Sweet bodements!° good!
    Rebellion's head, rise never till the wood
    Of Birnam rise, and our high-placed Macbeth
    Shall live the lease of nature,° pay his breath

---

68. *office:* thy function. * *an armed Head:* a symbol of Macduff. 74. *harped:* expressed. † *a bloody Child:* Macduff at birth. 84. *take . . . fate:* To be sure the prophecy turns out, he will kill Macduff. ‡ *a Child crowned:* symbol of Malcolm. 96. *bodements:* prophecies. 99. *lease of nature:* his allotted term of life; that is, he would die a natural death.

To time and mortal custom. Yet my heart   100
Throbs to know one thing: tell me, if your art
Can tell so much: shall Banquo's issue ever
Reign in this kingdom?

ALL.   Seek to know no more.

MACBETH. I will be satisfied; deny me this,
And an eternal curse fall on you! Let me know.   105
Why sinks that caldron? and what noise is this?   [*Hautboys.*

FIRST WITCH. Show!

SECOND WITCH. Show!

THIRD WITCH. Show!

ALL. Show his eyes, and grieve his heart;   110
Come like shadows, so depart!

[*A show of Eight* KINGS,* *the last with a glass* † *in his hand;*
BANQUO'S GHOST *following.*]

MACBETH. Thou art too like the spirit of Banquo; down!
Thy crown doth sear mine eyeballs. And thy hair,
Thou other gold-bound brow, is like the first.
A third is like the former. Filthy hags!   115
Why do you show me this? A fourth! Start, eyes!
What, will the line stretch out to the crack of doom?
Another yet! A seventh! I'll see no more.
And yet the eighth appears, who bears a glass
Which shows me many more; and some I see   120
That twofold balls and treble scepters° carry.
Horrible sight! Now, I see, 'tis true;
For the blood-boltered° Banquo smiles upon me,
And points at them for his.° [APPARITIONS *vanish.*] What, is this so?

FIRST WITCH. Ay, sir, all this is so; but why   125
Stands Macbeth thus amazedly?
Come, sisters, cheer we up his sprites,
And show the best of our delights.
I'll charm the air to give a sound,
While you perform your antic round;°   130
That this great king may kindly say,
Our duties did his welcome pay.
    [*Music. The* WITCHES *dance, and then vanish, with* HECATE.

MACBETH. Where are they? Gone? Let this pernicious hour
Stand aye accursèd in the calendar!
Come in, without there!

[*Enter* LENNOX.]

LENNOX.   What's your grace's will?   135

MACBETH. Saw you the weird sisters?

LENNOX.   No, my lord.

---

* *A show of Eight Kings:* a dumb show of figures passing across the stage silently, representing the eight Stuart kings of Scotland. † *glass:* mirror. 121. *twofold balls and treble scepters:* the insignia of James I, who united Scotland with England (1603) and later Ireland. 123. *blood-boltered:* his hair wet with blood. 124. *points at them for his:* James I was traditionally considered a descendant of Banquo. 130. *antic round:* fantastic dance.

MACBETH. Came they not by you?
LENNOX.   No, my lord.
MACBETH. Infected be the air whereon they ride;
          And damned all those that trust them! I did hear
          The galloping of horse: who was 't came by?   140
LENNOX. 'Tis two or three, my lord, that bring you word
          Macduff is fled to England.
MACBETH.   Fled to England!
LENNOX. Ay, my good lord.
MACBETH. Time, thou anticipatest my dread exploits;
          The flighty purpose never is o'ertook   145
          Unless the deed go with it. From this moment
          The very firstlings of my heart shall be
          The firstlings of my hand. And even now,
          To crown my thoughts with acts, be it thought and done.
          The castle of Macduff I will surprise;   150
          Seize upon Fife; give to the edge o' the sword
          His wife, and babes, and all unfortunate souls
          That trace him in his line. No boasting like a fool;
          This deed I'll do before this purpose cool.
          But no more sights! — Where are these gentlemen?   155
          Come, bring me where they are.   [*Exeunt.*

SCENE II. *Fife.* MACDUFF'S *castle.*

[*Enter* LADY MACDUFF, *her* SON, *and* ROSS.]

LADY MACDUFF. What had he done, to make him fly the land?
ROSS. You must have patience, madam.
LADY MACDUFF.   He had none;
          His flight was madness. When our actions do not,
          Our fears do make us traitors.
ROSS.   You know not
          Whether it was his wisdom or his fear.   5
LADY MACDUFF. Wisdom! to leave his wife, to leave his babes,
          His mansion and his titles in a place
          From whence himself does fly? He loves us not;
          He wants the natural touch; for the poor wren,
          The most diminutive of birds, will fight,   10
          Her young ones in her nest, against the owl.
          All is the fear and nothing is the love;°
          As little is the wisdom, where the flight
          So runs against all reason.
ROSS.   My dearest coz,
          I pray you, school yourself; but for your husband,   15
          He is noble, wise, judicious, and best knows
          The fits o' the season.° I dare not speak much further;
          But cruel are the times, when we are traitors

12. *All . . . love:* For Macduff, she says, fear is all-important and love means nothing. 17. *fits o'
the season:* disorders of the times.

And do not know ourselves, when we hold rumor
From what we fear, yet know not what we fear,　　　　　20
But float upon a wild and violent sea
Each way and move.° I take my leave of you;
Shall not be long but I'll be here again.
Things at the worst will cease, or else climb upward
To what they were before. My pretty cousin,°　　　　　25
Blessing upon you!
LADY MACDUFF. Fathered he is, and yet he's fatherless.
ROSS. I am so much a fool, should I stay longer,
　　It would be my disgrace and your discomfort.
　　I take my leave at once.　　　　　　　　　　[*Exit.*　30
LADY MACDUFF. Sirrah, your father's dead;
　　And what will you do now? How will you live?
SON. As birds do, mother.
LADY MACDUFF. What, with worms and flies?
SON. With what I get, I mean; and so do they.　　　　35
LADY MACDUFF. Poor bird! thou 'ldst never fear the net nor lime,
　　The pitfall nor the gin.°
SON. Why should I, mother? Poor birds they are not set for.
　　My father is not dead, for all your saying.
LADY MACDUFF. Yes, he is dead. How wilt thou do for a father?　40
SON. Nay, how will you do for a husband?
LADY MACDUFF. Why, I can buy me twenty at any market.
SON. Then you'll buy 'em to sell again.
LADY MACDUFF. Thou speak'st with all thy wit; and yet, i' faith,
　　With wit enough for thee.　　　　　　　　　45
SON. Was my father a traitor, mother?
LADY MACDUFF. Ay, that he was.
SON. What is a traitor?
LADY MACDUFF. Why, one that swears and lies.
SON. And be all traitors that do so?　　　　　　50
LADY MACDUFF. Every one that does so is a traitor, and must be hanged.
SON. And must they all be hanged that swear and lie?
LADY MACDUFF. Every one.
SON. Who must hang them?
LADY MACDUFF. Why, the honest men.　　　　　　55
SON. Then the liars and swearers are fools, for there are liars and swearers enow to
　　beat the honest men and hang up them.
LADY MACDUFF. Now, God help thee, poor monkey! But how wilt thou do for a
　　father?
SON. If he were dead, you 'ld weep for him; if you would not, it were a good　60
　　sign that I should quickly have a new father.
LADY MACDUFF. Poor prattler, how thou talk'st!

[*Enter a* MESSENGER.]

MESSENGER. Bless you, fair dame! I am not to you known,
　　Though in your state of honor I am perfect.°

---

　22. *Each way and move:* as a ship is tossed in a tempest. 25. *My pretty cousin:* addressed to the
boy, Macduff's son. 37. *gin:* trap. 64. *perfect:* perfectly acquainted with.

I doubt° some danger does approach you nearly.   65
If you will take a homely° man's advice,
Be not found here; hence, with your little ones.
To fright you thus, methinks, I am too savage;
To do worse to you were fell cruelty,
Which is too nigh your person. Heaven preserve you!   70
I dare abide no longer.   [*Exit.*

LADY MACDUFF.   Whither should I fly?
I have done no harm. But I remember now
I am in this earthly world; where to do harm
Is often laudable, to do good sometime
Accounted dangerous folly. Why then, alas,   75
Do I put up that womanly defense,
To say I have done no harm?

                    [*Enter* MURDERERS.]

                    What are these faces?
FIRST MURDERER. Where is your husband?
LADY MACDUFF. I hope, in no place so unsanctified
Where such as thou mayst find him.
FIRST MURDERER.   He's a traitor.   80
SON. Thou liest, thou shag-eared° villain!
FIRST MURDERER.   What, you egg!   [*Stabbing him.*
Young fry of treachery!
SON.   He has killed me, mother:
Run away, I pray you!   [*Dies.*
                    [*Exit* LADY MACDUFF, *crying* "Murder!"
                    [*Exeunt* MURDERERS, *following her.*

SCENE III. *England. Before the* KING'S *palace.*

                    [*Enter* MALCOLM *and* MACDUFF.]

MALCOLM. Let us seek out some desolate shade, and there
Weep our sad bosoms empty.
MACDUFF.   Let us rather
Hold fast the mortal° sword, and like good men
Bestride our downfall'n birthdom.° Each new morn
New widows howl, new orphans cry, new sorrows   5
Strike heaven on the face, that it resounds
As if it felt with Scotland and yelled out
Like syllable of dolor.°
MALCOLM.   What I believe, I'll wail,
What know, believe, and what I can redress,
As I shall find the time to friend, I will.   10
What you have spoke, it may be so perchance.

---

65. *doubt:* suspect. 66. *homely:* plain. 81. *shag-eared:* hairy eared.
3. *mortal:* deadly. 4. *birthdom:* native land. 6–8. *that . . . dolor:* The heavens resound as if they too felt Scotland's wrongs and echoed Scotland's lamentations.

This tyrant, whose sole name blisters our tongues,
Was once thought honest; you have loved him well;
He hath not touched you yet. I am young; but something
You may deserve of him through me, the wisdom   15
To offer up a weak poor innocent lamb
To appease an angry god.°
MACDUFF. I am not treacherous.
MALCOLM.   But Macbeth is.
A good and virtuous nature may recoil
In an imperial charge.° But I shall crave your pardon;   20
That which you are my thoughts cannot transpose.
Angels are bright still, though the brightest fell.
Though all things foul would wear the brows of grace,
Yet grace must still look so.°
MACDUFF.   I have lost my hopes.
MALCOLM. Perchance even there where I did find my doubts.   25
Why in that rawness left you wife and child,
Those precious motives, those strong knots of love,
Without leave-taking? I pray you,
Let not my jealousies be your dishonors,
But mine own safeties.° You may be rightly just,   30
Whatever I shall think.
MACDUFF.   Bleed, bleed, poor country!
Great tyranny! lay thou thy basis sure,
For goodness dare not check thee; wear thou thy wrongs;
The title is affeered!° Fare thee well, lord;
I would not be the villain that thou think'st   35
For the whole space that's in the tyrant's grasp,
And the rich East to boot.
MALCOLM.   Be not offended;
I speak not as in absolute fear of you.
I think our country sinks beneath the yoke;
It weeps, it bleeds; and each new day a gash   40
Is added to her wounds. I think withal
There would be hands uplifted in my right;
And here from gracious England have I offer
Of goodly thousands. But, for all this,
When I shall tread upon the tyrant's head,   45
Or wear it on my sword, yet my poor country
Shall have more vices than it had before,
More suffer and more sundry ways than ever,
By him that shall succeed.
MACDUFF.   What should he be?

14–17. *but something . . . god:* Malcolm fears that Macduff may be a tool of Macbeth seeking
to betray him — Malcolm. 19–20. *A good . . . charge:* In other words, Macduff may not be his own
master. His good and virtuous nature may be at the command of an evil king. 23–24. *Though . . .
look so:* Goodness must still appear as goodness even though wickedness sometimes clothes itself
in the same garb. In other words, Malcolm has no way of telling — so he says now, at least —
whether Macduff is to be trusted or not. 29–30. *Let not . . . safeties:* I am suspicious not in order to
dishonor you but to protect myself. 34. *affeered:* confirmed; that is, since goodness dares not oppose
tyranny, tyranny's title or right to power is confirmed.

MALCOLM. It is myself I mean; in whom I know   50
    All the particulars of vice so grafted
    That, when they shall be opened, black Macbeth
    Will seem as pure as snow, and the poor state
    Esteem him as a lamb, being compared
    With my confineless harms.
MACDUFF.   Not in the legions   55
    Of horrid hell can come a devil more damned
    In evils to top Macbeth.
MALCOLM.   I grant him bloody,
    Luxurious, avaricious, false, deceitful,
    Sudden, malicious, smacking of every sin
    That has a name; but there's no bottom, none,   60
    In my voluptuousness. Your wives, your daughters,
    Your matrons and your maids, could not fill up
    The cistern of my lust, and my desire
    All continent impediments° would o'erbear
    That did oppose my will. Better Macbeth   65
    Than such an one to reign.
MACDUFF.   Boundless intemperance
    In nature is a tyranny; it hath been
    The untimely emptying of the happy throne
    And fall of many kings. But fear not yet
    To take upon you what is yours. You may   70
    Convey your pleasures in a spacious plenty,
    And yet seem cold, the time you may so hoodwink.
    We have willing dames enough; there cannot be
    That vulture in you, to devour so many
    As will to greatness dedicate themselves,   75
    Finding it so inclined.
MALCOLM.   With this there grows
    In my most ill-composed affection such
    A staunchless avarice that, were I king,
    I should cut off the nobles for their lands,
    Desire his jewels and this other's house;   80
    And my more-having would be as a sauce
    To make me hunger more, that I should forge
    Quarrels unjust against the good and loyal,
    Destroying them for wealth.
MACDUFF.   This avarice
    Sticks deeper, grows with more pernicious root   85
    Than summer-seeming lust, and it hath been
    The sword of° our slain kings. Yet do not fear;
    Scotland hath foisons° to fill up your will,
    Of your mere own.° All these are portable,°
    With other graces weighed.   90
MALCOLM. But I have none. The king-becoming graces,
    As justice, verity, temperance, stableness,

---

64. *continent impediments:* restraints. 87. *The sword of:* that which has killed. 88. *foisons:* rich harvests. 89. *mere own:* own property; *portable:* endurable.

Bounty, perseverance, mercy, lowliness,
Devotion, patience, courage, fortitude,
I have no relish of them, but abound   95
In the division of each several crime,
Acting it many ways. Nay, had I power, I should
Pour the sweet milk of concord into hell,
Uproar the universal peace, confound
All unity on earth.

MACDUFF.   O Scotland, Scotland!   100

MALCOLM. If such a one be fit to govern, speak.
I am as I have spoken.

MACDUFF.   Fit to govern!
No, not to live. O nation miserable
With an untitled tyrant bloody-sceptered,
When shalt thou see thy wholesome days again,   105
Since that the truest issue of thy throne
By his own interdiction stands accursed,°
And does blaspheme his breed? Thy royal father
Was a most sainted king; the queen that bore thee,
Oftener upon her knees than on her feet,   110
Died every day she lived.° Fare thee well!
These evils thou repeat'st upon thyself
Have banished me from Scotland. O my breast,
Thy hope ends here!

MALCOLM.   Macduff, this noble passion,
Child of integrity, hath from my soul   115
Wiped the black scruples, reconciled my thoughts
To thy good truth and honor. Devilish Macbeth
By many of these trains hath sought to win me
Into his power, and modest wisdom plucks me
From overcredulous haste; but God above   120
Deal between thee and me! for even now
I put myself to thy direction, and
Unspeak mine own detraction,° here abjure
The taints and blames I laid upon myself,
For strangers to my nature. I am yet   125
Unknown to woman, never was foresworn,
Scarcely have coveted what was mine own,
At no time broke my faith, would not betray
The devil to his fellow, and delight
No less in truth than life; my first false speaking   130
Was this upon myself. What I am truly,
Is thine and my poor country's to command;
Whither indeed, before thy here-approach,
Old Siward, with ten thousand warlike men,
Already at a point,° was setting forth.   135
Now we'll together; and the chance of goodness

---

107. *By his . . . accursed:* Malcolm has accused himself of being unfit to govern. 110–111. *Oftener . . . lived:* The queen prepared in prayer for death. 123. *Unspeak mine own detraction:* take back the slander I uttered against myself. 135. *at a point:* ready for action.

Be like our warranted quarrel!° Why are you silent?
MACDUFF. Such welcome and unwelcome things at once
    'Tis hard to reconcile.

[Enter a DOCTOR.]

MALCOLM. Well; more anon. — Comes the king forth, I pray you?   140
DOCTOR. Ay, sir; there are a crew of wretched souls
    That stay his cure; their malady convinces
    The great assay of art; but at his touch —
    Such sanctity hath Heaven given his hand —
    They presently amend.
MALCOLM.   I thank you, Doctor.   *[Exit* DOCTOR.   145
MACDUFF. What's the disease he means?
MALCOLM.   'Tis called the evil;°
    A most miraculous work in this good king;
    Which often, since my here-remain in England,
    I have seen him do. How he solicits Heaven,
    Himself best knows; but strangely visited people,   150
    All swoln and ulcerous, pitiful to the eye,
    The mere despair of surgery, he cures,
    Hanging a golden stamp° about their necks,
    Put on with holy prayers; and 'tis spoken,
    To the succeeding royalty he leaves   155
    The healing benediction. With this strange virtue,
    He hath a heavenly gift of prophecy,
    And sundry blessings hang about his throne,
    That speak him full of grace.

[Enter ROSS.]

MACDUFF.   See, who comes here?
MALCOLM. My countryman; but yet I know him not.   160
MACDUFF. My ever-gentle cousin, welcome hither.
MALCOLM. I know him now. Good God, betimes remove
    The means that makes us strangers!°
ROSS.   Sir, amen.
MACDUFF. Stands Scotland where it did?
ROSS.   Alas, poor country!
    Almost afraid to know itself. It cannot   165
    Be called our mother, but our grave; where nothing,
    But who knows nothing, is once seen to smile;
    Where sighs and groans and shrieks that rend the air
    Are made, not marked; where violent sorrow seems
    A modern ecstasy.° The dead man's knell   170
    Is there scarce asked for who;° and good men's lives

136–137. *the chance . . . quarrel:* May our chance of success be as good as the outcome of our argument. 146. *evil:* This speech refers to the king's supposed power to cure scrofula, a dread skin disease, known at that time as the King's Evil. In Shakespeare's day, King James I at first refused to continue the practice of touching sufferers but later consented. This speech compliments him for his decision. 153. *stamp:* medal. 163. *The means . . . strangers:* Malcolm's exile has kept him out of touch with his countrymen. 170. *modern ecstasy:* a slight mental disturbance. 170–171. *The dead . . . who:* People can no longer keep track of Macbeth's victims.

Expire before the flowers in their caps,
Dying or ere they sicken.
MACDUFF.   O, relation°
Too nice,° and yet too true!
MALCOLM.   What's the newest grief?
ROSS. That of an hour's age doth hiss the speaker;°   175
Each minute teems a new one.
MACDUFF.   How does my wife?
ROSS. Why, well.
MACDUFF.   And all my children?
ROSS.   Well too.
MACDUFF. The tyrant has not battered at their peace?
ROSS. No; they were well at peace when I did leave 'em.
MACDUFF. Be not a niggard of your speech; how goes 't?   180
ROSS. When I came hither to transport the tidings,
Which I have heavily borne, there ran a rumor
Of many worthy fellows that were out;°
Which was to my belief witnessed the rather,
For that I saw the tyrant's power afoot.   185
Now is the time of help; your eye in Scotland
Would create soldiers, make our women fight,
To doff their dire distresses.
MALCOLM.   Be 't their comfort
We are coming thither. Gracious England hath
Lent us good Siward and ten thousand men;   190
An older and a better soldier none
That Christendom gives out.
ROSS.   Would I could answer
This comfort with the like! But I have words
That would be howled out in the desert air,
Where hearing should not latch° them.
MACDUFF.   What concern they?   195
The general cause? or is it a fee grief°
Due to some single breast?
ROSS.   No mind that's honest
But in it shares some woe; though the main part
Pertains to you alone.
MACDUFF.   If it be mine,
Keep it not from me, quickly let me have it.   200
ROSS. Let not your ears despise my tongue for ever,
Which shall possess them with the heaviest sound
That ever yet they heard.
MACDUFF.   Hum! I guess at it.
ROSS. Your castle is surprised; your wife and babes
Savagely slaughtered: to relate the manner,   205
Were, on the quarry of these murdered deer,
To add the death of you.
MALCOLM.   Merciful Heaven!

---

173. *relation:* account. 174. *nice:* exact. 175. *That . . . speaker:* Any grief an hour old is no longer
news. 183. *out:* up in arms. 195. *latch:* catch. 196. *fee grief:* private grief.

What, man! ne'er pull your hat upon your brows;
Give sorrow words. The grief that does not speak
Whispers the o'erfraught heart and bids it break.   210
MACDUFF. My children too?
ROSS.   Wife, children, servants, all
That could be found.
MACDUFF.   And I must be from thence!
My wife killed too?
ROSS.   I have said.
MALCOLM.   Be comforted.
Let's make us medicines of our great revenge,
To cure this deadly grief.   215
MACDUFF. He has no children. All my pretty ones?
Did you say all? O hell kite! All?
What, all my pretty chickens and their dam
At one fell swoop?
MALCOLM. Dispute it° like a man.
MACDUFF.   I shall do so;   220
But I must also feel it as a man.
I cannot but remember such things were,
That were most precious to me. Did Heaven look on,
And would not take their part? Sinful Macduff,
They were all struck for thee! naught that I am,   225
Not for their own demerits, but for mine,
Fell slaughter on their souls. Heaven rest them now!
MALCOLM. Be this the whetstone of your sword; let grief
Convert to anger; blunt not the heart, enrage it.
MACDUFF. O, I could play the woman with mine eyes   230
And braggart with my tongue! But, gentle heavens,
Cut short all intermission; front to front°
Bring thou this fiend of Scotland and myself;
Within my sword's length set him; if he 'scape,
Heaven forgive him too!
MALCOLM.   This tune goes manly.   235
Come, go we to the king; our power is ready;
Our lack is nothing but our leave. Macbeth
Is ripe for shaking, and the powers above
Put on their instruments.° Receive what cheer you may:
The night is long that never finds the day.   [*Exeunt.*   240

220. *Dispute it:* Resist your grief. 232. *front to front:* face to face. 238–239. *the powers . . . instruments:* The powers of heaven urge us, their agents, to battle.

"THIS DEED I'LL DO BEFORE THE PURPOSE COOL."

ACT IV

1. Name all of the devices Shakespeare uses in creating a feeling of horror and impending doom at the beginning of this act. What effects do the witches' enchantments have upon Macbeth's morale? What is his final reaction to the witches? What further moral degeneration does he show at the end of the scene?

2. In Scene iii, why does Malcolm misrepresent his own character to Macduff? What events reveal the strong points in the characters of both of these men?

ACT V

SCENE I. *Dunsinane. Anteroom in the castle.*

[*Enter a* DOCTOR OF PHYSIC *and a* WAITING-GENTLEWOMAN.]

DOCTOR. I have two nights watched with you, but can perceive no truth in your report. When was it she last walked?

GENTLEWOMAN. Since his majesty went into the field, I have seen her rise from her bed, throw her nightgown upon her, unlock her closet, take forth paper, fold it, write upon 't, read it, afterward seal it, and again return to bed;   5
yet all this while in a most fast sleep.

DOCTOR. A great perturbation in nature, to receive at once the benefit of sleep, and do the effects of watching! In this slumbery agitation, besides her walking and other actual performances, what, at any time, have you heard her say?

GENTLEWOMAN. That, sir, which I will not report after her.   10

DOCTOR. You may to me; and 'tis most meet you should.

GENTLEWOMAN. Neither to you nor any one; having no witness to confirm my speech

[*Enter* LADY MACBETH, *with a taper.*]

Lo you, here she comes! This is her very guise; and, upon my life, fast asleep. Observe her; stand close.   15

DOCTOR. How came she by that light?

GENTLEWOMAN. Why, it stood by her; she has light by her continually; 'tis her command.

DOCTOR. You see, her eyes are open.

GENTLEWOMAN. Ay, but their sense is shut.   20

DOCTOR. What is it she does now? Look, how she rubs her hands.

GENTLEWOMAN. It is an accustomed action with her, to seem thus washing her hands. I have known her continue in this a quarter of an hour.

LADY MACBETH. Yet here's a spot.

DOCTOR. Hark! She speaks. I will set down what comes from her, to satisfy my   25
remembrance the more strongly.

LADY MACBETH. Out, damned spot! out, I say! — One: two: why, then 'tis time to do 't. — Hell is murky! — Fie, my lord, fie! a soldier, and afeard? What need we fear who knows it, when none can call our power to account? — Yet who would have thought the old man to have had so much blood in him?   30

DOCTOR. Do you mark that?

LADY MACBETH. The thane of Fife had a wife; where is she now? — What, will these hands ne'er be clean? — No more o' that, my lord, no more o' that; you mar all with this starting.

DOCTOR. Go to, go to; you have known what you should not.   35

GENTLEWOMAN. She has spoke what she should not, I am sure of that; Heaven knows what she has known.

LADY MACBETH. Here's the smell of the blood still; all the perfumes of Arabia will not sweeten this little hand. Oh, oh, oh!

DOCTOR. What a sigh is there! The heart is sorely charged.°   40

GENTLEWOMAN. I would not have such a heart in my bosom for the dignity of the
    whole body.

DOCTOR. Well, well, well —

GENTLEWOMAN. Pray God it be, sir.

DOCTOR. This disease is beyond my practice; yet I have known those which   45
    have walked in their sleep who have died holily in their beds.

LADY MACBETH. Wash your hands, put on your nightgown; look not so pale. — I tell
    you yet again, Banquo's buried; he cannot come out on 's grave.

DOCTOR. Even so?

LADY MACBETH. To bed, to bed! There's knocking at the gate. Come, come,   50
    come, come, give me your hand. What's done cannot be undone. — To
    bed, to bed, to bed!   [*Exit.*

DOCTOR. Will she go now to bed?

GENTLEWOMAN. Directly.

DOCTOR. Foul whisperings are abroad; unnatural deeds   55
    Do breed unnatural troubles; infected minds
    To their deaf pillows will discharge their secrets.
    More needs she the divine than the physician.
    God, God forgive us all! Look after her;
    Remove from her the means of all annoyance,°   60
    And still keep eyes upon her. So, good night;
    My mind she has mated,° and amazed my sight.
    I think, but dare not speak.

GENTLEWOMAN.   Good night, good doctor.   [*Exeunt.*

SCENE II. *The country near Dunsinane.*

[*Drum and colors.* * *Enter* MENTEITH,† CAITHNESS,‡ ANGUS,
LENNOX, *and* SOLDIERS.]

MENTEITH. The English power is near, led on by Malcolm,
    His uncle Siward and the good Macduff.
    Revenges burn in them; for their dear causes
    Would to the bleeding and the grim alarm°
    Excite the mortified° man.

ANGUS.   Near Birnam wood   5
    Shall we well meet them; that way are they coming.

CAITHNESS. Who knows if Donalbain be with his brother?

LENNOX. For certain, sir, he is not; I have a file
    Of all the gentry. There is Siward's son,
    And many unrough youths that even now   10
    Protest their first of manhood.°

MENTEITH.   What does the tyrant?

CAITHNESS. Great Dunsinane he strongly fortifies.
    Some say he's mad; others that lesser hate him

---

40. *charged:* burdened. 60. *annoyance:* harm. 62. *mated:* overcome with amazement.
    Drum and colors: soldiers with a drum and a flag. † *Menteith* (mĕn·tēth′). ‡ *Caithness* (kāth′nĕs).
4. *alarm:* call to arms. 5. *mortified:* half dead. 11. *Protest . . . manhood:* have hardly reached manhood.

Do call it valiant fury; but, for certain,
He cannot buckle his distempered cause   15
Within the belt of rule.°
ANGUS.   Now does he feel
His secret murders sticking on his hands;
Now minutely° revolts upbraid his faith breach;°
Those he commands move only in command,
Nothing in love. Now does he feel his title   20
Hang loose about him, like a giant's robe
Upon a dwarfish thief.
MENTEITH.   Who then shall blame
His pestered senses to recoil and start,
When all that is within him does condemn
Itself for being there?
CAITHNESS.   Well, march we on,   25
To give obedience where 'tis truly owed.
Meet we the medicine of the sickly weal,°
And with him pour we in our country's purge
Each drop of us.
LENNOX.   Or so much as it needs,
To dew the sovereign flower° and drown the weeds.°   30
Make we our march toward Birnam.   [*Exeunt, marching.*

SCENE III. *Dunsinane. A room in the castle.*

[*Enter* MACBETH, DOCTOR, *and* ATTENDANTS.]

MACBETH. Bring me no more reports; let them fly all;°
Till Birnam wood remove to Dunsinane,
I cannot taint with fear. What's the boy Malcolm?
Was he not born of woman? The spirits that know
All mortal consequences have pronounced me thus: 5
"Fear not, Macbeth; no man that's born of woman
Shall e'er have power upon thee." Then fly, false thanes,
And mingle with the English epicures!°
The mind I sway by and the heart I bear
Shall never sag with doubt nor shake with fear.   10

[*Enter a* SERVANT.]

The devil damn thee black, thou cream-faced loon!
Where got'st thou that goose look?
SERVANT. There is ten thousand —
MACBETH.   Geese, villain?
SERVANT.   Soldiers, sir.
MACBETH. Go, prick thy face, and over-red thy fear,
Thou lily-livered boy. What soldiers, patch?°   15

15–16. *He cannot . . . rule:* Macbeth cannot keep his evil cause under control. 18. *minutely:* every minute; *faith breach:* disloyalty. 27. *the medicine of the sickly weal:* Malcolm and his army are the medicine which Scotland needs to heal the harassed commonwealth. 30. *sovereign flower:* Malcolm; *weeds:* Macbeth.
1. *let . . . all:* let them all desert me. 8. *epicures:* luxury seekers. 15. *patch:* fool.

Death of thy soul! those linen cheeks of thine
Are counselors to fear. What soldiers, whey-face?
SERVANT. The English force, so please you.
MACBETH. Take thy face hence.   [*Exit* SERVANT.
      Seyton!° — I am sick at heart,
When I behold — Seyton, I say! — This push   20
Will cheer me ever, or disseat me now.
I have lived long enough. My way of life
Is fall'n into the sear, the yellow leaf;
And that which should accompany old age,
As honor, love, obedience, troops of friends,   25
I must not look to have; but, in their stead,
Curses, not loud but deep, mouth honor, breath,
Which the poor heart would fain deny, and dare not.
Seyton!

     [*Enter* SEYTON.]

SEYTON. What is your gracious pleasure?
MACBETH.   What news more?   30
SEYTON. All is confirmed, my lord, which was reported.
MACBETH. I'll fight till from my bones my flesh be hacked.
  Give me my armor.
SEYTON.   'Tis not needed yet.
MACBETH. I'll put it on.
  Send out moe° horses; skirr° the country round;   35
  Hang those that talk of fear. Give me mine armor.
  How does your patient, doctor?
DOCTOR.   Not so sick, my lord,
  As she is troubled with thick-coming fancies,
  That keep her from her rest.
MACBETH.   Cure her of that.
  Canst thou not minister to a mind diseased,   40
  Pluck from the memory a rooted sorrow,
  Raze out the written troubles of the brain
  And with some sweet oblivious antidote
  Cleanse the stuffed bosom of that perilous stuff
  Which weighs upon the heart?
DOCTOR.   Therein the patient   45
  Must minister to himself.
MACBETH. Throw physic° to the dogs; I'll none of it.
  Come, put mine armor on; give me my staff.
  Seyton, send out. Doctor, the thanes fly from me.
  Come, sir, dispatch. If thou couldst, doctor, cast°   50
  The water of my land, find her disease,
  And purge it to a sound and pristine° health,
  I would applaud thee to the very echo,
  That should applaud again. — Pull 't off, I say.° —

---

  19. *Seyton* (sē′tŏn). 35. *moe:* more; *skirr:* scour. 47. *physic:* medicine. 50. *cast:* examine. 52. *pristine:* uncorrupted. 54. *Pull 't off, I say:* This sounds like an aside to Seyton, who has been told to pull off some pieces of Macbeth's armor, put on wrong in his haste.

What rhubarb, senna, or what purgative drug,　　　　55
　　　Would scour these English hence? Hear'st thou of them?
DOCTOR. Ay, my good lord; your royal preparation
　　　Makes us hear something.
MACBETH.　　　　　　　　　　　Bring it after me.
　　　I will not be afraid of death and bane,
　　　Till Birnam forest come to Dunsinane.　　　　60
DOCTOR [*Aside*] Were I from Dunsinane away and clear,
　　　Profit again should hardly draw me here.　　　　　　[*Exeunt.*

SCENE IV. *Country near Birnam wood.*

[*Drum and colors. Enter* MALCOLM, *old* SIWARD* *and his* SON, MACDUFF,
MENTEITH, CAITHNESS, ANGUS, LENNOX, ROSS, *and* SOLDIERS *marching.*]

MALCOLM. Cousins, I hope the days are near at hand
　　　That chambers will be safe.°
MENTEITH.　　　　　　　　　　We doubt it nothing.
SIWARD. What wood is this before us?
MENTEITH.　　　　　　　　　The wood of Birnam.
MALCOLM. Let every soldier hew him down a bough
　　　And bear it before him; thereby shall we shadow　　　　5
　　　The numbers of our host and make discovery
　　　Err in report of us.
SOLDIERS.　　　　　　　　It shall be done.
SIWARD. We learn no other but the confident tyrant
　　　Keeps still in Dunsinane, and will endure
　　　Our setting down before 't.°
MALCOLM.　　　　　　　　　'Tis his main hope;　　　　10
　　　For where there is advantage to be given,
　　　Both more or less have given him the revolt,°
　　　And none serve with him but constrainèd things
　　　Whose hearts are absent too.
MACDUFF.　　　　　　　　　　Let our just censures
　　　Attend the true event, and put we on　　　　15
　　　Industrious soldiership.°
SIWARD.　　　　　　　　　The time approaches
　　　That will with due decision make us know
　　　What we shall say we have and what we owe.
　　　Thoughts speculative their unsure hopes relate,
　　　But certain issue strokes must arbitrate;°　　　　20
　　　Toward which advance the war.　　　　[*Exeunt, marching.*

---

* *Siward* (sē′wärd). 1–2. *the days . . . safe:* Soon people will be able to sleep in peace. 8–10. *the confident . . . before 't:* Macbeth has fortified himself at Dunsinane and will endure siege. 11–12. *where . . . revolt:* Wherever there was opportunity (*advantage given*) both the higher and lower classes (*more or less*) have deserted Macbeth. 14–16. *Let . . . soldiership:* We can pass final judgment after we see what's happened. In the meantime, let's get on with the fighting. 16–20. *The time . . . arbitrate:* We shall soon know what the situation is, and whether our speculations are true, but action alone (*strokes*) will decide the issue for sure.

SCENE V. *Dunsinane. Within the castle.*

[*Enter* MACBETH, SEYTON, *and* SOLDIERS, *with drum and colors.*]

MACBETH. Hang out our banners on the outward walls;
      The cry is still "They come!" Our castle's strength
      Will laugh a siege to scorn; here let them lie
      Till famine and the ague eat them up.
      Were they not forced with those that should be ours,°   5
      We might have met them dareful, beard to beard,
      And beat them backward home.   [*A cry of women within.*
                   What is that noise?
SEYTON. It is the cry of women, my good lord.   [*Exit.*
MACBETH. I have almost forgot the taste of fears.
      The time has been, my senses would have cooled   10
      To hear a night-shriek; and my fell of hair°
      Would at a dismal treatise° rouse and stir
      As life were in 't. I have supped full with horrors;
      Direness, familiar to my slaughterous thoughts,
      Cannot once start me.

[*Re-enter* SEYTON.]

                 Wherefore was that cry?   15
SEYTON. The queen, my lord, is dead.
MACBETH. She should have died hereafter;°
      There would have been a time for such a word.
      Tomorrow, and tomorrow, and tomorrow,
      Creeps in this petty pace from day to day   20
      To the last syllable of recorded time,
      And all our yesterdays have lighted fools
      The way to dusty death. Out, out, brief candle!
      Life's but a walking shadow, a poor player
      That struts and frets his hour upon the stage   25
      And then is heard no more. It is a tale
      Told by an idiot, full of sound and fury,
      Signifying nothing.

[*Enter* MESSENGER.]

      Thou comest to use thy tongue; thy story quickly.
MESSENGER. Gracious my lord,   30
      I should report that which I say I saw,
      But know not how to do it.
MACBETH.   Well, say, sir.
MESSENGER. As I did stand my watch upon the hill,
      I looked toward Birnam, and anon, methought,
      The wood began to move.
MACBETH.   Liar and slave!   35

---

    5. *forced . . . ours:* reinforced with those who have deserted. 11. *my fell of hair:* the hair on my
scalp. 12. *dismal treatise:* gloomy story. 17. *She . . . hereafter:* She was bound to die sometime.

MESSENGER. Let me endure your wrath, if 't be not so.
     Within this three mile may you see it coming;
     I say, a moving grove.
MACBETH.   If thou speak'st false,
     Upon the next tree shalt thou hang alive,
     Till famine cling thee; if thy speech be sooth,°   40
     I care not if thou dost for me as much.
     I pull in resolution,° and begin
     To doubt the equivocation of the fiend
     That lies like truth: "Fear not, till Birnam wood
     Do come to Dunsinane." And now a wood   45
     Comes toward Dunsinane. Arm, arm, and out!
     If this which he avouches does appear,
     There is nor flying hence nor tarrying here.
     I 'gin to be aweary of the sun,
     And wish the estate o' the world were now undone.   50
     Ring the alarum bell! Blow, wind! come, wrack!
     At least we'll die with harness on our back.   [*Exeunt.*

SCENE VI. *Dunsinane. Before the castle.*

[*Drums and colors. Enter* MALCOLM, *old* SIWARD, MACDUFF,
and their ARMY, *with boughs.*]

MALCOLM. Now near enough; your leavy screens° throw down,
     And show like those you are. You, worthy uncle,
     Shall, with my cousin, your right noble son,
     Lead our first battle. Worthy Macduff and we
     Shall take upon 's else remains to do,   5
     According to our order.
SIWARD.   Fare you well.
     Do we but find the tyrant's power tonight,
     Let us be beaten, if we cannot fight.
MACDUFF. Make all our trumpets speak; give them all breath,
     Those clamorous harbingers° of blood and death.   [*Exeunt.* 10

SCENE VII. *Another part of the field.*

[*Alarums. Enter* MACBETH.]

MACBETH. They have tied me to a stake;° I cannot fly,
     But, bearlike, I must fight the course. What's he

---

40. *sooth:* truth. 42. *pull in resolution:* check courage; that is, Macbeth will not struggle against fate.
     1. *leavy screens:* the boughs used as camouflage. 10. *clamorous harbingers* (här′bĭn·jĕrz): noisy messengers.
     1. *They have tied me to a stake:* a reference to bear-baiting, a popular Elizabethan sport. Bears were tied to a stake and set upon by dogs.

That was not born of woman? Such a one
Am I to fear, or none.

[*Enter young* SIWARD.]

YOUNG SIWARD. What is thy name?
MACBETH.   Thou 'lt be afraid to hear it.   5
YOUNG SIWARD. No; though thou call'st thyself a hotter name
          Than any is in hell.
MACBETH.   My name's Macbeth.
YOUNG SIWARD. The devil himself could not pronounce a title
          More hateful to mine ear.
MACBETH.   No, nor more fearful.
YOUNG SIWARD. Thou liest, abhorrèd tyrant; with my sword   10
          I'll prove the lie thou speak'st.   [*They fight and young* SIWARD *is slain.*
MACBETH.   Thou wast born of woman.
          But swords I smile at, weapons laugh to scorn,
          Brandished by man that's of a woman born.   [*Exit.*

[*Alarums. Enter* MACDUFF.]

MACDUFF. That way the noise is. Tyrant, show thy face!
          If thou be'st slain and with no stroke of mine,   15
          My wife and children's ghosts will haunt me still.
          I cannot strike at wretched kerns,° whose arms
          Are hired to bear their staves; either thou, Macbeth,
          Or else my sword with an unbattered edge
          I sheathe again undeeded. There thou shouldst be;   20
          By this great clatter, one of greatest note
          Seems bruited.° Let me find him, fortune!
          And more I beg not.   [*Exit. Alarums.*

[*Enter* MALCOLM *and old* SIWARD.]

SIWARD. This way, my lord; the castle's gently rendered:°
          The tyrant's people on both sides do fight;°   25
          The noble thanes do bravely in the war;
          The day almost itself professes yours,
          And little is to do.
MALCOLM.   We have met with foes
          That strike beside us.°
SIWARD.   Enter, sir, the castle.   [*Exeunt. Alarums.*

SCENE VIII. *Another part of the field.*

[*Enter* MACBETH.]

MACBETH. Why should I play the Roman fool,° and die
          On mine own sword? Whiles I see lives, the gashes

17. *kerns:* common foot soldiers hired as mercenaries. 22. *bruited:* reported. 24. *gently rendered:*
surrendered without active defense. 25. *The tyrant's . . . fight:* Some of Macbeth's men are deserting
him. 29. *beside us:* on our side.
    1. *play the Roman fool:* Brutus and Cassius, ancient Romans who were also trapped, committed
suicide.

Do better upon them.

[*Enter* MACDUFF.]

MACDUFF.   Turn, hell-hound, turn!
MACBETH. Of all men else I have avoided thee.
    But get thee back; my soul is too much charged   5
    With blood of thine already.
MACDUFF.   I have no words;
    My voice is in my sword, thou bloodier villain
    Than terms can give thee out!   [*They fight.*
MACBETH.   Thou losest labor;
    As easy mayst thou the intrenchant air
    With thy keen sword impress as make me bleed.   10
    Let fall thy blade on vulnerable crests;°
    I bear a charmèd life, which must not yield
    To one of woman born.
MACDUFF.   Despair thy charm;
    And let the angel whom thou still hast served
    Tell thee, Macduff was from his mother's womb,   15
    Untimely ripped.
MACBETH. Accursèd be that tongue that tells me so,
    For it hath cowed my better part of man!
    And be these juggling fiends no more believed,
    That palter with us in a double sense;°   20
    That keep the word of promise to our ear,
    And break it to our hope. I'll not fight with thee.
MACDUFF. Then yield thee, coward,
    And live to be the show and gaze o' the time.
    We'll have thee, as our rarer monsters are,   25
    Painted upon a pole,° and underwrit,
    "Here may you see the tyrant."
MACBETH.   I will not yield,
    To kiss the ground before young Malcolm's feet,
    And to be baited with the rabble's curse.
    Though Birnam wood be come to Dunsinane,   30
    And thou opposed, being of no woman born,
    Yet I will try the last. Before my body
    I throw my warlike shield. Lay on, Macduff,
    And damned be him that first cries "Hold, enough!" [*Exeunt, fighting.*
                                                [*Alarums.*

[*Retreat. Flourish.* **Enter,** *with drum and colors,* MALCOLM, *old* SIWARD,
        ROSS, *the other* THANES, *and* SOLDIERS.]

MALCOLM. I would the friends we miss were safe arrived.   35
SIWARD. Some must go off;° and yet, by these I see,
    So great a day as this is cheaply bought.

---

  11. *vulnerable crests:* heads that can be wounded. 20. *palter with us in a double sense:* deceive us
by words that have a double meaning. 26. *Painted upon a pole:* that is, your picture painted on a
placard fastened to a pole. 36. *Some must go off:* In a battle it is inevitable that some should lose
their lives.

MALCOLM. Macduff is missing, and your noble son.
ROSS. Your son, my lord, has paid a soldier's debt.
          He only lived but till he was a man;   40
          The which no sooner had his prowess confirmed
          In the unshrinking station where he fought,
          But like a man he died.
SIWARD.   Then he is dead?
ROSS. Ay, and brought off the field. Your cause of sorrow
          Must not be measured by his worth, for then   45
          It hath no end.
SIWARD.   Had he his hurts before?°
ROSS. Ay, on the front.
SIWARD.   Why then, God's soldier be he!
          Had I as many sons as I have hairs,   [*Flourish.*
          I would not wish them to a fairer death.
          And so, his knell is knolled.
MALCOLM.   He's worth more sorrow,   50
          And that I'll spend for him.
SIWARD.   He's worth no more.
          They say he parted well, and paid his score;
          And so, God be with him! Here comes newer comfort.

          [*Re-enter* MACDUFF, *with* MACBETH's *head.*]

MACDUFF. Hail, king! for so thou art. Behold, where stands
          The usurper's cursèd head. The time is free.   55
          I see thee compassed with thy kingdom's pearl,°
          That speak my salutation in their minds;
          Whose voices I desire aloud with mine:
          Hail, King of Scotland!
ALL.   Hail, King of Scotland!   [*Flourish.*
MALCOLM. We° shall not spend a large expense of time   60
          Before we reckon with your several loves,
          And make us even with you. My thanes and kinsmen,
          Henceforth be earls, the first that ever Scotland
          In such an honor named. What's more to do,
          Which would be planted newly with the time,   65
          As calling home our exiled friends abroad
          That fled the snares of watchful tyranny;
          Producing forth the cruel ministers
          Of this dead butcher and his fiendlike queen,
          Who, as 'tis thought, by self and violent hands   70
          Took off her life; this, and what needful else
          That calls upon us, by the grace of Grace,
          We will perform in measure, time, and place;
          So, thanks to all at once and to each one,
          Whom we invite to see us crowned at Scone.   [*Flourish. Exeunt.* 75

46. *Had he his hurts before?:* If young Siward's wounds were in the front, it would indicate to his father that he died fighting, not fleeing. 56. *thy kingdom's pearl:* the nobility of the kingdom; that is, the nobles. 60. *We:* Malcolm now speaks of himself in the plural as befits a king.

"OF THIS DEAD BUTCHER AND HIS FIENDLIKE QUEEN."

ACT V

1. In Scene i, what words by Macbeth show that she has been brooding over the past crimes? Untangle the confused mixture of words to show which crime she dwells on most frequently. What is the reason for this?

2. What lines foreshadow Lady Macbeth's death? What do we learn later of her death?

3. In the series of short scenes trace the final mental state of Macbeth through significant speeches. Where does he show false bravery, masking underlying fear? dependence on the witches' prophecies? sense of betrayal by the witches? realization of his misspent life?

4. Do you feel pity for Macbeth at any of these points? Do you think he was any less responsible for his acts because the witches' prophecies tempted him?

5. Is the outcome of the plot satisfying to you? What note of hope ends the play?

READING DRAMA

Interest in the stage is inherent in all of us. We are constantly seeing movies, hearing radio plays, viewing television dramas, and attending legitimate stage productions. Drama is not a submerged art; it is a literary type to which many distinguished writers have given their talents. To study, to understand, and to interpret drama should appeal to people of all ages. The extent to which you are able to cultivate a critical appreciation of this literary form depends upon you.

The ideal approach to *Macbeth* or any other play is to see it performed on the stage. Since that is not always possible, a second-best approach is to see a good movie or television version of it. You may at least have access to a recording of parts of the play.

"The play's the thing," and you can read it with great enjoyment if you "set the stage," visualize the characters, follow the plot, and interpret the important scenes. The fun and flavor of *Macbeth* is not lost when you find pleasure in reading and reflecting on passages that are particularly poetic, dramatic, and profound in meaning.

As you read *Macbeth*, you will find it helpful to consider four key questions. You will find that these questions can be applied in reading almost all plays.

1. *How would this play look and sound on the stage?*

Take another look at the model of the Globe Theater on page 127. The Elizabethan stage was very different from our modern stage. Because there was no curtain in the Elizabethan theater, the action of the play was almost continuous. A scene was over when all the characters left the stage; a new scene began when another set of characters came on. This flowing of one scene into another speeds up the action and makes a Shakespearean drama somewhat like our modern movies. The opening of the play was announced by a trumpet. Since there was no "curtain going up," Shakespeare usually begins his plays with a bit of arresting action to quiet his audience. Does he follow this trick in *Macbeth*? How does Scene i establish the *atmosphere* of the play — that is, how does it suggest what the main tone or mood is likely to be?

The Elizabethan theater used magnificent costumes made of the finest and most costly fabrics, and many different kinds of properties were used. However, the stage was almost entirely bare of sets. The playwright therefore had to put descriptions of the setting into the mouths of the characters. What clues to stage "pictures" do you find in the dialogue? See, for example, Act I, Scene iii, line 77, and Scene vi, lines 1–10.

Although the Elizabethan theater had three main sections — the outer, or platform stage, the inner stage, and the upper stage or balcony — virtually all the action of an Elizabethan play took place on the large platform stage. As you go through the play, decide how you would place the characters on the stage. How would you use the trapdoor in the middle of the stage? How would you stage Lady Macbeth's famous sleepwalking scene (Act V, Scene i)? How would you use right and left entrances for various scenes, as that of the drunken porter, Act II, Scene iii, or the battle in Act V?

In the Elizabethan theater the audience received no program or playbill listing the names and relationships of the characters. Shakespeare therefore sometimes has the characters tell you *who* they are as well as *where* they are. Try to find several instances of this self-identification in *Macbeth*.

It is important, too, to visualize the appearance of the characters. There is usually little description of the way characters look, since the audience actually sees them. In Shakespeare's day, Elizabethan costumes were used for most plays, even if the setting was ancient Rome or eleventh-century Scotland. In the pictures on the following pages, however, the costuming is contemporary with the setting of the play. Do you think using modern dress instead of historical costuming detracts from the play's impact or simply emphasizes its enduring theme?

2. *Who are the main characters and what kinds of people are they?*

You can guess in advance that Macbeth is the chief character of the play. He is a good illustration of how a playwright creates a character and makes him come alive in our minds. There are at least four distinct ways in which a character is developed in a play. Each of these may be illustrated by a passage from Act I concerning Macbeth (there are, of course, many other such clues throughout the play).

a. Description of Macbeth's actions by others (Sergeant, Scene ii, lines 16–41).

b. Description of his personality or character traits by others (Lady Macbeth, Scene v, lines 11–26).

c. Macbeth's own thoughts in meditation (Scene iii, lines 129–44).

d. His talk and arguments with others (Scene vii, lines 28–82).

Review these passages and indicate what each tells you about Macbeth. Make a similar list of passages, from all five acts, that reveal the personalities or character traits of (*a*) Lady Macbeth, (*b*) Banquo, (*c*) Duncan, (*d*) Macduff, and (*e*) Malcolm.

Shakespeare is particularly clever at bringing out a character by contrast with other characters. What contrast did you notice between Duncan and Macbeth? What other characters can you contrast?

Shakespeare is a master of character development. Can you point out in this play the various stages by which the gallant soldier Macbeth turns into a butcher? How does Macbeth's hopefulness gradually turn into despair? Why?

Note how Macbeth and Lady Macbeth develop along different tracks. Both are ambitious, but notice that Lady Macbeth takes the initiative at the start and seems more bold and strong. How does this situation reverse itself during the play? Does Macbeth have more imagination or a more sensitive conscience than his wife?

3. *What is the main plot of the drama?*

A good plot is not just any story that comes along, but a story so arranged that it is an artistic whole. The many speeches and actions must all fit, piece by piece, into the complete plot. Each action by Macbeth must result from what has preceded it and take Macbeth further on his downward career. To see how the plot develops, write a short summary of each act.

The suspense of the plot comes from your uncertainty as to its outcome. It lies in these questions: to what will all these events lead? will justice be done in the end? Somewhere in the action is the turning point of the plot. Before this point in the play, Macbeth's crimes have brought him what he wanted; after this point, circumstances turn against him. Try to determine where this point is in *Macbeth*.

The last act of a play should bring all the threads of the plot together in conclusion; it should decide the fate of the main character and solve all the problems that have arisen in the play. How is this illustrated in *Macbeth?*

4. What is the meaning of the play?

The deterioration of Macbeth and his wife illustrates a profound moral truth: that the wages of sin is death and the way of the transgressor hard.

At the end of your first reading of the play, you are in a position to realize the point of the whole. In *Macbeth* it is evident that one of Shakespeare's purposes is to show the devastating effects of unrestrained ambition. How does this theme, or meaning, of the play affect you personally? Does it tell you something about the serious consequences of evil acts upon the persons who perform them? upon the persons who witness or are unwittingly involved in them? Does it make you realize the responsibility of a leader or ruler to the people under him? Does it sharpen your insight into human motives and desires?

The meaning of the play is found not only in its whole but also in its parts — in specific passages. How many powerful passages need to be clarified and thought over? What passages seem to you particularly significant in revealing Shakespeare's meaning?

LITERATURE AND THE ARTS

The photographs on the following pages, from a production of *Macbeth* seen nationally, illustrate the steadily growing relationship between literature and the newest of the communications arts — television. With the coming of age of this medium, more and more literary works have been presented. Productions of Shakespeare have been among the most popular of these presentations.

Never before, in fact, have there been so many productions of Shakespeare's plays, nor have so many people been able to enjoy them. In addition to television and the well-established festivals at Stratford (England, Connecticut, Ontario), small stock companies have sprung up everywhere. There have been adaptations for films and Broadway musicals. And Shakespeare is popular not only in English-speaking countries but throughout the world.

Television's *Macbeth,* starring Judith Anderson as Lady Macbeth and Maurice Evans as Macbeth, was filmed in Scotland in 1960 and won more awards that year than any other television production.

LEFT: *"All hail, Macbeth, that shall be king hereafter!"*

ABOVE: *"Will all great Neptune's ocean wash this blood clean from my hand?"*

BELOW: *"Awake, awake! Ring the alarum bell. Murder and treason!
. . . Up, up, and see the great doom's image!"*

ABOVE: *". . . Birnam wood do come to Dunsinane."*

BELOW: *". . . damned be him that first cries 'Hold, enough!'"*

Photographs by Robert Fuhrir

MACBETH: *An Afterword*

Macbeth, like *Hamlet, King Lear,* and *Othello,* was produced during what is generally called the third or tragic period of Shakespeare's life as a dramatist. It was a time when his stupendous powers were at their height, but when some inward conflict made him intensely aware of the contrast in our life between good and evil, light and dark, reasonable and peaceful order and chaotic violence. Some division in himself enabled him to give the fullest expression to these contrasts in hundreds of lines that haunt the mind like great tragic music. The world we discover in these tragedies is a terrible one.

Indeed, we might say that in *Macbeth,* a tragedy of tremendous power, Hell is let loose. Notice how much of it seems to take place at night, to be intimately concerned with darkness: it is a drama in black, edged with the crimson of spilled blood. Our actors used to be very superstitious, and one of their superstitions, which I can remember myself, was that it was very unlucky to produce *Macbeth,* as if the play attracted to the theater various accidents and misfortunes. This is probably only another tribute to its astonishing power as a piece of literature.

THE CHARACTER OF MACBETH

To this day, after knowing the play for fifty years, some of its speeches still make me feel my hair is standing on end. Macbeth himself is one of the great poets among Shakespeare's characters, for in line after line, speech after speech, he says wonderful things. And the fact that Shakespeare gives him such things to say, of a power and insight and poetry unmatched by any other character in the drama, proves definitely, to my mind, that Shakespeare saw it as Macbeth's play and nobody else's, not even Lady Macbeth's. The play is about what happened to Macbeth when ambition and the promptings of evil (represented by the witches) overcome the reluctance of an imaginative man — and Macbeth is essentially an imaginative man — to embark on a course of violent and criminal actions.

Many criminals, especially murderers, are people without imagination. They commit murder because other people, their victims, do not seem to them to be real persons like themselves, but mere obstacles to be got out of the way. They are so unimaginative and strongly self-centered that they, alone, really exist in a world of robots, dummies, shadows. Strictly speaking, such criminals are so far removed from ordinary personal and social relationships that they are mad. They do not defy their consciences because they have no consciences to defy.

But Macbeth is not one of these dreary criminal lunatics. He is an imaginative man, of unusual courage and ability, as Shakespeare makes us realize when Macbeth is first discussed in Act I, Scene ii. (These opening scenes are always very informative and important in Shakespeare.) But there is some weakness, some fatal flaw, in his character. We are made to realize this as soon as he enters and speaks his very first line: "So foul and fair a day I have not seen." This revealing line is spoken within hearing of the witches, who are aware of this flaw in his character. It suggests that already, in the hour of his triumph as a victorious general, there is in him some strange and dangerous confusion, bringing together and mingling what is "foul" and what is "fair." And notice that in this scene Banquo, a straightforward man, merely expresses a natural disgust for the witches, whereas Macbeth is fascinated by their prophecies, urging them to tell him more. There is more than impatient ambition

© 1961, by Harcourt, Brace & World, Inc.

here — though there is that too, and Shakespeare is always suspicious of such ambition — for behind it there is this fatal flaw, this inability to keep a strict watch along the border between good and evil, a weakness of the central and all-important conscience.

THE INFLUENCE OF LADY MACBETH

We do not know, however, how far Macbeth would have gone (for we soon discover that he cannot help recoiling in disgust and horror from criminal acts) if it had not been for his wife. It is she who encourages him by every feminine device, from wifely sympathy to artful scorn of what she calls his cowardice. Had his wife been an ordinary, tender-hearted woman, instead of being so ambitious, ruthless, and callous, then we feel that his career of crime — and that is what it is — would probably have been checked at the outset. But instead of pulling him out of it, she thrusts him further into it. Yet she is not really stronger than he is, for when he has reaped the full and terrible harvest of his crimes, she is no longer his partner, steeling his will, but a mere wreck of a woman, out of her mind.

What are we to make of this? It is all very difficult. My own view is that Shakespeare, beginning with the witches, felt so strongly impelled to hurry us into this atmosphere of darkness, evil, and doom that he omitted a scene that we need very badly. This scene, which would have had to be played chiefly between Macbeth and his wife, would have shown us what kind of relationship existed between them before any crime was committed or even considered. Lacking such a scene, and with it any knowledge of their normal relationship, we are naturally puzzled by the character of Lady Macbeth. Why did she urge him on so relentlessly? Why, having shown herself far more ruthless than he, does she break down so soon, leaving him alone to face the consequence of his actions?

THE CHARACTER OF LADY MACBETH

This bewilderment explains something that always happens when this play is produced. In spite of the fact that she breaks down and then disappears from the play before it is over, the part of Lady Macbeth, with its many powerful speeches and highly dramatic situations, is always assumed by actresses, producers, directors, and critics, to be a very fine part, a magnificent gift from Shakespeare to any leading actress able to play tragedy. Yet it is my experience that whenever the part is actually played, no matter how gifted the particular actress may be, the more intelligent drama critics always express some disappointment, as if something in the part had escaped the actress. But in my view it is Shakespeare and not the actresses who must be blamed. The part is, in fact, not a fine part, the character of Lady Macbeth not having been solidly established and not having been soundly welded into the action of the play. She is indeed its chief weakness.

We can only guess at what Shakespeare had in mind. Certainly, he needed some character, entirely in Macbeth's confidence and determined to egg him on, in order to show us that he was not all criminal, that he had scruples and terrible doubts, that he was very much a divided man. A wife would seem to be the best possible person to play this character. She could talk to Macbeth as nobody else could, playing confidently upon his feelings. And it is true that a very feminine woman, devoted to her husband and his career and ruthlessly ambitious both for herself and him, might overcome his doubts and scruples better than anybody else could. (There is a bad tradition in the theater that Lady Macbeth should be played as a commanding and rather masculine type of woman, but it is much better, truer to life, if she is seen to be a rather small, dainty, very feminine type, as pretty and soft but as cunning and ruthless as a cat.) But that he should have such a wife, instead of the more usual kind ready to protect him from his worse self, is simply bad luck for Macbeth, and true tragedy should be outside mere bad luck. Unless, of course, one argues that it is the fatal flaw in Macbeth that led him to fall in love with and then marry a woman like Lady Macbeth, a woman who, when the time came, would strengthen his darker, criminal side.

To be as utterly ruthless and callous as she appears to be at first, when she is ready to do things her husband shrinks from doing, means that Lady Macbeth has had to suppress all her natural womanly feelings. But she can do this only up to a point, and when one crime follows another and there is no end to the bloodshed and horror, the suppressed half of her takes its revenge by striking at her very sanity, finally taking her out of reality altogether. And by this time, as we discover, Macbeth has almost ceased to care whether she is mad or sane, living or dead, for no personal relationship means anything to him any longer, existing as he does in a kind of Hell where there are no such relationships, where nothing has any real meaning.

MACBETH'S TRAGEDY

Macbeth's great speech, one of the greatest in all dramatic literature, which follows the news of the Queen's death, offers us the key to the whole tragedy:

She should have died hereafter;
There would have been a time for such
   a word.
Tomorrow, and tomorrow, and tomor-
   row,
Creeps in this petty pace from day to
   day
To the last syllable of recorded time,
And all our yesterdays have lighted
   fools
The way to dusty death. Out, out,
   brief candle!

Life's but a walking shadow, a poor
   player
That struts and frets his hour upon
   the stage
And then is heard no more. It is a
   tale
Told by an idiot, full of sound and
   fury,
Signifying nothing.

Now much earlier, in Act II, Scene iii, after Duncan's death has been discovered and Macbeth is pretending to be as astonished and as much shaken as the others, we can find in Macbeth's speech on his re-entrance a curious foretaste of his final despair:

Had I but died an hour before this
   chance,
I had lived a blessèd time; for, from
   this instant,
There's nothing serious in mortality.
All is but toys: renown and grace is
   dead;
The wine of life is drawn, and the
   mere lees
Is left this vault to brag of.

He is largely pretending, yet there is something in him, some defeated goodness, that is already beginning to feel that "the wine of life is drawn."

Nor is Macbeth alone in this, for a little later in the play, at the beginning of Act III, Scene ii, Lady Macbeth, left alone for a moment, speaks to herself in this vein:

   Naught's had, all's spent,
Where our desire is got without con-
   tent.
'Tis safer to be that which we destroy
Than by destruction dwell in doubtful
   joy.

And very soon she will begin destroying herself, losing her wits in the attempt to lose a world no longer endurable.

As these two destroy life in others, they also destroy the life in themselves.

Macbeth the murderer is slowly murdering Macbeth. And being an imaginative man, not without some goodness in him, he knows this, and has known it from the moment he committed his first crime. Whatever is good, cherishing life, expands it, adds form and rich color to it, gives it bloom and flavor. But evil, despising and hating life, contracts it, diminishes and bleaches it, makes it formless and meaningless in the end. Macbeth's famous speech shows us the defeat of goodness, the triumph of evil in its terrible vision of a dusty nothingness and an endless idiocy.

We must not imagine that these ideas of good and evil apply only to life in Scotland in the eleventh century or in England early in the seventeenth century. They apply with equal force to our life here and now. Indeed, when reading about the more murderous types of American gangsters, I have often felt that their kind of life lacked precisely those qualities that stupid people imagined it to have: namely, excitement, zest,

enthusiasm. They seemed to live in that stale, dead atmosphere which we find in Macbeth's last despairing vision of existence. The evil to which they had given themselves had cut them off from everything that expands and enhances, colors and flavors life.

"Methought I heard a voice cry 'Sleep no more! Macbeth does murder sleep.' " Yes, and soon, before he has done, he has murdered honor and friendship, murdered all possibility of innocent pleasure and joy, murdered love and all satisfying human relationships. And his tragedy is that from first to last he is terribly aware of what he is losing, for he is neither a madman nor a dumb brute as so many murderers are, but a man who might have been great and good but for that fatal flaw in his nature. Through that crack in his conscience, as the witches perceived, the destructive forces of evil would invade his soul, giving him a crown that no longer meant anything, in a darkening ruin of a life on which the sun would never rise again.

J. B. P.

BEN JONSON
1572 – 1637

Folger Library

Next to Shakespeare, Ben Jonson was the most important dramatist of the Elizabethan era. But unlike Shakespeare, he was a quarrelsome and overbearing person who led a colorful and often turbulent life. In his early youth he ran away to fight the

Spaniards in Flanders because he had grown tired of laying bricks in London. In time, he returned, married, and became an actor and playwright. His quick temper got him into frequent trouble. One day he killed a fellow actor in a duel arising from a quarrel. He was thrown into prison and barely escaped hanging, but was branded on the left thumb in punishment. Another time, he almost had his nose and ears cut off when he confessed writing part of a comedy that offended the king.

Jonson was the first English dramatist to publish his plays. He was greatly loved and admired by his readers and by those who knew him personally. Among his friends were Raleigh, Marlowe, Shakespeare, and Sir Francis Bacon. A group of young writers became his devoted followers and called themselves "Sons of Ben." He was unofficial poet laureate of his day, and today he lies buried in Westminster Abbey, where his tombstone bears the words: "O Rare Ben Jonson."

Jonson was a distinguished scholar, as his plays show. In them he attacks human gullibility, exposes social abuses, scores the follies of the day, and satirizes the baseness of human nature. He pokes fun at the absurd fashions of the times by means of exaggerated characters and situations in his plays. He is satirical rather than sympathetic. His best-known play, *Volpone,* has several times been revived in the present day. It tells of an old miser (his name means "The Fox") who pretends to be dying in order to extract rich gifts from his greedy friends, who expect to be heirs. A less cynical side of Jonson is revealed in his poems, which are rich in appreciation of true beauty and nobility. "To Celia" is probably the only Elizabethan lyric well enough known to be sung by the general public today.

To the Memory of My Beloved Master,
William Shakespeare

To draw no envy, Shakespeare, on thy name,
Am I thus ample to thy book and fame;
While I confess thy writings to be such
As neither man nor muse can praise too much.
'Tis true, and all men's suffrage.° But these ways   5
Were not the paths I meant unto thy praise;
For silliest° ignorance on these may light,
Which, when it sounds at best, but echoes right;
Or blind affection, which doth ne'er advance
The truth, but gropes, and urgeth all by chance;   10
Or crafty malice might pretend this praise,
And think to ruin, where it seemed to raise. . . .
But thou art proof against them, and, indeed,
Above the ill fortune of them, or the need.
I therefore will begin. Soul of the age,   15
The applause, delight, the wonder of our stage,
My Shakespeare, rise! I will not lodge thee by
Chaucer, or Spenser, or bid Beaumont lie
A little further, to make thee a room.
Thou art a monument without a tomb,   20
And art alive still while thy book doth live,
And we have wits to read and praise to give. . . .

---

5. *suffrage:* vote; decision. 7. *silliest:* simplest, most innocent. In Elizabethan times, the adjective *silly* meant simply "rustic" or "plain."

Several lines which are omitted here point out the superiority of
Shakespeare to other dramatists of his day and compare him with a
number of classical poets of antiquity. This passage contains the
famous line: "He was not of an age, but for all time."

Or, for the laurel, he may gain a scorn;
For a good poet's made, as well as born.
And such wert thou; look how the father's face   25
Lives in his issue, even so the race
Of Shakespeare's mind and manners brightly shines
In his well turnèd and true filèd° lines,
In each of which he seems to shake a lance,°
As brandished at the eyes of ignorance.   30
Sweet Swan of Avon! what a sight it were
To see thee in our waters yet appear,
And make those flights upon the banks of Thames,
That so did take Eliza and our James!°
But stay, I see thee in the hemisphere   35
Advanced, and made a constellation there!
Shine forth, thou Star of poets, and with rage
Or influence chide or cheer the drooping stage,
Which, since thy flight from hence, hath mourned like night,
And despairs day, but for thy volume's light.   40

28. *filèd:* polished. 29. *shake a lance:* probably a pun on Shakespeare's name. 34. That so did
please Queen Elizabeth and King James.

The Noble Nature

It is not growing like a tree
In bulk, doth make Man better be;
Or standing long an oak, three hundred year,
To fall a log at last, dry, bald, and sere;
A lily of a day   5
Is fairer far in May,
Although it fall and die that night —
It was the plant and flower of Light.
In small proportions we just beauties see;
And in short measures life may perfect be.   10

To Celia

Drink to me only with thine eyes,
    And I will pledge with mine;
Or leave a kiss but in the cup
    And I'll not look for wine.
The thirst that from the soul doth rise   5
    Doth ask a drink divine;
But might I of Jove's nectar° sup,
    I would not change for thine.

I sent thee late a rosy wreath,
    Not so much honoring thee   10
As giving it a hope that there
    It could not withered be;
But thou thereon didst only breathe
    And sent'st it back to me;
Since when it grows, and smells,
    I swear,   15
Not of itself but thee!

7. *Jove's nectar:* the drink of the gods, a beverage of supernatural excellence.

A POET OF MANY MOODS

1. What is revealed about Jonson in his memorial tribute to Shakespeare? In what specific ways does he describe Shakespeare's greatness as a poet and dramatist?

2. How would you describe in your own words the central thought of "The Noble Nature"? Look carefully at Jonson's choice of words. What picture is called to mind by line 4? What figure of speech did the poet use throughout the poem?

3. You will enjoy hearing "To Celia" in a musical setting. Try to obtain a recording of it to determine whether the music fits the mood of the verse.

SUGGESTION FOR WRITING

These three poems by Jonson show different sides of his personality. Write a short essay on him as a person and a writer.

FRANCIS BACON

1561–1626

National Portrait Gallery

He was "the wisest, brightest, meanest of mankind," said the eighteenth-century poet Alexander Pope of Francis Bacon. Another picture of him is given by his contemporary, Ben Jonson: "He seemed to me ever, by his work, one of the greatest men, and most worthy of admiration that had been in many ages." All in all, Francis Bacon was a remarkable man, if a contradictory character. He was a scholar of tremendous learning and, as he himself said, took all knowledge for his province. He represents the first union in English literature of the man of letters and the man of science. He was, besides, an ambitious politician.

Until he was nineteen, Bacon had no financial worries. His father was Lord Keeper of the Seal to Queen Elizabeth, his mother a highborn lady known for her scholarship in Latin and Greek. When he was but twelve years old, Bacon went to Cambridge University; but he soon left, denouncing the educational system because it failed to challenge his mind. He then turned to travel, private study, and law. When his father died, Bacon found himself without funds. He resorted to moneylenders for help, and for the rest of his life he was hounded by creditors.

Bacon was not content to be a man of letters and learning. He had political ambitions and sought to gain Queen Elizabeth's favor, without much success. When King James ascended to the throne, however, Bacon's star rose rapidly. He became Lord Chancellor and was titled a baron and viscount. But he had enemies in court and was soon convicted of accepting bribes. Banished from Parliament, he was fined and imprisoned. Although he remained in prison but two days, his political career was at an end. He devoted the remainder of his life to writing and to scientific experiment.

Francis Bacon is regarded as the first

essayist in English literature. Much of his writing is philosophical, expressing his concern with men's understanding of themselves and the world they live in. One of his books, *The Advancement of Learning,* is a treatise about the divisions of knowledge. His essays cover a wide range of subjects, from such personal matters as "marriage and single life" to such abstractions as "truth." Bacon wrote more often in Latin than in English. His style in English, although sometimes difficult or obscure, is nevertheless full of grace and power.

Of Studies

STUDIES serve for delight, for ornament, and for ability. Their chief use for delight is in privateness and retiring; for ornament, is in discourse; and for ability, is in the judgment and disposition of business. For expert men [1] can execute, and perhaps judge of particulars, one by one; but the general counsels, and the plots and marshaling of affairs, come best from those that are learned. To spend too much time in studies is sloth; to use them too much for ornament is affectation; to make judgment wholly by their rules is the humor [2] of a scholar. They perfect nature, and are perfected by experience; for natural abilities are like natural plants, that need pruning by study; and studies themselves do give forth direction too much at large, except they be bounded in by experience. Crafty men [3] contemn studies, simple men admire them, [4] and wise men use them; for they teach not their own use; but that is a wisdom without them, and above them, won by observation. Read not to contradict and confute; nor to believe and take for granted; nor to find talk and discourse; but to weigh and consider. Some books are to be tasted, others to be swallowed, and some few to be chewed and digested; that is, some books are to be read only in parts; others to be read, but not curiously; [5] and some few to be read wholly, and with diligence and attention. Some books also may be read by deputy, and extracts made of them by others; but that would be only in the less important arguments, and the meaner sort of books; else distilled books are like common distilled waters, flashy [6] things. Reading maketh a full man; conference a ready man; and writing an exact man. And therefore, if a man write little, he had need have a great memory; if he confer little, he had need have a present wit; and if he read little, he had need have much cunning, to seem to know that [7] he doth not. Histories make men wise; poets witty; the mathematics subtile; natural philosophy deep; moral grave; logic and rhetoric able to contend. *Abeunt studia in mores.* [8] Nay, there is no stond [9] or impediment in the wit but may be wrought out by fit studies; like as diseases of the body may have appropriate exercises. Bowling is good for the stone and reins; [10] shooting for the lungs and breast; gentle walking for the stomach; riding for the head; and the like. So if a man's wit be wandering, let him

---

[1] *expert men:* men of practical skill and experience, as opposed to men of theoretical book learning. [2] *humor:* in the Elizabethan sense, whim or disposition. [3] *Crafty men:* men skilled in crafts, similar to "expert men." [4] *simple men admire them:* unlettered men wonder at them.

[5] *curiously:* thoroughly and carefully; with great attention. [6] *flashy:* insipid. [7] *that:* that which. [8] *Abeunt . . . mores:* "Studies are turned into habits." [9] *stond:* obstacle. [10] *stone and reins:* "stone," the old name for a disease of the kidneys ("reins").

study the mathematics; for in demonstrations, if his wit be called away never so little, he must begin again. If his wit be not apt to distinguish or find differences, let him study the Schoolmen; [1] for they are *cymini sectores.* If he be not apt to beat over matters, and to call up one thing to prove and illustrate another, let him study the lawyers' cases. So every defect of the mind may have a special receipt.

[1] *Schoolmen:* medieval scholars who were hairsplitters, or, as Bacon says in the Latin phrase following, splitters of cuminseeds in their prolonged arguments.

AN ELIZABETHAN STUDENT

1. In your own words give Bacon's definition of a scholar. Can you add to this definition? What does Bacon consider the main purposes of study? From your own experience, judging things in the light of the modern world, discuss Bacon's viewpoint pro and con. Do you agree with him that the study of a particular subject will have a specific effect on one's mind?

2. Name books that fall into each class of reading mentioned in Bacon's essay. Which type do you read most frequently? Can you add anything to the list Bacon gives of the *objectives* and *results* of reading?

SUGGESTION FOR WRITING

Try writing an essay of your own in Bacon's style — direct, concrete sentences marshaled one after another without particular attention to paragraphing or transitions. In 100 or 200 words take up a subject, such as athletics, schooling, or dating, about which you have personal opinions.

THE POWER OF WORDS

PREFIXES AND ROOTS

Bacon uses several words with the prefixes "con" and "contra" in talking about exchanging ideas. "Read not to contradict or confute," he says. In *contradict* the root is *dict,* to speak; the prefix is *contra,* against. When you contradict, you speak against another speaker. There is no suggestion in this word as to which view is the right one. But if you *confute* (prefix *con,* with or together; root *fute,* to make worthless), you prove that your side is right and the other is worthless.

Bacon says "conference maketh a ready man." We would probably express it, "Conversation makes a quick-witted man." Today *conference* is a more formal way of speaking together than Bacon probably meant. Look up its origin for an exact meaning of the word. How could you, during a *conference,* contradict another person or *confute* him by *refuting* his arguments? What is the difference between *confute* and *refute?*

The King James Bible

For many centuries the Bible was written in Latin and was therefore unknown to the ordinary English people. During the Middle Ages they depended for enlightenment upon the miracle and mystery plays and then upon the few translations available of the Bible by John Wyclif. Wyclif and his followers were responsible for the first complete translations of the Bible into English. Of the two Wyclif versions (1382 and 1388), the second or revised version is considered the more accurate and more readable. Later came William Tyndale (tĭn'dăl), who was fired with a desire to

bring the Bible to everyone, even "the boy that driveth the plow." Tyndale began printing his translation in 1525. However, religious wars and conflicts cut short his work of translating and made a martyr of him. Miles Coverdale later issued a translation, based partly on Tyndale's; and he supervised the preparation of the Great Bible, which in 1540 was finally established in all the churches.

During the reign of King James I, the need for a still better translation was recognized. Fifty-four scholars and churchmen assembled and worked for seven years to complete what is known as the King James Bible — perhaps the most familiar version among Protestants, although many other translations have since been made. The King James Version retains the vigor of the original Tyndale translation but is more poetic and colorful in language. Probably no other single book has had greater influence upon English literature than this translation of the Bible. Its literary value lies in its variety and wealth of material, which its writers have presented in a style that is stately and simple, direct and sometimes poetic.

The Prodigal Son

(A SHORT STORY)

LUKE 15:11–32

A CERTAIN man had two sons. And the younger of them said to his father, "Father, give me the portion of goods that falleth to me." And he divided unto them his living.

And not many days after, the younger son gathered all together and took his journey into a far country, and there wasted his substance with riotous living. And when he had spent all, there arose a mighty famine in that land, and he began to be in want. And he went and joined himself to a citizen of that country, and he sent him into his fields to feed swine. And he would fain have filled his belly with the husks that the swine did eat, and no man gave unto him.

And when he came to himself, he said, "How many hired servants of my father's have bread enough and to spare, and I perish with hunger! I will arise and go to my father, and will say to him, 'Father, I have sinned against Heaven and before thee, and am no more worthy to be called thy son. Make me as one of thy hired servants.' "

And he arose and came to his father. But when he was yet a great way off, his father saw him and had compassion, and ran, and fell on his neck, and kissed him. And the son said unto him. "Father, I have sinned against Heaven and in thy sight and am no more worthy to be called thy son."

But the father said to his servants, "Bring forth the best robe and put it on him; and put a ring on his hand, and shoes on his feet; and bring hither the fatted calf, and kill it; and let us eat, and be merry. For this my son was dead and is alive again; he was lost, and is found." And they began to be merry.

Now his elder son was in the field; and as he came and drew nigh to the house, he heard music and dancing. And he called one of the servants and asked what these things meant. And he said unto him, "Thy brother is come, and thy father has killed the fatted calf, because he hath received him safe and sound."

And he was angry and would not go in; therefore came his father out and entreated him. And he answering said to his father, "Lo, these many years do I serve thee, neither transgressed I at any time thy commandment; and yet thou never gavest me a kid, that I might make merry with my friends. But as soon as thy son was come, which hath devoured thy living, thou hast killed for him the fatted calf."

And he said unto him, "Son, thou art ever with me, and all that I have is thine. It was meet that we should make merry and be glad, for this thy brother was dead, and is alive again; and was lost, and is found."

But the Greatest of These Is Charity

(AN ESSAY)

ST. PAUL'S LETTER TO THE CORINTHIANS
(I, CHAPTER 13)

THOUGH I speak with the tongues of men and of angels and have not charity,[1] I am become as sounding brass or a tinkling cymbal. And though I have the gift of prophecy, and understand all mysteries, and all knowledge; and though I have all faith, so that I could remove mountains, and have not charity, I am nothing. And though I bestow all my goods to feed the poor, and though I give my body to be burned, and have not charity, it profiteth me nothing.

Charity suffereth long and is kind; charity envieth not; charity vaunteth not itself, is not puffed up; doth not behave itself unseemly, seeketh not her own, is not easily provoked, thinketh no evil, rejoiceth not in iniquity, but rejoiceth in the truth; beareth all things, believeth all things, hopeth all things, endureth all things. Charity never faileth; but whether there be prophecies, they shall fail; whether there be tongues, they shall cease; whether there be knowledge, it shall vanish away. For we know in part,[2] and we prophesy in part.

But when that which is perfect is come, then that which is in part shall be done away. When I was a child, I spake as a child, I understood as a child, I thought as a child; but when I became a man I put away childish things. For now we see through a glass darkly, but then face to face; now I know in part, but then shall I know even as also I am known.

And now abideth faith, hope, charity, these three; but the greatest of these is charity.

[1] *charity:* Throughout this essay, "charity" is used in the old sense of "love" rather than its more modern sense of "almsgiving." The modern revised versions usually substitute the word "love."

[2] *in part:* imperfectly

The Ideal Wife

(AN ESSAY)

PROVERBS 31:10–31

WHO CAN find a virtuous woman? For her price is far above rubies. The heart of her husband doth safely trust in her, so that he shall have no need of spoil. She will do him good and not evil all the days of her life. She seeketh wool, and flax, and worketh willingly with her hands. She is like the merchants' ships; she bringeth her food from afar. She riseth also while it is yet night, and giveth meat to her household, and a portion to her maidens. She considereth a field, and buyeth it; with the fruit of her hands she planteth a vineyard. She girdeth her loins with strength, and strengtheneth her arms. She perceiveth that her merchandise is good; her candle goeth not out by night. She layeth her hands to the spindle, and her hands hold the distaff. She stretcheth out her hand to the poor; yea, she reacheth forth her hands to the needy. She is not afraid of the snow for her household, for all her household are clothed with scarlet. She maketh herself coverings of tapestry; her clothing is silk and purple. Her husband is known in the gates, when he sitteth among the elders of the land. She maketh fine linen, and selleth it; and delivereth girdles unto the merchant. Strength and honor are her clothing, and she shall rejoice in time to come. She openeth her mouth with wisdom, and in her tongue is the law of kindness. She looketh well to the ways of her household, and eateth not the bread of idleness. Her children arise up, and call her blessed; her husband also, and he praiseth her. Many daughters have done virtuously, but thou excellest them all. Favor is deceitful, and beauty is vain, but a woman that feareth the Lord, she shall be praised. Give her of the fruit of her hands, and let her own works praise her in the gates.

Lyric Poems

The Bible is full of rich and beautiful lyric poetry. This is seen especially in the Book of Psalms. The psalms do not *look* like poetry as the Bible is usually printed. Ancient Hebrew poetry did not have the rhyme or the regular patterns of accented and unaccented syllables of the poetry we read today. Its rhythm is based largely on questions and answers and on repetitions of an idea with slightly different phrasing. The translators of the King James Version, wise enough not to try to squeeze this poetry into an English style, let it speak for itself in flowing rhythms.

The two psalms here given represent entirely different moods. The first is an exuberant hymn of praise to God. It is possible to think of this psalm as being sung by two great choruses, one asking the questions, the other answering, with the magnificent accompaniment of cymbals and trumpets. The second expresses quiet confidence in the protection of God even in the midst of danger and trouble.

Psalm 24

The earth is the Lord's, and the fullness thereof;
The world, and they that dwell therein.
For he hath founded it upon the seas,
And established it upon the floods.
Who shall ascend into the hill of the Lord?   5
Or who shall stand in his holy place?
He that hath clean hands and a pure heart;
Who hath not lifted up his soul unto vanity, nor sworn deceitfully.
He shall receive the blessing from the Lord,
And righteousness from the God of his salvation.   10
This is the generation of them that seek him,
That seek thy face, O God of Jacob.

Lift up your heads, O ye gates;
And be ye lifted up, ye everlasting doors;
And the King of glory shall come in.   15
Who is the King of glory?
The Lord strong and mighty, the Lord mighty in battle.
Lift up your heads, O ye gates;

Even lift them up, ye everlasting doors;
And the King of glory shall come in.   20
Who is this King of glory?
The Lord of hosts, he is the King of glory.

Psalm 121

I will lift up mine eyes unto the hills,
From whence cometh my help.
My help cometh from the Lord,
Which made heaven and earth.
He will not suffer thy foot to be moved;   5
He that keepeth thee will not slumber.
Behold, he that keepeth Israel
Shall neither slumber nor sleep.

The Lord is thy keeper;
The Lord is thy shade upon thy right hand.   10
The sun shall not smite thee by day,
Nor the moon by night.
The Lord shall preserve thee from all evil;
He shall preserve thy soul.
The Lord shall preserve thy going out and thy coming in   15
From this time forth, and even for evermore.

THE BIBLE AS LITERATURE

1. Why do you think the parable of "The Prodigal Son" is one of the best known and best loved in the New Testament? Just what is a parable? In what way was the father justified in acting as he did toward the two brothers? Do similar situations sometimes occur in modern families? What other famous parables do you know?

2. What is the importance of "charity" in a person's life? Which of the qualifications of charity as given in this essay are the hardest to live up to? What point does the author make about the place of childhood in life? What is the connection between this and charity? Is the word "charity" preferable to "love" in this selection? Why or why not?

3. Why are the psalms poetry even though they lack regular meter and rhyme? What is the main idea of each psalm? Point out a striking use of contrast.

4. Read these selections in one or more of the revised versions of the Bible. Do you get a different understanding of any of them by so doing? Which versions do you like best? Why?

LITERATURE AND THE ARTS

The art of staining glass reached its height in the great medieval cathedrals of Europe. As early techniques were refined, individual styles were developed and associated with different "schools." The angel musician on page 207 is an example of the type of stained glass made by the Norwich school of English glass painters of the fifteenth century, a school noted for its fine drawing and use of color, and its robust portrayals.

READING LIST FOR THE ELIZABETHAN AGE

Anderson, Maxwell, *Elizabeth the Queen* and *Mary of Scotland*
Two outstanding dramas about the famous cousins and rival queens.

Barnes, Margaret, *Tudor Rose*
A sympathetic picture of Elizabeth, the Princess of York, who was married to the Lancastrian Henry VII to settle the Wars of the Roses.

Burton, Elizabeth, *Pageant of Elizabethan England*
The architecture, music, costume, food, furniture, and medicine of Elizabethan England are reviewed for the reader.

Byrd, Elizabeth, *Immortal Queen*
This historical novel of the personal life of Mary Queen of Scots tells of her three marriages and of her conflicts with Elizabeth I.

Chidsey, Donald Barr, *Elizabeth I*
A short, briskly told story of Elizabeth as queen; the politics of her reign receives more attention than her personality.

Churchill, Winston S., *New World, 1485 to 1688*
Volume II of a four-volume history of the British Empire.

* Chute, Marchette, *Shakespeare of London*
A well-drawn portrait of Shakespeare's life, his theater, and his times.

Davis, William S., *Life in Elizabethan Days*
An excellent introduction to the period, showing a typical English community of the sixteenth century.

Irwin, Margaret, series of four novels on different periods in the life of Queen Elizabeth: *Young Bess, Elizabeth: Captive Princess, The Gay Galliard, Elizabeth and the Prince of Spain.*

——, *That Great Lucifer*
A portrait of Sir Walter Raleigh set against a background of the courts of Queen Elizabeth and James I.

Jenkins, Elizabeth, *Elizabeth the Great*
A popular biography and excellent characterization of Queen Elizabeth I, this book tells about Elizabeth's visits to her wealthy nobles and her courtship with Leicester.

Neale, J. E., *Queen Elizabeth*
Concise and readable biography.

Noyes, Alfred, "Forty Singing Seamen" and "Tales of the Mermaid Tavern" (both in his *Collected Poems*)
Narratives in verse told by famous persons of the period, the first by the voyagers, the second by the poets.

Scott, Sir Walter, *Kenilworth*
A vivid account, ending in tragedy, of the Earl of Leicester's elaborate entertaining of Queen Elizabeth at Kenilworth Castle.

Shellabarger, Samuel, *The King's Cavalier*
Intrigue in the court of Henry VII.

Strachey, Lytton, *Elizabeth and Essex*
Excellent fictionalized biography showing Elizabeth's struggle between her determination to control her kingdom and her love for the Earl of Essex.

Sutcliff, Rosemary, *Lady in Waiting*
Biographical novel about the lives of Sir Walter Raleigh and his wife, Bess Throckmorton. Their romance, secret marriage, and Raleigh's struggles to establish an English empire in the New World are recounted.

Twain, Mark, *The Prince and the Pauper*
Similar in appearance, the young Prince Edward VI and a slum boy exchange places. A vivid picture of contemporary London is given.

Westcott, Jan, *Queen's Grace*
Katryn was the sixth wife of Henry VIII. Her long romance with Thomas Seymour survived her three marriages; after Henry's death Katryn and Seymour are united.

*This biography is included in *Four English Biographies*, J. B. Priestley and O. B. Davis, eds. (Harcourt, Brace & World, Inc., 1961).

FOR LISTENING

The following selections have been recorded and are available on *Many Voices 6A:* Shakespeare's "Who Is Silvia?" "Full Fathom Five," Sonnets 18, 73, 29, 55, 116, *Macbeth:* Act I, Scene vii; Act V, Scene i; Act V, Scene v. A 45-minute recording of the five acts of *Macbeth* is available on *Many Voices 12B.* On *Many Voices 12A* are recorded Spenser's Sonnet 26, Jonson's "To the Memory of My Beloved Master, William Shakespeare," and Psalm 121 from the King James Bible.

ELIZABETHAN FRONTISPIECE: Pictured on page 104 are (1) an engraving of the battle between the English fleet and the Spanish Armada; (2) the Tudor coat of arms; (3) an eighteenth-century copy of Elizabethan damask fabric; (4) hemp rope of the type used by sailing vessels of the period; (5) an Elizabethan clay pipe; (6) an eighteenth-century copy of an Elizabethan silver bowl; (7) a map of the Americas, 1570.

THE GROWTH OF
THE ENGLISH LANGUAGE

The Elizabethan Age

Just as we say that the Elizabethan Age marked the flowering of English literature, so too we can see a parallel flowering of the English language. The two are inseparable. That buoyant, searching, investigating spirit that sent some men out to explore a New World, sent others back into the ancient world to relive the great days of antiquity, particularly Greek antiquity, through reading about them. New experiences need new words. When the Elizabethans could not find the words they wanted in an existing language, they coined new ones. They loved extravagant expression, elaborate figures of speech, and frequent allusions to classical mythology. The poets brought in new verse forms like the sonnet and blank verse, both developed in Italy, and created new forms like the Spenserian stanza. The great vogue of poetry in the sixteenth century brought into English the words *poem, ode, elegy, lyric, epic,* and *satire,* and, in fact, most of the terminology we now use in classifying poetry. Some of these were adopted directly from France or Italy, but all hark back to Greek roots, for ancient Greece was the cradle of our poetry.

The sudden popularity of drama tended to accentuate florid language. One of the best examples is in *Macbeth,* page 147, line 63 of Act II, Scene ii: "The multitudinous seas incarnadine." Two long words almost fill the line. In *Hamlet,* however, Shakespeare has the prince warn a strolling company of actors against mouthing great words and overacting.

One of Shakespeare's greatest gifts to our language was the tremendous number of phrases which have become familiar to our tongue. Here are a few:

laugh myself to death
brave new world
thereby hangs a tale
the tooth of time
the milk of human kindness
more in sorrow than in anger
more honored in the breach than the observance
one may smile and smile and be a villain
brevity is the soul of wit
the slings and arrows of outrageous fortune
the glass of fashion and the mold of form
we have seen better days.

A short session with Bartlett's *Familiar Quotations* will reveal dozens of others.

Like dress, language is subject to change of fashion. A great style-setter of Elizabethan days was a book by John Lyly called *Euphues* (ū'fū·ēz), intended to teach elegance of deportment and conversation to young courtiers. In language it was as full of frills and furbelows as one of Queen Elizabeth's costumes. At first Shakespeare, like everyone else, imitated its artificiality, but later he helped to laugh it out of style by his parodies on it. From the title of this book came the term *euphuism,* applied later to any highly mannered writing or speech.

Scholars and scientists used language with more restraint and orderliness than was customary among poets and playwrights. Bacon's essays show admirable neatness and balance of sentence structure. His thought is packed into small space and requires thinking over. Don't test your reading speed on a Bacon essay.

As a result of the work of the Humanists, education came to be more and more respected. Most people today remember Henry VIII as the man with six wives, but it is well to remember too that he was said to be the best-educated monarch that England had had up to that time. His daughter Elizabeth, who was well versed in Latin and Greek, carried on that tradition and proved that women were capable of higher learning. Schools where the study of Latin prevailed were now being rapidly established. The compiler of a Latin-English dictionary introduced Latin words into English as a means of expanding and beautifying the English tongue. Scholarly Sir Thomas More wrote his famous *Utopia* in Latin and expected his family to write letters to him in this language. The Humanists found English lacking in the abstract terms they needed for expressing their ideas, but Latin could supply them. Thus most of our abstract nouns come from Latin. The interest in man's relationship to other men and to the physical world around him brought in a whole new vocabulary. With innumerable Latin roots, prefixes, and suffixes to draw on, the possibilities for forming abstract words were endless. A few by way of illustration are *premise, deduction, reference, conclusion.*

In the schools Greek was now running a close second to Latin, and derivatives from Greek were appearing more and more. We have already mentioned poetic terms. *Criticism, rhetoric, philosophy* suggest other fields planted with Greek seeds. In fact most English words that begin with *rh* or that contain the roots *philo* (love), *tele* (far), *phon* (sound), to mention only a few, come from Greek sources. Ever since the Renaissance, Greek has been the gold mine from which to dig out scientific terms. He who discovers a species or makes an invention is likely to try a combination of Greek roots to name it.

Other languages that were drawn into the English stream in the sixteenth century were Spanish and American Indian. They entered chiefly by way of the New World. Spain had a foothold there before England and had already gathered names from the Indian tribes for various products. The best known in English today are *chocolate, cocoa, potato,* and *tobacco,* which have a flavor of both Indian and Spanish. Direct from Indian dialects strange words like *tomahawk, wampum,* and *wigwam* began to make their way across the Atlantic in the reports of the early settlers. Think of the new words that were to come pouring into English as discovery, commerce, and colonization developed in the centuries to come!

This woodcut, by the well-known English printer and illustrator Richard Pynson, is from an early hymnal. The switch leaning against the wall is for punishing disobedient students.

THE
SEVENTEENTH
CENTURY

1625–1700

T HIS is a very curious period, but it is only fair to add that many English historians and literary scholars prefer this age to any other. During most of it, England, though we should remember that now Scotland shared the same monarchy, steered both in her political and literary life a rather eccentric course entirely her own. Until the final years of this period, for example, what was being written in England was quite unlike what was being written elsewhere in Western Europe, just as public events in England did not reflect any general European pattern. It was a time when the English were out on their own, just going their own way.

POLITICAL UPHEAVAL

The English nowadays are considered a quiet, easygoing people, not given to fanaticism and violence. But in this period they horrified the rest of Europe. In the middle of it, they not only rebelled against their rightful sovereign, which was bad enough, but they then imprisoned and finally executed him. Later, disliking James II (1685–88), a militant Catholic in what was now a Protestant country, they got rid of him and invited a Dutch prince, William of Orange (1689–1702), who had married James' daughter Mary, to take the crown. But not on the same terms as those under which James and other Stuarts had ruled, for now the monarchy was a constitutional one, as it has been ever since.

◄ The items in the frontispiece are identified on page 269.

Welbeck Estates

Charles I

This means, broadly speaking, that the monarch reigns but does not rule, that real political power belongs not to the Crown but to Parliament.

The Civil War, which began in 1642, was a war between Charles I (1625–49) and those who sided with him, mostly landowners and country folk, and the Parliament forces, drawn mostly from London and the larger towns. It was a war between Cavaliers, long-haired, gay, and reckless, and the crop-headed, grimly determined Roundheads. (These are permanently opposed types of men, and you can find Cavaliers and Roundheads in any school or college group.) Victory went to Parliament in the end because it found in Oliver Cromwell a military leader of genius, whose New Model Army (known as "Ironsides") was probably the finest in Europe.

Calling himself the Protector, Cromwell (1653–58), ruling with the help of his major-generals, became in fact a dictator. He was extremely able and very soon raised the prestige of England abroad. But his Protectorate was unpopular with most of the English, whose idea of amusement was not psalm-singing and listening to very long sermons, and they were delighted when the monarchy was restored in 1660.

PURITANISM

Cromwell's triumph was really the triumph of Puritanism, the last it enjoyed on any great political scale in England. Serious and austere Christian believers, the Puritans, so-called because of their desire to purify their religion of the formal ceremonies practiced in the Church of England, wanted the freedom to follow their own consciences in matters of religious observance and the conduct of life. (Meanwhile, Puritanism had settled itself in New England, taking with it a trick of speaking in a nasal manner that the Puritans had had from the first. The later Elizabethan dramatists, who detested the Puritans, burlesqued this and other habits of theirs.) It is a mistake, however, to imagine that Puritanism vanished from the English scene after the Restoration of 1660. In a less exaggerated and aggressive form, discovered at its best in *Areopagitica,* Milton's noble plea for freedom of the press, it persisted throughout the next two-and-a-half centuries, influencing not only social legislation but also the development of literature. If the nineteenth-century English novelists were more restricted in their choice and handling of themes than French novelists were, this was due chiefly to the fact that the new large reading public in England had not escaped the influence of Puritanism.

But the original Puritans were very different from their nineteenth-century descendants. They were deeply religious, in a stern Old Testament

The Duke of Buccleuch
Oliver Cromwell

style, but condemned the church, the priesthood, and all ritualistic forms of worship, just as they also denounced playgoing, singing (except psalm-singing), dancing, and all popular amusements and pastimes. Macaulay said of them that they disliked bear-baiting not because it gave pain to the bear but because it gave pleasure to the spectators. Many of them were gloomy, bigoted, intolerant men, and some of them no doubt were as absurd as dramatists like Ben Jonson (1572–1637) made them out to be; but there was plenty of ability among them, and not only for trading and fighting. They produced writers of the stature of John Milton (1608–74) and John Bunyan (1628–88) and, in addition, some extremely original and audacious political theorists, chiefly known as "Levellers," because they wanted to make all men politically equal or level. There was indeed a great ferment of ideas among these English nonconformists and rebels.

SEVENTEENTH-CENTURY THEATER

The victorious Puritans closed the playhouses. (But troupes of actors still gave secret performances in large country houses, and it is surprising that no novelist or dramatist has ever made use of this amusing idea of a "bootlegged" theater.) It is easy, however, to make too much out of this closing of the playhouses. The glorious popular theater of the Elizabethans had disappeared years before the Puritans took action. The age of dramatic masterpieces had gone. Most of the popular enthusiasm had gone with it. The playhouses that were closed already existed in a kind of twilight. It was a drama in its decadence that was now forbidden to the public.

The theater came back with the Restoration, but it was very different from the Elizabethan theater. It was a theater for the court, the nobility, the men of fashion. Women's roles were now played by actresses, like the famous Nell Gwynn. Both the auditorium and the stage, quite unlike those of the Elizabethan playhouses, followed French and Italian models; and it is here, with a few differences, that the modern theater begins. That wonderful old stage, on which the action of Shakespearean drama passed so swiftly and imaginatively, was seen no more.

RESTORATION ENGLAND

The Restoration brought about many important changes, and to understand these we have to know something about the king himself, Charles II (1660-85). He was the eldest son of the unhappy Charles I; never were a father and son more unlike each other than these two. If the father had too much dignity

New York Public Library, Print Room

Charles II

and self-importance, his son had, if anything, too little. Tall, very swarthy, lazy, and dissipated, Charles II had great personal charm and plenty of intelligence, if not much conscience. His contemporaries declared that "he never said a foolish thing and never did a wise one." But this is unjust. He did many wise things, though he was anything but a dutiful, conscientious monarch, for he wasted money on trifles, secretly accepted a pension from Louis XIV, and, in spite of his oath to reign as a Protestant, was probably aways at heart a Catholic. But he was not a bigoted one, like his brother, afterwards James II.

During the reign of Charles II, the greatest European power was France, where the despotic if magnificent Louis XIV ruled from his new palace at Versailles. French influence in manners, literature, and the arts was now irresistible. The Restoration brought England out of its comparative isolation into this European orbit dominated by France. What was fashionable in Paris soon became fashionable in London, with the result that the French classical style and manner were soon imitated, in spite of the fact that London not long after the Restoration had terrible troubles entirely her own — namely, the Plague (1665) and the Great Fire (1666). The latter devastated the old city, which

BRITAIN
1485-1700

1 Site of royal palace in *Macbeth*.   2 Castle where Macbeth murdered Duncan.   3 Scottish kings crowned here.   4 Site of Macduff's castle.   5 York cycle of mystery plays given here, 15th–16th centuries.   6 Celebrated castle visited by Queen Elizabeth and described in Sir Walter Scott's *Kenilworth*.   7 Birth and burial place of William Shakespeare.   8 John Bunyan was imprisoned and wrote part of *Pilgrim's Progress* here.   9 Milton escaped from London plague here, 1665–66.   10 Famous school for boys; founded 1571.   11 Home of John Milton (1632–38).   12 Literary and cultural center. Shakespeare's plays, Sons of Ben, John Donne, Pepys flourished here.   13 Here stood the Globe Theater in which Shakespeare was actor and part owner.   14 Royal palace on the Thames; from time of Henry VIII, long a favorite residence of English kings.   15 Birthplace of Sir Philip Sidney (1564).   16 Robert Herrick was vicar here.   17 Pilgrims set sail for North America from here.

Guildhall Art Gallery

This painting by an unknown seventeenth-century artist suggests the great devastation wrought by the Great Fire of London of 1666.

was then rebuilt under the direction of the famous architect Christopher Wren.

We know a great deal about the intimate life of London in these times because Samuel Pepys (1633–1703), secretary of the navy, kept a diary, which was written in code shorthand and never intended to be published. Pepys is so completely candid about himself that he seems a rather quaint comic character (as most of us might seem if we put down the whole truth about ourselves), but he was in fact an excellent civil servant to whom the Royal Navy owed much. After his retirement he was made president of the Royal Society, composed of distinguished scientists, philosophers, and scholars, founded in London in 1662 under the direct patronage of Charles II, and still existing today.

INTELLECTUAL FERMENT

For all his indolence and frivolity, Charles II was interested in ideas, and he lived in the right time and place in which to discover them. This London of the Plague and the Great Fire, the city we discover so intimately and charmingly in Pepys' diary (you must pronounce his name as if it were spelled "peeps," by the way), was also the capital of the new scientific theories and experiments and philosophical ideas; the city of the great Isaac Newton (1642–1727), the mathematician and astronomer; of William Harvey (1578–1657), who discovered the circulation of the blood; of John Locke (1632–1704), whose *Essay concerning Human Understanding* described our mental processes, and whose influence on the eighteenth century was enormous. The new scientific and rational age was coming into existence in the London of Charles II.

Altogether, as we said at the beginning of this essay, this is a very curious period, not all of a piece as some other periods are, not confined to one great high road of thought and feeling, but breaking out, almost bursting, in many different directions. It is as if the instability and turbulence of the political scene set men thinking, feeling, writing, in widely different ways. There is no typical seventeenth-century outlook. Milton, the solemn Puritan, is a seventeenth-century poet; so is Robert Herrick (1591–1674), who wrote gay poems to pretty girls. They share only the time in which they lived.

THE NEW PROSE

But because there was this astonishing variety and because, under the pressure of dramatic events and new ideas, the men of this age went to extremes, literary forms were quick to change and develop during the seventeenth century. Prose writing offers us a particularly good example of this change and development. It moved in two different directions, though not quite at the same time. The earlier development, which can be found in Milton's prose or in the sermons of eloquent preachers like Jeremy Taylor (1613–67) and Sir Thomas Browne (1605–82), gives us writing of increasing complexity, in which sentences may branch out into dozens of relative clauses. It is prose quite unlike ordinary speech, elaborate in its structure, poetical in its richness of imagery, its tremendous sentences gleaming and glittering with images, like Christmas trees covered with glass ornaments and candles. The very richest English prose belongs to the seventeenth century.

The later development, taking place during the last twenty years of the century, is quite different, for instead of moving away from ordinary speech, it begins to reproduce much of the manner and rhythm of the best talk of the time. John Dryden (1631–1700), though primarily a poet, was an original master of this new kind of prose, and it could be argued that his exquisite perfection in it was really a greater achievement than anything he wrote in verse. The charm of Dryden's prose comes from the fact that while it seems to have the manner and rhythm of good talk, it has not entirely broken with the more poetical past and its bright imagery. Much earlier, Bacon in his essays had hammered out for himself a prose that suited him, but it is stiff and heavy compared with Dryden's prose, which dances and sparkles like the finest talk.

Late in the century, the dramatists, the creators of Restoration comedy, brought to the theater a similar prose style. As a stylist the master of this group was undoubtedly William Congreve (1670–1729), in spite of the fact that his comedies were written while he was still in his twenties, after which he gave up writing altogether. In other than stylistic respects Congreve was inferior to others in this group, notably William Wycherly (1640–1716) and later George Farquhar (1678–1707), for he was not as good as they in contriving acceptable plots and amusing situations. But at his best, in *The Way of the World*

(1700), which is still often played in the English theater, his dialogue is enchanting, wonderful prose for actors and actresses to speak. It is of course meant for the ear and not the eye, to be heard and not silently read, but this is in fact true of all good English prose, whether it is as solemn and stately as the Bible or Milton or as witty and frivolous as the dialogue of Congreve. To enjoy the best prose, you must *hear* it as you read it. Try to hear it and you will soon discover how much more alive and magical it is.

William and Mary

Welbeck Estates

THE GLORIOUS REVOLUTION

In 1688, James II had to flee the country, and his daughter Mary and her husband, William, ruler of Holland, jointly took the crown, reigning as the first constitutional monarchs, which, as we have seen already, meant that their power was severely limited. This was called the "Glorious Revolution," and was celebrated as such, quite justly too, because a complete and extremely important change had been made. The whole system of government had been reversed, and without violence and bloodshed. (And from now on, the English learned, as many other nations never did, that quiet revolutions are possible and that important political changes need not be violent and murderous.) The joint reign of William and Mary helped to create a new England.

FRENCH CULTURAL INFLUENCE

What it chiefly did was to put England squarely into the general European scene. William himself was the leading Protestant challenger of Louis XIV, easily the most powerful monarch in Europe and himself a militant Catholic. A little later, England, making full use of the military genius of the Duke of Marlborough (1650–1722), was able to attack and defeat the armies of Louis time after time, but the immediate social, cultural, and literary effect of England's taking her place in the European scene was that she inevitably came under the powerful influence of the French. The age ends, therefore, with the

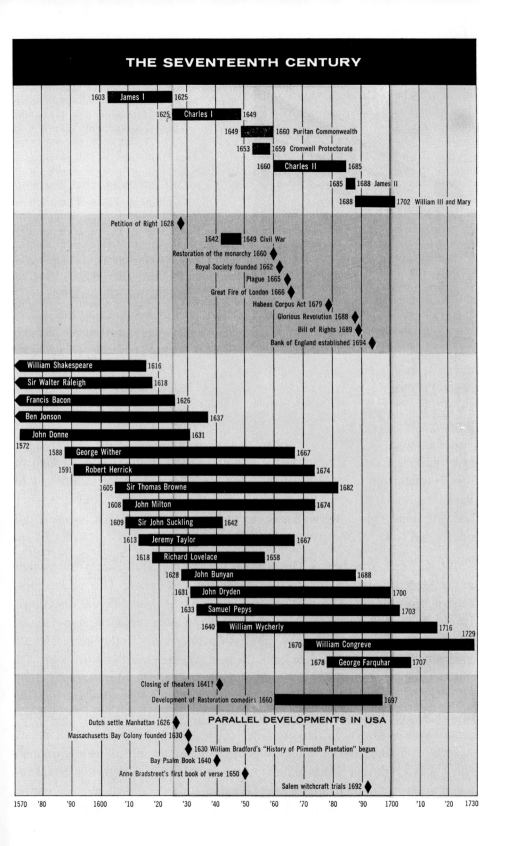

THE SEVENTEENTH CENTURY

1603 James I 1625
1625 Charles I 1649
1649 Puritan Commonwealth 1660
1653 Cromwell Protectorate 1659
1660 Charles II 1685
1685 James II 1688
1688 William III and Mary 1702

Petition of Right 1628
1642 Civil War 1649
Restoration of the monarchy 1660
Royal Society founded 1662
Plague 1665
Great Fire of London 1666
Habeas Corpus Act 1679
Glorious Revolution 1688
Bill of Rights 1689
Bank of England established 1694

William Shakespeare 1616
Sir Walter Ráleigh 1618
Francis Bacon 1626
Ben Jonson 1637
John Donne 1631
1572
1588 George Wither 1667
1591 Robert Herrick 1674
1605 Sir Thomas Browne 1682
1608 John Milton 1674
1609 Sir John Suckling 1642
1613 Jeremy Taylor 1667
1618 Richard Lovelace 1658
1628 John Bunyan 1688
1631 John Dryden 1700
1633 Samuel Pepys 1703
1640 William Wycherly 1716
1729
1670 William Congreve
1678 George Farquhar 1707

Closing of theaters 1641?
Development of Restoration comedies 1660 1697

PARALLEL DEVELOPMENTS IN USA

Dutch settle Manhattan 1626
Massachusetts Bay Colony founded 1630
1630 William Bradford's "History of Plimmoth Plantation" begun
Bay Psalm Book 1640
Anne Bradstreet's first book of verse 1650
Salem witchcraft trials 1692

1570   '80   '90   1600   '10   '20   '30   '40   '50   '60   '70   '80   '90   1700   '10   '20   1730

Christopher Wren, master architect of the seventeenth century, designed some of England's most beautiful buildings, among them St. Paul's Cathedral and the south side of Hampton Court Palace, which is pictured here.

Frank Monaco

triumph in London of what had long been triumphant in Paris. The French classical style and manners of Versailles were imitated in England. But there was always some difference, just because the English like to have at least something of their own way.

So the English poets, at the end of the century, were not *exactly* like the French poets. They obeyed some of the same rules, but not all. The dramatists, especially in tragedy, now kept one eye on the French, but not both eyes. And indeed in comedy, though the French (such as Corneille and Molière) were masters of the form, the English went very much their own way. And they began telling stories in their own way, which was chiefly a sober, realistic way, of which the master, soon to be discovered, was Daniel Defoe (1660?–1731). John Dryden, a kind of literary dictator, accepted much of what was dictated at Versailles and in Paris, but he too contrived to keep his essential Englishness. And in science and philosophy it was Paris that began to learn from London. Charles II did not found his Royal Society in vain.

We shall end as we began. This is a very curious period. It is surprisingly rich in the domestic arts, in architecture, furniture, and design. This period took English prose almost as far as it has ever gone, in two quite different directions. Its poetry, though rarely reaching the highest possible standard, shows us an astonishing variety, from the gay, careless Cavalier songs to the solemnities of Milton or the profound intricacies of the metaphysical and Platonist poets. Of these — poets like Cowley and Crashaw, Traherne and Vaughan — the earliest was also the greatest. This was John Donne (1572–1631), who was brought up as a Roman Catholic but later joined the Church of England and finally became Dean of St. Paul's. His sermons, often delivered in magnificent prose, were very popular, and certain passages from them are still frequently quoted. But it is as a poet that he has had the strongest influence, first during the seventeenth century and then, after a long period of almost complete neglect, on the poetry that followed immediately after World War I. Modern poets turned to him because he is both highly intellectual and impassioned and uses imagery in the modern manner, as if it were a kind of inspired shorthand. His chief weaknesses, which may be found in all his followers, are obscurity and a rather crabbed unmusical manner, song becoming argument.

Donne is often included among the Elizabethans. There is bound to be some confusion here, because many of the most famous Elizabethans — for example, Shakespeare and Ben Jonson — actually did their best work after James I had succeeded to the throne. But the true seventeenth century, as a literary period, arrives toward the end of James' reign, when the Elizabethan spirit in writing had vanished. This is how we have dealt with it here. It is a period that contains some of the most intimate records of ordinary life that we have ever had. It was a restless and often violent age, offering extremes and many contradictions, but nobody can deny that it was both fascinating and fruitful.

J. B. P.

JOHN DONNE
1572–1631

By gracious permission of Her Majesty Queen Elizabeth II

John Donne is more praised today than he was in any previous time. He is considered by some modern critics one of the great poets in English, although others complain that he twists both language and thought to an extreme. Donne was a nonconformist in literature. While the Elizabethans wrote of faithfulness in love, he praised inconstancy; while they celebrated beauty in life, Donne explored the dark paths of the mind; and while they depended on a fairly regular rhythm in verse, he varied lines, meter, and accent whenever he felt it necessary.

After attending Oxford, Donne led a gay, worldly life in London. He went on a military expedition to Spain and on his return was imprisoned for a time. Though he was born a Roman Catholic, later he was converted to the Church of England and became Dean of St. Paul's Cathedral, where he was famous as the most eloquent preacher of the day. His early poems are in the cynical, mundane vein of Cavalier writing; later he turned to metaphysical or philosophical themes and headed a group of Anglican poets who wrote intense poems that explore the intellectual and spiritual side of man. Donne and his followers were fond of writing an elaborate kind of verse, with farfetched and extravagant figures of speech, underlying paradoxes, and fanciful statements exaggerated for effect, called hyperboles (hī·pêr′bō·lēs).

Death Be Not Proud

Death be not proud, though some have called thee
Mighty and dreadful, for thou art not so;
For those whom thou think'st thou dost overthrow
Die not, poor Death; nor yet canst thou kill me.
From Rest and Sleep, which but thy picture be,   5
Much pleasure; then from thee much more must flow;
And soonest our best men with thee do go —
Rest of their bones and souls' delivery!

Thou 'rt slave to Fate, chance, kings, and desperate men,
And dost with poison, war, and sickness dwell;   10
And poppy° or charms can make us sleep as well
And better than thy stroke. Why swell'st° thou then?
One short sleep past, we wake eternally,
And Death shall be no more; Death, thou shalt die!

11. *poppy:* opium. 12. *swell'st:* that is, with pride.

The Tolling of the Bells

Meditation 17

"For whom the bell tolls" is a phrase that you know as the title of a novel by Ernest Hemingway. Did you know that it is a quotation from John Donne? While Donne was recovering from a serious illness, he recorded his daily thoughts. Later he used these notes for a book called *Devotions upon Emergent Occasions*. "For whom the bell tolls" comes from Meditation 17. Here, in Donne's prose, given in modern spelling, you find the same originality that you find in his poetry.

PERCHANCE he for whom this bell tolls may be so ill as that he knows not it tolls for him; and perchance I may think myself so much better than I am as that they who are about me and see my state may have caused it to toll for me, and I know not that.

The church is catholic, universal, so are all her actions; all that she does belongs to all. When she baptizes a child, that action concerns me; for that child is thereby connected to that body which is my head too, and ingrafted into that body whereof I am a member. And when she buries a man, that action concerns me.

All mankind is of one author, and is one volume; when one man dies, one chapter is not torn out of the book, but translated into a better language; and every chapter must be so translated. God employs several translators; some pieces are translated by age, some by sickness, some by war, some by justice; but God's hand is in every translation, and his hand shall bind up all our scattered leaves again for that library where every book shall lie open to one another.

As therefore the bell that rings to a sermon calls not upon the preacher only

[handwritten annotations: "High point of land or rock projecting into water", "bodily prominence."]

but upon the congregation to come, so this bell calls us all; but how much more me who am brought so near the door by this sickness! There was a contention as far as a suit — in which piety and dignity, religion and estimation, were mingled — which of the religious orders should ring to prayers first in the morning; and it was determined that they should ring first that rose earliest.

If we understand aright the dignity of this bell that tolls for our evening prayer, we would be glad to make it ours by rising early, in that application, that it might be ours as well as his, whose indeed it is.

The bell doth toll for him that thinks it doth; and though it intermit again, yet from that minute that that occasion wrought upon him he is united to God.

Who casts not up his eye to the sun when it rises? but who takes off his eye from a comet when that breaks out? Who bends not his ear to any bell which upon any occasion rings? but who can remove it from that bell which is passing a piece of himself out of this world?

No man is an island entire of itself; every man is a piece of the continent, a part of the main. If a clod be washed away by the sea, Europe is the less, as well as if a promontory were, as well as if a manor of thy friend's or of thine own were.

Any man's death diminishes me, because I am involved in mankind, and therefore never send to know for whom the bell tolls; it tolls for thee.

Neither can we call this a begging of misery or a borrowing of misery, as though we were not miserable enough of ourselves but must fetch in more from the next house, in taking upon us the misery of our neighbors. Truly it were an excusable covetousness if we did, for affliction is a treasure, and scarce any man hath enough of it. No man hath affliction enough that is not matured and ripened by it and made fit for God by that affliction.

If a man carry treasure in bullion or in a wedge of gold and have none coined into current money, his treasure will not defray him as he travels. Tribulation is treasure in the nature of it, but it is not current money in the use of it, except we get nearer and nearer our home, heaven, by it. Another man may be sick too, and sick to death, and this affliction may lie in his bowels as gold in a mine and be of no use to him; but this bell that tells me of his affliction digs out and applies that gold to me, if by this consideration of another's danger I take mine own into contemplation, and so secure myself by making my recourse to my God, who is our only security.

A PHILOSOPHICAL POET

1. What reasons does Donne give for believing death to be weak instead of powerful? How is sleep a "picture" of death? In what sense will death "die"?

2. Can you describe the verse form of this poem? Compare it for rhyme scheme with one of Shakespeare's poems on pages 121–26.

3. John Donne was seriously ill when he began composing Meditation 17. How did this illness affect his attitude toward death and life? How does Donne argue that affliction may benefit man? Do you agree?

4. Can you accept the statement that "no man is an island, entire of itself"? Defend your answer. What does Donne mean when he says "never send to know for whom the bell tolls; it tolls for thee"?

APPRECIATING FIGURATIVE LANGUAGE

After taking holy orders in 1614, John Donne became the most eloquent preacher in England. The prose style which characterized his sermons and devotions was unique. Since you have become familiar with similes and metaphors in the study of earlier selections, you should now realize that in both his poetry and prose Donne drew many comparisons with marked originality.

To express profound emotion in his sonnet "Death Be Not Proud," Donne uses personification, that figure of speech which gives to the lower animals, to inanimate objects, or to abstract ideas the characteristics of persons. Show how he has developed his theme by personifying death throughout the poem. What is the effect created by Donne in using this kind of device?

In the selection "The Tolling of the Bells," Donne uses a metaphor when he says, "All mankind is of one author, and is one volume." What is the implied comparison here? Notice that he proceeds to develop this metaphor in greater detail. How many additional comparisons does he add to the original one? Find another extended metaphor in this selection.

CAVALIER POETS

The lighter side of literature and life in the seventeenth century is reflected in the lyrics of the Cavalier poets. They sing of youth, love, happiness, and of beauty found in transient things; they take life as they find it — often with a mocking spirit.

GEORGE WITHER (1588–1667) was a curious combination of Cavalier and Puritan. Until the Civil War he apparently supported the Stuarts, and he wrote worldly poetry — love songs and pastoral lyrics. But he also wrote sharp social satires, and because of a poem attacking the government of Charles I, Wither was imprisoned for a long period. While in prison, he wrote an elaborate love poem containing the famous lyric "Shall I, Wasting in Despair." On being released he became a serious-minded Puritan and wrote hymns, psalms, and religious pamphlets.

RICHARD LOVELACE (1618–1658) was a gallant and handsome gentleman who spent his fortune and much of his time in prison for his king. He was born of a prominent and wealthy family and was educated at Oxford. For defending the deposed king, he was twice sent to prison, and while there composed a number of exquisite lyrics, including "To Althea, from Prison." Little is known of his last years, which were spent in poverty and obscurity. Lovelace's poetry and career are often paired with Suckling's. They were the perfect Cavaliers — brave soldiers, loyal courtiers, light of heart but sometimes satirical and mocking.

SIR JOHN SUCKLING (1609–1642) was a dashing and gifted young man who was knighted at twenty-one and became a leader in the court of Charles I. After leaving Cambridge, Suckling led an exciting life in London, gambling, cutting an elegant figure as a cavalier to the king, and joining a company of wits and poets who greatly admired Ben Jonson and called themselves "Sons of Ben." At the age of thrity-three Suckling was forced to flee to France, where he died mysteriously. One story says he committed suicide on losing all his money; another suggests he was murdered by a revengeful servant. The most colorful of the Cavalier poets, Suckling portrays the superficial and flippant attitudes of Stuart court life.

ROBERT HERRICK (1591–1674) was probably the greatest of the Cavalier poets. He wrote more than fourteen hundred poems that reflect his sunny disposition, his gaiety of manner, and also his often cynical view of the world. Herrick loved people. As one of the Sons of Ben, he spent carefree years in London. Then he took religious orders and became a vicar in Devonshire, where he found new enjoyment in the country festivals, feasts, and dances. Herrick was a strange clergyman, one whose love of nature and human pleasures was almost pagan. When the Commonwealth was established, Herrick lost his post, but with the restoration of Charles II in 1660, he returned to his vicarage to spend the rest of his life there.

Shall I, Wasting in Despair

GEORGE WITHER

Shall I, wasting in despair,
Die, because a woman's fair?
Or make pale my cheeks with care,
'Cause another's rosy are?
Be she fairer than the day,   5
Or the flowery meads in May,
  If she be not so to me,
  What care I how fair she be?

Should my heart be grieved or pined,
'Cause I see a woman kind?   10
Or a well-disposèd nature
Joinèd with a lovely feature?
Be she meeker, kinder than
Turtle dove, or pelican,°
  If she be not so to me,   15
  What care I how kind she be?

Shall a woman's virtues move
Me to perish for her love?
Or her well-deserving known,
Make me quite forget mine own?   20
Be she with that goodness blest
Which may gain her name of best,
  If she be not such to me,
  What care I how good she be?

'Cause her fortune seems too high,   25
Shall I play the fool and die?
Those that bear a noble mind,
Where they want° of riches find,
Think, "What, with them, they would do
That, without them, dare to woo!"   30
  And unless that mind I see,
  What care I though great she be?

Great, or good, or kind, or fair,
I will ne'er the more despair!
If she love me (this believe!)   35
I will die, ere she shall grieve;
If she slight me when I woo,
I can scorn, and let her go;
  For if she be not for me,
  What care I for whom she be?   40

14. *pelican:* a bird which was believed to tear open its breast in order to feed its offspring with its own blood. 28. *want:* lack.

To Althea,° from Prison

RICHARD LOVELACE

When Love with unconfinèd wings
  Hovers within my gates,
And my divine Althea brings
  To whisper at the grates;
When I lie tangled in her hair   5
  And fettered to her eye,
The birds that wanton° in the air
  Know no such liberty.

When flowing cups run swiftly round
  With no allaying Thames,°   10
Our careless heads with roses bound,
  Our hearts with loyal flames;
When thirsty grief in wine we steep,
  When healths and draughts go free —
Fishes that tipple in the deep   15
  Know no such liberty.

When, like committed linnets,° I
  With shriller throat shall sing
The sweetness, mercy, majesty,
  And glories of my king;°   20
When I shall voice aloud how good
  He is, how great should be,
Enlargèd° winds, that curl the flood,
  Know no such liberty.

Stone walls do not a prison make,   25
  Nor iron bars a cage;
Minds innocent and quiet take
  That for an hermitage;°
If I have freedom in my love
  And in my soul am free,   30
Angels alone, that soar above,
  Enjoy such liberty.

Title: *Althea* (ăl·thē′à). 7. *wanton* (wŏn′tŭn): play about. 9–10. *cups . . . Thames:* wine undiluted with water (from the river Thames). 17. *committed linnets:* caged birds. 20. *my king:* Charles I, in whose service Lovelace was "committed" to prison. Notice that his punishment did not dampen his enthusiasm for the king. 23. *Enlargèd:* set free or released. 27–28. *Minds . . . hermitage:* Even a prison may be suitable for quiet meditation.

*A young gallant,
as portrayed by
the English painter
Nicholas Hilliard.*

Victoria and Albert Museum

*To Lucasta,° on Going
to the Wars*

RICHARD LOVELACE

Tell me not, sweet, I am unkind,
  That from the nunnery
Of thy chaste breast and quiet mind
  To war and arms I fly.

True, a new mistress now I chase,   5
  The first foe in the field;
And with a stronger faith embrace
  A sword, a horse, a shield.

Yet this inconstancy is such
  As you, too, shall adore;   10
I could not love thee, dear, so much,
  Loved I not honor more.

Title: *Lucasta* (lṅ·kăs′tȧ).

The Constant Lover

SIR JOHN SUCKLING

Out upon it, I have loved
  Three whole days together!
And am like to love three more,
  If it prove fair weather.

Time shall molt away his wings   5
  Ere he shall discover
In the whole wide world again
  Such a constant lover.

But the spite on 't is, no praise
  Is due at all to me: 10
Love with me had made no stays,
  Had it any been but she.

Had it any been but she,
  And that very face,
There had been at least ere this   15
  A dozen dozen in her place.

Song from *Aglaura*°

SIR JOHN SUCKLING

Why so pale and wan, fond lover?
  Prithee, why so pale?
Will, when looking well can't move her,
  Looking ill prevail?
  Prithee, why so pale?   5

Why so dull and mute, young sinner?
  Prithee, why so mute?
Will, when speaking well can't win her,
  Saying nothing do 't?
  Prithee, why so mute?   10

Quit, quit for shame! This will not move;
  This cannot take her.
If of herself she will not love,
  Nothing can make her:
  The devil take her!   15

Title: *Aglaura* (á-glô′rä): a drama by Suckling, performed with great magnificence of scenery and costume at Blackfriars Theater.

Counsel to Girls

ROBERT HERRICK

Gather ye rosebuds while ye may,
  Old Time is still° aflying:
And this same flower that smiles today,
  Tomorrow will be dying.   4

The glorious Lamp of Heaven, the Sun,
  The higher he's agetting
The sooner will his race be run,
  And nearer he's to setting.   8

That age is best which is the first,
  When youth and blood are warmer;
But being spent, the worse, and worst
  Times, still succeed the former.   12

Then be not coy, but use your time;
  And while ye may, go marry:
For having lost but once your prime,
  You may forever tarry.   16

2. *still:* always.

LIGHT AND COURTLY LYRICS

1. In "To Althea," what three kinds of liberty are described? Note in the first three stanzas the comparison with something in nature. In what ways is the choice appropriate for each stanza? How does the fourth stanza form a climax to the three stanzas that precede it?

2. What subtle compliment does Lovelace pay Lucasta in the last stanza of the poem addressed to her? The last two lines summarize a Cavalier view of life. Why would this declaration be especially pleasing to a Cavalier lady?

3. "The Constant Lover" professes a lighthearted, even cynical attitude toward love. Do you find any evidence that this outward cynicism conceals a genuine emotion?

4. How does Herrick's point of view in "Counsel to Girls" accord with what you learned about Herrick on page 226?

5. Do you see any relation between the verse of Herrick and Lovelace and that of Ben Jonson? How would you compare and contrast the Elizabethan and Cavalier attitudes toward love, liberty, war, and duty?

Is there a difference between the mood and the singing quality of lyrics in the two periods?

6. Explain the difference in spirit between Lovelace's poems and those of Wither and Suckling.

7. Find, for reading aloud in class or for recording, additional Cavalier lyrics by these and other poets in an anthology like Palgrave's *Golden Treasury*.

8. What modern writers of light satiric verse do you know?

DRAWING CONCLUSIONS

1. What conclusion about the times do you draw from the fact that four of the seventeenth century's best-known writers — Wither, Lovelace, Suckling, and John Bunyan — were imprisoned at various periods? What effect might such times be expected to have on the production of literature?

2. Point out the lines from these lyrics which best reflect the attitudes and interests of the sophisticated court society to which the Cavalier poets belonged.

JOHN MILTON

1608–1674

New York Public Library

"Thy soul was like a star and dwelt apart," wrote Wordsworth of John Milton, who overshadowed all other poets of the seventeenth century and stands as one of the great figures of English literature. John Milton is known as the foremost representative of English Puritanism in literature, yet he was not the kind of person that the word "Puritan" might convey to you. The picture that many of us have of early American Puritans — black-frocked, joy-killing people who went about with gloomy thoughts and were given to witch hunting — certainly does not fit John Milton, who took great pleasure in living and in art and who defended freedom for all.

When the *Mayflower* landed in America in 1620, Milton was twelve years old. At this time he was studying at St. Paul's School in London to prepare himself for the ministry, the vocation to which his mother had directed him. Milton's parents provided a home in which the culture of the Renaissance was combined with the righteous life of the Puritans. His father, an accomplished musician and composer, played the organ and taught his son to play. From both his father and mother, John inherited the love for music that is reflected in his poetry. At the age of sixteen, Milton went to Cambridge, where he had an interesting and brilliant career. He won the esteem of his fellow students for his scholarship and for his skill in fencing and debating.

Milton's life seems to have revolved around three great decisions. The first one was taken at the university, where he gave up the idea of taking orders in the Anglican Church. He felt that he could not be bound by fixed creeds and doctrines but must be free to worship God in his own way. He always remained intensely religious, however, and he came to feel that poetry was a sacred calling, and the true poet, a priest.

After receiving his master's degree from Cambridge in 1632, Milton lived quietly for five years on his father's estate in Horton, twenty miles outside of London. Here he studied classical literature and prepared himself for a poet's career. During this period he wrote many of his shorter poems. It was in the small village of Horton that he led the idyllic life which he describes in the poem "L'Allegro," which you will read. Here in this peaceful valley of the Thames, where every sight and sound awoke in him thoughts of the classical mythology which he had studied, he took just such early morning walks as he describes in his poetry. On occasion, he went into London to see a play or buy a book.

In his poem "Il Penseroso," probably written about the same time and under the same circumstances as "L'Allegro," Milton recalls the joys of contemplation. However, it was probably at Cambridge, where Milton had enjoyed the beauty and the quiet of cloister and chapel, that he first experienced the meditative kind of happiness which he describes in "Il Penseroso."

At Horton, Milton also wrote "Comus," a masque (a special form of drama in verse) expressing the dedication of his life and talents to whatever service God had in store for him. In this poem Milton uses mythological characters in an idealized setting to develop the Puritan theme of the power of temperance over intemperance. In "Lycidas," written in the same period, he questions for the first time his own past, present, and future, and the religious meaning of life and death. Milton composed this pastoral elegy as his contribution to a collection of poems written by Cambridge students in memory of a classmate, Edward King, who had drowned in the Irish Sea shortly after graduation. "Lycidas" is an early attempt by Milton to justify the ways of God to man; its theme and emotional intensity are under the poet's strict artistic control.

In 1638 Milton left Horton and, supplied with introductions to the learned men of his time, went abroad to spend two years traveling in Europe. He particularly enjoyed his visit to Italy, the country whose melodious language and rich culture he came to know as did few men of his time. A highlight of his Italian sojourn was his introduction to Galileo, the famous scientist, who was now old and blind. Milton's travels were curtailed by news of religious and political trouble at home. On his return to England, he settled in London and took in private pupils. You can find theories about teaching in his tract *Of Education,* which includes an outline of a very ambitious course of study and an exposition of his theories as to the aims and purposes of education.

At this time, Milton was forced to make a second important decision. What part would he play in the civil war threatening England? Soon, putting aside most of his writing of poetry, he plunged into politics. He became a pamphleteer on behalf of church reform and joined the Puritans in Parliament who were then challenging the tyranny of King Charles I. The times were rough, and Milton used his literary weapons well, championing freedom and order in government and the personal rights of men. Unlike many Puritans of his time, he advocated granting religious freedom to certain minor sects. He pub-lished in 1644 his greatest work in English prose, the *Areopagitica* (ăr′ē·ŏp′á·jĭt′-ĭ·ká), a plea for freedom of the press — an early, perhaps the first, effective statement of a political ideal which is now recognized among all English-speaking peoples.

A third decision had to be made when Milton found himself threatened by blindness. His early years of constant study had weakened his eyesight, and now he was in danger of losing his sight entirely. Giving up his political work might have saved him from this, but the call of duty was powerful. Charles I, convicted of high treason by the parliamentary majority led by Oliver Cromwell, had been beheaded. Europe was aghast, and many Englishmen themselves were horrified by the deed. A few months later, England was declared a republic — a Commonwealth. Milton, as Cromwell's Latin Secretary, was left with the job of defending the course of the Commonwealth, and, despite his weakened eyesight, he continued to write tracts. At the age of forty-four, he went completely blind.

The last years of Milton's life were marked by tragedy. After the death of Cromwell, the Puritan political power declined. The monarchy was restored in 1660, and Charles II, the son of Charles I, came to the throne. With the regime of Charles II came the persecution and imprisonment of those who had aided in executing his father. As a defender of this execution, Milton was imprisoned for a time. He was released upon payment of a heavy fine and then retired from public life.

The early years of his retirement, however, were not happy ones. The restoration of the House of Stuart under Charles II destroyed everything for which Milton had fought. He was at the height of his literary powers, but he was blind and helpless and his family life was unsettled. His first wife, with whom he had lived happily, had died in 1652 and left him with three small girls. For three years he attempted to bring them up alone, but in 1655 he married again. His second wife died shortly after their marriage. Finally, in 1663 he married a third time. In this marriage Milton found the comfort, security, and happiness he needed for the completion of his work.

It was during these last ten years of his life that Milton, totally blind, completed his great long poems, often dictating them to his daughters. These poems, *Paradise Lost, Paradise Regained,* and *Samson Agonistes,* differ in their form and content, but they are related parts of a magnificent poetic theme to which Milton had dedicated himself while still a young man. *Paradise Lost* and *Paradise Regained* are epics having as their theme man's sins against God and his attempts to regain God's grace. *Samson Agonistes* is modeled on the form of the Greek tragedies but has a Biblical theme — the story of the heroic figure Samson, blinded and held in captivity by the Philistines. This theme closely parallels Milton's own misfortunes. Of these poems *Paradise Lost,* begun in 1658 and published in 1667, is the most famous. Its more than ten thousand lines of grand, vigorous, and marvelously varied blank verse constitute perhaps the finest artistic achievement of the Puritan Age in England.

L'Allegro and Il Penseroso

All of us are creatures of moods that color our thinking and our responses to the passing world. There are times when we enjoy the amusing companionship of friends, the noise of holiday crowds, laughter, lively music, dancing, exciting stories — the lighter things of life. Other times we feel less active and want to be alone, quiet, thoughtful. At such times we need music or reading that harmonizes with our pensive mood.

"L'Allegro" and "Il Penseroso" are twin poems that capture and contrast the moods of the cheerful man and the thoughtful man, as the Italian titles indicate. In the first title you will recognize the musical term *allegro,* meaning "quick" or "lively"; and in the second, you may detect the root for the word "pensive." In the first poem the poet addresses Mirth as a gay, dancing nymph and asks her to accompany him in the sunlit fields of the country. In the second poem, he dismisses "vain, deluding joys" and welcomes Melancholy, who is pictured as a nun, to be with him in the nightly solitude of his study. However, Milton does not speak of melancholy as a sorrowful thing but rather as a pleasantly reflective turn of mind. We can imagine that he himself enjoyed both moods at his country place at Horton, where he took part in the pastoral life, and where he was also able to shut himself up with his books and music.

It was the custom in Milton's day to introduce lyrics like these with a display of allusions to the classics. The opening lines of each poem, crammed with mythological references, have been omitted here.

L'Allegro

Haste thee, nymph, and bring with thee
Jest, and youthful Jollity,
Quips and cranks° and wanton wiles,°
Nods and becks and wreathèd smiles,
Such as hang on Hebe's° cheek,   5
And love to live in dimple sleek;
Sport that wrinkled Care derides,
And Laughter holding both his sides.
Come, and trip it as you go,
On the light fantastic toe;   10
And in thy right hand lead with thee

The mountain nymph, sweet Liberty;
And if I give thee honor due,
Mirth, admit me of thy crew,
To live with her, and live with thee,   15
In unreprovèd° pleasures free:

[COUNTRY SCENE AT MORN]

To hear the lark begin his flight,
And singing, startle the dull night,
From his watchtower in the skies,
Till the dappled dawn doth rise;   20
Then to come in spite of sorrow,

---

3. *cranks:* twists or turns in speech; *wanton wiles:* playful tricks. 5. *Hebe* (hē′bē): cupbearer to the Greek gods.

16. *unreprovèd:* not deserving of censure.

"A Young Man Playing on a Lute," attributed to Francis Barlow (1626–1702).

And at my window bid good morrow,
Through the sweetbrier or the vine,
Or the twisted eglantine;°
While the cock, with lively din,   25
Scatters the rear of darkness thin,
And to the stack, or the barn door,
Stoutly struts his dames before:
Oft listening how the hounds and horn°
Cheerly rouse the slumbering morn,   30
From the side of some hoar hill,
Through the high wood echoing shrill;
Sometime walking, not unseen,
By hedgerow elms,° on hillocks green,
Right against the eastern gate   35
Where the great sun begins his state,°
Robed in flames and amber light,
The clouds in thousand liveries dight;°
While the plowman, near at hand,
Whistles o'er the furrowed land,   40
And the milkmaid singeth blithe,
And the mower whets his scythe,
And every shepherd tells his tale°
Under the hawthorn° in the dale.
Straight mine eye hath caught new
    pleasures   45
Whilst the landskip° round it measures:

Russet lawns and fallows gray,
Where the nibbling flocks do stray;
Mountains on whose barren breast
The laboring clouds do often rest;   50
Meadows trim with daisies pied,°
Shallow brooks and river wide;
Towers and battlements it sees
Bosomed high in tufted trees,
Where perhaps some beauty lies,   55
The cynosure° of neighboring eyes.

[PLEASURES OF THE COUNTRY]

Hard by, a cottage chimney smokes
From betwixt two agèd oaks,
Where Corydon and Thyrsis° met
Are at their savory dinner set   60
Of herbs and other country messes,°
Which the neat-handed Phyllis dresses;
And then in haste her bower° she leaves,
With Thestylis to bind the sheaves;
Or, if the earlier season lead,   65
To the tanned haycock in the mead.
Sometimes, with secure delight,
The upland hamlets will invite,
When the merry bells ring round,
And the jocund rebecks° sound   70

24. *eglantine*: (ĕg′lăn·tĭn) honeysuckle.
29. *hounds and horn:* of hunters. 34. *hedgerow
elms:* elm trees planted in rows for enclosure or
separation of fields. 36. *state:* stately progress.
38. This line pictures the clouds dressed (*dight:*
dīt) in colors from the sun, as servants are
clothed in *liveries* by their master. 43. *tells his
tale:* counts his sheep. 44. *hawthorn:* a tree or
shrub with shiny leaves and white or pink
fragrant flowers. 46. *landskip:* landscape.

51. *pied* (pīd): of two or more colors.
56. *cynosure* (sī′nō·shōōr): the center of
attention. 59. *Corydon* (kŏr′ĭ·dŏn) *and Thyrsis*
(thûr′sĭs): conventional names for rustics or
shepherds in pastoral poetry, as *Phyllis* and
Thestylis (thĕs′tĭ·lĭs), in lines 62 and 64, are for
country maidens. 61. *messes:* dishes. 63. *bower:*
a rustic cottage or room. 70. *jocund rebecks*
(jŏk′ŭnd rē′bĕks): merry violins.

British Museum

To many a youth and many a maid
Dancing in the checkered shade;
And young and old come forth to play
On a sunshine holiday,
Till the livelong daylight fail: 75
Then to the spicy nut-brown ale,
With stories told of many a feat,
How faery Mab° the junkets° eat.
She° was pinched and pulled, she said;
And he, by friar's lantern° led,   80
Tells how the drudging goblin° sweat
To earn his cream bowl duly set,
When in one night, ere glimpse of morn,
His shadowy flail hath threshed the corn
That ten day laborers could not end;   85
Then lies him down, the lubber fiend,°
And, stretched out all the chimney's
    length
Basks at the fire his hairy strength,
And crop-full out of doors he flings,
Ere the first cock his matin° rings.   90
Thus done the tales, to bed they creep,
By whispering winds soon lulled asleep.

[PLEASURES OF THE CITY]

Towered cities please us then,
And the busy hum of men,
Where throngs of knights and barons
    bold,   95
In weeds° of peace high triumphs°
    hold,
With store of ladies, whose bright eyes
Rain influence,° and judge the prize

Of wits or arms, while both contend
To win her grace whom all commend.
There let Hymen° oft appear   101
In saffron robe, with taper clear,
And pomp and feast and revelry,
With mask and antique pageantry;
Such sights as youthful poets dream   105
On summer eves by haunted stream.
Then to the well-trod stage anon,
If Jonson's learnèd sock° be on.
Or sweetest Shakespeare, Fancy's child,
Warble his native wood-notes° wild.
And ever, against eating cares,°   111
Lap me in soft Lydian airs,°
Married to immortal verse,
Such as the meeting° soul may pierce,°
In notes with many a winding bout   115
Of linkèd sweetness long drawn out,
With wanton heed and giddy cunning,
The melting voice through mazes run-
    ning,
Untwisting all the chains that tie
The hidden soul of harmony;   120
That Orpheus'° self may heave his head
From golden slumber on a bed
Of heaped Elysian flowers, and hear
Such strains as would have won the ear
Of Pluto to have quite set free   125
His half-regained Eurydice.
    These delights if thou canst give,
    Mirth, with thee I mean to live.

78. *faery Mab:* probably a fairy of Welsh folklore. (A famous description of how she brings dreams is in *Romeo and Juliet,* Act I, Scene iv, lines 53–95); *junkets:* delicate sweetmeats, often made of curdled milk. 79. *She:* one of the rustic maids. 80. *friar's lantern:* sometimes called "will-o'-the-wisp" or "friar's rush"; a dancing light on marshy ground, supposed to lead travelers astray. 81. *drudging goblin:* Robin Goodfellow, who supposedly did chores at night to earn the food put out for him. 86. *lubber fiend:* awkward sprite. 90. *matin:* a morning song, or call to early prayers. 96. *weeds:* garments; *triumphs:* public shows or pageants. 97–98. *whose . . . influence:* The stars were once thought to affect human action; hence, the bright eyes of the ladies are compared to stars.

101. *Hymen* (hī′měn): Greek god of marriage. The smoking of his torch or taper was considered a bad omen; hence, *with taper clear* (line 102) would signify a happy marriage. 108. *sock:* symbolic of comedy, as the buskin or boot is of tragedy. 110. *native wood-notes:* implying that Shakespeare's verse is as natural as the singing of a bird, in contrast with the more "learned" poetry of Jonson. 111. *against eating cares:* as a protection against worries which eat up one's vitality. 112. *Lydian* (lĭd′ĭ·ăn) *airs:* soft melodies. Lydian is the name of one of the "modes" (varieties) of ancient Greek music. 114. *meeting:* responsive; *pierce:* comprehend. 121. *Orpheus* (ôr′fē·ŭs): the most famous musician of Greek mythology, who persuaded Pluto, king of the dead, to release his dead wife, *Eurydice* (û·rĭd′ĭ·sē). The condition was that Orpheus should not look back while leading her to the upper world; but he forgot himself at the last minute, and so lost her completely.

Il Penseroso

Come, pensive Nun, devout and pure,
Sober, steadfast, and demure,
All in a robe of darkest grain,°
Flowing with majestic train,
And sable stole of cypress lawn°   5
Over thy decent shoulders drawn.
Come, but keep thy wonted state,
With even step, and musing gait,
And looks commercing with the skies,
Thy rapt soul sitting in thine eyes: 10
There, held in holy passion still,
Forget thyself to marble,° till
With a sad leaden downward cast
Thou fix them on the earth as fast.
And join with thee calm Peace, and
    Quiet,   15
Spare° Fast, that oft with gods doth diet,
And hear the Muses in a ring
Aye round about Jove's altar sing;
And add to these retirèd Leisure,   19
That in trim gardens takes his pleasure;
But first, and chiefest, with thee bring
Him that yon soars on golden wing,
Guiding the fiery-wheelèd throne,
The cherub Contemplation.

[BEAUTIES OF A MOONLIT EVENING]

And the mute Silence hist along,   25
'Less Philomel° will deign a song,
In her sweetest, saddest plight,°
Smoothing the rugged brow of Night,
While Cynthia° checks her dragon yoke
Gently o'er the accustomed oak.   30
Sweet bird, that shunn'st the noise of
    folly,
Most musical, most melancholy!
Thee, chauntress,° oft the woods among,
I woo, to hear thy evensong;
And, missing thee, I walk unseen   35

The Pierpont Morgan Library

*"Melancholy," by William Blake, painted
expressly to illustrate "Il Penseroso."*

On the dry smooth-shaven green,
To behold the wandering moon
Riding near her highest noon,
Like one that had been led astray
Through the heaven's wide pathless
    way,   40
And oft, as if her head she bowed,
Stooping through a fleecy cloud.
Oft, on a plat of rising ground,
I hear the far-off curfew sound
Over some wide-watered shore,   45
Swinging slow with sullen roar.

[DELIGHTS OF THE FIRESIDE]

Or if the air will not permit,
Some still removèd place will fit,
Where glowing embers through the
    room
Teach light to counterfeit a gloom,   50
Far from all resort of mirth,
Save the cricket on the hearth,
Or the bellman's drowsy charm°
To bless the doors from nightly harm.

---

3. *grain:* dye. 5. *sable . . . lawn:* black veil of
crape. 12. *Forget thyself to marble:* become so
completely engrossed in thought that you seem
a marble statue. 16. *Spare:* an adjective, "lean."
26. *Philomel* (fĭl'ō-mĕl): the nightingale.
27. *plight:* mood. 29. *Cynthia* (sĭn'thĭ·à): or
Diana, the moon goddess, whose chariot was
drawn by dragons, and to whom the oak was
sacred. 33. *chauntress* (chôn'trĕs): a singer.

53. *bellman's drowsy charm:* night watchman's calling of the hours as he guarded the
streets.

[PLEASURES OF READING]

Or let my lamp, at midnight hour,   55
Be seen in some high lonely tower
Where I may oft outwatch the Bear°
With thrice-great Hermes,° or unsphere
The spirit of Plato,° to unfold   59
What worlds or what vast regions hold
The immortal mind that hath forsook
Her mansion in this fleshly nook;
And of those demons° that are found
In fire, air, flood, or underground,
Whose power hath a true consent,°   65
With planet or with element.
Sometime let gorgeous Tragedy
In sceptered pall° come sweeping by,
Presenting Thebes,° or Pelops'° line,
Or the tale of Troy° divine,   70
Or what (though rare) of later age
Ennobled hath the buskined stage.°
But, O sad Virgin! that thy power
Might raise Musaeus° from his bower;
Or bid the soul of Orpheus° sing   75
Such notes as, warbled to the string,
Drew iron tears down Pluto's cheek,
And made Hell grant what love did seek;
Or call up him that left half-told°
The story of Cambuscan bold,   80
Of Camball, and of Algarsife,
And who had Canace to wife
That owned the virtuous ring and glass,

And of the wondrous horse of brass,
On which the Tartar king did ride;   85
And if aught else great bards beside
In sage and solemn tunes have sung,
Of tourneys, and of trophies hung,
Of forests, and enchantments drear,
Where more is meant than meets the
    ear.   90

[BEAUTY OF A RAINY MORN]

Thus, Night, oft see me in thy pale ca-
    reer,
Till civil-suited° Morn appear,
Not tricked and frounced° as she was
    wont
With the Attic boy° to hunt,
But kerchiefed in a comely cloud,   95
While rocking winds are piping loud;
Or ushered with a shower still,
When the gust hath blown his fill,
Ending on the rustling leaves,   99
With minute drops from off the eaves.

[A SHADY WOOD]

And when the sun begins to fling
His flaring beams, me, Goddess, bring
To archèd walks of twilight groves,
And shadows brown, that Sylvan° loves,
Of pine, or monumental oak   105
Where the rude ax with heavèd stroke
Was never heard the nymphs to daunt,
Or fright them from their hallowed
    haunt.
There in close covert by some brook,
Where no profaner eye may look,   110
Hide me from day's garish eye,
While the bee, with honeyed thigh,
That at her flowery work doth sing,
And the waters murmuring,
With such consort as they keep,   115
Entice the dewy-feathered Sleep;
And let some strange mysterious dream

57. *outwatch the Bear:* to stay awake all night, for the constellation of the Bear never sets. 58, 59. *Hermes* (hûr'mēz): the Egyptian god of wisdom; *Plato* (plā'tō): a Greek philosopher who wrote on the immortality of the soul. 63. *demons:* According to Plato there were four elements: earth, water, air, fire. Later philosophers taught that each had its own presiding spirit, or "demon." 65. *consent:* harmony. 68. *sceptered pall:* a kingly robe or cloak. 69, 70. *Thebes* (thēbz), *Pelops'* (pē'lŏps) *line, Troy:* subjects of Greek tragedies. 72. *buskined stage:* Buskins were high boots worn by ancient actors to give dignity; hence, they are a symbol of tragedy as the sock was of comedy. 74. *Musaeus* (mū·zē'ŭs): a poet in mythology. 75. *soul of Orpheus:* See note on Orpheus for line 121 of "L'Allegro." 79. *him . . . half-told:* Chaucer never finished the Squire's Tale, a romantic, mysterious story described in the next few lines.

92. *civil-suited:* in the sober garb of a citizen. 93. *tricked and frounced:* dressed in gay robes, probably with hair curled. 94. *Attic boy:* Cephalus (sĕf'á·lŭs), a young huntsman of Attica, beloved by Aurora, the dawn. 104. *Sylvan:* Sylvanus (sĭl·vā'nŭs), god of the woodlands.

Wave at his wings in airy stream
Of lively portraiture displayed,
Softly on my eyelids laid;   120
And as I wake, sweet music breathe
Above, about, or underneath,
Sent by some spirit to mortals good,
Or the unseen Genius of the wood.°

[INSPIRATION WITHIN A CHURCH]

But let my due feet never fail   125
To walk the studious cloister's pale,°
And love the high embowèd roof,
With antique pillars massy proof,°
And storied windows richly dight,°
Casting a dim religious light.   130

124. *Genius . . . wood:* The ancient Greeks
believed that a benign deity dwelt in every
grove. 126. *pale:* boundary. 128. *massy proof:*
able to bear the weight they support.
129. *storied . . . dight:* richly colored stained-
glass windows telling Bible stories.

There let the pealing organ blow
To the full-voiced quire below
In service high and anthems clear
As may with sweetness, through mine
    ear,
Dissolve me into ecstasies,   135
And bring all Heaven before mine eyes.

[SATISFACTIONS OF OLD AGE]

And may at last my weary age
Find out the peaceful hermitage,
The hairy gown and mossy cell,
Where I may sit and rightly spell°   140
Of every star that heaven doth shew,
And every herb that sips the dew,
Till old experience do attain
To something like prophetic strain.   144
    These pleasures, Melancholy, give
    And I with thee will choose to live.

140. *spell:* learn the meaning by study.

TWIN POEMS

1. These poems are full of appeal to the senses, especially in their words of color and sound. Select some lines that seem especially rich in their pictures and sound effects. Did you find lines that you had heard quoted before you read the poem?

2. Analyze the characters of the cheerful man and the pensive man as Milton presents them. How are they different? Are they alike in any respect? Do you think they are young men or older men?

3. Would you consider these two poems examples of pastoral poetry? Why or why not? Are the country people treated romantically or realistically? Prove your points by referring to details in the poems.

4. What lines or words in the poems tell you that Milton was a musician? List some pieces of music that you feel harmonize with the moods of the two poems. If possible, bring records to play to the class and follow with a class discussion. What does the music contribute to your appreciation of the poems?

5. Note the many mythological references in these two poems and look up the stories behind these references.

RECOGNIZING MOOD IN POETRY

1. Examine the structure of the two poems carefully. They are written flawlessly in the same meter. Yet in one the words trip gaily; in the other they move in stately dignity. How does the poet achieve this effect? Point out how it is done by (*a*) choice of words, (*b*) characters, (*c*) scenes, (*d*) other devices.

2. Make two parallel columns and compare the resemblances and differences of the two poems on the following points: (*a*) time of day and the period of a man's life covered; (*b*) companions chosen; (*c*) references to objects in nature — birds, heavenly bodies, sounds, others; (*d*) references to literature and music.

SUGGESTIONS FOR WRITING

1. Write your own "L'Allegro" and "Il Penseroso," telling where you like to be and what you like to do when in these different moods.

2. Describe a country scene with which you are familiar, making it clearly American. Is there anything in the American scene that might correspond to the castle towers in the English landscape?

Short Poems

"On Shakespeare," the first short poem here, is to be found in the second edition of Shakespeare's plays and is the first of Milton's poems to be published. It is not likely that Milton ever saw Shakespeare (he was eight when Shakespeare died), and it may be that this tribute was inspired by Jonson's poem (see page 199), which appeared in the first edition of Shakespeare.

Like Shakespeare, Milton excelled in writing sonnets, though he did not produce as many or compose them in any sequence. "On His Having Arrived at the Age of Twenty-three" shows him as an earnest youth, on the threshold of his literary career. He wrote it at the time he was either writing or had just completed "L'Allegro" and "Il Penseroso."

The second sonnet was written twenty years later, when Milton was forty-four and blind but ready to embark on his greatest works. You will notice that the rhyme scheme is different from either Spenser's or Shakespeare's. This is the true Italian form — two quatrains (four-line stanzas) forming an octave (eight lines), always using the rhyme scheme *abba*. The concluding sestet (six lines) may have two or three rhymes, and they may fall in any order the poet chooses.

On Shakespeare

What needs my Shakespeare for his honored bones
The labor of an age in pilèd stones?
Or that his hallowed relics should be hid
Under a star-ypointing pyramid?
Dear son of memory, great heir of fame,   5
What need'st thou such weak witness of thy name?
Thou in our wonder and astonishment
Hast built thyself a livelong monument.
For whilst, to the shame of slow-endeavoring art,
Thy easy numbers flow, and that each heart   10
Hath from the leaves of thy unvalued° book
Those Delphic° lines with deep impression took,
Then thou, our fancy of itself bereaving,
Dost make us marble° with too much conceiving,
And so sepulchred° in such pomp dost lie   15
That kings for such a tomb would wish to die.

11. *unvalued:* beyond any fixed value. 12. *Delphic* (dĕl'fĭk): prophetic or inspired; relating to the oracle at ancient Delphi. 14. *Dost . . . marble:* as still as marble through our thoughtful attention. Milton uses the same figure in "Il Penseroso," line 12. 15. *sepulchred* (here, sĕp·ŭl'kĕrd, but usually accented on the first syllable): put in a tomb.

On His Having Arrived at the Age of Twenty-three

How soon hath Time, the subtle thief of youth,
Stolen on his wing my three-and-twentieth year!
My hasting days fly on with full career,
But my late spring no bud or blossom shew'th.
Perhaps my semblance might deceive the truth   5
That I to manhood am arrived so near;
And inward ripeness doth much less appear,
That some more timely-happy spirits endu'th.°
Yet be it less or more, or soon or slow,
It shall be still in strictest measure even   10
To that same lot, however mean or high,
Toward which Time leads me, and the will of **Heaven.**
All is, if I have grace to use it so,
As ever in my great Taskmaster's eye.

8. *endu'th:* endows.

On His Blindness

	Rhyme scheme	
When I consider how my light is spent	*a*	
Ere half my days, in this dark world and wide,	*b*	
And that one talent° which is death to hide	*b*	
Lodged with me useless, though my soul more bent	*a*	
To serve therewith my Maker, and present	*a*	5
My true account, lest He returning chide;	*b*	
"Doth God exact day labor, light denied?"	*b*	
I fondly° ask. But Patience, to prevent	*a*	
That murmur, soon replies, "God doth not need	*c*	
Either man's work or his own gifts. Who best	*d*	10
Bear his mild yoke, they serve him best. His state	*e*	
Is kingly: thousands at his bidding speed,	*c*	
And post o'er land and ocean without rest;	*d*	
They also serve who only stand and wait."	*e*	

3. *one talent:* see Matthew 25:14–30. 8. *fondly:* foolishly.

MILTON'S SHORT POEMS

1. Compare Milton's tribute to Shakespeare with Jonson's. Which poem reveals a better understanding of the dramatist? Which is more impressive? Why is this poem not a sonnet?

2. The two sonnets here offer an interesting study in contrast. What quality of the young man has been retained after twenty years? How has Milton kept his faith in God's direction of his talents? Apply these poems to your own experience.

Why is it a good habit to stop occasionally and take stock of your own personality and achievements?

3. In "On His Blindness" how does Milton apply the Biblical parable of the talents to himself? Describe in your own words the mental debate and final conclusion reached by Milton in this poem.

4. Reread a few Shakespearean sonnets for comparison with Milton's. How does the form differ? What difference in the division of thought within the sonnets do you notice?

Paradise Lost

Blindness is obviously a great handicap to a writer, yet curiously enough, it was a help toward Milton's completion of *Paradise Lost*. From his notebooks we know that Milton had for years planned a long poem that would tell the Biblical story of Creation. But not until he became blind was Milton relieved of the many tasks that had kept him from this work. *Paradise Lost*, which required seven years to write, is a literary epic, the greatest in the English language. Like a national or folk epic, such as *Beowulf*, a literary epic is a saga of grand and sweeping events. Milton adopted a grand and sweeping style to harmonize with the events he recounted. Part of the effect is gained by long sentences that build up to a climax, with essential parts at the very end, as in the very first sentence. Part is gained by the use of dignified, often majestic, diction.

Paradise Lost tells in twelve books the Biblical story of the temptation and fall of man at the hands of Satan. This much Milton took from the Book of Genesis, but to it he added pictures of Satan's expulsion from Heaven together with the rebel angels. The scene of the epic is the world of space, shifting between Heaven and Hell and the world. The characters are ones we know well — Adam, Eve, Satan, Michael, Gabriel, and others from the Old Testament. Satan emerges as a fearless leader, even though he leads in the wrong direction. The following passages are from the beginning of Book I of *Paradise Lost*.

Of Man's first disobedience, and the fruit
Of that forbidden tree whose mortal taste
Brought death into the World, and all our woe,
With loss of Eden, till one greater Man°
Restore us, and regain the blissful seat,   5
Sing, Heavenly Muse° . . .
             I thence
Invoke thy aid to my adventurous song,
That with no middle flight intends to soar
Above the Aonian mount,° while it pursues
Things unattempted yet in prose or rhyme.   10
And chiefly Thou, O Spirit,° that dost prefer
Before all temples the upright heart and pure,

The poet invokes the divine Spirit for inspiration to interpret God to man.

Instruct me, for Thou know'st; Thou from the first
Wast present, and, with mighty wings outspread,
Dovelike sat'st brooding on the vast Abyss,   15
And mad'st it pregnant: what in me is dark
Illumine, what is low raise and support;
That, to the height of this great argument,
I may assert Eternal Providence,
And justify the ways of God to men.   20

He searches for the cause of the fall of man.

     Say first — for Heaven hides nothing from thy view,
Nor the deep tract of Hell — say first what cause
Moved our grand Parents, in that happy state,

---

4. *one greater Man:* Christ. 6. *Heavenly Muse:* not the pagan Muse, but the Spirit that inspired the men of the Bible. 9. *Aonian* (ā·ō′nĭ·ăn) *mount:* Helicon in Greece, supposed to be the home of the Muses. Milton means that he intends to write on a theme higher than Greek poetry had attempted. 11. *Spirit:* divine inspiration.

Favored of Heaven so highly, to fall off
From their Creator, and transgress his will   25
For one restraint,° lords of the World besides.
Who first seduced them to that foul revolt?

*It was Satan who
deceived Eve,
"the mother of
mankind," in
revenge after he
with the rebel
angels was
thrown from
Heaven.*

   The infernal Serpent; he it was whose guile,
Stirred up with envy and revenge, deceived
The mother of mankind, what time his pride   30
Had cast him out from Heaven, with all his host
Of rebel Angels, by whose aid, aspiring
To set himself in glory above his peers,
He trusted to have equaled the Most High,
If he opposed, and, with ambitious aim   35
Against the throne and monarchy of God,
Raised impious war in Heaven, and battle proud,
With vain attempt. Him the Almighty Power
Hurled headlong flaming from the ethereal sky,
With hideous ruin and combustion, down   40
To bottomless perdition; there to dwell
In adamantine° chains and penal fire,
Who durst defy the Omnipotent to arms.
   Nine times the space that measures day and night
To mortal men, he with his horrid crew   45
Lay vanquished, rolling in the fiery gulf,
Confounded, though immortal. But his doom
Reserved him to more wrath; for now the thought
Both of lost happiness and lasting pain
Torments him; round he throws his baleful eyes,   50
That witnessed° huge affliction and dismay,
Mixed with obdurate pride and steadfast hate.
At once, as far as Angel's ken,° he views
The dismal situation waste and wild.
A dungeon horrible, on all sides round,   55
As one great furnace flamed; yet from those flames
No light; but rather darkness visible
Served only to discover sights of woe,
Regions of sorrow, doleful shades, where peace

*Satan and his
followers find
themselves in a
horrible Hell.*

And rest can never dwell, hope never comes   60
That comes to all; but torture without end
Still urges,° and a fiery deluge, fed
With ever-burning sulfur unconsumed.
Such place Eternal Justice had prepared
For those rebellious; here their prison ordained   65
In utter darkness, and their portion set,
As far removed from God and light of Heaven
As from the center thrice to the utmost pole.°
Oh, how unlike the place from whence they fell!
There the companions of his fall, o'erwhelmed   70

---

26. *one restraint:* that they should not eat of the fruit of the tree of knowledge. 42. *adamantine*
(ăd′á·mănt′ĭn): unbreakable, hard as a diamond. 51. *witnessed:* gave evidence of. 53. *ken:* sight.
62. *Still urges:* always presses. 68. *center . . . pole:* three times the distance from the earth (*center*)
to the furthest point in the universe.

With floods and whirlwinds of tempestuous fire,
He soon discerns; and, weltering by his side,
One next himself in power, and next in crime,
Long after known in Palestine, and named
Beelzebub.° To whom the Archenemy,   75
And thence in Heaven called Satan, with bold words
Breaking the horrid silence, thus began: —
   "If thou beest he — but, Oh, how fallen! how changed
From him! — who, in the happy realms of light,
Clothed with transcendent brightness, didst outshine   80
Myriads, though bright — if he whom mutual league,
United thoughts and counsels, equal hope
And hazard in the glorious enterprise,
Joined with me once, now misery hath joined
In equal ruin; into what pit thou seest   85
From what height fallen; so much the stronger proved
He with his thunder; and till then who knew
The force of those dire arms? Yet not for those,
Nor what the potent Victor in his rage
Can else inflict, do I repent, or change,   90
Though changed in outward luster, that fixed mind,
And high disdain from sense of injured merit,
That with the Mightiest raised me to contend,
And to the fierce contention brought along
Innumerable force of Spirits armed,   95
That durst dislike his reign, and, me preferring,
His utmost power with adverse power opposed
In dubious battle on the plains of Heaven,
And shook his throne. What though the field be lost?

Satan boldly says All is not lost; the unconquerable will,   100
"All is not lost" And study of revenge, immortal hate,
and declares
eternal war on And courage never to submit or yield:
Heaven with And what is else not to be overcome?
"immortal hate." That glory never shall his wrath or might
Extort from me. To bow and sue for grace   105
With suppliant knee, and deify his power
Who, from the terror of his arm, so late
Doubted° his empire — that were low indeed;
That were an ignominy and shame beneath
This downfall; since, by fate, the strength of gods,   110
And this empyreal° substance, cannot fail;
Since, through experience of this great event,
In arms not worse, in foresight much advanced,
We may with more successful hope resolve
To wage by force or guile eternal war,   115
Irreconcilable to our grand Foe,
Who now triumphs, and in the excess of joy

---

75. *Beelzebub* (bē·ĕl′zē·bŭb): In this poem the name is given to the fallen angel next in command to Satan, but in other connections it is often used as equivalent to Satan. 108. *Doubted:* feared for. 111. *empyreal* (ĕm·pĭr′ē·ăl): belonging to the highest heaven. The fallen angels still retain their immortality.

Sole reigning holds the tyranny of Heaven."
   So spake the apostate Angel, though in pain,
Vaunting aloud, but racked with deep despair;   120
And him thus answered soon his bold compeer:° —
   "O Prince, O Chief of many thronèd Powers
That led the embattled Seraphim° to war
Under thy conduct, and, in dreadful deeds
Fearless, endangered Heaven's perpetual King,   125
And put to proof his high supremacy,
Whether upheld by strength, or chance, or fate!
Too well I see and rue the dire event
That, with sad overthrow and foul defeat,
Hath lost us Heaven, and all this mighty host   130

Beelzebub regrets In horrible destruction laid thus low,
the loss of Heaven As far as gods and heavenly essences
and would now Can perish: for the mind and spirit remains
serve God as a Invincible, and vigor soon returns,
slave and obey Though all our glory extinct, and happy state   135
his will. Here swallowed up in endless misery.
But what if He our Conqueror (whom I now
Of force believe almighty, since no less
Than such could have o'erpowered such force as ours)
Have left us this our spirit and strength entire,   140
Strongly to suffer and support our pains,
That we may so suffice his vengeful ire,
Or do him mightier service as his thralls
By right of war, whate'er his business be,
Here in the heart of Hell to work in fire,   145
Or do his errands in the gloomy Deep?
What can it then avail though yet we feel
Strength undiminished, or eternal being
To undergo eternal punishment?"
   Whereto with speedy words the Archfiend replied: —   150
"Fallen Cherub, to be weak is miserable,
Doing or suffering:° but of this be sure —
To do aught good never will be our task,
But ever to do ill our sole delight,
As being the contrary to his high will   155
Whom we resist. If then his providence
Out of our evil seek to bring forth good,
Our labor must be to pervert that end,
And out of good still to find means of evil;
Which ofttimes may succeed so as perhaps   160
Shall grieve him, if I fail not, and disturb
His inmost counsels from their destined aim.
But see! the angry Victor hath recalled
His ministers of vengeance and pursuit
Back to the gates of Heaven: the sulfurous hail,   165
Shot after us in storm, o'erblown hath laid

---

121. *compeer:* companion, equal. 123. *Seraphim* (sĕr′a̐·fĭm): angels of the highest rank. 152. *Doing or suffering:* whether active or passive.

Satan denounces
Beelzebub's
weakness and
makes plans to
gather his forces
on a plain where
they may consult
on how to "offend
our enemy."

The fiery surge that from the precipice
Of Heaven received us falling; and the thunder,
Winged with red lightning and impetuous rage,
Perhaps hath spent his shafts, and ceases now   170
To bellow through the vast and boundless Deep.
Let us not slip the occasion, whether scorn
Or satiate° fury yield it from our Foe.
Seest thou yon dreary plain, forlorn and wild,
The seat of desolation, void of light,   175
Save what the glimmering of these livid flames
Casts pale and dreadful? Thither let us tend
From off the tossing of these fiery waves;
There rest, if any rest can harbor there;
And, reassembling our afflicted powers,   180
Consult how we may henceforth most offend
Our enemy, our own loss how repair,
How overcome this dire calamity,
What reinforcement we may gain from hope,
If not what resolution from despair."   185
     Thus Satan, talking to his nearest mate,
With head uplift above the wave, and eyes
That sparkling blazed; his other parts besides
Prone on the flood, extended long and large,
Lay floating many a rood.° . . .   190
So stretched out huge in length the Archfiend lay,
Chained on the burning lake; nor ever thence
Had risen, or heaved his head, but that the will

Heaven permits
Satan to carry
out his evil plans
and by so doing
reap his own ruin
and bring forth
good for Man.

And high permission of all-ruling Heaven
Left him at large to his own dark designs,   195
That with reiterated crimes he might
Heap on himself damnation, while he sought
Evil to others, and enraged might see
How all his malice served but to bring forth
Infinite goodness, grace, and mercy, shown   200
On Man by him seduced, but on himself
Treble confusion, wrath, and vengeance poured.
     Forthwith upright he rears from off the pool
His mighty stature; on each hand the flames
Driven backward slope their pointing spires, and, rolled   205
In billows, leave i' the midst a horrid vale.
Then with expanded wings he steers his flight
Aloft, incumbent° on the dusky air,
That felt unusual weight; till on dry land
He lights — if it were land that ever burned   210
With solid, as the lake with liquid fire,
And such appeared in hue as when the force
Of subterranean wind transports a hill
Torn from Pelorus,° or the shattered side

173. *satiate* (sā'shĭ·āt): satisfied. 190. *rood:* Milton conceived of the angels as being enormous in size. A *rood* is equal to seven or eight yards. 208. *incumbent:* lying. 214. *Pelorus* (pĕ·lōr'ŭs): a cape in Sicily, now Faro.

Giraudon

"Hurled headlong from the ethereal sky, With hideous ruin and combustion, down
To bottomless perdition; there to dwell In adamantine chains and penal fire . . ."

Satan and Beelzebub exult in escaping from the burning lake and recovering their strength without the aid of Heaven.

Of thundering Etna, whose combustible   215
And fueled entrails, thence conceiving fire,
Sublimed° with mineral fury, aid the winds,
And leave a singèd bottom all involved°
With stench and smoke.° Such resting found the sole
Of unblest feet. Him followed his next mate;   220
Both glorying to have scaped the Stygian° flood
As gods, and by their own recovered strength,
Not by the sufferance of supernal° power.
    "Is this the region, this the soil, the clime,"
Said then the lost Archangel, "this the seat   225
That we must change for Heaven? — this mournful gloom
For that celestial light? Be it so, since he
Who now is sovereign can dispose and bid
What shall be right: farthest from him is best,

Satan accepts the horrors of damnation and announces himself the ruler of Hell.

Whom reason hath equaled, force hath made supreme   230
Above his equals. Farewell, happy fields,
Where joy forever dwells! Hail, horrors! hail,
Infernal World! and thou, profoundest Hell,
Receive thy new possessor — one who brings
A mind not to be changed by place or time.   235
The mind is its own place, and in itself
Can make a Heaven of Hell, a Hell of Heaven.
What matter where, if I be still the same,
And what I should be, all but less than he
Whom thunder hath made greater? Here at least   240
We shall be free; the Almighty hath not built
Here for his envy, will not drive us hence:
Here we may reign secure; and, in my choice,
To reign is worth ambition, though in Hell:
Better to reign in Hell than serve in Heaven."   245

217. *Sublimed:* sublimated; i.e., turned into vapor by heat and solidified by cooling. 218. *involved:* enveloped. 212–219. *as when . . . smoke:* An example of the extended simile which Milton frequently uses to strengthen his pictures. This comparison to Mount Etna will be especially vivid to those who have seen moving pictures of volcanic eruptions. 221. *Stygian* (stĭj′ĭ·ăn): pertaining to the river Styx, which in Greek mythology surrounded the abode of the dead. Satan and Beelzebub, because they are of immortal substance, cannot die. 223. *supernal:* heavenly.

AN EPIC OF GOOD AND EVIL

1. Reread the story of the fall of man in the Old Testament and compare it with the account in Milton's poem. What has the poet added to the Biblical story? As a personification of evil, what attributes does Satan have? Wherein does his power lie?

2. What two beings carry on the dialogue in this selection? What differences are there in their attitudes?

3. Does Milton explain how Satan was able to continue in his evil deeds? What does he imply was the purpose of Heaven in so allowing him?

4. Select passages that appeal to you and read them aloud to the class. Show where Milton uses long words to obtain a sonorous, rolling effect.

5. Almost all literary epics open with an invocation to the Muse of Poetry to aid the poet in his task. Which of the opening lines comprise the invocation here? To whom are they addressed? What do the opening lines tell you about the poet's purpose?

6. Compare *Paradise Lost* with *Beowulf*. In what ways are they alike? different? Explain the difference between a literary epic and a folk or national epic.

APPRECIATING IMAGERY

The richness, power, and musical quality of Milton's poetic language are important elements in *Paradise Lost*.

Milton achieves his vivid description of Hell, his graphic portrayals of Satan and Beelzebub, by the skillful use of figurative language. In what kind of a Hell does Satan and his legion of angels find themselves? Read lines 44–77 which picture for you "their prison ordained in utter darkness." Milton gives Satan dignity and power and describes him as accepting his predicament with defiance. In what ways does the poet present Satan as a heroic figure? Point out lines which suggest that Beelzebub, "the next in crime," is different from Satan.

Milton uses many similes and allusions to set the stage for his epic work. In lines 212–19 the allusion to Mt. Etna's thundering volcanic eruptions makes especially vivid Satan's and Beelzebub's escape from the fiery lake. Point out other such comparisons and allusions.

LITERATURE AND THE ARTS

The manuscript illustration on page 245, from the *Très Riches Heures,* a pictorial religious calendar painted by Pol de Limbourg and his brothers for the Duc de Berry, is a fourteenth-century representation of the expulsion of Lucifer and his followers from heaven. As God and the celestial choir watch, the rebel angels are cast headlong into the fiery gulf below.

The mezzotint on page 247, done by John Martin in 1827 as one of a series made expressly for *Paradise Lost,* depicts a scene from Book III in which Satan (at the left) witnesses the ascent of angels to heaven. The grandeur and drama of Martin's portrayal in black and white is in sharp contrast to the brightly colored and dispassionate representation typical of the painting of Limbourg's day, when it was not the fashion to express mood or emotion as John Martin did in his engraving.

British Museum

JOHN BUNYAN

1628–1688

While Milton voiced the Puritan ideals for the educated classes, John Bunyan spoke for the common people.

Because Bunyan was one of the first authors to write his autobiography, we know more of his inner life than of that of most early writers. He was a village tinker and for a while a common soldier in the Parliamentary army. The intense religious emotions prevalent at that time seized the imaginative Bunyan and caused him frightful pangs of conscience about his swearing, his Sunday sports on the green, and his failure to attend church. He visualized his mental struggles as the conflict between angels and devils. He longed to perform miracles, but was afraid to try lest he should fail and lose his faith. He became a preacher and drew such crowds of laboring people to his outdoor services that his influence was greatly feared by the Royalists.

After the Restoration, an act was passed to forbid meetings hostile to the Established Church. Bunyan was brought to trial, and the judge urged him to give up his services. But, though he suffered agonies of spirit at the possibility of separation from his little blind daughter and the rest of his family, Bunyan would not yield his point. Consequently he spent almost twelve years in Bedford jail. He was, however, allowed considerable freedom to see his family and even to preach in the Baptist church. During these years his leisure enabled him to become a thorough student of two books — the only ones he had: the Bible and Fox's *Book of Martyrs.* Their influence is evident in his masterpiece, *The Pilgrim's Progress,* which, though probably written in jail, was not published until years after his release. The popularity of this book was truly remarkable. Today, next to the Bible, it has the largest number of translations into foreign languages of any book in the world.

Vanity Fair

The great allegory of *The Pilgrim's Progress* is told as if it were a dream. Christian, the hero, is seen as he leaves the City of Destruction to journey to the Celestial City. He carries a heavy burden of sin on his back and the Scriptures in his hand. One of his earliest difficulties is getting through the famous Slough of Despond, which proves too much for his companion, Pliable. But Christian, with the aid of Helpful, scrambles out and continues on his way. Further obstacles are encountered in the Hill of Difficulty, the Valley of Humiliation, the Valley of the Shadow, and the imprisonment at Doubting Castle by the Giant Despair. Through the first few of these adventures Christian is accompanied by Faithful, who suffers martyrdom at Vanity Fair. After that, Hopeful joins Christian, and the two finally reach the Heavenly Gates, where they are greeted by angels.

The following selection is one of the most significant passages in the book, partly because the term Vanity Fair is so often used as a symbol of worldliness.

THEN I SAW in my dream, that when they were got out of the wilderness, they presently saw a town before them, and the name of that town is Vanity. And at the town there is a fair kept, called Vanity Fair; it is kept all the year long; it beareth the name of Vanity Fair, because the town where 'tis kept is lighter than vanity; and also because all that is there sold, or that cometh thither, is vanity. As is the saying of the wise, "All that cometh is Vanity."

This fair is no new-erected business, but a thing of ancient standing; I will show you the original of it.

Almost five thousand years agone, there were pilgrims walking to the Celestial City, as these two honest persons are; and Beelzebub, Apollyon,[1] and Legion, with their companions, perceiving by the path that the pilgrims made, that their way to the City lay through this town of Vanity, they contrived here to set up a fair; a fair wherein should be sold all sorts of vanity, and that it should last all the year long; therefore at this fair are all such merchandise sold, as houses, lands, trades, places, honors, preferments, titles, countries, kingdoms, pleasures, and delights of all sorts, as wives, husbands, children, masters, servants, lives, blood, bodies, souls, silver, gold, pearls, precious stones, and what not.

And moreover, at this fair there is at all times to be seen jugglings, cheats, games, plays, fools, apes, knaves, and rogues, and that of all sorts.

Here are to be seen too, and that for nothing, thefts, murders, false swearers, and that of a blood-red color.

[1] *Beelzebub* (bē-ĕl'zē-bŭb): Satan; *Apollyon* (á-pŏl'yŭn): the angel of the bottomless pit.

[There follows a passage that identifies the streets and rows of Vanity Fair with the various nations of Europe and tells how Beelzebub tried in vain to win Jesus to Vanity Fair. The commotion aroused by the pilgrims Christian and Faithful is attributed to three causes: their strange clothing, their foreign language of Heaven, and their failure to be impressed by the wares at Vanity Fair.]

One chanced mockingly, beholding the carriages of the men, to say unto them, "What will ye buy?" But they, looking gravely upon him, answered, "We buy the Truth." At that there was an occasion taken to despise the men the more; some mocking, some taunting, some speaking reproachfully, and some calling upon others to smite them. At last things came to a hubbub and great stir in the fair, insomuch that all order was confounded.

Now was word presently brought to the Great One of the fair, who quickly came down and deputed some of his most trusty friends to take those men into examination, about whom the fair was almost overturned. So the men were brought to examination; and they that sat upon them, asked them whence they came, whither they went, and what they did there in such an unusual garb. The men told them that they were pilgrims and strangers in the world, and that they were going to their own country, which was the heavenly Jerusalem; and that they had given no occasion to the men of the town, nor yet to the merchandisers, thus to abuse them, and to let [1] them in their journey, except it was for that, when one asked them what they would buy, they said they would buy the Truth. But they that were appointed to examine them did not believe them to be any other than bedlams [2] and mad, or else such as came to put all things into a confusion

in the fair. Therefore they took them and beat them, and besmeared them with dirt, and then put them into the cage, that they might be made a spectacle to all the men of the fair. There, therefore, they lay for some time, and were made the objects of any man's sport, or malice, or revenge, the Great One of the fair laughing still at all that befell them.

But the men being patient, and not rendering railing for railing, but contrariwise blessing, and giving good words for bad, and kindness for injuries done, some men in the fair that were more observing, and less prejudiced than the rest, began to check and blame the baser sort for their continual abuses done by them to the men; they, therefore, in angry manner let fly at them again, counting them as bad as the men in the cage, and telling them that they seemed confederates, and should be made partakers of their misfortunes. The others replied, that for aught they could see, the men were quiet, and sober, and intended nobody any harm; and that there were many that traded in their fair that were more worthy to be put into the cage, yea, and pillory too, than were the men that they had abused. Thus, after divers words had passed on both sides (the men behaving themselves all the while very wisely and soberly before them), they fell to some blows among themselves, and did harm one to another.

Then were these two poor men brought before their examiners again, and there charged as being guilty of the late hubbub that had been in the fair. So they beat them pitifully and hung irons upon them, and led them in chains up and down the fair, for an example and a terror to others, lest any should speak in their behalf, or join themselves unto them. But Christian and Faithful behaved themselves yet more wisely, and received the ignominy and shame that was cast upon them, with so much meekness and patience, that it won to their side (though but few in comparison of the rest) several of the men in the fair.

---

[1] *let:* hinder. [2] *bedlams:* insane men. The word is a contraction of Bethlehem, from the name of a famous hospital for the insane, St. Mary of Bethlehem.

This put the other party yet into a greater rage, insomuch that they concluded the death of these two men. Wherefore they threatened, that the cage nor irons should serve their turn, but that they should die, for the abuse they had done, and for deluding the men of the fair.

Then were they remanded to the cage again, until further order should be taken with them. So they put them in, and made their feet fast in the stocks.

Here also they called again to mind what they had heard from their faithful friend Evangelist, and were the more confirmed in their way and sufferings, by what he told them would happen to them. They also now comforted each other, that whose lot it was to suffer, even he should have the best on 't; therefore each man secretly wished that he might have that preferment: but committing themselves to the all-wise disposal of Him that ruleth all things, with much content they abode in the condition in which they were, until they should be otherwise disposed of.

Then a convenient time being appointed, they brought them forth to their trial, in order to their condemnation. When the time was come, they were brought before their enemies, and arraigned. The judge's name was Lord Hategood. Their indictment was one and the same in substance, though somewhat varying in form, the contents whereof was this:

"That they were enemies to and disturbers of their trade; that they had made commotions and divisions in the town, and had won a party to their own most dangerous opinions, in contempt of the law of their prince."

Then Faithful began to answer, that he had only set himself against that which had set itself against Him that is higher than the highest. And said he, "As for disturbance, I make none, being myself a man of peace; the parties that were won to us, were won by beholding our truth and innocence, and they are only turned from the worse to the better. And

as to the king you talk of, since he is Beelzebub, the enemy of our Lord, I defy him and all his angels."

Then proclamation was made, that they that had aught to say for their Lord the King against the prisoner at the bar, should forthwith appear and give in their evidence. So there came in three witnesses, to wit, Envy, Superstition, and Pickthank.[1] They were then asked if they knew the prisoner at the bar; and what they had to say for their Lord the King against him.

Then stood forth Envy, and said to this effect: "My Lord, I have known this man a long time, and will attest upon my oath before this honorable Bench, that he is — "

Judge. "Hold! Give him his oath."

So they sware him. Then he said, "My Lord, this man, notwithstanding his plausible name, is one of the vilest men in our country. He neither regardeth prince nor people, law nor custom; but doth all that he can to possess all men with certain of his disloyal notions, which he in the general calls principles of faith and holiness. And in particular, I heard him once myself affirm that Christianity and the customs of our town of Vanity were diametrically opposite, and could not be reconciled. By which saying, my Lord, he doth at once not only condemn all our laudable doings, but us in the doing of them."

Then did the Judge say to him, "Hast thou any more to say?"

Envy. "My Lord, I could say much more, only I would not be tedious to the Court. Yet if need be, when the other gentlemen have given in their evidence, rather than anything shall be wanting that will dispatch him, I will enlarge my testimony against him." So he was bid stand by.

Then they called Superstition, and bid him look upon the prisoner. They also asked what he could say for their Lord

---

[1] *Pickthank:* an archaic word meaning one who seeks favor by flattery or by talebearing.

the King against him. Then they sware him; so he began:

Superstition. "My Lord, I have no great acquaintance with this man, nor do I desire to have further knowledge of him; however, this I know, that he is a very pestilent fellow, from some discourse that the other day I had with him in this town; for then talking with him, I heard him say that our religion was naught, and such by which a man could by no means please God. Which sayings of his, my Lord, your Lordship very well knows what necessarily thence will follow, to wit, that we still do worship in vain, are yet in our sins, and finally shall be damned; and this is that which I have to say."

Then was Pickthank sworn, and bid say that he knew, in behalf of their Lord the King, against the prisoner at the bar.

Pickthank. "My Lord, and you gentlemen all: This fellow I have known of a long time, and have heard him speak things that ought not to be spoke; for he hath railed on our noble Prince Beelzebub, and hath spoken contemptibly of his honorable friends, with all the rest of our nobility; and he hath said, moreover, that if all men were of his mind, if possible, there is not one of these noblemen should have any longer a being in this town; besides, he hath not been afraid to rail on you, my Lord, who are now appointed to be his judge, calling you an ungodly villain, with many other such-like vilifying terms, with which he hath bespattered most of the gentry of our town."

When this Pickthank had told his tale, the Judge directed his speech to the prisoner at the bar, saying, "Thou runagate, heretic, and traitor, hast thou heard what these honest gentlemen have witnessed against thee?"

Faithful. "May I speak a few words in my own defense?"

Judge. "Sirrah, sirrah, thou deservest to live no longer, but to be slain immediately upon the place; yet that all men may see our gentleness toward thee, let

us see what thou hast to say."

Faithful. "1. I say then, in answer to what Mr. Envy hath spoken, I never said ought but this, that what rule, or laws, or custom, or people, were flat against the Word of God, are diametrically opposite to Christianity. If I have said amiss in this, convince me of my error, and I am ready here before you to make my recantation.

"2. As to the second, to wit, Mr. Superstition, and his charge against me, I said only this, that in the worship of God there is required a divine faith; but there can be no divine faith without a divine revelation of the will of God; therefore whatever is thrust into the worship of God that is not agreeable to divine revelation, cannot be done but by an human faith, which faith will not profit to eternal life.

"3. As to what Mr. Pickthank hath said, I say (avoiding terms, as that I am said to rail, and the like) that the prince of this town, with all the rabblement his attendants, by this gentleman named, are more fit for a being in hell, than in this town and country; and so, the Lord have mercy upon me."

Then the Judge called to the jury (who all this while stood by, to hear and observe), "Gentlemen of the Jury, you see this man about whom so great an uproar hath been made in this town; you have also heard what these worthy gentlemen have witnessed against him; also you have heard this reply and confession. It lieth now in your breasts to hang him, or save his life; but yet I think meet to instruct you into our Law.

[The Judge then cites various laws enacted by kings of the Old Testament against the Israelites.]

"For that of Pharaoh,[1] his law was made upon a supposition, to prevent mischief, no crime being yet apparent; but here is a crime apparent. For the

---

[1] *Pharaoh:* The story of Pharaoh's measures against the Israelites is told in Exodus 1.

second and third, you see he disputeth against our religion; and for the treason he hath confessed, he deserveth to die the death."

Then went the jury out, whose names were, Mr. Blind-man, Mr. No-good, Mr. Malice, Mr. Love-lust, Mr. Live-loose, Mr. Heady, Mr. High-mind, Mr. Enmity, Mr. Liar, Mr. Cruelty, Mr. Hate-light, and Mr. Implacable; who every one gave in his private verdict against him among themselves, and afterwards unanimously concluded to bring him in guilty before the Judge. And first Mr. Blind-man the foreman, said, "I see clearly that this man is an heretic." Then said Mr. No-good, "Away with such a fellow from the earth." "Ay," said Mr. Malice, "for I hate the very looks of him." Then said Mr. Love-lust, "I could never endure him." "Nor I," said Mr. Live-loose, "for he would always be condemning my way." "Hang him, hang him," said Mr. Heady. "A sorry scrub," said Mr. High-mind. "My heart riseth against him," said Mr. Enmity. "He is a rogue," said Mr. Liar. "Hanging is too good for him," said Mr. Cruelty. "Let us dispatch him out of the way," said Mr. Hate-light. Then said Mr. Implacable, "Might I have all the world given me, I could not be reconciled to him; therefore let us forthwith bring him in guilty of death." And so they did; therefore he was presently condemned to be had from the place where he was, to the place from whence he came, and there to be put to the most cruel death that could be invented.

They therefore brought him out, to do with him according to their Law; and first they scourged him, then they buffeted him, then they lanced his flesh with knives; after that they stoned him with stones, then pricked him with their swords; and last of all they burned him to ashes at the stake.[1] Thus came Faithful to his end.

[1] The description of Faithful's execution is no great exaggeration of the kind of torture common in Europe during religious persecutions.

Mansell Collection

Illustration from the third edition of Pilgrim's Progress, *published in 1767.*

A PURITAN ALLEGORY

1. For what reasons do Christian and Faithful arouse the ire of the people at Vanity Fair? Which of these is probably the most serious cause of objection? Do the pilgrims have any sympathizers? If so, who are they?

2. Point out how the persons involved in the trial are particularly appropriate for Bunyan's purpose. Show how their words are in accordance with their names.

3. How does this selection reveal Bunyan's knowledge of the Bible? Do you know any men in the New Testament from whose experiences Bunyan may have derived some ideas for this experience of Christian and Faithful?

4. What teaching do you think Bunyan intended by the events at Vanity Fair? State his message as concisely as you can. Is it a message that is applicable to our own time? How do you account for the wide appeal of *The Pilgrim's Progress?*

SAMUEL PEPYS

1633-1703

National Portrait Gallery

Samuel Pepys (pēps) never considered himself a writer and, in fact, never intended to become one. Yet he wrote what is for the modern reader perhaps the most entertaining work of the seventeenth century. Throughout his life he was a busy man of affairs. His father was a poor tailor with ten other children to support, but Pepys managed to get to Cambridge with the aid of a relative and several scholarships. At twenty-two, with not a penny to start housekeeping, he married a girl of fifteen. With ambition and hard work he advanced quickly. He held an important position in the Navy Office and later became Secretary of the Admiralty. At fifty-five he retired into a pleasant and respected life, publishing a book about the Navy Office, receiving the honor of presidency of the Royal Society, and adding to his splendid library. This was, then, the career of a typical man of affairs, but with one

important difference — Pepys kept a diary.

Between the years 1660 and 1669, Samuel Pepys kept a diary which he wrote in a secret code or shorthand. Assured this security from prying eyes, he could be completely intimate and at ease in describing his personal life. More than one hundred years later, the six volumes of this diary were discovered among other books which Pepys had bequeathed to Cambridge University. It took several years to decipher and transcribe these volumes, but in 1825 the first edition of Pepys' *Diary* was finally published. Since then many editions of this work have appeared.

In the *Diary* we meet an extraordinary personality, Pepys himself, a great lover of music, a quick-tempered master, and a tireless worker. Here are Pepys' vanities, his vexations, and his prejudices. Nothing is concealed in the *Diary,* selections from which follow.

The Diary of Samuel Pepys

PERSONAL AFFAIRS

August 19, 1660. (Lord's Day.) This morning Sir W. Batten, Pen,[1] and my-

---

[1] *Sir W. Batten, Pen:* Sir William Batten and Sir William Pen (referred to later as "Sir Williams both") were members of the Navy Board of which Pepys was Clerk of the Acts.

self, went to church to the churchwardens, to demand a pew, which at present could not be given us, but we are resolved to have one built. So we stayed and heard Mr. Mills, a very good minister. Home to dinner, where my wife had on her new petticoat that she bought yesterday, which indeed is a very fine cloth, and a fine lace, but that being of a light color, and the lace all silver, it makes no great show. Mr. Creed and my brother Tom dined with me. After they were gone I went up to put my papers in order and finding my wife's clothes lie carelessly laid up, I was angry with her, which I was troubled for. After that my wife and I went and walked in the garden, and so home to bed.

November 21, 1660. This morning my wife and I went to Paternoster Row, and there we bought some green watered moire for a morning waistcoat. And after that we went to Mr. Cade's to choose some pictures for our house. After that my wife went home, and I to Pope's Head and bought me an agate-hafted knife, which cost me 5s. So home to dinner, and so to the office all the afternoon, and at night to my violin (the first time that I have played on it since I came to this house) in my dining room, and afterward to my lute there, and I took much pleasure to have the neighbors come forth into the yard to hear me. So up to bed.

January 3, 1661. To the Theater: and here the first time that I ever saw women come upon the stage.[1]

March 27, 1661. To the Dolphin to a dinner of Mr. Harris's where Sir Williams both and my Lady Batten and her two daughters, and other company, where a great deal of mirth, and there stayed until 11 o'clock at night, and in our mirth I sang and sometimes fiddled. At last we fell to dancing, the first time that ever I did in my life, which I did wonder to see myself do.

May 31, 1661. I went to my father's, but to my great grief I found my father and mother in a great deal of discontent one with another, and indeed my mother is now grown so pettish that I know not how my father is able to bear with it. I

did talk to her so as did not indeed become me, but I could not help it, she being so insufferably foolish and simple, so that my father, poor man, is become a very unhappy man.

December 31, 1661. My wife and I this morning to the painter's, and there she sat [2] the last time. After supper, and my barber had trimmed me, I sat down to end my journal for this year, and my condition at this time, by God's blessing, is thus: my health is very good, and so my wife's in all respects: my servants, W. Hewer, Sarah, Nell, and Wayneman: my house at the Navy Office. I suppose myself to be worth about £500 clear in the world, and my goods of my house my own, and what is coming to me from Brampton when my father dies, which God defer. My chiefest thought is now to get a good wife for Tom, there being one offered by the Joyces, a cousin of theirs, worth £200 in ready money. But my greatest trouble is that I have for this last half year been a very great spendthrift in all manner of respects, that I am afeared to cast up my accounts, though I hope I am worth what I say above. But I will cast them up very shortly. I have newly taken a solemn oath about abstaining from plays and wine, which I am resolved to keep according to the letter of the oath which I keep by me.

June 8, 1662. (Lord's Day.) To my Lady's, and there supped with her; and merry among other things, with the parrot which my Lord hath brought from the sea, which speaks very well, and cries Poll so pleasantly that made my Lord give it to Lady Paulina; but my Lady her mother do not like it. Home and observe my man Will to walk with his cloak flung over his shoulder like a ruffian, which, whether it was that he might not be seen to walk along with the footboy I know not, but I was vexed at it; and coming home and after prayers, I did ask him where he learned that immodest garb, and he answered me that it was not im-

---

[1] *women come upon the stage:* In Elizabethan times boys played the roles of women on the stage, and this custom continued until almost the end of the seventeenth century.

[2] *she sat:* She had been having her portrait painted.

modest, or some such slight answer, at which I did give him two boxes on the ears, which I never did before, and so was after a little troubled at it.

THE EXECUTION OF A REGICIDE

October 13, 1660. I went out to Charing Cross, to see Major General Harrison [1] hanged, drawn, and quartered; which was done there, he looking as cheerful as any man could do in that condition. He was presently cut down, and his head and heart shown to the people, at which there was great shouts of joy. It is said that he said that he was sure to come shortly at the right hand of Christ to judge them that now had judged him; and that his wife do expect his coming again. Thus it was my chance to see the King beheaded at Whitehall, [2] and to see the first blood shed in revenge for the blood of the King at Charing Cross. From thence to my Lord's, and took Captain Cuttance and Mr. Sheply to the Sun Tavern, and did give them some oysters. After that I went by water home, where I was angry with my wife for her things lying about, and in my passion kicked the little fine basket, which I bought her in Holland, and broke it, which troubled me after I had done it. Within all the afternoon setting up shelves in my study. At night to bed.

THE CORONATION OF CHARLES II

April 23, 1661. Coronation Day. About four I rose and got to the Abbey, where I followed Sir J. Denham, [3] the Surveyor, with some company that he was leading in. And with much ado, by the favor of Mr. Cooper, his man, did get up into a great scaffold across the north end of the Abbey, where with a great deal of patience I sat from past four till eleven before the King came in. And a great pleasure it was to see the Abbey raised in the middle, all covered with red, and a throne (that is a chair) and footstool on the top of it; and all the officers of all kinds, so much as the very fiddlers, in red vests.

At last comes in the Dean and Prebends [4] of Westminster, with the Bishops (many of them in cloth-of-gold copes), and after them the Nobility, all in their Parliament robes, which was a most magnificent sight. Then the Duke, and the King with a scepter (carried by my Lord Sandwich) and sword and mond [5] before him, and the crown too. The King in his robes, bare-headed, which was very fine. And after all had placed themselves, there was a sermon and the service; and then in the Choir at the high altar, the King passed through all the ceremonies of the Coronation, which to my great grief I and most in the Abbey could not see. The crown being put upon his head, a great shout began, and he came forth to the throne; and there passed more ceremonies: as taking the oath, and having things read to him by the Bishop; and his Lords (who put on their caps as soon as the King put on his crown) and bishops came, and kneeled before him. And three times the King at Arms [6] went to the three open places on the scaffold, and proclaimed, that if anyone could show any reason why Charles Stuart should not be King of England, that now he should come and speak. And a General Pardon also was read by the Lord Chancellor, and medals flung up and down by my Lord Cornwallis, of silver, but I could not come by any. But so great a noise that I could make but little of the music; and indeed, it was lost to everybody.

---

[1] *Major General Harrison:* one of the signers of the death warrant of Charles I. [2] King Charles I was beheaded in 1649 when, Pepys was sixteen. [3] *Sir J. Denham* was a popular poet as well as being in charge of government buildings.

[4] *Prebends* (prĕb′ĕndz): high officials in the church. [5] *mond:* an orb of gold, with a cross set with precious stones. [6] *King at Arms:* head of the heralds.

I went out a little while before the King had done all his ceremonies, and went round the Abbey to Westminster Hall, all the way within rails, and 10,000 people, with the ground covered with blue cloth; and scaffolds all the way. Into the Hall I got, where it was very fine with hangings and scaffolds one upon another full of brave ladies; and my wife in one little one, on the right hand. Here I stayed walking up and down, and at last, upon one of the side stalls, I stood and saw the King come in with all the persons (but the soldiers) that were yesterday in the cavalcade; and a most pleasant sight it was to see them in their several robes. And the King came in with his crown on, and his scepter in his hand, under a canopy borne up by six silver staves, carried by Barons of the Cinque Ports,[1] and little bells at every end.

And after a long time, he got up to the farther end, and all set themselves down at their several tables; and that was also a brave sight; and the King's first course carried up by the Knights of the Bath. And many fine ceremonies there was of the herald's leading up people before him, and bowing; and my Lord of Albemarle's going to the kitchen and eat a bit of the first dish that was to go to the King's table. But, above all, was these three Lords, Northumberland, and Suffolk, and the Duke of Ormond, coming before the courses on horseback, and staying so all dinnertime, and at last to bring up [2] [Dymock] the King's champion, all in armor on horseback, with his spear and target carried before him. And a herald proclaims, "That if any dare deny Charles Stuart to be lawful King of England, here was a champion that would fight with him"; and with these words, the champion flings

down his gauntlet, and all this he do three times in his going up toward the King's table. At last when he is come, the King drinks to him, and then sends him the cup, which is of gold, and he drinks it off, and then rides back again with the cup in his hand. I went from table to table to see the bishops and all others at their dinner, and was infinitely pleased with it. And at the Lords' table, I met with William Howe, and he spoke to my Lord for me, and he did give me four rabbits and a pullet, and so I got it and Mr. Creed and I got Mr. Michell to give us some bread, and so we at a stall eat [3] it, as everybody else did what they could get. I took a great deal of pleasure to go up and down, and look upon the ladies, and to hear the music of all sorts, but above all, the twenty-four violins.

THE LONDON FIRE

September 2, 1666. (Lord's Day.) Some of our maids sitting up late last night to get things ready against our feast today, Jane called us up about three in the morning, to tell us of a great fire they saw in the city. So I rose and slipped on my nightgown, and went to her window, and thought it to be on the back side of Mark Lane at the farthest; but, being unused to such fires as followed, I thought it far enough off; and so went to bed again and to sleep. About seven rose again to dress myself, and there looked out at the window, and saw the fire not so much as it was and farther off. So to my closet to set things to rights after yesterday's cleaning.

By and by Jane comes and tells me that she hears that above 300 houses have been burned down tonight by the fire we saw, and that it is now burning down all Fish Street, by London Bridge. So I made myself ready presently, and walked to the Tower,[4] and there got up

---

[1] *Cinque* (sĭngk) *Ports:* five ports on the English Channel: Hastings, Sandwich, Dover, Romney, and Hythe. [2] The ceremony here described is no longer observed as part of the coronation. It was a holdover from the days of chivalry.

[3] *eat* (ĕt): Americans would say *ate*. [4] *Tower:* the Tower of London.

upon one of the high places, Sir J. Robinson's little son going up with me; and there I did see the houses at that end of the bridge all on fire, and an infinite great fire on this and the other side the end of the bridge; which, among other people, did trouble me for poor little Michell and our Sarah on the bridge.[1] So down, with my heart full of trouble, to the Lieutenant of the Tower, who tells me that it begun this morning in the King's baker's house in Pudding Lane, and that it hath burned St. Magnus Church and most part of Fish Street already. So I down to the waterside, and there got a boat and through bridge, and there saw a lamentable fire. Poor Michell's house, as far as the Old Swan, already burned that way, and the fire running farther, that in a very little time it got as far as the Steel Yard, while I was there. Everybody endeavoring to remove their goods, and flinging into the river or bringing them into lighters that lay off; poor people staying in their houses as long as till the very fire touched them, and then running into boats, or clambering from one pair of stairs by the waterside to another. And among other things, the poor pigeons, I perceive, were loath to leave their houses, but hovered about the windows and balconies till they were, some of them burned, their wings, and fell down. Having stayed, and in an hour's time seen the fire rage every way, and nobody, to my sight, endeavoring to quench it, but to remove their goods, and leave all to the fire, and having seen it get as far as the Steel Yard, and the wind mighty high and driving it into the City;[2] and everything, after so long a drought, proving combustible, even the very stones of churches. I to Whitehall, and there up to the King's closet in the Chapel, where people come about me, and I did give them an account dismayed them all, and

word was carried in to the King. So I was called for, and did tell the King and Duke of York what I saw, and that unless his Majesty did command houses to be pulled down nothing could stop the fire. They seemed much troubled, and the King commanded me to go to my Lord Mayor from him, and command him to spare no houses, but to pull down before the fire every way. The Duke of York bid me tell him that if he would have any more soldiers he shall; and so did my Lord Arlington afterward, as a great secret. Here meeting with Captain Cocke, I in his coach, which he lent me, and Creed with me to Paul's,[3] and there walked along Watling Street, as well as I could, every creature coming away laden with goods to save, and here and there sick people carried away in beds. Extraordinary good goods carried in carts and on backs. At last met my Lord Mayor in Canning Street, like a man spent, with a handkerchief about his neck. To the King's message he cried, like a fainting woman, "Lord! what can I do? I am spent: people will not obey me. I have been pulling down houses; but the fire overtakes us faster than we can do it." That he needed no more soldiers and that, for himself, he must go and refresh himself, having been up all night.

So he left me, and I him, and walked home, seeing people all almost distracted, and no manner of means used to quench the fire. The houses, too, so very thick thereabouts, and full of matter for burning, as pitch and tar, in Thames Street; and warehouses of oil, and wines, and brandy, and other things. Here I saw Mr. Issake Houblon, the handsome man, prettily dressed and dirty, at his door at Dowgate, receiving some of his brothers' things, whose houses were on fire; and, as he says, have been removed twice already; and he doubts (as it soon proved) that they must be in a little time removed from his

---

[1] *on the bridge:* Old London Bridge was like a street with houses built on it (*see* engraving, p. 271). [2] *City:* the area of the original city of London, now its commercial center.

[3] *Paul's:* St. Paul's Cathedral.

house also, which was a sad consideration. And to see the churches all filling with goods by people who themselves should have been quietly there at this time.

By this time it was about twelve o'clock; and so home. Soon as dined, away, and walked through the city, the streets full of nothing but people and horses and carts laden with goods, ready to run over one another, and removing goods from one burned house to another. They now removing out of Canning Street (which received goods in the morning) into Lumbard Street, and farther; and among others I now saw my little goldsmith, Stokes, receiving some friend's goods, whose house itself was burned the day after. We parted at Paul's; he home, and I to Paul's Wharf, where I had appointed a boat to attend me, and took in Mr. Carcasse and his brother, whom I met in the street, and carried them below and above bridge, to and again to see the fire, which was now got farther, both below and above, and no likelihood of stopping it. Met with the King and Duke of York in their barge, and with them to Queenhithe, and there called Sir Richard Browne to them. Their order was only to pull down houses apace, and so below bridge at the waterside; but little was or could be done, the fire coming upon them so fast. Good hopes there was of stopping it at the Three Cranes above, and at Buttolph's Wharf below bridge, if care be used; but the wind carries it into the City, so as we know not by the waterside what it do there. River full of lighters and boats taking in goods, and good goods swimming in the water, and only I observed that hardly one lighter or boat in three that had the goods of a house in, but there was a pair of virginals [1] in it.

Having seen as much as I could now, I away to Whitehall by appointment and

---

¹ *virginal:* a keyed musical instrument popular in the sixteenth and seventeenth centuries.

there walked to St. James's Park, and there met my wife and Creed and walked to my boat; and there upon the water again, and to the fire up and down, it still increasing, and the wind great. So near the fire as we could for smoke; and all over the Thames, with one's face in the wind, you were almost burned with a shower of firedrops. This is very true; so as houses were burned by these drops and flakes of fire, three or four, nay, five or six houses, one from another. When we could endure no more upon the water, we to a little alehouse on the Bankside, over against the Three Cranes, and there stayed till it was dark almost, and saw the fire grow; and, as it grew darker, appeared more and more, and in corners and upon steeples, and between churches and houses, as far as we could see up the hill of the City, in a most horrid malicious bloody flame, not like the fine flame of an ordinary fire. Barbary and her husband away before us. We stayed till, it being darkish, we saw the fire as only one entire arch of fire from this to the other side of the bridge and in a bow up the hill for an arch of above a mile long: it made me weep to see it. The churches, houses, and all on fire and flaming at once; and a horrid noise the flames made, and the crackling of houses at their ruin.

So home with a sad heart, and there find everybody discoursing and lamenting the fire; and poor Tom Hater come with some few of his goods saved out of his house, which is burned upon Fish Street Hill. I invited him to lie at my house, and did receive his goods, but was deceived in his lying there, the news coming every moment of the growth of the fire; so as we were forced to begin to pack up our own goods, and prepare for their removal; and did by moonshine (it being brave dry, and moonshine, and warm weather) carry much of my goods into the garden, and Mr. Hater and I did remove my money and iron chests into my cellar, as thinking that the safest place. And got my bags of gold into my office, ready to carry away, and my chief papers of accounts also there, and my tallies into a box by themselves. So great was our fear, as Sir W. Batten hath carts come out of the country to fetch away his goods this night. We did put Mr. Hater, poor man, to bed a little; but he got but very little rest, so much noise being in my house, taking down of goods.

3rd. About four o'clock in the morning, my Lady Batten sent me a cart to carry away all my money, and plate, and best things, to Sir W. Rider's at Bednall Green. Which I did, riding myself in my nightgown in the cart; and, Lord! to see how the streets and the highways are crowded with people running and riding, and getting of carts at any rate to fetch away things. I find Sir W. Rider tired with being called up all night, and receiving things from several friends. His house full of goods, and much of Sir W. Batten's and Sir W. Pen's. I am eased at my heart to have my treasure so well secured. Then home, with much ado to find a way, nor any sleep all this night to me nor my poor wife.

THE DIARY OF SAMUEL PEPYS

1. What does the *Diary* tell you about Pepys as a husband, son, brother, master of the house, social companion, and "rising young man" in London?

2. What light does the *Diary* throw on life and customs of that day that differ from ours? In modern life in the United States what events do you think would attract the attention of a man like Pepys?

3. What, in your opinion, makes the *Diary* so interesting? Cite and discuss some rules for good reporting that you find illustrated in it.

LITERATURE AND THE ARTS ➤

The illustration opposite, by Wenceslaus Hollar, a well-known seventeenth-century engraver, depicts the coronation procession of Charles II. This great occasion took place on April 22, 1661, the day before the coronation in Westminster Abbey. Preceded by the richly dressed nobles of the realm, Charles rode through the crowded London streets giving his subjects what for most of them would be their only glimpse of their monarch during his reign.

BEHIND THE SCENES IN ENGLISH LITERATURE

Magdalene College, Cambridge

From Pepys' diary: his code and bookplate.

In order to secure complete privacy and freedom in describing his personal life, Pepys kept his diary in what was long thought to be a secret code or shorthand. He kept it from 1660 to 1669, from the ages of 27 to 36, at which time he stopped because he feared — groundlessly — that he was going blind.

After his death, Pepys' library and private papers went to Magdalene College, his old school at Cambridge University. Included were the secret diaries. Without a clue to the code, however, no one could read them. Thus they remained untouched for nearly a hundred years.

Then, in 1818, the master of Magdalene College remembered that his college library contained six mysterious volumes by Pepys. Upon examining them, how-

The Duke of Yorke

Sergants

The Earl of Lindſey
Lord great Chamberlain
of England

The Earl of Northumberland
Lord high Conſtable of Eng;
land

The Earl of Suffolk
Earl Marſhal of
England

...lemen Penſioners & Equeries

THE KING

Gentlemen Penſioners
& Equeries

Yeomen of the Guard

ever, and making nothing of them, he turned them over to Lord Grenville, a former Foreign Secretary who, from his work in deciphering foreign codes, knew something about cryptography. Grenville, managing to transcribe several pages, was so fascinated by what he found that he wanted the whole diary deciphered.

This job was given, with the few clues Grenville had discovered, to a student, John Smith, who, after three years of hard work, decoded the cipher completely. Upon completion of the transcript, Lord Braybrooke, a Magdalene official, published an edition of the work amounting to about a quarter of the whole. Thus, in 1825, the diary which its author never intended for publication made its appearance in public. Written by a man of affairs who moved in the mainstream of his day, it was instantly acclaimed as an extraordinary literary and historical document.

Since Lord Braybrooke's edition, many other editions have been issued. Later editors printed further passages, but never the whole work, and some of them, starting with Lord Braybrooke himself, altered the text to suit their own tastes. Fifty years after the Braybrooke edition appeared, Mynors Bright prepared a larger edition, and in the 1890's a fuller but still incomplete edition was presented. It was Mynors Bright, however, who discovered that John Smith's arduous labor could have been greatly simplified, for he recognized Pepys' code as a well-known system of seventeenth-century shorthand, which Pepys had used just as he found it. In Pepys' own library at Magdalene was a copy of Thomas Shelton's *Tachygraphy* (rapid writing). Poor John Smith had not noticed it.

Over the past several decades, scholars have been retranscribing the entire diary, eliminating the many errors and alterations of previous editions. When this work is finished, the most famous diary in world literature will finally be published in its entirety and exactly as Pepys wrote it.

JOHN DRYDEN

1631–1700

Beginning with the seventeenth century, English writers became more close-knit as a group, more intimate with one another *as writers*. Thus a figure like Ben Jonson in the early part of the century, or Dryden in the later part, could become the literary leader of a period. Today we often speak of the "Age of Dryden." Dryden was poet laureate, like Jonson before him. He wrote poetic plays, including the famous one about Antony and Cleopatra, *All for Love*, and many lyrics that established him as the first poet of his day. Dryden also wrote literary criticism and political satires, which were the outcome of the Puritan-Royalist controversies. He has often been called "the father of English prose."

Dryden was born in a Puritan family and educated at Cambridge. His allegiances, political and religious, shifted with the times. In his early poetry he defended the Commonwealth, but after the Restoration he praised Charles II. He wrote first in support of the Church of England but again, when a Catholic king came to the throne, Dryden became a Catholic and wrote the noted poem "The Hind and the Panther," which represents the Catholic Church as a "milk-white Hind" beset by all sorts of animals representing the Protestant sects. When the Catholic James II was driven from the throne in 1688, Dryden remained constant in his faith, thereby losing all his political advantages. He spent his last years mainly in writing translations of the classics. When he died, he was buried with honor at the side of Chaucer in Westminster Abbey.

Alexander's Feast, or the Power of Music

In 1683 the first choral society was formed in London. Every November 22 this society gave a concert in honor of St. Cecilia, the patron saint of music. The following ode is one of two Dryden wrote for these occasions. St. Cecilia was an early Christian martyr who, legend says, invented an arrangement of musical pipes, the forerunner of the organ, on which she played such exquisite music that an angel came down from heaven to listen.

In his tribute to music, Dryden chose as his central character Alexander the Great (356–323 B.C.), the powerful conqueror of the known world of his day. The scene is ancient Persia on a feast day. With the lovely young Thais (thā'ĭs) as companion, Alexander listens to his musician Timotheus (tĭ·mŏth'ē·ŭs) play the lyre. He is moved to pride, pity, love, anger; he is overcome by the music. But though Timotheus conquered a conqueror, Cecilia performed an equal or greater feat: she called an angel down from heaven.

'Twas at the royal feast for Persia won
  By Philip's warlike son —
 Aloft in awful state
 The godlike hero sate
  On his imperial throne;   5
His valiant peers were placed around,
Their brows with roses and with myrtles bound,
 (So should desert in arms be crowned);
The lovely Thais by his side
Sate like a blooming Eastern bride   10
In flower of youth and beauty's pride:
  Happy, happy, happy pair!
   None but the brave,
   None but the brave,
  None but the brave deserves the fair!   15

  Timotheus placed on high
  Amid the tuneful quire°
With flying fingers touched the lyre;
 The trembling notes ascend the sky
 And heavenly joys inspire.   20
The song began from Jove,°
Who left his blissful seats above —
Such is the power of mighty love!
A dragon's fiery form belied the god;°
Sublime on radiant spires he rode   25
When he to fair Olympia° pressed,
 And while he sought her snowy breast,
Then round her slender waist he curled,
And stamped an image of himself, a sovereign of the world.

---

17. *quire:* an old spelling of "choir." 21. Timotheus began by singing about Jove, the chief of the gods, who was supposed to be Alexander's father. In ancient days popular belief often acclaimed a ruler as a descendant of a god. In Dryden's own day the "divine right of kings" was a parallel superstition clung to by the Royalists. 24. *A dragon's . . . god:* Jove assumed the shape of a dragon. 26. *Olympia* (ô·lĭm'pĭ·à): The name of Alexander's mother was Olympias.

— The listening crowd admire the lofty sound.   30
  A present deity! they shout around;
  A present deity! the vaulted roofs rebound;
        With ravished ears
        The monarch hears,
        Assumes the god;   35
        Affects to nod
  And seems to shake the spheres.
The praise of Bacchus° then the sweet musician sung,
  Of Bacchus ever fair and ever young;
    The jolly god in triumph comes;   40
    Sound the trumpets, beat the drums!
        Flushed with a purple grace
        He shows his honest face
Now give the hautboys breath; he comes, he comes!
    Bacchus, ever fair and young,   45
      Drinking joys did first ordain;
    Bacchus' blessings are a treasure,
    Drinking is the soldier's pleasure;
      Rich the treasure,
      Sweet the pleasure,   50
    Sweet is pleasure after pain.

Soothed with the sound, the king grew vain;
    Fought all his battles o'er again,
And thrice he routed all his foes, and thrice he slew the slain!
  The master saw the madness rise,   55
  His glowing cheeks, his ardent eyes;
  And while he Heaven and Earth defied
Changed his hand and checked his pride.
    He chose a mournful Muse
    Soft pity to infuse;   60
    He sung Darius° great and good,
      By too severe a fate
    Fallen, fallen, fallen, fallen,
      Fallen from his high estate,
    And weltering in his blood;   65
    Deserted at his utmost need
    By those his former bounty fed;
    On the bare earth exposed he lies
    With not a friend to close his eyes.
    With downcast looks the joyless victor sate,   70
      Revolving in his altered soul
        The various turns of Chance below;
      And now and then a sigh he stole,
      And tears began to flow.

    The mighty master smiled to see   75
    That love was in the next degree;

38. *Bacchus* (băk′ŭs): the god of wine. 61. *Darius* (dȧ·rī′ŭs): the Persian king whom Alexander had just defeated.

'Twas but a kindred sound to move,
For pity melts the mind to love.
   Softly sweet, in Lydian° measures
   Soon he soothed his soul to pleasures.   80
War, he sung, is toil and trouble,
Honor but an empty bubble;
   Never ending, still beginning,
Fighting still, and still destroying;
   If the world be worth thy winning,   85
Think, O think, it worth enjoying;
   Lovely Thais sits beside thee,
   Take the good the gods provide thee!
— The many rend the skies with loud applause;
So Love was crowned, but Music won the cause.   90
The prince, unable to conceal his pain,
     Gazed on the fair
     Who caused his care,
And sighed and looked, sighed and looked,
Sighed and looked, and sighed again;   95
At length with love and wine at once oppressed
The vanquished victor sunk upon her breast.

Now strike the golden lyre again:
A louder yet, and yet a louder strain!
Break his bands of sleep asunder   100
And rouse him like a rattling peal of thunder.
   Hark, hark! the horrid sound
     Has raised up his head;
     As awaked from the dead
   And amazed he stares around.   105
Revenge, revenge, Timotheus cries,
   See the Furies° arise!
   See the snakes that they rear,
   How they hiss in their hair,
And the sparkles that flash from their eyes!   110
   Behold a ghastly band,
   Each a torch in his hand!
Those are Grecian ghosts, that in battle were slain,
    And unburied remain°
    Inglorious on the plain.   115
    Give the vengeance due
    To the valiant crew!
Behold how they toss their torches on high,
   How they point to the Persian abodes
And glittering temples of their hostile gods.   120
— The princes applaud with a furious joy;

79. *Lydian:* The music of Lydia, a province of Asia Minor, was of light and delicate quality.
107. *Furies:* the Greek avengers of crime, who were represented as furious creatures with snaky
hair. 114. *unburied remain:* The Greeks believed that the soul of an unburied person could not
cross the river Styx into the realms of the dead, but must wander piteously on the nearer shore
until burial. This belief gives special force to the vengeance of the next lines.

And the King seized a flambeau° with zeal to destroy;
Thais led the way
To light him to his prey,
And, like another Helen,° fired another Troy!   125

— Thus, long ago,
Ere heaving bellows learned to blow,
While organs yet were mute,
Timotheus, to his breathing flute
And sounding lyre   130
Could swell the soul to rage, or kindle soft desire.
At last divine Cecilia came,
Inventress of the vocal frame;°
The sweet enthusiast from her sacred store
Enlarged the former narrow bounds,   135
And added length to solemn sounds,
With Nature's mother wit, and arts unknown before.
— Let old Timotheus yield the prize
Or both divide the crown;
He raised a mortal to the skies;   140
She drew an angel down!

122. *flambeau:* a flaming torch. 125. *Helen:* the wife of the Greek king Menelaus who, by eloping to Troy with Paris, brought on the Trojan War, which resulted in the burning of Troy. 133. *vocal frame:* the organ.

An Essay on Dramatic Poesy

Dryden's prose style is often considered a model of grace and clarity. His influence on the English language was such that Dr. Samuel Johnson said of him: "He found it brick and he left it marble."

Before Dryden's time there was little of what we today call *literary criticism* — discussions of the importance or merits or interesting features of literature. Dryden's *Essay on Dramatic Poesy* is one of the first important works in English literary criticism. In the excerpt given here, he considers the ancients versus the moderns — always a favorite topic with critics. He discusses writers close to his own times, and he contrasts Shakespeare, who followed none of the old classical rules of writing drama, with Jonson, who wrote according to the principles of the ancient Greek and Roman dramatists. You will notice that Dryden sees value in both schools of thought.

To BEGIN, then, with Shakespeare. He was the man who of all modern, and perhaps ancient poets, had the largest and most comprehensive soul. All the images of Nature were still present in him, and he drew them, not laboriously, but luckily; when he describes anything, you more than see it, you feel it too. Those who accuse him to have wanted [1] learning give him the greater commendation: he was naturally learned. He needed not the spectacles of books to read Nature; he looked inwards, and found her there. I cannot say he is everywhere alike; were he so, I should do him injury to compare him with the greatest of mankind. He is many times flat, insipid; his comic wit degenerating into clenches,[2]

[1] *wanted:* lacked. [2] *clenches:* puns; now obsolete.

his serious swelling into bombast. But he is always great when some great occasion is presented to him; no man can say he ever had a fit subject for his wit [1] and did not raise himself as high above the rest of poets.

Quantum lenta solent inter viburna cupressi [2]

The consideration of this made Mr. Hales of Eton say, that there is no subject of which any poet ever writ, but he would produce it much better done in Shakespeare; and however others are now more generally preferred before him, yet the age wherein he lived, which had contemporaries with him Fletcher and Jonson, never equalled them to him in their esteem: and in the last King's court, when Ben's reputation was at highest, Sir John Suckling, and with him the greater part of the courtiers, set our Shakespeare far above him.

Beaumont and Fletcher,[3] of whom I am next to speak, had, with the advantage of Shakespeare's wit, which was their precedent, great natural gifts, improved by study. . . . The first play that brought Fletcher and him in esteem was their *Philaster:* for, before that, they had written two or three very unsuccessfully, as the like is reported of Ben Jonson, before he writ *Every Man in His Humor.* Their plots were generally more regular than Shakespeare's, especially those that were made before Beaumont's death; and they understood and imitated the conversation of gentlemen much better; whose wild debaucheries, and quickness of wit in repartees, no poet before them could paint as they have done. Humor, which Ben Jonson derived from particular persons, they made it their

Brítísh Museum

Frontispiece to Kirkman's "Drolls," a late seventeenth-century play.

business not to describe: they represented all the passions very lively, but above all, love. I am apt to believe the English language in them arrived to its highest perfection: what words have since been taken in are rather superfluous than ornamental. Their plays are now the most pleasant and frequent entertainments of the stage; two of theirs being acted through the year for one of Shakespeare's or Jonson's: the reason is, because there is a certain gaiety in their comedies, and pathos in their more serious plays, which suit generally with all men's humors. Shakespeare's language is likewise a little obsolete, and Ben Jonson's wit comes short of theirs.

As for Jonson, to whose character I am now arrived, if we look upon him while he was himself (for his last plays were but his dotages [4]), I think him the most learned and judicious writer which any theater ever had. He was a most severe judge of himself, as well as others. One cannot say he wanted wit, but rather that he was frugal of it. In his works you find little to retrench or alter. Wit, and language, and humor also in some measure we had before him; but something of art was wanting to the drama

---

[1] *wit:* Throughout, Dryden uses the word "wit" to mean "imaginative and inventive mind," rather than just "humor," as we tend today to define it. [2] *Quantum . . . cupressi:* as cypresses are accustomed to rise above bending shrubs. [3] *Beaumont and Fletcher:* English dramatists of the Elizabethan era who were joint authors of many plays.

[4] *dotages* (dō′tĭj·ĕz): products of a feeble old age.

till he came. He managed his strength to more advantage than any who preceded him. You seldom find him making love in any of his scenes, or endeavoring to move the passions; his genius was too sullen and saturnine [1] to do it gracefully, especially when he knew he came after those who had performed both to such a height. Humor was his proper sphere; and in that he delighted most to represent mechanic people.[2] He was deeply conversant in the ancients, both Greek and Latin, and he borrowed boldly from them: there is scarcely a poet or historian among the Roman authors of those times whom he has not translated in *Sejanus* and *Catiline*.[3] But he has done his robberies so openly, that one may see he fears not to be taxed by any law. He invades authors like a monarch; and what would be theft in other poets is only victory in him. With the spoils of these writers he so represents old Rome to us, in its rites, ceremonies, and customs, that if one of their poets had written either of his tragedies, we had seen less of it than in him. If there was any fault in his language, 'twas that he weaved it too closely and laboriously, in his comedies especially: perhaps, too, he did a little too much to Romanize our tongue, leaving the words which he translated almost as much Latin as when he found them: wherein, though he learnedly followed their language, he did not enough comply with the idiom of ours. If I would compare him with Shakespeare, I must acknowledge him the more correct poet, but Shakespeare the greater wit. Shakespeare was the Homer,[4] or father of our dramatic poets; Jonson was the Virgil,[5] the pattern of elaborate writing; I admire him, but I love Shakespeare. To conclude of him; as he has given us the most correct plays, so in the precepts which he has laid down in his *Discoveries,* we have as many and profitable rules for perfecting the stage, as any wherewith the French can furnish us. . . .

DRYDEN AS POET AND CRITIC

1. Give a brief picture of the setting of "Alexander's Feast" as you imagine it. What point does Dryden make about music? How is his poem a compliment to St. Cecilia?

2. The following musical selections will provide a good background for the poem:

Lines 21–37: "Ode to Joy," Beethoven's *Ninth Symphony,* last movement

Lines 38–51: "Soldier's Chorus" from Gounod's *Faust*

Lines 52–74: "The Death of Ase" by Grieg

Lines 75–97: "Serenade" by Schubert

Lines 98–115: Gluck's "Dance of the Furies"

Lines 126–41: *Largo* by Handel

What other music are you reminded of by the different moods of the poem?

3. In the *Essay on Dramatic Poesy* what differences do you find between Dryden's appraisal of Shakespeare and that of Ben Jonson in his poem on page 199? Why does one feel more confidence in a critic's judgment when he makes both favorable and unfavorable criticisms? Can you find in *Macbeth* or other plays some examples of Shakespeare's puns and bombast mentioned by Dryden? Wherein does he think Shakespeare's excellence lies?

4. According to Dryden, what are Jonson's strong and weak points? Does he condemn Jonson for borrowing from the ancients? Discuss "borrowing" in the present dramatic world.

READING LIST FOR THE SEVENTEENTH CENTURY

Abernethy, Cecil, *Mr. Pepys of Seething Lane*

A fascinating biography of a memorable seventeenth-century personality.

Ainsworth, William Harrison, *Old Saint Paul's: A Tale of the Plague and the Fire*

This story of a London family during the

---

[1] *saturnine* (săt′ẽr·nĭn): gloomy, dull. [2] *mechanic people:* people of the artisan class. [3] *Sejanus* (sē·jā′nŭs) and *Catiline* (kăt′ĭ·lĭn): plays by Jonson. [4] *Homer:* the reputed author of the *Iliad* and the *Odyssey,* the greatest of ancient epic poems. [5] *Virgil:* Roman author of the epic, the *Aeneid.*

Plague and the Fire presents a picture of the people of London in 1665–1666.

Barnes, Margaret, *Mary of Carisbrooke*
A blend of history, love, and adventure. The love story of the servant girl Mary is fictional, but the story of the imprisonment of Charles I on the Isle of Wight is based on historical data.

——, *With All My Heart*
Romantic story of Restoration times, based on the life of Catherine, wife of Charles II.

Blackmore, R. D., *Lorna Doone*
Set in southwestern England, this classic romance tells the story of a sturdy yeoman and the child of an outlaw family. Ruthless Judge Jeffreys is a vividly drawn historical character.

Bryher, Winifred, *The Player's Boy*
Not much plot, but a beautifully written story of the days following Queen Elizabeth.

Charques, Dorothy, *Dark Stranger*
An adventure story set during the political and religious strifes between the Royalists and Cromwell.

Churchill, Winston S., *New World, 1485 to 1688*
Volume II of a four-volume history of the British Empire, *History of the English-Speaking Peoples.*

Chute, Marchette, *Two Gentle Men: The Lives of George Herbert and Robert Herrick*
An entertaining narrative of the lives of two seventeenth-century poets. Their personalities are contrasted against a background of the political, social, and religious conflicts of the time.

Clark, J. Kent, *King's Agent*
The author combines mystery and social history in this fictional re-creation of the events surrounding the exile of James II.

Doyle, A. Conan, *Micah Clarke*
Doyle makes the stirring events of Monmouth's Rebellion in 1685 as exciting as his Sherlock Holmes stories.

Du Maurier, Daphne, *Frenchman's Creek*
The love story of a pirate and a lady of the Court of St. James, set on the Cornwall coast during the reign of Charles II.

——, *The King's General*
The love of a young Cornish lady and Sir Richard Grenville, a general under Charles I.

Fuller, Edmund, *John Milton*
In this book emphasis is placed on John Milton as a seventeenth-century man.

Goudge, Elizabeth, *White Witch*
Adventures during the civil wars.

Hawes, C. B., *Dark Frigate*
Thrilling adventures of an English runaway lad on the high seas. Excellent picture of seventeenth-century ships and sailing hazards.

Pepys, Samuel, *Everybody's Pepys*
An illustrated abridgment of the famous diary, describing life in England under Charles II.

Scott, Sir Walter, *Old Mortality*
A story about the Covenanters and Cavaliers of Scotland, as told by an eccentric cleaner of gravestones.

——, *Woodstock*
Many historical characters, such as Ben Jonson and Milton, enter into this tale of the disguises and escapes of Charles II during the Commonwealth.

Sutcliff, Rosemary, *Rider on a White Horse*
An account of a nobleman whose wife and daughter share his adventures in the rebel army during the uprising against King Charles.

FOR LISTENING

The following poems have been recorded and are available on *Many Voices 6A:* Donne's "Death Be Not Proud," Herrick's "Counsel to Girls," Suckling's "The Constant Lover," Lovelace's "To Althea, from Prison," Wither's "Shall I, Wasting in Despair," Milton's "On His Blindness." *Many Voices 12A* includes Donne's "Meditation 17," lines 1–44 from Milton's *Paradise Lost,* and a selection from Pepys' *Diary.*

SEVENTEENTH-CENTURY FRONTISPIECE: Pictured on page 212 are (1) an illustration of a staircase designed by Grinling Gibbons, a prominent sculptor of the period; (2) a Cavalier hat, Puritan hat, and Cavalier cape; (3) a seventeenth-century quadrant and armillary sphere, the former used for measuring altitudes, the latter an old astronomical device.

THE GROWTH OF
THE ENGLISH LANGUAGE

The Seventeenth Century

During the seventeenth century the sovereigns of England were members of the Stuart family — and the Stuarts were always strongly influenced by the French. Mary Queen of Scots, from whom the Stuarts were descended, spent her girlhood days in France as the wife of the French dauphin, who died in 1560. Because of this relationship between France and the Stuarts, French wielded a stronger influence on English language and literature during the seventeenth century than it had since the last part of the medieval period.

The Cavalier poets employ simplicity of wording, neatness of pattern, and sophistication of tone, all of which are characteristic of the French manner of expression. Playwriting, too, illustrates a marked shift in style. Early in the century, before the Puritans closed the theaters in 1642, plays were closely akin to Elizabethan drama — extravagant and colorful. Ben Jonson, however, in his devotion to the classical unities of time, place, and action, foreshadowed the comedies which followed the reopening of the theaters in 1660. Restoration plays might violate the code of morals, but never the code that prescribed a closely woven plot, wit, and worldliness.

Not all poetry followed French models, however. John Milton, greatest poet of the century, was a belated Elizabethan. His earlier poems continued the pastoral tradition of Spenser's *Shepherd's Calendar*. When *Paradise Lost* (page 240) whirls us into great spaces beyond the stars, we recall that Spenser's Faerie Queene lived in a sort of never-never land.

Prose style also wore two faces. Milton's prose showed the results of intensive study of Latin. The modern reader can easily get lost in Milton's involved sentences or weaken under his steady barrage of big words (Latin derivatives, of course). This ponderous style was not confined to Milton but was used by many theologians and scholars.

In the second half of the century we meet Dryden, who sensed that English speech was now quite different from what it had been a hundred years before. Many obsolete words and affectations had been trimmed off. Sentence structure had been greatly simplified. In Dryden's hands English became a precise instrument of thinking, more like French than like Latin. As he was practically a literary dictator in his day, Dryden's style was influential in forming the prose style of our own time as well as that of the seventeenth century. His essay on page 266, except for a few archaic words, might well be a product of our own day.

A third style might be called Biblical prose because it resulted from the widespread reading of the King James Version of the Bible, published at the beginning of the century. This was the one book of distinctive style read by the common people, and, like Shakespeare's writings, it has enriched our speech immensely. Here are some well-known phrases which you must have heard used entirely outside religious situations:

balm in Gilead
beat their swords into plowshares
sow the wind and reap the whirlwind
whited sepulchers full of dead men's bones
a house divided against itself

heap coals of fire on his head
thorn in the flesh
escaped with the skin of my teeth
the apple of his eye
a man after his own heart

The Bible added an element of dignity and beauty to the writing of many who had never attended Oxford and Cambridge. The best example of King James style in this volume is the selection from Bunyan's *The Pilgrim's Progress* (page 249). It is amazing that a totally uneducated tinker could produce a tale that has probably influenced more people than any other one book except the Bible. Bunyan used many of the older Saxon words, now on their way out, such as *befell, hubbub, runagate, cheapen* (to buy), *rabblement;* but side by side with them appear many Latin derivatives: *ignominy, commotion, heretic,* and *celestial.*

New words were constantly flowing into the language from various sources. With colonists flocking to America in great numbers, the small trickle of Spanish and American Indian words, noted in the preceding chapter, had grown into a rapid stream. Englishmen learned the meanings of *maize, tepee, canoe, squaw, papoose, chipmunk,* and countless others. Little did the Londoner realize that these outlandish words were just the beginning of a significant cleavage between English and American vocabulary, spelling, punctuation, idiom, and slang. Separate dictionaries became necessary eventually, and books came to be written about the American language.

Commercial rivalry, too, made its mark on the language. Already in the Middle Ages the Low Countries had attained a place of importance in navigation and trade. You remember that Chaucer's Wife of Bath could weave as well as the women of Flanders — a great distinction, for weaving was a specialty of the Low Countries. Many terms used in weaving come to us from the Dutch language: *curl, spool, stripe,*

tuck. When Charles I got England into an unpopular war with Holland, one result of the encounters on the sea was that we acquired words such as *bowsprit, freight,* and *keel* from the Dutch. More recently we continued the list with *dock, yacht,* and *yawl.*

In contrast to the words needed for business dealings came a whole new vocabulary in the realm of music. Toward the end of the century, Italian music swept London off its feet. With Italian musical styles came musical terms which have never left our language and are familiar to all students and lovers of music today: *opera, aria, oratorio, soprano, contralto, allegro, piano, fortissimo, sonata, cantata.* Look up the derivation of some of them.

Largo came from the same Latin root as *large,* but the two words entered our language five hundred years apart. *Large* came through the Norman French and is first recorded in English in 1175; *largo* came through the Italian and is first mentioned in 1683. You can find many examples of these "word immigrants" to English, some of which "came over on the *Mayflower*" while others are newly arrived.

London Bridge in the seventeenth century.

THE
EIGHTEENTH
CENTURY

1700 – 1800

Aт the beginning of this period the kingdoms of England and Scotland were officially united (1707), becoming the United Kingdom, their official title to this day. But here we shall follow the usual custom and refer to them as Britain. Notice, however, that we do not talk about "British literature" and also that an inhabitant of Britain is a Briton, not a "Britisher."

As several of the most brilliant writers of this century were Irishmen — notably, Jonathan Swift (1667–1745), Oliver Goldsmith (1728–74), and Richard Brinsley Sheridan (1751–1816) — it is time something is said about Ireland. Unlike Scotland, which shared the monarchy on equal terms with England, Ireland was a country that had been conquered by the English. The genuine Irish, mostly peasants, were Catholics and still spoke their own language, Gaelic. But most of the landowners and the professional class came from families of English settlers, and it is these Anglo-Irish, an unusually gifted, witty people, who gave English literature so many brilliant writers, from Jonathan Swift to Bernard Shaw.

THE REIGN OF THE HANOVERS

Something must be said too about the monarchy. After William and Mary came Mary's sister, Queen Anne, the last of the Stuarts, a fat, sleepy sort of woman who reigned from 1702 to 1714. On her death a difficult situation arose. The direct succession to the throne belonged to the line of the deposed

◀ The items in the frontispiece are identified on page 362.

James II, his son, and then his grandson, the famous "Bonnie Prince Charlie" of romantic legend. These Stuarts were waiting in France, just over the water, to be recalled by their still numerous supporters, known as "Jacobites." (When the king's health was drunk, if a man passed his glass of wine over the water jug, he was really drinking to "the king over the water" and was actually a Jacobite.) In order to avoid the Stuart succession, the crown was offered to a cousin of Queen Anne, the ruler of the small German kingdom of Hanover, who took the throne as George I. He reigned from 1714–27 and was followed by his son, George II (1727–60), an eccentric little man. George III, who was still reigning when the century ended, was the grandson of George II and for many years, toward the end of his life, was insane. His obstinacy, together with his attempt to increase the power of the Crown, had some unfortunate results, among them the loss to Britain of her American colonies.

New York Public Library, Print Room

George III

The Hanovers were not a very happy choice, but two attempts — in 1715 and 1745 — to restore the Stuarts were failures. (The one in 1745, however, nearly succeeded, for the wild Highland followers of "Bonnie Prince Charlie" reached the English Midlands before they were defeated. It is this '45 rebellion around which so many romantic stories have been written.) From now on the two-party political system, which America adopted later, came into being. The Whigs represented chiefly the financial and mercantile interests, the cities and towns, the progressive element, and were strongly opposed to any interference in politics by the monarchy. The Tories, many of them Jacobites in these earlier years, represented the country squires and their folk, all the people who favored old traditions. Though there were general elections then as now, only a comparatively small number of people were entitled to vote. Some quite large towns had no Member of Parliament at all, while some decaying little places, known as "rotten boroughs," were still able to elect two members. There was no real political democracy as we know it today, but, on the other hand, the ordinary people of the eighteenth century were public-spirited and often expressed their dissatisfaction by violent rioting that could be quelled only by military force.

A CENTURY OF WARS

From the beginning to the end of the century the great rival, the enemy, was France. At first the struggle was for European supremacy, and this produced the brilliant victories of John Churchill, Duke of Marlborough, an ancestor of Winston Churchill. But by the middle of the century, when Britain found a great war minister in William Pitt, afterwards Earl of Chatham (who, incidentally, sided with the colonists in the War of Independence), the struggle with France was for overseas empire. Here Britain had an advantage because she had the better navy and knew how to use her sea power. It was during these years that the huge British Empire, ranging from Gibraltar to India and Canada, was built up. In the last ten years of the century, the French had to be fought again because the British Tory ministers were afraid of the consequences of the French Revolution, an important historical event though not, as we know now, as important as the earlier and apparently less dramatic American Revolution.

It was a century of wars, fought in all manner of places and conditions, but they were not wars as we understand them now. They were usually fought by small professional armies (half the troops that Washington had to beat were not British but German), and the daily lives of most people in the nations concerned were affected hardly at all. Even when Britain and France were at war, trade and cultural exchanges continued between the two countries. There was no "total war," one whole nation trying to conquer another, such as we have had in the twentieth century. And in this respect the eighteenth century was far more civilized than our century has been.

THE INDUSTRIAL REVOLUTION

During the latter half of the century British prosperity was increasing rapidly because of what we have come to call the "Industrial Revolution" — that is, the increasing use of machinery and steam power in the manufacture of goods. What had previously been made by hand, often by people working at home, was now manufactured on an infinitely larger scale in mills and factories. Though the Industrial Revolution took place throughout the western world, Britain easily led the way because she had the necessary coal and iron ore, her inventors designed many of the new machines, and her growing empire gave her large overseas markets. This led to a rapid increase in population as well as in national wealth. But with all this sheer gain there came some sad losses, as many writers were quick to perceive.

For example, William Blake (1757–1827), the poet, artist, and mystic, re-

BRITAIN
1700-1800

SCOTLAND

1 SKYE

2 Bannockburn

Edinburgh

TWEED

3 Ayr   4 Auchinleck

DOON   AFTON

Dumfries

IRELAND

5 Dublin

ENGLAND

6 Lichfield

7 Cambridge

WALES

8 Oxford   9 Stoke Poges   10 London

Hampton Court   Twickenham

12 Bath   11

1 Johnson and Boswell visited Skye in their *Journey to the Hebrides.* 2 Site of famous battle (1314), celebrated by Burns, in which Robert the Bruce defeated the English. 3 Home of Robert Burns. 4 Family home of James Boswell. 5 Goldsmith attended college here. Birthplace of Swift (1667), who later became Dean of Dublin's St. Patrick's. 6 Birthplace of Joseph Addison (1672) and Samuel Johnson (1709). 7 Thomas Gray studied and became professor here. 8 Addison and Steele and Samuel Johnson attended the university here. 9 Vil-

lage identified with Gray's "Elegy in a Country Churchyard." 10 Coffeehouses flourished and *The Tatler, Spectator,* and Defoe's *Review* were published here. Center of elegant society; writers' mecca where Johnson's famous Literary Club met. 11 Home of Alexander Pope; Horace Walpole's Strawberry Hill. 12 Health resort, popular in eighteenth century. Visited by many literary figures, including Fielding, Smollett, Sheridan, Goldsmith, Southey, and Jane Austen; and the setting of much contemporary writing.

ferred with horror to "the dark, satanic mills." Much of England, especially in the north and the Midlands, was rapidly transformed into a blackened, ruined countryside of mine shafts, slag heaps, tall chimneys pouring out smoke, and horrible industrial towns in which people lived and worked in appalling conditions. All this, against which writer after writer protested, was not observed and felt in its full force until the next century, but already in the eighteenth century its shadow began to creep over the country.

THE AGE OF REASON

On the whole, however, this was a century very well pleased with itself. In this period Britain was free from the revolutionary, heated atmosphere of the seventeenth century and the growing doubts and dark divisions of the nineteenth century. The upper classes and the middle classes in Britain during this age felt more complacent than they had ever felt before or since. They felt that they were living in the best of all possible worlds, as the influential German philosopher Leibnitz (1646–1716) had proved to almost everybody's satisfaction. [But one who would not accept this smug notion was the great satirist, Voltaire (1694–1778), whose famous *Candide* is a savage attack on this complacency. Voltaire was, however, an open admirer of Britain, even though he said it had "fifty religions and only one sauce."] This eighteenth-century complacency was due partly to the work of the scientists and philosophers who really belonged to the previous century. They had announced in their various ways that the universe was a smoothly running machine first set in motion by a vaguely benevolent deity and that, so long as man understood the working of this machine, he could be said to be the master of it. This rational religion was known as Deism. Indeed, human reason and the watchword "common sense" played so large and significant a role in this period that it is often referred to as "the age of reason."

AN AGE OF ELEGANCE

Real civilization, not unlike but superior to the old, classical civilization of Greece and Rome, to which the eighteenth century compared itself, had been achieved at last, it was felt, and now society, by which was meant persons of position, wealth, and influence, could settle down to enjoy it. Never in European history do we see men and women so elaborately artificial, so far removed from natural appearance, as these men and women of the eighteenth century. The men wore wigs, which often had to be curled every day, and with them gaily colored and lace-trimmed satin coats and waistcoats, silk stockings, and

New York Public Library, Print Room

The Vauxhall Gardens, a fashionable eighteenth-century amusement place in London.

buckled shoes. The women often had immense coiffures of powdered hair and enormous hooped skirts and were carried to their parties in sedan chairs. An evening party in high society, taking place in a room lit with hundreds of candles, must have been an astonishingly impressive spectacle.

These people lived well, better in some ways than similar people have done before or since. The outward trappings of their lives were truly magnificent. We know this because the evidence is still with us, not only in pictures of the age but also in the houses, the furniture, the domestic utensils they left behind. It was in England especially that all these things were so exquisitely designed and made. The domestic architecture, from the Queen Anne style to the late Georgian, has probably never been equaled. The interior decoration of the Adams Brothers, the furniture designed by Chippendale, Hepplewhite, and Sheraton — all these were magnificent. Find if you can, if only reposing in some museum, a Georgian silver tankard or coffee pot. Remember that these people were surrounded by such things all day, and you will then realize with what style they lived.

Only a small minority, however, lived on this superb scale, waited upon by servants who were themselves often waited upon by humbler servants. (The footmen, with powdered hair and knee-breeches, who still exist in a few very large households in Britain, of course wear eighteenth-century costume. And the wigs still worn by judges and barristers in English courts of law are another direct link with the eighteenth century.) The mass of the people did not wear wigs (which cost a great deal of money) and satin coats and breeches and silk stockings; they did not sit on chairs designed by Chippendale and Hepplewhite, nor drink out of those beautiful silver tankards. They dressed plainly, wore their own hair unpowdered, and drank out of clumsy mugs and cups that were broken long ago. We do not have to guess how ordinary folk lived then, because not only have we the eighteenth-century authors to tell us, but we have

Boston Public Library

Merrymaking at the village fair provided rural folk with informal entertainment.

also an artist, William Hogarth (1697–1764), who had a great talent for exact realism and whose work offers us a panorama of the lives of all classes. What we learn from Hogarth, as we do from the novelists, is that the life of the poorer folk was often rough and rowdy, filled with crude sports and heavy drinking.

NEW RELIGIOUS DEVELOPMENTS

There was, however, another side to the picture. The official Church of England during the eighteenth century existed, for the most part, in a state of sleepy conformity. Many clergymen, some of them the younger sons of aristocratic landowners who could not provide for them out of their estates but could offer them church "livings," had several different and widely separated "parishes." They took the incomes attached to these "parishes" or "livings" and then appointed poor curates, at fifty pounds a year, to do the work. Even some of the bishops did not live within their dioceses or, if they did, they often concerned themselves more with scholarly research, antiquarianism, even chemistry, than they did with church work. Some of these eighteenth-century churchmen did not really believe in the Christian faith at all, regarding it as something intended for simple, uneducated minds. Laurence Sterne (1713–68), the great humorous novelist, was a parson, but he can hardly be accepted as a Christian believer. As soon as he became a successful writer he spent long periods hundreds of miles away from his church and his vicarage.

But such official indifference to the burning realities of religion inevitably produced a sharp reaction, and it is here that we come to the other side of the picture. Enthusiasts like the brothers Wesley began to convert ordinary people to a fervently evangelical type of Christianity. Throughout the century the various nonconformist sects were joined by more and more of the working folk and the members of the new middle classes created by the Industrial Revolution, especially in the Midlands and the north of England, where the growth of industry late in the period was to send the population figures soaring. We have then an elegant, complacent, skeptical, and cynical upper class, a rough and rowdy mob of poor folk (see Hogarth), and between them a growing number of earnestly pious and intensely respectable people belonging to the middle and artisan classes.

LITERATURE IN AN AGE OF FORMALITY

Literature at the beginning of this period, say, during the reign of Queen Anne, was created chiefly for a small and compact society of important and influential persons. It was very much a public literature, not representing the deeply felt impressions, hopes, or fears, of one individual, but the outlook and values of this limited society. It was literature that could be read aloud in a drawing room, enjoyed in a theater, or some other public place. Now, an atmosphere of this kind encourages comedy, satire in both verse and prose, pleasant little essays, and criticism, but it is fatal to poetry. Shakespeare's sonnets or Keats' odes would have seemed absurd to this society, which did not expect from literature anything so intensely private or intimately revealing. A man does not describe his most secret dreams to fifty people (many of them ready to snicker) in a drawing room. Poetry at its best comes out of an essentially individual inner life, out of what is private and not public. What these people believed in was not the inner life but rather what they felt to be civilized good taste, what persons of common sense and with reasonably nice feelings could enjoy together.

This is hopelessly cramping for the real poet, and so we cannot help feeling that a writer like Alexander Pope (1688–1744), at heart a real poet with a wonderful command of the smooth but often witty rhymed couplet, was never able to express himself as fully as he might have in another age. Within narrow limits he did wonderfully well. But, for example, in his translation of Homer, though done with great skill, we feel he is dressing the shaggy heroes of Greece and Troy in wigs, satin coats, and silk stockings, and giving them canes and snuffboxes to carry.

LITERARY PATRONAGE

But the writers of Queen Anne's reign, poets like John Gay (1685–1732) and Matthew Prior (1664–1721), and essayists like Joseph Addison (1672–1719) and Richard Steele (1672–1729), did not expect to be rewarded chiefly by the general reading public. Either they were rewarded directly by the

THE EIGHTEENTH CENTURY

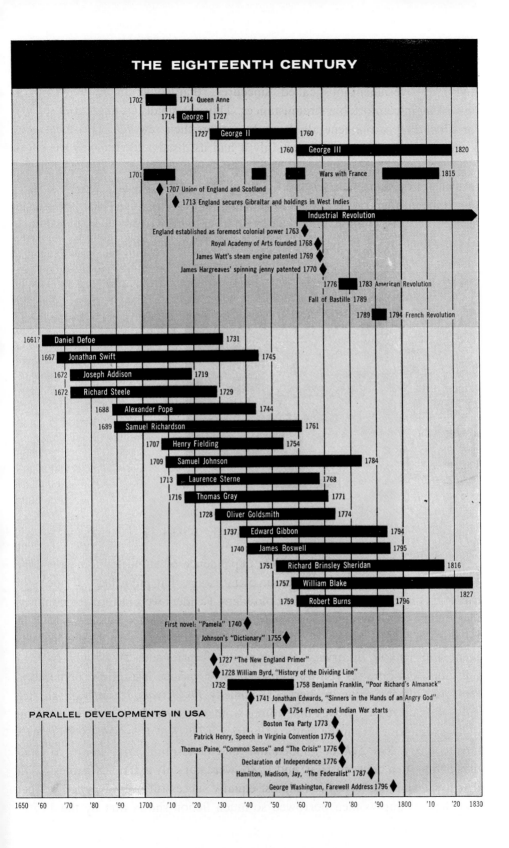

1702 ☐ 1714 Queen Anne

1714 George I 1727

1727 George II 1760

1760 George III 1820

1701 ☐ ☐ ☐ Wars with France ☐ 1815

◆ 1707 Union of England and Scotland

◆ 1713 England secures Gibraltar and holdings in West Indies

Industrial Revolution

England established as foremost colonial power 1763 ◆

Royal Academy of Arts founded 1768 ◆

James Watt's steam engine patented 1769 ◆

James Hargreaves' spinning jenny patented 1770 ◆

1776 ☐ 1783 American Revolution

Fall of Bastille 1789

1789 ☐ 1794 French Revolution

1661? Daniel Defoe 1731

1667 Jonathan Swift 1745

1672 Joseph Addison 1719

1672 Richard Steele 1729

1688 Alexander Pope 1744

1689 Samuel Richardson 1761

1707 Henry Fielding 1754

1709 Samuel Johnson 1784

1713 Laurence Sterne 1768

1716 Thomas Gray 1771

1728 Oliver Goldsmith 1774

1737 Edward Gibbon 1794

1740 James Boswell 1795

1751 Richard Brinsley Sheridan 1816

1757 William Blake 1827

1759 Robert Burns 1796

First novel: "Pamela" 1740 ◆

Johnson's "Dictionary" 1755 ◆

◆ 1727 "The New England Primer"

◆ 1728 William Byrd, "History of the Dividing Line"

1732 ☐ 1758 Benjamin Franklin, "Poor Richard's Almanack"

◆ 1741 Jonathan Edwards, "Sinners in the Hands of an Angry God"

◆ 1754 French and Indian War starts

PARALLEL DEVELOPMENTS IN USA

Boston Tea Party 1773 ◆

Patrick Henry, Speech in Virginia Convention 1775 ◆

Thomas Paine, "Common Sense" and "The Crisis" 1776 ◆

Declaration of Independence 1776 ◆

Hamilton, Madison, Jay, "The Federalist" 1787 ◆

George Washington, Farewell Address 1796 ◆

1650 '60 '70 '80 '90 1700 '10 '20 '30 '40 '50 '60 '70 '80 '90 1800 '10 '20 1830

wealthy patrons to whom they dedicated their work or they were given easy, well-paid government jobs, called "sinecures," that would enable them to keep on writing in comfortable circumstances. Thus the small but influential society for which they wrote generally brought authors their rewards. This may seem a very odd system to us and certainly it had its disadvantages — as we know from a famous bitter letter addressed by Samuel Johnson (1709–84) to his former patron, Lord Chesterfield (1694–1773) — but it had some advantages too. It meant that a writer could confidently address his work to cultivated, intelligent readers, could maintain a certain level in his writing, and did not have to cater to a mob as so many writers today feel they have to.

Bodleian Library

Coffeehouses were extremely popular in eighteenth-century London. They served not only as places for refreshment, but as meeting places where men gathered with friends and colleagues to discuss the events of the day.

THE NEW READING PUBLIC

Very soon, however, the complete dependence of authors upon patronage gave way to a system not unlike our own, except that publishers of books in those days were still themselves booksellers. Readers were no longer confined to a small class. The new middle class, especially its women members, took to buying and reading books. If they could not afford to buy them, they borrowed them from lending libraries, not free public libraries such as we now have in our cities, but libraries run by shopkeepers or various institutions demanding fees. An amusing scene in Sheridan's comedy *The Rivals*, set in Bath, the famous holiday resort, proves that young women visiting Bath borrowed fiction in large quantities from the lending libraries. (*The Rivals* as well as Sheridan's later comedy, *The School for Scandal*, and Goldsmith's *She Stoops to Conquer*, all written between 1770 and 1780, were not only extremely successful in their own time but have been almost equally successful ever since.) The fact that these young women borrowed so much fiction shows that by the 1770's the novel, though a comparatively new literary form, had won great popularity.

At any rate, outstanding novelists of the day, such as Samuel Richardson (1689–1761) and Henry Fielding (1707–54), Laurence Sterne and Tobias Smollett (1721–71), were almost entirely dependent upon this new and growing reading public. Authors of more weighty works, however — Samuel Johnson, for instance, or Edward Gibbon (1737–94), the great historian of the Roman Empire — usually brought out their works accompanied by a list of wealthy subscribers, whose support guaranteed that the books would at least pay for themselves.

Nevertheless, professional writers who had to earn their living and had no government pension (as Johnson finally had) often led desperate lives scribbling away day and night to keep themselves from starvation. They would often undertake, for miserable payment, to write long books on subjects they knew little about, just because these were what the "booksellers" (that is, the publishers) demanded from them. So for years a man of genius like Oliver Goldsmith (1730–74) — capable of writing comedy, fiction, and verse that would enchant future generations — wasted precious time and energy on this sort of hack work. If the rewards of good original work had been greater and more immediate than they were, the literature of this century might have been even richer than it is.

THE BEGINNINGS OF ROMANTICISM

In his masterpiece, the *Life of Samuel Johnson,* James Boswell (1740–95) tells about an old acquaintance of Johnson's who said that he too might have been a philosopher except that "cheerfulness kept breaking in." Now something had to break into this eighteenth century in Britain. For it was altogether too calm and complacent, too easily convinced that a new and superior classical age had arrived, too sure of itself and its standards, too contemptuous of the past and of all that earlier men had thought and felt, too certain that it lived in the best of all possible worlds. It ignored or denounced too often the secret inner life of men, their hidden dreams and desires and hopes, all that belonged essentially to men as individuals and not as members of a society. Even the writers who seem to us typically eighteenth-century figures show that the pressure of this conformity was too much for them: Jonathan Swift, for all his powerful intellect, has a suggestion of some dark madness in his savage satires, and Johnson, for all his sociability and delight in good talk, is at heart melancholy and fearful, enjoying the lighted dinner table all the more because of the threatening darkness.

What breaks through into this public literature of an ordered and complacent society is the other side of man's life, his inner world of wonder and strange feeling, all that cannot be expressed in a social mood of philosophic calm. This new literature belongs not to what is public and classical but to what is essentially private, and thus is called *romantic*. This breakthrough, which was gradual and began about the middle of the century, shows itself in various ways. It shows itself in the curious hothouse sentimentality of Richardson's novels, soon to conquer Europe, and in the strongly personal mixture of humor and sentiment in Laurence Sterne's work. It shows itself in the publication of the old ballads by Bishop Percy (1729–1811), ballads that will have a tremendous influence on the whole Romantic movement. It shows itself in the new taste, led by that apparently typical eighteenth-century dilettante, Horace Walpole (1717–97), for ruins and Gothic castles and tales of mystery. It shows itself in the fashion during the latter half of the century for founding strange, secret societies interested in magic and mysterious rites.

But this breakthrough is most obvious in poetry, which cannot possibly exist long as a public activity expressing not the individual poet but society itself. Though they are all in many ways typical eighteenth-century men, Thomas Gray (1716–71), Oliver Goldsmith, and William Cowper (1731–1800) in their best verse begin to show the other side of life. In Scotland, Robert Burns (1759–96), still regarded by the Scots as their national poet, alternates between verse in the acceptable eighteenth-century style and impassioned lyrics or comic-pathetic narrative poems about the peasantry that are undoubtedly Romantic in feeling. And then there is William Blake (1757–1827), an astonishing character and one of the world's great originals, who in his earliest poems seems like another Elizabethan but then flashes out, completely disregarding the taste of the time, in work that blazes with his own highly original genius. By this time the Romantic Age has almost arrived.

The last years of the eighteenth century were altogether different from its first years. Nothing was certain after the destructive fury of the French Revolution. Britain was sharply divided between those who had feared and denounced the French Revolution and those who had welcomed it. All the old values and standards vanished in the smoke of burning buildings and the roar of Napoleon's cannons. (At one time or another his armies successfully invaded Italy, the Low Countries, Austria and Germany, Spain and Poland.) Anything could happen now; it was that kind of world, that kind of universe. The social order was no longer as stable as it once had been. The old aristocracy was giving way to a rising middle class, and there was increasing sympathy for the underprivileged classes. Ideas of political freedom, of independence, of human brotherhood and man's "natural rights" had become more and more widespread, as revolutions on both sides of the Atlantic Ocean had attested. A new spirit was abroad. Gone were the philosophic calm, the complacency, the public good taste, the curled wigs and lacy satin coats, the coffeehouse wits and critics and their *Tatlers* and *Spectators:* the whole age was as dead as Queen Anne.

J. B. P.

DANIEL DEFOE

1661?–1731

National Portrait Gallery

Daniel Defoe, the first important English journalist, had a curious and colorful career. The brain of this versatile and prolific writer teemed with projects and reforms, many of which were far beyond the ideas of his day.

The son of a London butcher, he married, traveled on the Continent, and served in the army before he began to write. In 1704 he established the *Review,* one of the early London newspapers, which he ran almost singlehandedly for nine years. He also turned out political pamphlets by the score. In *The Shortest Way with Dissenters,* Defoe made the seemingly savage suggestion that death or violent penalties be meted out to members of dissenting churches, one of which he himself be-

longed to. Supporters of the Church of England accepted this as a serious solution but soon discovered that they had been tricked and ridiculed. When they had Defoe fined, imprisoned, and put in the pillory, he immediately composed a satiric "Hymn to the Pillory," which his friends sang in the streets while pelting him with flowers.

In 1719, after serving for a while as a government agent, Defoe turned from journalism to the writing of novels and fictitious history like *A Journal of the Plague Year*. In *Robinson Crusoe*, his best-known book, he describes the adventures of a shipwrecked sailor cast away on a desert island as if he were reporting a series of actual facts.

A Journal of the Plague Year

This book, written in 1722, is an example of Defoe's ability to persuade readers, by his direct style and careful reporting of details, that fiction is literal truth. With the accuracy of a historian and the graphic detail of an imaginative writer, he pictures

London in the grip of a horrible epidemic.

The *Journal* purports to be the diary of a Londoner who lived through the Great Plague of 1665, when thousands upon thousands of city dwellers were struck down by the rampant disease. Since Defoe was only about four years old at the time, he drew his information entirely from records and conversations. Early in the narrative the writer tells of his indecision about leaving London for the safety of the country. Because he feels an obligation to look after his servants and his business and because he finds consolation in the Bible ("Surely he shall deliver thee . . . from the noisome pestilence"), he decides to stay. Thus he is able to describe the day-by-day horrors of the epidemic. An excerpt from the *Journal* follows.

1665. It pleased God that I was still spared, and very hearty and sound in health, but very impatient of being pent up within doors without air, as I had been for fourteen days, or thereabouts; and I could not restrain myself, but I would go to carry a letter for my brother to the Posthouse. Then it was, indeed, that I observed a profound silence in the streets. When I came to the Posthouse, as I went to put in my letter, I saw a man stand in one corner of the yard, and talking to another at a window, and a third had opened a door belonging to the office. In the middle of the yard lay a small leather purse, with two keys hanging at it, and money in it, but nobody would meddle with it. I asked how long it had lain there; the man at the window said it had lain almost an hour, but they had not meddled with it, because they did not know but the person who dropped it might come back to look for it. I had no such need of money, nor was the sum so big that I had any inclination to meddle with it to get the money at the hazard it might be attended with; so I seemed to go away, when the man who had opened the door said he would take it up; but so that if the right owner came for it, he should be sure to have it. So he went in and fetched a pail of water, and set it down hard by the purse, then went again and fetched some gunpowder and cast a good deal of powder upon the purse, and then made a

train from that which he had thrown loose upon the purse; the train reached about two yards. After this he goes in a third time, and fetches out a pair of tongs red hot, and which he had prepared, I suppose, on purpose; and first setting fire to the train of powder, that singed the purse, and also smoked the air sufficiently. But he was not content with that; but he then takes up the purse with the tongs, holding it so long till the tongs burnt through the purse, and then he shook the money out into the pail of water, so he carried it in. The money, as I remember, was about thirteen shillings, and some smooth groats, and brass farthings.

There might, perhaps, have been several poor people, as I have observed above, that would have been hardy enough to have ventured for the sake of the money; but you may easily see, by what I have observed, that the few people who were spared were very careful of themselves at that time when the distress was so exceeding great. . . .

It would pierce the hearts of all that came by to hear the piteous cries of those infected people, who being thus out of their understandings by the violence of their pain, or the heat of their blood, were either shut in, or perhaps tied in their beds and chairs, to prevent their doing themselves hurt, and who would make a dreadful outcry at their being confined, and at their not being permitted to "die at large," as they called it, and as they would have done before.

This running of distempered people about the streets was very dismal, and the Magistrates did their utmost to prevent it; but as it was generally in the night and always sudden, when such attempts were made, the officers could not be at hand to prevent it, and even when they got out in the day, the officers appointed did not care to meddle with them, because, as they were all grievously infected, to be sure, when they were come to that height, so they were more than ordinarily infectious, and it was one of the most dangerous things that could be to touch them. On the other hand, they generally ran on, not knowing what they did, till they dropped down stark dead, or till they had exhausted their spirits so as that they would fall, and then die in perhaps half an hour or an hour; and what was most piteous to hear, they were sure to come to themselves entirely in that half-hour or hour, and then to make most grievous and piercing cries and lamentations in the deep afflicting sense of the condition they were in. This was much of it before the order for shutting up of houses was strictly put in execution, for at first the watchmen were not so rigorous and severe, as they were afterward, in the keeping the people in; that is to say, before they were, I mean some of them, severely punished for their neglect, failing in their duty, and letting people who were under their care slip away, or conniving at their going abroad, whether sick or well. But after they saw the officers appointed to examine into their conduct were resolved to have them do their duty, or be punished for the omission, they were more exact, and the people were strictly restrained; which was a thing they took so ill, and bore so impatiently, that their discontents can hardly be described; but there was an absolute necessity for it, that must be confessed, unless some other measures had been timely entered upon, and it was too late for that.

Had not this particular of the sick being restrained as above, been our case at that time,[1] London would have been the most dreadful place that ever was in the world; there would, for aught I know, have as many people died in the streets as died in their houses; for when the Distemper was at its height, it generally made them raving and delirious, and when they were so, they would never be persuaded to keep in their beds but by

force; and many, who were not tied, threw themselves out of windows, when they found they could not get leave to go out of their doors.

It was for want of people conversing one with another, in this time of calamity, that it was impossible any particular person could come at the knowledge of all the extraordinary cases that occurred in different families; and particularly I believe it was never known to this day how many people in their deliriums drowned themselves in the Thames, and in the river which runs from the marshes by Hackney, which we generally called Ware River, or Hackney River. As to those which were set down in the weekly bill,[2] they were indeed few; nor could it be known of any of those, whether they drowned themselves by accident or not. But I believe, I might reckon up more, who, within the compass of my knowledge or observation really drowned themselves in that year than are put down in the bill of all put together, for many of the bodies were never found, who yet were known to be so lost: and the like, in other methods of self-destruction. There was also one man, in or about Whitecross Street, who burnt himself to death in his bed; some said it was done by himself, others that it was by the treachery of the nurse that attended him; but that he had the Plague upon him was agreed by all. . . .

We that were Examiners [3] were often not able to come at the knowledge of the infection being entered into a house till it was too late to shut it up; and sometimes not till the people that were left were all dead. In Petticoat Lane two houses together were infected, and several people sick; but the Distemper was so well concealed that the Examiner, who was my neighbor, got no knowledge of it, till notice was sent him that the

---

[1] *Had not . . . time:* if we had not restrained the sick people in the manner described above.

[2] *bill:* a list of the dead in each parish and the cause of death. [3] *Examiners:* men whose job it was to determine which houses had been infected by the plague.

people were all dead, and that the carts [1] should call there to fetch them away. The two heads of the families concerted their measures, and so ordered their matters, as that when the Examiner was in the neighborhood, they appeared generally at a time, and answered, that is, lied for one another; or got some of the neighborhood to say they were all in health, and, perhaps, knew no better, till death making it impossible to keep it any longer as a secret, the Dead carts were called in the night to both houses, and so it became public; but when the Examiner ordered the constable to shut up the houses, there was nobody left in them but three people, two in one house, and one in the other, just dying, and a nurse in each house, who acknowledged that they had buried five before, that the houses had been infected nine or ten days, and that for all the rest of the two families, which were many, they were gone, some sick, some well, or whether sick or well, could not be known.

In like manner, at another house in the same lane, a man, having his family infected, but very unwilling to be shut up, when he could conceal it no longer, shut up himself; that is to say, he set the great Red Cross upon his door, with the words — "Lord have Mercy upon Us"; and so deluded the Examiner, who supposed it had been done by the constable by order of the other Examiner, for there were two Examiners to every district or precinct; by this means he had free egress and regress [2] into his house again, and out of it, as he pleased, notwithstanding it was infected; till at length his stratagem was found out, and then he, with the sound part of his servants and family, made off, and escaped; so they were not shut up at all. . . .

It is here, however, to be observed, that after the funerals became so many

that people could not toll the bell, mourn, or weep, or wear black for one another, as they did before; no, nor so much as make coffins for those that died; so after a while the fury of the Infection appeared to be so increased, that in short, they shut up no houses at all. It seemed enough that all the remedies of that kind had been used till they were found fruitless, and that the Plague spread itself with an irresistible fury; so that as the Fire, the succeeding year, spread itself, and burnt with such violence, that the citizens, in despair, gave over [3] their endeavors to extinguish it, so in the Plague, it came at last to such violence that the people sat still, looking at one another, and seemed quite abandoned to despair. Whole streets seemed to be desolated, and not to be shut up only, but to be emptied of their inhabitants; doors were left open, and windows stood shattering with the wind in empty houses for want of people to shut them. In a word, people began to give up themselves to their fears, and to think that all regulations and methods were in vain, and that there was nothing to be hoped for, but an universal Desolation; and it was even in the height of this general despair that it pleased God to stay his hand, and to slacken the fury of the Contagion, in such a manner as was even surprising (like its beginning), and demonstrated it to be his own particular Hand, and that above, if not without, the Agency of Means, as I shall take notice of in its proper place.

[3] over: up.

CREATING ATMOSPHERE

1. What evidence does Defoe give to show that London was in a state of panic during the plague? What attempts were made to maintain order? How successful were they? What examples are given of the orders being evaded during the plague?

2. In what way does this journal reveal that Defoe could move easily from fact to fiction? How does he create an atmosphere of horror?

[1] carts: The dead bodies were collected at night in carts and taken to a common burial ground, since the churchyards would not hold them all. [2] egress and regress: exit and entrance.

3. Defoe's description should be compared with Pepys' account of the Great Fire. Which do you consider more graphic, more realistic in impression? Why? In what way does Defoe's description remind you of present-day newspaper reporting?

CLASS ACTIVITY

Small groups of students may do some library research on the great plagues of the fourteenth and seventeenth centuries. What were their effects in England?

JOSEPH ADDISON 1672–1719
and
RICHARD STEELE 1672–1729

British Information

Joseph Addison

British Information

Richard Steele

The names of Addison and Steele are inevitably linked together. They were not only intimate friends but literary partners in one of the most significant enterprises in English literature: *The Spectator*. This modest little paper was the ancestor of our magazines and the feature articles in today's newspapers. It established a new style of writing in English literature — that of the familiar essay.

Though noticeably unlike in disposition, the two men were close friends from childhood. A year before Addison's death they quarreled over politics, which, strangely enough, had helped keep them together over the years. Both were Whigs and therefore opposed to Pope and Swift, who as Tories led a different literary group.

Joseph Addison and Richard Steele first met at the Charterhouse School in London, though Addison was born in England and Steele in Ireland. They continued together through Oxford, where Addison was an accomplished scholar and where Steele already began to show his lively but sometimes extravagant personality. Steele was good-natured, eloquent, versatile in mood, and inefficient. At various times he was captain of the Coldstream Guards, the manager of a theater for which he wrote several sentimental comedies, and official gazetteer for the Whig party, a job that Addison, a fellow Whig, secured for him. Later he turned to still more ventures as magazine publisher, poet, reformer, and Member of Parliament. Always impulsive, sometimes without funds, Steele cut a dashing figure in London. Though he was not as great a literary figure as Addison, he is remembered as a vigorous and original one.

Addison was quite a different person in many ways: elegant, quiet, and dignified. He was kindly, though shy and somewhat withdrawn. It is said that when he arose in Parliament to make his first speech, he was so embarrassed that he sat down without saying a word and never again tried to make a speech there. His triumphs were in literature instead. Though his enduring fame is as an essayist and stylist of English prose (Samuel Johnson once advised students of English to give their "days and nights" to reading Addison), he had one great success in the drama. His tragedy *Cato* was received with great acclaim, largely because the audience could read in its Roman scenes subtle suggestions of the political issues of the day. Three years before his death Addison married the Countess of Warwick and was appointed Secretary of State.

In 1709 Steele started a paper called *The Tatler,* his stated purpose in the first issue being to enliven mere news with gossip of the coffeehouses. In later issues, however, Steele embraced the more serious purpose of serving as a moral influence and speaking out against the negligence and improprieties of his contemporaries. Addison collaborated with Steele in this venture by contributing notes and articles.

When *The Tatler* was discontinued because of political difficulties, Addison and Steele decided to found together *The Spectator,* which would be devoted to literature, manners, and morals. Steele had written two-thirds of *The Tatler,* but Addison wrote more than half the essays in the new journal.

The Tatler (1709 – 1711)

When Steele launched his paper, *The Tatler,* he used the pen name of Isaac Bickerstaff. This name alone was enough to sell the paper because of a practical joke played the year before by Jonathan Swift. A quack astrologer and almanac maker named Partridge had been making a great deal of money out of gullible people by his predictions. To expose the faker, Swift had issued a rival almanac by an imaginary Isaac Bickerstaff, predicting "by the unerring stars" the death of Partridge on March 30. On that day the newspapers carried detailed accounts of the funeral of Partridge and an elegy on him. When Partridge protested that he was not dead, Bickerstaff retorted that his own stars had proved him so, and that these statements came from an impostor. When, therefore, Steele's new periodical appeared under the name of Bickerstaff, the town was naturally alert for further entertainment. It was clever advertising on Steele's part.

The following Prospectus gives the general plan of *The Tatler* and shows the importance of the coffeehouses as a gathering place for the social, political, and literary life of that day.

Steele began a good number of his essays with an appropriate classical motto, a practice which was continued in *The Spectator.* The motto accompanying the Prospectus was taken from Juvenal, a noted Roman poet of the second century. The motto appeared in Latin:

> *Quicquid agunt homines —*
> *nostri est farrago libelli.*
>
> JUVENAL's *Satires,* I, 85–86.

Pope's embellished translation of this motto reads:

> "Whate'er men do, or say, or think, or dream,
> Our motley paper seizes for its theme."

PROSPECTUS

No. 1. Tuesday, 12 April, 1709.

THOUGH the other papers, which are published for the use of the good people of England, have certainly very wholesome effects, and are laudable in their particular kinds, they do not seem to come up to the main design of such narrations, which, I humbly presume, should be principally intended for the use of politic persons, who are so public-spirited as to neglect their own affairs to look into transactions of state. Now these gentlemen, for the most part, being persons of strong zeal, and weak intellects, it is both a charitable and necessary work to offer something, whereby such worthy and well-affected members of the commonwealth may be instructed, after their reading, what to think; which shall be the end and purpose of this my paper, wherein I shall, from time to time, report and consider all matters of what kind soever that shall occur to me, and publish such my advices and reflections every Tuesday, Thursday, and Saturday in the week, for the convenience of the post. I resolve to have something which may be of entertainment to the fair sex, in honor of whom I have invented the title of this paper. I therefore earnestly desire all persons, without distinction, to take it in for the present *gratis*,[1] and hereafter at the price of one penny, forbidding all hawkers to take more for it at their peril. And I desire all persons to consider that I am at a very great charge [2] for the proper materials for this work, as well as that, before I resolved upon it, I had settled a correspondence in all parts of the known and knowing world. And forasmuch as this globe is not trodden upon by mere drudges of business only, but that men of spirit and genius are justly to be esteemed as considerable agents in it, we shall not, upon a dearth of news, present you with musty foreign edicts, and dull proclamations, but shall divide our relation of the passages which occur in action or discourse throughout this town, as well as elsewhere, under such dates of places as may prepare you for the matter you are to expect in the following manner.

All accounts of gallantry, pleasure, and entertainment shall be under the article of White's Chocolate House; poetry under that of Will's Coffeehouse; learning, under the title of Grecian; foreign and domestic news, you will have from St. James's Coffeehouse; and what else I have to offer on any other subject shall be dated from my own Apartment.

I once more desire my reader to consider, that as I cannot keep an ingenious man to go daily to Will's under twopence each day, merely for his charges; [3] to White's under sixpence; nor to the Grecian, without allowing him some plain Spanish,[4] to be as able as others at the learned table; and that a good observer cannot speak with even Kidney [5] at St. James's without clean linen; I say, these considerations will, I hope, make all persons willing to comply with my humble request (when my *gratis* stock is exhausted) of a penny apiece; especially since they are sure of some proper amusement, and that it is impossible for me to want means to entertain them, having, besides the force of my own parts,[6] the power of divination, and that I can, by casting a figure, tell you all that will happen before it comes to pass.

But this last faculty I shall use very sparingly, and speak but of few things until they are passed, for fear of divulging matters which may offend our superiors.

---

[3] *charges:* expenses. The twopence would buy him some coffee, presumably. [4] *Spanish:* wine. [5] *Kidney:* name of a waiter. [6] *force . . . parts:* the power of my own abilities.

[1] *gratis:* given without charge. [2] *charge:* pains.

The Spectator (1711 – 1712)

Two months after the appearance of the last number of *The Tatler,* the first number of *The Spectator* was issued. Its avowed purpose was "to enliven morality with wit, and to temper wit with morality." The extravagances and absurdities of the fashionable life of the day were gently yet pointedly satirized. The popularity of the little periodical was tremendous. From about three thousand, the circulation increased until as many as twenty thousand of certain issues were printed. Considering the size of London at that time and the limited number of possible readers, this was an astounding circulation. Altogether 555 issues of *The Spectator* were published.

Like our newspapers, this little paper appeared daily on the breakfast table and contained its "classified ads" of Wanted, Lost or Stolen, Amusements, and Merchandise, many of which offer amusing reading today. But it was written in a more finished literary style and was more limited in its scope than a newspaper, having only one main article to an issue. All the essays from *The Spectator* included here are by Addison. The essays are signed by the "Spectator," who is presented as a man of good sense, good breeding, and good nature, going quietly about London, saying little but seeing much. This might well serve as a picture of Addison himself.

To Steele is given credit for originating the club to which the Spectator was supposed to belong. This club consisted of a lawyer, a merchant, an ex-army captain, an elderly gallant, and a country baronet. The last of these appealed to Addison's imagination especially, and some of the most famous essays of *The Spectator* were devoted to this country gentleman, Sir Roger de Coverley. When printed together these essays form a running narrative, which is, in effect, a predecessor of the novel.

SIR ROGER AT CHURCH

No. 112. Monday, July 9, 1711.

First, in obedience to thy country's rites,
Worship th' immortal gods.[1]

I AM ALWAYS very well pleased with a country Sunday, and think, if keeping holy the seventh day were only a human institution, it would be the best method that could have been thought of for the polishing and civilizing of mankind. It is certain the country people would soon degenerate into a kind of savages and barbarians, were there not such frequent returns of a stated time, in which the whole village meet together with their best faces, and in their cleanliest habits, to converse with one another upon indifferent subjects, hear their duties explained to them, and join together in adoration of the Supreme Being. Sunday clears away the rust of the whole week, not only as it refreshes in their minds the notions of religion, but as it puts both the sexes upon appearing in their most agreeable forms, and exerting all such qualities as are apt to give them a figure in the eye of the village. A country fellow distinguishes himself as much in the churchyard as a citizen does upon the 'Change,[2] the whole parish politics being generally discussed in that place either after sermon or before the bell rings.

My friend Sir Roger, being a good

[1] The motto is from Pythagoras, a Greek philosopher of the sixth century B.C.

[2] *'Change:* Exchange, a place where business was transacted among merchants and brokers.

churchman, has beautified the inside of his church with several texts of his own choosing. He has likewise given a handsome pulpit cloth, and railed in the communion table at his own expense. He has often told me that at his coming to his estate he found his parishioners very irregular; and that in order to make them kneel and join in the responses, he gave every one of them a hassock and a common prayer book; and at the same time employed an itinerant singing master, who goes about the country for that purpose, to instruct them rightly in the tunes of the psalms; upon which they now very much value themselves, and indeed outdo most of the country churches that I have ever heard.

As Sir Roger is landlord to the whole congregation; he keeps them in very good order, and will suffer nobody to sleep in it besides himself; for if by chance he has been surprised into a short nap at sermon, upon recovering out of it he stands up and looks about him, and if he sees anybody else nodding, either wakes them himself, or sends his servant to them. Several other of the old knight's peculiarities break out upon these occasions. Sometimes he will be lengthening out a verse in the singing psalms, half a minute after the rest of the congregation have done with it; sometimes when he is pleased with the matter of his devotion, he pronounces Amen three or four times to the same prayer; and sometimes stands up when everybody else is upon their knees, to count the congregation, or see if any of his tenants are missing.

I was yesterday very much surprised to hear my old friend in the midst of the service calling out to one John Matthews to mind what he was about, and not disturb the congregation. This John Matthews it seems is remarkable for being an idle fellow, and at that time was kicking his heels for his diversion. This authority of the knight, though exerted in that odd manner which accompanies him in all circumstances of life, has a very good effect upon the parish, who

are not polite [1] enough to see anything ridiculous in his behavior; besides that the general good sense and worthiness of his character makes his friends observe these little singularities as foils that rather set off than blemish his good qualities.

As soon as the sermon is finished, nobody presumes to stir till Sir Roger is gone out of the church. The knight walks down from his seat in the chancel between a double row of his tenants, that stand bowing to him on each side; and every now and then inquires how such a one's wife, or mother, or son, or father do, whom he does not see at church; which is understood as a secret reprimand to the person that is absent.

The chaplain has often told me that upon a catechizing day, when Sir Roger has been pleased with a boy that answers well, he has ordered a Bible to be given him next day for his encouragement; and sometimes accompanies it with a flitch of bacon to his mother. Sir Roger has likewise added five pounds a year to the clerk's [2] place; and, that he may encourage the young fellows to make themselves perfect in the church service, has promised upon the death of the present incumbent, who is very old, to bestow it according to merit.

The fair understanding between Sir Roger and his chaplain, and their mutual concurrence in doing good, is the more remarkable, because the very next village is famous for the differences and contentions that rise between the parson and the squire, who live in a perpetual state of war. The parson is always preaching at the squire; and the squire, to be revenged on the parson, never comes to church. The squire has made all his tenants atheists and tithe stealers,[3] while the parson instructs them every Sunday in the dignity of his order, and insinuates to them almost in every ser-

[1] *polite:* versed in etiquette. [2] *clerk's:* refers to the parish clerk, a lay church official who assists in the services. [3] *tithe stealers:* persons who neglect to pay their church tax.

mon that he is a better man than his patron. In short, matters are come to such an extremity that the squire has not said his prayers either in public or private this half year; and that the parson threatens him, if he does not mend his manners, to pray for him in the face of the whole congregation.

Feuds of this nature, though too frequent in the country, are very fatal to the ordinary people; who are so used to be dazzled with riches that they pay as much deference to the understanding of a man of an estate as of a man of learning; and are very hardly brought to regard any truth, how important soever it may be, that is preached to them, when they know there are several men of five hundred a year [1] who do not believe it.

PARTY FEELING

No. 125. Tuesday, July 24, 1711.

*Ne, pueri, ne tanta animis assuescite
   bella;
Neu patriae validas in viscera vertite
   vires.* [2]

VIRGIL.

[1.] [3] My worthy friend, Sir Roger, when we are talking of the malice of parties, very frequently tells us an accident that happened to him when he was a high school boy, which was at a time when feuds ran high between Roundheads [4] and Cavaliers. This worthy

---

[1] *five . . . year:* with a yearly income of five hundred pounds. [2] "Do not, my children, make such wars familiar to your minds; nor turn your mighty strength against the life of your country." [3] The numbers at the beginning of each paragraph are not in the original, but are inserted to clarify references in the special study of the essay on page 299. [4] *Roundheads:* nickname for the short-haired Puritans. The anecdote which is related here illustrates the religious differences in the English Civil War (see pages 213–14). The Royalists (or Cavaliers) kept to the Episcopal belief, which recognized saints; the Puritans, however, rejected the idea of sainthood.

knight, being then but a stripling, had occasion to inquire which was the way to St. Anne's Lane, upon which the person whom he spoke to, instead of answering his question, called him a young popish cur and asked him who had made Anne a saint. The boy, being in some confusion, inquired of the next he met, which was the way to Anne's Lane; but was called a prick-eared cur for his pains and, instead of being shown the way, was told that she had been a saint before he was born, and would be one after he was hanged. "Upon this," says Sir Roger, "I did not think fit to repeat the former question but, going into every lane of the neighborhood, asked what they called the name of that lane." By which ingenious artifice he found the place he inquired after, without giving offense to any party. Sir Roger generally closes this narrative with reflections on the mischief that parties do in the country: how they spoil good neighborhood and make honest gentlemen hate one another; besides, that they manifestly tend to the prejudice of the land tax and the destruction of the game.

[2.] There cannot a greater judgment befall a country than such a dreadful spirit of division as rends a government into two distinct people and makes them greater strangers and more averse to one another than if they were actually two different nations. The effects of such a division are pernicious to the last degree, with regard not only to those advantages which they give the common enemy, but to those private evils which they produce in the heart of almost every particular person. This influence is very fatal to both men's morals and their understandings; it sinks the virtue of a nation — and not only so, but destroys even common sense.

[3.] A furious party spirit, when it rages in its full violence, exerts itself in civil war and bloodshed; and, when it is under its greatest restraints, naturally breaks out in falsehood, detraction, calumny, and a partial administration of justice. In a word, it fills a nation with spleen [1] and rancor and extinguishes all the seeds of good nature, compassion, and humanity.

[4.] Plutarch [2] says, very finely, that a man should not allow himself to hate even his enemies, because, says he, if you indulge this passion in some occasions it will rise of itself in others; if you hate your enemies you will contract such a vicious habit of mind as by degrees will break out upon those who are your friends, or those who are indifferent to you. I might here observe how admirably this precept of morality (which derives the malignity of hatred from the passion itself, and not from its object) answers to that great rule which was dictated to the world about a hundred years before this philosopher wrote; [3] but, instead of that, I shall only take notice, with a real grief of heart, that the minds of many good men among us appear sourced with party principles, and alienated from one another in such a manner as seems to me altogether inconsistent with the dictates of either reason or religion. Zeal for a public cause is apt to breed passions in the hearts of virtuous persons to which the regard of their own private interest would never have betrayed them.

[5.] If this party spirit has so ill an effect on our morals, it has likewise a very great one on our judgments. We often hear a poor insipid paper or pamphlet cried up, and sometimes a noble piece depreciated, by those who are of a different principle from the author. One who is actuated by this spirit is almost under an incapacity of discerning either real blemishes or beauties. A man of merit in a different principle is like an object seen in two different mediums — that appears crooked or broken, however

straight or entire it may be in itself. For this reason there is scarce a person of any figure in England who does not go by two contrary characters, as opposite to one another as light and darkness. Knowledge and learning suffer in a particular manner from this strange prejudice, which at present prevails amongst all ranks and degrees in the British nation. As men formerly became eminent in learned societies by their parts and acquisitions, they now distinguish themselves by the warmth and violence with which they espouse their respective parties. Books are valued upon the like considerations: an abusive, scurrilous style passes for satire, and a dull scheme of party notions is called fine writing.

[6.] There is one piece of sophistry practiced by both sides, and that is the taking any scandalous story that has ever been whispered or invented of a private man, for a known, undoubted truth, and raising suitable speculations upon it. Calumnies that have never been proved, or have been often refuted, are the ordinary postulatums [4] of these infamous scribblers — upon which they proceed as upon first principles granted by all men, though in their hearts they know they are false or at best very doubtful. When they have laid these foundations of scurrility, it is no wonder that their superstructure is every way answerable to them. If this shameless practice of the present age endures much longer, praise and reproach will cease to be motives of action in good men.

[7.] There are certain periods of time in all governments when this inhuman spirit prevails. Italy was long torn in pieces by the Guelphs and Ghibellines,[5] and France by those who were for and

---

[1] *spleen:* anger, spite. [2] *Plutarch* (plōō′tärk): writer of biographies of famous Greeks and Romans (46?–120). [3] The rule referred to is Jesus' command, "Love your enemies . . ." (Matthew 5:44).

[4] *postulatums* (pŏs′tū·lā′tŭmz): things assumed without proof. [5] *Guelphs* (gwĕlfs) *and Ghibellines* (gĭb′ĕlĭnz): Italian parties during the latter part of the Middle Ages. At first they had opposing principles of government, but they later fought largely over personal power.

against the league; [1] but it is very unhappy for a man to be born in such a stormy and tempestuous season. It is the restless ambition of artful men that thus breaks a people into factions, and draws several well-meaning persons to their interest by a specious concern for their country. How many honest minds are filled with uncharitable and barbarous notions, out of zeal for the public good! What cruelties and outrages would they not commit against men of an adverse party, whom they would honor and esteem if, instead of considering them as they are represented, they knew them as they are! Thus are persons of the greatest probity seduced into shameful errors and prejudices, and made bad men even by that noblest of principles — the love of their country. I cannot here forbear mentioning the famous Spanish proverb, "If there were neither fools nor knaves in the world, all people would be of one mind."

[8.] For my own part I could heartily wish that all honest men would enter into an association for the support of one another against the endeavors of those whom they ought to look upon as their common enemies, whatsoever side they may belong to. Were there such an honest body of neutral forces we should never see the worst of men in the great figures of life, because they are useful to a party; nor the best unregarded, because they are above practicing those methods which would be grateful to their faction. We should then single every criminal out of the herd and hunt him down, however formidable and overgrown he might appear. On the contrary we should shelter distressed innocence and defend virtue, however beset with contempt or ridicule, envy or defamation. In short, we should not any longer regard our fellow subjects as Whigs or Tories, but should make the man of merit our friend and the villain our enemy.

THE COQUETTE'S HEART

No. 281. Tuesday, January 22, 1712.

Pectoribus inhians spirantia consulit exta.[2]

VIRGIL.

Having already given an account of the dissection of a beau's head,[3] with the several discoveries made on that occasion, I shall here, according to my promise, enter upon the dissection of a coquette's heart, and communicate to the public such particularities as we observed in that curious piece of anatomy.

I should perhaps have waived this undertaking, had not I been put in mind of my promise by several of my unknown correspondents, who are very importunate with me to make an example of the coquette, as I have already done of the beau. It is therefore in compliance with the request of friends that I have looked over the minutes of my former dream, in order to give the public an exact relation of it, which I shall enter upon without further preface.

Our operator, before he engaged in this visionary dissection, told us that there was nothing in his art more difficult than to lay open the heart of a coquette, by reason of the many labyrinths and recesses which are to be found in it, and which do not appear in the heart of any other animal.

He desired us first of all to observe the pericardium, or outward case of the heart, which we did very attentively; and by the help of our glasses discerned in it

---

[1] *league:* probably a reference to the Holy, or Catholic, League, a successful alliance formed in 1576 by the Pope and leaders in Spain and France to prevent the Huguenots from gaining the French throne.

[2] "Anxious, the reeking entrails he consults." This is a reference to the ancient practice of divination by examining the entrails of sacrificial animals. [3] In an earlier essay the Spectator analyzed a young man of fashion.

millions of little scars, which seemed to have been occasioned by the points of innumerable darts and arrows, that from time to time had glanced upon the outward coat; though we could not discover the smallest orifice [1] by which any of them had entered and pierced the inward substance.

Every smatterer in anatomy knows that this pericardium, or case of the heart, contains in it a thin reddish liquor, supposed to be bred from the vapors which exhale out of the heart and, being stopped here, are condensed into this watery substance. Upon examining this liquor, we found that it had in it all the qualities of that spirit which is made use of in the thermometer to show the change of weather.

Nor must I here omit an experiment one of the company assured us he himself had made with this liquor, which he found in great quantity about the heart of a coquette whom he had formerly dissected. He affirmed to us that he had actually inclosed it in a small tube made after the manner of a weatherglass; but that, instead of acquainting him with the variations of the atmosphere, it showed him the qualities of those persons who entered the room where it stood. He affirmed also that it rose at the approach of a plume of feathers, an embroidered coat, or a pair of fringed gloves; and that it fell as soon as an ill-shaped periwig, a clumsy pair of shoes, or an unfashionable coat came into his house. Nay, he proceeded so far as to assure us that upon his laughing aloud when he stood by it, the liquor mounted very sensibly, and immediately sank again upon his looking serious. In short, he told us that he knew very well by this invention whenever he had a man of sense or a coxcomb in his room.

Having cleared away the pericardium, or the case, and liquor above mentioned, we came to the heart itself. The outward surface of it was extremely slippery, and the mucro, or point, so very

[1] *orifice* (ŏr'ĭ·fĭs): opening.

cold withal that upon endeavoring to take hold of it, it glided through the fingers like a smooth piece of ice.

The fibers were turned and twisted in a more intricate and perplexed manner than they are usually found in other hearts; insomuch that the whole heart was wound up together like a Gordian knot,[2] and must have had very irregular and unequal motions, while it was employed in its vital function.

One thing we thought very observable, namely, that upon examining all the vessels which came into it, or issued out of it, we could not discover any communication that it had with the tongue.

We could not but take notice likewise that several of those little nerves in the heart which are affected by the sentiments of love, hatred, and other passions, did not descend to this before us from the brain, but from the muscles which lie about the eye.

Upon weighing the heart in my hand, I found it to be extremely light, and consequently very hollow, which I did not wonder at, when, upon looking into the inside of it, I saw multitudes of cells and cavities running one within another, as our historians describe the apartments of Rosamond's bower.[3] Several of these little hollows were stuffed with innumerable sorts of trifles, which I shall forbear giving any particular account of, and shall, therefore, only take notice of what lay first and uppermost, which, upon our unfolding it, and applying our microscopes to it, appeared to be a flame-colored hood.

We are informed that the lady of this heart, when living, received the addresses of several who made love to her, and did not only give each of them encouragement, but made everyone she

[2] *Gordian knot:* a famous intricate knot in ancient history. The legend was that whoever could undo it would reign over the entire East. Alexander the Great, on hearing this, cut it in two with his sword. [3] *Rosamond's bower:* a labyrinth or maze which Henry II built for the fair Rosamond in order to hide her from his jealous wife.

conversed with believe that she regarded him with an eye of kindness; for which reason we expected to have seen the impression of multitudes of faces among the several plaits and foldings of the heart; but to our great surprise not a single print of this nature discovered itself till we came into the very core and center of it. We there observed a little figure, which, upon applying our glasses to it, appeared dressed in a very fantastic manner. The more I looked upon it, the more I thought I had seen the face before, but could not possibly recollect either the place or time; when at length one of the company, who had examined this figure more nicely [1] than the rest, showed us plainly by the make of its face, and the several turns of its features, that the little idol which was thus lodged in the very middle of the heart was the deceased beau, whose head I gave some account of in my last Tuesday's paper.

[1] *nicely:* carefully.

As soon as we had finished our dissection, we resolved to make an experiment of the heart, not being able to determine among ourselves the nature of its substance, which differed in so many particulars from that in the heart of other females. Accordingly, we laid it into a pan of burning coals, when we observed in it a certain salamandrine [2] quality that made it capable of living in the midst of fire and flame, without being consumed or so much as singed.

As we were admiring this strange phenomenon, and standing round the heart in a circle, it gave a most prodigious sigh, or rather crack, and dispersed all at once in smoke and vapor. This imaginary noise, which methought was louder than the burst of a cannon, produced such a violent shake in my brain, that it dissipated the fumes of sleep, and left me in an instant broad awake.

[2] *salamandrine* (săl'á·măn′drĭn): like the salamander, a little lizard supposedly able to live in fire.

Hymn

This majestic hymn by Addison expresses the eighteenth-century belief in the perfect order of the universe. It is based on the opening of the Nineteenth Psalm and is still sung in churches to the familiar tune adapted from Haydn's oratorio *The Creation*. Read the psalm and compare it with the hymn, noting how Addison has rephrased the thought.

> The spacious firmament on high,
> With all the blue ethereal sky,
> And spangled heavens, a shining frame,
> Their great Original proclaim.
> Th' unwearied Sun from day to day   5
> Does his Creator's power display;
> And publishes to every land
> The work of an Almighty hand.
>
> Soon as the evening shades prevail,
> The Moon takes up the wondrous tale;   10
> And nightly to the listening Earth
> Repeats the story of her birth:
> Whilst all the stars that round her burn,
> And all the planets in their turn,

Confirm the tidings as they roll,   15
And spread the truth from pole to pole.

What though in solemn silence all
Move round the dark terrestrial ball;
What though no real voice nor sound
Amidst their radiant orbs be found?   20
In Reason's ear they all rejoice,
And utter forth a glorious voice;
Forever singing as they shine,
"The Hand that made us is divine."

LITERARY PARTNERS

1. What information is given in the Prospectus of *The Tatler* as to the paper's purpose, frequency, price, subject matter, and the type of readers to whom it will appeal?

2. How did *The Spectator* differ from *The Tatler?* How do these papers resemble a modern newspaper? a magazine?

3. Describe Sir Roger on the basis of the impression you have of him from these essays. Which of his traits make you like him? Which are amusing? Do you know any person who resembles him?

4. Select passages from "The Coquette's Heart" which are particularly clever in suggesting the light-mindedness of the girl. How does Addison make the physical details of the heart illustrate the coquette's behavior? If you were to look up the manners of the Age of Elegance — as the eighteenth century is sometimes called — you would find how fashionable coquetry was. To what extent does Addison's criticism of the coquette apply to modern youth?

5. Note how Addison's "Hymn" differs from Psalm 19. Which version do you prefer? Why?

SUGGESTION FOR WRITING

In imitation of *The Spectator,* write a prospectus for a small paper to circulate in your school or neighborhood. In the manner of the Sir Roger papers, prepare character sketches of class members or town figures. Or write a satire on school life, such as "A Freshman's Head" or "A Senior's Heart."

READING THE ESSAY

It is not easy to agree on a definition of an essay. However, since you have read several essays by now, you should try to formulate a suitable definition for this type of writing. You can say that the essay is a short piece of prose, often gracefully informal, on a subject which interests the writer.

The essayist may approach his writing seriously or in an amusing manner; he may relate a story, record a personal reaction to a situation, or write impersonally on a thoughtful subject. What is required is that he point out some new ideas on a subject and unify his thoughts in both theme and mood. Readers, young and old, have found a good essayist delightful company.

As a literary form the essay was originated in the sixteenth century by the French writer Michel de Montaigne. He named it from the word *essai,* which means "trial" or "attempt," for his writing represented a modest endeavor to express his beliefs and meditations on a given subject.

You will find that the essay has two extremes: it can be either *formal* or *informal.* It can also fall at any point between these two extremes. In the formal essay, the writer, trying definitely to convince or to instruct, is dignified and often impersonal. As you recall, Bacon's "Of Studies" (page 202) is just such a thoughtful discussion. Looking ahead, Virginia Woolf's "Hours in a Library" (page 738) is a modern example of an appealing serious essay. Usually much lighter in subject and manner is the informal essay. Addison and Steele used this type of essay to express the absurdities of the fashionable world of their day. Illustrating another kind of informality, Charles Lamb in his "Dream Children" (page 419) relates his innermost thoughts in an easy, confidential style. Today J. B. Priestley and other contemporary essayists present us with further pleasant whimsicalities.

Though there are many ways of looking at the essay, this literary form can almost always be studied by considering three elements: idea, structure, and mood. Let us examine "Party Feeling" by Addison with these three points in mind.

IDEA

It is hard to miss Addison's main point, even on a quick reading. He believes that fanatical party politics are bad, since they injure men's morals and judgment and degrade the spirit of a nation. He presents this idea clearly and develops it through a logical consideration of relevant details. We know that this is an essay written to appeal to the intellect — a rational discussion on the subject of partisan political feeling.

STRUCTURE

Your enjoyment of any good essay is increased by seeing how it is put together. An analysis of "Party Feeling" in outline form will be enlightening. Such an outline is started here, with each numbered main topic representing a paragraph.

I. A particular anecdote may show the kind of mischief that party politics do in the country.

II. Partisan division is pernicious, since —
   A. It aids the enemy, and
   B. It harms each citizen in
     1. his morals, and
     2. his understanding or common sense.

III. Carried to an extreme, it can extinguish all good emotions in a nation and induce civil war and bloodshed.

IV. Morally, hatred or fanaticism against one's enemies harms a man because the hatred, springing from "the pas-

sion itself and not from its object," soon pervades his character.

Now complete the outline for the remaining four paragraphs.

This, then, is the argument. You can see that Addison writes forcefully and does not waste words. In a good essay the ideas follow in a logical development; all are relevant to one another and to the main thought. Is this true of "Party Feeling"? Could any part of this essay be omitted without weakening it?

In the last paragraph, Addison makes a proposal for avoiding the ill effects of party feeling. What else does he accomplish in this paragraph? How is it an effective conclusion to his argument?

MOOD AND TONE

Not all essays are logical arguments; many are significant not so much for *what* they say as for *how* the author expresses himself. In any personal essay, the writer's mood, or the tone that is apparent in his writing, is an important element.

Addison's tone here is intelligent, gentle, and sometimes humorous. It is hard to establish this light mood in an essay like "Party Feeling," which has a serious purpose throughout. But the introduction and conclusion get us into and out of the argument by smooth gradations. The first paragraph begins quite informally with the Spectator's reminiscence about his worthy friend, Sir Roger de Coverley. This catches our interest and is amusing in itself. Even here, Addison does not lose the thread of his thought, for he speaks of the "malice of parties" as his theme in the opening sentence.

Cleverest of all is the last phrase in the first paragraph, where we learn indirectly that Sir Roger, even when he is talking against party feeling, cannot help showing it himself: as a country gentleman he is against higher land taxes and against anything that might interfere with his hunting.

What indications of Addison's personal feeling do you find in the following paragraphs? What is the effect of his manner on the reader?

The last paragraph also lightens the argument, for it begins with the phrase "For my own part," whereupon the Spectator once more steps in, in his own person.

ALEXANDER POPE

1688–1744

Bodleian Library

Alexander Pope was a little, wizened, hunchbacked man, but the mind in his puny body was more than a match for the brilliant minds of a brilliant age. He was *the* poet of his day. Nowadays we don't think of Pope's writing as being highly poetic in an imaginative sense or in emotional appeal. Styles have changed. In Pope's day poetry was clipped, terse, and satiric. It had to be "correct" in form, which meant it had to be written in heroic couplets, with each of the two lines in iambic pentameter. No one has surpassed Pope in this kind of verse.

In the eighteenth century quarrels were frequently started — and settled — in satiric verse. Pope often used his poems like weapons against his political foes and literary rivals. His famous *Dunciad*, a mock epic of dunces, is a witty and often savage catalogue of the weaknesses and pretensions of scores of his fellow writers.

Though his quarrelsomeness and his physical deformity made life hard for Pope, he was unusually fortunate in other ways. Educated at home as a child, Pope was a prodigy. He began writing polished verses at eleven, and once said he had written his *Essay on Man* at the age of twelve. Because he was a Catholic, he was denied entrance into both Oxford and Cambridge and was unable to obtain the political preferment given to other writers. Yet, determined from childhood to be a famous poet, he achieved fame and influence at an early age and made a comfortable living as a professional writer.

He wrote *Pastorals* at sixteen; at twenty-three he published *An Essay on Criticism*, a didactic poem hailed for its clear, concise reasoning and praised by Joseph Addison in *The Spectator*. In 1712, when he was twenty-four, the appearance of *The Rape of the Lock*, Pope's lighthearted and gay mock epic, assured his reputation as the leading poet of his day. By the age of thirty-two Pope had made a fortune from his translation from the Greek of the *Iliad;* in another five years his translation of the *Odyssey* appeared, both of these works strengthening Pope's reputation and later earning him the praise of Dr. Samuel Johnson. Pope later concentrated on the writing of satires in which he assailed by means of his elegant, sharp, and witty couplets his various literary foes. *The Dunciad* is the best known of these.

Because of the ill health with which he had been plagued since childhood, Pope retired from London to the beautiful villa at Twickenham on the Thames in which the great financial success of the *Iliad* enabled him to establish himself. On this estate he cultivated a magnificent garden and avoided his literary enemies except in print. Here too he entertained a good deal, for, though referred to as "the wasp of Twickenham," Pope was by no means incapable of making many good and distinguished friends, among them the well-known Jonathan Swift.

Pope's age was primarily an age of prose, and he wrote only poetry; yet his influence over other writers was so great, both in his own day and later, that we speak today of the Age of Pope.

The Rape of the Lock

Though Pope was often quarrelsome, he had many friends to whom he showed the kindly side of his nature. On one notable occasion he attempted unsuccessfully to act as peacemaker. The result was a unique poem. A certain foppish young baron named Lord Petre had cut a curl from the head of Miss Arabella Fermor and refused to give it up. Out of this trivial incident there arose between the two families a quarrel which threatened to become a feud. A friend of Pope's named Caryll suggested that the author write a poem to show the absurdity of all this excitement. Pope, therefore, wrote a "mock heroic" poem. By treating his subject in the grand style of the old epic poems about the Greek heroes, he made it appear particularly ridiculous.

Here you will recognize some of the characteristics of *The Iliad* and *The Odyssey*. These early epics open with a statement of the theme of the poem, followed by an invocation to the Muse to inspire the writer. (You will remember that Milton opens *Paradise Lost* in this same way.) In the old epics, too, the lives of human beings are influenced throughout by the gods and goddesses, who protect their favorites by warning them in dreams of impending danger; they hover over them in battle and, in disguise, often enter directly into the fray. After a battle there are songs of triumph by the victors and great lamentations from the vanquished. In the end, mortals are often raised to the rank of gods. Notice how Pope applies these heroic devices to the trivialities of court life.

The poem is in five cantos, but, because of its great length, only a part of it is given here. Canto I opens with a formal statement of the theme — "what mighty contests rise from trivial things" — and invokes the Muse to inspire the poet. Then Belinda, heroine of the story, while sleeping late in the morning is visited by the sylph Ariel, who explains that fair ladies are guarded by sylphs and other supernatural creatures who were once living women. Ariel then warns her that some dread fate is hanging over her head, and closes:

"Beware of all, but most beware of man!"

Belinda, awakened by her lap dog, forgets all about the dream while reading a love letter and performing her morning worship before the dressing table, where she adores the heavenly image appearing in the mirror.

In Canto II, Belinda is seen in a pleasure boat on the Thames, being conducted with a group of other young fashionables to the palace of Hampton Court. An adventurous baron admires two curls of Belinda's hair lying upon her neck and determines to obtain them. Belinda's protecting sylph Ariel, greatly agitated at the danger, exhorts the other airy beings hovering about to protect her in every way. The closing lines of the canto are full of suspense:

"With beating hearts the dire event they wait,
Anxious and trembling for the birth of fate."

Canto III follows.

CANTO III

Close by those meads, forever crowned with flowers,
Where Thames with pride surveys his rising towers,
There stands a structure of majestic frame,°
Which from the neighboring Hampton takes its name.
Here Britain's statesmen oft the fall foredoom   5
Of foreign tyrants and of nymphs at home;
Here thou, great Anna! whom three realms obey,°
Dost sometimes counsel take — and sometimes tea.°

3. *structure . . . frame:* Hampton Court, a handsome royal residence near London. 7. Queen Anne was ruler of England, Scotland, and Ireland. 8. *tea:* pronounced tā.

Hither the heroes and the nymphs resort,
To taste awhile the pleasures of a court;   10

A gay party of young gentlemen and ladies go up the Thames to Hampton Court.

In various talk th' instructive hours they passed,
Who gave the ball, or paid the visit last;
One speaks the glory of the British Queen,
And one describes a charming Indian screen;
A third interprets motions, looks, and eyes;   15
At every word a reputation dies.
Snuff, or the fan,° supply each pause of chat,
With singing, laughing, ogling, and all that.
Meanwhile, declining from the noon of day,
The sun obliquely shoots his burning ray;   20
The hungry judges soon the sentence sign,
And wretches hang that jurymen may dine;
The merchant from th' Exchange° returns in peace,
And the long labors° of the toilet cease.

In the afternoon Belinda and two lords engage in a three-handed game of cards.

Belinda now, whom thirst of fame invites,   25
Burns to encounter two adventurous knights,
At omber° singly to decide their doom;
And swells her breast with conquests yet to come.
Straight the three bands prepare in arms to join,
Each band the number of the sacred nine.°   30
Soon as she spreads her hand, th' aerial guard
Descend, and sit on each important card:
First, Ariel perched upon a Matador,°
Then each, according to the rank they bore;
For sylphs, yet mindful of their ancient race,   35
Are, as when women, wondrous fond of place.
Behold, four kings in majesty revered,
With hoary whiskers and a forky beard;
And four fair queens whose hands sustain a flower,

The game is compared to a great battle among kings.

The expressive emblem of their softer power;   40
Four knaves in garbs succinct,° a trusty band,
Caps on their heads, and halberts° in their hand;
And particolored troops, a shining train,
Draw forth to combat on the velvet plain.
The skillful nymph reviews her force with care: 45
Let spades be trumps! she said, and trumps they were.
Now move to war her sable Matadors,
In show like leaders of the swarthy Moors.
Spadillio° first, unconquerable lord!
Led off two captive trumps and swept the board.   50
As many more Manillio° forced to yield

17. *Snuff, or the fan:* Snuff taking in the eighteenth century was almost as widespread among gentlemen as cigarette smoking is today. A lady was seldom without her fan to occupy her hands and often to help her flirtations. 23. *Exchange:* a place where merchants, brokers, and bankers met to transact business. 24. *long labors:* Because of the elaborate, towering headdresses of that time, ladies often spent most of the day at their dressing tables preparing for a ball in the evening. 27. *omber:* a fashionable card game. 30. *the sacred nine:* The nine cards in each player's hand are compared to the nine Muses of the Greeks. 33. *Matador:* a card that had power to take a trick, derived from the Spanish word for bullfighter. 41. *succinct* (sŭk·sĭngkt′): belted. 42. *halberts* (hăl′bĕrts): long-handled weapons with metal heads. 49. *Spadillio:* the ace of spades. 51. *Manillio:* another trump card.

And marched a victor from the verdant field.°
Him Basto° followed, but his fate more hard
Gained but one trump and one plebeian card.
With his broad saber next, a chief in years,   55
The hoary majesty of spades appears,
Puts forth one manly leg, to sight revealed,
The rest his many-colored robe concealed.
The rebel knave, who dares his prince engage,
Proves the just victim of his royal rage.   60
E'en mighty Pam,° that kings and queens o'erthrew,
And mowed down armies in the fights of Loo,
Sad chance of war! now destitute of aid,
Falls undistinguished by the victor spade!
   Thus far both armies to Belinda yield;   65
Now to the baron fate inclines the field.
His warlike Amazon her host invades,
The imperial consort of the crown of spades;
The club's black tyrant first her victim died,
Spite of his haughty mien, and barbarous pride.   70
What boots° the regal circle on his head,
His giant limbs, in state unwieldy spread;

Belinda's luck
changes. The   That long behind he trails his pompous robe,
baron's queen of And, of all monarchs, only grasps the globe?
spades takes her
king of clubs;   The baron now his diamonds pours apace;   75
his run of   Th' embroidered king who shows but half his face,
diamonds takes   And his refulgent° queen, with powers combined,
several tricks.   Of broken troops an easy conquest find.
Clubs, diamonds, hearts, in wild disorder seen,
With throngs promiscuous° strew the level green.   80
Thus when dispersed a routed army runs,
Of Asia's troops, and Afric's sable sons,
With like confusion different nations fly,
Of various habit, and of various dye,
The pierced battalions disunited fall,   85
In heaps on heaps; one fate o'erwhelms them all.
   The knave of diamonds tries his wily arts,
And wins (oh, shameful chance!) the queen of hearts.
At this the blood the virgin's cheek forsook,
A livid paleness spreads o'er all her look;   90
She sees, and trembles at the approaching ill,
Just in the jaws of ruin, and codille.°
And now (as oft in some distempered state)
On one nice trick depends the general fate.
An ace of hearts steps forth; the king unseen   95
Lurked in her hand, and mourned his captive queen:

---

52. *verdant field:* The omber table was covered with green cloth. 53. *Basto:* the ace of clubs.
61. *Pam:* In a card game called *Loo*, the knave of clubs, Pam, was the highest card and therefore
"o'erthrew kings and queens" and "mowed down armies." In omber, the game now being played,
the knave was less powerful. 71. *What boots:* of what benefit is. 77. *refulgent* (rĕ-fŭl′jĕnt): radiant,
resplendent. 80. *promiscuous:* mixed. 92. *codille:* a term meaning the defeat of the lone hand.

Belinda wins when her king of hearts takes the baron's ace of hearts.

He springs to vengeance with an eager pace,
And falls like thunder on the prostrate ace.
The nymph exulting fills with shouts the sky;
The walls, the woods, and long canals reply.   100
   O thoughtless mortals; ever blind to fate,
Too soon dejected, and too soon elate.
Sudden, these honors shall be snatched away,
And cursed forever this victorious day.
   For lo! the board with cups and spoons is crowned,   105
The berries crackle, and the mill turns round;°

The card game ended, coffee is served in a "rich repast."

On shining altars of Japan° they raise
The silver lamp; the fiery spirits blaze;
From silver spouts the grateful liquors glide,
While China's earth° receives the smoking tide.   110
At once they gratify their scent and taste,
And frequent cups prolong the rich repast.
Straight hover round the fair her airy band;
Some, as she sipped, the fuming liquor fanned,
Some o'er her lap their careful plumes displayed,   115
Trembling, and conscious of the rich brocade.
Coffee (which makes the politician wise,
And see through all things with his half-shut eyes)
Sent up in vapors to the baron's brain
New stratagems the radiant locks to gain.   120
Ah, cease, rash youth! desist ere 'tis too late,
Fear the just gods, and think of Scylla's fate!°
Changed to a bird, and sent to flit in air,
She dearly pays for Nisus' injured hair!
   But when to mischief mortals bend their will,   125
How soon they find fit instruments of ill!
Just then Clarissa drew with tempting grace
A two-edged weapon from her shining case:
So ladies in romance assist their knight,
Present the spear, and arm him for the fight.   130
He takes the gift with reverence, and extends
The little engine on his fingers' ends;

Clarissa, one of the ladies, helps the baron's plan by handing him her scissors. The sprites scurry to protect Belinda.

This just behind Belinda's neck he spread,
As o'er the fragrant steams she bends her head.
Swift to the lock a thousand sprites repair,   135
A thousand wings, by turns, blow back the hair;
And thrice they twitched the diamond in her ear;
Thrice she looked back, and thrice the foe drew near.
Just in that instant, anxious Ariel sought
The close recesses of the virgin's thought;   140
As on the nosegay in her breast reclined,
He watched th' ideas rising in her mind,

---

106. *The berries . . . round:* Prepared coffee could not be bought in those days, but the coffee berries were ground in a small hand mill at the table. 107. *altars of Japan:* Imported lacquered tables were popular at this time. 110. *China's earth:* The cups were earthenware imported from China. 122. *Scylla's* (sĭl′ăz) *fate:* Scylla betrayed her father, King Nisus, by sending the enemy a lock of his hair.

Sudden he viewed, in spite of all her art,
An earthly lover lurking at her heart.
Amazed, confused, he found his power expired,   145
Resigned to fate, and with a sigh retired.
　　The peer now spreads the glittering *forfex*° wide,
T' inclose the lock; now joins it, to divide.

Belinda's curl is E'en then, before the fatal engine closed,
severed — the A wretched sylph too fondly interposed: 150
rape of the lock! Fate urged the shears, and cut the sylph in twain,
(But airy substance soon unites again).
The meeting points the sacred hair dissever
From the fair head, forever, and forever!
　　Then flashed the living lightning from her eyes,   155
And screams of horror rend th' affrighted skies.
Not louder shrieks to pitying Heaven are cast,
When husbands, or when lap dogs breathe their last;
Or when rich China vessels, fallen from high,
In glittering dust and painted fragments lie!   160
　　"Let wreaths of triumph now my temples twine,"
The victor cried; "the glorious prize is mine!
While fish in streams, or birds delight in air,
Or in a coach and six the British fair,
As long as *Atalantis*° shall be read,   165
Or the small pillow grace a lady's bed,
While visits shall be paid on solemn days,
The baron exults When numerous wax lights in bright order blaze,
over the While nymphs take treats, or assignations give,
permanent fame So long my honor, name, and praise shall live!   170
he has won by What Time would spare, from steel receives its date,°
his conquest. And monuments, like men, submit to fate!
Steel could the labor of the gods destroy,
And strike to dust th' imperial towers of Troy;
Steel could the works of mortal pride confound,   175
And hew triumphal arches to the ground.
What wonder then, fair nymph! thy hairs should feel,
The conquering force of unresisted steel?"

147. *forfex* (fôr′fĕks): Latin for *shears.* 165. *Atalantis:* a popular book of scandalous gossip. 171. *receives its date:* is destroyed.

CANTO V

In Canto IV, Umbriel, a melancholy sprite, brings a bag (similar to the bag of winds once held by Ulysses) in which are contained "the force of female lungs, sighs, sobs, and passions, and the war of tongues." These he empties over the head of Belinda, who immediately bursts into loud lamentations on the loss of her lock. She then calls upon Sir Plume to aid her in regaining her lock. This ineffectual fop swears the favorite oaths of the time — "Zounds! Plague on 't! Prithee, pox!" — but fails to move the baron.
　　Then, in the beginning of Canto V, Clarissa urges good sense and good humor, but in vain. The story concludes with a mighty battle between the belles and the beaux.

"To arms, to arms!" the fierce virago cries,
And swift as lightning to the combat flies.
All side in parties, and begin th' attack;
Fans clap, silks rustle, and tough whalebones crack;
Heroes' and heroines' shouts confus'dly rise,   5
And bass and treble voices strike the skies.
No common weapons in their hands are found,
Like gods they fight, nor dread a mortal wound.°

*The lords and
ladies engage in
a battle — of
words and looks
— equal to those
described by
Homer in The
Iliad.*

So when bold Homer makes the gods engage,
And heavenly breasts with human passions rage;   10
'Gainst Pallas, Mars, Latona, Hermes° arms;
And all Olympus° rings with loud alarms:
Jove's thunder roars, Heaven trembles all around,
Blue Neptune storms, the bellowing deeps resound;
Earth shakes her nodding towers, the ground gives way,   15
And the pale ghosts start at the flash of day!
    Triumphant Umbriel on a sconce's° height
Clapped his glad wings, and sat to view the fight;
Propped on their bodkin spears,° the sprites survey
The growing combat, or assist the fray.   20
    While through the press enraged Thalestris° flies,
And scatters death around from both her eyes,
A beau and witling° perished in the throng,
One died in metaphor, and one in song.
"O cruel nymph! a living death I bear,"   25
Cried Dapperwit,° and sunk beside his chair.
A mournful glance Sir Fopling° upward cast,
"Those eyes are made so killing" — was his last.
Thus on Mæander's° flowery margin lies
Th' expiring swan, and as he sings he dies.   30
    When bold Sir Plume had drawn Clarissa down,
Chloe° stepped in and killed him with a frown;
She smiled to see the doughty hero slain,
But, at her smile, the beau revived again.

*The lock of hair
is found to be
heavier than the
intelligence of
the young lords.*

Now Jove suspends his golden scales in air,   35
Weighs the men's wits against the lady's hair;
The doubtful beam long nods from side to side;
At length the wits mount up, the hairs subside.
    See, fierce Belinda on the Baron flies,
With more than usual lightning in her eyes;   40
Nor feared the chief th' unequal fight to try,

---

8. The gods, being immortal, did not have to fear death in battle. 11. *Pallas, Mars, Latona, Hermes:* gods who directed the Trojan War. The first and fourth were on the side of the Greeks, the second and third on the Trojan side. 12. *Olympus:* the mountain in northern Greece on which the gods supposedly lived. 17. *sconce:* a candle holder attached to the wall. 19. *bodkin spears:* large needles. 21. *Thalestris* (thà·lĕs′trĭs): an Amazon who figured in medieval tales of Alexander the Great. 23. *witling:* a gentleman with empty pretensions to high intelligence. 26. *Dapperwit* and *Sir Fopling* (line 27) were names of humorous characters in sophisticated comedies of the time. 29. *Mæander's:* The Mæander was a winding river in Asia. 32. *Chloe* (klō′ē): a shepherdess loved by Daphnis in a Greek pastoral romance.

Who sought no more than on his foe to die.
But this bold lord with manly strength endued,
She with one finger and a thumb subdued:
Just where the breath of life his nostrils drew, 45
A charge of snuff the wily virgin threw;
The gnomes direct, to every atom just,
The pungent grains of titillating dust.
Sudden, with starting tears each eye o'erflows,
And the high dome re-echoes to his nose. 50
 "Now meet thy fate," incensed Belinda cried,
And drew a deadly bodkin from her side. . . .
 "Boast not my fall," he cried, "insulting foe!
Thou by some other shalt be laid as low;
Nor think to die dejects my lofty mind; 55
All that I dread is leaving you behind!
Rather than so, ah, let me still survive,
And burn in Cupid's flames — but burn alive."
 "Restore the lock!" she cries; and all around
"Restore the lock!" the vaulted roofs rebound. 60
Not fierce Othello in so loud a strain
Roared for the handkerchief that caused his pain.°
But see how oft ambitious aims are crossed,
And chiefs contend till all the prize is lost!
The lock, obtained with guilt, and kept with pain, 65
In every place is sought, but sought in vain.
With such a prize no mortal must be blessed,
So Heav'n decrees! with Heav'n who can contest?
 Some thought it mounted to the lunar sphere,
Since all things lost on earth are treasured there. 70
There heroes' wits are kept in ponderous vases,
And beaux' in snuffboxes and tweezer cases;
There broken vows and deathbed alms are found,
And lovers' hearts with ends of riband bound. . . .
 But trust the Muse — she saw it upward rise, 75
Though marked by none but quick, poetic eyes. . . .

Belinda's lost lock becomes a star in the sky; and the poet calls on Belinda to cease mourning, for the Muse of poetry will make the lock immortal.

A sudden star, it shot through liquid air,
And drew behind a radiant trail of hair. . . .
 Then cease, bright nymph! to mourn thy ravished hair,
Which adds new glory to the shining sphere! 80
Not all the tresses that fair head can boast,
Shall draw such envy as the lock you lost.
For, after all the murders of your eye,
When, after millions slain, yourself shall die;
When those fair suns shall set, as set they must, 85
And all those tresses shall be laid in dust:
This lock, the Muse shall consecrate to fame,
And 'midst the stars inscribe Belinda's name.

61–62. In Shakespeare's tragedy *Othello*, the hero is convinced of his wife's faithlessness when she cannot find a handkerchief which he had given her. The handkerchief had actually been stolen by an enemy to be used as evidence against her.

Pope's Epigrams

No authors except Shakespeare and Milton have given to our language so many quotable lines and phrases as Pope. His neat couplets are easy to remember, and his comments on life and learning are usually brief, clever, and exact. As their titles suggest, these poems are essays in verse.

1. Hope springs eternal in the human breast:
   Man never is, but always to be blest.
   An Essay on Man, Epistle I, lines 95–96.

2. All nature is but art, unknown to thee;
   All chance, direction, which thou canst not see;
   All discord, harmony not understood;
   All partial evil, universal good;
   And spite of pride, in erring reason's spite,
   One truth is clear, Whatever is, is right.
   Ibid., lines 289–94.

3. A wit's a feather, and a chief a rod;
   An honest man's the noblest work of God.
   Ibid., Epistle IV, lines 247–48.

4. 'Tis education forms the common mind:
   Just as the twig is bent the tree's inclined.
   Moral Essays, Epistle I, lines 149–50.

5. A little learning is a dangerous thing;
   Drink deep, or taste not the Pierian [1] spring:
   There shallow drafts intoxicate the brain,
   And drinking largely [2] sobers us again.
   An Essay on Criticism, Part II, lines 15–18.

6. True ease in writing comes from art, not chance,
   As those move easiest who have learned to dance.
   'Tis not enough no harshness gives offense —
   The sound must seem an echo to the sense.
   Ibid., lines 162–65.

7. To err is human, to forgive divine.
   Ibid., line 325.

8. For fools rush in where angels fear to tread.
   Ibid., Part III, line 66.

---

[1] *Pierian* (pĭ·er′ĭ·ăn): Pieria was the region where the Muses were first worshiped; hence, the spring represents the understanding of the arts and sciences. [2] *largely:* deeply.

THE WIT OF TWICKENHAM

THE RAPE OF THE LOCK

1. Select several passages to show how Pope makes unimportant incidents of social life sound like world-shaking events. What effect does he produce by linking something serious with something trivial?

2. In the description of the card game, what is the extended metaphor that is used? Is it an effective comparison? Do any of the details of behavior of the gentlemen and ladies remind you of behavior of young people today?

3. How is the battle between the beaux and belles made to appear ridiculous? What details suggest the fashions of the day?

4. Point out lines and passages where Pope is imitating the old heroic poems. For what kind of verse is the heroic couplet (the form Pope uses) appropriate?

5. How does the coquette in Addison's "The Coquette's Heart" compare with the young ladies in *The Rape of the Lock?* Which do you consider the more enjoyable satire, Pope's or Addison's?

EPIGRAMS

1. Do you agree with Pope's ideas in all of these sayings? From your experience, can you support or attack these ideas?

2. Which quotation expresses one of Pope's standards for literature? Is this standard still considered important by poets today?

UNDERSTANDING SATIRE

Satire in verse and in prose was the fashion of the eighteenth century. Although almost every possible kind of writing was turned out during this period, satire was the vehicle for many critics of etiquette, fashion, education, government, and religion. Satire ranges from light, impersonal mockery to bitter, cruel ridicule, and you should learn to recognize these various degrees.

From what you have read of Pope, how would you describe him as a satirist? What specifically is he ridiculing? In what manner does he criticize? What events in Pope's life might have influenced him to write satire?

You have already been introduced to the satire of Addison (p. 292) and Steele (p. 290). After you read Swift, another satirist of this period, you will want to compare the kind of satire written by these four men. Note the differences between the satire of Addison and Steele and that of Pope and Swift. Addison and Steele, with a polished and restrained satire, criticized fashions and types of individuals, not specific persons. In contrast, behind the writing of Pope and Swift was spite, and their ridicule, directed at certain men and women, was intended to antagonize and to denounce certain individuals and practices. Can you point to examples of satire today, either in books, magazines, or newspapers; or in the theater, motion pictures, or television?

THE POWER OF WORDS

UNUSUAL COLOR WORDS

The description of the card game gives Pope an opportunity to introduce some color words. Beginning with line 38 of Canto III we see the four kings each with *hoary* (silvery white) whiskers. *Hoary* (from the Old English for *frost*) suggests both color and age and is usually applied to hair, not to skin or to garments. In contrast to the white beards there are the *sable Matadors* and *swarthy Moors*. Look up the derivations of these words.

The card table is referred to as a *verdant* field. *Verdant* goes back through French to Latin, where it means *green*. Card tables in the eighteenth century were likely to be covered with a green cloth, which prompted its comparison to a grassy battlefield.

LITERATURE AND THE ARTS

The illustration on page 307 depicts the most dramatic moment in *The Rape of the Lock.* The painting, done especially for this anthology by Isadore Seltzer, shows that crucial and amusing scene in which the baron has just snipped off a lock of Belinda's hair.

Pope took great pains to establish atmosphere in his poem. It is interesting to note how the creator of this painting, through his own medium, has rendered the charm of an afternoon at Hampton Court.

JONATHAN
SWIFT

1667–1745

Bodleian Library

Swift and Pope were congenial as friends and writers. Both had sharp tongues and sharper pens; both hated dullness and sentimentality. Swift was born in Dublin, of English parents, aristocratic but poor. After his father's death, Swift became dependent upon an uncle for his education at Dublin University, and later upon Sir William Temple, a relative in England who employed him as a private secretary. The proud, independent young man found this position hard to bear. He passed several years, at two different times, at the beck and call of his employer, whom he thought pretentious, and he suffered such indignities as being forced to eat in the servants' hall. Finally, he struck out for himself by taking religious orders in the Church of England and entering politics as a writer. Because of his brilliant party writings, Swift rose rapidly and gained great influence among the Tories, then ruling England. In 1713 he was appointed dean of St. Patrick's in Dublin. He had hoped to become a bishop, but when the Tories lost power his chances were ruined, and he remained in Dublin as dean for thirty-two years.

Swift was a moody, self-tortured, and often despondent man. While at Sir William's estate in Surrey he developed his friendship with Esther Johnson, who was considerably younger than he. His numerous letters to her were published under the title *Journal to Stella* (*Esther* is the Hebrew word for *star, Stella* is the Latin). He loved her deeply but somewhat hopelessly; whether they married is one of the unsolved mysteries in English literary history. Late in life Swift grew increasingly despondent until he finally suffered a mental breakdown.

Swift is best known for his satires; he was the most versatile of English satirists. His first great success, published anonymously in 1704, was *A Tale of a Tub,* a biting satire on the various sects of the church which, though it alienated Queen Anne and many others in power, won its author acclaim as a remarkable and highly able writer. *The Battle of the Books,* in the same volume, was a contribution to a literary controversy. *A Modest Proposal* — in which Swift suggests that English absentee landlords might fatten Irish children to serve on their dinner tables as a new luxury — represents his political defense of the Irish and reflects his deep hatred of human cruelty and exploitation. For this and other pieces of writing protesting English policies, Swift won the undying gratitude of the Irish who, on one of his returns from England to Dublin, treated him as a national hero. *Gulliver's Travels,* his masterpiece, is a satire on humanity in general and shows the truth of Swift's observation about himself: that he hated mankind but loved men as individuals.

Gulliver's Travels

It is ironic that a book written to satirize everything from the king to all mankind should today be looked on by most people as a book for young readers. Because Swift made use of pygmies and giants, the first part of the book can easily be read as an entertaining fairy tale for children, who like it for its strange adventure. Swift's main purpose in this tale, however, was to poke fun at human vanities. Through his clever use of a story which can stand alone on its own merits, the author produced a book which can thus be read on two levels, one of storytelling interest and one of underlying, symbolic meaning.

Gulliver's Travels was published anonymously, purporting to be the true adventures of one Lemuel Gulliver. The opening chapter contributes to the illusion of reality by its details of Gulliver's past life and the circumstances of the voyage and shipwreck, all told in the most matter-of-fact way. Then Gulliver suddenly finds himself in the land of the Lilliputians (lĭl·ĭ·pū'-shănz), who are only six inches tall. The narrative moves with such directness and simplicity and with such careful attention to mathematical proportions that it becomes almost plausible in its absurdity.

THE VOYAGE TO LILLIPUT

In the first two chapters Gulliver is discovered in his sleep by the Lilliputians. He is transported with great difficulty to their capital, where he is housed in a deserted temple. He wins favor with the emperor, is taught their language, but is deprived of his sword and pistols. The satire in this adventure becomes more evident in Chapter III, which follows, where the pretensions of English politicians and the royal court are made ridiculous by reduction to a tiny scale.

M Y GENTLENESS and good behavior had gained so far on the emperor and his court, and indeed upon the army and people in general, that I began to conceive hopes of getting my liberty in a short time. I took all possible methods to cultivate this favorable disposition. The natives came by degrees to be less apprehensive of any danger from me. I would sometimes lie down and let five or six of them dance on my hand; and at last the boys and girls would venture to come and play at hide-and-seek in my hair. I had now made a good progress in understanding and speaking their language.

The emperor had a mind, one day, to entertain me with several of the country shows, wherein they exceed all nations I have known, both for dexterity and magnificence. I was diverted with none so much as that of the rope dancers, performed upon a slender white thread, extended about two feet and twelve inches from the ground. Upon which I shall desire liberty, with the reader's patience, to enlarge a little.

This diversion is only practiced by those persons who are candidates for great employments and high favor at court. They are trained in this art from their youth, and are not always of noble birth or liberal education. When a great office is vacant, either by death or disgrace (which often happens), five or six of those candidates petition the emperor to entertain his majesty and the court with a dance on the rope; and whoever jumps the highest, without falling, succeeds in the office. Very often the chief ministers themselves are commanded to show their skill, and to convince the emperor that they have not lost their faculty. Flimnap,[1] the treasurer, is allowed to cut a caper on the strait rope at least an inch higher than any other lord in the

[1] *Flimnap:* probably meant to be Sir Robert Walpole, a famous eighteenth-century Whig statesman.

whole empire. I have seen him do the somersault several times together upon a trencher,[1] fixed on a rope, which is no thicker than a common packthread in England. My friend Reldresal, principal secretary for private affairs, is, in my opinion, if I am not partial, the second after the treasurer; the rest of the great officers are much upon a par.

These diversions are often attended by fatal accidents, whereof great numbers are on record. I myself have seen two or three candidates break a limb. But the danger is much greater when the ministers themselves are commanded to show their dexterity! for, by contending to excel themselves and their fellows, they strain so far that there is hardly one of them who hath not received a fall,[2] and some of them two or three. I was assured that a year or two before my arrival, Flimnap would have infallibly broke his neck if one of the king's cushions, that accidentally lay on the ground, had not weakened the force of his fall.

There is likewise another diversion, which is only shown before the emperor and empress and first minister, upon particular occasions. The emperor lays on the table three fine silken threads,[3] of six inches long; one is blue, the other red, and the third green. These threads are proposed as prizes for those persons whom the emperor hath a mind to distinguish by a peculiar mark of his favor. The ceremony is performed in his majesty's great chamber of state, where the candidates are to undergo a trial of dexterity very different from the former, and such as I have not observed the least resemblance of in any other country

of the old or the new world.

The emperor holds a stick in his hands, both ends parallel to the horizon, while the candidates, advancing one by one, sometimes leap over the stick, sometimes creep under it backward and forward several times, according as the stick is advanced or depressed. Sometimes the emperor holds one end of the stick, and his first minister the other; sometimes the minister has it entirely to himself. Whoever performs his part with most agility, and holds out the longest in leaping and creeping, is rewarded with the blue colored silk; the red is given to the next, and the green to the third, which they all wear girt twice round about the middle; and you see few great persons about this court who are not adorned with one of these girdles.

The horses of the army, and those of the royal stables, having been daily led before me, were no longer shy, but would come up to my very feet without starting. The riders would leap them over my hand as I held it on the ground; and one of the emperor's huntsmen, upon a large courser, took my foot, shoe and all, which was indeed a prodigious leap.

I had the good fortune to divert the emperor one day after a very extraordinary manner. I desired he would order several sticks of two feet high, and the thickness of an ordinary cane, to be brought me; whereupon his majesty commanded the master of his woods to give directions accordingly; and the next morning six woodmen arrived with as many carriages, drawn by eight horses to each.

I took nine of these sticks, and fixing them firmly in the ground in a quadrangular figure, two feet and a half square, I took four other sticks and tied them parallel at each corner, about two feet from the ground; then I fastened my handkerchief to the nine sticks that stood erect, and extended it on all sides, till it was as tight as the top of a drum; and the four parallel sticks, rising about five inches

---

[1] *trencher:* a wooden platter. [2] *a fall:* that is, a loss of office. At this time there was considerable shifting of power between Whigs and Tories. Walpole had been deprived of his office previous to the publication of this book. The "cushion" referred to, a few lines down, is a reference to the intervention by the king on behalf of one of his favorites. [3] *three . . . threads:* a suggestion of the badges of the Orders of the Garter, Bath, and Thistle, which were often given as political awards.

higher than the handkerchief, served as ledges on each side.

When I had finished my work, I desired the emperor to let a troop of his best horse, twenty-four in number, come and exercise upon this plain. His majesty approved of the proposal, and I took them up one by one in my hands, ready mounted and armed, with the proper officers to exercise them. As soon as they got into order, they divided into two parties, performed mock skirmishes, discharged blunt arrows, drew their swords, fled and pursued, attacked and retired, and, in short, discovered the best military discipline I ever beheld. The parallel sticks secured them and their horses from falling over the stage; and the emperor was so much delighted that he ordered this entertainment to be repeated several days, and once was pleased to be lifted up and give the word of command; and, with great difficulty, persuaded even the empress herself to let me hold her in her close chair within two yards of the stage, from whence she was able to take a full view of the whole performance.

It was my good fortune that no ill accident happened in these entertainments; only once a fiery horse, that belonged to one of the captains, pawing with his hoof, struck a hole in my handkerchief, and his foot slipping, he overthrew his rider and himself; but I immediately relieved them both, and covering the hole with one hand, I set down the troop with the other, in the same manner as I took them up. The horse that fell was strained in the left shoulder, but the rider got no hurt, and I repaired my handkerchief as well as I could; however, I would not trust to the strength of it any more in such dangerous enterprises.

About two or three days before I was set at liberty, as I was entertaining the court with these kinds of feats, there arrived an express to inform his majesty that some of his subjects riding near the place where I was first taken up had seen a great black substance lying on the ground, very oddly shaped, extending its edges round as wide as his majesty's bedchamber, and rising up in the middle as high as a man; that it was no living creature, as they at first apprehended, for it lay on the grass without motion; and some of them had walked round it several times; that, by mounting upon each other's shoulders, they had got to the top, which was flat and even, and, stamping upon it, they found it was hollow within; that they humbly conceived it might be something belonging to the man-mountain; and if his majesty pleased, they would undertake to bring it with only five horses.

I presently knew what they meant, and was glad at heart to receive this intelligence.[1] It seems, upon my first reaching the shore after our shipwreck, I was in such confusion that, before I came to the place where I went to sleep, my hat, which I had fastened with a string to my head while I was rowing, and had stuck on all the time I was swimming, fell off after I came to land; the string, as I conjecture, breaking by some accident which I never observed, but thought my hat had been lost at sea. I entreated his imperial majesty to give orders it might be brought to me as soon as possible, describing to him the use and nature of it; and the next day the wagoners arrived with it, but not in a very good condition; they had bored two holes in the brim, within an inch and a half of the edge, and fastened two hooks in the holes; these hooks were tied by a long cord to the harness, and thus my hat was dragged along for above half an English mile; but the ground in that country being extremely smooth and level, it received less damage than I expected.

Two days after this adventure, the emperor, having ordered that part of the army which quarters in and about his metropolis to be in readiness, took a fancy of diverting himself in a very singular manner. He desired I would stand like a colossus,[2] with my legs as far asun-

---

[1] *intelligence:* news, information. [2] *colossus:* an enormous statue.

der as I conveniently could. He then commanded his general (who was an old, experienced leader and a great patron of mine) to draw up the troops in close order and march them under me; the foot by twenty-four in a breast and the horse by sixteen, with drums beating, colors flying, and pikes advanced. This body consisted of three thousand foot and a thousand horse. . . .

I had sent so many memorials and petitions for my liberty that his majesty at length mentioned the matter, first in the cabinet, and then in a full council; where it was opposed by none, except Skyresh Bolgolam who was pleased, without any provocation, to be my mortal enemy. But it was carried against him by the whole board, and confirmed by the emperor. That minister was *galbet,* or admiral of the realm, very much in his master's confidence, and a person well versed in affairs, but of a morose and sour complexion.[1] However, he was at length persuaded to comply; but prevailed that the articles and conditions upon which I should be set free, and to which I must swear, should be drawn up by himself.

These articles were brought to me by Skyresh Bolgolam in person, attended by two undersecretaries, and several persons of distinction. After they were read, I was demanded to swear to the performance of them, first in the manner of my own country, and afterward in the method prescribed by their laws; which was, to hold my right foot in my left hand, and to place the middle finger of my right hand on the crown of my head, and my thumb on the tip of my right ear.

But because the reader may be curious to have some idea of the style and manner of expression peculiar to that people, as well as to know the articles upon which I recovered my liberty, I have made a translation of the whole instrument, word for word, as near as I

was able, which I here offer to the public.

"Golbasto Momaren Evlame Gurdilo Shefin Mully Ully Gue, most mighty Emperor of Lilliput, delight and terror of the universe, whose dominions extend five thousand *blustrugs* (about twelve miles in circumference) to the extremities of the globe; monarch of all monarchs, taller than the sons of men; whose feet press down to the center, and whose head strikes against the sun; at whose nod the princes of the earth shake their knees; pleasant as the spring, comfortable as the summer, fruitful as autumn, dreadful as winter. His most sublime Majesty proposeth to the man-mountain, lately arrived to our celestial dominions, the following articles, which by a solemn oath he shall be obliged to perform.

"1. The man-mountain shall not depart from our dominions without our license under our great seal.

"2. He shall not presume to come into our metropolis without our express order; at which time the inhabitants shall have two hours' warning to keep within their doors.

"3. The said man-mountain shall confine his walks to our principal high roads, and not offer to walk or lie down in a meadow or field of corn.

"4. As he walks the said roads, he shall take the utmost care not to trample upon the bodies of any of our loving subjects, their horses or carriages, nor take any of our said subjects into his hands without their own consent.

"5. If an express requires extraordinary dispatch, the man-mountain shall be obliged to carry in his pocket the messenger and horse a six days' journey once in every moon, and return the said messenger back (if so required) safe to our imperial presence.

"6. He shall be our ally against our enemies in the island of Blefuscu, and do his utmost to destroy their fleet, which is now preparing to invade us.

"7. That the said man-mountain shall at his times of leisure be aiding and as-

---

[1] *complexion:* In the eighteenth century this word often referred to temperament rather than to the coloring and texture of the face.

sisting to our workmen, in helping to raise certain great stones toward covering the wall of the principal park, and other our royal buildings.

"8. That the said man-mountain shall, in two moons' time, deliver in an exact survey of the circumference of our dominions, by a computation of his own paces round the coast.

"9. That upon his solemn oath to observe all the above articles, the said man-mountain shall have a daily allowance of meat and drink sufficient for the support of 1,728 of our subjects, with free access to our royal person, and other marks of our favor. Given at our palace at Belfaborac the twelfth day of the ninety-first moon of our reign."

I swore and subscribed to these articles with great cheerfulness and content, although some of them were not so honorable as I could have wished; which proceeded wholly from the malice of Skyresh Bolgolam the high admiral; whereupon my chains were immediately unlocked, and I was at full liberty; the emperor himself in person did me the honor to be by at the whole ceremony. I made my acknowledgments by prostrating myself at his majesty's feet; but he commanded me to rise; and after many gracious expressions, which to avoid the censure of vanity, I shall not repeat, he added that he hoped I should prove a useful servant, and well deserve all the favors he had already conferred upon me, or might do for the future.

The reader may please to observe that in the last article for the recovery of my liberty the emperor stipulates to allow me a quantity of meat and drink sufficient for the support of 1,728 Lilliputians. Sometime after, asking a friend at court how they came to fix on that determined number, he told me that his majesty's mathematicians having taken the height of my body by the help of a quadrant, and finding it to exceed theirs in the proportion of twelve to one, they concluded, from the similarity of their bodies, that mine must contain at least 1,728 of theirs, and consequently would require as much food as was necessary to support that number of Lilliputians. By which the reader may conceive an idea of the ingenuity of that people, as well as the prudent and exact economy of so great a prince.

[Gulliver's greatest service to Lilliput is his capture of the fleet of the enemy country, Blefuscu. By cutting the anchor ropes with his knife and attaching fifty ships to a central cable, he is able to drag them after him as he wades across the channel between the two countries.

The jealousy of Skyresh Bolgolam, mentioned in Chapter III, finally results in the proposed impeachment of Gulliver, of which he is warned in time to escape to Blefuscu. Here he is kindly received in spite of his previous treatment of this nation. (This is a satire on the impeachment and escape to France of Bolingbroke, a leader of the Tory party and an intimate friend of Swift.) Soon after, Gulliver discovers a derelict lifeboat. He manages to get away in the lifeboat, and he carries home in his pocket some cattle and sheep as proof that his strange experiences actually did happen.]

SUMMARIES OF SUCCEEDING VOYAGES

VOYAGE TO BROBDINGNAG [1]

Gulliver's second voyage takes him to a land of giants, where the situation of the previous trip is exactly reversed. The inhabitants are twelve times as tall as Gulliver, instead of one-twelfth his height. Here again the king's court is satirized, partly through the contempt the giant king feels for England as described by Gulliver. Man is also made ridiculous through the misadventures of Gulliver, who is almost devoured by the baby, torn to pieces by the rats, drowned in the cream pitcher by the queen's jealous dwarf, and dropped from the roof of the gigantic palace by a playful monkey. Finally his little cagelike house is carried away by a great eagle, and he is

[1] *Brobdingnag* (brŏb′dĭng·năg): The inhabitants were Brobdingnagians (brŏb·dĭng·năg′ĭănz).

dropped in the ocean, rescued by a passing vessel, and returned to his native country. Back home again, he has great difficulty in readjusting himself to the fact that people are of his own size.

VOYAGE TO LAPUTA [1] AND BALNIBARBI [2]

The third voyage is a satire on learned people. Gulliver is drawn up into a flying island, Laputa, inhabited by musicians, mathematicians, and philosophers. They are so absent-minded that they must be attended by servants who dutifully recall their masters' attention to practical affairs. Later Gulliver is lowered to the mainland, Balnibarbi, where he visits the academy at Lagado, the metropolis. Here the satire is on scientific experimentation, with which Swift was not in sympathy.

THE COUNTRY OF THE HOUYHNHNMS [3]

The account of Gulliver's last voyage is the most biting satire of all. He finds a land governed by horses of the highest intelligence and uprightness. Their name and the occasional words of their language quoted by Gulliver are intended to represent the whinnying of horses. After learning this language Gulliver is able to converse with the king, but in describing the affairs of Europe he discovers that the horse-people have no words for many evils of personal character or government. Gulliver's account of a European war so horrifies the noble Houyhnhnm that he condemns Gulliver's countrymen as worse than the repulsive Yahoos, creatures in the shape of men who serve the horses without pretense of intelligence. Gulliver pictures the land of the horses as one where peace and contentment are never marred by disease, bribery, flattery, fraud, politics, courtiers, lords, fiddlers, judges, or dancing masters. In short, the land of the horses is an ideal state.

[1] *Laputa* (là·pūt′á). [2] *Balnibarbi* (bàl·nĭ-bär′bĭ). [3] *Houyhnhnms* (hōō·ĭn′ŭmz).

GULLIVER'S TRAVELS

1. To what individuals and groups did Swift direct his satire?
2. Make a list of the different aspects of life satirized by Swift in these selections.

How many of them might still be criticized today? Which of them no longer exist?

3. How did the Lilliputians arrive at the figure they gave as the necessary amount of food for Gulliver?
4. Does Swift go beyond the limits of reason in condemning his country? What circumstances of his life made him bitter toward the government and the church?

THE POWER OF WORDS

PRECISION

In describing the skills of the Lilliputians, Swift says the candidates for honors in the court undergo a trial of *dexterity* in leaping over or creeping under a stick held by the emperor, and that the one showing the greatest *agility* is given the highest award. Though both *dexterity* and *agility* describe speed and skill of action, there is a difference in their precise meanings. *Agility* applies specifically to the suppleness of the limbs. *Dexter* is the Latin word for *right hand;* therefore *dexterity* is especially appropriate for hand skills. A related word is *ambidextrous,* "using both hands with equal ease."

Swift speaks of the *ingenuity* of the Lilliputians in calculating the amount of food needed by Gulliver. *Ingenuity* is mental agility — quickness to find solutions for new problems or to contrive new devices.

List synonyms for *dexterity, agility,* and *ingenuity;* discuss their precise use.

LITERATURE AND THE ARTS ➤

In Jonathan Swift's "The Voyage to Brobdingnag," the second of Gulliver's travels, the King of Brobdingnag expresses his contempt for European society — its politics, education, manners, and government. In the drawing opposite, James Gillray, a leading cartoonist of his day, adapts the King of Brobdingnag's remark and uses it as commentary on current international politics. Napoleon Bonaparte, by his political maneuvering, had been threatening Britain with invasion. This cartoon appeared in June 1803, about a month after England decided to declare war on France. The figure at the left represents Napoleon; the one at the right, George III.

"My little friend Grildrig, you have made a most admirable panegyric upon Yourself and Country, but from what I can gather from your own relation & the answers I have with much pains wringed & extorted from you, I cannot but conclude you to be, one of the most pernicious, little odious reptiles that nature ever suffered to crawl upon the surface of the Earth."

The KING of BROBDINGNAG, and GULLIVER.

Vide Swift's Gulliver Voyage to Brobdingnag

SAMUEL JOHNSON 1709–1784

and

JAMES BOSWELL 1740–1795

National Portrait Gallery

Samuel Johnson

National Portrait Gallery

James Boswell

Doctor Samuel Johnson was the literary dictator of the last half of the eighteenth century. A picturesque figure — huge, shambling, scarred of face, thunderous of voice, and slovenly of dress — Johnson drew about him the most talented men of his age. He was the oracle of the famous Literary Club, which included David Garrick, the actor; Sir Joshua Reynolds, the painter; Oliver Goldsmith, the poet and novelist; Richard Sheridan, the dramatist; Edmund Burke, the statesman and defender of America; Adam Smith, the economist; Edward Gibbon, the historian — and James Boswell, his biographer. Today we know Johnson best through Boswell's biography. In fact, Boswell is far more widely read than Johnson himself, whose importance resided mainly in his personal influence. Johnson could talk fluently and learnedly on practically any subject, and he molded the taste of his age with his conversation. To this day we prize his critical judgments on men of letters.

Samuel Johnson in his early career waged a constant struggle against poverty. He was brought up in the country town of Lichfield, where his father was a bookseller, poor in money but rich in reading fare. Sam was a proud young man. At Oxford he once threw away a much-needed pair of shoes given to him by a fellow student because he did not wish to accept charity. He worked for a time as a schoolteacher at Lichfield but, after less than two years, finally left for London, sharing a horse with his pupil, David Garrick.

In London Johnson was unsuccessful in selling his writings, which included poetry, biography, and essays, and he took to hack writing. Slowly he gained recognition, mainly from his famous *Dictionary,* his paper *The Rambler,* and his *Lives of the English Poets.* Yet he remained poor, and his one novel, *Rasselas,* was written in four days to pay the expense of his mother's funeral. At the age of fifty-three he was relieved by a pension from George III.

From Boswell's *The Life of Samuel Johnson* we get a rounded picture of Johnson: he was a gruff and stern man but a kindly one. He supported in his house a number of poor and unfortunate people, including Miss Williams, his old, half-blind housekeeper, who is reputed to have used her thumb to judge whether the guests' tea-cups needed refilling! All in all, he deserved to have the literary period named for him and to be the subject of Boswell's famous biography, which records his life and times for posterity.

James Boswell is recognized as one of the greatest biographers in English literature. A Scotsman of wealthy family who came to London to get a commission in the army, Boswell was ambitious, impulsive, and often lacking in judgment. Yet he had a true gift for writing and the rare insight to recognize his life work on meeting Samuel Johnson. For years, whenever the two men met, Boswell recorded Johnson's conversation, his habits, his peculiarities. The biographer submerged his own personality in that of his subject, but Boswell was a personality in his own right. His journals, not discovered until the twentieth century, reveal him as a vain, sometimes ridiculous youth, yet in many ways an appealing one. He was a delightful writer with a keen sense of observation and a lively humor that never failed him.

Letter to
Lord Chesterfield

The significance of this letter is in its relation to the system of patronage prevalent in England in Johnson's time. Since the reading public was small, the only way a man could obtain any substantial financial return from writing was by securing a patron among the wealthy nobility. It was understood that the author would dedicate his work to the patron, who in return saw to the author's welfare. When the *Dictionary* was first contemplated, Johnson requested the support of Lord Chesterfield,

the most elegant gentleman of his day. The result is told in the following letter. Johnson showed his native independence of spirit and is said to have thereby sounded the death knell of the whole patronage system. In connection with this letter, you should read the selection "The Dictionary" from Boswell's *Life* which appears on page 323.

February 7, 1755

To the Right Honorable the Earl of Chesterfield.

My Lord:

I have been lately informed by the proprietor of the *World* [1] that two papers, in which my Dictionary is recommended to the public, were written by your Lordship. To be so distinguished is an honor which, being very little accustomed to favors from the great, I know not well how to receive, or in what terms to acknowledge.

When, upon some slight encouragement, I first visited your Lordship, I was overpowered, like the rest of mankind, by the enchantment of your address, and could not forbear to wish that I might boast myself *Le vainqueur du vainqueur de la terre* [2] — that I might obtain that regard for which I saw the world contending; but I found my attendance so little encouraged that neither pride nor modesty would suffer me to continue it. When I had once addressed your Lordship in public, I had exhausted all the art of pleasing which a retired and uncourtly scholar can possess. I had done all that I could; and no man is well pleased to have his all neglected, be it ever so little.

Seven years, my Lord, have now passed since I waited in your outward rooms, or was repulsed from your door; during which time I have been pushing

---

[1] *the* World: a newspaper run by Edward Moore, a friend of Johnson's. [2] "The conqueror of the conqueror of the world."

on my work through difficulties, of which it is useless to complain, and have brought it, at last, to the verge of publication without one act of assistance, one word of encouragement, or one smile of favor. Such treatment I did not expect, for I never had a Patron before.

The shepherd in Virgil grew at last acquainted with Love, and found him a native of the rocks.[1]

Is not a Patron, my Lord, one who looks with unconcern on a man struggling for life in the water, and when he has reached ground, encumbers him with help? The notice which you have been pleased to take of my labors, had it been early, had been kind; but it has been delayed till I am indifferent, and cannot enjoy it; till I am solitary, and cannot impart it; till I am known, and do not want it. I hope it is no very cynical asperity not to confess obligations where no benefit has been received, or to be unwilling that the Public should consider me as owing that to a Patron which Providence has enabled me to do for myself.

Having carried on my work thus far with so little obligation to any favorer of learning, I shall not be disappointed though I should conclude it, if less be possible, with less; for I have been long wakened from that dream of hope, in which I once boasted myself with so much exultation.

My Lord,
Your Lordship's most humble,
Most obedient servant,

Sam: Johnson.

---

[1] *The shepherd . . . rocks:* a reference to a passage in Virgil's eighth Eclogue (a pastoral poem in which shepherds converse on the cruelty and inhumanity of love).

Definitions from Johnson's Dictionary

Some of Johnson's definitions are famous for showing his prejudices, his errors, his use of big words to define a fairly simple term, and, at times, his humor.

Excise duty: a hateful tax levied by wretches hired by those to whom excise is paid.

Oats: a grain which in England is generally given to horses, but in Scotland [1] supports the people.

Pension: an allowance made to anyone without an equivalent.[2] In England it is generally understood to mean pay given to a state hireling for treason to his country.

Pensioner: a slave of state hired by a stipend to obey his master. [Later, when Johnson himself became a pensioner, he replied to the critics who reminded him of this definition: "I wish my pension were twice as large that they might make twice as much noise."]

Tory: one who adheres to the ancient constitution of the State and the apostolical hierarchy of the Church of England; opposed to a Whig.

Whig: the name of a faction.

Lexicographer: a writer of dictionaries, a harmless drudge.

Grub Street: the name of a street in London, much inhabited by writers of small histories, dictionaries, and temporary poems: whence any mean production is called *Grub Street.*

Pastern: the knee of a horse. [On being asked by a lady why he defined it thus, he said, "Ignorance, madam, pure ignorance."]

Network: anything reticulated or decussated at equal distances with interstices between the intersections.

---

[1] You will learn later of Johnson's dislike of the Scots. [2] *equivalent* (ĕ·kwĭv′á·lĕnt): here, service of equal value.

The Life of Samuel Johnson

JAMES BOSWELL

Through his *Life of Samuel Johnson* James Boswell ensured the immortality of a great personality whose role in the literary circles of his time and whose importance in the history of English literature may otherwise have been obscured. At the same time, Boswell ensured his own immortality as a personality and a biographer.

It is interesting to note that Boswell's association with Samuel Johnson was, from the outset, frowned upon by Boswell's stern Scottish father. Indeed, capricious, extravagant, and irresponsible, Boswell, who as eldest son was heir to his father's estate, was considered the disgrace of his family. In 1762, having made temporary peace at home, he left Scotland for London. Twenty-two years old, alternately conceited and self-doubting, Boswell was markedly unstable in personality. For many reasons, his meeting and subsequent friendship with Johnson was probably the luckiest event of his life. Johnson brought out the good side of Boswell and in many respects served as substitute for Boswell's severe parent. The advantages of this relationship were mutual, however, for Boswell in turn complemented Johnson's personality. Boswell's famous biography illuminates the personalities of both men and serves as a unique testimony of this celebrated friendship.

[THE DICTIONARY]

The following excerpt is from the first part of the biography, covering the period before Boswell became acquainted with Johnson.

How long this immense undertaking had been the object of his contemplation, I do not know. I once asked him by what means he had attained to that astonishing knowledge of our language by which he was enabled to realize a design of such extent and accumulated difficulty. He told me that "it was not the effect of particular study; but that it had grown up in his mind insensibly." . . .

That he was fully aware of the arduous nature of the undertaking, he acknowledges; and shows himself perfectly sensible of it in the conclusion of his "Plan"; but he had a noble consciousness of his own abilities, which enabled him to go on with undaunted spirit.

Dr. Adams found him one day busy at his Dictionary, when the following dialogue ensued:

Adams: "This is a great work, Sir. How are you to get all the etymologies?" [1]

Johnson: "Why, Sir, here is a shelf with Junius, and Skinner,[2] and others; and there is a Welsh gentleman who has published a collection of Welsh proverbs, who will help me with the Welsh."

Adams: "But, Sir, how can you do this in three years?"

Johnson: "Sir, I have no doubt that I can do it in three years."

Adams: "But the French Academy, which consists of forty members, took forty years to compile their Dictionary."

Johnson: "Sir, thus it is. This is the proportion. Let me see: forty times forty is sixteen hundred. As three to sixteen hundred so is the proportion of an Englishman to a Frenchman."

With so much ease and pleasantry could he talk of that prodigious labor which he had undertaken to execute.

While the Dictionary was going forward, Johnson lived part of the time in Holborn, part in Gough Square, Fleet Street; and he had an upper room fitted up like a countinghouse for the purpose, in which he gave to the copyists their several tasks. The words, partly taken from other Dictionaries, and partly supplied by himself, having been first written down with spaces left between them,

---

[1] *etymologies* (ĕt'ĭ·mŏl'ŏ·jĭz): origins and derivations of words. [2] *Junius, and Skinner:* seventeenth-century English scholars, both of whom wrote books on etymology. Skinner was also a physician.

he delivered in writing their etymologies, definitions, and various significations. The authorities were copied from the books themselves, in which he had marked the passages with a black-lead pencil, the traces of which could be easily effaced. I have seen several of them in which that trouble had not been taken; so that they were just as when used by the copyists. It is remarkable that he was so attentive in the choice of the passages in which words were authorized that one may read page after page of his Dictionary with improvement and pleasure; and it should not pass unobserved that he has quoted no author whose writings had a tendency to hurt sound religion and morality.

The necessary expense of preparing a work of such magnitude for the press must have been a considerable deduction from the price stipulated to be paid for the copyright.[1] I understand that nothing was allowed by the booksellers on that account; and I remember his telling me that a large portion of it having, by mistake, been written upon both sides of the paper, so as to be inconvenient for the compositor, it cost him twenty pounds to have it transcribed upon one side only.

[BOSWELL'S FIRST MEETING WITH DR. JOHNSON]

Mr. Thomas Davies, the actor, who then kept a bookseller's shop in Russell Street, Covent Garden, told me that Johnson was very much his friend, and came frequently to his house, where he more than once invited me to meet him: but by some unlucky accident or other he was prevented from coming to us. . . .

At last, on Monday the 16th of May, when I was sitting in Mr. Davies' back parlor, after having drunk tea with him and Mrs. Davies, Johnson unexpectedly came into the shop; and Mr. Davies having perceived him through the glass door in the room in which we were sitting, ad-

---

[1] The price was £1,575.

vancing toward us — he announced his awful approach to me, somewhat in the manner of an actor in the part of Horatio, when he addresses Hamlet on the appearance of his father's ghost, "Look, my Lord, it comes." I found that I had a very perfect idea of Johnson's figure, from the portrait of him painted by Sir Joshua Reynolds soon after he had published his Dictionary, in the attitude of sitting in his easy chair in deep meditation; which was the first picture his friend did for him, which Sir Joshua very kindly presented to me, and from which an engraving has been made for this work. Mr. Davies mentioned my name, and respectfully introduced me to him. I was much agitated; and recollecting his prejudice against the Scotch, of which I had heard much, I said to Davies, "Don't tell him where I come from."

"From Scotland," cried Davies, roguishly.

"Mr. Johnson (said I), I do indeed come from Scotland, but I cannot help it."

I am willing to flatter myself that I meant this as light pleasantry to soothe and conciliate him, and not as an humiliating abasement at the expense of my country. But however that might be, this speech was somewhat unlucky; for with that quickness of wit for which he was so remarkable, he seized the expression "come from Scotland," which I used in the sense of being of that country; and, as if I had said that I had come away from it, or left it, retorted, "That, Sir, I find, is what a very great many of your countrymen cannot help."

This stroke stunned me a good deal; and when we had sat down, I felt myself not a little embarrassed, and apprehensive of what might come next.

He then addressed himself to Davies: "What do you think of Garrick? He has refused me an order for the play for Miss Williams, because he knows the house will be full, and that an order would be worth three shillings."

Eager to take any opening to get into

conversation with him, I ventured to say, "O, Sir, I cannot think Mr. Garrick would grudge such a trifle to you."

"Sir (said he, with a stern look), I have known David Garrick longer than you have done; and I know no right you have to talk to me on the subject."

Perhaps I deserved this check; for it was rather presumptuous in me, an entire stranger, to express any doubt of the justice of his animadversion [1] upon his old acquaintance and pupil. I now felt myself much mortified, and began to think that the hope which I had long indulged of obtaining his acquaintance was blasted. And, in truth, had not my ardor been uncommonly strong, and my resolution uncommonly persevering, so rough a reception might have deterred me forever from making any further attempts. Fortunately, however, I remained upon the field not wholly discomfited; and was soon rewarded by hearing some of his conversation. . . .

A few days afterward I called on Davies, and asked him if he thought I might take the liberty of waiting on Mr. Johnson at his Chambers in the Temple.[2] He said I certainly might, and that Mr. Johnson would take it as a compliment. So on Tuesday the 24th of May, after having been enlivened by the witty sallies of Messieurs Thornton, Wilkes, Churchill, and Lloyd,[3] with whom I had passed the morning, I boldly repaired to Johnson. His Chambers were on the first floor of No. 1, Inner Temple-lane, and I entered them with an impression given me by the Reverend Dr. Blair, of Edinburgh, who had been introduced to him not long before, and described his having "found the Giant in his den"; an expression which, when I came to be pretty well acquainted with Johnson, I repeated to him, and he was diverted at this picturesque account of himself.

He received me very courteously: but it must be confessed that his apartment, and furniture, and morning dress were sufficiently uncouth. His brown suit of clothes looked very rusty: he had on a little old shriveled unpowdered wig, which was too small for his head; his shirt neck and knees of his breeches were loose; his black worsted stockings ill drawn up; and he had a pair of unbuckled shoes by way of slippers. But all these slovenly particularities were forgotten the moment that he began to talk. Some gentlemen, whom I do not recollect, were sitting with him; and when they went away, I also rose; but he said to me, "Nay, don't go."

"Sir (said I), I am afraid that I intrude upon you. It is benevolent to allow me to sit and hear you."

He seemed pleased with this compliment, which I sincerely paid him, and answered, "Sir, I am obliged to any man who visits me." . . .

When I rose a second time, he again pressed me to stay, which I did.

He told me that he generally went abroad at four in the afternoon and seldom came home till two in the morning. I took the liberty to ask if he did not think it was wrong to live thus, and not make more use of his great talents. He owned it was a bad habit. On reviewing, at the distance of many years, my journal of this period, I wonder how, at my first visit, I ventured to talk to him so freely, and that he bore it with so much indulgence.

Before we departed, he was so good as to promise to favor me with his company one evening at my lodgings; and, as I took my leave, shook me cordially by the hand. It is almost needless to add that I felt no little elation at having now so happily established an acquaintance of which I had been so long ambitious.

My readers will, I trust, excuse me for being thus minutely circumstantial, when it is considered that the acquaintance of Dr. Johnson was to me a most valuable acquisition, and laid the foundation of

---

[1] *animadversion* (ăn′ĭ·măd·vûr′shŭn): criticism, usually adverse. [2] *Temple:* an area of London in which lawyers lived and where law courts are located. [3] *Thornton . . . Lloyd:* literary wits and friends of Boswell.

whatever instruction and entertainment they may receive from my collections concerning the great subject of the work which they are now perusing.

[DR. JOHNSON'S PECULIARITIES]

He had another particularity,[1] of which none of his friends even ventured to ask an explanation. It appeared to me some superstitious habit, which he had contracted early, and from which he had never called upon his reason to disentangle him. This was his anxious care to go out or in at a door or passage by a certain number of steps from a certain point, or at least so as that either his right or his left foot (I am not certain which) should constantly make the first actual movement when he came close to the door or passage. Thus I conjecture: for I have, upon innumerable occasions, observed him suddenly stop, and then seem to count his steps with a deep earnestness; and when he had neglected or gone wrong in this sort of magical movement, I have seen him go back again, put himself in a proper posture to begin the ceremony, and, having gone through it, break from his abstraction, walk briskly on, and join his companion. Sir Joshua Reynolds has observed him to go a good way about, rather than cross a particular alley in Leicester [2] Fields; but this Sir Joshua imputed to his having had some disagreeable recollections associated with it.

That the most minute singularities which belonged to him, and made very observable parts of his appearance and manner, may not be omitted, it is requisite to mention that while talking or even musing as he sat in his chair, he commonly held his head to one side toward his right shoulder, and shook it in a tremulous manner, moving his body backward and forward, and rubbing his left knee in the same direction, with the

palm of his hand. In the intervals of articulating he made various sounds with his mouth; sometimes giving a half whistle, sometimes as if ruminating, or what is called chewing the cud, sometimes making his tongue play backward from the roof of his mouth, as if clucking like a hen, and sometimes protruding it against his upper gums in front, as if pronouncing quickly under his breath, too, too, too: all this accompanied sometimes with a thoughtful look, but more frequently with a smile. Generally when he had concluded a period,[3] in the course of a dispute, by which time he was a good deal exhausted by violence and vociferation, he used to blow out his breath like a whale. This I suppose was a relief to his lungs; and seemed in him to be a contemptuous mode of expression, as if he had made the arguments of his opponents fly like chaff before the wind.

[JOHNSON AND GOLDSMITH]

The following incident takes place at dinner at the home of two booksellers, where about a dozen gentlemen, including Johnson, Boswell, and Goldsmith, are assembled. A long conversation is first reported.

During this argument, Goldsmith sat in restless agitation, from a wish to get in and shine. Finding himself excluded, he had taken his hat to go away, but remained for some time with it in his hand, like a gamester, who, at the close of a long night, lingers for a little while, to see if he can have a favorable opening to finish with success. Once when he was beginning to speak, he found himself overpowered by the loud voice of Johnson, who was at the opposite end of the table, and did not perceive Goldsmith's attempt. Thus disappointed of his wish to obtain the attention of the company, Goldsmith in a passion threw down his hat, looking angrily at Johnson, and exclaimed in a bitter tone, "Take it." When Toplady was going to speak, Johnson ut-

---

[1] *another particularity:* The first one described was his habit of talking to himself. [2] *Leicester* (lĕs'tẽr).

[3] *concluded a period:* ended a sentence.

tered some sound, which led Goldsmith to think that he was beginning again, and taking the words from Toplady. Upon which, he seized this opportunity of venting his own envy and spleen, under the pretext of supporting another person: "Sir (said he to Johnson), the gentleman has heard you patiently for an hour: pray allow us now to hear him."

Johnson (*sternly*): "Sir, I was not interrupting the gentleman. I was only giving him a signal of my attention. Sir, you are impertinent." Goldsmith made no reply, but continued in the company for some time.

He and Mr. Langton and I went together to the Club, where we found Mr. Burke, Mr. Garrick, and some other members, and among them our friend Goldsmith, who sat silently brooding over Johnson's reprimand to him after dinner. Johnson perceived this, and said aside to some of us, "I'll make Goldsmith forgive me"; and then called to him in a loud voice, "Dr. Goldsmith — something passed today where you and I dined: I ask your pardon." Goldsmith answered placidly, "It must be much from you, Sir, that I take ill." And so at once the difference was over, and they were on as easy terms as ever, and Goldsmith rattled away as usual.

In our way to the Club tonight, when I regretted that Goldsmith would, upon every occasion, endeavor to shine, by which he often exposed himself, Mr. Langton observed that he was not like Addison, who was content with the fame of his writings, and did not aim also at excellency in conversation, for which he found himself unfit: and that he said to a lady who complained of his having talked little in company, "Madam, I have but ninepence in ready money, but I can draw for a thousand pounds." I observed that Goldsmith had a great deal of gold in his cabinet, but not content with that, was always taking out his purse. Johnson: "Yes, Sir, and that so often an empty purse!"

Goldsmith's incessant desire of being conspicuous in company was the occasion of his sometimes appearing to such disadvantage as one should hardly have supposed possible in a man of his genius. When his literary reputation had risen deservedly high, and his society was much courted, he became very jealous of the extraordinary attention which was everywhere paid to Johnson. One evening, in a circle of wits, he found fault with me for talking of Johnson as entitled to the honor of unquestionable superiority. "Sir (said he), you are for making a monarchy of what should be a republic."

He was still more mortified, when talking in a company with fluent vivacity, and, as he flattered himself, to the admiration of all who were present; a German who sat next him, and perceived Johnson rolling himself as if about to speak, suddenly stopped him, saying, "Stay, stay — Toctor Shonson is going to say something." This was, no doubt, very provoking, especially to one so irritable as Goldsmith, who frequently mentioned it with strong expressions of indignation.

It may also be observed that Goldsmith was sometimes content to be treated with an easy familiarity, but upon occasions would be consequential and important. An instance of this occurred in a small particular. Johnson had a way of contracting the names of his friends: as Beauclerk, Beau; Boswell, Bozzy; Langton, Lanky; Murphy, Mur; Sheridan, Sherry. I remember one day, when Tom Davies was telling that Dr. Johnson said, "We are all in labor for a name to Goldy's play," Goldsmith seemed displeased that such a liberty should be taken with his name, and said, "I have often desired him not to call me Goldy." Tom was remarkably attentive to the most minute circumstance about Johnson. I recollect his telling me once, on my arrival in London, "Sir, our great friend has made an improvement on his appellation of old Mr. Sheridan. He calls him now Sherry derry."

Boswell's London Journal, 1762 – 1763

Boswell's journal, secreted or neglected by the Boswell family over the centuries, finally found its way to Yale University in 1949, and a year later the first of many projected volumes was published. Its detailed account of the life of a gallant young eighteenth-century man-about-town — alternately naïve and sophisticated, fun-loving and earnest — delighted contemporary readers. Boswell's journal became a literary sensation and a best seller.

The journal throws further light not only upon Boswell himself, but also upon his unusual friendship with Johnson. The following selections show how Boswell sought Johnson's advice in the affairs of his private life and the kindly spirit in which Johnson replied. The first entry here quoted also illustrates Boswell's habit of jotting down unconnected sentences he remembered from conversations with his friend.

Saturday 25 June [*1763*] . . . I told him all my story. "Sir," said he, "your father has been wanting to make the man of you at twenty which you will be at thirty. Sir, let me tell you that to be a Scotch landlord,[1] where you have a number of families dependent upon and attached to you, is perhaps as high a situation as humanity can arrive at. A merchant upon 'Change with a hundred thousand pounds is nothing. The Duke of Bedford with all his immense fortune is but a little man in reality. He has no tenants who consider themselves as under his patriarchal care.

"Sir, a father and a son should part at a certain time of life. I never believed what my father said. I always thought that he spoke ex officio,[2] as a priest does.

"Sir, I am a friend to subordination. It is most conducive to the happiness of society. There is a reciprocal pleasure in governing and being governed.

"Sir, I think your breaking off idle connections by going abroad is a matter of importance. I would go where there are courts and learned men."

I then complained to him how little I knew, and mentioned study. "Sir," said he, "don't talk of study just now. I will put you upon a plan. It will require some time to talk of that." I put out my hand. "Will you really take a charge of me? It is very good in you, Mr. Johnson, to allow me to sit with you thus. Had I but thought some years ago that I should pass an evening with the Author of *The Rambler!*" These expressions were all from the heart, and he perceived that they were; and he was very complacent and said, "Sir, I am glad we have met. I hope we shall pass many evenings and mornings too together."

Thursday 14 July. Mr. Johnson and I met at the Mitre by ourselves. He was in most excellent humor, though the night was very rainy. I said it was good for the vegetable part of the creation. "Ay, Sir," said he, "and for the animals who eat those vegetables, and for the animals who eat those animals." We had a good supper, which made us very comfortable.

I said, "You and I, Sir, are very good companions, but my father and I are not so. Now what can occasion this? For you are as old a man as my father, and you are certainly as learned and as knowing." "Sir," said he, "I am a man of the world. I live in the world, and I take in some measure the color of the world as it moves along. But your father is a judge in a remote part of the country, and all his notions are taken

---

[1] Boswell's father was Laird of Auchinleck (ŏ′kĭn·lĕk′), a Scotch landowner and jurist. Boswell, the eldest son, was due to inherit his father's lands and responsibilities. [2] *ex officio* (ĕks ŏ·fĭsh′ĭ·ō): because of his office (here as a father).

From *Boswell's London Journal, 1762–1763*, edited by Frederick A. Pottle. Published by McGraw-Hill Book Company. Copyright, 1950, by Yale University.

from the old world. Besides, there must always be a struggle between a father and son, while the one aims at power and the other at independency." I told him that I was afraid of my father's forcing me to be a lawyer. "Why, Sir," said he, "you need not be afraid of his forcing you to be a laborious practicing lawyer. That is not in his power. For, as the proverb says, 'One man may lead a horse to the water, but twenty cannot make him drink.' He may be displeased, but it will not go far. If he only insists on your having as much law as is necessary for a man of property, and endeavors to get you into Parliament, he is quite in the right."

Saturday 16 July . . . He advised me to keep a journal of my life, fair and undisguised. He said it would be a very good exercise, and would yield me infinite satisfaction when the ideas were faded from my remembrance. I told him that I had done so ever since I left Scotland. He said he was very happy that I pursued so good a plan. And now, O my journal! art thou not highly dignified? Shalt thou not flourish tenfold? No former solicitations or censures could tempt me to lay thee aside; and now is there any argument which can outweigh the sanction of Mr. Samuel Johnson? He said indeed that I should keep it private, and that I might surely have a friend who would burn it in case of my death. For my own part, I have at present such an affection for this my journal that it shocks me to think of burning it. I rather encourage the idea of having it carefully laid up among the archives of Auchinleck. However, I cannot judge fairly of it now. Some years hence I may. I told Mr. Johnson that I put down all sorts of little incidents in it. "Sir," said he, "there is nothing too little for so little a creature as man. It is by studying little things that we attain the great knowledge of having as little misery and as much happiness as possible."

Six lively volumes of "The Private Papers of James Boswell" have resulted from the long-hidden manuscript of Boswell's journal. They are:

Boswell's London Journal, 1762–1763
Boswell in Holland, 1763–1764
Boswell on the Grand Tour: Germany and Switzerland, 1764
Boswell on the Grand Tour: Italy, Corsica, and France, 1765–1766
Boswell in Search of a Wife, 1766–1769
Boswell for the Defense, 1769–1774

A UNIQUE LITERARY PAIR

1. What light is thrown on Johnson's character by his conduct toward Lord Chesterfield?

2. Compare with others your impressions of Johnson's personality and attitude toward people. Is your impression favorable or unfavorable? Why was he so much admired in spite of his peculiarities?

3. Contrast Johnson and Goldsmith. Which of the two appeals to you more? Do you think Boswell gives an objective picture of Goldsmith? Why or why not?

4. Boswell submerged himself in the personality of Dr. Johnson, a man thirty years older than he was. Does he seem to you to be impartial or partial as a biographer? Why? Specifically, what do you notice in his biography that you do not find in most biographies?

5. On what basis did Johnson gain such great influence over his age? How does he typify the eighteenth century? Do we have literary dictators today? What do literary dictators have in common with political dictators?

6. How would you describe the friendship of Boswell and Johnson as it is shown in Boswell's journal? What was Johnson's attitude toward Boswell? Was there mutual admiration and respect between these men?

CLASS ACTIVITIES

1. Write and enact a short play or dramatized conversation of the Literary Club for presentation before the class.

2. Plan brief oral reports on the following members of the Literary Club: Sir Joshua Reynolds, David Garrick, Edmund Burke, Oliver Goldsmith.

LITERATURE AND THE ARTS

The renown of Dr. Samuel Johnson, ensured in print by his enthusiastic young friend Boswell, is also perpetuated by the two engravings opposite. At the top of the page, Dr. Johnson waits to see Lord Chesterfield with the hope of obtaining his patronage. Johnson's famous letter to Lord Chesterfield (page 321) relates the outcome of his petition. The second engraving shows a gathering of Johnson and some of the most distinguished figures of the day. Seated around the table, from left to right, are Boswell, Johnson, Sir Joshua Reynolds, David Garrick, Edmund Burke, General Pasquale de Paoli, Dr. Charles Burney, Sr., the Rev. Thomas Warton, and Oliver Goldsmith.

BEHIND THE SCENES IN ENGLISH LITERATURE

Boswell's *Life of Johnson,* considered a masterpiece from the moment of publication, did nothing to diminish its author's reputation as something of a fool. Playing down his own role to enhance that of his hero, Boswell often deliberately showed himself at a disadvantage. Perhaps, however, he was not quite as foolish as he made himself out to be.

In the *Life* Boswell mentions his "archives," so from the beginning scholars assumed they must contain material not used in the *Life* that might prove highly interesting. Boswell's will, though, directed that the "archives" be kept in the family. Though his literary executors were instructed to publish as they thought best, they published nothing whatsoever, and when later scholars tried to investigate, Boswell's Victorian descendants refused access to the papers and failed to deny a story that they had been destroyed. So the matter rested for over a century.

In the 1920's, Professor Chauncey B. Tinker of Yale, in bringing out the first edition of all the private Boswell letters available, revealed that there was more than one side to Boswell's personality. In addition to the familiar vices, there was deep remorse, noble resolution, and a profound and earnest introspection. Clearly, Boswell seemed worth studying for his own sake.

Acting on an anonymous tip, Professor Tinker visited at Malahide Castle, near Dublin, Boswell's great-great grandson, Lord Talbot, to whom Boswell's possessions had passed after the death of his Scottish relatives. To his amazed delight, Tinker was shown a wealth of unpublished material on Johnson, Boswell, and others of their circle. The "archives" still existed; Tinker, however, was unable to make arrangements to study them.

Then, after much persuasion, Lt. Col. Ralph H. Isham, a New York financier and ardent Johnsonian, induced Talbot to part with his treasure. From these papers — many letters and, above all, an intimate diary revealing with utmost candor the complexities of his inner life — we can know Boswell as few historical or literary figures can be known. Still the buffoon, he is also a gifted reporter and psychological observer.

Talbot's collection, however, contained neither the manuscript of the *Life* itself, letters from Johnson or others of his circle, nor that part of the journal covering Boswell's early acquaintance with Johnson. Prematurely, scholars resigned themselves to these losses.

Then, in 1930, someone at Malahide Castle found an old croquet box in which were still more Boswell papers, plus the uncensored manuscript of the well-known *Journal of a Tour to the Hebrides.* Also in 1930, a British scholar visiting Fettercairn House in Scotland chanced upon masses of unsorted papers and — the

missing portion of Boswell's diary.

Finally, during the last war, when all facilities for storing grain were needed, an old barn at Malahide was pressed into service. When cleared out, the barn loft yielded a further collection of papers, including nearly 3,000 letters and, at long last, the manuscript of the *Life* itself, which in revealing Boswell's methods of working up his quickly jotted notes, shows that the biographer was a discerning and sophisticated artist.

All these discoveries were acquired by Colonel Isham, and in 1949 the entire Boswell collection was presented to Yale University. Altogether, it is said, there is enough material to keep fifty scholars busy for fifty years.

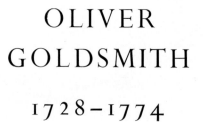

OLIVER GOLDSMITH

1728-1774

National Portrait Gallery

Johnson's friend "Goldy" was an irresponsible, lovable, witty Irishman whose life presents a combination of pathos and absurdity. His boyhood in the little Irish village of Lissoy is accurately pictured in *The Deserted Village*. At school the awkward, pock-marked boy was regarded as a dunce; and at Trinity College, Dublin, he came out at the foot of his class. Money given him by relatives so that he could study law or emigrate to America he lost in gambling. For a time he studied medicine at Edinburgh and later on the Continent. Returning to England, he tried acting, working in a chemist's shop, teaching in a boys' school, and even begging, before finally taking up literature.

Here at last he found something he could do superbly. Goldsmith has the unique distinction among eighteenth-century writers of having produced a poem (*The Deserted Village*), a comedy (*She Stoops to Conquer*), and a novel (*The Vicar of Wakefield*) that are still read and enjoyed today. The story goes that when Goldsmith was about to be imprisoned for not paying his rent, Johnson rescued him by selling the manuscript of *The Vicar of Wakefield* to a bookseller for sixty pounds.

Goldsmith made a better income from his hack writing than from his literary work. He turned out textbooks of history with astounding rapidity and inaccuracy. Some of the statements in his *Animated Nature* justify the remark made by one of his friends that he didn't know one fowl from another until it appeared cooked on the table.

With greater prosperity, Goldsmith spent most of his time with the members of the famous Literary Club. There he was usually the butt of the jokes. On one occasion when he was late as usual, they all wrote epitaphs on him. Garrick's ran thus:
"Here lies Nolly Goldsmith, for shortness called 'Noll,'
Who wrote like an angel and talked like poor Poll."

Nevertheless, Goldsmith had a certain sly wit in conversation, too. Once when he and Johnson were looking at the tombs in Westminster Abbey, Johnson quoted a Latin sentence that meant, "Perhaps our names also will be mingled with these." On the way home they passed Temple Bar, where heads of criminals used to be exposed. Goldsmith thereupon repeated in Latin with different emphasis: "Perhaps our names also will be mingled with *these*." Fortunately it was the first rather than the second prophecy that came true. Johnson wrote the inscription for the memorial to Goldsmith in the Abbey: "He touched nothing that he did not adorn."

The Deserted Village

Three well-known poems of the eighteenth century portray the life of the common people — *The Deserted Village,* Thomas Gray's "Elegy Written in a Country Churchyard," and Robert Burns' "The Cotter's Saturday Night." Curiously enough, each represents a different country of the British Isles. Gray depicts England, Burns Scotland, while Goldsmith writes of Auburn, a fictitious name for an Irish village, probably similar to Lissoy. In contrast to the strict and sophisticated writing of Pope and Johnson, all three of these poems express the growing interest in the middle and late eighteenth century in rural settings and humble lives. The style of Goldsmith's poem is not markedly different from that of earlier eighteenth-century writers, but the subject matter and sentiment of *The Deserted Village* point forward to the Romantic movement.

The last part of the poem, a prolonged lamentation over the woes of the peasants, has been omitted here.

Sweet Auburn! loveliest village of the plain,
Where health and plenty cheered the laboring swain,
Where smiling spring its earliest visit paid,
And parting summer's lingering blooms delayed;
Dear lovely bowers of innocence and ease,   5
Seats of my youth, when every sport could please,
How often have I loitered o'er thy green,°
Where humble happiness endeared each scene!
How often have I paused on every charm,
The sheltered cot,° the cultivated farm,   10
The never-failing brook, the busy mill,
The decent church that topped the neighboring hill,
The hawthorn bush, with seats beneath the shade
For talking age and whispering lovers made!
How often have I blest the coming day,   15
When toil remitting lent its turn to play,
And all the village train, from labor free,
Led up their sports beneath the spreading tree,
While many a pastime circled in the shade,
The young contending as the old surveyed;   20

7. *green:* an open lawn in the middle of a village, a center for recreation. 10. *cot:* cottage.

And many a gambol frolicked o'er the ground,
And sleights of art° and feats of strength went round.
And still, as each repeated pleasure tired,
Succeeding sports the mirthful band inspired;
The dancing pair that simply sought renown   25
By holding out to tire each other down;
The swain mistrustless° of his smutted face,
While secret laughter tittered round the place;
The bashful virgin's sidelong looks of love,
The matron's glance that would those looks reprove.   30
These were thy charms, sweet village! sports like these,
With sweet succession, taught even toil to please;
These round thy bowers their cheerful influence shed;
These were thy charms — but all these charms are fled.

    Sweet smiling village, loveliest of the lawn,   35
Thy sports are fled, and all thy charms withdrawn;
Amidst thy bowers the tyrant's hand is seen,
And desolation saddens all thy green;
One only master grasps the whole domain,°
And half a tillage stints thy smiling plain.   40
No more thy glassy brook reflects the day,
But, choked with sedges, works its weedy way;
Along the glades, a solitary guest,
The hollow sounding bittern guards its nest;
Amidst thy desert walks the lapwing flies,   45
And tires their echoes with unvaried cries.
Sunk are thy bowers in shapeless ruin all,
And the long grass o'ertops the moldering wall;
And trembling, shrinking from the spoiler's hand,
Far, far away thy children leave the land.   50

    Ill fares the land, to hastening ills a prey,
Where wealth accumulates, and men decay.
Princes and lords may flourish, or may fade;
A breath can make them, as a breath has made;
But a bold peasantry, their country's pride,   55
When once destroyed, can never be supplied.

---

22. *sleights of art:* skillful turns. We still use the word in *sleight of hand.* 27. *mistrustless:* unaware.
39. This line refers to the process known as "enclosure," whereby the common grazing lands of villages were taken over by wealthy landowners.

A time there was, ere England's griefs began,
When every rood° of ground maintained its man;
For him light labor spread her wholesome store,
Just gave what life required, but gave no more;   60
His best companions, innocence and health;
And his best riches, ignorance of wealth.

But times are altered; trade's unfeeling train
Usurp the land and dispossess the swain;°
Along the lawn, where scattered hamlets rose,   65
Unwieldy wealth and cumbrous pomp repose,
And every want to opulence allied,
And every pang that folly pays to pride.
These gentle hours that plenty bade to bloom,
Those calm desires that asked but little room,   70
Those healthful sports that graced the peaceful scene,
Lived in each look, and brightened all the green;
These, far departing, seek a kinder shore,
And rural mirth and manners are no more.

Sweet Auburn! parent of the blissful hour,   75
Thy glades forlorn confess the tyrant's power.
Here, as I take my solitary rounds
Amidst thy tangling walks and ruined grounds,
And, many a year elapsed, return to view
Where once the cottage stood, the hawthorn grew,   80
Remembrance wakes with all her busy train,
Swells at my breast, and turns the past to pain.

In all my wanderings round this world of care,
In all my griefs — and God has given my share —
I still had hopes, my latest° hours to crown,   85
Amidst these humble bowers to lay me down;
To husband out life's taper at the close,
And keep the flame from wasting by repose;
I still had hopes, for pride attends us still,
Amidst the swains to show my book-learned skill,   90
Around my fire an evening group to draw,
And tell of all I felt, and all I saw;
And, as a hare whom hounds and horns pursue
Pants to the place from whence at first she flew,
I still had hopes, my long vexations past,   95
Here to return — and die at home at last.

O blest retirement, friend to life's decline,
Retreats from care, that never must be mine,
How happy he who crowns in shades like these
A youth of labor with an age of ease;   100
Who quits a world where strong temptations try,

58. *rood:* one-fourth of an acre. 63–64. *trade's . . . swain:* a reference to the effects of the Industrial
Revolution on village life. 85. *latest:* last.

And, since 'tis hard to combat, learns to fly!
For him no wretches, born to work and weep,
Explore the mine, or tempt the dangerous deep;
No surly porter stands in guilty state,   105
To spurn imploring famine from the gate;
But on he moves to meet his latter end,
Angels around befriending virtue's friend;
Bends to the grave with unperceived decay,
While resignation gently slopes the way;   110
And, all his prospects brightening to the last,
His heaven commences ere the world be past!

   Sweet was the sound, when oft at evening's close
Up yonder hill the village murmur rose;
There, as I passed with careless steps and slow,   115
The mingling notes came softened from below;
The swain responsive as the milkmaid sung,
The sober herd that lowed to meet their young,
The noisy geese that gabbled o'er the pool,
The playful children just let loose from school,   120
The watchdog's voice that bayed the whispering wind,
And the loud laugh that spoke the vacant mind —
These all in sweet confusion sought the shade,
And filled each pause the nightingale had made.
But now the sounds of population fail,   125
No cheerful murmurs fluctuate in the gale,
No busy steps the grass-grown footway tread,
For all the bloomy flush of life is fled.
All but yon widowed, solitary thing,
That feebly bends beside the plashy° spring;   130
She, wretched matron, forced in age, for bread,
To strip the brook with mantling cresses° spread,
To pick her wintry faggot from the thorn,
To seek her nightly shed, and weep till morn;
She only left of all the harmless train,   135
The sad historian of the pensive plain.

   Near yonder copse, where once the garden smiled,
And still where many a garden flower grows wild;
There, where a few torn shrubs the place disclose,
The village preacher's° modest mansion rose.   140
A man he was to all the country dear,
And passing rich with forty pounds a year;
Remote from towns he ran his godly race,
Nor e'er had changed, nor wished to change his place;
Unpracticed he to fawn, or seek for power,   145
By doctrines fashioned to the varying hour;

---

130. *plashy* (plăsh′ĭ): marshy. 132. *mantling cresses:* plants spreading over a surface. 140. *village preacher:* The following portrait is perhaps a composite portrait of Goldsmith's father and brother, both of whom were preachers.

Far other aims his heart had learned to prize,
More skilled to raise the wretched than to rise.
His house was known to all the vagrant train;
He chid their wanderings but relieved their pain.　　　　150
The long-remembered beggar was his guest,
Whose beard descending swept his aged breast;
The ruined spendthrift, now no longer proud,
Claimed kindred there, and had his claims allowed;

　The broken soldier, kindly bade to stay,　　　　155
Sat by the fire, and talked the night away,
Wept o'er his wounds or, tales of sorrow done,
Shouldered his crutch and showed how fields were won.
Pleased with his guests, the good man learned to glow,
And quite forgot their vices in their woe;　　　　160
Careless their merits or their faults to scan,
His pity gave ere charity began.

　Thus to relieve the wretched was his pride,
And e'en his failings leaned to virtue's side;
But in his duty prompt at every call,　　　　165
He watched and wept, he prayed and felt for all;
And, as a bird each fond endearment tries
To tempt its new-fledged offspring to the skies,
He tried each art, reproved each dull delay,
Allured to brighter worlds, and led the way.　　　　170

　Beside the bed where parting life was laid,
And sorrow, guilt, and pain by turns dismayed,
The reverend champion stood. At his control
Despair and anguish fled the struggling soul;
Comfort came down the trembling wretch to raise,　　　　175
And his last faltering accents whispered praise.

At church, with meek and unaffected grace,
His looks adorned the venerable place;
Truth from his lips prevailed with double sway,
And fools, who came to scoff, remained to pray.   180
The service past, around the pious man,
With steady zeal, each honest rustic ran;
Even children followed with endearing wile,
And plucked his gown to share the good man's smile.
His ready smile a parent's warmth expressed;   185
Their welfare pleased him, and their cares distressed;
To them his heart, his love, his griefs were given,
But all his serious thoughts had rest in heaven.
As some tall cliff that lifts its awful form,
Swells from the vale, and midway leaves the storm,   190
Though round its breast the rolling clouds are spread,
Eternal sunshine settles on its head.

Beside yon straggling fence that skirts the way,
With blossomed furze unprofitably gay,
There, in his noisy mansion, skilled to rule,   195
The village master° taught his little school.
A man severe he was, and stern to view;
I knew him well, and every truant knew;
Well had the boding tremblers learned to trace
The day's disasters in his morning face;   200
Full well they laughed with counterfeited glee
At all his jokes, for many a joke had he;
Full well the busy whisper circling round
Conveyed the dismal tidings when he frowned.
Yet he was kind, or, if severe in aught,   205
The love he bore to learning was in fault;
The village all declared how much he knew;
'Twas certain he could write, and cipher too;
Lands he could measure, terms and tides presage,°
And even the story ran that he could gauge;°   210
In arguing, too, the parson owned his skill,
For, even though vanquished, he could argue still;
While words of learned length and thundering sound
Amazed the gazing rustics ranged around;
And still they gazed, and still the wonder grew,   215
That one small head could carry all he knew.
But past is all his fame. The very spot
Where many a time he triumphed is forgot.

Near yonder thorn that lifts its head on high,
Where once the signpost caught the passing eye,   220

---

196. *The village master:* thought to be a portrait of Goldsmith's own schoolmaster. 209. *terms and tides presage:* figure out in advance the time for law sessions and church festivals, such as Easter. 210. *gauge:* measure the capacity of casks.

Low lies that house where nut-brown draughts° inspired,
Where graybeard mirth and smiling toil retired,
Where village statesmen talked with looks profound,
And news much older than their ale went round.
Imagination fondly stoops to trace   225
The parlor splendors of that festive place:
The whitewashed wall, the nicely sanded floor,
The varnished clock that clicked behind the door;
The chest contrived a double debt to pay,
A bed by night, a chest of drawers by day;   230
The pictures placed for ornament and use,
The twelve good rules,° the royal game of goose;°
The hearth, except when winter chilled the day,
With aspen boughs and flowers and fennel° gay;
While broken teacups, wisely kept for show,   235
Ranged o'er the chimney, glistened in a row.

   Vain transitory splendors! could not all
Reprieve the tottering mansion from its fall?
Obscure it sinks, nor shall it more impart
An hour's importance to the poor man's heart.   240
Thither no more the peasant shall repair
To sweet oblivion of his daily care;
No more the farmer's news, the barber's tale,
No more the woodman's ballad shall prevail;
No more the smith his dusky brow shall clear,   245
Relax his ponderous strength, and lean to hear;
The host himself no longer shall be found
Careful to see the mantling bliss° go round;
Nor the coy maid, half willing to be pressed,
Shall kiss the cup to pass it to the rest.   250

   Yes! let the rich deride, the proud disdain,
These simple blessings of the lowly train;
To me more dear, congenial to my heart,
One native charm, than all the gloss of art.
Spontaneous joys, where nature has its play,   255
The soul adopts, and owns their first-born sway;
Lightly they frolic o'er the vacant mind,
Unenvied, unmolested, unconfined.
But the long pomp, the midnight masquerade,
With all the freaks° of wanton wealth arrayed —   260
In these, ere trifles half their wish obtain,
The toiling pleasure sickens into pain;
And, even while fashion's brightest arts decoy,
The heart distrusting asks if this be joy.

---

221. *nut-brown draughts:* drinks of ale. 232. *twelve good rules:* brief rules such as "Reveal no secrets" and "Pick no quarrels" which were attributed to Charles I and often hung up in inns; *goose:* a game played with checkers and dice, somewhat like parchesi. 234. *fennel:* a garden herb. 248. *mantling bliss:* foaming ale. Compare with the use of *mantling* in line 132. 260. *freaks:* whims.

Elegy on the Death
of a Mad Dog

As a contrast to the melancholy note struck by the merry Oliver Goldsmith in *The Deserted Village,* here is a neat absurdity showing the poet in a lighter vein. You will find this quite different from other elegies you have read.

Good people all, of every sort,
  Give ear unto my song;
And if you find it wondrous short,
  It cannot hold you long.

In Islington there was a man   5
  Of whom the world might say
That still a godly race° he ran,
  Whene'er he went to pray.

A kind and gentle heart he had,
  To comfort friend and foes;   10
The naked every day he clad,
  When he put on his clothes.

And in that town a dog was found,
  As many dogs there be,
Both mongrel, puppy, whelp, and
    hound   15
  And cur of low degree.

This dog and man at first were friends;
  But when a pique began,
The dog to gain his private ends,
  Went mad and bit the man.   20

Around from all the neighboring streets
  The wondering people ran,

7. *godly race:* Compare with line 143 of *The Deserted Village.*

And swore the dog had lost his wits,
  To bite so good a man.

The wound it seemed both sore and sad
  To every Christian eye;   26
And while they swore the dog was mad,
  They swore the man would die.

But soon a wonder came to light,
  That showed the rogues they lied;   30
The man recovered of the bite;
  The dog it was that died.

INFERRING CHARACTER
AND SETTING

1. How does Goldsmith idealize plain country folk? How realistic is his picture, do you think? What passages express an attitude toward people of humble position different from that of the early eighteenth century? Point out specific passages which show that Goldsmith also had characteristics of the classical school of Pope.

2. How do subject matter and sentiment in the poem point to the Romantic movement?

3. Which scenes and persons in *The Deserted Village* stand out in your mind most vividly? Compare the pictures of the parson and schoolmaster with those of some of Chaucer's characters. Which author's descriptions seem more realistic? Which do you prefer?

4. What kind of sentiment do you usually find expressed in an elegy? How does Goldsmith's "Elegy on the Death of a Mad Dog" differ from those with which you are familiar?

CLASS ACTIVITIES

1. Read the complete version of *The Deserted Village* and sum up — in a panel discussion — Goldsmith's opinions on Irish farm conditions, on the value of farmers to a nation and to city life, on Irish immigration, and on living conditions in America. Evaluate his opinions in the light of subsequent history.

2. Goldsmith's lively play *She Stoops to Conquer* contains some good scenes for class dramatization.

3. Compare the vicar in *The Vicar of Wakefield* with the parson in *The Deserted Village.* Which seems more credible to you?

Forerunners of the Romantic Age

National Portrait Gallery

THOMAS GRAY

1716-1771

In his day Thomas Gray was recognized as the foremost English poet; he was offered (but declined to accept) the position of poet laureate. Today he is remembered chiefly as the author of one of the best-known poems in the English language, "Elegy Written in a Country Churchyard."

By keeping a shop, Gray's mother earned enough money to send her son to fashionable Eton and later to Cambridge, where he steeped himself in classical literature. With his former schoolmate Horace Walpole, Gray spent three years on a tour of the Continent. It was an adventurous experience, and both he and Walpole left a vivid record of it in letters. Thereafter, Gray, who never married, lived the quiet life of a Cambridge professor. He was an enthusiastic student of Anglo-Saxon and Welsh folklore, and in this respect foreshadowed the great interest that the nineteenth-century Romantic poets took in old

English and Scottish ballads. Gray's poems are few in number but were painstakingly composed and polished. His "Elegy Written in a Country Churchyard" was nine years in the writing.

Gray represents the transition from classical to romantic literature in England — from the strictly patterned verse and sophisticated ideas of Pope and Johnson to the simpler, freer verse forms and the depiction of nature and common life found in later Romantic poets like Wordsworth. His verse form is only slightly varied from Pope's, but his poetry reveals a romantic spirit in its personal tone and in its emotional expressions on nature and death. Dr. Johnson thought Gray a dull poet, but General Wolfe, who won Quebec from the French in 1763, said of the "Elegy Written in a Country Churchyard" before entering the great battle: "I would rather be the author of those lines than take Quebec."

Elegy Written in a Country Churchyard

The curfew tolls the knell of parting day,
    The lowing herd wind slowly o'er the lea,
The plowman homeward plods his weary way,
    And leaves the world to darkness and to me.

Now fades the glimmering landscape on the sight,
    And all the air a solemn stillness holds,

5

Save where the beetle wheels his droning flight,
    And drowsy tinklings lull the distant folds;

Save that from yonder ivy-mantled tower
    The moping owl does to the moon complain   10
Of such, as wandering near her secret bower,
    Molest her ancient solitary reign.

Beneath those rugged elms, that yew tree's shade,
    Where heaves the turf in many a moldering heap,
Each in his narrow cell forever laid,   15
    The rude forefathers of the hamlet sleep.

The breezy call of incense-breathing morn,
    The swallow twittering from the straw-built shed,
The cock's shrill clarion, or the echoing horn,°
    No more shall rouse them from their lowly bed.   20

For them no more the blazing hearth shall burn,
    Or busy housewife ply her evening care:
No children run to lisp their sire's return,
    Or climb his knee the envied kiss to share.

Oft did the harvest to their sickle yield,   25
    Their furrow oft the stubborn glebe° has broke;
How jocund did they drive their team afield!
    How bowed the woods beneath their sturdy stroke!

Let not ambition mock their useful toil,
    Their homely joys, and destiny obscure;   30
Nor grandeur hear with a disdainful smile,
    The short and simple annals of the poor.

The boast of heraldry,° the pomp of power,
    And all that beauty, all that wealth e'er gave,
Awaits alike the inevitable hour.   35
    The paths of glory lead but to the grave.

Nor you, ye proud, impute to these the fault,
    If memory o'er their tomb no trophies raise,
Where through the long-drawn aisle and fretted vault°
    The pealing anthem swells the note of praise.   40

19. *horn:* the horn of a hunter. 26. *glebe:* ground. 33. *The boast of heraldry:* Heraldry is the study
of family coats of arms; hence, this phrase refers to the pride of having a great family. 39. *fretted
vault:* church roof ornamented by elaborate design.

The photograph opposite was taken in the churchyard at Stoke Poges, a small village ▶
in Buckinghamshire. Here, in 1742, after the death of a dear friend, Thomas Gray is
supposed to have written his famous "Elegy." Members of Gray's family lived in Stoke
Poges, and Gray and his mother were buried here.

Can storied urn° or animated° bust
    Back to its mansion call the fleeting breath?
Can honor's voice provoke° the silent dust,
    Or flatt'ry soothe the dull cold ear of Death?

Perhaps in this neglected spot is laid   45
    Some heart once pregnant with celestial fire;
Hands, that the rod of empire might have swayed,
    Or waked to ecstasy the living lyre.

But knowledge to their eyes her ample page
    Rich with the spoils of time did ne'er unroll;   50
Chill penury repressed their noble rage,
    And froze the genial° current of the soul.

Full many a gem of purest ray serene,
    The dark unfathomed caves of ocean bear;
Full many a flower is born to blush unseen,   55
    And waste its sweetness on the desert air.

Some village Hampden° that with dauntless breast
    The little tyrant of his fields withstood,
Some mute inglorious Milton here may rest,
    Some Cromwell guiltless of his country's blood.   60

The applause of listening senates to command,
    The threats of pain and ruin to despise,
To scatter plenty o'er a smiling land,
    And read their history in a nation's eyes,°

Their lot forbade: nor circumscribed alone   65
    Their growing virtues, but their crimes confined;
Forbade to wade through slaughter to a throne,
    And shut the gates of mercy on mankind,

The struggling pangs of conscious truth to hide,
    To quench the blushes of ingenuous shame,   70
Or heap the shrine of luxury and pride
    With incense kindled at the Muse's flame.

Far from the madding° crowd's ignoble strife,
    Their sober wishes never learned to stray;
Along the cool sequestered vale of life   75
    They kept the noiseless tenor° of their way.

---

41. *storied urn:* an urn inscribed with pictures that tell the story of the deceased; *animated:* lifelike. 43. *provoke:* arouse. 52. *genial:* warm or living. 57. *Hampden:* a landowner who resisted one of the tax assessments of Charles I and thus made the matter of unjust taxes a public issue. 61–64. This whole stanza is the object of *forbade* in the first line of the next stanza. 73. *madding:* wild, furious. 76. *tenor* (tĕn′ēr): even course.

Yet ev'n these bones from insult to protect,
   Some frail memorial still erected nigh,
With uncouth rhymes and shapeless sculpture decked,
   Implores the passing tribute of a sigh.   80

Their name, their years, spelt by the unlettered Muse,
   The place of fame and elegy supply;
And many a holy text around she strews,
   That teach the rustic moralist to die.

For who to dumb forgetfulness a prey,   85
   This pleasing anxious being e'er resigned,
Left the warm precincts of the cheerful day,
   Nor cast one longing lingering look behind?

On some fond breast the parting soul relies,
   Some pious drops the closing eye requires;   90
Ev'n from the tomb the voice of nature cries,
   Ev'n in our ashes live their wonted fires.

For thee,° who mindful of the unhonored dead
   Dost in these lines their artless tale relate;
If chance, by lonely contemplation led,   95
   Some kindred spirit shall inquire thy fate,

Haply some hoary-headed swain may say,
   "Oft have we seen him at the peep of dawn
Brushing with hasty steps the dews away,
   To meet the sun upon the upland lawn.   100

"There at the foot of yonder nodding beech
   That wreathes its old fantastic roots so high,
His listless length at noontide would he stretch,
   And pore upon the brook that babbles by.

"Hard by yon wood, now smiling as in scorn,   105
   Muttering his wayward fancies he would rove,
Now drooping, woeful wan, like one forlorn,
   Or crazed with care, or crossed in hopeless love.

"One morn I missed him on the customed hill,
   Along the heath and near his favorite tree,   110
Another came; nor yet beside the rill,
   Nor up the lawn, nor at the wood was he;

"The next, with dirges due in sad array
   Slow through the church-way path we saw him borne.
Approach and read (for thou canst read)° the lay,   115
   Graved on the stone beneath yon aged thorn."°

   93. *thee:* Gray himself. 115. *thou canst read:* In the eighteenth century, a large proportion of the country people were unable to read. 116. *thorn:* hawthorn.

THE EPITAPH

Here rests his head upon the lap of earth
A youth to fortune and to fame unknown.
Fair science frowned not on his humble birth,°
And melancholy marked him for her own.   120

Large was his bounty, and his soul sincere,
Heaven did a recompense as largely send;
He gave to misery all he had, a tear;
He gained from Heaven ('twas all he wished) a friend.

No farther seek his merits to disclose,   125
Or draw his frailties from their dread abode,
(There they alike in trembling hope repose)
The bosom of his Father and his God.

119. His humble birth had not prevented his having a good education.

GRAY'S "ELEGY"

1. The "Elegy" falls into clear-cut divisions of thought. What stanzas would you include in each of these three beginning divisions: (*a*) the setting, (*b*) the imagined life of the villagers, (*c*) death, the common end of all classes, rich and poor? The remainder of the poem can be divided into four sections. How would you divide the stanzas and what descriptions would you give to each division?

2. With what details does Gray represent happiness in the life of the country folk?

3. Line 47 suggests a possible statesman or ruler. What other hidden potentialities in the lives of the common people does Gray suggest? Why were these potentialities not fulfilled?

4. What picture of himself does Gray paint from line 98 on? Does it correspond with what you know of Gray's life?

5. How does Gray's verse form — rhyme scheme and stanza division — differ from that of Pope? What elements of the new, romantic trend in literature do you find in this poem?

RECOGNIZING MOOD

Words which suggest pictures usually set the mood of a piece of writing. If you were a painter, how many pictures could you paint by using the first seven stanzas of Gray's elegy as your subject matter?

The first three stanzas of this poem are introductory. What mood is set in these lines? What do you see? Analyze how Gray puts the reader in a particular mood by the use of carefully chosen details. What effect does he create with the words *tolls, plods, fades,* and *lull.* Find a few short phrases which also suggest mood. Now choose three adjectives of your own to describe the kind of mood set by the first three stanzas.

Recall how Milton achieves mood in "L'Allegro" and "Il Penseroso." Which poem by Milton is similar in mood to Gray's? Compare.

THE POWER OF WORDS

WORDS EASILY CONFUSED

In line 70 Gray uses the word *ingenuous* (ĭn·jĕn'u·ŭs), which is easily confused with *ingenious* (ĭn·jēn'yŭs). An ingenuous person may be one of high character, noble and honest. The word is also used to suggest candor, frankness, and naïveté. Which quality does Gray probably have in mind when he says that the villagers' humble lot kept them from quenching "the blushes of ingenuous shame"? How would you rephrase this line?

How does *ingenuous* differ from *ingenious*? List several fictitious or actual characters you have encountered in this book that you would consider ingenuous and several that were ingenious.

ROBERT
BURNS
1759–1796

British Information

Burns might be called the national poet of Scotland. Among the many writers that that country has produced, no name sets afire the loyalty and pride of Scots as "Bobbie Burns" does. Their own idiom of speech is made musical in his lyrics. The hard lives and poverty of some of their people is glorified through the laurels won by a peasant boy. Their essentially independent spirit is proclaimed to the world in the ringing lines of "A man's a man for a' that."

Burns was born in a two-room clay cottage built by his father near Ayr in southwestern Scotland. Poverty pursued the family from one stony farm to another. The father gave his sons the best education available to peasants, but it was meager. Robert supplemented his schooling by ardently reading the Bible, *The Spectator,* Pope's poems, and a book of lyrics that first inspired him to write songs. His mother taught him old Scottish songs and stories, and he spent spare hours reading Scottish and English literature.

As the plowboy developed into a lively, handsome young man, he was often in scrapes resulting from too much drinking, satires on ministers, and numerous romances. Finally, the father of his sweetheart, Jean Armour, made life so miserable for him that he decided to sail for Jamaica.

To raise money for his passage he published his first volume, *Poems: Chiefly in Scottish Dialect,* in 1786. It won immediate success. Instead of going to Jamaica, Burns went to Edinburgh in triumph. Edinburgh society lionized him, but after a time turned away from the young poet because he remained an earthy peasant — friendly, genial, but not given to polite ways. Back he went to the farm, married Jean Armour, and wrote some of his finest poetry. He served as tax collector to add to his meager income, a job he nearly lost because of his sympathy for the French Revolution. His health, never strong because of his poor childhood, weakened. He increasingly took to drink; and poverty, as always, plagued him and his family. Burns died at the early age of thirty-seven.

No sooner had he breathed his last than the whole country united to honor him. Ten thousand persons are said to have followed him to his grave at Dumfries. Contributions poured in for his destitute family. Two handsome marble monuments were eventually erected, one at Dumfries and the other at Ayr, not far from the banks of the bonnie Doon. But cold marble is a poor memorial for warmhearted, impulsive, generous Robert Burns. His real monument is his poetry, which keeps ever alive his best self.

Songs

Scotland gave to English literature a great song writer in Robert Burns. No one else has combined quite the same lilting melody and warm human emotion. In the following songs he sings of exuberance, sorrow, faithful affection, patriotism, and sturdy independence. Some are sung in his own person; some are dramatically put into the mouths of imaginary or historical characters; in others, the poet makes shrewd observations on his fellow humans. Many of them were set to old Scotch airs already in existence; some have since been set to music.

Sweet Afton

Flow gently, sweet Afton! among thy green braes,°
Flow gently, I'll sing thee a song in thy praise;
My Mary's asleep by thy murmuring stream,
Flow gently, sweet Afton, disturb not her dream.

Thou stock dove whose echo resounds through the glen,   5
Ye wild whistling blackbirds in yon thorny den,
Thou green-crested lapwing, thy screaming forbear,
I charge you, disturb not my slumbering Fair.

How lofty, sweet Afton, thy neighboring hills,
Far marked with the courses of clear, winding rills;   10
There daily I wander as noon rises high,
My flocks and my Mary's sweet cot in my eye.

How pleasant thy banks and green valleys below,
Where, wild in the woodlands, the primroses blow;
There oft, as mild ev'ning weeps over the lea,   15
The sweet-scented birk° shades my Mary and me.

Thy crystal stream, Afton, how lovely it glides,
And winds by the cot where my Mary resides;
How wanton thy waters her snowy feet lave,
As, gathering sweet flowerets, she stems thy clear wave.   20

Flow gently, sweet Afton, among thy green braes,
Flow gently, sweet river, the theme of my lays;
My Mary's asleep by thy murmuring stream,
Flow gently, sweet Afton, disturb not her dream.

1. *braes* (brāz): hillsides. 16. *birk:* birch.

The Banks o' Doon

Ye flowery banks o' bonnie Doon,
  How can ye blume sae fair!
How can ye chant, ye little birds,
  And I sae fu' o' care!

Thou'lt break my heart, thou bonnie
    bird,   5
  That sings upon the bough;
Thou minds me o' the happy days,
  When my fause° luve was true.

Thou'lt break my heart, thou bonnie
    bird,
  That sings beside thy mate;   10
For sae I sat, and sae I sang,
  And wist na° o' my fate.

Aft hae I roved by bonnie Doon
  To see the woodbine twine,
And ilka° bird sang o' its luve,   15
  And sae did I o' mine.

Wi' lightsome heart I pu'd° a rose,
  Frae aff its thorny tree;
And my fause luver staw° my rose
  But left the thorn wi' me.   20

8. *fause:* false. 12. *wist na:* knew not. 15. *ilka:*
every. 17. *pu'd:* pulled. 19. *staw:* stole.

John Anderson My Jo

John Anderson my jo,° John,
  When we were first acquent,°
Your locks were like the raven,
  Your bonnie brow was brent;°
But now your brow is beld,° John,   5
  Your locks are like the snaw;
But blessings on your frosty pow,°
  John Anderson my jo.

John Anderson my jo, John,
  We clamb the hill thegither;   10
And mony a canty° day, John,
  We've had wi' ane anither.
Now we maun° totter down, John,
  And hand in hand we'll go,
And sleep thegither at the foot,   15
  John Anderson my jo.

1. *jo:* joy, sweetheart. 2. *acquent:* acquainted.
4. *brent:* smooth. 5. *beld:* bald. 7. *pow:* head.
11. *canty:* cheerful. 13. *maun:* must.

Bannockburn

Robert the Bruce carried on the work begun by Wallace of freeing Scotland from
English domination in the days of Edward I. The battle of Bannockburn (băn'-
ŭk·bûrn), fought in 1314 in central Scotland, was a critical engagement. The English far outnumbered the Scots; but Bruce,
by digging pits in the plain and covering
them with leaves, caused the English cavalry to be overcome by panic, and thus won
the day. The occasion is looked on by
Scots as one of the great milestones in their
history. This poem is supposed to be Bruce's
address to his army before the battle.
Through the Scottish leader, Burns voices
a characteristic desire for freedom. It is
said that he composed the poem while galloping over a moor in a thunderstorm.

Scots, wha hae° wi' Wallace bled,
Scots, wham Bruce has aften led;
Welcome to your gory bed,
    Or to victory!

Now's the day, and now's the hour;   5
See the front o' battle lour;°
See approach proud Edward's power —
    Chains and slavery!

Wha will be a traitor knave?
Wha can fill a coward's grave?   10
Wha sae base as be a slave?
    Let him turn and flee!

Wha for Scotland's king and law
Freedom's sword will strongly draw,
Freeman stand, or Freeman fa',   15
    Let him follow me!

By oppression's woes and pains!
By your sons in servile chains!
We will drain our dearest veins,
    But they shall be free!   20

Lay the proud usurpers low!
Tyrants fall in every foe!
Liberty's in every blow! —
    Let us do or die!°

1. *wha hae:* who have. 6. *lour:* lower, threaten.
24. *die:* Scottish pronunciation is dē.

A Man's a Man for A' That

Here speaks a prophetic voice for the coming acceptance of the brotherhood of man. As the first clear note of democracy, this poem is one of the most significant written in the eighteenth century.

Is there, for honest poverty,
   That hings his head, an' a' that?
The coward slave, we pass him by,
   We dare be poor for a' that!
     For a' that, an' a' that,   5
      Our toils obscure, an' a' that;
     The rank is but the guinea's stamp;°
     The man's the gowd° for a' that.

What tho' on hamely fare we dine,
   Wear hodden-gray,° an' a' that;   10
Gie fools their silks, and knaves their wine,
   A man's a man for a' that.
     For a' that, an' a' that,
      Their tinsel show, an' a' that;
     The honest man, though e'er sae poor,   15
     Is king o' men for a' that.

Ye see yon birkie,° ca'd a lord,
   Wha struts, an' stares, an' a' that;
Tho' hundreds worship at his word,
   He's but a coof° for a' that.   20
     For a' that, an' a' that,
      His riband, star,° an' a' that,
     The man o' independent mind,
      He looks and laughs at a' that.

A prince can mak' a belted knight,   25
   A marquis, duke, an' a' that;
But an honest man's aboon° his might,
   Guid faith he mauna fa' that!°
     For a' that, an' a' that,
      Their dignities, an' a' that,   30
     The pith o' sense, an' pride o' worth,
     Are higher rank than a' that.

7. *guinea's stamp:* mold for stamping out gold coins. 8. *gowd:* gold. 10. *hodden-gray:* coarse cloth. 17. *birkie:* fellow. 20. *coof:* fool. 22. *riband, star:* insignia of titles and honors. 27. *aboon:* above. 28. *he . . . that:* he can't make that.

Then let us pray that come it may,
   As come it will for a' that,
That sense and worth, o'er a' the earth,
   May bear the gree,° an' a' that.   36
     For a' that, an' a' that,
      It's coming yet, for a' that,
     That man to man, the warld o'er,
      Shall brothers be for a' that.   40

36. *bear the gree:* take the prize.

To a Mouse

ON TURNING HER UP IN HER NEST
WITH THE PLOW, NOVEMBER, 1785

This and the following poem form an interesting pair in several respects: they have unusual meter, unconventional subjects, and frequently quoted lines. Their moods are in strong contrast: on the one hand, the despair of thwarted ambition is expressed; on the other, the rollicking humor of an irrepressible wag.

Wee, sleekit,° cowrin', tim'rous beastie,
O, what a panic's in thy breastie!
Thou need na start awa sae hasty
   Wi' bickering brattle!°
I wad be laith° to rin an' chase thee   5
   Wi' murd'rin pattle!°

I'm truly sorry man's dominion
Has broken nature's social union,
And justifies that ill opinion
   Which makes thee startle   10
At me, thy poor, earthborn companion,
   An' fellow mortal!

I doubt na, whyles,° but thou may thieve;
What then? poor beastie, thou maun live!
A daimen icker in a thrave°   15
   'S a sma' request;
I'll get a blessin' wi' the lave,°
   An' never miss 't!

1. *sleekit:* sleek. 4. *bickering brattle:* hasty scamper. 5. *laith* (lāth): loath, reluctant. 6. *pattle:* plowstaff. 13. *whyles:* at times. 15. *A daimen . . . thrave:* an occasional head of grain in a shock. 17. *lave:* rest.

Thy wee bit housie, too, in ruin!
It's silly wa's° the win's are strewin'!   20
An' naething, now, to big a new ane,°
    O' foggage° green!
An' bleak December's winds ensuin',
    Baith snell° an' keen!

Thou saw the fields laid bare and waste,
An' weary winter comin' fast,   26
An' cozie here, beneath the blast,
    Thou thought to dwell,
Till crash! the cruel coulter° passed
    Out through thy cell.   30

That wee bit heap o' leaves an' stibble
Has cost thee mony a weary nibble!
Now thou's turn'd out, for a' thy trouble,
    But house or hald,°
To thole° the winter's sleety dribble   35
    An' cranreuch° cauld!

But, Mousie, thou art no thy lane°
In proving foresight may be vain;
The best laid schemes o' mice an' men
    Gang aft agley,°   40
An' lea'e us nought but grief an' pain,
    For promis'd joy.

Still thou art blest, compared wi' me,
The present only toucheth thee;
But och! I backward cast my e'e   45
    On prospects drear!
An' forward, though I canna see,
    I guess an' fear!

20. *silly wa's:* weak walls. 21. *big . . . ane:*
build a new one. 22. *foggage:* herbage. 24. *snell:*
sharp. 29. *coulter* (kōl'tĕr): plow. 34. *But house
or hald:* without a dwelling place. 35. *thole:*
endure. 36. *cranreuch* (krȧn'rŭk): hoarfrost.
37. *no thy lane:* not alone. 40. *Gang aft agley*
(ȧ·glē'): oft go astray.

To a Louse

ON SEEING ONE
ON A LADY'S BONNET AT CHURCH

Ha! wh' are ye gaun, ye crowlin' ferlie!°
Your impudence protects you sairly;°
I canna say but ye strunt° rarely,
    Owre gauze and lace;
Though faith! I fear ye dine but sparely
    On sic a place.   6

Ye ugly, creepin', blastit wonner,°
Detested, shunned by saunt an' sinner!
How dare ye set your fit° upon her,
    Sae fine a lady?   10
Gae somewhere else, and seek your din-
    ner
    On some poor body.

Swith, in some beggar's haffet squattle;°
There ye may creep, and sprawl, and
    sprattle°
Wi' ither kindred jumping cattle,   15
    In shoals and nations;
Where horn nor bane° ne'er dare un-
    settle
    Your thick plantations.

Now haud ye there,° ye're out o' sight,
Below the fatt'rels,° snug an' tight;   20
Na, faith ye yet! ye'll no be right
    Till ye've got on it,
The very tapmost tow'ring height
    O' Miss's bonnet.

My sooth! right bauld ye set your nose
    out,   25
As plump and gray as onie grozet;°
O for some rank mercurial rozet,°
    Or fell red smeddum!°

1. *crowlin' ferlie* (fĕr'lĭ): crawling wonder.
2. *sairly:* greatly. 3. *strunt:* strut. 7. *blastit
wonner:* blasted wonder. 9. *fit:* foot. 13. *Swith
. . . squattle:* Be off with you! Sprawl in some
beggar's temple. 14. *sprattle:* struggle. 17. *horn
nor bane:* comb nor poison. 19. *haud ye there:*
stay where you are. 20. *fatt'rels:* ribbon ends.
26. *onie grozet* (grŏz'ĭt): any gooseberry. 27. *rozet:* rosin. 28. *smeddum:* powder.

I'd gie you sic a hearty dose o't,
    Wad dress your droddum!°   30

I wad na been surprised to spy
You on an auld wife's flannen toy;°
Or aiblins some bit duddie boy,°
    On's wyliecoat;°
But Miss's fine Lunardi!° fie,   35
    How daur ye do 't?

30. *Wad . . . droddum:* would put an end to
you. 32. *flannen toy:* flannel headdress. 33. *Or
. . . boy:* or perhaps on some little ragged boy.
34. *wyliecoat* (wī'lǐ'kōt'): flannel vest. 35. *Lunardi:* a bonnet named for an aeronaut of that
day, probably with winglike ribbons.

O Jenny, dinna toss your head,
An' set your beauties a' abroad!°
Ye little ken what cursèd speed
    The blastie's makin'!   40
Thae winks and finger ends, I dread,
    Are notice takin'!

O wad some Pow'r the giftie gie us
To see oursels as ithers see us!
It wad frae mony a blunder free us,   45
    And foolish notion:
What airs in dress an' gait wad lea'e us,
    And e'en devotion!

38. *abread:* abroad.

The Cotter's Saturday Night

This well-known poem, which takes us back in spirit to
"Elegy Written in a Country Churchyard" and *The Deserted Village*, was published in Burns' first volume. An interesting comment comes from Robert's brother Gilbert:
"Robert had frequently remarked to me that he thought
there was something peculiarly venerable in the phrase,
'Let us worship God,' used by a decent, sober head of a
family, introducing family worship. To this sentiment of
the author the world is indebted for 'The Cotter's Saturday
Night.' The cotter is an exact copy of my father, in his
manners, his family devotion, and exhortations. . . ."

INSCRIBED TO ROBERT AIKEN, ESQ.°

Let not ambition mock their useful toil,
    Their homely joys, and destiny obscure;
Nor grandeur hear, with a disdainful smile,
    The short and simple annals of the poor.
                    Gray.

My loved, my honored, much respected friend!
No mercenary bard this homage pays;°
With honest pride, I scorn each selfish end,
My dearest meed, a friend's esteem and praise;
To you I sing, in simple Scottish lays,   5
The lowly train in life's sequestered scene,
The native feelings strong, the guileless ways,
What Aiken in a cottage would have been;
Ah! though his worth unknown, far happier there, I ween!

Inscription *Robert Aiken:* a warm friend of Burns in Ayr, who had helped to make his poems
known. 2. Burns says he is not dedicating his poem to Aiken for hope of reward. See note on Johnson's letter to Chesterfield (page 321) for explanation of the patronage system.

November chill blaws loud wi' angry sugh;° 10
The shortening winter day is near a close;
The miry beasts retreating frae the pleugh;°
The blackening trains o' craws to their repose:
The toilworn Cotter° frae his labor goes, —
This night his weekly moil° is at an end, — 15
Collects his spades, his mattocks, and his hoes,
Hoping the morn in ease and rest to spend,
And weary, o'er the moor, his course does hameward bend.

At length his lonely cot appears in view,
Beneath the shelter of an aged tree; 20
The expectant wee things, toddlin', stacher° through
To meet their dad, wi' flichterin' noise an' glee.
His wee bit ingle,° blinkin' bonnilie,°
His clean hearthstane, his thrifty wifie's smile,
The lisping infant prattling on his knee, 25
Does a' his weary kiaugh° and care beguile,
An' makes him quite forget his labor an' his toil.

Belyve,° the elder bairns° come drappin' in,
At service out, amang the farmers roun';
Some ca' the pleugh,° some herd, some tentie rin 30
A cannie errand° to a neibor town.
Their eldest hope, their Jenny, woman-grown,
In youthfu' bloom, love sparkling in her e'e,
Comes hame, perhaps to shew a braw° new gown,
Or deposit her sair-won penny fee, 35
To help her parents dear, if they in hardship be.

With joy unfeigned, brothers and sisters meet,
And each for other's weelfare kindly spiers.°
The social hours, swift-winged, unnoticed fleet;
Each tells the uncos° that he sees or hears. 40
The parents, partial, eye their hopeful years;
Anticipation forward points the view;
The mother, wi' her needle an' her shears,
Gars° auld claes look amaist as weel's the new;
The father mixes a' wi' admonition due. 45

Their master's an' their mistress's command
The yonkers a' are warnèd to obey;
An' mind their labors wi' an eydent° hand,
An' ne'er, though out o' sight, to jauk° or play;
"An' O! be sure to fear the Lord alway, 50

10. *sugh* (sōōк; the Scotch *gh* represents a blowing out of breath between an *h* and a *k*): sough;
moan. 12. *pleugh* (plūк): plow. 14. *Cotter:* cottager. 15. *moil:* labor. 21. *stacher* (stȧк'ēr): stagger.
23. *ingle:* fire, fireplace; *bonnilie:* prettily. 26. *kiaugh* (kyäh): trouble, anxiety. 28. *Belyve:* by
and by; *bairns:* children. 30. *ca' the pleugh:* drive the plow. 30–31. *tentie . . . errand:* heedfully run
a careful errand. 34. *braw:* handsome. 38. *spiers* (spērz): inquires. 40. *uncos:* strange things; news.
44. *Gars:* makes. This line means: makes old clothes look almost as good as new. 48. *eydent* (ī'dĕnt):
industrious. 49. *jauk* (jäk): waste time.

An' mind your duty, duly, morn an' night;
Lest in temptation's path ye gang astray,
Implore His counsel and assisting might;
They never sought in vain that sought the Lord aright!"

But hark! a rap comes gently to the door;   55
Jenny, wha kens the meaning o' the same,
Tells how a neibor lad cam o'er the moor,
To do some errands, and convoy her hame.
The wily mother sees the conscious flame
Sparkle in Jenny's e'e, and flush her cheek;   60
Wi' heart-struck, anxious care, inquires his name,
While Jenny hafflins° is afraid to speak;
Weel pleased the mother hears it's nae wild worthless rake.

Wi' kindly welcome Jenny brings him ben,°
A strappin' youth; he takes the mother's eye;   65
Blythe Jenny sees the visit's no ill taen;
The father cracks° of horses, pleughs, and kye,°
The youngster's artless heart o'erflows wi' joy,
But blate and laithfu',° scarce can weel behave;
The mother, wi' a woman's wiles, can spy   70
What makes the youth sae bashfu' and sae grave,
Weel pleased to think her bairn's respected like the lave.°

O happy love! where love like this is found!
O heartfelt raptures! bliss beyond compare!
I've pacèd much this weary, mortal round,   75
And sage experience bids me this declare —
"If Heaven a draft of heavenly pleasure spare,
One cordial in this melancholy vale,
'Tis when a youthful, loving, modest pair
In other's arm breathe out the tender tale,   80
Beneath the milk-white thorn that scents the evening gale."

Is there, in human form, that bears a heart,
A wretch! a villain! lost to love and truth!
That can, with studied, sly, ensnaring art,
Betray sweet Jenny's unsuspecting youth?   85
Curse on his perjured arts! dissembling smooth!
Are honor, virtue, conscience, all exiled?
Is there no pity, no relenting ruth,
Points to the parents fondling o'er their child;
Then paints the ruined maid, and their distraction wild?   90

But now the supper crowns their simple board,
The halesome parritch,° chief of Scotia's food;

62. *hafflins:* partly. 64. *ben:* into the parlor. The Scotch peasant's house had two rooms called *but an' ben,* kitchen and parlor. 67. *cracks:* talks. Compare our use in the slang "wisecracks"; *kye:* cows. 69. *blate and laithfu':* shy and bashful. 72. *lave:* rest. 92. *halesome parritch:* wholesome porridge, i.e., oatmeal.

The sowpe° their only hawkie° does afford,
That yont the hallam° snugly chows her cood.
The dame brings forth, in complimental mood,   95
To grace the lad, her weel-hained kebbuck fell;°
An' aft he's prest, an' aft he ca's it guid.
The frugal wifie, garrulous, will tell
How 'twas a towmond auld, sin' lint was i' the bell.°

The cheerfu' supper done, wi' serious face,   100
They round the ingle form a circle wide;
The sire turns o'er with patriarchal grace
The big ha' Bible,° ance his father's pride.
His bonnet reverently is laid aside,
His lyart haffets° wearing thin and bare;   105
Those strains that once did sweet in Zion glide,
He wales° a portion with judicious care;
And "Let us worship God!" he says with solemn air.

  · · · · · · · · · · · · · ·

From scenes like these old Scotia's grandeur springs,
That makes her loved at home, revered abroad: 110
Princes and lords are but the breath of kings,
"An honest man's the noblest work of God";°
And certes, in fair Virtue's heavenly road,
The cottage leaves the palace far behind.
What is a lordling's pomp? a cumbrous load,   115
Disguising oft the wretch of human kind,
Studied in arts of hell, in wickedness refined!

O Scotia! my dear, my native soil!
For whom my warmest wish to Heaven is sent,
Long may thy hardy sons of rustic toil   120
Be blest with health, and peace, and sweet content!
And oh! may Heaven their simple lives prevent
From luxury's contagion, weak and vile!
Then, howe'er crowns and coronets be rent,
A virtuous populace may rise the while,   125
And stand a wall of fire around their much-loved isle.

O Thou! who poured the patriotic tide
That streamed through Wallace's undaunted heart,
Who dared to nobly stem tyrannic pride,
Or nobly die, the second glorious part — °   130
(The patriot's God peculiarly thou art,
His friend, inspirer, guardian, and reward!)
O never, never Scotia's realm desert,
But still the patriot, and the patriot-bard,
In bright succession raise, her ornament and guard!   135

---

93. *sowpe:* sup of milk; *hawkie:* cow. 94. *yont the hallam:* beyond the partition, in the same house.
96. *weel-hained kebbuck fell:* well-kept sharp cheese. 99. *a . . . bell:* a year old since flax was in flower.
103. *ha' Bible:* hall or family Bible. 105. *lyart haffets* (lī′ĕrt hàf′ĕts): gray temples. 107. *wales:*
selects. 112. This line is quoted from Pope's *Essay on Man.* 130. *part:* alternative.

SCOTLAND'S SPOKESMAN

THE SONGS

1. Decide what is the prevalent emotion of each of these lyrics — love, sorrow, joy, patriotism? State the situation and the point of each. Practice reading these songs aloud to bring out their rhythmic quality.

THREE LONGER POEMS

1. How does "A Man's a Man for A' That" reveal the new democratic spirit that was emerging in the eighteenth century? What ideas and customs does Burns challenge? What is the significance of the poem in Burns' own life?

2. What points of similarity do you find in "To a Mouse" and "To a Louse"? what marked contrast in mood? What Scottish words provide a humorous touch in "To a Louse"? Show how the point made at the end of each poem is a natural outgrowth of the situation. What frequently quoted lines come at the close of each?

3. How do the subject matter and meter of these three poems show that Burns was far removed from the classical school of Pope? Compare Burns with Pope, Goldsmith, and Gray. What characteristics of the Romantic school does Burns display?

THE COTTER'S SATURDAY NIGHT

1. What similarity can you find between the opening description in the second and third stanzas and the opening of Gray's "Elegy"? What are some differences?

2. Describe the different members of the family. What were the Saturday night pleasures of the family? What lines show respect of members of the family for one another? Why was Saturday night probably the happiest time for this family? What characteristics attributed to Scotland as a nation are evident in the description of this home?

3. What are Burns' own comments on Scottish peasant life? How do his ideas compare with those of Goldsmith on the Irish peasants in *The Deserted Village*? What change do you note in Burns' language when he begins to philosophize?

National Portrait Gallery

WILLIAM
BLAKE
1757–1827

William Blake, an unusual figure in English literature, was the complete opposite of writers of the classical school. He was a religious mystic in an age of reason, a unique creator who ignored the strict poetic rules of the classicist to follow his own original style.

Born of a poor family, Blake received practically no formal education, though he struggled to attend a drawing school. At fourteen he was apprenticed to an engraver, and that trade became an important means of livelihood, for his pictures and poetry were not widely accepted dur-

Opening page of The Book of Urizen, *written and illustrated by William Blake.* ▶

PRELUDIUM

TO

THE

BOOK OF

URIZEN

Of the primeval Priests assum'd power,
When Eternals spurn'd back his religion:
And gave him a place in the north,
Obscure, shadowy, void, solitary.

Eternals I hear your call gladly,
Dictate swift winged words, & fear not
To unfold your dark visions of torment.

ing his lifetime. He employed his talent for sketching by producing some powerful drawings to illustrate not only his own poems but also Milton's *Paradise Lost,* Dante's *Divine Comedy,* and the Book of Job from the Bible. All his life Blake devoted himself to expressing his mystical faith and his visions of a heavenly world. He was encouraged by his handsome, uneducated wife, who learned to draw and paint so that she could help him in his work. On one occasion Mrs. Blake is reported to have said, "I have very little of Mr. Blake's company. He is always in Paradise."

Although readers in his own day were confused by the symbolism and hidden meanings in his prophetic books like *The Marriage of Heaven and Hell,* the delicate images and fancifulness of his earlier *Songs of Innocence* and *Songs of Experience* appealed to the later Romantic poets. Blake's intensity and beauty of language are more appreciated today than ever before, as are his exceptional qualities as artist and poet.

The Lamb

Little Lamb, who made thee?
　Dost thou know who made thee?
Gave thee life, and bid thee feed,
By the stream and o'er the mead;
Gave thee clothing of delight,　　5
Softest clothing, woolly, bright;
Gave thee such a tender voice,
Making all the vales rejoice?
　Little Lamb, who made thee?
　Dost thou know who made thee?　10

Little Lamb, I'll tell thee,
Little Lamb, I'll tell thee:
He is callèd by thy name,
For He calls Himself a Lamb,
He is meek, and He is mild;　　15
He became a little child.
I a child, and thou a lamb,
We are callèd by His name.
　Little Lamb, God bless thee!
　Little Lamb, God bless thee!　20

The Tiger

Tiger, tiger, burning bright
In the forest of the night,
What immortal hand or eye
Could frame thy fearful symmetry?

In what distant deeps or skies　　5
Burnt the fire of thine eyes?
On what wings dare he aspire?
What the hand dare seize the fire?

And what shoulder, and what art,
Could twist the sinews of thy heart?　10

When thy heart began to beat,
What dread hand forged thy dread feet?

What the hammer? What the chain?
In what furnace was thy brain?
What the anvil? What dread grasp　　15
Dared its deadly terrors clasp?

When the stars threw down their spears,
And watered heaven with their tears,
Did He smile his work to see?
Did He who made the lamb make thee?

Tiger, tiger, burning bright　　21
In the forest of the night,
What immortal hand or eye
Dare frame thy fearful symmetry?

The Clod
and the Pebble

"Love seeketh not itself to please,
　Nor for itself hath any care,
But for another gives its ease,
　And builds a Heaven in Hell's despair."

So sung a little Clod of Clay,　　5
　Trodden with the cattle's feet,
But a Pebble of the brook
　Warbled out these meters meet:

"Love seeketh only Self to please,
　To bind another to Its delight,　　10
Joys in another's loss of ease,
　And builds a Hell in Heaven's despite."

In this typical Blake engraving, God appears to Job out of a whirlwind.

UNDERSTANDING SYMBOLISM

The poetry of William Blake appeals not only to our imagination but to our minds and often conveys meaning by the use of symbols.

The use of symbols is a practice common to all of us. We often explain an idea, a quality, something invisible, by using a conventional sign or familiar relationship. For example, the lion has become for most of us the symbol of courage; the eagle, the sign of strength; the donkey, the mark of stupidity.

1. Blake's lamb and tiger can be thought of as real animals, but the emphasis should be on their function as symbols: the lamb as the symbol of the innocence of childhood, the tiger as the symbol of the fearful power that worldly experience brings. What lines in both poems picture the two as animals and as symbols?

2. State in your own words the central thought in "The Tiger." Blake wrote "The Tiger" after "The Lamb." Can you point out a relationship between the poems?

3. In "The Clod and the Pebble" two kinds of love are symbolized. Explain Blake's symbolism in this poem. How does the use of symbols help you to understand the three poems presented here?

4. In "The Clod and the Pebble" Blake suggests that love varies in its nature. Do you agree? In what human relationships might you find the two kinds of love?

LITERATURE AND THE ARTS

William Blake, a solitary figure in English painting as well as in English literature, is a classic example of a man who was outstanding as both artist and poet.

Possessed with an unusually vivid imagination, Blake began his long life as a visionary when only a child. His artistic talents were also evident at an early age. In 1789, after experimenting with a new method of printing from etched copperplates, Blake published a volume of original poetry illustrated with his own designs, the first of many similar volumes. The title page of *Urizen* (page 357), one of his books of mystical poems, exemplifies Blake's combining of his artistic and literary talents. Blake etched his poetry and decorations on a copperplate and then, usually with water paints, added the colors by hand.

Blake's output was incredibly large. But his imaginative genius, uncomprehended and unrecognized in an age which valued reason above all, went unacknowledged until half a century after his death. Since then he has been acclaimed as one of the truly great figures in English art and poetry.

THE GROWTH OF
THE ENGLISH LANGUAGE

The Eighteenth Century

In the early part of the eighteenth century there were two cross-currents at work in the stream of the English language. One was a continuation of the growth that had occurred during the Elizabethan Age and the Restoration. The other force sought to confine language within neat limitations. The noncritical members of the population, careless of technical niceties of grammar and spelling, were eager to bring in new and exhilarating words. But many literary men believed that the time had come to give the language shape and stability, even at the cost of expansion and liveliness.

We have seen what Dryden did at the end of the seventeenth century to trim the language into an admirable prose style. Of the same mind, but with more specific proposals for attaining the end, were Defoe, Swift, and Addison. They all bemoaned the indifference and often scorn of the court for *correctness* (a word that was not heard of before their time). Defoe ridiculed the misspelling that was characteristic of the nobility, citing the example of a lord who described the accidental drowning of a servant as "a mollinkolli accidence be happen'd in our house."

Swift wrote a scathing paper for *The Tatler* on the state of the language, which Addison followed up in his milder manner by occasional comments in *The Spectator*. But Swift's most famous dictum on language came in a letter addressed to the Lord Treasurer and containing a Proposal for Correcting, Improving, and Ascertaining [limiting] the English Tongue. Here he said that the language had reached its highest point

from Queen Elizabeth's day to the beginning of the Restoration, and that it had been degenerating ever since in the mouths of the fashionable figures of court and town and in the writing of stupid poets. He blamed the poets for the contraction of words to suit their meter, as in such forms as *drudg'd, disturb'd, fledg'd,* in which the *ed* was originally pronounced as a separate syllable. (Note that modern English keeps both the clipped pronunciation and the *e* instead of an apostrophe, to show the eye that *ed* is the past or participial ending.) Swift condemned the new idea that we ought to spell as we speak, on the ground that so many styles of pronunciation in different classes, different localities, and different times would make any printed standards impossible. He predicted that without some definite regulation of present tendencies, two hundred years hence (which would be 1912) the world would be unable to read the writings of the eighteenth century. To avoid this sad outcome Swift proposed that an Academy of suitable persons be appointed to "ascertain and fix" our language forever. Such an unrealistic proposal, had it been followed, would have created a literary "dictatorship" whose function would have been to prohibit all future life and growth in the language.

Swift's idea was approved by the Lord Treasurer and a sum of money was appropriated for it, but no Academy ever materialized. The nobility continued to misspell; the town and college wits continued to coin new words and abbreviate old ones; the criminal classes still slyly introduced their cant phrases into the best society.

The word *slang,* which then applied only to the special vocabularies of the underworld, has now come to be a general term for all words and phrases not yet admitted into formal usage. But today such words are not looked upon askance as often as they were by older purists, for we realize that if a new word fills a real need it will soon become a part of the language. To show the folly of totally condemning all new or strangely formed words, we need only look back to the eighteenth century when the following words were frowned upon in polite usage: *mob* (abbreviation of the Latin *mobile vulgus*), *enthusiasm, extra, fun, gambling, humbug, nervous, shabby, fop.* There were many others.

At the end of the seventeenth century came the first suggestion that English literature would be better than Latin declamations for study in schools. In the eighteenth century, the old grammar schools, teaching Greek and Latin only, were gradually superseded by charity schools and private schools where the study of English was introduced. This innovation raised the standard of English used by both the aristocratic and the humble classes.

As a parallel development, this period became a great age for the appearance of dictionaries. In the fifteenth and sixteenth centuries there had been two-language dictionaries, but it was not till the very end of the sixteenth century that we find one with explanations of words in the mother tongue. In the seventeenth century a new type of vernacular dictionary with two separate lists was introduced, one list containing choice words, the other vulgar words.

Of the rash of dictionaries which appeared in the eighteenth century, the greatest in attempt, in accomplishment, and in influence was the one written by Dr. Samuel Johnson. Johnson intended to make a complete list of words in English, give definitions, and show how the words had been used by citing quotations from literature. He did not try to indicate pronunciation except for accent. When in doubt about accepting a word as good English, he often decided on the basis of the word's ancestry. Thus *sherbet,* traceable through Arabic to Persian, was admitted; but *punch,* apparently without a family tree, was branded as a cant word.

Later the whole matter of acceptability of words was more successfully solved by Dr. George Campbell, a Scottish schoolmaster, who established three tests for standard English, which are still generally accepted: *national* (not only local), *reputable* (used by reputable people), and *present* (not fallen into disuse). Campbell, however, was scornful of words "betraying some frivolous humor in the formation of them," such as *bamboozle, topsy-turvy, helter-skelter,* and *hurly-burly.* He was somewhat lacking in a sense of humor.

Fewer borrowings from foreign languages appeared in the eighteenth century than in earlier periods, but there were some. The emphasis on classical architecture accounted for the addition of words from Greek: *porch* and *attic* (from the state Attica), for example. With the advent of George I to the throne, French became the court language. But French words came into use more via the New World than the court; *prairie, crevasse, shanty,* and *bayou* became familiar at this time.

It was during the eighteenth century that the real deviation between English and American usage and pronunciation began to be evident, especially after American independence reduced communication across the Atlantic. The influx into the middle Atlantic states of German and Scandinavian colonists brought into American English words and sounds that never became accepted in the old country. Then too, America was still a frontier land and new words had to be devised for phenomena not seen in England. So we have *landslide, snowplow, basswood, catbird, mudhen, bobolink, ground hog, rattlesnake.*

READING LIST FOR
THE EIGHTEENTH CENTURY

Balderston, John L., *Berkeley Square*
A three-act play about an American in eighteenth-century London.

* Boswell, James, *The Life of Samuel Johnson*
One of the best-known biographies in the English language.

Clifford, James L., *Young Sam Johnson*
A readable biography of Sam Johnson's early years in Lichfield to his life in London in 1749, after he had completed his *Dictionary*.

Falkner, John M., *Moonfleet*
A tale of smugglers in which orphaned John Trenchard follows the lure of a valuable diamond along a path of violence.

Frye, Pearl, *Game for Empires*
A superior biographical novel of Nelson, from his command of the *Agamemnon* to the French defeat in the Battle of the Nile.

Goldsmith, Oliver, *She Stoops to Conquer*
A comedy of love in disguise. A bashful young man mistakes a squire's home for an inn.

Nordhoff, Charles B., and Hall, James Norman, *Mutiny on the Bounty*
Rebellion aboard the *Bounty* from England to the South Seas in 1787, a famous trial, and what became of the mutineers. For a continuation of the story read *Men Against the Sea* and *Pitcairn's Island*.

Norman, Charles, *The Pundit and the Player*
The life stories of two outstanding personalities — David Garrick and Samuel Johnson — are interwoven.

Orczy, Baroness Emmuska, *The Scarlet Pimpernel*
A titled Englishman calling himself the "Scarlet Pimpernel" assists condemned or suspected Frenchmen to escape from France during the Reign of Terror.

Pearson, Hesketh, *Johnson and Boswell: The Story of Their Lives*
Pearson introduces two famous writers in this readable and informative biography.

Sabatini, Raphael, *Scaramouche*
A colorful and romantic story of intrigue in the early days of the French Revolution.

Scott, Sir Walter, *Guy Mannering*
Gypsy life and smuggling as it was practiced in the late eighteenth century.

——, *Waverly*
During the rebellion of 1745–46, exiled Prince Charles Edward and his followers, the Jacobites, try to gain the English throne.

Shellabarger, Samuel, *Lord Chesterfield and His World*
Portrait of an extraordinary figure of eighteenth-century England.

Sheridan, Richard B., *The Rivals* and *The School for Scandal*
Two famous satirical plays on eighteenth-century society, still popular on the stage.

Stevenson, Robert L., *Kidnapped*
The story of many exciting adventures which take place in the highlands of Scotland during the Jacobite rebellion.

Tarkington, Booth, *Monsieur Beaucaire*
At Bath, an English resort, a French nobleman masquerades as a barber and falls in love with an English girl.

Thackeray, William M., *Henry Esmond*
A story of a Cavalier and Jacobite. Addison, Steele, and others are introduced.

NOTE: See also "Notable English Novels," pages 370–71.

* This biography (abridged) is included in *Four English Biographies,* J. B. Priestley and O. B. Davis, eds. (Harcourt, Brace & World, Inc., 1961).

FOR LISTENING

Burns' "A Man's a Man for A' That" and "To a Mouse" have been recorded and are available on *Many Voices 6A*. Included on *Many Voices 12A* are a selection from Boswell's *Life of Samuel Johnson* and Blake's "The Lamb," "The Tiger," and "The Clod and the Pebble."

EIGHTEENTH–CENTURY FRONTISPIECE: Pictured on page 272 are (1) an engraving of the interior of an eighteenth-century coffeehouse; (2) modern copies of Regency striped wallpaper and a gilt frame mirror; (3) a wig dressed in the fashion of the day; (4) a silver candlestick; (5) an eighteenth-century wooden box for silverware; (6) a pewter inkstand with quill pen; (7) a bone snuffbox and an enamel snuffbox; (8) a British Army officer's red coat.

THE ENGLISH NOVEL

It is hard to decide exactly what a novel is. It is of course prose fiction, but not all pieces of prose fiction can be reasonably classed as novels. For example, Swift's *Gulliver's Travels* (1726), which is equally successful as a savage satire on humanity and as a story for children, is prose fiction, but nobody would call it a novel. Is *Robinson Crusoe* (1719), Defoe's masterpiece, a novel, or is it simply a tale of adventure? Where do we draw the line between adventure tales, fantasies, romances, science fiction, and novels? It is difficult to decide, but at least we can agree that in the novel proper we are concerned with men and women who are related to some sort of society in a fairly realistic fashion. A story about monsters living at the back of the moon would not be a novel. We can say, then, that a novel is a prose narrative that offers us imaginary characters and events set in some particular and recognizable society.

MAJOR PERIODS OF THE ENGLISH NOVEL

The novel was a comparatively late arrival in English literature; Italy, Spain, and France produced what we are entitled to call novels long before England did. The Elizabethans, for example, found it easy to tell a story in dramatic form for the stage, but could not manage prose fiction. But once English literature really got hold of the novel, in the eighteenth century, it became famous for its fiction and influenced writers in many different countries. From the middle of the eighteenth century onward, more and more English novels were written and read; but in this literary form, like others (the drama is a striking example), there was a mysterious ebb and flow of greatness. Excellent English novels have been published continually during the last two hundred years, but some are better than others. We might say that Eng-

lish fiction reached its highest level in three separate periods — roughly, 1740–1770, 1840–1890, and 1905–1930. It is during these years especially that we find English novelists of genius producing acknowledged masterpieces. Now let us take a look at them.

DEFOE: PIONEER IN FICTION

A word first, though, about Daniel Defoe, whose best-known book, *Robinson Crusoe,* appeared in 1719. Defoe was an important originator of realism in English fiction. He had to be realistic because while actually creating fiction, though usually with some basis of fact, he was pretending to offer his readers memoirs and autobiographies. Many authors have claimed to be important novelists when they have been mere journalists, but here in Defoe we have a journalist who was secretly a storyteller of quite remarkable talent. And just because his stories had to seem solidly real, he did some valuable pioneer work for English fiction. His best characters, after his famous shipwrecked sailor, are raffish types like Moll Flanders and Captain Singleton.

FOUR EIGHTEENTH-CENTURY NOVELISTS

The 1740–1770 group of English novelists consists of Samuel Richardson, Henry Fielding, Laurence Sterne, and Tobias Smollett. After Richardson, a smug little man and a retired printer, was commissioned to do a book of letters which readers could use as samples, he contrived a novel in the form of letters, all about a virtuous serving girl, Pamela, who repulsed her master until he consented to marry her. Though *Pamela* (1740) is often referred to as the first English novel, it was Richardson's second and much longer novel, *Clarissa Harlowe,* also written in letter form, that

British Information

Henry Fielding

became the rage not only in England but all over the continent. This narrative-in-letters method is entirely unreal, at least as Richardson used it (for his chief characters would be spending twelve hours a day writing letters). However, it has the great advantage, which Richardson made use of very artfully, of giving in turn everybody's points of view, thoughts, feelings, hopes, and fears. The hothouse sentimentality and piety of these novels are not to our taste today, but Richardson's reputation in his own time was tremendous, and he undoubtedly had a great deal of influence on the development of fiction.

Henry Fielding, a very different type of man, detested Richardson and all his works. It was like a dog looking at a cat. Fielding came from an old landed family, lived riotously, and then took to writing (plays at first) to earn a living, finally becoming a city magistrate — a very good one too. His masterpiece is *Tom Jones* (1749), which is both a magnificent panorama of eighteenth-century life and the expression, unusual in the novel, of a powerful masculine intellect, quick to observe all the ironies, absurdities, and hypocrisies of social life. Nineteenth-century critics considered him one

of the great masters of the novel, but during the last fifty years he has been somewhat neglected and undervalued.

Laurence Sterne's reputation has had a different history. He was enormously popular in his own time. Later his faults of taste and manner alienated many critics, but now he is warmly praised again. One reason for this is that his highly original method, ruthlessly cutting out everything that is not essential to our understanding of a character and a situation, is very "modern," like his extremely artful, intimate, and conversational style. His humor is "modern" too, but not his sentiment, which is too often forced and false. *Tristram Shandy* (1760), his masterpiece, is a wonderful study of a family in which nobody understands anybody else.

Tobias Smollett, a Scot who had been a surgeon's mate in the navy, wrote long novels crammed with rough humor and knockabout incidents. He had a very solid reputation for some fifty years after his death and had considerable influence upon Dickens in the latter's earlier years. But now Smollett is no longer regarded as one of the eighteenth-century masters. Nor is Goldsmith's one novel, *The Vicar of Wakefield* (1766), read as often as it used to be; for, though equally charming in its humor and sentiment, the story it tells is hardly convincing, too obviously contrived.

JANE AUSTEN AND WALTER SCOTT

Between the two peaks of 1740–1770 and 1840–1890 come two important novelists, Jane Austen (1775–1817) and Sir Walter Scott (1771–1832). Jane Austen, with her very acute and exquisitely feminine sense of character and scene, has probably never been equaled within her deliberately limited range. Her novels are classics of the art of fiction, and once enjoyed they are our friends for life. Scott is a curious case, for in his own time, when he had stupendous success and very wide influence, he was thought to be not so much a novelist as a historical romancer. In point of fact, however, he has many weaknesses as a historical romancer and a good deal of enduring strength and appeal as a novelist. His finest stories are those with an eighteenth-century background. These are far superior to *Ivanhoe* (1819) and the other medieval romances.

MASTERS OF NINETEENTH-CENTURY FICTION

The 1840–1890 group begins with Charles Dickens (1812–70), one of the acknowledged world masters of fiction. Dickens began to write in a slapdash, improvising way, mixing glorious fun with unreal melodrama; then he gradually planned his work more and more and, while keeping the inimitable humor, filled his writings with a searching criticism of mid-Victorian society. He was a strange, divided man, but for the art of fiction he had a blazing genius. William Makepeace Thackeray (1811–63) had no such genius, but he had great qualities of his own: a wide knowledge of social life, a wonderful eye and ear for charac-

Culver

William Makepeace Thackeray

ter and scene, and an easy narrative style that could rise to passages of great force and beauty. These qualities are perhaps found at their best in *Vanity Fair,* although many critics consider his historical novel, *Esmond,* his masterpiece. (Its sequel, *The Virginians,* takes us to America.) Anthony Trollope (1815–82), who was one of Thackeray's most enthusiastic admirers, is less distinguished in style and lacks Thackeray's flashes of insight, but his solid novels about mid-Victorian churchmen and politicians, after being almost forgotten, are now being widely read and appreciated in Britain.

The chief women in this group are Charlotte Brontë (1816–55), who brought an intense and strongly feminine realism into fiction; her sister, Emily (1818–48), whose *Wuthering Heights* (1847) is hardly a novel at all in the ordinary sense but rather an impassioned and symbolic prose poem; and Marian Evans (1819–80), who wrote under the name of George Eliot. The latter was a deeply serious woman with a good intellect as well as a sound knowledge of English provincial life; her very solid virtues are found at their best in *Middle-*

Jane Austen

British Information

march (1871), which thoroughly analyzes a certain type of society and which is one of the best examples in English of a highly organized novel.

George Meredith (1828–1909) and Thomas Hardy (1840–1928) both preferred their poetry to their fiction, although they wrote many long novels. They are both philosophical novelists, making their fiction express certain ideas about life. But whereas Meredith is a high-spirited if rather affected comic-romantic, Hardy is broodingly pessimistic, at his best when his characters are rustic types surrounded by the heaths and vales of the author's native Wessex. With them may be mentioned Robert Louis Stevenson (1850–94), who died too young — at forty-four — to fulfill completely all his promise, but who has retained his hold on successive generations of readers by the romantic zest of his narrative and a curious charm of style.

BROADENED HORIZONS

Before we reach the next high tableland of the English novel, 1905–1930, we must note that during the intervening period, from 1890 onward, English prose fiction suddenly began to travel to very distant places. Before this time, from Richardson to Hardy, every major novel, except for a few chapters here and there, had been concerned with the British scene itself. Now came a much wider sweep. Stevenson began it with his tales of the South Seas. Then Rudyard Kipling (1865–1936) arrived from India, W. H. Hudson (1841–1922) from South America, and Joseph Conrad (1852–1924) from world-wide travels. The last, a Pole by birth who became a captain in the British merchant marine, is the most important of these three as a novelist. Conrad is often thought to be simply a romantic storyteller just because he shows us so many sailors and ships in far-off places. However, he is really a novelist who happens to be indifferent to

the usual social themes but who is deeply concerned with character, with men's behavior in moments of great stress, and with the fundamental nature of man's life and destiny. These themes he often treats in a symbolical way, as poets are apt to do, so that in reading Conrad we must always try to be aware of depths of meaning below the surface of the narrative.

SOCIOLOGICAL NOVELISTS

The beginning of the 1905–1930 period shows us three very successful English writers who might be described as "sociological" novelists. By this we mean that their chief concern is with society itself — its organization, outlook, values, and tone. H. G. Wells (1866–1946), Arnold Bennett (1867–1931), and John Galsworthy (1867–1933), the three writers in question, are far from being alike either as men or as writers, but they have this sociological foundation in common in their fiction. Wells, the most brilliant, never thought of himself as a literary artist (though he was), and made no secret of the fact that he made use of the novel as a critic of society. But his genius in the creation of character and scene often triumphs over his sociology, as in *Mr. Polly* (1910) and *Tono-Bungay* (1909). Bennett's fiction is varied and uneven, but the best of it is a solidly realistic record of the society he knew as a boy in that provincial region known, because it was the center of the pottery industry, as "The Potteries." There is, however, in Bennett an easy, unforced charm as well as a solid realism, which he learned from French novelists during the years he lived in France. Bennett's masterpiece is *The Old Wives' Tale* (1908). John Galsworthy made his reputation in Britain before World War I, not only by his novels, which were sharply critical studies of the property-owning class to which he himself belonged, but also by his realistic and well-constructed plays. It was, however, with the publication of *The Forsyte Saga* (1906–21) that he achieved during the 1920's a world-wide body of admiring readers, who felt that his wide social range, his honest criticism of his own class, his deep compassion, his essential Englishness, made him the representative English novelist of his time. He was the first English writer of fiction after Kipling to be awarded the Nobel Prize.

Although Galsworthy achieved international fame after World War I, he, Wells, and Bennett really belong to the period that ended in 1914, at the outbreak of that war. And here it must be remembered that for Britain the war lasted over four years, killed nearly a million young men, and caused an unimaginable amount of suffering and grief. Because these years 1914–1918 represent a break in the history of the English novel, we shall pause here to take a wider view of the writing, publishing, and reading of fiction.

GROWING POPULARITY OF THE NOVEL

During most of the nineteenth century, novels of any importance were originally published in three volumes and at prices that only wealthier readers and libraries could afford to pay. (Dickens and Thackeray, however, brought out most of their novels first in what were called "parts," that is, in separate installments published every month. Dickens sent Martin Chuzzlewit, in the novel of that name, off to America just because the "parts" were not selling briskly and the story needed a new interest added to it.) But cheap one-volume editions began to be published, chiefly for the benefit of railroad travelers. Then in the 1890's enterprising publishers brought out one-volume editions of new novels, at a quarter of the price of the old three-volume editions. Libraries could now afford to buy more copies, ordinary readers became novel-buyers, and the trade in fiction increased enormously.

All manner of readers were now catered to by all manner of novelists specializing in humorous stories, or historical romances, or tales of crime and detection, like the famous Sherlock Holmes stories by Arthur Conan Doyle (1859–1930). Many of these popular novelists were excellent craftsmen [for example, the humorist, W. W. Jacobs (1863–1943)]. Your reading lists will include many of their works, which you are bound to enjoy. By 1914 the output of fiction in London was so large that really excellent writers like Maurice Hewlett (1861–1923), George Moore (1852–1933), and William de Morgan (1839–1917) cannot be considered in this chronicle. And in the years just before the war, a whole group of young novelists, including Compton Mackenzie (1883–   ), Frank Swinnerton (1884–   ), and Hugh Walpole (1884–1941), arrived on the scene. But the big names were still Wells, Bennett, Galsworthy — all of them, as we have seen, sociological novelists.

TWENTIETH-CENTURY NOVELISTS

Now what the war did was to remove the interest of the more literary critics of fiction from the sociological novel and to fix that interest on novels and novelists of a very different kind. Instead of looking outward toward society itself, these new novelists tended to look inward and describe what was happening in the minds of their characters. So Virginia Woolf (1882–1941), one of these new novelists and a very brilliant woman, could attack Bennett because he did not seem to her to bring any illusion of life into the novel. (But this was true only from her own point of view, and if a Bennett novel is weak in its inward life, a Virginia Woolf novel is weak in its outward life, in the relation of its characters to society.) Literary fashion in London, following a general European movement, now insisted that fiction, to be of any significance, should explore the depths and recesses of personality, revealing an unending stream of impressions, feelings, and thoughts, and showing us fewer people if necessary, but telling us everything about them.

A master of this method, which he finally carried to an extreme that lies outside the novel proper, was James Joyce (1882–1941), whose genius especially in *Ulysses* (1922) cannot be questioned, but whose stature and influence simply as a novelist have been wildly overestimated. Joyce is best regarded as a kind of humorous prose-poet with an astonishing passion for and knowledge of language — a master of words.

E. M. Forster (1879–   ) published most of his novels well before World War I, but his finest novel, *A Passage to India* (1924), did not arrive until the 'twenties, and he stands quite apart from the older sociological novelists. His work is easier to enjoy than to describe. He cares nothing for any broad picture of man and society. His own point of view shapes and colors all his novels, and he tries — as a rule very successfully — to give the reader certain supremely important, all-revealing moments in the lives of his characters. There is a kind of magic in Forster at his best, but he can also be oddly improbable and unconvincing.

Virginia Woolf, as we have seen, be-

E. M. Forster

Culver

lieved that the significant modern novel should reflect the inner life of its characters, and with this aim in mind, she made several difficult, subtle, and not always successful experiments. But in novels like *To the Lighthouse* (1927) and *Between the Acts* (1941), she succeeds triumphantly, creating fiction of deep human interest and strange beauty. Elsewhere, character and situation almost seem to vanish, and she is more like a prose poet than a real novelist.

There can be no doubt that D. H. Lawrence (1885–1930), especially in his earlier work, was a real novelist. He too looks inward, but not to show us a stream of impressions as Virginia Woolf does, but to explore those mysterious areas of feeling of which we are hardly conscious but which can strongly influence our lives. Lawrence was certainly a man of genius, and his writing reveals a marvelously sensitive feeling for nature and a gift for description.

Younger novelists who made their first appearance in the 'twenties are Aldous Huxley (1894–   ), who succeeds in fiction by sheer intelligence but who is really more a philosophical essayist than a novelist proper; Evelyn Waugh (1903–   ), who in his first two stories, *Decline and Fall* (1928) and *Vile Bodies* (1930), achieved something very rare — namely a new kind of humor that quickly became fashionable and much imitated; and Graham Greene (1904–   ), whose best work (which came later) is concerned with good and evil and is haunted by a feeling of guilt that many of his readers cannot help sharing. Among the women novelists first published during this decade were Elizabeth Bowen (1899–   ), Rosamund Lehmann (1903–   ), and Ivy Compton-Burnett (1892–   ).

THE CONTEMPORARY SCENE

We made 1930 the outside limit of this third important period in English fiction. This date, which might be pushed forward a few years without doing any harm, does not imply that after 1930 there was a sharp decline in the standard of new English fiction. Good novelists — as for example, Joyce Cary (1888–1957), Liam O'Flaherty (1896–), and C. P. Snow (1905–) — were bringing out excellent new work. But it is difficult not to feel that sometime not long after 1930 much of the earlier excitement about the English novel began to subside. Most of the experiments had already been made. Man's inner life had been explored and recorded up to a point beyond which fiction would become unreadable. Novels were being written and read, but the form itself seemed to lose its primary importance. Moreover, as the various dictators in Europe became ever more powerful and menacing, political events and books dealing with those events attracted more and more attention. Fiction has always been at its best during comparatively peaceful eras, and this period, which ended with World War II, was anything but peaceful.

English fiction has produced some good new names and good new work since the second World War. Angus Wilson (1913–), Kingsley Amis (1922–), Iris Murdoch (1919–), Pamela Hansford Johnson (1912–), and John Braine (1922–) are some of these names. The craftsmanship, the writing, are on a high level. But this contemporary fiction lacks size and weight, profound originality, and the kind of urgency that makes the novel seem important. These shortcomings may be due to a change of attitude in the reading public itself, for it will be found that it is precisely at those times when people are passionately eager to read fiction — as they were, for example, during the middle years of the nineteenth century, not only in England but all over Europe and in America — that the novel reaches toward greatness.

Finally, it must be understood that much excellent fiction has made its ap-

British Information

C. P. Snow

pearance outside Britain, in the various dominions of the British Commonwealth. From Canada we have had the successful novels about the Whiteoaks family by Mazo de la Roche; regional fiction by F. P. Grove, Thomas Raddall, W. O. Mitchell; Morley Callaghan's stories of city life; Hugh McLennan's novels and well-written lighter fiction by Robertson Davies. Australia, which is increasingly productive in fiction, has given us novelists like Katherine Susannah Pritchard, Kylie Tennant and Henry Handel Richardson, whose trilogy of novels, *Richard Mahony,* is outstanding. Among the most vigorous and powerful of the newer Australian novelists is Patrick White. New Zealand writers of fiction include the famous short-story writer Katherine Mansfield, Jane Mander, and Robin Hyde, who died before he could become widely known outside his own country. The peasant life of India has found its way into the stories of Mulk Raj Anand, and now George Lamming's books are bringing the West Indies into the ever-widening panorama of Dominion life. It is impossible, however, to do even the barest justice to the fiction of these Dominion writers in a brief survey.

J. B. P.

NOTABLE ENGLISH NOVELS

1719 Daniel Defoe's *Robinson Crusoe*
A strange and fascinating tale of a shipwrecked mariner who lives on a desert island off the east coast of South America.

1740 Samuel Richardson's *Pamela*
In letters that reveal the "sentiments" of the age, a maidservant tells how she resisted her young master until he offered marriage.

1749 Henry Fielding's *Tom Jones*
A realistic novel, richly filled with characters and adventurers, which tells the story of a lively hero from childhood to marriage.

1760 Laurence Sterne's *Tristram Shandy*
Comic domestic episodes, written in all sorts of styles — extravagant, digressive, and whimsical.

1766 Oliver Goldsmith's *The Vicar of Wakefield*
The unworldly Dr. Primrose and his family are the subject of this delightful story of English country life.

1813 * Jane Austen's *Pride and Prejudice*
A mother tries to find husbands for her five daughters among the quiet country gentlefolk.

1818 Sir Walter Scott's *The Heart of Midlothian*
A story rich in homely characterization and emotional intensity, centering about the struggle of Jeanie Deans to save her erring sister.

1847 Charlotte Brontë's *Jane Eyre*
In this well-known novel, Jane falls in love with her employer, a strange but fascinating man.

1847 Emily Brontë's *Wuthering Heights*
A wild tale of love and hate among the rough people of the Yorkshire moors.

1847 William Makepeace Thackeray's *Vanity Fair*
A satirical novel relating the story of Becky Sharp, an ambitious young girl who uses every trick she knows to get ahead in society.

1849 Charles Dickens' *David Copperfield*
Many of Dickens' best-known characters are in this story based on his own life.

1857 Anthony Trollope's *Barchester Towers*
A story of the intrigues and gossip of petty church officialdom found in the small-town, middle-class life of Victorian England.

1859 George Meredith's *The Ordeal of Richard Feverel*
The hero bitterly resents the smug inhumanity of his father's educational system.

1861 George Eliot's *Silas Marner*
The sentimental story of a victim of deceit who is restored to happiness through the love of a child.

1878 * Thomas Hardy's *The Return of the Native*
Fatal misunderstandings between relatives and a subtle yielding to temptation lead a strong person to a tragic death.

1886 Robert Louis Stevenson's *The Strange Case of Dr. Jekyll and Mr. Hyde*
A strange alteration in personality symbolizes the conflict between the good and evil in man.

1900 Joseph Conrad's *Lord Jim*
A psychological study of a young Englishman who loses his honor, settles in a Malay village, and finally regains his courage.

1901 Rudyard Kipling's *Kim*
A vivid picture of Indian life centered on the story of the orphaned son of an Irish soldier in India who is adopted by his father's regiment and ultimately works for the secret service.

1904 W. H. Hudson's *Green Mansions*
A beautifully written fantasy of the love of a Venezuelan for Rima,

a birdlike creature, in a South American forest.

1908 Arnold Bennett's *Old Wives' Tale*
Life in a small English industrial town and in Paris, described with sympathy and humor.

1909 H. G. Wells' *Tono-Bungay*
The story of the rise and fall of the promoters of a patent-medicine fraud, with perceptive sidelights on the evils of commercialism.

1915 W. Somerset Maugham's *Of Human Bondage*
The hero comes to the realization of his individual identity through suffering, defeat, and tragic love.

1922 John Galsworthy's *The Forsyte Saga*
This trilogy, centering on the affairs of a large, wealthy, middle-class family from 1886 to 1920, traces the effect on the Forsytes of property and the possessive instinct.

1924 E. M. Forster's *A Passage to India*
A potent story, subtle and powerful, about Moslems, Hindus, and Englishmen.

1927 Virginia Woolf's *To the Lighthouse*
A symbolic novel showing Mrs. Ramsay and her ever-increasing influence, even after death, on the lives that touch hers.

1929 J. B. Priestley's *The Good Companions*
A diverting, picaresque tale involving a troupe of wandering English players.

1932 Aldous Huxley's *Brave New World*
A satire on the mechanized, dehumanized world of the future.

SOME MODERN NOVELS

1934 James Hilton's *Good-bye, Mr. Chips*
A moving story of an English schoolmaster and his associations with boys of three generations.

1937 A. J. Cronin's *The Citadel*
A young doctor struggles against mediocrity, forgets honor and ideals, and is brought to his senses by a tragic error.

1939 Elizabeth **Bowen's** *The Death of the Heart*
A deeply moving tragedy of adolescence, brought about by adult cruelty and insensitivity.

1940 Richard Llewellyn's *How Green Was My Valley*
An old man, recalling the green valley of his youth, depicts alternately the tragedy and comedy of a Welsh mining village.

1946 Evelyn Waugh's *Brideshead Revisited*
Dissipation, boredom, and insurmountable hopelessness is presented as the only alternative to faith and works.

1948 Alan Paton's *Cry, the Beloved Country*
After the murder of his son, a European works with a Zulu parson, the father of the murderer, to bring new understanding to the South African scene.

1950 Joyce Cary's *The Horse's Mouth*
The exuberant story of Gulley Jimson, a visionary painter, told by himself.

1951 C. P. Snow's *The Masters*
An account of the events leading up to the election of a new master of a large English university.

1953 Nadine Gordimer's *The Lying Days*
The first twenty-four years of a girl brought up by conventional parents in a mining suburb of Johannesburg, South Africa.

1956 Rebecca West's *The Fountain Overflows*
An absorbing novel, vividly characterized, of a family in London about fifty years ago.

1960 Elizabeth Goudge's *Dean's Watch*
In a nineteenth-century cathedral town the lives of many people are changed by a talented clockmaker and the dean of the cathedral.

* Included in *Four English Novels,* J. B. Priestley and O. B. Davis, eds. (Harcourt, Brace & World, Inc., 1960).

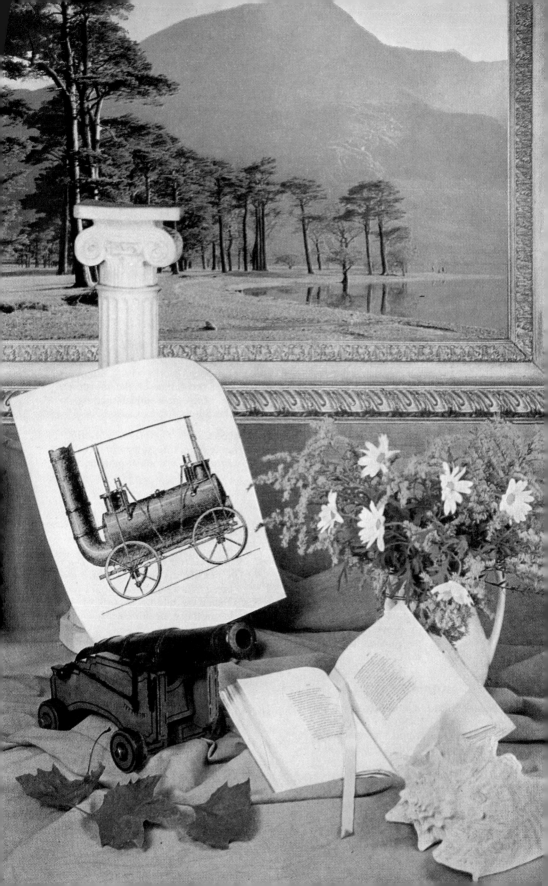

THE ROMANTIC AGE

1800 – 1837

Romance, Romantic, Romanticism — we shall be always coming across these terms, but they are very hard to define. They have in fact been given quite different meanings by people at different times. But clearly we cannot introduce the Romantic Age without some idea of what it means to be Romantic and what kind of writing belongs to Romanticism.

THE CHARACTERISTICS OF ROMANTICISM

From what we know already about the spirit of the eighteenth century, especially in its earlier, more confident, and classical period, we can surmise that Romanticism will be its opposite. Romanticism will be the other side — the hidden and suppressed side, the formerly unfashionable and frowned-upon side — bursting out, breaking through.

Therefore if one side — one spirit, really — is reasonable, calm, and smugly confident, the other will be unreasonable or irrational, agitated, dubious, and troubled. If one side likes company, the other will love solitude. If one side flourishes only in cities, then the other will not only want the country but also the least inhabited parts of the country — the mountains, the forests, the desert. If one side believes in a highly civilized and artificial style of life, the other will turn away from it in disgust and praise all that is simple, natural, even primitive. If one side believes there is no mystery left in the universe, the other will see mystery everywhere — in a flower, a tree, a cloud, a star. If the writing

◀ The items in the frontispiece are identified on page 477.

of one side is a kind of public performance, the writing of the other will be intensely private. And so it goes on.

This "other" side which is breaking through is Romanticism. And though the breakthrough was inevitable sooner or later, it came sooner than it might have otherwise, owing to the extraordinary influence of one eighteenth-century man of genius, Jean-Jacques Rousseau (1712–1778), a Swiss who lived and worked mostly in France. It is impossible to overestimate the influence of Rousseau, who denounced with passionate eloquence everything the eighteenth century believed in and hurried on both the French Revolution and the whole Romantic movement. Almost everything in this movement can be found, much earlier, in Rousseau. All the English Romantics read him with enthusiasm, at least when they were young.

New York Public Library, Print Room

Jean-Jacques Rousseau

We should note in passing that Romanticism was a European movement, though it did not succeed in all countries at the same time. It was seen first in Germany, then in England, then in Russia and elsewhere, and then, belatedly but brilliantly, in France as late as 1830. Its main influence on both North and South America was later still. As a period in English literature, Romanticism can be said to extend from about 1798, which marks the publication of Wordsworth's and Coleridge's *Lyrical Ballads,* to the mid-1830's, when Queen Victoria began her reign and most of the major Romantic poets, with the exception of Wordsworth, had died.

To return to Rousseau, he was so far from being a balanced human being that the last years of his life were threatened and then darkened by insanity. But then the Romanticism he so largely helped to create was itself unbalanced. It was one-sided, just as the earlier eighteenth-century attitude of mind was one-sided in the opposite fashion. It was as if a pendulum had been set in motion, taking writers from one extreme to the other.

A balanced man looks neither entirely outward nor entirely inward; he considers both the outer world and his own inner world. Sometimes he wants society; at other times he prefers solitude, enjoying in turn both the city and the quiet countryside. He does not believe that everything is a mystery, but he also refuses to believe that nothing is a mystery. Shakespeare and nearly all the earlier great writers were balanced men of this sort. They were quite unlike the writers of the Romantic Age, who were one-sidedly correcting something that had itself been too one-sided.

THE LIMITED INFLUENCE OF ROMANTICISM

There is another important point that must be made. We have called this *the Romantic Age,* but what we really mean is *the Romantic Age in English literature.* For the age itself, outside literature, was not "romantic." The Prince Regent (who was accorded this title because his father, George III, was out of his mind); and William Pitt, the Prime Minister; and the Duke of Wellington, who commanded the British forces — these men were not Romantics. It was only the poets and their friends and some of the younger people who could be said to belong to the Romantic movement. The politicians, bankers, merchants, soldiers, editors, even most of the literary critics, remained quite untouched by Romanticism.

Now this is important because it is new. In the time of Queen Elizabeth it was not simply the poets who were Elizabethan in spirit; almost everybody was. In the days of Queen Anne the writers shared the outlook, morals, manners, and tastes of the society for which they wrote. But now in

By gracious permission of Her Majesty Elizabeth II

The Prince of Wales, son of George III and named Prince Regent by Parliament, in 1820 came to the throne in his own right as George IV.

the Romantic Age we arrive at a very different state of things. It is only the comparatively small literary part of society, not the whole of society, that belongs to Romanticism. And this means, in effect, that literature no longer occupies a central position in society. What is being written by the most gifted men of the age no longer expresses what most people are thinking and feeling, as it did in former ages.

The loss of a central position for literature signals our arrival in the modern world. For nowadays it never occurs to us that the poet is the typical man, the man who is speaking for everybody. He seems to us now the odd and exceptional man, who is speaking only for himself. We should be surprised if newspaper editors, in time of national crisis, hurried to discover and print the opinions of poets. If leaders of political parties spent most of their evenings in the company of poets, they would soon be considered too eccentric to be fit for political leadership. Yet if the poet, the man with unusual depth of insight and feeling, is not speaking for our society, then something is wrong either with our poetry or with our society. But to this we shall have to return later, when we consider our own age.

THE POLITICAL BACKGROUND

The political events of this period, 1800–1837, cannot be ignored. They played an important part in the development of the English literature of the time. Revolutionary France, compelled to fight to defend its very existence, badly needed a commander capable of organizing victory. It found one in Napoleon Bonaparte, an astonishing military and organizing genius, one of the greatest commanders of all time, though unscrupulous and the victim of unresting ambition. Unable to invade Britain because his navy was destroyed by Lord Nelson at the Battle of Trafalgar, Napoleon proceeded to conquer most of Western Europe and organized its resources to aid him in his ceaseless struggle against Britain, his most determined and formidable enemy.

Although Emperor now, with unlimited powers, Napoleon was in some respects still a man of the French Revolution, inheriting some of its liberating ideas, which were already triumphant in America. The Whigs in Britain recognized this fact and were in favor of trying to come to terms with Napoleon.

At the Battle of Trafalgar (1805), one of the great landmarks in British history, the British navy under Admiral Lord Nelson resoundingly defeated the French fleet.

New York Public Library, Print Room

But the Tories, who saw in him a threat to their political and social system, carried the country. Making full use of the invasion scare and allying themselves with the despotic monarchies in Europe, they finally succeeded in defeating Napoleon in 1815 at the Battle of Waterloo. At the famous Congress of Vienna, which met to settle the political problems of Europe, any good that Napoleon had done was soon undone. England, together with Russia and the Germans, set up a "Holy Alliance" which, though it secured a long period of peace for Europe, discouraged further reform. All traces of liberating influences were removed; the Congress was a triumph of reaction.

As it was abroad, so it was at home in Britain, which was held fast in the grip of reactionary and shortsighted Toryism. Liberal opinions were dangerous, any spirited expression of them being liable to drive a writer into exile or land him in prison. [One of the minor Romantics, the poet and essayist Leigh Hunt (1784–1859), was sentenced to two years' imprisonment for calling the Prince Regent, among other things, "a fat Adonis."] Meetings of laborers, shockingly overworked and underpaid, were broken up by dragoons. There were riots and much popular agitation for reform. Toward the end of the period the Whigs passed the Reform Bill (1832) which helped to abolish the worst inequalities in Parliamentary representation by increasing the number of those eligible to vote. Further reforms — against child labor, to lighten prison sentences, improve education, broaden freedom of the press, and abolish the slave trade — were also made. Until these reforms had been achieved, however, London was an uncomfortable place for any outspoken lover of liberty.

THE ROMANTICS AS CHAMPIONS OF FREEDOM

The older poets, William Wordsworth (1770–1850), Samuel Taylor Coleridge (1772–1834), and Robert Southey (1774–1843), were eager revolutionaries in their youth. With many other Romantics, they believed in individual liberty and the brotherhood of man and sympathized with those who rebelled against injustice and tyranny. Later, when the France they had admired became Napoleon's empire and Britain herself seemed to be in danger, they renounced these early opinions, taking what was more or less the Tory line. William Hazlitt (1778–1830), the finest critic and essayist of the age, was a passionate anti-Tory and Radical — he wrote a biography of Napoleon chiefly to defy official and popular opinion — and though he greatly admired Wordsworth and Coleridge, he never ceased to denounce them as renegades to the cause of freedom.

Among the younger poets, George Gordon, Lord Byron (1788–1824) was famous throughout Europe as a champion of liberty, and Percy Bysshe Shelley (1792–1822) was an out-and-out revolutionary with a special brand of anarchy all his own. John Keats (1795–1821) was not politically minded, but because he was one of the young Romantics, he was viciously attacked in the *Quarterly Review*, the chief organ of Tory literary opinion. Indeed, this attack was so savage and outrageous that many people believed that it was the cause of his severe illness and early death. We know this to be untrue, however, for Keats was already a victim of tuberculosis and, in fact, faced this attack in a cheerful, manly fashion.

But the stupidity and savagery of much of its criticism represent an important feature of this Romantic Age. Reviewers like William Gifford (1756–1826) and John Wilson Croker (1780–1857) were inflamed against the Romantics by two different sets of prejudices. One was literary, for these men still had eighteenth-century ideas about literature and really did not begin to understand what Romantic poetry was trying to do. With them the "breakthrough" already described never took place. They wanted tame public verses from men who were writing intensely emotional poetry inspired by their inner lives. The other set of prejudices was political in origin, for these reviewers were all hidebound Tories who regarded the Romantics as dangerous liberals, radicals, and revolutionaries.

INTEREST IN THE PAST

Tory Romanticism is possible, however, and a writer like Sir Walter Scott (1771–1832) is offered as an outstanding example of it. Oddly enough, in view of the fact that Scott was accepted as an outstanding figure of the whole European Romantic movement, this levelheaded Scots lawyer was not really a true Romantic. The inner world is not breaking through with him. There is nothing of Rousseau's influence here. Scott was really an eighteenth-century man who, as you can tell from novels such as *Ivanhoe, The Talisman,* and *The Heart of Midlothian,* happened to have a great love of the past in its more picturesque aspects.

Although the true Romantic poets, from Coleridge to Keats, appeared to be always writing about the past, they had not in fact the solid interest in it that Scott had and that historians and antiquaries and archaeologists have. This is an important point without which Romanticism cannot be properly understood. Scott wrote about the Middle Ages because he was genuinely interested in the Middle Ages and wanted to tell stories about them. But the real Romantic poets and storytellers all over Europe who began to give their poems and stories a medieval background were not so much turning to the past as deliberately turning away from the outward scene of their own time. What they wanted to explore and then express was their own inner world of dream and desire, of mysterious hopes and fears; in order to separate this inner world from the ordinary outer world, to make it all different, they used a kind of medieval dreamland. Their poems and tales are not really *about* the Middle Ages but are concerned with their own inner selves.

The Romantics made frequent use of rather vague medieval settings just because the Middle Ages of their imagination were so entirely different from the complicated and rather ugly industrial society which was growing up all around them. The earlier times were simpler yet more picturesque and, what was more important, they seemed more *magical*. (Our inner world seems — and indeed is — magical to us because we cannot really understand it.) But the medieval spirit was not essential to Romanticism. Any setting that was strange, remote in time or space, served its purpose.

Thus Shelley and Keats turned to Greek mythology, giving a new significance to ancient figures of legend. Byron and lesser poets like Thomas Moore (1779–1852) made use of the people and landscapes of what we now call the Near and Middle East. If Wordsworth, who was not at all a typical Romantic, was able to stay at home a good deal, that was because he had made his home in the north of England in the heart of the Lake District, at that time not often visited and not easily accessible. In any case, Wordsworth was not concerned with immediate effects of picturesque strangeness. He wanted to brood over the real, outward scene, though always some remote aspect of it far removed from the effects of the Industrial Revolution, so that at last the outer world and his inner world fused together, so to speak, making one whole. It is usually this process that his best poems describe so magnificently. Where other Romantic poets ransack mythology, legend, or folk beliefs for enchantment, Wordsworth waits for the sound of the cuckoo in spring to transform the real world into a magical place.

THE IDEALIZING OF WOMEN

Again, in Romanticism women can hardly ever be simply fellow creatures of the opposite sex, seeking a lasting relationship, a home, and children; instead, they must be strange and magical. So Romantic love poetry is not addressed to the girl next door. It is filled with mysterious beings — nymphs, water sprites, Oriental queens and princesses, savage gypsy girls — in fact, with any beautiful feminine creatures who could not possibly live next door. This does not mean that the Romantics were indifferent to ordinary girls and women; far from it. What they were doing was dramatizing and overemphasiz-

Photo Researchers, Inc.

The elaborate Regent's Pavilion at Brighton, built before George IV became king, accommodated the Prince Regent and his court during stays at the seaside resort.

ing the aspects of real womanhood that appear strange and magical to a man's inner life. The Romantics pictured women in the same way that even the girl next door might appear in the inner world of dream of a young man who falls in love with her. And all this was instinctively understood by the feminine readers of the Romantic poets and storytellers. These enthusiastic but often tearful readers felt that they themselves were not unlike the nymphs, water sprites, Oriental princesses, and gypsy girls described.

ROMANTIC MELANCHOLY

Because it is itself one-sided, never moving toward a balance between the outer and inner worlds, between what is real and what we feel ought to be real, Romanticism always tends, as it loses itself in the inner dream world and longing, to find existence less and less satisfying. This is why poets such as Wordsworth are always praising the lost kingdom of childhood, where dream and reality are not yet separated. The real, outward world remains obstinately itself, refusing to be shaped and colored by what the Romantic feels. So the literature of Romanticism, as we can easily discover in the poetry of this age, is filled with melancholy and regret and hopelessly unsatisfied longing. This mood is more characteristic of young men than older men, who ought to know better and arrive at some balance. It is significant that Coleridge stopped

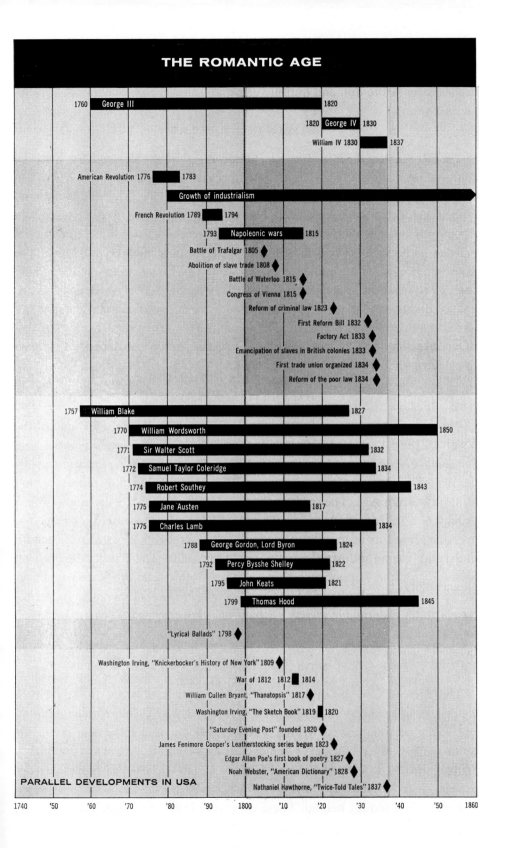

THE ROMANTIC AGE

1760 George III 1820

1820 George IV 1830

William IV 1830 1837

American Revolution 1776 1783

Growth of industrialism

French Revolution 1789 1794

1793 Napoleonic wars 1815

Battle of Trafalgar 1805 ◆

Abolition of slave trade 1808 ◆

Battle of Waterloo 1815 ◆

Congress of Vienna 1815 ◆

Reform of criminal law 1823 ◆

First Reform Bill 1832 ◆

Factory Act 1833 ◆

Emancipation of slaves in British colonies 1833 ◆

First trade union organized 1834 ◆

Reform of the poor law 1834 ◆

1757 William Blake 1827

1770 William Wordsworth 1850

1771 Sir Walter Scott 1832

1772 Samuel Taylor Coleridge 1834

1774 Robert Southey 1843

1775 Jane Austen 1817

1775 Charles Lamb 1834

1788 George Gordon, Lord Byron 1824

1792 Percy Bysshe Shelley 1822

1795 John Keats 1821

1799 Thomas Hood 1845

"Lyrical Ballads" 1798 ◆

Washington Irving, "Knickerbocker's History of New York" 1809 ◆

War of 1812 1812 1814

William Cullen Bryant, "Thanatopsis" 1817 ◆

Washington Irving, "The Sketch Book" 1819 1820

"Saturday Evening Post" founded 1820 ◆

James Fenimore Cooper's Leatherstocking series begun 1823 ◆

Edgar Allan Poe's first book of poetry 1827 ◆

Noah Webster, "American Dictionary" 1828 ◆

PARALLEL DEVELOPMENTS IN USA

Nathaniel Hawthorne, "Twice-Told Tales" 1837 ◆

1740 '50 '60 '70 '80 '90 1800 '10 '20 '30 '40 '50 1860

writing poetry as he grew older; that Wordsworth, except for a few occasional flashes, later wrote dull and dutiful verses; and that Keats, Shelley, and Byron all died young.

ROMANTIC POETRY

The Romantic Age in English literature, though glorious for what it achieved, was unusually strong in some forms of writing and curiously weak in others. Though most of the poets wrote verse dramas, the wonderful command of the theater that the Elizabethans had was not recaptured. We are often told that if only poets would write for the theater our drama would be great again, but this is too simple. To succeed on the stage poets must be dramatists too. There must also be an audience like the one the Elizabethans had, eager to respond to what the true dramatic poet offers them. Even if Shelley and Keats had lived long enough to write poetic drama, the necessary audience might still have been missing. As it was, the Romantic poets were at their wonderful best in lyrical poetry and, as a good second best, they often succeeded with narrative poetry too, as we know to our delight.

ROMANTIC FICTION

The age was also not uniformly successful in its prose forms. In spite of the novels of Jane Austen (1775–1817) such as *Emma, Pride and Prejudice,* and *Sense and Sensibility,* and those of Sir Walter Scott which were mentioned earlier, its fiction as a whole was inferior to that of the eighteenth century or that of the Victorian Age. The truth is, the novel on a grand scale demands a background of a fairly settled society. This stability the Regency, with its wars and invasion scares, its deep political divisions and unrest, its rapid transformation of a rural into an industrial society, could not offer. There was, however, an increasing output of popular fiction — either Gothic tales of mystery and horror such as Horace Walpole's *The Castle of Otranto* or sentimental and satirical novels about fashionable society — that might have helped to lay a foundation for the greater fiction that was to come.

THE TRIUMPH OF THE PERSONAL ESSAY

This age can show no masterpieces of biography and history to equal Boswell's *Life of Johnson* and Gibbon's *Decline and Fall of the Roman Empire.* But in the personal essay, written with an intimacy and force that the eighteenth-century essay had never achieved, the Romantic Age was triumphant. William Hazlitt (1778–1830) and Charles Lamb (1775–1834) were its two masters, with Thomas de Quincey (1785–1859), Leigh Hunt (1784–1859), and others not too far behind. These men were critics too — Romantic critics to keep pace with the Romantic poets. Their criticism, unlike that of the eighteenth century, was not so much cold judgment on behalf of society, but was essentially personal and intimate, suggesting first-class talk among friends about books and authors. Here Hazlitt, offering a wide range of criticism from Shakespeare onwards, was the master, but Lamb too did valuable service, especially in his selections from and notes on the lesser Elizabethan and Jacobean dramatists. Finally, in his numerous notes, Coleridge was perhaps the most subtle and profound critic in this or any other age.

The Romantic period was particularly rich in fascinating characters, in and out of literature. There was William Cobbett (1763–1835), who, in his *Rural Rides,* was equally forthright in both his admiration and denunciation of the English scene. There was Shelley's witty friend, Thomas Love Peacock (1785–1866), who, as we can judge from *Nightmare Abbey,* wrote novels like nobody else's. There was Sydney Smith (1771–1845), clergyman, humorist, wit, reformer — a rich character. This age is crammed with remarkable characters, and fortunately it is equally rich in journals, memoirs, and diaries that reveal these characters to us. Whole libraries of works have been concerned with this period. It provides a never-ending feast for the literary historian, the critic, and the student of human nature. Any reader who falls under its spell will discover in it a lifelong fascination and charm.

J. B. P.

WILLIAM WORDSWORTH

1770–1850

New York Public Library, Print Room

To understand Wordsworth, it is important to know something of the natural surroundings among which he lived. In a section of northwestern England known as the Lake District, nature has been lavish not only with lakes, but also with mountains, streams, and waterfalls over which the shifting lights and shades and seasonal colors play with ever-varying effect. Wordsworth has left us a vivid record of his long life here.

In part of his long poem *The Prelude,*

Wordsworth gave a full account of his boyhood in the Cumberland hills. It is significant that, more than any other English poet up to his day, he studied the thoughts, feelings, and reactions of children and traced the part played by childhood in the total development of a person's life. "The child is father of the man," is one of his most famous lines. His love of outdoor life as a boy deepened and matured until he became the great interpreter of nature in poetry. He sensed a divine spirit within all forms of nature. Even birds and flowers, he believed, were aware of pleasure in being alive. To Wordsworth, nature was mankind's best moral teacher. Nature was, in fact, his religion, and he has been called "nature's high priest."

At Cambridge another dominant interest came into Wordsworth's life. The world was seething with new political ideas. The Americans had recently won their independence; now the French masses were rising against the tyranny of the aristocrats. While on a trip to France in 1791, young Wordsworth enthusiastically adopted the side of the French revolutionists, but when his family cut off his allowance at the end of a year, he was forced to return to England. Later, feeling that the revolution had fallen short of its early ideals, he turned against the radical democratic ideas of the time and became conservative, much to the distaste of some of his admirers. Robert Browning reproachfully called him a "lost leader."

A close companionship with his sister Dorothy was one of the abiding influences of Wordsworth's life. Another was his long friendship with Coleridge. The two men had met in their twenties, when Wordsworth and Dorothy were living in southern England. The three young people found an immediate bond in their ardent discussions of poetry while on long hikes through the Somerset hills. Out of this association came *Lyrical Ballads*, the book which marks the beginning of the Romantic movement.

In these poems the two men put into practice their poetic principles. They believed that poetry — which they thought of as "emotion recollected in tranquillity" — should deal with simple subjects and everyday people, that feelings rather than plot or action should be presented, and that the ordinary, daily language of the people should be used to impart these feelings. The simple, musical lyrics in this volume, so different from the polished, formal verse of the eighteenth century, were unfavorably received at first, but later their profound importance was recognized.

For fifty years Wordsworth lived near Grasmere in the Lake District, with his wife, his devoted sister, and a circle of congenial literary friends. Sir Walter Scott and Ralph Waldo Emerson were among his famous visitors. Wordsworth's last thirty years were largely unproductive poetically, but his fame and greatness were already established. At the age of seventy-three he was made poet laureate. He died seven years later and was buried in the little churchyard at Grasmere.

She Dwelt among the Untrodden Ways

This is one of five "Lucy Poems" centering upon an imaginary girl of the English countryside. In these lyrics the poet praises the influence of nature on a young girl and describes his emotion at her death.

She dwelt among the untrodden ways
  Beside the springs of Dove;°
A maid whom there were none to praise,
  And very few to love.

2. *Dove:* a river in the Midlands of England.

lieved by a pension from George III.

From Boswell's *The Life of Samuel Johnson* we get a rounded picture of Johnson: he was a gruff and stern man but a kindly one. He supported in his house a number of poor and unfortunate people, including Miss Williams, his old, half-blind housekeeper, who is reputed to have used her thumb to judge whether the guests' tea-cups needed refilling! All in all, he deserved to have the literary period named for him and to be the subject of Boswell's famous biography, which records his life and times for posterity.

James Boswell is recognized as one of the greatest biographers in English literature. A Scotsman of wealthy family who came to London to get a commission in the army, Boswell was ambitious, impulsive, and often lacking in judgment. Yet he had a true gift for writing and the rare insight to recognize his life work on meeting Samuel Johnson. For years, whenever the two men met, Boswell recorded Johnson's conversation, his habits, his peculiarities. The biographer submerged his own personality in that of his subject, but Boswell was a personality in his own right. His journals, not discovered until the twentieth century, reveal him as a vain, sometimes ridiculous youth, yet in many ways an appealing one. He was a delightful writer with a keen sense of observation and a lively humor that never failed him.

Letter to
Lord Chesterfield

The significance of this letter is in its relation to the system of patronage prevalent in England in Johnson's time. Since the reading public was small, the only way a man could obtain any substantial financial return from writing was by securing a patron among the wealthy nobility. It was understood that the author would dedicate his work to the patron, who in return saw to the author's welfare. When the *Dictionary* was first contemplated, Johnson requested the support of Lord Chesterfield,

the most elegant gentleman of his day. The result is told in the following letter. Johnson showed his native independence of spirit and is said to have thereby sounded the death knell of the whole patronage system. In connection with this letter, you should read the selection "The Dictionary" from Boswell's *Life* which appears on page 323.

February 7, 1755

To the Right Honorable the Earl of Chesterfield.

My Lord:

I have been lately informed by the proprietor of the *World* [1] that two papers, in which my Dictionary is recommended to the public, were written by your Lordship. To be so distinguished is an honor which, being very little accustomed to favors from the great, I know not well how to receive, or in what terms to acknowledge.

When, upon some slight encouragement, I first visited your Lordship, I was overpowered, like the rest of mankind, by the enchantment of your address, and could not forbear to wish that I might boast myself *Le vainqueur du vainqueur de la terre* [2] — that I might obtain that regard for which I saw the world contending; but I found my attendance so little encouraged that neither pride nor modesty would suffer me to continue it. When I had once addressed your Lordship in public, I had exhausted all the art of pleasing which a retired and uncourtly scholar can possess. I had done all that I could; and no man is well pleased to have his all neglected, be it ever so little.

Seven years, my Lord, have now passed since I waited in your outward rooms, or was repulsed from your door; during which time I have been pushing

---

[1] *the* World: a newspaper run by Edward Moore, a friend of Johnson's. [2] "The conqueror of the conqueror of the world."

on my work through difficulties, of which it is useless to complain, and have brought it, at last, to the verge of publication without one act of assistance, one word of encouragement, or one smile of favor. Such treatment I did not expect, for I never had a Patron before.

The shepherd in Virgil grew at last acquainted with Love, and found him a native of the rocks.[1]

Is not a Patron, my Lord, one who looks with unconcern on a man struggling for life in the water, and when he has reached ground, encumbers him with help? The notice which you have been pleased to take of my labors, had it been early, had been kind; but it has been delayed till I am indifferent, and cannot enjoy it; till I am solitary, and cannot impart it; till I am known, and do not want it. I hope it is no very cynical asperity not to confess obligations where no benefit has been received, or to be unwilling that the Public should consider me as owing that to a Patron which Providence has enabled me to do for myself.

Having carried on my work thus far with so little obligation to any favorer of learning, I shall not be disappointed though I should conclude it, if less be possible, with less; for I have been long wakened from that dream of hope, in which I once boasted myself with so much exultation.

My Lord,
Your Lordship's most humble,
Most obedient servant,

Sam: Johnson.

---

[1] *The shepherd . . . rocks:* a reference to a passage in Virgil's eighth Eclogue (a pastoral poem in which shepherds converse on the cruelty and inhumanity of love).

Definitions from Johnson's Dictionary

Some of Johnson's definitions are famous for showing his prejudices, his errors, his use of big words to define a fairly simple term, and, at times, his humor.

Excise duty: a hateful tax levied by wretches hired by those to whom excise is paid.

Oats: a grain which in England is generally given to horses, but in Scotland[1] supports the people.

Pension: an allowance made to anyone without an equivalent.[2] In England it is generally understood to mean pay given to a state hireling for treason to his country.

Pensioner: a slave of state hired by a stipend to obey his master. [Later, when Johnson himself became a pensioner, he replied to the critics who reminded him of this definition: "I wish my pension were twice as large that they might make twice as much noise."]

Tory: one who adheres to the ancient constitution of the State and the apostolical hierarchy of the Church of England; opposed to a Whig.

Whig: the name of a faction.

Lexicographer: a writer of dictionaries, a harmless drudge.

Grub Street: the name of a street in London, much inhabited by writers of small histories, dictionaries, and temporary poems: whence any mean production is called *Grub Street*.

Pastern: the knee of a horse. [On being asked by a lady why he defined it thus, he said, "Ignorance, madam, pure ignorance."]

Network: anything reticulated or decussated at equal distances with interstices between the intersections.

---

[1] You will learn later of Johnson's dislike of the Scots. [2] *equivalent* (ê·kwĭv′á·lĕnt): here, service of equal value.

The Life of Samuel Johnson

JAMES BOSWELL

Through his *Life of Samuel Johnson* James Boswell ensured the immortality of a great personality whose role in the literary circles of his time and whose importance in the history of English literature may otherwise have been obscured. At the same time, Boswell ensured his own immortality as a personality and a biographer.

It is interesting to note that Boswell's association with Samuel Johnson was, from the outset, frowned upon by Boswell's stern Scottish father. Indeed, capricious, extravagant, and irresponsible, Boswell, who as eldest son was heir to his father's estate, was considered the disgrace of his family. In 1762, having made temporary peace at home, he left Scotland for London. Twenty-two years old, alternately conceited and self-doubting, Boswell was markedly unstable in personality. For many reasons, his meeting and subsequent friendship with Johnson was probably the luckiest event of his life. Johnson brought out the good side of Boswell and in many respects served as substitute for Boswell's severe parent. The advantages of this relationship were mutual, however, for Boswell in turn complemented Johnson's personality. Boswell's famous biography illuminates the personalities of both men and serves as a unique testimony of this celebrated friendship.

[THE DICTIONARY]

The following excerpt is from the first part of the biography, covering the period before Boswell became acquainted with Johnson.

How LONG this immense undertaking had been the object of his contemplation, I do not know. I once asked him by what means he had attained to that astonishing knowledge of our language by which he was enabled to realize a design of such extent and accumulated difficulty. He told me that "it was not the effect of particular study; but that it had grown up in his mind insensibly." . . .

That he was fully aware of the arduous nature of the undertaking, he acknowledges; and shows himself perfectly sensible of it in the conclusion of his "Plan"; but he had a noble consciousness of his own abilities, which enabled him to go on with undaunted spirit.

Dr. Adams found him one day busy at his Dictionary, when the following dialogue ensued:

Adams: "This is a great work, Sir. How are you to get all the etymologies?" [1]

Johnson: "Why, Sir, here is a shelf with Junius, and Skinner,[2] and others; and there is a Welsh gentleman who has published a collection of Welsh proverbs, who will help me with the Welsh."

Adams: "But, Sir, how can you do this in three years?"

Johnson: "Sir, I have no doubt that I can do it in three years."

Adams: "But the French Academy, which consists of forty members, took forty years to compile their Dictionary."

Johnson: "Sir, thus it is. This is the proportion. Let me see: forty times forty is sixteen hundred. As three to sixteen hundred so is the proportion of an Englishman to a Frenchman."

With so much ease and pleasantry could he talk of that prodigious labor which he had undertaken to execute.

While the Dictionary was going forward, Johnson lived part of the time in Holborn, part in Gough Square, Fleet Street; and he had an upper room fitted up like a countinghouse for the purpose, in which he gave to the copyists their several tasks. The words, partly taken from other Dictionaries, and partly supplied by himself, having been first written down with spaces left between them,

---

[1] *etymologies* (ĕt′ĭ·mŏl′ō·jĭz): origins and derivations of words. [2] *Junius, and Skinner:* seventeenth-century English scholars, both of whom wrote books on etymology. Skinner was also a physician.

he delivered in writing their etymologies, definitions, and various significations. The authorities were copied from the books themselves, in which he had marked the passages with a black-lead pencil, the traces of which could be easily effaced. I have seen several of them in which that trouble had not been taken; so that they were just as when used by the copyists. It is remarkable that he was so attentive in the choice of the passages in which words were authorized that one may read page after page of his Dictionary with improvement and pleasure; and it should not pass unobserved that he has quoted no author whose writings had a tendency to hurt sound religion and morality.

The necessary expense of preparing a work of such magnitude for the press must have been a considerable deduction from the price stipulated to be paid for the copyright.[1] I understand that nothing was allowed by the booksellers on that account; and I remember his telling me that a large portion of it having, by mistake, been written upon both sides of the paper, so as to be inconvenient for the compositor, it cost him twenty pounds to have it transcribed upon one side only.

[BOSWELL'S FIRST MEETING WITH DR. JOHNSON]

Mr. Thomas Davies, the actor, who then kept a bookseller's shop in Russell Street, Covent Garden, told me that Johnson was very much his friend, and came frequently to his house, where he more than once invited me to meet him: but by some unlucky accident or other he was prevented from coming to us. . . .

At last, on Monday the 16th of May, when I was sitting in Mr. Davies' back parlor, after having drunk tea with him and Mrs. Davies, Johnson unexpectedly came into the shop; and Mr. Davies having perceived him through the glass door in the room in which we were sitting, ad-

vancing toward us — he announced his awful approach to me, somewhat in the manner of an actor in the part of Horatio, when he addresses Hamlet on the appearance of his father's ghost, "Look, my Lord, it comes." I found that I had a very perfect idea of Johnson's figure, from the portrait of him painted by Sir Joshua Reynolds soon after he had published his Dictionary, in the attitude of sitting in his easy chair in deep meditation; which was the first picture his friend did for him, which Sir Joshua very kindly presented to me, and from which an engraving has been made for this work. Mr. Davies mentioned my name, and respectfully introduced me to him. I was much agitated; and recollecting his prejudice against the Scotch, of which I had heard much, I said to Davies, "Don't tell him where I come from."

"From Scotland," cried Davies, roguishly.

"Mr. Johnson (said I), I do indeed come from Scotland, but I cannot help it."

I am willing to flatter myself that I meant this as light pleasantry to soothe and conciliate him, and not as an humiliating abasement at the expense of my country. But however that might be, this speech was somewhat unlucky; for with that quickness of wit for which he was so remarkable, he seized the expression "come from Scotland," which I used in the sense of being of that country; and, as if I had said that I had come away from it, or left it, retorted, "That, Sir, I find, is what a very great many of your countrymen cannot help."

This stroke stunned me a good deal; and when we had sat down, I felt myself not a little embarrassed, and apprehensive of what might come next.

He then addressed himself to Davies: "What do you think of Garrick? He has refused me an order for the play for Miss Williams, because he knows the house will be full, and that an order would be worth three shillings."

Eager to take any opening to get into

---

[1] The price was £1,575.

conversation with him, I ventured to say, "O, Sir, I cannot think Mr. Garrick would grudge such a trifle to you."

"Sir (said he, with a stern look), I have known David Garrick longer than you have done; and I know no right you have to talk to me on the subject."

Perhaps I deserved this check; for it was rather presumptuous in me, an entire stranger, to express any doubt of the justice of his animadversion [1] upon his old acquaintance and pupil. I now felt myself much mortified, and began to think that the hope which I had long indulged of obtaining his acquaintance was blasted. And, in truth, had not my ardor been uncommonly strong, and my resolution uncommonly persevering, so rough a reception might have deterred me forever from making any further attempts. Fortunately, however, I remained upon the field not wholly discomfited; and was soon rewarded by hearing some of his conversation. . . .

A few days afterward I called on Davies, and asked him if he thought I might take the liberty of waiting on Mr. Johnson at his Chambers in the Temple. [2] He said I certainly might, and that Mr. Johnson would take it as a compliment. So on Tuesday the 24th of May, after having been enlivened by the witty sallies of Messieurs Thornton, Wilkes, Churchill, and Lloyd, [3] with whom I had passed the morning, I boldly repaired to Johnson. His Chambers were on the first floor of No. 1, Inner Temple-lane, and I entered them with an impression given me by the Reverend Dr. Blair, of Edinburgh, who had been introduced to him not long before, and described his having "found the Giant in his den"; an expression which, when I came to be pretty well acquainted with Johnson, I repeated to him, and he was diverted at this picturesque account of himself.

He received me very courteously: but it must be confessed that his apartment, and furniture, and morning dress were sufficiently uncouth. His brown suit of clothes looked very rusty: he had on a little old shriveled unpowdered wig, which was too small for his head; his shirt neck and knees of his breeches were loose; his black worsted stockings ill drawn up; and he had a pair of unbuckled shoes by way of slippers. But all these slovenly particularities were forgotten the moment that he began to talk. Some gentlemen, whom I do not recollect, were sitting with him; and when they went away, I also rose; but he said to me, "Nay, don't go."

"Sir (said I), I am afraid that I intrude upon you. It is benevolent to allow me to sit and hear you."

He seemed pleased with this compliment, which I sincerely paid him, and answered, "Sir, I am obliged to any man who visits me." . . .

When I rose a second time, he again pressed me to stay, which I did.

He told me that he generally went abroad at four in the afternoon and seldom came home till two in the morning. I took the liberty to ask if he did not think it was wrong to live thus, and not make more use of his great talents. He owned it was a bad habit. On reviewing, at the distance of many years, my journal of this period, I wonder how, at my first visit, I ventured to talk to him so freely, and that he bore it with so much indulgence.

Before we departed, he was so good as to promise to favor me with his company one evening at my lodgings; and, as I took my leave, shook me cordially by the hand. It is almost needless to add that I felt no little elation at having now so happily established an acquaintance of which I had been so long ambitious.

My readers will, I trust, excuse me for being thus minutely circumstantial, when it is considered that the acquaintance of Dr. Johnson was to me a most valuable acquisition, and laid the foundation of

[1] *animadversion* (ăn′ĭ·măd·vûr′shŭn): criticism, usually adverse. [2] *Temple:* an area of London in which lawyers lived and where law courts are located. [3] *Thornton . . . Lloyd:* literary wits and friends of Boswell.

whatever instruction and entertainment they may receive from my collections concerning the great subject of the work which they are now perusing.

[DR. JOHNSON'S PECULIARITIES]

He had another particularity,[1] of which none of his friends even ventured to ask an explanation. It appeared to me some superstitious habit, which he had contracted early, and from which he had never called upon his reason to disentangle him. This was his anxious care to go out or in at a door or passage by a certain number of steps from a certain point, or at least so as that either his right or his left foot (I am not certain which) should constantly make the first actual movement when he came close to the door or passage. Thus I conjecture: for I have, upon innumerable occasions, observed him suddenly stop, and then seem to count his steps with a deep earnestness; and when he had neglected or gone wrong in this sort of magical movement, I have seen him go back again, put himself in a proper posture to begin the ceremony, and, having gone through it, break from his abstraction, walk briskly on, and join his companion. Sir Joshua Reynolds has observed him to go a good way about, rather than cross a particular alley in Leicester[2] Fields; but this Sir Joshua imputed to his having had some disagreeable recollections associated with it.

That the most minute singularities which belonged to him, and made very observable parts of his appearance and manner, may not be omitted, it is requisite to mention that while talking or even musing as he sat in his chair, he commonly held his head to one side toward his right shoulder, and shook it in a tremulous manner, moving his body backward and forward, and rubbing his left knee in the same direction, with the palm of his hand. In the intervals of articulating he made various sounds with his mouth; sometimes giving a half whistle, sometimes as if ruminating, or what is called chewing the cud, sometimes making his tongue play backward from the roof of his mouth, as if clucking like a hen, and sometimes protruding it against his upper gums in front, as if pronouncing quickly under his breath, too, too, too: all this accompanied sometimes with a thoughtful look, but more frequently with a smile. Generally when he had concluded a period,[3] in the course of a dispute, by which time he was a good deal exhausted by violence and vociferation, he used to blow out his breath like a whale. This I suppose was a relief to his lungs; and seemed in him to be a contemptuous mode of expression, as if he had made the arguments of his opponents fly like chaff before the wind.

[JOHNSON AND GOLDSMITH]

The following incident takes place at dinner at the home of two booksellers, where about a dozen gentlemen, including Johnson, Boswell, and Goldsmith, are assembled. A long conversation is first reported.

During this argument, Goldsmith sat in restless agitation, from a wish to get in and shine. Finding himself excluded, he had taken his hat to go away, but remained for some time with it in his hand, like a gamester, who, at the close of a long night, lingers for a little while, to see if he can have a favorable opening to finish with success. Once when he was beginning to speak, he found himself overpowered by the loud voice of Johnson, who was at the opposite end of the table, and did not perceive Goldsmith's attempt. Thus disappointed of his wish to obtain the attention of the company, Goldsmith in a passion threw down his hat, looking angrily at Johnson, and exclaimed in a bitter tone, "Take it." When Toplady was going to speak, Johnson ut-

---

[1] *another particularity:* The first one described was his habit of talking to himself. [2] *Leicester* (lĕs'tĕr).

[3] *concluded a period:* ended a sentence.

tered some sound, which led Goldsmith to think that he was beginning again, and taking the words from Toplady. Upon which, he seized this opportunity of venting his own envy and spleen, under the pretext of supporting another person: "Sir (said he to Johnson), the gentleman has heard you patiently for an hour: pray allow us now to hear him."

Johnson (*sternly*): "Sir, I was not interrupting the gentleman. I was only giving him a signal of my attention. Sir, you are impertinent." Goldsmith made no reply, but continued in the company for some time.

He and Mr. Langton and I went together to the Club, where we found Mr. Burke, Mr. Garrick, and some other members, and among them our friend Goldsmith, who sat silently brooding over Johnson's reprimand to him after dinner. Johnson perceived this, and said aside to some of us, "I'll make Goldsmith forgive me"; and then called to him in a loud voice, "Dr. Goldsmith — something passed today where you and I dined: I ask your pardon." Goldsmith answered placidly, "It must be much from you, Sir, that I take ill." And so at once the difference was over, and they were on as easy terms as ever, and Goldsmith rattled away as usual.

In our way to the Club tonight, when I regretted that Goldsmith would, upon every occasion, endeavor to shine, by which he often exposed himself, Mr. Langton observed that he was not like Addison, who was content with the fame of his writings, and did not aim also at excellency in conversation, for which he found himself unfit: and that he said to a lady who complained of his having talked little in company, "Madam, I have but ninepence in ready money, but I can draw for a thousand pounds." I observed that Goldsmith had a great deal of gold in his cabinet, but not content with that, was always taking out his purse. Johnson: "Yes, Sir, and that so often an empty purse!"

Goldsmith's incessant desire of being conspicuous in company was the occasion of his sometimes appearing to such disadvantage as one should hardly have supposed possible in a man of his genius. When his literary reputation had risen deservedly high, and his society was much courted, he became very jealous of the extraordinary attention which was everywhere paid to Johnson. One evening, in a circle of wits, he found fault with me for talking of Johnson as entitled to the honor of unquestionable superiority. "Sir (said he), you are for making a monarchy of what should be a republic."

He was still more mortified, when talking in a company with fluent vivacity, and, as he flattered himself, to the admiration of all who were present; a German who sat next him, and perceived Johnson rolling himself as if about to speak, suddenly stopped him, saying, "Stay, stay — Toctor Shonson is going to say something." This was, no doubt, very provoking, especially to one so irritable as Goldsmith, who frequently mentioned it with strong expressions of indignation.

It may also be observed that Goldsmith was sometimes content to be treated with an easy familiarity, but upon occasions would be consequential and important. An instance of this occurred in a small particular. Johnson had a way of contracting the names of his friends: as Beauclerk, Beau; Boswell, Bozzy; Langton, Lanky; Murphy, Mur; Sheridan, Sherry. I remember one day, when Tom Davies was telling that Dr. Johnson said, "We are all in labor for a name to Goldy's play," Goldsmith seemed displeased that such a liberty should be taken with his name, and said, "I have often desired him not to call me Goldy." Tom was remarkably attentive to the most minute circumstance about Johnson. I recollect his telling me once, on my arrival in London, "Sir, our great friend has made an improvement on his appellation of old Mr. Sheridan. He calls him now Sherry derry."

Boswell's London Journal, 1762 – 1763

Boswell's journal, secreted or neglected by the Boswell family over the centuries, finally found its way to Yale University in 1949, and a year later the first of many projected volumes was published. Its detailed account of the life of a gallant young eighteenth-century man-about-town — alternately naïve and sophisticated, fun-loving and earnest — delighted contemporary readers. Boswell's journal became a literary sensation and a best seller.

The journal throws further light not only upon Boswell himself, but also upon his unusual friendship with Johnson. The following selections show how Boswell sought Johnson's advice in the affairs of his private life and the kindly spirit in which Johnson replied. The first entry here quoted also illustrates Boswell's habit of jotting down unconnected sentences he remembered from conversations with his friend.

Saturday 25 June [1763] . . . I told him all my story. "Sir," said he, "your father has been wanting to make the man of you at twenty which you will be at thirty. Sir, let me tell you that to be a Scotch landlord,[1] where you have a number of families dependent upon and attached to you, is perhaps as high a situation as humanity can arrive at. A merchant upon 'Change with a hundred thousand pounds is nothing. The Duke of Bedford with all his immense fortune is but a little man in reality. He has no tenants who consider themselves as under his patriarchal care.

"Sir, a father and a son should part at a certain time of life. I never believed what my father said. I always thought that he spoke ex officio,[2] as a priest does.

[1] Boswell's father was Laird of Auchinleck (ô'kĭn·lĕk'), a Scotch landowner and jurist. Boswell, the eldest son, was due to inherit his father's lands and responsibilities. [2] *ex officio* (ĕks ŏ·fĭsh'ĭ·ō): because of his office (here as a father).

"Sir, I am a friend to subordination. It is most conducive to the happiness of society. There is a reciprocal pleasure in governing and being governed.

"Sir, I think your breaking off idle connections by going abroad is a matter of importance. I would go where there are courts and learned men."

I then complained to him how little I knew, and mentioned study. "Sir," said he, "don't talk of study just now. I will put you upon a plan. It will require some time to talk of that." I put out my hand. "Will you really take a charge of me? It is very good in you, Mr. Johnson, to allow me to sit with you thus. Had I but thought some years ago that I should pass an evening with the Author of *The Rambler!*" These expressions were all from the heart, and he perceived that they were; and he was very complacent and said, "Sir, I am glad we have met. I hope we shall pass many evenings and mornings too together."

Thursday 14 July. Mr. Johnson and I met at the Mitre by ourselves. He was in most excellent humor, though the night was very rainy. I said it was good for the vegetable part of the creation. "Ay, Sir," said he, "and for the animals who eat those vegetables, and for the animals who eat those animals." We had a good supper, which made us very comfortable.

I said, "You and I, Sir, are very good companions, but my father and I are not so. Now what can occasion this? For you are as old a man as my father, and you are certainly as learned and as knowing." "Sir," said he, "I am a man of the world. I live in the world, and I take in some measure the color of the world as it moves along. But your father is a judge in a remote part of the country, and all his notions are taken

From *Boswell's London Journal, 1762–1763,* edited by Frederick A. Pottle. Published by McGraw-Hill Book Company. Copyright, 1950, by Yale University.

from the old world. Besides, there must always be a struggle between a father and son, while the one aims at power and the other at independency." I told him that I was afraid of my father's forcing me to be a lawyer. "Why, Sir," said he, "you need not be afraid of his forcing you to be a laborious practicing lawyer. That is not in his power. For, as the proverb says, 'One man may lead a horse to the water, but twenty cannot make him drink.' He may be displeased, but it will not go far. If he only insists on your having as much law as is necessary for a man of property, and endeavors to get you into Parliament, he is quite in the right."

Saturday 16 July . . . He advised me to keep a journal of my life, fair and undisguised. He said it would be a very good exercise, and would yield me infinite satisfaction when the ideas were faded from my remembrance. I told him that I had done so ever since I left Scotland. He said he was very happy that I pursued so good a plan. And now, O my journal! art thou not highly dignified? Shalt thou not flourish tenfold? No former solicitations or censures could tempt me to lay thee aside; and now is there any argument which can outweigh the sanction of Mr. Samuel Johnson? He said indeed that I should keep it private, and that I might surely have a friend who would burn it in case of my death. For my own part, I have at present such an affection for this my journal that it shocks me to think of burning it. I rather encourage the idea of having it carefully laid up among the archives of Auchinleck. However, I cannot judge fairly of it now. Some years hence I may. I told Mr. Johnson that I put down all sorts of little incidents in it. "Sir," said he, "there is nothing too little for so little a creature as man. It is by studying little things that we attain the great knowledge of having as little misery and as much happiness as possible."

Six lively volumes of "The Private Papers of James Boswell" have resulted from the long-hidden manuscript of Boswell's journal. They are:

Boswell's London Journal, 1762–1763
Boswell in Holland, 1763–1764
Boswell on the Grand Tour: Germany and Switzerland, 1764
Boswell on the Grand Tour: Italy, Corsica, and France, 1765–1766
Boswell in Search of a Wife, 1766–1769
Boswell for the Defense, 1769–1774

A UNIQUE LITERARY PAIR

1. What light is thrown on Johnson's character by his conduct toward Lord Chesterfield?

2. Compare with others your impressions of Johnson's personality and attitude toward people. Is your impression favorable or unfavorable? Why was he so much admired in spite of his peculiarities?

3. Contrast Johnson and Goldsmith. Which of the two appeals to you more? Do you think Boswell gives an objective picture of Goldsmith? Why or why not?

4. Boswell submerged himself in the personality of Dr. Johnson, a man thirty years older than he was. Does he seem to you to be impartial or partial as a biographer? Why? Specifically, what do you notice in his biography that you do not find in most biographies?

5. On what basis did Johnson gain such great influence over his age? How does he typify the eighteenth century? Do we have literary dictators today? What do literary dictators have in common with political dictators?

6. How would you describe the friendship of Boswell and Johnson as it is shown in Boswell's journal? What was Johnson's attitude toward Boswell? Was there mutual admiration and respect between these men?

CLASS ACTIVITIES

1. Write and enact a short play or dramatized conversation of the Literary Club for presentation before the class.

2. Plan brief oral reports on the following members of the Literary Club: Sir Joshua Reynolds, David Garrick, Edmund Burke, Oliver Goldsmith.

LITERATURE AND THE ARTS

The renown of Dr. Samuel Johnson, ensured in print by his enthusiastic young friend Boswell, is also perpetuated by the two engravings opposite. At the top of the page, Dr. Johnson waits to see Lord Chesterfield with the hope of obtaining his patronage. Johnson's famous letter to Lord Chesterfield (page 321) relates the outcome of his petition. The second engraving shows a gathering of Johnson and some of the most distinguished figures of the day. Seated around the table, from left to right, are Boswell, Johnson, Sir Joshua Reynolds, David Garrick, Edmund Burke, General Pasquale de Paoli, Dr. Charles Burney, Sr., the Rev. Thomas Warton, and Oliver Goldsmith.

BEHIND THE SCENES IN ENGLISH LITERATURE

Boswell's *Life of Johnson,* considered a masterpiece from the moment of publication, did nothing to diminish its author's reputation as something of a fool. Playing down his own role to enhance that of his hero, Boswell often deliberately showed himself at a disadvantage. Perhaps, however, he was not quite as foolish as he made himself out to be.

In the *Life* Boswell mentions his "archives," so from the beginning scholars assumed they must contain material not used in the *Life* that might prove highly interesting. Boswell's will, though, directed that the "archives" be kept in the family. Though his literary executors were instructed to publish as they thought best, they published nothing whatsoever, and when later scholars tried to investigate, Boswell's Victorian descendants refused access to the papers and failed to deny a story that they had been destroyed. So the matter rested for over a century.

In the 1920's, Professor Chauncey B. Tinker of Yale, in bringing out the first edition of all the private Boswell letters available, revealed that there was more than one side to Boswell's personality. In addition to the familiar vices, there was deep remorse, noble resolution, and a profound and earnest introspection. Clearly, Boswell seemed worth studying for his own sake.

Acting on an anonymous tip, Professor Tinker visited at Malahide Castle, near Dublin, Boswell's great-great grandson, Lord Talbot, to whom Boswell's possessions had passed after the death of his Scottish relatives. To his amazed delight, Tinker was shown a wealth of unpublished material on Johnson, Boswell, and others of their circle. The "archives" still existed; Tinker, however, was unable to make arrangements to study them.

Then, after much persuasion, Lt. Col. Ralph H. Isham, a New York financier and ardent Johnsonian, induced Talbot to part with his treasure. From these papers — many letters and, above all, an intimate diary revealing with utmost candor the complexities of his inner life — we can know Boswell as few historical or literary figures can be known. Still the buffoon, he is also a gifted reporter and psychological observer.

Talbot's collection, however, contained neither the manuscript of the *Life* itself, letters from Johnson or others of his circle, nor that part of the journal covering Boswell's early acquaintance with Johnson. Prematurely, scholars resigned themselves to these losses.

Then, in 1930, someone at Malahide Castle found an old croquet box in which were still more Boswell papers, plus the uncensored manuscript of the well-known *Journal of a Tour to the Hebrides.* Also in 1930, a British scholar visiting Fettercairn House in Scotland chanced upon masses of unsorted papers and — the

missing portion of Boswell's diary.

Finally, during the last war, when all facilities for storing grain were needed, an old barn at Malahide was pressed into service. When cleared out, the barn loft yielded a further collection of papers, including nearly 3,000 letters and, at long last, the manuscript of the *Life* itself, which in revealing Boswell's methods of working up his quickly jotted notes, shows that the biographer was a discerning and sophisticated artist.

All these discoveries were acquired by Colonel Isham, and in 1949 the entire Boswell collection was presented to Yale University. Altogether, it is said, there is enough material to keep fifty scholars busy for fifty years.

OLIVER GOLDSMITH

1728-1774

National Portrait Gallery

Johnson's friend "Goldy" was an irresponsible, lovable, witty Irishman whose life presents a combination of pathos and absurdity. His boyhood in the little Irish village of Lissoy is accurately pictured in *The Deserted Village*. At school the awkward, pock-marked boy was regarded as a dunce; and at Trinity College, Dublin, he came out at the foot of his class. Money given him by relatives so that he could study law or emigrate to America he lost in gambling. For a time he studied medicine at Edinburgh and later on the Continent. Returning to England, he tried acting, working in a chemist's shop, teaching in a boys' school, and even begging, before finally taking up literature.

Here at last he found something he could do superbly. Goldsmith has the unique distinction among eighteenth-century writers of having produced a poem (*The Deserted Village*), a comedy (*She Stoops to Conquer*), and a novel (*The Vicar of Wakefield*) that are still read and enjoyed today. The story goes that when Goldsmith was about to be imprisoned for not paying his rent, Johnson rescued him by selling the manuscript of *The Vicar of Wakefield* to a bookseller for sixty pounds.

Goldsmith made a better income from his hack writing than from his literary work. He turned out textbooks of history with astounding rapidity and inaccuracy. Some of the statements in his *Animated Nature* justify the remark made by one of his friends that he didn't know one fowl from another until it appeared cooked on the table.

With greater prosperity, Goldsmith spent most of his time with the members of the famous Literary Club. There he was usually the butt of the jokes. On one occasion when he was late as usual, they all wrote epitaphs on him. Garrick's ran thus:
"Here lies Nolly Goldsmith, for shortness called 'Noll,'
Who wrote like an angel and talked like poor Poll."

Nevertheless, Goldsmith had a certain sly wit in conversation, too. Once when he and Johnson were looking at the tombs in Westminster Abbey, Johnson quoted a Latin sentence that meant, "Perhaps our names also will be mingled with these." On the way home they passed Temple Bar, where heads of criminals used to be exposed. Goldsmith thereupon repeated in Latin with different emphasis: "Perhaps our names also will be mingled with *these.*" Fortunately it was the first rather than the second prophecy that came true. Johnson wrote the inscription for the memorial to Goldsmith in the Abbey: "He touched nothing that he did not adorn."

The Deserted Village

Three well-known poems of the eighteenth century portray the life of the common people — *The Deserted Village,* Thomas Gray's "Elegy Written in a Country Churchyard," and Robert Burns' "The Cotter's Saturday Night." Curiously enough, each represents a different country of the British Isles. Gray depicts England, Burns Scotland, while Goldsmith writes of Auburn, a fictitious name for an Irish village, probably similar to Lissoy. In contrast to the strict and sophisticated writing of Pope and Johnson, all three of these poems express the growing interest in the middle and late eighteenth century in rural settings and humble lives. The style of Goldsmith's poem is not markedly different from that of earlier eighteenth-century writers, but the subject matter and sentiment of *The Deserted Village* point forward to the Romantic movement.

The last part of the poem, a prolonged lamentation over the woes of the peasants, has been omitted here.

Sweet Auburn! loveliest village of the plain,
Where health and plenty cheered the laboring swain,
Where smiling spring its earliest visit paid,
And parting summer's lingering blooms delayed;
Dear lovely bowers of innocence and ease,   5
Seats of my youth, when every sport could please,
How often have I loitered o'er thy green,°
Where humble happiness endeared each scene!
How often have I paused on every charm,
The sheltered cot,° the cultivated farm,   10
The never-failing brook, the busy mill,
The decent church that topped the neighboring hill,
The hawthorn bush, with seats beneath the shade
For talking age and whispering lovers made!
How often have I blest the coming day,   15
When toil remitting lent its turn to play,
And all the village train, from labor free,
Led up their sports beneath the spreading tree,
While many a pastime circled in the shade,
The young contending as the old surveyed;   20

7. *green:* an open lawn in the middle of a village, a center for recreation. 10. *cot:* cottage.

And many a gambol frolicked o'er the ground,
And sleights of art° and feats of strength went round.
And still, as each repeated pleasure tired,
Succeeding sports the mirthful band inspired;
The dancing pair that simply sought renown   25
By holding out to tire each other down;
The swain mistrustless° of his smutted face,
While secret laughter tittered round the place;
The bashful virgin's sidelong looks of love,
The matron's glance that would those looks reprove.   30
These were thy charms, sweet village! sports like these,
With sweet succession, taught even toil to please;
These round thy bowers their cheerful influence shed;
These were thy charms — but all these charms are fled.

Sweet smiling village, loveliest of the lawn,   35
Thy sports are fled, and all thy charms withdrawn;
Amidst thy bowers the tyrant's hand is seen,
And desolation saddens all thy green;
One only master grasps the whole domain,°
And half a tillage stints thy smiling plain.   40
No more thy glassy brook reflects the day,
But, choked with sedges, works its weedy way;
Along the glades, a solitary guest,
The hollow sounding bittern guards its nest;
Amidst thy desert walks the lapwing flies,   45
And tires their echoes with unvaried cries.
Sunk are thy bowers in shapeless ruin all,
And the long grass o'ertops the moldering wall;
And trembling, shrinking from the spoiler's hand,
Far, far away thy children leave the land.   50

Ill fares the land, to hastening ills a prey,
Where wealth accumulates, and men decay.
Princes and lords may flourish, or may fade;
A breath can make them, as a breath has made;
But a bold peasantry, their country's pride,   55
When once destroyed, can never be supplied.

22. *sleights of art:* skillful turns. We still use the word in *sleight of hand.* 27. *mistrustless:* unaware.
39. This line refers to the process known as "enclosure," whereby the common grazing lands of
villages were taken over by wealthy landowners.

A time there was, ere England's griefs began,
When every rood° of ground maintained its man;
For him light labor spread her wholesome store,
Just gave what life required, but gave no more;   60
His best companions, innocence and health;
And his best riches, ignorance of wealth.

But times are altered; trade's unfeeling train
Usurp the land and dispossess the swain;°
Along the lawn, where scattered hamlets rose,   65
Unwieldy wealth and cumbrous pomp repose,
And every want to opulence allied,
And every pang that folly pays to pride.
These gentle hours that plenty bade to bloom,
Those calm desires that asked but little room,   70
Those healthful sports that graced the peaceful scene,
Lived in each look, and brightened all the green;
These, far departing, seek a kinder shore,
And rural mirth and manners are no more.

Sweet Auburn! parent of the blissful hour,   75
Thy glades forlorn confess the tyrant's power.
Here, as I take my solitary rounds
Amidst thy tangling walks and ruined grounds,
And, many a year elapsed, return to view
Where once the cottage stood, the hawthorn grew,   80
Remembrance wakes with all her busy train,
Swells at my breast, and turns the past to pain.

In all my wanderings round this world of care,
In all my griefs — and God has given my share —
I still had hopes, my latest° hours to crown,   85
Amidst these humble bowers to lay me down;
To husband out life's taper at the close,
And keep the flame from wasting by repose;
I still had hopes, for pride attends us still,
Amidst the swains to show my book-learned skill,   90
Around my fire an evening group to draw,
And tell of all I felt, and all I saw;
And, as a hare whom hounds and horns pursue
Pants to the place from whence at first she flew,
I still had hopes, my long vexations past,   95
Here to return — and die at home at last.

O blest retirement, friend to life's decline,
Retreats from care, that never must be mine,
How happy he who crowns in shades like these
A youth of labor with an age of ease;   100
Who quits a world where strong temptations try,

58. *rood:* one-fourth of an acre. 63–64. *trade's . . . swain:* a reference to the effects of the Industrial
Revolution on village life. 85. *latest:* last.

And, since 'tis hard to combat, learns to fly!
For him no wretches, born to work and weep,
Explore the mine, or tempt the dangerous deep;
No surly porter stands in guilty state,   105
To spurn imploring famine from the gate;
But on he moves to meet his latter end,
Angels around befriending virtue's friend;
Bends to the grave with unperceived decay,
While resignation gently slopes the way;   110
And, all his prospects brightening to the last,
His heaven commences ere the world be past!

   Sweet was the sound, when oft at evening's close
Up yonder hill the village murmur rose;
There, as I passed with careless steps and slow,   115
The mingling notes came softened from below;
The swain responsive as the milkmaid sung,
The sober herd that lowed to meet their young,
The noisy geese that gabbled o'er the pool,
The playful children just let loose from school,   120
The watchdog's voice that bayed the whispering wind,
And the loud laugh that spoke the vacant mind —
These all in sweet confusion sought the shade,
And filled each pause the nightingale had made.
But now the sounds of population fail,   125
No cheerful murmurs fluctuate in the gale,
No busy steps the grass-grown footway tread,
For all the bloomy flush of life is fled.
All but yon widowed, solitary thing,
That feebly bends beside the plashy° spring;   130
She, wretched matron, forced in age, for bread,
To strip the brook with mantling cresses° spread,
To pick her wintry faggot from the thorn,
To seek her nightly shed, and weep till morn;
She only left of all the harmless train,   135
The sad historian of the pensive plain.

   Near yonder copse, where once the garden smiled,
And still where many a garden flower grows wild;
There, where a few torn shrubs the place disclose,
The village preacher's° modest mansion rose.   140
A man he was to all the country dear,
And passing rich with forty pounds a year;
Remote from towns he ran his godly race,
Nor e'er had changed, nor wished to change his place;
Unpracticed he to fawn, or seek for power,   145
By doctrines fashioned to the varying hour;

---

130. *plashy* (plăsh′ĭ): marshy. 132. *mantling cresses:* plants spreading over a surface. 140. *village preacher:* The following portrait is perhaps a composite portrait of Goldsmith's father and brother, both of whom were preachers.

Far other aims his heart had learned to prize,
More skilled to raise the wretched than to rise.
His house was known to all the vagrant train;
He chid their wanderings but relieved their pain.   150
The long-remembered beggar was his guest,
Whose beard descending swept his aged breast;
The ruined spendthrift, now no longer proud,
Claimed kindred there, and had his claims allowed;

   The broken soldier, kindly bade to stay,   155
Sat by the fire, and talked the night away,
Wept o'er his wounds or, tales of sorrow done,
Shouldered his crutch and showed how fields were won.
Pleased with his guests, the good man learned to glow,
And quite forgot their vices in their woe;   160
Careless their merits or their faults to scan,
His pity gave ere charity began.

   Thus to relieve the wretched was his pride,
And e'en his failings leaned to virtue's side;
But in his duty prompt at every call,   165
He watched and wept, he prayed and felt for all;
And, as a bird each fond endearment tries
To tempt its new-fledged offspring to the skies,
He tried each art, reproved each dull delay,
Allured to brighter worlds, and led the way.   170

   Beside the bed where parting life was laid,
And sorrow, guilt, and pain by turns dismayed,
The reverend champion stood. At his control
Despair and anguish fled the struggling soul;
Comfort came down the trembling wretch to raise,   175
And his last faltering accents whispered praise.

At church, with meek and unaffected grace,
His looks adorned the venerable place;
Truth from his lips prevailed with double sway,
And fools, who came to scoff, remained to pray.   180
The service past, around the pious man,
With steady zeal, each honest rustic ran;
Even children followed with endearing wile,
And plucked his gown to share the good man's smile.
His ready smile a parent's warmth expressed;   185
Their welfare pleased him, and their cares distressed;
To them his heart, his love, his griefs were given,
But all his serious thoughts had rest in heaven.
As some tall cliff that lifts its awful form,
Swells from the vale, and midway leaves the storm,   190
Though round its breast the rolling clouds are spread,
Eternal sunshine settles on its head.

Beside yon straggling fence that skirts the way,
With blossomed furze unprofitably gay,
There, in his noisy mansion, skilled to rule,   195
The village master° taught his little school.
A man severe he was, and stern to view;
I knew him well, and every truant knew;
Well had the boding tremblers learned to trace
The day's disasters in his morning face;   200
Full well they laughed with counterfeited glee
At all his jokes, for many a joke had he;
Full well the busy whisper circling round
Conveyed the dismal tidings when he frowned.
Yet he was kind, or, if severe in aught,   205
The love he bore to learning was in fault;
The village all declared how much he knew;
'Twas certain he could write, and cipher too;
Lands he could measure, terms and tides presage,°
And even the story ran that he could gauge;°   210
In arguing, too, the parson owned his skill,
For, even though vanquished, he could argue still;
While words of learned length and thundering sound
Amazed the gazing rustics ranged around;
And still they gazed, and still the wonder grew,   215
That one small head could carry all he knew.
But past is all his fame. The very spot
Where many a time he triumphed is forgot.

Near yonder thorn that lifts its head on high,
Where once the signpost caught the passing eye,   220

---

196. *The village master:* thought to be a portrait of Goldsmith's own schoolmaster. 209. *terms and tides presage:* figure out in advance the time for law sessions and church festivals, such as Easter. 210. *gauge:* measure the capacity of casks.

Low lies that house where nut-brown draughts° inspired,
Where graybeard mirth and smiling toil retired,
Where village statesmen talked with looks profound,
And news much older than their ale went round.
Imagination fondly stoops to trace   225
The parlor splendors of that festive place:
The whitewashed wall, the nicely sanded floor,
The varnished clock that clicked behind the door;
The chest contrived a double debt to pay,
A bed by night, a chest of drawers by day;   230
The pictures placed for ornament and use,
The twelve good rules,° the royal game of goose;°
The hearth, except when winter chilled the day,
With aspen boughs and flowers and fennel° gay;
While broken teacups, wisely kept for show,   235
Ranged o'er the chimney, glistened in a row.

    Vain transitory splendors! could not all
Reprieve the tottering mansion from its fall?
Obscure it sinks, nor shall it more impart
An hour's importance to the poor man's heart.   240
Thither no more the peasant shall repair
To sweet oblivion of his daily care;
No more the farmer's news, the barber's tale,
No more the woodman's ballad shall prevail;
No more the smith his dusky brow shall clear,   245
Relax his ponderous strength, and lean to hear;
The host himself no longer shall be found
Careful to see the mantling bliss° go round;
Nor the coy maid, half willing to be pressed,
Shall kiss the cup to pass it to the rest.   250

    Yes! let the rich deride, the proud disdain,
These simple blessings of the lowly train;
To me more dear, congenial to my heart,
One native charm, than all the gloss of art.
Spontaneous joys, where nature has its play,   255
The soul adopts, and owns their first-born sway;
Lightly they frolic o'er the vacant mind,
Unenvied, unmolested, unconfined.
But the long pomp, the midnight masquerade,
With all the freaks° of wanton wealth arrayed —   260
In these, ere trifles half their wish obtain,
The toiling pleasure sickens into pain;
And, even while fashion's brightest arts decoy,
The heart distrusting asks if this be joy.

---

221. *nut-brown draughts:* drinks of ale. 232. *twelve good rules:* brief rules such as "Reveal no secrets" and "Pick no quarrels" which were attributed to Charles I and often hung up in inns; *goose:* a game played with checkers and dice, somewhat like parchesi. 234. *fennel:* a garden herb. 248. *mantling bliss:* foaming ale. Compare with the use of *mantling* in line 132. 260. *freaks:* whims.

Elegy on the Death
of a Mad Dog

As a contrast to the melancholy note struck by the merry Oliver Goldsmith in *The Deserted Village,* here is a neat absurdity showing the poet in a lighter vein. You will find this quite different from other elegies you have read.

Good people all, of every sort,
  Give ear unto my song;
And if you find it wondrous short,
  It cannot hold you long.

In Islington there was a man   5
  Of whom the world might say
That still a godly race° he ran,
  Whene'er he went to pray.

A kind and gentle heart he had,
  To comfort friend and foes;   10
The naked every day he clad,
  When he put on his clothes.

And in that town a dog was found,
  As many dogs there be,
Both mongrel, puppy, whelp, and
    hound   15
  And cur of low degree.

This dog and man at first were friends;
  But when a pique began,
The dog to gain his private ends,
  Went mad and bit the man.   20

Around from all the neighboring streets
  The wondering people ran,

7. *godly race:* Compare with line 143 of *The Deserted Village.*

And swore the dog had lost his wits,
  To bite so good a man.

The wound it seemed both sore and sad
  To every Christian eye;   26
And while they swore the dog was mad,
  They swore the man would die.

But soon a wonder came to light,
  That showed the rogues they lied;   30
The man recovered of the bite;
  The dog it was that died.

INFERRING CHARACTER
AND SETTING

1. How does Goldsmith idealize plain country folk? How realistic is his picture, do you think? What passages express an attitude toward people of humble position different from that of the early eighteenth century? Point out specific passages which show that Goldsmith also had characteristics of the classical school of Pope.

2. How do subject matter and sentiment in the poem point to the Romantic movement?

3. Which scenes and persons in *The Deserted Village* stand out in your mind most vividly? Compare the pictures of the parson and schoolmaster with those of some of Chaucer's characters. Which author's descriptions seem more realistic? Which do you prefer?

4. What kind of sentiment do you usually find expressed in an elegy? How does Goldsmith's "Elegy on the Death of a Mad Dog" differ from those with which you are familiar?

CLASS ACTIVITIES

1. Read the complete version of *The Deserted Village* and sum up — in a panel discussion — Goldsmith's opinions on Irish farm conditions, on the value of farmers to a nation and to city life, on Irish immigration, and on living conditions in America. Evaluate his opinions in the light of subsequent history.

2. Goldsmith's lively play *She Stoops to Conquer* contains some good scenes for class dramatization.

3. Compare the vicar in *The Vicar of Wakefield* with the parson in *The Deserted Village.* Which seems more credible to you?

Forerunners of the Romantic Age

THOMAS GRAY

1716–1771

National Portrait Gallery

In his day Thomas Gray was recognized as the foremost English poet; he was offered (but declined to accept) the position of poet laureate. Today he is remembered chiefly as the author of one of the best-known poems in the English language, "Elegy Written in a Country Churchyard."

By keeping a shop, Gray's mother earned enough money to send her son to fashionable Eton and later to Cambridge, where he steeped himself in classical literature. With his former schoolmate Horace Walpole, Gray spent three years on a tour of the Continent. It was an adventurous experience, and both he and Walpole left a vivid record of it in letters. Thereafter, Gray, who never married, lived the quiet life of a Cambridge professor. He was an enthusiastic student of Anglo-Saxon and Welsh folklore, and in this respect foreshadowed the great interest that the nineteenth-century Romantic poets took in old English and Scottish ballads. Gray's poems are few in number but were painstakingly composed and polished. His "Elegy Written in a Country Churchyard" was nine years in the writing.

Gray represents the transition from classical to romantic literature in England — from the strictly patterned verse and sophisticated ideas of Pope and Johnson to the simpler, freer verse forms and the depiction of nature and common life found in later Romantic poets like Wordsworth. His verse form is only slightly varied from Pope's, but his poetry reveals a romantic spirit in its personal tone and in its emotional expressions on nature and death. Dr. Johnson thought Gray a dull poet, but General Wolfe, who won Quebec from the French in 1763, said of the "Elegy Written in a Country Churchyard" before entering the great battle: "I would rather be the author of those lines than take Quebec."

Elegy Written in a Country Churchyard

The curfew tolls the knell of parting day,
    The lowing herd wind slowly o'er the lea,
The plowman homeward plods his weary way,
    And leaves the world to darkness and to me.

Now fades the glimmering landscape on the sight,   5
    And all the air a solemn stillness holds,

Save where the beetle wheels his droning flight,
  And drowsy tinklings lull the distant folds;

Save that from yonder ivy-mantled tower
  The moping owl does to the moon complain   10
Of such, as wandering near her secret bower,
  Molest her ancient solitary reign.

Beneath those rugged elms, that yew tree's shade,
  Where heaves the turf in many a moldering heap,
Each in his narrow cell forever laid,   15
  The rude forefathers of the hamlet sleep.

The breezy call of incense-breathing morn,
  The swallow twittering from the straw-built shed,
The cock's shrill clarion, or the echoing horn,°
  No more shall rouse them from their lowly bed.   20

For them no more the blazing hearth shall burn,
  Or busy housewife ply her evening care:
No children run to lisp their sire's return,
  Or climb his knee the envied kiss to share.

Oft did the harvest to their sickle yield,   25
  Their furrow oft the stubborn glebe° has broke;
How jocund did they drive their team afield!
  How bowed the woods beneath their sturdy stroke!

Let not ambition mock their useful toil,
  Their homely joys, and destiny obscure;   30
Nor grandeur hear with a disdainful smile,
  The short and simple annals of the poor.

The boast of heraldry,° the pomp of power,
  And all that beauty, all that wealth e'er gave,
Awaits alike the inevitable hour.   35
  The paths of glory lead but to the grave.

Nor you, ye proud, impute to these the fault,
  If memory o'er their tomb no trophies raise,
Where through the long-drawn aisle and fretted vault°
  The pealing anthem swells the note of praise.   40

19. *horn:* the horn of a hunter. 26. *glebe:* ground. 33. *The boast of heraldry:* Heraldry is the study of family coats of arms; hence, this phrase refers to the pride of having a great family. 39. *fretted vault:* church roof ornamented by elaborate design.

The photograph opposite was taken in the churchyard at Stoke Poges, a small village ▶ in Buckinghamshire. Here, in 1742, after the death of a dear friend, Thomas Gray is supposed to have written his famous "Elegy." Members of Gray's family lived in Stoke Poges, and Gray and his mother were buried here.

Can storied urn° or animated° bust
    Back to its mansion call the fleeting breath?
Can honor's voice provoke° the silent dust,
    Or flatt'ry soothe the dull cold ear of Death?

Perhaps in this neglected spot is laid   45
    Some heart once pregnant with celestial fire;
Hands, that the rod of empire might have swayed,
    Or waked to ecstasy the living lyre.

But knowledge to their eyes her ample page
    Rich with the spoils of time did ne'er unroll;   50
Chill penury repressed their noble rage,
    And froze the genial° current of the soul.

Full many a gem of purest ray serene,
    The dark unfathomed caves of ocean bear;
Full many a flower is born to blush unseen,   55
    And waste its sweetness on the desert air.

Some village Hampden° that with dauntless breast
    The little tyrant of his fields withstood,
Some mute inglorious Milton here may rest,
    Some Cromwell guiltless of his country's blood.   60

The applause of listening senates to command,
    The threats of pain and ruin to despise,
To scatter plenty o'er a smiling land,
    And read their history in a nation's eyes,°

Their lot forbade: nor circumscribed alone   65
    Their growing virtues, but their crimes confined;
Forbade to wade through slaughter to a throne,
    And shut the gates of mercy on mankind,

The struggling pangs of conscious truth to hide,
    To quench the blushes of ingenuous shame,   70
Or heap the shrine of luxury and pride
    With incense kindled at the Muse's flame.

Far from the madding° crowd's ignoble strife,
    Their sober wishes never learned to stray;
Along the cool sequestered vale of life   75
    They kept the noiseless tenor° of their way.

---

41. *storied urn:* an urn inscribed with pictures that tell the story of the deceased; *animated:* lifelike. 43. *provoke:* arouse. 52. *genial:* warm or living. 57. *Hampden:* a landowner who resisted one of the tax assessments of Charles I and thus made the matter of unjust taxes a public issue. 61–64. This whole stanza is the object of *forbade* in the first line of the next stanza. 73. *madding:* wild, furious. 76. *tenor* (tĕn'ēr): even course.

Yet ev'n these bones from insult to protect,
    Some frail memorial still erected nigh,
With uncouth rhymes and shapeless sculpture decked,
    Implores the passing tribute of a sigh.   80

Their name, their years, spelt by the unlettered Muse,
    The place of fame and elegy supply;
And many a holy text around she strews,
    That teach the rustic moralist to die.

For who to dumb forgetfulness a prey,   85
    This pleasing anxious being e'er resigned,
Left the warm precincts of the cheerful day,
    Nor cast one longing lingering look behind?

On some fond breast the parting soul relies,
    Some pious drops the closing eye requires;   90
Ev'n from the tomb the voice of nature cries,
    Ev'n in our ashes live their wonted fires.

For thee,° who mindful of the unhonored dead
    Dost in these lines their artless tale relate;
If chance, by lonely contemplation led,   95
    Some kindred spirit shall inquire thy fate,

Haply some hoary-headed swain may say,
    "Oft have we seen him at the peep of dawn
Brushing with hasty steps the dews away,
    To meet the sun upon the upland lawn.   100

"There at the foot of yonder nodding beech
    That wreathes its old fantastic roots so high,
His listless length at noontide would he stretch,
    And pore upon the brook that babbles by.

"Hard by yon wood, now smiling as in scorn,   105
    Muttering his wayward fancies he would rove,
Now drooping, woeful wan, like one forlorn,
    Or crazed with care, or crossed in hopeless love.

"One morn I missed him on the customed hill,
    Along the heath and near his favorite tree,   110
Another came; nor yet beside the rill,
    Nor up the lawn, nor at the wood was he;

"The next, with dirges due in sad array
    Slow through the church-way path we saw him borne.
Approach and read (for thou canst read)° the lay,   115
    Graved on the stone beneath yon aged thorn."°

  93. *thee:* Gray himself. 115. *thou canst read:* In the eighteenth century, a large proportion of the country people were unable to read. 116. *thorn:* hawthorn.

THE EPITAPH

Here rests his head upon the lap of earth
A youth to fortune and to fame unknown.
Fair science frowned not on his humble birth,°
And melancholy marked him for her own.   120

Large was his bounty, and his soul sincere,
Heaven did a recompense as largely send;
He gave to misery all he had, a tear;
He gained from Heaven ('twas all he wished) a friend.

No farther seek his merits to disclose,   125
Or draw his frailties from their dread abode,
(There they alike in trembling hope repose)
The bosom of his Father and his God.

119. His humble birth had not prevented his having a good education.

GRAY'S "ELEGY"

1. The "Elegy" falls into clear-cut divisions of thought. What stanzas would you include in each of these three beginning divisions: (a) the setting, (b) the imagined life of the villagers, (c) death, the common end of all classes, rich and poor? The remainder of the poem can be divided into four sections. How would you divide the stanzas and what descriptions would you give to each division?

2. With what details does Gray represent happiness in the life of the country folk?

3. Line 47 suggests a possible statesman or ruler. What other hidden potentialities in the lives of the common people does Gray suggest? Why were these potentialities not fulfilled?

4. What picture of himself does Gray paint from line 98 on? Does it correspond with what you know of Gray's life?

5. How does Gray's verse form — rhyme scheme and stanza division — differ from that of Pope? What elements of the new, romantic trend in literature do you find in this poem?

RECOGNIZING MOOD

Words which suggest pictures usually set the mood of a piece of writing. If you were a painter, how many pictures could you paint by using the first seven stanzas of Gray's elegy as your subject matter?

The first three stanzas of this poem are introductory. What mood is set in these lines? What do you see? Analyze how Gray puts the reader in a particular mood by the use of carefully chosen details. What effect does he create with the words *tolls, plods, fades,* and *lull.* Find a few short phrases which also suggest mood. Now choose three adjectives of your own to describe the kind of mood set by the first three stanzas.

Recall how Milton achieves mood in "L'Allegro" and "Il Penseroso." Which poem by Milton is similar in mood to Gray's? Compare.

THE POWER OF WORDS

WORDS EASILY CONFUSED

In line 70 Gray uses the word *ingenuous* (ĭn·jĕn'u·ŭs), which is easily confused with *ingenious* (ĭn·jēn'yŭs). An ingenuous person may be one of high character, noble and honest. The word is also used to suggest candor, frankness, and naïveté. Which quality does Gray probably have in mind when he says that the villagers' humble lot kept them from quenching "the blushes of ingenuous shame"? How would you rephrase this line?

How does *ingenuous* differ from *ingenious?* List several fictitious or actual characters you have encountered in this book that you would consider ingenuous and several that were ingenious.

ROBERT
BURNS
1759–1796

British Information

Burns might be called the national poet of Scotland. Among the many writers that that country has produced, no name sets afire the loyalty and pride of Scots as "Bobbie Burns" does. Their own idiom of speech is made musical in his lyrics. The hard lives and poverty of some of their people is glorified through the laurels won by a peasant boy. Their essentially independent spirit is proclaimed to the world in the ringing lines of "A man's a man for a' that."

Burns was born in a two-room clay cottage built by his father near Ayr in southwestern Scotland. Poverty pursued the family from one stony farm to another. The father gave his sons the best education available to peasants, but it was meager. Robert supplemented his schooling by ardently reading the Bible, *The Spectator,* Pope's poems, and a book of lyrics that first inspired him to write songs. His mother taught him old Scottish songs and stories, and he spent spare hours reading Scottish and English literature.

As the plowboy developed into a lively, handsome young man, he was often in scrapes resulting from too much drinking, satires on ministers, and numerous romances. Finally, the father of his sweetheart, Jean Armour, made life so miserable for him that he decided to sail for Jamaica.

To raise money for his passage he published his first volume, *Poems: Chiefly in Scottish Dialect,* in 1786. It won immediate success. Instead of going to Jamaica, Burns went to Edinburgh in triumph. Edinburgh society lionized him, but after a time turned away from the young poet because he remained an earthy peasant — friendly, genial, but not given to polite ways. Back he went to the farm, married Jean Armour, and wrote some of his finest poetry. He served as tax collector to add to his meager income, a job he nearly lost because of his sympathy for the French Revolution. His health, never strong because of his poor childhood, weakened. He increasingly took to drink; and poverty, as always, plagued him and his family. Burns died at the early age of thirty-seven.

No sooner had he breathed his last than the whole country united to honor him. Ten thousand persons are said to have followed him to his grave at Dumfries. Contributions poured in for his destitute family. Two handsome marble monuments were eventually erected, one at Dumfries and the other at Ayr, not far from the banks of the bonnie Doon. But cold marble is a poor memorial for warmhearted, impulsive, generous Robert Burns. His real monument is his poetry, which keeps ever alive his best self.

347

Songs

Scotland gave to English literature a great song writer in Robert
Burns. No one else has combined quite the same lilting melody and
warm human emotion. In the following songs he sings of exuberance, sorrow, faithful affection, patriotism, and sturdy independence.
Some are sung in his own person; some are dramatically put into
the mouths of imaginary or historical characters; in others, the poet
makes shrewd observations on his fellow humans. Many of them
were set to old Scotch airs already in existence; some have since been
set to music.

Sweet Afton

Flow gently, sweet Afton! among thy green braes,°
Flow gently, I'll sing thee a song in thy praise;
My Mary's asleep by thy murmuring stream,
Flow gently, sweet Afton, disturb not her dream.

Thou stock dove whose echo resounds through the glen,   5
Ye wild whistling blackbirds in yon thorny den,
Thou green-crested lapwing, thy screaming forbear,
I charge you, disturb not my slumbering Fair.

How lofty, sweet Afton, thy neighboring hills,
Far marked with the courses of clear, winding rills;   10
There daily I wander as noon rises high,
My flocks and my Mary's sweet cot in my eye.

How pleasant thy banks and green valleys below,
Where, wild in the woodlands, the primroses blow;
There oft, as mild ev'ning weeps over the lea,   15
The sweet-scented birk° shades my Mary and me.

Thy crystal stream, Afton, how lovely it glides,
And winds by the cot where my Mary resides;
How wanton thy waters her snowy feet lave,
As, gathering sweet flowerets, she stems thy clear wave.   20

Flow gently, sweet Afton, among thy green braes,
Flow gently, sweet river, the theme of my lays;
My Mary's asleep by thy murmuring stream,
Flow gently, sweet Afton, disturb not her dream.

1. *braes* (brāz): hillsides. 16. *birk:* birch.

The Banks o' Doon

Ye flowery banks o' bonnie Doon,
  How can ye blume sae fair!
How can ye chant, ye little birds,
  And I sae fu' o' care!

Thou'lt break my heart, thou bonnie
    bird,   5
  That sings upon the bough;
Thou minds me o' the happy days,
  When my fause° luve was true.

Thou'lt break my heart, thou bonnie
    bird,
  That sings beside thy mate;   10
For sae I sat, and sae I sang,
  And wist na° o' my fate.

Aft hae I roved by bonnie Doon
  To see the woodbine twine,
And ilka° bird sang o' its luve,   15
  And sae did I o' mine.

Wi' lightsome heart I pu'd° a rose,
  Frae aff its thorny tree;
And my fause luver staw° my rose
  But left the thorn wi' me.   20

8. *fause:* false. 12. *wist na:* knew not. 15. *ilka:*
every. 17. *pu'd:* pulled. 19. *staw:* stole.

John Anderson My Jo

John Anderson my jo,° John,
  When we were first acquent,°
Your locks were like the raven,
  Your bonnie brow was brent;°
But now your brow is beld,° John,   5
  Your locks are like the snaw;
But blessings on your frosty pow,°
  John Anderson my jo.

John Anderson my jo, John,
  We clamb the hill thegither;   10
And mony a canty° day, John,
  We've had wi' ane anither.
Now we maun° totter down, John,
  And hand in hand we'll go,
And sleep thegither at the foot,   15
  John Anderson my jo.

1. *jo:* joy, sweetheart. 2. *acquent:* acquainted.
4. *brent:* smooth. 5. *beld:* bald. 7. *pow:* head.
11. *canty:* cheerful. 13. *maun:* must.

Bannockburn

Robert the Bruce carried on the work begun by Wallace of freeing Scotland from
English domination in the days of Edward I. The battle of Bannockburn (băn'-
ŭk·bûrn), fought in 1314 in central Scotland, was a critical engagement. The English far outnumbered the Scots; but Bruce,
by digging pits in the plain and covering
them with leaves, caused the English cavalry to be overcome by panic, and thus won
the day. The occasion is looked on by
Scots as one of the great milestones in their
history. This poem is supposed to be Bruce's
address to his army before the battle.
Through the Scottish leader, Burns voices
a characteristic desire for freedom. It is
said that he composed the poem while galloping over a moor in a thunderstorm.

Scots, wha hae° wi' Wallace bled,
Scots, wham Bruce has aften led;
Welcome to your gory bed,
  Or to victory!

Now's the day, and now's the hour;   5
See the front o' battle lour;°
See approach proud Edward's power —
  Chains and slavery!

Wha will be a traitor knave?
Wha can fill a coward's grave?   10
Wha sae base as be a slave?
  Let him turn and flee!

Wha for Scotland's king and law
Freedom's sword will strongly draw,
Freeman stand, or Freeman fa',   15
  Let him follow me!

By oppression's woes and pains!
By your sons in servile chains!
We will drain our dearest veins,
  But they shall be free!   20

Lay the proud usurpers low!
Tyrants fall in every foe!
Liberty's in every blow! —
  Let us do or die!°

1. *wha hae:* who have. 6. *lour:* lower, threaten.
24. *die:* Scottish pronunciation is dē.

A Man's a Man for A' That

Here speaks a prophetic voice for the coming acceptance of the brotherhood of man. As the first clear note of democracy, this poem is one of the most significant written in the eighteenth century.

Is there, for honest poverty,
    That hings his head, an' a' that?
The coward slave, we pass him by,
    We dare be poor for a' that!
        For a' that, an' a' that,   5
          Our toils obscure, an' a' that;
        The rank is but the guinea's stamp;°
        The man's the gowd° for a' that.

What tho' on hamely fare we dine,
    Wear hodden-gray,° an' a' that;   10
Gie fools their silks, and knaves their wine,
    A man's a man for a' that.
        For a' that, an' a' that,
          Their tinsel show, an' a' that;
        The honest man, though e'er sae poor,   15
        Is king o' men for a' that.

Ye see yon birkie,° ca'd a lord,
    Wha struts, an' stares, an' a' that;
Tho' hundreds worship at his word,
    He's but a coof° for a' that.   20
        For a' that, an' a' that,
          His riband, star,° an' a' that,
        The man o' independent mind,
        He looks and laughs at a' that.

A prince can mak' a belted knight,   25
    A marquis, duke, an' a' that;
But an honest man's aboon° his might,
    Guid faith he mauna fa' that!°
        For a' that, an' a' that,
          Their dignities, an' a' that,   30
        The pith o' sense, an' pride o' worth,
        Are higher rank than a' that.

7. *guinea's stamp:* mold for stamping out gold coins. 8. *gowd:* gold. 10. *hodden-gray:* coarse cloth. 17. *birkie:* fellow. 20. *coof:* fool. 22. *riband, star:* insignia of titles and honors. 27. *aboon:* above. 28. *he . . . that:* he can't make that.

Then let us pray that come it may,
    As come it will for a' that,
That sense and worth, o'er a' the earth,
    May bear the gree,° an' a' that.   36
        For a' that, an' a' that,
          It's coming yet, for a' that,
        That man to man, the warld o'er,
        Shall brothers be for a' that.   40

36. *bear the gree:* take the prize.

To a Mouse

ON TURNING HER UP IN HER NEST WITH THE PLOW, NOVEMBER, 1785

This and the following poem form an interesting pair in several respects: they have unusual meter, unconventional subjects, and frequently quoted lines. Their moods are in strong contrast: on the one hand, the despair of thwarted ambition is expressed; on the other, the rollicking humor of an irrepressible wag.

Wee, sleekit,° cowrin', tim'rous beastie,
O, what a panic's in thy breastie!
Thou need na start awa sae hasty
    Wi' bickering brattle!°
I wad be laith° to rin an' chase thee   5
    Wi' murd'rin pattle!°

I'm truly sorry man's dominion
Has broken nature's social union,
And justifies that ill opinion
    Which makes thee startle   10
At me, thy poor, earthborn companion,
    An' fellow mortal!

I doubt na, whyles,° but thou may thieve;
What then? poor beastie, thou maun live!
A daimen icker in a thrave°   15
    'S a sma' request;
I'll get a blessin' wi' the lave,°
    An' never miss 't!

1. *sleekit:* sleek. 4. *bickering brattle:* hasty scamper. 5. *laith* (lāth): loath, reluctant. 6. *pattle:* plowstaff. 13. *whyles:* at times. 15. *A daimen . . . thrave:* an occasional head of grain in a shock. 17. *lave:* rest.

Thy wee bit housie, too, in ruin!
It's silly wa's° the win's are strewin'!　　20
An' naething, now, to big a new ane,°
　　O' foggage° green!
An' bleak December's winds ensuin',
　　Baith snell° an' keen!

Thou saw the fields laid bare and waste,
An' weary winter comin' fast,　　26
An' cozie here, beneath the blast,
　　Thou thought to dwell,
Till crash! the cruel coulter° passed
　　Out through thy cell.　　30

That wee bit heap o' leaves an' stibble
Has cost thee mony a weary nibble!
Now thou's turn'd out, for a' thy trouble,
　　But house or hald,°
To thole° the winter's sleety dribble　　35
　　An' cranreuch° cauld!

But, Mousie, thou art no thy lane°
In proving foresight may be vain;
The best laid schemes o' mice an' men
　　Gang aft agley,°　　40
An' lea'e us nought but grief an' pain,
　　For promis'd joy.

Still thou art blest, compared wi' me,
The present only toucheth thee;
But och! I backward cast my e'e　　45
　　On prospects drear!
An' forward, though I canna see,
　　I guess an' fear!

To a Louse

ON SEEING ONE
ON A LADY'S BONNET AT CHURCH

Ha! wh' are ye gaun, ye crowlin' ferlie!°
Your impudence protects you sairly;°
I canna say but ye strunt° rarely,
　　Owre gauze and lace;
Though faith! I fear ye dine but sparely
　　On sic a place.　　6

Ye ugly, creepin', blastit wonner,°
Detested, shunned by saunt an' sinner!
How dare ye set your fit° upon her,
　　Sae fine a lady?　　10
Gae somewhere else, and seek your din-
　　ner
　　On some poor body.

Swith, in some beggar's haffet squattle;°
There ye may creep, and sprawl, and
　　sprattle°
Wi' ither kindred jumping cattle,　　15
　　In shoals and nations;
Where horn nor bane° ne'er dare un-
　　settle
　　Your thick plantations.

Now haud ye there,° ye're out o' sight,
Below the fatt'rels,° snug an' tight;　　20
Na, faith ye yet! ye'll no be right
　　Till ye've got on it,
The very tapmost tow'ring height
　　O' Miss's bonnet.

My sooth! right bauld ye set your nose
　　out,　　25
As plump and gray as onie grozet;°
O for some rank mercurial rozet,°
　　Or fell red smeddum!°

20. *silly wa's:* weak walls. 21. *big . . . ane:* build a new one. 22. *foggage:* herbage. 24. *snell:* sharp. 29. *coulter* (kōl'tẽr): plow. 34. *But house or hald:* without a dwelling place. 35. *thole:* endure. 36. *cranreuch* (krȧn'rŭk): hoarfrost. 37. *no thy lane:* not alone. 40. *Gang aft agley* (ȧ·glē'): oft go astray.

1. *crowlin' ferlie* (fẽr'lĭ): crawling wonder. 2. *sairly:* greatly. 3. *strunt:* strut. 7. *blastit wonner:* blasted wonder. 9. *fit:* foot. 13. *Swith . . . squattle:* Be off with you! Sprawl in some beggar's temple. 14. *sprattle:* struggle. 17. *horn nor bane:* comb nor poison. 19. *haud ye there:* stay where you are. 20. *fatt'rels:* ribbon ends. 26. *onie grozet* (grŏz'ĭt): any gooseberry. 27. *rozet:* rosin. 28. *smeddum:* powder.

I'd gie you sic a hearty dose o't,
    Wad dress your droddum!°   30

I wad na been surprised to spy
You on an auld wife's flannen toy;°
Or aiblins some bit duddie boy,°
    On's wyliecoat;°
But Miss's fine Lunardi!° fie,   35
    How daur ye do 't?

30. *Wad . . . droddum:* would put an end to you. 32. *flannen toy:* flannel headdress. 33. *Or . . . boy:* or perhaps on some little ragged boy. 34. *wyliecoat* (wī′lǐ′kōt′): flannel vest. 35. *Lunardi:* a bonnet named for an aeronaut of that day, probably with winglike ribbons.

O Jenny, dinna toss your head,
An' set your beauties a' abread!°
Ye little ken what cursèd speed
    The blastie's makin'!   40
Thae winks and finger ends, I dread,
    Are notice takin'!

O wad some Pow'r the giftie gie us
To see oursels as ithers see us!
It wad frae mony a blunder free us,   45
    And foolish notion:
What airs in dress an' gait wad lea'e us,
    And e'en devotion!

38. *abread:* abroad.

The Cotter's Saturday Night

This well-known poem, which takes us back in spirit to "Elegy Written in a Country Churchyard" and *The Deserted Village*, was published in Burns' first volume. An interesting comment comes from Robert's brother Gilbert: "Robert had frequently remarked to me that he thought there was something peculiarly venerable in the phrase, 'Let us worship God,' used by a decent, sober head of a family, introducing family worship. To this sentiment of the author the world is indebted for 'The Cotter's Saturday Night.' The cotter is an exact copy of my father, in his manners, his family devotion, and exhortations. . . ."

INSCRIBED TO ROBERT AIKEN, ESQ.°

Let not ambition mock their useful toil,
    Their homely joys, and destiny obscure;
Nor grandeur hear, with a disdainful smile,
    The short and simple annals of the poor.
                Gray.

My loved, my honored, much respected friend!
No mercenary bard this homage pays;°
With honest pride, I scorn each selfish end,
My dearest meed, a friend's esteem and praise;
To you I sing, in simple Scottish lays,   5
The lowly train in life's sequestered scene,
The native feelings strong, the guileless ways,
What Aiken in a cottage would have been;
Ah! though his worth unknown, far happier there, I ween!

Inscription *Robert Aiken:* a warm friend of Burns in Ayr, who had helped to make his poems known. 2. Burns says he is not dedicating his poem to Aiken for hope of reward. See note on Johnson's letter to Chesterfield (page 321) for explanation of the patronage system.

Coleridge had in abundance, together with the poet's ability to verbalize his vision.

A revealing approach to the poem is Professor John Livingston Lowes' study, *The Road to Xanadu,* in which the author tracks down most of the individual images that reappear, transformed, in both *The Rime of the Ancient Mariner* and "Kubla Khan." Coleridge was a voracious reader, and his passion for early travelers' accounts of strange lands and seas was only one of many. Professor Lowes, guided by Coleridge's scribbled notes here and there, set out to read everything that Coleridge had read or might have read; he found the albatross, the Arctic ice, the bright-colored sea creatures, in fact, nearly all the germinating details of both these poems. The book over which Coleridge fell asleep after taking laudanum and just prior to writing "Kubla Khan" was *Purchas his Pilgrimage,* an early seventeenth-century book of travels by the Elizabethan writer Samuel Purchas. The passage he was reading is as follows:

In Xamdu did Cublai Can build a stately Palace, encompassing sixteene miles of plaine ground with a wall, wherein are fertile Meddowes, pleasant springs, delightful Streames, and all sorts of beasts of chase and game, and in the middest thereof a sumptuous house of pleasure, which may be removed from place to place.

Here is the beginning of Coleridge's poem. Purchas had also told the same story in another book, which Coleridge had previously read, and in which the place is spelled "Xandu," a form the poet would naturally prefer and felicitously expand. In Purchas, in Bartram's *Travels,* in Bruce's *Travels to Discover the Sources of the Nile,* in dozens of other works, crop up details which, through the mysterious processes of association, fuse to become the Abyssinian maid, the caves of ice, the sacred river, and so on. And they were all in the poet's head when he dozed off. The opium had only put him to sleep.

CHARLES

LAMB

1775–1834

National Portrait Gallery

Unlike his friends Wordsworth and Coleridge, Charles Lamb was a product and admirer of the city. Once when he visited the Lake Poets in their beautiful countryside he confessed that he missed the chimney pots of London and was eager to return to the city's crowded, bustling streets.

For thirty-three years Lamb worked as an accountant in the East India House. When someone asked him once what he had written, he pointed to the long row of ledgers about his desk and jokingly added that they were all manuscript copies of his works. This whimsical outlook on life made Lamb a great conversationalist, a choice letter writer, and a friend to be cherished. His personality lent itself perfectly to the writing of familiar essays, which were assembled at various times under the title *Essays of Elia* (ē'lĭ·à). Through these he won his immortality. Many of them are autobiographical, with fictitious names supplied for his family and friends: Elia is Lamb himself, and Cousin Bridget is his sister Mary.

Between the lines of these essays we can read some of the privations and sorrows of Lamb's life, but his difficulties never rise to the surface in the form of bitterness or complaint. Poverty sent him to the charity school of Christ's Hospital. Here he met Coleridge and began what became a lifelong friendship. Real tragedy was brought into Lamb's family by the recurring mental illness of his sister Mary. When Lamb was only twenty-one, Mary, while out of her mind, stabbed her mother to death. Under ordinary circumstances Mary would have been sent to an asylum, but since Charles promised to guard her, she was committed to his care. For thirty-eight long years his brotherly care continued, interrupted several times when Mary's malady returned and she was forced to enter an institution. In her lucid periods Mary was a charming companion and added to the pleasure of the weekly gatherings of congenial friends around the Lamb fireplace. Together the brother and sister wrote *Tales from Shakespeare,* Charles retelling in prose for young readers the tragedies and Mary the comedies. Charles never married, fearing the family insanity hereditary.

At the age of fifty Lamb retired on pension. In his essay "The Superannuated Man" he tells of his strange feeling on retirement that every day was Sunday. The essays following are among his most famous: the first for delicate, restrained pathos, the second for its gentle philosophy.

Dream Children

CHILDREN love to listen to stories about their elders, when *they* were children; to stretch their imagination to the conception of a traditionary great-uncle, or grandame, whom they never saw. It was in this spirit that my little ones crept about me the other evening to hear about their great-grandmother Field,[1] who lived in a great house in Norfolk (a hundred times bigger than that in which they and papa lived) which had been the scene (so at least it was generally believed in that part of the country) of the tragic incidents which they had lately become familiar with from the ballad of the "Children in the Wood." Certain it is that the whole story of the children and their cruel uncle was to be seen fairly carved out in wood upon the chimney piece of the great hall, the whole story down to the Robin Redbreasts;[2] till a foolish rich person pulled it down to set up a marble one of modern invention in its stead, with no story upon it. Here Alice put out one of her dear mother's looks, too tender to be called upbraiding.

Then I went on to say how religious and how good their great-grandmother Field was, how beloved and respected by everybody, though she was not indeed the mistress of this great house, but had only the charge of it (and yet in some respects she might be said to be the mistress of it too) committed to her by the owner, who preferred living in a newer and more fashionable mansion which he had purchased somewhere in the adjoin-

[1] *great-grandmother Field:* a reference to Mary Field, Lamb's grandmother, a housekeeper at a country home in Hertfordshire.

[2] *Robin Redbreasts:* At the end of the ballad, the robins cover the bodies of the children with leaves.

ing county; but still she lived in it in a manner as if it had been her own, and kept up the dignity of the great house in a sort while she lived, which afterward came to decay, and was nearly pulled down, and all its old ornaments stripped and carried away to the owner's other house, where they were set up, and looked as awkward as if someone were to carry away the old tombs they had seen lately at the Abbey, and stick them up in Lady C.'s tawdry gilt drawing room. Here John smiled, as much as to say, "that would be foolish indeed."

And then I told how, when she came to die, her funeral was attended by a concourse of all the poor, and some of the gentry too, of the neighborhood for many miles round, to show their respect for her memory, because she had been such a good and religious woman; so good indeed that she knew all the Psaltery [1] by heart, ay, and a great part of the Testament besides. Here little Alice spread her hands.

Then I told what a tall, upright, graceful person their great-grandmother Field once was; and how in her youth she was esteemed the best dancer — here Alice's little right foot played an involuntary movement, till, upon my looking grave, it desisted — the best dancer, I was saying, in the county, till a cruel disease, called a cancer, came, and bowed her down with pain; but it could never bend her good spirits, or make them stoop, but they were still upright, because she was so good and religious.

Then I told how she was used to sleep by herself in a lone chamber of the great lone house; and how she believed that an apparition of two infants was to be seen at midnight gliding up and down the great staircase near where she slept, but she said, "those innocents would do her no harm"; and how frightened I used to be, though in those days I had my maid to sleep with me, because I was never

half so good or religious as she; and yet I never saw the infants. Here John expanded all his eyebrows and tried to look courageous.

Then I told how good she was to all her grandchildren, having us to the great house in the holidays, where I in particular used to spend many hours by myself, in gazing upon the old busts of the Twelve Caesars, that had been Emperors of Rome, till the old marble heads would seem to live again, or I to be turned into marble with them; how I never could be tired with roaming about that huge mansion, with its vast empty rooms, with their worn-out hangings, fluttering tapestry, and carved oaken panels, with the gilding almost rubbed out — sometimes in the spacious old-fashioned gardens, which I had almost to myself, unless when now and then a solitary gardening man would cross me — and how the nectarines and peaches hung upon the walls, without my ever offering to pluck them, because they were forbidden fruit, unless now and then — and because I had more pleasure in strolling about among the old melancholy-looking yew trees, or the firs, and picking up the red berries, and the fir apples,[2] which were good for nothing but to look at — or in lying about upon the fresh grass with all the fine garden smells around me — or basking in the orangery, till I could almost fancy myself ripening too along with the oranges and the limes in that grateful warmth — or in watching the dace that darted to and fro in the fishpond, at the bottom of the garden, with here and there a great sulky pike hanging midway down the water in silent state, as if it mocked at their impertinent friskings — I had more pleasure in these busy-idle diversions than in all the sweet flavors of peaches, nectarines, oranges, and suchlike common baits for children. Here John slyly deposited back upon the plate a bunch of grapes, which, not unobserved by Alice, he had meditated di-

---

[1] *Psaltery:* Psalms of David, as used in the Book of Common Prayer.

[2] *fir apples:* fir cones.

viding with her, and both seemed willing to relinquish them for the present as irrelevant.

Then, in somewhat a more heightened tone, I told how, though their great-grandmother Field loved all her grandchildren, yet in an especial manner she might be said to love their uncle, John L———,[1] because he was so handsome and spirited a youth, and a king to the rest of us; and, instead of moping about in solitary corners, like some of us, he would mount the most mettlesome horse he could get, when but an imp no bigger than themselves, and make it carry him half over the county in a morning, and join the hunters when there were any out — and yet he loved the old great house and gardens too, but had too much spirit to be always pent up within their boundaries — and how their uncle grew up to man's estate as brave as he was handsome, to the admiration of everybody, but of their great-grandmother Field most especially; and how he used to carry me upon his back when I was a lame-footed boy — for he was a good bit older than me — many a mile when I could not walk for pain; and how in after life he became lame-footed too, and I did not always (I fear) make allowances enough for him when he was impatient and in pain, nor remember sufficiently how considerate he had been to me when I was lame-footed; and how when he died, though he had not been dead an hour, it seemed as if he had died a great while ago, such a distance there is betwixt life and death; and how I bore his death as I thought pretty well at first, but afterward it haunted and haunted me; and though I did not cry or take it to heart as some do, and as I think he would have done if I had died, yet I missed him all day long, and knew not till then how much I had loved him. I missed his kindness, and I missed his crossness, and wished him to be alive again, to be quarreling with him (for we quarreled sometimes) rather than not have him again, and was as uneasy without him as he, their poor uncle, must have been when the doctor took off his limb.[2] Here the children fell a-crying, and asked if their little mourning which they had on was not for uncle John, and they looked up, and prayed me not to go on about their uncle, but to tell them some stories about their pretty dead mother.

Then I told how for seven long years, in hope sometimes, sometimes in despair, yet persisting ever, I courted the fair Alice W———n;[3] and, as much as children could understand, I explained to them what coyness, and difficulty, and denial, meant in maidens — when suddenly, turning to Alice, the soul of the first Alice looked out at her eyes with such a reality of representment,[4] that I became in doubt which of them stood there before me, or whose that bright hair was; and while I stood gazing, both the children gradually grew fainter to my view, receding, and still receding, till nothing at last but two mournful features were seen in the uttermost distance, which, without speech, strangely impressed upon me the effects of speech: "We are not of Alice, nor of thee, nor are we children at all. The children of Alice call Bartrum father. We are nothing; less than nothing, and dreams. We are only what might have been, and must wait upon the tedious shores of Lethe [5] millions of ages before we have existence and a name" — and immediately awaking, I found myself quietly seated in my bachelor armchair, where I had fallen asleep, with the faithful Bridget unchanged by my side — but John L. (or James Elia) was gone forever.

---

[1] *John L———:* John Lamb, Charles Lamb's elder brother who died shortly before this essay was written. His lameness, mentioned later, was due to an injury.

[2] *doctor . . . limb:* an imaginary detail. [3] *Alice W———n:* Alice Winterton, probably Ann Simmons, whom Lamb loved when he was a young man. She married a Mr. Bartrum. [4] *representment:* portrayal, picturing. [5] *Lethe* (lē'-thē): in Greek mythology, the river of forgetfulness.

Old China

In a simple, conversational style, Lamb gives free rein to his feelings in "Old China." In his love of old literature and old things and in his attitudes toward life, Lamb is a Romantic. This essay not only provides a glimpse into his life, but it also reveals a delineation of the blessings of poverty.

I HAVE an almost feminine partiality for old china. When I go to see any great house, I inquire for the china-closet, and next for the picture gallery. I cannot defend the order of preference, but by saying, that we have all some taste or other, of too ancient a date to admit of our remembering distinctly that it was an acquired one. I can call to mind the first play, and the first exhibition, that I was taken to; but I am not conscious of a time when china jars and saucers were introduced into my imagination.

I had no repugnance then — why should I now have? — to those little, lawless, azure-tinctured grotesques, that under the motion of men and women, float about, uncircumscribed by any element, in that world before perspective — a china tea-cup.

I like to see my old friends — whom distance cannot diminish — figuring up in the air (so they appear to our optics), yet on *terra firma* still — for so we must in courtesy interpret that speck of deeper blue, which the decorous artist, to prevent absurdity, had made to spring up beneath their sandals.

I love the men with women's faces, and the women, if possible, with still more womanish expressions.

Here is a young and courtly Mandarin, handing tea to a lady from a salver — two miles off. See how distance seems to set off respect! And here the same lady, or another — for likeness is identity on tea-cups — is stepping into a little fairy boat, moored on the hither side of this calm garden river, with a dainty mincing foot, which in a right angle of incidence (as angles go in our world) must infallibly land her in the midst of a flowery mead — a furlong off on the other side of the same strange stream!

Farther on — if far or near can be predicated of their world — see horses, trees, pagodas, dancing the hays.[1]

Here — a cow and rabbit couchant, and coextensive — so objects show, seen through the lucid atmosphere of fine Cathay.[2]

I was pointing out to my cousin last evening, over our Hyson [3] (which we are old fashioned enough to drink unmixed still of an afternoon), some of these *speciosa miracula* [4] upon a set of extraordinary old blue china (a recent purchase) which we were now for the first time using; and could not help remarking how favorable circumstances had been to us of late years, that we could afford to please the eye sometimes with trifles of this sort — when a passing sentiment seemed to over-shade the brows of my companion. I am quick at detecting these summer clouds in Bridget.

"I wish the good old times would come again," she said, "when we were

---

[1] *hays:* country dances. [2] *Cathay:* the old name for China. [3] *Hyson:* a kind of tea. [4] *speciosa miracula:* Latin for "shining wonders."

not quite so rich. I do not mean that I want to be poor; but there was a middle state" —so she was pleased to ramble on — "in which I am sure we were a great deal happier. A purchase is but a purchase, now that you have money enough to spare. Formerly it used to be a triumph. When we coveted a cheap luxury (and, O! how much ado I had to get you to consent in those times!) we were used to have a debate two or three days before, and to weigh the *for* and *against,* and think what we might spare it out of, and what saving we could hit upon, that should be an equivalent. A thing was worth buying then, when we felt the money that we paid for it.

"Do you remember the brown suit, which you made to hang upon you till all your friends cried shame upon you, it grew so threadbare — and all because of that folio Beaumont and Fletcher,[1] which you dragged home late at night from Barker's in Covent Garden? Do you remember how we eyed it for weeks before we could make up our minds to the purchase, and had not come to a determination till it was near ten o'clock of the Saturday night, when you set off from Islington, fearing you should be too late — and when the old bookseller with some grumbling opened his shop, and by the twinkling taper (for he was setting bedwards) lighted out the relic from his dusty treasures — and when you lugged it home, wishing it were twice as cumbersome — and when you presented it to me — and when we were exploring the perfectness of it (*collating,* you called it) — and while I was repairing some of the loose leaves with paste, which your impatience would not suffer to be left till daybreak — was there no pleasure in being a poor man? Or can those neat black clothes which you wear now, and are so careful to keep brushed, since we have become rich and finical — give you half the honest vanity with which you flaunt-

ed it about in that over-worn suit — your old corbeau [2] — for four or five weeks longer than you should have done, to pacify your conscience for the mighty sum of fifteen — or sixteen shillings was it? — a great affair we thought it then — which you had lavished on the old folio? Now you can afford to buy any book that pleases you, but I do not see that you ever bring me home any nice old purchases now.

"When you came home with twenty apologies for laying out a less number of shilling upon that print after Lionardo, which we christened the 'Lady Blanch'; when you looked at the purchase, and thought of the money — and thought of the money, and looked again at the picture — was there no pleasure in being a poor man? Now, you have nothing to do but to walk into Colnaghi's, and buy a wilderness of Lionardos. Yet do you?

"Then, do you remember our pleasant walks to Enfield, and Potter's Bar, and Waltham, when we had a holyday — holydays and all other fun are gone now we are rich — and the little handbasket in which I used to deposit our day's fare of savory cold lamb and salad — and how you would pry about at noon-tide for some decent house, where we might go in, and produce our store — only paying for the ale that you must call for — and speculate upon the looks of the landlady, and whether she was likely to allow us a table-cloth — and wish for such another honest hostess as Izaak Walton has described many a one on the pleasant banks of the Lea, when he went a-fishing — and sometimes they would prove obliging enough, and sometimes they would look grudgingly upon us — but we had cheerful looks still for one another, and would eat our plain food savorily, scarcely grudging Piscator [3] his Trout Hall? Now — when we go out a day's pleasuring, which is seldom moreover, we *ride* part of the way — and go

---

[1] *folio Beaumont and Fletcher:* the plays of Beaumont and Fletcher, Elizabethan dramatists, bound in a large book.

[2] *corbeau:* dark greenish-black color. [3] *Piscator:* a character in Walton's *Compleat Angler.*

into a fine inn, and order the best of dinners, never debating the expense — which, after all, never has half the relish of those chance country snaps, when we were at the mercy of uncertain usage, and a precarious welcome.

"You are too proud to see a play anywhere now but in the pit. Do you remember where it was we used to sit, when we saw the battle of Hexham, and the Surrender of Calais, and Bannister and Mrs. Bland in the Children in the Wood — when we squeezed out our shillings a-piece to sit three or four times in a season in the one-shilling gallery — where you felt all the time that you ought not to have brought me — and more strongly I felt obligation to you for having brought me — and the pleasure was the better for a little shame — and when the curtain drew up, what cared we for our place in the house, or what mattered it where we were sitting, when our thoughts were with Rosalind in Arden, or with Viola at the Court of Illyria? [1] You used to say, that the gallery was the best place of all for enjoying a play socially — that the relish of such exhibitions must be in proportion to the infrequency of going — that the company we met there, not being in general readers of plays, were obliged to attend the more, and did attend to what was going on, on the stage — because a word lost would have been a chasm, which it was impossible for them to fill up. With such reflections we consoled our pride then — and I appeal to you whether, as a woman, I met generally with less attention and accommodation than I have done since in more expensive situations in the house? The getting in indeed, and the crowding up those inconvenient staircases, was bad enough — but there was still a law of civility to woman recognized to quite as great an extent as we ever found in the other passages — and how a little difficulty overcome heightened the snug seat

[1] *Rosalind . . . Illyria:* characters and scenes in *As You Like It* and *Twelfth Night,* respectively.

and the play, afterwards! Now we can only pay our money and walk in. You cannot see, you say, in the galleries now. I am sure we saw, and heard too, well enough then — but sight, and all, I think, is gone with our poverty.

"There was pleasure in eating strawberries, before they became quite common — in the first dish of peas, while they were yet dear — to have them for a nice supper, a treat. What treat can we have now? If we were to treat ourselves now — that is, to have dainties a little above our means, it would be selfish and wicked. It is the very little more that we allow ourselves beyond what the actual poor can get at, that makes what I call a treat — when two people, living together, as we have done, now and then indulge themselves in a cheap luxury, which both like; while each apologizes, and is willing to take both halves of the blame to his single share. I see no harm in people making much of themselves in that sense of the word. It may give them a hint how to make much of others. But now — what I mean by the word — we never do make much of ourselves. None but the poor can do it. I do not mean the veriest poor of all, but persons as we were, just above poverty.

"I know what you were going to say, that it is mighty pleasant at the end of the year to make all meet — and much ado we used to have every Thirty-first Night of December to account for our exceedings — many a long face did you make over your puzzled accounts, and in contriving to make out how we had spent so much — or that we had not spent so much — or that it was impossible that we should spend so much next year — and still we found our slender capital decreasing — but then, betwixt ways, and projects, and compromises of one sort or another, and talk of curtailing this charge, and doing without that for the future — and the hope that youth brings, and laughing spirits (in which you were never poor till now) we pocketed up our loss, and in conclusion, with 'lusty brimmers' (as you used to quote it out of *hearty cheerful Mr. Cotton,* as you called him), we used to welcome in the 'coming guest.' Now we have no reckoning at all at the end of the old year — no flattering promises about the new year doing better for us."

Bridget is so sparing of her speech on most occasions, that when she gets into a rhetorical vein, I am careful how I interrupt it. I could not help, however, smiling at the phantom of wealth which her dear imagination had conjured up out of a clear income of poor —— hundred pounds a year. "It is true we were happier when we were poorer, but we were also younger, my cousin. I am afraid we must put up with the excess, for if we were to shake the superflux into the sea, we should not much mend ourselves. That we had much to struggle with, as we grew up together, we have reason to be most thankful. It strengthened, and knit our compact closer. We could never have been what we have been to each other, if we had always had the sufficiency which you now complain of. The resisting power — those natural dilations of the youthful spirit, which circumstances cannot straiten — with us are long since passed away. Competence to age is supplementary youth, a sorry supplement indeed, but I fear the best that is to be had. We must ride where we formerly walked: live better, and lie softer — and shall be wise to do so — than we had means to do in those good old days you speak of. Yet could those days return — could you and I once more walk our thirty miles a day — could Bannister and Mrs. Bland again be young, and you and I be young to see them — could the good old one-shilling gallery days return — they are dreams, my cousin, now — but could you and I at this moment, instead of this quiet argument, by our well-carpeted fireside, sitting on this luxurious sofa — be once more about, and squeezed, and elbowed by the poorest rabble of poor gallery scramblers — could I once more hear those anxious shrieks of yours — and the delicious *Thank God, we are safe,* which always followed when the topmost stair, conquered, let in the first light of the whole cheerful theater down beneath us — I know not the fathom line that ever touched a descent so deep as I would be willing to bury more wealth in than Croesus had, or the great R—— is supposed to have, to purchase it. And now do just look at that merry little Chinese waiter holding an umbrella, big enough for a bed-tester, over the head of that pretty insipid half-Madonnaish chit of a lady in that very blue summer-house."

FAMILIAR ESSAYS

DREAM CHILDREN

1. Which passages of this essay give actual facts of Lamb's life? Which are fictitious? Where does Lamb show restraint in suggesting but not bewailing some of the misfortunes of his life? How does this affect your feeling toward Lamb?

2. What details make John and Alice seem like real children?

3. What is the general tone and style of this essay? Notice how the repeated phrase, "Then I told" gives a certain rhythmic quality to the style.

4. Do you think Lamb wanted you to recognize the essay as a dream at the beginning or to be surprised when it was shown to be only a dream? Compare this essay with another famous dream, "Kubla Khan." Which seems to you to resemble more nearly an actual dream? Why?

OLD CHINA

1. Was Lamb an accurate observer?

2. What were some of the blessings of being poor, in Lamb's view? What part did youth play in their pleasures when they were poorer? In your opinion, when is poverty more intensely felt — in youth or in old age?

SUGGESTION FOR WRITING

Imitating in part Lamb's method, write an original familiar essay on conversations with dream characters, book characters, or other imaginary persons.

SIR WALTER SCOTT

1771–1832

National Portrait Gallery

As a boy Walter Scott was fascinated by the tales of Scotland's past told him by his mother and grandfather. In accordance with his father's wishes, young Scott studied law at the University of Edinburgh and practiced it for a time. But his interest in writing grew, and at the age of thirty-one he published a collection of old Scottish folk ballads. In the next few years this book was followed by three long original narrative poems, of which *The Lady of the Lake* is the most famous. The supposed scene of the story, Loch Katrine, with its little Ellen's Isle, the home of the heroine, marks the center of the "Scott country" to which tourists flock today.

For a time Scott was the most popular poet in England. Then he turned to prose and produced the long series of Waverley novels, the authorship of which he kept secret for several years. Many of these popular, romantic novels are widely read today. They are remarkable for their high level of excellence and for their re-creation of the past with vigor and great richness of colorful detail.

With the fortune that he reaped from these books, Scott bought Abbotsford, a handsome manor house on the Tweed River, south of Edinburgh. In 1820 he was made a baronet. For about twelve years he enjoyed at Abbotsford the life of a medieval Scots "laird," with his faithful retainers, hunting preserves, and hearty hospi-

tality. But the publishing house that was to support all this grandeur failed in 1826, and Scott and his partners were confronted with a debt of more than $600,000. In this crisis, though a silent partner and not legally responsible, Scott undertook to pay off the entire debt himself by writing still more novels. Though handicapped by failing health, at times writing in extreme pain, he paid over half the debt. So highly esteemed was Scott that the government sent a naval vessel to take him to the Mediterranean, away from the rigors of a winter in Scotland. After cruising for about a year, he felt that death was approaching and returned to die at his beloved Abbotsford, in the heart of the Lowlands he had described so well.

My Native Land

The love of homeland inspired Scott to write these stirring lines in *The Lay of the Last Minstrel,* Canto VI, Stanza I.

Breathes there the man, with soul so dead,
Who never to himself hath said,
    This is my own, my native land!
Whose heart hath ne'er within him
    burned,

4

As home his footsteps he hath turned,
   From wandering on a foreign strand!
If such there breathe, go, mark him well;
For him no Minstrel raptures swell;
High though his titles, proud his name,
Boundless his wealth as wish can claim;
Despite those titles, power, and pelf,   11
The wretch, concentered all in self,
Living, shall forfeit fair renown,
And, doubly dying, shall go down
To the vile dust, from whence he sprung,
Unwept, unhonored, and unsung.   16

Proud Maisie

Scott, like Shakespeare, often scattered little bursts of song throughout his longer writings. This song is from the novel *The Heart of Midlothian,* Chapter XL. Observe the skill with which the little tragedy is developed in brief space. The second stanza gives the hint, the third the direct statement, the fourth interprets in a different way the lights and the singing which would normally be part of a wedding.

Proud Maisie is in the wood,
   Walking so early;
Sweet Robin sits on the bush,
   Singing so rarely.

"Tell me, thou bonny bird,   5
   When shall I marry me?"
"When six braw° gentlemen
   Kirkward° shall carry ye."

"Who makes the bridal bed,
   Birdie, say truly?"   10
"The gray-headed sexton
   That delves the grave duly.

"The glowworm o'er grave and stone
   Shall light thee steady.
The owl from the steeple sing,   15
   'Welcome, proud lady.'"

7. *braw:* fine; smartly dressed. 8. *Kirkward:* churchward; toward the church.

Jock o' Hazeldean

"Why weep ye by the tide, ladie?
   Why weep ye by the tide?
I'll wed ye to my youngest son,
   And ye sall be his bride.
And ye sall be his bride, ladie,   5
   Sae comely to be seen" —
But aye she loot the tears down fa'°
   For Jock o' Hazeldean.

"Now let this willfu' grief be done,
   And dry that cheek so pale;   10
Young Frank is chief of Errington,
   And lord of Langley dale;
His step is first in peaceful ha',°
   His sword in battle keen" —
But aye she loot the tears down fa'   15
   For Jock o' Hazeldean.

"A chain of gold ye sall not lack,
   Nor braid to bind your hair;
Nor mettled hound,° nor managed
   hawk,°
   Nor palfrey° fresh and fair;   20
And you, the foremost o' them a',
   Shall ride our forest queen" —
But aye she loot the tears down fa'
   For Jock o' Hazeldean.

The kirk was decked at morningtide,   25
   The tapers glimmered fair;
The priest and bridegroom wait the
   bride,
   And dame and knight are there.
They sought her baith by bower and
   ha' —
   The ladie was not seen!   30
She's o'er the Border,° and awa'
   Wi' Jock o' Hazeldean.

7. *aye . . . fa':* ever she continued to weep. 13. *ha':* hall. 19. *mettled hound:* a spirited hunting dog; *managed hawk:* a hawk trained for hunting. 20. *palfrey:* a horse trained for ladies. 31. *Border:* the boundary between Scotland and England. She has fled from Scotland to escape pursuit.

A LOYAL SCOTSMAN

1. In "My Native Land," what is Scott's attitude toward his homeland? What question is the poet asking in the first six lines? How does he answer it?

2. Explain "doubly dying" in line 14. What is the effect of the three words in the last line?

3. In "Proud Maisie," what is the prophecy of the bird? Who are the "six braw gentlemen"? Compare this passage with the famous ninth stanza of Gray's "Elegy" (see page 342).

4. What ballad characteristics mark "Jock o' Hazeldean"? Who is the speaker in the first three stanzas? What effect is gained through the refrain?

SUGGESTION FOR WRITING

You have read and sung many ballads, old and new. Now try writing a ballad with a modern setting.

GEORGE GORDON, LORD BYRON

1788–1824

New York Public Library, Print Room

The most dashing figure among the Romantic poets, Byron was a titled lord — handsome, athletic, and courageous. Endowed with literary genius, he was acclaimed throughout Europe as the leading English poet of his day. He had a stormy, proud, sensitive disposition, and a love of personal liberty that led him to defy most of the conventions of society. His whole life was "tempest-tossed."

To understand Byron, we must consider his upbringing. His father, a spendthrift army captain, called "Mad Jack" Byron, died when the boy was three years old. His mother was emotional, unstable, and tyrannical. She resented their poverty but prized their noble ancestry. At times she overindulged her son, but she also railed at him and taunted him for his clubfoot, his one physical blemish. At the age of ten, he inherited his great-uncle's estate, Newstead Abbey. Afterward he had a good education, and at twenty-one was by birthright seated in the House of Lords.

Byron's literary career began at eighteen while he was at Cambridge. His first volume of verse was attacked and ridiculed by the influential literary quarterly *Edinburgh Review*. The indignant poet retaliated with a biting satire, "English Bards and Scotch Reviewers." His next literary venture, however, made his name.

After two years of touring on the Continent, he produced an astounding travelogue, *Childe Harold's Pilgrimage*, written in the difficult Spenserian stanza. After its publication Byron said, "I awoke one morning to find myself famous." Later he wrote many long poems or poetic dramas with lonely, romantic, mysterious heroes, subtly suggesting portraits of himself. He was now at the height of his popularity, a celebrity throughout Europe, eclipsing even the well-known Walter Scott.

But after a few years the attitude of the public changed. Whispers of his love affairs and his unconventional behavior were increasing; his wife left him suddenly after a year of marriage. Angered and embittered by the public's censure, and unsettled as always, he left England forever. He wandered from one place to another on the Continent, and for a time joined Shelley's little group in Italy. His restless life ended with a generous and noble act. Greece was fighting to gain independence from Turkey. This conflict aroused all Byron's strong instincts to champion the oppressed, and he gave both his money and his entire effort to the cause. He became an officer in the Greek army, and though he wished to die in battle, he fell ill in the little Greek town of Missolonghi and died of a fever at the age of thirty-six.

Byron's dramatic, vigorous, and colorful poems with their romantic pictures of castles and prisons, mountains and sea, make their appeal to all readers, but especially to young people. His narrative verse — the greatest since Milton — and his poetic satires like *Don Juan* make him stand out among the Romantics. Generations of readers have recognized him as a poet of energy and magnificence.

Stanzas Written on the Road Between Florence and Pisa°

In this poem one can almost hear the hoofbeats of the horse
Byron was riding. This meter was one of Byron's favorites,
for it conveyed the vigor and exuberance which contributed
to his great popularity as a poet.

Oh, talk not to me of a name great in story —
The days of our youth are the days of our glory;
And the myrtle and ivy of sweet two-and-twenty
Are worth all your laurels, though ever so plenty.

What are garlands and crowns to the brow that is wrinkled?   5
'Tis but a dead flower with May dew besprinkled:
Then away with all such from a head that is hoary!
What care I for the wreaths that can *only* give glory?

Oh Fame! — if I e'er took delight in thy praises,
'Twas less for the sake of thy high-sounding phrases   10
Than to see the bright eyes of the dear one discover
She thought that I was not unworthy to love her.

There chiefly I sought thee, *there* only I found thee;
Her glance was the best of the rays that surround thee;
When it sparkled o'er aught that was bright in my story,   15
I knew it was love, and I felt it was glory.

Title: *Pisa* (pē′zà).

The Destruction of Sennacherib

Sennacherib,[1] king of Assyria in the seventh century B.C.,
led his army into Judea and besieged Jerusalem. According
to the Bible story in II Kings 19:35–37, an angel of the
Lord smote the Assyrians in camp during the night. With
a mere remnant of his forces, Sennacherib retreated in haste
to his own country. Jerusalem was saved. Byron's portrayal
of this event is both stirring and beautiful.

The Assyrian came down like the wolf on the fold,
And his cohorts were gleaming in purple and gold;
And the sheen of their spears was like stars on the sea,
When the blue wave rolls nightly on deep Galilee.

Like the leaves of the forest when Summer is green,   5
That host with their banners at sunset were seen;
Like the leaves of the forest when Autumn hath blown,
That host on the morrow lay withered and strown.°

For the Angel of Death spread his wings on the blast,
And breathed in the face of the foe as he passed;   10
And the eyes of the sleepers waxed deadly and chill,
And their hearts but once heaved, and for ever grew still!

And there lay the steed with his nostril all wide,
But through it there rolled not the breath of his pride;
And the foam of his gasping lay white on the turf,   15
And cold as the spray of the rock-beating surf.

And there lay the rider distorted and pale,
With the dew on his brow, and the rust on his mail;
And the tents were all silent, the banners alone,
The lances unlifted, the trumpet unblown.   20

And the widows of Ashur° are loud in their wail,
And the idols are broke in the temple of Baal;°
And the might of the Gentile,° unsmote by the sword,
Hath melted like snow in the glance of the Lord!

[1] *Sennacherib* (sĕ·năk′ĕr·ĭb) is also called the Assyrian. It was a custom in early times to identify
the king by the name of the country he ruled. 8. *strown:* strewn, scattered. 21. *Ashur:* Assyria.
22. *Baal* (bā′ăl): one of the Assyrian gods. 23. *Gentile:* Sennacherib; so called because he was a
stranger to the Hebrew beliefs.

The Prisoner of Chillon

In Switzerland in June 1816, Byron visited the castle of Chillon (shē·yôn'), where during the sixteenth century François Bonnivard, a Swiss patriot and reformer who wished to make Geneva a republic, was held as a prisoner for six years. This castle is built on a rock just off the northeastern shore of Lake Leman (now commonly called Lake Geneva), with the great peaks of the Alps towering behind it. Byron was impressed by the picturesque surroundings, the massive walls, and the dungeon with its romance of long-dead prisoners.

Byron wrote this long poem in two days when he was detained in the neighborhood by a storm. Although his descriptions of the settings are exact, he did not adhere strictly to historical fact, for Bonnivard had no brothers imprisoned with him.

Byron's intense sympathy with the cause of liberty is reflected here. To him Bonnivard is not merely a single prisoner; he represents all martyrs in the onward march of freedom throughout the ages.

My hair is gray, but not with years,
  Nor grew it white
  In a single night,
As men's have grown from sudden
  fears;
My limbs are bowed, though not with
  toil,   5
 But rusted with a vile repose,
For they have been a dungeon's spoil,
 And mine has been the fate of those
To whom the goodly earth and air
Are banned, and barred — forbidden
  fare;   10
But this was for my father's faith
I suffered chains and courted death;
That father perished at the stake
For tenets he would not forsake;
And for the same his lineal race° 15
In darkness found a dwelling-place;
We were seven — who now are one,
 Six in youth, and one in age,
Finished as they had begun,
 Proud of Persecution's rage; 20
One in fire, and two in field
Their belief with blood have sealed,
Dying as their father died,
For the God their foes denied;
Three were in a dungeon cast, 25
Of whom this wreck is left the last.

  15. *lineal race:* children.

There are seven pillars of Gothic° mold,
In Chillon's dungeons deep and old,
There are seven columns, massy and
  gray,
Dim with a dull imprisoned ray, 30
A sunbeam which hath lost its way
And through the crevice and the cleft
Of the thick wall is fallen and left;
Creeping o'er the floor so damp,
Like a marsh's meteor lamp.° 35
And in each pillar there is a ring,
 And in each ring there is a chain;
That iron is a cankering thing,
 For in these limbs its teeth remain,
With marks that will not wear away, 40
Till I have done with this new day,
Which now is painful to these eyes,
Which have not seen the sun to rise
For years — I cannot count them o'er,
I lost their long and heavy score 45
When my last brother drooped and
  died,
And I lay living by his side.

27. *Gothic:* a medieval form of architecture. Byron's description of this dungeon is exact; the rings that attached the prisoners' chains to the column and their footprints on the pavement are still to be seen. Byron carved his name on one of the pillars. 35. *marsh's meteor lamp:* the will-o'-the-wisp.

They chained us each to a column stone,
And we were three — yet, each alone.
We could not move a single pace,   50
We could not see each other's face,
But with that pale and livid light
That made us strangers in our sight.
And thus together — yet apart,
Fettered in hand, but joined in heart,   55
'Twas still some solace, in the dearth
Of the pure elements of earth,
To hearken to each other's speech,
And each turn comforter to each
With some new hope, or legend old,   60
Or song heroically bold;
But even these at length grew cold.
Our voices took a dreary tone,
An echo of the dungeon stone,
    A grating sound, not full and free, 65
    As they of yore were wont to be;
It might be fancy, but to me
They never sounded like our own.

I was the eldest of the three,
    And to uphold and cheer the rest   70
    I ought to do — and did my best —
And each did well in his degree.
    The youngest, whom my father loved,
Because our mother's brow was given
To him, with eyes as blue as heaven —
    For him my soul was sorely moved;
And truly might it be distressed   77
To see such bird in such a nest;
For he was beautiful as day —
    When day was beautiful to me   80
    As to young eagles, being free —
A polar day, which will not see
A sunset till its summer's gone,°
    Its sleepless summer of long light,
The snow-clad offspring of the sun;   85
    And thus he was as pure and bright,
And in his natural spirit gay,
With tears for naught but others' ills,
And then they flowed like mountain rills,
Unless he could assuage the woe   90
Which he abhorred to view below.

The other was as pure of mind,
But formed to combat with his kind;

Strong in his frame, and of a mood
Which 'gainst the world in war had
        stood   95
And perished in the foremost rank
    With joy° — but not in chains to pine;
His spirit withered with their clank;
    I saw it silently decline —
    And so perchance in sooth° did mine;
But yet I forced it on to cheer   101
Those relics of a home so dear.
He was a hunter of the hills,
    Had followed there the deer and wolf;
    To him this dungeon was a gulf,   105
And fettered feet the worst of ills.

    Lake Leman lies by Chillon's walls;
A thousand feet in depth below
Its massy° waters meet and flow;
Thus much the fathom line was sent   110
From Chillon's snow-white battlement,
    Which round about the wave en-
        thralls;°
A double dungeon wall and wave
Have made — and like a living grave,
Below the surface of the lake   115
The dark vault lies wherein we lay;
We heard it ripple night and day;
    Sounding o'er our heads it knocked;
And I have felt the winter's spray
Wash through the bars when winds were
        high   120
And wanton in the happy sky;
    And then the very rock hath rocked,
    And I have felt it shake, unshocked,
Because I could have smiled to see
The death that would have set me free.

I said my nearer brother pined,   126
I said his mighty heart declined,
He loathed and put away his food;
It was not that 'twas coarse and rude,
For we were used to hunter's fare,   130
And for the like had little care.
The milk drawn from the mountain goat
Was changed for water from the moat;

82–83. Near the poles the day lasts the whole season.

95–97. *had stood . . . joy:* would have stood and would have perished with joy. 100. *sooth:* truth. 109. *massy:* massive or heavy. 112. *enthralls:* holds captive.

Our bread was such as captives' tears
Have moistened many a thousand years,
Since man first pent his fellow men   136
Like brutes within an iron den;
But what were these to us or him?
These wasted not his heart or limb;
My brother's soul was of that mold   140
Which in a palace had grown cold,
Had his free breathing been denied
The range of the steep mountain's side;
But why delay the truth? — he died.
I saw, and could not hold his head,   145
Nor reach his dying hand — nor dead —
Though hard I strove, but strove in vain
To rend and gnash my bonds in twain.
He died, and they unlocked his chain,
And scooped for him a shallow grave
Even from the cold earth of our cave.
I begged them as a boon to lay   152
His corse in dust whereon the day
Might shine — it was a foolish thought,
But then within my brain it wrought,
That even in death his free-born breast
In such a dungeon could not rest.   157
I might have spared my idle prayer —
They coldly laughed, and laid him there,
The flat and turfless earth above   160
The being we so much did love;
His empty chain above it leant,
Such murder's fitting monument!

But he, the favorite and the flower,
Most cherished since his natal hour,
His mother's image in fair face,   166
The infant love of all his race,
His martyred father's dearest thought,
My latest° care, for whom I sought
To hoard my life, that his might be   170
Less wretched now, and one day free;
He, too, who yet had held untired
A spirit natural or inspired —
He, too, was struck, and day by day
Was withered on the stalk away.   175
Oh, God! it is a fearful thing
To see the human soul take wing
In any shape, in any mood;
I've seen it rushing forth in blood;
I've seen it on the breaking ocean   180
Strive with a swol'n convulsive motion,

169. *latest:* last.

TWA

*The medieval castle of Chillon stands on
the shores of Lake Geneva.*

I've seen the sick and ghastly bed
Of sin, delirious with its dread;
But these were horrors — this was woe
Unmixed with such — but sure and slow.
He faded, and so calm and meek,   186
So softly worn, so sweetly weak,
So tearless, yet so tender — kind
And grieved for those he left behind;
With all the while a cheek whose
   bloom   190
Was as a mockery of the tomb,
Whose tints as gently sunk away
As a departing rainbow's ray;
An eye of most transparent light,
That almost made the dungeon bright;
And not a word of murmur, not   196
A groan o'er his untimely lot —
A little talk of better days,
A little hope my own to raise,
For I was sunk in silence — lost   200
In this last loss, of all the most;
And then the sighs he would suppress
Of fainting nature's feebleness,
More slowly drawn, grew less and less;
I listened, but I could not hear;   205
I called, for I was wild with fear;
I knew 'twas hopeless, but my dread
Would not be thus admonishèd;
I called, and thought I heard a sound —
I burst my chain with one strong bound,
And rushed to him — I found him not,
I only stirred in this black spot,

I only lived, *I* only drew
The accursèd breath of dungeon dew;
The last, the sole, the dearest link   215
Between me and the eternal brink,°
Which bound me to my failing race,
Was broken in this fatal place.
One on the earth, and one beneath —
My brothers — both had ceased to
    breathe.   220
I took that hand which lay so still,
Alas! my own was full as chill;
I had not strength to stir, or strive,
But felt that I was still alive —
A frantic feeling, when we know   225
That what we love shall ne'er be so.
       I know not why
       I could not die,
I had no earthly hope — but faith,
And that forbade a selfish° death.   230

What next befell me then and there
    I know not well — I never knew —
First came the loss of light, and air,
    And then of darkness too.
I had no thought, no feeling — none —
Among the stones I stood a stone,   236
And was scarce conscious what I wist,
As shrubless crags within the mist;
For all was blank, and bleak, and gray;
It was not night, it was not day;   240
It was not even the dungeon light,
So hateful to my heavy sight,
But vacancy absorbing space,
And fixedness without a place;
There were no stars, no earth, no time,
No check,° no change, no good, no
    crime,   246
But silence, and a stirless breath
Which neither was of life nor death;
A sea of stagnant idleness,
Blind, boundless, mute, and motionless!

A light broke in upon my brain —   251
    It was the carol of a bird;
It ceased, and then it came again,
    The sweetest song ear ever heard,
And mine was thankful till my eyes   255

216. *eternal brink:* death. 230. *selfish:* self-
inflicted. His religion forbade taking his own
life. 246. *No check:* no stopping or halting.

Ran over with the glad surprise,
And they that moment could not see
I was the mate of misery;
But then by dull degrees came back
My senses to their wonted track;   260
I saw the dungeon walls and floor
Close slowly round me as before,
I saw the glimmer of the sun
Creeping as it before had done,
But through the crevice where it came
That bird was perched, as fond and
    tame,   266
    And tamer than upon the tree;
A lovely bird, with azure wings,
And song that said a thousand things,
    And seemed to say them all for me!
I never saw its like before,   271
I ne'er shall see its likeness more;
It seemed like me to want a mate,
But was not half so desolate,
And it was come to love me when   275
None lived to love me so again,
And cheering from my dungeon's brink,
Had brought me back to feel and think.
I know not if it late were free,
    Or broke its cage to perch on mine,
But knowing well captivity,   281
    Sweet bird; I could not wish for thine!
Or if it were, in wingèd guise,
A visitant from Paradise;
For — Heaven forgive that thought! the
    while   285
Which made me both to weep and
    smile —
I sometimes deemed that it might be
My brother's soul come down to me;
But then at last away it flew,
And then 'twas mortal well I knew,   290
For he would never thus have flown,
And left me twice so doubly lone,
Lone as the corse within its shroud,
Lone as a solitary cloud —
    A single cloud on a sunny day,   295
While all the rest of heaven is clear,
A frown upon the atmosphere,
That hath no business to appear
    When skies are blue, and earth is gay.

A kind of change came in my fate;   300
My keepers grew compassionate;

I know not what had made them so,
They were inured to sights of woe,
But so it was — my broken chain
With links unfastened did remain,   305
And it was liberty to stride
Along my cell from side to side,
And up and down, and then athwart,
And tread it over every part;
And round the pillars one by one,   310
Returning where my walk begun,
Avoiding only, as I trod,
My brothers' graves without a sod;
For if I thought with heedless tread
My step profaned their lowly bed,   315
My breath came gaspingly and thick,
And my crushed heart fell blind and
    sick.

I made a footing in the wall,
  It was not therefrom to escape,
For I had buried one and all   320
  Who loved me in a human shape;
And the whole earth would henceforth
  be
A wider prison unto me.
No child, no sire, no kin had I,
No partner in my misery;   325
I thought of this, and I was glad,
For thought ot them had made me mad;
But I was curious to ascend
To my barred windows, and to bend
Once more, upon the mountains high,
The quiet of a loving eye.   331

I saw them, and they were the same,
They were not changed like me in frame;
I saw their thousand years of snow
On high — their wide long lake below,
And the blue Rhone in fullest flow;   336
I heard the torrents leap and gush
O'er channeled rock and broken bush;
I saw the white-walled distant town,
And whiter sails go skimming down;
And then there was a little isle,   341
Which in my very face did smile,
  The only one in view;
A small green isle; it seemed no more,
Scarce broader than my dungeon floor,
But in it there were three tall trees,   346
And o'er it blew the mountain breeze,

And by it there were waters flowing,
And on it there were young flowers
  growing,
  Of gentle breath and hue.   350
The fish swam by the castle wall,
And they seemed joyous each and all;
The eagle rode the rising blast,
Methought he never flew so fast
As then to me he seemed to fly;   355
And then new tears came in my eye,
And I felt troubled — and would fain°
I had not left my recent chain;
And when I did descend again,
The darkness of my dim abode   360
Fell on me as a heavy load;
It was as is a new-dug grave,
Closing o'er one we sought to save —
And yet my glance, too much op-
  pressed°
Had almost need of such a rest.   365
It might be months, or years, or days;
  I kept no count, I took no note,
I had no hope my eyes to raise,
  And clear them of their dreary mote;
At last men came to set me free;   370
  I asked not why, and recked° not
  where;
It was at length the same to me,
Fettered or fetterless to be,
  I learned to love despair.
And thus when they appeared at last,
And all my bonds aside were cast,   376
These heavy walls to me had grown
A hermitage — and all my own,
And half I felt as they were come
To tear me from a second home;   380
With spiders I had friendship made,
And watched them in their sullen trade,
Had seen the mice by moonlight play,
And why should I feel less than they?
We were all inmates of one place,   385
And I, the monarch of each race,
Had power to kill — yet, strange to tell!
In quiet we had learned to dwell.
My very chains and I grew friends,
So much a long communion tends   390
To make us what we are — even I
Regained my freedom with a sigh.

357. *would fain*: wished. 364. *oppressed*: that
is, with the unaccustomed sights. 371. *recked*:
cared.

She Walks in Beauty

This lyric, which has been set to music, was inspired by the
poet's first meeting with his cousin by marriage, Mrs. Wilmot. The occasion of their meeting was an evening party at
which Mrs. Wilmot appeared in a black dress with spangles.

She walks in beauty, like the night
    Of cloudless climes and starry skies;
And all that's best of dark and bright
    Meet in her aspect° and her eyes:
Thus mellowed to that tender light   5
    Which heaven to gaudy day denies.

One shade the more, one ray the less,
    Had half impaired the nameless grace
Which waves in every raven tress,
    Or softly lightens o'er her face;   10
Where thoughts serenely sweet express
    How pure, how dear their dwelling place.

And on that cheek, and o'er that brow,
    So soft, so calm, so eloquent,
The smiles that win, the tints that glow,   15
    But tell of days in goodness spent,
A mind at peace with all below,
    A heart whose love is innocent!

4. *aspect:* countenance.

"Mrs. Richard Brinsley Sheridan," by Thomas Gainsborough. ▶

Apostrophe to the Ocean

These stanzas (178–84 of Canto IV of *Childe Harold's Pilgrimage*), considered among Byron's most sublime lines, are a worthy tribute not only to the time-defying ocean but to its effects on the empires which border it. Byron observes that great empires of the past, once centers of art, religion, and law, are now ruins washed by the ever-changing yet changeless sea.

Characteristically, Byron delighted in the grand aspects of nature, such as mountain ranges and the turbulent ocean. His enduring love of the sea can be paralleled with that of both earlier and later English writers.

There is a pleasure in the pathless woods,
There is a rapture on the lonely shore,
There is society, where none intrudes,
By the deep sea, and music in its roar;
I love not man the less, but nature more,   5
From these our interviews, in which I steal
From all I may be, or have been before,
To mingle with the universe, and feel
What I can ne'er express, yet cannot all conceal.

Roll on, thou deep and dark blue Ocean — roll!   10
Ten thousand fleets sweep over thee in vain;
Man marks the earth with ruin — his control
Stops with the shore — upon the watery plain
The wrecks are all thy deed, nor doth remain
A shadow of man's ravage, save his own,°   15
When for a moment, like a drop of rain,
He sinks into thy depths with bubbling groan —
Without a grave, unknelled, uncoffined, and unknown.

His steps are not upon thy path — thy fields
Are not a spoil for him — thou dost arise   20
And shake him from thee; the vile strength he wields
For earth's destruction thou dost all despise,
Spurning him from thy bosom to the skies,
And send'st him, shivering in thy playful spray
And howling, to his gods, where haply° lies   25
His petty hope in some near port or bay,
And dashest him again to earth; there let him lay.°

15. *save his own:* except his own destruction (*ravage*). 25. *haply:* perhaps. 27. *lay:* Byron's note on his galley proof suggests that he made this grammatical error purposely, for the sake of the rhyme.

The armaments which thunderstrike the walls
Of rock-built cities, bidding nations quake
And monarchs tremble in their capitals,   30
The oak leviathans,° whose huge ribs make
Their clay creator° the vain title take
Of lord of thee, and arbiter of war —
These are thy toys, and as the snowy flake,
They melt into thy yeast of waves, which mar   35
Alike the Armada's° pride, or spoils of Trafalgar.°

Thy shores are empires, changed in all save thee —
Assyria, Greece, Rome, Carthage, what are they?
Thy waters washed them power while they were free,
And many a tyrant since;° their shores obey   40
The stranger, slave, or savage; their decay
Has dried up realms to deserts — not so thou,
Unchangeable save to thy wild waves' play.
Time writes no wrinkle on thine azure brow;
Such as creation's dawn beheld, thou rollest now.   45

Thou glorious mirror, where the Almighty's form
Glasses itself in tempest; in all time,
Calm or convulsed — in breeze, or gale, or storm,
Icing the pole, or in the torrid clime
Dark-heaving — boundless, endless, and sublime;   50
The image of eternity, the throne
Of the Invisible; even from out thy slime
The monsters of the deep are made; each zone
Obeys thee; thou goest forth, dread, fathomless, alone.

And I have loved thee, Ocean! and my joy   55
Of youthful sports was on thy breast to be
Borne, like thy bubbles, onward; from a boy
I wantoned with thy breakers° — they to me
Were a delight; and if the freshening sea
Made them a terror — 'twas a pleasing fear,   60
For I was as it were a child of thee,
And trusted to thy billows far and near,
And laid my hand upon thy mane — as I do here.

31. *leviathans* (lĕ·vī′à·thănz): monstrous sea animals, described several times in the Old Testament. Here the word means huge ships. 32. *clay creator:* man. 36. *Armada* (är·mä′dà): refers to the defeat of the Spanish Armada in 1588; *Trafalgar* (trà·făl′gĕr, but here must be accented on the first syllable for the meter): Nelson's memorable victory over the French and Spanish fleets in 1805. 39–40. The ocean brought power to these empires, and, when they had fallen, it brought tyrants to rule them. 58. Byron was a famous swimmer. He succeeded in swimming across the Hellespont (now called the Dardanelles) to verify the possibility of the Greek myth that Leander had done so to meet Hero.

POEMS OF A "GLORIOUS APOLLO"

TWO SHORT POEMS

1. In "Stanzas Written on the Road Between Florence and Pisa," what does Byron mean by the word "glory"?

2. In "The Destruction of Sennacherib," note the swift panorama of pictures. How many distinct pictures can you find? What sharp contrasts are there? Read the Bible story on which the poem is based.

THE PRISONER OF CHILLON

1. Recount the persecution of the Bonnivard family as given in the first stanza. How does this make you feel toward the prisoner at the outset? What details of the imprisonment increase this feeling?

2. Differentiate the personalities of the three brothers. Compare the speaker's emotions on the death of each brother. Which lines show the climax of his despair?

3. How does Byron create a strong impression of the lapse of years? How does the bird affect the prisoner's mental state? What other creatures are in the prison?

4. What changes come about in the prisoner's condition? Can you account for the change in the keepers?

5. How does the prisoner feel when released? Do you regard this as natural or unnatural under the circumstances?

6. In connection with this poem, you should read Byron's moving "Sonnet on Chillon," which expresses in beautiful form his passionate devotion to liberty — the "Eternal Spirit of the chainless Mind." Swinburne, a celebrated poet of the Victorian Age, regarded that sonnet as one of Byron's "noblest and completest poems."

SHE WALKS IN BEAUTY

Compare "She Walks in Beauty" with "She Was a Phantom of Delight" (page 385) as to both the physical and the spiritual qualities of the women described. In the mind of each poet, what constitutes a woman's chief beauty?

APOSTROPHE TO THE OCEAN

What theme unifies these stanzas into a complete poem? Compare Byron's view of nature with Wordsworth's. Which lines identify Byron as a Romantic writer?

APPRECIATING FIGURATIVE LANGUAGE

To read poetry well is, in one sense, to borrow the highly gifted imagination of a poet and to see the world with the poet's insight. Because the accomplished poet is usually highly sensitive to the appearance as well as the inner meaning of what he sees and because he is also sufficiently skilled to communicate both of these aspects of good poetry, he awakens his readers to new experiences; and he often does this by using figurative language.

1. Byron shows an ability to use figurative language with powerful effect. There are six striking similes in "The Destruction of Sennacherib." Explain the figure of speech with which Byron describes the attack. How does he suggest the size of the attacking army? How does he characterize the army before and after the pestilence? Find the other three similes in the poem.

2. Byron uses another figure of speech when he says in the selection from *Childe Harold's Pilgrimage,* "Roll on, thou deep and dark blue Ocean — roll!" This effective figure of speech, called an *apostrophe,* can be direct address; address to the dead as if living; to the absent as if present; and to animals, objects, or ideas as if they were persons. Find other lines in which the poet speaks directly to the ocean. What is Byron's attitude toward the sea? Why is the apostrophe effective as used here?

LITERATURE AND THE ARTS

Mrs. Richard Brinsley Sheridan (page 437), one of the outstanding beauties of her day, could easily have been the inspiration for a poem such as Byron's "She Walks in Beauty." As a singer, the toast of London at the age of nineteen, and the wife of Richard Brinsley Sheridan, the well-known dramatist and statesman, Mrs. Sheridan moved in London's most fashionable and literary circles and was a fit subject for the great eighteenth-century English portraitist, Thomas Gainsborough.

Both Byron's poetry and Gainsborough's portrait reflect the lyricism of the English Romantics.

PERCY BYSSHE SHELLEY

1792–1822

Bodleian Library

"Tameless, and swift, and proud" wrote Shelley, describing himself as resembling the west wind. Indeed, he spent much of his life struggling rebelliously against conventions of the society in which he was born. His conflict began at Eton, where the older boys goaded this gentle-looking, imaginative boy by chasing him with mud balls and branding him "Mad Shelley." It continued at Oxford, where he was expelled for writing a pamphlet "On the Necessity of Atheism." He antagonized his wealthy father by eloping at nineteen with a sixteen-year-old girl, Harriet Westbrook. A few years later he fell in love with the beautiful and talented Mary Godwin, daughter of William Godwin, whose home was a center for the political radicals and free thinkers of London. Harriet, then only twenty-one, drowned herself in despair. Shelley and Mary were then married.

Two years later they moved to Italy. Byron joined them for a time, and together with other English friends they formed a small, congenial colony. Here in the short space of four years Shelley produced his best poetry. Not long before his thirtieth birthday, while he and two companions were crossing the Gulf of Leghorn in a small yacht, a raging storm arose and the three men were drowned. When their bodies were later washed ashore, Shelley's friends burned his body on a great funeral pyre on the beach. Byron swam far out to sea to watch the flames that marked the end of his fellow exile.

Shelley had an innate gentleness and sweetness of disposition. He was a generous and loyal friend, an idealist who never lost faith in the power of love and good will. He was passionately devoted to the idea of personal freedom and unconcerned with the individual's responsibilities to society. He maintained that human conduct would always be good if based on sincere convictions and not bound by laws and social conventions.

Shelley was a prolific writer. His long poems — *Adonais* (an elegy on the death of Keats) and *Prometheus Unbound* — are intense pleas for freeing the human spirit from the conditions of life that enchain it. His shorter lyrics have a rhythmic beauty and ethereal quality of spirit that lift Shelley to a high pinnacle in the realm of English lyric poetry.

To Night

Swiftly walk o'er the western wave,
   Spirit of Night!
Out of the misty eastern cave,
Where, all the long and lone daylight,
Thou wovest dreams of joy and fear,   5

441

Which make thee terrible and dear —
   Swift be thy flight!

Wrap thy form in a mantle gray,
   Star-inwrought!°
Blind with thine hair the eyes of Day;
Kiss her until she be wearied out;   11
Then wander o'er city and sea and land,
Touching all with thine opiate wand° —
   Come, long-sought!

When I arose and saw the dawn,   15
   I sighed for thee;
When light rode high, and the dew was
   gone,
And noon lay heavy on flower and tree,

9. *Star-inwrought:* with stars woven into it.
13. *opiate wand:* sleep-producing power.

And the weary Day turned to his rest,
Lingering like an unloved guest,   20
   I sighed for thee.

Thy brother Death came, and cried,
   "Wouldst thou me?"
Thy sweet child Sleep, the filmy-eyed,
Murmured like a noontide bee,   25
   "Shall I nestle near thy side?
Wouldst thou me?" — And I replied,
   "No, not thee!"

Death will come when thou art dead,
   Soon, too soon —   30
Sleep will come when thou art fled;
Of neither would I ask the boon
I ask of thee, belovèd Night —
Swift be thine approaching flight,
   Come soon, soon!   35

The Cloud

"The poet," writes Mary Godwin Shelley, "marked the cloud as it
sped across the heavens, while he floated in his boat on the Thames."
The cloud, personified, is speaking throughout the poem; therefore
Shelley's personal emotions are not in evidence as in the poems
addressed to the skylark and the west wind which follow it. These
three are often grouped as Shelley's great trilogy. In all of them we
feel the lift and rush of flight in an element purer than air.

I bring fresh showers for the thirsting flowers,
   From the seas and the streams;
I bear light shade for the leaves when laid
   In their noonday dreams.
From my wings are shaken the dews that waken   5
   The sweet buds every one,
When rocked to rest on their mother's breast,
   As she dances about the sun.
I wield the flail of the lashing hail,
   And whiten the green plains under,   10
And then again I dissolve it in rain,
   And laugh as I pass in thunder.

I sift the snow on the mountains below,
   And their great pines groan aghast;
And all the night 'tis my pillow white,   15
   While I sleep in the arms of the blast.

Sublime on the towers of my skyey° bowers
    Lightning my pilot sits;
In a cavern under is fettered the thunder,
    It struggles and howls at fits;   20
Over earth and ocean, with gentle motion,
    This pilot is guiding me,
Lured by the love of the genii that move
    In the depths of the purple sea;
Over the rills, and the crags, and the hills,   25
    Over the lakes and the plains,
Wherever he dream, under mountain or stream,
    The Spirit he loves remains;
And I all the while bask in Heaven's blue smile,
    Whilst he is dissolving in rains.   30

The sanguine° Sunrise, with his meteor eyes,
    And his burning plumes outspread,
Leaps on the back of my sailing rack,°
    When the morning star shines dead;
As on the jag of a mountain crag,   35
    Which an earthquake rocks and swings,
An eagle alit one moment may sit
    In the light of its golden wings.
And when Sunset may breathe, from the lit sea beneath,
    Its ardors of rest and of love,   40
And the crimson pall of eve may fall
    From the depth of Heaven above,
With wings folded I rest, on mine airy nest,
    As still as a brooding dove.
That orbèd maiden with white fire laden,   45
    Whom mortals call the Moon,
Glides glimmering o'er my fleecelike floor,
    By the midnight breezes strewn;
And wherever the beat of her unseen feet,
    Which only the angels hear,   50
May have broken the woof of my tent's thin roof,
    The stars peep behind her and peer;
And I laugh to see them whirl and flee,
    Like a swarm of golden bees,
When I widen the rent in my wind-built tent,   55
    Till the calm rivers, lakes, and seas,
Like strips of the sky fallen through me on high,
    Are each paved with the moon and these.

I bind the Sun's throne with a burning zone,°
    And the Moon's with a girdle of pearl;   60
The volcanoes are dim, and the stars reel and swim
    When the whirlwinds my banner unfurl.
From cape to cape, with a bridgelike shape,

---

17. *skyey* (skī′ĭ): of the sky. 31. *sanguine:* blood-red (the root meaning of the word). 33. *sailing rack:* broken clouds, floating through the air. 59. *zone:* girdle, belt.

Over a torrent sea,
Sunbeam-proof, I hang like a roof —   65
    The mountains its columns be.
The triumphal arch through which I march
    With hurricane, fire, and snow,
When the Powers of the air are chained to my chair,
    Is the million-colored bow;   70
The sphere fire° above its soft colors wove,
    While the moist Earth was laughing below.

I am the daughter of Earth and Water,
    And the nursling of the Sky;
I pass through the pores of the ocean and shores,   75
    I change, but I cannot die.
For after the rain when with never a stain
    The pavilion of Heaven is bare,
And the winds and sunbeams with their convex gleams
    Build up the blue dome of air,   80
I silently laugh at my own cenotaph,°
    And out of the caverns of rain,
Like a child from the womb, like a ghost from the tomb,
    I arise and unbuild it again.

71. *sphere fire:* the light of the heavens. 81. *cenotaph:* a monument erected in honor of the dead buried elsewhere; here, the cloud's cenotaph is the "blue dome of air."

To a Skylark

Of the origin of this poem, Mary Shelley wrote: "It was a beautiful summer evening, while wandering along the lanes whose myrtle hedges were the bowers of the fireflies, that we heard the caroling of the skylark which inspired one of the most beautiful of his poems." Notice how the verse form suggests the motion of the bird. The first four short lines represent the swift upward dart of the bird; the fifth long line corresponds to the long, steady, graceful sweep of the soaring bird.

    Hail to thee, blithe spirit!
      Bird thou never wert,
    That from heaven, or near it,
      Pourest thy full heart
In profuse strains of unpremeditated art.   5

    Higher still and higher
      From the earth thou springest
    Like a cloud of fire;
      The blue deep thou wingest,
And singing still dost soar, and soaring ever singest.   10

    In the golden lightning
      Of the sunken sun,

O'er which clouds are bright'ning,
   Thou dost float and run;
Like an unbodied joy whose race is just begun.   15

The pale purple even°
   Melts around thy flight;
Like a star of heaven
   In the broad daylight
Thou art unseen, but yet I hear thy shrill delight,   20

Keen as are the arrows
   Of that silver sphere,°
Whose intense lamp narrows
   In the white dawn clear,
Until we hardly see, we feel that it is there.   25

All the earth and air
   With thy voice is loud,
As, when night is bare,
   From one lonely cloud
The moon rains out her beams, and heaven is overflowed.   30

What thou art we know not;
   What is most like thee?
From rainbow clouds there flow not
   Drops so bright to see,
As from thy presence showers a rain of melody.   35

Like a poet hidden
   In the light of thought,
Singing hymns unbidden,
   Till the world is wrought
To sympathy with hopes and fears it heeded not;   40

Like a high-born maiden
   In a palace tower,
Soothing her love-laden
   Soul in secret hour
With music sweet as love, which overflows her bower;   45

Like a glowworm golden
   In a dell of dew,
Scattering unbeholden
   Its aerial hue
Among the flowers and grass, which screen it from the view;   50

Like a rose embowered
   In its own green leaves,

16. *even:* evening. 22. *silver sphere:* the morning star.

By warm winds deflowered,
　　Till the scent it gives
Makes faint with too much sweet those heavy-wingèd thieves;　　55

Sound of vernal showers
　　On the twinkling grass,
Rain-awakened flowers,
　　All that ever was
Joyous, and clear, and fresh, thy music doth surpass.　　60

Teach us, sprite or bird,
　　What sweet thoughts are thine;
I have never heard
　　Praise of love or wine
That panted forth a flood of rapture so divine.　　65

Chorus Hymeneal,°
　　Or triumphal chant,
Matched with thine, would be all
　　But an empty vaunt,
A thing wherein we feel there is some hidden want.　　70

What objects are the fountains°
　　Of thy happy strain?
What fields, or waves, or mountains?
　　What shapes of sky or plain?
What love of thine own kind? what ignorance of pain?　　75

With thy clear keen joyance
　　Languor cannot be;
Shadow of annoyance
　　Never came near thee;
Thou lovest, but ne'er knew love's sad satiety.　　80

Waking or asleep,
　　Thou of death must deem°
Things more true and deep
　　Than we mortals dream,
Or how could thy notes flow in such a crystal stream?　　85

We look before and after,
　　And pine for what is not;
Our sincerest laughter
　　With some pain is fraught;
Our sweetest songs are those that tell of saddest thought.　　90

Yet if° we could scorn
　　Hate, and pride, and fear;

---

66. *Chorus Hymeneal* (hĭ'mĕ·nē'ăl): marriage chant. Hymen was the Greek god of marriage.
71. *fountains:* sources, or inspiration. 82. *deem:* know. 91. *if:* even if.

> If we were things born
> Not to shed a tear,
> I know not how thy joy we ever should come near.   95
>
> Better than all measures
> Of delightful sound
> Better than all treasures
> That in books are found,
> Thy skill to poet were,° thou scorner of the ground!   100
>
> Teach me half the gladness
> That thy brain must know,
> Such harmonious madness
> From my lips would flow,
> The world should listen then, as I am listening now.   105

100. *were:* would be.

Ode to the West Wind

The construction of this poem is beautifully precise. Each of the first three parts invokes the powerful west wind, which in the first part is shown driving the leaves, in the second the clouds, and in the third the waves. In the fourth part the poet imagines himself as each of these three playthings of the wind and calls for inspiration in his personal despondency. In the fifth, he prays that his ideas be given the power of the wind, and spread throughout the world. The oft-quoted last line is an expression of hope.

I

> O wild West Wind, thou breath of Autumn's being,
> Thou, from whose unseen presence the leaves dead
> Are driven, like ghosts from an enchanter fleeing,
>
> Yellow, and black, and pale, and hectic red,
> Pestilence-stricken multitudes: O thou,   5
> Who chariotest to their dark wintry bed
>
> The wingèd seeds, where they lie cold and low,
> Each like a corpse within its grave, until
> Thine azure sister of the Spring° shall blow
>
> Her clarion° o'er the dreaming earth, and fill   10
> (Driving sweet buds like flocks to feed in air)
> With living hues and odors plain and hill;
>
> Wild Spirit, which art moving everywhere;
> Destroyer and preserver; hear, Oh, hear!

9. *sister of the Spring:* south wind. 10. *clarion:* a trumpet with a pure, clear tone.

II

Thou on whose stream, 'mid the steep sky's commotion,   15
Loose clouds like earth's decaying leaves are shed,
Shook from the tangled boughs of Heaven and Ocean,

Angels° of rain and lightning; there are spread
On the blue surface of thine airy surge,
Like the bright hair uplifted from the head   20

Of some fierce Maenad,° even from the dim verge
Of the horizon to the zenith's° height,
The locks of the approaching storm. Thou dirge

Of the dying year, to which this closing night
Will be the dome of a vast sepulcher,   25
Vaulted with all thy congregated might

Of vapors, from whose solid atmosphere
Black rain, and fire, and hail will burst: Oh, hear!

III

Thou who didst waken from his summer dreams
The blue Mediterranean, where he lay,   30
Lulled by the coil of his crystalline streams,

Beside a pumice° isle in Baiae's bay,°
And saw in sleep old palaces and towers
Quivering within the wave's intenser day,

18. *Angels:* messengers (from the Greek *angelos*). 21. *Maenad* (mē′năd): a priestess of Bacchus, *fierce* because she engaged in wild and frenzied ceremonies in honor of the god. 22. *zenith:* the point in the heavens directly overhead. 32. *pumice* (pŭm′ĭs): formed from lava; *Baiae's* (bä′yäz) *bay,* near Naples, is close to nearly extinct volcanoes which still rumble and erupt occasionally. The area was famous as a resort of the ancient Romans.

All overgrown with azure moss and flowers   35
So sweet, the sense faints picturing them! Thou
For whose path the Atlantic's level powers°

Cleave themselves into chasms, while far below
The sea blooms and the oozy woods which wear
The sapless foliage of the ocean, know   40

Thy voice and suddenly grow gray with fear,
And tremble and despoil themselves: Oh, hear!

IV

If I were a dead leaf thou mightest bear;
If I were a swift cloud to fly with thee;
A wave to pant beneath thy power, and share   45

The impulse of thy strength, only less free
Than thou, O uncontrollable! If even
I were as in my boyhood, and could be

The comrade of thy wanderings over heaven,
As then, when to outstrip thy skyey speed   50
Scarce seemed a vision;° I would ne'er have striven

As thus with thee in prayer in my sore need.
Oh, lift me as a wave, a leaf, a cloud!
I fall upon the thorns of life! I bleed!

A heavy weight of hours has chained and bowed   55
One too like thee: tameless, and swift, and proud.

V

Make me thy lyre, even as the forest is;
What if my leaves are falling like its own!
The tumult of thy mighty harmonies

Will take from both a deep, autumnal tone,   60
Sweet though in sadness. Be thou, spirit fierce,
My spirit! Be thou me, impetuous one!

Drive my dead thoughts over the universe
Like withered leaves to quicken a new birth!
And, by the incantation of this verse,   65

Scatter, as from an unextinguished hearth
Ashes and sparks, my words among mankind!
Be through my lips to unawakened earth

The trumpet of a prophecy! O wind,
If Winter comes, can Spring be far behind?   70

37. *level powers:* surfaces. 51. *vision:* that is, something impossible to attain.

Ozymandias°

In reading an ancient Greek historian, Shelley had learned of the gigantic statue described here. In this poem, he expresses two ideas that occur frequently in his verse — the vainglory of kings and the inconstancy of life.

I met a traveler from an antique land
Who said: "Two vast and trunkless legs of stone
Stand in the desert. . . . Near them, on the sand,
Half sunk, a shattered visage lies, whose frown,
And wrinkled lip, and sneer of cold command   5
Tell that its sculptor well those passions read
Which yet survive, stamped on these lifeless things,
The hand that mocked them, and the heart that fed;
And on the pedestal these words appear;
'My name is Ozymandias, king of kings;   10
Look on my works, ye Mighty, and despair!'
Nothing beside remains. Round the decay
Of that colossal wreck, boundless and bare
The lone and level sands stretch far away."

Title: *Ozymandias* (ŏz′ĭ·măn′dĭ·ăs): a corruption of a name of Rameses II (1324?–1258? B.C.), a famous Egyptian king and great builder of palaces and temples. Many statues of him are found in Egypt; the one referred to here is probably near Thebes.

A Lament

This poem and the one that follows were written in the last two years of Shelley's life and published in *Posthumous Poems* (1824), two years after his death. Both of them suggest the troubled and tempestuous spirit of Shelley's last days. He seems even to have had a premonition of his early tragic death.

O world! O life! O time!
On whose last steps° I climb,
  Trembling at that where I had stood
    before;
When will return the glory of your
    prime?°
No more — oh, nevermore!   5

2. *last steps:* The poet compares life to a stairway, whose end he is nearing. 4. *prime:* the beginning of life.

Out of the day and night
A joy has taken flight;
  Fresh spring, and summer, and winter
    hoar,
Move my faint heart with grief, but with
    delight
No more — oh, nevermore!   10

A Dirge

Rough wind, that moanest loud
Grief too sad for song;
Wild wind, when sullen cloud
  Knells all the night long;
Sad storm, whose tears are vain,   5
Bare woods, whose branches strain,
Deep caves and dreary main,
  Wail, for the world's wrong!

SHELLEY'S POETRY

TO A SKYLARK

1. The thought divisions of this poem are indicated by the following outline: (*a*) lines 1–30, where and when the bird's song is heard; (*b*) lines 31–60, description of the bird's song by a series of comparisons; (*c*) lines 61–75, the sources and nature of its song; (*d*) lines 76–105, the disparity between the lark's joy and man's troubled state. What does each stanza contribute to these main ideas?

2. To what different things is the skylark compared? What quality do all these things have in common with the bird? Why are they less lovely to the poet than the bird is?

3. Compare this poem with Wordsworth's poems on the skylark (page 387) for similar words used to describe the effect of the bird's song on the hearer. What is the effect which each poet emphasizes? In what way is Shelley's reaction to the skylark's song different from that of Shakespeare, of Milton, and of Wordsworth?

4. Is it true that "our sweetest songs are those that tell of saddest thought"? Give some examples in both music and poetry. Are the greatest works of literature tragedies?

ODE TO THE WEST WIND

1. How well did Shelley understand his own nature? What incidents in his life illustrate the adjectives by which he describes himself in this poem?

2. Study carefully the interlocking rhyme scheme. Interlocking means that the middle rhyme of each triplet becomes the first and third rhyme of the next triplet: a-b-a, b-c-b, c-d-c, d-e-d, e-e. This is an old form called *terza rima,* derived from Italian poetry. Chaucer also used it. The couplet at the end of each part is Shelley's addition to the old form.

3. You may recall that an ode is a lyric poem characterized by noble feeling and dignity of style. What distinguishes this ode in tone and form from Wordsworth's "Intimations of Immortality"?

SONNET AND LYRICS

1. Compare Shelley's "To Night" with Longfellow's "Hymn to the Night," written several years later. What mood is common to both poems?

2. What in the situation of the statue of Ozymandias would appeal especially to a man of Shelley's temperament? Wherein lies the irony of the inscription?

3. Write out the rhyme scheme of the sonnet to discover how unusual it is. Even in this restricted form Shelley showed his love of freedom.

4. Which of the two posthumous lyrics seems to you the more despairing? Why? Which lines seem to foretell Shelley's death?

CLASS ACTIVITY

Look up and report to the class on the origin of *terza rima* and its use in English literature through the ages. Compare its use by some of the leading English poets.

SUGGESTION FOR WRITING

Browse through a collection of Romantic poets, reading further lyrics, and then try your hand at writing a lyric of your own.

THE POWER OF WORDS

SIMILES

In the "Ode to the West Wind" Shelley's rich imagination weaves simile after simile into an intricate pattern of figurative language. In the first stanza, the autumn wind is compared to an enchanter and the dry leaves to ghosts which he drives before him. (Aside from its importance to the meter, why is *ghosts* a more suitable word here than any of its synonyms?) Two lines down, the leaves are called *pestilence-stricken multitudes.* Then the seeds driven into the ground are called *corpses.* So far, everything contributes to the idea of death. But with the coming of spring the whole metaphor shifts its emphasis to new life. What may be the purpose of a clarion? Why are buds likened to flocks?

Make a similar analysis of the rest of the poem to show how the figures interlock and reinforce the alternately despondent and hopeful mood of the poet. What else in nature besides the West Wind is personified (given human attributes or form)?

READING LYRIC POETRY

This is not the first time you have read lyric poetry. In fact, you have been hearing, reading, and singing lyric poems all your life. Children — and primitive civilizations — have a keen sense of rhythm, and for them simple verses are a natural form of expression. As man — or a civilization — matures and becomes more complex in personality, the lyric poetry through which he speaks (or sings) also becomes more complex — more subtly imaginative in its content, more varied in its rhythms, more intricate in its language. The Romantic Age brought English lyric poetry to a climax of richness and beauty. Since in its highest forms lyric poetry may sometimes baffle the reader by its difficulties, it may be well to consider here some of the ways to approach a lyric poem.

APPROACHING THE LYRIC

You already know, of course, that a lyric poem does not tell a story about people as a narrative or dramatic poem does. We are not, then, looking for a sequence of events or analyzing character. We are dealing entirely with more intangible things — thoughts, emotions, fine shades of meaning. One of the first requisites in approaching a lyric poem is to open our minds willingly to the thoughts of another person and be ready to identify ourselves as far as possible with that person's experience. A striking example of this identification can be found in "The Cloud." In reading this poem you must for a moment cease to be a mortal on earth looking *up* at a cloud. You must, instead, become that cloud, free in the heavens, looking *down* on the earth. Then only can you appreciate the cloud's song as Shelley sings it. Similarly, you may recall that Robert Burns' lyrics offer many good examples of how a poet utters the thoughts of different kinds of people — an old wife, a gentle lover, Bruce addressing his army. A good lyric poem indicates to the reader the type of person speaking or the circumstances that called forth the poem. Sometimes these may not be obvious on first reading, but usually they become clear on a careful rereading.

Another requisite for gaining the full value of a lyric poem is first to hear or read it as a whole. Detailed study — by looking up words in a dictionary or by trying to understand each sentence fully before continuing — should come *after* the first reading. Let the poem have a chance to make a total first impression on you. Don't reject a poem or become disturbed if you do not completely understand it on the first reading. A good poem must often be lived with for a while before its meaning is fully revealed to you.

METER AND ALLITERATION

The *sound* of any poem, of course, should never be overlooked. In a lyric poem the metrical form is especially important because it contributes greatly to the total effect, matching both mood and meaning. Reading lyric poetry with the eye alone is almost like trying to read sheet music with the eye alone. A favorable approach, then, is to read aloud. In "The Cloud," consider the unusual meter and the internal rhymes in alternate lines. What swing and gusto these give to the constantly shifting life of the cloud! The whole poem moves with the speed of racing clouds on a windy day:

"The triumphal arch through which I
     march
   With hurricane, fire, and snow,
 When the Powers of the air are chained
     to my chair,
   Is the million-colored bow . . ."

In the next Shelley poem, "To a Skylark," an entirely different tempo is given by the meter. How do the first four lines suggest the swift upward flight of the bird? How does the fifth line suggest a different kind of motion?

Lyric poetry is a broad term including everything from deeply thoughtful philosophic poems like Wordsworth's odes to flippant little songs like those of the Cavalier poets. It is fortunate that English poetry has such varied meters to voice these different moods. The dignified blank verse of "Tintern Abbey" establishes a mood of serious meditation. Not all lyrics create definite musical effects, yet some employ a pronounced rhythmic meter. The "feet" of "The Destruction of Sennacherib" gallop; those of "Flow Gently, Sweet Afton" tiptoe.

The Romantic poets were eagerly searching for new meters to produce new emotional effects. The nineteenth century is therefore the best period in which to study different verse forms. The eighteenth century was bound by the classical convention of the rhymed couplet, while the twentieth tends to break away into free verse. You have now had enough experience in meters to build up your own list of metrical forms with illustrations from the poetry in this volume. Such a project would be valuable to continue through the rest of this year's study.

Other devices besides meter add to the sound-value of a poem. One of the oldest in English poetry is alliteration, harking back to Anglo-Saxon days. In "The Cloud" not a stanza is without this effective repetition of initial sounds. To see how alliteration adds to the smoothness and swiftness of a line, try substituting nonalliterative words for those with a common consonant in these lines:

"I sift the snow on the mountains below,
   And their great pines groan aghast"

                 or

"The stars peep behind her and peer . . ."

IMAGERY

Probably the most important single element in reading a lyric poem is to grasp its imaginative quality, which, along with meter, distinguishes a poem from a piece of prose that might express the same thought. The imagination takes fire largely from the imagery of a poem. In "The Cloud" notice how much the word *flail* accomplishes toward an instantaneous picture in the line "I wield the flail of the lashing hail." How superbly the cloud is personified in the phrase, "And laugh as I pass in thunder." Again, we have a sense of great height in "Sublime on the towers of my skyey bowers, Lightning my pilot sits," or an impression of calm beauty in the following lines:

"That orbèd maiden with white fire laden,
   Whom mortals call the Moon,
Glides glimmering o'er my fleecelike floor,
   By the midnight breezes strewn."

Imagery results not only from personification (assigning human feelings or actions to inanimate things) but also from metaphor, or comparisons. The cloud's surface is called a "tent's thin roof"; the stars are said to move "like a swarm of golden bees." Look at the poem closely to discover how many other examples of personification and metaphor you can find. Note in your reading of lyrics that when the poet wishes to convey abstract emotions and thoughts he uses concrete images.

DESIGN OF THE POEM

There remains one more point to consider — the general design of the poem. A poet does not just string together a series of imaginative lines in a chosen meter; he writes a poem to express something. You may not associate anything as prosaic as an outline with lyric poetry, but you may be sure that a good poet has in mind something like an outline — a definite progression of ideas to a conclusion. This is evident in the three stanzas of Wordsworth's "She Was a Phantom of Delight" (page 385). A sonnet may show its design in a clear division between octave and sestet.

How does the design of thoughts develop in "The Cloud"? First we see the action of the cloud under various weather conditions — in light summer storms, in more menacing mountain storms, at sunrise, at sunset, in the moonlight. Then a stanza summarizes the force and magnificence of the cloud as it relates to all the elements of the heavens. Finally, the last stanza analyzes the very nature of the cloud and explains its immortality. You can easily see how the design of the poem would be weakened by changing the order of these topics.

One of the most carefully designed lyric poems in literature is Shelley's "Ode to the West Wind." It will repay thorough study on all the points touched upon in this discussion — identifying yourself with the speaker and grasping the thought or emotion he expresses, reading the poem as a whole before studying its details, examining its unusual meter, looking for other devices which enhance its musical sound, letting your imagination be stirred by its figurative language, and noting the design of its elements into a perfect whole.

JOHN KEATS

1795–1821

National Portrait Gallery

It may truly be said of Keats that one over-powering idea shaped his work. He was a man preoccupied with beauty; in beauty he perceived love, power, truth. He gave expression to this philosophy in some of the most beautiful lyric poetry in English.

In contrast to the aristocratic Byron and Shelley, Keats was of humble origin. His father kept a stable in London, and Keats was born in the family quarters in the same building. He had some schooling before he was left an orphan at the age of fifteen. Shortly thereafter he was apprenticed to an apothecary-surgeon in London. During the seven years that he studied to become a surgeon, he eagerly read the Greek myths and Spenser's *The Faerie Queene*. With the encouragement of new-found literary friends he eventually forsook medicine to devote himself to poetry. Between the ages of twenty-two and twenty-five he published three volumes, the total output on which his fame rests. Though he was a vigorous youth, he developed a bad case of tuberculosis and, after several years of fighting the disease unsuccessfully, was finally forced to seek the warmer climate of Italy. Less than five months after his arrival there, at the age of twenty-five, he died in Rome. Little did he know that his poetry would eventually receive world recognition, for during his life the critics had given his volumes scathing reviews. There is pathos in the epitaph he wrote for himself: "Here lies one whose name was writ in water."

Besides his literary disappointment,

Keats had other anxieties. His younger brother Tom, to whom he was devoted, died in 1818 of tuberculosis, a disease which hovered like a shadow over Keats' whole family. In the same year Keats fell in love with a young neighbor, Fanny Brawne, whom he characterized on first meeting as "beautiful and elegant, graceful, silly, fashionable, and strange." She proved to be an unsympathetic and self-centered girl, who throughout their engagement brought as much distress as happiness to her lover.

The names of Shelley and Keats are often linked, partly because of a certain exquisite quality they have in common, partly because Shelley wrote one of the most famous of all elegies, *Adonais,* on the death of Keats. In disposition, however, the two men were quite different. Although few of Keats' published poems reveal that he had a jovial, whimsical side, more like Lamb than Shelley, this fact comes out in his letters, especially those written to his sister Fanny, eight years his junior. Nor did he share Shelley's ideas of the evils of society and religion. If life proved hard, he could always find solace in the world of literature and art where —

A thing of beauty is a joy forever:
Its loveliness increases; it will never
Pass into nothingness; but still will keep
A bower quiet for us, and a sleep
Full of sweet dreams, and health, and
    quiet breathing.

        — *Endymion*

Ode on a Grecian Urn

Though there are several large vases among the fine Greek collection
at the British Museum, no one of these could have served as an
exact model for Keats' poem. In fact, much scholarly research has
failed to uncover any vase with just such scenes as he describes. His
picture is a composite one, put together from typical Greek carvings
he had seen. He shows us a clear picture of one side of the urn in
the first three stanzas and of the other side in the fourth stanza. Two
moments of ancient times have thus been given immortality.

Thou still unravished bride of quietness,
    Thou foster child of silence and slow time,
Sylvan historian, who canst thus express
    A flowery tale more sweetly than our rhyme:
What leaf-fringed legend haunts about thy shape   5
    Of deities or mortals, or of both,
        In Tempe° or the dales of Arcady?°
What men or gods are these? What maidens loath?
    What mad pursuit? What struggle to escape?
        What pipes and timbrels?° What wild ecstasy?   10

Heard melodies are sweet, but those unheard
    Are sweeter; therefore, ye soft pipes, play on;
Not to the sensual ear, but, more endeared,
    Pipe to the spirit ditties of no tone.
Fair youth, beneath the trees, thou canst not leave   15
    Thy song, nor ever can those trees be bare;
        Bold Lover, never, never canst thou kiss,
Though winning near the goal — yet, do not grieve;
    She cannot fade, though thou hast not thy bliss,
        Forever wilt thou love, and she be fair!   20

Ah, happy, happy boughs! that cannot shed
    Your leaves, nor ever bid the Spring adieu;
And, happy melodist, unwearièd,
    Forever piping songs forever new;
More happy love! more happy, happy love!   25
    Forever warm and still to be enjoyed,
        Forever panting, and forever young;
All breathing human passion far above,
    That leaves a heart high-sorrowful and cloyed,
        A burning forehead, and a parching tongue.   30

Who are these coming to the sacrifice?
    To what green altar, O mysterious priest,
Lead'st thou that heifer lowing at the skies,

7. *Tempe:* a lovely valley in Thessaly, Greece; *Arcady* (är′kȧ·dĭ): a picturesque region of Greece, characterized by its beauty and by the contentment of those who dwelt there. 10. *timbrels:* tambourines.

And all her silken flanks with garlands dressed?
What little town by river or sea shore,   35
   Or mountain-built with peaceful citadel,
     Is emptied of this folk, this pious morn?
And, little town, thy streets for evermore
   Will silent be; and not a soul to tell
     Why thou art desolate, can e'er return.   40

O Attic° shape! Fair attitude! with brede°
   Of marble men and maidens overwrought,
With forest branches and the trodden weed;
   Thou, silent form, dost tease us out of thought
As doth eternity. Cold Pastoral!°   45
   When old age shall this generation waste,
     Thou shalt remain, in midst of other woe
Than ours, a friend to man, to whom thou say'st,
   "Beauty is truth, truth beauty" — that is all
     Ye know on earth, and all ye need to know.   50

41. *Attic:* pertaining to Attica, a kingdom of ancient Greece; *brede:* embroidery. 45. *Cold Pastoral:* Keats compares the urn to a pastoral poem (a poem that deals with shepherds and the countryside), which was a favorite verse form of the ancient Greeks.

British Museum

LITERATURE AND THE ARTS ➤

Pictured on page 457 is one of the many Greek vases in the British Museum, whose collection Keats admired. This vase, or amphora, as vases of this particular shape were called, is in the classical "red-figure" style of Greek pottery which was developed late in the sixth century B.C., a departure from the earlier style of painting black figures on a red background. The scene is a musical one. Seated in the center and playing a triangular harp is Terpsichore, the muse of dancing and choral song. Standing before and behind her are minor musical deities. On the reverse side (see left) stand a woman and two youths.

Although these vases are carefully shaped works of art and although we today may view them as chiefly decorative, they were designed and used, aside from their function in certain religious ceremonies, for very practical purposes. Amphorae, for instance, were used to store wine, corn, oil, and honey. Due to steadily growing trade, pottery-making, by 700 B.C., flourished in Greece as never before.

Ode to a Nightingale

Keats wrote this poem in the spring of 1819 when a nightingale, in
whose song he took great pleasure, built its nest next to his house.
The death of Keats' younger brother Tom, which had occurred the
previous December, is referred to in the third stanza.

My heart aches, and a drowsy numbness pains
  My sense, as though of hemlock I had drunk,
Or emptied some dull opiate to the drains
  One minute past, and Lethe-wards° had sunk;
'Tis not through envy of thy happy lot,   5
  But being too happy in thine happiness —
    That thou, light-wingèd Dryad° of the trees,
      In some melodious plot
  Of beechen green, and shadows numberless,
    Singest of summer in full-throated ease.   10

O for a draught of vintage! that hath been
  Cooled a long age in the deep-delved earth,
Tasting of Flora° and the country green,
  Dance, and Provençal° song, and sunburnt mirth!
O for a beaker full of the warm South,   15
  Full of the true, the blushful Hippocrene,°
    With beaded bubbles winking at the brim,
      And purple-stainèd mouth;
  That I might drink, and leave the world unseen,
    And with thee fade away into the forest dim;   20

Fade far away, dissolve, and quite forget
  What thou among the leaves hast never known,
The weariness, the fever, and the fret
  Here, where men sit and hear each other groan;
Where palsy shakes a few, sad, last gray hairs;   25
  Where youth grows pale and specter-thin, and dies;
    Where but to think is to be full of sorrow
      And leaden-eyed despairs;
  Where Beauty cannot keep her lustrous eyes
    Or new Love pine at them beyond tomorrow.   30

Away! away! for I will fly to thee,
  Not charioted by Bacchus and his pards,°
But on the viewless° wings of Poesy,
  Though the dull brain perplexes and retards:
Already with thee! tender is the night,   35
  And haply the Queen Moon is on her throne,

4. *Lethe-wards:* toward the Greek river of forgetfulness, whose waters prepared the good to enter
the bliss of the Elysian Fields. 7. *Dryad:* a wood nymph. 13. *Flora:* goddess of flowers. 14. *Provençal*
(prŏv'ĕn·säl'; in this line, however, the meter requires an accent on the second syllable): pertaining
to Provence in southern France, home of the medieval troubadours. 16. *Hippocrene* (hĭp'ō·krēn):
a fountain on Mount Helicon, sacred to the Muses. 32. *Bacchus and his pards:* The god of wine
rode in a chariot drawn by leopards. 33. *viewless:* invisible.

Clustered around by all her starry Fays;°
　　But here there is no light,
Save what from heaven is with the breezes blown
　　Through verdurous glooms and winding mossy ways.   40

I cannot see what flowers are at my feet,
　　Nor what soft incense hangs upon the boughs,
But, in embalmèd° darkness, guess each sweet
　　Wherewith the seasonable month endows
The grass, the thicket, and the fruit tree wild;   45
　　White hawthorn, and the pastoral eglantine;
　　　　Fast fading violets covered up in leaves;
　　　　　　And mid-May's eldest child,
　　The coming musk rose, full of dewy wine,
　　　　The murmurous haunt of flies on summer eves.   50

Darkling° I listen; and, for many a time
　　I have been half in love with easeful Death,
Called him soft names in many a musèd rhyme,
　　To take into the air my quiet breath;
Now more than ever seems it rich to die,   55
　　To cease upon the midnight with no pain,
　　　　While thou art pouring forth thy soul abroad
　　　　　　In such an ecstasy!
　　Still wouldst thou sing, and I have ears in vain —
　　　　To thy high requiem become a sod.   60

Thou wast not born for death, immortal Bird!
　　No hungry generations tread thee down;
The voice I hear this passing night was heard
　　In ancient days by emperor and clown;
Perhaps the selfsame song that found a path   65
　　Through the sad heart of Ruth,° when, sick for home,
　　　　She stood in tears amid the alien corn;
　　　　　　The same that ofttimes hath
　　Charmed magic casements, opening on the foam
　　　　Of perilous seas, in fairylands forlorn.   70

Forlorn! the very word is like a bell
　　To toll me back from thee to my sole self!
Adieu! the fancy cannot cheat so well
　　As she is famed° to do, deceiving elf.
Adieu! adieu! thy plaintive anthem fades   75
　　Past the near meadows, over the still stream,
　　　　Up the hillside; and now 'tis buried deep
　　　　　　In the next valley glades.
　　Was it a vision, or a waking dream?
　　　　Fled is that music — Do I wake or sleep?   80

37. *Fays:* fairies. The moon is here identified with the queen of the fairies. 43. *embalmèd:* balmy.
51. *Darkling:* in the dark. 66. *Ruth:* heroine of the Book of Ruth in the Bible. For this part of her
story, see the second chapter. 74. *famed:* reported.

When I Have Fears

Written when the poet was twenty-two years old, this sonnet shows how long Keats dreaded the disease that afflicted his family.

When I have fears that I may cease to be
Before my pen has gleaned my teeming brain,
Before high-pilèd books, in charactery,°
Hold like rich garners the full ripened grain;
When I behold, upon the night's starred face,   5
Huge cloudy symbols of a high romance,
And think that I may never live to trace
Their shadows, with the magic hand of chance;°
And when I feel, fair creature of an hour,°
That I shall never look upon thee more,   10
Never have relish in the fairy power
Of unreflecting love — then on the shore
Of the wide world I stand alone, and think
Till love and fame to nothingness do sink.

3. *charactery:* letters. 8. *chance:* inspiration. 9. *fair creature of an hour:* perhaps, idealized woman. This sonnet was written before Keats had met Fanny Brawne.

Bright Star! Would I Were Steadfast As Thou Art

The autumn before his death Keats sailed for Italy with a companion, Joseph Severn. Becalmed off the coast of England, the poet watched the evening star — pure, radiant, alone. It awakened in him the grief and yearning expressed in these lines.

Bright star! would I were steadfast as thou art —
    Not in lone splendor hung aloft the night
And watching, with eternal lids apart,
    Like nature's patient, sleepless Eremite,°
The moving waters at their priestlike task   5
    Of pure ablution round earth's human shores,
Or gazing on the new soft-fallen mask
    Of snow upon the mountains and the moors —
No — yet still steadfast, still unchangeable,
    Pillowed upon my fair love's ripening breast,   10
To feel forever its soft fall and swell,
    Awake forever in a sweet unrest,
Still, still to hear her tender-taken breath,
And so live ever — or else swoon to death.

4. *Eremite* (ĕr'ē·mīt): a religious recluse; a hermit.

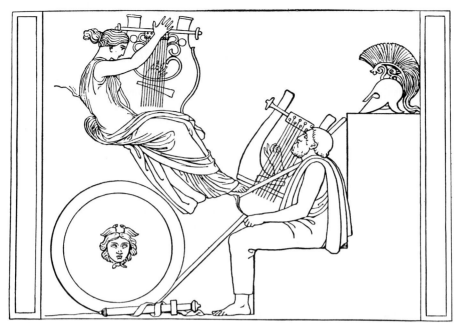

New York Public Library, Print Room

"Homer invoking the Muse," by Flaxman, used in editions of Chapman's Homer.

On First Looking into Chapman's Homer

Although Keats knew no Greek, he loved Greek mythology. When he was about twenty-one he borrowed a translation of Homer by George Chapman, an Elizabethan poet. He and a lifelong friend, Charles C. Clarke, sat up till daylight reading it, "Keats shouting with delight as some passage of special energy struck his imagination." The next morning his friend found this sonnet on his breakfast table.

> Much have I traveled in the realms of gold,°
> And many goodly states and kingdoms seen;
> Round many western islands have I been
> Which bards in fealty to Apollo° hold.
> Oft of one wide expanse had I been told   5
> That deep-browed Homer ruled as his demesne;°
> Yet did I never breathe its pure serene°
> Till I heard Chapman speak out loud and bold.
> Then felt I like some watcher of the skies
> When a new planet swims into his ken;   10
> Or like stout Cortez° when with eagle eyes
> He stared at the Pacific — and all his men
> Looked at each other with a wild surmise —
> Silent, upon a peak in Darien.°

1. The terms *realms of gold, goodly states and kingdoms* (line 2), and *western islands* (line 3) are here used metaphorically to represent the range of literature in which Keats had read. 4. *Apollo:* the Greek god of poetry and music. 6. *demesne* (dĕ-mān', but here dĕ-mēn): domain; land over which one rules. 7. *serene:* air. 11. *Cortez* (kôr'tĕz): It was Balboa, not Cortez, who discovered the Pacific Ocean from a mountain in Central America. 14. *Darien* (dâr'ĭ-ĕn'): the eastern part of the Isthmus of Panama.

The Eve of St. Agnes

In this metrical romance the poet uses as his setting a castle in medieval Italy. The chapel with its stone images of lords and ladies, the great hall, and the chamber of Madeline with its triple-arched casement are pictured in vivid detail. The medieval characters of beadsman (an old man supported by a family in return for his regular prayers), nurse, warrior guests, and romantic lovers combine with archaic language to weave a spell of rare, unearthly beauty. The theme, like that of *Romeo and Juliet,* is the flowering of young love against a background of age, death, and human intolerance.

St. Agnes was an early Christian martyr who, after her death, appeared to her parents in a vision with a lamb. Thereafter the white lamb, symbol of purity, was sacred to her. The legend on which this story is based is that a maiden, by observing certain rites on St. Agnes' Eve, which occurs on January 20, may have a glimpse of her future husband.

St. Agnes' Eve — Ah, bitter chill it was!
The owl, for all his feathers, was acold;
The hare limped trembling through the frozen grass,
And silent was the flock in wooly fold;
Numb were the Beadsman's fingers, while he told   5
His rosary, and while his frosted breath,
Like pious incense from a censer old,
Seemed taking flight for heaven, without a death,
Past the sweet Virgin's picture, while his prayer he saith.

His prayer he saith, this patient, holy man;   10
Then takes his lamp, and riseth from his knees,
And back returneth, meager, barefoot, wan,
Along the chapel aisle by slow degrees;
The sculptured dead, on each side, seem to freeze,
Imprisoned in black, purgatorial rails;°   15
Knights, ladies, praying in dumb orat'ries,°
He passeth by; and his weak spirit fails
To think how they may ache in icy hoods and mails.°

Northward he turneth through a little door,
And scarce three steps, ere Music's golden tongue   20
Flattered to tears this aged man and poor;
But no — already had his deathbell rung;
The joys of all his life were said and sung;
His was harsh penance on St. Agnes' Eve;
Another way he went, and soon among   25
Rough ashes sat he for his soul's reprieve,
And all night kept awake, for sinners' sake to grieve.

That ancient Beadsman heard the prelude soft;
And so it chanced, for many a door was wide,
From hurry to and fro. Soon, up aloft,   30

---

15. *purgatorial rails:* burial robes. 16. *orat'ries:* oratories, small chapels for private prayers.
18. *mails:* coats of armor.

The silver, snarling trumpets 'gan to chide;
The level chambers, ready with their pride,
Were glowing to receive a thousand guests;
The carvèd angels, ever eager-eyed,
Stared, where upon their heads the cornice rests,   35
With hair blown back, and wings put crosswise on their breasts.

At length burst in the argent revelry,°
With plume, tiara, and all rich array,
Numerous as shadows, haunting fairily
The brain, new stuffed, in youth, with triumphs gay   40
Of old romance. These let us wish away,
And turn, sole-thoughted, to one Lady there,
Whose heart had brooded, all that wintry day,
On love, and winged St. Agnes' saintly care,
As she had heard old dames full many times declare.   45

They told her how, upon St. Agnes' Eve,
Young virgins might have visions of delight,
And soft adorings from their loves receive
Upon the honeyed middle of the night,
If ceremonies due they did aright;   50
As, supperless to bed they must retire,
And couch supine° their beauties, lily white;
Nor look behind, nor sideways, but require
Of Heaven with upward eyes for all that they desire.

Full of this whim was thoughtful Madeline;   55
The music, yearning like a god in pain,
She scarcely heard; her maiden eyes divine,
Fixed on the floor, saw many a sweeping train
Pass by — she heeded not at all; in vain
Came many a tiptoe, amorous cavalier,   60
And back retired; not cooled by high disdain,
But she saw not; her heart was otherwhere;
She sighed for Agnes' dreams, the sweetest of the year.

She danced along with vague, regardless eyes,
Anxious her lips, her breathing quick and short;   65
The hallowed hour was near at hand; she sighs
Amid the timbrels, and the thronged resort
Of whisperers in anger, or in sport;
'Mid looks of love, defiance, hate, and scorn,
Hoodwinked with fairy fancy; all amort,°   70
Save to St. Agnes and her lambs unshorn,°
And all the bliss to be before tomorrow morn.

---

37. *argent revelry:* shining group of revelers. **52.** *couch supine* (sū·pīn′): lay flat. **70.** *amort:* as if dead. **71.** *lambs unshorn:* In honor of St. Agnes, the symbol of youth and innocence, two lambs were sacrificed annually in the church on her eve. The wool was later spun and woven by the nuns into garments for the poor.

So, purposing each moment to retire,
She lingered still. Meantime, across the moors,
Had come young Porphyro,° with heart on fire   75
For Madeline. Beside the portal doors,
Buttressed from moonlight,° stands he, and implores
All saints to give him sight of Madeline,
But for one moment in the tedious hours,
That he might gaze and worship all unseen;   80
Perchance speak, kneel, touch, kiss — in sooth such things have been.

He ventures in; let no buzzed whisper tell;
All eyes be muffled, or a hundred swords
Will storm his heart, Love's feverous citadel;
For him, those chambers held barbarian hordes,   85
Hyena foemen, and hot-blooded lords,
Whose very dogs would execrations howl
Against his lineage; not one breast affords
Him any mercy, in that mansion foul,
Save one old beldame,° weak in body and in soul.   90

Ah, happy chance! the aged creature came,
Shuffling along with ivory-headed wand,
To where he stood, hid from the torch's flame,
Behind a broad hall pillar, far beyond
The sound of merriment and chorus bland.   95
He startled her; but soon she knew his face,
And grasped his fingers in her palsied hand,
Saying, "Mercy, Porphyro! hie thee from this place;
They are all here tonight, the whole bloodthirsty race!

"Get hence; get hence! there's dwarfish Hildebrand;   100
He had a fever late, and in the fit
He cursèd thee and thine, both house and land;
Then there's that old Lord Maurice, not a whit
More tame for his gray hairs — Alas me! flit!
Flit like a ghost away." — "Ah, Gossip° dear,   105
We're safe enough; here in this armchair sit
And tell me how" — "Good Saints! not here, not here;
Follow me, child, or else these stones will be thy bier."

He followed through a lowly archèd way,
Brushing the cobwebs with his lofty plume;   110
And as she muttered, "Wella — welladay!"
He found him in a little moonlight room,
Pale, latticed, chill, and silent as a tomb.
"Now tell me where is Madeline," said he,
"O tell me, Angela, by the holy loom   115
Which none but secret sisterhood may see,
When they St. Agnes' wool are weaving piously."

---

75. *Porphyro* (pôr′fĭ·rō). 77. *Buttressed from moonlight:* He is standing in the shadow of one
of the buttresses which supported the walls of the castle. 90. *beldame* (bĕl′dăm): an old woman.
105. *Gossip:* godmother.

"St. Agnes! Ah! it is St. Agnes' Eve —
Yet men will murder upon holy days.
Thou must hold water in a witch's sieve,°   120
And be liege lord of all the Elves and Fays,
To venture so: it fills me with amaze
To see thee, Porphyro! — St. Agnes' Eve!
God's help! my lady fair the conjurer plays
This very night; good angels her deceive!   125
But let me laugh awhile, I've mickle° time to grieve."

Feebly she laugheth in the languid moon,
While Porphyro upon her face doth look,
Like puzzled urchin on an aged crone
Who keepeth closed a wondrous riddle book,   130
As spectacled she sits in chimney nook.
But soon his eyes grew brilliant, when she told
His lady's purpose; and he scarce could brook
Tears, at the thought of those enchantments cold,
And Madeline asleep in lap of legends old.   135

Sudden a thought came like a fullblown rose,
Flushing his brow, and in his painèd heart
Made purple riot; then doth he propose
A stratagem, that makes the beldame start.
"A cruel man and impious thou art.   140
Sweet lady, let her pray, and sleep, and dream
Alone with her good angels, far apart
From wicked men like thee. Go, go! — I deem
Thou canst not surely be the same that thou didst seem."°

"I will not harm her, by all saints I swear,"   145
Quoth Porphyro: "O may I ne'er find grace
When my weak voice shall whisper its last prayer,
If one of her soft ringlets I displace,
Or look with ruffian passion in her face.
Good Angela, believe me by these tears;   150
Or, I will, even in a moment's space,
Awake, with horrid shout, my foemen's ears,
And beard them, though they be more fanged than wolves and bears."

"Ah! why wilt thou affright a feeble soul?
A poor, weak, palsy-stricken churchyard thing,   155
Whose passing bell may ere the midnight toll;
Whose prayers for thee, each morn and evening,
Were never missed." Thus plaining,° doth she bring
A gentler speech from burning Porphyro;
So woeful, and of such deep sorrowing,   160
That Angela gives promise she will do
Whatever he shall wish, betide her weal or woe.°

120. *hold . . . sieve:* have supernatural powers. 126. *mickle:* much (a Scottish expression).
144. You cannot be as honorable as I thought you were. 158. *plaining:* complaining. 162. *betide . . .*
woe: whether good or evil come of it.

Which was, to lead him, in close secrecy,
Even to Madeline's chamber, and there hide
Him in a closet, of such privacy   165
That he might see her beauty unespied,
And win perhaps that night a peerless bride,
While legioned fairies paced the coverlet,
And pale enchantment held her sleepy-eyed.
Never on such a night have lovers met,   170
Since Merlin° paid his Demon all the monstrous debt.

"It shall be as thou wishest," said the Dame;
"All cates° and dainties shall be storèd there
Quickly on this feast night; by the tambour frame°
Her own lute thou wilt see; no time to spare,   175
For I am slow and feeble, and scarce dare
On such a catering trust my dizzy head.
Wait here, my child, with patience; kneel in prayer
The while. Ah! thou must needs the lady wed,
Or may I never leave my grave among the dead."   180

So saying, she hobbled off with busy fear.
The lover's endless minutes slowly passed;
The dame returned, and whispered in his ear
To follow her; with aged eyes aghast
From fright of dim espial. Safe at last,   185
Through many a dusky gallery, they gain
The maiden's chamber, silken, hushed, and chaste;
Where Porphyro took covert, pleased amain.°
His poor guide hurried back with agues° in her brain.

Her faltering hand upon the balustrade,   190
Old Angela was feeling for the stair,
When Madeline, St. Agnes' charmèd maid,
Rose, like a missioned spirit, unaware:
With silver taper's light, and pious care,
She turned, and down the aged gossip led   195
To a safe level matting. Now prepare,
Young Porphyro, for gazing on that bed;
She comes, she comes again, like ringdove frayed° and fled.

Out went the taper as she hurried in;
Its little smoke, in pallid moonshine, died;   200
She closed the door, she panted, all akin
To spirits of the air, and visions wide;
No uttered syllable or woe betide!
But to her heart, her heart was voluble,

---

171. *Merlin:* a magician, the offspring of demons, who was at last overpowered by means of one of his own spells reversed. 173. *cates:* dainty, choice food. 174. *tambour frame:* embroidery hoops, shaped like a tambour or drum. 188. *amain:* greatly. 189. *agues* (ā′gūz): An ague causes one to shake from either fever or cold; in other words, she was frightened. 198. *frayed:* frightened.

Paining with eloquence her balmy side;   205
As though a tongueless nightingale should swell
Her throat in vain, and die, heart-stifled, in her dell.

A casement high and triple-arched there was,
All garlanded with carven imageries
Of fruits, and flowers, and bunches of knotgrass,   210
And diamonded with panes of quaint device,
Innumerable of stains and splendid dyes,
As are the tiger moth's deep-damasked° wings;
And in the midst, 'mong thousand heraldries,
And twilight saints, and dim emblazonings,   215
A shielded scutcheon blushed with blood of queens and kings.°

Full on this casement shone the wintry moon,
And threw warm gules° on Madeline's fair breast,
As down she knelt for heaven's grace and boon;
Rose bloom fell on her hands, together pressed,   220
And on her silver cross soft amethyst,
And on her hair a glory, like a saint:
She seemed a splendid angel, newly dressed,
Save wings, for heaven; Porphyro grew faint;
She knelt, so pure a thing, so free from mortal taint.   225

Anon his heart revives; her vespers done,
Of all its wreathèd pearls her hair she frees;
Unclasped her warmèd jewels one by one;
Loosens her fragrant bodice; by degrees
Her rich attire creeps rustling to her knees;   230
Half-hidden, like a mermaid in seaweed,
Pensive awhile she dreams awake, and sees,
In fancy, fair St. Agnes in her bed,
But dares not look behind, or all the charm is fled.

Soon, trembling in her soft and chilly nest,   235
In sort of wakeful swoon, perplexed she lay,
Until the poppied° warmth of sleep oppressed
Her soothèd limbs, and soul fatigued away;
Flown, like a thought, until the morrow day;
Blissfully havened both from joy and pain;   240
Clasped like a missal° where swart Paynims° pray;
Blinded alike from sunshine and from rain,
As though a rose should shut, and be a bud again.

Stolen to this paradise, and so entranced,
Porphyro gazed upon her empty dress,   245
And listened to her breathing, if it chanced

213. *deep-damasked:* patterned. 216. A coat of arms shaped like a shield was colored red to indicate a royal family. 218. *gules* (gūlz): red, represented in heraldry by parallel lines. 237. *poppied:* druglike. 241. *missal:* Mass book; *Paynims:* pagans. Her eyes were as tightly closed in sleep as a prayer book would be in pagan lands.

To wake into a slumberous tenderness;
Which when he heard, that minute did he bless,
And breathed himself; then from the closet crept,
Noiseless as fear in a wide wilderness,   250
And over the hushed carpet, silent, stepped,
And 'tween the curtains peeped, where, lo! how fast she slept.

Then by the bedside, where the faded moon
Made a dim, silver twilight, soft he set
A table, and half-anguished, threw thereon   255
A cloth of woven crimson, gold, and jet —
O for some drowsy Morphean amulet!°
The boisterous, midnight, festive clarion,
The kettledrum, and far-heard clarinet,
Affray° his ears, though but in dying tone —   260
The hall door shuts again, and all the noise is gone.

And still she slept an azure-lidded sleep,
In blanchèd linen, smooth, and lavendered,°
While he from forth the closet brought a heap
Of candied apple, quince, and plum, and gourd;   265
With jellies soother° than the creamy curd,
And lucent° sirups, tinct° with cinnamon;
Manna and dates, in argosy transferred
From Fez;° and spicèd dainties, every one,
From silken Samarkand° to cedared Lebanon.°   270

These delicates he heaped with glowing hand
On golden dishes and in baskets bright
Of wreathèd silver; sumptuous they stand
In the retirèd quiet of the night,
Filling the chilly room with perfume light.—   275
"And now, my love, my seraph fair, awake!
Thou art my heaven, and I thine eremite;
Open thine eyes, for meek St. Agnes' sake,
Or I shall drowse beside thee, so my soul doth ache."

Thus whispering, his warm, unnervèd arm   280
Sank in her pillow. Shaded was her dream
By the dusk curtains — 'twas a midnight charm
Impossible to melt as icèd stream;
The lustrous salvers in the moonlight gleam;
Broad golden fringe upon the carpet lies;   285
It seemed he never, never could redeem
From such a steadfast spell his lady's eyes;
So mused awhile, entoiled in woofèd° phantasies.

---

257. *Morphean amulet:* a charm pertaining to the god of dreams; that is, one to keep her asleep.
260. *Affray:* frighten. 263. *lavendered:* perfumed with lavender. 266. *soother:* smoother. 267. *lucent*
(lū′sĕnt): clear; *tinct:* delicately flavored. 269. *Fez:* a city in Morocco. 270. *Samarkand:* a city of
Turkestan, famous for its manufacture of silk; *Lebanon:* a country at the eastern end of the Mediterranean. From it came the timbers of cedar which were used in Solomon's temple. 288. *woofèd:*
intertwined, as the threads are in weaving.

Awakening up, he took her hollow lute —
Tumultuous — and, in chords that tenderest be,   290
He played an ancient ditty, long since mute,
In Provence called "La belle dame sans merci";°
Close to her ear touching the melody;
Wherewith disturbed, she uttered a soft moan;
He ceased — she panted quick — and suddenly   295
Her blue affrayèd eyes wide open shone;
Upon his knees he sank, pale as smooth-sculptured stone.

Her eyes were open, but she still beheld,
Now wide awake, the vision of her sleep;
There was a painful change, that night expelled   300
The blisses of her dream so pure and deep,
At which fair Madeline began to weep,
And moan forth witless words with many a sigh;
While still her gaze on Porphyro would keep;
Who knelt, with joinèd hands and piteous eyes,   305
Fearing to move or speak, she looked so dreamingly.

"Ah, Porphyro!" said she, "but even now
Thy voice was at sweet tremble in mine ear,
Made tunable with every sweetest vow;
And those sad eyes were spiritual and clear;   310
How changed thou art! how pallid, chill, and drear!
Give me that voice again, my Porphyro,
Those looks immortal, those complainings dear!
Oh, leave me not in this eternal woe,
For if thou diest, my Love, I know not where to go."   315

Beyond a mortal man impassioned far
At these voluptuous accents, he arose,
Ethereal, flushed, and like a throbbing star
Seen mid the sapphire heaven's deep repose;
Into her dream he melted, as the rose   320
Blendeth its odor with the violet —
Solution sweet; meantime the frost wind blows
Like Love's alarum pattering the sharp sleet
Against the windowpanes; St. Agnes' moon hath set.

'Tis dark; quick pattereth the flaw-blown° sleet;   325
"This is no dream, my bride, my Madeline!"
'Tis dark; the icèd gusts still rave and beat.
"No dream, alas! alas! and woe is mine!
Porphyro will leave me here to fade and pine. —
Cruel! what traitor could thee thither bring?   330
I curse not, for my heart is lost in thine,
Though thou forsakest a deceivèd thing —
A dove forlorn and lost with sick unprunèd wing."

---

292. *"La belle dame sans merci"*: the beautiful lady without mercy. 325. *flaw-blown*: squall-blown.

"My Madeline; sweet dreamer! lovely bride!
Say, may I be for aye thy vassal° blest?   335
Thy beauty's shield, heart-shaped and vermeil-dyed?°
Ah, silver shrine, here will I take my rest
After so many hours of toil and quest,
A famished pilgrim — saved by miracle.
Though I have found, I will not rob thy nest   340
Saving of thy sweet self; if thou think'st well
To trust, fair Madeline, to no rude infidel.

"Hark! 'tis an elfin storm from fairyland,
Of haggard seeming,° but a boon indeed.
Arise — arise! the morning is at hand —   345
The bloated wassailers will never heed —
Let us away, my love, with happy speed;
There are no ears to hear, or eyes to see —
Drowned all in Rhenish° and the sleepy mead.°
Awake! arise! my love, and fearless be,   350
For o'er the southern moors I have a home for thee."

She hurried at his words, beset with fears,
For there were sleeping dragons all around,
At glaring watch, perhaps, with ready spears —
Down the wide stairs a darkling way they found —   355
In all the house was heard no human sound.
A chain-drooped lamp° was flickering by each door;
The arras,° rich with horseman, hawk, and hound,
Fluttered in the besieging wind's uproar;
And the long carpets rose along the gusty floor.   360

They glide, like phantoms, into the wide hall;
Like phantoms, to the iron porch, they glide;
Where lay the porter, in uneasy sprawl,
With a huge empty flagon by his side.
The wakeful bloodhound rose, and shook his hide,   365
But his sagacious eye an inmate owns;°
By one and one, the bolts full easy slide —
The chains lie silent on the footworn stones —
The key turns, and the door upon its hinges groans.

And they are gone; ay, ages long ago   370
These lovers fled away into the storm.
That night the Baron dreamt of many a woe,
And all his warrior guests, with shade and form
Of witch, and demon, and large coffin worm,
Were long benightmared. Angela the old   375

---

335. *vassal:* in feudal times, a knight who pledged allegiance to his overlord. 336. *vermeil-dyed*
(vûr′mĭl): vermilion, bright red. 344. *haggard seeming:* wild in aspect. 349. *Rhenish* (rĕn′ĭsh): wine
made near the Rhine River; *mead:* a drink made of fermented honey. 357. *chain-drooped lamp:*
lamp hanging on a chain. 358. *arras* (ăr′ăs): tapestry hanging on the wall to keep out drafts.
366. *owns:* recognizes.

Died palsy-twitched, with meager face deform;
The Beadsman, after thousand aves told,
For aye unsought-for slept among his ashes cold.

A FAMOUS AMERICAN NOVELIST ON KEATS

Poetry is either something that lives like fire inside of you . . . or else it is nothing, an empty, formalized bore around which pedants can endlessly drone their notes and explanations. "The Grecian Urn" is unbearably beautiful with every syllable as inevitable as the notes in Beethoven's Ninth Symphony, *or it's just something you don't understand. It is what it is because an extraordinary genius passed at that point in history and touched it. I suppose I've read it a hundred times. About the tenth time I began to know what it is about, and caught the chime in it and the exquisite inner mechanics. Likewise with the "Nightingale" which I can never read through without tears in my eyes; likewise the "Pot of Basil" with its great stanzas about the two brothers; and "The Eve of Saint Agnes" which has the richest, most sensuous imagery in English, not excepting Shakespeare. And finally his three or four great sonnets, "Bright Star" and the others.*

Knowing those things young and granted an ear, one can scarcely ever afterwards be unable to distinguish between gold and dross in what one reads. In themselves those eight poems are a scale of workmanship for anybody who wants to know truly about words, their most utter value for evocation, persuasion, or charm. For a while after you quit Keats all other poetry seems to be only whistling or humming.

F. SCOTT FITZGERALD

From a letter quoted in the Princeton Alumni Weekly, *March 9, 1956. Used by permission of Frances Scott Fitzgerald Lanahan.*

POEMS FROM "REALMS OF GOLD"

ODE ON A GRECIAN URN

1. Explain the significance of the various names Keats gives the urn in the first three lines. In your own words, give a clear picture of the two scenes on the urn, showing what is happening at the moment the artist has caught and preserved the action.

2. What in Keats' own life helps us to grasp his emotion in the third stanza?

3. In giving the urn's message at the end, Keats uses both *thou* and *ye*. To what different persons or things do they refer? Discuss whether you think the poet means to apply this message to all of life. Do you agree with him? Give some examples to support your opinion.

ODE TO A NIGHTINGALE

1. What emotions are aroused in the poet by the song of the nightingale? What similarities and what differences do you find between Keats' response in this poem and Shelley's in "To a Skylark"?

2. What line refers to the death of Keats' brother Tom? What lines may refer to his feeling for Fanny Brawne, whom he met at about this time?

3. Discuss the contrast made in this poem between the world of reality and the world of fancy. How does the word *forlorn* in line 71 bring him back to reality?

4. How does the seventh stanza recall the "Ode on a Grecian Urn"?

SONNETS

1. In "When I Have Fears," what two great longings are expressed? What metaphor does the poet use to describe creative writing?

2. In "Bright Star," how does Keats wish to resemble the star? How would he differ from it?

3. In "On First Looking into Chapman's Homer," point out how Keats compares geographical discovery with discovery in literature. What feeling is shown in the last lines? What books have given you the same feeling?

THE EVE OF ST. AGNES

1. How many details can you discover which give a medieval flavor to the story, setting it apart from modern times?

2. At the end of the story, what becomes of the lovers, the beadsman, the nurse, the baron, and the guests? How is a veil of mystery thrown over the conclusion? Does this add to the romantic appeal of the poem, in your opinion?

3. How does Keats' handling of an elopement story differ from Scott's in "Jock o' Hazeldean"? In what way is this difference characteristic of the two poets?

4. What stanza form does Keats use in this poem? What other poems that you have read in this book are written in this form?

APPRECIATING IMAGERY

Keats is a master of language; his magical phrasing and his harmoniously flowing lines are comparable to those of Shakespeare. What sets Keats apart from most poets, however, is his sensuous imagery. In appealing to the senses, he does not describe an object — he actually presents it. For example, in "Ode to a Nightingale" the evening is not directly described. Specific, concrete objects are presented as they appear in the increasing darkness; both the kind of evening and its effect on the poet are implied.

I cannot see what flowers are at my feet,
   Nor what soft incense hangs upon the
     boughs,
But, in embalmèd darkness, guess each
   sweet
Wherewith the seasonable month endows
The grass, the thicket, and the fruit tree
   wild . . .

It is Keats' skillful use of concrete objects that achieves the sensuous imagery that is so characteristic of his poetry. He is thus able to stimulate our senses as they would be if the objects depicted were physically present.

Keats' masterful appeal to the senses is also illustrated by two pairs of contrasting stanzas from "The Eve of St. Agnes." In the opening stanza of the poem the reader cannot escape the dominant note of cold. Many lines have at least one word to add to the sensation: *bitter chill, acold, limped trembling, frozen, silent, numb, frosted.* The crowning simile suggests a striking image by likening the Beadsman's frosted breath to the cloud of incense from an old censer rising toward heaven.

The cold of the outside world is contrasted to the richness and beauty of the scene in Madeline's chamber. The two stanzas from lines 253 to 270 appeal to every one of the five senses:

sight: a dim silver twilight; a cloth of woven crimson, gold, and jet; azure-lidded sleep; blanchèd linen, smooth; all the foods in lines 265–69; silken Samarkand and cedared Lebanon.

sound: the musical instruments "affray his ears," then are silent.

smell and taste: the fruits, jellies, and sirups mentioned appeal to *three* senses, smell, taste, and sight; lavendered linen; spicèd dainties.

touch: smooth linen (to the hands); jellies soother than the creamy curd (to the tongue).

Make a list of the images appealing to the senses that the poet uses in the next three stanzas (ll. 271–297).

LITERATURE AND THE ARTS

The painting on page 469, an artistic interpretation by Isadore Seltzer of the late medieval atmosphere of "The Eve of St. Agnes," evokes, with its gay color and strict artistic outline, something of the luxury and austerity of medieval life as Madeline and Porphyro might have known it. It also recalls Keats' great skill in combining rich imagery with a strict poetic form.

ROBERT SOUTHEY 1774–1843

The Battle of Blenheim

Robert Southey, the third of the trio of Lake Poets, was a popular poet laureate of his time. His verse lacks the genius of Wordsworth's and Coleridge's, but the vigorous ballad style of his many narrative and descriptive poems is highly readable. A greatly praised writer of both poetry and prose, Southey was also an excellent and prolific letter writer.

Southey's treatment of the battle of Blenheim (blĕn′ĭm) is an early expression against the cruelty and futility of war. That battle, fought in 1704 in a town in Bavaria, was a decisive victory for the English and Austrians over the French and Bavarians. The war grew out of the rivalries and jealousies of several ruling families of Europe. In the poem Kaspar stands for the older generation that took war for granted. The children voice questions about the famous battle of 1704 — which Addison once glorified in a poem — that serve to reveal the futility of war.

It was a summer evening,
  Old Kaspar's work was done,
And he before his cottage door
  Was sitting in the sun;
And by him sported on the green   5
  His little grandchild Wilhelmine.

She saw her brother Peterkin
  Roll something large and round
Which he beside the rivulet
  In playing there had found;   10
He came to ask what he had found
That was so large and smooth and
    round.

Old Kaspar took it from the boy
  Who stood expectant by;
And then the old man shook his head,
  And with a natural sigh   16
" 'Tis some poor fellow's skull," said he,
"Who fell in the great victory.

"I find them in the garden,
  For there's many here about;   20
And often when I go to plow
  The plowshare turns them out.
For many thousand men," said he,
"Were slain in that great victory."

"Now tell us what 'twas all about,"   25
  Young Peterkin he cries;
And little Wilhelmine looks up
  With wonder-waiting eyes;
"Now tell us all about the war,   29
And what they fought each other for."

"It was the English," Kaspar cried,
  "Who put the French to rout;
But what they fought each other for
  I could not well make out.
But everybody said," quoth he,   35
"That 'twas a famous victory.

"My father lived at Blenheim then,
  Yon little stream hard by;
They burnt his dwelling to the ground,
  And he was forced to fly;   40
So with his wife and child he fled,
Nor had he where to rest his head.

"With fire and sword the country round
  Was wasted far and wide,
And many a childing mother then   45
  And newborn baby died;
But things like that, you know, must be
At every famous victory.

"They say it was a shocking sight
  After the field was won;   50
For many thousand bodies here
  Lay rotting in the sun;
But things like that, you know, must be
After a famous victory.

"Great praise the Duke of Marlbro'°
   won   55
And our good Prince Eugene";°

55. *Duke of Marlbro':* The Duke of Marlborough was the commander of the British
forces. 56. *Prince Eugene:* commander of the
Austrian forces. Notice that Kaspar bore him
no ill will though he was on the side that burned
Kaspar's father's home. This attitude indicates
that there were no issues in the campaign which
were clear to the country people.

"Why, 'twas a very wicked thing!"
   Said little Wilhelmine.
"Nay — nay — my little girl," quoth he,
"It was a famous victory.   60

"And everybody praised the Duke
   Who this great fight did win."
"But what good came of it at last?"
   Quoth little Peterkin.
"Why that I cannot tell," said he,   65
"But 'twas a famous victory."

THOMAS HOOD 1799–1845

The Song of the Shirt

Thomas Hood experienced such poverty
and sickness himself that he had great sympathy with the suffering of others. A Londoner, he edited several magazines, and
was acquainted with Lamb and other literary men. He is remembered for his humorous poetry, as well as serious poems like
"The Song of the Shirt." Like "The Battle
of Blenheim," this poem expresses the
growing humanitarian spirit of the times.

The origin of "The Song of the Shirt" was
a newspaper account concerning a woman
on trial for pawning articles that belonged
to her employer. Evidence presented at the
trial showed that she received only seven
shillings a week for making trousers at
home. On this small sum (see page 842)
she had to support her family. The timely
appearance of this poem had a decided effect in improving labor legislation.

With fingers weary and worn,
   With eyelids heavy and red,
A woman sat, in unwomanly rags,
   Plying her needle and thread —
Stitch! stitch! stitch!   5
   In poverty, hunger, and dirt,
And still with a voice of dolorous pitch
   She sang the "Song of the Shirt."

"Work! work! work!
   While the cock is crowing aloof!   10
And work — work — work,
   Till the stars shine through the roof!
It's Oh! to be a slave
   Along with the barbarous Turk,
Where woman has never a soul to save,°
   If this is Christian work!   16

15. *woman . . . save:* refers to a Moslem
belief.

"Work — work — work,
   Till the brain begins to swim;
Work — work — work,
   Till the eyes are heavy and dim!   20
Seam, and gusset,° and band,
   Band, and gusset, and seam,
Till over the buttons I fall asleep,
   And sew them on in a dream!

"O, Men, with Sisters dear!   25
   Oh, Men, with Mothers and Wives!
It is not linen you're wearing out,
   But human creatures' lives!
Stitch — stitch — stitch,
   In poverty, hunger, and dirt,   30

21. *gusset:* an extra strip inserted to
strengthen or widen a garment.

Sewing at once, with a double thread,
  A shroud° as well as a Shirt.

"But why do I talk of Death?
  That Phantom of grisly bone,
I hardly fear its terrible shape,   35
  It seems so like my own —
It seems so like my own,
  Because of the fasts I keep;
Oh, God! that bread should be so dear
  And flesh and blood so cheap!   40

"Work — work — work!
  My labor never flags;
And what are its wages? A bed of straw,
  A crust of bread — and rags.
That shattered roof — this naked floor —
  A table — a broken chair —   46
And a wall so blank, my shadow I thank
  For sometimes falling there!

"Work — work — work!
  From weary chime to chime,   50
Work — work — work,
  As prisoners work for crime!
Band, and gusset, and seam,
  Seam, and gusset, and band,
Till the heart is sick, and the brain be-
  numbed,   55
  As well as the weary hand.

"Work — work — work,
  In the dull December light,
And work — work — work,
  When the weather is warm and
    bright —   60
While underneath the eaves
  The brooding swallows cling
As if to show me their sunny backs
  And twit me with the spring.

"Oh, but to breathe the breath   65
  Of the cowslip and primrose sweet —
With the sky above my head,
  And the grass beneath my feet;
For only one short hour
  To feel as I used to feel,   70

Before I knew the woes of want
  And the walk that costs a meal.

"Oh! but for one short hour!
  A respite however brief!
No blessèd leisure for Love or Hope,   75
  But only time for Grief!
A little weeping would ease my heart,
  But in their briny bed
My tears must stop, for every drop
  Hinders needle and thread!"   80

With fingers weary and worn,
  With eyelids heavy and red,
A woman sat, in unwomanly rags,
  Plying her needle and thread —
Stitch! stitch! stitch!   85
  In poverty, hunger, and dirt,
And still with a voice of dolorous
  pitch, —
Would that its tone could reach the
  Rich! —
  She sang this "Song of the Shirt!"

TWO HUMANITARIANS

1. Robert Southey's poem is a study in contrasts. What contrasts can you find between persons, between attitudes, between ideas about war? What other poems have you read that show the cruelty and futility of war?

2. By what means did Hood hope that he might "reach the Rich"? "The Song of the Shirt" has been translated into several foreign languages; do you understand its wide appeal?

CLASS ACTIVITIES

1. Compare "The Song of the Shirt" with Elizabeth Barrett Browning's "The Cry of the Children," Edwin Markham's "The Man with the Hoe," and Margaret Widdemer's "Factories."

2. Investigate working conditions for women and children in England in the early nineteenth century and the reforms which followed. Compare conditions of that time with present working conditions in England and the United States.

---

32. *shroud:* a garment in which to wrap the dead. In other words, this cruel situation will cause the seamstress' death.

READING LIST FOR
THE ROMANTIC AGE

Austen, Jane, *Emma*
Emma is the focal point in a maze of personal relationships set against a background of life in a quiet English town.

——, *Sense and Sensibility*
A satire directed against commonplace foolishness. Two sisters of different temperaments are contrasted.

Brighouse, Harold, *The Night of "Mr. H."*
A one-act play showing Charles Lamb's bravery when his play *Mr. H.* was a failure at the Drury Lane Theater in London.

Brontë, Charlotte, *Shirley*
Capital and labor and the emancipation of women are issues in this moorland story.

Carr, John D., *Bride of Newgate*
Continuous suspense in the story of Darwent's marriage one hour before he is to die, his escape, and his life afterward.

Collins, Norman, *Black Ivory*
In 1829 off the African coast, a fourteen-year-old boy encounters highjacking, mutiny, and violence.

Forester, C. S., *Hornblower and the Atropos*
Young Captain Hornblower journeys across England, takes part in Nelson's funeral, and recovers a huge treasure in an English sunken ship.

——, *Lord Hornblower*
Horatio leaves Lady Barbara, concludes his private war with Napoleon, quiets a mutiny, and is made a peer by his grateful sovereign.

Gaskell, Elizabeth, *Cranford*
A pleasing story of small-community life in Cranford where some spinsters live in a genteel manner on inherited money.

Goudge, Elizabeth, *Gentian Hill*
An irresistible romance, based on an old Devonshire legend, in which a princess living in a peasant's home falls in love with a young midshipman in Lord Nelson's fleet.

Gray, Elizabeth Janet, *Young Sir Walter Scott*
A detailed biography of Sir Walter Scott. Some of the people in the biography were fictionalized in Scott's novels.

Hardy, Thomas, *Trumpet Major*
Suspense prevails in this story of family life and love during the Napoleonic terror.

Lamb, Charles, *Essays of Elia* and *Last Essays of Elia*
Essays written purely for fun and entertainment. Read "A Chapter on Ears" and "The Praise of Chimney Sweeps" in the first volume, and "The Superannuated Man" and "Poor Relations" in the second.

——, *Tales from Shakespeare*
Twenty plays of Shakespeare transposed into prose — the comedies by Mary Lamb and the tragedies by Charles Lamb.

Pearson, Hesketh, *Sir Walter Scott*
This book follows Scott through his lameness, his struggle against monetary problems, his happiness in marriage, and his literary successes.

Shelley, Mary W., *Frankenstein: or, The Modern Prometheus*
A tale of horror. Mrs. Shelley wrote *Frankenstein* in competition with her husband and Byron. Frankenstein creates a mechanical man without a soul.

Trollope, Anthony, *The Eustace Diamonds*
The story of the unscrupulous Lady Eustace and her diamonds.

Winwar, Frances, *The Romantic Rebels*
Excellent biographical studies of Byron, Shelley, and Keats.

NOTE: See also "Notable English Novels," pages 370–371.

FOR LISTENING

The following poems have been recorded and are available on *Many Voices 6A:* Coleridge's "The Rime of the Ancient Mariner" (ll. 1-82, Part I), Wordsworth's "She Dwelt among the Untrodden Ways," "Composed upon Westminster Bridge," "The World Is Too Much with Us." On *Many Voices 6B* are Byron's "Apostrophe to the Ocean," Shelley's "Ode to the West Wind," Keats' "Ode on a Grecian Urn" and "On First Looking into Chapman's Homer."

ROMANTIC AGE FRONTISPIECE: Pictured on page 372 are (1) a photograph of Buttermere in the English Lake District; (2) an engraving of Stephenson's locomotive; (3) a Greek column; (4) a conch shell; (5) a facsimile of the first edition of the Wordsworth-Coleridge *Lyrical Ballads* (see text, pages 374, 384, 397); and (6) model of cannon.

THE GROWTH OF
THE ENGLISH LANGUAGE

The Romantic Age

Have you ever read a book that was actually *printed* before the nineteenth century? If so, you have probably been aware of certain peculiarities which may have hindered your understanding. For instance, the letter *s* used to have a long line somewhat resembling the letter *f* today: the word *wise* looked like *wife*. The modern reader frequently finds himself caught with a wrong interpretation of a sentence until he learns to recognize that *s*. Then too, the paragraphs and sentences are much longer than we are accustomed to and are sprinkled with colons and semicolons. As a convenience for those reading aloud, the last word of each page is repeated at the top of the next page. Spelling is different, though Dr. Johnson's *Dictionary* so stabilized spelling that variations in the last part of the eighteenth century are not so noticeable as in books printed earlier, and capital letters are used with a freer hand than nowadays. During the late eighteenth century and first half of the nineteenth century these peculiarities were gradually abandoned and the present style definitely established.

The period covered by this chapter shows in many ways the results of attempts by previous writers and grammarians to standardize the language. Grammars were published in greater numbers than ever before and reached the public through increasing numbers of schools. The ambition to speak "correctly" took hold of the middle classes as the reading public rapidly increased.

One of the most interesting language developments of this period came in America, which now, as a free country, asserted its linguistic independence.

Certain words and phrases, originating in the United States, became known as Americanisms. Englishmen who respected their mother tongue did not use these American expressions, which they considered to be uncouth. Ironically, in America there persisted among rural people many of the pronunciations and constructions which had characterized the speech of the upper classes in England in the seventeenth century. A telling example of this is James Russell Lowell's *Biglow Papers,* in which the Yankee Horatio Biglow uses many a pronunciation which scholars have attributed to the casual colloquial style of the Restoration aristocrats.

Chief advocate of a standardized American style was Noah Webster, whose first spelling book, appearing in 1783, was quite radical in some of its suggested changes. But he became more conservative as time went on. His great work, the first real American dictionary (1828) was eclipsed by that of William Worcester (Wooster) in 1831; but later Webster's dictionary won a place that has been maintained by groups of linguists who have carried on his work long after his death.

Three innovations by Webster are noteworthy. He used American authors such as Franklin and Irving for his examples of usage, instead of confining himself to British authors. He gave preference to American cultivated pronunciation where it deviated from British, and was more lenient in allowing alternate pronunciations. He advocated certain simpler forms of spelling, some of which have become accepted nationally: *-or* instead of *-our* (as in *honor*), *-er* for *-re* (as in *theater*), and no doubling of final consonants retained where there is no change of accent (as in *traveling*). The original forms prevail in England.

Meanwhile, across the sea the English purists, with their grammars based largely on Latin grammar, were wielding more and more influence. One British "authority" on language said he would use no words not used by Dryden. A curious grammar of 1823 intended for "Use of Schools and of Young Persons in General, but more especially for the Use of Soldiers, Sailors, Apprentices, and Ploughboys" must have been a comfort to all such persons, for it disapproved of irregular verbs and advocated such regular forms as *blowed, springed, sweeped,* and *throwed!*

Let us turn to the effects of Romanticism on the English language. In the first place, the Romantics believed in being guided by instincts and emotions rather than by rules; thus they were not language purists. They believed in writing new kinds of literature, in seeking new verse forms, in finding new language to express their thoughts. Sometimes their interest in coining words led to ridiculous extremes. Southey concocted *critickasting, fuzzgig,* and *evangelizationeer!* Thomas De Quincey, far from recognizing the authority of grammarians, thought the best examples of the use of the mother tongue were to be heard by listening to mothers and young children (and he did not intend a pun). Wordsworth wanted to get away from so-called poetic language and use "the very language of men," meaning that of humble men, not pedants. He believed, however, in "purifying" that language.

Much of this was reaction against the formal style of conversation at that time. To realize the difference a hundred years can make in the ordinary daily talk of human beings, one need only read the novels of Jane Austen, who faithfully reproduced the speech of the early nineteenth century.

We are greatly indebted to the Eng-

lish novel for the light it throws on English speech in general. Before the rise of the novel in the eighteenth century, there were only plays and poetry to reveal to modern linguists the ordinary speech habits of bygone days. Neither of these presented a wholly natural mode of communication.

Scott's novels made an additional contribution. They served to add to the interest in Scottish dialect which Burns' poems had aroused in the late eighteenth century. The Northern dialect now attained a place in literature which it had not held since medieval times. Indeed the whole Romantic movement brought the distant past back to life, and some of the language of the past came back with it. Scott made the terms of chivalry understood by the man on the street. To smaller groups of readers Gray had already introduced the old Welsh and Norse legends, and Keats echoed the overtones of Spenser. Coleridge's criticism stimulated new interest in Shakespeare. In "The Rime of the Ancient Mariner" Coleridge also uses some obsolete Old English words, such as *wot* and *ween*. While such words never returned to active use, they at least returned to the reader's understanding and have often appeared since to create an archaic atmosphere.

In general, the Romantics were a fortunate foil to the purists, for they brought back something of the freedom and vitality of Elizabethan days.

This small woodcut and the one on page 384 are the work of the nineteenth-century engraver, Thomas Bewick. Bewick's designs were used as decorative head- and end-pieces in many books of this period.

THE

VICTORIAN

AGE

1837 – 1900

(A Personal Note by J.B.P.   Perhaps I should warn my readers that I have very personal views about this period because I am a Victorian myself. True, I am a very late one, being born in 1894, but for seven years I was one of Queen Victoria's subjects. Unfortunately, living in the north of England as I did, I never saw the old lady, but I well remember her death in 1901. And of course all the people who brought me up, all the adults I knew as a child, were completely Victorian.

Though I never saw the old Queen herself I have had the privilege of being presented to several of her descendants. And twenty-odd years ago, when I was first living in the Isle of Wight, my family and I were visited by the then Governor of the Island, who was none other than old Princess Beatrice, a daughter of Queen Victoria. And I remember thinking, as I watched my small son make his bow to her, that my son might easily live into the 2000's and be able to say that he once made his bow to Queen Victoria's daughter. Because I have many personal associations with the history and literature of this period, please remember: I am a Victorian.)

VICTORIA, daughter of the Duke of Kent, one of the sons of George III, succeeded her uncle, William IV, in 1837 when she was a girl of eighteen. She died in 1901 a fabulous old lady, having celebrated her Jubilee in 1887 after fifty years on the throne, and then her Diamond Jubilee in 1897, after sixty

◀ The items in the frontispiece are identified on page 599.

years as sovereign. These two Jubilees, which were celebrated with enormous pomp and ceremony and with princes and chiefs of every race and color in the processions, represented the British Empire at its height.

THE REIGN OF QUEEN VICTORIA

Queen Victoria was extremely popular in the opening years of her reign and during her marriage to the Prince Consort, Albert of Saxe-Coburg, a minor German prince. Prince Albert was very earnest, conscientious, and industrious, but perhaps too German in manner and outlook to please all the British. (Many German customs, such as decorating trees at Christmas, became widespread in Britain, probably through the influence of Albert.) After the early death of her adored Albert in 1861, Victoria remained in mourning for years and virtually retired from public life. This led to some unpopularity, and sev-

National Portrait Gallery

Queen Victoria near the end of her reign.

eral prominent radicals during the next twenty years did not hesitate to declare themselves in favor of Britain becoming a republic. But the two Jubilees, her return to public life, and the great courage of the little old lady (who insisted upon visiting Ireland when there was real danger of her assassination by Irish Republicans) brought Victoria's reign to a close in a blaze of popularity. She was not a clever woman like the great Elizabeth I and was limited in her tastes and outlook, but she had character, a great sense of public duty and responsibility, and was perhaps the best possible monarch for nineteenth-century Britain.

BRITAIN AS A WORLD POWER

During most of Victoria's reign, Britain held the position of world leadership now occupied by the United States. Britain, the center of a vast empire which included Canada, Australia, New Zealand, India, South Africa, and many other parts of Africa and Asia, was in those years the wealthiest, the most productive, and the most powerful country in the world. Her military power did not rest on her army, which was much smaller than the armies of France, Germany, and Russia, but on her navy, which was so much stronger than any other that it acted as a kind of police force throughout the world. Though frequently engaged in small colonial wars and punitive expeditions, Britain all during this time kept clear of any major wars on the scale of the American War Between the States or the Franco-Prussian War of 1870–71. The Crimean War of 1854–56, when Britain and France together invaded the Russian Crimea, was not really a war on a major scale, though the troops who took part in it suffered terribly because everything was so badly organized.

(It was a determined upper-class Englishwoman, Florence Nightingale, who insisted upon organizing a proper nursing service in the Crimea, a progressive step of some importance, for her example was followed in many different countries. If only to show the interdependence of things, here are two other results of the Crimean War. Beards became fashionable in Britain, as we may see in portraits of Victorian authors, because the soldiers returning from the Crimea still wore the beards they had grown there where shaving was difficult. And it was the Crimean War that introduced cigarette smoking into Britain, for the men out there had picked up the habit from their Turkish allies.)

MATERIAL PROGRESS AND SCIENTIFIC ADVANCES

The great wealth and unequaled productiveness of Victorian Britain were due to the fact that she was still ahead in the Industrial Revolution and had a world market for Lancashire cotton goods, Yorkshire woolens, and the metal products of Birmingham and Sheffield. And London was the financial capital of the nineteenth-century world, the center of banking, insurance, shipping, and so forth. Most of the railroads that were being built outside Western Europe and the United States were financed by British capital and organized by British engineers. The Great Exhibition held in London in 1851 was the first of these ambitious international exhibitions and represented the British commercial and industrial triumph at its height.

The material progress of these years was tremendous. The country was covered with an intricate network of railroads. Industrial cities and towns grew like mushrooms. With factories being built everywhere, plenty of employment, and some attention at last to public health, the population figures went leaping up. And there was progress on other than material fronts. Science and invention went forward at the same pace. The Victorian Age is studded with famous names, from Michael Faraday (1791–1867), who experimented successfully with electricity, to Charles Darwin (1809–82), whose researches in biology were responsible for the theory of evolution. Britain's massive contribution to modern civilization belongs mostly to this period.

The opening of the Liverpool and Manchester Railway, 31 miles long, in September 1830, marked the advent of what may be called the "railroad age." Twenty-five years later, 9000 miles of track had been constructed throughout the country.

William B. Parsons Collection, Columbia University

This is not surprising. The Victorian felt himself to be — in a phrase then still to be originated — "on top of the world." Compared with men of today he was astoundingly self-confident, and with this confidence came tremendous energy. So he was ready to sweep aside all obstacles, to undertake anything anywhere, convinced beyond doubt that he was the representative figure of progress and civilization. Wherever he went, he felt, benefits must follow him. It should be obvious now that the typical Victorian Englishman and the typical American of today have much in common, cutting the same kind of figure in their respective worlds. There is, however, one important difference. The American, coming from a social democracy with a tradition of friendly neighborliness, expects to be liked wherever he goes in the world and is disappointed when he is not liked. The Victorian Englishman, generally a member of a ruling class cool and reserved in its manner, did not expect to be liked, did not care a rap whether he was liked or not. This also meant that he did not suffer a feeling of disappointment. Fortunately we have not to decide here which is the better of these two attitudes of mind.

THE VICTORIAN SPIRIT

The typical Victorian outlook is well expressed in the essays of Thomas Babington Macaulay (1800–59), the most popular historian of the mid-Victorian period, and in the kind of verse that Alfred, Lord Tennyson (1809–92) wrote in his official capacity as Victoria's Poet Laureate. Macaulay was a Whig who believed that the "Glorious Revolution" of 1688, which created a constitutional monarchy, and the Reform Bill of 1832, which increased the number of voters, were the greatest political triumphs of the human race. With such examples of wisdom to follow, together with all the material improvements that the age, led by Britain, was devising, the world had only to be sensible to assure itself forever of peace, prosperity, and progress. Macaulay's influence was enormous and, in spite of all the catastrophes of the present century, there are still people who believe more or less that Macaulay was right.

The thought expressed in Tennyson's official verse, actually his weakest verse though it rarely fails in craftsmanship, follows the same pattern as Macaulay's. Everything, with Britain serving as a shining example, is surely, if slowly, getting better and better. In this official verse Tennyson seems to be forcing himself to be almost as insensitively and blindly optimistic as Macaulay. But the real Tennyson, a magnificent poet, breaks through in finer works — those of a belated Romantic. This poetry is steeped in longing and regret and dreamy melancholy, often expressed in lines of the most exquisite and haunting beauty. It is not when he is celebrating Victoria as Queen-Empress or offering Britain's "broadening freedom" as an example to the world that Tennyson is a magical poet. His magical appeal shines through when he is writing about the aging Ulysses or the lotus eaters or the dark sorrows of Guinevere and Lancelot.

PROTESTS AGAINST VICTORIAN OPTIMISM

Indeed, Victorian literature as a whole represents a protest and rebellion against the Victorianism of Macaulay and of Tennyson in his official mood, against all that is characteristic of the self-confidence, complacency, and optimism of the age. For there is another side to the bright medal this period awarded itself. This is true even on the lowest material level. A country is not a commercial firm, to be judged by the amount of trade it does or by its balance sheets and profits. It cannot exist without business enterprise just as it cannot exist without water, but it itself is something more than so much business enterprise just as it is something more than so much water in reservoirs, pipes, and faucets. A country is the home of thousands of people. If it is a good home, if people are enjoying satisfactory lives, then the country is really prospering and making genuine progress. This — not the total amount of trade or the annual turnover in figures of money — is the real test.

Now although Victorian Britain was increasing its trade and getting richer every year, the great mass of industrial workers, crammed into the dark, ugly towns of the Midlands and the North, led appalling lives working in factories and mines from dawn to dusk — not only men and women but children as well

The town of Hanley, with its factories, chimneys, black smoke, and long rows of rooftops, was typical of many another industrial center in Victorian England.

Pictorial Parade

— for wages that barely kept them alive. Industrial England was so horrible that more than one foreign visitor compared it to hell. The countryside was blackened and ruined to produce wealth that vanished and reappeared elsewhere as country mansions, estates like parks, houses in London, and extravagant, fashionable living. This difference was so marked that even a Tory like Benjamin Disraeli (1804–81), an outstanding Prime Minister of the day, could declare that the English were divided into "two nations."

THE GROWING MIDDLE CLASS

Moreover, securely situated above this dark mass of industrial workers toiling to keep themselves alive, was a large and growing middle class. It was from this class that the Victorian writers, especially the novelists, drew most of their readers. Indeed, when we think of ordinary Victorian life, we think of it in terms of this segment of society, picturing to ourselves some comfortable middle-class family living in a villa with a servant or two, sitting around the drawing-room fire. (Outside it is probably foggy. There is a good reason why there is so much fog in the London of the Victorian novelists. Coal was cheap then, and every house had several coal fires burning in winter. When all the black smoke met the mists of the Thames Valley, the result was often a thick, yellow, choking fog.) Too many of the people belonging to this class were typically Victorian in a bad sense; that is, they were smugly complacent, prudish, hypocritical, disinclined to disturb themselves over people less fortunate than they were. It was these middle-class Victorians whom Dickens, who began with a prejudice in their favor, finally came to detest and to satirize savagely.

"ANTI-VICTORIAN" LITERATURE

Good writers are sensitive men and women, and it is not easy for them to pretend that all is well when they see quite clearly that all is not well. Furthermore, they are easily angered by the pretense of people who deliberately shut their eyes and close their minds so that they can go on feeling cozy, comfortable, and piously optimistic. Typical Victorians had much to be proud of, for the achievements of this age were beyond question and there was genuine and steady progress in many directions. However, they undoubtedly had a bad habit of ignoring what was unpleasant and might make them feel uncomfortable. It is against all this that so much of Victorian literature is a sharp protest. A great deal of Victorian literature is really anti-Victorian in the sense that it angrily denies what was thought to be true by newspaper editors, popular clergymen, self-congratulating businessmen, speechmaking politicians and officials, and second-rate writers trying to please their readers. When the smiling question went up: "Are we all happy?", the great writers said "No!"

Thomas Carlyle (1795–1881) said "No" over and over again, refusing to accept anything that even faintly resembled Macaulay's cheerful conclusions. He believed that the society of his time was steadily going from bad to worse, that its belief in its own progress was nonsensical, and that a true civilization based chiefly on trade and profit was impossible. John Stuart Mill (1806–73), the liberal philosopher and economist, though much politer than Carlyle, had his doubts. John Ruskin (1819–1900) was held to be a wonderful art critic, but when he later began to criticize the whole spirit of the age he was thought to be affected and absurd. Some people believe, however, that his social criticism is much sounder than his art criticism. Following Carlyle in spirit, Ruskin pointed out that the real test of a community is not how much wealth it is producing but what kind of people it is producing. And, following Ruskin, William Morris (1834–96), who himself combined various skills in handicrafts with his writing, condemned the whole industrial age for its ugliness, its mean products, and its joyless work. Samuel Butler (1835–1902),

Benjamin Disraeli, nicknamed "Dizzy," brilliant leader of the Conservative Party, first Earl of Beaconsfield, statesman, prime minister, and man of letters.

National Portrait Gallery

a highly original satirist from whom Bernard Shaw learned a great deal, turned upside down and inside out everything the Victorians held to be sacred, from family life to banking. Even an author of hugely successful light operas, W. S. Gilbert (1836–1911), was constantly and often very sharply satirical.

But, after all, these men were Victorians too, products of the same age, and must therefore be allowed this very valuable faculty of self-criticism. Here again there is some likeness between the Victorians and the Americans of our day, who through their writers so often attack their own complacency and are so often able to laugh at themselves. It is when such criticism is forbidden, when rebellious writers are silenced, that a society is in real danger, and this did not happen in Victorian Britain.

THE SOCIAL NOVEL

The chief Victorian novelists were also social critics and did not hesitate to show much of contemporary society in a very unfavorable light. Charles Dickens (1812–70), the master of the social novelists, is increasingly critical — and indeed almost despairing — as his fiction comes closer and closer to reality. Thackeray (1811–63) launches attack after attack upon the snobbery and bad social values of the time. George Eliot (1819–80), herself a radical, is essentially a social critic. And later, George Meredith (1828–1909), in a spirit of sharp mockery, and Thomas Hardy (1840–1928), in his slow, brooding, tragic fashion, turn their fiction into an instrument of philosophical social criticism. Even the easygoing Anthony Trollope (1815–82) can show us society, whether parsons or politicians are in the foreground, in terms of unsavory intrigues and power plots. And lesser novelists such as Charles Reade, Charles Kingsley, and Benjamin Disraeli almost turn their novels into what we would now call "social propaganda."

THE POETS' PROTEST

The poets reacted against this central complacent Victorianism in another fashion. Tennyson, as we have seen, turned out official verse in the prevailing mood of optimism, but when he was writing to please himself he became a wistful, melancholy Romantic. Robert (1812–89) and Elizabeth Barrett (1806–61) Browning did not even live in England, and Robert, though capable of writing very sharply about his own time, preferred on the whole to escape into Italy of the Renaissance. Algernon Charles Swinburne (1837–1909) in his

Illustrated here is the lavishly ornamented opening page of the Kelmscott Chaucer, William Morris' edition of Chaucer's Canterbury Tales *and one of the most famous English books. Morris, founder of the Kelmscott Press and one of the notable poets of his time, approached printing as an artist and craftsman, designed his own type and decorative borders, and used specially prepared paper and ink.*

productive and successful earlier years was an out-and-out rebel who scandalized everybody. Dante Gabriel Rossetti (1828–82), also a painter and one of the founders of the Pre-Raphaelite Brotherhood, and William Morris were defiant Romantics who paid no tribute to their age,

The Pierpont Morgan Library

from which they were obviously glad to escape in their poetry. George Meredith and Thomas Hardy condensed into their poetry the interpretation of life, alien to most Victorian thought and feeling, that also shaped their fiction.

INDIVIDUALISM OF VICTORIAN WRITERS

Apart from this common protest against Victorian smugness and hypocrisy, the major writers of the age have little in common. We have seen how the eighteenth-century writers, especially during the early years of the century, formed a compact group which shared the same outlook and held the same values. And later, the Romantics, though by no means a compact group, were at least members of the same general literary movement. But now, in the Victorian Age, writers do not seem to be moving together in any particular direction. Not only is it impossible to say that there is a Victorian movement, but it is also difficult to agree that there is a definitely Victorian manner or style. The major Victorian writers cannot be criticized as a literary group; they are highly individualistic almost to the point of eccentricity.

"FAMILY" LITERATURE

At the same time the Victorian reading public as a whole had certain tastes which writers respected or defied according to their desire for popularity. The middle-class Victorians, who made up the bulk of the reading public, had a

BRITAIN
1800-1900

SCOTLAND

1
Edinburgh

Abbotsford
2 TWEED RIVER

3
Craigenputtock
4
Ecclefechan

5
Keswick
LAKE
DISTRICT
6
Grasmere
YORKSHIRE
MOORS

IRELAND

8
Haworth

7
Dublin
Liverpool

ENGLAND

Newstead Abbey

9
Shrewsbury
WALES

10
Rugby

Cambridge

12
Oxford

11
Tintern Abbey

13
London

Bristol

15
Salisbury

Gadshill
14

Dover

16
Dorchester

Portsmouth

ISLE OF WIGHT

1 Birthplace of Sir Walter Scott (1771) and R. L. Stevenson (1850). **2** Sir Walter Scott's home. **3** Home of Thomas Carlyle. **4** Birthplace of Carlyle (1795). **5** Coleridge and Southey lived here. **6** Wordsworth's long-time home and burial place. **7** Cardinal Newman was university rector and Hopkins taught Greek here. **8** Home of the Brontës. **9** Mr. Pickwick and his friends dined at the Hop Pole Inn here. **10** Well-known school where Matthew Arnold studied and taught and his father was headmaster. **11** Famous ruins near which Words-worth wrote his well-known ode. **12** Lewis Carroll taught here. **13** Literary and cultural center. Lamb and Keats lived and worked here. Macaulay served in Parliament; Carlyle lived in Cheyne Row, Rossetti nearby; Dickens lived and worked in the city, and Browning was lionized here. Gilbert and Sullivan's operettas were first produced by London's D'Oyly Carte Company. **14** Home of Charles Dickens. **15** The "Barchester" of Anthony Trollope's novels. **16** The "Casterbridge" of Thomas Hardy's "Wessex" novels.

very definite liking for what may be called "family" literature. There was a good deal of reading aloud in the evenings and, even when this custom was not observed, parents preferred books that could be read and enjoyed by all the family. This meant, first, that it was impossible for novelists with a large public, like Dickens and Thackeray, to be as frank as they wished to be or as novelists have been during the past fifty years. (Dickens savagely satirizes the attitude of the typical middle-class father of a family in the character of Mr. Podsnap in *Our Mutual Friend*.) But that was not all. A popular novelist was expected to provide something for each member of the family — something pathetic for Mother, dramatic for Father, sentimental for the girls, comic for the boys. A popular Victorian novel is like a Christmas hamper intended for the whole family.

The poets, perhaps envying the novelists their popularity, tried to capture the reading public which had such a large appetite for fiction. Tennyson's "The Princess" and "Maud" might reasonably be described as novels in verse, with the real poetry blazing out in the beautiful lyrics within the narratives. Browning and Arthur Hugh Clough (1819–61), though aiming at a smaller and more highbrow public, followed Tennyson's example. Even Matthew Arnold (1822–88), though more critical and fastidious still, does not altogether disdain a narrative interest in his poetry.

EDUCATION

Matthew Arnold was a poet, but he was also an inspector of schools for thirty-five years. The spread of popular education was one of the best features of the Victorian Age. It took several forms. The most important dates from 1870, when the government authorized the creation of "board schools" (the equivalent then of American public schools) for elementary education. It was not until 1890, however, that free elementary education was established in England. At the same time the needs of older students were being met. Colleges, which afterwards became universities (and so had the power of giving degrees), were created in London, Manchester, and elsewhere. University Extension lectures, in which scholars appointed by the older universities gave courses of lectures to groups of ordinary citizens, came into existence. There was a strong and successful movement to remove the control of education, from the level of Oxford and Cambridge down to that of the elementary schools, from the Church of England. I know from personal experience what great strides were made in popular education during this age. My father's father was a mill worker who probably never earned more than the equivalent (but in those days when money bought far more) of about eight dollars a week. Yet

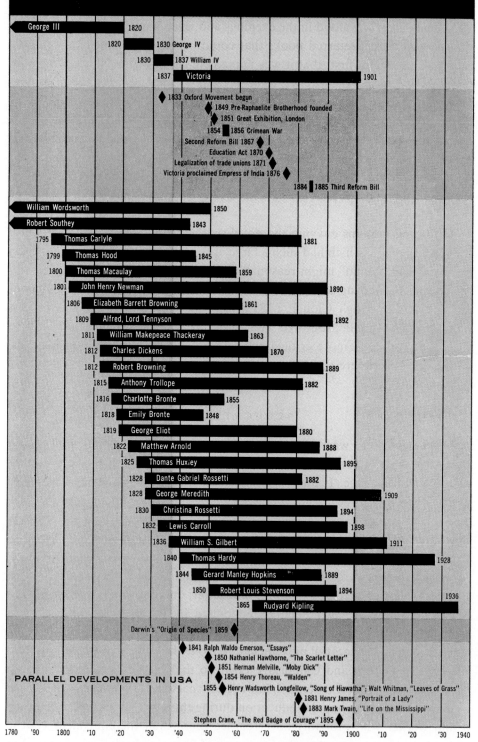

VICTORIAN TIMES

George III — 1820
1820 — 1830 George IV
1830 — 1837 William IV
1837 Victoria 1901

◆ 1833 Oxford Movement begun
◆ 1849 Pre-Raphaelite Brotherhood founded
◆ 1851 Great Exhibition, London
1854 ■ 1856 Crimean War
Second Reform Bill 1867 ◆
Education Act 1870 ◆
Legalization of trade unions 1871 ◆
Victoria proclaimed Empress of India 1876 ◆
1884 ■ 1885 Third Reform Bill

William Wordsworth — 1850
Robert Southey — 1843
1795 Thomas Carlyle 1881
1799 Thomas Hood 1845
1800 Thomas Macaulay 1859
1801 John Henry Newman 1890
1806 Elizabeth Barrett Browning 1861
1809 Alfred, Lord Tennyson 1892
1811 William Makepeace Thackeray 1863
1812 Charles Dickens 1870
1812 Robert Browning 1889
1815 Anthony Trollope 1882
1816 Charlotte Bronte 1855
1818 Emily Bronte 1848
1819 George Eliot 1880
1822 Matthew Arnold 1888
1825 Thomas Huxley 1895
1828 Dante Gabriel Rossetti 1882
1828 George Meredith 1909
1830 Christina Rossetti 1894
1832 Lewis Carroll 1898
1836 William S. Gilbert 1911
1840 Thomas Hardy 1928
1844 Gerard Manley Hopkins 1889
1850 Robert Louis Stevenson 1894
1865 Rudyard Kipling 1936

Darwin's "Origin of Species" 1859 ◆

1841 Ralph Waldo Emerson, "Essays"
◆ 1850 Nathaniel Hawthorne, "The Scarlet Letter"
◆ 1851 Herman Melville, "Moby Dick"
◆ 1854 Henry Thoreau, "Walden"

PARALLEL DEVELOPMENTS IN USA

1855 ◆ Henry Wadsworth Longfellow, "Song of Hiawatha"; Walt Whitman, "Leaves of Grass"
◆ 1881 Henry James, "Portrait of a Lady"
◆ 1883 Mark Twain, "Life on the Mississippi"
Stephen Crane, "The Red Badge of Courage" 1895 ◆

1780 '90 1800 '10 '20 '30 '40 '50 '60 '70 '80 '90 1900 '10 '20 '30 1940

his son, my father, was able to spend at least two years at a teachers' training college in London. My father, who eventually became headmaster of a large new elementary school, had a passionate belief in education. He was a fairly typical Victorian.

VICTORIAN TASTES

It must be understood that what is typically "Victorian" really belongs to the years 1837–77, the first forty years of the period. The late Victorian period — the 1880's and 1890's — is quite different from the early and mid-Victorian periods. These later Victorians lived in a larger world and in a more sophisticated fashion than did the earlier Victorians. Rudyard Kipling (1865–1936), who was already famous when he was in his twenties, introduced readers to this larger world through his tales and ballads of British India. He was essentially the poet and storyteller of the spirit of the new imperialism, the pride in controlling and managing a vast empire, which flourished between 1880 and 1900. The sophistication of the late Victorian period was well represented by Oscar Wilde (1854–1900), whose masterful comedy, *The Importance of Being Earnest,* is still frequently produced. Wilde, however, was always more talked about than read and enjoyed in England, where he has never had the reputation that he gained, rather mysteriously, on the European continent. In any event, when, as below, we refer to the taste of the time, it is not these later Victorians but the earlier Victorians that we have in mind.

These people are remarkable for two things, the first of which is a preoccupation with disease and death that is so strong that we consider it morbid. In characteristically Victorian fiction and verse, we cannot escape from the sickroom, the death bed, and the cemetery. Even in the most popular stories of school life whole chapters are given up to death beds and funerals. It is true that the Victorians saw far more of death than we do now (except of course in war) because they had large families and many children died young. The "wasting sickness" from which so many Victorian heroines suffered was probably tuberculosis, all the more dangerous and infectious in those days because its victims were kept indoors. But even allowing for these facts in their lives, the Victorian taste for fatal illnesses, lingering death, funerals, and graveyards remains extraordinary. They seem to have enjoyed having "a good cry," and novelists anxious to please their public, like the early Dickens with his Little Nell and poor Paul Dombey, did not hesitate to set their tears flowing. Tough public men, who seem to have been unmoved by all the appalling sights of real life, would often spend an evening weeping over these pathetic chapters.

On the other hand, the Victorians had an even stronger desire to laugh.

Nobody can complain that Victorian literature is without humor. It is crammed, from Dickens on, with comic scenes and characters, some of them among the finest in English literature. The readers of the day had a special taste, which is very English as well as being Victorian, for the literature of sheer absurdity and wild nonsense. In this spirit the Rev. Charles L. Dodgson (1832–98), an Oxford mathematics tutor hiding himself behind the pen name "Lewis Carroll," produced masterpieces of elaborate and fascinating absurdity in the famous *Alice in Wonderland, Through the Looking Glass,* and (please don't miss it!) *The Hunting of the Snark.* Edward Lear (1812–88), the artist, and W. S. Gilbert of operetta fame, were also original and fertile in this field, and behind them were dozens of lesser humorists, many of them, like Francis Cowley Burnand and Jerome K. Jerome, still worth reading today.

Illness and death, comic characters and nonsense, a new realism in fiction, a fading, wistful Romanticism in verse, science and industry triumphant, thus encouraging complacency and a confident belief in unchecked progress; against these the doubts, protests, and often savage social criticism of the writers, each of them, however, going his or her own way — such is the richly varied, immensely productive, strangely contradictory Victorian Age.

J. B. P.

THOMAS CARLYLE

1795–1881

National Portrait Gallery

Thomas Carlyle, like his fellow Scotsman Robert Burns, had a hard struggle against poverty. His father, a stonemason with nine children, was determined that his brilliant son should study for the ministry at Edinburgh University. Thomas, then fifteen years old, walked the hundred miles from his birthplace, Ecclefechan (ĕk″l·fĕk′ăn), to Edinburgh. Of his five years of painful economy there, he writes: "I was without friends, experience, or connection in the sphere of human business, was of sly humor, proud enough and to spare, and had begun my long curriculum of dyspepsia." This nagging and persistent illness contributed to his irritable temperament, for which he was known and feared all his life. Influenced by his study of German philosophy, Carlyle developed a marked pessimism about mankind. He was a reformer, but history rather than religion became his teacher.

While tutoring in London he married Jane Welsh, a beautiful Scottish girl, who fortunately had a farm in southern Scotland where they could live at little expense. Her letters to her friends describing their none-too-easy life were written in delightful style and have since been published in several editions. In 1834 the Carlyles moved to London, and their house in Cheyne Row became a center for the gathering of literary people, as Lamb's home had been earlier. (Lamb died the year the Carlyles moved to London.) In spite of his gruff and thorny exterior, Carlyle had the power to make warm friends among those who recognized his sincerity and his genius. Dickens, Thackeray, and Tennyson greatly admired him, and when Emerson first went to Europe, his most earnest desire was to meet Carlyle. Their thirty-year friendship won for each a reading public in the other's country.

The Fall of the Bastille

A tragic circumstance was connected with the writing of Carlyle's famous history *The French Revolution*. Carlyle had given his manuscript to his friend, the economist John Stuart Mill, to read, and Mill's servant accidentally used the sheets to build a fire one morning. Carlyle had kept no notes and at first could not recall any of his writing. He spent a week reading novels to calm his mind; then he laboriously rewrote the whole book.

The following selection illustrates Carlyle's highly individual style, with its broken, exclamatory sentences. He gives the reader the feeling of being present and experiencing the excitement and suspense of the scene.

The gloomy Bastille (băs·tēl') prison, surrounded by a moat, had stood since the fourteenth century at one of the gates of Paris. With its long history of unjust imprisonments and forgotten prisoners, it had become a symbol of the oppressions of the French monarchy. The day of its destruction, July 14, 1789, became the date for the annual celebration of national independence, just as July 4 is Independence Day in America.

T HE BASTILLE is besieged! On, then, all Frenchmen that have hearts in your bodies! Roar with all your throats of cartilage and metal, ye sons of liberty; stir spasmodically whatsoever of utmost faculty is in you, soul, body, or spirit, for it is the hour! Smite thou, Louis Tournay, cartwright of the Marais,[1] old soldier of the Régiment Dauphiné;[2] smite at that outer drawbridge chain, though the fiery hail whistles around thee! Never, over nave[3] or felloe,[4] did thy ax strike such a stroke. Down with it, man; down with it to Orcus;[5] let the whole accursed edifice sink thither, and tyranny be swallowed up forever! Mounted, some say, on the roof of the guardroom, some "on bayonets stuck into joints of the wall," Louis Tournay smites, brave Aubin Bonnemère[6] (also an old soldier) seconding him. The chain yields, breaks; the huge drawbridge slams down, thundering. Glorious! and yet, alas! it is still but the outworks. The eight grim towers with their invalide[7] musketry, their paving stones and can-

---

[1] *Marais* (mä·rā'): a manufacturing quarter of Paris. [2] *Régiment Dauphiné* (rā·zhē·mäN' dō-fē·nā'): regiment of the Dauphin, or king's son. [3] *nave:* the hub of a wheel. [4] *felloe:* a segment of the rim of a wooden wheel. [5] *Orcus:* in Roman mythology, the home of the dead; the underworld. [6] *Bonnemère* (bŏn·mĕr'). [7] *invalide* (ăn·vä·lēd'): veteran (originally, wounded soldier).

non mouths, still soar aloft intact; ditch yawning impassable, stonefaced; the inner drawbridge with its *back* toward us; the Bastille is still to take! . . .

Paris, wholly, has got to the acme of its frenzy, whirled all ways by panic madness. At every street barricade there whirls, simmering, a minor whirlpool, strengthening the barricade, since God knows what is coming; and all minor whirlpools play distractedly into that grand fire maelstrom [1] which is lashing round the Bastille.

And so it lashes and roars. Cholat,[2] the wine merchant, has become an impromptu cannoneer. See Georget,[3] of the marine service, fresh from Brest,[4] play the King of Siam's cannon. Singular (if we were not used to the like). Georget lay last night taking his ease at his inn; the King of Siam's cannon also lay, knowing nothing of *him* for a hundred years; yet now, at the right instant, they have got together, and discourse eloquent music; for, hearing what was toward, Georget sprang from the Brest diligence,[5] and ran. Gardes Françaises,[6] also, will be here with real artillery. Were not the walls so thick! Upward from the esplanade, horizontally from all neighboring roofs and windows, flashes one irregular deluge of musketry, without effect. The invalides lie flat, firing comparatively at their ease from behind stone; hardly through portholes show the tip of a nose. We fall, shot, and make no impression!

Let conflagration rage of whatsoever is combustible! Guardrooms are burnt, invalides messrooms. A distracted "peruke-maker with two fiery torches" is for burning "the saltpeters of the arsenal," had not a woman run screaming, had not a patriot, with some tincture of natural

philosophy, instantly struck the wind out of him (butt of musket on pit of stomach), overturned barrels, and stayed the devouring element. A young, beautiful lady seized, escaping, in these outer courts, and thought, falsely, to be De Launay's [7] daughter, shall be burnt in De Launay's sight; she lies, swooned, on a paillasse; [8] but, again, a patriot — it is brave Aubin Bonnemère, the old soldier — dashes in, and rescues her. Straw is burnt; three cartloads of it, hauled hither, go up in white smoke, almost to the choking of patriotism itself; so that Elie had, with singed brows, to drag back one cart, and Réole, the "gigantic haberdasher," another. Smoke as of Tophet,[9] confusion as of Babel,[10] noise as of the crack of doom!

Blood flows, the aliment of new madness. The wounded are carried into houses of the Rue Cerisaie; [11] the dying leave their last mandate not to yield till the accursed stronghold fall. And yet, alas! how fall? The walls are so thick! Deputations, three in number, arrive from the Hôtel-de-Ville.[12] . . . These wave their town flag in the arched gateway, and stand, rolling their drum, but to no purpose. In such crack of doom De Launay cannot hear them, dare not believe them; they return, with justified rage, the whew of lead still singing in their ears. What to do? The firemen are here, squirting with their fire pumps on the invalides' cannon to wet the touchholes; they unfortunately cannot squirt so high, but produce only clouds of spray. Individuals of classical knowledge propose *catapults*. Santerre, the sonorous brewer of the suburb Saint-Antoine, advises rather that the place be fired by "a mixture of phosphorus and

---

[1] *maelstrom* (māl'strŏm): a whirlpool off the northwest coast of Norway; used figuratively, any turmoil of resistless movement or influence. [2] *Cholat* (shō·lä'). [3] *Georget* (zhôr·zhĕ'). [4] *Brest:* a naval station in northwest France. [5] *diligence* (dē·lē·zhäns'): stagecoach. [6] *Gardes Françaises* (gärd frän·sĕz'): French guards.

[7] *De Launay* (dĕ lō·nā'): governor of the Bastille; slain after its capture. [8] *paillasse* (päl·yäs'): a straw mattress. [9] *Tophet* (tō'fĕt): a place near Jerusalem used for burning sacrifices and, later, refuse. [10] *Babel* (bā'bĕl): a confusion of many voices; from the Tower of Babel (Genesis 11:9). [11] *Rue Cerisaie* (rū sĕr·ē·sā'): a street in Paris. [12] *Hôtel-de-Ville* (ō·tĕl·dĕ·vēl'): City Hall.

oil of turpentine spouted up through forcing pumps." O Spinola-Santerre,[1] has thou the mixture *ready?* Every man his own engineer! And still the fire deluge abates not; even women are firing, and Turks — at least one woman (with her sweetheart) and one Turk. Gardes Françaises have come; real cannon, real cannoneers. Usher Maillard is busy; half-pay Elie, half-pay Hulin, rage in the midst of thousands.

How the great Bastille clock ticks (inaudible) in its inner court, there, at its ease, hour after hour; as if nothing special, for it or the world, were passing! It tolled one when the firing began, and is now pointing toward five, and still the firing slakes not. Far down in their vaults, the seven prisoners hear muffled din as of earthquakes; their turnkeys answer vaguely.

Woe to thee, De Launay, with thy poor hundred invalides! . . .

What shall De Launay do? One thing only De Launay could have done — what he said he would do. Fancy him sitting, from the first, with lighted taper, within arm's length of the powder magazine; motionless, like an old Roman senator, or bronze lamp holder; coldly apprising all manner of men, by a slight motion of his eye, what his resolution was. Harmless he sat there, while unharmed; but the king's fortress, meanwhile, could, might, would, or should in nowise be surrendered, save to the king's messengers; one old man's life is worthless, so it be lost with honor; but think, ye brawling *canaille,*[2] how will it be when a whole Bastille springs skyward? In such statuesque, taper-holding attitude, one fancies De Launay might have left Thuriot, the red clerks of the Basoche, curé[3] of St. Stephen, and all the tagrag and bobtail of the world, to work their will.

And yet, withal, he could not do it. . . . Distracted he hovers between two — hopes in the middle of despair; surrenders not his fortress; declares that he will blow it up, seizes torches to blow it up, and does not blow it. Unhappy old De Launay, it is the death agony of the Bastille and thee! Jail, jailoring, and jailor, all three, such as they may have been, must finish.

For four hours now has the world bedlam roared; call it the world chimera[4] blowing fire! The poor invalides have sunk under their battlements, or rise only with reversed muskets; they have made a white flag of napkins, go beating the chamade,[5] or seeming to beat, for one can hear nothing. The very Swiss at the portcullis[6] look weary of firing, disheartened in the fire deluge; a porthole at the drawbridge is opened, as by one that would speak. See Huissier Maillard, the shifty man! On his plank, swinging over the abyss of that stoned ditch, plank resting on parapet, balanced by weight of patriots, he hovers perilous — such a dove toward such an ark! Deftly, thou shifty usher; one man already fell and lies smashed, far down there against the masonry! Usher Maillard falls not; deftly, unerringly, he walks, with outspread palm. The Swiss holds a paper through the porthole; the shifty usher snatches it and returns. Terms of surrender: Pardon, immunity to all! Are they accepted? *"Foi d'officier* (on the word of an officer)," answers half-pay Hulin, or half-pay Elie — for men do not agree on it — "they are!" Sinks the drawbridge, Usher Maillard bolting it when down; rushes in the living deluge; the Bastille is fallen!

Victoire! La Bastille est prise![7]

[1] *Spinola-Santerre* (spĭ·nō′là-sàn·târ′): Santerre, a leader of the Parisian Revolutionary mob, is likened to General Spinola, who captured a fortress in Holland in 1625. [2] *canaille* (kà′nä′y′): the vulgar multitude; the mob. [3] *curé* (kū·rā′): parish priest.

[4] *chimera* (kī·mēr′à): a mythical fire-breathing animal. [5] *chamade* (shà·mäd′): a drum or trumpet signal for a parley. [6] *Swiss at the portcullis:* The French hired Swiss mercenaries as guards. The portcullis was an iron grating at the entrance. [7] Victory! The Bastille is taken!

CARLYLE'S HISTORY

1. Describe in your own words the outer appearance of the Bastille and just what happened to cause it to surrender. What descriptive touches make the scene vivid and dramatic?

2. What is the attitude of the mob toward the aristocrats? What do you learn about mob psychology? Does Carlyle show sympathy with either side? Support your answer with specific references.

3. Some class members should read Dickens' account of the fall of the Bastille in *A Tale of Two Cities* (Book II, Chapter 21) and tell the class what likenesses and what differences they find in the two versions. Dickens based his narrative largely on Carlyle's.

THOMAS BABINGTON MACAULAY

1800–1859

National Portrait Gallery

Carlyle and Macaulay are often coupled as the greatest writers of history and essay during the Victorian Age. Yet how unlike are their lives and their talents! Carlyle was a rough-hewn, gloomy, often secluded man who scolded against the times; Macaulay was a bland, confident, earnest public figure, whose writings were extremely popular.

Thomas Macaulay was a child prodigy who read at the age of three and wrote a *Compendium of Universal Knowledge* at eight. He later embarked on his formal literary career with an essay on Milton. Later he entered Parliament, where he spoke brilliantly in behalf of the Reform Bill to extend suffrage and where he championed the cause of Negro slaves in the West Indies. He also served the British government in India for four years. During these active years of public service, young Macaulay was constantly writing prose, and he even ventured into the field of poetry with *Lays of Ancient Rome*, which are still popular narrative poems. At thirty-nine he began his *History of England*, a work that has since become standard. (It brought him more than $150,-000 in royalties, but twice that amount was lost to him by the inadequate copyright laws of the day, which prevented his receiving royalties from sales in America.) At fifty-seven he was made Lord Macaulay, one of many other honors he received. Two years later he died and was buried in Westminster Abbey.

Such a career points to the sturdy qualities of honesty, industry, perseverance, and devotion to public welfare. Macaulay was sometimes criticized for his lack of deep insight into human problems, his prejudice, and his apparent inability to see all sides of a question. "I wish," said one of his contemporaries in government, "that I could be as sure of anything as Lord Macaulay is of everything."

London Streets

Macaulay's smooth, direct style is in sharp contrast to the jagged sentences and headlong style of Thomas Carlyle. Both writers use graphic details to hold the attention of the reader, but the effect produced is entirely different. As a result of the detail in which Macaulay pictured the bygone ages, he covered in five volumes of his *History of England* only sixteen years, from James II to Queen Anne. London as described in these excerpts was much the same throughout the late seventeenth and eighteenth centuries.

THE POSITION of London, relatively to the other towns of the empire, was, in the time of Charles II, far higher than at present. For at present the population of London is little more than six times the population of Manchester or of Liverpool. In the days of Charles II the population of London was more than seventeen times the population of Bristol or of Norwich. It may be doubted whether any other instance can be mentioned of a great kingdom in which the first city was more than seventeen times as large as the second. There is reason to believe that in 1685 London had been, during about half a century, the most populous capital in Europe. The inhabitants, who are now at least nineteen hundred thousand, were then probably little more than half a million. . . .

We should greatly err if we were to suppose that any of the streets and squares then bore the same aspect as at present. The great majority of the houses, indeed, have, since that time, been wholly, or in great part, rebuilt. If the most fashionable parts of the capital could be placed before us, such as they then were, we should be disgusted by their squalid appearance, and poisoned by their noisome atmosphere. In Covent Garden a filthy and noisy market was held close to the dwellings of the great. Fruit women screamed, carters fought, cabbage stalks and rotten apples accumulated in heaps at the thresholds of the Countess of Berkshire and of the Bishop of Durham.

The center of Lincoln's Inn Fields [1] was an open space where the rabble congregated every evening, within a few yards of Cardigan House and Winchester House, to hear mountebanks harangue, to see bears dance, and to set dogs at oxen. Rubbish was shot in every part of the area. Horses were exercised there. The beggars were as noisy and importunate as in the worst-governed cities of the Continent. A Lincoln's Inn mumper [2] was a proverb. The whole fraternity knew the arms and liveries of every charitably disposed grandee in the neighborhood, and, as soon as his lordship's coach and six appeared, came hopping and crawling in crowds to persecute him. These disorders lasted, in spite of many accidents, and of some legal proceedings, till, in the reign of George II, Sir Joseph Jekyll, Master of the Rolls, was knocked down and nearly killed in the middle of the square. Then at length palisades were set up, and a pleasant garden laid out.

Saint James' Square [3] was a receptacle for all the offal and cinders, for all the dead cats and dead dogs of Westminster. [4] At one time a cudgel player [5] kept the ring there. At another time an impudent squatter settled himself there, and built a shed for rubbish under the windows of the gilded saloons in which the first magnates of the realm, Norfolk, Ormond, Kent, and Pembroke, gave banquets and balls. It was not till these nuisances had lasted through a whole generation, and till much had been written about them, that the inhabitants ap-

[1] *Lincoln's Inn Fields:* the largest square in London, surrounded by lawyers' offices and old mansions. [2] *mumper:* a beggar and impostor. [3] *Saint James' Square:* later a fashionable district. [4] *Westminster:* the section of London where the government houses are located. [5] *cudgel player:* a man skilled in defending himself with cudgel or staff.

"The Stagecoach," by Eugene Lami, a mode of travel common in early Victorian times.

New York Public Library, Print Room

plied to Parliament for permission to put up rails, and to plant trees.

When such was the state of the region inhabited by the most luxurious portion of society, we may easily believe that the great body of the population suffered what would now be considered as insupportable grievances. The pavement was detestable; all foreigners cried shame upon it. The drainage was so bad that in rainy weather the gutters soon became torrents. Several facetious poets have commemorated the fury with which these black rivulets roared down Snow Hill and Ludgate Hill, bearing to Fleet Ditch a vast tribute of animal and vegetable filth from the stalls of butchers and greengrocers. This flood was profusely thrown to right and left by coaches and carts. To keep as far from the carriage road as possible was therefore the wish of every pedestrian. The mild and timid gave the wall. The bold and athletic took it. If two roisterers met, they cocked their hats in each other's faces, and pushed each other about till the weaker was shoved toward the kennel.[1] If he was a mere bully he sneaked off, muttering that he should find a time. If he was pugnacious, the encounter probably ended in a duel behind Montague House.[2]

The houses were not numbered. There would indeed have been little advantage in numbering them; for of the coachmen, chairmen,[3] porters, and errand boys of London, a very small proportion could read. It was necessary to use marks which the most ignorant could understand. The shops were therefore distinguished by painted or sculptured signs, which gave a gay and grotesque aspect to the streets. The walk from Charing Cross to Whitechapel lay through an endless succession of Saracens' Heads, Royal Oaks, Blue Bears, and Golden Lambs, which disappeared when they were no longer required for the direction of the common people.

When the evening closed in, the difficulty and danger of walking about London became serious indeed. The garret windows were opened, and pails were emptied, with little regard to those who were passing below. Falls, bruises, and broken bones were of constant occurrence. For, till the last year of the reign of Charles II, most of the streets were left in profound darkness. Thieves and robbers plied their trade with impunity; yet they were hardly so terrible to peaceable citizens as another class of ruffians. It was a favorite amusement of dissolute young gentlemen to swagger by night about the town, breaking windows, upsetting sedans, beating quiet men, and offering rude caresses to pretty women. Several dynasties of these tyrants had, since the Restoration, domineered over the streets. The Muns and Tityre Tus had given place to the Hectors, and the Hectors had been recently succeeded by

---

[1] *kennel:* street gutter. [2] *Montague* (mŏn′tá-gū) *House:* a government building in Whitehall.

[3] *chairmen:* men who carried the sedan chairs.

the Scourers. At a later period rose the Nicker, the Hawcubite, and the yet more dreaded name of Mohawk. The machinery for keeping the peace was utterly contemptible. There was an act of Common Council which provided that more than a thousand watchmen should be constantly on the alert in the city, from sunset to sunrise, and that every inhabitant should take his turn of duty. But this act was negligently executed. Few of those who were summoned left their homes; and those few generally found it more agreeable to tipple in alehouses than to pace the streets. . . .

London Coffeehouses

THE COFFEEHOUSE must not be dismissed with a cursory mention. It might indeed at that time have been not improperly called a most important political institution. No Parliament had sat for years. The municipal council of the city had ceased to speak the sense of the citizens. Public meetings, harangues, resolutions, and the rest of the modern machinery of agitation had not yet come into fashion. Nothing resembling the modern newspaper existed. In such circumstances the coffeehouses were the chief organs through which the public opinion of the metropolis vented itself.

The first of these establishments had been set up, in the time of the Commonwealth, by a Turkey merchant, who had acquired among the Mohammedans a taste for their favorite beverage. The convenience of being able to make appointments in any part of the town, and of being able to pass evenings socially at a very small charge, was so great that the fashion spread fast. Every man of the upper or middle class went daily to his coffeehouse to learn the news and to discuss it. Every coffeehouse had one or more orators to whose eloquence the crowd listened with admiration, and who

soon became what the journalists of our own time have been called, a fourth Estate of the realm. The court had long seen with uneasiness the growth of this new power in the state. An attempt had been made, during Danby's [1] administration, to close the coffeehouses. But men of all parties missed their usual places of resort so much that there was an universal outcry. The government did not venture, in opposition to a feeling so strong and general, to enforce a regulation of which the legality might well be questioned. Since that time ten years had elapsed, and during those years the number and influence of the coffeehouses had been constantly increasing. Foreigners remarked that the coffeehouse was that which especially distinguished London from all other cities; that the coffeehouse was the Londoner's home, and that those who wished to find a gentleman commonly asked, not whether he lived in Fleet Street or Chancery Lane, but whether he frequented the Grecian or the Rainbow. Nobody was excluded from these places who laid down his penny at the bar. Yet every rank and profession, and every shade of religious and political opinion, had its own headquarters. There were houses near Saint James' Park where fops congregated, their heads and shoulders covered with black or flaxen wigs, not less ample than those which are now worn by the Chancellor and by the Speaker of the House of Commons. The wig came from Paris; and so did the rest of the fine gentleman's ornaments, his embroidered coat, his fringed gloves, and the tassel which upheld his pantaloons. The conversation was in that dialect which, long after it had ceased to be spoken in fashionable circles, continued, in the mouth of Lord Foppington,[2] to excite the mirth of theaters. The atmosphere was like that of a

[1] *Danby:* Thomas Osborn, Lord Danby; Lord Treasurer under Charles II. [2] *Foppington:* a character in *The Relapse,* by Vanbrugh; he pronounced "Lord" as "Lard."

perfumer's shop. Tobacco in any other form than that of richly scented snuff was held in abomination. If any clown, ignorant of the usages of the house, called for a pipe, the sneers of the whole assembly and the short answers of the waiters soon convinced him that he had better go somewhere else. Nor, indeed, would he have had far to go. For, in general, the coffeerooms reeked with tobacco like a guardroom; and strangers sometimes expressed their surprise that so many people should leave their own firesides to sit in the midst of eternal fog and stench.

Nowhere was the smoking more constant than at Will's. That celebrated house, situated between Covent Garden and Bow Street, was sacred to polite letters. There the talk was about poetical justice and the unities of place and time. There was a faction for Perrault[1] and the moderns, a faction for Boileau[2] and the ancients. One group debated whether *Paradise Lost* ought not to have been in rhyme. To another an envious poetaster demonstrated that *Venice Preserved*[3] ought to have been hooted from the stage. Under no roof was a greater variety of figures to be seen. There were earls in stars and garters, clergymen in cassocks and bands, pert Templars,[4] sheepish lads from the universities, translators and index makers in ragged coats of frieze. The great press was to get near the chair where John Dryden sat. In winter that chair was always in the warmest nook by the fire; in summer it stood in the balcony. To bow to the Laureate, and to hear his opinion of Racine's[5] last tragedy or of Bossu's[6] treatise on epic

poetry, was thought a privilege. A pinch from his snuffbox was an honor sufficient to turn the head of a young enthusiast. There were coffeehouses where the first medical men might be consulted. Doctor John Radcliffe, who, in the year 1685, rose to the largest practice in London, came daily, at the hour when the Exchange was full, from his house in Bow Street, then a fashionable part of the capital, to Garaway's, and was to be found, surrounded by surgeons and apothecaries, at a particular table. There were Puritan coffeehouses where no oath was heard, and where lank-haired men discussed election and reprobation through their noses; Jew coffeehouses where dark-eyed money-changers from Venice and from Amsterdam greeted each other; and Popish coffeehouses where, as good Protestants believed, Jesuits planned, over their cups, another great fire, and cast silver bullets to shoot the King.

These gregarious habits had no small share in forming the character of the Londoner of that age. He was, indeed, a different being from the rustic Englishman. There was not then the intercourse which now exists between the two classes. Only very great men were in the habit of dividing the year between town and country. Few esquires came to the capital thrice in their lives. Nor was it yet the practice of all citizens in easy circumstances to breathe the fresh air of the fields and woods during some weeks of every summer. A cockney, in a rural village, was stared at as much as if he had intruded into a kraal[7] of Hottentots. On the other hand, when the Lord of a Lincolnshire or Shropshire manor appeared in Fleet Street, he was as easily distinguished from the resident population as a Turk or a lascar.[8] His dress, his gait, his accent, the manner in which he stared at the shops, stumbled into the gutters, ran against the porters, and

---

[1] *Perrault* (pě'rō'): French writer (1628–1703); member of the French Academy. [2] *Boileau* (bwȧ'lō'): French satirist and critic (1636–1711); member of the French Academy. The two disputed the merits of ancient and modern literature. [3] *Venice Preserved:* a play by Thomas Otway (1652–1685). It was produced in London in 1953. [4] *Templars:* lawyers and law students, who resided in the Temple. [5] *Racine* (rȧ'sēn'): French poet (1639–1699). [6] *Bossu* (bô'sü'): French critic (1631–1680).

[7] *kraal* (kräl): a stockaded village of South African natives. [8] *lascar:* East Indian sailor.

stood under the waterspouts, marked him out as an excellent subject for the operations of swindlers and banterers. Bullies jostled him into the kennel. Hackney coachmen splashed him from head to foot. Thieves explored with perfect security the huge pockets of his horseman's coat, while he stood entranced by the splendor of the Lord Mayor's show. Money droppers, sore from the cart's tail,[1] introduced themselves to him, and appeared to him the most honest, friendly gentlemen that he had ever seen. Painted women, the refuse of Lewkner Lane and Whetstone Park, passed themselves on him for countesses and maids of honor. If he asked his way to Saint James', his informants sent him to Mile End.[2] If he went into a shop, he was instantly discerned to be a fit purchaser of everything that nobody else would buy, of secondhand embroidery, copper rings, and watches that would not go. If he rambled into any fashionable coffeehouse, he became a mark for the insolent derision of fops and the grave waggery of Templars. Enraged and mortified, he soon returned to his mansion, and there, in the homage of his tenants, and the conversation of his boon companions, found consolation for the vexations and humiliations which he had undergone. There he was once more a great man, and saw nothing above himself except when at the assizes[3] he took his seat on the bench, near the Judge, or when at the muster of the militia he saluted the Lord Lieutenant.

[1] *Money droppers . . . tail:* cheats, who had been tied to a cart and whipped through the streets. [2] *Mile End:* a poor district in the east end of London. [3] *assizes* (ă·sīz'ĕz): sessions of the county court.

MACAULAY'S HISTORY

1. Explain briefly conditions in London in the late seventeenth century as to street cleanliness, identification of shops, the troubles of pedestrians. What different groups were to be found in the coffeehouses?

2. Judging Carlyle and Macaulay by the selections in this book, what differences do you observe in their style (sentence structure, choice of words, use of detail, etc.)? How do these selections differ from the historical writing familiar to you?

CLASS ACTIVITIES

1. In a panel, discuss the great improvements in city conditions that have been made since the time this history describes. Would you have enjoyed living in the London of those days? Why, or why not? In a modern city what various institutions take care of those needs and interests to which the coffeehouses once catered?

2. Some students might read and report to the class on the interesting passage on travel conditions in Chapter 3 of Volume I of Macaulay's *History of England.* If possible, illustrate your talk with pictures.

THE POWER OF WORDS

EXPRESSIVE ADJECTIVES

Macaulay uses three adjectives which are good ones to add to your vocabulary: *facetious* (fà·sē'shŭs), *pugnacious* (pŭg·nā'shŭs), and *gregarious* (grĕ·gâr'ĭ·ŭs). Macaulay says that several facetious poets have written about the bad drainage system of old London. If you did not know the word, the context might lead you to think that they wrote indignantly, but no, they wrote with intent to make the reader laugh. This intent is always important in the word *facetious.* A person may be unconsciously funny, or naturally witty, or mildly humorous, but if he is purposely taking a light attitude about some serious matter, he is being facetious. What poems have you read in this book to which the word *facetious* might be applied?

Though the poets might treat the drainage system lightly, the pedestrians did not always do so. If people who tried to get next to the wall at the same moment happened to be *pugnacious,* there might have been a duel. The origin of this word clearly explains its meaning. Look it up.

In the coffeehouses men were *gregarious:* that is, they liked to mingle with others. The original root means a *flock* or *herd.* Of the authors you have studied, which could you call gregarious?

JOHN HENRY NEWMAN

1801–1890

and

THOMAS HENRY HUXLEY

1825–1895

Oriel College, Oxford

John Henry Newman

National Portrait Gallery

Thomas Henry Huxley

Newman and Huxley, leading essayists of the period, reflect the Victorians' absorbing interest in two fields: religion and science. With typical earnestness, writers and thinkers of the time were examining both the spiritual and the natural realms of life. Often their religious beliefs and their scientific beliefs clashed, but just as often they sought to reconcile them in a broad view of education. For the Victorians were above all energetic teachers and learners; both Newman and Huxley were not only essayists but educators.

John Henry Newman typified the personal earnestness of the Victorians. He found his answers the hard way, through much soul searching and a marked break with his past. The first half of his life was spent chiefly at Oxford, as a student to be-

gin with, later as a teacher and clergyman. Early in his career as rector of St. Mary's Church he met differences of opinion which led him to resign and to go to the Continent for a while.

During the next dozen years he became closely associated with the Oxford Movement, which he helped to found. His many sermons and tracts in behalf of this movement pleaded for firmer belief in the early doctrines of the Christian church. In 1845, the halfway point in his life, he left the Anglican Church for the Roman Catholic Church. As the prime minister at the time said, "England reeled under the shock." In answer to much criticism, Newman wrote an autobiography, *Apologia pro Vita Sua*, to explain and justify this step. Late in life he was made a cardinal.

In 1854 Newman was sent to Dublin as

504

rector of a newly established Catholic university. During his few years there, he prepared a series of lectures, *The Idea of a University Defined,* from which the following essays are taken. The thoughtful style and noble standards of these two famous definitions show why Newman was able to win back those whom he had previously antagonized. Today his memory is honored by both Roman Catholics and Protestants.

Thomas Henry Huxley reflects the tremendous growth of interest in science during the Victorian Age. Today it is hard to realize that only a hundred years ago universities almost ignored science in favor of classical languages and literatures. Had Huxley gone to Oxford or Cambridge, his career might have been quite different. But the meager income of his parents forbade higher education, and he was placed on the naval vessel *Rattlesnake* to learn medicine from the ship's surgeon. Four years later he left the navy to become a Fellow of the Royal Society. Thereafter his life was spent as an essayist, lecturer, and experimenter in such varied fields as physiology, biology, and paleontology (the study of fossils).

With a fine gift for wit, clear organization, and simple, direct style, Huxley did great service in making science understandable to the masses. At a time when England was split into two camps over the theory of evolution, Huxley became the great defender and popularizer of Darwin's *The Origin of Species.* Against the attackers of Darwin who feared that the new discoveries of science would undermine religion, Huxley argued for more freedom in research so that truth could be known.

The Educated Man

JOHN HENRY NEWMAN

A UNIVERSITY is not a birthplace of poets or of immortal authors, of founders of schools, leaders of colonies, or conquerors of nations. It does not promise a generation of Aristotles or Newtons, of Napoleons or Washingtons, of Raphaels or Shakespeares, though such miracles of nature it has before now contained within its precincts. Nor is it content on the other hand with forming the critic or the experimentalist, the economist or the engineer, though such too it includes within its scope. But a university training is the great ordinary means to a great but ordinary end; it aims at raising the intellectual tone of society, at cultivating the public mind, at purifying the national taste, at supplying true principles to popular enthusiasm and fixed aims to popular aspiration, at giving enlargement and sobriety to the ideas of the age, at facilitating the exercise of political power, and refining the intercourse of private life. It is the education which gives a man a clear conscious view of his own opinions and judgments, a truth in developing them, an eloquence in expressing them, and a force in urging them. It teaches him to see things as they are, to get right to the point, to disentangle a skein of thought, to detect what is sophistical, and to discard what is irrelevant. It prepares him to fill any post with credit, and to master any subject with facility. It shows him how to accommodate himself to others, how to throw himself into their state of mind, how to bring before them his own, how to influence them, how to come to an understanding with them, how to bear with them. He is at home in any society, he has common ground with every class; he knows when to speak and when to be silent; he is able to converse, he is able to listen; he can ask a question pertinently, and gain a lesson seasonably, when he has nothing to impart himself; he is ever ready, yet never in the way; he is a pleasant companion, and a comrade you can depend upon; he knows when to be serious and when to trifle, and he has a sure tact which enables him to trifle with gracefulness and to be serious with effect. He has the repose of mind which lives in itself, while it lives in the world, and which has resources for its happiness at home when it cannot go abroad. He has a gift which serves him in public, and supports him in retirement, without which good fortune is but vulgar, and with which failure and disappointment have a charm.

The Gentleman

IT IS almost a definition of a gentleman to say he is one who never inflicts pain. This description is both refined and, as far as it goes, accurate. He is mainly occupied in merely removing the obstacles which hinder the free and unembarrassed action of those about him, and he concurs with their movements rather than takes the initiative himself. His benefits may be considered as parallel to what are called comforts or conveniences in arrangements of a personal nature; like an easy chair or a good fire, which do their part in dispelling cold and fatigue, though nature provides both means of rest and animal heat without them. The true gentleman in like manner carefully avoids whatever may cause a jar or a jolt in the minds of those with whom he is cast — all clashing of opinion, or collision of feeling, all restraint, or suspicion, or gloom, or resentment; his great concern being to make everyone at their ease and at home. He has his eyes on all his company; he is tender toward the bashful, gentle toward the distant, and merciful toward the absurd; he can recollect to whom he is speaking; he guards against unreasonable allusions, or topics which may irritate; he is seldom prominent in conversation, and never wearisome. He makes light of favors while he does them, and seems to be receiving when he is conferring. He never speaks of himself except when compelled, never defends himself by a mere retort, he has no ears for slander or gossip, is scrupulous in imputing motives to those who interfere with him, and interprets everything for the best. He is never mean or little in his disputes, never takes unfair advantage, never mistakes personalities or sharp sayings for arguments, or insinuates evil which he dare not say out. From a long-sighted prudence, he observes the maxim of the ancient sage, that we should ever conduct ourselves toward our enemy as if he were one day to be our friend. He has too much good sense to be affronted at insults, he is too well employed to remember injuries, and too indolent to bear malice. He is patient, forbearing, and resigned, on philosophical principles; he submits to pain because it is inevitable, to bereavement because it is irreparable, and to death because it is his destiny. If he engages in controversy of any kind, his disciplined intellect preserves him from the blundering discourtesy of better, perhaps, but less educated minds, who, like blunt weapons, tear and hack, instead of cutting clean, who mistake the point in argument, waste their strength on trifles, misconceive their adversary, and leave the question more involved than they find it. He may be right or wrong in his opinion, but he is too clearheaded to be unjust; he is as simple as he is forcible, and as brief as he is decisive. Nowhere shall we find greater candor, consideration, indulgence; he throws himself into the minds of his opponents; he accounts for their mistakes. He knows the weakness of human reason as well as its strength, its province and its limits. If he be an unbeliever, he will be too profound and large-minded to ridicule religion or to act against it; he is too wise to be a dogmatist or fanatic in his infidelity. He respects piety and devotion; he even supports institutions as venerable, beautiful, or useful, to which he does not assent; he honors the ministers of religion, and it contents him to decline its mysteries without assailing or denouncing them. He is a friend of religious toleration, and that not only because his philosophy has taught him to look on all forms of faith with an impartial eye, but also from the gentleness and effeminacy of feeling which is the attendant on civilization.

Lick Observatory

Lead, Kindly Light

In richly figurative poetry, this hymn expresses the serene faith that Newman found in religion. It was written before his conversion, as he was returning to England from Sicily.

Lead, kindly Light, amid the encircling
    gloom,
  Lead thou me on;
The night is dark, and I am far from
    home,
  Lead thou me on.
Keep thou my feet; I do not ask to see 5
The distant scene; one step enough for
  me.

I was not ever thus, nor prayed that thou
  Should'st lead me on;
I loved to choose and see my path, but
  now
  Lead thou me on.   10
I loved the garish day; and spite of fears,
Pride ruled my will; remember not past
  years.

So long thy power has blessed me, sure
  it still
  Will lead me on,
O'er moor and fen, o'er crag and torrent,
  till   15
  The night is gone,
And with the morn those angel faces
  smile,
Which I have loved long since, and lost
  awhile.

A Liberal Education

THOMAS HENRY HUXLEY

Huxley was not a scientist in a narrow sense only; he believed in applying the laws of science to the whole of life. The following statement of his views is part of a long address delivered to the South London Working Men's College in 1868. This college, founded in 1854, was one evidence of the growing interest in popular education during the Victorian Age. Compulsory education was not yet established, but it was on its way. In the first part of this address Huxley says: "I believe we should have compulsory education in the course of [the] next session [of Parliament] if there were the least probability that half a dozen leading statesmen of different parties would agree what that education should be." He then goes on to show what he believes to be the purpose and scope of a liberal education.

SUPPOSE it were perfectly certain that the life and fortune of every one of us would, one day or other, depend upon his winning or losing a game of chess. Don't you think that we should all consider it to be a primary duty to learn at least the names and the moves of the pieces; to have a notion of a gambit, and a keen eye for all the means of giving and getting out of check? Do you not think that we should look with a disapprobation amounting to scorn upon the father who allowed his son, or the state which allowed its members, to grow up without knowing a pawn from a knight?

Yet it is a very plain and elementary truth, that the life, the fortune, and the happiness of every one of us, and, more or less, of those who are connected with us, do depend upon our knowing something of the rules of a game infinitely more difficult and complicated than chess. It is a game which has been played for untold ages, every man and woman of us being one of the two players in a game of his or her own. The chessboard is the world, the pieces are the phenomena of the universe, the rules of the game are what we call the laws of Nature. The player on the other side is hidden from us. We know that his play is always fair, just, and patient. But also we know, to our cost, that he never overlooks a mistake, or makes the smallest allowance for ignorance. To the man who plays well, the highest stakes are paid, with that sort of overflowing generosity with which the strong shows delight in strength. And one who plays ill is checkmated — without haste, but without remorse.

My metaphor will remind some of you of the famous picture in which Retzsch has depicted Satan playing at chess with man for his soul. Substitute for the mocking fiend in that picture, a calm, strong angel who is playing for love, as we say, and would rather lose than win — and I should accept it as an image of human life.

Well, what I mean by Education is learning the rules of this mighty game. In other words, education is the instruction of the intellect in the laws of Nature, under which name I include not merely things and their forces but men and their ways; and the fashioning of the affections and of the will into an earnest and loving desire to move in harmony with those laws. For me education means neither more nor less than this. Anything which professes to call itself education must be tried by this standard, and if it fails to stand the test, I will not call it education, whatever may be the force of authority, or of numbers, upon the other side.

It is important to remember that, in strictness, there is no such thing as an uneducated man. Take an extreme case.

Suppose that an adult man, in the full vigor of his faculties, could be suddenly placed in the world, as Adam is said to have been, and then left to do as he best might. How long would he be left uneducated? Not five minutes. Nature would begin to teach him, through the eye, the ear, the touch, the properties of objects. Pain and pleasure would be at his elbow telling him to do this and avoid that; and by slow degrees the man would receive an education, which, if narrow, would be thorough, real, and adequate to his circumstances, though there would be no extras and very few accomplishments.

And if to this solitary man entered a second Adam, or better still, an Eve, a new and greater world, that of social and moral phenomena, would be revealed. Joys and woes, compared with which all others might seem but faint shadows, would spring from the new relations. Happiness and sorrow would take the place of the coarser monitors, pleasure and pain; but conduct would still be shaped by the observation of the natural consequences of actions; or, in other words, by the laws of the nature of man.

To every one of us the world was once as fresh and new as to Adam. And then, long before we were susceptible of any other mode of instruction, Nature took us in hand, and every minute of waking life brought its educational influence, shaping our actions into rough accordance with Nature's laws, so that we might not be ended untimely by too gross disobedience. Nor should I speak of this process of education as past for anyone, be he as old as he may. For every man the world is as fresh as it was at the first day, and as full of untold novelties for him who has the eyes to see them. And Nature is still continuing her patient education of us in that great university, the universe, of which we are all members — Nature having no Test-Acts.[1]

[1] *Test-Acts:* acts which at that time excluded from English universities all those who did not profess the established religion.

Those who take honors in Nature's university, who learn the laws which govern men and things and obey them, are the really great and successful men in this world. The great mass of mankind are the "Poll," [2] who pick up just enough to get through without much discredit. Those who won't learn at all are plucked; [3] and then you can't come up again. Nature's pluck means extermination.

Thus the question of compulsory education is settled so far as Nature is concerned. Her bill on that question was framed and passed long ago. But, like all compulsory legislation, that of Nature is harsh and wasteful in its operation. Ignorance is visited as sharply as willful disobedience — incapacity meets with the same punishment as crime. Nature's discipline is not even a word and a blow, and the blow first; but the blow without the word. It is left to you to find out why your ears are boxed.

The object of what we commonly call education — that education in which man intervenes and which I shall distinguish as artificial education — is to make good these defects in Nature's methods; to prepare the child to receive Nature's education, neither incapably nor ignorantly, nor with willful disobedience; and to understand the preliminary symptoms of her displeasure, without waiting for the box on the ear. In short, all artificial education ought to be an anticipation of natural education. And a liberal education is an artificial education, which has not only prepared a man to escape the great evils of disobedience to natural laws, but has trained him to appreciate and to seize upon the rewards, which Nature scatters with as free a hand as her penalties.

[2] *"Poll":* The poll degree at Cambridge was the common degree, without honors. The term was derived from a Greek word, οἱ πολλοί (hoi polloi), meaning "the many." We still use this term today to mean "the common people."
[3] *plucked:* English college slang, same as "flunked" in America.

That man, I think, has had a liberal education, who has been so trained in youth that his body is the ready servant of his will, and does with ease and pleasure all the work that, as a mechanism, it is capable of; whose intellect is a clear, cold, logic engine, with all its parts of equal strength, and in smooth working order; ready, like a steam engine, to be turned to any kind of work, and spin the gossamers as well as forge the anchors of the mind; whose mind is stored with a knowledge of the great and fundamental truths of Nature and of the laws of her operations; one who, no stunted ascetic, is full of life and fire, but whose passions are trained to come to heel by a vigorous will, the servant of a tender conscience; who has learned to love all beauty, whether of Nature or of art, to hate all vileness, and to respect others as himself.

Such an one and no other, I conceive, has had a liberal education; for he is, as completely as a man can be, in harmony with Nature. He will make the best of her, and she of him. They will get on together rarely; she as his ever beneficent mother; he as her mouthpiece, her conscious self, her minister and interpreter.

VICTORIAN ESSAYISTS

1. What are the chief characteristics of a gentleman according to Newman's definition? Can a person be a great man and still not be a gentleman? Conversely, can a person be a gentleman and not be a great man? Are gentlemen in Newman's sense of the word common or uncommon among your acquaintances?

2. What characteristics of Newman's gentleman would also fit a lady? What requirements would you add?

3. What does Huxley say about an uneducated man? Would Newman agree with him on this, do you think? How would you relate the idea of a self-made man, so often mentioned in America, to Huxley's ideas on this subject?

4. What are Huxley's standards for a liberal education? What does he consider to be the reward of such an education?

UNDERSTANDING THE DEVELOPMENT OF IDEAS

Study each author's method of presenting an argument. Notice that Newman begins "The Educated Man" by stating purposes that are *not* those of a university. Likewise, the first statement in his definition of a gentleman is a negative one. Then, in a thoughtful and straightforward manner, he lists the chief purposes of education in the first essay and the characteristics of a gentleman in the second.

Huxley gains the reader's attention by asking him questions. His writing is clearly organized; he gives a certain display of facts; but the force of his humor is what interests the reader. Try analyzing Huxley's witty comparison of life to a game of chess in the second paragraph.

Newman and Huxley can also be compared as stylists. Which style do you prefer? In addition to those already suggested, what devices to gain the reader's attention do you find? How does each writer arrive at conclusions?

CLASS ACTIVITY

Present a panel discussion on "Education for Living." Let one student present Newman's ideas, another Huxley's, a third describe his own school experiences toward this end, a fourth what is lacking in his school experience.

LITERATURE AND THE ARTS ➤

The watercolor opposite of Magdalen College and Bridge illustrates one of the most familiar scenes at Oxford University, where John Henry Newman spent so much of his life and where so many other of the great men of English literature received their education. J. M. W. Turner, one of the leading exponents of nineteenth-century English painting, did this watercolor when he was only twenty. The creator of thousands of oils, watercolors, and drawings, Turner was most famous for his landscapes, of which this is an early example. With the exception of the people shown, this scene could be duplicated today in a photograph, for very little has changed since Turner painted it over a century and a half ago.

ALFRED, LORD TENNYSON

1809–1892

National Portrait Gallery

Born into a large family, Tennyson grew up in Somersby, Lincolnshire, where his father was rector. Most of his early education was received directly from his scholarly father, who recognized and encouraged the boy's precocity. Alfred, who had been writing poetry since the age of five, collaborated with his brother Charles in writing and publishing *Poems of Two Brothers* the year before they entered Cambridge together.

In college the shy, reserved Alfred found a close friend in brilliant, vivacious Arthur Hallam, thought to be the most promising youth of the class. A few years after leaving college Hallam died suddenly. Tennyson was stunned by the cruel fate that had taken one so young, so talented, and so beloved; and in his sorrow, he began to have personal and religious doubts. In a series of poems which, during seventeen years, recorded the stages of his grief, doubt, resignation, and finally, faith, Tennyson wrote his masterpiece, published in 1850 as *In Memoriam*. The immediate success of this work and his award of a pension and appointment as poet laureate in the same year made it financially possible for Tennyson to marry Emily Sellwood, to whom he had been engaged fourteen years earlier. Afterward, his long poems, like *The Idylls of the King,* were eagerly awaited.

Assured financially, Tennyson built a house for himself and his wife on the Isle of Wight. Fifteen years later he built another beautiful home in Surrey. Once established as a poet, Tennyson lived almost in seclusion and pursued his craft unceasingly. A writer of world-wide reputation, he was persuaded to accept a peerage late in life. Even as an old man he was a striking figure — "a great black, shaggy man" — who looked the part of a poet.

Flower in the Crannied Wall

This miniature poem and the one which follows reveal two important aspects of Tennyson's poetry: his responsiveness to the scientific thinking of his day, and his close observation of nature.

Flower in the crannied wall,
I pluck you out of the crannies,
I hold you here, root and all, in my
    hand,
Little flower — but *if* I could understand
What you are, root and all, and all in
    all,   5
I should know what God and man is.

512

The Eagle

He clasps the crag with crooked hands,
Close to the sun in lonely lands,
Ringed with the azure world, he stands.

The wrinkled sea beneath him crawls,
He watches from his mountain walls,   5
And like a thunderbolt he falls.

Locksley Hall

A PROPHECY

"Locksley Hall" is a monologue spoken by a rejected lover
who seeks to drown his private sorrows by active participation in public affairs. This famous prophetic passage is
remarkable because the poem was published in 1842, long
before man had succeeded in the first steps of conquering
the air (except by simple balloons). Within a century two
great world wars have fulfilled the prophecy of the "airy
navies." Tennyson's other prophecy, "the federation of
the world," brings to mind the establishment of the United
Nations.

For I dipped into the future, far as human eye could see,
Saw the vision of the world, and all the wonder that would be;

Saw the heavens fill with commerce, argosies° of magic sails,
Pilots of the purple twilight, dropping down with costly bales;

Saw the heavens fill with shouting, and there rained a ghastly dew,   5
From the nations' airy navies grappling in the central blue;

Far along the world-wide whisper of the south wind rushing warm,
With the standards of the peoples plunging through the thunderstorm;

Till the war drum throbbed no longer, and the battle flags were furled
In the parliament of man, the federation of the world.   10

There the common sense of most shall hold a fretful realm in awe,
And the kindly earth shall slumber, lapped in universal law.

3. *argosies:* fleets of ships laden with vast riches.

Ulysses°

In this poem Tennyson draws his subject from ancient Greek sources. Ulysses, the famous hero of many adventures in *The Odyssey*, is pictured years after the time described in that epic. Here the old man expresses his urge to go out again into the world to accomplish something worth-while, rather than to rust away in a life of ease at home. To Tennyson's generation this poem symbolized the constant striving onward and upward of civilized man. It is said that "Ulysses" was the deciding factor in the government's choice of Tennyson to receive a pension.

It little profits that an idle king,
By this still hearth, among these barren crags,
Matched with an aged wife, I mete and dole°
Unequal laws° unto a savage race,
That hoard, and sleep, and feed, and know not me.   5
I cannot rest from travel; I will drink
Life to the lees. All times I have enjoyed
Greatly, have suffered greatly, both with those
That loved me, and alone; on shore, and when
Through scudding drifts the rainy Hyades°   10
Vexed the dim sea. I am become a name;
For always roaming with a hungry heart
Much have I seen and known — cities of men
And manners, climates, councils, governments,
Myself not least, but honored of them all —   15
And drunk delight of battle with my peers,
Far on the ringing plains of windy Troy.
I am a part of all that I have met;
Yet all experience is an arch wherethrough
Gleams that untraveled world whose margin fades   20
Forever and forever when I move.°
How dull it is to pause, to make an end,
To rust unburnished, not to shine in use!
As though to breathe were life! Life piled on life
Were all too little, and of one to me   25
Little remains; but every hour is saved
From that eternal silence, something more,
A bringer of new things; and vile it were
For some three suns to store and hoard myself,
And this gray spirit yearning in desire   30
To follow knowledge like a sinking star,
Beyond the utmost bound of human thought.

Title: *Ulysses* (û·lĭs′ēz). 3. *mete and dole:* measure and give out. 4. *Unequal laws:* unfair laws. The people were not civilized enough to be governed by the kind of laws Ulysses approved. 10. *Hyades* (hī′á·dēz): stars in the constellation Taurus, supposed to bring rain. 19–21. All experience beckons me on to more experiences lying beyond.

This is my son, mine own Telemachus,
To whom I leave the scepter and the isle° —
Well-loved of me, discerning to fulfill   35
This labor, by slow prudence to make mild
A rugged people, and through soft degrees
Subdue them to the useful and the good.
Most blameless is he, centered in the sphere
Of common duties, decent not to fail   40
In offices of tenderness, and pay
Meet adoration to my household gods,
When I am gone. He works his work, I mine.

There lies the port; the vessel puffs her sail;
There gloom the dark, broad seas. My mariners,   45
Souls that have toiled, and wrought, and thought with me —
That ever with a frolic welcome took
The thunder and the sunshine, and opposed
Free hearts, free foreheads — you and I are old;
Old age hath yet his honor and his toil.   50
Death closes all; but something ere the end,
Some work of noble note, may yet be done,
Not unbecoming men that strove with Gods.
The lights begin to twinkle from the rocks;
The long day wanes; the slow moon climbs; the deep   55
Moans round with many voices. Come, my friends,
'Tis not too late to seek a newer world.
Push off, and sitting well in order smite
The sounding furrows; for my purpose holds
To sail beyond the sunset, and the baths   60
Of all the western stars, until I die.
It may be that the gulfs will wash us down;
It may be we shall touch the Happy Isles,°
And see the great Achilles,° whom we knew.
Though much is taken, much abides; and though   65
We are not now that strength which in old days
Moved earth and heaven, that which we are, we are —
One equal temper of heroic hearts,
Made weak by time and fate, but strong in will
To strive, to seek, to find, and not to yield.   70

---

34. *isle:* Ulysses' kingdom was Ithaca, an island off the west coast of Greece. Telemachus (tĕ·lĕm′ȧ·kŭs) a youth in *The Odyssey*, is now a mature man, well suited to rule the kingdom. 63. *Happy Isles:* the place where heroes went after death. 64. *Achilles* (ȧ·kĭl′ēz): the strongest hero of the Trojan War, in which Ulysses had taken part before his long series of adventures on the return journey.

The Lady of Shalott

In his boyhood Tennyson was fascinated by the stories of King Arthur's knights, and it was natural for him to turn to them later as subjects for poetry. The twelve metrical tales included in *The Idylls of the King* were composed over a period of twenty-six years (1859–1885). But long before that time the poet had written this legend of the Lady of Shalott (1832). The melodious and magic quality of this version is often preferred to the more elaborate story of Elaine and Lancelot, one of the knights of the Round Table, in the *Idylls*.

Tennyson explains the symbolism of the Lady thus: "The newborn love for something, for someone in the wide world from which she has been so long excluded takes her out of the region of shadows into that of realities."

PART I

On either side the river lie
Long fields of barley and of rye,
That clothe the wold° and meet the sky;
And through the field the road runs by
 To many-towered Camelot;°   5
And up and down the people go,
Gazing where the lilies blow
Round an island there below,
 The island of Shalott.

Willows whiten,° aspens quiver, 10
Little breezes dusk and shiver
Through the wave that runs forever
By the island in the river
 Flowing down to Camelot.
Four gray walls, and four gray towers,
Overlook a space of flowers, 16
And the silent isle embowers
 The Lady of Shalott.

By the margin, willow-veiled,
Slide the heavy barges° trailed 20
By slow horses; and unhailed

3. *wold:* an open stretch of rising ground.
5. *Camelot:* a mysterious city where King Arthur and his knights held court in medieval romances. 10. *whiten:* Leaves turned by the breeze show their underside, which is white. 20. *barges:* roomy, flat-bottomed freight boats; here drawn by horses along the river banks.

The shallop° flitteth silken-sailed
 Skimming down to Camelot.
But who hath seen her wave her hand?
Or at the casement seen her stand? 25
Or is she known in all the land,
 The Lady of Shalott?

Only reapers, reaping early
In among the bearded barley,
Hear a song that echoes cheerly 30
From the river winding clearly
 Down to towered Camelot:
And by the moon the reaper weary,
Piling sheaves in uplands airy,
Listening, whispers, " 'Tis the fairy 35
 Lady of Shalott."

PART II

There she weaves by night and day
A magic web with colors gay.
She has heard a whisper say,
A curse is on her if she stay 40
 To look down to Camelot.
She knows not what the curse may be,
And so she weaveth steadily,
And little other care hath she,
 The Lady of Shalott. 45

And moving through a mirror clear
That hangs before her all the year,
Shadows of the world appear.
There she sees the highway near
 Winding down to Camelot: 50
There the river eddy whirls,
And there the surly village churls,°
And the red cloaks of market girls,
 Pass onward from Shalott.

Sometimes a troop of damsels glad, 55
An abbot on an ambling pad,°
Sometimes a curly shepherd lad,
Or long-haired page in crimson clad,
 Goes by to towered Camelot:
And sometimes through the mirror blue
The knights come riding two and two:

22. *shallop:* a light pleasure boat. 52. *churls:* country folk. 56. *pad:* an easy-paced riding horse.

She hath no loyal knight and true,   62
   The Lady of Shalott.

But in her web she still delights
To weave the mirror's magic sights,   65
For often through the silent nights
A funeral, with plumes and lights
   And music, went to Camelot:
Or when the moon was overhead,
Came two young lovers lately wed;   70
"I am half sick of shadows," said
   The Lady of Shalott.

PART III

A bow-shot from her bower eaves,
He rode between the barley sheaves,
The sun came dazzling through the
   leaves,   75
And flamed upon the brazen greaves°
   Of bold Sir Lancelot.
A red-cross knight° forever kneeled
To a lady in his shield,
That sparkled on the yellow field,   80
   Beside remote Shalott.

The gemmy° bridle glittered free,
Like to some branch of stars we see
Hung in the golden Galaxy.°
The bridle bells rang merrily   85
   As he rode down to Camelot:
And from his blazoned baldric° slung,
A mighty silver bugle hung,
And as he rode his armor rung,
   Beside remote Shalott.   90

All in the blue unclouded weather
Thick-jeweled shone the saddle leather,
The helmet and the helmet feather
Burned like one burning flame together
   As he rode down to Camelot.   95
As often through the purple night,
Below the starry clusters bright,

76. *greaves:* armor for the legs below the
knees. 78. *red-cross knight:* a symbol of St.
George, patron saint of England. He slew the
dragon, and thus saved a maiden from sacrifice.
82. *gemmy:* studded with jewels. 84. *Galaxy:* the
Milky Way, a pathway of myriad stars stretching across the middle heavens. 87. *blazoned
baldric:* a decorated belt worn diagonally across
the chest.

Some bearded meteor, trailing light,
   Moves over still Shalott.

His broad clear brow in sunlight
   glowed;   100
On burnished hoofs his war horse trode;
From underneath his helmet flowed
His coal-black curls as on he rode,
   As he rode down to Camelot.
From the bank and from the river   105
He flashed into the crystal mirror,
"Tirra lirra," by the river
   Sang Sir Lancelot.

She left the web, she left the loom,
She made three paces through the room,
She saw the water lily bloom,   111
She saw the helmet and the plume,
   She looked down to Camelot.
Out flew the web and floated wide;
The mirror cracked from side to side;
"The curse is come upon me," cried
   The Lady of Shalott.   117

PART IV

In the stormy east wind straining,
The pale yellow woods were waning,
The broad stream in his banks com-
   plaining,   120
Heavily the low sky raining
   Over towered Camelot;
Down she came and found a boat
Beneath a willow left afloat,
And round about the prow she wrote
   The Lady of Shalott.   126

And down the river's dim expanse —
Like some bold seër in a trance,
Seeing all his own mischance —
With a glassy countenance   130
   Did she look to Camelot.
And at the closing of the day
She loosed the chain, and down she lay;
The broad stream bore her far away,
   The Lady of Shalott.   135

Lying, robed in snowy white
That loosely flew to left and right —
The leaves upon her falling light —
Through the noises of the night

She floated down to Camelot: 140
And as the boathead wound along
The willowy hills and fields among,
They heard her singing her last song,
   The Lady of Shalott.

Heard a carol, mournful, holy,   145
Chanted loudly, chanted lowly,
Till her blood was frozen slowly,
And her eyes were darkened wholly,
   Turned to towered Camelot.
For ere she reached upon the tide   150
The first house by the waterside,
Singing in her song she died,
   The Lady of Shalott.

Under tower and balcony,
By garden wall and gallery,   155

A gleaming shape she floated by,
Dead-pale between the houses high,
   Silent into Camelot.
Out upon the wharves they came   159
Knight and burgher,° lord and dame,
And round the prow they read her name,
   The Lady of Shalott.

Who is this? and what is here?
And in the lighted palace near
Died the sound of royal cheer;   165
And they crossed themselves for fear,
   All the knights at Camelot:
But Lancelot mused a little space;
He said, "She has a lovely face;
God in his mercy lend her grace,   170
   The Lady of Shalott."

160. *burgher:* citizen.

Songs from *The Princess*

Tennyson wrote a long narrative poem, *The Princess,* to defend higher education for women, an idea much challenged in the middle of his century. Between the cantos of this poem he later inserted lyrics.

"The Bugle Song," written the year of Tennyson's marriage, is said to have been suggested to him while he and his bride were visiting beautiful Lake Killarney in Ireland. The dying echoes of a bugle blown at sunset are effectively contrasted with the living echoes sent from one soul to another.

"Tears, Idle Tears" was written on a visit to Tintern Abbey when, he writes, "the woods were all yellowing with autumn, seen through the ruined windows. . . . It is distance that charms the past." The melancholy mood of this poem in recalling vanished days shows Tennyson to have been a true follower of the romantic tradition.

The Bugle Song

The splendor falls on castle walls
   And snowy summits old in story;
The long light shakes across the lakes,
   And the wild cataract leaps in glory.
Blow, bugle, blow, set the wild echoes flying,   5
Blow, bugle; answer, echoes, dying, dying, dying.

Oh, hark, oh, hear! how thin and clear,
   And thinner, clearer, farther going!
Oh, sweet and far from cliff and scar°
   The horns of Elfland faintly blowing!   10
Blow, let us hear the purple glens replying;
Blow, bugle; answer, echoes, dying, dying, dying.

9. *scar:* bare rock.

◀ *Elaine, the Lady of Shalott, as shown in a fourteenth-century French manuscript.*

O love, they die in yon rich sky,
   They faint on hill or field or river;
Our echoes roll from soul to soul,   15
   And grow forever and forever.
Blow, bugle, blow, set the wild echoes flying,
And answer, echoes, answer, dying, dying, dying.

Tears, Idle Tears

Tears, idle tears, I know not what they mean,
Tears from the depth of some divine despair
Rise in the heart, and gather to the eyes,
In looking on the happy autumn fields,
And thinking of the days that are no more.   5

Fresh as the first beam glittering on a sail,
That brings our friends up from the underworld,°
Sad as the last which reddens over one
That sinks with all we love below the verge;
So sad, so fresh, the days that are no more.   10

Ah, sad and strange as in dark summer dawns
The earliest pipe of half-awakened birds
To dying ears, when unto dying eyes
The casement slowly grows a glimmering square;
So sad, so strange, the days that are no more.   15

Dear as remembered kisses after death,
And sweet as those by hopeless fancy feigned
On lips that are for others; deep as love,
Deep as first love, and wild with all regret;
O Death in Life, the days that are no more.   20

7. *underworld:* the other side of the globe.

Break, Break, Break

Just as the stories of King Arthur come into Tennyson's poetry again and again, so also he finds a constantly recurring theme in another Arthur, his college friend Hallam (see page 512). The four poems that follow reveal Tennyson's change of attitude toward this tragic loss over a period of years. The first published expression (1842) is this poignant lyric "Break, Break, Break." The poet hears sad sounds played by the breakers as he stands upon the shore.

Break, break, break,
   On thy cold gray stones, O Sea!
And I would that my tongue could utter
   The thoughts that arise in me.

Oh, well for the fisherman's boy,   5
   That he shouts with his sister at play!
Oh, well for the sailor lad,
   That he sings in his boat on the bay!

And the stately ships go on
   To their haven under the hill;   10
But oh, for the touch of a vanished
   hand,
   And the sound of a voice that is still!

Break, break, break,
   At the foot of thy crags, O Sea!
But the tender grace of a day that is
   dead   15
   Will never come back to me.

In Memoriam

Common consent has named the three greatest elegies (poems of mourning for the dead) in English literature: Milton's "Lycidas," on Edward King, a college friend drowned before the completion of his studies; Shelley's *Adonais,* on John Keats; Tennyson's *In Memoriam,* on Arthur Hallam. The similarity in the situations that called forth these elegies is apparent. Each poem mourns a young man of great talent cut off before he is able to fulfill the promise of his youth. However, *In Memoriam* differs from the others in two respects. The personal tie between Tennyson and Hallam was the strongest friendship of the three. Besides being warm college friends, they had traveled together, and Hallam was engaged to Tennyson's sister. *In Memoriam* is a series of one hundred and thirty-one short meditations on the meaning of life and death, written through seventeen years of thought and spiritual struggle. It represents Tennyson's most mature poetry.

The Proem, which always appears first in the printed editions, was the last part to be composed. It is a prayer asking for greater faith in divine love and immortal life though we are confronted with confusion and change.

Section XXVII presents the idea that it is better for a man to bear sorrow and loss than to exist with a complete lack of sensitiveness and feeling.

Section LIV declares that good can eventually come out of ill even though we are confused by seeming injustice at the moment, for there is a divine plan to be accepted with faith.

Section CVI, a complete song in itself, shows the New Year's bells as a symbol of the progress from old outworn practices and evils to the new era of peace and goodness based on the example of Christ.

PROEM

Strong Son of God, immortal Love,
  Whom we, that have not seen thy
    face,
  By faith, and faith alone, embrace,
Believing where we cannot prove;   4

Thine are these orbs of light and shade;
  Thou madest Life in man and brute;
  Thou madest Death; and lo, thy foot
Is on the skull which thou hast made.°

Thou wilt not leave us in the dust;
  Thou madest man, he knows not why,
  He thinks he was not made to die;   11
And thou hast made him; thou art just.°

Thou seemest human and divine,
  The highest, holiest manhood, thou;
  Our wills are ours, we know not how;
Our wills are ours, to make them thine.

Our little systems have their day;   17
  They have their day and cease to be;
  They are but broken lights° of thee,
And thou, O Lord, art more than they.

We have but faith; we cannot know;   21
  For knowledge is of things we see;
  And yet we trust it comes from thee,
A beam in darkness; let it grow.

Let knowledge grow from more to
    more,   25
  But more of reverence in us dwell;
  That mind and soul, according well,
May make one music as before,

But vaster. We are fools and slight;
  We mock thee when we do not fear;
  But help thy foolish ones to bear;   31
Help thy vain worlds to bear thy light.°

Forgive what seemed my sin° in me;
  What seemed my worth° since I began;
  For merit lives from man to man,   35
And not from man, O Lord, to thee.

6–8. Thou dost control life and death. 9–12. Death cannot be the end of everything, for thou (God) art just. 19. *broken lights:* colored or prismatic lights; the partial truth obtainable in this world. 32. *light:* the perfect truth. 33. *sin:* mourning for the dead. 34. *worth:* devotion to the memory of Hallam. Tennyson asks forgiveness for both his grief and his devotion.

Forgive my grief for one removed,
  Thy creature, whom I found so fair.
  I trust he lives in thee, and there
I find him worthier to be loved.   40

Forgive these wild and wandering cries,
  Confusions of a wasted youth;
  Forgive them where they fail in truth,
And in thy wisdom make me wise.

XXVII

I envy not in any moods
  The captive void of noble rage,
  The linnet born within the cage,
That never knew the summer woods;

I envy not the beast that takes   5
  His license in the field of time,
  Unfettered by the sense of crime,
To whom a conscience never wakes;

Nor, what may count itself as blest,   9
  The heart that never plighted troth
  But stagnates in the weeds of sloth;
Nor any want-begotten rest.°

I hold it true, whate'er befall;
  I feel it, when I sorrow most;
  'Tis better to have loved and lost   15
Than never to have loved at all.

LIV

Oh, yet we trust that somehow good
  Will be the final goal of ill,
  To pangs of nature, sins of will,
Defects of doubt, and taints of blood;°

That nothing walks with aimless feet;   5
  That not one life shall be destroyed,
  Or cast as rubbish to the void,
When God hath made the pile complete;

9–12. (I envy not) the kind of rest or peace that comes from absence (want) of human ties or affections.

3–4. Four kinds of ills are specified: physical, moral, spiritual, and inherited.

That not a worm is cloven in vain;
  That not a moth with vain desire   10
  Is shriveled in a fruitless fire,
Or but subserves another's gain.

Behold, we know not anything;
  I can but trust that good shall fall
  At last — far off — at last, to all,   15
And every winter change to spring.

So runs my dream; but what am I?
  An infant crying in the night;
  An infant crying for the light;
And with no language but a cry.°   20

CVI

Ring out, wild bells, to the wild sky,
  The flying cloud, the frosty light;
  The year is dying in the night;
Ring out, wild bells, and let him die.

Ring out the old, ring in the new,   5
  Ring, happy bells, across the snow;
  The year is going, let him go;
Ring out the false, ring in the true.

Ring out the grief that saps the mind,
  For those that here we see no more;
  Ring out the feud of rich and poor,
Ring in redress to all mankind.   12

Ring out a slowly dying cause,
  And ancient forms of party strife;
  Ring in the nobler modes of life,   15
With sweeter manners, purer laws.

Ring out the want, the care, the sin,
  The faithless coldness of the times;
  Ring out, ring out my mournful rhymes,
But ring the fuller minstrel in.   20

Ring out false pride in place and blood,
  The civic slander and the spite;
  Ring in the love of truth and right,
Ring in the common love of good.

17–20. Man is as helpless as an infant in the presence of mysteries he does not understand.

Ring out old shapes of foul disease; 25
  Ring out the narrowing lust of gold;
  Ring out the thousand wars of old,
Ring in the thousand years of peace.

Ring in the valiant man and free,
  The larger heart, the kindlier hand;
  Ring out the darkness of the land, 31
Ring in the Christ that is to be.

In the Valley of Cauteretz

Eleven years after the publication of *In Memoriam,* Tennyson wrote this poem on his second visit to the beautiful valley of Cauteretz in the Pyrenees, where he had traveled with Arthur Hallam thirty-two years before. The memory of his friend is here brought back to him with renewed vividness.

All along the valley, stream that flashest white,
Deepening thy voice with the deepening of the night,
All along the valley, where thy waters flow,
I walked with one I loved two and thirty years ago.
All along the valley, while I walked today, 5
The two and thirty years were a mist that rolls away;
For all along the valley, down thy rocky bed,
Thy living voice to me was as the voice of the dead,
And all along the valley, by rock and cave and tree,
The voice of the dead was a living voice to me. 10

Crossing the Bar

Tennyson tells us that this lyric, written in his eighty-first year, "came in a moment." That evening, when the poet read it aloud, his son said enthusiastically, "It is the crown of your life's work." A few days before his death Tennyson said to his son, "Mind you put 'Crossing the Bar' at the end of my poems." The request has always been observed in the many editions of Tennyson's poetry.

Sunset and evening star,
  And one clear call for me!
And may there be no moaning° of the
    bar,
  When I put out to sea,

But such a tide as moving seems asleep,
  Too full for sound and foam, 6
When that which drew from out the
    boundless deep
  Turns again home.

Twilight and evening bell,
  And after that the dark! 10
And may there be no sadness of fare-
    well,
  When I embark;

For though from out our bourne° of
    Time and Place
  The flood may bear me far,
I hope to see my Pilot face to face 15
  When I have crossed the bar.

3. *moaning:* It is a popular belief that the ebbing tide moans when a death has occurred.

13. *bourne:* bounded territory, referring here to earthly life. Compare with "the boundless deep" (of eternity), line **7.**

THOUGHTFUL AND MELODIOUS POEMS

THE SHORT LYRICS

1. For each of the short lyrics, indicate in a sentence Tennyson's prevailing mood or the main idea he expresses. What words or details in the poem convey the mood?

2. In "The Bugle Song" show how each stanza represents a stage in the life of an echo. Which single word in each of the last two stanzas recalls the sunset glory of the first one?

3. In "Tears, Idle Tears" show how the difference in the refrain at the end of each stanza grows out of the thought of that stanza. Why are these tears "idle"?

LOCKSLEY HALL

In what is the rejected lover seeking solace? Approximately how many years has it taken to fulfill Tennyson's prophecies? To what extent has his last prophecy been fulfilled? Discuss.

ULYSSES

1. Review the chief incidents in the career of Ulysses after the Trojan War was over. Who was his "aged wife"?

2. Discuss the way in which the spirit of Ulysses represents all civilization.

3. Select the lines in the poem which best bring out these main ideas:

a. Life is a series of experiences, each one of which leaves its mark.

b. Life's possibilities are endless.

c. No individual lives long enough to experience all that life has to offer.

d. Life must be activity, not mere being. It must be met, in spite of its sorrows, with hope and courage.

THE LADY OF SHALOTT

1. The Lady is a symbol of someone who has experienced life indirectly only. To what extent is this possible? What does her final end symbolize, in your opinion? Can you think of other possible situations the Lady might represent?

2. Why is so much stress laid on the splendor of Lancelot and his equipment? How has the Lady's reaction toward him been prepared for in Part II? Explain the pathos of his words in the last stanza.

BREAK, BREAK, BREAK

What is the prevailing mood of the poem? How does the setting enhance the mood? Find lines which best express the poet's feelings. What is the significance of the second stanza?

IN MEMORIAM

In Memoriam is a thoughtful analysis of one of life's greatest problems. Use this outline to help you follow the beliefs expressed in the Proem.

Lines 1–8. God in wisdom has made all things, including death.

Lines 9–12. He will not let the soul perish.

Lines 13–16. Human beings have the will to do right.

Lines 17–20. Our systems and organizations are but imperfect reflections of God's spirit.

Lines 21–32. Greater knowledge will bring greater reverence for life's mysteries.

Lines 33–44. The poet prays for greater faith and for divine mercy.

1. In section XXVII why does the poet not envy the captive bird and the beast without a conscience, even though they are spared his distress? Do you agree that it is better to have had painful experiences than no deeply moving experiences at all?

2. What in section LIV suggests that Tennyson was troubled by the new scientific doctrines derived from evolutionary theories, such as the "struggle for existence" and "survival of the fittest"? Is his conclusion on the matter hopeful or despairing?

3. In section CVI what evils does the poet wish to see disappear? What good things does he want to see come in? In what way is the mood of this section different from that of earlier sections?

IN THE VALLEY OF CAUTERETZ

How many years have elapsed since Tennyson visited this valley with his friend? Compare the mood of this poem with that of "Break, Break, Break." Explain the last line, "The voice of the dead was a living voice to me."

CROSSING THE BAR

1. Of "Crossing the Bar," Professor R. M. Alden wrote: "It is a pure lyrical

allegory, in which every word has a double meaning, substance, and shadow, each contributing to and taking nothing from the other." Find examples of this double meaning in the details of setting out to sea.

2. Compare Tennyson's attitude toward approaching death in "Crossing the Bar" with that of Keats in "When I Have Fears" and Shelley in "A Lament."

RESPONDING TO WORDS AND IMAGES

In Part III of "The Lady of Shalott" there is a fine example of Tennyson's skill in using words to produce a desired effect. Sir Lancelot is the center of the picture. As in an actual painting, the central figure holds our eye by the intensity of light that

is concentrated upon it. Tennyson uses two kinds of words. There are the direct words full of the vitality of light: *dazzling, flamed, sparkled, glittered, shone, burned, burning, flame, glowed, flashed* — ten within the space of thirty lines. Then there are the *indirect* words which add to the effect because our experience tells us what sunlight does to certain colors, metals, and jewels. So we find the colors: *red, yellow, golden, blue, purple*, with a dash of *coal-black* for contrast. The reflecting surfaces are seen in *brazen* greaves, *gemmy* bridle, *blazoned* baldric, *silver* bugle, *thick-jeweled* saddle leather.

Trace in Part IV words that directly state an emotion of grief and those that contribute indirectly to the mood through color, sound, or condition of nature.

ELIZABETH BARRETT BROWNING 1806–1861
and
ROBERT BROWNING 1812–1889

Both portraits from National Portrait Gallery

The Brownings are perhaps the most famous couple in English literature. Robert Browning is now recognized as the greater poet of the two, but before Elizabeth and Robert met, she was better known than he.

During her girlhood Elizabeth Barrett showed a marked bent toward classical studies and wrote several ambitious poems. Then at sixteen, while tightening the girth on her saddle horse, she suffered a back injury which caused her to be bedridden. Now deprived of the world at large, she retreated to the refuge of her studies and her writing.

In the meantime Robert Browning, six years younger, was growing up in Camberwell, a suburb of London. He was fortunate in his home background, for his father combined business success with scholarly tastes, while his mother was a woman of high ideals and considerable musical talent. Robert, an only son, was given every possible advantage — private tutoring, travel, and a workshop of his own where he assembled a small menagerie and began the close study of nature so evident in his writing. Recognition of his talent came slowly. His early poems were hard to understand, and the public seemed to prefer the simple, melodious verses of Tennyson.

Then came the dramatic meeting of the two poets, their intense love affair, and their elopement to Italy. Their fifteen years of married life, spent mostly in Florence, brought health to Elizabeth, and to both of them the happiness of congenial interests and creative work together.

After Elizabeth's death Browning returned to England with their only child. The poet was an energetic, handsome man who enjoyed the pleasures of society, but he continued regular hours of writing as well. He wrote a number of poetic dramas for Macready, the famous actor, but these were not successful on the stage.

Browning's poetry won increasing favor with the public during the latter part of his life. He was lionized in London; indeed, Browning Societies which met to interpret the obscurities of many of his poems became an intellectual fad of the day. The poet died in Italy, a land he associated with his love of his wife, and was buried in the Poet's Corner of Westminster Abbey.

Sonnets from the Portuguese

ELIZABETH BARRETT BROWNING

Elizabeth Barrett Browning's *Sonnets from the Portuguese* are the best example of a true sonnet sequence since Elizabethan times. She wrote these forty-four sonnets during Browning's courtship of her, but did not show them to him until after their marriage. One day she slipped them into his pocket and told him to destroy them if he did not like them. Later he said, "I dared not reserve to myself the finest sonnets in any language since Shakespeare."

Mrs. Browning's admiration for one of the classic poets of Portugal had led her husband to nickname her "the little Portugee." This suggested the title chosen for the sequence.

Sonnet 1

I thought once how Theocritus° had sung
Of the sweet years, the dear and wished-for years,
Who each one in a gracious hand appears
To bear a gift for mortals, old or young;
And, as I mused it in his antique tongue,   5
I saw, in gradual vision through my tears,
The sweet, sad years, the melancholy years,
Those of my own life, who by turns° had flung
A shadow across me. Straightway I was 'ware,
So weeping, how a mystic Shape° did move   10

1. *Theocritus* (thē͞ŏk′rĭ·tŭs): a Sicilian poet of the third century B.C.; the first writer of pastoral idyls. 8. *by turns:* This phrase refers to the loss of her mother and the tragic death of her brother by drowning. 10. *Shape:* Destiny or Fate.

Behind me, and drew me backward by the hair;
And a voice said in mastery, while I strove —
"Guess now who holds thee?" — "Death," I said. But, there,
The silver answer rang — "Not Death, but Love."

Sonnet 6

Go from me. Yet I feel that I shall stand
Henceforth in thy shadow. Nevermore
Alone upon the threshold of my door
Of individual life, I shall command
The uses of my soul, nor lift my hand   5
Serenely in the sunshine as before,
Without the sense of that which I forebore . . .
Thy touch upon the palm. The widest land
Doom takes to part us, leaves thy heart in mine
With pulses that beat double. What I do   10
And what I dream include thee, as the wine
Must taste of its own grapes. And when I sue
God for myself, He hears that name of thine,
And sees within my eyes the tears of two.

Sonnet 14

If thou must love me, let it be for nought
Except for love's sake only. Do not say,
"I love her for her smile — her look — her way
Of speaking gently — for a trick of thought
That falls in well with mine, and certes° brought   5
A sense of pleasant ease on such a day" —
For these things in themselves, Belovèd, may
Be changed, or change for thee — and love, so wrought,
May be unwrought so. Neither love me for
Thine own dear pity's wiping my cheeks dry —   10
A creature might forget to weep, who bore
Thy comfort long, and lose thy love thereby!
But love me for love's sake, that evermore
Thou may'st love on, through love's eternity.

5. *certes:* certainly.

Sonnet 43

How do I love thee? Let me count the ways.
I love thee to the depth and breadth and height
My soul can reach, when feeling out of sight
For the ends of Being and ideal Grace.
I love thee to the level of every day's   5

Most quiet need, by sun and candlelight.
I love thee freely, as men strive for Right;
I love thee purely, as they turn from Praise.
I love thee with the passion put to use
In my old griefs, and with my childhood's faith.   10
I love thee with a love I seemed to lose
With my lost saints — I love thee with the breath,
Smiles, tears, of all my life! — and, if God choose,
I shall but love thee better after death.

Poems by Robert Browning

Browning's poetical genius flowered in many directions. He could write delicate lyrics as well as rousing marching songs. Perhaps he was most successful with his dramatic lyrics. They are usually in the form of a monologue, in which a single speaker supplies through the delicate play of his emotions the whole background of a dramatic situation, and even suggests the presence and dialogue of other characters. The short monologues, such as "My Last Duchess," are most often read today, but Browning's masterpiece is a combination of dramatic monologues into one unified poem, *The Ring and the Book.* In this long poem the story of a horrible murder is told through the monologues of twelve different persons, a perfect illustration of how point of view affects the telling of a story.

The first two poems which follow are reminiscent of Cavalier times. From your study of the seventeenth century, you know the contrasting traits of the Roundheads and Cavaliers. Browning here conveys typical moods of the Cavaliers.

Boot and Saddle

Boot, saddle, to horse, and away!
Rescue my castle before the hot day
Brightens to blue from its silvery gray,
CHORUS: *Boot, saddle, to horse, and away!*

Ride past the suburbs, asleep as you'd say;   5
Many's the friend there, will listen and pray,
"God's luck to gallants that strike up the lay —
CHORUS: *Boot, saddle, to horse, and away!"*

Forty miles off, like a roebuck at bay,
Flouts Castle Brancepeth the Roundheads' array;°   10
Who laughs, "Good fellows ere this, by my fay,°
CHORUS: *Boot, saddle, to horse, and away!"*

Who? My wife Gertrude; that, honest and gay,
Laughs when you talk of surrendering, "Nay!
I've better counselors; what counsel they?   15
CHORUS: *Boot, saddle, to horse, and away!"*

10. Castle Brancepeth mocks at the attacking forces of the Roundheads. This castle is in Northumberland. 11. *fay:* faith.

Give a Rouse

King Charles, and who'll do him right now?
King Charles, and who's ripe for fight now?
Give a rouse; here's, in hell's despite now,
King Charles!
Who gave me the goods that went since?   5
Who raised me the house that sank once?
Who helped me to gold I spent since?
Who found me in wine you drank once?

CHORUS:
King Charles, and who'll do him right now?
King Charles, and who's ripe for fight now?   10
Give a rouse; here's, in hell's despite now,
King Charles!

To whom used my boy George quaff else,
By the old fool's side that begot him?
For whom did he cheer and laugh else,   15
While Noll's° damned troopers shot him?

CHORUS:
King Charles, and who'll do him right now?
King Charles, and who's ripe for fight now?
Give a rouse; here's, in hell's despite now,
King Charles!   20

16. *Noll:* an abbreviation for Oliver, a term of contempt for Oliver Cromwell.

Love among the Ruins

The scene of this monologue is the Roman Campagna (kȧm·pȧn′yȧ), the open country surrounding the capital city. The speaker is a shepherd who eagerly anticipates his return to his young wife. Their home is a ruined turret, on the spot where, in ancient days, stood a loftier tower from which the Roman emperor watched the chariot races.

The poem contrasts the quiet campagna with the tumult of the ancient city, the temporary nature of all earthly things with the realization that "love is best."

Where the quiet-colored end of evening smiles
     Miles and miles
On the solitary pastures where our sheep
     Half-asleep
Tinkle homeward through the twilight, stray or stop   5
     As they crop —
Was the site once of a city great and gay
     (So they say),°

8. *they say:* The archæologists alone can determine this fact; so the shepherd takes his data from them.

Of our country's very capital, its prince
          Ages since   10
Held his court in, gathered councils, wielding far
          Peace or war.

Now — the country does not even boast a tree,
          As you see,
To distinguish slopes of verdure, certain rills   15
          From the hills
Intersect and give a name to (else they run
          Into one),
Where the domed and daring palace shot its spires
          Up like fires   20
O'er the hundred-gated circuit of a wall
          Bounding all,
Made of marble, men might march on nor be pressed,
          Twelve abreast.

And such plenty and perfection, see, of grass   25
          Never was!
Such a carpet as, this summertime, o'erspreads
          And embeds
Every vestige of the city, guessed alone,°
          Stock or stone —   30
Where a multitude of men breathed joy and woe
          Long ago;
Lust of glory pricked their hearts up, dread of shame
          Struck them tame;
And that glory and that shame alike, the gold   35
          Bought and sold.

Now — the single little turret that remains
          On the plains,
By the caper° overrooted, by the gourd
          Overscored,°   40
While the patching houseleek's° head of blossom winks
          Through the chinks —
Marks the basement whence a tower in ancient time
          Sprang sublime,
And a burning ring, all round, the chariots traced   45
          As they raced,
And the monarch and his minions° and his dames
          Viewed the games.

And I know — while thus the quiet-colored eve
          Smiles to leave   50

29. *guessed alone:* Now one can only guess where the city was because the site is covered by grass.
39. *caper:* a Mediterranean shrub, abundant on old walls and rocks. Its flower buds are often used as a seasoning. 39–40. *gourd overscored:* The climbing vine, overrunning the turret, has marked or scored it as if with lines. 41. *houseleek:* a common plant with thick, fleshy leaves and yellow or purple flowers, frequently found on old walls and roofs. 47. *minions:* attendants; more strictly, favorites.

Photo Researchers, Inc.

To their folding, all our many tinkling fleece
    In such peace,
And the slopes and rills in undistinguished gray
    Melt away —
That a girl with eager eyes and yellow hair   55
    Waits me there
In the turret whence the charioteers caught soul
    For the goal,
When the king looked, where she looks now, breathless, dumb
    Till I come.   60

But he looked upon the city, every side,
    Far and wide,
All the mountains topped with temples, all the glades'
    Colonnades,°
All the causeys,° bridges, aqueducts — and then,   65
    All the men!
When I do come, she will speak not, she will stand,
    Either hand
On my shoulder, give her eyes the first embrace
    Of my face,   70
Ere we rush, ere we extinguish sight and speech
    Each on each.

In one year they sent a million fighters forth
    South and North,
And they built their gods a brazen pillar high   75
    As the sky,
Yet reserved a thousand chariots in full force —
    Gold, of course.
O heart! O blood that freezes, blood that burns!
    Earth's returns°   80
For whole centuries of folly, noise and sin!
    Shut them in,
With their triumphs and their glories and the rest!
    Love is best.

63–64. *glades' Colonnades:* The open spaces in the woods are enclosed by trees, just as a large building is often enclosed by a series of columns. 65. *causeys:* Ruins of old causeways, or raised sidewalks, and aqueducts may still be seen in the Roman Campagna. 80. *Earth's returns:* the rewards of temporal or earthly efforts.

Home Thoughts, from the Sea

Browning made his first voyage to Italy in 1838. While passing along
the coast of Portugal and Spain, he was filled with gratitude toward
England for her past struggles for freedom and longed to repay her
in some way. Three places caught his eye as he mused: *Cape Saint
Vincent* (line 1): a promontory on the southwest coast of Portugal;
Cadiz (here kā′dĭz) *Bay* (line 2): a gulf southeast of Cape Saint
Vincent, where the Spanish fleets that threatened England were de-
feated by Drake in 1587, and again by Essex and Raleigh in 1596;
and *Trafalgar* (trȧ·făl′gẽr) (line 3): a point on the southwest coast of
Spain where Nelson defeated the French and Spanish navies in 1805.

Nobly, nobly Cape Saint Vincent to the Northwest died away;
Sunset ran, one glorious blood-red, reeking into Cadiz Bay;
Bluish 'mid the burning water, full in face Trafalgar lay;
In the dimmest Northeast distance dawned Gibraltar grand and gray;
"Here and here did England help me: how can I help England?" — say,   5
Whoso turns as I, this evening, turns to God to praise and pray,
While Jove's planet° rises yonder, silent over Africa.

7. *Jove's planet:* Jupiter, an evening star.

Home Thoughts, from Abroad

The poet, now in Italy, longs for the beauty of early spring in England.

Oh, to be in England
Now that April's there,
And whoever wakes in England
Sees, some morning, unaware,
That the lowest boughs and the brushwood sheaf   5
Round the elm tree bole° are in tiny leaf,
While the chaffinch° sings on the orchard bough
In England — now!

And after April, when May follows,
And the whitethroat° builds, and all the swallows!   10
Hark, where my blossomed pear tree in the hedge
Leans to the field and scatters on the clover
Blossoms and dewdrops — at the bent spray's edge —
That's the wise thrush! he sings each song twice over,
Lest you should think he never could recapture   15
The first fine careless rapture!
And though the fields look rough with hoary dew,
All will be gay when noontide wakes anew
The buttercups, the little children's dower
— Far brighter than this gaudy melon flower!   20

6. *bole:* tree trunk. 7. *chaffinch:* a common European songbird. 10. *whitethroat:* a European warbler.

Song from *Pippa Passes*

This lyric, perhaps Browning's most perfect, is one of four songs of Pippa, a young worker in the silk mills at Asolo, Italy. On her one holiday in the year, she passes around the town singing, and, unknown to herself, her songs — at morning, noon, evening, and night — help four important people of her city at a crisis in each of their lives. This short song gives the philosophy of the whole poem.

The year's at the spring
And day's at the morn;
Morning's at seven;
The hillside's dew-pearled;

The lark's on the wing;   5
The snail's on the thorn;
God's in his heaven —
All's right with the world!

Prospice°

These lines were written in 1861, seven months after the death of Mrs. Browning. They express Browning's undaunted spirit in the face of death and his firm belief in eventual reunion with his beloved wife. As he had faced the joyous contest of living, so he would meet the final struggle with death.

Fear death? — to feel the fog in my throat,
    The mist in my face,
When the snows begin, and the blasts denote
    I am nearing the place,
The power of the night, the press of the storm,   5
    The post of the foe;
Where he stands, the Arch Fear in a visible form,
    Yet the strong man must go;
For the journey is done and the summit attained,
    And the barriers fall,   10
Though a battle's to fight ere the guerdon be gained
    The reward of it all.
I was ever a fighter, so — one fight more,
    The best and the last!
I would hate that death bandaged my eyes, and forbore, 15
    And bade me creep past.
No! let me taste the whole of it, fare like my peers,
    The heroes of old,
Bear the brunt, in a minute pay glad life's arrears°
    Of pain, darkness, and cold.   20
For sudden the worst turns the best to the brave,
    The black minute's at end,
And the elements' rage, the fiend-voices° that rave,
    Shall dwindle, shall blend,
Shall change, shall become first a peace out of pain,   25
    Then a light, then thy breast,
O thou soul of my soul! I shall clasp thee again,
    And with God be the rest!

Title: *Prospice* (prō·spĭk′ĭ): look forward (Latin). 17–20. His life had been so happy that he had avoided pain, darkness, and cold — the common lot of man. He would pay these debts (*arrears*) all at once in the moment of dying. 23. *fiend-voices:* This term refers to a legend that fiends try to snatch the soul away from the powers of light as it leaves the body.

My Last Duchess

This poem is perhaps the most popular of Browning's dramatic monologues. A *dramatic monologue* is a piece in which there is only one speaker, not soliloquizing, but directly addressing another person or group, whose responses or gestures are often suggested by the words of the speaker.

The scene is in the castle of the Duke of Ferrara, an arrogant Italian nobleman of the Renaissance period. The duke is showing a painting of his first wife to an envoy who has been sent to arrange the details of a second marriage. With keen dramatic skill, wherein every detail is significant, Browning shows us the true character of the duke, revealed through his discussion of his artless young wife. Browning's skill at portraying character — rare in lyric poets — is here clearly exhibited.

> That's my last Duchess painted on the wall,
> Looking as if she were alive; I call
> That piece a wonder, now; Fra Pandolf's° hands
> Worked busily a day, and there she stands.
> Will 't please you sit and look at her? I said   5
> "Fra Pandolf" by design, for never read
> Strangers like you that pictured countenance,
> The depth and passion of its earnest glance,
> But to myself they turned (since none puts by
> The curtain I have drawn for you, but I)   10
> And seemed as they would ask me, if they durst,
> How such a glance came there; so, not the first
> Are you to turn and ask thus. Sir, 'twas not
> Her husband's presence only, called that spot
> Of joy into the Duchess' cheek: perhaps   15
> Fra Pandolf chanced to say, "Her mantle laps
> Over my lady's wrist too much," or, "Paint
> Must never hope to reproduce the faint
> Half flush that dies along her throat"; such stuff
> Was courtesy, she thought, and cause enough   20
> For calling up that spot of joy. She had
> A heart . . . how shall I say? . . . too soon made glad,
> Too easily impressed; she liked whate'er
> She looked on, and her looks went everywhere.
> Sir, 'twas all one! My favor at her breast,   25
> The dropping of the daylight in the West,
> The bough of cherries some officious fool
> Broke in the orchard for her, the white mule
> She rode with round the terrace — all and each
> Would draw from her alike the approving speech,   30
> Or blush, at least. She thanked men — good; but thanked
> Somehow . . . I know not how . . . as if she ranked
> My gift of a nine-hundred-year-old name
> With anybody's gift. Who'd stoop to blame
> This sort of trifling? Even had you skill   35

3. *Fra Pandolf:* an imaginary monk and painter of the Italian Renaissance period. "Fra" means "Brother."

In speech — which I have not — to make your will
Quite clear to such an one, and say, "Just this
Or that in you disgusts me; here you miss
Or there exceed the mark" — and if she let
Herself be lessoned so, nor plainly set   40
Her wits to yours, forsooth, and made excuse
— E'en then would be some stooping, and I choose
Never to stoop. Oh, sir, she smiled, no doubt,
Whene'er I passed her; but who passed without
Much the same smile? This grew; I gave commands;   45
Then all smiles stopped together. There she stands
As if alive. Will 't please you rise? We'll meet
The company below, then. I repeat,
The Count your Master's known munificence
Is ample warrant that no just pretense   50
Of mine for dowry will be disallowed;
Though his fair daughter's self, as I avowed
At starting, is my object. Nay, we'll go
Together down,° sir! Notice Neptune,° though,
Taming a sea horse, thought a rarity,   55
Which Claus of Innsbruck° cast in bronze for me.

53–54. *we'll go together down:* The envoy, out of respect, has dropped behind the duke, who calls
him forward to a position of equality. 54. *Neptune:* the Greek god of the sea. 56. *Claus of Innsbruck:* an imaginary sculptor.

THE BROWNINGS' POETRY

SONNETS FROM THE PORTUGUESE

1. From evidence within the sonnets show (a) that they were written by a woman, (b) that their author was familiar with Greek literature, (c) that they represent a definite series of steps in a courtship, (d) that the one courted had been ill or an invalid.

2. How does Elizabeth Barrett Browning's concept of love compare with that revealed in the sonnets of William Shakespeare (pages 124–26)? How does it compare with that in the Marlowe and Raleigh poems (page 118)?

ROBERT BROWNING'S POEMS

1. What differences in the meter of the two Cavalier lyrics produce the effect of cheering in the first and of riding in the second? What characteristics of the Cavaliers are emphasized in these lyrics?

2. In "Love among the Ruins," how is the contrast between the past grandeur and the present bareness emphasized and made effective? In this same poem, how do the motives behind the sports, buildings, and wars of the vanished civilization compare with the emotions of the two young people, in value? in permanence?

3. What mood is common to the two "Home Thoughts" poems? What happened at Trafalgar that would especially stir the heart of an Englishman of Browning's day? What details of an English spring differ from spring as you have experienced it? Where does the last line of "Home Thoughts, from Abroad" suggest that Browning is at the time of writing? Pick out vivid bits of local color in this poem. When you are homesick, for what sights and sounds do you long?

4. In Pippa's song, how do lines 4–6 relate to the first three lines? Contrast the spirit of this song, especially the last line, with the spirit expressed in Shelley's "Dirge" (page 450). How is each typical of the general attitude of its author?

MY LAST DUCHESS

1. Contrast the characters of the husband and wife as Browning discloses both. What was it in his wife that annoyed the duke?

2. What possible interpretations might be given to lines 45 and 46: "I gave commands; Then all smiles stopped together"? What happened to the duchess?

3. What do you think was the purpose of the duke's interview? What impression do you suppose the duke made on the envoy? Why does the duke prize the painting of his wife?

4. Contrast Browning's use of the heroic couplet with Pope's in "The Rape of the Lock."

UNDERSTANDING THE POET'S PERSONALITY

"Prospice" undoubtedly came from the depths of the poet's heart. How is the title (see footnote, page 533) in harmony with Browning's personality and philosophy, as judged from his other poems?

In "Prospice" Browning regards death as a challenge, a last fight. He is exultant with certainty of victory, glowing with the prospective joy of reunion with his wife. For Browning, fighting death involved not fear, but struggling against weakness and pain of the flesh. Find the lines that reveal this philosophy.

Compare this poem on death in movement, imagery, climax, and spirit with Tennyson's "Crossing the Bar" (page 523) and with the other poems mentioned for comparison on page 525. How does Browning differ from the other poets in what he most eagerly anticipates in immortality?

THE POWER OF WORDS

MONOSYLLABLES

In contrast to the smoothness of Tennyson's writing, Browning's style often seems abrupt and harsh. He achieves tremendous power and drive by his use of monosyllables. In "Give a Rouse" you will find only three or four words of two syllables and none of more than two. (The short Anglo-Saxon words in English make it easy to use monosyllables alone.) How is this style appropriate to the situation and to the singers in the poem? Not only are the words short, but the very construction of the sentences is awkward and rough. Could Tennyson have used this style for a poem like "The Lady of Shalott"? Where else in the Browning poems is this style found?

BEHIND THE SCENES IN ENGLISH LITERATURE

One of the most famous forgeries is the fake "first" printing, for private circulation only, of the "Sonnets of EBB" — that is, Elizabeth Barrett Browning's *Sonnets from the Portuguese*. This was known as the "Reading 1847" pamphlet because of the purported date and place of publication. For over forty years after their first appearance on the market, these pamphlets were accepted as genuine and brought prices as high as $1,250 until, in the 1930's, two British bibliographers, Graham Pollard and John Carter, became suspicious and began investigating.

Browning lovers are fond of the story of how Mrs. Browning shyly slipped her sonnets into her husband's pocket one morning and then hurried off to her room, and of how Browning afterwards insisted that they be published. This story was related in 1894 in an essay by the popular critic Edmund Gosse. Gosse went on to tell how Mrs. Browning (then living in Italy), after consenting to publication, dispatched the poems to a friend in England, who having a few copies printed at Reading, sent them to the Brownings to distribute among friends. Gosse said this little episode occurred in Pisa in 1847. But Carter and Pollard knew that Browning and his friends claimed it had occurred elsewhere, in 1849. More suspicion. When, then, had the pamphlet been printed?

Turning to the weighty Browning bibliographies by Thomas J. Wise, the foremost authority of the early twentieth century on Victorian bibliography, Carter and Pollard found Gosse's story repeated with the additional information that Mrs. Browning's friend had kept back a few copies and given them to a certain Dr. Bennett, who, "about 1885," had sold one to Thomas J. Wise and others to other Browning enthusiasts. So that was how about a dozen of them came on the market. Yet in 1932 at least twenty-nine copies were known to exist, all new when sold, none showing signs of having been in Italy or associated with the Brownings.

Carter and Pollard now turned to scientific detective work. They discovered that the paper on which the Reading pamphlet was printed was made by a process not used before the 1880's and that the typeface was of a design first used in 1880, which, in this pamphlet, exhibited certain peculiarities. The forgery was proved. But who was the forger?

By a lucky coincidence, Carter and Pollard soon discovered the name of the printer, an eminently respectable firm which specialized in producing limited facsimile editions. Unfortunately, however, the printer could shed no light on the publication of the Reading pamphlet, though they knew they had printed the book for Thomas J. Wise as a collector's item, just as they had printed many another book for Wise, all presumably legitimate facsimiles.

Ever since the bogus pamphlets had begun to appear, they had been listed by bibliographers and bought by book collectors, most of whom acknowledged the assistance of Thomas J. Wise. Since they first appeared on the market in small groups, it seemed likely that they originated from a common source. This turned out to be a certain bookseller, who had once worked in Wise's office, and who, convinced that the pamphlets were genuine, had resold hundreds of them after buying them from Thomas J. Wise.

In 1934, Carter and Pollard published all their findings and claimed to have "no conclusive evidence of the forger's identity." Their deliberately understated case, however, pointed clearly to Wise, and this became the most sensational literary scandal of the century. Wise denied the implication, but years later a confession of his guilt was found in his own writing.

CHARLES
DICKENS

1812 – 1870

British Information

In the early years of the nineteenth century the great majority of public institutions in England — schools, courts, prisons, hospitals, and poorhouses — were in a deplorable condition. The spirit of reform aroused by these abuses found its most able and effective champion in Charles Dickens.

The son of a government clerk who became bankrupt and was thrown into prison, Dickens received little education and was forced to work in a factory at an early age. Many of the unhappy experiences of his youth are related in the semi-autobiographical *David Copperfield*. While working as a newspaper reporter in London at the age of 22, Dickens began his *Sketches by Boz*. Soon afterward he achieved fame and fortune through the publication of *Pickwick Papers*, another series of rambling adventures, which appeared in a monthly magazine. Acclaimed as the most popular fiction writer of his day, he succeeded Sir Walter Scott in the affection of the reading public in both Great Britain and the United States and soon became well known for platform readings from his works throughout Europe and in this country.

Though Dickens was primarily a novelist, he also made a contribution to the development of the short story form, which evolved more rapidly in this country than in England. While Poe and Hawthorne were producing beautifully constructed stories on this side of the Atlantic, Dickens was writing his *Sketches by Boz*. In both *Sketches by Boz* and *Pickwick Papers* there is more of the short story than of the sustained narrative; in both, the tales are only loosely connected by featuring the same characters. *A Christmas Carol,* one of Dickens' best known writings, and *Christmas Stories* are further contributions to short fiction.

Pickwick Papers, with its illustrations by "Phiz" (H. K. Browne, a popular cartoonist of the day), took London by storm. Everyone waited breathlessly for the next monthly installment which would relate the adventures of the kindly, naïve Mr. Pickwick and his three friends who formed the Pickwick Club. These three absurd gentlemen — Tupman, Snodgrass, and Winkle — accompany their leader on a tour of "scientific" investigation and discovery through England. With Mr. Pickwick is his servant, Sam Weller, whose broad Cockney dialect produces much of the humor in the stories. In the course of their travels, the Pickwickians become acquainted with Mr. Wardle, a hospitable country squire who invites them to spend Christmas with him at Manor Farm, where they are in the following account. Each of the Pickwickians has his particular pride — as well as his particular folly. Mr. Winkle, for instance, has boasted of his athletic prowess.

Mr. Pickwick on the Ice

OLD WARDLE led the way to a pretty large sheet of ice; and the fat boy and Mr. Weller having shoveled and swept away the snow which had fallen on it during the night, Mr. Bob Sawyer adjusted his skates with a dexterity which to Mr. Winkle was perfectly marvelous, and described circles with his left leg, and cut figures of eight, and inscribed upon the ice, without once stopping for breath, a great many other pleasant and astonishing devices, to the excessive satisfaction of Mr. Pickwick, Mr. Tupman, and the ladies, which reached a pitch of positive enthusiasm when old Wardle and Benjamin Allen, assisted by the aforesaid Bob Sawyer, performed some mystic evolutions which they called a reel.

All this time Mr. Winkle, with his face and hands blue with the cold, had been forcing a gimlet into the soles of his feet, and putting his skates on with the points behind, and getting the straps into a very complicated and entangled state, with the assistance of Mr. Snodgrass, who knew rather less about skates than a Hindu. At length, however, with the assistance of Mr. Weller, the unfortunate skates were firmly screwed and buckled on, and Mr. Winkle was raised to his feet.

"Now, then, sir," said Sam, in an encouraging tone; "off with you, and show 'em how to do it."

"Stop, Sam, stop!" said Mr. Winkle, trembling violently, and clutching hold of Sam's arm with the grasp of a drowning man. "How slippery it is, Sam!"

"Not an uncommon thing upon ice, sir," replied Mr. Weller. "Hold up, sir!"

This last observation of Mr. Weller's bore reference to a demonstration Mr. Winkle made, at the instant, of a frantic desire to throw his feet in the air and dash the back of his head on the ice.

"These — these — are very awkward skates; ain't they, Sam?" inquired Mr. Winkle, staggering.

"I'm afeerd there's a orkard gen'l'm'n in 'em, sir," replied Sam.

"Now, Winkle," cried Mr. Pickwick, quite unconscious that there was anything the matter. "Come; the ladies are all anxiety."

"Yes, yes," replied Mr. Winkle, with a ghastly smile; "I'm coming."

"Just agoin' to begin," said Sam, endeavoring to disengage himself. "Now, sir, start off!"

"Stop an instant, Sam," gasped Mr. Winkle, clinging most affectionately to Mr. Weller. "I find I've got a couple of coats at home that I don't want, Sam. You may have them, Sam."

"Thank'ee, sir," replied Mr. Weller.

"Never mind touching your hat, Sam," said Mr. Winkle, hastily; "you needn't take your hand away to do that. I meant to have given you five shillings this morning for a Christmas box, Sam. I'll give it you this afternoon, Sam."

"You're wery good, sir," replied Mr. Weller.

"Just hold me at first, Sam; will you?" said Mr. Winkle. "There — that's right. I shall soon get in the way of it, Sam. Not too fast, Sam; not too fast."

Mr. Winkle, stooping forward with his body half doubled up, was being assisted over the ice by Mr. Weller, in a very singular and unswanlike manner, when Mr. Pickwick most innocently shouted from the opposite bank, —

"Sam!"

"Sir?" said Mr. Weller.

"Here. I want you."

"Let go, sir," said Sam. "Don't you hear the governor acallin'? Let go, sir."

With a violent effort, Mr. Weller disengaged himself from the grasp of the agonized Pickwickian, and in so doing administered a considerable impetus to the unhappy Mr. Winkle. With an accuracy which no degree of dexterity or practice could have insured, that unfortunate gentleman bore swiftly down into the center of the reel, at the very moment when Mr. Bob Sawyer was performing a flourish of unparalleled beauty. Mr. Winkle struck wildly against him, and with a loud crash they both fell heavily down. Mr. Pickwick ran to the spot. Bob Sawyer had risen to his feet, but Mr. Winkle was far too wise to do anything of the kind in skates. He was seated on the ice making spasmodic efforts to smile; but anguish was depicted on every lineament of his countenance.

"Are you hurt?" inquired Mr. Benjamin Allen, with great anxiety.

"Not much," said Mr. Winkle, rubbing his back very hard.

"I wish you'd let me bleed [1] you," said Mr. Benjamin, with great eagerness.

"No, thank you," replied Mr. Winkle, hurriedly.

"I really think you had better," said Allen.

"Thank you," replied Mr. Winkle, "I'd rather not."

"What do *you* think, Mr. Pickwick?" inquired Bob Sawyer.

Mr. Pickwick was excited and indignant. He beckoned to Mr. Weller and said, in a stern voice, "Take his skates off."

"No; but really I had scarcely begun," remonstrated Mr. Winkle.

"Take his skates off," repeated Mr. Pickwick, firmly.

The command was not to be resisted. Mr. Winkle allowed Sam to obey it in silence.

"Lift him up," said Mr. Pickwick. Sam assisted him to rise.

Mr. Pickwick retired a few paces apart from the bystanders, and beckoning his friend to approach, fixed a searching look upon him, and uttered, in a low but distinct and emphatic tone, these remarkable words —

[1] *bleed:* a common treatment by doctors in those days. Benjamin Allen and Bob Sawyer were young medical students.

"You're a humbug, sir."

"A what?" said Mr. Winkle, starting.

"A humbug, sir. I will speak plainer, if you wish it. An impostor, sir."

With these words Mr. Pickwick turned slowly on his heel, and rejoined his friends.

While Mr. Pickwick was delivering himself of the sentiment just recorded, Mr. Weller and the fat boy, having by their joint endeavors cut out a slide, were exercising themselves thereupon in a very masterly and brilliant manner. Sam Weller, in particular, was displaying that beautiful feat of fancy sliding which is currently denominated "knocking at the cobbler's door," and which is achieved by skimming over the ice on one foot, and occasionally giving a two-penny postman's knock upon it with the other. It was a good long slide, and there was something in the motion which Mr. Pickwick, who was very cold with standing still, could not help envying.

"It looks a nice, warm exercise that, doesn't it?" he inquired of Wardle, when that gentleman was thoroughly out of breath by reason of the indefatigable manner in which he had converted his legs into a pair of compasses, and drawn complicated problems on the ice.

"Ah, it does indeed," replied Wardle. "Do you slide?"

"I used to do so, on the gutters, when I was a boy," replied Mr. Pickwick.

"Try it now," said Wardle.

"Oh, do, please, Mr. Pickwick!" cried all the ladies.

"I should be very happy to afford you any amusement," replied Mr. Pickwick, "but I haven't done such a thing these thirty years."

"Pooh, pooh! Nonsense!" said Wardle, dragging off his skates with the impetuosity which characterized all his proceedings. "Here; I'll keep you company. Come along!" And away went the good-tempered old fellow down the slide with a rapidity which came very close upon Mr. Weller, and beat the fat boy all to nothing.

Mr. Pickwick paused, considered, pulled off his gloves and put them in his hat; took two or three short runs, balked himself as often, and at last took another run, and went slowly and gravely down the slide, with his feet about a yard and a quarter apart, amidst the gratified shouts of all the spectators.

"Keep the pot abilin', sir!" said Sam; and down went Wardle again, and then Mr. Pickwick, and then Sam, and then Mr. Winkle, and then Mr. Bob Sawyer, and then the fat boy, and then Mr. Snodgrass, following closely upon each other's heels, and running after each other with as much eagerness as if all their future prospects in life depended on their expedition.

It was the most intensely interesting thing to observe the manner in which Mr. Pickwick performed his share in the ceremony: to watch the torture of anxiety with which he viewed the person behind, gaining upon him at the imminent hazard of tripping him up; to see him gradually expend the painful force which he had put on at first, and turn slowly round on the slide, with his face toward the point from which he had started; to contemplate the playful smile which mantled on his face when he had accomplished the distance, and the eagerness with which he turned round when he had done so and ran after his predecessor — his black gaiters tripping pleasantly through the snow, and his eyes beaming cheerfulness and gladness through his spectacles. And when he was knocked down (which happened upon the average every third round), it was the most invigorating sight that can possibly be imagined to behold him gather up his hat, gloves, and handkerchief with a glowing countenance, and resume his station in the rank with an ardor and enthusiasm that nothing could abate.

The sport was at its height, the sliding was at the quickest, the laughter was at the loudest, when a sharp, smart crack was heard. There was a quick rush toward the bank, a wild scream from the ladies, and a shout from Mr. Tupman. A large mass of ice disappeared; the water bubbled up over it; Mr. Pickwick's hat, gloves, and handkerchief were floating on the surface; and this was all of Mr. Pickwick that anybody could see.

Dismay and anguish were depicted on every countenance; the males turned pale, and the females fainted; Mr. Snodgrass and Mr. Winkle grasped each other by the hand, and gazed at the spot where their leader had gone down, with frenzied eagerness; while Mr. Tupman, by way of rendering the promptest assistance, and at the same time conveying to any persons who might be within hearing the clearest possible notion of the catastrophe, ran off across the country at his utmost speed, screaming "Fire!" with all his might.

It was at this very moment, when old Wardle and Sam Weller were approaching the hole with cautious steps, and Mr. Benjamin Allen was holding a hurried consultation with Mr. Bob Sawyer on the advisability of bleeding the company generally, as an improving little bit of professional practice — it was at this very moment that a face, head, and shoulders emerged from beneath the water, and disclosed the features and spectacles of Mr. Pickwick.

"Keep yourself up for an instant — for only one instant!" bawled Mr. Snodgrass.

"Yes, do; let me implore you — for my sake!" roared Mr. Winkle, deeply affected. The adjuration was rather unnecessary — the probability being that if Mr. Pickwick had declined to keep himself up for anybody else's sake, it would have occurred to him that he might as well do so for his own.

"Do you feel the bottom there, old fellow?" said Wardle.

"Yes, certainly," replied Mr. Pickwick, wringing the water from his head and face, and gasping for breath. "I fell upon my back. I couldn't get on my feet at first."

The clay upon so much of Mr. Pickwick's coat as was yet visible bore testimony to the accuracy of this statement; and as the fears of the spectators were still further relieved by the fat boy's suddenly recollecting that the water was nowhere more than five feet deep, prodigies of valor were performed to get him out. After a vast quantity of splashing, and cracking, and struggling, Mr. Pickwick was at length fairly extricated from his unpleasant position, and once more stood on dry land.

"Oh, he'll catch his death of cold," said Emily.

"Dear old thing!" said Arabella. "Let me wrap this shawl round you, Mr. Pickwick."

"Ah, that's the best thing you can do," said Wardle; "and when you've got it on, run home as fast as your legs can carry you, and jump into bed directly."

A dozen shawls were offered on the instant. Three or four of the thickest having been selected, Mr. Pickwick was wrapped up, and started off, under the guidance of Mr. Weller — presenting the singular phenomenon of an elderly gentleman, dripping wet, and without a hat, with his arms bound down to his sides, skimming over the ground without any clearly defined purpose, at the rate of six good English miles an hour.

But Mr. Pickwick cared not for appearances in such an extreme case, and urged on by Sam Weller, he kept at the very top of his speed until he reached the door of Manor Farm, where Mr. Tupman had arrived some five minutes before, and had frightened the old lady into palpitations of the heart by impressing her with the unalterable conviction that the kitchen chimney was on fire — a calamity which always presented itself in glowing colors to the old lady's mind when anybody about her evinced the smallest agitation.

Mr. Pickwick paused not an instant until he was snug in bed. Sam Weller lighted a blazing fire in the room, and took up his dinner; a bowl of punch was carried up afterward, and a grand carouse held in honor of his safety. Old Wardle would not hear of his rising, so they made the bed the chair, and Mr. Pickwick presided. A second and a third bowl were ordered in. And when Mr. Pickwick awoke next morning there was not a symptom of rheumatism about him; which proves, as Mr. Bob Sawyer very justly observed, that there is nothing like hot punch in such cases; and that if ever hot punch did fail to act as a preventative, it was merely because the patient fell into the vulgar error of not taking enough of it.

THE PICKWICKIANS

1. Characterize Mr. Pickwick, Mr. Winkle, Bob Sawyer, and Sam Weller. How do their personalities add to the humor of the situations?

2. To give the class a more complete picture of the Pickwick Club's adventures, some students might describe other amusing adventures from *Pickwick Papers*.

SUGGESTION FOR WRITING

Write a narrative showing yourself or someone else in an absurd predicament.

THE POWER OF WORDS

EXAGGERATION FOR EFFECT

Dickens frequently uses big words to enhance the humor of his tale. They give a mock-heroic touch to simple incidents. For example, *catastrophe* and *calamity*, usually reserved for train wrecks, earthquakes, and the like, are here applied to Mr. Pickwick's breaking through the ice and to an old lady's belief that the chimney was on fire. Mr. Winkle roared an *adjuration* to his supposedly drowning friend. The word denotes a serious appeal to someone; Winkle's appeal is of course ridiculous.

Find other examples of humor created by using big words. In Dickens' style, write about a simple school "calamity."

Mr. Pickwick's skating party at Manor Farm in a drawing by Alfred Crowquill (1837). ▶

Sir you're a Humbug!

The Slide.

MATTHEW
ARNOLD
1822–1888

National Portrait Gallery

Matthew Arnold, poet, essayist, and critic, was the eldest son of Dr. Thomas Arnold, the well-known headmaster of Rugby, one of the most famous boys' schools in England. Following family traditions, Matthew attended Rugby and Oxford. He later began his teaching career at Rugby, developing an interest in education through his father. The meaning and content of a good education were the concern of many Victorian writers. You have already noted the ideas of Newman and Huxley; and Dickens, through his novels, was instrumental in bringing about reforms in boarding schools. Arnold, however, was the only one of the major Victorian writers who became a professional educator. For thirty-five years he led a busy life as government inspector of schools and was especially well-known in his day for his reports on European school systems, which he studied in his work as foreign assistant commissioner on education.

In literature, Arnold's first interest was poetry, but after his first two volumes were coldly received, he turned to the writing of essays. Later he received a pension from the government and toured both England and the United States as a lecturer. A versatile and learned man, Arnold, like Carlyle, was an earnest critic of his age. He was particularly concerned with the growing materialism and complacency of his times and called for a pursuit of culture — of "the best that has been thought and said in the world." In *Essays in Criticism* he wrote: "Culture is the study of perfection, and looks beyond machinery and coal; hates hatred and all sham; has one great passion, the passion for sweetness and light."

Much of Arnold's poetry is tinged with sadness and pessimism, traceable often to the conflict in the thinking of his day between science and religion. Yet there is always a clear and simple beauty in his lines, reminiscent of the Greek poetry in which he was widely read. In "Dover Beach," one of his best-loved poems, both these elements are strongly marked.

Dover Beach

The sea is calm tonight.
The tide is full, the moon lies fair
Upon the Straits° — on the French coast, the light

3. *Straits:* the Strait of Dover, the shortest distance between England and the Continent.

Gleams, and is gone; the cliffs of England stand,
Glimmering and vast, out in the tranquil bay.   5
Come to the window, sweet is the night air!
Only, from the long line of spray
Where the sea meets the moon-blanched sand,
Listen! you hear the grating roar
Of pebbles which the waves suck back, and fling,   10
At their return, up the high strand,
Begin, and cease, and then again begin,
With tremulous cadence slow, and bring
The eternal note of sadness in.

Sophocles° long ago   15
Heard it on the Aegean,° and it brought
Into his mind the turbid ebb and flow
Of human misery; we
Find also in the sound a thought,
Hearing it by this distant northern sea.   20

The sea of faith
Was once, too, at the full, and round earth's shore
Lay like the folds of a bright girdle furled;
But now I only hear
Its melancholy, long, withdrawing roar,   25
Retreating to the breath
Of the night wind down the vast edges drear
And naked shingles° of the world.

Ah, love, let us be true
To one another! for the world, which seems   30
To lie before us like a land of dreams,
So various, so beautiful, so new,
Hath really neither joy, nor love, nor light,
Nor certitude, nor peace, nor help for pain;
And we are here as on a darkling plain   35
Swept with confused alarms of struggle and flight,
Where ignorant armies clash by night.

15. *Sophocles* (sŏf′ŏ-klēz): an Athenian writer (496?–406 B.C.), one of the three greatest tragedians in the golden age of Greek drama. 16. *Aegean* (ē-jē′ăn): an arm of the Mediterranean Sea, between Greece and Asia Minor. 28. *shingles:* pebbly shores, common in England.

ARNOLD'S PESSIMISM

1. State in your own words the problem, or doubt, in the poet's mind. How does this poem illustrate the conflict between science and religion in Victorian times? Into what two main divisions of thought does the poem fall? Contrast the thoughts expressed in the subdivisions of the second half of the poem.

2. What link does the poet feel between himself and Sophocles? In what way are the troubled thoughts of the two poets like the sea? What consolation does he find in the midst of a confused world? Is the last stanza descriptive of our situation today?

CHRISTINA ROSSETTI
1830–1894

and

DANTE GABRIEL ROSSETTI
1828–1882

Love of poetry was a natural inheritance in the family of Dante Gabriel and Christina Rossetti. Their father was an exiled Italian who, besides teaching his native language in Kings College, London, wrote commentaries on the great Italian poet Dante, for whom he named his son. All four children in the family did some writing, and Dante and Christina earned a secure place in the roll of English poets.

Christina Rossetti, one of the masters of the English sonnet, led a life of self-sacrifice. A devout Anglican, she refused to marry two suitors because of religious differences. The first of these love affairs caused her intense grief, as some of her poems show. After devoting much of her life to the care of her mother and two elderly aunts, she herself became a semi-invalid for her last twenty years. She found consolation in her poetry and in prose writings of a religious nature. It has been said that all we know of her is that she was a great saint and a great poet.

Dante Gabriel Rossetti thought of himself more as a painter than a poet, and practiced the two arts throughout his life. In both he expressed his love of beauty and of rich color and his desire to "encourage the simplicity of nature in all things." He was an influential member of the Pre-Raphaelite Brotherhood of painters and writers, a romantic revival which, turning against contemporary conventions in art and literature, desired a return to art forms which prevailed in the fifteenth century, before the time of Raphael. In some of Rossetti's early paintings we see the face of Christina. Later, the central figure was usually his wife, the beautiful Elizabeth Siddal. After only two years of marriage, Elizabeth, who was tubercular, tragically died. Rossetti, in despair, buried all his unpublished poems beside her, but several years later his friends induced the poet to allow them to recover the poems for publication. The success of this volume encouraged him to continue writing during the last twenty years of his life. His sonnet sequence of 101 poems, called *The House of Life,* is among the greatest in English literature.

A Birthday

CHRISTINA ROSSETTI

My heart is like a singing bird
    Whose nest is in a watered shoot;
My heart is like an apple tree
    Whose boughs are bent with thickset
      fruit;
My heart is like a rainbow shell   5
    That paddles in a halcyon sea;°
My heart is gladder than all these
    Because my love is come to me.

Raise me a dais of silk and down;   9
    Hang it with vair° and purple dyes;

6. *halcyon* (hăl′sĭ·ŭn) *sea:* calm, peaceful sea, which is supposed to exist for fourteen days each winter when the kingfisher, or halcyon, nests on the waves. 10. *vair:* a kind of fur used in the Middle Ages.

Carve it in doves, and pomegranates,
  And peacocks with a hundred eyes;
Work it in gold and silver grapes
  In leaves, and silver fleurs-de-lys;
Because the birthday of my life   15
  Is come, my love is come to me.

Remember

CHRISTINA ROSSETTI

Remember me when I am gone away,
Gone far away into the silent land;
When you can no more hold me by the
  hand,
Nor I half turn to go, yet turning stay.
Remember me when no more, day by
  day,   5
You tell me of our future that you
  planned;
Only remember me; you understand
It will be late to counsel then or pray.
Yet if you should forget me for a while
And afterward remember, do not grieve;
For if the darkness and corruption leave
A vestige of the thoughts that once I had,
Better by far you should forget and smile
Than that you should remember and be
  sad.

The Woodspurge

DANTE GABRIEL ROSSETTI

The grieving poet chances upon a three-
blossomed woodspurge, which becomes the
image of his despair.

The wind flapped loose, the wind was
  still,
Shaken out dead from tree and hill;
I had walked on at the wind's will —
I sat now, for the wind was still.

Between my knees my forehead was —
My lips, drawn in, said not Alas!   6
My hair was over in the grass,
My naked ears heard the day pass.

My eyes, wide open, had the run
Of some ten weeds to fix upon;   10
Among those few, out of the sun,
The woodspurge flowered, three cups in
  one.

From perfect grief there need not be
Wisdom or even memory:
One thing then learned remains to me,
The woodspurge has a cup of three.   16

Silent Noon

DANTE GABRIEL ROSSETTI

Your hands lie open in the long fresh grass,
The finger points look through like rosy blooms;
Your eyes smile peace. The pasture gleams and glooms
'Neath billowing skies that scatter and amass.
All round our nest, far as the eye can pass,   5
Are golden kingcup fields with silver edge
Where the cow parsley skirts the hawthorn hedge.
'Tis visible silence, still as the hourglass.
Deep in the sun-searched growths the dragonfly
Hangs like a blue thread loosened from the sky —   10
So this winged hour is dropped to us from above.
Oh! clasp we to our hearts, for deathless dower,
This close-companioned inarticulate hour
When twofold silence was the song of love.

Spring

DANTE GABRIEL ROSSETTI

Soft-littered is the new year's lambing fold,
And in the hollowed haystack at its side
The shepherd lies o' nights now, wakeful-eyed
At the ewes' travailing call through the dark cold.
The young rooks cheep 'mid the thick caw o' the old: 5
And near unpeopled streamsides, on the ground,
By her spring-cry the moor hen's nest is found,
Where the drained floodlands flaunt their marigold,
Chill are the gusts to which the pastures cower,
And chill the current where the young reeds stand   10
As green and close as the young wheat on land:
Yet here the cuckoo and the cuckoo flower
Plight to the heart Spring's perfect imminent hour
Whose breath shall soothe you like your dear one's hand.

THE ROSSETTIS

CHRISTINA

1. In what sense is the word "birthday" used in the first poem? Contrast the pictures of natural beauty in the first stanza with the details of oriental splendor and luxury in the second.

2. How is the mood of "Remember" different from that of "A Birthday"? What do the two together suggest of the author's experience?

DANTE GABRIEL

1. Find evidence from Rossetti's poems that he was a painter with a trained eye for color and design. Show also that sound — and the suggestion of silence — are important elements in these poems.

2. By what details does the poet suggest utter despair in "The Woodspurge"? Can you think of an instance when some trivial detail impressed itself on your mind during an important or moving experience?

SUGGESTION FOR REPORT

Present to the class a report on the Pre-Raphaelite Brotherhood. What was the role of Christina and Dante Gabriel Rossetti in the Brotherhood, and with what other writers and painters were they associated? What was the group's contribution to the art of its day?

LITERATURE AND THE ARTS →

The most influential member of the Pre-Raphaelites, D. G. Rossetti, like William Blake, is a classic example of a man who practiced both literary and applied art.

An association of painters and writers, the Pre-Raphaelite Brotherhood was founded by Rossetti in 1849. It was, in essence, a protest movement, a reaction against the unsettling influences which the Industrial Revolution had had on England socially and economically as well as artistically. Most important to the Brotherhood was the restoration to English art of the old traditions of simplicity and high standards of workmanship. The movement was as short-lived as it was controversial, but though it disbanded a short three years after its foundation, it had a considerable influence on Victorian painting and poetry.

The illustration opposite — "The Day Dream" — is an example of Rossetti's style as a painter and reflects the pictorial quality of his verse. To accompany this painting, Rossetti wrote a poem, also called "The Day Dream," the closing lines of which are as follows:

Lo! tow'rd deep skies, not deeper than her look,
She dreams; till now on her forgotten book
Drops the forgotten blossom from her hand.

LEWIS CARROLL

1832–1898

Bettmann

Lewis Carroll is a name known to all children who have delighted in the story of *Alice in Wonderland* and its sequel *Through the Looking Glass*. Few of them have guessed that hiding behind this pen name was a learned professor of mathematics at Oxford, the Reverend Charles Lutwidge Dodgson. During the quarter century he was teaching at Oxford and writing books on mathematics, Dodgson found expression for the other side of his nature by writing nonsense verse and gay fanciful sto-

ries for children. There is more meaning behind the strange characters in the distorted world of the Alice books than first appears. Adults find that the upside-down world of Alice reflects almost uncannily the true nature of life.

"A Sea Dirge" (not from the Alice books) is in marked contrast to many other poems on the sea which occur in English literature. With characteristic drollery Lewis Carroll denounces the sea as his "pet peeve."

A Sea Dirge

There are certain things — as, a spider, a ghost,
    The income tax, gout, an umbrella for three —
That I hate, but the thing that I hate the most
    Is a thing they call the Sea.

Pour some salt water over the floor —   5
    Ugly I'm sure you'll allow it to be;
Suppose it extended a mile or more,
    That's very like the Sea.

Beat a dog till he howls outright —
    Cruel, but all very well for a spree;   10
Suppose that he did so day and night,
    That would be like the Sea.

I had a vision of nurserymaids;
    Tens of thousands passed by me —
All leading children with wooden spades,   15
    And this was by the Sea.

Who invented those spades of wood?
  Who was it cut them out of the tree?
None, I think, but an idiot could —
    Or one that loved the Sea.   20

It is pleasant and dreamy, no doubt, to float
  With "thoughts as boundless, and souls as free";
But, suppose you are very unwell in the boat —
    How do you like the Sea?

There is an insect that people avoid   25
  (Whence is derived the verb "to flee").
Where have you been by it most annoyed?
    In lodgings by the Sea.

If you like your coffee with sand for dregs,
  A decided hint of salt in your tea,   30
And a fishy taste in the very eggs —
    By all means choose the Sea.

And if, with these dainties to drink and eat,
  You prefer not a vestige of grass or tree,
And a chronic state of wet in your feet,   35
    Then — I recommend the Sea.

For *I* have friends who dwell by the coast —
  Pleasant friends they are to me!
It is when I am with them I wonder most
    That anyone likes the Sea.   40

They take me a walk; though tired and stiff,
  To climb the heights I madly agree;
And, after a tumble or so from the cliff,
    They kindly suggest the Sea.

I try the rocks, and I think it cool   45
  That they laugh with such an excess of glee,
As I heavily slip into every pool
    That skirts the cold, cold Sea.

A DIFFERENT SEA POEM

1. In "A Sea Dirge" what various aspects of the sea arouse Carroll's distaste? Which comparisons are most amusing to you? What are your own reactions to the sea? Are they based on firsthand experience or on what you have heard and read about the sea?

2. Contrast the moods created in the following poems on the sea: "The Seafarer" (page 32), "The Rime of the Ancient Mariner" (page 398), "Apostrophe to the Ocean (page 438), "Break, Break, Break" (page 520), "Crossing the Bar" (page 523), "Home Thoughts, from the Sea" (page 532). What can you conclude from this variety of poetry on the sea?

W. S. GILBERT 1836–1911

William Schwenck Gilbert is rarely spoken of alone; his name is invariably coupled with that of Arthur Sullivan. But before meeting Sullivan, Gilbert had made a name as the witty author of satirical verses in *Bab Ballads*. He wrote the librettos and Sullivan the music for a series of light operas which are still as popular as they were back in the seventies and eighties. Today high school students continue to stage *H.M.S. Pinafore*, *The Mikado*, and others. Traveling professional companies specializing in Gilbert and Sullivan still go up and down the land. The most famous of these companies is the D'Oyly Carte, which was organized by Richard D'Oyly Carte, an astute theater producer who brought Gilbert and Sullivan together and first produced their works.

Much of Gilbert's humor lies in his unexpected rhymes and many-syllabled words that ripple along. His lines read almost as well as they sing. He was a master of satire. He knew how to ridicule the army, the navy, and the government without offending the public.

On page 709 you will find a chapter from Hesketh Pearson's *Gilbert and Sullivan*, which points out some of Gilbert's personal peculiarities and tells of the beginnings of *H.M.S. Pinafore*. Two songs from that operetta are given here.

He Is an Englishman

BOATSWAIN: He is an Englishman!
    For he himself has said it,
    And it's greatly to his credit
    That he is an Englishman!
CHORUS: *That he is an Englishman!*
BOATSWAIN: For he might have been a
    Roosian,   6
    A French or Turk or Proosian,
    Or perhaps Italian!
CHORUS: *Or perhaps Italian!*
BOATSWAIN: But in spite of all temptations   10
    To belong to other nations,
    He remains an Englishman!
    He remains an Englishman!
Chorus repeats last four lines.

When I Was a Lad

When I was a lad I served a term
As office boy to an attorney's firm.
I cleaned the windows and I swept the floor,
And I polished up the handle of the big front door.
CHORUS: *He polished up the handle of the big front door.* 5

I polished up the handle so carefullee
That now I am the ruler of the Queen's Navee!
CHORUS: *He polished up the handle so carefullee*
    That now he is the ruler of the Queen's Navee!

[For each stanza the chorus repeats three lines,
as shown in the first stanza.]

As office boy I made such a mark   10
That they gave me the post of a junior clerk.°
I served the writs with a smile so bland,
And I copied all the letters in a big round hand.

I copied all the letters in a hand so free
That now I am the ruler of the Queen's Navee!   15

In serving writs I made such a name
That an articled clerk I soon became;
I wore clean collars and a brand-new suit
For the pass examination at the Institute.

That pass examination did so well for me   20
That now I am the ruler of the Queen's Navee!

Of legal knowledge I acquired such a grip
That they took me into the partnership.
And that junior partnership, I ween,
Was the only ship that I ever had seen.   25

But that kind of ship so suited me
That now I am the ruler of the Queen's Navee!

I grew so rich that I was sent
By a pocket borough° into Parliament.
I always voted at my party's call,   30
And I never thought of thinking for myself at all.

I thought so little they rewarded me
By making me the ruler of the Queen's Navee!

Now landsmen all, whoever you may be,
If you want to rise to the top of the tree,   35
If your soul isn't fettered to an office stool,
Be careful to be guided by this golden rule,

Stick close to your desks and never go to sea,
And you all may be rulers of the Queen's Navee!

11. *clerk:* The British pronounce this to rhyme with *mark.* 29. *pocket borough:* Before the election reforms of the nineteenth century, certain boroughs had become so reduced in population that they could be easily controlled or "put in the pocket" by a wealthy or powerful candidate.

VICTORIANS RIDICULED
1. In "He Is an Englishman" Gilbert is poking fun at exaggerated national pride. In the selection on page 709 about *H.M.S. Pinafore,* you will find an amusing parody on this song, proposed as an adaptation of the idea to the United States.

2. In "When I Was a Lad" Gilbert satirizes two different things: the "self-made man" type of biography, and the British Navy. Give specific lines which most clearly ridicule each of these. Show why both these songs from *H.M.S. Pinafore* arouse laughter instead of resentment.

ROBERT
LOUIS
STEVENSON

1850–1894

National Portrait Gallery

You probably come upon Robert Louis Stevenson as an old friend. Nearly every teen-age boy and girl reads *Treasure Island,* and many have seen a motion-picture version of it. Probably when you were younger you read (or listened to) *A Child's Garden of Verses.* Stevenson has something to interest every age. Now you are ready for his essays and psychological stories, which appeal to adults.

Stevenson's whole life was a struggle against tuberculosis, yet his literary output was greatly enriched by this misfortune. He was nursed through a sickly childhood by a devoted Scottish nurse, to whom he dedicated *A Child's Garden of Verses.* From his walking tours in Scotland he got background material for the descriptions of bleak moors and lonely hills in *Kidnapped* and other romances. A similar journey through southern France, taken for his health, resulted in *Travels with a Donkey* and other books of essays. In France he met a charming American, Mrs. Fanny Osbourne, whom, after her divorce, he later married in California. The long trip across an ocean and a continent to join her played havoc with his weak constitution, but his wife's nursing saved his life. After a number of years spent in various parts of the United States and Europe, the Stevensons moved, again for his health, to Vailima, Samoa. His "Vailima Letters" to his many friends show this gifted writer

as a master of the art of letter writing.

The variety of Stevenson's work has been indicated by the mention so far of novels, poetry, essays, and letters. One other type is necessary to complete the picture — the short story. Stevenson's contribution to this literary form is of the greatest importance. Up to his time the short story had not been developed in England as it had in America. You will notice that "Markheim" is the first short story in the modern manner to appear in this book. It strikes a new note in its emphasis on the psychological approach to character and to the personal problem of right and wrong.

Stevenson is remembered and loved for his personality as well as for his books. The kindliness, the humor, and the sheer pluck of the man in his long fight against disease gave all who knew him a feeling of close friendship with him. Even in remote Samoa, where he spent his last years, he won the friendship of the natives. They named him "Tusitala" (teller of tales) and revered him as a chieftain. On his death, to do him signal honor, sixty natives cut a path through heavy underbrush to the top of Mount Vailima, where they buried him. When Mrs. Stevenson died, she was buried beside him. On the monument are two bronze tablets: Stevenson's bearing the epitaph "Requiem," which he wrote for himself; and hers, the closing stanza of "My Wife," his affectionate tribute to her.

My Wife

Trusty, dusky, vivid, true,
With eyes of gold and bramble-dew,
   Steel-true and blade-straight,
The great Artificer
   Made my mate.   5

Honor, anger, valor, fire;
A love that life could never tire,
   Death quench, or evil stir,
The mighty Master
   Gave to her.   10

Teacher, tender,° comrade, wife,
A fellow farer true through life,
   Heart-whole and soul-free,
The august Father
   Gave to me.   15

11. *tender:* an attendant or nurse.

Requiem

Under the wide and starry sky
Dig the grave and let me lie.
Glad did I live and gladly die,
   And I laid me down with a will.

This be the verse you grave for me: 5
Here he lies where he longed to be;
Home is the sailor, home from sea,
   And the hunter home from the hill.

New York Public Library, Rare Book Room

This woodcut, by Robert Louis Stevenson, appears in one of the several small volumes of his poetry (called the Davos-Platz books) which Stevenson and a friend printed themselves in Switzerland.

El Dorado

Stevenson's buoyant, courageous nature speaks through this essay from his collection *Virginibus Puerisque* (For Girls and Boys). "El Dorado" means "The Golden," a name originally given to a fabulous king in a wealthy city, supposedly in South America. Later the name came to mean any visionary quest.

Iᴛ sᴇᴇᴍs as if a great deal were attainable in a world where there are so many marriages and decisive battles, and where we all, at certain hours of the day, and with great gusto and dispatch, stow a portion of victuals finally and irretrievably into the bag which contains us. And it would seem also, on a hasty view, that the attainment of as much as possible was the one goal of man's contentious life. And yet, as regards the spirit, this is but a semblance. We live in an ascending scale when we live happily, one thing leading to another in an endless series. There is always a new horizon for onward-looking men, and although we dwell on a small planet, immersed in petty business and not enduring beyond a brief period of years, we are so constituted that our hopes are inaccessible, like stars, and the term of hoping is prolonged until the term of life. To be truly happy is a question of how we begin and not of how we end, of what we want and not of what we have. An aspiration is a joy forever, a possession as solid as a landed estate, a fortune which we can never exhaust and which gives us year by year a revenue of pleasurable activity. To have many of these is to be spiritually rich. Life is only a very dull and ill-directed theater unless we have some interests in the piece; and to those who have neither art nor science, the world is a mere arrangement of colors, or a rough footway where they may very well break their shins. It is in virtue of his own desires and curiosities that any man continues to exist with even patience, that he is charmed by the look of things and people, and that he wakens every morning with a renewed appetite for work and pleasure. Desire and curiosity are the two eyes through which he sees the world in the most enchanted colors; it is they that make women beautiful or fossils interesting; and the man may squander his estate and come to beggary, but if he keeps these two amulets he is still rich in the possibilities of pleasure. Suppose he could take one meal so compact and comprehensive that he should never hunger any more; suppose him, at a glance, to take in all the features of the world and allay the desire for knowledge; suppose him to do the like in any province of experience — would not that man be in a poor way for amusement ever after?

One who goes touring on foot with a single volume in his knapsack reads with circumspection, pausing often to reflect, and often laying the book down to contemplate the landscape or the prints in the inn parlor; for he fears to come to an end of his entertainment, and be left companionless on the last stages of his journey. A young fellow recently finished the works of Thomas Carlyle, winding up, if we remember aright, with the ten notebooks upon Frederick the Great. "What!" cried the young fellow, in consternation, "is there no more Carlyle? Am I left to the daily papers?" A more celebrated instance is that of Alexander, who wept bitterly because he had no more worlds to subdue. And when Gibbon had finished the *Decline and Fall*,[1] he had only a few moments of joy; and it was with a "sober melancholy" that he parted from his labors.

Happily we all shoot at the moon with ineffectual arrows; our hopes are set on inaccessible El Dorado; we come to an end of nothing here below. Interests are only plucked up to sow themselves again, like mustard. You would think, when the child was born, there would be an end to trouble; and yet it is only the beginning of fresh anxieties; and when you have seen it through its teething and its education, and at last its marriage, alas! it is only to have new fears, new quivering sensibilities, with every day; and the health of your children's children grows as touching a concern as that of your own. Again, when you have married your wife, you would think you were got upon a hilltop, and might begin to go downward by an easy slope. But you have only ended courting to begin marriage. Falling in love and winning love are often difficult tasks to overbearing and rebellious spirits; but to keep in love is also a business of some importance, to which both man and wife must bring kindness and good will. The true love story commences at the altar, when there lies before the married pair a most beautiful contest of wisdom and generosity, and a lifelong struggle toward an unattainable ideal. Unattainable? Ay, surely unattainable, from the very fact that

[1] *Decline and Fall:* This work on the Roman Empire occupied Gibbon twenty-four years.

they are two instead of one.

"Of making books there is no end," complained the Preacher; [1] and did not perceive how highly he was praising letters as an occupation. There is no end, indeed, to making books or experiments, or to travel, or to gathering wealth. Problem gives rise to problem. We may study forever, and we are never as learned as we would. We have never made a statue worthy of our dreams. And when we have discovered a continent, or crossed a chain of mountains, it is only to find another ocean or another plain upon the further side. In the infinite universe there is room for our swiftest diligence and to spare. It is not like the works of Carlyle, which can be read to an end. Even in a corner of it, in a private park, or in the neighborhood of a single hamlet, the weather and the seasons keep so deftly changing that although we walk there for a lifetime there will be always something new to startle and delight us.

There is only one wish realizable on

[1] *Preacher:* Ecclesiastes 12:12.

the earth; only one thing that can be perfectly attained: Death. And from a variety of circumstances we have no one to tell us whether it be worth attaining.

A strange picture we make on our way to our chimeras,[2] ceaselessly marching, grudging ourselves the time for rest; indefatigable, adventurous pioneers. It is true that we shall never reach the goal; it is even more than probable that there is no such place; and if we lived for centuries and were endowed with the powers of a god, we should find ourselves not much nearer what we wanted at the end. O toiling hands of mortals! O unwearied feet, traveling ye know not whither! Soon, soon, it seems to you, you must come forth on some conspicuous hilltop, and but a little way further, against the setting sun, descry the spires of El Dorado. Little do ye know your own blessedness; for to travel hopefully is a better thing than to arrive, and the true success is to labor.

[2] *chimeras* (kĭ·mē′räz): The word *chimera* originally meant an imaginary monster, but it has come to mean a vain or foolish fancy.

Markheim

In the 1880's, short stories in the modern manner began to appear in England, where writers were following Edgar Allan Poe's definition of the short story as an art form. In a short space, Poe said, a story should make a single, clear-cut impression without deviations and side plots, and it should maintain a dominant mood from the first word to the last. "Markheim" was one of the most successful of early stories in this manner. It was printed along with others, some of them considerably longer, in Stevenson's volume *The Merry Men* (1887), and it still holds its place as one of the great short stories of the nineteenth century. Its emphasis on the psychological aspect of crime gave new treatment to an old subject. In the same volume appeared the longer tale "Dr. Jekyll and Mr. Hyde," which personified the dual nature of man

so dramatically that these names have passed into common speech as representing the good and bad sides of an individual. Twentieth-century writers have since made wide use of the new sources of story interest which Stevenson tapped late in the nineteenth century.

Y ES," said the dealer, "our windfalls are of various kinds. Some customers are ignorant, and then I touch a dividend on my superior knowledge. Some are dishonest," and here he held up the candle, so that the light fell strongly on his visitor, "and in that case," he continued, "I profit by my virtue."

Markheim had but just entered from

the daylight streets, and his eyes had not yet grown familiar with the mingled shine and darkness in the shop. At these pointed words, and before the near presence of the flame, he blinked painfully and looked aside.

The dealer chuckled. "You come to me on Christmas Day," he resumed, "when you know that I am alone in my house, put up my shutters, and make a point of refusing business. Well, you will have to pay for that; you will have to pay for my loss of time, when I should be balancing my books; you will have to pay, besides, for a kind of manner that I remark in you today very strongly. I am the essence of discretion, and ask no awkward questions; but when a customer cannot look me in the eye, he has to pay for it." The dealer once more chuckled; and then, changing to his usual business voice, though still with a note of irony, "You can give, as usual, a clear account of how you came into the possession of the object?" he continued. "Still your uncle's cabinet? A remarkable collector, sir!"

And the little pale, round-shouldered dealer stood almost on tiptoe, looking over the top of his gold spectacles, and nodding his head with every mark of disbelief. Markheim returned his gaze with one of infinite pity, and a touch of horror.

"This time," said he, "you are in error. I have not come to sell, but to buy. I have no curios to dispose of; my uncle's cabinet is bare to the wainscot; even were it still intact, I have done well on the Stock Exchange, and should more likely add to it than otherwise, and my errand today is simplicity itself. I seek a Christmas present for a lady," he continued, waxing more fluent as he struck into the speech he had prepared; "and certainly I owe you every excuse for thus disturbing you upon so small a matter. But the thing was neglected yesterday; I must produce my little compliment at dinner; and, as you very well know, a rich marriage is not a thing to be neglected."

There followed a pause, during which the dealer seemed to weigh this statement incredulously. The ticking of many clocks among the curious lumber of the shop, and the faint rushing of the cabs in a near thoroughfare, filled up the interval of silence.

"Well, sir," said the dealer, "be it so. You are an old customer after all; and if, as you say, you have the chance of a good marriage, far be it from me to be an obstacle. Here is a nice thing for a lady, now," he went on, "this hand glass — fifteenth-century, warranted; comes from a good collection, too; but I reserve the name, in the interests of my customer, who was just like yourself, my dear sir, the nephew and sole heir of a remarkable collector."

The dealer, while he thus ran on in his dry and biting voice, had stooped to take the object from its place; and, as he had done so, a shock had passed through Markheim, a start both of hand and foot, a sudden leap of many tumultuous passions to the face. It passed as swiftly as it came, and left no trace beyond a certain trembling of the hand that now received the glass.

"A glass," he said hoarsely, and then paused, and repeated it more clearly. "A glass? For Christmas? Surely not."

"And why not?" cried the dealer. "Why not a glass?"

Markheim was looking upon him with an indefinable expression. "You ask me why not?" he said. "Why, look here — look in it — look at yourself! Do you like to see it? No! nor I — nor any man."

The little man had jumped back when Markheim had so suddenly confronted him with the mirror; but now, perceiving there was nothing worse on hand, he chuckled. "Your future lady, sir, must be pretty hard-favored," said he.

"I ask you," said Markheim, "for a Christmas present, and you give me this — this damned reminder of years and sins and follies — this hand conscience! Did you mean it? Had you a thought in your mind? Tell me. It will be better for you if you do. Come, tell me about yourself. I hazard a guess now, that you are in secret a very charitable man?"

The dealer looked closely at his companion. It was very odd, Markheim did not appear to be laughing; there was something in his face like an eager sparkle of hope, but nothing of mirth.

"What are you driving at?" the dealer asked.

"Not charitable?" returned the other, gloomily. "Not charitable; not pious; not scrupulous; unloving; unbeloved; a hand to get money, a safe to keep it. Is that all? Dear Lord, man, is that all?"

"I will tell you what it is," began the dealer, with some sharpness, and then broke off again with a chuckle. "But I see this is a love match of yours, and you have been drinking the lady's health."

"Ah!" cried Markheim, with a strange curiosity. "Ah, have you been in love? Tell me about that."

"I!" cried the dealer. "I in love! I never had the time, nor have I the time today for all this nonsense. Will you take the glass?"

"Where is the hurry?" returned Markheim. "It is very pleasant to stand here talking; and life is so short and insecure that I would not hurry away from any pleasure — no, not even from so mild a one as this. We should rather cling, cling to what little we can get, like a man at a cliff's edge. Every second is a cliff, if you think upon it — a cliff a mile high — high enough, if we fall, to dash us out of every feature of humanity. Hence it is best to talk pleasantly. Let us talk of each other; why should we wear this mask? Let us be confidential. Who knows, we might become friends?"

"I have just one word to say to you," said the dealer. "Either make your purchase, or walk out of my shop."

"True, true," said Markheim. "Enough fooling. To business. Show me something else."

The dealer stooped once more, this time to replace the glass upon the shelf,

his thin blond hair falling over his eyes as he did so. Markheim moved a little nearer, with one hand in the pocket of his greatcoat; he drew himself up and filled his lungs; at the same time many different emotions were depicted together on his face — terror, horror, and resolve, fascination, and a physical repulsion; and through a haggard lift of his upper lip, his teeth looked out.

"This, perhaps, may suit," observed the dealer; and then, as he began to rearise, Markheim bounded from behind upon his victim. The long, skewerlike dagger flashed and fell. The dealer struggled like a hen, striking his temple on the shelf, and then tumbled on the floor in a heap.

Time had some score of small voices in that shop, some stately and slow as was becoming to their great age, others garrulous and hurried. All these told out the seconds in an intricate chorus of tickings. Then the passage of a lad's feet, heavily running on the pavement, broke in upon these smaller voices and startled Markheim into the consciousness of his surroundings. He looked about him awfully. The candle stood on the counter, its flame solemnly wagging in a draft; and by that inconsiderable movement, the whole room was filled with noiseless bustle and kept heaving like a sea: the tall shadows nodding, the gross blots of darkness swelling and dwindling as with respiration, the faces of the portraits and the china gods changing and wavering like images in water. The inner door stood ajar, and peered into that leaguer of shadows with a long slit of daylight like a pointing finger.

From these fear-stricken rovings, Markheim's eyes returned to the body of his victim, where it lay both humped and sprawling, incredibly small and strangely meaner than in life. In these poor, miserly clothes, in that ungainly attitude, the dealer lay like so much sawdust. Markheim had feared to see it, and, lo! it was nothing. And yet, as he gazed, this bundle of old clothes and pool of blood began to find eloquent voices. There it must lie; there was none to work the cunning hinges or direct the miracle of locomotion — there it must lie till it was found. Found! ay, and then? Then would this dead fish lift up a cry that would ring over England, and fill the world with the echoes of pursuit. Ay, dead or not, this was still the enemy. "Time was that when the brains were out," [1] he thought; and the first word struck into his mind. Time, now that the deed was accomplished — time, which had closed for the victim, had become instant and momentous for the slayer.

The thought was yet in his mind, when, first one and then another, with every variety of pace and voice — one deep as the bell from a cathedral turret, another ringing on its treble notes the prelude of a waltz — the clocks began to strike the hour of three in the afternoon.

The sudden outbreak of so many tongues in that dumb chamber staggered him. He began to bestir himself, going to and fro with the candle, beleaguered by moving shadows, and startled to the soul by chance reflections. In many rich mirrors, some of home designs, some from Venice or Amsterdam, he saw his face repeated and repeated, as it were an army of spies; his own eyes met and detected him; and the sound of his own steps, lightly as they fell, vexed the surrounding quiet. And still as he continued to fill his pockets, his mind accused him, with a sickening iteration, of the thousand faults of his design. He should have chosen a more quiet hour; he should have prepared an alibi; he should not have used a knife; he should have been more cautious, and only bound and gagged the dealer, and not killed him; he should have been more bold, and killed the servant also; he should have done all things otherwise; poignant regrets, weary, incessant toiling of the mind to change what was unchangeable, to plan what was now useless, to be the

[1] See *Macbeth*, Act III, Scene 4, lines 78–79.

architect of the irrevocable past. Meanwhile, and behind all this activity, brute terrors, like the scurrying of rats in a deserted attic, filled the more remote chambers of his brain with riot; the hand of the constable would fall heavy on his shoulder, and his nerves would jerk like a hooked fish; or he beheld, in galloping defile, the dock, the prison, the gallows, and the black coffin. Terror of the people in the street sat down before his mind like a besieging army. It was impossible, he thought, but that some rumor of the struggle must have reached their ears and set on edge their curiosity; and now, in all the neighboring houses, he divined them sitting motionless and with uplifted ear — solitary people, condemned to spend Christmas dwelling alone on memories of the past, and now startlingly recalled from that tender exercise; happy family parties, struck into silence round the table, the mother still with raised finger: every degree and age and humor, but all, by their own hearths, prying and hearkening and weaving the rope that was to hang him. Sometimes it seemed to him he could not move too softly; the clink of the tall Bohemian goblets rang out loudly like a bell; and alarmed by the bigness of the ticking, he was tempted to stop the clocks. And then, again, with a swift transition of his terrors, the very silence of the place appeared a source of peril, and a thing to strike and freeze the passer-by; and he would step more boldly, and bustle aloud among the contents of the shop, and imitate, with elaborate bravado, the movements of a busy man at ease in his own house.

But he was now so pulled about by different alarms that, while one portion of his mind was still alert and cunning, another trembled on the brink of lunacy. One hallucination in particular took a strong hold on his credulity. The neighbor hearkening with white face beside his window, the passer-by arrested by a horrible surmise on the pavement — these could at worst suspect, they could not know; through the brick walls and shuttered windows only sounds could penetrate. But here, within the house, was he alone? He knew he was; he had watched the servant set forth sweethearting, in her poor best, "out for the day" written in every ribbon and smile. Yes, he was alone, of course; and yet, in the bulk of empty house about him, he could surely hear a stir of delicate footing — he was surely conscious, inexplicably conscious, of some presence. Ay, surely; to every room and corner of the house his imagination followed it; and now it was a faceless thing, and yet had eyes to see with; and again it was a shadow of himself! and yet again behold the image of the dead dealer, reinspired with cunning and hatred.

At times, with a strong effort, he would glance at the open door which still seemed to repel his eyes. The house was tall, the skylight small and dirty, the day blind with fog; and the light that filtered down to the ground story was exceedingly faint, and showed dimly on the threshold of the shop. And yet, in that strip of doubtful brightness, did there not hang wavering a shadow?

Suddenly, from the street outside, a very jovial gentleman began to beat with a staff on the shop door, accompanying his blows with shouts and railleries in which the dealer was continually called upon by name. Markheim, smitten into ice, glanced at the dead man. But no! he lay quiet still; he was fled away far beyond earshot of these blows and shoutings; he was sunk beneath seas of silence; and his name, which would once have caught his notice above the howling of a storm, had become an empty sound. And presently the jovial gentleman desisted from his knocking and departed.

Here was a broad hint to hurry what remained to be done, to get forth from this accusing neighborhood, to plunge into a bath of London multitudes, and to reach, on the other side of day, that haven of safety and apparent innocence — his bed. One visitor had come; at any moment another might follow and be more obstinate. To have done the deed, and yet not to reap the profit, would be too abhorrent a failure. The money, that was now Markheim's concern; and as a means to that, the keys.

He glanced over his shoulder at the open door, where the shadow was still lingering and shivering; and with no conscious repugnance of the mind, yet with a tremor of the belly, he drew near the body of his victim. The human character had quite departed. Like a suit half-stuffed with bran, the limbs lay scattered, the trunk doubled, on the floor; and yet the thing repelled him. Although so dingy and inconsiderable to the eye, he feared it might have more significance to the touch. He took the body by the shoulders, and turned it on its back. It was strangely light and supple, and the limbs, as if they had been broken, fell into the oddest postures. The face was robbed of all expression; but it was as pale as wax, and shockingly smeared with blood about one temple. That was, for Markheim, the one displeasing circumstance. It carried him back, upon the instant, to a certain fair day in a fishers' village: a gray day, a piping wind, a crowd upon the street, the blare of brasses, the booming of drums, the nasal voice of a ballad singer; and a boy going to and fro, buried over head in the crowd and divided between interest and fear, until, coming out upon the chief place of concourse, he beheld a booth and a great screen with pictures, dismally designed, garishly colored: Brownrigg with her apprentice; the Mannings with their murdered guest; Weare in the death grip of Thurtell;[1] and a score besides of famous crimes. The thing was as clear as an illusion; he was once again that little boy; he was looking once

[1] *Brownrigg, Mannings, Thurtell:* Elizabeth Brownrigg was a murderess of the eighteenth century; the Mannings and Thurtell were murderers of a later date. The pictures were probably to advertise waxworks of notorious criminals, which were formerly a popular form of side show at country fairs.

again, and with the same sense of physical revolt, at these vile pictures; he was still stunned by the thumping of the drums. A bar of that day's music returned upon his memory; and at that, for the first time, a qualm came over him, a breath of nausea, a sudden weakness of the joints, which he must instantly resist and conquer.

He judged it more prudent to confront than to flee from these considerations; looking the more hardily in the dead face, bending his mind to realize the nature and greatness of his crime. So little a while ago that face had moved with every change of sentiment, that pale mouth had spoken, that body had been all on fire with governable energies; and now, and by his act, that piece of life had been arrested, as the horologist, with interjected finger, arrests the beating of the clock. So he reasoned in vain; he could rise to no more remorseful consciousness; the same heart which had shuddered before the painted effigies of crime, looked on its reality unmoved. At best, he felt a gleam of pity for one who had been endowed in vain with all those faculties that can make the world a garden of enchantment, one who had never lived and who was now dead. But of penitence, no, not a tremor.

With that, shaking himself clear of these considerations, he found the keys and advanced toward the open door of the shop. Outside, it had begun to rain smartly; and the sound of the shower upon the roof had banished silence. Like some dripping cavern, the chambers of the house were haunted by an incessant echoing, which filled the ear and mingled with the ticking of the clocks. And, as Markheim approached the door, he seemed to hear, in answer to his own cautious tread, the steps of another foot withdrawing up the stair. The shadow still palpitated loosely on the threshold. He threw a ton's weight of resolve upon his muscles, and drew back the door.

The faint, foggy daylight glimmered dimly on the bare floor and stairs; on the bright suit of armor posted, halbert in hand, upon the landing; and on the dark wood carvings and framed pictures that hung against the yellow panels of the wainscot. So loud was the beating of the rain through all the house that, in Markheim's ears, it began to be distinguished into many different sounds. Footsteps and sighs, the tread of regiments marching in the distance, the chink of money in the counting, and the creaking of doors held stealthily ajar, appeared to mingle with the patter of the drops upon the cupola and the gushing of the water in the pipes. The sense that he was not alone grew upon him to the verge of madness. On every side he was haunted and begirt by presences. He heard them moving in the upper chambers; from the shop, he heard the dead man getting to his legs; and as he began with a great effort to mount the stairs, feet fled quietly before him and followed stealthily behind. If he were but deaf, he thought, how tranquilly he would possess his soul! And then again, and hearkening with ever fresh attention, he blessed himself for that unresting sense which held the outposts and stood a trusty sentinel upon his life. His head turned continually on his neck; his eyes, which seemed starting from their orbits, scouted on every side, and on every side were half rewarded as with the tail of something nameless vanishing. The four and twenty steps to the first floor were four and twenty agonies.

On that first story the doors stood ajar, three of them like three ambushes, shaking his nerves like the throats of cannon. He could never again, he felt, be sufficiently immured and fortified from men's observing eyes; he longed to be home, girt in by walls, buried among bedclothes, and invisible to all but God. And at that thought he wondered a little, recollecting tales of other murderers and the fear they were said to entertain of heavenly avengers. It was not so, at least, with him. He feared the laws of nature, lest, in their callous and immutable procedure, they should preserve some damning evidence of his crime. He feared tenfold more, with a slavish, superstitious terror, some scission in the continuity of man's experience, some willful illegality of nature. He played a game of skill, depending on the rules, calculating consequence from cause; and what if nature, as the defeated tyrant overthrew the chessboard, should break the mold of their succession? The like had befallen Napoleon (so writers said) when the winter changed the time of its appearance. The like might befall Markheim: the solid walls might become transparent and reveal his doings like those of bees in a glass hive; the stout planks might yield under his foot like quicksands and detain him in their clutch; ay, and there were soberer accidents that might destroy him: if, for instance, the house should fall and imprison him beside the body of his victim; or the house next door should fly on fire, and the firemen invade him from all sides. These things he feared; and, in a sense, these things might be called the hands of God reached forth against sin. But about God himself he was at ease; his act was doubtless exceptional, but so were his excuses, which God knew; it was there, and not among men, that he felt sure of justice.

When he got safe into the drawing room, and shut the door behind him, he was aware of a respite from alarms. The room was quite dismantled, uncarpeted besides, and strewn with packing cases and incongruous furniture; several great pier glasses, in which he beheld himself at various angles, like an actor on a stage; many pictures, framed and unframed, standing, with their faces to the wall; a fine Sheraton [1] sideboard, a cabinet of marquetry, and a great old bed, with tapestry hangings. The windows opened to the floor; but by great good fortune the lower part of the shutters had been closed, and this concealed him

from the neighbors. Here, then, Markheim drew in a packing case before the cabinet, and began to search among the keys. It was a long business, for there were many; and it was irksome, besides; for, after all, there might be nothing in the cabinet, and time was on the wing. But the closeness of the occupation sobered him. With the tail of his eye he saw the door — even glanced at it from time to time directly, like a besieged commander pleased to verify the good estate of his defenses. But in truth he was at peace. The rain falling in the street sounded natural and pleasant. Presently, on the other side, the notes of a piano were wakened to the music of a hymn, and the voices of many children took up the air and words. How stately, how comfortable was the melody! How fresh the youthful voices! Markheim gave ear to it smilingly, as he sorted out the keys; and his mind was thronged with answerable ideas and images; churchgoing children and the pealing of the high organ; children afield, bathers by the brookside, ramblers on the brambly common, kitefliers in the windy and cloud-navigated sky; and then, at another cadence of the hymn, back again to church and the somnolence of summer Sundays, and the high, genteel voice of the parson (which he smiled a little to recall), and the painted Jacobean [2] tombs, and the dim lettering of the Ten Commandments in the chancel.

And as he sat thus, at once busy and absent, he was startled to his feet. A flash of ice, a flash of fire, a bursting gush of blood, went over him, and then he stood transfixed and thrilling. A step mounted the stair slowly and steadily, and presently a hand was laid upon the knob, and the lock clicked, and the door opened. Fear held Markheim in a vise. What to expect he knew not, whether the dead man walking, or the official ministers of human justice, or some chance witness blindly stumbling in to consign

[1] *Sheraton:* Thomas Sheraton (1751–1806), a famous English furniture maker.

[2] *Jacobean:* from the seventeenth-century reign of the Jameses.

him to the gallows. But when a face was thrust into the aperture, glanced round the room, looked at him, nodded and smiled as if in friendly recognition, and then withdrew again, and the door closed behind it, his fear broke loose from his control in a hoarse cry. At the sound of this the visitant returned.

"Did you call me?" he asked pleasantly, and with that he entered the room and closed the door behind him.

Markheim stood and gazed at him with all his eyes. Perhaps there was a film upon his sight, but the outlines of the newcomer seemed to change and waver like those of the idols in the wavering candlelight of the shop; and at times he thought he knew him; and at times he thought he bore a likeness to himself; and always, like a lump of living terror, there lay in his bosom the conviction that this thing was not of the earth and not of God.

And yet the creature had a strange air of the commonplace, as he stood looking on Markheim with a smile; and when he added: "You are looking for the money, I believe?" it was in the tones of everyday politeness.

Markheim made no answer.

"I should warn you," resumed the other, "that the maid has left her sweetheart earlier than usual and will soon be here. If Mr. Markheim be found in this house I need not describe to him the consequences."

"You know me?" cried the murderer.

The visitor smiled. "You have long been a favorite of mine," he said; "and I have long observed and often sought to help you."

"What are you?" cried Markheim: "the devil?"

"What I may be," returned the other, "cannot affect the service I propose to render you."

"It can," cried Markheim; "it does! Be helped by you? No, never; not by

you! You do not know me yet; thank God, you do not know me!"

"I know you," replied the visitant, with a sort of kind severity or rather firmness. "I know you to the soul."

"Know me!" cried Markheim. "Who can do so? My life is but a travesty and slander on myself. I have lived to belie my nature. All men do; all men are better than this disguise that grows about and stifles them. You see each dragged away by life, like one whom bravos have seized and muffled in a cloak. If they had their own control — if you could see their faces, they would be altogether different, they would shine out for heroes and saints! I am worse than most; my self is more overlaid; my excuse is known to me and God. But, had I the time, I could disclose myself."

"To me?" inquired the visitant.

"To you before all," returned the murderer. "I supposed you were intelligent. I thought — since you exist — you would prove a reader of the heart. And yet you would propose to judge me by my acts! Think of it; my acts! I was born and I have lived in a land of giants; giants have dragged me by the wrists since I was born out of my mother — the giants of circumstance. And you would judge me by my acts! But can you not look within? Can you not understand that evil is hateful to me? Can you not see within me the clear writing of conscience, never blurred by any willful sophistry although too often disregarded? Can you not read me for a thing that surely must be common as humanity — the unwilling sinner?"

"All this is very feelingly expressed," was the reply, "but it regards me not. These points of consistency are beyond my province, and I care not in the least by what compulsion you may have been dragged away, so as you are but carried in the right direction. But time flies; the servant delays, looking in the faces of

In this drawing by Isadore Seltzer, Markheim is confronted by his disquieting visitor. ▶

the crowd and at the pictures on the hoardings, but still she keeps moving nearer; and remember, it is as if the gallows itself were striding toward you through the Christmas streets! Shall I help you — I, who know all? Shall I tell you where to find the money?"

"For what price?" asked Markheim.

"I offer you the service for a Christmas gift," returned the other.

Markheim could not refrain from smiling with a kind of bitter triumph. "No," said he, "I will take nothing at your hands; if I were dying of thirst, and it was your hand that put the pitcher to my lips, I should find the courage to refuse. I may be credulous, but I will do nothing to commit myself to evil."

"I have no objection to a deathbed repentance," observed the visitant.

"Because you disbelieve their efficacy!" Markheim cried.

"I do not say so," returned the other; "but I look on these things from a different side, and when the life is done my interest falls. The man has lived to serve me, to spread black looks under color of religion, or to sow tares in the wheat field, as you do, in a course of weak compliance with desire. Now that he draws so near to his deliverance, he can add but one act of service — to repent, to die smiling, and thus to build up in confidence and hope the more timorous of my surviving followers. I am not so hard a master. Try me. Accept my help. Please yourself in life as you have done hitherto; please yourself more amply, spread your elbows at the board; and when the night begins to fall and the curtains to be drawn, I tell you, for your greater comfort, that you will find it even easy to compound your quarrel with your conscience, and to make a truckling peace with God. I came but now from such a deathbed, and the room was full of sincere mourners, listening to the man's last words; and when I looked into that face, which had been set as a flint against mercy, I found it smiling with hope."

"And do you, then, suppose me such a creature?" asked Markheim. "Do you think I have no more generous aspirations than to sin, and sin, and sin, and, at last, sneak into heaven? My heart rises at the thought. Is this, then, your experience of mankind? or is it because you find me with red hands that you presume such baseness? and is this crime of murder indeed so impious as to dry up the very springs of good?"

"Murder is to me no special category," replied the other. "All sins are murder, even as all life is war. I behold your race, like starving mariners on a raft, plucking crusts out of the hands of famine and feeding on each other's lives. I follow sins beyond the moment of their acting; I find in all that the last consequence is death; and to my eyes, the pretty maid who thwarts her mother with such taking graces on a question of a ball, drips no less visibly with human gore than such a murderer as yourself. Do I say that I follow sins? I follow virtues also; they differ not by the thickness of a nail, they are both scythes for the reaping angel of Death. Evil, for which I live, consists not in action but in character. The bad man is dear to me; not the bad act, whose fruits, if we could follow them far enough down the hurtling cataract of the ages, might yet be found more blessed than those of the rarest virtues. And it is not because you have killed a dealer, but because you are Markheim, that I offered to forward your escape."

"I will lay my heart open to you," answered Markheim. "This crime on which you find me is my last. On my way to it I have learned many lessons; itself is a lesson, a momentous lesson. Hitherto I have been driven with revolt to what I would not; I was a bond-slave to poverty, driven and scourged. There are robust virtues that can stand in these temptations; mine was not so: I had a thirst of pleasure. But today, and out of this deed, I pluck both warning and riches — both the power and a fresh resolve to be myself. I become in all things a free actor in the world; I begin to see myself all changed, these hands the agents of good, this heart at peace. Something comes over me out of the past; something of what I have dreamed on Sabbath evenings to the sound of the church organ, of what I forecast when I shed tears over noble books, or talked, an innocent child, with my mother. There lies my life; I have wandered a few years, but now I see once more my city of destination."

"You are to use this money on the Stock Exchange, I think?" remarked the visitor; "and there, if I mistake not, you have already lost some thousands?"

"Ah," said Markheim, "but this time I have a sure thing."

"This time, again you will lose," replied the visitor, quietly.

"Ah, but I keep back the half!" cried Markheim.

"That also you will lose," said the other.

The sweat started upon Markheim's brow. "Well, then, what matter?" he exclaimed. "Say it be lost, say I am plunged again in poverty, shall one part of me, and that the worse, continue until the end to override the better? Evil and good run strong in me, haling me both ways. I do not love the one thing, I love all. I can conceive great deeds, renunciations, martyrdoms; and though I be fallen to such a crime as murder, pity is no stranger to my thoughts. I pity the poor; who knows their trials better than myself? I pity and help them; I prize love, I love honest laughter; there is no good thing nor true thing on earth but I love it from my heart. And are my vices only to direct my life, and my virtues to lie without effect, like some passive lumber of the mind? Not so; good, also, is a spring of acts."

But the visitant raised his finger. "For six and thirty years that you have been in this world," said he, "through many changes of fortune and varieties of humor, I have watched you steadily fall. Fifteen years ago you would have started at a theft. Three years back you would have blenched at the name of murder. Is there any crime, is there any cruelty or meanness, from which you still recoil? — five years from now I shall detect you in the fact! Downward, downward lies your way; nor can anything but death avail to stop you."

"It is true," Markheim said huskily, "I have in some degree complied with evil. But it is so with all: the very saints, in the mere exercise of living, grow less dainty, and take on the tone of their surroundings."

"I will propound to you one simple question," said the other; "and as you answer, I shall read to you your moral horoscope. You have grown in many things more lax; possibly you do right to be so; and at any account, it is the same with all men. But granting that, are you in any one particular, however trifling, more difficult to please with your own conduct, or do you go in all things with a looser rein?"

"In any one?" repeated Markheim, with an anguish of consideration. "No," he added, with despair, "in none! I have gone down in all."

"Then," said the visitor, "content yourself with what you are, for you will never change; and the words of your part on this stage are irrevocably written down."

Markheim stood for a long while silent, and indeed it was the visitor who first broke the silence. "That being so," he said, "shall I show you the money?"

"And grace?" cried Markheim.

"Have you not tried it?" returned the other. "Two or three years ago, did I not see you on the platform of revival meetings, and was not your voice the loudest in the hymn?"

"It is true," said Markheim; "and I see clearly what remains for me by way of duty. I thank you for these lessons from my soul; my eyes are opened, and I behold myself at last for what I am."

At this moment, the sharp note of the doorbell rang through the house; and the visitant, as though this were some concerted signal for which he had been waiting, changed at once in his demeanor.

"The maid!" he cried. "She has returned, as I forewarned you, and there is now before you one more difficult passage. Her master, you must say, is ill; you must let her in, with an assured but rather serious countenance — no smiles, no overacting, and I promise you success! Once the girl within, and the door closed, the same dexterity that has already rid you of the dealer will relieve you of this last danger in your path. Thenceforward you have the whole evening — the whole night, if needful — to ransack the treasures of the house and to make good your safety. This is help that comes to you with the mask of danger. Up!" he cried: "up, friend; your life hangs trembling in the scales: up, and act!"

Markheim steadily regarded his counselor. "If I be condemned to evil acts," he said, "there is still one door of freedom open — I can cease from action. If my life be an ill thing, I can lay it down. Though I be, as you say truly, at the beck of every small temptation, I can yet, by one decisive gesture, place myself beyond the reach of all. My love of good is damned to barrenness; it may, and let it be! But I have still my hatred of evil; and from that, to your galling disappointment, you shall see that I can draw both energy and courage."

The features of the visitor began to undergo a wonderful and lovely change: they brightened and softened with a tender triumph; and, even as they brightened, faded and dislimned. But Markheim did not pause to watch or understand the transformation. He opened the door and went downstairs very slowly, thinking to himself. His past went soberly before him; he beheld it as it was, ugly and strenuous like a dream, random as chance medley — a scene of defeat. Life, as he thus reviewed it, tempted him no longer; but on the farther side he perceived a quiet haven for his bark.

He paused in the passage, and looked into the shop, where the candle still burned by the dead body. It was strangely silent. Thoughts of the dealer swarmed into his mind, as he stood gazing. And then the bell once more broke out into impatient clamor.

He confronted the maid upon the threshold with something like a smile.

"You had better go for the police," said he: "I have killed your master."

POET AND TELLER OF TALES

POEMS

1. Compare Stevenson's poem to his wife with Wordsworth's "She Was a Phantom of Delight" (page 385). Does one seem to you a finer tribute than the other?

2. How did Stevenson achieve a happy outlook on life in spite of his handicaps?

EL DORADO

1. How does the title of the essay relate to its theme? Where is the main idea stated? What illustrations does Stevenson use to prove his point?

2. From your own experience give examples that cause you to agree or disagree with Stevenson's theory of the real satisfactions in life.

FOLLOWING THE PLOT

1. What details does the author use early in *Markheim* to build up the two characters? Why is a secondhand shop a particularly appropriate place to create the atmosphere desired in this story? Which element — setting, character, action — has Stevenson made most important?

2. Where and how is the idea of conscience first introduced? At what point does the working of conscience become the main part of the story?

3. Discuss the various thoughts that pass through Markheim's mind while he is alone in the shop. What kind of man do they show him to be?

4. How do you explain the presence of the stranger? What purpose does he serve in the story?

5. Notice carefully the conversation between Markheim and the stranger. The stranger submits him to a series of tempta-

tions to further evil. What are they? How does Markheim react toward each? Why does the stranger's face undergo a change at the very end? In what ways is Markheim's final act a solution to the problem?

6. Compare this story with Poe's "The Tell-Tale Heart," in which a murderer also gives himself up to the police. What noticeable differences are there in the situations in the two stories?

GERARD MANLEY HOPKINS

1844–1889

Educated from childhood for a career in the English church, Hopkins, a brilliant student, at the age of twenty-two was converted to Roman Catholicism and was received into that church by Cardinal Newman. Two years later he became a Jesuit priest and in this capacity served successively as preacher and teacher. In 1884 he was appointed to the chair of Greek at the Royal University of Ireland in Dublin, where he remained until his death.

Hopkins' poetry was long hidden from the world; Robert Bridges, a close friend of Hopkins at Oxford and later poet laureate of England, was responsible for its first publication in 1918, twenty-nine years after the poet's death.

Among the Victorians, Hopkins seems much like a modern poet. His sparkling images, his condensed thought, his skillful innovations in rhythm are the marks of a fresh and original talent. Hopkins' highly individual way of expression reveals a mind that darts rapidly from image to image, sometimes leaving the reader to ponder, more slowly, on the idea behind the words. His influence on twentieth-century poets has been considerable.

Pied Beauty

Glory be to God for dappled things —
    For skies of couple-color as a brinded cow;
      For rose-moles all in stipple upon trout that swim;
Fresh-firecoal chestnut-falls; finches' wings;
    Landscape plotted and pieced — fold, fallow, and plow;   5
    And all trades, their gear and tackle and trim.

All things counter, original, spare, strange;
    Whatever is fickle, freckled (who knows how?)
      With swift, slow; sweet, sour; adazzle, dim;
He fathers-forth whose beauty is past change: 10
    Praise him.

"Pied Beauty" from *Poems of Gerard Manley Hopkins.* Third edition. Edited by W. H. Gardner. Copyright 1948 by Oxford University Press, Inc. Reprinted by permission.

Heaven-Haven

A nun takes the veil

I have desired to go
Where springs not fail,
To fields where flies no sharp and sided hail
And a few lilies blow.

And I have asked to be   5
Where no storms come,
Where the green swell is in the havens dumb,
And out of the swing of the sea.

"Heaven-Haven" from *Poems of Gerard Manley Hopkins*. Third Edition. Edited by W. H. Gardner. Copyright 1948 by Oxford University Press, Inc. Reprinted by permission.

IMAGERY AND IDEA

1. What does the title "Pied Beauty" mean? What are the "dappled things" that attract the poet? Describe the mood of this poem. Does it seem to you an appropriate expression of deep religious feeling?

2. Hopkins compares the active outside world with the sequestered world of a nunnery in "Heaven-Haven." Pick out the several ways in which he makes the comparison. From what realm do his images come?

3. Both of these poems illustrate Hopkins' original style of expression. Notice the sharply breaking sounds, and the unusual position of words, as in "Where the green swell is in the havens dumb," and "For rose-moles all in stipple upon trout that swim." What is the effect of this style? Point out rarely used or archaic words and examples of alliterative language.

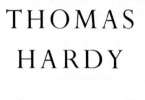

THOMAS HARDY

1840–1928

National Portrait Gallery

Though he was born before the mid-point of the nineteenth century, Thomas Hardy seems almost a modern writer. More than any other author, he is a link between the Victorian era and modern times. Hardy's literary career falls into two distinct periods — that as fiction writer and that as poet — divided almost at the turn of the century. In the last decades of the nineteenth century he wrote many notable novels, including *The Return of the Native* and *Far from the Madding Crowd*. At that time he and George Meredith were undoubtedly the greatest living English novelists.

From 1904 to 1908 Hardy published various parts of a long dramatic poem, *The Dynasts*. Though it was written apparently to show England's part in the Napoleonic wars, it is actually a great study of man's destiny and represents the thinking of the modern world as Milton's *Paradise Lost* represents that of the seventeenth century. With the publication of this work, Hardy's reputation as a poet was at once established.

The setting of both Hardy's fiction and poetry is "Wessex," a name he used to characterize the six southwest counties of England, including his home county of Dorset. Here he worked as a young church architect before turning to writing, and here he spent his honored last years. Hardy's death was an occasion for national mourning. His ashes were buried in Westminster Abbey, but in accordance with his last wish his heart was returned to his own parish churchyard in the little Dorsetshire village of Stinsford.

In his short stories, as in his novels and poems, Hardy is repeatedly concerned with the circumstances that often defeat people and with the part that chance, or fate, plays in their lives. The setting of "The Three Strangers" is the remote and wind-swept downs of Wessex. Hardy's rich use of local color acquaints us with a rural festivity — with the mead-drinking, the singing and dancing, the Wessex dialect, and the homely philosophy of the people.

The Three Strangers

AMONG the few features of agricultural England which retain an appearance but little modified by the lapse of centuries may be reckoned the high, grassy and furzy downs, coombs,[1] or ewe-leases, as they are indifferently called, that fill a large area of certain counties in the south and southwest. If any mark of human occupation is met with hereon, it usually takes the form of the solitary cottage of some shepherd.

Fifty years ago such a lonely cottage stood on such a down, and may possibly be standing there now. In spite of its loneliness, however, the spot, by actual measurement, was not more than five miles from a county-town. Yet that affected it little. Five miles of irregular upland, during the long inimical seasons, with their sleets, snows, rains, and mists, afford withdrawing space enough to isolate a Timon[2] or a Nebuchadnezzar;[3]

much less, in fair weather, to please that less repellent tribe, the poets, philosophers, artists, and others who "conceive and meditate of pleasant things."

Some old earthen camp or barrow,[4] some clump of trees, at least some starved fragment of ancient hedge is usually taken advantage of in the erection of these forlorn dwellings. But, in the present case, such a kind of shelter has been disregarded. Higher Crowstairs, as the house was called, stood quite detached and undefended. The only reason for its precise situation seemed to be the crossing of two footpaths at right angles hard by, which may have crossed there and thus for a good five hundred years. Hence the house was exposed to the elements on all sides. But, though the wind up here blew unmistakably when it did blow, and the rain hit hard whenever it fell, the various weathers of the winter season were not quite so formidable on the coomb as they were imagined to be by dwellers on low ground. The raw

[1] *coombs* (ko͞oms): hollows in the side of a hill or mountain. [2] *Timon* (tī'mŏn): a Greek of the fifth century who hated people and preferred to live in a cave. [3] *Nebuchadnezzar* (nĕb'ū·kăd·nĕz'ēr): a Babylonian king who went to live alone in the fields when he became insane.

[4] *barrow:* a hill or mound, often an ancient burial ground.

"The Three Strangers" from *Wessex Tales* by Thomas Hardy. Reprinted by permission of the Trustees of the Hardy Estate, St. Martin's Press, Inc., Macmillan Company of Canada, Ltd., and Macmillan and Company Limited, London, England.

rimes [1] were not so pernicious as in the hollows, and the frosts were scarcely so severe. When the shepherd and his family who tenanted the house were pitied for their sufferings from the exposure, they said that upon the whole they were less inconvenienced by "wuzzes and flames" (hoarses and phlegms) than when they had lived by the stream of a snug neighboring valley.

The night of March 28, 182–, was precisely one of the nights that were wont to call forth these expressions of commiseration. The level rainstorm smote walls, slopes, and hedges like the clothyard shafts of Senlac [2] and Crecy.[3] Such sheep and outdoor animals as had no shelter stood with their buttocks to the winds; while the tails of little birds trying to roost on some scraggy thorn were blown inside-out like umbrellas. The gable-end of the cottage was stained with wet, and the eavesdroppings flapped against the wall. Yet never was commiseration for the shepherd more misplaced. For that cheerful rustic was entertaining a large party in glorification of the christening of his second girl.

The guests had arrived before the rain began to fall, and they were all now assembled in the chief or living room of the dwelling. A glance into the apartment at eight o'clock on this eventful evening would have resulted in the opinion that it was as cosy and comfortable a nook as could be wished for in boisterous weather. The calling of its inhabitant was proclaimed by a number of highly polished sheep crooks without stems that were hung ornamentally over the fireplace, the curl of each shining crook varying from the antiquated type engraved in the patriarchal pictures of old

family Bibles to the most approved fashion of the last local sheep fair. The room was lighted by half a dozen candles having wicks only a trifle smaller than the grease which enveloped them, in candlesticks that were never used but at highdays, holy-days, and family feasts. The lights were scattered about the room, two of them standing on the chimney piece. This position of candles was in itself significant. Candles on the chimney piece always meant a party.

On the hearth, in front of a backbrand to give substance, blazed a fire of thorns, that crackled "like the laughter of the fool."

Nineteen persons were gathered here. Of these, five women, wearing gowns of various bright hues, sat in chairs along the wall; girls shy and not shy filled the window-bench; four men, including Charley Jake, the hedge-carpenter, Elijah New, the parish-clerk, and John Pitcher, a neighboring dairyman, the shepherd's father-in-law, lolled in the settle; a young man and maid, who were blushing over tentative *pour-parlers* [4] on a life-companionship, sat beneath the corner-cupboard; and an elderly engaged man of fifty or upward moved restlessly about from spots where his betrothed was not to the spot where she was. Enjoyment was pretty general, and so much the more prevailed in being unhampered by conventional restrictions. Absolute confidence in each other's good opinion begat perfect ease, while the finishing stroke of manner, amounting to a truly princely serenity, was lent to the majority by the absence of any expression or trait denoting that they wished to get on in the world, enlarge their minds, or do any eclipsing thing whatever — which nowadays so generally nips the bloom and bonhomie [5] of all except the two extremes of the social scale.

Shepherd Fennel had married well, his wife being a dairyman's daughter

---

[1] *rimes* (rīms): white frost. [2] *Senlac:* hill near Hastings in southeastern England where the Normans defeated the Saxons in 1066. [3] *Crecy* (krā'sē'): town in northern France where English archers defeated the French in 1346 during the Hundred Years War between France and England. The *clothyard shafts* referred to are the yard-long arrows of the English archers.

[4] *pour-parlers* (poōr'pår'lāz'): informal discussions (*French*). [5] *bonhomie* (bôn'ô'·mē'): good nature (*French*).

from a vale at a distance, who brought fifty guineas in her pocket — and kept them there, till they should be required for ministering to the needs of a coming family. This frugal woman had been somewhat exercised as to the character that should be given to the gathering. A sit-still party had its advantages; but an undisturbed position of ease in chairs and settles was apt to lead on the men to such an unconscious deal of toping that they would sometimes fairly drink the house dry. A dancing-party was the alternative; but this, while avoiding the foregoing objection on the score of good drink, had a counterbalancing disadvantage in the matter of good victuals, the ravenous appetites engendered by the exercise causing immense havoc in the buttery. Shepherdess Fennell fell back upon the intermediate plan of mingling short dances with short periods of talk and singing, so as to hinder any ungovernable rage in either. But this scheme was entirely confined to her own gentle mind: the shepherd himself was in the mood to exhibit the most reckless phases of hospitality.

The fiddler was a boy of those parts, about twelve years of age, who had a wonderful dexterity in jigs and reels, though his fingers were so small and short as to necessitate a constant shifting for the high notes, from which he scrambled back to the first position with sounds not of unmixed purity of tone. At seven the shrill tweedle-dee of this youngster had begun, accompanied by a booming ground-bass from Elijah New, the parish-clerk, who had thoughtfully brought with him his favorite musical instrument, the serpent.[1] Dancing was instantaneous, Mrs. Fennel privately enjoining the players on no account to let the dance exceed the length of a quarter of an hour.

But Elijah and the boy, in the excitement of their position, quite forgot the injunction. Moreover, Oliver Giles, a

man of seventeen, one of the dancers, who was enamored of his partner, a fair girl of thirty-three rolling years, had recklessly handed a new crown-piece to the musicians, as a bribe to keep going as long as they had muscle and wind. Mrs. Fennel, seeing the steam begin to generate on the countenances of her guests, crossed over and touched the fiddler's elbow and put her hand on the serpent's mouth. But they took no notice, and fearing she might lose her character of genial hostess if she were to interfere too markedly, she retired and sat down helpless. And so the dance whizzed on with cumulative fury, the performers moving in their planet-like courses, direct and retrograde, from apogee to perigee,[2] till the hand of the well-kicked clock at the bottom of the room had traveled over the circumference of an hour.

While these cheerful events were in course of enactment within Fennel's pastoral dwelling, an incident having considerable bearing on the party had occurred in the gloomy night without. Mrs. Fennel's concern about the growing fierceness of the dance corresponded in point of time with the ascent of a human figure to the solitary hill of Higher Crowstairs from the direction of the distant town. This personage strode on through the rain without a pause, following the little-worn path which, further on in its course, skirted the shepherd's cottage.

It was nearly the time of full moon, and on this account, though the sky was lined with a uniform sheet of dripping cloud, ordinary objects out of doors were readily visible. The sad, wan light revealed the lonely pedestrian to be a man of supple frame; his gait suggested that he had somewhat passed the period of perfect and instinctive agility, though not so far as to be otherwise than rapid of motion when occasion required. At a

[1] *serpent:* an obsolete bass wind instrument of the trumpet type.

[2] *apogee and perigee:* the points at which the moon is, respectively, farthest and nearest to the earth.

rough guess, he might have been about forty years of age. He appeared tall, but a recruiting sergeant, or other person accustomed to the judging of men's heights by the eye, would have discerned that this was chiefly owing to his gauntness, and that he was not more than five-feet-eight or nine.

Notwithstanding the regularity of his tread, there was caution in it, as in that of one who mentally feels his way; and despite the fact that it was not a black coat nor a dark garment of any sort that he wore, there was something about him which suggested that he naturally belonged to the black-coated tribes [1] of men. His clothes were of fustian,[2] and his boots hobnailed, yet in his progress he showed not the mud-accustomed bearing of hobnailed and fustianed peasantry.

By the time that he had arrived abreast of the shepherd's premises the rain came down, or rather came along, with yet more determined violence. The outskirts of the little settlement partially broke the force of wind and rain, and this induced him to stand still. The most salient of the shepherd's domestic erections was an empty sty at the forward corner of his hedgeless garden, for in these latitudes the principle of masking the homelier features of your establishment by a conventional frontage was unknown. The traveler's eye was attracted to this small building by the pallid shine of the wet slates that covered it. He turned aside, and, finding it empty, stood under the pent-roof for shelter.

While he stood, the boom of the serpent within the adjacent house, and the lesser strains of the fiddler, reached the spot as an accompaniment to the surging hiss of the flying rain on the sod, its louder beating on the cabbage leaves of the garden, on the eight or ten beehives just discernible by the path, and its dripping from the eaves into a row of buckets and pans that had been placed under

[1] *black-coated tribe:* middle class. [2] *fustian:* a type of coarse cotton.

the walls of the cottage. For at Higher Crowstairs, as at all such elevated domiciles, the grand difficulty of housekeeping was an insufficiency of water; and a casual rainfall was utilized by turning out, as catchers, every utensil that the house contained. Some queer stories might be told of the contrivances for economy in suds and dishwaters that are absolutely necessitated in upland habitations during the droughts of summer. But at this season there were no such exigencies; a mere acceptance of what the skies bestowed was sufficient for an abundant store.

At last the notes of the serpent ceased and the house was silent. This cessation of activity aroused the solitary pedestrian from the reverie into which he had elapsed, and, emerging from the shed, with an apparently new intention, he walked up the path to the house door. Arrived here, his first act was to kneel down on a large stone beside the row of vessels, and to drink a copious draught from one of them. Having quenched his thirst, he rose and lifted his hand to knock, but paused with his eye upon the panel. Since the dark surface of the wood revealed absolutely nothing, it was evident that he must be mentally looking through the door, as if he wished to measure thereby all the possibilities that a house of this sort might include, and how they might bear upon the question of his entry.

In his indecision he turned and surveyed the scene around. Not a soul was anywhere visible. The garden path stretched downward from his feet, gleaming like the track of a snail; the roof of the little well (mostly dry), the well-cover, the top rail of the garden gate, were varnished with the same dull liquid glaze; while, far away in the vale, a faint whiteness of more than usual extent showed that the rivers were high in the meads. Beyond all this winked a few bleared lamplights through the beating drops — lights that denoted the situation of the county-town from which he had appeared to come. The absence of all notes of life in that direction seemed to clinch his intentions, and he knocked at the door.

Within, a desultory chat had taken the place of movement and musical sound. The hedge-carpenter was suggesting a song to the company, which nobody just then was inclined to undertake, so that the knock afforded a not unwelcome diversion.

"Walk in!" said the shepherd, promptly.

The latch clicked upward, and out of the night our pedestrian appeared upon the door mat. The shepherd arose, snuffed two of the nearest candles, and turned to look at him.

Their light disclosed that the stranger was dark in complexion and not unprepossessing as to feature. His hat, which for a moment he did not remove, hung low over his eyes, without concealing that they were large, open, and determined, moving with a flash rather than a glance round the room. He seemed pleased with his survey, and, baring his shaggy head, said, in a rich, deep voice: "The rain is so heavy, friends, that ask leave to come in and rest awhile."

"To be sure, Stranger," said the shepherd. "And faith, you've been lucky in choosing your time, for we are having a bit of a fling for a glad cause — though, to be sure, a man could hardly wish that glad cause to happen more than once a year."

"Nor less," spoke up a woman. "For 'tis best to get your family over and done with, as soon as you can, so as to be all the earlier out of the fag o't."

"And what may be this glad cause?" asked the stranger.

"A birth and christening," said the shepherd.

The stranger hoped his host might not be made unhappy either by too many or too few of such episodes and, being invited by a gesture to a pull at the mug, he readily acquiesced. His manner, which, before entering, had been so dubious, was now altogether that of a careless and candid man.

"Late to be traipsing athwart this coomb — hey?" said the engaged man of fifty.

"Late it is, Master, as you say. — I'll take a seat in the chimney corner, if you have nothing to urge against it, Ma'am; for I am a little moist on the side that was next the rain."

Mrs. Shepherd Fennel assented, and made room for the self-invited comer, who, having got completely inside the chimney corner, stretched out his legs and arms with the expansiveness of a person quite at home.

"Yes, I am rather cracked in the vamp,"[1] he said freely, seeing that the eyes of the shepherd's wife fell upon his boots, "and I am not well fitted either. I have had some rough times lately, and have been forced to pick up what I can get in the way of wearing, but I must find a suit better fit for working-days when I reach home."

"One of hereabouts?" she inquired.

"Not quite that — further up the country."

"I thought so. And so be I; and by your tongue you come from my neighborhood."

"But you would hardly have heard of me," he said quickly. "My time would be long before yours, Ma'am, you see."

This testimony to the youthfulness of his hostess had the effect of stopping her cross-examination.

"There is only one thing more wanted to make me happy," continued the newcomer, "and that is a little baccy, which I am sorry to say I am out of."

"I'll fill your pipe," said the shepherd.

"I must ask you to lend me a pipe likewise."

"A smoker, and no pipe about 'ee?"

"I have dropped it somewhere on the road."

The shepherd filled and handed him a new clay pipe, saying, as he did so,

_____

[1] *vamp:* the part of a shoe above the sole and in front of the ankle seam.

"Hand me your baccy-box — I'll fill that too, now I am about it."

The man went through the movement of searching his pockets.

"Lost that too?" said his entertainer, with some surprise.

"I am afraid so," said the man with some confusion. "Give it to me in a screw of paper." Lighting his pipe at the candle with a suction that drew the whole flame into the bowl, he resettled himself in the corner and bent his looks upon the faint steam from his damp legs, as if he wished to say no more.

Meanwhile the general body of guests had been taking little notice of this visitor by reason of an absorbing discussion in which they were engaged with the band about a tune for the next dance. The matter being settled, they were about to stand up when an interruption came in the shape of another knock at the door.

At sound of the same the man in the chimney corner took up the poker and began stirring the brands as if doing it thoroughly were the one aim of his existence; and a second time the shepherd said, "Walk in!" In a moment another man stood upon the straw-woven doormat. He too was a stranger.

This individual was one of a type radically different from the first. There was more of the commonplace in his manner, and a certain jovial cosmopolitanism sat upon his features. He was several years older than the first arrival, his hair being slightly frosted, his eyebrows bristly, and his whiskers cut back from his cheeks. His face was rather full and flabby, and yet it was not altogether a face without power. A few grog-blossoms marked the neighborhood of his nose. He flung back his long drab greatcoat, revealing that beneath it he wore a suit of cinder-gray shade throughout, large heavy seals, of some metal or other that would take a polish, dangling from his fob as his only personal ornament. Shaking the water drops from his low-crowned glazed hat, he said, "I must ask for a few minutes' shelter, comrades, or I shall be wetted to my skin before I get to Casterbridge."

"Make yourself at home, Master," said the shepherd, perhaps a trifle less heartily than on the first occasion. Not that Fennel had the least tinge of niggardliness in his composition; but the room was far from large, spare chairs were not numerous, and damp companions were not altogether desirable at close quarters for the women and girls in their bright-colored gowns.

However, the second comer, after taking off his greatcoat, and hanging his hat on a nail in one of the ceiling-beams as if he had been specially invited to put it there, advanced and sat down at the table. This had been pushed so closely into the chimney corner, to give all available room to the dancers, that its inner edge grazed the elbow of the man who had ensconced himself by the fire; and thus the two strangers were brought into close companionship. They nodded to each other by way of breaking the ice of unacquaintance, and the first stranger handed his neighbor the family mug — a huge vessel of brown ware, having its upper edge worn away like a threshold by the rub of whole generations of thirsty lips that had gone the way of all flesh, and bearing the following inscription burnt upon its rotund side in yellow letters:

THERE IS NO FUN
UNTiL i CUM.

The other man, nothing loth,[1] raised the mug to his lips, and drank on, and on, and on — till a curious blueness overspread the countenance of the shepherd's wife, who had regarded with no little surprise the first stranger's free offer to the second of what did not belong to him to dispense.

"I knew it!" said the toper to the shepherd with much satisfaction. "When I walked up your garden before coming in, and saw the hives all of a row, I said

[1] *nothing loth:* not reluctant.

to myself, 'Where there's bees there's honey, and where there's honey there's mead.' But mead of such a truly comfortable sort as this I really didn't expect to meet in my older days." He took yet another pull at the mug, till it assumed an ominous elevation.

"Glad you enjoy it!" said the shepherd warmly.

"It is goodish mead," assented Mrs. Fennel, with an absence of enthusiasm which seemed to say that it was possible to buy praise for one's cellar at too heavy a price. "It is trouble enough to make — and really I hardly think we shall make any more. For honey sells well, and we ourselves can make shift with a drop o' small mead and metheglin [1] for common use from the comb-washings."

"Oh, but you'll never have the heart!" reproachfully cried the stranger in cinder-gray, after taking up the mug a third time and setting it down empty. "I love mead, when 'tis old like this, as I love to go to church o' Sundays, or to relieve the needy any day of the week."

"Ha, ha, ha!" said the man in the chimney corner, who, in spite of the taciturnity induced by the pipe of tobacco, could not or would not refrain from this slight testimony to his comrade's humor.

Now the old mead of those days, brewed of the purest first-year or maiden honey, four pounds to the gallon — with its due complement of white of eggs, cinnamon, ginger, cloves, mace, rosemary, yeast, and processes of working, bottling, and cellaring — tasted remarkably strong; but it did not taste so strong as it actually was. Hence presently, the stranger in cinder-gray at the table, moved by its creeping influence, unbuttoned his waistcoat, threw himself back in his chair, spread his legs, and made his presence felt in various ways.

"Well, well, as I say," he resumed, "I am going to Casterbridge, and to Caster-

[1] *small mead and metheglin:* a beverage made of fermented honey and water, but weaker than the mead being served at the christening.

bridge I must go. I should have been almost there by this time; but the rain drove me into your dwelling, and I'm not sorry for it."

"You don't live in Casterbridge?" said the shepherd.

"Not as yet; though I shortly mean to move there."

"Going to set up in trade, perhaps?"

"No, no," said the shepherd's wife. "It is easy to see that the gentleman is rich, and don't want to work at anything."

The cinder-gray stranger paused, as if to consider whether he would accept that definition of himself. He presently rejected it by answering. "Rich is not quite the word for me, Dame. I do work, and I must work. And even if I only get to Casterbridge by midnight I must begin work there at eight tomorrow morning. Yes, het or wet, blow or snow, famine or sword, my day's work tomorrow must be done."

"Poor man! Then, in spite o' seeming, you be worse off than we," replied the shepherd's wife.

" 'Tis the nature of my trade, men and maidens. 'Tis the nature of my trade more than my poverty. . . . But really and truly I must up and off, or I shan't get a lodging in the town." However, the speaker did not move, and directly added, "There's time for one more draught of friendship before I go; and I'd perform it at once if the mug were not dry."

"Here's a mug o' small," said Mrs. Fennel. "Small, we call it, though to be sure 'tis only the first wash o' the combs."

"No," said the stranger, disdainfully. "I won't spoil your first kindness by partaking o' your second."

"Certainly not," broke in Fennel. "We don't increase and multiply every day, and I'll fill the mug again." He went away to the dark place under the stairs where the barrel stood. The shepherdess followed him.

"Why should you do this?" she said, reproachfully, as soon as they were alone. "He's emptied it once, though it held enough for ten people; and now he's not contented wi' the small, but must needs call for more o' the strong! And a stranger unbeknown to any of us. For my part, I don't like the look o' the man at all."

"But he's in the house, my honey; and 'tis a wet night, and a christening. Daze it, what's a cup of mead more or less? There'll be plenty more next bee-burning."

"Very well — this time, then," she answered, looking wistfully at the barrel. "But what is the man's calling, and where is he one of, that he should come in and join us like this?"

"I don't know. I'll ask him again."

The catastrophe of having the mug drained dry at one pull by the stranger in cinder-gray was effectually guarded against this time by Mrs. Fennel. She poured out his allowance in a small cup, keeping the large one at a discreet distance from him. When he had tossed off his portion the shepherd renewed his inquiry about the stranger's occupation.

The latter did not immediately reply, and the man in the chimney corner, with sudden demonstrativeness, said, "Anybody may know my trade — I'm a wheelwright."

"A very good trade for these parts," said the shepherd.

"And anybody may know mine — if they've the sense to find it out," said the stranger in cinder-gray.

"You may generally tell what a man is by his claws," observed the hedge-carpenter, looking at his own hands. "My fingers be as full of thorns as an old pincushion is of pins."

The hands of the man in the chimney corner instinctively sought the shade, and he gazed into the fire as he resumed his pipe. The man at the table took up the hedge-carpenter's remark, and added smartly, "True; but the oddity of my trade is that, instead of setting a mark upon me, it sets a mark upon my customers."

No observation being offered by anybody in elucidation of this enigma, the shepherd's wife once more called for a song. The same obstacles presented themselves as at the former time — one had no voice, another had forgotten the first verse. The stranger at the table, whose soul had now risen to a good working temperature, relieved the difficulty by exclaiming that, to start the company, he would sing himself. Thrusting one thumb into the armhole of his waistcoat, he waved the other hand in the air, and, with an extemporizing gaze at the shining sheep-crooks above the mantelpiece, began:

O my trade it is the rarest one,
        Simple shepherds all —
My trade is a sight to see;
For my customers I tie, and take
    them up on high,
And waft 'em to a far countree!

The room was silent when he had finished the verse — with one exception, that of the man in the chimney corner, who at the singer's word, "Chorus!" joined him in a deep bass voice of musical relish:

    And waft 'em to a far countree!

Oliver Giles, John Pitcher the dairyman, the parish-clerk, the engaged man of fifty, the row of young women against the wall, seemed lost in thought not of the gayest kind. The shepherd looked meditatively on the ground, the shepherdess gazed keenly at the singer, and with some suspicion; she was doubting whether this stranger were merely singing an old song from recollection, or was composing one there and then for the occasion. All were as perplexed at the obscure revelation as the guests at Belshazzar's Feast,[1] except the man in the chimney corner, who quietly said, "Second verse, stranger," and smoked on.

The singer thoroughly moistened him-

[1] *Belshazzar's Feast:* according to the Old Testament, writing appeared on the wall prophesying the destruction of Babylonia.

self from his lips inward, and went on with the next stanza as requested:

My tools are but common ones,
  Simple shepherds all —
My tools are no sight to see:
A little hempen string, and a post
  whereon to swing,
Are implements enough for me!

Shepherd Fennel glanced round. There was no longer any doubt that the stranger was answering his question rhythmically. The guests one and all started back with suppressed exclamations. The young woman engaged to the man of fifty fainted halfway, and would have proceeded, but finding him wanting in alacrity for catching her she sat down trembling.

"Oh, he's the — !" whispered the people in the background, mentioning the name of an ominous public officer. "He's come to do it! 'Tis to be at Casterbridge jail tomorrow — the man for sheep-stealing — the poor clockmaker we heard of, who used to live away at Shottsford and had no work to do — Timothy Summers, whose family were astarving, and so he went out of Shottsford by the highroad, and took a sheep in open daylight, defying the farmer and the farmer's wife and the farmer's lad, and every man jack among 'em. He" (and they nodded toward the stranger of the deadly trade) "is come from up the country to do it because there's not enough to do in his own county-town, and he's got the place here now our own county-man's dead; he's going to live in the same cottage under the prison wall."

The stranger in cinder-gray took no notice of this whispered string of observations, but again wetted his lips. Seeing that his friend in the chimney corner was the only one who reciprocated his joviality in any way, he held out his cup toward that appreciative comrade, who also held out his own. They clinked together, the eyes of the rest of the room hanging upon the singer's actions. He parted his lips for the third verse; but at that moment another knock was audible upon the door. This time the knock was faint and hesitating.

The company seemed scared; the shepherd looked with consternation toward the entrance, and it was with some effort that he resisted his alarmed wife's deprecatory glance, and uttered for the third time the welcoming words, "Walk in!"

The door was gently opened, and another man stood upon the mat. He, like those who had preceded him, was a stranger. This time it was a short, small personage, of fair complexion, and dressed in a decent suit of dark clothes.

"Can you tell me the way to — ?" he began: when, gazing round the room to observe the nature of the company among whom he had fallen, his eyes lighted on the stranger in cinder-gray. It was just at the instant when the latter, who had thrown his mind into his song with such a will that he scarcely heeded the interruption, silenced all whispers and inquiries by bursting into his third verse:

Tomorrow is my working day,
  Simple shepherds all —
Tomorrow is a working day for me:
For the farmer's sheep is slain, and
  lad who did it ta'en,
And on his soul may God ha' merc-y!

The stranger in the chimney corner, waving cups with the singer so heartily that his mead splashed over the hearth, repeated in his bass voice as before:

And on his soul may God ha' merc-y!

All this time the third stranger had been standing in the doorway. Finding now that he did not come forward or go on speaking, the guests particularly regarded him. They noticed to their surprise that he stood before them the picture of abject terror — his knees trembling, his hand shaking so violently that the door-latch by which he supported himself rattled audibly: his white lips were parted, and his eyes fixed on the merry officer of justice in the middle of the room. A moment more and he had turned, closed the door, and fled.

"What a man can it be?" said the shepherd.

The rest, between the awfulness of their late discovery and the odd conduct of this third visitor, looked as if they knew not what to think, and said nothing. Instinctively they withdrew further and further from the grim gentleman in their midst, whom some of them seemed to take for the Prince of Darkness himself, till they formed a remote circle, an empty space of floor being left between them and him — . . . *circulus, cujus centrum diabolus.*[1] The room was so silent — though there were more than twenty people in it — that nothing could be heard but the patter of the rain against the window-shutters, accompanied by the occasional hiss of a stray drop that fell down the chimney into the fire, and the steady puffing of the man in the corner, who had now resumed his pipe of long clay.

The stillness was unexpectedly broken. The distant sound of a gun reverberated through the air — apparently from the direction of the county-town.

"Be jiggered!" cried the stranger who had sung the song, jumping up.

"What does that mean?" asked several.

"A prisoner escaped from the jail — that's what it means."

All listened. The sound was repeated, and none of them spoke but the man in the chimney corner, who said quietly, "I've often been told that in this county they fire a gun at such times; but I never heard it till now."

"I wonder if it is *my* man?" murmured the personage in cinder-gray.

"Surely it is!" said the shepherd involuntarily. "And surely we've zeed him! That little man who looked in at the door by now, and quivered like a leaf

[1] *circulus . . . diabolus:* a circle with the devil at its center.

when he zeed ye and heard your song!"

"His teeth chattered, and the breath went out of his body," said the dairyman.

"And his heart seemed to sink within him like a stone," said Oliver Giles.

"And he bolted as if he'd been shot at," said the hedge-carpenter.

"True — his teeth chattered, and his heart seemed to sink; and he bolted as if he'd been shot at," slowly summed up the man in the chimney corner.

"I didn't notice it," remarked the hangman.

"We were all awondering what made him run off in such a fright," faltered one of the women against the wall, "and now 'tis explained!"

The firing of the alarm-gun went on at intervals, low and sullenly, and their suspicions became a certainty. The sinister gentleman in cinder-gray roused himself. "Is there a constable here?" he asked, in thick tones. "If so, let him step forward."

The engaged man of fifty stepped quavering out from the wall, his betrothed beginning to sob on the back of the chair.

"You are a sworn constable?"

"I be, Sir."

"Then pursue the criminal at once, with assistance, and bring him back here. He can't have gone far."

"I will, Sir, I will — when I've got my staff. I'll go home and get it, and come sharp here, and start in a body."

"Staff! — never mind your staff; the man'll be gone!"

"But I can't do nothing without my staff — can I, William, and John, and Charles Jake? No; for there's the king's royal crown apainted on en in yaller and gold, and the lion and the unicorn, so as when I raise en up and hit my prisoner, 'tis made a lawful blow thereby. I wouldn't 'tempt to take up a man without my staff — no, not I. If I hadn't the law to gie me courage, why, instead o' my taking up him he might take up me!"

"Now, I'm a king's man myself, and

can give you authority enough for this," said the formidable officer in gray. "Now then, all of ye, be ready. Have ye any lanterns?"

"Yes — have ye any lanterns? — I demand it!" said the constable.

"And the rest of you able-bodied — "

"Able-bodied men — yes — the rest of ye!" said the constable.

"Have you some good stout staves and pitchforks — "

"Staves and pitchforks — in the name o' the law! And take 'em in yer hands and go in quest, and do as we in authority tell ye!"

Thus aroused, the men prepared to give chase. The evidence was, indeed, though circumstantial, so convincing, that but little argument was needed to show the shepherd's guests that after what they had seen it would look very much like connivance if they did not instantly pursue the unhappy third stranger, who could not as yet have gone more than a few hundred yards over such uneven country.

A shepherd is always well provided with lanterns; and, lighting these hastily, and with hurdle-staves in their hands, they poured out of the door, taking a direction along the crest of the hill, away from the town, the rain having fortunately a little abated.

Disturbed by the noise, or possibly by unpleasant dreams of her baptism, the child who had been christened began to cry heartbrokenly in the room overhead. These notes of grief came down through the chinks of the floor to the ears of the women below, who jumped up one by one, and seemed glad of the excuse to ascend and comfort the baby, for the incidents of the last half-hour greatly oppressed them. Thus in the space of two or three minutes the room on the ground-floor was deserted quite.

But it was not for long. Hardly had the sound of footsteps died away when a man returned round the corner of the house from the direction the pursuers had taken. Peeping in at the door, and seeing nobody there, he entered leisurely. It was the stranger of the chimney corner, who had gone out with the rest. The motive of his return was shown by his helping himself to a cut piece of skimmer-cake that lay on a ledge beside where he had sat, and which he had apparently forgotten to take with him. He also poured out half a cup more mead from the quantity that remained, ravenously eating and drinking these as he stood. He had not finished when another figure came in just as quietly — his friend in cinder-gray.

"Oh — you here?" said the latter, smiling. "I thought you had gone to help in the capture." And this speaker also revealed the object of his return by looking solicitously round for the fascinating mug of old mead.

"And I thought you had gone," said the other, continuing his skimmer-cake with some effort.

"Well, on second thoughts, I felt there were enough without me," said the first confidentially, "and such a night as it is, too. Besides, 'tis the business o' the Government to take care of its criminals — not mine."

"True; so it is. And I felt as you did, that there were enough without me."

"I don't want to break my limbs running over the humps and hollows of this wild country."

"Nor I neither, between you and me."

"These shepherd-people are used to it — simple-minded souls, you know, stirred up to anything in a moment. They'll have him ready for me before the morning, and no trouble to me at all."

"They'll have him, and we shall have saved ourselves all labor in the matter."

"True, true. Well, my way is to Casterbridge; and 'tis as much as my legs will do to take me that far. Going the same way?"

"No, I am sorry to say! I have to get home over there" (he nodded indefinitely to the right), "and I feel as you do, that it is quite enough for my legs to do before bedtime."

The other had by this time finished the mead in the mug, after which, shaking hands heartily at the door, and wishing each other well, they went their several ways.

In the meantime the company of pursuers had reached the end of the hog's-back elevation which dominated this part of the down. They had decided on no particular plan of action; and, finding that the man of the baleful trade was no longer in their company, they seemed quite unable to form any such plan now. They descended in all directions down the hill, and straightway several of the party fell into the snare set by Nature for all misguided midnight ramblers over this part of the cretaceous [1] formation. The "lanchets," or flint slopes, which belted the escarpment at intervals of a dozen yards, took the less cautious ones unawares, and losing their footing on the rubbly steep they slid sharply downward, the lanterns rolling from their hands to the bottom, and there lying on their sides till the horn [2] was scorched through.

When they had again gathered themselves together, the shepherd, as the man who knew the country best, took the lead, and guided them round these treacherous inclines. The lanterns, which seemed rather to dazzle their eyes and warn the fugitive than to assist them in the exploration, were extinguished, due silence was observed; and in this more rational order they plunged into the vale. It was a grassy, briery, moist defile, affording some shelter to any person who had sought it; but the party perambulated it in vain, and ascended on the other side. Here they wandered apart, and after an interval closed together again to report progress. At the second time of closing in they found themselves near a lonely ash, the single tree on this part of the coomb, probably sown there by a passing bird some fifty years before. And here, standing a little to one side of the trunk, as motionless as the trunk itself

[1] cretaceous: chalky. [2] horn: scraped horn which is used instead of glass in lanterns.

appeared the man they were in quest of, his outline being well defined against the sky beyond. The band noiselessly drew up and faced him.

"Your money or your life!" said the constable sternly to the still figure.

"No, no," whispered John Pitcher. " 'Tisn't our side ought to say that. That's the doctrine of vagabonds like him, and we be on the side of the law."

"Well, well," replied the constable, impatiently; "I must say something, mustn't I? and if you had all the weight o' this undertaking upon your mind, perhaps you'd say the wrong thing, too! — Prisoner at the bar, surrender in the name of the Father — the Crown, I mane!"

The man under the tree seemed now to notice them for the first time, and, giving them no opportunity whatever for exhibiting their courage, he strolled slowly toward them. He was, indeed, the little man, the third stranger; but his trepidation had in a great measure gone.

"Well, travelers," he said, "did I hear you speak to me?"

"You did; you've got to come and be our prisoner at once!" said the constable. "We arrest 'ee on the charge of not biding in Casterbridge jail in a decent proper manner to be hung tomorrow morning. Neighbors, do your duty, and seize the culpet!"

On hearing the charge, the man seemed enlightened, and, saying not another word, resigned himself with preternatural civility to the search-party, who, with their staves in their hands, surrounded him on all sides, and marched him back toward the shepherd's cottage.

It was eleven o'clock by the time they arrived. The light shining from the open door, a sound of men's voices within, proclaimed to them as they approached the house that some new events had arisen in their absence. On entering they discovered the shepherd's living-room to be invaded by two officers from Casterbridge jail, and a well-known magistrate who lived at the nearest country-seat, intelligence of the escape having become generally circulated.

"Gentlemen," said the constable, "I have brought back your man — not without risk and danger; but every one must do his duty! He is inside this circle of able-bodied persons, who have lent me useful aid, considering their ignorance of Crown work. — Men, bring forward your prisoner!" And the third stranger was led to the light.

"Who is this?" said one of the officials.

"The man," said the constable.

"Certainly not," said the turnkey; and the first corroborated his statement.

"But how can it be otherwise?" asked the constable. "Or why was he so terrified at sight o' the singing instrument of the law who sat there?" Here he related the strange behavior of the third stranger on entering the house during the hangman's song.

"Can't understand it," said the officer coolly. "All I know is that it is not the condemned man. He's quite a different character from this one; a gauntish fellow, with dark hair and eyes, rather good-looking, and with a musical bass voice that if you heard it once you'd never mistake as long as you lived."

"Why, souls — 'twas the man in the chimney corner!"

"Hey — what?" said the magistrate, coming forward after inquiring particulars from the shepherd in the background. "Haven't you got the man after all?"

"Well, Sir," said the constable, "he's the man we were in search of, that's true; and yet he's not the man we were in search of. For the man we were in search of was not the man we wanted, Sir, if you understand my everyday way; for 'twas the man in the chimney corner!"

"A pretty kettle of fish altogether!" said the magistrate. "You had better start for the other man at once."

The prisoner now spoke for the first time. The mention of the man in the chimney corner seemed to have moved him as nothing else could do. "Sir," he said, stepping forward to the magistrate, "take no more trouble about me. The time is come when I may as well speak. I have done nothing; my crime is that the condemned man is my brother. Early this afternoon I left home at Shottsford to tramp it all the way to Casterbridge jail to bid him farewell. I was benighted, and called here to rest and ask the way. When I opened the door I saw before me the very man, my brother, that I thought to see in the condemned cell at Casterbridge. He was in this chimney corner; and jammed close to him, so that he could not have got out if he had tried, was the executioner who'd come to take his life, singing a song about it and not knowing that it was his victim who was close by, joining in to save appearances. My brother looked a glance of agony at me, and I know he meant, 'Don't reveal what you see; my life depends on it.' I was so terror-struck that I could hardly stand, and, not knowing what I did, I turned and hurried away."

The narrator's manner and tone had the stamp of truth, and his story made a great impression on all around. "And do you know where your brother is at the present time?" asked the magistrate.

"I do not. I have never seen him since I closed this door."

"I can testify to that, for we've been between ye ever since," said the constable.

"Where does he think to fly to? — what is his occupation?"

"He's a watch-and-clock-maker, Sir."

" 'A said 'a was a wheelwright — a wicked rogue," said the constable.

"The wheels of clocks and watches he meant, no doubt," said Shepherd Fennel. "I thought his hands were palish for's trade."

"Well, it appears to me that nothing can be gained by retaining this poor man in custody," said the magistrate; "your business lies with the other, unquestionably."

And so the little man was released off-hand; but he looked nothing the less sad on that account, it being beyond the power of magistrate or constable to raze out the written troubles in his brain, for they concerned another whom he regarded with more solicitude than himself. When this was done, and the man had gone his way, the night was found to be so far advanced that it was deemed useless to renew the search before the next morning.

Next day, accordingly, the quest for the clever sheep-stealer became general and keen, to all appearance at least. But the intended punishment was cruelly disproportioned to the transgression, and the sympathy of a great many country-folk in that district was strongly on the side of the fugitive. Moreover, his marvelous coolness and daring in hob-and-nobbing with the hangman, under the unprecedented circumstances of the shepherd's party, won their admiration. So that it may be questioned if all those who ostensibly made themselves so busy in exploring woods and fields and lanes were quite so thorough when it came to the private examination of their own lofts and out-houses.

Stories were afloat of a mysterious figure being occasionally seen in some old overgrown trackway or other, remote from turnpike roads, but when a search was instituted in any of these suspected quarters nobody was found. Thus the days and weeks passed without tidings.

In brief, the bass-voiced man of the chimney corner was never recaptured. Some said that he went across the sea, others that he did not, but buried himself in the depths of a populous city. At any rate, the gentleman in cinder-gray never did his morning's work at Caster-bridge, nor met anywhere at all, for business purposes, the genial comrade with whom he had passed an hour of relaxation in the lonely house on the coomb.

The grass has long been green on the graves of Shepherd Fennel and his frugal wife; the guests who made up the christening party have mainly followed their entertainers to the tomb; the baby in whose honor they all had met is a matron in the sere and yellow leaf. But the arrival of the three strangers at the shepherd's that night, and the details connected therewith, is a story as well-known as ever in the country about Higher Crowstairs.

The Darkling Thrush

I leant upon a coppice gate
  When Frost was specter-gray,
And Winter's dregs made desolate
  The weakening eye of day.
The tangled vine-stems scored the sky   5
  Like strings of broken lyres,
And all mankind that haunted nigh
  Had sought their household fires.

The land's sharp features seemed to be
  The Century's corpse outleant,   10
His crypt the cloudy canopy,
  The wind his death lament.
The ancient pulse of germ and birth
  Was shrunken hard and dry,
And every spirit upon earth   15
  Seemed fervorless as I.

At once a voice arose among
  The bleak twigs overhead
In a fullhearted evensong
  Of joy illimited;   20
An aged thrush, frail, gaunt, and small,
  In blast-beruffled plume,
Had chosen thus to fling his soul
  Upon the growing gloom.

So little cause for carolings   25
  Of such ecstatic sound
Was written on terrestrial things
  Afar or nigh around,
That I could think there trembled through
  His happy good-night air   30
Some blessèd Hope, whereof he knew
  And I was unaware.

"The Darkling Thrush" reprinted with the permission of The Macmillan Company, Macmillan and Company Limited, and the Trustees of the Hardy Estate from *Collected Poems* by Thomas Hardy. Copyright 1925 by The Macmillan Company.

Weathers

This is the weather the cuckoo likes,
 And so do I;
When showers betumble the chestnut spikes,
 And nestlings fly;
And the little brown nightingale bills his best,   5
And they sit outside the Traveler's Rest,
And maids come forth sprig muslin dressed,
And citizens dream of the South and West,
 And so do I.

This is the weather the shepherd shuns,   10
 And so do I;
When beeches drip in browns and duns,
 And thresh, and ply;
And hill-hid tides throb, throe on throe,
And meadow rivulets overflow,   15
And drops on gate bars hang in a row,
And rooks in families homeward go,
 And so do I.

Afterward

When the Present has latched its postern behind my tremulous stay,
 And the May month flaps its glad green leaves like wings,
Delicate-filmed as new-spun silk, will the neighbors say,
 "He was a man who used to notice such things"?

If it be in the dusk when, like an eyelid's soundless blink,   5
 The dewfall hawk comes crossing the shades to alight
Upon the wind-warped upland thorn, a gazer may think,
 "To him this must have been a familiar sight."

If I pass during some nocturnal blackness, mothy and warm,
 When the hedgehog travels furtively over the lawn,   10
One may say, "He strove that such innocent creatures should come to no harm,
 But he could do little for them; and now he is gone."

If, when hearing that I have been stilled at last, they stand at the door,
 Watching the full-starred heavens that winter sees,
Will this thought rise on those who will meet my face no more,   15
 "He was one who had an eye for such mysteries"?

And will any say when my bell of quittance is heard in the gloom,
 And a crossing breeze cuts a pause in its outrollings,
Till they rise again, as they were a new bell's boom,
 "He hears it not now, but used to notice such things"?   20

"Weathers," and "Afterward" reprinted with the permission of The Macmillan Company, Macmillan and Company Limited, and the Trustees of the Hardy Estate from *Collected Poems* by Thomas Hardy. Copyright 1925 by The Macmillan Company.

In Time of
"The Breaking of Nations"

Only a man harrowing clods
  In a slow silent walk,
With an old horse that stumbles and
      nods
  Half asleep as they stalk.

Only thin smoke without flame   5
  From the heaps of couch grass:
Yet this will go onward the same
  Though dynasties pass.

Yonder a maid and her wight °
  Come whispering by;   10
War's annals will fade into night
  Ere their story die.

9. *wight:* an archaic or jocose word for *man.*

HARDY'S PROSE AND POETRY

THE THREE STRANGERS

1. Hardy first describes the setting for his story. What effect on subsequent happenings do each of the following details have?
a. The house "stood quite detached and undefended. The only reason for its precise situation seemed to be the crossing of two footpaths."
b. "The level rainstorm smote walls, slopes, and hedges."
c. "That cheerful rustic was entertaining a large party in glorification of the christening of his second girl."
2. All the characters in the story are natives of Wessex. They have gathered in the home of the Fennels to celebrate a joyous occasion. How do they enjoy themselves? What evidences of local color can you find throughout the story?
3. What interests you about the first stranger when he begins to ascend the solitary hill of Higher Crowstairs? How does he impress the guests?
4. The second stranger was "one of a type radically different from the first." Compare the two. Why does Mrs. Fennel

dislike him? How does he arouse the curiosity of the guests? In what way does he reveal his identity?
5. Why do the guests conclude that the third stranger is the prisoner? Explain their reaction to this stranger. What is the captured man's explanation of his hurried departure?
6. At what point in the story did you first recognize the hangman and the prisoner? Point out phrases and sentences in which Hardy prepares you to rejoice at the escape of the condemned man? Why do you feel that his escape is justified?

POEMS

1. What is the tone of "The Darkling Thrush" and by what details does the poet establish it? What is the significance of the thrush in the development of the mood of the poem? How does this poem compare in its outlook on life with "Dover Beach" (page 544)?
2. Which seasons does Hardy depict in "Weathers"? How do you feel about these two kinds of weather?
3. In "Afterward" note the different phrases used to describe the coming of death. By what characteristic does the poet wish to be remembered after death?
4. Look up the Biblical passage from which the title "In Time of 'The Breaking of Nations' " is derived (Jeremiah 51:20). In this poem, what universal experiences of men are contrasted with war? What is the poet's purpose in making the contrast?

LITERATURE AND THE ARTS

As in the case of William Wordsworth, among other English writers, the writings of Thomas Hardy are strongly associated with a specific region of Britain (see page 7). "Hardy country," or "Wessex," as Hardy himself called it, is in the southwest of England. Here, set against the Wessex downs, most of Hardy's writing — fiction and poetry — unfolds. The photograph opposite shows the countryside near Shaftesbury, renamed "Shaston" in Hardy's novels, and quite near his Dorsetshire home.

"In Time of 'The Breaking of Nations' " reprinted with the permission of The Macmillan Company, Macmillan and Company Limited, and the Trustees of the Hardy Estate from *Collected Poems* by Thomas Hardy. Copyright 1925 by The Macmillan Company.

RUDYARD KIPLING

1865–1936

Bettmann

Like Hardy, Kipling belongs to both the Victorian and the modern age. His life was at mid-point at the turn of the century, and while his reputation was definitely established during the eighties and nineties, he was probably the most widely read British author in the first decades of the twentieth century. In both verse and fiction Kipling has been a favorite storyteller of millions. Children treasure the animal stories of India told in *The Jungle Book,* and later they thrill to the excitement of *Kim,* his best-known novel. Readers of all ages enjoy the quick sketching of his army ballads such as "Danny Deever" and "Gunga Din." But Kipling's fame rests most securely on his numerous volumes of short stories, filled with the hilarious antics and sometimes strange fates of the British soldier.

Rudyard Kipling was born in Bombay, and he is always associated with India, though he was educated and lived in England most of his life. At seventeen he became editor of a newspaper in Lahore, and

for the next nine years he gathered material for many of his later books — exotic Indian backgrounds of dusty villages and colonial military posts, of lush jungles and remote mountain passes. In 1892 Kipling married an American girl from Vermont and spent five years there. One of his novels, *Captains Courageous,* has a New England setting. Travel was one of Kipling's delights; there are few places "east and west" he did not visit and write about.

Kipling was out of favor with officialdom in his own day and with critics of later days. Though he was the most eligible of poets, Queen Victoria kept him from becoming poet laureate because of his satiric descriptions (he called her the "Widow of Windsor" in *Barrack-Room Ballads*). However, Kipling won the Nobel Prize in Literature in 1907. Afterward, he was criticized as a defender of British imperialism. But that issue, at least since India has been granted independence, has passed, and readers continue to enjoy Kipling as a master storyteller.

Miss Youghal's *Sais*°

This story from *Plain Tales from the Hills* illustrates in small space several points about Kipling's stories. It deals with British

Title: *Youghal* (youl); *sais* (sīs): a sais is a servant in charge of horses.

official and army life in India, and suggests that Kipling himself must have been, like Strickland, capable of "going native" so completely that he was lost in the crowd. At the end of this story of the *sais* we find

"Miss Youghal's *Sais*" from *Plain Tales from the Hills* by Rudyard Kipling. Reprinted by permission of A. P. Watt and Son, Macmillan Company of Canada, Ltd., and Mrs. George Bambridge.

a typical mannerism of the author. Because his brain was overflowing with so many stories, he seldom concluded one tale without hinting that he had another good story up his sleeve. He often ends — "But that is another story."

"Miss Youghal's *Sais*" is preceded by a motto:

When Man and Woman are agreed, what can the Kazi* do?
— MOHAMMEDAN PROVERB

Some people say that there is no romance in India. Those people are wrong. Our lives hold quite as much romance as is good for us. Sometimes more.

Strickland was in the police, and people did not understand him; so they said he was a doubtful sort of man and passed by on the other side. Strickland had himself to thank for this. He held the extraordinary theory that a policeman in India should try to know as much about the natives as the natives themselves. Now, in the whole of upper India, there is only *one* man who can pass for Hindu or Mohammedan, *chamar* [1] or *faquir*,[2] as he pleases. He is feared and respected by the natives from the Ghor Kathri to the Jamma Musjid; and he is supposed to have the gift of invisibility and executive control over many devils. But what good has this done him with the government? None in the world. He has never got Simla [3] for his charge; and his name is almost unknown to Englishmen.

Strickland was foolish enough to take that man for his model; and, following out his absurd theory, dabbled in unsavory places no respectable man would think of exploring — all among the native riffraff. He educated himself in this peculiar way for seven years, and people could not appreciate it. He was per-petually "going Fantee" among natives, which, of course, no man with any sense believes in. He was initiated into the *Sat Bhai* at Allahabad [4] once, when he was on leave; he knew the Lizard Song of the Sansis, and the *Hálli-Hukk* dance, which is a religious cancan of a startling kind. When a man knows who dances the *Hálli-Hukk,* and how, and when, and where, he knows something to be proud of. He has gone deeper than the skin. But Strickland was not proud, though he had helped once, at Jagadhri, at the Painting of the Death Bull, which no Englishman must even look upon; had mastered the thieves' patter of the *chángars;* had taken a Eusufzai horse thief alone near Attock; and had stood under the *mimbar* board [5] of a Border mosque and conducted service in the manner of a Sunni Mollah.

His crowning achievement was spending eleven days as a *faquir* in the gardens of Baba Atal at Amritsar,[6] and there picking up the threads of the great Nasiban murder case. But people said, justly enough, "Why on earth can't Strickland sit in his office and write up his diary, and recruit, and keep quiet, instead of showing up the incapacity of his seniors?" So the Nasiban murder case did him no good departmentally; but, after his first feeling of wrath, he returned to his outlandish custom of prying into native life. By the way, when a man once acquires a taste for this particular amusement, it abides with him all his days. It is the most fascinating thing in the world; Love not excepted. Where other men took ten days to the Hills, Strickland took leave for what he called *shikar,*[7] put on the disguise that appealed to him at the time, stepped down into the brown crowd, and was swal-

---

*Kazi: Military judge of the Ottoman Empire.
[1] *chamar* (shă·mär′): skin dresser. [2] *faquir* (fä·kēr′): priest. [3] *Simla:* the summer capital of India; situated in the Himalayas.

[4] *Allahabad* (ăl′ά·hä·bäd′): an important city on the Ganges at the foot of the Himalayas. The other places mentioned in this paragraph are in northern India. [5] *mimbar board:* sounding board, a structure over a pulpit. [6] *Amritsar* (ŭm·rĭt′sĕr): a city in the Punjab, the Northwest Province of India. [7] *shikar* (shē·kär′): hunting.

lowed up for a while. He was a quiet, dark young fellow — spare; black eyes — and, when he was not thinking of something else, a very interesting companion. Strickland on Native Progress as he had seen it was worth hearing. Natives hated Strickland; but they were afraid of him. He knew too much.

When the Youghals came into the station, Strickland — very gravely, as he did everything — fell in love with Miss Youghal; and she, after a while, fell in love with him because she could not understand him. Then Strickland told the parents; but Mrs. Youghal said she was not going to throw her daughter into the worst-paid department in the Empire, and old Youghal said, in so many words, that he mistrusted Strickland's ways and works, and would thank him not to speak or write to his daughter any more. "Very well," said Strickland, for he did not wish to make his ladylove's life a burden. After one long talk with Miss Youghal he dropped the business entirely.

The Youghals went up to Simla in April.

In July Strickland secured three months' leave on "urgent private affairs." He locked up his house — though not a native in the province would wittingly have touched "Estreekin Sahib's" gear for the world — and went down to see a friend of his, an old dyer, at Tarn Taran.

Here all trace of him was lost, until a *sais* met me on the Simla Mall with this extraordinary note:

DEAR OLD MAN,

Please give bearer a box of cheroots — Supers, No. 1, for preference. They are freshest at the Club. I'll repay when I reappear; but at present I'm out of society.

Yours,
E. STRICKLAND.

I ordered two boxes, and handed them over to the *sais* with my love. That *sais* was Strickland, and he was in old Youghal's employ, attached to Miss Youghal's Arab. The poor fellow was suffering for an English smoke, and knew that, whatever happened, I should hold my tongue till the business was over.

Later on, Mrs. Youghal, who was wrapped up in her servants, began talking at houses where she called of her paragon among *saises* — the man who was never too busy to get up in the morning and pick flowers for the breakfast table, and who blacked — actually *blacked* — the hoofs of his horse like a London coachman! The turnout of Miss Youghal's Arab was a wonder and a delight. Strickland — Dulloo, I mean — found his reward in the pretty things that Miss Youghal said to him when she went out riding. Her parents were pleased to find she had forgotten all her foolishness for young Strickland and said she was a good girl.

Strickland vows that the two months of his service were the most rigid mental discipline he has ever gone through. Quite apart from the little fact that the wife of one of his fellow *saises* fell in love with him and then tried to poison him with arsenic because he would have nothing to do with her, he had to school himself into keeping quiet when Miss Youghal went out riding with some man who tried to flirt with her, and he was forced to trot behind, carrying the blanket and hearing every word! Also, he had to keep his temper when he was slanged in Benmore porch [1] by a policeman — especially once when he was abused by a Naik he had himself recruited from Isser Jang village — or, worse still, when a young subaltern called him a pig for not making way quickly enough.

But the life had its compensations. He obtained great insight into the ways and thefts of *saises* — enough, he says, to have summarily convicted half the *cha-*

[1] *Benmore porch:* entrance to the recreation center.

mar population of the Punjab if he had been on business. He became one of the leading players at knucklebones, which all *jampanis* [1] and many *saises* play while they are waiting outside the Government House or the Gaiety Theater of nights; he learned to smoke tobacco that was three-fourths cow-dung; and he heard the wisdom of the grizzled *Jemadar* [2] of the Government Houses *saises,* whose words are valuable. He saw many things which amused him; and he states, on honor, that no man can appreciate Simla properly till he has seen it from the *sais's* point of view. He also says that if he chose to write all he saw, his head would be broken in several places.

Strickland's account of the agony he endured on wet nights, hearing the music and seeing the lights in "Benmore," with his toes tingling for a waltz and his head in a horse blanket, is rather amusing. One of these days, Strickland is going to write a little book on his experiences. That book will be worth buying; and even more worth suppressing.

Thus, he served faithfully as Jacob served for Rachel; [3] and his leave was nearly at an end when the explosion came. He had really done his best to keep his temper in the hearing of the flirtations I have mentioned; but he broke down at last. An old and very distinguished general took Miss Youghal for a ride, and began that specially offensive "you're-only-a-little-girl" sort of flirtation — most difficult for a woman to turn aside deftly, and most maddening to listen to. Miss Youghal was shaking with fear at the things he said in the hearing of her *sais.* Dulloo — Strickland — stood it as long as he could. Then he caught hold of the general's bridle, and, in most fluent English, invited him to step off and be heaved over the cliff. Next minute Miss Youghal began crying; and Strickland saw that he had hopelessly given himself away, and everything was over.

The general nearly had a fit, while Miss Youghal was sobbing out the story of the disguise and the engagement that was not recognized by the parents. Strickland was furiously angry with himself, and more angry with the general for forcing his hand; so he said nothing, but held the horse's head and prepared to thrash the general as some sort of satisfaction. But when the general had thoroughly grasped the story, and knew who Strickland was, he began to puff and blow in the saddle, and nearly rolled off with laughing. He said Strickland deserved a V. C.,[4] if it were only for putting on a *sais's* blanket. Then he called himself names, and vowed that he deserved a thrashing, but he was too old to take it from Strickland. Then he complimented Miss Youghal on her lover. The scandal of the business never struck him; for he was a nice old man, with a weakness for flirtations. Then he laughed again, and said that old Youghal was a fool. Strickland let go of the cob's head, and suggested that the general had better help them, if that was his opinion. Strickland knew Youghal's weakness for men with titles and letters after their names and high official position. "It's rather like a forty-minute farce," said the general, "but, begad, I *will* help, if it's only to escape that tremendous thrashing I deserve. Go along to your home, my *sais*-policeman, and change into decent kit, and I'll attack Mr. Youghal. Miss Youghal, may I ask you to canter home and wait?"

About seven minutes later, there was a wild hurroosh at the club. A *sais,* with blanket and headrobe, was asking all the men he knew: "For Heaven's sake lend me decent clothes!" As the men did not

[1] *jampanis* (jăm·pà·nēz'): bearers of a jampan — like a sedan chair. [2] *Jemadar* (jĕm·à·där'): a native sergeant. [3] The story of Jacob and Rachel is in Genesis 29:15–30.

[4] *V. C.:* Victoria Cross, the highest crown award for military valor.

recognize him, there were some peculiar scenes before Strickland could get a hot bath, with soda in it, in one room, a shirt here, a collar there, a pair of trousers elsewhere, and so on. He galloped off, with half the club wardrobe on his back, and an utter stranger's pony under him, to the house of old Youghal. The general, arrayed in purple and fine linen, was before him. What the general had said Strickland never knew, but Youghal received Strickland with moderate civility; and Mrs. Youghal, touched by the devotion of the transformed Dulloo, was almost kind. The general beamed and chuckled, and Miss Youghal came in, and almost before old Youghal knew where he was, the parental consent had been wrenched out, and Strickland had departed with Miss Youghal to the telegraph office to wire for his kit. The final embarrassment was when a stranger attacked him on the Mall and asked for the stolen pony.

So, in the end, Strickland and Miss Youghal were married, on the strict understanding that Strickland should drop his old ways, and stick to departmental routine, which pays best and leads to Simla. Strickland was far too fond of his wife, just then, to break his word, but it was a sore trial to him; for the streets and the bazaars, and the sounds in them, were full of meaning to Strickland, and these called to him to come back and take up his wanderings and his discoveries. Someday I will tell you how he broke his promise to help a friend. That was long since, and he has, by this time, been nearly spoiled for what he would call *shikar*. He is forgetting the slang, and the beggar's cant, and the marks, and the signs, and the drift of the undercurrents, which, if a man would master, he must always continue to learn.

But he fills in his departmental returns beautifully.

Recessional

This hymn was written in honor of Queen Victoria's Diamond Jubilee. A "recessional" is a hymn sung as the choir and clergy leave the chancel after the service.

God of our fathers, known of old,
    Lord of our far-flung battle line,
Beneath whose awful Hand we hold
    Dominion over palm and pine —
Lord God of Hosts, be with us yet,   5
Lest we forget — lest we forget!

The tumult and the shouting dies;
    The captains and the kings depart;
Still stands Thine ancient sacrifice,
    An humble and a contrite heart.   10
Lord God of Hosts, be with us yet,
Lest we forget — lest we forget!

Far-called, our navies melt away;
    On dune and headland sinks the fire;°
Lo, all our pomp of yesterday   15
    Is one with Nineveh and Tyre!°
Judge of the nations, spare us yet,
Lest we forget — lest we forget!"

If drunk with sight of power, we loose
    Wild tongues that have not Thee in
    awe,   20
Such boasting as the Gentiles° use,
    Or lesser breeds without the Law —
Lord God of Hosts, be with us yet,
Lest we forget — lest we forget!

For heathen heart that puts her trust
    In reeking tube ° and iron shard,°   26
All valiant dust that builds on dust,
    And guarding calls not Thee to guard,
For frantic boast and foolish word —
Thy mercy on Thy people, Lord!   30

14. As a part of the opening ceremonies of the Jubilee, bonfires "on dune and headland" were lighted one by one on signal until the island of Great Britain was encircled with a wall of protecting fire, which the poet now sees fading away. 16. *Nineveh and Tyre:* ancient cities, long since destroyed. 21. *Gentiles:* here used in the Biblical sense — not belonging to the chosen people of God. 26. *tube:* the barrel of a gun; *shard:* destructive fragments of the bombshell.

"Recessional" from *The Five Nations* by Rudyard Kipling. Reprinted by permission of A. P. Watt and Son, Macmillan Company of Canada, Ltd., and Mrs. George Bambridge.

The Ballad of East and West

This virile ballad recounts the meeting of two young heroes — the Englishman, representative of Western civilization, and the Afghan, representing Eastern civilization. The setting is the northwest frontier of India, where the British troops in the border forts were constantly fighting against the depredations of the native outlaws. Published in 1890, this poem with its swinging meter, vivid imagery, and powerful diction brought Kipling immediate acclaim.

Oh, East is East, and West is West, and never the twain shall meet,
Till Earth and Sky stand presently at God's great Judgment Seat;
But there is neither East nor West, Border, nor Breed, nor Birth,
When two strong men stand face to face, though they come from the ends of the
earth!

Kamal° is out with twenty men to raise the Border side,   5
And he has lifted the Colonel's mare that is the Colonel's pride.
He has lifted her out of the stable-door between the dawn and the day,
And turned the calkins° upon her feet, and ridden her far away.
Then up and spoke the Colonel's son that led a troop of the Guides:°
"Is there never a man of all my men can say where Kamal hides?"   10
Then up and spoke Mohammed Khan, the son of the Ressaldar:°
"If ye know the track of the morning mist, ye know where his pickets are.
At dusk he harries the Abazai° — at dawn he is into Bonair,°
But he must go by Fort Bukloh to his own place to fare.
So if ye gallop to Fort Bukloh as fast as a bird can fly,   15
By the favor of God ye may cut him off ere he win the Tongue of Jagai.
But if he be past the Tongue of Jagai, right swiftly turn ye then,
For the length and the breadth of that grisly plain is sown with Kamal's men.
There is rock to the left, and rock to the right, and low lean thorn between,
And ye may hear a breech-bolt snick where never a man is seen."   20
The Colonel's son has taken horse, and a raw rough dun was he,
With the mouth of a bell and the heart of Hell and the head of a gallows-tree.
The Colonel's son to the Fort has won, they bid him stay to eat —
Who rides at the tail of a Border thief, he sits not long at his meat.
He's up and away from Fort Bukloh as fast as he can fly,   25
Till he was aware of his father's mare in the gut of the Tongue of Jagai,
Till he was aware of his father's mare with Kamal upon her back,
And when he could spy the white of her eye, he made the pistol crack.
He has fired once, he has fired twice, but the whistling ball went wide.
"Ye shoot like a soldier," Kamal said. "Show now if ye can ride!"   30
It's up and over the Tongue of Jagai, as blown dust-devils go,
The dun he fled like a stag of ten, but the mare like a barren doe.

5. *Kamal* (kä′mål): the leader of the Afghans. 8. *calkins* (kôk′ĭnz): bent metal pieces on a horseshoe to prevent slipping. 9. *Guides:* trusted native troops, who served with the English as guides and interpreters. 11. *Ressaldar* (rĕs-ăl-där′): a native Indian commander of a troop of cavalry. 13. *Abazai* (à-bà-zī′), *Bonair* (bō-nâr′): settlements about forty miles apart on the frontier of the Punjab district.

"The Ballad of East and West" from *Barrack-Room Ballads* by Rudyard Kipling. Reprinted by permission of A. P. Watt and Son, Macmillan Company of Canada, Ltd., and Mrs. George Bambridge.

The dun he leaned against the bit and slugged his head above,
But the red mare played with the snaffle bars,° as a maiden plays with a glove.
There was rock to the left and rock to the right, and low lean thorn between,   35
And thrice he heard a breech-bolt snick tho' never a man was seen.
They have ridden the low moon out of the sky, their hoofs drum up the dawn,
The dun he went like a wounded bull, but the mare like a new-roused fawn.
The dun he fell at a watercourse — in a woeful heap fell he,
And Kamal has turned the red mare back, and pulled the rider free.   40
He has knocked the pistol out of his hand — small room was there to strive,
" 'Twas only by favor of mine," quoth he, "ye rode so long alive:
There was not a rock for twenty mile, there was not a clump of tree,
But covered a man of my own men with his rifle cocked on his knee.
If I had raised my bridle hand, as I have held it low,   45
The little jackals that flee so fast were feasting all in a row.
If I had bowed my head on my breast, as I have held it high,
The kite that whistles above us now were gorged till she could not fly."
Lightly answered the Colonel's son: "Do good to bird and beast,
But count who come for the broken meats before thou makest a feast.   50
If there should follow a thousand swords to carry my bones away,
Belike the price of jackal's meal were more than a thief could pay.
They will feed their horse on the standing crop, their men on the garnered grain.
The thatch of the byres° will serve their fires when all the cattle are slain.
But if thou thinkest the price be fair, — thy brethren wait to sup,   55
The hound is kin to the jackal-spawn — howl, dog, and call them up!
And if thou thinkest the price be high, in steer and gear and stack,
Give me my father's mare again, and I'll fight my own way back!"
Kamal has gripped him by the hand and set him upon his feet.
"No talk shall be of dogs," said he, "when wolf and gray wolf meet.   60
May I eat dirt if thou hast hurt of me in deed or breath;
What dam of lances brought thee forth to jest at the dawn with Death?"
Lightly answered the Colonel's son: "I hold by the blood of my clan:
Take up the mare for my father's gift — by God, she has carried a man!"
The red mare ran to the Colonel's son, and nuzzled against his breast;   65
"We be two strong men," said Kamal then, "but she loveth the younger best.
So she shall go with a lifter's dower, my turquoise-studded rein,
My 'broidered saddle and saddlecloth, and silver stirrups twain."
The Colonel's son a pistol drew, and held it muzzle end,
"Ye have taken the one from a foe," said he. "Will ye take the mate from a
    friend?"   70
"A gift for a gift," said Kamal straight: "a limb for the risk of a limb.
Thy father has sent his son to me, I'll send my son to him!"
With that he whistled his only son, that dropped from a mountain crest —
He trod the ling° like a buck in spring, and he looked like a lance in rest.
"Now here is thy master," Kamal said, "who leads a troop of the Guides,   75
And thou must ride at his left side as shield on shoulder rides.
Till Death or I cut loose the tie, at camp and board and bed,
Thy life is his — thy fate it is to guard him with thy head.
So, thou must eat the White Queen's meat, and all her foes are thine,
And thou must harry thy father's hold for the peace of the Border-line.   80

34. *snaffle bars:* jointed bridles without curbs. 54. *byres:* cow barns. 74. *ling:* heather.

And thou must make a trooper tough and hack thy way to power —
Belike they will raise thee to Ressaldar when I am hanged in Peshawur!"°
They have looked each other between the eyes, and there have found no fault.
They have taken the Oath of the Brother-in-Blood on leavened bread and salt;
They have taken the Oath of the Brother-in-Blood on fire and fresh-cut sod,   85
On the hilt and the haft of the Khyber knife,° and the Wondrous Names of God.°

The Colonel's son he rides the mare and Kamal's boy the dun,
And two have come back to Fort Bukloh where there went forth but one.
And when they drew to the Quarter-Guard, full twenty swords flew clear —
There was not a man but carried his feud with the blood of the mountaineer.   90
"Ha' done! ha' done!" said the Colonel's son. "Put up the steel at your sides!
Last night ye had struck at a Border thief — tonight 'tis a man of the Guides!"

Oh, East is East, and West is West, and never the twain shall meet,
Till Earth and Sky stand presently at God's great Judgment Seat;
But there is neither East nor West, Border, nor Breed, nor Birth,   95
When two strong men stand face to face, though they come from the ends of the
    earth!

82. *Peshawur* (pĕ·shä′wár): the seat of the British government in Northwest Frontier Province.
86. *Khyber* (kī′bĕr) *knife:* a knife used in Khyber Pass, a narrow road between India and
Afghanistan; *Wondrous Names of God:* one hundred Mohammedan names given to God, one
revealed only to the priests, the others given in the Koran.

L'Envoi°

When Earth's last picture is painted, and the tubes are twisted and dried,
When the oldest colors have faded, and the youngest critic has died,
We shall rest, and, faith, we shall need it — lie down for an aeon or two,
Till the Master of All Good Workmen shall put us to work anew.

And those that were good shall be happy: they shall sit in a golden chair;   5
They shall splash at a ten-league canvas with brushes of comets' hair.
They shall find real saints to draw from — Magdalene, Peter, and Paul;
They shall work for an age at a sitting and never be tired at all!

And only the Master shall praise us, and only the Master shall blame;
And no one shall work for money and no one shall work for fame,   10
But each for the joy of the working, and each, in his separate star,
Shall draw the Thing as he sees It for the God of Things as They are!

Title: *L'Envoi:* a postscript to a poem, book, or essay. Kipling wrote this poem to close his
book *The Seven Seas.*

"L'Envoi" from *The Seven Seas* by Rudyard Kipling. Reprinted by permission of A. P. Watt and Son, Macmillan Company of
Canada, Ltd., and Mrs. George Bambridge.

Tommy

From his years of residence in India and his journalistic work on the *Military Gazette,* Kipling knew the Anglo-Indian soldier intimately. In Kipling's day the professional soldier was often regarded as an undesirable character. In this characteristic poem from *Barrack-Room Ballads,* written long before World War I, a typical "Tommy Atkins" speaks his mind and presents the grievances of his lot.

I went into a public 'ouse° to get a pint o' beer,
The publican° 'e up an' sez, "We serve no redcoats here."
The girls be'ind the bar they laugh an' giggled fit to die,
I outs into the street again an' to myself sez I:
    Oh, it's Tommy this, an' Tommy that, an' "Tommy, go away";   5
    But it's "Thank you, Mister Atkins," when the band begins to play —
    The band begins to play, my boys, the band begins to play,
    Oh, it's "Thank you, Mister Atkins," when the band begins to play.

I went into a theater as sober as could be,
They gave a drunk civilian room, but 'adn't none for me;   10
They sent me to the gallery or round the music 'alls,
But when it comes to fightin', Lord! they'll shove me in the stalls!°
    For it's Tommy this, an' Tommy that, an' "Tommy, wait outside";
    But it's "Special train for Atkins" when the trooper's on the tide —
    The troopship's on the tide, my boys, the troopship's on the tide,   15
    Oh, it's "Special train for Atkins" when the trooper's on the tide.

Yes, makin' mock o' uniforms that guard you while you sleep
Is cheaper than them uniforms, an' they're starvation cheap;
An' hustlin' drunken soldiers when they're goin' large a bit
Is five times better business than paradin' in full kit.°   20
    Then it's Tommy this, an' Tommy that, an' "Tommy, 'ow's yer soul?"
    But it's "Thin red line of 'eroes" when the drums begin to roll —
    The drums begin to roll, my boys, the drums begin to roll,
    Oh, it's "Thin red line of 'eroes" when the drums begin to roll.

We aren't no thin red 'eroes, nor we aren't no blackguards too,   25
But single men in barricks, most remarkable like you;

1. *public 'ouse:* a tavern. 2. *publican:* the innkeeper. 12. *stalls:* the best seats in English theaters. 20. *paradin' in full kit:* marching with the heavy load of the infantryman.

"Tommy" from *Barrack-Room Ballads* by Rudyard Kipling. Reprinted by permission of A. P. Watt and Son, Macmillan Company of Canada, Ltd., and Mrs. George Bambridge.

An' if sometimes our conduck isn't all your fancy paints,
Why, single men in barricks don't grow into plaster saints;
   While it's Tommy this, an' Tommy that, an' "Tommy, fall be'ind,"
   But it's "Please to walk in front, sir," when there's trouble in the wind —   30
   There's trouble in the wind, my boys, there's trouble in the wind,
   Oh, it's "Please to walk in front, sir," when there's trouble in the wind.

You talk o' better food for us, an' schools, an' fires, an' all;
We'll wait for extry rations if you treat us rational.
Don't mess about the cookroom slops, but prove it to our face   35
The Widow's uniform is not the soldier-man's disgrace.
   For it's Tommy this, an' Tommy that, an' "Chuck him out, the brute!"
   But, it's "Savior of 'is country" when the guns begin to shoot;
   An' it's Tommy this, an' Tommy that, an' anything you please;
   An' Tommy ain't a bloomin' fool — you bet that Tommy sees!   40

SPOKESMAN FOR THE EMPIRE

MISS YOUGHAL'S *SAIS*

1. In what kind of predicament did Strickland find himself? What personal qualities and past experience enabled him to carry out his plan? Did his conduct in any way differ from that of a native *sais?*

2. What do you learn of Indian life and customs from this story? Does the life of the English colony sound pleasant or unpleasant as described? What traits of the English in India during the time of the Empire do you observe?

POETRY

1. What great fear and what fervent prayer are expressed in "Recessional"? In your own words restate the moral Kipling draws in this hymn. Why are the title and the warning appropriate for the occasion (Victoria's Diamond Jubilee)? How may the life of a nation be compared to that of an individual?

2. The theme of "The Ballad of East and West" is clearly stated at the beginning. Recount briefly what happens in the story that carries out the theme. How do present world conditions have bearing on this theme?

3. In "L'Envoi" how does Kipling picture heaven? What ideals of art, work, and life are realized in this heaven? Can they ever be realized on earth?

4. In "Tommy" does the soldier have a legitimate complaint to make or not? Discuss the public attitude toward soldiers during peacetime, with particular reference to our own country.

SUGGESTIONS FOR WRITING

1. Adapt "Miss Youghal's *Sais*" for radio or television. Present it to the class with proper sound effects.

2. Describe a predicament that you were able to get out of because of an earlier experience.

READING LIST FOR
THE VICTORIAN AGE

Bennett, Arnold, *Clayhanger*
A realistic approach to the life of Edwin Clayhanger from his schooldays to his marriage.

Besier, Rudolph, *The Barretts of Wimpole Street*
A three-act play about Elizabeth Barrett's life before her marriage, her courtship by Browning, and their elopement.

Blackmore, Richard D., *Lorna Doone*
John Ridd, a farmer of Exmoor, falls in love with the daughter of an outlawed family.

Bonnet, Theodore, *The Mudlark*
A ragamuffin from the London streets eludes the guards and gains admittance to Windsor Castle to see Queen Victoria.

Burnett, Constance, *The Silver Answer*
Re-creation of Elizabeth Barrett's life in the home of her strict and possessive father, her courtship, marriage to Robert Browning, and their life together.

Butler, Samuel, *The Way of All Flesh*
An account of an artist's rebellion against the conventions of the Victorian Age.

Carroll, Lewis, *Alice in Wonderland*
A subtle and complex nonsense tale in which the familiar rules of life go for nothing.

Cary, Joyce, *House of Children*
A childhood spent on the coast of Ireland in the 1890's seen through a double vision, that of the child and that of the man he becomes.

Collins, Wilkie, *The Moonstone*
The first detective novel in English — and one of the best.

De La Roche, Mazo, *Mary Wakefield*
A turbulent love story set in a Canadian locale of the 1890's.

Dickens, Charles, *Oliver Twist*
After a boy from an English workhouse is trained to be a pickpocket, he struggles against severe obstacles to escape from an environment of crime.

*———, *Pickwick Papers*
One of Dickens' most amusing and best loved novels.

Du Maurier, Daphne, *My Cousin Rachel*
Philip Ashley meets his uncle's widow, succumbs to her charms, but learns what may be the truth about his uncle's death.

Eliot, George, *Adam Bede*
A man of high character finds himself in many perplexing situations.

———, *Mill on the Floss*
In a tragic story of affection and antipathy between a sister and brother, some humor is provided by three comic aunts.

Field, Isobel, *This Life I've Loved*
Robert Louis Stevenson seen through the eyes of his stepdaughter.

Fielding, Kenneth Joshua, *Charles Dickens*
Brief but a lucid and compact study showing the close relationship between Dickens' work and his life.

Fulford, Roger, *Hanover to Windsor*
An intimate study of William IV, Victoria, Edward VII, and George V, who, among them, ruled England from 1830–1936.

Gaskell, Elizabeth C., *The Life of Charlotte Brontë*
An excellent picture of Charlotte Brontë and her place among Victorian novelists.

Gerin, Winifred, *Anne Brontë*
The youngest of the three talented Brontë sisters is presented as the bravest and most resolute of the family, both as a writer and a person.

Grahame, Kenneth, *Wind in the Willows*
Half animal story, half allegory presumably written for children, but appealing to adults who enjoy imaginative literature.

Grover, Eulalie Osgood, *Robert Louis Stevenson: Teller of Tales*
Because of his weak lungs, Stevenson spent much time in bed and amused himself by telling stories to himself or his cousin.

Hardy, Thomas, *The Mayor of Casterbridge*
A moving story of a man of distinction who eventually pays for a mistake made in his youth.

Haycraft, Molly C., *Queen Victoria*
A fictional biography of Queen Victoria that reads like a romance.

Hinkley, Laura L., *The Stevensons: Louis and Fanny*
A biography of Stevenson's childhood in Scotland, Fanny's early life in Indianapolis, their marriage in San Francisco, and their travels around the world.

Holt, Victoria, *Mistress of Mellyn*
A Victorian melodrama of a governess in a mysterious Cornwall manor house.

Housman, Laurence, *Victoria Regina*
A brilliant play of outstanding episodes in Queen Victoria's life from girlhood to her Diamond Jubilee.

Kipling, Rudyard, *Captains Courageous*
Harvey, a wealthy young brat, is washed overboard from an ocean liner. Picked up by a fishing vessel, he becomes a hardworking young man before he reaches home.

Leonowens, Anna, *The English Governess at the Siamese Court*
A story, a film, and a musical have been made from this account of teaching the king's children in Siam (Thailand) in the 1860's.

Maugham, W. S., *Maugham's Choice of Kipling's Best*
Sixteen Kipling stories and an introductory essay by Maugham.

Pearson, Hesketh, *Dizzy*
A colorful picture of an outstanding Prime Minister, a true Englishman, and a great friend to Queen Victoria.

Postgate, Raymond, *Every Man Is God*
A Victorian plot of murder and retribution with period detail of furniture and dress.

Stephens, Eve, *Victoria and Albert*
Beginning with the young Victoria, this historical novel tells about Victoria's life with Albert.

Stern, Gladys B., *Robert Louis Stevenson*
A vigorous personality is presented in an informal style in this brief, straightforward biography.

Stevenson, Robert Louis, *Travels with a Donkey*
Accompanied by his burden-bearer, Modestine, Stevenson, as an unconventional traveler, records his twelve-day "walking tour" through South Central France.

† Strachey, Lytton, *Queen Victoria*
A well-written biography of Queen Victoria and her times, including excellent portraits of Gladstone, Disraeli, and others.

Trollope, Anthony, *The Eustace Diamonds*
The story of the unscrupulous Lady Eustace and her diamonds.

Waite, Helen E., *How Do I Love Thee?*
The moving story of Elizabeth Barrett, whose courage and love have thrilled generations and whose marriage stirred the Victorian world.

White, T. H., *Farewell Victoria*
A recent biography of the famous queen.

Woodham-Smith, Cecil, *Lonely Crusader*
An exciting and inspiring shortened version of an earlier biography of Florence Nightingale.

Woolf, Virginia, *Flush*
The romance of Elizabeth Barrett and Robert Browning is told as if by Elizabeth's cocker spaniel.

NOTE: See also "Notable English Novels," pp. 370–71.

* This novel (abridged) is available in *Four English Novels*, J. B. Priestley and O. B. Davis, eds. (Harcourt, Brace & World, Inc., 1960).
† This biography is available in *Four English Biographies*, J. B. Priestley and O. B. Davis, eds. (Harcourt, Brace & World, Inc., 1961).

FOR LISTENING

The following poems have been recorded and are available on *Many Voices 6B:* Browning's "My Last Duchess," Tennyson's "Bugle Song," C. Rossetti's "Remember," and E. B. Browning's "How Do I Love Thee?" On *Many Voices 12A* are recorded Hopkins' "Pied Beauty," Housman's "To an Athlete Dying Young," Yeats' "The Lake Isle of Innisfree."

VICTORIAN FRONTISPIECE: Pictured on page 480 are a Victorian leaded glass lamp shade, a portrait of Queen Victoria in a gilt frame, a nineteenth-century telephone, and a nineteenth-century globe symbolizing the British Empire. The potted fern and Paisley shawl were familiar items in this period.

THE GROWTH OF
THE ENGLISH LANGUAGE

The Victorian Age

The Victorian Age continued and accentuated the tendencies we have already noted in the Romantic Age. There were still two schools of thought on language usage: on the one hand were the conservatives — grammarians, school masters, the newly rich middle class who were not sure of their "correctness," the ambitious merchants who wished to mingle easily with the upper classes. On the other hand were the writers who, with the heritage of the Romantic tradition, were unafraid of innovations, and the aristocracy, who spoke as they heard the language used in their own class, without regard for formal rules of grammar.

New styles in pronunciation came in largely through this second group, but new styles in punctuation and spelling came in chiefly through the printers. Many authors were indifferent to such matters. It is said that Dickens left his punctuation entirely to the printer, but some writers who had had more schooling kept a watchful eye on the "points." Gradually the colon and semicolon, which had been all too obvious in earlier printing, thinned out. The system of modern punctuation slowly evolved in the Victorian era.

In the earlier part of the nineteenth century, the wide study of English grammar (influenced by Latin forms) tended to result in long, formal sentences, in which every part fitted perfectly with every other part, and a neat diagram could be made of the whole. Macaulay's writings illustrate the perfection of sentence structure which made him the idol of the schoolmaster; yet he was astute enough to realize the value of the contrasting short sentence for relief. On the other hand, Carlyle's sentences have no rhyme or reason. They change direction, break off suddenly, and defy analysis. Carlyle, too, was a great coiner of words. For his unique style it was necessary to coin another new word — Carlylese.

In general, the style of mid-Victorian conversation revealed by the novels of the day was heavy and formal. Husbands and wives used the titles Mr. and Mrs. in addressing each other. Proposals of marriage were oratorical masterpieces. Lofty sentiments abounded on all occasions. It is hard for us today to believe that people ever talked in that way, but they undoubtedly did on some occasions at least.

Of course, revolt was bound to follow such extremes. In the last two or three decades of the century even the language of literature began to limber up. Stevenson and Kipling came in like a breath of fresh air. Gilbert and Sullivan made people laugh at their own follies. The young George Bernard Shaw began to shock the public out of its complacency.

Meanwhile the English language had been growing rapidly all through the century. The opening up of trade with the Orient brought in words like *pongee* from China, *bamboo* from Malaya, *kimono* from Japan. The extension of the British Empire familiarized Britons with words pertaining to the life of distant peoples. India, with the help of Kipling's genius, supplied the largest number (*rajah* and *pundit,* for example). Australia and New Zealand sent a trickle of strange terms (such as *boomerang*). The Boer War flooded London with words from Africa, many of which were originally Dutch (*veldt*). And of course, Americanisms poured in with every boatload of visitors from the New World.

Then there were new words, not names of anything, but strange adjectives or other parts of speech that came from no one knows where. These caused great distress to particular people. Macaulay objected to *talented, influential,* and *gentlemanly.* Other much-criticized newcomers were *reliable* and *environment. Lengthy* fought a long battle for admittance and is still to be found on some taboo lists. (*Taboo* itself came from the Samoan.) It is enlightening to read lists of objectionable neologisms (new terms) compiled fifty years ago and find how large a proportion of them are now unquestionably accepted.

Some new developments on the American side of the ocean should be pointed out. In the years preceding the War Between the States, the United States received great numbers of immigrants from Germany, Switzerland, Scandinavia, Scotland, and Ireland, most of whom settled in the vast midland plains and gradually made their way west. It is interesting to note that the borrowing from Germany and the Scandinavian countries often pertained to food (*wieners, frankfurters, smörgåsbord*).

This mixture of nationalities west of the Alleghenies tended to produce there a speech somewhat different from that of New England and the South Atlantic coast — areas more exclusively influenced by England. But surprisingly enough, there developed over the width of a continent a uniformity of language greater than England has in her much smaller territory. An Englishman traveling in this country expressed his amazement at finding he could understand and be understood in all parts of the United States more easily than in many counties of his own Great Britain. This speaks well both for public education in the United States and for the high development of swift communications. Of course, differences of pronunciation can be easily detected in different localities, but they add interest to conversation rather than detracting from our comprehension.

We must also recognize the contributions of science and invention to the language — they were far greater than in any previous century. Medicine, physics, chemistry, biology, mathematics, transportation, new machines for the factory and the home were adding new words all the time. The purists balked at many of these, especially if a Greek root was combined with a word from another language. They also objected to the suffix *-ize* being added to all kinds of nouns and verbs to identify the many new processes. Even proper names were so treated as in "to *macadamize* roads." But this concern with linguistic origins made no difference to the general public, and if a word was needed it was accepted.

Viewed as a whole, the Victorian Age witnessed great expansion, and at the same time standardization, of the English language.

A detail from the Kelmscott Chaucer (see page 489), designed and printed by the Victorian poet and artist, William Morris.

The Pierpont Morgan Library

Τ̄HΑΤ Aprille with his shoures soote
The droghte of March hath perced to the roote,
And bathed every veyne in swich licour,
Of which vertu engendred is the flour;
Whan Zephirus eek with his swete breeth
Inspired hath in every holt and heeth

THE TWENTIETH CENTURY

1900 –

THIS AGE of ours represents the triumph of science, invention, technology, and social welfare. Man travels faster and faster, further and further. He is able to invent machines that do more and more work for him. By means of public health services and the use of antibiotics he has been able to save countless millions of lives that would have been lost in any former age. The mass of people in Western Europe and North America are better fed, housed, clothed, and educated than ever before in history. On all this — and much more — we can congratulate ourselves.

SOME MODERN PROBLEMS

But there is another side to the picture, and unless we take a look at it we cannot understand our age and the literature it has produced. This century has known already the two most destructive and terrible wars in all history, and it is not yet out of danger of a third world war that would destroy our whole civilization. Science can save lives but, with two-thirds of the world's inhabitants threatened with starvation, does not yet know any quick way of producing food for the steadily increasing populations of the earth. It may be important to reach the moon and travel through space, but it is even more important to make sure that all the people on this planet are adequately fed, housed, and clothed, and that they have at least a chance of good health.

◀ The items in the frontispiece are identified on page 830.

THE MODERN TEMPER

In spite of our wonderful scientific and technological advances, we in this century are curiously lacking in big new ideas. It is a fact that almost all the ideas that have shaped both our thought and our history in the twentieth century actually belong to the nineteenth century. This is true of Communism, Socialism, Fascism, Anarchism, in politics. The theory of evolution, which has had immense influence on modern thought, also originated in the nineteenth century. No great new religious idea has been developed in our own age. Even Freud, the father of psychoanalysis and depth psychology, is more a nineteenth- than a twentieth-century figure. In all the ideas that relate men to one another or to some spiritual principle in the universe, this age has owed almost everything to the past.

What is most startlingly new and belongs essentially to this time of ours is what men are discovering not on the human scale but in the immensely large and the unimaginably tiny realms of galaxies and stars, atoms, electrons and protons. The mathematicians and astronomers and their theory of relativity, and the nuclear physicists, who may either destroy us with their H-bombs or save us by offering us new sources of energy, are in the forefront of our picture of contemporary life. Both sets of scientists deal with highly abstract and difficult ideas so far removed from any human scale that it is difficult to relate them to our own lives. This situation, in which man no longer seems at home in his world but merely poised perilously between gigantic stars and whirling atoms, is not easily accepted even by imaginative men and women and has been partly responsible for introducing into literature more than a suggestion of bewilderment, doubt, and despair. We wonder who and what we are.

TWENTIETH-CENTURY BRITAIN

In this age three important things have happened to Britain. She has lost the dominant position she had during the nineteenth century and now must accept third place, behind the United States and Russia. Secondly, she has had to face two ruinous wars which have cost her lives (chiefly of young healthy men) she could ill spare, the destruction and loss of much property, especially during World War II (1939–45), and the continued loss of investments abroad that had once made London the financial capital of the world. Thirdly — a gain now instead of a loss — first through the Liberal Party, then through the Labor Party, she has raised the standard of life of the working people and has finally created a welfare state, which makes itself responsible for the health, employment, housing, education, and pensions of the great mass of the population. Everybody makes some kind of contribution to finance this welfare program. Much of it would be impossible without exceptionally heavy taxation — directly through income and surtaxes and indirectly through high duties on tobacco, liquor, imported luxuries, and what are really sales taxes (much heavier than any in America) on a variety of goods.

FROM EMPIRE TO COMMONWEALTH

During the first half of the century what had been the British Empire became the British Commonwealth. This is not merely a change of name. Ireland, except for Ulster, declared itself an independent republic in 1921. In 1947 so did India and Pakistan, though nominally remaining within the Commonwealth. In the early years of the century, Canada, Australia, and New Zealand became dominions — self-governing and independent nations — within the Commonwealth. And now the people in West Africa and elsewhere are, with British help, creating states of their own, like Ghana and Nigeria. People who have a prejudice against Britain often sneer at her for "losing her Empire," but this is to misjudge the more liberal British attitude toward her former possessions. The more liberal and progressive idea was always that Britain had been holding these territories in trust for their inhabitants, who when they were ready to govern themselves should be encouraged to do so. Many brutal and stupid things have been done in the name of British imperialism — and such things have always been denounced by the more enlightened British themselves — but the idea behind the British Commonwealth of gradually bringing new states and nations into existence is one of the noblest and most creative political ideas that history can show us, fit companion to the idea that inspired the American Constitution.

No doubt in earlier years Britain's colonial possessions were exploited for commercial purposes and were financially beneficial to Britain. Today the heavily-taxed Briton finds himself helping to run these areas at a financial loss. Not only is he still responsible for their protection (adding to the size and cost of Army, Navy, and Air Force), but he must also subsidize their development into independent and economically strong nations. Moreover, the large dominions have no financial responsibility to Britain herself. Canada, the wealthiest of them, is not even within "the sterling area" (that is, the area using the British pound sterling) but has her own dollar currency. The ties between Britain and the dominions are in fact more sentimental than economic. Nevertheless, in each of the two world wars, the dominions hastened to support Britain with men and materials as well as with financial assistance.

INFLUENCE OF THE WARS ON LITERATURE

The influence of the two great wars, even upon English literature, has been so great that something must be said about them. This is all the more important because Americans cannot help regarding these wars as being much shorter and less crippling than they seemed, and actually were, to the British.

For Britain, World War I began in August 1914 and ended in November 1918. During that time almost a million young Britons were killed outright. The slaughter was terrible, especially during the Battle of the Somme, which began in July 1916. (In that month, more than half the young men I had known as boys were killed.) Since many battalions had been recruited largely from single cities, after which they were named, these cities were plunged at once into mourning when their battalions were mowed down by machine guns. The effect of these ghastly casualties was powerful and lasting, both on surviving soldiers themselves — poets like Siegfried Sassoon (1886–   ) and Robert Graves (1895–   ) — and on the civilians at home. A certain optimism, the nineteenth-century conviction that progress must forever continue, which can also be found in twentieth-century figures such as Shaw (1856–1950) and Wells (1866–1946) and Arnold Bennett (1867–1931), vanished from Britain.

The younger creative writers and critics from 1919 onward turned in disgust from public affairs (from which the war developed), and, much influenced by writers abroad, turned from man in society to man in the inner world of his mind. Whatever was associated with the world before the war was condemned or ignored because it was that world which had produced the war. Even rebels like Shaw and Wells never recovered the popularity among "advanced" young writers and critics that they had had before 1914.

THE NEW WRITING

Literature had now a much narrower base. It was regarded as something that could appeal only to a very small minority, the cultured few. The old idea that good literature could be enjoyed by almost everybody did not survive into the 1920's, which was very much a period of new writing that might be called "highbrow" and "precious." The work of these writers — T. S. Eliot (1888–   ), James Joyce (1882–1941), Virginia Woolf (1882–1941), for example — was often difficult and deliberately obscure. If ordinary people could not understand such writing, then so much the worse for ordinary people, who, anyhow, had plenty of rubbish to amuse them. This was the more extreme literary attitude during the 1920's.

BRITAIN
1900-1960

1 Kirriemuir

SCOTLAND

Edinburgh

2
YORKSHIRE

IRELAND

3
Dublin

ENGLAND

4
Ludlow

WALES

8
Cambridge

5
Laugharne

6
Oxford

7
CHILTERN
HILLS

9
Ayot St. Lawrence

London
10

1 Birthplace of James M. Barrie (1860).
2 Setting of "All Yankees Are Liars" and
Eric Knight's native country. 3 Birthplace
of G. B. Shaw (1856) and W. B. Yeats
(1865). Site of Abbey (Irish National) Theater. 4 A. E. Housman born near here
(1859) in county of Shropshire, the setting
of almost all his poetry. 5 Home of Dylan
Thomas. 6 Housman, Galsworthy, Betjeman studied here; Spender and "new school"
of poets met here. 7 Coppard retired to
country to write here. 8 Housman, well-

known classical scholar, was professor of
Latin here. Rupert Brooke and Lytton
Strachey were at university here. 9 Long-
time home of George Bernard Shaw.
10 Katherine Mansfield attended college
here. Home of John Galsworthy, John Mase-
field, Walter de la Mare, T. S. Eliot, and
Stephen Spender. W. Somerset Maugham
worked as doctor in Lambeth slums; George
Bernard Shaw gave speeches in Hyde Park;
Virginia Woolf, Lytton Strachey, and the
"Bloomsbury Group" met here.

One reason for this defiant and rather "snooty" attitude was the enormous development throughout the 1920's and 30's (and, indeed, down to this day) of what are generally referred to as "mass media." These are the popular press, including both newspapers and magazines with large circulations; films; radio; and, of course more recently, television. All these were held to be the enemies of real literature. Young creative writers felt themselves in danger of being overwhelmed by these mass media. So they had to keep a long way off and do something very different. If so much was being made easily acceptable to the ordinary public, then real literature, not meant for such people, could afford to be difficult, could even glory in its difficulty.

(A personal note: It was impossible, during the 1920's and 30's, for a youngish writer in England to have both a large and enthusiastic public and a good literary reputation at the same time. So when I published *The Good Companions,* which sold about a million copies, I immediately lost any literary reputation I had had and did not get it back for years. I mention this to show that here, in this introduction, I am writing about what I know from personal experience.)

WORLD WAR II

For Britain World War II lasted from 1939 to 1945. During most of 1940 and most of 1941 Britain was alone facing Hitler, who first threatened invasion and then launched bombing attacks on London and many other English cities. The destruction in this war was staggering (in a single night millions and millions of books were destroyed by fire, the result of incendiary bombs in the city of London), but the loss of life among the armed forces was less than that in the previous war, though the *civilian* casualties, those killed or severely wounded, numbered about 250,000. There was nothing like the growing disillusionment and bitterness of the first war, if only because few illusions remained when the second war began. Indeed many of us feel that the spirit of the English was higher

British Information

Sir Winston Churchill served his government for a half-century and, as Prime Minister, led Britain during World War II.

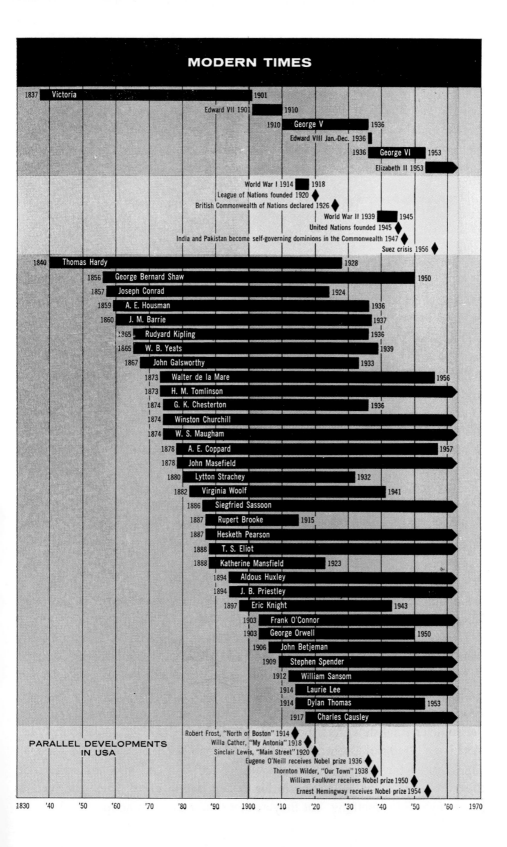

MODERN TIMES

1837 Victoria — 1901

Edward VII 1901 — 1910

1910 George V 1936

Edward VIII Jan.-Dec. 1936

1936 George VI 1953

Elizabeth II 1953

World War I 1914 — 1918

League of Nations founded 1920

British Commonwealth of Nations declared 1926

World War II 1939 — 1945

United Nations founded 1945

India and Pakistan become self-governing dominions in the Commonwealth 1947

Suez crisis 1956

1840 Thomas Hardy 1928

1856 George Bernard Shaw 1950

1857 Joseph Conrad 1924

1859 A. E. Housman 1936

1860 J. M. Barrie 1937

1865 Rudyard Kipling 1936

1865 W. B. Yeats 1939

1867 John Galsworthy 1933

1873 Walter de la Mare 1956

1873 H. M. Tomlinson

1874 G. K. Chesterton 1936

1874 Winston Churchill

1874 W. S. Maugham

1878 A. E. Coppard 1957

1878 John Masefield

1880 Lytton Strachey 1932

1882 Virginia Woolf 1941

1886 Siegfried Sassoon

1887 Rupert Brooke 1915

1887 Hesketh Pearson

1888 T. S. Eliot

1888 Katherine Mansfield 1923

1894 Aldous Huxley

1894 J. B. Priestley

1897 Eric Knight 1943

1903 Frank O'Connor

1903 George Orwell 1950

1906 John Betjeman

1909 Stephen Spender

1912 William Sansom

1914 Laurie Lee

1914 Dylan Thomas 1953

1917 Charles Causley

PARALLEL DEVELOPMENTS IN USA

Robert Frost, "North of Boston" 1914

Willa Cather, "My Antonia" 1918

Sinclair Lewis, "Main Street" 1920

Eugene O'Neill receives Nobel prize 1936

Thornton Wilder, "Our Town" 1938

William Faulkner receives Nobel prize 1950

Ernest Hemingway receives Nobel prize 1954

1830 '40 '50 '60 '70 '80 '90 1900 '10 '20 '30 '40 '50 '60 1970

during World War II than it had been before or has been since. Among other things, there was a tremendous demand for good reading and theater, for music and the visual arts. It was during the war that what is now called the British Arts Council was born. By dispensing government grants to worthy nonprofit cultural projects which otherwise would be unable to exist, this organization has done much to encourage the arts in Britain.

THE POLITICAL SCENE

As a result of the Parliamentary reform bills passed during the later years of Victoria's reign and the growth of stronger local self-government and increasingly widened suffrage, control of the government, both in Britain and in her colonies, passed more and more from royalty and the aristocracy to the middle and lower classes. Accompanying the more popular form of government was more extensive social legislation which continued throughout the following years, characterizing the period both before and after World War I, and indeed before and after World War II, during which Winston Churchill as prime minister did so much to marshal the country's forces for survival and final victory.

Many Americans are surprised that in the General Election of 1945 Winston Churchill was defeated. But the point is that Churchill (whose personal popularity was as high as ever) was the head of the Conservative Party, and it was Clement Attlee and the opposing Labor Party that answered the mood of the time, especially for the younger people. The result was the welfare state, which the Conservatives kept intact when Churchill led them back to power again in 1951. Churchill served as prime minister until 1955 when, at the age of 81, he retired from public life. Government leadership and the leadership of the Conservative Party was then placed in the hands of Anthony Eden, who in 1957 was in turn succeeded by Harold Macmillan.

Despite the fact that the original welfare state represented for Britain a completely new approach to economic and social affairs, certain hopes of some of the younger people, who wanted a more radical social democracy, were never realized. This defeat, together with an increasingly materialistic outlook among people in general, explains the basic dissatisfaction, the cynicism, of many of the younger English writers such as Kingsley Amis (1922–   ), John Wain (1925–   ), John Osborne (1929–   ), and John Braine (1922–   ). They dislike the complacent, materialistic, selfish mood and atmosphere of their time, so obviously lacking in ideals and public spirit. They, too, would like to fight for something, but they cannot find a cause to adopt.

THE ARTS IN CONTEMPORARY BRITAIN

Although there is a reasonably high level of accomplishment in most literary forms — poetry, fiction, drama — in postwar Britain, there is still a disappointing lack of really outstanding figures, figures ready to belong to world literature. The giants are very slow to arrive. But this may have something to do with the state of the public mind, for, as we have already seen, it is when some form of literature (like the drama in the Elizabethan Age, the novel in the Victorian) is important and exciting to people in general that great work is achieved in those forms. A public that is more concerned about "television personalities" than it is about authors is in no condition to nourish great literature.

Certain modern developments should be noted. The wide popularity of paperbacks, beginning with the *Penguin* series that originally sold for about a dime, brought good reading to a very large public. These paperbacks, however, were of little or no financial help to young authors, and they killed the more literary magazines and the market for short stories. Also, as in America, with the costs of publishing rising all the time, it was more and more difficult for young poets to find publishers. (On the other hand, poets and playwrights have been not ungenerously assisted by the British Broadcasting Corporation, and, to a lesser extent, by the Arts Council.) As for the theater, it is always about to become much better but on the whole remains much the same. Just as it began to recover from the triumphant competition of the films, it had to meet the challenge of television. It is true that London probably has more plays running at any time than any other city in the world. Nevertheless, too high a proportion of these plays have no literary nor even dramatic value.

At this time of writing — for the situation can easily change — contemporary English literature and the production of good new work suffer from certain handicaps. One is that the former middle class, which liked to buy books and literary reviews and seats for good plays, is dwindling and is comparatively hard up, whereas the very large working class, which at last has leisure and some money to spend, has not yet discovered an interest in books and authors. Perhaps a more serious handicap, though it might disappear any time, is that the contemporary atmosphere, tone, mood, flavor, of Britain as a society possesses a certain staleness and want of imagination and inspiration. This does not encourage the creation of fine literature on any scale. England, like the rest of the world, is now sadly short of great and illuminating ideas. But when they come, they will be reflected, as they have so often been before, in English literature.

J. B. P.

MODERN SHORT STORIES

ALTHOUGH Dickens at the height of his popularity wrote some short stories, the modern English short story makes its appearance some years after his death, beginning in the 1880's. The interest in this form was strongest probably from 1885–1930. The names associated with the short story would include Stevenson, Hardy, Kipling, H. G. Wells, Conrad, Somerset Maugham, Lawrence, O'Connor, Katherine Mansfield, and A. E. Coppard.

Clearly there has been no lack of work in the short story in Britain. Yet literary and critical interest in the short story has never been as great in Britain as it has been in the United States, France, and possibly Germany. Although writers like Stevenson, Kipling, and Wells still enjoy large sales for their short stories, it is a fact, which many British publishers have been reluctantly compelled to acknowledge, that it is very difficult to sell volumes of short stories by new writers to the British reading public, which has never really taken the short story to its heart. (Coppard, an excellent writer and widely praised by critics, had comparatively small sales in Britain, in spite of his fine reputation.) This public indifference to the short story is probably due to the fact that English readers enjoy a leisurely display and development of character, something which is impossible in the short story form.

We must make a distinction, however, between the true short story, which really is short, and much longer tales — long short stories — that come somewhere between the true short story and the novel. (There is no proper term for this kind of fiction in English, but, borrowing from the Italian, *novella* might do.) Both Conrad and Maugham, for example, have done some of their best work in these longer tales, which are particularly suitable for stories with exotic backgrounds, if only because they are not too short for some elaborate descriptive passages and the creation of a special atmosphere. Quite often, three or four of these tales together are sufficient to make up a fair-sized volume.

Both Kipling and Wells made admirable use of the shorter short story form. The stories of neither of these writers, however, are usually very short, both men needing a certain length in order to develop an action. The short story in their hands tends to be a fully realized tale in miniature, complete with characters, action, atmosphere, and background. In the stories they write, something definitely happens. [A minor master of this form of tale, which he always most cunningly plotted, was the humorist W. W. Jacobs (1846–1943), who could also on occasion write a convincing tale of horror. And so, with even more force and subtlety, could the poet Walter de la Mare.] There can be no doubt that it is this type of short story, which keeps us in suspense, that the British reading public prefers to any other.

A later and generally shorter kind of story, which has little or no action, no plot in the old sense of the term, but depends instead on insight into character, the ability to suggest a mood or atmosphere, can be found in the work of Katherine Mansfield. She did not invent it, for stories of this kind were being written in the 1890's, but she gave it emotional intensity and poetic feeling. She and her contemporaries, all writing about the time of World War I, were very much under the influence of Anton Chekhov (1860–1904), the Russian master of the short story, whose work was first appearing at that time in English translations.

A friend and contemporary of Katherine Mansfield was D. H. Lawrence (1885–1930), many of whose short stories are more satisfying than all but two or three of his novels. Lawrence is able to combine something of the emotional intensity and poetic feeling of the Mansfield type of story with the plot development of the older short story writers. Many of his stories are based on real incidents and characters who were friends and acquaintances.

A. E. Coppard at his best has much in common with both Mansfield and Lawrence, though he tends to write more elaborately. But what distinguishes him from them is a kind of sly and almost rustic humor. A self-educated man, who in his time tried all manner of jobs, Coppard had a great knowledge of all the byways and out-of-the-way places of southern England, almost like that of a gypsy, and he put this knowledge to good use in his short stories. There is a rather similar rustic background in many of the early stories of the novelist H. E. Bates.

Some of the more distinguished women writers, like Rebecca West (1892–   ) and Elizabeth Bowen (1899–   ), have turned occasionally, and with success, to the short story. But there are very few women writers since Katherine Mansfield who have specialized in this form. Irish writers, male and female, have produced fine short stories; it is a form that seems to suit the Irish.

Few things are easier to write than a mediocre short story, especially when nothing much happens in it. But good short stories, giving us so much in so little space, are very hard indeed to write. Their authors are more like poets than like novelists. There is, however, one trap that even good short story writers are rarely able to avoid. This might be called "false finality," which tries to persuade us that all is over forever with a character because he or she does, or fails to do, something or other. "As he closed the door, he knew that life could never be the same again" — that kind of thing, true enough at the moment but false in its finality. But at its best the short story offers us a wonderfully clear little window through which we can see something of the lights and shadows, the heights and depths, of life in this world.

J. B. P.

Magnum

The Lagoon

JOSEPH CONRAD 1857–1924

Joseph Conrad was the pen name of a Polish youth who became one of the most remarkable figures in twentieth-century English literature. Until he was twenty-one, he could speak no English. He did not begin his writing career until he was thirty, and yet became one of England's great novelists. His real name was Teodor Józef Konrad Korzeniowski. Born in the Ukraine, where his aristocratic and highly cultured parents were political exiles, he was educated at Cracow, Poland, under the guidance of an uncle. He liked to read and was fortunate to find in his father's

"The Lagoon" by Joseph Conrad, copyright, 1898, 1920, by Doubleday and Co., Inc. Reprinted by permission of Doubleday and Co., Inc., and J. M. Dent & Sons Limited.

library translations of Shakespeare, Cervantes, Hugo, and other classics.

From early youth, Conrad yearned for a life at sea and when seventeen left home to become a sailor. Within a short time he was a seaman, mate, and then master of French and British merchant vessels. He said later that he picked up English from the sailors and from newspapers. Though he never studied grammar in his life, at twenty-three he passed an examination to show that he had "mastered" English. Joseph Conrad also wanted to *write* in English. While on shipboard on a Congo river steamer, he began his first novel, *Almayer's Folly*. Later, retiring from the merchant marine, he began to write steadily. He was constantly goaded by debt, the need to support his family, and a relentless desire to succeed.

The sea is never far away in a Conrad story. Like Herman Melville in American literature, Conrad is the great storyteller of the sea in English fiction. In novels (*The Secret Sharer, Victory, Lord Jim*, and others), in long stories ("Youth," "The End of the Tether"), and in short stories like "The Lagoon," the sounds and moods of the sea run through his writing. But Conrad stories are not travelogues. Vigorously and with keen psychological insight, he is always probing into the hidden motives and problems of men. The grandeur of the sea and the mystery of tropic shores or shady riverbanks are typical Conrad settings for memorable character studies.

T HE WHITE MAN, leaning with both arms over the roof of the little house in the stern of the boat, said to the steersman:

"We will pass the night in Arsat's clearing. It is late."

The Malay only grunted, and went on looking fixedly at the river. The white man rested his chin on his crossed arms and gazed at the wake of the boat. At the end of the straight avenue of forests cut by the intense glitter of the river, the sun appeared unclouded and dazzling, poised low over the water that shone smoothly like a band of metal.

The forests, somber and dull, stood motionless and silent on each side of the broad stream. At the foot of big, towering trees, trunkless nipa palms rose from the mud of the bank, in bunches of leaves enormous and heavy, that hung unstirring over the brown swirl of eddies. In the stillness of the air every tree, every leaf, every bough, every tendril of creeper and every petal of minute blossoms seemed to have been bewitched into an immobility perfect and final. Nothing moved on the river but the eight paddles that rose flashing regularly, dipped together with a single splash, while the steersman swept right and left with a periodic and sudden flourish of his blade describing a glinting semicircle above his head. The churned-up water frothed alongside with a confused murmur. And the white man's canoe, advancing upstream in the short-lived disturbance of its own making, seemed to enter the portals of a land from which the very memory of motion had forever departed.

The white man, turning his back upon the setting sun, looked along the empty and broad expanse of the sea reach. For the last three miles of its course the wandering, hesitating river, as if enticed irresistibly by the freedom of an open horizon, flows straight into the sea, flows straight to the east — to the east that harbors both light and darkness. Astern of the boat the repeated call of some bird, a cry discordant and feeble, skipped along over the smooth water and lost itself, before it could reach the other shore, in the breathless silence of the world.

The steersman dug his paddle into the stream, and held hard with stiffened arms, his body thrown forward. The water gurgled aloud; and suddenly the long straight reach seemed to pivot on its center, the forests swung in a semicircle, and the slanting beams of sunset touched the broadside of the canoe with a fiery glow, throwing the slender and distorted shadows of its crew upon the streaked glitter of the river. The white man turned to look ahead. The course of the boat had been altered at right angles to the stream, and the carved dragonhead on its prow was pointing now at a gap in the fringing bushes of the bank. It glided through, brushing the overhanging twigs, and disappeared from the river like some slim and amphibious creature leaving the water for its lair in the forests.

The narrow creek was like a ditch: tortuous, fabulously deep; filled with gloom under the thin strip of pure and shining blue of the heaven. Immense trees soared up, invisible behind the festooned draperies of creepers. Here and there, near the glistening blackness of the water, a twisted root of some tall tree showed among the tracery of small ferns, black and dull, writhing and motionless, like an arrested snake. The short words of the paddlers reverberated loudly between the thick and somber walls of vegetation. Darkness oozed out from between the trees, through the tangled maze of the creepers, from behind the great fantastic and unstirring leaves; the darkness, mysterious and invincible; the darkness scented and poisonous of impenetrable forests.

The men poled in the shoaling water. The creek broadened, opening out into a wide sweep of a stagnant lagoon. The forests receded from the marshy bank, leaving a level strip of bright green, reedy grass to frame the reflected blueness of the sky. A fleecy pink cloud drifted high above, trailing the delicate coloring of its image under the floating leaves and the silvery blossoms of the lotus. A little house, perched on high piles, appeared black in the distance. Near it, two tall nibong palms, that seemed to have come out of the forests in the background, leaned slightly over the ragged roof, with a suggestion of sad tenderness and care in the droop of their leafy and soaring heads.

The steersman, pointing with his paddle, said, "Arsat is there. I see his canoe fast between the piles."

The polers ran along the sides of the boat glancing over their shoulders at the end of the day's journey. They would have preferred to spend the night somewhere else than on this lagoon of weird aspect and ghostly reputation. Moreover, they disliked Arsat, first as a stranger, and also because he who repairs a ruined house, and dwells in it, proclaims that he is not afraid to live amongst the spirits that haunt the places abandoned by mankind. Such a man can disturb the course of fate by glances or words; while his familiar ghosts are not easy to propitiate by casual wayfarers upon whom they long to wreak the malice of their human master. White men care not for such things, being unbelievers and in league with the Father of Evil, who leads them unharmed through the invisible dangers of this world. To the warnings of the righteous they oppose an offensive pretense of disbelief. What is there to be done?

So they thought, throwing their weight on the end of their long poles. The big canoe glided on swiftly, noiselessly, and smoothly, toward Arsat's clearing, till, in a great rattling of poles thrown down, and the loud murmurs of "Allah be praised!" it came with a gentle knock against the crooked piles below the house.

The boatmen with uplifted faces shouted discordantly, "Arsat! O Arsat!" Nobody came. The white man began to climb the rude ladder giving access to the bamboo platform before the house. The juragan [1] of the boat said sulkily, "We will cook in the sampan,[2] and sleep on the water."

"Pass my blankets and the basket," said the white man, curtly.

He knelt on the edge of the platform to receive the bundle. Then the boat shoved off, and the white man, standing up, confronted Arsat, who had come out

[1] *juragan:* native leader or captain. [2] *sampan:* flat-bottomed boat, used in river and harbor traffic.

through the low door of his hut. He was a man young, powerful, with broad chest and muscular arms. He had nothing on but his sarong.[1] His head was bare. His big, soft eyes stared eagerly at the white man, but his voice and demeanor were composed as he asked, without any words of greeting:

"Have you medicine, Tuan?" [2]

"No," said the visitor in a startled tone. "No. Why? Is there sickness in the house?"

"Enter and see," replied Arsat, in the same calm manner, and turning short round, passed again through the small doorway. The white man, dropping his bundles, followed.

In the dim light of the dwelling he made out on a couch of bamboos a woman stretched on her back under a broad sheet of red cotton cloth. She lay still, as if dead; but her big eyes, wide open, glittered in the gloom, staring upward at the slender rafters, motionless and unseeing. She was in a high fever, and evidently unconscious. Her cheeks were sunk slightly, her lips were partly open, and on the young face there was the ominous and fixed expression — the absorbed, contemplating expression of the unconscious who are going to die. The two men stood looking down at her in silence.

"Has she been long ill?" asked the traveler.

"I have not slept for five nights," answered the Malay, in a deliberate tone. "At first she heard voices calling her from the water and struggled against me who held her. But since the sun of today rose she hears nothing — she hears not me. She sees nothing. She sees not me — me!"

He remained silent for a minute, then asked softly:

"Tuan, will she die?"

"I fear so," said the white man, sorrowfully. He had known Arsat years ago,

in a far country in times of trouble and danger, when no friendship is to be despised. And since his Malay friend had come unexpectedly to dwell in the hut on the lagoon with a strange woman, he had slept many times there, in his journeys up and down the river. He liked the man who knew how to keep faith in council and how to fight without fear by the side of his white friend. He liked him — not so much perhaps as a man likes his favorite dog — but still he liked him well enough to help and ask no questions, to think sometimes vaguely and hazily in the midst of his own pursuits, about the lonely man and the long-haired woman with audacious face and triumphant eyes, who lived together hidden by the forests — alone and feared.

The white man came out of the hut in time to see the enormous conflagration of sunset put out by the swift and stealthy shadows that, rising like a black and impalpable vapor above the tree-tops, spread over the heaven, extinguishing the crimson glow of floating clouds and the red brilliance of departing daylight. In a few moments all the stars came out above the intense blackness of the earth and the great lagoon gleaming suddenly with reflected lights resembled an oval patch of night sky flung down into the hopeless and abysmal night of the wilderness. The white man had some supper out of the basket, then collecting a few sticks that lay about the platform, made up a small fire, not for warmth, but for the sake of the smoke, which would keep off the mosquitoes. He wrapped himself in the blankets and sat with his back against the reed wall of the house, smoking thoughtfully.

Arsat came through the doorway with noiseless steps and squatted down by the fire. The white man moved his outstretched legs a little.

"She breathes," said Arsat in a low voice, anticipating the expected question. "She breathes and burns as if with

[1] sarong: skirt or kilt worn by both sexes in the Malay Peninsula. [2] Tuan: term of respect, like Sir, used by natives to white men.

a great fire. She speaks not; she hears not — and burns!"

He paused for a moment, then asked in a quiet, incurious tone:

"Tuan . . . will she die?"

The white man moved his shoulders uneasily and uttered in a hesitating manner:

"If such is her fate."

"No, Tuan," said Arsat, calmly. "If such is my fate. I hear, I see, I wait. I remember . . . Tuan, do you remember the old days? Do you remember my brother?"

"Yes," said the white man. The Malay rose suddenly and went in. The other, sitting still outside, could hear the voice in the hut. Arsat said: "Hear me! Speak!" His words were succeeded by a complete silence. "O Diamelen!" he cried, suddenly. After that cry there was a deep sigh. Arsat came out and sank down again in his old place.

They sat in silence before the fire. There was no sound within the house, there was no sound near them; but far away on the lagoon they could hear the voices of the boatmen ringing fitful and distinct on the calm water. The fire in the bow of the sampan shone faintly in the distance with a hazy red glow. Then it died out. The voices ceased. The land and the water slept invisible, unstirring, and mute. It was as though there had been nothing left in the world but the glitter of stars streaming, ceaseless and vain, through the black stillness of the night.

The white man gazed straight before him into the darkness with wide-open eyes. The fear and fascination, the inspiration and the wonder of death — of death near, unavoidable, and unseen, soothed the unrest of his race and stirred the most indistinct, the most intimate of his thoughts. The ever-ready suspicion of evil, the gnawing suspicion that lurks in our hearts, flowed out into the stillness round him — into the stillness profound and dumb, and made it appear untrustworthy and infamous, like the placid and impenetrable mask of an unjustifiable violence. In that fleeting and powerful disturbance of his being, the earth, enfolded in the starlight peace, became a shadowy country of inhuman strife, a battlefield of phantoms terrible and charming, august or ignoble, struggling ardently for the possession of our helpless hearts. An unquiet and mysterious country of inextinguishable desires and fears.

A plaintive murmur rose in the night; a murmur saddening and startling, as if the great solitudes of surrounding woods had tried to whisper into his ear the wisdom of their immense and lofty indifference. Sounds hesitating and vague floated in the air round him, shaped themselves slowly into words; and at last flowed on gently in a murmuring stream of soft and monotonous sentences. He stirred like a man waking up and changed his position slightly. Arsat, motionless and shadowy, sitting with bowed head under the stars, was speaking in a low and dreamy tone:

". . . for where can we lay down the heaviness of our trouble but in a friend's heart? A man must speak of war and of love. You, Tuan, know what war is, and you have seen me in time of danger seek death as other men seek life! A writing may be lost; a lie may be written; but what the eye has seen is truth and remains in the mind!"

"I remember," said the white man, quietly. Arsat went on with mournful composure:

"Therefore I shall speak to you of love. Speak in the night. Speak before both night and love are gone — and the eye of day looks upon my sorrow and my shame; upon my blackened face; upon my burnt-up heart."

A sigh, short and faint, marked an almost imperceptible pause, and then his words flowed on, without a stir, without a gesture.

"After the time of trouble and war was over and you went away from my country in the pursuit of your desires, which we, men of the islands, cannot understand, I and my brother became again, as we had been before, the sword-bearers of the Ruler. You know we were men of family, belonging to a ruling race, and more fit than any to carry on our right shoulder the emblem of power. And in the time of prosperity Si Dendring showed us favor, as we, in time of sorrow, had showed to him the faithfulness of our courage. It was a time of peace. A time of deer hunts and cockfights; of idle talks and foolish squabbles between men whose bellies are full and weapons are rusty. But the sower watched the young rice shoots grow up without fear, and the traders came and went, departed lean and returned fat into the river of peace. They brought news, too. Brought lies and truth mixed together, so that no man knew when to rejoice and when to be sorry. We heard from them about you also. They had seen you here and had seen you there. And I was glad to hear, for I remembered the stirring times, and I always remembered you, Tuan, till the time came when my eyes could see nothing in the past, because they had looked upon the one who is dying there — in the house."

He stopped to exclaim in an intense whisper, "O Mara bahia! O Calamity!" then went on speaking a little louder:

"There's no worse enemy and no better friend than a brother, Tuan, for one brother knows another, and in perfect knowledge is strength for good or evil. I loved my brother. I went to him and told him that I could see nothing but one face, hear nothing but one voice. He told me: 'Open your heart so that she can see what is in it — and wait. Patience is wisdom. Inchi Midah may die or our Ruler may throw off his fear of a woman!' . . . I waited — . . . You remember the lady with the veiled face, Tuan, and the fear of our Ruler before her cunning and temper. And if she wanted her servant, what could I do? But I fed the hunger of my heart on short glances and stealthy words. I loitered on the path to the bathhouses in the daytime, and when the sun had fallen behind the forest I crept along the jasmine hedges of the women's courtyard. Unseeing, we spoke to one another through the scent of flowers, through the veil of leaves, through the blades of long grass that stood still before our lips; so great was our prudence, so faint was the murmur of our great longing. The time passed swiftly . . . and there were whispers among women — and our enemies watched — my brother was gloomy, and I began to think of killing and of a fierce death. . . . We are of a people who take what they want — like you whites. There is a time when a man should forget loyalty and respect. Might and authority are given to rulers, but to all men is given love and strength and courage. My brother said, 'You shall take her from their midst. We are two who are like one.' And I answered, 'Let it be soon, for I find no warmth in sunlight that does not shine upon her.' Our time came when the Ruler and all the great people went to the mouth of the river to fish by torchlight. There were hundreds of boats, and on the white sand, between the water and the forests, dwellings of leaves were built for the households of the Rajahs. The smoke of cooking fires was like a blue mist of the evening, and many voices rang in it joyfully. While they were making the boats ready to beat up the fish, my brother came to me and said, 'Tonight!' I looked to my weapons, and when the time came our canoe took its place in the circle of boats carrying the torches. The lights blazed on the water, but behind the boats there was darkness. When the shouting began and the excitement made them like mad we dropped out. The water swallowed our fire, and we floated back to the shore that was dark with only here and there the glimmer of embers. We could hear the talk of slave girls among the sheds. Then we found a place deserted and silent. We waited there. She came. She came running along the shore, rapid and leaving no trace, like a leaf driven by the wind into the sea. My brother said gloomily, 'Go and take her; carry her into our boat.' I lifted her in my arms. She panted. Her heart was beating against my breast. I said, 'I take you from those people. You came to the cry of my heart, but my arms take you into my boat against the will of the great!' 'It is right,' said my brother. 'We are men who take what we want and can hold it against many. We should have taken her in daylight.' I said, 'Let us be off'; for since she was in my boat I began to think of our Ruler's many men. 'Yes. Let us be off,' said my brother. 'We are cast out and this boat is our country now — and the sea is our refuge.' He lingered with his foot on the shore, and I entreated him to hasten, for I remembered the strokes of her heart against my breast and thought that two men cannot withstand a hundred. We left, paddling downstream close to the bank; and as we passed by the creek where they were fishing, the great shouting had ceased, but the murmur of voices was loud like the humming of insects flying at noonday. The boats floated, clustered together, in the red light of torches, under a black roof of smoke; and men talked of their sport. Men that boasted, and praised, and jeered — men that would have been our friends in the morning, but on that night were already our enemies. We paddled swiftly past. We had no more friends in the country of our birth. She sat in the middle of the canoe with covered face; silent as she is now; unseeing as she is now — and I had no regret at what I was leaving because I could hear her breathing close to me — as I can hear her now."

He paused, listened with his ear turned to the doorway, then shook his head and went on:

"My brother wanted to shout the cry of challenge — one cry only — to let the people know we were freeborn robbers who trusted our arms and the great sea. And again I begged him in the name of our love to be silent. Could I not hear her breathing close to me? I knew the pursuit would come quick enough. My brother loved me. He dipped his paddle without a splash. He only said, 'There is a half a man in you now — the other half is in that woman. I can wait. When you are a whole man again, you will come back with me here to shout defiance. We are sons of the same mother.' I made no answer. All my strength and all my spirit were in my hands that held the paddle — for I longed to be with her in a safe place beyond the reach of men's anger and of women's spite. My love was so great, that I thought it could guide me to a country where death was unknown, if I could only escape from Inchi Midah's fury and from our Ruler's sword. We paddled with haste, breathing through our teeth. The blades bit deep into the smooth water. We passed out of the river; we flew in clear channels among the shallows. We skirted the black coast; we skirted the sand beaches where the sea speaks in whispers to the land; and the gleam of white sand flashed back past our boat, so swiftly she ran upon the water. We spoke not. Only once I said, 'Sleep, Diamelen, for soon you may want all your strength.' I heard the sweetness of her voice, but I never turned my head. The sun rose and still we went on. Water fell from my face like rain from a cloud. We flew in the light and heat. I never looked back, but I knew that my brother's eyes, behind me, were looking steadily ahead, for the boat went as straight as a bushman's dart, when it leaves the end of the sumpitan [1] There was no better paddler, no better steersman than my brother. Many times, together, we had won races in that canoe. But we never had put out our strength as we did then — then, when for the last time we paddled to-

[1] *sumpitan:* a kind of blowgun for discharging a dart, used by natives of Borneo and adjacent islands.

gether! There was no braver or stronger man in our country than my brother. I could not spare the strength to turn my head and look at him, but every moment I heard the hiss of his breath getting louder behind me. Still he did not speak. The sun was high. The heat clung to my back like a flame of fire. My ribs were ready to burst, but I could no longer get enough air into my chest. And then I felt I must cry out with my last breath, 'Let us rest!' . . . 'Good!' he answered; and his voice was firm. He was strong. He was brave. He knew not fear and no fatigue. . . . My brother!"

A murmur powerful and gentle, a murmur vast and faint; the murmur of trembling leaves, of stirring boughs, ran through the tangled depths of the forests, ran over the starry smoothness of the lagoon, and the water between the piles lapped the slimy timber once with a sudden splash. A breath of warm air touched the two men's faces and passed on with a mournful sound — a breath loud and short like an uneasy sigh of the dreaming earth.

Arsat went on in an even, low voice. "We ran our canoe on the white beach of a little bay close to a long tongue of land that seemed to bar our road; a long wooded cape going far into the sea. My brother knew that place. Beyond the cape a river has its entrance, and through the jungle of that land there is a narrow path. We made a fire and cooked rice. Then we lay down to sleep on the soft sand in the shade of our canoe, while she watched. No sooner had I closed my eyes than I heard her cry of alarm. We leaped up. The sun was halfway down the sky already, and coming in sight in the opening of the bay we saw a prau [1] manned by many paddlers. We knew it at once; it was one of our Rajah's praus. They were watching the shore, and saw us. They beat the gong, and turned the head of the prau into the bay. I felt my

[1] *prau:* swift Malayan vessel with sharp prow and stern, which can sail equally well prow or stern first.

heart become weak within my breast. Diamelen sat on the sand and covered her face. There was no escape by sea. My brother laughed. He had the gun you had given him, Tuan, before you went away, but there was only a handful of powder. He spoke to me quickly: 'Run with her along the path. I shall keep them back, for they have no firearms, and landing in the face of a man with a gun is certain death for some. Run with her. On the other side of that wood there is a fisherman's house — and a canoe. When I have fired all the shots I will follow. I am a great runner, and before they can come up we shall be gone. I will hold out as long as I can, for she is but a woman — that can neither run nor fight, but she has your heart in her weak hands.' He dropped behind the canoe. The prau was coming. She and I ran, and as we rushed along the path I heard shots. My brother fired — once — twice — and the booming of the gong ceased. There was silence behind us. That neck of land is narrow. Before I heard my brother fire the third shot I saw the shelving shore, and I saw the water again; the mouth of a broad river. We crossed a grassy glade. We ran down to the water. I saw a low hut above the black mud, and a small canoe hauled up. I heard another shot behind me. I thought, 'That is his last charge.' We rushed down to the canoe; a man came running from the hut, but I leaped on him, and we rolled together in the mud. Then I got up, and he lay still at my feet. I don't know whether I had killed him or not. I and Diamelen pushed the canoe afloat. I heard yells behind me, and I saw my brother run across the glade. Many men were bounding after him. I took her in my arms and threw her into the boat, then leaped in myself. When I looked back I saw that my brother had fallen. He fell and was up again, but the men were closing round him. He shouted, 'I am coming!' The men were close to him. I looked. Many men. Then I looked at her. Tuan, I pushed the canoe! I pushed it into deep water. She was kneeling forward looking at me, and I said, 'Take your paddle,' while I struck the water with mine. Tuan, I heard him cry. I heard him cry my name twice; and I heard voices shouting, 'Kill! Strike!' I never turned back. I heard him calling my name again with a great shriek, as when life is going out together with the voice — and I never turned my head. My own name! . . . My brother! Three times he called — but I was not afraid of life. Was she not there in that canoe? And could I not with her find a country where death is forgotten — where death is unknown!"

The white man sat up. Arsat rose and stood, an indistinct and silent figure above the dying embers of the fire. Over the lagoon a mist drifting and low had crept, erasing slowly the glittering images of the stars. And now a great expanse of white vapor covered the land: it flowed cold and gray in the darkness, eddied in noiseless whirls round the tree trunks and about the platform of the house, which seemed to float upon a restless and impalpable illusion of a sea. Only far away the tops of the trees stood outlined on the twinkle of heaven, like a somber and forbidding shore — a coast deceptive, pitiless and black.

Arsat's voice vibrated loudly in the profound peace.

"I had her there! I had her! To get her I would have faced all mankind. But I had her — and — "

His words went out ringing into the empty distances. He paused, and seemed to listen to them dying away very far — beyond help and beyond recall. Then he said quietly:

"Tuan, I loved my brother."

A breath of wind made him shiver. High above his head, high above the silent sea of mist the drooping leaves of the palms rattled together with a mournful and expiring sound. The white man stretched his legs. His chin rested on his chest, and he murmured sadly without lifting his head:

"We all love our brothers."

Arsat burst out with an intense whispering violence —

"What did I care who died? I wanted peace in my own heart."

He seemed to hear a stir in the house — listened — then stepped in noiselessly. The white man stood up. A breeze was coming in fitful puffs. The stars shone paler as if they had retreated into the frozen depths of immense space. After a chill gust of wind there were a few seconds of perfect calm and absolute silence. Then from behind the black and wavy line of the forests a column of golden light shot up into the heavens and spread over the semicircle of the eastern horizon. The sun had risen. The mist lifted, broke into drifting patches, vanished into thin flying wreaths; and the unveiled lagoon lay, polished and black, in the heavy shadows at the foot of the wall of trees. A white eagle rose over it with a slanting and ponderous flight, reached the clear sunshine and appeared dazzlingly brilliant for a moment, then soaring higher, became a dark and motionless speck before it vanished into the blue as if it had left the earth forever. The white man, standing gazing upward before the doorway, heard in the hut a confused and broken murmur of distracted words ending with a loud groan. Suddenly Arsat stumbled out with outstretched hands, shivered, and stood still for some time with fixed eyes. Then he said:

"She burns no more."

Before his face the sun showed its edge above the treetops rising steadily. The breeze freshened; a great brilliance burst upon the lagoon, sparkled on the rippling water. The forests came out of the clear shadows of the morning, became distinct, as if they had rushed nearer — to stop short in a great stir of leaves, of nodding boughs, of swaying branches. In the merciless sunshine the whisper of unconscious life grew louder, speaking in an incomprehensible voice round the dumb darkness of that human sorrow. Arsat's eyes wandered slowly, then stared at the rising sun.

"I can see nothing," he said half aloud to himself.

"There is nothing," said the white man, moving to the edge of the platform and waving his hand to his boat. A shout came faintly over the lagoon and the sampan began to glide toward the abode of the friend of ghosts.

"If you want to come with me, I will wait all the morning," said the white man, looking away upon the water.

"No, Tuan," said Arsat, softly. "I shall not eat or sleep in this house, but I must first see my road. Now I can see nothing — see nothing! There is no light and no peace in the world; but there is death — death for many. We are sons of the same mother — and I left him in the midst of enemies; but I am going back now."

He drew a long breath and went on in a dreamy tone:

"In a little while I shall see clear enough to strike — to strike. But she has died, and . . . now . . . darkness."

He flung his arms wide open, let them fall along his body, then stood still with unmoved face and stony eyes, staring at the sun. The white man got down into his canoe. The polers ran smartly along the sides of the boat, looking over their shoulders at the beginning of a weary journey. High in the stern, his head muffled up in white rags, the juragan sat moody, letting his paddle trail in the water. The white man, leaning with both arms over the grass roof of the little cabin, looked at the shining ripple of the boat's wake. Before the sampan passed out of the lagoon into the creek he lifted his eyes. Arsat had not moved. He stood lonely in the searching sunshine; and he looked beyond the great light of a cloudless day into the darkness of a world of illusions.

READING THE SHORT STORY

Short stories are often read for enjoyment only. Although enjoyment is always important, reading short stories becomes an even more satisfying experience if we examine this literary type from the point of view of form and technique. For many readers the answers to two questions are often enlightening: *Why* was this short story written? *How* does it achieve its effects? You will find that these questions can be used in evaluating any short story you read. Try to answer them by examining Joseph Conrad's "The Lagoon."

THE PURPOSE OF THE STORY

Conrad's story is the death of Arsat's wife and the events leading up to it. But what is the idea behind the story? What are Arsat's values and standards of behavior? What conflict does he face in the situation he describes? Why has Arsat failed to find that peace which he said he wanted in his own heart? Is the story a tragedy because of the failure of a faithful, courageous man to act courageously and faithfully in a moment of crisis? To answer such questions we must go beyond the plot of the story and look at its structure, its characters, its atmosphere.

STRUCTURE

This story is unusual in its development. Try dividing it into the following sections: (1) *introduction,* the arrival of the white trader to spend the night with Arsat; (2) *transition,* illness of Diamelen; (3) *big scene,* Arsat's story of the winning of Diamelen and his brother's death; (4) *transition,* death of Diamelen; (5) *final scene,* Arsat's poignant grief.

If you were planning a television production of this story, how much time out of a total of thirty minutes would you give to each part of it? What method would you use to convey a single impression of the first scene? While telling of their last hours together, Conrad uses the "flashback" technique to explain why Arsat and Diamelen are living on the isolated lagoon. At what point in the story is the flashback completed? How does Arsat react to his wife's death? Is Diamelen's death the real tragedy of Arsat's life? What attitude toward Arsat does Conrad seem to have? How do the answers to these questions help you to see why Conrad constructed the story as he did?

CHARACTERS

Arsat's love for Diamelen and the intensity of his grief at her death can be traced throughout the story. His first words to the visitor are, "Have you medicine, Tuan?" Later he asks, "Tuan, will she die?" About to lose what he holds most dear, Arsat is in the depths of despair. His character has also been revealed in a crisis he himself describes. He must be judged both by his actions toward his brother and toward Diamelen. What evidence is there that Arsat is essentially a courageous man?

A complex individual, Arsat's character is revealed through *conversation, action, direct description,* and *interaction with other characters.* Notice how he speaks to the white trader, how he refers to his brother. Where does Conrad indicate what is going on in Arsat's mind by describing

what he is doing? Point out short passages that describe Arsat to the reader.

What do you learn about the character of Arsat's brother? How is his character important to the story?

Although Diamelen is a somewhat ephemeral character, her relationship with Arsat should be considered. She never speaks, only cries out during the escape. However, the fact remains that she loved Arsat enough to risk her life for him.

ATMOSPHERE

Conrad's poetic descriptions of remote waters and forests create a sense of mystery. They not only furnish clear pictures for the reader but also establish a mood. Conrad takes care to create the actual physical setting of his story and to suggest its influence on the characters. In his first few paragraphs he conveys a sense of awe by his descriptions of the deep silence and the beauty of the scene. It is by choosing significant details that the author sets the tone and creates the atmosphere. Reread the second paragraph of the story, beginning "The Malay . . . ," and note Conrad's method of conveying a single impression of a scene — in this case, its stillness.

Go over the story again pointing out how Conrad uses specific details to convey a single impression.

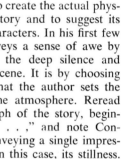

Photo Researchers, Inc.

The Old Venerable

A. E. COPPARD 1878–1957

Alfred Edgar Coppard, a recognized master of the short story, was born in Folkestone, Kent, of a tailor and a housemaid. At the age of nine he left school and was apprenticed to a London tailor. Later, as an errand boy, he began reading poetry. While he was employed in Oxford as an accountant for an engineering firm, he be-

"The Old Venerable" from *The Selected Tales of A. E. Coppard* by A. E. Coppard. Copyright 1927, 1955 by Alfred A. Knopf, Inc. Reprinted by permission of Alfred A. Knopf, Inc. and Jonathan Cape Limited.

came the friend of Aldous Huxley and other student writers at the University there.

This group of eager writers gave him the inspiration and encouragement he needed to become a writer himself. Giving up his job, Coppard moved to a hut in the Chiltern Hills, northwest of London, and for two years devoted all his time to writing. He endured extreme poverty, but was justified when *Adam and Eve and Pinch Me,* his first volume of short stories, appeared. This book, published by the Golden Cockerel Press, is already a collector's item. Other collections which followed are *Fishmonger's Fiddle, The Field of Mustard,* and *Tapster's Tapestry.* At the time of his death, Coppard was working on an autobiography, which has been published posthumously under the title *It's Me, O Lord.*

For many years, A. E. Coppard was neglected by the reading public, but today he is praised for both his poetry and short stories. He has been influenced considerably by folk literature. Because he began writing seriously after World War I, he is often included among the postwar writers. He really is not one of them, however, for he has no psychological answers to give, no sociological theories to advance, simply a story to tell. In "The Old Venerable," Coppard demonstrates that he is at his best in realistic, robust tales of rural life.

Down in the village the women called him "the dirty old man," the childen did not seem to notice him, and their fathers called him "the Owd Venrable," or old Dick, with a sigh as of vague envy. There was little cause for that, he living in a wood in a little old tent shanty built of boughs and string and tarpaulin, with a heap of straw to sleep on. Outside the tent was his fire, and he had dwelt there so long that the mound of wood ash had grown almost as big as his house. Seventy years old he was, an old venerable ragged crippled man using two sticks, with a cheery voice and a truculent spirit, but honest as spring water, sharing his last drop with the last man or the first — he invariably shared theirs. When he was drunk he sang, when he was not drunk he talked for evermore about nothing, to nobody, for his tent was in a wood, a little clearing in a great wood, and the wood was away, a long way, from anywhere, so that he lived, as you might say, on air and affability and primed his starved heart with hope. A man like that could hope for anything, and a mere anything — twopence — would bring him bliss, but his undeviating aspiration, an ambition as passionate as it was supine, was to possess a donkey. He had pestered many sympathetic people who had the means; often he had sent out that dove of his fancy from the ark of his need, but it had never returned, at least not with a donkey; and never an ass fell like a bolt from heaven. If it had done, it would surely have taken no hurt, such a grand wood it was, miles of it, growing up and down the hills and hills, and so thickly bosomed that if you had fallen from a balloon into the top of that wood it would have been at the last like sinking into a feather bed. And full of birds and game. And gamekeepers. The keepers did not like him to be there, it was unnatural to them, but keepers come and go, the shooting was let to a syndicate, and he had been there so long that new keepers found him where the old ones had left him. They even made use of him; he swept the rides and alley-ways for the shooters, marked down the nests of pheasants. and kept observation on rabbits and weasels and the flocks of pigeons which anybody was welcome to shoot. Sometimes he earned a few shillings by plashing [1] hedgerows or hoeing a field of roots, but mostly he was a "kindler," he gathered firewood and peddled it on a hand truck around the villages. That was why he dreamed of donkey and

---

[1] *plashing:* cutting and intertwining branches to make a hedge.

nothing but donkey; a creature whose four feet together were not so big as one of its ears, would carry double and treble the load of kindling and make him a rich man.

One day he tramped right over to the head keeper's house to deliver a message, and there Tom Hussey had shown him a litter of retriever puppies he was tending. They had a pedigree, Tom Hussey said, as long as the shafts of a cart; the mother herself was valued at fifty golden guineas,[1] but the sire belonged to Lord Camover and bank notes wouldn't buy that dog, nor love nor money — not even the crown of England. There they were, six puppies just weaned and scrambling about, beautiful bouncing creatures, all except one that seemed quiet and backward.

"That one?" Tom Hussey said; "I be going to kill her. Sha's got a sort of rupture in her navel."

"Don't do that," said old Dick, for he knew a lot about dogs as well as birds and lambs and donkeys. "Give it to I." And Tom Hussey gave him the pup then and there, and he took it home to his tent and bandaged it artfully with a yard strip of canvas, and called it Sossy because it was so pert.

Every day the old man attended to that bandage round Sossy's stomach — he knew a whole lot about dogs — and the dog throve and grew, and every night nuzzled in the straw beside him; and Dick rejoiced. They lived heartily, for Dick was a nimble hand with a wire, and rabbits were plentiful, and he was always begging for bones and suchlike for his Sossy. Everywhere in that wood he took Sossy with him and he trained her so in the arts of obedience that she knew what he wanted even if he only winked one eye. After about six months of this he took off her bandage for the last time and threw it away. There she was, cured and fit and perfect, a fine sweet flourishing thing. What a glossy

coat! What a bushy tail! And her eyes — they made you dream of things!

Awhile after that Tom Hussey came into the wood to shoot some pigeons. There was always a great flock of them somewhere in the wood, and when they rose up from the trees the whirr of their thousand wings was like the roar of a great wave. Well, Tom Hussey came, and as he passed near the tent he called out the good of the morning to old Dick.

"Come here," cried Dick, and Tom Hussey went, and when he saw that dog you could have split him with a lath of wood he was so astonished. Sossy danced round him in a rare flurry, nuzzling at his pockets.

"She's hungry," he said.

"No, she ain't. Get down, you great devil! No, she ain't hungry, she's just had a saucepan ful o' shackles — get down! — that saucepan there what I washes myself in."

When Tom Hussey shot a pigeon she stood to the gun and brought the bird back like an angel.

"Dick, you can swap that dog for a donkey whenever you've a mind to," Tom Hussey said.

"Ain't she got a mouth? I tell you," Dick cried joyfully.

"Like silk," was the rejoinder.

"It's a gift."

"Born," chanted Tom Hussey.

"It's a gift, I tell you."

"Born. She's worth twenty pounds. You sell that bitch and get you a donkey, quick."

"No," deliberated the veteran, "I shan't do that."

"Twenty pound she's worth, of good money."

"I shan't have 'ee, I tell you."

"You sell that bitch and get you a donkey. That's my last word to you," Tom Hussey said as he stalked away.

But that "Owd Venrable" was a far-seeing sagacious creature, a very artful old man he was, and when the time came for it he and Tom Hussey conjured up a deal between themselves. It

---

[1] *guineas:* see note on British money, p. 842.

would have been risky for Tom Hussey, but as he was changing to another estate he chanced it and he connived and Sossy was mated on the sly to one of his master's finest retrievers, as good as ever stepped into a covert, and by all accounts the equal of Lord Camover's dog that had begot Sossy. So when Tom Hussey departed, there was old Dick with his valuable dog, looking forward to the few weeks hence when Sossy would have the finest bred puppies of their kind in the land. He scarcely dared to compute their value, but it would surely be enough to relegate the idea of a donkey to the limbo of outworn and mean conceits. No, if all went well he would have a change of life altogether. He would give up the old tent; it was rotting, he was tired of it. If things came wonderful well he would buy a nag and a little cart and a few cokernuts and he would travel the round of the fairs and see something of the world again. Nothing like cokernuts for a profitable trade.

This roseate [1] dream so tinted every moment of his thoughts that he lived, as you might say, like a poet, cherishing the dog, the source and promise of these ideals, with fondness and joy. The only cloud on the horizon of bliss was the new gamekeeper, a sprag young fellow, who had taken a deep dislike to him. Old Dick soon became aware of this animosity, for the new keeper kept a strict watch upon his neighborhood and walked about kicking over Dick's snares, impounding his wires, and complaining of his dirty habits and his poaching. And it was true, he *was* dirty, he had lost his pride, and he *did* poach, just a little, for he had a belly that hungered like any other man's, and he had a dog.

Early one morning as Dick was tending his fire the new keeper strolled up. He was a wry-mouthed, slow-speaking young chap, and he lounged there with his gun under his arm and his hands in his pockets. Neither spoke for a while,

[1] *roseate:* tinged with the color rose; used figuratively to mean optimistic.

but at last the keeper said:

"It burns well."

"Huh, and so would you burn well," grinned the old man, "if I cut you atop of it."

For fully two minutes the young keeper made no retort, he was a rather enraging young keeper. Then he said: "Ah, and what do you think you may be doing round here?"

The old man flung a few pinches of tea into a can of boiling water.

"You get on with your job, young feller, and I'll get on with mine."

"What *is* your job?"

The "Owd Venrable" eyed him angrily.

"My job? I'll tell you — it's to mind my own business. You'll learn that for yourself later on, I 'spects, when you get the milk outer your mouth — you ought to, however. Wait till yer be as old as I."

"Ah," drawled the keeper, "I don't mind waiting."

"I met chaps like you before," the old man began to thunder. "Thousands on 'em. D'you know what happened to the last one?"

"Died of fleabites, I shouldn't wonder," was the placid rejoinder.

"I had him on the hop. When he warn't thinking," the old man, ruminating, grinned, "I wuz! I give him a kick o' the stomach as fetched him atween wind and water, and down he went, clean as a smelt. D'you know what I did then?"

"Picked his pocket, I shouldn't wonder."

"Yah! Never stole nothing from no man, 'cept it was my own. Clean as a smelt, I tell you."

"Well," the new keeper slowly said, shifting his gun from the left arm to the right, "I can take a hiding from any man. . . ."

"Ah, and from any old woman, too, I should say."

". . . from any man," continued the imperturbable one, "as can give it me

— if you know of one." He began to pick his teeth with a matchstick. "Did you get my message?" he more briskly added.

"What message?"

"I sent you a message."

"Then you sent it by a wet hen. I ain't had no message."

"I know you had it, but I'll tell you again. I've got orders to clear you out of this wood, you and your dog. You can take your time, don't want to be hard on you, but out you goes, and soon, you and your dog."

"Well, we can go, my cunning feller, we can go."

"That's right, then."

"We can go — when we've a mind to. But who's a-going to look arter my job?"

"What job's that?"

"Huh, what job!" the old man disgustedly groaned. "Why, who's a-going to keep an eye on things, and they poachers, thousands on 'em, just waiting for to catch I asleep! But they can't do it."

"Naw, I shouldn't think anyone *could* sleep in a hole like that!"

"Yah, I could sleep, I could sleep a sack o' taters rotten! And who's a-going to clear up when the storms been shamracking about the place? I cleans up the paths, I cleans 'em for one and all, and I cleans 'em for you. Some I does it right for and some I does it wrong. If I did it right for all, I'd be out of this world, seemly."

"Who asked you to? Nobody asked you to, we can do without it, and we can do without you. So now I've told you." With that the young keeper sauntered airily away.

"Yah!" the Old Venerable called after him. "Clean as a smelt, I tell you, clean as a smelt"; and as long as his adversary remained in view he continued to remind him of that excellent conclusion.

But despite his contempt the old man was perturbed; he knew the game was up, he would have to seek a lodging elsewhere. By the grace of fortune the blow had come just when it could least concern him; all he wanted was time for Sossy to rear her pups, and then he would go; then he would gaily, driving his horse and cart like a man of property all over that Berkshire and that Oxfordshire.

A week later Sossy was safely delivered of nine puppies. Miracles are possible — they must be — but it is not possible to anticipate a miracle: a litter of nine! They were born in the tent beside the man, and they all — Dick, Sossy, and the nine morsels — slept together, and in a few days, although Sossy, despite heroic feeding, began to grow lean, the pups were fat as slugs.

When they were seven days old the man got up one morning to go to a job of hedging. It was a bright, draughty [1] March morn, and he noted the look of the early pink clouds. A fine day promised, though some of the clouds had a queer shape like a goose with its head turned backwards. That boded something! The blackies and thrushers sang beautiful. After Sossy had fed somewhat daintily from the same pot of "shackles" as himself, old Dick hung the sack over the tent opening and left her mothering the pups. He limped off to work. The hedge he was laying was on an upland farm that overlooked his wood. At midday when he lunched he could sit and stare over the vast stern brownness that was so soon to unbend in unbelievable trellises of leaves. Already the clearings and banks were freckled with primroses, the nut thickets hung with showers of yellow pods, and the pilewort's cresset in the hedge was a beam to wandering bees. In all that vastitude there was one tiny hole into which he had crept like a snail for years and years, but it was too small to hide him for ever and ever. So now they would go, he and Sossy.

[1] *draughty:* drafty.

Just beside him was a pond and the barns of the farm. Two white horses were nuzzling each other in the croft, and a magpie watched them from the cone of a stack. A red ox at the pond snuffled in the water, and as it lifted its head to stare at the old man, streams of water pattered back from its hairy lips. Deftly the ox licked with its tongue first one nostril, then the other, but water still dribbled from its mouth in one long glutinous [1] stripe. A large cloud hung above the scene, brooding, white and silent as a swan. Old Dick rose and stretched himself; the wind had died. When the afternoon had worn on he ceased work and turned home. Half-way through the woods he came to a clearing full of primroses, and on a bank, with her muzzle in a rich clump of the blooms, lay his dog, shot through the breast. The old man knelt down beside his dog, but there was nothing he could do, she had been dead a long time. He recalled hearing the shot of a gun, hours ago, not a sharp report, but sullen. Perhaps she had gone out for a scamper and had been chasing a rabbit, or perhaps she had left her litter in order to come to him. The keeper had shot her, shot a poor man's dog, shot her dead. There was nothing he could do, the doom had come crushing even time in its swiftness.

"Fizzled and mizzled I am now," he said forlornly, "and that's a fact."

He left there and, conversing angrily, pottered home to his tent. Two of the pups were already dead. The others were helpless, and he was helpless; there was nothing he could do for them, they were too young to feed by hand, and he had nothing to feed them with. He crawled out of the tent to suck a long drink from the bucket of water that stood outside, and then he knelt there gazing without vision at the smoldering fire.

[1] glutinous (gloō'tǐ·nŭs): gluey in nature.

"I know, yes, I know what I can do," he mumbled, picking up his long, heavy billhook.[2] "Just a smack o' that behind his earhole and he won't take no more hidings from e'er a man or a woman neither. Tipet, I says, and he'd be done, he'd be done in a couple o' minutes, ah, quicker, quicker'n you could say smoke." He dashed the billhook to the earth and groaned. "Oh I be fair fizzled and mizzled now, I be, ah." He sat up and pulled the bucket between his legs. Picking up one of the pups he plopped it into the bucket. "There's your donkey," he gurgled, "huh, huh, huh! And there" — as he plopped the others in one by one — "goes your cob and your cart and your cokernuts. And there" — as he dashed the last one violently in.

After a while the old man rose and emptied the drowned bodies into a heap of bushes; the clash of the bucket as he flung it back only fretted [3] the silence of the wood for a few moments.

[2] billhook: a cutting or pruning instrument with a hooked point. [3] fretted: disturbed.

A REALISTIC TALE

1. First, check the exact meaning of the word *venerable*. Who used this word in reference to the old man? Explain how they used it. Does the word really describe him? Why do you think the author chose this word? What did the other members of the village think of the old man?

2. Why was the old man allowed to stay in the wood? Explain how he lived "on air and affability and primed his starved heart with hope." What became of his "roseate dream"?

3. Give reasons for the antagonism which develops between the old man and the new gamekeeper. Where in the story do you first become aware of the gamekeeper's plan of revenge?

4. Describe the old man's feelings when he first finds his dog. How do these feelings change from this point to the end of the story? Has the old man been treated unjustly?

ANALYZING CONFLICT

In Robert Louis Stevenson's "Markheim" (page 557) we were especially interested in the character's reaction to his conscience. Where in that story does the working of the conscience become the main part of the narrative? From that point on, we are engaged in analyzing the conflict created by Stevenson between Markheim and his conscience. Markheim's final act is a solution to the conflict.

The conflict in a short story is often what most easily captures the interest of the reader. Consider the conflict in "The Lagoon" — the problem Arsat faces in the situation he describes to the white man. Can you describe his struggle? This conflict becomes important to you, the reader. Whether or not you agree with the decision he makes is determined by your own analysis of the conflict.

What is conflict? Conflict can be discord between personalities, ideas, interests, and even cultures. Man can be in conflict with nature. There can be conflict between characters — in a clash of worldly wisdom with unworldly innocence, for example. Because of the many different kinds of conflict to be found — as many kinds as there are in life itself — it is important for you to learn to recognize the conflict in the particular story that you are reading.

In "The Old Venerable" there is a conflict that for the old man moves toward tragedy. Where is the conflict first set in motion? Find the paragraph in which the first warning of tragedy appears. Describe the conflict at this point in the story. Now consider how the old man's antagonism toward the gamekeeper is developed. Does the conflict become just a clash of the personalities of the gamekeeper and the Old Venerable, or is it more than this? Note the Old Venerable's lack of struggle at the end, his complete defeat, the end of the conflict. Try to state briefly in your own words what you believe to be the major conflict in this story.

The Japanese Quince

JOHN GALSWORTHY 1867–1933

The year before his death John Galsworthy was awarded the Nobel Prize for Literature. It was a well-deserved honor, for Galsworthy had been writing distinguished fiction and drama for a third of a century.

In his person, Galsworthy represented the best tradition of England — descent from a cultivated family of Surrey, education at Harrow and Oxford, and training in the law. Though he did not practice his profession, his legal turn of mind emerges in his writings. Concerned with the problems his characters must face, he is always the unbiased judge, not the prosecuting attorney. No other modern writer gives quite the same impression of sane and balanced judgment of his characters. He shows so clearly why people act as they do that the reader can scarcely condemn even the most unpleasant of them. His great social

"The Japanese Quince" from *A Motley* by John Galsworthy, copyright 1910 by Charles Scribner's Sons: renewal 1938 Ada Galsworthy. Reprinted with the permission of Charles Scribner's Sons, and William Heinemann Ltd. as publishers of the British Commonwealth edition.

dramas suggest the nature of their conflicts by their titles: *Justice* — the irony of how the process of law wrecks the life of a weak character; *Strife* — the devastating results of capital-labor troubles; *Escape* — the emotional experiences of an escaped convict; *Loyalties* — the cross-purposes of allegiances when a crime is involved.

As a writer of novels, Galsworthy created the Forsyte family and followed their fortunes through several generations, beginning with the Victorians. Three of his novels were combined into *The Forsyte Saga,* one of the best-loved works of this century. A later volume, *A Modern Comedy,* brings the younger Forsytes through World War I.

Galsworthy was always keenly aware of the tastes of his time. He was one of the first playwrights to use natural, colloquial speech in his plays rather than the stilted speech prevalent in earlier drama.

Although you are given only a brief glimpse of Mr. Nilson in "The Japanese Quince," Galsworthy provides considerable illumination of his character's life. There are passages which give you clues to an understanding of what Mr. Nilson's life is like and of the social class to which he belongs. Watch for these as you read.

As MR. NILSON, well known in the City,[1] opened the window of his dressing room on Campden Hill, he experienced a peculiar sweetish sensation in the back of his throat, and a feeling of emptiness just under his fifth rib. Hooking the window back, he noticed that a little tree in the Square Gardens had come out in blossom, and that the thermometer stood at sixty. "Perfect morning," he thought; "spring at last!"

Resuming some meditations on the price of Tintos,[2] he took up an ivory-backed handglass and scrutinized his face. His firm, round, well-opened, clear gray eyes, wore a reassuring appearance of good health. Putting on his black frock coat, he went downstairs.

In the dining room his morning paper was laid out on the sideboard. Mr. Nilson had scarcely taken it in his hand when he again became aware of that queer feeling. Somewhat concerned, he went to the French window and descended the scrolled iron steps into the fresh air. A cuckoo clock struck eight.

"Half an hour to breakfast," he thought; "I'll take a turn in the Gardens."

He had them to himself, and proceeded to pace the circular path with his morning paper clasped behind him. He had scarcely made two revolutions, however, when it was borne in on him that, instead of going away in the fresh air, the feeling had increased. He drew several deep breaths, having heard deep breathing recommended by his wife's doctor; but they augmented rather than diminished the sensation — as of some sweetish liquor in course within him, together with a faint aching just above his heart. Running over what he had eaten the night before, he could recollect no unusual dish, and it occurred to him that it might possibly be some smell affecting him. But he could detect nothing except a faint sweet lemony scent, rather agreeable than otherwise, which evidently emanated from the bushes budding in the sunshine. He was on the point of resuming his promenade, when a blackbird close by burst into song, and, looking up, Mr. Nilson saw at a distance of perhaps five yards a little tree, in the heart of whose branches the bird was perched. He stood staring curiously at this tree, recognizing it for that which he had noticed from his window. It was covered with young blossoms, pink and white, and little bright green leaves both round and spiky; and on all this blossom and these leaves the sunlight glistened. Mr. Nilson smiled; the little tree was so alive and pretty! And instead of passing on, he stayed there smiling at the tree.

---

[1] *City:* the financial and commercial section of London. [2] *Tintos:* red Madeira wines.

"Morning like this!" he thought; "and here I am the only person in the Square who has the — to come out and —!" But he had no sooner conceived this thought than he saw quite near him a man with his hands behind him, who was also staring up and smiling at the little tree. Rather taken aback, Mr. Nilson ceased to smile, and looked furtively at the stranger. It was his next-door neighbor, Mr. Tandram, well known in the City, who had occupied the adjoining house for some five years. Mr. Nilson perceived at once the awkwardness of his position, for, being married, they had not yet had occasion to speak to one another. Doubtful as to his proper conduct, he decided at last to murmur: "Fine morning!" and was passing on, when Mr. Tandram answered: "Beautiful, for the time of year!" Detecting a slight nervousness in his neighbor's voice, Mr. Nilson was embolded to regard him openly. He was of about Mr. Nilson's own height, with firm, well-colored cheeks, neat brown moustaches, and round, well-opened, clear gray eyes; and he was wearing a black frock coat. Mr. Nilson noticed that he had his morning paper clasped behind him as he looked up at the little tree. And, visited somehow by the feeling that he had been caught out, he said abruptly:

"Er — can you give me the name of that tree?"

Mr. Tandram answered:

"I was about to ask you that," and stepped toward it. Mr. Nilson also approached the tree.

"Sure to have its name on, I should think," he said.

Mr. Tandram was the first to see the little label, close to where the blackbird had been sitting. He read it out.

"Japanese quince!"

"Ah!" said Mr. Nilson, "thought so. Early flowerers."

"Very," assented Mr. Tandram, and added: "Quite a feelin' in the air to-day."

Mr. Nilson nodded.

"It was a blackbird singin'," he said.

"Blackbirds," answered Mr. Tandram. "I prefer them to thrushes myself; more body in the note." And he looked at Mr. Nilson in an almost friendly way.

"Quite," murmured Mr. Nilson. "These exotics, they don't bear fruit. Pretty blossom!" and he again glanced up at the blossom, thinking: "Nice fellow, this, I rather like him."

Mr. Tandram also gazed at the blossom. And the little tree, as if appreciating their attention, quivered and glowed. From a distance the blackbird gave a loud, clear call. Mr. Nilson dropped his eyes. It struck him suddenly that Mr. Tandram looked a little foolish; and, as if he had seen himself, he said: "I must be going in. Good morning!"

A shade passed over Mr. Tandram's face, as if he, too, had suddenly noticed something about Mr. Nilson.

"Good morning," he replied, and clasping their journals to their backs they separated.

Mr. Nilson retraced his steps toward his garden window, walking slowly so as to avoid arriving at the same time as his neighbor. Having seen Mr. Tandram mount his scrolled iron steps, he ascended his own in turn. On the top step he paused.

With the slanting spring sunlight darting and quivering into it, the Japanese quince seemed more living than a tree. The blackbird had returned to it, and was chanting out his heart.

Mr. Nilson sighed; again he felt that queer sensation, that choky feeling in his throat.

The sound of a cough or sigh attracted his attention. There, in the shadow of his French window, stood Mr. Tandram, also looking forth across the Gardens at the little quince tree.

Unaccountably upset, Mr. Nilson turned abruptly into the house, and opened his morning paper.

A GLIMPSE OF LIFE

1. Find the clues which suggest what Mr. Nilson's life is like. What really is troubling him? Find the words which define his "ailment."

2. Of what significance are the similarities of Mr. Nilson and Mr. Tandram in appearance, manner, and situation? What abstractions or qualities does the quince tree seem to represent?

3. "The Japanese Quince" contains little action, but it dramatizes a conflict. Decide exactly what that conflict is. How is it resolved? In a sentence, state the purpose of the story.

All Yankees
Are Liars

ERIC KNIGHT 1897–1943

Photo Researchers, Inc.

Few modern English authors have lived a more varied life than Eric Knight. He was a man of two cultures — an Anglo-American; for him, going across the Atlantic was almost like going across the street. Knight was born in Yorkshire, in the north of England, but he married an American and lived in this country intermittently. His experiences here and abroad provided a broad background for a writer of fiction. At different periods of his life he was an art student in New York, a factory worker in Manchester, a screen writer in Hollywood, a critic for the Philadelphia *Ledger,* a major in the United States Army, and a soldier in a Canadian regiment in World War I. During World War II he was killed in an airplane crash.

Eric Knight's stories reflect his sympathetic understanding of the lives of ordinary people. His *Song on Your Bugles* and his last novel, *This Above All,* are moving stories about the working people of England; and *The Flying Yorkshireman,* while a delightful fantasy, is also a shrewd appraisal of the foibles and strengths of his countrymen. The following story illustrates Knight's ability to weave local color into fiction. Its setting is his native Yorkshire, the characters are village folk, and their dialect and mannerisms are those with which the author was fondly familiar. But the influence of America is also apparent in the story. Knight knew this country, and he proves in humorous fashion that "all Yankees are liars."

> *You can always tell the Irish,*
> *You can always tell the Dutch.*
> *You can always tell a Yankee;*
> *But you cannot tell him much.*

M R. SMITH was pleased with The Spread Eagle. He was pleased with Polkingthorpe Brig. The village was off the beaten track — the truly rural sort of English village the American always wants to see.

The inn was low and rambling, with great sloping roofs. Over the door swung the sign — a darksome bird in a weatherbeaten setting.

Everything justified his decision to take this bicycle trip up into the north

"All Yankees Are Liars" from *Sam Small Flies Again* by Eric Knight. Copyright © 1938 by The Curtis Publishing Co. Reprinted by permission of the Author's Estate.

— the mullioned ¹ windows, the roaring fire, the Yorkshire accents of the men who shuffled over the sanded stone floor of the low-ceilinged room as they played darts. Mr. Smith was almost beginning to understand what they were talking about. During his excellent high tea he had sorted out the four men playing darts. One was Saw Cooper, a farmer; a small old man was referred to as Sam; a young, bright-faced lad who played darts left-handed was Gollicker Pearson; and the fourth, a huge man, was just called Ian.

Mr. Smith watched them play, listening to the endless thwock of the darts in the cork board as he finished his meal. The barmaid, plump, corn-haired, came toward him, her apron rustling stiffly.

"Would there be owt else?"

"No. It was a very good meal." Mr. Smith smiled. He wanted to make the girl talk some more. "Er — what do they do for fun in this place of an evening?"

"Foon?" she repeated. "Well, they sit here — or o' Sat'day neights lots o' fowk goa ovver to Wuxley to t' pictures." She waited. "They gate Boock D'Arcy i' T' Singing Cowboy," she added suggestively.

Mr. Smith had already become acquainted with British cinemas in small towns. Also he was a Southern Californian, and had that familiarity with movies that belongs to all Southern Californians. He had no inclination to go four miles to see a last year's Class B Western. "No. I think I'll have another ale and sit here," he said.

"If tha'll sit ovver by t' fire, Ah'll bring it to thee theer. Then Ah can clean opp here."

Mr. Smith sat on the bench by the generous fire and nursed his ale. The dart game came to an end with Saw Cooper losing and paying for the round. The men brought their mugs to the fire. Mr. Smith shifted politely. The men, in

¹ *mullioned* (mŭl'yŭnd): windows whose panes are divided by slender vertical bars.

the presence of a stranger, grew quiet. Mr. Smith decided to put them at ease.

"Pretty chilly for an October evening, isn't it?"

The men considered the remark, as if looking at both sides of it. Finally Saw Cooper spoke.

"Aye," he said.

The others nodded. There was silence, and the five regarded the fire. Then, suddenly, young Gollicker smiled.

"Tha shouldn't heed t' cowd, being a Yankee," he said.

"Ah, but I'm not a Yankee," Mr. Smith said.

They stared at him in disbelief.

"Yankees," explained Mr. Smith, "come from New England."

They looked from Mr. Smith to one another. The big man named Ian took a deep breath.

"Yankees," he said, "coom fro' t' United States."

"Well, yes. New England is a part of the United States," Mr. Smith said. "But it's thousands of miles away from where I live. In fact, believe it or not, I should think you're closer to the Yankees than I am. You see, the United States is a big country. In the part where the Yankees come from, it gets very cold in the winter. Where I am — in Southern California — it never snows. Why, I've never known it to snow there in all my life."

"No snow?" Gollicker breathed.

Mr. Smith smiled. For, after all, he was a Southern Californian — and they were discussing climate. "No snow," he said. "In wintertime we have a bit of a rainy season, but after February it clears, and then it doesn't even rain for nine months — not a drop."

"Noa rain for a nine month — noan at all?" Saw Cooper asked.

"Not a drop. Day after day, the sun comes out, clear skies, never a drop of rain for nine months. Never!"

"Whet do ye graw theer, lad?" Saw asked slyly.

"Lots of things. Truck vegetables,

oranges — all kinds of things."

There was a silence again. Big Ian took a breath.

"Orinjis," he said, and then took another breath, "graw i' Spain."

He looked at Mr. Smith so emphatically that Mr. Smith nodded.

"Oh, yes," he said. "They grow in Spain, too, I understand."

"Orinjis," Ian repeated, "graw i' Spain."

That seemed to settle the question. They all looked in the fire in silence. Saw Cooper sniffed.

"Whet else graws theer?"

"Well, I have a ranch there; we grow alfalfa."

"Whet's that off to be?"

"Alfalfa? We use it for hay. It's a desert plant originally, but it thrives in California. We get eight cuttings a year."

"Eight cuttings o' hay a year?"

"Eight cuttings a year."

The little man, Sam, spoke for the first time: "Mister, if it doan't rain for a nine month, how can ye get eight cuttings o' hay a year?"

"Oh, that's easy," Mr. Smith said. "We irrigate the land." He went into a short but conclusive description of irrigating.

"Heh," Saw Cooper said. "Wheer's this here watter coom fro'?"

"In the San Fernando Valley we buy it from the water company, just like you do in your homes."

"Wheer do they get it?"

"From reservoirs."

"If it doan't rain, where's t' reservoys get t' watter?"

"Oh, we pipe it down from five hundred miles north. It rains a lot up there."

"And ye sprinkle t' farming land out o' t' watter tap. How many acres hesta?"

"It isn't like sprinkling from the tap, of course. I used that to illustrate. The pipes are large — we have fourteen-inch valves on our pipes. We flood the land — cover it right over with water."

Saw looked in the fire. "Does corn graw theer?"

"Well, generally our land is too valuable to put into corn. But it will grow corn fourteen feet high."

They made noises in their throats and shifted their feet.

"Fohteen foot," Saw breathed. "Eigh, ba gum!"

"Mister," Sam said, "once Ah were oop to see t' Firth o' Forth brig. Ah suppose they hev bigger brigs i' Yankee-land?"

Mr. Smith should have touched on the new Oakland bridge, but then, he was a *Southern* Californian.

"We have bridges, but they're building vehicular tunnels under the rivers now."

"Whet for?"

"Well, there's so much motor traffic."

"How many moatorcars goa through 'em?"

Mr. Smith lit his pipe happily. They seemed quite interested in America.

"I couldn't say. The way they turn 'em out, I should say there's hundreds of thousands."

"How fast do they turn 'em out?" Gollicker asked.

"I don't know. I think they roll out finished at the rate of one every couple of minutes."

"And they goa i' tunnels, not i' brigs?" Sam commented.

"Oh, we have some bridges."

"Big uns, Ah suppose."

"Well," Mr. Smith said modestly, thinking of the Pulaski Skyway coming into New York, "we have some that go right over entire towns. You're practically on one bridge for miles."

Saw Cooper spat in the fire. "How many fowk is there in all America?"

Mr. Smith didn't know, but he felt expansive. And after all, there was South America, too.

"A quarter of a billion, I should say," he hazarded.

"A quarter of a billion," they repeated. Then they stared at Mr. Smith, and he became aware of their disbelief.

"Wait a moment," he said. "I think a billion is different in America from here. It's a thousand million in America and a million million here, isn't it?"

"A billion," said Ian slowly, "is a billion."

The others nodded, and then Ian stood. The others rose, too.

"Oh — er — wait a minute. Won't you all have a drink with me?" Mr. Smith invited.

"Us is off to play darts for a round — us four," Ian said meaningly.

The other three laughed.

"Ah knew them theer brigs o' thine'd hev to be big," Saw Cooper said as a parting shot as he swung over the bench. "That's so's they'd be able to goa ovver wheat what graws fohteen foot high when ye sprinkle it fro' t' watter tap."

He grinned at the others in victory.

"I didn't say wheat; I said corn," Mr. Smith protested.

"Same thing," Saw snapped.

"It isn't. Wheat grows in an ear. Corn grows on a cob; it has broad long leaves."

"Heh! That's maize," Saw said.

Big Ian stepped between Saw Cooper and Mr. Smith.

"Now, lad," he said flatly, "tha said corn, and Ah heeard thee. Thee and thy orinjis, and farming out o' t' watter tap, and brigs ovver cities, and it nivver rains, and denying th' art a Yankee, and a billion is a billion and yet it ain't. Tha's tripped thysen oop a dozen times, it seems to me. Now, hesta owt to say?"

Mr. Smith looked at Big Ian, standing belligerently with legs widespread and his thumbs in the waistband of his corduroy trousers. He looked round and saw everyone in the inn waiting, silent.

Then a curious thing happened. In that minute the smell of soft-coal smoke and pig-twist tobacco and ale was gone, and instead Mr. Smith was smelling the mixed odor of sun-baked land and citrus blossom and jasmine and eucalyptus trees, just as you smell it on the cool darkness coming across the San Fer-nando Valley. And he was homesick. Suddenly it felt unreal that he should be so far from home, sitting in an English inn with these men about him. He looked up at the faces, forbidding in their expression of disapproval. And he began to laugh.

It was all so unreal that he laughed until he cried. Every time he looked up he saw the faces, now even more comical in their bewilderment than they had been in their disapproval. They stared at him, and then Big Ian began to laugh.

"Eigh, Ah'll be jiggered!" he roared. "Drat ma buttons if Ah won't!"

It was Mr. Smith's turn to be puzzled now.

Big Ian roared, and suddenly slapped Mr. Smith on the back so heartily that his chin flew up in the air and then banged back on his chest. The others looked on in amazement.

"Why, whet's oop, Ian?" Saw asked.

"Why, ye gowks!" Ian roared. "He's laughing at ye! He's been heving us on! Sitting theer for an hour, keeping his mug straight and telling us the tale! And us swallering it, thinking he was serious!"

"But," Mr. Smith said — "but you don't —— "

"Nay, now no moar on it!" Ian roared. "Ye've codded us for fair, and done it champion! Lewk at owd Sam's face!"

The others regarded Ian and scratched their heads and grinned sheepishly, and finally looked at Mr. Smith in admiration.

"But — " Mr. Smith began again.

"Nay, now, ye copped us napping," Ian said, "and here's ma hand on it. Soa we'll hev noa moar — onless ye'd like to tell us whet Yankeeland's rightly like."

Mr. Smith drew a deep breath. "Well, what would you like to hear about?"

"About cowboys," young Gollicker breathed. "Werta ivver a cowboy?"

For a moment Mr. Smith stood on a brink, and then an imp pushed him over.

"Of course I've been a cowboy — naturally," Mr. Smith said. "What would you like to hear about it?"

"Wait a minute," Gollicker said. They all adjusted themselves on the bench. " Now," he went on, "tell us about a roundup — tha knaws, 'Ah'm yeading for t' last roundup,' like Bing Crosby sings."

Mr. Smith held his mental breath and plunged.

"Ah," he said. "A roundup and the life of a cowboy. Up at the crack of dawn, mates, and down to the corral. There you rope your horse —— "

"A mustang?" Gollicker asked.

"A mustang," Mr. Smith agreed.

"A wild one off'n the prairies, happen?"

"Indeed a wild one from off the prairies," Mr. Smith agreed. "I see you know America yourself."

Gollicker grinned modestly. "Doan't let me interrupt, measter," he apologized.

Mr. Smith drew another breath. He saw he was up against at least one expert, so he made it very good. Inwardly he thanked fate for what he had hitherto regarded as two entirely misspent weeks on a Nevada dude ranch. He gave them, in more senses than one, a moving picture of the cowboy's life.

When he was done, Gollicker sighed and Big Ian nodded.

"Now," Sam said, "how about them bloody buffalo?"

"Ah, the buffalo," Mr. Smith said. "The thundering herd! The bison! For a while there was danger — or thought to be — that the herds were dying out. But now, I am glad to say — and no doubt you are just as glad to hear — the herds are increasing, and ere long, again the crack of a rifle will bring down a bull in full gallop."

"But how about them bloody Indians?" Saw put in.

Mr. Smith considered the Indians at the station in Santa Fe. They didn't seem at all satisfactory. But he was in-

spired. He drew himself up.

"You will pardon me if I do not speak of that," he said. "We have not too much love for the paleface who stole our lands. I say 'we,' for my mother was Yellow Blanket, a princess of the Blackfoot tribe. Therefore, let us not speak of the white man and the red man."

He stared into the fire — majestically, he hoped.

"Now, see what tha's done?" Ian said to Saw. "Happen it'll learn thee to keep thy yapper shut once in a while. . . . Tha maun excuse him, measter. Tell us about gangsters instead. Didta ivver run into any gangsters?"

"Run into them? Why, how could you help it?" Mr. Smith asked.

Swiftly and graphically he painted for them an America in which here was the town where the bullets of the gangs cracked day and night. Here was the last street, and on it the last house, and beyond that was the trackless prairie where the buffalo thundered, the cowboy rode, and the Indian ever lurked.

As he finished, he looked up. Everyone in the inn was listening. Men had gathered behind him silently. At the bar, the maid leaned on her elbows, entranced.

"Ah, I talk too much," Mr. Smith said.

"Nay, goa on, lad," they said. "Goa on."

"Well, it's dry work. How about a drink?"

"Champion," said Saw.

"Owd on," Big Ian said. "Us'll play darts for a round."

"Now, Ian, if the lad wants to buy — "

"Ah said," Ian repeated, "us'll play darts — onybody that wishes to be in on t' round. And t' loser will pay."

Mr. Smith paid anyhow, for the dart game was trickier than he had thought, and they all seemed to be experts.

He was getting very much better when the barmaid called: "Time, gentlemen, please."

Mr. Smith was sorry. It had been a

good evening. They all said good night cheerfully. Big Ian shook him by the hand.

"Well, soa long, lad. We had a champion time. But Ah just want to say, tha didn't fool me when tha were kidding us at first. Tha sees, for one thing, us goas to t' pictures and so us knaws whet America's really like. And then Ah'd allus heeard tell that all Yankees were liars."

"Yes," Mr. Smith said, regarding his conscience, "I did tell some lies."

"Aye, but Ah suppose it's a way ye Yankees hev," Ian said. "But it's all right as long as tha told us t' trewth finally."

YANKEES AND YORKSHIREMEN

1. How does the four-line jingle at the beginning fit the story? What does the name "Yankee" mean as Mr. Smith uses it? as the Yorkshiremen use it?

2. What is the central idea of the story? When do the Yorkshiremen begin to disbelieve Mr. Smith? How does Mr. Smith finally win their favor? How do the Yorkshiremen remind you of people in general?

3. In what part of England is Yorkshire? This story is full of what is usually called "local color" — descriptions of setting and characters and use of dialect that build up an impression of a particular place. Find several examples of local color.

4. How does Knight achieve his humor? Select passages that illustrate his humor.

The Ballroom

WILLIAM SANSOM 1912–

Like some earlier English writers, William Sansom substituted travel for a university degree. He has traveled in Europe; he has lived in France, Germany, Spain, and Hungary. During World War II, he joined the London Fire Service, which helped the city survive the tremendous bombing attacks. Sansom's first book, *Fireman Flower and Other Stories*, reflects wartime London.

After the war Sansom worked as a script writer for a time and then left his job to devote himself entirely to writing. Since then he has enjoyed literary recognition with the publication of short story collections such as *A Contest of Ladies, Among the Dahlias*, and *A Touch of the Sun*. Some of his recent novels are *A Bed of Roses, The Loving Eye*, and *The Cautious*

Heart. As a member of the new generation of British storytellers, he has also written for such magazines as *Horizon, New Writing*, and *Cornhill*, all English literary periodicals. In acknowledgment of his literary talent, he has been awarded prizes by the Society of Authors and elected a Fellow of the Royal Society of Literature.

Like Katherine Mansfield and Virginia Woolf of an earlier generation, Sansom prefers to concentrate on the feelings and thoughts of a character over a short period of time rather than to spin out a long narrative. In such stories time seems to stand still while the storyteller probes into the character's emotions. He also tries to arouse in us a sense of pity and understanding. See if he succeeds.

"The Ballroom" from *A Contest of Ladies* by William Sansom, published in 1956 by The Hogarth Press Ltd. Reprinted by permission of The Hogarth Press Ltd. and Russell & Volkening, Inc..

Strange weather! A warm morning, with all the windows open and the sunlight making a pale fool of the big log fire. Wet and warm in the garden outside, muddy and fresh: and inside the Christmas cards looked like invitations to a summer rout, the holly and mistletoe hung like the morning after some May-Day-night-before, cotton-wool snow looked particularly like cotton-wool and nothing like snow, the tinsel glittered in the sun with the tarnished tang of old seaside souvenirs. Two or three flies Hoovered [1] a Monday buzz about the ceiling and in the garden a red-hot robin stamped its dislike of such an unseasonable Christmas Morning.

Snow and ice are seldom to be hoped for. The least that might be expected is a touch of the magic of frost, a winter glitter and a brisk raw bite in the air, something to match the glowing coals and the good rich food. However . . . on that morning there was no hope left, and as Lesseps went to look out over the garden it was in a mood of ill-ease — he felt that he ought to be scrambling the deck-chairs out for an early airing, not thinking of sherry and turkey and the rest of whatever conviviality lay ahead. There was a steam in the air, no wind, and across the hedge at the garden's end the steam thickened to mist above the warm mysterious depths of the Chine. Beyond this lay a wilderness of trees and the ivy-clad walls of Waltham.

The sun struck gold on the topmost windows of this great Victorian house that then belonged to the lady we only knew as "Miss Amery" — and it was perhaps the sudden illumination of a turreted and gabled edifice so in keeping with the idea of an old-fashioned Christmas that led Lesseps once again that morning to wonder about this Miss Amery. The sun struck the topmost windows — and even these had their white blinds drawn — but he knew that in the shadowed wilderness of dripping and overgrown trees and ivy below all the rest of the house would lie in a kind of dead shuttered dusk cut off absolutely from this wide-lit morning. Within the padlocked gates, up the bough-hung drive and under the peeling gables lay a darker world: Miss Amery was what they call a recluse. She had not left the house for fifteen years.

Many the theories. But only one thing is certain about such a secret life, and that is a final uncertainty of anyone getting to know exactly how it is lived. The houses of such solitaries have been examined after death — a litter of filth, a wilderness of papers, hoards of money have been found: and once even a house within a house, corridors and rooms lined with the empty tins of a decade, each immaculately shined. But whatever is found, people can only suppose how life was actually lived; nobody *knows*, the germ of the bitter or the radiant secret dies with its conceiver.

So with Miss Amery. But she still lived, and the theories with her. Some said The War. Others that she had always been queer, from a young girl. Others spoke of something that had happened in her childhood. But nobody knew. And few people ever saw her. There were tales that she had occasional guests — once a schoolgirl had been seen in the park: but that might have been any apple-happy intruder of the afternoon.

At all events she was no terrifying figure. No pig-faced woman suffering within her black veil; no wild-eyed brooder over dark religions; no tall, soured châtelaine [2] with the big hands of a stranger. None of these. The few who saw or had seen her, like the postman, talked simply of a little "frail"

---

[1] *Hoover:* a brand name for a vacuum cleaner.

[2] *châtelaine:* the mistress of a château.

old lady. Pale eyes, white skin, fragile, timid; a very ordinary picture of lavender and lace.

Yet a vague picture. And on that Christmas Morning, thinking of her all alone somewhere beneath her sunblinded tower — Lesseps suddenly felt a longing to visit her. Don't be a fool, he told himself, she'd hate it. You're just restless. You're just lonely yourself for your white snow and frost.

But the idea persisted. And late that afternoon he excused himself from warm port on the verandah and "went for a walk." As he passed over the Chine bridge he pretended: I'll just get into the grounds and look around. I won't disturb the old girl.

But he never really hesitated; and certainly not on that giddying thin iron bridge that overhung such a sudden rocky drop and its weird wet growth of fern far beneath.

Then the wall of Waltham faced him. Higher than a man, it leaned its old red brickness for as far as he could see to either side: it came from mist and vanished into mist, and this made it seem to go on for ever. It was old, silent, decayed — it kept the eyes from seeing what was beyond, it sat there saying as all walls say: "Keep out." The only sound was the dripping of trees. He felt uneasy. But nevertheless measured its height, the crumbling of its mossed bricks, the inward tilt it took from the roots of trees that would one day overturn its foundation. Would it take his weight? He heard the crash of brick, a sudden thunderclap dying again into the wet silence of the trees. He put his left foot in a crevice, pulled himself up and over, dropped soundlessly on to thick black leaves the other side.

Over. When he had put his foot up, he had felt as guilty and small as a child: now, the deed done and in forbidden territory, he was suddenly instead big as a child feeling itself big as a man, on its mettle. In that deserted overgrown wilderness, even in such quiet, he held his breath and listened. What a different world inside! The sun was sinking — it must have been nearly four o'clock; but those trees were already dark with moss and age, everything creaked and dripped and hung at broken levels, and as he now walked forward in the direction of the house the sky seemed to disappear altogether in a depth of long-fingering arms interlaced above. It was like entering the gloom that masses before a fog in a great town; the air peculiarly still, no fog yet, but all light gone. Yet in its way, at that time, it was preferable to the world outside — this darkness and mystery more matched the mood of Christmas.

He walked on. No twigs snapped, everything too old, rotten, wet. Beneath the trees a thick undergrowth of elder and nettles had grown; he had to snake his way through — once he stopped suddenly, holding his breath: a statue, an eyeless youth in Greek drapery, was watching him from the thicket; mossed and in half-shadow, it stood still as life. He coughed — no echo — and went on. He came up against a huge high bank of overgrown laurel. He had to walk some way to skirt it; it was like a high green wall within the walled garden: but at last he rounded it — and there suddenly was the house itself. He drew back against the laurel. The house accused him with its immense, sudden presence. But then he saw how utterly dead it was — or how deeply asleep. White blinds were drawn over all the upper windows. Creeper hung thick about the lower reaches, a gabled porch and Gothic buttresses, tall stone-framed downstairs windows. From where he stood he could see the rusted bellpull — and wondered how it could possibly work. Wondering, he found himself going toward it — and then quickly ran the last few yards across the open, weed-grown gravel.

Now he stood in the porch, among wind-blown leaves and littered paper, as if in a deserted wind shelter on a sea front, and looked at that bellpull. It was dead with rust. Thick spider webs, heavy with rotted seed, hung across it. Suddenly he thought, and his stomach dropped — perhaps the old lady was dead? Perhaps no one knows? But then he remembered how groceries and food were still delivered, probably at a back door. They would soon have known in the village. Yet this was a holiday; Christmas is a busy time, the shops had been shut a day already. At the thought again of Christmas it passed absurdly through his mind that if anyone caught him there in the porch he could start singing a carol; but at the same time he decided to go round the house and see if there was a back door that might look more used. But — his mind whispered — with a pile of groceries never taken in?

He never went round.

He held his breath, wondering what so suddenly had happened. Sound? Movement? Something had happened: and everything was changed. But there was no sound, nothing had moved in the porch. What . . . ? And then he realized. The most obvious thing, so obvious that it had passed his notice. All the lights of one of the rooms facing the drive had been turned on — the great dark bank of laurel was now a high pale emerald mass, leaf upon leaf of green and gold, a high theatrical screen of leaf, and across the gravel itself the tall garden windows had thrown their giant rectangular shapes.

Yet no shadow crossed this great new light, no sound echoed its muffling from within the house. It was like an empty theater lit by a dead man's hand.

Lesseps hardly waited.

He moved quickly out of the porch and in again to the wall, creeping like a thief, turning his coat collar up to hide his white shirt, sprung on the toes of his shoes that made no sound on such wet mold, rounding the big buttress until he could squeeze against the stone window frame and peer carefully round, using one eye.

Every chandelier in that room was lit.

The windows reached nearly to the ground and all inside, as in a huge glass-case, was light. The floor had been freshly polished and shone with light: tall mirrors on all the walls reflected it further, and the twists and coils of their gilt frames winked and glittered: and then the mirrors reflected each other, one mirror within another within another, until the room receded for ever in corridors of mirror on every side: in each mirror shone a crystal wealth of chandelier, and wherever it struck, either in a leaping of shadows or a red-gilt flaming tongue, there rose and fell the effigy of a great log fire blazing to one end of the room in a richly marbled fireplace. Heavy curtains hung undrawn by the windows. Lesseps's one eye came round by a large gilt-tassel. It must have been the old ballroom.

But old? It was as alive as it had ever been. And in its very center stood a tall Christmas Tree bright with yellow candles. Colored globes caught the fire-shadow, tinsel laced its sparkling snow about the dark branches, and all danced with light; the yellow candles burned steadily upwards, yet sometimes shuddered — it must have been a draught from the fire — leaning afraid all one way, and then as suddenly resuming their solid upward flame.

He stood there held with wonder. It was a magical scene — all polish, wealth, and warmth . . . but empty, no sign of a single person.

And the minutes passed. The last of the red evening sun fell down through the black wet trees outside. Lesseps thought: How exactly like the colored plates in a book of fairy stories, there is no difference, the old red sun casts its strange winter light and the trees become huge, you can still see the drip and drab of ordinary life, but it recedes, light and shadow are really in charge, you're more in an old book than anywhere else. Then he smelled life again, as the sun flashed down and the first sharp nose of a winter's chill envigored the night. Soon he would see his breath.

He peered back into the window. Nobody had come. Nothing had moved but the candles, the fire flames, and the shadows that were always moving. And this motionless moving, this empty liveliness, gave the room more death than if the house had been shut and dark and truly dead; as with a ghost-ship, all sails set, all lights ablaze — empty on an empty ocean; or the shop-window stage of a room, playing the dead life of dummies and never-used furniture, all lights on and nothing, nothing ever to happen. But behind the doors of such rooms people wait: the doors hold back unbelievable crowds waiting to burst in.

And that, then, was what actually happened, unbelievably, exactly in front of Lesseps' one peering eye. So startling him that he drew this back behind the window frame.

Abruptly the room had poured full of children!

A dam of children had burst, it was like that moment in the empty street when a morning of children breaks out of the cinema and the street is stopped with arms and legs and voices whirling and screaming over every inch. He quickly drew back. Where? How? How did they get there . . . ? And all those children had been little girls! Ten, twenty, thirty little girls in white party dresses flooded in through the door! And all had been dressed, he thought, surely alike? All in white, all in sashes alive in the light, blue bows bobbing in each head of curls; all dancing.

He peered round the window frame again. With the air chilling, the window glass was beginning to mist: safe enough, he would never be seen now.

He saw instantly what a mistake he had made — this was after all no room full of girls, it was of course one child only, one child reflected in a dozen mirrors.

And now that one pretty little child, so small and alone among her dozen glittering shadows in so large-lit a hall of a room — the one little child approached on tiptoe the Christmas Tree and bravely, beautifully, dropped a curtsy.

All alone she began to dance.

Lesseps watched charmed and fascinated through the pale mist beading the window. It was growing much colder with the sun down, it was dark now and he shivered out there among the dripping trees — but he only remembered feeling a sense of great gladness and warmth that after all, in that huge lonely shuttered house, the old lady did have her secret friends. Who they might be, he hardly considered — the scene was so warm, friendly, well-lit, a picture of festive content.

Then, as he told us afterwards, a sense of uneasiness grew upon him. He could not say what it was, he tried to push it aside. He thought it was some previous association with the house. Or even his lowered spirits out there in the chill garden. But the feeling persisted, and he began to wonder: had it something to do with such a little girl all alone in so great a room? For as the minutes passed, no one came to be with her — and it began to seem that she, the little one, was the only life in that huge house. A dreadful notion came to him, which he put quickly aside — had the old lady died upstairs and was this child who had come to stay, simply, in her innocence thinking her grand-aunt asleep, dancing on with the fun?

For she never stopped dancing. To and fro, up to the great fireplace, down the polished wood to the mirrors, pirouetting, pointing a toe, weaving her arms into some pretty arabesque,[1] greeting the image of herself in a dozen long mirrors — and always returning, for it was the most special place, to the Christmas Tree.

Lesseps grew more aware — perhaps because it was the central point of her

[1] *arabesque:* a ballet position in which the dancer bends forward on one leg, extends the corresponding arm horizontally forward, and the other arm and leg backward.

dancing — of that Christmas Tree. It seemed in presence to become taller; and it held now a quiet imminence of movement, the feeling tall wardrobes have, standing so very still and forbidding, that they might at any moment move. . . . He thought: Nonsense. This is only the uneasy memory of old Christmases, old toys, as garish toys can terrify: the nightmare quality of toys and trees that some children carry with them for ever. And of course, Lesseps concluded, I was such a child. Puppets, golliwogs, even the Happy Family cards, frightened me.

But he felt a sudden wish to get away, to get back behind that bank of wet laurels bathed in their high golden light.

He did the opposite.

He went straight forward and pressed his face against the window.

It was misting now beyond the brightness of the light. He thought he would never be seen. He was holding his breath to see.

But he was seen.

Almost instantly the little girl, in the middle of a pirouette, stopped, stared into his eyes, screamed a hand up to her mouth, and fled back straight into that Christmas Tree.

In a second her dress was blazing.

He had his boot off and was smashing through the glass. The draught of sudden air fanned the flame higher — but he got to her quickly and muffled her in his coat and rolled this poor little bundle on the floor. Then he picked her up and quietly held her in his arms.

She was not badly burned. But she was dead. She must have died of shock.

And then, Lesseps said, his voice was raised to cry for help, to hoarse his wretched stupid sickened heart out — but he never breathed a word . . . for only then did his eyes realize, slowly, the thin blue-veined leg in his hand, the gray-gold hair, the old enameled face — and a mouth set now not in anguish but in sleeping peace, the shade of a smile of childhood dreams on her thin shriveled lips.

A SURPRISE ENDING

1. Did the ending of this story come as a shock to you? The outcome of a story must be made to seem plausible in terms of the information which the author provides. Find clues in the story which helped you to accept the climax.

2. To what extent does the author reveal the personality of Miss Amery? How much does Lesseps really know about her? In what ways are Waltham and Miss Amery alike?

3. Review Lesseps' feelings as he views the ballroom. Describe the emotional impact of the final incident on Lesseps. What specifically appeals to you in this story? What do you learn from "The Ballroom" about the way to end a story?

REACTING TO SUSPENSE

When you are uncertain what will happen next and anxious to find out, you are reacting to an important element of the short story: suspense. What is going to happen to the main character? Can a situation be improved? These and many other questions are in your mind as the writer prepares you for the climax of the action. A story which creates in you this sense of anticipation or suspense will hold your attention. As the British critic E. M. Forster says, the "and then" is what keeps the reader interested. The skillful use of suspense is certainly one way to judge a writer's skill.

The suspense in "The Ballroom" begins almost immediately — in the second paragraph with the garden "in a mood of illease." From that point on, trace the suspense as Sansom builds it: (1) the sudden illumination of Waltham, (2) theories about Miss Amery's life, (3) the decision to visit Miss Amery, (4) scaling the wall of Waltham, (5) entering "that deserted overgrown wilderness," (6) arrival at the house, (7) the turning on of the lights, (8) viewing "a magical scene," (9) watching the dancing child, (10) being seen at the window, (11) entering the blazing room, (12) making a shocking discovery.

The Verger

W. SOMERSET MAUGHAM 1874–

The early life of W. Somerset Maugham (môm) was unhappy. He was born in France of English parents who both died when he was still a boy. Thereafter he went to England to live in the cold, stern atmosphere of his uncle's home. This setting appears in Maugham's novel *Cakes and Ale,* in which he describes a boy like himself: shy, uncertain, afflicted with a stammer, but also imaginative and responsive. Maugham studied in English schools and at the University of Heidelberg. He wanted to be a writer but at the insistence of his uncle studied medicine instead. After a year's internship in the Lambeth slums of London, Maugham suffered an attack of tuberculosis and soon left to travel on the Continent, where he began writing. He worked steadily for years; success did not come easily. In his most famous novel, *Of Human Bondage,* he tells the moving story of a young medical student much like himself.

Somerset Maugham has become perhaps the most accomplished storyteller of our time. He has traveled the world over and gathered tales along the way — stories and novels and plays with strange incidents, odd characters, often exotic settings. Possibly one secret of his popularity lies in his stated purpose in writing — entertainment. "Pleasure," he says, "is in itself good." Yet Maugham writes of neither the pleasant nor the pretty. While he does not plead for the poor, he depicts the upper classes with an irony that is often malicious.

THERE had been a christening that afternoon at St. Peter's, Neville Square, and Albert Edward Foreman still wore his verger's [1] gown. He kept his new one, its folds as full and stiff as though it were made not of alpaca but of perennial bronze, for funerals and weddings (St. Peter's, Neville Square, was a church much favored by the fashionable for these ceremonies), and now he wore only his second best. He wore it with complacence; for it was the dignified symbol of his office, and without it (when he took it off to go home) he had the disconcerting sensation of being somewhat insufficiently clad. He took pains with it; he pressed it and ironed it himself. During the sixteen years he had been verger of this church he had had a succession of such gowns; but he had never been able to throw them away when they were worn out, and the complete series, neatly wrapped up in brown paper, lay in the bottom drawer of the wardrobe in his bedroom.

The verger busied himself quietly, replacing the painted wooden cover on the marble font, taking away a chair that had been brought for an infirm old lady,

[1] *verger:* an employee, or official, who takes care of the interior of a church building and exhibits it to visitors.

"The Verger" from *The Cosmopolitans* by W. Somerset Maugham, copyright, 1923, 1924, 1925, 1926, 1927, 1928, 1929, 1936, by Doubleday and Co., Inc. Reprinted by permission of Doubleday and Co., Inc.; A. P. Watt and Son; William Heinemann Limited; and the author.

and waited for the vicar to have finished in the vestry so that he could tidy up in there and go home. Presently he saw him walk across the chancel, genuflect in front of the high altar, and come down the aisle; but he still wore his cassock.

"What's he 'anging about for?" the verger said to himself. "Don't 'e know I want my tea?"

The vicar had been but recently appointed, a red-faced, energetic man in his early forties, and Albert Edward still regretted his predecessor, a clergyman of the old school who preached leisurely sermons in a silvery voice and dined out a great deal with his more aristocratic parishioners. He liked things in church to be just so, but he never fussed; he was not like this new man who wanted to have his finger in every pie. But Albert Edward was tolerant. St. Peter's was in a very good neighborhood and the parishioners were a very nice class of people. The new vicar had come from the East End, and he couldn't be expected to fall in all at once with the discreet ways of his fashionable congregation.

"All this 'ustle," said Albert Edward. "But give 'im time; he'll learn."

When the vicar had walked down the aisle so far that he could address the verger without raising his voice more than was becoming in a place of worship, he stopped.

"Foreman, will you come into the vestry for a minute? I have something to say to you."

"Very good, sir."

The vicar waited for him to come up and they walked up the church together.

"A very nice christening, I thought, sir. Funny 'ow the baby stopped cryin' the moment you took him."

"I've noticed they very often do," said the vicar, with a little smile. "After all, I've had a good deal of practice with them."

It was a source of subdued pride to him that he could nearly always quiet a whimpering infant by the manner in which he held it, and he was not unconscious of the amused admiration with which mothers and nurses watched him settle the baby in the crook of his surpliced arm. The verger knew that it pleased him to be complimented on his talent.

The vicar preceded Albert Edward into the vestry. Albert Edward was a trifle surprised to find the two churchwardens there. He had not seen them come in. They gave him pleasant nods.

"Good afternoon, my lord. Good afternoon, sir," he said to one after the other.

They were elderly men, both of them, and they had been churchwardens almost as long as Albert Edward had been verger. They were sitting now at a handsome refectory table that the old vicar had brought many years before from Italy, and the vicar sat down in the vacant chair between them. Albert Edward faced them, the table between him and them, and wondered with slight uneasiness what was the matter. He remembered still the occasion on which the organist had got into trouble and the bother they had had to hush things up. In a church like St. Peter's, Neville Square, they couldn't afford a scandal. On the vicar's red face was a look of resolute benignity, but the others bore an expression that was slightly troubled.

"He's been naggin' them, he 'as," said the verger to himself. "He's jockeyed them into doin' something, but they don't 'alf like it. That's what it is; you mark my words."

But his thoughts did not appear on Albert Edward's clean-cut and distinguished features. He stood in a respectful but not obsequious attitude. He had been in service before he was appointed to his ecclesiastical office, but only in very good houses, and his deportment was irreproachable. Starting as a page boy in the household of a merchant prince, he had risen by due degrees from the position of fourth to first footman; for a year he had been singlehanded butler to a widowed peeress and, till the vacancy occurred at St. Peter's, butler with two men under him in the house of a retired ambassador. He was tall, spare, grave, and dignified. He looked, if not like a duke, at least like an actor of the old school who specialized in dukes' parts. He had tact, firmness, and self-assurance. His character was unimpeachable.

The vicar began briskly.

"Foreman, we've got something rather unpleasant to say to you. You've been here a great many years, and I think his lordship and the general agree with me that you've fulfilled the duties of your office to the satisfaction of everybody concerned."

The two churchwardens nodded.

"But a most extraordinary circumstance came to my knowledge the other day and I felt it my duty to impart it to the churchwardens. I discovered to my astonishment that you could neither read nor write."

The verger's face betrayed no sign of embarrassment.

"The last vicar knew that, sir," he replied. "He said it didn't make no difference. He always said there was a great deal too much education in the world for 'is taste."

"It's the most amazing thing I ever heard," cried the general. "Do you mean to say that you've been verger of this church for sixteen years and never learned to read or write?"

"I went into service when I was twelve, sir. The cook in the first place tried to teach me once; but I didn't seem to 'ave the knack for it, and then what with one thing and another I never seemed to 'ave the time. I've never really found the want of it. I think a lot of these young fellows waste a lot of time readin' when they might be doin' something useful."

"But don't you want to know the news?" said the other churchwarden. "Don't you ever want to write a letter?"

"No, me lord, I seem to manage very well without. And of late years, now they've all these pictures in the papers, I get to know what's goin' on pretty well. Me wife's quite a scholar, and if I want to write a letter she writes it for me. It's not as if I was a bettin' man."

The two churchwardens gave the vicar a troubled glance and then looked down at the table.

"Well, Foreman, I've talked the matter over with these gentlemen and they quite agree with me that the situation is impossible. At a church like St. Peter's, Neville Square, we cannot have a verger who can neither read nor write."

Albert Edward's thin, sallow face reddened and he moved uneasily on his feet, but he made no reply.

"Understand me, Foreman, I have no complaint to make against you. You do your work quite satisfactorily. I have the highest opinion both of your character and of your capacity, but we haven't the right to take the risk of some accident that might happen owing to your lamentable ignorance. It's a matter of prudence as well as of principle."

"But couldn't you learn, Foreman?" asked the general.

"No, sir, I'm afraid I couldn't — not now. You see, I'm not as young as I was, and, if I couldn't seem able to get the letters in me 'ead when I was a nipper,[1] I don't think there's much chance of it now."

"We don't want to be harsh with you, Foreman," said the vicar. "But the churchwardens and I have quite made up our minds. We'll give you three months, and if at the end of that time you cannot read and write I'm afraid you'll have to go."

Albert Edward had never liked the new vicar. He'd said from the beginning that they'd made a mistake when they gave him St. Peter's. He wasn't the type of man they wanted with a classy congregation like that. And now he straightened himself a little. He knew his value

[1] *nipper:* English slang for small boy.

and he wasn't going to allow himself to be put upon.

"I'm very sorry, sir; I'm afraid it's no good. I'm too old a dog to learn new tricks. I've lived a good many years without knowin' 'ow to read and write, and without wishin' to praise myself — self-praise is no recommendation — I don't mind sayin' I've done my duty in that state of life in which it 'as pleased a merciful providence to place me, and if I *could* learn now I don't know as I'd want to."

"In that case, Foreman, I'm afraid you must go."

"Yes, sir, I quite understand. I shall be 'appy to 'and in my resignation as soon as you've found somebody to take my place."

But when Albert Edward, with his usual politeness, had closed the church door behind the vicar and the two churchwardens, he could not sustain the air of unruffled dignity with which he had borne the blow inflicted upon him, and his lips quivered. He walked slowly back to the vestry and hung up on its proper peg his verger's gown. He sighed as he thought of all the grand funerals and smart weddings it had seen. He tidied everything up, put on his coat, and hat in hand walked down the aisle. He locked the church door behind him. He strolled across the square; but, deep in his sad thoughts, he did not take the street that led him home, where a nice strong cup of tea awaited him — he took the wrong turning.

He walked slowly along. His heart was heavy. He did not know what he should do with himself. He did not fancy the notion of going back to domestic service; after being his own master for so many years — for the vicar and churchwardens could say what they liked; it was he that had run St. Peter's, Neville Square — he could scarcely demean himself by accepting a situation. He had saved a tidy sum, but not enough to live on without doing something; and life seemed to cost more every year. He had never thought to be troubled with such questions. The vergers of St. Peter's, like the popes of Rome, were there for life. He had often thought of the pleasant reference the vicar would make, in his sermon at evensong the first Sunday after his death, to the long and faithful service and the exemplary character of their late verger Albert Edward Foreman.

He sighed deeply. Albert Edward was a nonsmoker and a total abstainer, but with a certain latitude; that is to say, he liked a glass of beer with his dinner and when he was tired he enjoyed a cigarette. It occurred to him now that one would comfort him and, since he did not carry them, he looked about him for a shop where he could buy a packet of Gold Flakes. He did not at once see one and walked on a little. It was a long street, with all sorts of shops in it; but there was not a single one where you could buy cigarettes.

"That's strange," said Albert Edward.

To make sure, he walked right up the street again. No, there was no doubt about it. He stopped and looked reflectively up and down.

"I can't be the only man as walks along this street and wants a fag," he said. "I shouldn't wonder but what a fellow might do very well with a little shop here. Tobacco and sweets, you know."

He gave a sudden start.

"That's an idea," he said. "Strange 'ow things come to you when you least expect it."

He turned, walked home, and had his tea.

"You're very silent this afternoon, Albert," his wife remarked.

"I'm thinkin'," he said.

He considered the matter from every point of view, and next day he went along the street and by good luck found a little shop to let that looked as though it would exactly suit him. Twenty-four hours later he had taken it and, when a month after that he left St. Peter's,

Neville Square, forever, Albert Edward Foreman set up in business as a tobacconist and newsagent. His wife said it was a dreadful comedown after being verger of St. Peter's; but he answered that you had to move with the times, the church wasn't what it was, and 'enceforeward he was going to render unto Caesar [1] what was Caesar's. Albert Edward did very well. He did so well that in a year or so it struck him that he might take a second shop and put a manager in. He looked for another long street that hadn't got a tobacconist in it and when he found it, and a shop to let, took it and stocked it. This was a success too. Then it occurred to him that if he could run two he could run half a dozen; so he began walking about London, and whenever he found a long street that had no tobacconist, and a shop to let, he took it. In the course of ten years he had acquired no less than ten shops and he was making money hand over fist. He went round to all of them himself every Monday, collected the week's takings and took them to the bank.

One morning when he was there, paying in a bundle of notes and a heavy bag of silver, the cashier told him that the manager would like to see him. He was shown into an office and the manager shook hands with him.

"Mr. Foreman, I wanted to have a talk to you about the money you've got on deposit with us. D'you know exactly how much it is?"

"Not within a pound or two, sir; but I've got a pretty rough idea."

"Apart from what you paid in this morning, it's a little over thirty thousand pounds. That's a very large sum to have on deposit and I should have thought you'd do better to invest it."

"I wouldn't want to take no risk, sir. I know it's safe in the bank."

"You needn't have the least anxiety. We'll make you out a list of absolutely

[1] *render unto Caesar:* see Matthew 22:21.

gilt-edged securities. They'll bring you in a better rate of interest than we can possiby afford to give you."

A troubled look settled on Mr. Foreman's distinguished face.

"I've never 'ad anything to do with stocks and shares and I'd 'ave to leave it all in your 'ands," he said.

The manager smiled.

"We'll do everything. All you'll have to do next time you come in is just to sign the transfers."

"I could do that all right," said Albert uncertainly. "But 'ow should I know what I was signin'?"

"I suppose you can read," said the manager a trifle sharply.

Mr. Foreman gave him a disarming smile.

"Well, sir, that's just it. I can't. I know it sounds funny like, but there it is! I can't read or write — only me name, an' I only learned to do that when I went into business."

The manager was so surprised that he jumped up from his chair.

"That's the most extraordinary thing I ever heard."

"You see, it's like this, sir — I never 'ad the opportunity until it was too late, and then some'ow I wouldn't. I got obstinate like."

The manager stared at him as though he were a prehistoric monster.

"And do you mean to say that you've built up this important business and amassed a fortune of thirty thousand pounds without being able to read or write? Good Lord, man, what would you be now if you had been able to?"

"I can tell you that, sir," said Mr. Foreman, a little smile on his still aristocratic features. "I'd be verger of St. Peter's, Neville Square."

MEMORABLE CHARACTER

1. Why is the conversation of the verger with the vicar and the two churchwardens the big scene in the story? Compare this scene with the final scene between the

principal character and the bank manager. Is the verger a changed man at the end of the story? Give reasons for your answer.

2. What part of the story is a flashback? What do you learn of the verger's earlier life? What do you infer about his lifetime's savings as a verger? About his smoking and drinking habits? Notice that a period of ten years is condensed into a single paragraph.

3. The comic spirit of the story does not mean that Maugham is without a serious purpose. What is that purpose?

FOLLOWING CHARACTER DEVELOPMENT

"The Verger" illustrates Maugham's chief interest as a storyteller: characterization. His technique here is an example of what he meant when he said in his book *The Summing Up:* "I think what has chiefly struck me in human beings is their lack of consistency. . . . It has amazed me that the most incongruous traits should exist in the same person and for all that yield a plausible harmony."

The interest in the story you have just read revolves around the verger: what kind of a man he is, what happens to him, and why he acts as he does. There are several ways to suggest character, and Maugham uses many of them to develop the character of Albert Edward Foreman. Character may be revealed by *conversation* and *action*. Recall everything that Foreman says. Why does Maugham have Foreman talk to himself in a lower-class dialect? In how many places throughout the story does Maugham indicate what is going on in someone's mind by describing what he is doing? Here is one example: "Albert Edward's thin, sallow face reddened and he moved uneasily on his feet, but he made no reply."

One of the verger's two principal actions is his decision *not* to meet the conditions imposed by his superiors. What is his other principal decision, and how do both decisions show his independence as well as his confidence in his own worth?

Character may also be presented, of course, in *direct description*. Find as many short descriptions — phrases or words —

as you can that build up your picture of Foreman. Can you find a single statement in the story which might serve to sum up Foreman's character?

Finally, character may often be revealed by showing the *interaction between two persons*. What is the effect of the contrast between the verger and the bank manager? Watching the verger and the manager together, what conclusions can you draw about the extent to which they understand each other?

SUGGESTION FOR WRITING

The topsy-turvy standards found in "The Verger" make us look again at some of our ideas. Is there a necessary connection between learning and virtue? Can an education be used for harmful ends as well as for good? Write your thoughts on one of the following subjects: "Learning Is a Dangerous Thing," "Virtue Is Always Rewarded," "Respect for Our Superiors."

LITERATURE AND THE ARTS ➤

The painting opposite is a detail from "Fulham by Moonlight," by the contemporary British artist, Bateson Mason, and depicts a working-class neighborhood in southwest London, the city which figures in many of Somerset Maugham's stories.

Indeed, as Britain's leading city through the ages, London has figured in the background of much of English literature — from the fourteenth-century days of Geoffrey Chaucer, who in *The Canterbury Tales* immortalized Southwark and the Tabard Inn, to the nineteenth- and twentieth-century days of George Bernard Shaw, who in *Pygmalion* (page 759) did the same for the bustling Covent Garden market area. Through the five hundred years intervening, we can see London through the eyes of England's poets, essayists, novelists, biographers, and social critics; and such landmarks as Trafalgar Square, Drury Lane, London Bridge, Wimpole Street, Piccadilly, Hyde Park, and Westminster Abbey, among many others, have thus become familiar wherever English literature is read. Turning to the map (pages 18–19), review the city's many literary associations.

The Doll's House

KATHERINE MANSFIELD
1888–1923

In spite of ill-health and a tragically short life, Katherine Mansfield wrote short stories that won her a secure place in modern English literature. Her real name was Kathleen Beauchamp. Born of a wealthy family in Wellington, New Zealand, she attended Queen's College, London, as a young girl. Her urge to write was great, and on returning to New Zealand she was restless and unhappy. After many conflicts with her domineering father, she returned to London. At first she lived recklessly. Impetuously she married her music teacher and left him almost immediately. An attack of tuberculosis forced her to go to Germany to recuperate, and here she began to write stories. In England once again, she married the editor and critic J. Middleton Murry and became known as a literary reviewer and story writer. But appreciation of her work came too late for her to enjoy. Constantly ill, she spent most of her last years trying to regain her health in the warmer climates of France and Italy. She died at the age of thirty-five while living in France.

In "The Doll's House" one finds the human touch, the keen insight into human nature, and the strong character analysis that are typical of the stories of Katherine Mansfield. Here she condenses the meaning of life into poignant episodes. Her vivid presentation of the situation, her intermingling of pathos and irony, and her sharp contrast of characters reveal her as a deeply emotional writer. Although this story is about children, you will discover that it is not a childish story.

WHEN dear old Mrs. Hay went back to town after staying with the Burnells she sent the children a doll's house. It was so big that the carter and Pat carried it into the courtyard, and there it stayed, propped up on two wooden boxes beside the feed-room door. No harm could come to it; it was summer. And perhaps the smell of paint would have gone off by the time it had to be taken in. For, really, the smell of paint coming from that doll's house ("Sweet of old Mrs. Hay, of course; most sweet and generous!") — but the smell of paint was quite enough to make anyone seriously ill, in Aunt Beryl's opinion. Even before the sacking was taken off. And when it was. . . .

There stood the doll's house, a dark, oily, spinach green, picked out with bright yellow. Its two solid little chimneys, glued onto the roof, were painted red and white, and the door, gleaming with yellow varnish, was like a little slab of toffee. Four windows, real windows, were divided into panes by a broad streak of green. There was actually a tiny porch too, painted yellow, with big lumps of congealed paint hanging along the edge.

But perfect, perfect little house! Who could possibly mind the smell? It was part of the joy, part of the newness.

"Open it quickly, someone!"

The hook at the side was stuck fast.

"The Doll's House" from *The Short Stories of Katherine Mansfield* by Katherine Mansfield. Copyright 1923, 1937 by Alfred A. Knopf, Inc. Reprinted by permission of Alfred A. Knopf, Inc., and The Society of Authors as the literary representative of the Estate of the late Miss Katherine Mansfield.

Pat pried it open with his penknife, and the whole house front swung back, and — there you were, gazing at one and the same moment into the drawing room and dining room, the kitchen and two bedrooms. That is the way for a house to open! Why don't all houses open like that? How much more exciting than peering through the slit of a door into a mean little hall with a hatstand and two umbrellas! That is — isn't it — what you long to know about a house when you put your hand on the knocker. Perhaps it is the way God opens houses at dead of night when He is taking a quiet turn with an angel. . . .

"O-oh!" The Burnell children sounded as though they were in despair. It was too marvelous; it was too much for them. They had never seen anything like it in their lives. All the rooms were papered. There were pictures on the walls, painted on the paper, with gold frames complete. Red carpet covered all the floors except the kitchen; red plush chairs in the drawing room, green in the dining room; tables, beds with real bedclothes, a cradle, a stove, a dresser with tiny plates and one big jug. But what Kezia liked more than anything, what she liked frightfully, was the lamp. It stood in the middle of the dining-room table, an exquisite little amber lamp with a white globe. It was even filled all ready for lighting, though, of course, you couldn't light it. But there was something inside that looked like oil, and that moved when you shook it.

The father and mother dolls, who sprawled very stiff as though they had fainted in the drawing room, and their two little children asleep upstairs, were really too big for the doll's house. They didn't look as though they belonged. But the lamp was perfect. It seemed to smile at Kezia, to say: "I live here." The lamp was real.

The Burnell children could hardly walk to school fast enough the next morning. They burned to tell everybody, to describe, to — well — to boast about

their doll's house before the school bell rang.

"I'm to tell," said Isabel, "because I'm the eldest. And you two can join in after. But I'm to tell first."

There was nothing to answer. Isabel was bossy, but she was always right, and Lottie and Kezia knew too well the powers that went with being eldest. They brushed through the thick buttercups at the road edge and said nothing.

"And I'm to choose who's to come and see it first. Mother said I might."

For it had been arranged that while the doll's house stood in the courtyard they might ask the girls at school, two at a time, to come and look. Not to stay to tea, of course, or to come traipsing through the house. But just to stand quietly in the courtyard while Isabel pointed out the beauties, and Lottie and Kezia looked pleased. . . .

But hurry as they might, by the time they had reached the tarred palings of the boys' playground the bell had begun to jangle. They only just had time to whip off their hats and fall into line before the roll was called. Never mind, Isabel tried to make up for it by looking very important and mysterious and by whispering behind her hand to the girls near her: "Got something to tell you at playtime."

Playtime came and Isabel was surrounded. The girls of her class nearly fought to put their arms round her, to walk away with her, to beam flatteringly, to be her special friend. She held quite a court under the huge pine trees at the side of the playground. Nudging, giggling together, the little girls pressed up close. And the only two who stayed outside the ring were the two who were always outside, the little Kelveys. They knew better than to come anywhere near the Burnells.

For the fact was that the school the Burnell children went to was not at all the kind of place their parents would have chosen if there had been any choice. But there was none. It was the only school for miles. And the consequence was all the children in the neighborhood, the Judge's little girls, the doctor's daughters, the storekeeper's children, the milkman's, were forced to mix together. Not to speak of there being an equal number of rude, rough little boys as well. But the line had to be drawn somewhere. It was drawn at the Kelveys. Many of the children, including the Burnells, were not allowed even to speak to them. They walked past the Kelveys with their heads in the air, and as they set the fashion in all matters of behavior, the Kelveys were shunned by everybody. Even the teacher had a special voice for them, and a special smile for the other children when Lil Kelvey came up to her desk with a bunch of dreadfully common-looking flowers.

They were the daughters of a spry, hardworking little washerwoman, who went about from house to house by the day. This was awful enough. But where was Mr. Kelvey? Nobody knew for certain. But everybody said he was in prison. So they were the daughters of a washerwoman and a jailbird. Very nice company for other people's children! And they looked it. Why Mrs. Kelvey made them so conspicuous was hard to understand. The truth was they were dressed in "bits" given to her by the people for whom she worked. Lil, for instance, who was a stout, plain child, with big freckles, came to school in a dress made from a green art-serge tablecloth of the Burnells', with red plush sleeves from the Logans' curtains. Her hat, perched on top of her high forehead, was a grown-up woman's hat, once the property of Miss Lecky, the postmistress. It was turned up at the back and trimmed with a large scarlet quill. What a little guy she looked! It was impossible not to laugh. And her little sister, our Else, wore a long white dress, rather like a nightgown, and a pair of little boy's boots. But whatever our Else wore, she would have looked strange. She was a tiny wishbone of a child, with cropped

hair and enormous solemn eyes — a little white owl. Nobody had ever seen her smile; she scarcely ever spoke. She went through life holding on to Lil, with a piece of Lil's skirt screwed up in her hand. Where Lil went our Else followed. In the playground, on the road going to and from school, there was Lil marching in front and our Else holding on behind. Only when she wanted anything, or when she was out of breath, our Else gave Lil a tug, a twitch, and Lil stopped and turned round. The Kelveys never failed to understand each other.

Now they hovered at the edge; you couldn't stop them listening. When the little girls turned round and sneered, Lil, as usual, gave her silly, shamefaced smile, but our Else only looked.

And Isabel's voice, so very proud, went on telling. The carpet made a great sensation, but so did the beds with real bedclothes, and the stove with an oven door.

When she finished, Kezia broke in. "You've forgotten the lamp, Isabel."

"Oh, yes," said Isabel, "and there's a teeny little lamp, all made of yellow glass, with a white globe, that stands on the dining-room table. You couldn't tell it from a real one."

"The lamp's best of all," cried Kezia. She thought Isabel wasn't making half enough of the little lamp. But nobody paid any attention. Isabel was choosing the two who were to come back with them that afternoon and see it. She chose Emmie Cole and Lena Logan. But when the others knew they were all to have a chance, they couldn't be nice enough to Isabel. One by one they put their arms round Isabel's waist and walked her off. They had something to whisper to her, a secret. "Isabel's my friend."

Only the little Kelveys moved away forgotten; there was nothing more for them to hear.

Days passed, and as more children saw the doll's house, the fame of it spread. It became the one subject, the rage. The one question was: "Have you seen Burnells' doll's house? Oh, ain't it lovely!" "Haven't you seen it? Oh, I say!"

Even the dinner hour was given up to talking about it. The little girls sat under the pines eating their thick mutton sandwiches and big slabs of johnnycake spread with butter. While always, as near as they could get, sat the Kelveys, our Else holding on to Lil, listening too, while they chewed their jam sandwiches out of a newspaper soaked with large red blobs. . . .

"Mother," said Kezia, "can't I ask the Kelveys just once?"

At last everybody had seen it except them. On that day the subject rather flagged. It was the dinner hour. The children stood together under the pine trees, and suddenly, as they looked at the Kelveys eating out of their paper, always by themselves, always listening, they wanted to be horrid to them. Emmie Cole started the whisper.

"Lil Kelvey's going to be a servant when she grows up."

"O-oh, how awful!" said Isabel Burnell, and she made eyes at Emmie.

Emmie swallowed in a very meaning way and nodded to Isabel as she'd seen her mother do on those occasions.

"It's true — it's true — it's true," she said.

Then Lena Logan's little eyes snapped. "Shall I ask her?" she whispered.

"Bet you don't," said Jessie May.

"Pooh, I'm not frightened," said Lena. Suddenly she gave a little squeal and danced in front of the other girls. "Watch! Watch me! Watch me now!" said Lena. And sliding, gliding, dragging one foot, giggling behind her hand, Lena went over to the Kelveys.

Lil looked up from her dinner. She wrapped the rest quickly away. Our Else stopped chewing. What was coming now?

"Is it true you're going to be a servant when you grow up, Lil Kelvey?" shrilled Lena.

Dead silence. But instead of answering, Lil only gave her silly, shamefaced smile. She didn't seem to mind the question at all. What a sell for Lena! The girls began to titter.

Lena couldn't stand that. She put her hands on her hips; she shot forward. "Yah, yer father's in prison!" she hissed, spitefully.

This was such a marvelous thing to have said that the little girls rushed away in a body, deeply, deeply excited, wild with joy. Someone found a long rope, and they began skipping. And never did they skip so high, run in and out so fast, or do such daring things as on that morning.

In the afternoon Pat called for the Burnell children with the buggy and they drove home. There were visitors. Isabel and Lottie, who liked visitors, went upstairs to change their pinafores. But Kezia thieved out at the back. Nobody was about; she began to swing on the big white gates of the courtyard. Presently, looking along the road, she saw two little dots. They grew bigger, they were coming toward her. Now she could see that one was in front and one close behind. Now she could see that they were the Kelveys. Kezia stopped swinging. She slipped off the gate as if she was going to run away. Then she hesitated. The Kelveys came nearer, and beside them walked their shadows, very long, stretching right across the road with their heads in the buttercups. Kezia clambered back on the gate; she had made up her mind; she swung out.

"Hullo," she said to the passing Kelveys.

They were so astounded that they stopped. Lil gave her silly smile. Our Else stared.

"You can come and see our doll's house if you want to," said Kezia, and she dragged one toe on the ground. But at that Lil turned red and shook her head quickly.

"Why not?" asked Kezia.

Lil gasped, then she said: "Your ma told our ma you wasn't to speak to us."

"Oh, well," said Kezia. She didn't know what to reply. "It doesn't matter. You can come and see our doll's house all the same. Come on. Nobody's looking."

But Lil shook her head still harder.

"Don't you want to?" asked Kezia.

Suddenly there was a twitch, a tug at Lil's skirt. She turned round. Our Else was looking at her with big, imploring eyes; she was frowning; she wanted to go. For a moment Lil looked at our Else very doubtfully. But then our Else twitched her skirt again. She started forward. Kezia led the way. Like two little stray cats they followed across the courtyard to where the doll's house stood.

"There it is," said Kezia.

There was a pause. Lil breathed loudly, almost snorted; our Else was still as a stone.

"I'll open it for you," said Kezia kindly. She undid the hook and they looked inside.

"There's the drawing room and the dining room, and that's the ——"

"Kezia!"

Oh, what a start they gave!

"Kezia!"

It was Aunt Beryl's voice. They turned round. At the back door stood Aunt Beryl, staring as if she couldn't believe what she saw.

"How dare you ask the little Kelveys into the courtyard?" said her cold, furious voice. "You know as well as I do you're not allowed to talk to them. Run away, children, run away at once. And don't come back again," said Aunt Beryl. And she stepped into the yard and shooed them out as if they were chickens.

"Off you go immediately!" she called, cold and proud.

They did not need telling twice. Burning with shame, shrinking together, Lil huddling along like her mother, our Else dazed, somehow they crossed the big courtyard and squeezed through the white gate.

"Wicked, disobedient little girl!" said Aunt Beryl bitterly to Kezia, and she slammed the doll's house to.

The afternoon had been awful. A letter had come from Willie Brent, a terrifying, threatening letter, saying if she did not meet him that evening in Pulman's Bush, he'd come to the front door and ask the reason why! But now that she had frightened those little rats of Kelveys and given Kezia a good scolding, her heart felt lighter. That ghastly pressure was gone. She went back to the house humming.

When the Kelveys were well out of sight of Burnells', they sat down to rest on a big red drainpipe by the side of the road. Lil's cheeks were still burning; she took off the hat with the quill and held it on her knee. Dreamily they looked over the hay paddocks, past the creek, to the group of wattles where Logan's cows stood waiting to be milked. What were their thoughts?

Presently our Else nudged up close to her sister. But now she had forgotten the cross lady. She put out a finger and stroked her sister's quill; she smiled her rare smile.

"I seen the little lamp," she said, softly.

Then both were silent once more.

A STORY OF DEEP FEELING

1. Who notices the little lamp first? What do you think it meant to her? How do the other children regard it? To whom does it also have added meaning? What does the little lamp symbolize?

2. Why did the doll house make the Burnell sisters feel so important? Why are the children cruel to the Kelveys? Are children at this age usually cruel? Why? What truth is the author illustrating here?

ANALYZING MOOD

Mood, not actually an ingredient in the construction of a short story, is somewhat like a filter through which the elements of setting, characters, and action are viewed. Because of Katherine Mansfield's skill in creating an emotional atmosphere or mood, the reader reacts to both the lightheartedness and the pathos which pervade "The Doll's House."

Analyze the change of mood in this story. When the doll's house arrives, the Burnell children are overjoyed. Describe their enthusiasm when they first look at the gift. When does this mood first shift, although momentarily, to a less lighthearted response? Which character helps you to notice this change in emotional attitude? How has Kezia been affected by the doll's house?

The next day on their way to school, the three sisters are joyously anticipating their announcement to their friends. The mood of lightheartedness still pervades the story. But shortly the emotional response changes. Where do you find the definite shift in mood? How are the Kelveys affected by the news?

Notice at this point the intermingling of lightheartedness with that of sadness. How are the elements of pathos then introduced into the story? Recall the incidents which have resulted in a shift in mood. To contrast the mood at the opening of the story with that at the end, do not fail to consider Else's remark, "I seen the little lamp."

SUGGESTION FOR WRITING

Write about a personal incident in which you experienced a change in contrasting moods. You might use happiness and sorrow, love and hate, or anticipation and disappointment. Be sure to show what brought about the change in mood.

Pix

The Man of the House

FRANK O'CONNOR 1903–

Frank O'Connor is the pseudonym of Michael O'Donovan. Born in Cork, Ireland, of poor parents, he grew up in that city. Although he left school at an early age, he educated himself further in the public library and began to write poems and essays while still a boy. In the bitter civil war of the 1920's, O'Connor joined the Republicans, who were fighting for an independent and united Ireland. Arrested by the government and imprisoned for a year, he spent his time studying languages and writing. After his release, he became a librarian first in County Cork and then in Dublin. Through this profession he had the welcome opportunity to continue his education and develop as a writer. A former director of the famous Abbey Theatre,

O'Connor, who lives in the United States, is today recognized as a scholar, critic, and linguist as well as one of the leading contemporary writers of short stories. He has taught writing at Harvard and Northwestern University, and has published frequently in American magazines. Today he spends time revising the stories for which he wants to be remembered.

O'Connor's Ireland is that of the small shopkeeper, the teacher, and the clerk. His stories, surprisingly varied and original, seem to tell themselves. They follow no single pattern, although most of his tales have a moral or a theme that the reader recognizes as the author's purpose in writing. Following is a good example of O'Connor's lilting Irish-English.

"The Man of the House" by Frank O'Connor. Copyright 1949 by Frank O'Connor. Originally appeared in *The New Yorker.* Reprinted by permission of Alfred A. Knopf, Inc. from *More Stories by Frank O'Connor.*

WHEN I woke, I heard my mother coughing, below in the kitchen. She had been coughing for days, but I had paid no attention. We were living on the Old Youghal Road at the time, the old hilly coaching road into East Cork. The coughing sounded terrible. I dressed and went downstairs in my stocking feet, and in the clear morning light I saw her, unaware that she was being watched, collapsed into a little wickerwork arm-chair, holding her side. She had made an attempt to light the fire, but it had gone against her. She looked so tired and helpless that my heart turned over with compassion. I ran to her.

"Are you all right, Mum?" I asked.

"I'll be all right in a second," she replied, trying to smile. "The old sticks were wet, and the smoke started me coughing."

"Go back to bed and I'll light the fire," I said.

"Ah, how can I, child?" she said anxiously. "Sure, I have to go to work."

"You couldn't work like that," I said. "I'll stop at home from school and look after you."

It's a funny thing about women, the way they'll take orders from anything in trousers, even if it's only ten.

"If you could make yourself a cup of tea, I might be all right later on," she said guiltily, and she rose, very shakily, and climbed back up the stairs. I knew then she must be feeling really bad.

I got more stick out of the coalhole, under the stairs. My mother was so economical that she never used enough, and that was why the fire sometimes went against her. I used a whole bundle, and I soon had the fire roaring and the kettle on. I made her toast while I was about it. I was a great believer in hot buttered toast at all hours of the day. Then I made the tea and brought her up a cup on the tray. "Is that all right?" I asked.

"Would you have a sup of boiling water left?" she asked doubtfully.

" 'Tis too strong," I agreed cheerfully, remembering the patience of the saints in their many afflictions. "I'll pour half of it out."

"I'm an old nuisance," she sighed.

" 'Tis my fault," I said, taking the cup. "I can never remember about tea. Put the shawl round you while you're sitting up. Will I shut the skylight?"

"Would you be able?" she asked doubtfully.

" 'Tis no trouble," I said, getting the chair to it. "I'll do the messages after."

I had my own breakfast alone by the window, and then I went out and stood by the front door to watch the kids from the road on their way to school.

"You'd better hurry or you'll be killed, Sullivan," they shouted.

"I'm not going," I said. "My mother is sick, and I have to mind the house."

I wasn't a malicious child, by any means, but I liked to be able to take out my comforts and study them by the light of others' misfortunes. Then I heated another kettle of water and cleared up the breakfast things before I washed my face and came up to the attic with my shopping basket, a piece of paper, and a lead pencil.

"I'll do the messages now if you'll write them down," I said. "Would you like me to get the doctor?"

"Ah," said my mother impatiently, "he'd only want to send me to hospital, and how would I go to hospital? You could call in at the chemist's and ask him to give you a good, strong cough bottle."

"Write it down," I said. "If I haven't it written down, I might forget it. And put 'strong' in big letters. What will I get for the dinner? Eggs?"

As boiled eggs were the only dish I could manage, I more or less knew it would be eggs, but she told me to get sausages as well, in case she could get up.

I passed the school on my way. Opposite it was a hill, and I went up a short distance and stood there for ten minutes in quiet contemplation. The schoolhouse and yard and gate were revealed as in a painted picture, detached and peaceful except for the chorus of voices through the opened windows and the glimpse of Danny Delaney, the teacher, passing the front door with his cane behind his back, stealing a glance at the world outside. I could have stood there all day. Of all the profound and simple pleasures of those days, that was the richest.

When I got home, I rushed upstairs and found Minnie Ryan sitting with my mother. She was a middle-aged woman, very knowledgeable, gossipy, and pious.

"How are you, Mum?" I asked.

"Grand," said my mother, with a smile.

"You can't get up today, though," said Minnie Ryan.

"I'll put the kettle on and make a cup of tea for you," I said.

"Sure, I'll do that," said Minnie.

"Ah, don't worry, Miss Ryan," I said lightly. "I can manage it all right."

"Wisha, isn't he very good?" I heard her say in a low voice to my mother.

"As good as gold," said my mother.

"There's not many like that, then," said Minnie. "The most of them that's going now are more like savages than Christians."

In the afternoon, my mother wanted me to run out and play, but I didn't go far. I knew if once I went a certain distance from the house, I was liable to stray into temptation. Below our house, there was a glen, the drill field of the barracks perched high above it on a chalky cliff, and below, in a deep hollow, the millpond and millstream running between wooded hills — the Rockies, the Himalayas, or the Highlands, according to your mood. Once down there, I tended to forget the real world, so I sat on a wall outside the house, running in every half hour to see how the mother was and if there was anything she wanted.

Evening fell; the street lamps were lit, and the paper boy went crying up the road. I bought a paper, lit the lamp in the kitchen and the candle in my mother's attic, and tried to read to her, not very successfully, because I was only at words of one syllable, but I had a great wish to please, and she to be pleased, so we got on quite well, considering.

Later, Minnie Ryan came again, and as she was going, I saw her to the door.

"If she's not better in the morning, I think I'd get the doctor, Flurry," she said, over her shoulder.

"Why?" I asked, in alarm. "Do you think is she worse, Miss Ryan?"

"Ah, I wouldn't say so," she replied with affected nonchalance, "but I'd be frightened she might get pneumonia."

"But wouldn't he send her to hospital, Miss Ryan?"

"Wisha, he mightn't," she said with a shrug, pulling her old shawl about her. "But even if he did, wouldn't it be better than neglecting it? Ye wouldn't have a drop of whiskey in the house?"

"I'll get it," I said at once. I knew what might happen to people who got pneumonia, and what was bound to happen afterward to their children.

"If you could give it to her hot, with a squeeze of lemon in it, it might help to shake it off," said Minnie.

My mother said she didn't want the whiskey, dreading the expense, but I had got such a fright that I wouldn't be put off. When I went to the public house, it was full of men, who drew aside to let me reach the bar. I had never been in a public house before, and I was frightened.

"Hullo, my old flower," said one man, grinning diabolically at me. "It must be ten years since I seen you last. What are you having?"

My pal, Bob Connell, had told me how he once asked a drunk man for a half crown and the man gave it to him. I always wished I could bring myself to do the same, but I didn't feel like it just then.

"I want a half glass of whiskey for

my mother," I said.

"Oh, the thundering ruffian!" said the man. "Pretending 'tis for his mother, and the last time I seen him he had to be carried home."

"I had not," I shouted indignantly. "And 'tis for my mother. She's sick."

"Ah, let the child alone, Johnnie," said the barmaid. She gave me the whiskey, and then, still frightened of the men in the public house, I went off to a shop for a lemon.

When my mother had drunk the hot whiskey, she fell asleep, and I quenched the lights and went to bed, but I couldn't sleep very well. I was regretting I hadn't asked the man in the pub for a half crown. I was wakened several times by the coughing, and when I went into my mother's room her head felt very hot, and she was rambling in her talk. It frightened me more than anything else when she didn't know me, and I lay awake, thinking of what would happen to me if it were really pneumonia.

The depression was terrible when, next morning, my mother seemed not to be any better. I had done all I could do, and I felt helpless. I lit the fire and got her breakfast, but this time I didn't stand at the front door to see the other fellows on their way to school. I should have been too inclined to envy them. Instead, I went over to Minnie Ryan and reported.

"I'd go for the doctor," she said firmly. "Better be sure than sorry."

I had first to go to the house of a Poor Law Guardian, for a ticket to show we couldn't pay. Then I went down to the dispensary, which was in a deep hollow beyond the school. After that I had to go back to ready the house for the doctor. I had to have a basin of water and soap and a clean towel laid out for him, and I had to get the dinner, too.

It was after dinner when he called. He was a fat, loud-voiced man and supposed to be "the cleverest doctor in Cork, if only he'd mind himself." He hadn't been minding himself much that

morning, it seemed.

"How are you going to get this now?" he grumbled, sitting on the bed with the prescription pad on his knee. "The only place open is the North Dispensary."

"I'll go, Doctor," I said at once, relieved that he had said nothing about hospital.

" 'Tis a long way," he said, doubtfully. "Do you know where it is?"

"I'll find it," I said.

"Isn't he a great little fellow?" he said to my mother.

"Oh, the best in the world, Doctor!" she said. "A daughter couldn't be better to me."

"That's right," said the doctor. "Look after your mother; she'll be the best for you in the long run. We don't mind them when we have them," he added, to my mother, "and then we spend the rest of our lives regretting it."

I wished he hadn't said that; it tuned in altogether too well with my mood. To make it worse, he didn't even use the soap and water I had laid ready for him.

My mother gave me directions how to reach the dispensary, and I set off with a bottle wrapped in brown paper under my arm. The road led uphill, through a thickly populated poor locality, as far as the barracks, which was perched on the very top of the hill, over the city, and then descended, between high walls, till it suddenly almost disappeared in a stony path, with red brick corporation houses to one side of it, that dropped steeply, steeply, to the valley of the little river, where a brewery stood, and the opposite hillside, a murmuring honeycomb of houses, rose to the gently rounded top, on which stood the purple sandstone tower of the cathedral and the limestone spire of Shandon church, on a level with your eye.

It was so wide a view that it was never all lit up together, and the sunlight wandered across it as across a prairie, picking out first a line of roofs with a brightness like snow, and then delving into the depth of some dark street and outlining in shadow figures of climbing carts and straining horses. I leaned on the low wall and thought how happy a fellow could be, looking at that, if he had nothing to trouble him. I tore myself from it with a sigh, slithered without stopping to the bottom of the hill, and climbed up a series of shadowy and stepped lanes around the back of the cathedral, which now seemed enormous. I had a penny, which my mother had given me by way of encouragement, and I made up my mind that when I had done my business, I should go into the cathedral and spend it on a candle to the Blessed Virgin, to make my mother better quick. I felt sure it would be more effective in a really big church like that, so very close to Heaven.

The dispensary was a sordid little hallway with a bench to one side and a window like the one in a railway ticket office at the far end. There was a little girl with a green plaid shawl about her shoulders sitting on the bench. I knocked at the window, and a seedy, angry-looking man opened it. Without waiting for me to finish what I was saying, he grabbed bottle and prescription from me and banged the shutter down again without a word. I waited for a moment and then lifted my hand to knock again.

"You'll have to wait, little boy," said the girl quickly.

"What will I have to wait for?" I asked.

"He have to make it up," she explained. "You might as well sit down."

I did, glad of anyone to keep me company.

"Where are you from?" she asked. "I live in Blarney Lane," she added when I had told her. "Who's the bottle for?"

"My mother," I said.

"What's wrong with her?"

"She have a bad cough."

"She might have consumption," she said thoughtfully. "That's what my sister that died last year had. This is a tonic for my other sister. She have to have tonics all the time. Is it nice where you live?"

I told her about the glen, and then she told me about the river near their place. It seemed to be a nicer place than ours, as she described it. She was a pleasant, talkative little girl, and I didn't notice the time until the window opened again and a red bottle was thrust out.

"Dooley!" shouted the seedy man, and closed the window again.

"That's me," said the little girl. "Yours won't be ready for a good while yet. I'll wait for you."

"I have a penny," I said boastfully.

She waited until my bottle was thrust out, and then she accompanied me as far as the steps leading down to the brewery. On the way, I bought a pennyworth of sweets, and we sat on the other steps, beside the infirmary, to eat them. It was nice there, with the spire of Shandon in shadow behind us, the young trees overhanging the high walls, and the sun, when it came out in great golden blasts, throwing our linked shadows onto the road.

"Give us a taste of your bottle, little boy," she said.

"Why?" I asked. "Can't you taste your own?"

"Mine is awful," she said. "Tonics is awful to taste. You can try it if you like."

I took a taste of it and hastily spat out. She was right; it was awful. After that, I couldn't do less than let her taste mine.

"That's grand," she said enthusiastically, after taking a swig from it. "Cough bottles are nearly always grand. Try it, can't you?"

I did, and saw she was right about that, too. It was very sweet and sticky.

"Give us another," she said excitedly, grabbing at it.

" 'Twill be all gone," I said.

"Erra, 'twon't," she replied with a laugh. "You have gallons of it."

Somehow, I couldn't refuse her. I was swept from my anchorage into an unfamiliar world of spires and towers, trees, steps, shadowy laneways, and little girls with red hair and green eyes. I took a drink myself and gave her another. Then I began to panic. " 'Tis nearly gone," I said. "What am I going to do now?"

"Finish it and say the cork fell out," she replied, and again, as she said it, it sounded plausible enough. We finished the bottle between us, and then, slowly, as I looked at it in my hand, empty as I had brought it, and remembered that I had not kept my word to the Blessed Virgin and had spent her penny on sweets, a terrible despondency swept over me. I had sacrificed everything for the little girl and she didn't even care for me. It was my cough bottle she had coveted all the time. I saw her guile too late. I put my head in my hands and began to cry.

"What are you crying for?" the little girl asked in astonishment.

"My mother is sick, and we're after drinking her medicine," I said.

"Ah, don't be an old crybaby!" she said contemptuously. "You have only to say the cork fell out. Sure, that's a thing could happen to anybody."

"And I promised the Blessed Virgin a candle, and I spent the money on you!" I screamed, and, suddenly grabbing the empty bottle, I ran up the road from her, wailing. Now I had only one refuge and one hope — a miracle. I went back to the cathedral, and, kneeling before the shrine of the Blessed Virgin, I begged her pardon for having spent her penny, and promised her a candle from the next penny I got, if only she would work a miracle and make my mother better before I got back. After that, I crawled miserably homeward, back up the great hill, but now all the light had gone out of the day, and the murmuring hillside had become a vast, alien, cruel world. Besides, I felt very sick. I thought I might be going to die. In one way it would be better.

When I got back into the house, the silence of the kitchen and then the sight of the fire gone out in the grate smote me with the cruel realization that the Blessed Virgin had let me down. There was no miracle, and my mother was still in bed. At once, I began to howl.

"What is it at all, child?" she called in alarm from upstairs.

"I lost the medicine," I bellowed, and rushed up the stairs to throw myself on the bed and bury my face in the clothes.

"Oh, wisha, if that's all that's a trouble to you!" she exclaimed with relief, running her hand through my hair. "Is anything the matter?" she added, after a moment. "You're very hot."

"I drank the medicine," I bawled.

"Ah, what harm?" she murmured soothingly. "You poor, unfortunate child! 'Twas my own fault for letting you go all that way by yourself. And then to have your journey for nothing. Undress yourself now, and you can lie down here."

She got up, put on her slippers and coat, and unlaced my boots while I sat on the bed. But even before she had finished I was fast asleep. I didn't see her dress herself or hear her go out, but some time later I felt a hand on my forehead and saw Minnie Ryan peering down at me, laughing.

"Ah, 'twill be nothing," she said, giving her shawl a pull about her. "He'll sleep it off by morning. The dear knows, Mrs. Sullivan, 'tis you should be in bed."

I knew that was a judgment on me, but I could do nothing about it. Later I saw my mother come in with the candle and her paper, and I smiled up at her. She smiled back. Minnie Ryan might despise me as much as she liked, but there were others who didn't. The miracle had happened, after all.

A STORY WITH A VIEW

1. What does the title "The Man of the House" mean to you after you have finished the story? With what idea is O'Connor mainly concerned?

2. Do you think the boy is a typical child of ten? What incidents in the story help to answer this question? What does the boy mean when he says "I liked to be able to take out my comforts and study them by the light of others' misfortunes"? During the first day of his mother's illness, what was the boy's richest pleasure?

3. Describe the girl that the boy meets at the dispensary. Why is she successful in her plan? What was his "one refuge and one hope"? How do you explain "the miracle" that happened?

READING LIST FOR MODERN FICTION

SHORT STORIES

Chesterton, G. K., *Father Brown Omnibus*
Fifty stories in which a priest-detective, Father Brown, solves mystery after mystery.

Coppard, A. E., *Collected Tales*
Stories ranging from naturalism to fantasy and symbolism.

Doyle, A. Conan, *The Adventures of Sherlock Holmes*
Some of the best mystery and detective stories by a world favorite.

Galsworthy, John, *Caravan*
Here are the outstanding stories by a master craftsman.

Garrity, Devin A. (editor), *Forty-four Irish Short Stories*
An anthology, from Yeats to Frank O'Connor.

Goodman, Jack (editor), *Fireside Book of Dog Stories*
A dog fancier will enjoy especially the stories by Galsworthy, Kipling, D. H. Lawrence, and Eric Knight.

Mansfield, Katherine, *Short Stories*
Portraits of situations and characters of English life.

O'Connor, Frank, *Stories*
Stories that present the charm and tragedy of everyday life.

O'Faoláin, Seán, *The Man Who Invented Sin*
The essence of Ireland with very real Irishmen transmitted in fifteen stories.

Priestley, J. B., *The Other Place and Other Stories of the Same Sort*
How the supernatural seems to play a part in everyday life is found in all nine stories.

Pritchett, V. S., *The Sailor, Sense of Humour, and Other Stories*
The double lives of middle-class Britishers tormented by changing social forces.

Schweikert, Harry C. (editor), *Short Stories*
Jacobs, Hardy, Conrad, Kipling, Bennett, Barrie, Galsworthy, and Katherine Mansfield are represented with a story and biographical sketch.

Ustinov, Peter, *Add a Dash of Pity*
Eight amusing satires by a playwright, actor, and television personality.

NOTE: For a listing of modern novels, see pages 370–71.

MODERN POETRY

INCLUDED among the poets in this section are A. E. Housman and Dylan Thomas. Now Housman was born in 1859, Dylan Thomas in 1914. So between these two men is a gap of fifty-five years. This is important to remember, for much can happen in the world over a space of fifty-five years. The world that Dylan Thomas knew in his boyhood and youth was very different from the one that Housman knew in the latter half of Victoria's reign. For example, although Housman wrote about young men killed in battle, he grew up in an era of peace, whereas Dylan Thomas, though he wrote little about it, lived in the very shadow of war — total and terrible war.

Even a first quick reading of the work of these two fine and highly original poets reveals at once a profound difference between them as artists. They offer us two quite different kinds of poetry. Housman's "To an Athlete Dying Young" (page 664) has a comparatively simple central theme that we understand at once. The imagery in the sharply chiselled lines, typical of his work, gives his idea a compelling force and a certain haunting beauty. This is the classical manner in poetry; and indeed, Housman, a famous classical scholar, owes much to his study of Greek and Roman poetry.

Turn to Dylan Thomas' magnificent "Do Not Go Gentle into That Good Night" (page 695) and you find something very different, something at once newer and yet at the same time even older. It is newer because, being very modern in its manner (following to some extent the French Symbolist Movement), it depends entirely for its effect on a rapid succession of images, making great demands on the reader's imagination before the poem can be understood and appreciated. And at the same time it is older because Dylan Thomas, not only a Welshman but a very Welsh Welshman, is returning in spirit to the oldest traditions of his people, to the ancient bards and their magical chants. To hear Dylan Thomas read his poetry — and there was no better reader of poetry in our time — was to return with him to this ancient magical tradition. He made your hair stand on end.

Taking Housman and Dylan Thomas for comparison, we have the two extremes, but the difference between them well illustrates the whole modern movement in English poetry, a half century filled with restless experiment and changes in poetical art. There has been both gain and loss, which is of course what always happens when one of the arts is on the move. And the quickest and easiest way to understand what

changes have taken place is this — to try to strike a balance between rough estimates of these gains and losses, if the poets will forgive us for dealing with them in bookkeeping terms.

There was first an immense gain in what might be called the subject matter of poetry. When this period began there were still set "poetical" subjects. A poet could write about This but not about That. But the poets in the modern movement felt they could write about anything, that nothing was barred. They were prepared to consider every possible aspect of the world in which they lived. Consequently, there was a sudden and tremendous gain in breadth.

Along with this was a corresponding gain in depth. Just as modern poets ventured into the outer world, so too they delved further into the inner world of the mind and imagination. The new freedom in poetry encouraged them to explore the recesses, no matter how dimly illuminated, of their own being. What they found there could often be communicated only by means of symbolic imagery, if only because these mysterious depths are beyond the reach of conscious thought. This demanded a new attitude on the part of the reader, who could no longer stand away from poetry and ask himself what it meant in terms of conscious thought. The reader had to give himself to the poem and allow it to take possession of him. When I was at school, half a century ago, we had to write paraphrases of poetry. Truly modern poetry cannot be paraphrased. A poem is a poem, existing entirely in its own right, and cannot be turned into anything else without being destroyed.

These gains in breadth, depth, and independence seem very impressive, as indeed they are. It might seem difficult, therefore, to discover what counterbalancing losses there might be. There are losses, however, especially in the relation between poetry and the general reading public. To begin with, the newer poets seem far more obscure and "difficult" than the older ones were. Some of their work suggests a series of riddles, and, although solving riddles can be an entertaining pastime, it seems far removed from the joyful appreciation of poetry. Undoubtedly a great many people, not necessarily stupid, have ceased to read new poetry, preferring to return to older work.

Again, in the change from old to new, there was a definite loss in what can be called the memorable quality of poetry. It is easy to remember given lines of Housman's poetry and very difficult to remember Dylan Thomas', however much we may admire it. And if earlier poetry had often seemed too public in theme and manner, as if written to be declaimed on the steps of the local town hall, now the newer poetry seemed often altogether too private, too much like something muttered among members of a secret society. This too was a loss, reducing the stature and influence of the poet in the community.

One last word. The truly great poet — a man of outstanding genius like W. B. Yeats — cannot be confined within such estimates of gains and losses. He has the good qualities of both the older and newer poets but is free from their respective weaknesses. He can be public and memorable and yet also private, searching, and subtle. He can explore his own inner world without disappearing from the outer world and is able to describe in the market place his most secret and strangest dreams. But this takes us well outside mere literary fashions and movements, for what it demands is original poetic genius.

J. B. P.

A. E. HOUSMAN

1859–1936

National Portrait Gallery

Alfred Edward Housman's reputation as a poet rests on the high quality of comparatively few poems. In 1896 he published *A Shropshire Lad*, containing sixty-three simple lyrics. They were the meditations of a young man, many of them tinged with a wistful, ironic, or pessimistic tone, but others filled with the joyousness of a farm boy during springtime in the country. So distinctive was the flavor of these poems that Housman was immediately established as a leader among the new poets of the twentieth century. He did not publish again for twenty-six years.

Then an even smaller volume called *Last Poems* appeared. A third volume, *More Poems,* was published by his brother Laurence after the poet's death.

By profession A. E. Housman was a gifted and eminent classical scholar. After leaving Oxford, he worked for ten years in the British patent office, a job which he left in order to become a professor of Latin first at the University of London and later at Cambridge. His carefully wrought lyrics — simple, beautiful, and highly polished — reveal the influence of his lifelong interest in classical studies.

Loveliest of Trees

Loveliest of trees, the cherry now
Is hung with bloom along the bough,
And stands about the woodland ride°
Wearing white for Eastertide.

Now, of my three score years and ten, 5
Twenty will not come again,
And take from seventy springs a score,
It only leaves me fifty more.

And since to look at things in bloom
Fifty springs are little room, 10
About the woodlands I will go
To see the cherry hung with snow.

3. *ride:* a road intended for horseback travel.

Far in a Western Brookland

Far in a western brookland
    That bred me long ago
The poplars stand and tremble
    By pools I used to know.

There, in the windless nighttime, 5
    The wanderer, marveling why,
Halts on the bridge to hearken
    How soft the poplars sigh.

He hears: no more remembered
    In fields where I was known, 10
Here I lie down in London
    And turn to rest alone.

There, by the starlit fences,
    The wanderer halts and hears
My soul that lingers sighing 15
    About the glimmering weirs.

To an Athlete Dying Young

The time you won your town the race
We chaired you through the market-
    place;
Man and boy stood cheering by,
And home we brought you shoulder-
    high.

Today, the road all runners come, 5
Shoulder-high we bring you home,
And set you at your threshold down,
Townsman of a stiller town.

Smart lad, to slip betimes away
From fields where glory does not stay,
And early though the laurel grows, 11
It withers quicker than the rose.

Eyes the shady night has shut
Cannot see the record cut,
And silence sounds no worse than
    cheers 15
After earth has stopped the ears:

Now you will not swell the rout
Of lads that wore their honors out,
Runners whom renown outran
And the name died before the man. 20

So set, before its echoes fade,
The fleet foot on the sill of shade,
And hold to the low lintel up
The still-defended challenge-cup.

And round that early-laureled head 25
Will flock to gaze the strengthless dead,
And find unwithered on its curls
The garland briefer than a girl's.

LYRICS FROM SHROPSHIRE

1. Each of the lyrics expresses a different mood. For each one, state the mood the poet is trying to convey, and in a sentence or two express the central thought of the poem.

2. Where in these poems do you find sharp contrasts, sometimes wistful, sometimes ironical?

3. Notice that Housman uses a ballad measure. Are these poems ballads? How do they illustrate almost perfectly the usual definition of a lyric poem?

"Loveliest of Trees" by A. E. Housman. Reprinted by permission of The Society of Authors and Jonathan Cape Limited.
"Far in a Western Brookland" from *A Shropshire Lad* by A. E. Housman. "To an Athlete Dying Young" from *Collected Poems of A. E. Housman.* Copyright, 1940, by Henry Holt and Company, Inc. Both poems reprinted by permission of Henry Holt and Company, Inc., and The Society of Authors as the Literary Representative of the Trustees of the Estate of the late A. E. Housman, and Messrs. Jonathan Cape Limited, publishers of A. E. Housman's *Collected Poems.*

WILLIAM
BUTLER
YEATS

1865-1939

Brown Bros.

In contrast to the meager output of Housman, the total output of William Butler Yeats (yāts) is tremendous. This is due partly to patriotic as well as poetic fervor, for Yeats took an active part in the Celtic Renaissance, and he was a senator in the newly established Irish Free State. Much of his poetry was inspired by these two consuming interests. Born in Dublin and educated in London, he lived during his early years with his grandparents in the Irish coastal town of Sligo (slī'gō). Here he became acquainted with Irish folklore, which influenced him greatly throughout his life.

One of the founders of the Irish National Abbey Theater in Dublin, Yeats' special interest was poetic drama. When the theater began to produce realistic prose plays, Yeats proved that he could write effectively in either medium. *The Land of Heart's Desire* is an example of his richly symbolical verse dramas; *The Pot of Broth,* of a successful prose play. Yeats was also an essayist and critic. He is best known, though, for his early lyrics, richly embroidered with metaphors and symbols. In 1923 he received the Nobel Prize for Literature for "his consistently emotional poetry, which in the strictest artistic form expresses a people's spirit."

The Wild Swans at Coole°

The trees are in their autumn beauty,
The woodland paths are dry,
Under the October twilight the water
Mirrors a still sky;
Upon the brimming water among the stones   5
Are nine-and-fifty swans.

The nineteenth autumn has come upon me
Since I first made my count;
I saw, before I had well finished,
All suddenly mount   10
And scatter wheeling in great broken rings
Upon their clamorous wings.

Title: *Coole* (kōōʻlĭ): the estate of Yeats' friend and fellow dramatist Lady Gregory.

"The Wild Swans at Coole" from *The Collected Poems of W. B. Yeats* by W. B. Yeats. Copyright 1919 by The Macmillan Company. Copyright 1946 by Bertha Georgie Yeats. Reprinted with the permission of The Macmillan Company, A. P. Watt and Son, and Macmillan and Company of Canada Limited.

I have looked upon those brilliant creatures,
And now my heart is sore.
All's changed since I, hearing at twilight,   15
The first time on this shore,
The bell-beat of their wings above my head,
Trod with a lighter tread.

Unwearied still, lover by lover,
They paddle in the cold   20
Companionable streams or climb the air;
Their hearts have not grown old;
Passion or conquest, wander where they will,
Attend upon them still.

But now they drift on the still water   25
Mysterious, beautiful;
Among what rushes will they build,
By what lake's edge or pool
Delight men's eyes when I awake some day
To find they have flown away?   30

The Lake Isle of Innisfree

The Celtic spirit, with its yearning for the remote, the beautiful, the
ideal, is melodiously caught in this poem. Of its origin the author
says: "I had still the ambition, formed . . . in my teens, of living
in imitation of Thoreau on Innisfree [a little island in Lough Gill,
Ireland] . . . and when walking through Fleet Street [London],
very homesick, I heard a little tinkle of water and saw a fountain in
a shopwindow . . . and began to remember lake water. From the
sudden remembrance came my poem, 'Innisfree.' "

I will arise and go now, and go to Innisfree,
    And a small cabin build there, of clay and wattles° made;
Nine bean rows will I have there, a hive for the honeybee,
    And live alone in the bee-loud glade.

And I shall have some peace there, for peace comes dropping slow,   5
    Dropping from the veils of the morning to where the cricket sings;
There midnight's all aglimmer, and noon a purple glow,
    And evening full of the linnet's wings.

I will arise and go now, for always night and day
    I hear lake water lapping with low sounds by the shore;   10
While I stand on the roadway, or on the pavements gray,
    I hear it in the deep heart's core.

2. *wattles:* twigs and pliable rods woven together.

"The Lake Isle of Innisfree" from *Early Poems and Stories* by William Butler Yeats. Reprinted by permission of The Macmillan Company, New York; Macmillan Company of Canada, Ltd.; and A. P. Watt and Son.

The Fiddler of Dooney

From the earliest days of singers and storytellers, the Irish have held
their musicians and poets in high esteem. Although this ballad has
a light tone, underneath is the fiddler's strong belief in the sacredness
of his important calling.

When I play on my fiddle in Dooney,°
Folk dance like the wave of the sea;
My cousin is priest in Kilvarnet,°
My brother in Moharabuiee.°

I passed by brother and cousin;   5
They read in their books of prayer;
I read in my book of songs
I bought at the Sligo fair.

When we come to the end of time,
To Peter° sitting in state,   10
He will smile on the three old spirits,
But call me first through the gate;

For the good are always the merry,
Save by an evil chance,
And the merry love the fiddle,   15
And the merry love to dance;

And when the folk there spy me,
They will all come up to me,
With "Here is the fiddler of Dooney!"
And dance like a wave of the sea.   20

1, 3, 4. *Dooney, Kilvarnet, Moharabuiee* (mō-
hä·rä·bū·ē′): hamlets on the west coast of
Ireland. 10. *Peter:* Saint Peter, keeper of the
gates of Heaven.

YEATS' POEMS

1. In "The Wild Swans at Coole" at
what season of the year and what time of
day does the poet describe the swans?
What contrast does he feel between himself and the swans after nineteen years?
2. What details in "The Lake Isle of
Innisfree" suggest the peace of spirit to be
found there? To which poem of Housman's does it have some resemblance in
mood?
3. Why does the fiddler of Dooney
mention the occupation of his two relatives? Why does he think he will be given
preference on entering Heaven? Do you
agree with the philosophy in the fourth
stanza?

WALTER DE LA MARE

1873 – 1956

"Walter de la Mare's *Collected Poems*
would be my first choice," said a critic
once, "if I were to make a present to a
child, or a sweetheart, or an old gentleman, or in general, to any happily constituted person. From the first page to the
last, one is in the land of poetry, in the
atmosphere of genuine folklore, in the age
of creative faith."

One would scarcely suspect that the subject of this tribute spent twenty years in
the London office of the Anglo-American
Oil Company. A grant from the Crown
enabled him to withdraw from this prosaic
work in 1908 and give free rein to that
rare imaginative gift which he displayed
in his prose work as well as in his poetry.
His *The Memoirs of a Midget* shows a
distorted world as seen from the position
of a midget — like Gulliver among the
giants, only with pathetic rather than satirical effect. His poems for and about children have taken their place as classics beside Stevenson's *A Child's Garden of
Verses*. "The Listeners" and "Silver" are
De la Mare's most-quoted poems.

"The Fiddler of Dooney" from *Later Poems* by William Butler Yeats. Reprinted by permission of The Macmillan Company,
New York; Macmillan Company of Canada, Ltd.; and A. P. Watt and Son.

The Listeners

The poet takes you into a strange world of echoes and eerie fancies.
With details of sound, silence, and light, the desired mood is created
and a story suggested.

"Is there anybody there?" said the Traveler,
    Knocking on the moonlit door;
And his horse in the silence champed the grasses
    Of the forest's ferny floor;
And a bird flew up out of the turret,   5
    Above the Traveler's head;
And he smote upon the door again a second time;
    "Is there anybody there?" he said.
But no one descended to the Traveler;
    No head from the leaf-fringed sill   10
Leaned over and looked into his gray eyes,
    Where he stood perplexed and still.
But only a host of phantom listeners
    That dwelt in the lone house then
Stood listening in the quiet of the moonlight   15
    To that voice from the world of men;
Stood thronging the faint moonbeams on the dark stair,
    That goes down to the empty hall,
Hearkening in an air stirred and shaken
    By the lonely Traveler's call.   20
And he felt in his heart their strangeness,
    Their stillness answering his cry,
While his horse moved, cropping the dark turf,
    'Neath the starred and leafy sky;
For he suddenly smote on the door, even   25
    Louder, and lifted his head —
"Tell them I came, and no one answered,
    That I kept my word," he said.
Never the least stir made the listeners,
    Though every word he spake   30
Fell echoing through the shadowiness of the still house
    From the one man left awake.
Ay, they heard his foot upon the stirrup,
    And the sound of iron on stone,
And how the silence surged softly backward,   35
    When the plunging hoofs were gone.

"The Listeners" from *Collected Poems, 1901–1918*, by Walter de la Mare. Copyright, 1920, by Henry Holt and Company, Inc.
Copyright, 1948, by Walter de la Mare. Used by permission of the publishers.

Silver

Slowly, silently, now the moon
Walks the night in her silver shoon;
This way, and that, she peers, and sees
Silver fruit upon silver trees;
One by one the casements catch   5
Her beams beneath the silvery thatch;
Couched in his kennel, like a log,
With paws of silver sleeps the dog;
From their shadowy cote the white
   breasts peep
Of doves in a silver-feathered sleep;   10
A harvest mouse goes scampering by,
With silver claws and a silver eye;
And moveless fish in the water gleam,
By silver reeds in a silver stream.

A Widow's Weeds

Walter de la Mare's imaginative gift
touches even the ordinary person. The
widow is old; she is dressed in her
"weeds," her mourning garments. Sorrow
has touched her life. She sows her garden,
and it grows. The poet says that "all she
has is all she needs."

A poor old Widow in her weeds
Sowed her garden with wild-flower
   seeds;
Not too shallow, and not too deep,
And down came April — drip — drip
   — drip.
Up shone May, like gold, and soon   5
Green as an arbour grew leafy June.
And now all summer she sits and sews
Where willow-herb, comfrey, bougloss
   blows,
Teasel and tansy, meadowsweet,   9
Campion, toadflax, and rough hawksbit;
Brown bee orchis, and Peals of Bells;
Clover, burnet, and thyme she smells;
Like Oberon's° meadows her garden is

13. *Oberon* (ō′bĕr·ŏn): in medieval folklore,
king of the fairies.

Drowsy from dawn till dusk with bees.
Weeps she never, but sometimes sighs,
And peeps at her garden with bright
   brown eyes;   16
And all she has is all she needs —
A poor old Widow in her weeds.

SCENES AND STORIES

1. What is your interpretation of the
story which the poet suggests in "The
Listeners"? By what details of sight, sound,
and silence is the atmosphere created?
What is unusual about its rhythm? Contrast the meter of the odd and even lines.

2. "Silver" presents an unusual picture.
How many times is the word *silver* used?

3. How would you describe the old lady
in "A Widow's Weeds"? What details in
the poem help you best to establish a mental image? Explain the significance of
line 17.

APPRECIATING FANTASY

De la Mare, a master of fantasy, has a
strange freshness of imagination that often
carries us into a mysterious and enchanting world. "The Listeners" is marked by its
imaginative beauty and excellent craftsmanship. You may read it either of two ways:
for the sheer delight of its eerie mystery
and haunting music or for the deeper
meaning hidden in its strange story.

To appreciate this fantasy fully, you
should realize that the poet is concerned
with life and universal experience. What
does the traveler stand for? He came from
the "world of men." He also seems to be
expected. Why is his knock unanswered?
Who are the listeners? Does the house
stand for something? Behind these questions lies the meaning of the fantasy in
"The Listeners."

THE POWER OF WORDS

CREATING EFFECT

In "The Listeners" we find a variety of
words (e.g., *phantom, lone, quiet, dark*)
leading to the climax in the last two lines.
In "Silver" effect is created by repeating
one word. Of the two methods, is variety
or intensity most effective?

"Silver" from *Collected Poems, 1901–1918*, by Walter de la Mare. Copyright, 1920, by Henry Holt and Company, Inc. Copyright, 1948, by Walter de la Mare. Used by permission of the publishers. "A Widow's Weeds" from *Collected Poems* by Walter de la Mare. Reprinted by permission of the Literary Trustees of Walter de la Mare and The Society of Authors as their representative.

G. K. CHESTERTON

1874–1936

The versatile Gilbert Keith Chesterton had many interests, only one of which is represented here. Besides poetry he wrote essays and a series of detective stories. His Father Brown stories, in which a priest-detective is always able to solve the mystery, make absorbing reading.

An energetic and enthusiastic person, Chesterton's first interest was art, and after graduating from art school, he began his career as a reviewer of art books. His manifold activities ranged from art and literature to politics, economics, and philosophy. He traveled and lectured extensively.

In some ways Chesterton resembled Dr. Samuel Johnson. He was large in frame, indifferent to his personal appearance, agile in conversation, prolific in essay writing, and keenly analytic in his studies of writers such as Robert Browning and G. B. Shaw. A writer who thought in terms of contradiction, he is referred to as a master of paradox. You will see examples of this technique in "The World State."

Lepanto

Out of a sixteenth-century battle Chesterton created one of the finest of modern chants. Banging, clanging, colorful, its music beats until we feel in our own pulses the marching song of the mighty host of warriors. This battle was fought in the Gulf of Lepanto (between central and southern Greece) on October 7, 1571. Because the capture of Cyprus by the Turks threatened the end of Venetian trade and even the stability of Spain, Pope Pius V had called for the gathering of a fleet from all the Christian nations. Don John of Austria, a brilliant strategist, was in command of the two hundred and eight vessels of the Christian powers which opposed two hundred and seventy-three small and more poorly equipped Turkish vessels. Both sides depended on galleys manned by prisoners. (This was the last important historical engagement in which galleys were used.) Through their heavier vessels and superior discipline the Christians won the battle, only a few of the Turkish vessels escaping capture or destruction. The Christians lost some eight thousand men; the Turks, more than twenty thousand. Moreover, the Turkish naval power was so broken that it never again threatened the peace of Christian Europe. These historical details are enlivened and glorified by the virile lines of Chesterton's poem.

White founts falling in the Courts of the Sun,
And the Soldan of Byzantium° is smiling as they run;
There is laughter like the fountains in that face of all men feared,
It stirs the forest darkness, the darkness of his beard;
It curls the blood-red crescent, the crescent of his lips;   5
For the inmost sea° of all the earth is shaken with his ships.
They have dared the white republics on the capes of Italy,
They have dashed the Adriatic round the Lion of the Sea,°

2. *Soldan of Byzantium* (sŏl'dăn . . . bĭ·zăn'shĭ·ŭm): Sultan of Constantinople. 6. *inmost sea:* the Mediterranean. 8. *Lion of the Sea:* The winged lion of St. Mark is the emblem of Venice.

"Lepanto" by G. K. Chesterton, copyright by and reprinted by permission of Dodd, Mead & Company, Inc., and by permission of A. P. Watt and Son and Miss Collins.

And the Pope has cast his arms abroad for agony and loss,
And called the kings of Christendom for swords about the Cross. 10
The cold queen° of England is looking in the glass;
The shadow of the Valois° is yawning at the Mass;
From evening isles fantastical rings faint the Spanish gun,
And the Lord upon the Golden Horn° is laughing in the sun.

Dim drums throbbing, in the hills half heard, 15
Where only on a nameless throne a crownless prince° has stirred,
Where, risen from a doubtful seat and half-attained stall,
The last knight of Europe takes weapons from the wall,
The last and lingering troubadour to whom the bird has sung,
That once went singing southward when all the world was young. 20
In that enormous silence, tiny and unafraid,
Comes up along a winding road the noise of the Crusade.
Strong gongs groaning as the guns boom far,
Don John of Austria is going to the war;
Stiff flags straining in the night blasts cold 25
In the gloom black-purple, in the glint old-gold,
Torchlight crimson on the copper kettledrums,
Then the tuckets,° then the trumpets, then the cannon, and he comes.
Don John laughing in the brave beard curled,
Spurning of his stirrups like the thrones of all the world, 30
Holding his head up for a flag of all the free.
Love light of Spain — hurrah!
Death light of Africa!
Don John of Austria
Is riding to the sea. 35

Mahound° is in his paradise above the evening star;
(*Don John of Austria is going to the war.*)
He moves a mighty turban on the timeless houri's° knees,
His turban that is woven of the sunsets and the seas.
He shakes the peacock gardens as he rises from his ease, 40
And he strides among the treetops and is taller than the trees;
And his voice through all the garden is a thunder sent to bring
Black Azrael° and Ariel° and Ammon° on the wing.
Giants and the Genii,
Multiplex of wing and eye, 45
Whose strong obedience broke the sky
When Solomon° was king.

---

11. *cold queen:* Elizabeth of England did not take part in this expedition. 12. *shadow of the Valois* (vȧ´lwȧ´): Charles IX was nominally King of France, but actually he was in the power of Catherine de Medici, the Duchess of Valois. 14. *Lord upon the Golden Horn:* The Sultan's palace in Constantinople overlooks an arm of the Bosporus called the Golden Horn. 16. *crownless prince:* Don John of Austria. 28. *tuckets:* a flourish of trumpets. 36. *Mahound* (mȧ·hound´): Mohammed. 38. *timeless houri* (hōō´rǐ): In the Mohammedan paradise, the faithful were rewarded with the companionship of beautiful women (*houris*) throughout eternity. 43. *Azrael* (ăz´rȧ·ĕl): the angel of death; *Ariel:* the spirit of the air; *Ammon:* the highest god of the Egyptians. 47. *Solomon:* According to Mohammedan legend, Solomon had a ring inscribed with the name of God which gave him control over demons and genii of the underworld.

They rush in red and purple from the red clouds of the morn,
From the temples where the yellow gods shut up their eyes in scorn;
They rise in green robes roaring from the green hells of the sea   50
Where fallen skies and evil hues and eyeless creatures be,
On them the sea valves cluster and the gray sea forests curl,
Splashed with a splendid sickness, the sickness of the pearl;
They swell in sapphire smoke out of the blue cracks of the ground —
They gather and they wonder and give worship to Mahound.   55
And he saith, "Break up the mountains where the hermitfolk can hide,
And sift the red and silver sands lest bone of saint abide,
And chase the Giaours° flying night and day, not giving rest,
For that which was our trouble comes again out of the west.
We have set the seal of Solomon on all things under sun,   60
Of knowledge and of sorrow and endurance of things done.
But a noise is in the mountains, in the mountains, and I know
The voice that shook our palaces — four hundred years ago:°
It is he that saith not 'Kismet';° it is he that knows not Fate;
It is Richard,° it is Raymond,° it is Godfrey° at the gate!   65
It is he whose loss is laughter when he counts the wager worth,
Put down your feet upon him, that our peace be on the earth."
For he heard drums groaning and he heard guns jar,
(*Don John of Austria is going to the war.*)
Sudden and still — hurrah!   70
Both from Iberia!°
Don John of Austria
Is gone by Alcalar.

St. Michael's on his Mountain° in the sea roads of the north
(*Don John of Austria is girt and going forth.*)   75
Where the gray seas glitter and the sharp tides shift
And the seafolk labor and the red sails lift.
He shakes his lance of iron and he claps his wings of stone;
The noise is gone through Normandy; the noise is gone alone;
The North is full of tangled things and texts and aching eyes,   80
And dead is all the innocence of anger and surprise,
And Christian killeth Christian in a narrow dusty room,
And Christian dreadeth Christ that hath a newer face of doom,
And Christian hateth Mary that God kissed in Galilee —
But Don John of Austria is riding to the sea.   85
Don John calling through the blast and the eclipse
Crying with the trumpet, with the trumpet of his lips,
Trumpet that sayeth *ha!*
    Domino gloria!°
Don John of Austria   90
Is shouting to the ships.

---

58. *Giaours* (jourz): unbelievers; an insulting name used by Mohammedans for anyone not of their faith. 63. *four hundred years ago:* at the time of the early Crusades. 64. *Kismet:* Fate. 65. *Richard, Raymond, Godfrey:* leaders in early Crusades. 71. *Iberia:* Spain. 74. *St. Michael's on his Mountain:* Mont St. Michel, a rocky islet off the coast of France, sacred to St. Michael. 89. *Domino gloria* (dō′mǐ·nō glō′rǐ·à): Glory be to God!

The Pope was in his chapel before day or battle broke,
(*Don John of Austria is hidden in the smoke.*)
The hidden room in man's house where God sits all the year,
The secret window whence the world looks small and very dear.   95
He sees as in a mirror on the monstrous twilight sea
The crescent of his cruel ships whose name is mystery;
They fling great shadows foe-wards, making Cross and Castle° dark;
They veil the plumèd lions on the galleys of St. Mark;°
And above the ships are palaces of brown, black-bearded chiefs,   100
And below the ships are prisons, where with multitudinous griefs,
Christian captives° sick and sunless, all a laboring race repines
Like a race in sunken cities, like a nation in the mines.
They are lost like slaves that swat,° and in the skies of morning hung
The stairways of the tallest gods when tyranny was young.   105
They are countless, voiceless, hopeless as those fallen or fleeing on
Before the high Kings' horses in the granite of Babylon.
And many a one grows witless in his quiet room in hell
Where a yellow face looks inward through the lattice of his cell,
And he finds his God forgotten, and he seeks no more a sign —   110
(*But Don John of Austria has burst the battle line!*)
Don John pounding from the slaughter-painted poop,
Purpling all the ocean like a bloody pirate's sloop,
Scarlet running over on the silvers and the golds,
Breaking of the hatches up and bursting of the holds,   115
Thronging of the thousands up that labor under sea
White for bliss and blind for sun and stunned for liberty.

98. *Cross and Castle:* the arms of Aragon and of Castile. 99. *galleys of St. Mark:* the Venetian ships. 102. *Christian captives:* galley slaves in the Turkish fleet. 104. *swat:* obsolete form of *sweated.*

Vivat Hispania!°
Domino gloria!
Don John of Austria   120
Has set his people free!

Cervantes° on his galley sets the sword back in the sheath
(*Don John of Austria rides homeward with a wreath.*)
And he sees across a weary land a straggling road in Spain,
Up which a lean and foolish knight° forever rides in vain,   125
And he smiles, but not as Sultans smile, and settles back the blade. . . .
(*But Don John of Austria rides home from the Crusade.*)

118. *Vivat Hispania:* Long live Spain! 122. *Cervantes* (sẽr·văn′tēz): Miguel de Cervantes (1547–1616), the author of *Don Quixote* (dŏn kwĭk′sŏt), Spain's great satirical classic. 125. *a lean and foolish knight:* Don Quixote.

The World State

One tendency of Chesterton's prose style is his use of the paradox, an apparent contradiction of terms that nevertheless throws new light on the truth. In "The World State" he expresses one of the world's problems by means of a paradox.

Oh, how I love Humanity,
    With love so pure and pringlish,°
And how I hate the horrid French,
    Who never will be English!

The International Idea,   5
    The largest and the clearest,
Is welding all the nations now,
    Except the one that's nearest.

This compromise has long been known,
    This scheme of partial pardons,   10
In ethical societies
    And small suburban gardens —

The villas and the chapels where
    I learned with little labor
The way to love my fellow man   15
    And hate my next-door neighbor.

2. *pringlish:* a pure invention. What does the word suggest to you?

CHESTERTON'S POETRY

1. Report on the battle of Lepanto as described in a history book. How closely does Chesterton follow actual occurrences?

2. "The World State" shows that it is easier to talk about brotherly love than to practice it. Can you illustrate Chesterton's point from affairs in today's world? in the United States? in your own community?

ANALYZING IDEAS

You will find that it sometimes takes careful review and study to see the order and the form of ideas that a writer is attempting to present. The very dash and surge of "Lepanto" tend to obscure the orderly progress of the thought. A good technique to follow in this and similar cases is to go back and outline the main ideas. Your analysis of "Lepanto" might look like this:

   a. The Soldan's arrogant laughter;
   b. Rumors of the gathering of the Christian hosts;
   c. Mohammed's summons to his helpers;
   d. Their arrival and Mohammed's orders to them;
   e. The rally of the Christians, forgetful of internal strifes, to the call;
   f. The Pope's scrutiny of the battle of the galleys;
   g. The thoughts of one combatant — Cervantes.

Complete each scene for color and detail.

"The World State" from *The Collected Poems* of G. K. Chesterton, copyright, 1932, by Dodd, Mead & Company, Inc. Reprinted by permission of Dodd, Mead & Company, Inc.; A. P. Watt and Son; Miss Collins; and Methuen and Company.

JOHN MASEFIELD

1878 –

John Masefield has been England's poet laureate since 1930. Interested in common people and everyday concerns, he is a down-to-earth and robust writer.

Orphaned as a child, Masefield was at fourteen apprenticed as a cabin boy on a merchant ship. Between voyages he tramped about in various countries and for several months worked in a New York barroom. Then a reading of Chaucer reawakened in him a childhood love of poetry. He determined to return to England and devote his life to literature. His *Salt-Water Ballads* (1902) and his later book-length poem *Dauber* struck the keynote of his writing. The tang and terror of the sea, as well as its beauty, were there. His reputation was established with a long poem, *The Everlasting Mercy,* in which a brutal boxer tells of his religious conversion. This poem shocked the public by its frank language and at the same time fascinated readers by its powerful narrative.

During a long life of active writing, Masefield has produced novels, boys' adventure stories, plays, essays, biographies, and accounts of his war experiences; but his poetry tops them all in importance.

In his younger years, Masefield lectured and read his poems in America and was often seen among the literary people of London. At present he leads a retired life at Penbury, Gloucestershire. In person he is gentle, modest, and somewhat shy — quite different from the rough and rugged characters in his poems.

A Consecration

In this poem, the introduction to *Salt-Water Ballads,* the poet consecrates himself and his poetic efforts to the toilers and sufferers of the world.

Not of the princes and prelates with periwigged charioteers
Riding triumphantly laureled to lap the fat of the years —
Rather the scorned — the rejected — the men hemmed in with the spears;

The men of the tattered battalion which fights till it dies,
Dazed with the dust of the battle, the din, and the cries,   5
The men with the broken heads and the blood running into their eyes.

Not the bemedaled Commander, beloved of the throne,
Riding cockhorse to parade when the bugles are blown,
But the lads who carried the koppie° and cannot be known.

Not the ruler for me, but the ranker, the tramp of the road,   10
The slave with the sack on his shoulders pricked on with the goad,
The man with too weighty a burden, too weary a load.

9. *koppie:* from *kopje,* a hill; a term used by the British during the Boer War in South Africa.

"A Consecration" from *Collected Poems* by John Masefield. Reprinted by permission of The Macmillan Company, New York.

The sailor, the stoker of steamers, the man with the clout,°
The chanteyman° bent at the halliards putting a tune to the shout,
The drowsy man at the wheel and the tired lookout.   15

Others may sing of the wine and the wealth and the mirth,
The portly presence of potentates goodly in girth —
Mine be the dirt and the dross, the dust and scum of the earth!

Theirs be the music, the color, the glory, the gold;
Mine be a handful of ashes, a mouthful of mold.   20
Of the maimed, of the halt and the blind in the rain and the cold —
Of these shall my songs be fashioned, my tales be told.

13. *clout:* a rag or cloth, here used for cleaning. 14. *chanteyman:* the sailor who leads in a song called a chantey, used to lighten the labor at the *halliards* (ropes for hoisting).

Laugh and Be Merry

Laugh and be merry; remember, better the world with a song,
Better the world with a blow in the teeth of a wrong.
Laugh, for the time is brief, a thread the length of a span,
Laugh and be proud to belong to the old proud pageant of man.

Laugh and be merry; remember, in olden time,   5
God made heaven and earth, for joy He took in a rime,
Made them, and filled them full with the strong red wine of His mirth,
The splendid joy of the stars, the joy of the earth.

So we must laugh and drink from the deep blue cup of the sky,
Join the jubilant song of the great stars sweeping by,   10
Laugh, and battle, and work, and drink of the wine outpoured
In the dear green earth, the sign of the joy of the Lord.

Laugh and be merry together, like brothers akin,
Guesting awhile in the rooms of a beautiful inn,
Glad till the dancing stops, and the life of the music ends.   15
Laugh till the game is played; and be you merry, my friends.

ENGLAND'S POET LAUREATE

1. What types of people inspire the poet in "A Consecration"? How does this poem (written at the beginning of the twentieth century) suggest the new trend in all forms of writing that makes the literature of our century different from that which preceded it? How does the rhyme scheme of this poem resemble the rhyme scheme in Shelley's "Ode to the West Wind" (page 447)?

2. From "Laugh and Be Merry" what do you discover about the poet's disposition and philosophy of life? Be specific in your answer.

"Laugh and Be Merry" from *Collected Poems* by John Masefield. Reprinted by permission of The Macmillan Company, New York.

SIEGFRIED SASSOON

1886 –

The terrible toll that World War I took of young poets was not only in the loss of promising young lives but also in the bitterness it left with the survivors. "Let no one from henceforth," said Siegfried Sassoon, "say one word countenancing war." Sassoon was a young man of wealthy family, an Oxford graduate who wrote poetry and loved hunting and music. His life was abruptly changed by military service — as were the lives of hundreds of men. He was made a captain and was later awarded the Military Cross for bravery. His experiences convinced him of the fundamental baseness and futility of war, and his poems painted it with uncompromising realism. Much of Sassoon's writing in the twenties and thirties was milder in tone, but he will probably be best remembered for his invectives against war.

Dreamers

Soldiers are citizens of death's gray land,
    Drawing no dividend from time's tomorrows.
In the great hour of destiny they stand,
    Each with his feuds, and jealousies, and sorrows.
Soldiers are sworn to action; they must win   5
    Some flaming, fatal climax with their lives.
Soldiers are dreamers; when the guns begin
    They think of firelit homes, clean beds, and wives.

I see them in foul dugouts, gnawed by rats,
    And in the ruined trenches, lashed with rain.   10
Dreaming of things they did with balls and bats,
    And mocked by hopeless longing to regain
Bank holidays, and picture shows, and spats,
    And going to the office in the train.

Everyone Sang

The armistice of World War I came on November 11, 1918. Imagine how the sudden news affected soldiers who had gone through four hard years of fighting!

Everyone suddenly burst out singing;
And I was filled with such delight
As prisoned birds must find in freedom
Winging wildly across the white
Orchards and dark green fields; on; on; and out of sight.   5

"Dreamers" from *Counter-Attack* by Siegfried Sassoon, published by E. P. Dutton & Company, Inc. Copyright, 1918, by Siegfried Sassoon. "Everyone Sang" from *Picture Show* by Siegfried Sassoon, copyright, 1920, by E. P. Dutton & Company, Inc. Both reprinted by permission of Brandt and Brandt.

Everyone's voice was suddenly lifted,
And beauty came like the setting sun.
My heart was shaken with tears, and horror
Drifted away. . . . O, but everyone
Was a bird; and the song was wordless; the singing will never be done.   10

A SOLDIER'S POEMS

1. How does Sassoon show his feeling toward war in "Dreamers"? What does the second line mean? (In the business world, what are dividends?) In what sense do we, in times of peace, draw dividends from the future?

2. How do some of the dreams of these soldiers suggest the difference between the fighters of the two great wars of the twentieth century and those of earlier wars?

3. Is this poem a sonnet? Prove your answer. What do you notice that is unusual about the rhyme scheme?

4. In "Everyone Sang" why is Sassoon's comparison of a soldier with a free-winging bird so appropriate? Why was the song "wordless"? In what way will the singing "never be done"?

RUPERT BROOKE

1887–1915

Sidgewick and Jackson

Rupert Brooke was outstanding among several young poets who died in World War I. "A golden young Apollo," as a friend called him, he started out life with everything in his favor: good looks, a keen mind, athletic prowess, and fine family background (his father was assistant headmaster of the Rugby school). After college he traveled extensively in 1913–14 throughout Europe, America, and the South Seas. When war broke out, he enlisted and was sent to the Dardanelles, but he never reached this destination. Death by blood poisoning overtook him on the way. The little island of Skyros in the Aegean Sea is the "corner of a foreign field that is forever England" which Brooke mentions in his sonnet "The Soldier." The manuscript of this sonnet is kept in the British Museum as a memorial of a whole generation of young men.

Brooke managed to live intensely during his few years, as is shown by the following poem, which lists all the simple things of our common life which gave him especial joy. Through perpetuating them in this much-prized poem, he did indeed "cheat drowsy Death."

"The Great Lover" by Rupert Brooke. Copyright ©, 1915, by Dodd, Mead & Company, Inc. Renewal, 1943, by Edward Marsh. Reprinted by permission of Dodd, Mead & Company, Inc., and McClelland and Stewart Limited.

The Great Lover

I have been so great a lover: filled my days
So proudly with the splendor of Love's praise,
The pain, the calm, the astonishment,
Desire illimitable, and still content,
And all dear names men use, to cheat despair,   5
For the perplexed and viewless streams that bear
Our hearts at random down the dark of life.
Now, ere the unthinking silence on that strife
Steals down, I would cheat drowsy Death so far,
My night shall be remembered for a star   10
That outshone all the suns of all men's days.
Shall I not crown them with immortal praise
Whom I have loved, who have given me, dared with me
High secrets, and in darkness knelt to see
The inenarrable° godhead of delight?   15
Love is a flame — we have beaconed the world's night;
A city — and we have built it, these and I;
An emperor — we have taught the world to die.
So, for their sakes I loved, ere I go hence,
And the high cause of Love's magnificence,   20
And to keep loyalties young, I'll write those names
Golden forever, eagles, crying flames,
And set them as a banner, that men may know,
To dare the generations, burn, and blow
Out on the wind of Time, shining and streaming.   25

These I have loved:
                    White plates and cups, clean-gleaming,
Ringed with blue lines; and feathery, fairy dust;
Wet roofs, beneath the lamplight; the strong crust
Of friendly bread; and many-tasting food;
Rainbows; and the blue bitter smoke of wood;   30
And radiant raindrops couching in cool flowers;
And flowers themselves, that sway through sunny hours,
Dreaming of moths that drink them under the moon;
Then, the cool kindliness of sheets, that soon
Smooth away trouble; and the rough male kiss   35
Of blankets; grainy wood; live hair that is
Shining and free; blue-massing clouds; the keen
Unpassioned beauty of a great machine;
The benison of hot water; furs to touch;
The good smell of old clothes; and other such —   40
The comfortable smell of friendly fingers,
Hair's fragrance, and the musty reek that lingers
About dead leaves and last year's ferns —
                              Dear names,
And thousand others throng to me! Royal flames;

15. *inenarrable* (ĭn′ĕ·năr′á·b'l): unspeakable; indescribable.

Sweet water's dimpling laugh from tap or spring;   45
Holes in the ground; and voices that do sing —
Voices in laughter, too; and body's pain,
Soon turned to peace; and the deep-panting train;
Firm sands; the little dulling edge of foam
That browns and dwindles as the wave goes home;   50
And washen stones, gay for an hour; the cold
Graveness of iron; moist black earthen mold;
Sleep; and high places; footprints in the dew;
And oaks; and brown horse chestnuts, glossy-new;
And new-peeled sticks; and shining pools on grass —   55
All these have been my loves. And these shall pass.
Whatever passes not, in the great hour,
Nor all my passion, all my prayers, have power
To hold them with me through the gate of Death.
They'll play deserter, turn with the traitor breath,   60
Break the high bond we made, and sell Love's trust
And sacramental covenant to the dust.
— Oh, never a doubt but, somewhere, I shall wake,
And give what's left of love again, and make
New friends, now strangers —
                      But the best I've known,   65
Stays here, and changes, breaks, grows old, is blown
About the winds of the world, and fades from brains
Of living men, and dies.
                    Nothing remains.

O dear my loves, O faithless, once again
This one last gift I give: that after men   70
Shall know, and later lovers, far-removed,
Praise you, "All these were lovely"; say, "He loved."

The Soldier

If I should die, think only this of me:
    That there's some corner of a foreign field
That is forever England. There shall be
    In that rich earth a richer dust concealed;
A dust whom England bore, shaped, made aware,   5
    Gave, once, her flowers to love, her ways to roam,
A body of England's, breathing English air,
    Washed by the rivers, blest by suns of home.

And think, this heart, all evil shed away,
    A pulse in the eternal mind, no less   10
        Gives somewhere back the thought by England given;
Her sights and sounds; dreams happy as her day;
    And laughter, learnt of friends; and gentleness,
        In hearts at peace, under an English heaven.

"The Soldier" by Rupert Brooke. Copyright ©, 1915, by Dodd, Mead & Company, Inc. Renewal, 1943, by Edward Marsh Reprinted by permission of Dodd, Mead & Company, Inc. and McClelland and Stewart Limited.

LIFE AND IMMORTALITY

1. Note in "The Great Lover" the keen awareness and the vigorous enthusiasm that the poet brought to the everyday experiences of living. How many of the things listed in the poem would you choose for your personal list of "loves"? What other things would you include?

2. Look through the list to discover some original metaphors, such as the "cool kindliness" of sheets and raindrops "couching" in cool flowers.

3. In "The Soldier" how is the poet's idea of immortality linked with his ideal of patriotism? Why do you think this poem is especially prized? In what way can it be said to have universal appeal, even though the feeling expressed is toward England?

4. In both of these poems, Brooke has touched in some way on immortality. Compare his ideas on the subject with those expressed in Tennyson's *In Memoriam* (page 521) and Wordsworth's "Ode on Immortality" (page 394). Which presentation seems to you most effective?

SUGGESTIONS FOR WRITING

1. Write a description of familiar objects or scenes in your life that you would consider your "loves." (If you prefer to try poetry, go ahead.) To give the reader a quick picture or a sympathetic reaction to the thing described, try to use fresh and striking metaphors as Brooke does.

2. The converse of Brooke's theme — things you hate — also makes for natural expression. A sample of this theme is Carroll's "A Sea Dirge" (page 550). Which subject — your likes or your dislikes — lends itself best to humorous treatment?

JOHN
BETJEMAN
1906 –

British Information

In 1959 the British literary world claimed John Betjeman (bĕtch'à·măn) as the next poet laureate. This prediction came when the rush for his *Collected Poems,* selling as many as one thousand copies a day, was said to be unmatched since the publication of Byron's *Childe Harold* in 1812.

Born of Quaker parents, Betjeman grew up in London; he was educated at Oxford but failed to get a degree because of an intense dislike for his chief instructor. As an assistant editor of *Architectural Review,* he became known for his wealth of knowledge and appreciation of English places. His guidebooks are described as "glowing." Betjeman describes the English landscape lyrically, sentimentally, and sometimes satirically.

The poet's nostalgia for the Victorian Age is evident. His poetry reveals his dislike for the planned progress of the future. He is interested in small, local, and personal things and asserts, "I write about the things I care about."

Although Betjeman is not chiefly a poet of humor, he at times delights the reader with amusing descriptions of people and scenes. *Slick But Not Streamlined* is a collection of light verse with concrete and witty observations about his country.

As a devoted member of the Anglican Church, Betjeman writes of religion with earnestness and simplicity, and sometimes with a chuckle. At times he can move from mockery to fierce satire. While working at the Ministry of Information during World War II, he wrote the frequently-quoted sardonic prayer which closes with: "But gracious Lord, whate'er shall be, Don't let anyone bomb me."

Today John Betjeman writes book reviews for the London *Daily Telegraph*. He spends most of his time, however, enjoying the countryside around his Berkshire home in Wantage; here, he says, he produces about one poem every six weeks.

The Planster's Vision

Betjeman's love for the past compels him not only to question the desecration of "the old" but also to distrust those who are responsible for planning for "the new." The satire is lacking in cruelty and spite, but Betjeman realistically pictures a state which to him is deplorable.

> Cut down that timber! Bells, too many and strong,
>   Pouring their music through the branches bare,
>   From moon-white church-towers down the windy air
> Have pealed the centuries out with Evensong.
> Remove those cottages, a huddled throng!   5
>   Too many babies have been born in there,
>   Too many coffins, bumping down the stair,
> Carried the old their garden paths along.
>
> I have a Vision of The Future, chum,
>   The workers' flats in fields of soya beans   10
>   Tower up like silver pencils, score on score:
> And Surging Millions hear the Challenge come
>   From microphones in communal canteens
>   "No Right! No Wrong! All's perfect, evermore."

Hertfordshire

> I had forgotten Hertfordshire,
>   The large unwelcome fields of roots
> Where with my knickerbockered sire
>   I trudged in syndicated shoots;
>
> And that unlucky day when I   5
>   Fired by mistake into the ground
> Under a Lionel Edwards° sky
>   And felt disapprobation round.

7. *Lionel Edwards:* British watercolorist (1878–   ).

"The Planster's Vision" and "Hertfordshire" from *Collected Poems* by John Betjeman. Reprinted by permission of John Murray (Publishers) Ltd., and Houghton Mifflin Company.

The slow drive home by motor-car,
    A heavy Rover Landaulette,°   10
Through Welwyn, Hatfield, Potters Bar,
    Tweed and cigar smoke, gloom and wet:

"How many times must I explain
    The way a boy should hold a gun?"
I recollect my father's pain   15
    At such a milksop for a son.

And now I see these fields once more
    Clothed, thank the Lord, in summer green,
Pale corn waves rippling to a shore
    The shadowy cliffs of elm between,   20

Color-washed cottages reed-thatched
    And weather-boarded water mills,
Flint churches, brick and plaster patched,
    On mildly undistinguished hills —

They still are there. But now the shire   25
    Suffers a devastating change,
Its gentle landscape strung with wire,
    Old places looking ill and strange.

One can't be sure where London ends,
    New towns have filled the fields of root   30
Where father and his business friends
    Drove in the landaulette to shoot;

Tall concrete standards line the lane,
    Brick boxes glitter in the sun:
Far more would these have caused him pain   35
    Than my mishandling of a gun.

10. *Landaulette* (lăn'dô·lĕt'): an automobile having an enclosed rear section with a collapsible roof and an open driver's seat.

LANDSCAPE PAINTER IN WORDS

1. What fears does Betjeman express in "The Planster's Vision"? Why does he seem to dislike planned progress? Where in the poem is there a satirical note? Describe what he foresees as future living conditions. Do you agree with the poet's point of view? Give reasons for your answer.

2. In "Hertfordshire," how many years do you think have elapsed since the incident mentioned by the poet? On revisiting Hertfordshire, what does Betjeman find unchanged? In what ways has the area changed since his boyhood?

SUGGESTION FOR WRITING

Recall a place that you knew well as a child but that has changed considerably in the last five to seven years. How has it changed? What forces have brought about these changes? Write a comparison of this place as you once knew it and as it appears to you now. Include in the composition your reaction to the changes that have occurred.

T. S. ELIOT

1888 –

British Information

The literary career of Thomas Stearns Eliot is a marked example of the changes a man's thinking may undergo with the shifting experiences of life. By birth he was a Middle Westerner from St. Louis, Missouri. After graduating from Harvard University in 1910, he attended the Sorbonne in Paris and later studied Greek philosophy at Oxford as a Rhodes scholar. The English way of life so appealed to him that he continued to live abroad and in 1927 became a naturalized British subject.

In his early poems Eliot revolted against the cheerfulness, smoothness, and obviousness of preceding poets. He wrote poetry that was hard and brittle. In design, these poems are zigzags of classical allusions, wit, obscure symbols, and cryptic phrases. In mood, they convey the impression that life is futile — hardly worth the effort of drawing breath. Note the titles of his most famous early poems — *The Waste Land* and "The Hollow Men."

But his next long poem, *Ash Wednesday* (1930), shows a change in Eliot's attitude. The note of despair is gradually replaced by one of religious faith. From that time on, Eliot's work takes on a more hopeful and affirmative tone.

With the two plays *Murder in the Cathedral* (1935) and *The Family Reunion* (1939), Eliot revived the poetic tradition in the theater. In recent years he has produced other successful plays in verse — *The Cocktail Party* (1950), *The Confidential Clerk* (1953), and *The Elder Statesman* (1959). The dialogue in his plays is patterned in a loose metrical form somewhat like *Beowulf*. All his writing — drama, poetry, and prose — has subtle underlying meanings which are not apparent from a superficial reading. Considered the most famous, one of the most controversial, and perhaps the most influential poet of the twentieth century, Eliot, though often difficult, repays thoughtful study.

Preludes

Eliot's poetry throughout his long career shows a progression in technique as well as in content. "Preludes," written in 1915 and published in his first collection, *Prufrock and Other Observations,* represents his early period. In this piece, Eliot uses the free verse broken by occasional rhymes which is found in most of his early poems.

"Preludes" is an experiment in the use of imagery which employs as its subject matter scenes of everyday life. The speaker in these poems appears to be an objective observer. However, his very choice of certain scenes and images shows that he is emotionally concerned and that he has a definite point of view.

"Preludes" from *Collected Poems 1909–1935* by T. S. Eliot, copyright, 1936, by Harcourt, Brace & World, Inc. Reprinted by permission of Harcourt, Brace & World, Inc., and Faber and Faber Ltd.

I

The winter evening settles down
With smell of steaks in passageways.
Six o'clock.
The burnt-out ends of smoky days.
And now a gusty shower wraps   5
The grimy scraps
Of withered leaves about your feet
And newspapers from vacant lots;
The showers beat
On broken blinds and chimney-pots,   10
And at the corner of the street
A lonely cab-horse steams and stamps.
And then the lighting of the lamps.

II

The morning comes to consciousness
Of faint stale smells of beer   15
From the sawdust-trampled street
With all its muddy feet that press
To early coffee-stands.
With the other masquerades
That time resumes,   20
One thinks of all the hands
That are raising dingy shades
In a thousand furnished rooms.

III

You tossed a blanket from the bed,
You lay upon your back, and waited;   25
You dozed, and watched the night revealing
The thousand sordid images
Of which your soul was constituted;
They flickered against the ceiling.
And when all the world came back   30
And the light crept up between the shutters
And you heard the sparrows in the gutters,
You had such a vision of the street
As the street hardly understands;
Sitting along the bed's edge, where   35
You curled the papers from your hair,
Or clasped the yellow soles of feet
In the palms of both soiled hands.

IV

His soul stretched tight across the skies
That fade behind a city block,   40
Or trampled by insistent feet
At four and five and six o'clock;

And short square fingers stuffing pipes,
And evening newspapers, and eyes
Assured of certain certainties,   45
The conscience of a blackened street
Impatient to assume the world.

I am moved by fancies that are curled
Around these images, and cling:
The notion of some infinitely gentle   50
Infinitely suffering thing.

Wipe your hand across your mouth, and laugh;
The worlds revolve like ancient women
Gathering fuel in vacant lots.

The Hollow Men

"The Hollow Men" (1925) depicts the citizens of modern Western culture, synthetically stuffed with ideas, opinions, and faiths which they cannot feel. Eliot's chief purpose in the poem is to create a mood of frustration, emptiness, and despair. Conveying the mood of despair, for example, are the striking phrases "rats' feet over broken glass," "this is cactus land."

The childish nursery rhyme which begins Section V indicates the pointlessness of modern man's daily round. Man is impotent, inactive; the world ends "not with a bang but a whimper."

Mistah Kurtz — he dead.
A penny for the Old Guy.*

I

We are the hollow men
We are the stuffed men
Leaning together
Headpiece filled with straw. Alas!
Our dried voices, when   5
We whisper together
Are quiet and meaningless
As wind in dry grass
Or rats' feet over broken glass
In our dry cellar   10

Shape without form, shade without color,

Paralyzed force, gesture without motion;°

Those who have crossed
With direct eyes, to death's other Kingdom°
Remember us — if at all — not as lost
Violent souls, but only   16
As the hollow men
The stuffed men.

II

Eyes I dare not meet in dreams
In death's dream kingdom   20
These do not appear:

* *Mistah Kurtz:* a character in Joseph Conrad's novel *Heart of Darkness,* a cultivated philosopher who dies unremembered in the African jungle. *A penny for the Old Guy:* This is a cry used by children on Guy Fawkes Day in England to obtain handouts, much as is done in America on Halloween.

12. These are descriptions, or suggestions, of modern man's lack of power and usefulness. 13–14. The dead, who stare (*with direct eyes*); *death's other Kingdom* implies that this life is a kind of death also.

"The Hollow Men" from *Collected Poems 1909–1935* by T. S. Eliot, copyright, 1936, by Harcourt, Brace & World, Inc. Reprinted by permission of Harcourt, Brace & World, Inc., and Faber and Faber Ltd.

There, the eyes are
Sunlight on a broken column
There, is a tree swinging
And voices are   25
In the wind's singing
More distant and more solemn
Than a fading star.

Let me be no nearer
In death's dream kingdom   30
Let me also wear
Such deliberate disguises
Rat's coat, crowskin, crossed staves
In a field
Behaving as the wind behaves   35
No nearer —

Not that final meeting
In the twilight kingdom

III

This is the dead land
This is cactus land   40
Here the stone images
Are raised, here they receive
The supplication of a dead man's hand°
Under the twinkle of a fading star.

Is it like this   45
In death's other kingdom
Waking alone
At the hour when we are
Trembling with tenderness
Lips that would kiss   50
Form prayers to broken stone.

IV

The eyes are not here
There are no eyes here
In this valley of dying stars
In this hollow valley   55
This broken jaw of our lost kingdoms

In this last of meeting places
We grope together

And avoid speech
Gathered on this beach of the tumid
    river   60

Sightless, unless
The eyes reappear
As the perpetual star°
Multifoliate rose
Of death's twilight kingdom   65
The hope only
Of empty men.

V

Here we go round the prickly pear
Prickly pear prickly pear
Here we go round the prickly pear 70
At five o'clock in the morning.°

Between the idea
And the reality
Between the motion
And the act   75
Falls the Shadow°
            For Thine is the Kingdom

Between the conception
And the creation
Between the emotion   80
And the response
Falls the Shadow
            Life is very long

Between the desire
And the spasm   85
Between the potency
And the existence
Between the essence
And the descent

43. Men pray (*supplication*) to outworn tradition (*stone images*). In the next stanza the poet says that men desire the vigor and warmth of life (*would kiss*) but can only pray fearfully, because of their lack of faith.

63. That is, men will be ineffectual (*sightless*) unless they regain their faith (*eyes reappear as the perpetual star*). 71. This is, of course, a familiar nursery rhyme. *Prickly pear* is desert cactus and thus is appropriately substituted for the usual "mulberry bush." Contrasted with the Lord's Prayer line that follows (*For Thine is the Kingdom*), the nursery rhyme suggests the meaninglessness of modern life. 76. Once again the poet indicates man's lack of power and usefulness. He feels that man has lost the power to achieve, to accomplish, to build; always the *Shadow* of lost faith and failure falls between what he seeks and what he obtains.

<table>
<tr><td>Falls the Shadow   90</td><td>This is the way the world ends   95</td></tr>
</table>

Falls the Shadow   90

     For Thine is the Kingdom

  For Thine is
Life is
For Thine is the

This is the way the world ends   95
This is the way the world ends
This is the way the world ends
Not with a bang but a whimper.

FROM *Murder in the Cathedral*

Murder in the Cathedral, a drama dealing with the assassination of
Thomas à Becket, was originally written for production at the
Canterbury Festival of 1935. Since that time this play has been
often performed — sometimes in regular church settings — and a
film version using the crypt of the Canterbury Cathedral was made.

   In dramatizing the death of Thomas à Becket, Archbishop of
Canterbury at the time of Henry II, Eliot presents the Christian
martyr as a man torn with suffering. England is the scene of a
power struggle between the king and the barons and bishops. Fearing the power of the archbishop, knights arrive in Canterbury to
pronounce the king's sentence: Thomas à Becket and his retinue
must leave England. The archbishop refuses; in the cathedral proper
he is slain. The only solace of the priests and populace who mourn
his death is that so long as men will die for their faith the Church
will reign supreme. The following words conclude a dramatic and
climactic scene when Thomas à Becket commands the door to be
opened for the knights who have come to slay him.

Thomas: Unbar the door!
   You think me reckless, desperate and mad.
   You argue by results, as this world does,
   To settle if an act be good or bad.
   You defer to the fact. For every life and every act   5
   Consequence of good and evil can be shown.
   And as in time results of many deeds are blended
   So good and evil in the end become confounded.
   It is not in time that my death shall be known;
   It is out of time that my decision is taken   10
   If you call that decision
   To which my whole being gives entire consent.
   I give my life
   To the law of God above the Law of Man.
   Those who do not the same   15

From *Murder in the Cathedral* by T. S. Eliot, copyright, 1935, by Harcourt, Brace & World, Inc. Reprinted by permission of Harcourt, Brace & World, Inc., and Faber and Faber Ltd.

In this photograph taken in Canterbury Cathedral, the clergyman is standing on ▶
the approximate spot in the Trinity Chapel where Thomas à Becket was murdered.
The stairs at top center are the "Pilgrim's Steps," worn from centuries of use. The
gilt copper effigy at the left is of Edward, the Black Prince (1330–76).

How should they know what I do?
How should you know what I do? Yet how much more
Should you know than these madmen beating on the door.
Unbar the door! unbar the door!
We are not here to triumph by fighting, by stratagem, or by
    resistance,   20
Not to fight with beasts as men. We have fought the beast
And have conquered. We have only to conquer
Now, by suffering. This is the easier victory.
Now is the triumph of the Cross, now
Open the door! I command it. OPEN THE DOOR!   25

THE POETRY OF T. S. ELIOT

1. Describe the images found in "Preludes." What feelings of the poet are conveyed through the images he has chosen? Do you find in these poems a satiric observation of life? Explain the metaphor at the end of the fourth prelude.

2. Try to state in simple, direct words the thought of each section of "The Hollow Men." Besides the symbols explained in the footnotes, look for other symbols which you can interpret yourself. Compare expressions like "a headpiece filled with straw" with the slang phrase "a stuffed shirt." Do these phrases describe the same or different types of men?

3. What prominent men of today would you class as "hollow men"? Which are the opposite, full of character and purpose?

4. Compare "The Hollow Men" with Shakespeare's famous lines in *Macbeth*, "Out, out, brief candle" (page 184, lines 23–28). Which poet do you think better conveys the idea that life is meaningless? Eliot arrives at this conclusion at the beginning of his life, Macbeth at the end. What differences do you see in the causes that made each arrive at this opinion?

5. What does Thomas à Becket have to say about good and evil? Does he expect his decision to be understood? Explain. Why does he choose to give his life?

STEPHEN SPENDER

1909 –

British Information

At seventeen Stephen Spender had his own printing press and was earning money by printing druggists' labels. Later he put the press to good use in printing his own poems. He did not need to depend on it for an income, however, for his father, a journalist and lecturer at Oxford, was well-to-do. Spender was able to devote himself to poetry and later to literary magazines.

At Oxford he associated with a small

group of poets of the "new school," of which W. H. Auden was the leader. In its active life as well as in its poetry, this highly politically and socially conscious group interested itself in the major issues of the day. Spender's emphasis has since changed. Though still concerned with contemporary social and moral problems, today poetry for him has a far broader scope. He is not so satirical as some of the other poets of his generation, nor does he seek poetry as an escape. He thinks that poetry should say to the reader, "This is what life is like. It is even realer, less to be evaded than you thought. But I offer you an example of acceptance and under-standing. Now, go back and live!"

The poetry of Brooke and Sassoon is the work of men who experienced World War I. Rupert Brooke's poems sound the note of anticipation of war's terrible price; Siegfried Sassoon gives us the full realization of it. Stephen Spender lived through World War II, during which he worked for the Churchill government. The following poem is from "Part Six 1940–1944: Poems about War" in his *Collected Poems.* An epilogue is usually a speech addressed to the audience after the conclusion of a play. This is a different kind of epilogue. The poet creates a powerful impression of the aftermath of war.

Epilogue to a Human Drama

When pavements were blown up, exposing nerves,
And the gas mains burned blue and gold,
And stucco and brick were pulverized to a cloud
Pungent with smells of mice, dust, garlic, anxiety:
When the reverberant emptied façades   5
Of the West End palaces of commerce
Isolated in a vacuum of silence, suddenly
Cracked and blazed and fell, with the seven-maned
Lions of Wrath licking the stony fragments —

Then the one voice through deserted streets   10
Was the Cassandra ° bell which rang and rang and rang
Released at last by Time
To seek those fires that burst through many walls —
Prophetic doom laid bare under the nostrils,
Blood and fire streaming from the stones.   15

London burned with unsentimental dignity
Of resigned kingship: those stores and Churches
Which had glittered century-long in dusty gold
Stood near the throne of domed St. Paul's
Like courtiers round the Royal sainted martyr.   20
August shadows of night
And bursting of concentrated light
Dropped from the skies to paint a final scene
Illuminated agony of frowning stone.
Who then can wonder that every word   25
In burning London, stepped out of a play?

11. *Cassandra* (kǎ·sǎn′drà): daughter of Troy; Apollo gave her the gift of prophecy but afterwards, in anger, decreed that no one should believe her prophecies. The word has come to mean any prophetess of evil who is not believed.

"Epilogue to a Human Drama" Copyright 1940 by Stephen Spender. Reprinted from *Collected Poems 1928–1953*, by Stephen Spender. Reprinted by permission of Random House, Inc., and Faber and Faber Ltd.

On the stage, there were heroes, maidens, fools,
Victims, a Chorus. The heroes were brave,
The fools spat jokes into the skull of death,
The victims waited with the humble patience 30
Of animals trapped behind a wall
For the pickaxes to break, with light and water.
The Chorus assisted, bringing cups of tea,
Praising the heroes, deploring the morals of the wicked,
Underlining punishment, justifying Doom to Truth. 35

The Express

In this poem you can feel the speed and force of a modern express
train.

After the first powerful plain manifesto
The black statement of pistons, without more fuss
But gliding like a queen, she leaves the station.
Without bowing and with restrained unconcern
She passes the houses which humbly crowd outside, 5
The gasworks and at last the heavy page
Of death, printed by gravestones in the cemetery.
Beyond the town there lies the open country
Where, gathering speed, she acquires mystery,
The luminous self-possession of ships on ocean. 10
It is now she begins to sing — at first quite low,
Then loud, and at last with a jazzy madness —
The song of her whistle screaming at curves,
Of deafening tunnels, brakes, innumerable bolts.
And always light, aerial, underneath 15
Goes the elate meter of her wheels.
Steaming through metal landscape on her lines,
She plunges new eras of wild happiness
Where speed throws up strange shapes, broad curves,
And parallels clean like the steel of guns. 20
At last, further than Edinburgh or Rome,
Beyond the crest of the world, she reaches night
Where only a low streamline brightness
Of phosphorus on the tossing hills is white.
Ah, like a comet through flame, she moves entranced 25
Wrapt in her music no bird song, no, nor bough
Breaking with honey buds, shall ever equal.

"The Express" from *Poems* by Stephen Spender. Copyright 1934, by Modern Library, Inc. Reprinted by permission of Random House, Inc., and Faber and Faber Ltd

AN OBSERVER OF MODERN LIFE

1. Describe Spender's feelings toward war as they are expressed in "Epilogue to a Human Drama." What is the toll of war in the city? In what way is the scene a drama for the poet? Compare his reaction to war with that of Brooke and Sassoon.

2. Is the poem "The Express" purely pictorial or does it offer comments on modern living as well? Older poets, like Wordsworth, for example, looked on the railroad as an ugly intrusion on the beauties of nature. What do you think is Spender's view on this matter?

UNDERSTANDING FIGURATIVE LANGUAGE

Did you notice the comparisons that Spender uses in "The Express"? There are fresh combinations of noun and modifier that label accurately what was noted. Some of the comparisons are direct; that is, they are similes beginning with *like*, as in line 3 and line 20. Others are indirect and are worth seeking out, like "the heavy page of death, printed by gravestones" in lines 6–7; "the luminous self-possession of ships" in line 10. Analyze the comparisons made in nearly every line of the poem.

DYLAN THOMAS

1914 – 1953

Marion Morehouse

Dylan (dĭl'ăn) Thomas is one of the most celebrated poets of the twentieth century. New and dynamic language, remarkably fierce vigor of speech, vibrant imagery, and unusual rhythmical cadences characterize the poetry of this highly talented Welshman. A lecturer at Cambridge said of Dylan Thomas, "He was the most poetical poet of our time. He talked and dressed and behaved and lived like a poet; he was innocent, reckless, flamboyant, and irreverent. And his verse, too, had a romantic wildness about it that even the readers who could make nothing of it recognized as 'poetic.' " His poetry is rich with symbolism and original images. A poet who often demands much of his readers, he has been hailed as the most original and refreshing lyric genius of our time.

Thomas was born in Swansea, a seacoast town in southern Wales. Here he enjoyed a happy childhood, which he writes about in *Quite Early One Morning*, a collection of his prose and poetry. In Part I of this work the prose is especially exuberant in style. Dylan in Welsh means "sea," and he was haunted by it all his life. He lived with his wife and children in the Welsh seacoast village of Laugharne, immortalized in his radio drama *Under Milk Wood*, a play depicting life in a small Welsh village.

Writing documentary films and reading poetry for the British Broadcasting Company gave Thomas some financial security. He was most successful, however, in his American poetry-reading tours. It was while he was on his third tour that he died in New York City at the age of thirty-nine. Not long before his death he published his *Collected Poems 1934–53*. Fortunately, we can still experience the magnificent voice of Dylan Thomas by listening to the recordings he made of many of his writings.

Fern Hill

"Fern Hill," a bright and joyful picture of summer on a Welsh
farm, is an echo of Dylan Thomas' youth. Childhood experiences
made a deep impression on him. The carefree happiness of a young
boy is suggested repeatedly throughout this poem.

Now as I was young and easy under the apple boughs
About the lilting house and happy as the grass was green,
   The night above the dingle° starry,
     Time let me hail and climb
   Golden in the heydays of his eyes,   5
And honored among wagons I was prince of the apple towns
And once below a time I lordly had the trees and leaves
    Trail with daisies and barley
   Down the rivers of the windfall light.

And as I was green and carefree, famous among the barns   10
About the happy yard and singing as the farm was home,
   In the sun that is young once only,
     Time let me play and be
   Golden in the mercy of his means,
And green and golden I was huntsman and herdsman, the calves   15
Sang to my horn, the foxes on the hills barked clear and cold,
    And the sabbath rang slowly
   In the pebbles of the holy streams.

All the sun long it was running, it was lovely, the hay
Fields high as the house, the tunes from the chimneys, it was air   20
   And playing, lovely and watery
     And fire green as grass.
   And nightly under the simple stars
As I rode to sleep the owls were bearing the farm away,
All the moon long I heard, blessed among stables, the nightjars°   25
   Flying with the ricks,° and the horses
    Flashing into the dark.

And then to awake, and the farm, like a wanderer white
With the dew, come back, the cock on his shoulder: it was all
   Shining, it was Adam and maiden,   30
    The sky gathered again
   And the sun grew round that very day.
So it must have been after the birth of the simple light
In the first, spinning place, the spellbound horses walking warm
   Out of the whinnying green stable   35
    On to the fields of praise.

---

3. *dingle:* little valley. 25. *nightjars:* a kind of night bird. 26. *ricks:* haystacks.

"Fern Hill" from *Collected Poems of Dylan Thomas.* Copyright, 1953, by Dylan Thomas and published by New Directions.

And honored among foxes and pheasants by the gay house
Under the new made clouds and happy as the heart was long,
   In the sun born over and over,
     I ran my heedless ways,   40
   My wishes raced through the house high hay
And nothing I cared, at my sky blue trades, that time allows
In all his tuneful turning so few and such morning songs
   Before the children green and golden
     Follow him out of grace,   45

Nothing I cared, in the lamb white days, that time would take me
Up to the swallow thronged loft by the shadow of my hand,
   In the moon that is always rising,
     Nor that riding to sleep
I should hear him fly with the high fields   50
And wake to the farm forever fled from the childless land.
Oh as I was young and easy in the mercy of his means,
   Time held me green and dying
   Though I sang in my chains like the sea.

Do Not Go Gentle into That Good Night

A defiant attitude toward death is found in the following poem,
which Thomas wrote when his father was dying.

      Do not go gentle into that good night,
      Old age should burn and rave at close of day;
      Rage, rage against the dying of the light.

      Though wise men at their end know dark is right,
      Because their words had worked no lightning they   5
      Do not go gentle into that good night.

      Good men, the last wave by, crying how bright
      Their frail deeds might have danced in a green bay,
      Rage, rage against the dying of the light.

      Wild men who caught and sang the sun in flight,   10
      And learn, too late, they grieved it on its way,
      Do not go gentle into that good night.

      Grave men, near death, who see with blinding sight
      Blind eyes could blaze like meteors and be gay,
      Rage, rage against the dying of the light.   15

      And you, my father there on the sad height,
      Curse, bless, me now with your fierce tears, I pray.
      Do not go gentle into that good night.
      Rage, rage against the dying of the light.

"Do Not Go Gentle into That Good Night" from *Collected Poems of Dylan Thomas*. Copyright, 1953, by Dylan Thomas and published by New Directions.

The Hand that Signed the Paper Felled a City

The hand that signed the paper felled a city;
Five sovereign fingers taxed the breath,
Doubled the globe of dead and halved a country;
These five kings did a king to death.

The mighty hand leads to a sloping shoulder,   5
The finger joints are cramped with chalk;
A goose's quill has put an end to murder
That put an end to talk.

The hand that signed the treaty bred a fever,
And famine grew, and locusts came;   10
Great is the hand that holds dominion over
Man by a scribbled name.

The five kings count the dead but do not soften
The crusted wound nor pat the brow;
A hand rules pity as a hand rules heaven;   15
Hands have no tears to flow.

POEMS OF VIGOR AND SUBTLETY

1. In "Fern Hill" what are the specific scenes and childhood activities which the poet mentions? Do any of them recall experiences you yourself have had?

2. "Fern Hill" is full of striking images and of sounds that are particularly memorable. Select phrases or lines that you like — why are they effective? How does the poet create the mood of exhilaration and joy? What is the thought in the last stanza that changes the mood?

3. What is the poet's central thought in "Do Not Go Gentle into That Good Night"? To whom is he speaking? What do "good night" and "the dying of the light" symbolize? What other symbols in the poem can you interpret? Do you think this poem could have been written by an old man? Explain the reasons for your answer.

4. What does the poet say about the responsibility of a ruler? What results of signing the paper or document are mentioned? Explain the metaphor used for the five fingers of the hand.

APPRECIATING POETIC LANGUAGE

Dylan Thomas was obsessed with words that produce unusual effects. The ordinary person, although he often finds Thomas' play of words puzzling, finds himself responding to the words and phrases which this poet uses in unfamiliar ways. In "Fern Hill" you can find examples of the poet's use of original expressions. What would you normally say instead of "once below a time" (line 7); "all the sun long" (line 19); "all the moon long" (line 25); "riding to sleep" (line 49)?

Thomas' use of metaphor and simile is particularly striking. In "Fern Hill," which is rich in these vivid figures of speech, the poet helps you to see sharp images of what he is describing. Consider the comparisons which are made in the following: "prince of the apple towns" (line 6); "in the lamb white days" (line 46); "sang in my chains like the sea" (line 54). Do you enjoy seeing some common thing in a new way? Find other comparisons in Thomas' poetry which show a fresh use of words. No other poet is better able to use poetic language.

"The Hand that Signed the Paper Felled a City" from *The Collected Poems of Dylan Thomas* by Dylan Thomas. Copyright 1952, 1953 by Dylan Thomas. Reprinted by permission of New Directions, and J. M. Dent & Sons Limited.

LAURIE LEE

1914 –

In 1960 Laurie Lee gained recognition in the United States when his autobiography, *Edge of Day,* was widely acclaimed. Published a year earlier in England as *Cider with Rosie,* this work is the delightful story of Lee's boyhood in the west of England.

Before the first publication in 1944 of his poems, *The Sun My Monument,* many of Lee's poems were published in magazines such as *Horizon* and *The Listener.*

Two other collections which followed are *The Blooms of Candles* (1947) and *My Many-Coated Man* (1955).

In much of his writing, Lee seems to be aware of the world's disharmony and of the necessity to correct its disorder. Both city and country figure in "Town Owl." "Field of Autumn," in its use of rural rather than urban images, is perhaps more typical of Lee's poetry.

Town Owl

On eves of cold, when slow coal fires,
rooted in basements, burn and branch,
brushing with smoke the city air;

When quartered moons pale in the sky,
and neons glow along the dark   5
like deadly nightshade on a briar;

Above the muffled traffic then
I hear the owl, and at his note
I shudder in my private chair.

For like an augur he has come   10
to roost among our crumbling walls,
his blooded talons sheathed in fur.

Some secret lure of time it seems
has called him from his country wastes
to hunt a newer wasteland here.   15

And where the candelabra swung,
bright with the dancers' thousand eyes,
now his black, hooded pupils stare,

And where the silk-shoed lovers ran
with dust of diamonds in their hair,   20
he opens now his silent wing,

And, like a stroke of doom, drops down,
and swoops across the empty hall,
and plucks a quick mouse off the stair . . .

"Town Owl" from *My Many-Coated Man* by Laurie Lee. Reprinted by permission of Andre Deutsch Limited.

Field of Autumn

Slow moves the acid breath of noon
over the copper-coated hill,
slow from the wild crab's bearded breast
the palsied apples fall.

Like colored smoke the day hangs fire,   5
taking the village without sound;
the vulture-headed sun lies low
chained to the violet ground.

The horse upon the rocky height
rolls all the valley in his eye,   10
but dares not raise his foot or move
his shoulder from the fly.

The sheep, snail-backed against the wall,
lifts her blind face but does not know
the cry her blackened tongue gives forth   15
is the first bleat of snow.

Each bird and stone, each roof and well,
feels the gold foot of autumn pass;
each spider binds with glittering snare
the splintered bones of grass.   20

Slow moves the hour that sucks our life,
slow drops the late wasp from the flower,
the rose tree's thread of scent draws thin —
and snaps upon the air.

IMAGERY AND REALISM

1. What incident does the poet describe in "Town Owl"? See if you can discover a deeper meaning to the poem. Why does the owl come "like an augur" (line 10)? What has happened to the city? Can you attach any significance to the last three lines? Discuss.

2. Contrast the scenery of Lee's "Field of Autumn" with that in Betjeman's "Hertfordshire" (page 682). By what details of sight and sound does Lee create the atmosphere of his poem?

"Field of Autumn" from *The Sun My Monument*, by Laurie Lee. Copyright 1944 by Laurie Lee. Reprinted by permission of Doubleday & Company, Inc.

CHARLES CAUSLEY

1917–

Charles Causley — poet, teacher, and broadcaster — was in the communications branch of the Royal Navy during World War II, and a good share of his poems deal with war in one or another of its phases. From 1953–56 he was literary editor of the British Broadcasting Company's West Region radio magazines: *Apollo in the West* and *Signature*. A recent collection of his poetry is entitled *Union Street*.

Causley lived for many years in Cornwall, near the seacoast, and writes of the sea with a lyrical beauty, a clearness, and freshness that has a flavor all its own. He likes to use the ballad form, and in much of his poetry, particularly his later poems, there is a sharp originality in his use of ballad meters. At times, he uses a very strict metrical form as a contrast to the emotion expressed in the poem.

Edith Sitwell, a well-known critic, characterizes "At the British War Cemetery, Bayeux," one of Causley's most powerful war poems, as "magnificent, moving, terrible." In "The Seasons in North Cornwall" are feelings, images, and musical lines not often found today in younger English poets.

At the British War Cemetery, Bayeux°

I walked where in their talking graves
And shirts of earth five thousand lay,
When history with ten feasts of fire
Had eaten the red air away.

I am Christ's boy, I cried, I bear   5
In iron hands the bread, the fishes.°
I hang with honey and with rose
This tidy wreck of all your wishes.

On your geometry of sleep
The chestnut and the fir-tree fly,   10
And lavender and marguerite
Forge with their flowers an English sky.

Turn now toward the belling town
Your jigsaws of impossible bone,
And rising read your rank of snow   15
Accurate as death upon the stone.

About your easy heads my prayers
I said with syllables of clay.
What gift, I asked, shall I bring now
Before I weep and walk away?   20

Take, they replied, the oak and laurel.
Take our fortune of tears and live
Like a spendthrift lover. All we ask
Is the one gift you cannot give.

Title: *Bayeux* (bä·yû'): small community in northwest France. 6. *the bread, the fishes:* (Matthew 14: 15–21) parable of the five thousand fed by Jesus with five loaves and two fishes.

"At the British War Cemetery, Bayeux" from *Union Street* by Charles Causley. Reprinted by permission of Rupert Hart-Davis Limited.

Photo Researchers, Inc.

The Seasons in North Cornwall

O spring has set off her green fuses
    Down by the Tamar° today,
And careless, like tidemarks, the hedges
    Are bursting with almond and may.

Here lie I, waiting for old summer,   5
    A red face and straw-colored hair has
      he:
I shall meet him on the road from
      Marazion°
    And the Mediterranean Sea.

September has flung a spray of rooks
    On the sea chart of the sky,   10
The tall shipmasts crack in the forest
    And the banners of autumn fly.

My room is a bright glass cabin,
    All Cornwall thunders at my door,
And the white ships of winter lie   15
    In the sea roads of the moor.

2. *Tamar* (tā′mēr): a river in southwest England, flowing between Cornwall and Devonshire. 7. *Marazion:* a small seaport of Cornwall.

A CORNISH POET

1. Describe Causley's feelings toward war in "At the British War Cemetery, Bayeux." Point to references in the poem which suggest World War II. What is the one gift that the poet is unable to give? Compare his reaction to war with that of Brooke, Sassoon, and Spender.

2. In "The Seasons in North Cornwall" how is each season pictured by the poet? What images are especially effective in the poem? Which season do you think Causley prefers? Why?

READING LIST FOR
MODERN POETRY

In addition to the following titles, many other anthologies of modern poetry are available. See also the collected works of the poets you have just read.

Cecil, Lord David and Allen Tate (editors), *Modern Verse in English*
A reasonably wide choice of poets, with representative selections arranged chronologically. Biographical notes on the fifty-five British poets included.

Cole, William (editor), *Fireside Book of Humorous Poetry*
This collection includes old favorites, blandly funny poems, and others for more sophisticated taste.

Conquest, Robert (editor), *New Lines*
The newest group of British poets, who call themselves the New Movement or simply the Movement, has published its own anthology.

Garrity, D. A. (editor), *New Irish Poets*

Gillis, Adolph, and W. R. Benét (editors), *Poems for Modern Youth*
Easily understood poems.

"The Seasons in North Cornwall" from *Union Street* by Charles Causley. Reprinted by permission of Rupert Hart-Davis Limited.

Ledward, P., and C. Strang (editors), *Poems of This War*
Poetry of World War II.

Le Gallienne, Richard (editor), *A Modern Book of English Verse*

Lucy, Sean, *T. S. Eliot and the Idea of Tradition*
An examination of Eliot's influence on those who in turn have influenced him.

Parker, Elinor (editor), *100 More Story Poems*
The humorous verse of Hillaire Belloc and W. S. Gilbert is especially enjoyable in this volume focusing on narrative poetry.

Sitwell, Dame Edith (editor), *The Atlantic Book of British and American Poetry*

An anthology prepared by an outstanding poet and critic of poetry.

Untermeyer, Louis (editor), *Modern British Poetry*
Editions of this comprehensive anthology have been coming out since 1920. Excellent biographical and critical materials are included.

Yeats, W. B. (editor), *The Oxford Book of Modern Verse*

FOR LISTENING

Eliot's "The Hollow Men," and Thomas' "Do Not Go Gentle into That Good Night" have been recorded on *Many Voices 6B*. Spender's "Epilogue to a Human Drama" and Lee's "Field of Autumn" are available on *Many Voices 12A*.

MODERN BIOGRAPHY

BOSWELL'S *Life of Samuel Johnson* is an enduring masterpiece because it gives us everything we want from a biography. It tells what we want to know about the life of a remarkable man; it is a work of art as well — that is, it is deliberately shaped and colored to produce a definite effect; and its detailed scenes and exact dialogue make it as dramatically entertaining as a good novel. There are three different kinds of excellence here, and these are very rarely found together in one biography. What we usually have instead are biographies or pseudo-biographies offering us only one of these virtues.

The supply of what we may call "standard" or "official" biographies continues, simply telling us what we ought to know about the lives of statesmen, famous authors, successful generals, and other important personages. There are plenty of these, to be read casually by the general reader and with greater interest by the historian or literary critic. But few of them make any contribution to literature.

The biography-as-work-of-art is of course far less common. In modern English literature it is chiefly associated with Lytton Strachey, whose *Eminent Victorians* and *Queen Victoria* are extremely successful examples of this form. The witty historian, Philip Guedalla (1889–1944), was not far behind Strachey, though his work is not so well known. A prolific biographer like Hesketh Pearson, with his *Gilbert and Sullivan, Shaw, Oscar Wilde,* and other informative and entertaining biographies, is somewhere between the standard type of biographer and the biographer-as-artist.

A few biographers-as-artists have succeeded not only because of the skill and talent they have brought to their work but also because they were very close, as people, to their subjects. One fascinating example of this kind of biography is the life of her father, the actor Sir Gerald du Maurier, by his daughter, Daphne, (1907–   ), the well-known novelist. Called *Gerald: A Portrait,* it is an intimate, candid, very moving account of a father by his daughter and is probably the best thing Daphne du

Maurier has ever written. Oddly enough, a more recent and nearly as successful biography of this kind takes us into the theater too, for it is the life of the playwright, Frederick Lonsdale (1881–1954), also by his daughter.

It is one thing when a genuine biography, like Boswell's, offers us scenes and dialogue as entertaining as those of a good novel, and it is quite another thing when biography and fiction are inextricably mingled in one book. This "biographical fiction" or "fictionalized biography" — and both terms have been often used for it — is a very dubious form, though obviously there is a large public for it, especially in America.

In this type of book, all the more important facts of a man's life may be included, but a great many scenes, together with the dialogue they involve, are simply invented by the author. The result is a doubtful mixture, neither real biography nor out-and-out fiction, and it is all too easy, when composing a book in this fashion, to present a man in such a way that the average reader is sharply prejudiced for or against him. Although the authors of such books may do a great deal of honest research to find as much genuine biographical material as they can, their work should not be classed as biography but as fiction.

The two world wars produced a large crop of diaries, journals, memoirs, and autobiography of all kinds. But in Britain, World War I produced more literature in this form than did World War II, which offered more in quantity but less in quality. Many established English writers have experimented with semi-autobiographical books, like Somerset Maugham's *The Summing Up*. But very few have published detailed journals such as Arnold Bennett (1867–1931) did, in three volumes based on his actual diaries. Some years after her death, a selection from Virginia Woolf's diaries was made. But the great autobiography covering, let us say, the last fifty years has still to make its appearance.

J. B. P.

Queen Victoria's Accession

LYTTON STRACHEY 1880–1932

Like a breath of fresh air, Lytton Strachey (lĭt″n strā′chĭ) blew the dust off the dull shelves of biography. "It is perhaps as difficult to write a good life as to live one," he said. "To preserve in a becoming brevity which excludes everything that is redundant, and nothing that is significant — that surely is the first duty of a biographer. The second, no less surely, is to maintain his own freedom of speech." These two duties he followed consistently.

Strachey was a member of a distinguished family; his father, Sir Richard Strachey, was a general and an Indian administrator, and his cousin John is a writer and a leader in England's Labor party.

After his Cambridge days Lytton became a writer of reviews and magazine articles, but his name was little known when in 1918 he published *Eminent Victorians*. In this book he "maintained his freedom of speech" by frank appraisals of four nineteenth-century figures who had become objects of hero worship. By so doing, Strachey launched a new type of biography, which brought forth many imitators. Strachey's reputation was firmly established by *Elizabeth and Essex*, a full-length biography about the sixteenth-century queen and her ill-fated lover. His best-known work is *Queen Victoria*, from which the following selection is taken.

"Queen Victoria's Accession" from *Queen Victoria* by Lytton Strachey, copyright, 1921, by Harcourt, Brace & World, Inc., renewed 1949 by James Strachey. Reprinted by permission of Harcourt, Brace & World, Inc.

THE NEW QUEEN was almost entirely unknown to her subjects. In her public appearances her mother had invariably dominated the scene. Her private life had been that of a novice in a convent: hardly a human being from the outside world had ever spoken to her; and no human being at all, except her mother and the Baroness Lehzen,[1] had ever been alone with her in a room. Thus it was not only the public at large that was in ignorance of everything concerning her; the inner circles of statesmen and officials and highborn ladies were equally in the dark. When she suddenly emerged from this deep obscurity, the impression that she created was immediate and profound. Her bearing at her first Council filled the whole gathering with astonishment and admiration; the Duke of Wellington, Sir Robert Peel, even the savage Croker, even the cold and caustic Greville [2] — all were completely carried away. Everything that was reported of her subsequent proceedings seemed to be of no less happy augury. Her perceptions were quick, her decisions were sensible, her language was discreet; she performed her royal duties with extraordinary facility. Among the outside public there was a great wave of enthusiasm. Sentiment and romance were coming into fashion; and the spectacle of the little girl-queen, innocent, modest, with fair hair and pink cheeks, driving through her capital, filled the hearts of the beholders with raptures of affectionate loyalty. What, above all, struck everybody with overwhelming force was the contrast between Queen Victoria and her uncles.[3] The nasty old men, debauched and selfish, pigheaded and ridiculous, with their perpetual burden of debts, confusions, and disreputabilities — they had vanished like the snows of winter, and here at last, crowned and radiant was the spring. Lord John Russell,[4] in an elaborate oration, gave voice to the general sentiment. He hoped that Victoria might prove an Elizabeth without her tyranny, an Anne without her weakness. He asked England to pray that the illustrious Princess who had just ascended the throne with the purest intentions and the justest desires might see slavery abolished, crime diminished, and education improved. He trusted that her people would henceforward derive their strength, their conduct, and their loyalty from enlightened religious and moral principles, and that, so fortified, the reign of Victoria might prove celebrated to posterity and to all the nations of the earth.

Very soon, however, there were signs that the future might turn out to be not quite so simple and roseate as a delighted public dreamed. The "illustrious Princess" might perhaps, after all, have something within her which squared ill with the easy vision of a well-conducted heroine in an edifying storybook. The purest intentions and the justest desires? No doubt; but was that all? To those who watched closely, for instance, there might be something ominous in the curious contour of that little mouth. When, after her first Council, she crossed the anteroom and found her mother waiting for her, she said, "And now, Mamma, am I really and truly Queen?" "You see, my dear, that it is

---

[1] *Baroness Lehzen* (lā'tzĕn): Victoria's governess, a clergyman's daughter from Hanover, Germany. [2] *Duke of Wellington* (1769–1852): victor over Napoleon at the battle of Waterloo, and an important leader of the Conservative party. *Sir Robert Peel* (1788–1850): a leader of the Conservative party and later Prime Minister (1841–46). *Croker:* John Wilson Croker (1780–1857), at this time retired secretary of the Admiralty, prominent member of the Conservative party, and a literary critic. *Greville* (grĕv'il): Charles C. F. Greville (1794–1865), clerk of the council, writer of a famous diary published after his death.

[3] *her uncles:* Victoria's father, who died when she was less than a year old, was the Duke of Kent, one of the four sons of George III. Two of these sons became kings as George IV and William IV. When William died in 1837, Victoria was heir to the throne. [4] *Lord John Russell* (1792–1878): a leader of the Liberal party.

so." "Then, dear Mamma, I hope you will grant me the first request I make to you, as Queen. Let me be by myself for an hour." For an hour she remained in solitude. Then she reappeared, and gave a significant order: her bed was to be moved out of her mother's room. It was the doom of the Duchess of Kent. The long years of waiting were over at last; the moment of a lifetime had come; her daughter was Queen of England; and that very moment brought her own annihilation. She found herself, absolutely and irretrievably, shut off from every vestige of influence, of confidence, of power. She was surrounded, indeed, by all the outward signs of respect and consideration; but that only made the inward truth of her position the more intolerable. Through the mingled formalities of court etiquette and filial duty she could never penetrate to Victoria. She was unable to conceal her disappointment and rage. *Il n'y a plus d'avenir pour moi,"* she exclaimed to Madame de Lieven; *"je ne suis plus rien."* [1] For eighteen years, she said, this child had been the sole object of her existence, of her thoughts, her hopes, and now — no! she would not be comforted, she had lost everything, she was to the last degree unhappy. Sailing, so gallantly and so pertinaciously, through the buffeting storms of life, the stately vessel, with sails still swelling and pennons flying, had put into harbor at last; to find nothing — a land of bleak desolation.

Within a month of the accession the realities of the new situation assumed a visible shape. The whole royal household moved from Kensington to Buckingham Palace, and, in the new abode, the Duchess of Kent was given a suite of apartments entirely separate from the Queen's. By Victoria herself the change was welcomed, though, at the moment of departure, she could afford to be sentimental. "Though I rejoice to go into

[1] *il . . . rien:* "There is no more future for me. I am no longer anything."

B. P. for many reasons," she wrote in her diary, "it is not without feeling of regret that I shall bid adieu forever to this my birthplace, where I have been born and bred, and to which I am really attached!" Her memory lingered for a moment over visions of the past: her sister's wedding, pleasant balls and delicious concerts . . . and there were other recollections. "I have gone through painful and disagreeable scenes here, 'tis true," she concluded, "but still I am fond of the poor old palace."

[Here follows a long discussion of two of the Queen's advisers, Baroness Lehzen and Baron Stockmar, a German doctor who had proved his sagacity as adviser to Victoria's Uncle Leopold, brother of Victoria's mother and king of Belgium.]

With Lehzen to supervise every detail of her conduct, with Stockmar in the next room, so full of wisdom and experience of affairs, with her uncle Leopold's letters, too, pouring out so constantly their stream of encouragements, general reflections, and highly valuable tips, Victoria, even had she been without other guidance, would have stood in no lack of private counselors. But other guidance she had; for all these influences paled before a new star, of the first magnitude, which, rising suddenly upon her horizon, immediately dominated her life.

William Lamb, Viscount Melbourne, was fifty-eight years of age, and had been for the last three years Prime Minister of England. In every outward respect he was one of the most fortunate of mankind. He had been born into the midst of riches, brilliance, and power. Nature had given him beauty and brains; the unexpected death of an elder brother brought him wealth, a peerage, and the possibility of high advancement. Bound to succeed, and to succeed easily, he was gifted with so fine a nature that his success became him. His mind, at once supple and copious, his temperament, at once calm and sensitive, enabled him not merely to work, but to live with perfect facility and with the grace of strength. In society he was a notable talker, a captivating companion, a charming man. If one looked deeper, one saw at once that he was not ordinary, that the piquancies of his conversation and his manner — his free-and-easy vaguenesses, his abrupt questions, his lollings and loungings, his innumerable oaths — were something more than an amusing ornament, were the outward manifestations of an individuality that was fundamental. . . .

And now, with old age upon him, his life took a sudden, new, extraordinary turn. He became, in the twinkling of an eye, the intimate adviser and the daily companion of a young girl who had stepped all at once from a nursery to a throne. . . . However, he was used to delicacies, and he met the situation with consummate success. His behavior was from the first moment impeccable. His manner toward the young Queen mingled, with perfect facility, the watchfulness and the respect of a statesman and a courtier with the tender solicitude of a parent. He was at once reverential and affectionate, at once the servant and the guide. At the same time the habits of his life underwent a surprising change. His comfortable, unpunctual days became subject to the unaltering routine of a palace; no longer did he sprawl on sofas; not a single "damn" escaped his lips. The man of the world who had been the friend of Byron and the Regent, the talker whose paradoxes had held Holland House enthralled, the cynic whose ribaldries had enlivened so many deep potations, the lover whose soft words had captivated such beauty and such passion and such wit, might now be seen, evening after evening, talking with infinite politeness to a schoolgirl, bolt upright, amid the silence and the rigidity of court etiquette.

On her side Victoria was instantaneously fascinated by Lord Melbourne. The good report of Stockmar had no doubt prepared the way; Lehzen was wisely propitiated; and the first highly favorable impression was never afterward belied. She found him perfect; and perfect in her sight he remained. Her absolute and unconcealed adoration was very natural; what innocent young creature could have resisted, in any circumstances, the charm and the devotion of such a man? But, in her situation, there was a special influence which gave a peculiar glow to all she felt. After years of emptiness and dullness and suppression she had come suddenly, in the heyday of youth, into freedom and power. She was mistress of herself, of great domains and palaces; she was Queen of England. Responsibilities and difficulties she might have, no doubt, and in heavy measure; but one feeling dominated and absorbed all others — the feeling of joy. Everything pleased her. She was in high spirits from morning till night. Mr. Creevey,[1] grown old now, and very near his end, catching a glimpse of her at Brighton, was much amused, in his sharp fashion, by the ingenuous gaiety of "little Vic." — "A more homely [2] little being you never beheld, when she is at her ease, and she is evidently dying to be always more so. She laughs in real earnest, opening her mouth as wide as it can go, showing not very pretty gums. . . . She eats quite as heartily as she laughs, I think I may say she gobbles. . . . She blushes and laughs every instant in so natural a way as to disarm anybody." But it was not merely when she was laughing or gobbling that she enjoyed herself; the performance of her official duties gave her intense satisfaction. "I really have immensely to do," she wrote in her *Journal* a few days after her accession; "I receive so many communi-

---

[1] *Mr. Creevey:* Thomas Creevey (1764–1838), well-known London Whig (earlier name for Liberal). His journals give a valuable picture of the late Georgian era. [2] *homely:* In English usage, this word means informal or unaffected in manners.

cations from my Ministers, but I like it very much." And again, a week later, "I repeat what I said before that I have so many communications from the Ministers, and from me to them, and I get so many papers to sign every day, that I have always a very great deal to do. I delight in this work." Through the girl's immaturity the vigorous predestined tastes of the woman were pushing themselves into existence with eager velocity, with delicious force.

One detail of her happy situation deserves particular mention. Apart from the splendor of her social position and the momentousness of her political one, she was a person of great wealth. As soon as Parliament met, an annuity of £385,000 was settled upon her. When the expenses of her household had been discharged, she was left with £68,000 a year of her own. She enjoyed, besides, the revenues of the Duchy of Lancaster, which amounted annually to over £27,000. The first use to which she put her money was characteristic: she paid off her father's debts. In money matters, no less than in other matters, she was determined to be correct. She had the instincts of a man of business; and she never could have borne to be in a position that was financially unsound.

With youth and happiness gilding every hour, the days passed merrily enough. And each day hinged upon Lord Melbourne. Her diary shows us, with undiminished clarity, the life of the young sovereign during the early months of her reign — a life satisfactorily regular, full of delightful business, a life of simple pleasures, mostly physical — riding, eating, dancing — a quick, easy, highly unsophisticated life, sufficient unto itself. The light of the morning is upon it; and, in the rosy radiance, the figure of "Lord M." emerges, glorified and supreme. If she is the heroine of the story, he is the hero; but indeed they are more than hero and heroine, for there are no other characters at all. Lehzen, the Baron,

Uncle Leopold, are unsubstantial shadows — the incidental supers of the piece. Her paradise was peopled by two persons, and surely that was enough. One sees them together still, a curious couple, strangely united in those artless pages, under the magical illumination of that dawn of eighty years ago; the polished high fine gentleman with the whitening hair and the whiskers and the thick dark eyebrows and the mobile lips and the big expressive eyes; and beside him the tiny Queen — fair, slim, elegant, active, in her plain girl's dress and little tippet, looking up at him earnestly, adoringly, with eyes blue and projecting, and half-open mouth. So they appear upon every page of the *Journal;* upon every page Lord M. is present, Lord M. is speaking, Lord M. is being amusing, instructive, delightful, and affectionate at once, while Victoria drinks in the honeyed words, laughs till she shows her gums, tries hard to remember, and runs off, as soon as she is left alone, to put it all down. Their long conversations touched upon a multitude of topics. Lord M. would criticize books, throw out a remark or two on the British Constitution, make some passing reflections on human life, and tell story after story of the great people of the eighteenth century. Then there would be business — a dispatch perhaps from Lord Durham in Canada, which Lord M. would read. But first he must explain a little. "He said that I must know that Canada originally belonged to the French, and was only ceded to the English in 1760, when it was taken in an expedition under Wolfe: 'a very daring enterprise,' he said. Canada was then entirely French, and the British only came afterward. . . . Lord M. explained this very clearly (and much better than I have done) and said a good deal more about it. He then read me Durham's dispatch, which is a very long one and took him more than ½ an hour to read. Lord M. read it beautifully with that fine soft voice of his, and with so much expression, so that it is needless to say I was much interested by it." And then the talk would take a more personal turn. Lord M. would describe his boyhood, and she would learn that "he wore his hair long, as all boys then did, till he was 17 (how handsome he must have looked!)." Or she would find out about his queer tastes and habits — how he never carried a watch, which seemed quite extraordinary. " 'I always ask the servant what o'clock it is, and then he tells me what he likes,' said Lord M." Or, as the rooks wheeled about round the trees, "in a manner which indicated rain," he would say that he could sit looking at them for an hour, and "was quite surprised at my disliking them. . . . Lord M. said, 'The rooks are my delight.' "

The day's routine, whether in London or at Windsor, was almost invariable. The morning was devoted to business and Lord M. In the afternoon the whole court went out riding. The Queen, in her velvet riding habit, and a top hat with a veil draped about the brim, headed the cavalcade; and Lord M. rode beside her. The lively troupe went fast and far, to the extreme exhilaration of Her Majesty. Back in the palace again, there was still time for a little more fun before dinner — a game of battledore and shuttlecock, perhaps, or a romp along the galleries with some children. Dinner came, and the ceremonial decidedly tightened. The gentleman of highest rank sat on the right hand of the Queen; on her left — it soon became an established rule — sat Lord Melbourne. After the ladies had left the dining room, the gentlemen were not permitted to remain behind for very long; indeed, the short time allowed them for their wine drinking formed the subject — so it was rumored — of one of the very few disputes between the Queen and her Prime Minister; but her determination carried the day, and from that moment after-dinner drunkenness began to go out of fashion. When the company was reassembled in the drawing room the etiquette was stiff. For a few moments the Queen spoke in turn to each one of her guests; and during these short uneasy colloquies the aridity of royalty was likely to become painfully evident. One night, Mr. Greville, the Clerk of the Privy Council, was present; his turn soon came; the middle-aged, hard-faced *viveur* [1] was addressed by his young hostess. "Have you been riding today, Mr. Greville?" asked the Queen. "No, Madam, I have not," replied Mr. Greville. "It was a fine day," continued the Queen. "Yes, Madam, a very fine day," said Mr. Greville. "It was rather cold, though," said the Queen. "It was rather cold, Madam," said Mr. Greville. "Your sister, Lady Frances Egerton, rides, I think, doesn't she?" said the Queen. "She does ride sometimes Madam," said Mr. Greville. There was a pause, after which Mr. Greville ventured to take the lead, though he did not venture to change the subject. "Has your Majesty been riding today?" asked Mr. Greville. "Oh, yes, a very long ride," answered the Queen with animation. "Has your Majesty got a nice horse?" said Mr. Greville. "Oh, a very nice horse," said the Queen. It was over. Her Majesty gave a smile and an inclination of the head, Mr. Greville a profound bow, and the next conversation began with the next gentleman. When all the guests had been disposed of, the Duchess of Kent sat down to her whist, while everybody else was ranged about the round table. Lord Melbourne sat beside the Queen, and talked pertinaciously — very often apropos to the contents of one of the large albums of engravings with which the round table was covered — until it was half-past eleven and time to go to bed.

Occasionally, there were little diversions: the evening might be spent at the

---

[1] *viveur* (vē·vûr'): one who lives at a fast and reckless pace.

opera or at the play. Next morning the royal critic was careful to note down her impressions. "It was Shakespeare's tragedy of *Hamlet,* and we came in at the beginning of it. Mr. Charles Kean (son of old Kean) acted the part of Hamlet, and I must say beautifully. His conception of this very difficult, and I may almost say incomprehensible, character is admirable; his delivery of all the fine long speeches quite beautiful; he is excessively graceful and all his actions and attitudes are good, though not at all goodlooking in face. . . . I came away just as *Hamlet* was over." Later on, she went to see Macready in *King Lear.* The story was new to her; she knew nothing about it, and at first she took very little interest in what was passing on the stage; she preferred to chatter and laugh with the Lord Chamberlain. But, as the play went on, her mood changed; her attention was fixed, and then she laughed no more. Yet she was puzzled; it seemed a strange, a horrible business. What did Lord M. think? Lord M. thought it was a very fine play, but to be sure, "a rough, coarse play, written for those times, with exaggerated characters." "I'm glad you've seen it," he added. But, undoubtedly, the evenings which she enjoyed most were those on which there was dancing. She was always ready enough to seize any excuse — the arrival of cousins — a birthday — a gathering of young people — to give the command for that. Then, when the band played, and the figures of the dancers swayed to the music, and she felt her own figure swaying too, with youthful spirits so close on every side — then her happiness reached its height, her eyes sparkled, she must go on and on into the small hours of the morning. For a moment Lord M. himself was forgotten.

The months flew past. The summer was over: "the pleasantest summer I ever passed in my life, and I shall never forget this first summer of my reign." With surprising rapidity, another summer was upon her. The coronation came and went — a curious dream. The antique, intricate, endless ceremonial worked itself out as best it could, like some machine of gigantic complexity which was a little out of order. The small central figure went through her gyrations. She sat; she walked; she prayed; she carried about an orb that was almost too heavy to hold; the Archbishop of Canterbury came and crushed a ring upon the wrong finger, so that she was ready to cry out with the pain; old Lord Rolle tripped up in his mantle and fell down the steps as he was doing homage; she was taken into a side chapel, where the altar was covered with a tablecloth, sandwiches, and bottles of wine; she perceived Lehzen in an upper box and exchanged a smile with her as she sat, robed and crowned, on the Confessor's throne.[1] "I shall ever remember this day as the proudest of my life," she noted. But the pride was soon merged once more in youth and simplicity. When she returned to Buckingham Palace at last she was not tired; she ran up to her private rooms, doffed her splendors, and gave her dog Dash its evening bath.

Life flowed on again with its accustomed smoothness — though, of course, the smoothness was occasionally disturbed. . . .

[1] *the Confessor's throne:* the coronation throne of Edward the Confessor, next to the last of the Saxon kings before the Norman Conquest.

A YOUNG QUEEN

1. What does Victoria's relationship with her mother, as briefly described here, suggest to you about her character? about the demands of being a country's ruler?

2. Summarize your impression of Victoria and Lord Melbourne together. Why did Melbourne appeal to Victoria so greatly? Do you think she would become critical of him as she grew older? Why or why not?

3. In what ways did Victoria show the common sense of a mature woman? In what ways, the lively disposition of a

young girl? Can you point out examples of the use of irony in describing her?

4. What do you think of the usual evening activities at the palace? What qualities that we think of as characteristically "Victorian" did they have?

5. How does Strachey's account of Victoria's coronation compare with Pepys' description of that of Charles II (see page 256)? What very human touch comes at the end of Victoria's coronation day?

6. The interest of the whole world was centered on the coronation of Elizabeth II of England in June 1953. What reasons can you give for the interest of other nations in this event? How did this coronation differ from that of all preceding monarchs? What parts of the coronation ritual mentioned by Strachey were observed in 1953?

SUGGESTION FOR WRITING

As a project requiring some outside reading, compare and contrast the personalities of Elizabeth I, Victoria, and Elizabeth II on their accession to the throne. Also compare briefly their participation in national affairs.

The Launching of *H. M. S. Pinafore*

HESKETH PEARSON 1887–

After finishing Bedford Grammar School, Pearson "wasted" (as he said) two years as a clerk in a London shipping office. In 1911 he went on the stage, where he remained for many years, except for the brief interval of World War I. Since his theatrical experience brought him in touch with many of the leading producers of the time, it was natural that several subjects of his biographies should have been persons connected with the stage.

In 1931 Pearson gave up acting for writing. He has produced an imposing array of books, mainly biographies, but also some essays of travel and criticism. Among his best-known books are *Tom Paine, G.B.S.: A Full Length Portrait* (George Bernard Shaw), and biographies of Benjamin Disraeli (entitled *Dizzy*) and Sir Walter Scott.

You have already met W. S. Gilbert on page 552, where you read two of the famous songs from that perennial favorite, *H.M.S. Pinafore*. In earlier chapters of his double biography *Gilbert and Sullivan*, Pearson brings out the difference in background of these partners: Gilbert, of the comfortable middle class, with opportunities for attending Oxford and studying law

— Sullivan, the son of a poorly paid clarinet player in a theater orchestra. Their particular talents were evident early in life. Gilbert had written fifteen plays by the time he was twenty-five. Sullivan entered the choir of Chapel Royal at twelve years of age and composed madrigals in bed after lights were out. Through scholarships he was able to attend the Royal Academy of Music and the Conservatory at Leipzig, where he began to compose seriously.

In disposition the two men were quite different. Gilbert had a sharp tongue and often "carried a chip on his shoulder." The rehearsals of his plays were sometimes punctuated by his outbursts of temper. On the other hand, the handsome, sweet-tempered Sullivan charmed everyone who met him and was constantly being helped to new opportunities by his friends. He became a great favorite of the royal family and was knighted in 1883 on the recommendation of Prime Minister Gladstone.

Gilbert and Sullivan began their collaboration in 1870 at the suggestion of Richard D'Oyly Carte, a theater manager. *Trial by Jury* was the first of their famous light operas. *H.M.S. Pinafore* was launched in 1877.

"The Launching of *H. M. S. Pinafore*," from *Gilbert and Sullivan* by Hesketh Pearson, published by Hamish Hamilton Ltd. Reprinted by permission of the author.

JUST BEFORE the end of the year Sullivan received the scenario *H.M.S. Pinafore* from Gilbert, who said: "I have little doubt whatever but that you will be pleased with it." Sullivan was so much pleased with it that, returning home, he began to work on it at once, in spite of the most violent attacks of illness. Throughout the entire period of composition he was racked with pain, and only managed to complete the work between paroxysms of agony which almost left him insensible.

Paroxysms of a different kind were taking place on the stage during rehearsals. Gilbert was already enforcing those methods of production which were to make his name a byword in the profession and revolutionize the art of dramatic presentation. He had learned from Robertson that, in drama, the whole was greater than the part, and he was busy subordinating his actors to the play. He regarded each of his librettos as a composer regards a symphony, which can be wrecked by the playing of a single false note, and he determined from the outset to achieve perfect harmony from his orchestra of actors. Every word had to be said with a certain inflection. Every movement had to be made in a certain manner, every position had to be judged to a square inch, every piece of "business" had to be considered in its relation to the scene. The actors were not allowed, as in the old days, to emerge for an instant from the frame of the picture he was trying to create. They were like chessmen on a board, to be moved at the discretion of the player-producer; they were like marionettes, whose motions were governed by the master; they were the members of a team, under the strict discipline of its captain.

For this reason he preferred his actors to be novices, who could be taught by himself and would not resent the teaching. For this reason, too, he arrived at the first rehearsal with a fairly complete mental picture of all the moves, all the inflections, all the "business," and all the positions of all the actors at every moment of the play. For hour after hour before the commencement of rehearsals, he would sit at his desk with replicas of the scenes on a scale of half an inch to a foot, with blocks of wood three inches high representing the males, two and a half inches high representing the females, and work out every detail of the production. It was not likely therefore that he was going to stand any nonsense from an actor who was solely concerned with his part and who did not mind what happened to the play so long as he made a personal success. At the rehearsals of *Pinafore* a player of the older school refused to repeat for perhaps the fiftieth time a piece of "business" which Gilbert was patiently instructing him to do.

"No, sir, I object," said the actor warmly. "I have been on the stage quite long enough."

"Quite," agreed Gilbert, and dismissed him on the spot.

Gilbert could never see eye-to-eye with people who considered that their proper place was in the center of the stage, and when a lady who was rehearsing the part of Josephine in *Pinafore* pointed out that she had always occupied that position in Italian opera, he remarked:

"Unfortunately this is not Italian opera, but only a low burlesque of the worst possible kind."

The lady continued her career in Italian opera.

Another well-known actress who was cast for a part in *Pinafore* walked out of the theater when she heard that a newcomer with no experience named Jessie Bond was to play in her scenes. Though upsetting at the time, it turned out luckily for Gilbert and Sullivan, as Jessie Bond became one of the most popular Savoy favorites.

Explosions between producer and actors were frequent in the early days, though when Gilbert had gained the complete ascendancy over his actors that had always been his aim, their occurrence was rare. His anger only flashed out when anyone questioned his authority, and his wit was usually confined to such harmless squibs as that recorded by Barrington:

"Cross left on that speech, I think, Barrington, and sit on the skylight over the saloon, pensively," advised Gilbert at a rehearsal of *Pinafore*.

The actor did so, but the stage carpenter had sewn the skylight with packthread and it collapsed under Barrington's fourteen stone.[1]

"That's expensively," remarked Gilbert.

H.M.S. Pinafore was produced on May 25th, 1878, and, its merits apart, caused something of a sensation because of the caricature of W. H. Smith, the publisher, who had recently been appointed First Lord of the Admiralty by Disraeli. For some of the lyrics Gilbert had drawn on the *Bab Ballads*,[2] one of which he adapted for his present purpose. This cutting ridicule of the political game, together with the satire on blatant patriotism in the same opera, reveals a vital aspect of Gilbert's character and explains why he had to wait so long for a knighthood.

It must be repeated that the qualities of wariness and daring were mixed in his nature in about equal proportions; and also, it may be added, stupidity and insight. He was a typical Briton with a streak of genius, possibly the only known example. He could see through a thing, but he could not see around it. He was visited with sudden flashes of reality, but he was not gifted with a steady vision. He had acute perceptions,

but no guiding philosophy. He was a respectable man who made fun of respectability, a sentimentalist who laughed at sentiment, a patriot who ridiculed patriotism. Again and again, at the bidding of some powerful intuition, he exposed a social or national absurdity, but as often as not he failed to see the point of his exposure and fell back upon a piece of conventional claptrap which was equally typical of him. His sudden exhibitions of daring and insight, coupled with his native caution and conventionality, made his work uneven and incalculable, and it was Sullivan's music that rendered it wholly palatable to the Victorians. The Englishman is perhaps the only man in the world who can laugh at himself; add music to the satire and he brings the house down, for music removes the sting of reality. Nevertheless, the chief powers in the land never quite got over the "contempt of court" shown in *Trial by Jury,* the contempt in *Pinafore,* and the continuous digs at authority in the rest of the operas, culminating with the contempt of the Royal Court in *Utopia;* and they took their only possible revenge. The average Englishman laughed, applauded, and whistled the delectable tunes; the important Englishman watched, smiled wryly, and sometimes writhed inwardly.

Owing to the fact that London was visited by a heat wave that summer, the audiences at the Opera Comique varied in size and the directors had periodical fits of panic. They announced the withdrawal of the piece about once a fortnight and canceled the announcement whenever the receipts went up. D'Oyly Carte calmed them to the best of his ability, but both he and the company were kept on tenterhooks for months owing to the nervous condition of his codirectors. Then two things happened to give the show a fillip. Sullivan, who was conducting the Promenade Concerts at Covent Garden, included an arrangement of the *Pinafore* music in one evening's program. It was liked so much

---

[1] *fourteen stone:* 196 pounds. The British use the unit *stone* (14 pounds) for heavy weights.
[2] *Bab Ballads:* verses written and illustrated by Gilbert for *Fun* magazine in 1869. Cleverly written, they satirize amiably the violence and crime so evident in London at that time. The collection made Gilbert famous as a literary figure.

that crowds of concertgoers visited the opera, which was running to good houses by the end of August. Next came the news that *Pinafore* had taken New York by storm and was playing to enormous business at no less than eight theaters; and since England was just beginning to model her taste on that of America, and America was just beginning to accept everything English as a model of taste, *Pinafore* soon became the rage in both countries.

Of course it was pirated in America. There was no copyright agreement between the two countries; and unless the author of a play could produce it on the spot, before anyone else could steal it and produce it first, he could whistle for his royalties. American publishers and theatrical managers made fortunes out of *Pinafore* while Gilbert and Sullivan gnashed their teeth in impotence. Adding insult to injury, the Americans put in a number of local "gags," songs about "pants" (which they have an incurable habit of rhyming with "dance") [1] and suchlike unsuitable sallies. Gilbert, Sullivan, and Carte decided that something had to be done about it, and the latter sailed for America to take stock of the situation.

In the summer of that year, a long report from Carte persuaded Gilbert and Sullivan to visit America in order to give their authorized version of *Pinafore* in New York. Before leaving, Sullivan underwent an operation for crushing the stone in the kidney, and received felicitations upon its success from the Prince of Wales and the Duke of Edinburgh. Gilbert was suffering from a different complaint. "I will not have another libretto of mine produced if the Americans are going to steal it," he declared, "not that I need the money so much, but it upsets my digestion."

Reporters swooped down upon them the instant their boat reached New

[1] *pants:* The British used only the word *trousers*, and pronounced *dance* as *däns*, so that *pants* (pănts) and *dance* (dăns) seemed crude.

York, and the American public, through the medium of its press, was quickly introduced to the two famous visitors: the librettist, a tall military-looking gentleman, with fair hair, rosy complexion, bright blue eyes and high massive forehead, who spoke quickly and jerkily in a deep hearty voice; the composer, a short, plump, daintily-clad person, with a thick neck, dark hair and eyes, olive-tinted mobile face, sensuous lips, and tender expression, whose voice was wistful and full of feeling. They were interviewed so thoroughly that Sullivan wondered "Where do all these Americans end? " and Gilbert ceased to wonder. Each of them took pains to make it known that he had done far better work than *Pinafore* unaided by the other. Gilbert said it was a little mortifying to find that a trifle like *Pinafore* should so far exceed in success the plays he held in more serious estimation. Sullivan regretted that his oratorios and other compositions of a more classical and ambitious style had not received the popular approval accorded to *Pinafore*. Neither of them felt unduly flattered when some judge, in an after-dinner speech, hoped they would be brought before him on the charge of being drunk and disorderly, so that he might repay the pleasure *Pinafore* had given him by letting them off. Nor was Gilbert altogether pleased when an American impresario had the bright idea that they might heap up a pile of dollars if only they would prepare an American version of the piece.

"Say now, Mr. Gilbert," said this gentleman, "all you've got to do is to change H.M.S. to U.S.S., pull down the British ensign, hoist the stars and stripes, and anchor your ship off Jersey beach. Then, in place of your First Lord of the Admiralty, introduce our navy boss. All the rewriting you'd want would be some new words to Bill Bobstay's song — just let him remain an American instead of an Englishman. Now ain't that a cute notion, sir?"

"Well, yes," replied Gilbert thoughtfully, "perhaps your suggestion is a good one, but I see some difficulties in carrying it out. In the first place I'm afraid I'm not sufficiently versed in your vernacular to translate my original English words. The best I could do would be something like this:

> He is Ameri-can!
> Though he himself has said it,
> 'Tis not much to his credit,
> That he is Ameri-can!
> For he might have been a Dutchman,
> An Irish, Scotch, or such a man,
> Or perhaps an Englishman!
> But in spite of hanky-panky,
> He remains a true-born Yankee,
> A cute Ameri-can." [1]

The impresario was delighted; he swore it would save the situation and set New York ablaze. After a few moments' reflection Gilbert gravely abandoned the notion, on the ground that such words might impair the friendly relations between the two countries.

While Gilbert and Sullivan were rehearsing their opera and being entertained and interviewed until their heads swam, the barrel organs of New York were churning out the tunes of *Pinafore,* the music shops were flooded with its scores, most of the theaters were playing it, and such was the demand for it throughout the States that one paper announced: "At present there are forty-two companies playing *Pinafore* about the country. Companies formed after six p.m. yesterday are not included." The authorized edition of the work appeared on December 1st at the Fifth Avenue Theater and received an ovation. Everyone in the audience was of course already familiar with the airs, but the orchestration, with which the numerous American bands had not troubled their heads, was a revelation. It was greeted as a comparatively new work and it looked as if a ninth company were about to coin money in the

city. Gilbert, in his speech before the curtain after the first performance, said: "It has been our purpose to produce something that should be innocent but not imbecile." That was the slogan of the collaborators: clean but clever fun.

FAMOUS COLLABORATORS

1. What differences between Gilbert and Sullivan in appearance and disposition are brought out here? Is it surprising that these two men worked so well together? Discuss.

2. Would you have liked being an actor under Gilbert's direction? If you have had any experience in amateur dramatics, discuss whether actors should be allowed to have some part in the stage direction.

3. Show how the two songs from *Pinafore* on pages 552–53 illustrate Gilbert's ridicule of the English ruling classes. What would this have to do with Gilbert's having to "wait so long for a knighthood"? If you have seen other Gilbert and Sullivan operettas, discuss wherein the ridicule lies.

4. What do you think of the proposed American version of *Pinafore?* How do you suppose Americans would have reacted to the words suggested for "He is an Englishman"? Pearson says the English are the only people who can laugh at themselves. Do you think Americans also have this faculty? Give some examples.

THE POWER OF WORDS

WORD DISCRIMINATION

Pearson uses five words descriptive of various kinds of humor. A *caricature* is an exaggerated picture in writing or in drawing. It most commonly applies to a person, as the caricature of the First Lord of the Admiralty in *H.M.S. Pinafore.* *Ridicule* is a more general word. It may be applied to a specific person, an idea, or a whole social system, as in "ridicule of the political game." *Satire* is a special kind of ridicule, employing subtlety and cleverness. This word is also used to describe a type of literature. *Absurdity* applies to the innate quality in something that lays it open to ridicule. (Gilbert exposed national absurdities.) A *sally* is a witty remark. Which of these words can be used as verbs? From which can adjectives be made?

[1] See the original version on page 552.

Go Where Glory Waits Thee

FRANK O'CONNOR 1903–

You already know Frank O'Connor ("The Man of the House," page 655) as one of the best contemporary Irish short-story writers. In the following autobiographical selection he tells with dry and subtle humor of his own fears, disappointments, aspirations, and faith as a young man who discovered that he was to become a writer. Here is an unusual opportunity to learn firsthand of the background and early trials of a man whose work you have studied and to compare O'Connor's treatment in two quite different literary forms. After reading this selection, you may be able to judge how much — and in what ways — O'Connor has drawn upon his own background for "The Man of the House."

Since it first appeared in print, "Go Where Glory Waits Thee" has been published as part of a full-length autobiography entitled *An Only Child,* which was published in 1961 and met with immediate critical acclaim.

ALL I ever wanted from life was an education. Apart from any liking I may have had for it, I knew it was the key to success. Everyone admitted that. They said you could get nowhere without an education. They blamed their own failure in life on the lack of it. You should learn everything, they said, because it all came in useful — every scrap of it. If Father was no more than a casual laborer and never earned more than fourteen or fifteen shillings a week, that was because he hadn't the education like Mr. Moynihan down the road had it. If Mother was only a charwoman who went out every day to work in the big houses on the river in Cork, it was because she hadn't the education, either. So I knew it was up to me to get the education, and, by the Lord, when I

did, things were going to be different in the home. Father would have to treat me with proper respect, and Mother, instead of going out to work, would stay at home and look after me. As for me, I'd look after everybody.

But the difficulty was to get started. It seemed to be extremely hard to get an education, or even — at the level on which we lived — to find out what education was. Education, of course, implied nice manners as opposed to coarse ones — I could see that for myself — and I set out to be a polite and good-living boy, which in the main I was, except when the business of getting an education became too much for me and I had to go to confession and tell the priest that I had been disobedient and rude to my parents. Education was also speaking correctly, and I listened with great admiration to the priest on Sunday and then came home and imitated him in front of the mirror. But in moments of depression I realized that these were only the things that went with education, not education itself. The priest not only spoke well but he also knew Latin. Latin was clearly a great part of education, so I got Mother to teach me the Latin hymns she knew, like the "Stabat Mater" and the "Ave Maris Stella," and at intervals I had the excited feeling that I really was getting somewhere at last, but those fits of exultation rarely lasted for more than an evening, and I woke next morning with the foreboding that I was never going to get any education.

All that anybody seemed able to tell you about how you got an education was that you should "stick to the books." Now, I didn't have any books, but I

"Go Where Glory Waits Thee" by Frank O'Connor. Copyright 1960 by Frank O'Connor. Originally appeared in *The New Yorker.* Reprinted by permission of Harold Matson Co.

did read comics and boy's weeklies, and I stuck to them with great enthusiasm. I don't mean that I didn't enjoy them for their own sakes, for I did. I lived in a sort of social vacuum between the kids of my own class, who had no ambitions to be educated, and the class above ours — policemen and minor officials — whose sons got educated whether they wanted to or not. The latter lived down the Ballyhooley Road, and the boys gathered at night by the gas lamp. Between them, they produced all those indications of a proper education I learned to recognize from the boy's weeklies — a bicycle, or a stamp album, or a real football, or boxing gloves, or a cricket bat, or occasionally even a copy of *The Boy's Own Paper,* which cost sixpence and had halftone illustrations, as compared with the weeklies I could afford, which cost a penny and only had line drawings. To both of those groups I must have seemed a freak — to the poorer kids because I spoke in what probably sounded like an affected accent, and used strange words I had picked up from my reading and didn't even know how to pronounce; to the others because I was only a ragged laney boy who put on airs and tried to force his company on them. So, though I was a fairly normal child who did his best to fit in with others, the others could never fit in with me, and for a lot of the time I had to live in my fantasy. It wasn't such a bad place to live if only the bottom weren't always falling out of it.

There was nothing exclusive about my approach to the world of make-believe — cops and robbers, cowboys and Indians, sailors and pirates — but more than anything else I loved the penny school stories. I don't think they appealed to me for any snobbish reason, for though English boys might recognize that there were remote originals for such schools, and that being given a hundred lines on the day of a cricket match might be a cruel punishment, and that "playing the game" and "keeping a stiff upper lip"

were desirable things socially, with me all this was an act of faith. I had never seen or heard of anything in the least resembling an English public school. The appeal of these stories, which has kept them fresh in my mind to this day, was that the characters were getting an education, and I could watch them at it with the certainty that some of the education was bound to brush off on me. If only the authors had identified the particular hundred lines of Latin that the hero was compelled to write out during the last cricket match of the season, how gladly I would have written them for him! As it was, I had to be content with the odd snatches of Latin and French that emerged from the narrative.

But education was hard. To be properly educated, you had to have a father who didn't drink and a mother who didn't work; you had to have long trousers and a short jacket and a top hat; you had to have footballs and cricket bats and shorts and a suit with white trousers, and the best people had uncles who came to the school in racing cars and tipped them five pounds, a sum of money I had never seen all together, so that they could blow it all in the tuckshop and have a feed in the dormitory after dark. The only rich relative I could get certain tidings of was a patrolman in the Chicago police force, know as Big Tim Fahy. He was a cousin of Mother, and so tall and powerful that Father, who was a six-footer, admitted he felt like a small boy beside him. He had a photograph of him on the sideboard in his uniform, wearing a sword, and the photographs and clippings the Fahys showed us proved that he was highly regarded in Chicago. A man like that would, I thought, go far in the States, and might eventually help me.

Meanwhile, even if you couldn't afford a top hat, you could play cricket with an old piece of board and a raggy ball against a wicket you had chalked on the blank end wall of a block of houses.

You could get papers that gave you tips about the Noble Art of Self-Defense and practice a straight left in front of the mirror. You could even abide by the public-school code, and not tell lies, or betray a friend when he'd done something wrong, or yell when you got punished in school. All the boys I knew screamed that their wrist was broken and went back to their desks sobbing and nursing their hand between their knees.

I was always fond of heights, and afterward it struck me that reading was only another form of height. It was a way of looking beyond one's own back yard, and seeing into the neighbors'. Our yard — the real one — had a high back wall, and by early afternoon it had made the whole kitchen dark, but when the evening was fine I climbed the door of the outdoor toilet and onto the top of the wall. It was on a level with the respectable terrace behind ours, which had front gardens and a fine view, and there I sat for hours, on terms of relative equality with the policemen and their children, and watched the opposite hillside that fell headlong toward the valley of the city, with its terraces of tall houses and its crest of dark trees. It was all lit up when our little house was in darkness. In the mornings, the first thing I did when I got up was to put a chair under my attic window and push up the window sash to see the same hillside when it was still in shadow and its colors had the stiffness of early-morning light.

The best place for a good view was the quarry that fell sheer from the neighborhood of the Barrack to the Ballyhooley Road. It was a noisome place, where people dumped their rubbish and gangs of wild kids held stoning matches after school and poor people from lanes around the Barrack poked among the rubbish for treasure; but all that meant nothing to me, and I picked my way through the discarded bully-beef tins and climbed till I found a ledge of rock or a hollow in the quarry face that could be promoted to the rank of a cave, and

after carefully placing an old penknife or a heavy stone beside me as a weapon to use against imaginary pursuers, I sat happily surveying the whole neighborhood, from Mayfield Chapel, which rode the extreme top of the hillside on the edge of the open country, to the spire of St. Luke's Church, which lay beneath me, and beyond which, dim in the distance, were the hills at the other side of the River Lee. Lord knows what I should think of it now, but then it seemed to me a wonderful view: the Ballyhooley Road winding up the hill from St. Luke's Cross, with its little houses and their tiny front gardens, and, on the side of the road nearest me, the back yards where the women came to hang out their washing. And all the time the shadow moved with a chill one could almost feel, and the isolated spots of sunlight grew brighter. Up there I felt like some sort of wild bird, secure from everything and observing everything: a horse and cart coming up the road, or a little girl with her skipping rope on the pavement, or an old man staggering along on his stick — all of them unaware of the eagle eyes that watched them from above.

Cork on its hills was full of such spots. Not far from our house was Goulding's Glen, in those days a valley with a stream that led from the clean open country by Ballyvolane to a manure factory in Blackpool where Father worked for a time. It skirted the base of the hill on which the Barrack stood, with the Barrack itself the highest spot, and for hours each day young buglers practiced on the sandy bluff that overlooked the second terrace, known as the Black Patch. Here the British had their rifle range and the local boys played football, and on the third level was the Glen itself, which led from the Big Pond, where we skated in wintertime, past the Mill House, which always looked dank and sinister between its trees, and along by the crimson sluice gates that controlled the factory stream under the steep hills which in those days were still covered in trees. This deep cutting was the first to fill with shadow, and I liked to sit somewhere high up, watching the workmen come home in the evening. Once I began to read, I needed no other landscape for dreaming. It was a pretty dirty hole even then, but for me it contained everything that the books told of — the Rocky Mountains, the Alps, the Castle on the Hill, the Haunted House, and the playing fields of whichever imaginary school I was then reading about.

But whatever the height, whether that of the storybook or the quarry, the eagle had to descend. Even eagles get cold and hungry, and nobody has taught the human eagle to feed off its own heights. Mother would soon be finished work. At some houses she did half a day, which ended at three o'clock, and for which she was paid ninepence or a shilling, and at others she did a whole day, which did not end till six, and for which she was paid one and sixpence. Depending on the humor of the maid she worked for, I might be allowed to call for her half an hour or so before she was finished work. In one house not only was I admitted to the kitchen after school and given my tea, but — if the family was out or on holiday — I was allowed up to the lumber room in the attic, which was filled with old pamphlets, guidebooks, phrase books in German and French, heavenly old dance programs with tassels and tiny pencils, a number of old schoolbooks, including a French primer, and — greatest treasure of all — a text of the Oberammergau Passion Play, in English and German. It was junk that would have meant nothing to almost anyone else in the world, and indeed the maid eventually let me take my pick of it before she cleared it out, but it filled my mind with ravishing glimpses of how educated people lived, the places they saw, the things they did, and the way they spoke to hotel managers and railway porters. "From which platform does the train start for Köln." "We wish a carriage for non-smokers." "We have two trunks and five bags." "That is for you, young man." It was only another aspect of the vision I had caught in the master bedrooms. In these rooms there were mirrors in which you could see yourself twice over in profile, silver-handled brushes with engraved designs, and curiously shaped bottles that contained hair oil and scents that I experimented with recklessly when Mother's back was turned. Sometimes since then, when I stay in such a house, I wonder what small black face has studied itself in the mirror of the dressing table, what grubby little paw has used the silver-handled brushes to rub in the bay rum, and turn round almost expecting to see a tiny figure dash past me down the stairs toward the kitchen.

So I scampered down the quarry face to the snug suburban road, with its gas lamps and smooth pavements, and went to the tram stop at St. Luke's Cross, where I could be sure Mother would not escape me. In the dusk I sat, swinging my legs on the wall that overlooked the church, afraid to look behind me for fear I might grow dizzy, and when a tram came wheezing up the hill and discharged its load of passengers, I chased the men for cigarette pictures, terrified at the same time that I might miss her, a small, grave figure in a black shawl. Sometimes she had only her day's wages, but occasionally a maid would give her a bit of meat or a slice of apple pie for my supper, and then if she could spare me a penny for a boy's weekly, my day was almost saved. Saved it would be if for any reason Father was working late and we could sit in the dusk over the fire while I explained to her my plans for taking her abroad, and got her to sing for me "Farewell, but Whenever You Welcome the Hour" and "How Dear to Me the Hour When Daylight Dies." She was very fond of "Go Where Glory Waits Thee," and I put up with the rather dull tune for the sake of the words, which were beautiful and held such a personal appeal to myself that I could barely listen to them without tears:

> Go where glory waits thee,
> But while fame elates thee,
>   Oh, then remember me!
> When the praise thou meetest
> To thine ear is sweetest,
>   Oh, still remember me.

But often it was misery to return from the heights. It wasn't only that I might find Father drunk or quarrelsome, or that the rent collector might turn up and take a shilling of what Mother had earned, or that I might be sent for a loaf of bread and be refused it without the money. It was also that sometimes I ran into some happy group of boys amusing themselves at a lamppost, and, drawn by the clublike atmosphere of the pool of light and the shadowy figures, I tried to join them. Everything went well for a minute or two, till I suddenly said something wrong or used a word no one recognized and the whole group began to jeer me and call me "Four-eyes," and I would realize that once again I had been talking the language of the heights.

The trouble was that I was always a little bit of what I had picked up from whatever source — book or picture or glimpse of a different sort of life — always half in and half out of the world of reality, like Moses descending the mountain, or a dreamer waking. I couldn't see a picture of Robin Hood in a storybook but I had to make myself a long bow out of a curtain pole; and when I got a couple of younger kids to assist me at cricket and stood with a make-believe bat before a make-believe wicket, I was always the Dark Horse of the school, emerging to save its honor when all seemed lost. Once when we were playing cricket in the square in front of our house, a policeman came up the road and the others ran home. I didn't run, though I was as scared as they were. I rested on my hurling stick and waited for him to speak. "What do you mean, playing ball on the public street?" he demanded. "Excuse me," I replied politely. "This is not a public street. This square is private property." The bobby was so surprised at being checked by a small spectacled boy with an imitation cricket bat that he let me get away with it. But it wasn't often I got away with it, and sometimes I got in trouble for being cheeky when all I was doing was acting out a part, and at other times I was accused of being a liar when I was still only half in, half out of the dream and telling the truth as best I could; and then I slunk back in tears to my heights and my loneliness.

I couldn't keep from brooding on suffering and injustice, or from making a fool of myself about them. I don't know what age I was when I heard that a wild and handsome boy up the road, whose father beat him savagely, had run away from home and was being searched for by the police. The story was told in whispers. He would eventually be found, people said, and sent to the reformatory. That evening I found him myself, lurking in an alleyway, his long face filthy with tears, and begged him to come home. He would not come, and I would not leave him. At last he agreed to come, on condition that I go with him and plead for him. While I knocked at his door, he stood against the wall, his head down. His elder sister opened the door and I made my little speech. She promised to see that he was not punished, and I went home in a glow of exaltation, feeling that I had saved him from a terrible fate — the fate I was always dreading, of finding myself without a mother and a home. I thought that after this he and I might be friends. When we met again, he wouldn't even look at me but turned away with a sneer, and I knew that his father had beaten him again and that it was all my fault. As a protector of the weak I never was worth much.

As a result of this queer existence, half real and half fantastic, I who was always standing up for truth and justice never learned to fight; I who was always winning games for the school when everything seemed lost never learned to play any game; I who was always swimming flooded rivers to escape my pursuers never could swim at all till I was thirty. I never even got to be an acolyte [1] in the parish church or learned to ride a bicycle. The distance between the dream and the reality, between the private and the public personality, was always too great.

By the time I was fourteen or fifteen, it had become altogether clear that education was something I could not afford. Not that even then I had any intention of giving it up. I was just looking for a job that would enable me to buy the books from which I could pick up the education myself. So with the rest of the unemployed I went to the newsroom of the Carnegie Library, where on wet days the central heating warmed the perished bodies in the broken boots and made the dirty rags steam and smell. I read carefully through the advertisements and applied for every job that demanded "a smart boy." Sometimes, as a sort of bonus from Providence, I found a new number of *The Times Literary Supplement, The Spectator, The New Statesman,* or *The Studio* free, and I sat there and read reviews of books I would never be able to read and discussions of paintings I would never see, but usually some hungry old man would have toppled asleep over it and I was cheated. The real out-of-works always favored the high-class magazines, at which they were not likely to be disturbed. After a while, I got up and went out and wandered aimlessly round town till hunger or darkness or rain sent me home.

When it became clear that I would never be a priest, Mother's only ambi-

tion was for me to become a clerk: someone who would wear a white collar and be called "Mister." Knowing no better but always willing, I went to the Technical School and the School of Commerce at night to learn arithmetic, bookkeeping, and shorthand-typing. Of bookkeeping all I remember is a saying quoted approvingly on the first page of our textbook: "In business there is no such thing as an out-and-out free gift." And the very first thing I was asked to type in the School of Commerce threw me into a fresh fever, for it was Tennyson's "Blow, Bugle, Blow," presented as an example of advanced punctuation. To me it was merely fresh material for fantasy. I also worked hard at a Self-Educator, a big blue book that contained courses in everything, which I had picked up. From my reading I had deduced that German was the real language of culture, and that the greatest of cultured persons was Goethe, so I read Goethe right through in English and studied German out of the Self-Educator to read him in the original. I also made an attempt to learn Greek, which struck me as a very important cultural medium, but as I had never learned the rudiments of grammar in any language, I didn't get far with Greek.

I got my first job through my confessor, a gentle old priest who regarded me as a very saintly boy, and if innocence and sanctity are related, he was probably not so far wrong. The job was in a pious wholesale drapery business, where every single member of the staff seemed to have been recommended by his confessor, but I hated my immediate boss — a small, smug, smooth, greasy man, who tried hard to teach me that whenever he called my name I was instantly to drop whatever I was doing and reply smartly "Yessir." I never minded dropping whatever I was doing, which was usually folding shirts — the two arms neatly across the breast, as if I were laying out a corpse

[1] *acolyte* (ăk'ō·lĭt): a boy who assists a priest at Mass.

— and I had no objection to calling anybody "sir," but it was several seconds before my armor of daydreaming was penetrated by any voice from outside, and several seconds more before I realized that it was the voice to which I should reply "Yessir;" so at the end of a fortnight I stopped folding shirts and saying yessir and went home to do some more work at Greek. Then I tried a spell in a chemist's shop that was looking for a smart boy, but I soon discovered that I was only wanted to deliver messages. I have a vivid recollection of the end of this job, with myself, a small boy looking up at a tall counter, and a still taller man, refreshed by a visit to the pub next door, looking down at me pityingly and begging me in a thick Dublin accent to get out of this for my own good. There was an even briefer spell at a job printer's. While I was being shown the ropes, the printer asked me if I could spell and I replied airily "Oh, that's my forte!" which was the sort of language we used on the heights and I saw nothing wrong with it. That evening I met the man who had recommended me to the printer, and he repeated my reply with a good deal of laughter, and I realized that as usual I had made a fool of myself. I was so mortified that I never went back. I was sorry about that, because I really was quite good at spelling, and I still think I might have made an excellent typesetter.

I went to the railway as a messenger boy, because I despaired of ever becoming anything better, and, besides, though the hours — eight to seven — were cruelly long for a growing boy, the pay was good — a pound a week — and with money like that coming in I could buy a lot of books and get a lot of education. My job was to assist the invoice and claims clerks, bringing in dockets from the warehouse, and going to the warehouse to inquire for missing goods. All transport companies have colossal claims for missing goods, most of which were not really missing at all but lying around forgotten. Whiskey and tobacco were easy to trace, as they had to be loaded into sealed wagons in the presence of one of the old railway policemen, who recorded them in his book. But nobody took much responsibility for other articles, and it depended on the uncertain memory of checkers whether or not you could find out what had happened to them. A friendly checker could often remember a particular consignment, and if he were in really good humor, find it where it had lain for weeks in a corner, covered by a mountain of fresh merchandise. Usually, nobody remembered anything at all, and you solemnly marked your memorandum or wire with some code word, like "Bison," which signified "Certainly forwarded please say if since received." Back came a wire saying "Moose," meaning that it hadn't been received, and you had to go to the file room, where the dockets were stored, and search through scores of dusty files to find the original docket and the name of the porter or checker who had signed for the goods.

Sheehy and Cremin, the two other tracers, were the sons of railwaymen and protected by their fathers' presence from anything worse than good-natured ragging, but, apart from the patience and kindness of two or three checkers, I had to depend on my wits, which were all but nonexistent. I hated the file room, and when I worked there with Cremin or Sheehy I realized that they found six dockets in the time it took me to find one. I had bad sight, and often failed to see a docket properly, particularly when it was written in the semi-literate scrawl of carters or porters, and even when I should have seen it I was daydreaming, and when I wasn't daydreaming I was harassed by panic,

A view of Cork, Ireland, settled since Anglo-Saxon times. ▶

shyness, and ignorance. Sheehy sneered all the time; Cremin sneered only some of the time, because he had a sort of impatient pity for my stupidity, and occasionally, smiling as I bogged myself deeper in some job I couldn't do, he took it from me with a complacent air and did it himself in a moment.

One of my jobs was to answer the telephone, and I did it with such intensity that I could never hear a word the other person said, and usually I was too ashamed to admit that I hadn't understood. When I did admit it, it was worse, for the person at the other end grew furious — a fatal thing to do with me, as it deprives me of the last shred of my wits. The trouble was that I couldn't believe in the telephone or the messages that came by it. I couldn't believe that the missing goods I was supposed to trace had ever existed, or if they had, that their loss meant anything to anybody. All I could believe in was words. I would read the word "unsophisticated" and at once I would want to know what the Irish for it was. In those days I didn't ask to be a writer. All I wanted was to translate, to feel the unfamiliar become familiar, the familiar take on all the mystery of some dark foreign face one glimpsed in the street.

I had taken a checker's discarded notebook from the railway storeroom and, having patiently rubbed out all the pencil notes, begun a poem book of my own. And though I was stupid, I really did care madly about poetry, good and bad, without understanding why I cared. More even than music it is the universal speech, but it is spoken fluently only by those whose existence is already all aflame with emotion, for then the beauty and order of language are the only beauty and order possible. Above all, it is the art of the boy and girl overburdened by the troubles of their sex and station, for as Jane Austen wistfully noted, poetry can be best appreciated by those who should taste it most sparingly.

It was a strange double life, and small wonder if it comes back to me as hallucination. Each morning when I made my way across the tracks from the passenger station to the goods station, I said good-by to a part of myself, and at seven that evening, when I returned across the dark railway yard and paused in the well-lit passenger station to see the new books in the bookstall, he rejoined me, a boy exactly like myself except that no experience had dinged or dented him.

When my first wretched effort at composition appeared in a boy's paper and word of it got round the office, everyone was astonished, but most of all my boss. Sitting at his high desk with the paper open before him and a frown on his bulgy forehead, he asked, "Did you write this, Native?"

"Yes, sir," I said, feeling sure I had done it again. Everything I did only seemed to get me into fresh trouble.

"Nobody help you?" he asked suspiciously.

"No, sir," I replied warmly, because it looked as though someone else might have fallen under suspicion, and I still hung on to the code of the boy's weeklies and was always prepared to own up sooner than see another suffer.

The frown deepened on his fat face. "Then for God's sake, stick to writing!" he snapped. "You'll never be any good on the Great Southern & Western Railway."

And that, as we used to say in Cork, was one sure five. Looking for models of fine conduct as usual, I had lit on a Left Wing timekeeper, who knew all the Italian operas by heart and made it a point of honor not to take off his cap when speaking to the bosses. Thinking that anyone who knew so much about Italian operas must know the correct thing for other situations, I decided not to take my cap off, either. Even then I should probably have been let off with a reprimand, because my boss realized that I had no self-confidence and went about imitating everybody in the wild hope that I might accidentally strike on the right thing. But with my bad sight, I fell over a hand truck and injured my shin, so that I couldn't walk for weeks. On the railway, bad sight was more serious than bad manners, because it might result in a claim, and transport companies have a thing about claims.

On the Saturday night I was sacked, I read my first paper before the Gaelic League. It was in Irish, and the subject was Goethe. For me, my whole adolescence is summed up in that extraordinary evening — so much that even yet I can't laugh at it in comfort. I didn't know much about Irish, and I knew practically nothing about Goethe, and that little was wrong. In a truly anthropomorphic spirit, I re-created Goethe in my own image and likeness, as a patriotic young fellow who merely wished to revive the German language, which I considered to have been gravely threatened by the use of French. I drew an analogy between the French culture that dominated eighteenth-century Germany and the English culture by which we in Ireland were dominated.

While I was reading, it was suddenly borne in on me that I no longer had a job, or a penny in the world, or even a home I could return to without humiliation, and that the neighbors would say again, as they had so often said before, that I was mad and a good-for-nothing. And I knew they would be right, for here I was committing myself absolutely and publicly to vague words and vaguer impressions. I could barely control my voice, because the words and impressions no longer mattered. All that mattered to me now was the act of faith, the hope that somewhere, somehow I would be able to prove that I was neither mad nor a good-for-nothing, because now I realized that there was no turning back. I had tossed my cap over the wall of life, and I must follow wherever it had fallen.

A YOUNG IRISHMAN

1. What were O'Connor's reasons as a young boy for wanting an education? How do his reasons differ from what you want from your education? Explain the author's statement that he "lived in a sort of social vacuum." Why did he think that it was hard to get an education?

2. Explain O'Connor's fondness for heights. What do you learn about the neighborhood which the author knew as a boy? What were his favorite pastimes?

3. What does O'Connor's relationship with his mother suggest to you about her character? Explain the significance of "Go where glory waits thee" to the boy and as title of this selection.

4. Do you agree with the author that poetry is the universal speech? Explain. How did he live "a strange double life"? Why did his boss think he should stick to writing? Cite three or four of O'Connor's boyhood experiences which you think really helped him in becoming a writer.

COMPARING WORKS
BY THE SAME AUTHOR

What new understanding and appreciation does this selection give you of the short story "The Man of the House" (page 655)? Does the child in "The Man of the House" seem to have anything in common with O'Connor as a young boy in "Go Where Glory Waits Thee"? What comparisons are you able to make between these two selections — about O'Connor as a writer of fiction and of autobiography?

LITERATURE AND THE ARTS

The illustration on page 721, which shows a view of Cork, Frank O'Connor's birthplace, also points up the relationship between literature and the art of photography. Through this modern art, our understanding of literature and its creators can be greatly enhanced, for true-to-life representations of the places where authors lived and wrote can contribute much toward giving the reader a new understanding of a writer as a person and artist. You may want to collect photographs illustrating, for example, the locale or the mood of other literature you are studying.

READING LIST FOR
MODERN BIOGRAPHY

Brickhill, Paul, *Reach for the Sky*
A thrilling account of Douglas Bader, the legless air ace of the Battle of Britain, who was shot down and who escaped from German prisons.

Cecil, Lord David, *Melbourne*
Queen Victoria's first prime minister, to whom Strachey has already introduced you; one of the best-written biographies of our century.

Hudson, William H., *Far Away and Long Ago*
The South American boyhood of an Englishman who not only studied nature but could also paint it in colorful words.

* Lee, Laurie, *The Edge of Day*
A contemporary British poet recounts the story of his childhood in western England.

Maugham, W. Somerset, *The Summing Up*
The popular Mr. Maugham's observations on himself as a writer and as a man.

Montgomery, Bernard Law, *Montgomery of Alamein*
Montgomery's autobiography is an important contribution to the history of World War II and to postwar problems.

Pearson, Hesketh, *Merry Monarch: The Life and Likeness of Charles II*
A modern, lifelike portrait of Charles II as a wise and personable ruler.

——, *Sir Walter Scott, His Life and Personality*
The romantic life of one of Scotland's greatest poets and novelists, by a major modern biographer.

Pippett, Aileen, *The Moth and the Star*
An admirer of Virginia Woolf assesses her life and art.

Raverat, Gwen, *Period Piece*
A granddaughter of Charles Darwin, gifted with a lively style, sketches her famous relatives and describes the life of English young people in the early days of this century.

Tuckerman, Arthur, *The Old School Tie*
If you want to see the difference between English and American secondary schools, you will enjoy this man's account of his youth.

* Available in *Four English Biographies,* J. B. Priestley and O. B. Davis, eds. (Harcourt, Brace & World, Inc., 1961).

MODERN ESSAYS

THE ESSAY must not be confused with the *article*. The latter belongs to journalism, and its chief purpose is to inform. The article tells you something about the world. The essay, on the other hand, is a literary form and may tell you little or nothing about the world but a great deal about its author. An essay is just as much the expression of a personality as a lyric poem. All good essayists have a very personal manner and style.

By an odd coincidence the essay has best flourished at the beginning of each century: with Bacon early in the seventeenth; Addison and Steele early in the eighteenth; William Hazlitt, Charles Lamb, and Leigh Hunt early in the nineteenth; while the best English essayists of this century, Max Beerbohm, Hilaire Belloc, G. K. Chesterton, Edward Lucas, really belonged to the period ending in 1914.

In the years before 1914, as some of us well remember, essays — real essays, not articles — were regularly published in daily newspapers, which then were still edited for readers who enjoyed good writing. But the leisurely essayist had no place in the later newspapers, which were influenced by the dictates of mass circulation and a standard of taste largely determined by their advertising managers. After World War I, the essayists were restricted to the weekly reviews and monthly magazines, and soon there were fewer and fewer of these. And as the "familiar" (as it was once called) or light essay was always intended for periodical publication first, soon there were fewer and fewer essayists.

But the great tradition was not allowed to die: Robert Lynd, H. M. Tomlinson, and C. E. Montague all produced volumes of essays of enduring merit, and many fine essays were written by authors distinguished in other fields, such as Virginia Woolf, Aldous Huxley, and George Orwell.

The essay, to be successful, demands not only a good writer but also a good reader, somebody with an eye and ear for fine prose and both the taste and leisure to enjoy it. The great mass public for "best sellers" in fiction has never enjoyed essayists. Nevertheless, there has been an interesting develop-ment in Britain, thanks to the British Broadcasting Corporation, the noncommercial organization responsible for all radio and half the television of the country. For the essay, which looked as if it might disappear altogether, has had a new lease of life on the air, generally on radio but occasionally on television. Several of the older essayists, notably Max Beerbohm, were able to adapt their art to this new medium, with excellent results. So the essayist may still be with us for some time yet, pleasing a much larger public than the old essayists ever knew.

The essays you will read in this section are both serious and humorous, personal and social, concerned with large issues and the tiny details of ordinary life. They may tell a story; they may discuss a topic; but all express an individual point of view.

J. B. P.

The Pit Mouth

H. M. TOMLINSON 1873–1958

H. M. Tomlinson was born in the East End of London and grew up on the docks of the Thames River, where he mingled with stevedores and sailors from the far corners of the world. At the age of twelve he started to work as a clerk for a shipping company, and though he also began writing at an early age, was unable to secure a more literary job until he was over thirty. After working for a while on the staff of a London newspaper, Tomlinson left England to take a 2,000-mile trip up the Amazon on a tramp steamer of which his brother-in-law was captain. *The Sea and the Jungle* is an exciting travel story of this voyage. Returning to Europe, Tomlinson served as a war correspondent during World War I and worked subsequently on literary magazines. Among his works are *Gallions Reach,* a novel which is largely autobiographical, and *Old Junk,* in which appear some of his best essays.

Christopher Morley has said that reading the best essays of H. M. Tomlinson and surrendering oneself to the "moving music and magic of that prose, so simple and yet so subtle, one wonders whether poetry is not, after all, an inferior and more mechanic form." The following essay is considered one of Tomlinson's best. To witness the Great Barr fire and transmit its significance into words requires both literary skill and genuine compassion.

THERE was Great Barr, idle, still, and quiet. Through the Birmingham suburbs, out into the raw, bleak winter

"The Pit Mouth" by H. M. Tomlinson. Reprinted by permission of the Society of Authors as the literary representative of the Estate of the late H. M. Tomlinson.

roads between the hedges, quite beyond the big town smoking with its enterprising labors, one approached the village of calamity with some awe and diffidence. You felt you were intruding; that you were a mere gross interloper, coming through curiosity, that was not excused by the compunction you felt, to see the appearance of a place that had tragedy in nearly all its homes. Young men streamed by on bicycles in the same direction, groups were hurrying there on foot.

The road rose in a mound to let the railway under, and beyond the far dip was the village, an almost amorphous[1] group of mean red dwellings stuck on ragged fields about the dominant colliery[2] buildings. Three high, slim chimneys were leisurely pouring smoke from the grotesque black skeleton structures above the pits. The road ran by the boundary and was packed with people, all gazing absorbed and quiet into the grounds of the colliery; they were stacked up the hedge banks, and the walls and trees were loaded with boys.

A few empty motorcars of the colliery directors stood about. A carriage horse champed its bit, and the still watchers turned at once to that intrusive sound. Around us a lucid winter landscape (for it had been raining) ran to the distant encompassing hills which lifted like low ramparts of cobalt and amethyst to a sky of luminous saffron and ice green, across which leaden clouds were moving. The country had that hard, coldly radiant appearance which always impresses a sad man as this world's frank expression of its alien disregard; this world not his, on which he has happened, and must endure with his trouble for a brief time.

As I went through the press of people to the colliery gates, the women in shawls turned to me, first with annoyance that their watching should be disturbed, and then with some dull interest.

My assured claim to admittance probably made them think I was the bearer of new help outside their little knowledge; and they willingly made room for me to pass. I felt exactly like the interfering fraud I was. What would I not have given then to be made, for a brief hour, a nameless miracle worker.

In the colliery itself was the same seeming apathy. There was nothing to show in that yard, black with soddened cinders and ash muck, where the new red-brick enginehouses stood, that somewhere half a mile beneath our feet were thirty men, their only exit to the outer world barred by a subterranean fire. Nothing showed of the fire but a whitish smoke from a ventilating shaft; and a stranger would not know what that signified. But the women did. Wet with the rain showers, they had been standing watching that smoke all night, and were watching it still, for its unceasing pour to diminish. Constant and unrelenting, it streamed steadily upward, as though it drew its volume from central fires that would never cease.

The doors of the office were thrown open, and three figures emerged. They broke into the listlessness of that dreary place, where nothing seemed to be going on, with a sudden real purpose, fast but unhurried, and moved toward the shaft. Three Yorkshire rescue experts — one of them to die later — with the Hamstead manager explaining the path they should follow below with eager seriousness. "Figures of fun!" They had muzzles on their mouths and noses, goggles on their eyes, fantastic helms,[3] and queer cylinders and bags slung about them. As they went up the slope of wet ash, quick and full of purpose, their comical gear and coarse dress became suddenly transfigured; and the silent crowd cheered emotionally that little party of forlorn hope.

They entered the cage, and down they went. Still it was difficult for me to think that we were fronting tragedy, for no

[1] *amorphous* (á·môr′fŭs): shapeless. [2] *colliery* (kŏl′yer·ĭ): a coal mine.

[3] *helms:* helmets.

danger showed. An hour and more passed in nervous and dismal waiting. There was a signal. Some men ran to the pit head carrying hot bricks and blankets. The doctors took off their coats, and arranged bottles and tinkling apparatus on chairs stuck in the mud. The air smelt of iodoform.[1] A cloth was laid on the ground from the shaft to the enginehouse, and stretchers were placed handy. The women, some carrying infants, broke rank. That quickly uprunning rope was bringing the first news. The rope stopped running and the cage appeared. Only the rescue party came out, one carrying a moribund [2] cat. They knew nothing; and the white-faced women, with hardly repressed hysteria, took again their places by the enginehouse. So we passed that day, watching the place from which came nothing but disappointment. Occasionally a child, too young to know it was adding to its mother's grief, would wail querulously. There came a time when I and all there knew that to go down that shaft was to meet with death. The increasing exhaustion and pouring sweat of the returning rescue parties showed that. Yet the miners who were not selected to go down were angry; they violently abused the favoritism of the officials who would not let all risk their lives.

I have a new regard for my fellows since Great Barr. About you and me there are men like that. There is nothing to distinguish them. They show no signs of greatness. They have common talk. They have coarse ways. They walk with an ugly lurch. Their eyes are not eager. They are not polite. Their clothes are dirty. They live in cheap houses on cheap food. They call you "sir." They are the great unwashed, the mutable [3] many, the common people. The common people! Greatness is as common as that. There are not enough honors and

decorations to go round. Talk of the soldier! *Vale* [4] to Welsby of Normanton! He was a common miner. He is dead. His fellows were in danger, their wives were white-faced and their children were crying, and he buckled on his harness and went to the assault with no more thought for self than great men have in a great cause; and he is dead. I saw him go to his death. I wish I could tell you of Welsby of Normanton.

I left that place where the starshine was showing the grim skeleton of the shaftwork overhead in the night, and where men moved about below in the indeterminate dark like dismal gnomes. There was a woman whose cry, when Welsby died, was like a challenge.

Next morning, in Great Barr, some blinds were down, the street was empty. Children, who could see no reason about them why their fathers should not return as usual, were playing football by the tiny church. A group of women were still gazing at the grotesque ribs and legs of the pit head staring as though it were a monster without ruth.[5]

[4] *Vale* (vā'lē): farewell. [5] *ruth:* pity.

A VILLAGE OF CALAMITY

1. What details in the first three paragraphs point to the fact that the author is approaching a "village of calamity"? How do the women at the colliery gates respond to the author? How does he respond to them?

2. Describe the scene at the pit when the author first arrives, when the rescue experts go underground, and when the signal comes from below. What gave Tomlinson a new regard for his fellows? Note the details in the last paragraph which picture Great Barr the next morning. In what respect was the pit head like a monster?

ANALYZING AN AUTHOR'S STYLE

"The Pit Mouth" is more than just a record of what Tomlinson observed at the fire. The tragedy is witnessed by an individual who has a certain attitude toward life; the compassionate way in which he writes

[1] *iodoform* (ī·ō'dō·fôrm): a healing and antiseptic dressing for wounds and sores. [2] *moribund* (mŏr'ĭ·bŭnd): near death. [3] *mutable:* changeable.

about this calamity reflects the man himself.

Imagine that you are to report the pit fire at Great Barr. What are the items of "news value" that you would look for? In addition to his factual reporting, what else characterizes Tomlinson's style of writing? Is the essay written in long or short sentences? Do you notice any relationship between the length of Tomlinson's sentences and what he chooses to say? Can you find examples of unusual word choice and phraseology? Find specific passages that you think illustrate Tomlinson's ability to write effective prose.

SUGGESTION FOR WRITING

After you have discussed the ideas found in "The Pit Mouth" and have analyzed the style of the writer, be ready to write an essay on a scene of tragedy familiar to you. Choose an incident from which you gathered more than simply the items of news value.

Music at Night

ALDOUS HUXLEY 1894–

Aldous Huxley — novelist, essayist, and critic — is the grandson of Thomas Huxley, the eminent Victorian scientist, educator, and writer. On his mother's side, he is the grandnephew of Matthew Arnold, the famous critic, poet, and essayist. Huxley became interested in writing while he was at Eton. His intention of going into medicine was never realized because of eye trouble which left him almost blind.

After several government jobs during World War I, Huxley worked on the staff of the London *Athenaeum* and the *Westminster Gazette,* writing critical essays on drama, art, and music. In 1921 he gave up journalism to support himself by writing; he also traveled extensively in Italy, France, India, and what was then the Dutch East Indies. For special treatment to improve his eyesight, he visited the United States in 1937 and since that time has lived in California. Here he writes fiction, articles and essays, and an occasional motion-picture script. A well-rounded person who is interested in many fields, Huxley has made a special study of Vedanta and other mystic religions, the influence of which is evident in his fiction. In his novels Huxley presents a somewhat exaggerated portrait of the evil tendencies in modern life. In *Point Counter Point,* probably his masterpiece, *Brave New World,* and *Eyeless in Gaza,* these tendencies are shown as extreme forms of perversity. *Brave New World Revisited,* published in 1955, depicts in fictional form Huxley's concept of the world of the future. His imaginative conception has become a contemporary nightmare.

You will find Huxley to be a stimulating essayist. In "Music at Night" he sets down the thoughts which come to him as he listens to a piece of music. His essay shows him to be a person who possesses a delicate sensitivity to combinations and sequences of sound, a writer who has the ability to translate his impressions into appropriate words. Note the frequent allusions touching on many branches of knowledge. You may wish to investigate some of these references further after finishing the essay.

MOONLESS, this June night is all the more alive with stars. Its darkness is perfumed with faint gusts from the blossoming lime trees, with the smell of wetted earth and the invisible greenness of the vines. There is silence; but a silence that breathes with the soft breathing of the sea and, in the thin shrill noise of a cricket, insistently, incessantly harps on the fact of its own deep perfection. Far away, the passage of a train is like a long caress, moving gently, with an in-

"Music at Night" from *Music at Night and Other Essays* by Aldous Huxley, reprinted by permission of Harper & Brothers, and Chatto and Windus Ltd. Copyright, 1930, 1931, by Aldous Huxley. Copyright R, 1958, 1959 by Aldous Huxley.

exorable gentleness, across the warm living body of the night.

Music, you say; it would be a good night for music. But I have music here in a box, shut up, like one of those bottled djinns [1] in the *Arabian Nights,* and ready at a touch to break out of its prison. I make the necessary mechanical magic, and suddenly, by some miraculously appropriate coincidence (for I had selected the record in the dark, without knowing what music the machine would play), suddenly the introduction to the *Benedictus* in Beethoven's *Missa Solemnis* [2] begins to trace its patterns on the moonless sky.

The *Benedictus.* Blessed and blessing, this music is in some sort the equivalent of the night, of the deep and living darkness, into which, now in a single jet, now in a fine interweaving of melodies, now in pulsing and almost solid clots of harmonious sound, it pours itself, stanchlessly pours itself, like time, like the rising and falling, falling trajectories [3] of a life. It is the equivalent of the night in another mode of being, as an essence is the equivalent of the flowers from which it is distilled.

There is, at least there sometimes seems to be, a certain blessedness lying at the heart of things, a mysterious blessedness, of whose existence occasional accidents or providences (for me, this night is one of them) make us obscurely, or it may be intensely, but always fleetingly, alas, always only for a few brief moments aware. In the *Benedictus* Beethoven gives expression to this awareness of blessedness. His music is the equivalent of this Mediterranean night, or rather of the blessedness at the heart of the night, of the blessedness as

it would be if it could be sifted clear of irrelevance and accident, refined and separated out into its quintessential [4] purity.

"Benedictus, benedictus . . ." One after another the voices take up the theme propounded by the orchestra and lovingly meditated through a long and exquisite solo (for the blessedness reveals itself most often to the solitary spirit) by a single violin. *"Benedictus, benedictus . . ."* And then, suddenly, the music dies; the flying djinn has been rebottled. With a stupid insect-like insistence, a steel point rasps and rasps the silence.

At school, when they taught us what was technically known as English, they used to tell us to "express in our own words" some passage from what ever play of Shakespeare was at the moment being rammed, with all its annotations — particularly the annotations — down our reluctant throats. So there we would sit, a row of inky urchins, laboriously translating "now silken dalliance in the wardrobe lies" into "now smart silk clothes lie in the wardrobe," or "To be or not to be" into "I wonder whether I ought to commit suicide or not." When we had finished, we would hand in our papers, and the presiding pedagogue would give us marks, more or less, according to the accuracy with which "our own words" had "expressed" the meaning of the Bard.

He ought, of course, to have given us naught [5] all round with a hundred lines to himself for ever having set us the silly exercise. Nobody's "own words," except those of Shakespeare himself, can possibly "express" what Shakespeare meant. The substance of a work of art is inseparable from its form; its truth and its beauty are two and yet, mysteriously, one. The verbal expression of even a metaphysic [6] or a system of

---

[1] *djinns* (jĭns): in Mohammedan belief, one of a class of supernatural beings, subject to magic control. [2] *Beethoven* (bā′tō′vĕn): German composer (1770–1827); *Missa Solemnis* (mĭs′ȧ sō·lĕm′nĭs): High Mass. [3] *trajectories* (trȧ-jĕk′tō·rĭz): a curve or path which a body describes in space, as a planet or comet in its orbit.

[4] *quintessential* (kwĭn′tĕ·sĕn′shăl): highest and most concentrated. [5] *naught:* zero. [6] *metaphysic:* here, a theory or philosophy explaining the nature of reality or existence.

ethics is very nearly as much of a work of art as a love poem. The philosophy of Plato expressed in the "own words" of Jowett [1] is not the philosophy of Plato; nor in the "own words" of, say, Billy Sunday,[2] is the teaching of St. Paul's teaching.

"Our own words" are inadequate even to express the meaning of other words; how much more inadequate, when it is a matter of rendering meanings which have their original expression in terms of music or one of the visual arts! What, for example, does music "say"? You can buy at almost any concert an analytical program that will tell you exactly. Much too exactly; that is the trouble. Every analyst has his own version. Imagine Pharaoh's dream interpreted successively by Joseph, by the Egyptian soothsayers, by Freud, by Rivers, by Adler, by Jung, by Wohlgemuth: [3] it would "say" a great many different things. Not nearly so many, however, as the Fifth Symphony has been made to say in the verbiage [4] of its analysts. Not nearly so many as the Virgin of the Rocks [5] and the Sistine Madonna [6] have no less lyrically said.

Annoyed by the verbiage and this absurd multiplicity of attributed "meanings," some critics have protested that music and painting signify nothing but themselves; that the only things they "say" are things, for example, about modulations and fugues,[7] about color

values and three-dimensional forms. That they say anything about human destiny or the universe at large is a notion which these purists dismiss as merely nonsensical.

If the purists were right, then we should have to regard painters and musicians as monsters. For it is strictly impossible to be a human being and not to have views of some kind about the universe at large, very difficult to be a human being and not to express those views, at any rate by implication. Now, it is a matter of observation that painters and musicians are *not* monsters. Therefore . . . The conclusion follows, unescapably.

It is not only in program music [8] and problem pictures [9] that composers and painters express their views about the universe. The purest and most abstract artistic creations can be, in their own peculiar language, as eloquent in this respect as the most deliberately tendentious.[10] . . .

The limits of criticism are very quickly reached. When he has said "in his own words" as much, or rather as little, as "own words" can say, the critic can only refer his readers to the original work of art: let them go and see for themselves. Those who overstep the limit are either rather stupid, vain people, who love their "own words" and imagine that they can say in them more than "own words" are able in the nature of things to express. Or else they are intelligent people who happen to be philosophers or literary artists and who find it convenient to make the criticism of other men's work a jumping-off place for their own creativity.

What is true of painting is equally true of music. Music "says" things about

---

[1] *Jowett:* Benjamin Jowett (1817–1893), an English scholar and professor of Greek at Oxford University who wrote what many consider to be the finest translation of the works of the Greek philosopher Plato. [2] *Billy Sunday:* American evangelist (1862–1935) well known for his conducting of religious revivals. [3] *Freud . . . Wohlgemuth:* five famous psychologists whose theories lead to somewhat different explanations of dreams. [4] *verbiage:* wordiness. [5] *Virgin of the Rocks:* a tempera panel, now hanging in the Louvre, Paris, painted around 1487 by the celebrated Florentine painter, Leonardo da Vinci. [6] *Sistine Madonna:* a painting done by Raphael in 1515 for the Church of St. Sixtus at Piacenza, Italy. [7] *fugue* (fūg): a musical composition in several harmonizing parts which are independent in melody.

[8] *program music:* music inspired by something outside itself, such as a person, place, thing, or a concept of literary, historical, geographical, religious character. [9] *problem picture:* a picture dealing usually with sociological or philosophical questions. [10] *tendentious* (tĕn·dĕn'-shŭs): argumentative.

the world, but in specifically musical terms. Any attempts to reproduce these musical statements "in our own words" is necessarily doomed to failure. We cannot isolate the truth contained in a piece of music; for it is a beauty-truth and inseparable from its partner. The best we can do is to indicate in the most general terms the nature of the musical beauty-truth under consideration and to refer curious truth-seekers to the original. Thus, the introduction to the *Benedictus* in the *Missa Solemnis* is a statement about the blessedness that is at the heart of things. But this is about as far as "own words" will take us. If we were to start describing in our "own words" exactly what Beethoven felt about this blessedness, how he conceived it, what he thought its nature to be, we should very soon find ourselves writing lyrical nonsense in the style of the analytical program makers. Only music, and only Beethoven's music, and only this particular music of Beethoven, can tell us with any precision what Beethoven's conception of the blessedness at the heart of things actually was. If we want to know, we must listen — on a still June night, by preference, with the breathing of the invisible sea for background, to the music and the scent of lime trees drifting through the darkness, like some exquisite soft harmony apprehended by another sense.

THE POWER OF MUSIC

1. Reread the first paragraph of this essay. What sense impressions contribute to the picture you visualize in this paragraph? Where do you think Huxley was writing?

2. What is the real message of the *Benedictus* for the author?

3. What is the main point that Huxley makes about music in this essay? Do you agree? Why or why not?

CLASS ACTIVITY

Appoint a committee to do research and report to the class on Beethoven's *Missa Solemnis* or on any of the other works of art mentioned in Huxley's essay.

SUGGESTIONS FOR WRITING

1. Select a piece of music, a play, poem, painting, or piece of sculpture which you particularly like and write a composition on how it affects you.

2. Write your thoughts and feelings on one of the following subjects: "The Best Place to Listen to Music," "Why I Like (a certain composer)," "Pictures and Music," "Hearing Poetry Read Aloud."

Shooting an Elephant

GEORGE ORWELL 1903–1950

England lost one of her most original writers in the untimely death of George Orwell. Always a provocative writer, with keen insight into social and political situations, Orwell was a skillful and entertaining novelist as well as an essayist. Because he was so astute a critic of his times, a contemporary called him "the conscience of his generation."

Orwell was born in India, but at an early age was sent to boarding school in England. After finishing his education at Eton, he served briefly with the Imperial Police in Burma. The following essay narrates an exciting incident of his service there and shows how his thinking about world problems was beginning to develop. Greatly concerned with the political and social

"Shooting an Elephant" from *Shooting an Elephant* by George Orwell, copyright, 1945, 1946, 1949, 1950, by Sonia Brownell Orwell. Reprinted by permission of Harcourt, Brace & World Inc., and Secker and Warburg, London.

issues of his day, Orwell stated that it was his aim "to make political writing into an art."

When he decided to become a writer he went to Paris, where he lived through several years of extreme poverty. Just as he began to become known, his health failed him. He died in London from tuberculosis at the age of forty-six. In 1949 he received the *Partisan Review* award for distinguished writing, with a citation for "singular directness and honesty, a scrupulous fidelity to his experience that has placed him in that very valuable clan of the writer who is a witness to his time."

I N MOULMEIN, in lower Burma, I was hated by large numbers of people — the only time in my life that I have been important enough for this to happen to me. I was subdivisional police officer of the town, and in an aimless, petty kind of way an anti-European feeling was very bitter. No one had the guts to raise a riot, but if a European woman went through the bazaars alone somebody would probably spit betel juice over her dress. As a police officer I was an obvious target and was baited whenever it seemed safe to do so. When a nimble Burman tripped me up on the football field and the referee (another Burman) looked the other way, the crowd yelled with hideous laughter. This happened more than once. In the end the sneering yellow faces of young men that met me everywhere, the insults hooted after me when I was at a safe distance, got badly on my nerves. The young Buddhist priests were the worst of all. There were several thousands of them in the town and none of them seemed to have anything to do except stand on street corners and jeer at Europeans.

All this was perplexing and upsetting. For at that time I had already made up my mind that imperialism was an evil thing and the sooner I chucked up my job and got out of it the better. Theoretically — and secretly, of course — I

was all for the Burmese and all against their oppressors, the British. As for the job I was doing, I hated it more bitterly than I can perhaps make clear. In a job like that you see the dirty work of Empire at close quarters. The wretched prisoners huddling in the stinking cages of the lockups, the gray, cowed faces of the long-term convicts, the scarred buttocks of men who had been flogged with bamboos — all these oppressed me with an intolerable sense of guilt. But I could get nothing into perspective. I was young and ill-educated and I had to think out my problems in the utter silence that is imposed on every Englishman in the East. I did not know that the British Empire is dying, still less did I know that it is a great deal better than the younger empires that are going to supplant it. All I knew was that I was stuck between my hatred of the empire I served and my rage against the evil-spirited little beasts who tried to make my job impossible. With one part of my mind I thought of the British Raj as an unbreakable tyranny, as something clamped down, in *saecula saeculorum*,[1] upon the will of prostrate peoples; with another part I thought that the greatest joy in the world would be to drive a bayonet into a Buddhist priest's guts. Feelings like these are the normal by-product of imperialism; ask any Anglo-Indian official, if you can catch him off duty.

One day something happened which in a roundabout way was enlightening. It was a tiny incident in itself, but it gave me a better glimpse than I had had before of the real nature of imperialism — the real motives for which despotic governments act. Early one morning the subinspector at a police station the other end of the town rang me up on the phone and said that an elephant was ravaging the bazaar. Would I please come and do something about it? I did not know what I could do, but I wanted

---

[1] *saecula* (sĕk'ū·lá) *saeculorum:* forever and ever.

to see what was happening and I got onto a pony and started out. I took my rifle, an old .44 Winchester and much too small to kill an elephant, but I thought the noise might be useful *in terrorem*.[1] Various Burmans stopped me on the way and told me about the elephant's doings. It was not, of course, a wild elephant, but a tame one which had gone "must." [2] It had been chained up, as tame elephants always are when their attack of "must" is due, but on the previous night it had broken its chain and escaped. Its mahout,[3] the only person who could manage it when it was in that state, had set out in pursuit, but had taken the wrong direction and was now twelve hours' journey away, and in the morning the elephant had suddenly reappeared in the town. The Burmese population had no weapons and were quite helpless against it. It had already destroyed somebody's bamboo hut, killed a cow, and raided some fruit stalls and devoured the stock; also it had met the municipal rubbish van and, when the driver jumped out and took to his heels, had turned the van over and inflicted violences upon it.

The Burmese subinspector and some Indian constables were waiting for me in the quarter where the elephant had been seen. It was a very poor quarter, a labyrinth of squalid huts, thatched with palm leaf, winding all over a steep hillside. I remember it was a cloudy, stuffy morning at the beginning of the rains. We began questioning the people where the elephant had gone and, as usual, failed to get any definite information. That is invariably the case in the East; a story always sounds clear enough at a distance, but the nearer you get to the scene of events the vaguer it becomes. Some of the people said that the elephant had gone in one direction, some said that it had gone in another, some professed not even to have heard of any

elephant. I had made up my mind that the whole story was a pack of lies, when I heard yells a little distance away. There was a loud, scandalized cry of "Go away, child! Go away this instant!" and an old woman with a switch in her hand came round the corner of a hut, violently shooing away a crowd of naked children. Some more women followed, clicking their tongues and exclaiming; evidently there was something the children ought not to have seen. I rounded the hut and saw a man's dead body sprawling in the mud. He was an Indian, a black Dravidian [4] coolie, almost naked, and he could not have been dead many minutes. The people said that the elephant had come suddenly upon him round the corner of the hut, caught him with its trunk, put its foot on his back, and ground him into the earth. This was the rainy season and the ground was soft, and his face had scored a trench a foot deep and a couple of yards long. He was lying on his belly with his arms crucified and head sharply twisted to one side. His face was coated with mud, the eyes wide open, the teeth bared and grinning with an unendurable agony. (Never tell me, by the way, that the dead look peaceful. Most of the corpses I have seen looked devilish.) The friction of the great beast's foot had stripped the skin from his back as neatly as one skins a rabbit. As soon as I saw the dead man I sent an orderly to a friend's house nearby to borrow an elephant rifle. I had already sent back the pony, not wanting it to go mad with fright and throw me if it smelt the elephant.

The orderly came back in a few minutes with a rifle and five cartridges, and meanwhile some Burmans had arrived and told us that the elephant was in the paddy fields [5] below, only a few hundred yards away. As I started forward practically the whole white population of the quarter flocked out of the houses and

---

[1] *in terrorem:* in a case of fright. [2] *"must":* a condition of dangerous frenzy. [3] *mahout* (má-hout'): the keeper and driver of an elephant.

[4] *Dravidian* (drá·vĭd′ĭ·ăn): belonging to an ancient race of India, numerous in the south. [5] *paddy fields:* rice fields.

followed me. They had seen the rifle and were all shouting excitedly that I was going to shoot the elephant. They had not shown much interest in the elephant when he was merely ravaging their homes, but it was different now that he was going to be shot. It was a bit of fun to them, as it would be to an English crowd; besides they wanted the meat. It made me vaguely uneasy. I had no intention of shooting the elephant — I had merely sent for the rifle to defend myself if necessary — and it is always unnerving to have a crowd following you. I marched down the hill, looking and feeling a fool, with the rifle over my shoulder and an ever growing army of people jostling at my heels. At the bottom, when you got away from the huts, there was a metaled road and beyond that a miry waste of paddy fields a thousand yards across, not yet plowed but soggy from the first rains and dotted with coarse grass. The elephant was standing eight yards from the road, his left side toward us. He took not the slightest notice of the crowd's approach. He was tearing up bunches of grass, beating them against his knees to clean them, and stuffing them into his mouth.

I had halted on the road. As soon as I saw the elephant I knew with perfect certainty that I ought not to shoot him. It is a serious matter to shoot a working elephant — it is comparable to destroying a huge and costly piece of machinery — and obviously one ought not to do it if it can possibly be avoided. And at that distance, peacefully eating, the elephant looked no more dangerous than a cow. I thought then and I think now that his attack of "must" was already passing off; in which case he would merely wander harmlessly about until the mahout came back and caught him. Moreover, I did not want in the least to shoot him. I decided that I would watch him a little while to make sure that he did not turn savage again, and then go home.

But at that moment I glanced round at the crowd that had followed me. It was an immense crowd, two thousand at the least and growing every minute. It blocked the road for a long distance on either side. I looked at the sea of yellow faces above the garish clothes — faces all happy and excited over this bit of fun, all certain that the elephant was going to be shot. They were watching me as they would watch a conjurer about to perform a trick. They did not like me, but with the magical rifle in my hand I was momentarily worth watching. And suddenly I realized that I would have to shoot the elephant after all. The people expected it of me and I had got to do it; I could feel their two thousand wills pressing me forward irresistibly. And it was at this moment, as I stood there with the rifle in my hands, that I first grasped the hollowness, the futility of the white man's dominion in the East. Here was I, the white man with his gun, standing in front of the unarmed crowd — seemingly the leading actor of the piece; but in reality I was only an absurd puppet pushed to and fro by the will of those yellow faces behind. I perceived in this moment that when the white man turns tyrant it is his own freedom that he destroys. He becomes a sort of hollow, posing dummy, the conventionalized figure of a sahib.[1] For it is the condition of his rule that he shall spend his life in trying to "impress the natives," and so in every crisis he has got to do what the "natives" expect of him. He wears a mask, and his face grows to fit it. I had got to shoot the elephant. I had committed myself to doing it when I sent for the rifle. A sahib has got to act like a sahib; he has got to appear resolute, to know his own mind and do definite things. To come all that way, rifle in hand, with two thousand people marching at my heels, and then to trail feebly away, having done nothing — no, that was impossible. The crowd would laugh

[1] *sahib* (sä'Ib): native term for a European gentleman.

at me. And my whole life, every white man's in the East, was one long struggle not to be laughed at.

But I did not want to shoot the elephant. I watched him beating his bunch of grass against his knees, with that preoccupied grandmotherly air that elephants have. It seemed to me that it would be murder to shoot him. At that age I was not squeamish about killing animals, but I had never shot an elephant and never wanted to. (Somehow it always seems worse to kill a large animal.) Besides, there was the beast's owner to be considered. Alive, the elephant was worth at least a hundred pounds; dead, he would only be worth the value of his tusks, five pounds, possibly. But I had got to act quickly. I turned to the experienced-looking Burmans who had been there when we arrived, and asked them how the elephant had been behaving. They all said the same thing; he took no notice of you if you left him alone, but he might charge if you went too close to him.

It was perfectly clear to me what I ought to do. I ought to walk up to within, say, twenty-five yards of the elephant and test his behavior. If he charged, I could shoot; if he took no notice of me, it would be safe to leave him until the mahout came back. But I also knew that I was going to do no such thing. I was a poor shot with a rifle and the ground was soft mud into which one would sink at every step. If the elephant charged and I missed him, I should have about as much chance as a toad under a steam roller. But even then I was not thinking particularly of my own skin, only of the watchful yellow faces behind. For at that moment, with the crowd watching me, I was not afraid in the ordinary sense, as I would have been if I had been alone. A white man mustn't be frightened in front of "natives"; and so, in general, he isn't frightened. The thought in my mind was that if anything went wrong those two thousand Burmans would see me pursued, caught, trampled

on, and reduced to a grinning corpse like that Indian up the hill. And if that happened it was quite probable that some of them would laugh. That would never do. There was only one alternative. I shoved the cartridges into the magazine and lay down on the road to get a better aim.

The crowd grew very still, and a deep, low, happy sigh, as of people who see the theater curtain go up at last, breathed from innumerable throats. They were going to have their bit of fun after all. The rifle was a beautiful German thing with cross-hair sights. I did not know then that in shooting an elephant one would shoot to cut an imaginary bar running from earhole to earhole. I ought, therefore, as the elephant was sideways on, to have aimed straight at his earhole; actually I aimed several inches in front of this, thinking the brain would be further forward.

When I pulled the trigger I did not hear the bang or feel the kick — one never does when a shot goes home — but I heard the devilish roar of glee that went up from the crowd. In that instant, in too short a time, one would have thought, even for the bullet to get there, a mysterious, terrible change had come over the elephant. He neither stirred nor fell, but every line of his body had altered. He looked suddenly stricken, shrunken, immensely old, as though the frightful impact of the bullet had paralyzed him without knocking him down. At last, after what seemed a long time — it might have been five seconds, I dare say — he sagged flabbily to his knees. His mouth slobbered. An enormous senility seemed to have settled upon him. One could have imagined him thousands of years old. I fired again into the same spot. At the second shot he did not collapse but climbed with desperate slowness to his feet and stood weakly erect, with legs sagging and head drooping. I fired a third time. That was the shot that did for him. You could see the agony of it jolt his whole body

and knock the last remnant of strength from his legs. But in falling he seemed for a moment to rise, for as his hind legs collapsed beneath him he seemed to tower upward like a huge rock toppling, his trunk reaching skywards like a tree. He trumpeted for the first and only time. And then down he came, his belly toward me, with a crash that seemed to shake the ground even where I lay.

I got up. The Burmans were already racing past me across the mud. It was obvious that the elephant would never rise again, but he was not dead. He was breathing very rhythmically with long rattling gasps, his great mound of a side painfully rising and falling. His mouth was wide open — I could see far down into caverns of pink throat. I waited a long time for him to die, but his breathing did not weaken. Finally I fired my two remaining shots into the spot where I thought his heart must be. The thick blood welled out of him like red velvet, but still he did not die. His body did not even jerk when the shots hit him, the tortured breathing continued without a pause. He was dying, very slowly and in great agony, but in some world remote from me where not even a bullet could damage him further. I felt that I had got to put an end to that dreadful noise. It seemed dreadful to see the great beast lying there, powerless to move and yet powerless to die, and not even to be able to finish him. I sent back for my small rifle and poured shot after shot into his heart and down his throat. They seemed to make no impression. The tortured gasps continued as steadily as the ticking of a clock.

In the end I could not stand it any longer and went away. I heard later that it took him half an hour to die. Burmans were bringing dahs [1] and baskets

[1] *dahs* (däz): bowls.

even before I left, and I was told they had stripped his body almost to the bones by afternoon.

Afterwards, of course, there were endless discussions about the shooting of the elephant. The owner was furious, but he was only an Indian and could do nothing. Besides, legally I had done the right thing, for a mad elephant has to be killed, like a mad dog, if its owner fails to control it. Among the Europeans, opinion was divided. The older men said I was right, the younger men said it was a shame to shoot an elephant for killing a coolie, because an elephant was worth more than any Coringhee [2] coolie. And afterwards I was very glad that the coolie had been killed; it put me legally in the right and gave me a sufficient pretext for shooting the elephant. I often wondered whether any of the others grasped that I had done it solely to avoid looking a fool.

[2] *Coringhee* (kô·rĭn'gē).

BRITISH OFFICER IN THE EAST

1. Why was Orwell hated by many people in Burma? In what little ways was this hatred shown? Summarize the author's ideas about imperialism.
2. What characteristics common to human nature everywhere are shown by the Burmese townspeople on hearing that an elephant is to be shot?
3. Why did Orwell think that he should not shoot the elephant? Why did he feel he must do it? What did this paradox show him of the weakness of imperialism?
4. What different opinions were expressed by various people as to whether he should have shot the elephant? How do you feel about this matter?

RECOGNIZING AN AUTHOR'S PURPOSE

To determine the central purpose of the Orwell essay, go beyond the story related and look at this quote from paragraph 2:

◄ *The mixture of old and new in modern Burma is typified by this present-day street scene near the golden spire of the Shwedagon Pagoda in Rangoon.*

"I did not know that the British Empire is dying, still less did I know that it is a great deal better than the younger empires that are going to supplant it." Now ask yourself: Why does the incident described become so important to the author? How does a predicament arise from the situation? Is it moral or physical courage which helps solve Orwell's dilemma? Consider your answers to these questions before stating what you think the author's purpose is in "Shooting an Elephant."

CLASS ACTIVITY

Several students may wish to read Orwell's *Animal Farm* and present a report to the class in the form of a panel discussion. Discussion can center on two things: (1) the social and political implications of the book, (2) *Animal Farm* as a twentieth-century satire. Compare the satire in *Animal Farm* with the satire found in the writings of Addison and Steele, Pope, and Swift.

Hours in a Library

VIRGINIA WOOLF 1882–1941

Virginia Woolf was the daughter of Sir Leslie Stephen, a distinguished scholar, critic, and biographer. Throughout her childhood her natural talents were stimulated by association with poets, artists, musicians, and novelists who were friends of her father. After her marriage in 1912 to Leonard Woolf, a London editor, the two set up a hand press for publishing limited editions of modern literature. This venture later developed into a full-fledged publishing house, The Hogarth Press. At their home in the Bloomsbury section of London, the Woolfs were part of the remarkable intellectual circle called the "Bloomsbury Group," which included Lytton Strachey, E. M. Forster, and others in the literary and art world.

It is difficult to say whether Virginia Woolf was more distinguished as a novelist or as an essayist and critic. In fiction, as one of the early advocates of "stream of consciousness" stories, she blazed new trails in technique. Her novels, such as *To the Lighthouse* and *Mrs. Dalloway,* emphasize the psychology and personal motivation of the characters rather than plot. Using some of the methods of the novel, Mrs. Woolf also wrote a unique biography, *Flush.* Here, in telling the story of Elizabeth Barrett's cocker spaniel, she gives a "dog's-eye view" of the famous Browning courtship.

In the essay, Virginia Woolf showed her talent for literary criticism. She was an enthusiastic reader whose interests ranged from medieval to modern literature, and though she could be as scholarly and as discriminating as the best of critics, she preferred to think of herself as the "common reader." Some of the authors mentioned in this essay will be familiar to you; others you may want to look up and perhaps sample.

LET US begin by clearing up the old confusion between the man who loves learning and the man who loves reading, and point out that there is no connection whatever between the two. A learned man is a sedentary, concentrated, solitary enthusiast, who searches through books to discover some particular grain of truth upon which he has set his heart. If the passion for reading conquers him, his gains dwindle and vanish between his fingers. A reader, on the other hand, must check the desire for learning at the outset; if knowledge sticks to him well and good, but to go in pursuit of it, to read on a system, to become a specialist or an authority, is

"Hours in a Library" from *Granite and Rainbow* by Virginia Woolf, © 1958 by Leonard Woolf. Reprinted by permission of Leonard Woolf, and Harcourt, Brace & World, Inc.

very apt to kill what it suits us to consider the more humane passion for pure and disinterested reading.

In spite of all this we can easily conjure up a picture which does service for the bookish man and raises a smile at his expense. We conceive a pale, attenuated [1] figure in a dressing gown, lost in speculation, unable to lift a kettle from the hob,[2] or address a lady without blushing, ignorant of the daily news, though versed in the catalogues of the secondhand booksellers, in whose dark premises he spends the hours of sunlight — a delightful character, no doubt, in his crabbed simplicity, but not in the least resembling that other to whom we would direct attention. For the true reader is essentially young. He is a man of intense curiosity; of ideas; openminded and communicative, to whom reading is more of the nature of brisk exercise in the open air than of sheltered study; he trudges the high road, he climbs higher and higher upon the hills until the atmosphere is almost too fine to breathe in; to him it is not a sedentary pursuit at all.

But, apart from general statements, it would not be hard to prove by an assembly of facts that the great season for reading is the season between the ages of eighteen and twenty-four. The bare list of what is read then fills the heart of older people with despair. It is not only that we read so many books, but that we had such books to read. If we wish to refresh our memories, let us take down one of those old notebooks which we have all, at one time or another, had a passion for beginning. Most of the pages are blank, it is true; but at the beginning we shall find a certain number very beautifully covered with a strikingly legible handwriting. Here we have written down the names of great writers in their order of merit; here we have copied out fine passages from

the classics; here are lists of books to be read; and here, most interesting of all, lists of books that have actually been read, as the reader testifies with some youthful vanity by a dash of red ink.

The old lists are there to make us smile and perhaps to sigh a little, but we would give much to recall also the mood in which this orgy of reading was done. Happily, this reader was no prodigy, and with a little thought we can most of us recall the stages at least of our own initiation. The books we read in childhood, having purloined [3] them from some shelf supposed to be inaccessible, have something of the unreality and awfulness of a stolen sight of the dawn coming over quiet fields when the household is asleep. Peeping between the curtains we see strange shapes of misty trees which we hardly recognize, though we may remember them all our lives; for children have a strange premonition of what is to come.

But the later reading is quite a different matter. For the first time, perhaps, all restrictions have been removed, we can read what we like; libraries are at our command, and, best of all, friends who find themselves in the same position. For days upon end we do nothing but read. It is a time of extraordinary excitement and exaltation. We seem to rush about recognizing heroes. There is a sort of wonderment in our minds that we ourselves are really doing this, and mixed with it an absurd arrogance and desire to show our familiarity with the greatest human beings who have ever lived in the world. The passion for knowledge is then at its keenest or at least most confident, and we have, too, an intense singleness of mind which the great writers gratify by making it appear that they are at one with us in their estimate of what is good in life. And as it is necessary to hold one's own against some one who has adopted Pope, let us

---

[1] *attenuated:* thin. [2] *hob* (hŏb): a projection at the back or side of a fireplace.

[3] *purloined:* stolen.

say, instead of Sir Thomas Browne,[1] for a hero, we conceive a deep affection for these men, and feel that we know them not as other people know them, but privately by ourselves. We are fighting under their leadership, and almost in the light of their eyes. So we haunt the old bookshops and drag home folios and quartos, Euripides in wooden boards, and Voltaire in eighty-nine volumes octavo.

But these lists are curious documents, in that they seem to include scarcely any of the contemporary writers. Meredith and Hardy and Henry James were of course alive when this reader came to them, but they were already accepted among the classics. There is no man of his own generation who influences him as Carlyle, or Tennyson, or Ruskin influenced the young of their day. And this we believe to be very characteristic of youth, for unless there is some admitted giant he will have nothing to do with the smaller men, although they deal with the world he lives in. He will rather go back to the classics, and consort entirely with minds of the very first order. For the time being he holds himself aloof from all the activities of men, and, looking at them from a distance, judges them with superb severity.

Indeed, one of the signs of passing youth is the birth of a sense of fellowship with other human beings as we take our place among them. We should like to think that we keep our standard as high as ever; but we certainly take more interest in the writings of our contemporaries and pardon their lack of inspiration for the sake of something that brings them nearer to us. It is even arguable that we get actually more from the living, although they may be much inferior, than from the dead. In the first

place there can be no secret vanity in reading our contemporaries, and the kind of admiration which they inspire is extremely warm and genuine because in order to give way to our belief in them we have often to sacrifice some very respectable prejudice which does us credit. We have also to find our own reasons for what we like and dislike, which acts as a spur to our attention, and is the best way of proving that we have read the classics with understanding.

Thus to stand in a great bookshop crammed with books so new that their pages almost stick together, and the gilt on their backs is still fresh, has an excitement no less delightful than the old excitement of the secondhand bookstall. It is not perhaps so exalted. But the old hunger to know what the immortals thought has given place to a far more tolerant curiosity to know what our own generation is thinking. What do living men and women feel, what are their houses like and what clothes do they wear, what money have they and what food do they eat, what do they love and hate, what do they see of the surrounding world, and what is the dream that fills the spaces of their active lives? They tell us all these things in their books. In them we can see as much both of the mind and of the body of our times as we have eyes for seeing.

When such a spirit of curiosity has fully taken hold of us, the dust will soon lie thick upon the classics unless some necessity forces us to read them. For the living voices are, after all, the ones we understand the best. We can treat them as we treat our equals; they are guessing our riddles, and, what is perhaps more important, we understand their jokes. And we soon develop another taste, unsatisfied by the great — not a valuable taste, perhaps, but certainly a very pleasant possession — the taste for bad books. Without committing the indiscretion of naming names, we

---

[1] *Sir Thomas Browne* (1605–82): well-known physician, philosopher, and man of letters of the seventeenth century. Author of *Religio Medici*, an exposition of the religious principles of a young and scientifically-minded physician.

know which authors can be trusted to produce yearly (for happily they are prolific) a novel, a book of poems or essays, which affords us indescribable pleasure. We owe a great deal to bad books; indeed, we come to count their authors and their heroes among those figures who play so large a part in our silent life.

Something of the same sort happens in the case of the memoir writers and autobiographers, who have created almost a fresh branch of literature in our age. They are not all of them important people, but strangely enough, only the most important, the dukes and the statesmen, are even really dull. The men and women who set out, with no excuse except perhaps that they saw the Duke of Wellington once, to confide to us their opinions, their quarrels, their aspirations, and their diseases, generally end by becoming, for the time at least, actors in those private dramas with which we beguile our solitary walks and our sleepless hours. Refine all this out of our consciousness and we should be poor indeed. And then there are the books of facts and history, books about bees and wasps and industries and gold mines and Empresses and diplomatic intrigues, about rivers and savages, trade unions, and Acts of Parliament, which we always read and always, alas! forget.

Perhaps we are not making out a good case for a bookshop when we have to confess that it gratifies so many desires which have apparently nothing to do with literature. But let us remember that here we have a literature in the making. From these new books our children will select the one or two by which we shall be known for ever. Here, if we could recognize it, lies some poem, or novel, or history which will stand up and speak with other ages about our age when we lie prone and silent as the crowd of Shakespeare's day is silent and lives for us only in the pages of his poetry.

It is oddly difficult in the case of new books to know which are the real books and what it is that they are telling us, and which are the stuffed books which will come to pieces when they have lain about for a year or two. We can see that there are many books, and we are frequently told that every one can write nowadays. That may be true; yet we do not doubt that at the heart of this immense volubility this flood and foam of language, this irreticence [1] and vulgarity and triviality, there lies the heat of some great passion which only needs the accident of a brain more happily turned than the rest to issue in a shape which will last from age to age. It should be our delight to watch this turmoil, to do battle with the ideas and visions of our own time, to seize what we can use, to kill what we consider worthless, and above all to realize that we must be generous to the people who are giving shape as best they can to the ideas within them.

No age of literature is so little submissive to authority as ours, so free from the dominion of the great; none seems so wayward with its gift of reverence, or so volatile in its experiments. It may well seem, even to the attentive, that there is no trace of school or aim in the work of our poets and novelists. But the pessimist is inevitable, and he shall not persuade us that our literature is dead, or prevent us from feeling how true and vivid a beauty flashes out as the young writers draw together, to form their new vision, the ancient words of the most beautiful of living languages. Whatever we may have learned from reading the classics we need now in order to judge the work of our contemporaries, for whenever there is life in them they will be casting their net out over some unknown abyss to snare new shapes, and we must throw our imaginations after them if we are to accept with understanding the strange gifts

[1] *irreticence:* frankness.

they bring back to us.

But if we need all our knowledge of the old writers in order to follow what the new writers are attempting, it is certainly true that we come from adventuring among new books with a far keener eye for the old. It seems that we should now be able to surprise their secrets; to look deep down into their work and see the parts come together, because we have watched the making of new books, and with eyes clear of prejudice can judge more truly what it is that they are doing, and what is good and what bad. We shall find, probably, that some of the great are less venerable than we thought them. Indeed, they are not so accomplished or so profound as some of our own time. But if in one or two cases this seems to be true, a kind of humiliation mixed with joy overcomes us in front of others. Take Shakespeare, or Milton, or Sir Thomas Browne. Our little knowledge of how things are done does not avail us much here, but it does lend an added zest to our enjoyment. Did we ever in our youngest days feel such amazement at their achievement as that which fills us now that we have sifted myriads of words and gone along uncharted ways in search of new forms for our new sensations? New books may be more stimulating and in some ways more suggestive than the old, but they do not give us that absolute certainty of delight which breathes through us when we come back again to *Comus*, or *Lycidas, Urn Burial,* or *Antony and Cleopatra.*

Far be it from us to hazard any theory as to the nature of art. It may be that we shall never know more about it than we know by nature, and our longer experience of it teaches us this only — that of all our pleasures those we get from the great artists are indisputably among the best; and more we may not know. But, advancing no theory, we shall find one or two qualities in such works as these which we can hardly expect to find in books made within the span of our lifetime. Age itself may have an alchemy of its own. But this is true: you can read them as often as you will without finding that they have yielded any virtue and left a meaningless husk of words; and there is a complete finality about them. No cloud of suggestions hangs about them teasing us with a multitude of irrelevant ideas. But all our faculties are summoned to the task, as in the great moments of our own experience; and some consecration descends upon us from their hands which we return to life, feeling it more keenly and understanding it more deeply than before.

THE TRUE READER

1. In "Hours in a Library" Virginia Woolf first compares the man who loves learning with the one who loves reading. In what ways does she say they differ? How does she describe the "true reader"? Do you agree with her that "the great season for reading" is "between the ages of eighteen and twenty-four"? Give reasons for your answer.

2. Can you recall your early initiation to books and libraries? Does it compare with that of the author? In what ways does reading change from this first stage? In the opinion of the writer, why do people go back to the classics?

3. Why do we eventually turn to reading contemporary writers? What are the reasons given for this change? How can the taste for bad books be a "pleasant possession"? Explain.

4. What kind of a case does the essayist make for bookshops? In judging today's writers, why is the knowledge of old writers important? Explain: "Age itself may have an alchemy of its own."

SUGGESTION FOR WRITING

Take a look at your reading tastes and determine what kind of a reader you are. Do you read the classics, or the writings of contemporary authors? Have you spent considerable time reading the works of one author in particular? Do you prefer reading many examples of one type of writing? Decide on a suitable title and write an essay in answer to one of these questions.

A Churchill Sampler

SIR WINSTON CHURCHILL 1874–

We need not await the verdict of history to place Sir Winston Churchill among England's greatest men. His leadership carried England through the darkest period of her entire history — from the summer of 1940 to the autumn of 1941. During this time England stood alone, with a formidable enemy massed across the English Channel ready to attack.

This man who led England through her hour of greatest peril is the descendant of the famous Duke of Marlborough. His father was Lord Randolph Churchill; his mother, a brilliant and beautiful American, was the former Jennie Jerome. Churchill's early career included army service in India, Egypt, and South Africa, and a brief period as a war correspondent. In 1900 he entered the House of Commons as a member of the Conservative party. He was in government service almost continuously from that time until he retired in 1955. At the outbreak of World War II he became First Lord of the Admiralty (the equivalent of our Secretary of the Navy), and in 1940 he was made Prime Minister. Here his magnificent qualities of mind and spirit inspired the English people with the unparalleled courage to fight to victory.

In 1953 Churchill received two notable honors. Queen Elizabeth knighted him and presented him with the Order of the Garter. Later in the year he was awarded the Nobel Prize for Literature for his six volumes of memoirs, *The Second World War*. In 1954, on his eightieth birthday, he was acclaimed by Queen and country as "the greatest living Briton."

All his life, in the midst of a busy public career, Churchill has been a writer. As a young Army officer and later when in government service, he published much nonfiction — on his travels and war experiences, the Marlborough family, and international politics — and one novel. A collection of his speeches during World War II, *Blood, Sweat, and Tears,* takes its title from a sentence in his first speech as Prime Minister, which he delivered just as Hitler was approaching through Holland: "I have nothing to offer but blood, toil, tears, and sweat."

Since his retirement in 1955 he has completed work on the long-contemplated *History of the English-Speaking Peoples: The Birth of Britain* (to 1485), *The New World* (1485–1688), *The Age of Revolution* (1688–1815), and *The Great Democracies* (1815–1900). Sir Winston now divides his time between his home in England and the warm Mediterranean, where one of his hobbies is oil painting.

The Nature of Modern War

In *The Gathering Storm*, Churchill reviews some of his earlier impressions of the world tensions which World War I had failed to settle. This passage (written in 1928) on the meaning of war in our century is significant in the light of what followed. It is still pertinent for readers today in our far-from-peaceful world.

IT WAS NOT until the dawn of the twentieth century of the Christian Era that war began to enter into its kingdom as the potential destroyer of the human race. The organization of mankind into great states and empires, and the rise of nations to full collective consciousness,

"The Nature of Modern War" from *The Gathering Storm* by Winston Churchill. Copyright, 1948. Reprinted by permission of and arrangement with Houghton Mifflin Company, the authorized publishers, and Thomas Allen and Company Ltd.

enabled enterprises of slaughter to be planned and executed upon a scale and with a perseverance never before imagined. All the noblest virtues of individuals were gathered together to strengthen the destructive capacity of the mass. Good finances, the resources of world-wide credit and trade, the accumulation of large capital reserves made it possible to divert for considerable periods the energies of whole peoples to the task of devastation. Democratic institutions gave expression to the will power of millions. Education not only brought the course of the conflict within the comprehension of everyone, but rendered each person serviceable in a high degree for the purpose in hand. The press afforded a means of unification and of mutual stimulation. Religion, having discreetly avoided conflict on the fundamental issues, offered its encouragements and consolations, through all its forms, impartially to all the combatants. Lastly, Science unfolded her treasures and her secrets to the desperate demands of men, and placed in their hand agencies and apparatus almost decisive in their character.

In consequence many novel features presented themselves. Instead of fortified towns being starved, whole nations were methodically subjected, or sought to be subjected, to the process of reduction by famine. The entire population in one capacity or another took part in the war; all were equally the object of attack. The air opened paths along which death and terror could be carried far behind the lines of the actual armies, to women, children, the aged, the sick, who in earlier struggles would perforce have been left untouched. Marvelous organization of railroads, steamships, and motor vehicles placed and maintained tens of millions of men continuously in action. Healing and surgery in their exquisite developments returned them again and again to the shambles. Nothing was wasted that could contribute to the process of waste. The last dying kick was brought into military utility.

But all that happened in the four years of the Great War was only a prelude to what was preparing for the fifth year. The campaign of the year 1919 would have witnessed an immense accession to the powers of destruction. Had the Germans retained the morale to make good their retreat to the Rhine, they would have been assaulted in the summer of 1919 with forces and by methods incomparably more prodigious than any yet employed. Thousands of airplanes would have shattered their cities. Scores of thousands of cannon would have blasted their front. Arrangements were being made to carry simultaneously a quarter of a million men, together with all their requirements, continuously forward across country in mechanical vehicles moving ten or fifteen miles each day. Poison gases of incredible malignity, against which only a secret mask (which the Germans could not obtain in time) was proof, would have stifled all resistance and paralyzed all life on the hostile front subjected to attack. No doubt the Germans too had their plans. But the hour of wrath had passed. The signal of relief was given, and the horrors of 1919 remained buried in the archives of the great antagonists.

The war stopped as suddenly and as universally as it had begun. The world lifted its head, surveyed the scene of ruin, and victors and vanquished alike drew breath. In a hundred laboratories, in a thousand arsenals, factories and bureaus, men pulled themselves up with a jerk, and turned from the task in which they had been absorbed. Their projects were put aside unfinished, unexecuted; but their knowledge was preserved; their data, calculations, and discoveries were hastily bundled together and docketed "for future reference" by the War Office in every country. The campaign of 1919 was never fought; but its ideas go marching along. In every army they are being explored, elaborated, refined, under the surface of peace, and should war come again to the world, it is not with the weapons and agencies prepared for 1919 that it will be fought, but with developments and extensions of these which will be incomparably more formidable and fatal.

It is in these circumstances that we entered upon that period of exhaustion which has been described as Peace. It gives us at any rate an opportunity to consider the general situation. Certain somber facts emerge, solid, inexorable, like the shapes of mountains from drifting mist. It is established that henceforward whole populations will take part in war, all doing their utmost, all subjected to the fury of the enemy. It is established that nations who believe their life is at stake will not be restrained from using any means to secure their existence. It is probable — nay, certain — that among the means which will next

time be at their disposal will be agencies and processes of destruction wholesale, unlimited, and perhaps, once launched, uncontrollable.

Mankind has never been in this position before. Without having improved appreciably in virtue or enjoying wiser guidance, it has got into its hands for the first time the tools by which it can unfailingly accomplish its own extermination. That is the point in human destinies to which all the glories and toils of men have at last led them. They would do well to pause and ponder upon their new responsibilities. Death stands at attention, obedient, expectant, ready to serve, ready to shear away the peoples *en masse;* ready, if called on, to pulverize, without hope of repair, what is left of civilization. He awaits only the word of command. He awaits it from a frail, bewildered being, long his victim, now — for one occasion only — his Master.

The Miracle of Dunkirk

On June 4, 1940, Winston Churchill, Prime Minister of Great Britain, stood before the House of Commons to deliver this account of the successful evacuation of some three hundred thousand men of the British Expeditionary Forces. The position of the British Army, trapped on the beaches of northern France with its back to the English Channel, appeared hopeless and tragic. The Belgian Army had already surrendered; the French Army had ceased to be a fighting organization. For the British the choice seemed to be suicidal defense or humiliating surrender. A plan for rescue was hastily conceived. It demanded the concerted effort of all branches of the British armed services, aided by hundreds of volunteers manning small boats of every type. The achievement at Dunkirk has already taken its place among the heroic episodes of history.

THE GERMAN eruption swept like a sharp scythe around the right and rear of the Armies of the north. Eight or nine armored divisions, each of about four hundred armored vehicles of different kinds, but carefully assorted to be complementary and divisible into small self-contained units, cut off all communications between us and the main French Armies. It severed our own communications for food and ammunition, which ran first to Amiens and afterward through Abbeville, and it shoved its way up the coast to Boulogne and Calais and almost to Dunkirk. Behind this armored and mechanized onslaught came a number of German divisions in lorries, and behind them again there plodded comparatively slowly the dull

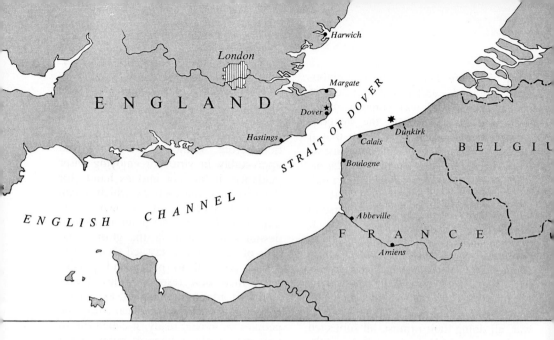

brute mass of the ordinary German Army and German people, always so ready to be led to the trampling down in other lands of liberties and comforts which they have never known in their own land.

I have said this armored scythe-stroke almost reached Dunkirk — almost but not quite. Boulogne and Calais were the scenes of desperate fighting. The Guards defended Boulogne for a while and were then withdrawn by orders from this country. The Rifle Brigade, the 60th Rifles, and the Queen Victoria's Rifles, with a battalion of British tanks and one thousand Frenchmen, in all about four thousand strong, defended Calais to the last. The British Brigadier was given an hour to surrender. He spurned the offer, and four days of intense street fighting passed before silence reigned over Calais, which marked the end of a memorable resistance. Only thirty unwounded survivors were brought off by the Navy, and we do not know the fate of their comrades. Their sacrifice, however, was not in vain. At least two armored divisions, which otherwise would have been turned against the British Expeditionary Force, had to be sent to overcome them. They have added another page to the glories of the light divisions, and the time gained enabled the Gravelines water lines to be flooded and to be held by the French troops.

Thus it was that the port of Dunkirk was kept open. When it was found impossible for the Armies of the north to reopen their communications to Amiens with the main French Armies, only one choice remained. It seemed, indeed, forlorn. The Belgian, British, and French Armies were almost surrounded. Their sole line of retreat was to a single port and to its neighboring beaches. They were pressed on every side by heavy attacks and far outnumbered in the air.

When, a week ago today, I asked the House to fix this afternoon as the occasion for a statement, I feared it would be my hard lot to announce the greatest military disaster in our long history. I thought — and some good judges agreed with me — that perhaps twenty thousand or thirty thousand men might be re-embarked. But it certainly seemed that the whole of the French First Army and the whole of the British Expeditionary Force north of the Amiens-Abbeville gap would be broken up in the open field or else would have to capitulate for lack of food and ammunition.

These were the hard and heavy tidings for which I called upon the House and the nation to prepare themselves a week ago. The whole root and core and brain of the British Army, on which and around which we were to build, and are to build, the great British Armies in the later years of the war, seemed about to perish upon the field or to be led into an ignominious and starving captivity. . . .

The enemy attacked on all sides with great strength and fierceness, and their main power, the power of their far more numerous Air Force, was thrown into the battle or else concentrated upon Dunkirk and the beaches. Pressing in upon their narrow exit, both from the east and from the west, the enemy began to fire with cannon upon the beaches by which alone the shipping could approach or depart. They sowed magnetic mines in the channels and seas; they sent repeated waves of hostile aircraft, sometimes more than a hundred strong in one formation, to cast their bombs upon the single pier that remained, and upon the sand dunes upon which the troops had their eyes for shelter. Their U-boats, one of which was sunk, and their motor launches took their toll of the vast traffic which now began. For four days or five days an intense struggle reigned. All their armored divisions — or what was left of them — together with great masses of infantry and artillery, hurled themselves in vain upon the ever-narrowing, ever-contracting appendix within which the British and French Armies fought.

Meanwhile the Royal Navy, with the willing help of countless merchant seamen, strained every nerve to embark the British and Allied troops; 220 light warships and 650 other vessels were engaged. They had to operate upon the difficult coast, often in adverse weather, under an almost ceaseless hail of bombs and an increasing concentration of artillery fire. Nor were the seas, as I have said, themselves free from mines and torpedoes. It was in conditions such as these that our men carried on, with little or no rest, for days and nights on end, making trip after trip across the dangerous waters, bringing with them always men whom they had rescued. The numbers they have brought back are the measure of their devotion and their courage. The hospital ships, which brought off many thousands of British and French wounded, being so plainly marked, were a special target for Nazi bombs; but the men and women on board them never faltered in their duty.

The Royal Air Force, which had already been intervening in the battle, so far as its range would allow, from home bases, now used part of its main metropolitan fighter strength and struck at the German bombers and at the fighters which in large numbers protected them. This struggle was protracted and fierce. Suddenly the scene was cleared; the crash and thunder has for the moment — but only for the moment — died away. A miracle of deliverance, achieved by valor, by perseverance, by perfect discipline, by faultless service, by resource, by skill, by unconquerable fidelity, is manifest to us all. The enemy was hurled back by the retreating British and French troops. He was so roughly handled that he did not hurry their departure seriously. The Royal Air Force engaged the main strength of the German Air Force, and inflicted upon them losses of at least four to one; and the Navy, using nearly one thousand ships of all kinds, carried over three hundred and thirty-five thousand men, French and British, out of the jaws of death and shame, to their native land and to the tasks which lie immediately ahead. We must be very careful not to assign to this deliverance the attributes of a victory. Wars are not won by evacuations. But there was a victory inside this deliverance, which should be noted. It was gained by the Air Force. Many of our soldiers coming back have not seen the Air Force at work; they saw only the bombers which escaped its protective attacks. They underrate its achievements. I have heard much talk of this; that is why I go out of my way to say this. I will tell you about it.

This was a great trial of strength between the British and German Air Forces. Can you conceive a greater objective for the Germans in the air than to make evacuation from these beaches impossible and to sink all these ships which were displayed, almost to the extent of thousands? Could there have been an objective of greater military importance and significance for the whole purpose of the war than this? They tried hard, and they were beaten back; they were frustrated in their task. We got the Army away and they have paid fourfold for any losses which they have inflicted. Very large formations of German airplanes — and we know that they are a very brave race — have turned on several occasions from the attack of one-quarter of their number of the Royal Air Force, and have dispersed in different directions. Twelve airplanes have been hunted by two. One airplane was driven into the water and cast away by the mere charge of a British airplane, which had no more ammunition. All of our types — the Hurricane, the Spitfire, and the new Defiant — and all our pilots have been vindicated as superior to what they have at present to face.

When we consider how much greater would be our advantage in defending the air above this island against an overseas attack, I must say that I find in these facts a sure basis upon which practical and reassuring thoughts may rest. I will pay my tribute to these young airmen. The great French Army was very largely, for the time being, cast back and disturbed by the onrush of a few thousands of armored vehicles. May it not also be that the cause of civilization itself will be defended by the skill and devotion of a few thousand airmen? There never has been, I suppose, in all the world, in all the history of war,

such an opportunity for youth. The Knights of the Round Table, the Crusaders, all fall back into the past — not only distant but prosaic; these young men, going forth every morn to guard their native land and all that we stand for, holding in their hands these instruments of colossal and shattering power, of whom it may be said that

Every morn brought forth a noble chance
And every chance brought forth a noble
  knight

deserve our gratitude, as do all of the brave men who, in so many ways and on so many occasions, are ready, and continue ready, to give life and all for their native land.

I return to the Army. In the long series of very fierce battles, now on this front, now on that, fighting on three fronts at once, battles fought by two or three divisions against an equal or somewhat larger number of the enemy, and fought fiercely on some of the old grounds that so many of us knew so well — in these battles our losses in men have exceeded thirty thousand killed, wounded, and missing. I take occasion to express the sympathy of the House to all who have suffered bereavement or who are still anxious. The President of the Board of Trade is not here today. His son has been killed, and many in the House have felt the pangs of affliction in the sharpest form. But I will say this about the missing: we have had a large number of wounded come home safely to this country, but I would say about the missing that there may be very many reported missing who will come back home, someday, in one way or another. In the confusion of this fight it is inevitable that many have been left in positions where honor required no further resistance from them.

Against this loss of over thirty thousand men, we can set a far heavier loss certainly inflicted upon the enemy. But our losses in material are enormous. We have perhaps lost one-third of the men we lost in the opening days of the battle of 21st March, 1918, but we have lost nearly as many guns — nearly one thousand — and all our transport, all the armored vehicles that were with the Army in the north. This loss will impose a further delay on the expansion of our military strength. That expansion had not been proceeding as fast as we had hoped. The best of all we had to give had gone to the British Expeditionary Force; and although they had not the numbers of tanks and some articles of equipment which were desirable, they were a very well and finely equipped Army. They had the first fruits of all that our industry had to give, and that is gone. And now here is this further delay. How long it will be, how long it will last, depends upon the exertions which we make in this island. An effort the like of which has never been seen in our records is now being made. Work is proceeding everywhere, night and day, Sundays and weekdays. Capital and Labor have cast aside their interests, rights, and customs and put them into the common stock. Already the flow of munitions has leaped forward. There is no reason why we should not in a few months overtake the sudden and serious loss that has come upon us, without retarding the development of our general program.

Nevertheless, our thankfulness at the escape of our Army and so many men, whose loved ones have passed through an agonizing week, must not blind us to the fact that what has happened in France and Belgium is a colossal military disaster. The French Army has been weakened; the Belgium Army has been lost; a large part of those fortified lines upon which so much faith had been reposed is gone; many valuable mining districts and factories have passed into the enemy's possession; the whole of the Channel ports are in his hands, with all the tragic consequences that follow from that, and we must ex-

pect another blow to be struck almost immediately at us or at France. We are told that Herr Hitler has a plan for invading the British Isles. This has often been thought of before. When Napoleon lay at Boulogne for a year with his flat-bottomed boats and his Grand Army, he was told by someone, "There are bitter weeds in England." There are certainly a great many more of them since the British Expeditionary Force returned.

I would observe that there has never been a period in all these long centuries of which we boast when an absolute guarantee against invasion, still less against serious raids, could have been given to our people. In the days of Napoleon the same wind which would have carried his transports across the Channel might have driven away the blockading fleet. There was always the chance, and it is that chance which has excited and befooled the imaginations of many Continental tyrants. Many are the tales that are told. We are assured that novel methods will be adopted, and when we see the originality of malice, the ingenuity of aggression, which our enemy displays, we may certainly prepare ourselves for every kind of novel stratagem and every kind of brutal and treacherous maneuver. I think that no idea is so outlandish that it should not be considered and viewed with a searching, but at the same time, I hope, with a steady eye. We must never forget the solid assurances of sea power and those which belong to air power if it can be locally exercised.

I have, myself, full confidence that if all do their duty, if nothing is neglected, and if the best arrangements are made, as they are being made, we shall prove ourselves once again able to defend our island home, to ride out the storm of war, and to outlive the menace of tyranny, if necessary for years, if necessary alone. At any rate, that is what we are going to try to do. That is the resolve of His Majesty's Government — every man of them. That is the will of Parliament and the nation. The British Empire and the French Republic, linked together in their cause and in their need, will defend to the death their native soil, aiding each other like good comrades to the utmost of their strength. Even though large tracts of Europe and many old and famous states have fallen or may fall into the grip of the Gestapo and all the odious apparatus of Nazi rule, we shall not flag or fail. We shall go on to the end: we shall fight in France; we shall fight on the seas and oceans; we shall fight with growing confidence and growing strength in the air; we shall defend our island, whatever the cost may be — we shall fight on the beaches; we shall fight on the landing grounds, we shall fight in the fields and in the streets; we shall fight in the hills. We shall never surrender, and even if, which I do not for a moment believe, this island or a large part of it were subjugated and starving, then our Empire beyond the seas, armed and guarded by the British Fleet, would carry on the struggle until, in God's good time, the New World with all its power and might, steps forth to the rescue and the liberation of the old.

Churchill on War and Peace

What General Weygand has called the Battle of France is over. The Battle of Britain is about to begin. Upon this battle depends the survival of Christian civilization. Upon it depends our own British life and the long continuity of our institutions and our empire. The whole fury and might of the enemy must very soon be turned on us. Hitler knows that he will have to break us in this island or lose the war. If we can stand up to him, all Europe may be free, and the life of the world may move forward into broad sunlit uplands. But if we fail, then the whole world, including the United States, including all that we have known and cared for, will sink into the abyss of a new dark age, made more sinister and perhaps more protracted by the light of perverted science. Let us therefore brace ourselves to our duty and so bear ourselves that if the British Empire and its Commonwealth last for a thousand years, men will still say "This was their finest hour."

(Speech in the House, June 18, 1940 — the day of the French capitulation.)

THe problems of victory are more agreeable than those of defeat, but they are no less difficult.

(Speech in the House, November 1942.)

THE VOICE OF A LEADER

1. Outline the major ways in which, according to Churchill, twentieth-century warfare is different from that of earlier times. Give some specific illustrations of techniques of warfare used in World War I which were quite unlike those used in nineteenth-century wars.

2. The author foresaw great changes in methods of conducting later wars. Give examples of the fulfillment of his prophecy in World War II. What does Churchill's prophecy say to us about current problems?

3. In "The Miracle of Dunkirk" how did the circumstances under which the speech was delivered affect the nature of Churchill's account of what had happened?

4. With a map to help you, study the progress of events so that you can give a clear account of (a) the position of the opposing forces, (b) the effect of the British and French delaying action at Calais,

(c) the battle of Dunkirk, (d) the co-opera-tive participation of the Royal Navy and the Royal Air Force.

5. To what extent was the prophecy of the closing lines fulfilled?

APPRECIATING AN AUTHOR'S STYLE

Being aware of how a man reflects himself in his writing will help you to improve your own writing ability. You already have analyzed the writing of many authors, and by doing so, you have developed an appreciation for those elements which characterize effective written expression.

There are few readers who fail to respond to the style of Sir Winston Churchill, a master of prose. His incisive manner and ready wit lift his style far above that of most men in public life. Study the qualities of Churchill's style by noting (a) the directness and clarity of his sentences, (b) his use of repetition for emphasis, (c) his use of parallel construction and balanced sentences, (d) his emotional appeal.

Delight

J. B. PRIESTLEY 1894–

Karsh, Ottawa-Pix

People are always asking me which are my favorites among the many novels, plays, and books of essays I have written. It is only when the question refers strictly to books of essays that I find it easy to answer. My own favorite here is undoubtedly *Delight,* from which the following short pieces have been chosen. Perhaps I like it best because writing it gave me so much pleasure. *Delight* consists entirely of short pieces, like those printed here, and I wrote them not one after the other but at odd times, whenever I felt like doing one. Very few books by experienced professional writers are composed in this random fashion. Generally we just stick at a job until it is done; we cannot afford to write things just when we think we would enjoy writing them. But this is how *Delight* was done, and probably this was the only way it could have been done. In the days when these pieces were written I still had my family living at home or frequently returning home, and when I had done a few of these pieces I would read them aloud in the evenings. I always felt, when writing them, that they should be read aloud, and some years after the book was published I filled two sides of a long-playing record with readings from it. Though books are handier things than records, I hope this particular record can still be obtained, because it does suggest the way I feel these pieces should be read, even by people who are reading to themselves. I have always felt that all good prose should read easily and effectively, have always tried to write through my ear and not my eye. These little *Delight* pieces in particular, however, seem to me to be essentially *spoken* prose, asking to be read aloud. So I hope readers of this volume will try the experiment. If they do not enjoy my pieces, they might at least enjoy the sound of their own voices and find delight that way, which is a good and well-tried way.

J. B. P.

From *Delight* by J. B. Priestley, copyright, 1949, by J. B. Priestley. Reprinted by permission of Harold Matson and A. D. Peters.

Women and Clothes

WOMEN who say they are indifferent to clothes, like men who say they do not mind what they eat, should be distrusted: there is something wrong. And men who sneer at woman's passionate concern about dress should be banished to the woods. For my part I delight in women when they go into a conference huddle over new clothes. They seem to me then most themselves and the furthest removed from my sex. They are at such times completely in their own world. They are half children, half witches. Note their attitude during these clothes conferences. For example, their absolutely clear-sighted realism about themselves. We chaps always peer at ourselves through a haze of good will. We never believe we are as fat or as thin and bony as other people say we are. The ladies are free of all such illusions. (Notice the direct level glances they give each other on these occasions.) So in their clothes conference, unlike all masculine conferences, there is no clash of illusions. All of them meet on the firm ground of fact. What is known is immediately taken into account: Kate's left shoulder is higher than her right; Meg is very broad across the hips; Phyllis has very short legs. The conference line — and very sensible too — is that we are all imperfect creatures, so how do we make the best of ourselves? (If politicians and their senior officials tried the same line at international conferences, they could change the whole world in a week.) Yet the whole clothes huddle is not simply so much grim realism. There is one grand illusion that they all share and never dream of challenging. It is the belief that out of these clothes, with necessary swaps and alterations, beauty and witchery can emerge, that somewhere here is the beginning of an enchanted life. And I for one find this altogether delightful.

No School Report

WE FATHERS of families have one secret little source of delight that is closed to other men. As we read the school reports upon our children, we realize with a sense of relief that can rise to delight that — thank Heaven — nobody is reporting in this fashion upon us. What a nightmare it would be if our personalities were put through this mincing machine![1] I can imagine my own report: *"Height and weight at beginning of term* — 5 feet, 9 inches: 13 stone, 10 pounds. At end of term — 5 feet, 8 inches: 14 stone, 2 pounds. Note: Through greed and lack of exercise, J.B. is putting on weight and is sagging. He must get out more and eat and drink less. *Conduct* — Not satisfactory. J.B. is increasingly irritable, inconsiderate, and unco-operative. He is inclined to blame others for faults in himself. He complains of lack of sleep but persists in remaining awake to finish rubbishy detective stories. He smokes far too much, and on several occasions has been discovered smoking in bed. There is no real harm in him but at the present time he tends to be self-indulgent, lazy, vain, and touchy. He should be encouraged to spend some weeks this summer with the Sea Scouts or at a Harvest Camp. *English Language and Literature:* Fair but inclined to be careless. *French:* A disappointing term. *History:* Has not made the progress here that we expected of him. Should read more. *Mathematics:* Very poor. *Art:* Has made some attempts both at oils and water color but shows little aptitude. Has been slack in his Appreciation and did not attend Miss Mulberry's excellent talks on the Italian Primitives.[2] *Music:* Fair, but will not practice. *Natural History:* Still professes an interest but finds it impossible

---

[1] *mincing machine:* British for *meat grinder.*
[2] *Italian Primitives:* early Italian painters.

to remember names of birds, butterflies, flowers. Has not joined in the Rambles this term. *Chemistry:* Clearly has no interest in this subject. *Physics:* Poor, though occasionally shows interest. Fails to comprehend basic laws. *Physical Culture:* Sergeant Beefer reports that J.B. has been frequently absent and is obviously far from keen. A bad term. *General Reports:* J.B. is not the bright and helpful member of our little community that he once promised to be. He lacks self-discipline and does not try to cultivate a cheery outlook. There are times when he still exerts himself — e.g., he made a useful contribution to the end of term production of *A Comedy of Errors* — but he tends to be lazy and egoistical. His housemaster has had a talk with him, but I suggest that stronger parental guidance would be helpful, and is indeed necessary." And then I would be asked to see my father, and would find him staring and frowning at this report, and then he would stare and frown at me and would begin asking me, in his deep and rather frightening voice, what on earth was the matter with me. But it can't happen, not this side of the grave. I am knee-deep in the soggy world of graying hair and rotting teeth, of monstrous taxes and overdrafts, of vanishing friends and fading sight; but at least, I can tell myself delightedly, nobody is writing a school report upon me.

Cooking Picnics

Like most men and unlike nearly all women, those atavistic[1] creatures, I detest picnics. One reason is that I am usually very hungry out in the open and I dislike the kind of food provided by picnics. Thus, there are few things to eat better than a properly dressed salad in a fine salad bowl, but there are few things less appetizing than an undressed salad out of a paper bag or cardboard box. Then, except for thick slices of ham between thin slices of bread, I have a growing distaste for the whole sandwich family, especially paste, egg, or cheese sandwiches. Again, anything with jam in it or on it is a curse on a summer's day. Finally, there is a peculiarly hard, green, sour little apple that must be grown specially for picnic boxes. Nevertheless, I have delighted in my time — and am not yet past it — in one kind of picnic, namely, the cooking picnic. This is for great souls. The instrumental basis of it is the frying pan. Sausages will do, though steak of course is better. Fried potatoes are essential, and persons whose stomachs shrink from a greasy chip rather underdone should stay at home and nibble health foods. Coffee, which stands up to wood smoke better than tea, is the beverage. The cooking picnic is, I will admit, a smoky job, at least in this damp climate of ours. I have superintended cooking picnics — and I am a natural superintendent on all these occasions — with inflamed and streaming eyes and every sinus wrecked, spluttering and coughing and choking, damning and blasting, glaring at would-be helpful children until they ran away and howled. I have stoked, and fried and stewed and dished out portions until there was nothing left for me but a few bits of greasy muck

---

[1] *atavistic* (ăt'á·vĭst'ĭk): showing characteristics of remote or primitive ancestors.

and a half a cup of coffee grounds. And even my pipe has tasted all wrong in the inferno of wood smoke. Yet I would not have missed a moment of it for a five-pound lunch in a private room on somebody else's expense sheet. Somewhere among the damp obstinate sticks, the dwindling sausages, the vanishing fat, the potatoes that would not brown and the water that would not boil, the billowing smoke on the hillside, the monstrous appetites of the company, there has been delight like a crumb of gold.

THE AUTHOR ASKS SOME QUESTIONS

1. How can you explain what, in "Women and Clothes," I have called women's "absolutely clear-sighted" and "grim realism" about themselves in some respects and their "grand illusion" in another respect?

2. One important ingredient of a sense of humor is the ability to laugh at oneself. Do you think I deserve a better grade in this respect for "No School Report" than I would receive in the subjects listed in my essay? Try writing a humorous report about yourself — not limiting yourself to academic subjects.

3. Do you agree with what I say in "Cooking Picnics" about the relative merits of basket picnics and cooking picnics? How do you account for the fact that some men who never want to cook on the kitchen stove are delighted to cook on an outdoor grill? Why do you think many men enjoy officiating at outdoor cooking occasions?

J. B. P.

SUGGESTION FOR WRITING

Using a light touch with an underlying purpose, write an essay or series of observations or brief comments on some of your own "delights."

READING LIST FOR MODERN ESSAYS

Browsing through the collections of essays in your library is a good way to find entertaining essays. Such books may include the work of both English and American writers as well as essays by writers of many other nationalities.

Bowen, Elizabeth, *A Time in Rome*
If you have been, or want to go, to Rome, you will be delighted with this beautifully written commentary on the Eternal City.

Cooke, Alistair, *One Man's America*
A newspaperman, formerly English but now American, takes an inquiring look at our country.

Eliot, T. S., *Selected Essays*
The poet surveys literature and religion in a classic of modern criticism.

Fairbrother, Nan, *An English Year*
There is real British flavor in these delightful reflections made around the calendar.

Highet, Gilbert, *People, Places, and Books*
Mr. Highet, a Scotsman, has recorded his radio talks on the subjects indicated by the title.

Jameson, Robert U. (editor), *Essays Old and New,* 3rd edition
This collection includes Forster, Leacock, Churchill, Stevenson, and others.

Macaulay, Rose, *Personal Pleasures*
Akin to the mood of Priestley's *Delight*.

Maugham, W. Somerset, *Points of View*
Essays, mostly on writers and writing.

Orwell, George, *A Collection of Essays*
The author discusses books, humor, language, and politics.

Struther, Jan, *A Pocketful of Pebbles*
The tradition of the informal, personal essay is perpetuated in this " Pocketful," written by the author of *Mrs. Miniver.*

Yeats, William Butler, *Mythologies*
A collection of revised and rewritten essays based on Irish country beliefs.

FOR LISTENING

A selection from Churchill's speech of June 18, 1940, has been recorded and is available on *Many Voices 6B.* Priestley's "No School Report" is available on *Many Voices 12A.*

MODERN DRAMA

THERE is a simple reason why there are so few periods of really great theater in our whole western world. Too many things have to come right at the very same time. The dramatists must have the right actors, the actors must have the right playhouses, the playhouses must have the right audiences. We must remember that plays exist to be performed, not merely to be read. (Even when you read a play to yourself, try to perform it, to put it on a stage, as you go along.) As soon as a play has to be performed, then some kind of theatrical organization must be there to take charge of the production and to bring in the audience.

The audience is very important. The dramatist shapes his play; the director and his actors shape it too; but the final shaping is done by the audience. The audience is a kind of giant character in any play. Whenever the theater has been great, the audience has been great. At the present time the theater in London and New York is not more than second-rate, but then the audiences are second-rate too.

People should go to see plays as they go to concerts or to picture galleries, to experience some work of dramatic art. Most playgoing in European countries is undertaken in this spirit. But all too often in London and New York people see a play as one item in an evening's long program of celebration, coming between dinner and supper-and-dancing at a night club. The stage to many of these people is not a place where talented players work hard in a difficult art, but a sort of glittering shop window of "glamour." Why have we British and Americans this foolish, rather childish, attitude toward the theater? Perhaps because, unlike Continental people, we are still being influenced by the puritan-ism of our ancestors, and so secretly expect the theater to be gay and wicked. If we could all go to see the plays of Shakespeare or Shaw in exactly the same spirit in which we go to hear Bach suites or Brahms' symphonies, our drama would soon show some improvement.

POST-ELIZABETHAN DRAMA

As we have already seen, the Elizabethan theater reached a height that we have never reached since. The theater of the Restoration and the eighteenth century had their minor triumphs, especially in a type of comedy imitated partly from the French theater (where Molière was the supreme master of comedy) though given a fresher and broader humor, particularly by Farquhar, Goldsmith, and Sheridan. Comedies by these three playwrights still have a place on the English stage.

The nineteenth century is noteworthy chiefly for the failure of the great poets, from Coleridge and Byron to Tennyson and Swinburne, to establish themselves in the theater. Somehow the wonderful fusion of poetry and true drama eluded all their efforts. They did their best, but their best was not good enough; not one of their poetic dramas is performed today.

THE EVOLUTION OF MODERN DRAMA

From the point of view of modern prose drama, a far more important figure is T. W. Robertson (1829–1871), a member of a theatrical family, and an actor himself, who took to playwriting. He had a curious fondness for short titles: *Ours, Caste, School,* and so forth. He was no genius, but he was an extremely successful playwright, with an excellent command of both pathos and humor. He is important because he can be regarded as the father of realism on the English stage. To begin with, his plays themselves were more realistic than other contemporary works. Then he insisted upon realistic scenery, rooms that looked like rooms, gardens that looked like gardens, solid sets in place of the old painted backcloths and wings; and he introduced many realistic effects — falling leaves, whirling snowflakes, and that kind of thing. Finally, instead of having a few days of sketchy rehearsals conducted by the chief actor and the stage manager, he demanded several weeks of careful rehearsing under his own direction. Thus, so far as the London theater is concerned, he became the first director of the modern type.

But it is doubtful if Robertson's innovations, sensible as they seemed at the time, benefited the theater ultimately. His elaborately realistic sets, rooms looking exactly like real rooms, had one grave disadvantage: it took time and money to put them up and take them down. The old scenery consisted of painted cloths that could easily be raised to or lowered from "the flies" (high above the stage, well out of sight of the audience). This meant there was no difficulty about playing one piece on Monday, another on Tuesday, a third on Wednesday, and so on. This was the true "repertory" system, adopted by all great theaters throughout the world. It is true that these theaters now make use of heavy realistic sets, but they do it at enormous expense and so most of them have to be subsidized. However, the use of such sets in the commercial playhouses of London and New York, which are operated to make a profit, brought an end to the repertory system, and put in its place the "long run," in which the play is kept on as long as it shows a profit. The repertory system is much better for dramatists, actors, and audiences.

SHAW, BARRIE, AND GALSWORTHY

Modern realistic prose drama reached its peak during the latter half of the nineteenth century, and curiously enough all three masters of it came from the North. They were Ibsen, Strindberg, and Chekhov. Against these, as outstanding figures of world theater, Britain can offer only Bernard Shaw, the master of modern comedy, whose characteristics are discussed at the end of *Pygmalion.* Contemporary with him in the Edwardian theater — that is, the theater as it was just after the beginning of the century to almost the beginning of World War I — were J. M. Barrie and John Galsworthy. Barrie was immensely popular in Britain and America but never became an important figure in world theater. He is an astonishingly skillful playwright, a wonderful technician, with a whimsical humor and wistful pathos entirely his own, but his themes lack both the depth and the breadth of appeal necessary for world drama. Perhaps his most characteristic and artful piece is *Dear Brutus,* though his *Mary Rose,* too often regarded as being merely sentimental, has unusual psychological depth and subtlety. His *Peter Pan,* marred by sentimentality but glorious in its humor, is one of the few children's classics in the theater. Galsworthy is important in the history of English drama because of his severely realistic method and his handling of social themes, seen at its best perhaps in *The Silver Box,* an early play, and later in *The Skin Game.* But his is a drama entirely devoid of poetry.

IRISH AND SCOTTISH DRAMA

It was across the Irish Sea, in Dublin, that poetry re-entered English-speaking drama. W. B. Yeats, the great poet, and his friend Lady Gregory, herself the author of many excellent plays of peasant life, together created an Irish theater, which had its home, a very modest home, in the small Abbey Theater in Dublin. They were fortunate, first, in finding a number of local actors and actresses of remarkable talent and strong individuality. They were equally fortunate in discovering in John Millington Synge a highly original dramatic genius. Though Synge writes in prose, an elaborate prose based on the speech of the peasants of western Ireland, his genius is essentially poetic. His masterpiece, *The Playboy of the Western World,* defies analysis, being both satirical and romantic, comic and tragic. His one-act *Riders to the Sea* is a good example of his highly individual manner in a tragic key. Much later, the Abbey Theater saw the first productions of Sean O'Casey, not the original genius that Synge was, but a dramatist of great talent, force, and wonderful humor, whose best early work is *Juno and the Paycock.*

After Barrie had done his best work, Scotland was represented during the 1930's and 40's by James Bridie, an unequal dramatist, not always sound in his construction, but one who brought a strong intellect, an original outlook, and something of Shaw's brilliance in debate to the theater. His *Sleeping Clergyman,* in which he makes use of his knowledge of medicine (he had been a doctor), is a good example of his work.

MODERN ENGLISH DRAMA

The London theater has long been attached to what is called "light comedy," rather frivolous witty pieces about people in drawing rooms, for which the unusually polished acting of London players is especially suited. In this particular vein, Somerset Maugham (*The Circle*) and then later, Noel Coward (*Blithe Spirit*) have been notable. Terence Rattigan (*The Browning Version*) began in this easy style but has since broadened his method and added some depth to his plays.

From the late 30's onward, T. S. Eliot has made a gallant but not altogether successful attempt to bring back poetry to the theater, contriving a rather flat, low-toned kind of poetic dialogue that would not seem too far away from ordinary speech. Though some later plays, notably *The Cocktail Party,* were more successful at the box office, it is likely that posterity will recognize an earlier play, *The Family Reunion,* as his best all-round piece of dramatic writing. Christopher Fry (*The Lady's Not for Burning, Venus Observed*) attempts, not without success but with some loss of clarity, a richer poetic style; but though Fry is an experienced man of the theater he tends to be weak on the purely dramatic side of his work. Though other poets, from W. H. Auden to Ronald Duncan, have also attempted poetic drama, no really successful schools of dramatists in this form have been established.

The younger prose dramatists like John Osborne (*Look Back in Anger, The Entertainer*) have a fine ear for effective dialogue and an eye for significant contemporary types of character, but generally they seem to show less interest in and capacity for construction, for the architecture of playwriting, than the older dramatists did. But here they have been encouraged by the younger drama critics, who also tend to be less interested in dramatic form than the older generation of critics.

Both the B.B.C. and the various commercial television networks have shown themselves anxious to use — and, if necessary, to train — new young dramatists who wish to write plays for television. There are signs that a distinct talent for this form — a form quite different from drama for the stage, much more intimate — is beginning to be found among young writers just as it is among young actors and actresses. And here such writers are certain of a vast audience willing to listen to anything they have to say. So drama continues.

J. B. P.

Pygmalion

GEORGE BERNARD SHAW
1856–1950

George Bernard Shaw became a legend in his own lifetime, and his death on November 2, 1950, marked the end of the last of the early pioneers in modern literature. His life spanned almost a century, and he was actively writing drama of a vigorous and original kind almost to the end of his days. Although his sharp tongue and satiric attitude toward conventional thinking made him many enemies, he was generally acknowledged during his last quarter century to be England's greatest living writer.

Shaw was born in Dublin of Irish gentry but from early manhood lived in London. Here he became one of the first socialists in England and served as pamphleteer and speaker for the Fabian Society.

During the eighties and nineties, Shaw became a journalist, writing criticism of music, drama, books, and art for various newspapers. Thus he became known to the literary world. Journalistic criticism fascinated him because it gave him the opportunity to express his ideas to a wide public.

Because he grew disgusted with the poor quality of plays being presented, Shaw began writing plays himself. He interested Ellen Terry, the leading romantic actress of the time, in modern drama; she was the inspiration for several of his plays and a lifelong friend and correspondent.

Like Dr. Samuel Johnson, Shaw was known for the peculiarities of his personality as well as for his literary ability. His active mind was full of theories: he was, for instance, a staunch vegetarian and a great attacker of standard English spelling, leaving, at his death, a large fortune to promote its "reform." But his reputation rests securely on the enduring qualities of his writing, which transcend personal idiosyncrasies. In 1925 he was awarded the Nobel Prize for Literature, and now, several decades later, is still one of the most widely read and admired modern English writers.

Pygmalion, written in 1912, has been a successful play on stage, screen, and television. Shaw took its title from a Greek myth, in which the sculptor Pygmalion carved an ivory statue of a maiden and then fell in love with it. He entreated the goddess Aphrodite for a wife resembling the statue, and she brought the statue to life. Shaw's Pygmalion is Professor Higgins, a phonetician who makes a business as well as a hobby of recording and studying various dialects. Higgins changes the cockney speech of an illiterate, bedraggled flower girl of the London streets into English that is acceptable to the upper classes. But more than that, through the strong influence of her new environment upon her character, a sensitive woman emerges from what had been a "squashed cabbage leaf." You will find that *Pygmalion* is a satire in Shaw's most amusing manner.

In the first act what happens is more important than who the main characters are. Most of these are not even identified by name during the early part of this act. As these persons become increasingly important to the play, however, you will learn to identify them as:

Miss Eynsford Hill, the daughter Clara
Mrs. Eynsford Hill, the mother
Mr. Eynsford Hill, the son Freddy
Eliza Doolittle, the flower girl
Professor Henry Higgins, the note taker and teacher of phonetics
Colonel Pickering, the gentleman and student of Indian dialects.

In the second act, two new characters are introduced:

Mrs. Pearce, Henry Higgins' housekeeper
Alfred Doolittle, Eliza's father.

In the third act, you will meet:

Mrs. Higgins, Henry Higgins' mother.

Pygmalion, copyright 1913 by George Bernard Shaw. Renewal copyright 1941 by George Bernard Shaw. Used by permission of the Public Trustees, The Society of Authors, and Dodd, Mead & Company, Inc. All rights reserved.

◄ *Professor Higgins teaches Eliza Doolittle in this scene from* My Fair Lady.

759

ACT I

Covent Garden [1] at 11:15 P.M. Torrents of heavy summer rain. Cab whistles blowing frantically in all directions. Pedestrians running for shelter into the market and under the portico [2] of St. Paul's Church, where there are already several people, among them a lady and her daughter in evening dress. They are all peering out gloomily at the rain, except one man with his back turned to the rest, who seems wholly preoccupied with a notebook in which he is writing busily.

The church clock strikes the first quarter.

THE DAUGHTER (*in the space between the central pillars, close to the one on her left*). I'm getting chilled to the bone. What can Freddy be doing all this time? He's been gone twenty minutes.

THE MOTHER (*on her daughter's right*). Not so long. But he ought to have got us a cab by this.

A BYSTANDER (*on the lady's right*). He won't get no cab not until half-past eleven, missus, when they come back after dropping their theater fares.

THE MOTHER. But we must have a cab. We can't stand here until half-past eleven. It's too bad.

THE BYSTANDER. Well, it ain't my fault, missus.

THE DAUGHTER. If Freddy had a bit of gumption, he would have got one at the theater door.

THE MOTHER. What could he have done, poor boy?

THE DAUGHTER. Other people got cabs. Why couldn't he?

---

[1] *Covent Garden:* a site north of the Strand, London, occupied by the principal fruit, flower, and vegetable market. Covent Garden Theater is the most important place for grand opera in London. [2] *portico* (pōr'tǐ·kō): a platform with a protecting roof.

[FREDDY *rushes in out of the rain from the Southampton Street side, and comes between them closing a dripping umbrella. He is a young man of twenty, in evening dress, very wet round the ankles.*]

THE DAUGHTER. Well, haven't you got a cab?

FREDDY. There's not one to be had for love or money.

THE MOTHER. Oh, Freddy, there must be one. You can't have tried.

THE DAUGHTER. It's too tiresome. Do you expect us to go and get one ourselves?

FREDDY. I tell you they're all engaged. The rain was so sudden: nobody was prepared; and everybody had to take a cab. I've been to Charing Cross one way and nearly to Ludgate Circus the other; and they were all engaged.

THE MOTHER. Did you try Trafalgar Square?

FREDDY. There wasn't one at Trafalgar Square.

THE DAUGHTER. Did you try?

FREDDY. I tried as far as Charing Cross Station. Did you expect me to walk to Hammersmith?

THE DAUGHTER. You haven't tried at all.

THE MOTHER. You really are very helpless, Freddy. Go again; and don't come back until you have found a cab.

FREDDY. I shall simply get soaked for nothing.

THE DAUGHTER. And what about us? Are we to stay here all night in this draught, with next to nothing on? You selfish pig —

FREDDY. Oh, very well! I'll go, I'll go.

[*He opens his umbrella and dashes off Strandwards, but comes into collision with a flower girl, who is hurrying in for shelter, knocking her basket out of*

her hands. *A blinding flash of lightning, followed instantly by a rattling
peal of thunder, orchestrates the incident.*]

THE FLOWER GIRL. Nah then, Freddy,
look why' y' gowin, deah.
FREDDY. Sorry. (*He rushes off.*)
THE FLOWER GIRL (*picking up her
scattered flowers and replacing them in
the basket*). There's menners f' yer!
Te-oo banches o' voylets trod into the
mad.[1] (*She sits down on the plinth[2] of
the column, sorting her flowers, on the
lady's right. She is not at all an attractive person. She is perhaps eighteen,
perhaps twenty, hardly older. She wears
a little sailor hat of black straw that has
long been exposed to the dust and soot
of London and has seldom if ever been
brushed. Her hair needs washing rather
badly: its mousy color can hardly be
natural. She wears a shoddy black coat
that reaches nearly to her knees and is
shaped to her waist. She has a brown
skirt with a coarse apron. Her boots are
much the worse for wear. She is no
doubt as clean as she can afford to be;
but compared to the ladies she is very
dirty. Her features are no worse than
theirs; but their condition leaves something to be desired; and she needs the
services of a dentist.*)
THE MOTHER. How do you know that
my son's name is Freddy, pray?
THE FLOWER GIRL. Ow, eez ye-ooa
san, is e? Wal, fewd dan y' de-ooty
bawmz a mather should, eed now bet-
tern to spawl a pore gel's flahrzn than
ran awy athaht pyin. Will ye-oo py me
f'them?[3]

(*Here, with apologies, this desperate attempt to represent her dialect without a
phonetic alphabet must be abandoned as
unintelligible outside London.*)

THE DAUGHTER. Do nothing of the
sort, Mother. The idea!
THE MOTHER. Please allow me, Clara.
Have you any pennies?
THE DAUGHTER. No. I've nothing
smaller than sixpence.
THE FLOWER GIRL (*hopefully*). I can
give you change for a tanner,[4] kind
lady.
THE MOTHER (*to Clara*). Give it to
me. (*Clara parts reluctantly.*) Now (*to
the girl*) this is for your flowers.
THE FLOWER GIRL. Thank you kindly,
lady.
THE DAUGHTER. Make her give you
the change. These things are only a
penny a bunch.
THE MOTHER. Do hold your tongue,
Clara. (*To the girl*) You can keep the
change.
THE FLOWER GIRL. Oh, thank you,
lady.
THE MOTHER. Now tell me how you
know that young gentleman's name.
THE FLOWER GIRL. I didn't.
THE MOTHER. I heard you call him
by it. Don't try to deceive me.
THE FLOWER GIRL (*protesting*).
Who's trying to deceive you? I called
him Freddy or Charlie same as you
might yourself if you was talking to a
stranger and wished to be pleasant. (*She
sits down beside her basket.*)
THE DAUGHTER. Sixpence thrown
away! Really, Mamma, you might have
spared Freddy *that.* (*She retreats in disgust behind the pillar.*)

[*An elderly gentleman of the amiable
military type rushes into the shelter,
and closes a dripping umbrella. He is
in the same plight as* FREDDY, *very*

---

[1] "There is manners for you! Two bunches of
violets trod in the mud." The girl speaks with a
cockney accent. [2] *plinth* (plĭnth): lowest
member of the base of a column. [3] "Oh, he is
your son, is he? Well, if you had done your duty
by him as a mother should, he would know
better than to spoil a poor girl's flowers and
then run away without paying. Will you pay
me for them?"

[4] *tanner:* English slang for a sixpence. (For
the value of this coin and other denominations
of English money, see page 842.)

wet about the ankles. He is in evening dress, with a light overcoat. He takes the place left vacant by the DAUGHTER'S *retirement.*]

THE GENTLEMAN. Phew!

THE MOTHER (*to the* GENTLEMAN). Oh, sir, is there any sign of its stopping?

THE GENTLEMAN. I'm afraid not. It started worse than ever about two minutes ago. (*He goes to the plinth beside the* FLOWER GIRL; *puts up his foot on it; and stoops to turn down his trouser end.*)

THE MOTHER. Oh dear! (*She retires sadly and joins her daughter.*)

THE FLOWER GIRL (*taking advantage of the military gentleman's proximity to establish friendly relations with him*). If it's worse, it's a sign it's nearly over. So cheer up, Captain; and buy a flower off a poor girl.

THE GENTLEMAN. I'm sorry. I haven't any change.

THE FLOWER GIRL. I can give you change, Captain.

THE GENTLEMAN. For a sovereign? I've nothing less.

THE FLOWER GIRL. Garn! [1] Oh do buy a flower off me, Captain. I can change half-a-crown. Take this for tuppence.

THE GENTLEMAN. Now don't be troublesome: there's a good girl. (*Trying his pockets*) I really haven't any change — Stop! Here's three hapence, if that's any use to you. (*He retreats to the other pillar.*)

THE FLOWER GIRL (*disappointed, but thinking three halfpence better than nothing*). Thank you, sir.

THE BYSTANDER (*to the girl*). You be careful; give him a flower for it. There's a bloke [2] here behind taking down every blessed word you're saying. (*All turn to the man who is taking notes.*)

THE FLOWER GIRL (*springing up terrified*). I ain't done nothing wrong by speaking to the gentleman. I've a right

to sell flowers if I keep off the curb. (*Hysterically*) I'm a respectable girl. So help me, I never spoke to him except to ask him to buy a flower off me. (*General hubbub, mostly sympathetic to the* FLOWER GIRL *but deprecating [3] her excessive sensibility. Cries of* Don't start hollerin. Who's hurting you? Nobody's going to touch you. What's the good of fussing? Steady on. Easy easy, *etc., come from the elderly staid spectators, who pat her comfortingly. Less patient ones bid her shut her head, or ask her roughly what is wrong with her. A remoter group, not knowing what the matter is, crowd in and increase the noise with question and answer:* What's the row? What's he do? Where is he? A tec [4] taking her down. What! him? Yes! Him over there. Took money off the gentleman, *etc. The* FLOWER GIRL, *distraught and mobbed, breaks through them to the* GENTLEMAN, *crying wildly*) Oh, sir, don't let him charge me. You dunno what it means to me. They'll take away my character and drive me on the streets for speaking to gentlemen. They —

THE NOTE TAKER (*coming forward on her right, the rest crowding after him*). There, there, there, there! Who's hurting you, you silly girl? What do you take me for?

THE BYSTANDER. It's all right; he's a gentleman. Look at his boots. (*Explaining to the* NOTE TAKER) She thought you was a copper's nark, sir.

THE NOTE TAKER (*with quick interest*). What's a copper's nark?

THE BYSTANDER (*inapt at definition*). It's a — well, it's a copper's nark, as you might say. What else would you call it? A sort of informer.

THE FLOWER GIRL (*still hysterical*). I take my Bible oath I never said a word —

THE NOTE TAKER (*overbearing but good-humored*). Oh, shut up, shut up.

[1] *Garn:* expression of disappointment and anger. [2] *bloke:* slang name for a person.

[3] *deprecating* (dĕp'rē·kā'tĭng): deploring; disapproving. [4] *tec:* detective.

Do I look like a policeman?

THE FLOWER GIRL (*far from reassured*). Then what did you take down my words for? How do I know whether you took me down right? You just show me what you've wrote about me. (*The* NOTE TAKER *opens his book and holds it steadily under her nose, though the pressure of the mob trying to read it over his shoulders would upset a weaker man.*) What's that? That ain't proper writing. I can't read that.

THE NOTE TAKER. I can. (*Reads, reproducing her pronunciation exactly*) "Cheer ap, Keptin; n' baw ye flahr orf a pore gel."

THE FLOWER GIRL (*much distressed*). It's because I called him Captain. I meant no harm. (*To the* GENTLEMAN) Oh, sir, don't let him lay a charge agen me for a word like that. You —

THE GENTLEMAN. Charge! I make no charge. (*To the* NOTE TAKER) Really, sir, if you are a detective, you need not begin protecting me against molestation by young women until I ask you. Anybody could see that the girl meant no harm.

THE BYSTANDERS GENERALLY (*demonstrating against police espionage*). Course they could. What business is it of yours? You mind your own affairs. He wants promotion, he does. Taking down people's words! Girl never said a word to him. What harm if she did? Nice thing a girl can't shelter from the rain without being insulted, etc., etc., etc. (*She is conducted by the more sympathetic demonstrators back to her plinth, where she resumes her seat and struggles with her emotion.*)

THE BYSTANDER. He ain't a tec. He's a blooming busybody: that's what he is. I tell you, look at his boots.

THE NOTE TAKER (*turning on him genially*). And how are all your people down at Selsey?

THE BYSTANDER (*suspiciously*). Who told you my people come from Selsey?

THE NOTE TAKER. Never you mind. They did. (*To the girl*) How do you come to be up so far east? You were born in Lisson Grove.

THE FLOWER GIRL (*appalled*). Oh, what harm is there in my leaving Lisson Grove? It wasn't fit for a pig to live in; and I had to pay four-and-six a week. (*In tears*) Oh, boo — hoo — oo —

THE NOTE TAKER. Live where you like; but stop that noise.

THE GENTLEMAN (*to the girl*). Come, come! he can't touch you: you have a right to live where you please.

A SARCASTIC BYSTANDER (*thrusting himself between the* NOTE TAKER *and the* GENTLEMAN). Park Lane, for instance. I'd like to go into the Housing Question with you, I would.

THE FLOWER GIRL (*subsiding into a brooding melancholy over her basket, and talking very low-spiritedly to herself*). I'm a good girl, I am.

THE SARCASTIC BYSTANDER (*not attending to her*). Do you know where I come from?

THE NOTE TAKER (*promptly*). Hoxton.

[*Titterings. Popular interest in the* NOTE TAKER'S *performance increases.*]

THE SARCASTIC ONE (*amazed*). Well, who said I didn't? Bly me! You know everything, you do.

THE FLOWER GIRL (*still nursing her sense of injury*). Ain't no call to meddle with me, he ain't.

THE BYSTANDER (*to her*). Of course he ain't. Don't you stand it from him. (*To the* NOTE TAKER) See here! What call have you to know about people what never offered to meddle with you? Where's your warrant?

SEVERAL BYSTANDERS (*encouraged by this seeming point of law*). Yes, where's your warrant?

THE FLOWER GIRL. Let him say what he likes. I don't want to have no truck with him.

THE BYSTANDER. You take us for dirt under your feet, don't you? Catch you taking liberties with a gentleman!

THE SARCASTIC BYSTANDER. Yes, tell

him where he comes from if you want to go fortune-telling.

THE NOTE TAKER. Cheltenham, Harrow, Cambridge, and India.

THE GENTLEMAN. Quite right. (*Great laughter. Reaction in the* NOTE TAKER'S *favor. Exclamations of* He knows all about it. Told him proper. Hear him tell the toff [1] where he come from? etc.) May I ask, sir, do you do this for your living at a music hall?

THE NOTE TAKER. I've thought of that. Perhaps I shall some day.

[*The rain has stopped; and the persons on the outside of the crowd begin to drop off.*]

THE FLOWER GIRL (*resenting the reaction*). He's no gentleman, he ain't, to interfere with a poor girl.

THE DAUGHTER (*out of patience, pushing her way rudely to the front and displacing the* GENTLEMAN, *who politely retires to the other side of the pillar*). What on earth is Freddy doing? I shall get pneumonia if I stay in this draught any longer.

THE NOTE TAKER (*to himself, hastily making a note of her pronunciation of "monia"*). Earl's Court.

THE DAUGHTER (*violently*). Will you please keep your impertinent remarks to yourself.

THE NOTE TAKER. Did I say that out loud? I didn't mean to. I beg your pardon. Your mother's Epsom, unmistakably.

THE MOTHER (*advancing between her daughter and the* NOTE TAKER). How very curious! I was brought up in Largelady Park, near Epsom.

THE NOTE TAKER (*uproariously amused*). Ha! ha! What a devil of a name! Excuse me. (*To the* DAUGHTER) You want a cab, do you?

THE DAUGHTER. Don't dare speak to me.

THE MOTHER. Oh please, please, Clara. (*Her daughter repudiates her*

with an angry shrug and retires haughtily.*) We should be so grateful to you, sir, if you found us a cab. (*The* NOTE TAKER *produces a whistle.*) Oh, thank you. (*She joins her daughter.*)

[*The* NOTE TAKER *blows a piercing blast.*]

THE SARCASTIC BYSTANDER. There! I knowed he was a plain-clothes copper.

THE BYSTANDER. That ain't a police whistle. That's a sporting whistle.

THE FLOWER GIRL (*still preoccupied with her wounded feelings*). He's no right to take away my character. My character is the same to me as any lady's.

THE NOTE TAKER. I don't know whether you've noticed it, but the rain stopped about two minutes ago.

THE BYSTANDER. So it has. Why didn't you say so before? And us losing our time listening to your silliness! (*He walks off toward the Strand.*)

THE SARCASTIC BYSTANDER. I can tell where *you* come from. You come from Anwell. Go back there.

THE NOTE TAKER (*helpfully*). Hanwell. [2]

THE SARCASTIC BYSTANDER (*affecting great distinction of speech*). Thenk you, teacher. Haw haw! So long. (*He touches his hat with mock respect and strolls off.*)

THE FLOWER GIRL. Frightening people like that! How would he like it himself?

THE MOTHER. It's quite fine now, Clara. We can walk to a motor bus. Come. (*She gathers her skirts above her ankles and hurries off toward the Strand.*)

THE DAUGHTER. But the cab — (*her mother is out of hearing*). Oh, how tiresome! (*She follows angrily.*)

[*All the rest have gone except the* NOTE TAKER, *the* GENTLEMAN, *and the* FLOWER GIRL, *who sits arranging her basket and still pitying herself in murmurs.*]

[1] *toff* (tŏf): slang for a dandy.

[2] *Hanwell:* location of a mental hospital.

THE FLOWER GIRL. Poor girl! Hard enough for her to live without being worrited and chivied.[1]

THE GENTLEMAN (*returning to his former place on the* NOTE TAKER'S *left*). How do you do it, if I may ask?

THE NOTE TAKER. Simply phonetics. The science of speech. That's my profession: also my hobby. Happy is the man who can make a living by his hobby! You can spot an Irishman or a Yorkshireman by his brogue. *I* can place any man within six miles. I can place him within two miles in London. Sometimes within two streets.

THE FLOWER GIRL. Ought to be ashamed of himself, unmanly coward!

THE GENTLEMAN. But is there a living in that?

THE NOTE TAKER. Oh, yes. Quite a fat one. This is an age of upstarts. Men begin in Kentish Town with £80 a year, and end in Park Lane with a hundred thousand. They want to drop Kentish Town; but they give themselves away every time they open their mouths. Now I can teach them —

THE FLOWER GIRL. Let him mind his own business and leave a poor girl —

THE NOTE TAKER (*explosively*). Woman! Cease this detestable boohooing instantly, or else seek the shelter of some other place of worship.

THE FLOWER GIRL (*with feeble defiance*). I've a right to be here if I like, same as you.

THE NOTE TAKER. A woman who utters such depressing and disgusting sounds has no right to be anywhere — no right to live. Remember that you are a human being with a soul and the divine gift of articulate speech — that your native language is the language of Shakespeare and Milton and the Bible — and don't sit there crooning like a bilious pigeon.

THE FLOWER GIRL (*quite overwhelmed, looking up at him in mingled wonder and deprecation without daring to raise her head*). Ah-ah-ah-ow-ow-ow-oo!

THE NOTE TAKER (*whipping out his book*). Heavens! what a sound! (*He writes; then holds out the book and reads, reproducing her vowels exactly.*) Ah-ah-ah-ow-ow-ow-oo!

THE FLOWER GIRL (*tickled by the performance, and laughing in spite of herself*). Garn!

THE NOTE TAKER. You see this creature with her curbstone English: the English that will keep her in the gutter to the end of her days. Well, sir, in three months I could pass that girl off as a duchess at an ambassador's garden party. I could even get her a place as lady's maid or shop assistant, which requires better English. That's the sort of thing I do for commercial millionaires. And on the profits of it I do genuine scientific work in phonetics, and a little as a poet on Miltonic lines.

THE GENTLEMAN. I am myself a student of Indian dialects; and —

THE NOTE TAKER (*eagerly*). Are you? Do you know Colonel Pickering, the author of *Spoken Sanscrit?* [2]

THE GENTLEMAN. I *am* Colonel Pickering. Who are you?

THE NOTE TAKER. Henry Higgins, author of *Higgins' Universal Alphabet.*[3]

PICKERING (*with enthusiasm*). I came from India to meet you.

HIGGINS. I was going to India to meet you.

PICKERING. Where do you live?

HIGGINS. 27A Wimpole Street. Come and see me tomorrow.

PICKERING. I'm at the Carlton. Come with me now and let's have a jaw over some supper.

HIGGINS. Right you are.

THE FLOWER GIRL (*to* PICKERING, *as he passes her*). Buy a flower, kind gentleman. I'm short for my lodging.

PICKERING. I really haven't any

[1] *worrited and chivied:* a cockney expression, meaning worried and tormented.

[2] *Sanscrit* (săn′skrĭt): ancient language of the Hindus of India. [3] *Universal Alphabet:* Shaw is speaking here. He felt that a universal alphabet would help to solve many problems.

change. I'm sorry. (*He goes away.*)

HIGGINS (*shocked at the girl's mendacity*). Liar. You said you could change half-a-crown.

THE FLOWER GIRL (*rising in desperation*). You ought to be stuffed with nails, you ought. (*Flinging the basket at his feet*) Take the whole blooming basket for sixpence.

[*The church clock strikes the second quarter.*]

HIGGINS (*hearing in it the voice of God, rebuking him for his Pharisaic* [1] *want of charity to the poor girl*). A reminder. (*He raises his hat solemnly; then throws a handful of money into the basket and follows* PICKERING.)

THE FLOWER GIRL (*picking up a half-crown*). Ah-ow-ooh! (*Picking up a couple of florins*) Aaah-ow-ooh! (*Picking up several coins*) Aaaaaah-ow-ooh! (*Picking up a half-sovereign*) Aaaaaaa-aaaaah-ow-ooh!!!

FREDDY (*springing out of a taxicab*). Got one at last. Hallo! (*To the girl*) Where are the two ladies that were here?

THE FLOWER GIRL. They walked to the bus when the rain stopped.

FREDDY. And left me with a cab on my hands! Damnation!

THE FLOWER GIRL (*with grandeur*). Never mind, young man. I'm going home in a taxi. (*She sails off to the cab. The driver puts his hand behind him and holds the door firmly shut against her. Quite understanding his mistrust,*

[1] *Pharisaic* (făr′ĭ·sā′ĭk): The Pharisees were a group among the ancient Jews known for their formality and strictness. Higgins realizes his strictness of thought and lack of charity toward the flower girl.

she shows him her handful of money). Eightpence ain't no object to me, Charlie. (*He grins and opens the door.*) Angel Court, Drury Lane, round the corner of Micklejohn's oil shop. Let's see how fast you can make her hop it. (*She gets in and pulls the door to with a slam as the taxicab starts.*)

FREDDY. Well, I'm dashed!

MEETING THE CHARACTERS

1. Major characters of a play generally are identified by name when they first appear. Why are the characters not identified in the opening of Act I? Notice what types of people are represented in this act. How would you describe them? How do the mother and her daughter differ in character? What kind of man is Freddy?

2. Why does the crowd stir up a dispute between the flower girl and the note taker? Whose side does the group take? Why? What do you learn about the flower girl that helps you to understand what kind of person she is? How does she react to the sudden possession of money?

3. The flower girl speaks a cockney dialect. Look up "cockney" to determine what kind of dialect it is and what people speak it. Why do you think Shaw includes some speeches written in cockney? What reason does he give for not continuing to write the cockney dialect?

4. Why is the note taker referred to as a detective? What is his profession? What kind of people does he teach? Can you tell what his feelings are toward his pupils? What is his attitude toward the flower girl?

5. What do Higgins, the note taker, and Colonel Pickering, the gentleman, have in common? At this point in the play, try to formulate some idea of the kind of men Higgins and Pickering are. Are they both gentlemen? Give reasons for your answers.

ACT II

Next day at 11 A.M. HIGGINS' *laboratory in Wimpole Street. It is a room on the first floor, looking on the street, and was meant for the drawing room. The*

double doors are in the middle of the back wall; and persons entering find in the corner to their right two tall file cabinets at right angles to one another against the walls. In this corner stands a flat writing table, on which are a phonograph, a laryngoscope,[1] a row of tiny organ pipes with bellows, a set of lamp chimneys for singing flames with burners attached to a gas plug in the wall by an indiarubber tube, several tuning forks of different sizes, a life-size image of half a human head, showing in section the vocal organs, and a box containing a supply of wax cylinders for the phonograph.

Further down the room, on the same side, is a fireplace, with a comfortable leather-covered easy chair at the side of the hearth nearest the door, and a coal scuttle. There is a clock on the mantelpiece. Between the fireplace and the phonograph table is a stand for newspapers.

On the other side of the central door, to the left of the visitor, is a cabinet of shallow drawers. On it is a telephone and the telephone directory. The corner beyond, and most of the side wall, is occupied by a grand piano, with the keyboard at the end furthest from the door, and a bench for the player extending the full length of the keyboard. On the piano is a dessert dish heaped with fruit and sweets, mostly chocolates.

The middle of the room is clear. Besides the easy chair, the piano bench, and two chairs at the phonograph table, there is one stray chair. It stands near the fireplace. On the walls, engravings: mostly Piranesis[2] and mezzotint portraits. No paintings.

PICKERING *is seated at the table, putting down some cards and a tuning fork which he has been using.* HIGGINS *is standing up near him, closing two or three file drawers which are hanging out. He appears in the morning light as a robust, vital, appetizing sort of man of forty or thereabouts, dressed in a professional-looking black frock coat with a* white linen collar and black silk tie. He is of the energetic, scientific type, heartily, even violently interested in everything that can be studied as a scientific subject, and careless about himself and other people, including their feelings. He is, in fact, but for his years and size, rather like a very impetuous baby "taking notice" eagerly and loudly, and requiring almost as much watching to keep him out of unintended mischief. His manner varies from genial bullying when he is in a good humor to stormy petulance when anything goes wrong; but he is so entirely frank and void of malice that he remains likable even in his least reasonable moments.*

HIGGINS (*as he shuts the last drawer*). Well, I think that's the whole show.

PICKERING. It's really amazing. I haven't taken half of it in, you know.

HIGGINS. Would you like to go over any of it again?

PICKERING (*rising and coming to the fireplace, where he plants himself with his back to the fire*). No, thank you; not now. I'm quite done up for this morning.

HIGGINS (*following him, and standing beside him on his left*). Tired of listening to sounds?

PICKERING. Yes. It's a fearful strain. I rather fancied myself because I can pronounce twenty-four distinct vowel sounds, but your hundred and thirty beat me. I can't hear a bit of difference between most of them.

HIGGINS (*chuckling, and going over to the piano to eat sweets*). Oh, that comes with practice. You hear no difference at first; but you keep on listening, and presently you find they're all as different as A from B. (MRS. PEARCE *looks in; she is* HIGGINS' *housekeeper.*) What's the matter?

MRS. PEARCE (*hesitating, evidently perplexed*). A young woman wants to see you, sir.

HIGGINS. A young woman! What does she want?

---

[1] *laryngoscope* (lă·rĭng′gō·skōp): an instrument for examining the voice. [2] *Piranesi:* Italian engraver of the eighteenth century.

MRS. PEARCE. Well, sir, she says you'll be glad to see her when you know what she's come about. She's quite a common girl, sir. Very common indeed. I should have sent her away, only I thought perhaps you wanted her to talk into your machines. I hope I've not done wrong, but really you see such queer people sometimes — you'll excuse me, I'm sure, sir —

HIGGINS. Oh, that's all right, Mrs. Pearce. Has she an interesting accent?

MRS. PEARCE. Oh, something dreadful, sir, really. I don't know how you can take an interest in it.

HIGGINS (*to* PICKERING). Let's have her up. Show her up, Mrs. Pearce. (*He rushes across to his working table and picks out a cylinder to use on the phonograph.*)

MRS. PEARCE (*only half resigned to it*). Very well, sir. It's for you to say. (*She goes downstairs.*)

HIGGINS. This is rather a bit of luck. I'll show you how I make records. We'll set her talking; and I'll take it down first in Bell's Visible Speech; then in broad Romic; and then we'll get her on the phonograph so that you can turn her on as often as you like with the written transcript before you.

MRS. PEARCE (*returning*). This is the young woman, sir.

[*The* FLOWER GIRL *enters in state. She has a hat with three ostrich feathers — orange, sky-blue, and red. She has a nearly clean apron, and the shoddy coat has been tidied a little. The pathos of this deplorable figure, with its innocent vanity and consequential air, touches* PICKERING, *who has already straightened himself in the presence of* MRS. PEARCE. *But as to* HIGGINS, *the only distinction he makes between men and women is that when he is neither bullying nor exclaiming to the heavens against some featherweight cross, he coaxes women as a child coaxes its nurse when it wants to get anything out of her.*]

HIGGINS (*brusquely,*[1] *recognizing her with unconcealed disappointment, and at once, babylike, making an intolerable grievance of it*). Why, this is the girl I jotted down last night. She's no use: I've got all the records I want of the Lisson Grove lingo [2]; and I'm not going to waste another cylinder on it. (*To the girl*) Be off with you: I don't want you.

THE FLOWER GIRL. Don't you be so saucy. You ain't heard what I come for yet. (*To* MRS. PEARCE, *who is waiting at the door for further instructions*) Did you tell him I come in a taxi?

MRS. PEARCE. Nonsense, girl! What do you think a gentleman like Mr. Higgins cares what you came in?

THE FLOWER GIRL. Oh, we *are* proud! He ain't above giving lessons, not him. I heard him say so. Well, I ain't come here to ask for any compliment; and if my money's not good enough I can go elsewhere.

HIGGINS. Good enough for what?

THE FLOWER GIRL. Good enough for ye-oo. Now you know, don't you? I'm come to have lessons, I am. And to pay for 'em too; make no mistake.

HIGGINS (*stupefied*). Well!!! (*Recovering his breath with a gasp*) What do you expect me to say to you?

THE FLOWER GIRL. Well, if you was a gentleman, you might ask me to sit down, I think. Don't I tell you I'm bringing you business?

HIGGINS. Pickering, shall we ask this baggage to sit down, or shall we throw her out of the window?

THE FLOWER GIRL (*running away in terror to the piano, where she turns at bay*). Ah-ah-oh-ow-ow-ow-oo! (*Wounded and whimpering*) I won't be called a baggage when I've offered to pay like any lady.

[*Motionless, the two men stare at her from the other side of the room, amazed.*]

---

[1] *brusquely* (brŭsk'lĭ): abruptly.　[2] *lingo* (lĭng'gō): dialect.

PICKERING (*gently*). What is it you want, my girl?

THE FLOWER GIRL. I want to be a lady in a flower shop 'stead of selling at the corner of Tottenham [1] Court Road. But they won't take me unless I can talk more genteel. He said he could teach me. Well, here I am ready to pay him — not asking any favor — and he treats me as if I was dirt.

MRS. PEARCE. How can you be such a foolish ignorant girl as to think you could afford to pay Mr. Higgins?

THE FLOWER GIRL. Why shouldn't I? I know what lessons cost as well as you do, and I'm ready to pay.

HIGGINS. How much?

THE FLOWER GIRL (*coming back to him, triumphant*). Now you're talking! I thought you'd come off it when you saw a chance of getting back a bit of what you chucked at me last night. (*Confidentially*) You'd had a drop in, hadn't you?

HIGGINS (*peremptorily*). Sit down.

THE FLOWER GIRL. Oh, if you're going to make a compliment of it —

HIGGINS (*thundering at her*). Sit down.

MRS. PEARCE (*severely*). Sit down, girl. Do as you're told. (*She places the stray chair near the hearthrug between* HIGGINS *and* PICKERING, *and stands behind it waiting for the girl to sit down.*)

THE FLOWER GIRL. Ah-ah-ah-ow-ow-oo! (*She stands, half rebellious, half bewildered.*)

PICKERING (*very courteous*). Won't you sit down?

LIZA (*coyly*). Don't mind if I do. (*She sits down.* PICKERING *returns to the hearthrug.*)

HIGGINS. What's your name?

THE FLOWER GIRL. Liza Doolittle.

HIGGINS (*declaiming gravely*).
Eliza, Elizabeth, Betsy and Bess,
They went to the woods to get a bird's nes':

¹ *Tottenham* (tŏt'năm).

PICKERING. They found a nest with four eggs in it:

HIGGINS. They took one apiece, and left three in it.

[*They laugh heartily at their own wit.*]

LIZA. Oh, don't be silly.

MRS. PEARCE. You mustn't speak to the gentleman like that.

LIZA. Well, why won't he speak sensible to me?

HIGGINS. Come back to business. How much do you propose to pay me for the lessons?

LIZA. Oh, I know what's right. A lady friend of mine gets French lessons for eighteenpence an hour from a real French gentleman. Well, you wouldn't have the face to ask me the same for teaching me my own language as you would for French; so I won't give more than a shilling. Take it or leave it.

HIGGINS (*walking up and down the room, rattling his keys and his cash in his pockets*). You know, Pickering, if you consider a shilling, not as a simple shilling, but as a percentage of this girl's income, it works out as fully equivalent to sixty or seventy guineas from a millionaire.

PICKERING. How so?

HIGGINS. Figure it out. A millionaire has about £150 a day. She earns about half-a-crown.

LIZA (*haughtily*). Who told you I only —

HIGGINS (*continuing*). She offers me two-fifths of her day's income for a lesson. Two-fifths of a millionaire's income for a day would be somewhere about £60. It's handsome. By George, it's enormous! It's the biggest offer I ever had.

LIZA (*rising, terrified*). Sixty pounds! What are you talking about? I never offered you sixty pounds. Where would I get —

HIGGINS. Hold your tongue.

LIZA (*weeping*). But I ain't got sixty pounds. Oh —

MRS. PEARCE. Don't cry, you silly girl.

Sit down. Nobody is going to touch your money.

HIGGINS. Somebody is going to touch you, with a broomstick, if you don't stop sniveling. Sit down.

LIZA (*obeying slowly*). Ah-ah-ah-ow-oo-o! One would think you was my father.

HIGGINS. If I decide to teach you, I'll be worse than two fathers to you. Here! (*He offers her his silk handkerchief.*)

LIZA. What's this for?

HIGGINS. To wipe your eyes. To wipe any part of your face that feels moist. Remember: that's your handkerchief; and that's your sleeve. Don't mistake the one for the other if you wish to become a lady in a shop.

[LIZA, *utterly bewildered, stares helplessly at him.*]

MRS. PEARCE. It's no use talking to her like that, Mr. Higgins. She doesn't understand you. Besides, you're quite wrong. She doesn't do it that way at all. (*She takes the handkerchief.*)

LIZA (*snatching it*). Here! You give me that handkerchief. He give it to me, not to you.

PICKERING (*laughing*). He did. I think it must be regarded as her property, Mrs. Pearce.

MRS. PEARCE (*resigning herself*). Serve you right, Mr. Higgins.

PICKERING. Higgins, I'm interested. What about the ambassador's garden party? I'll say you're the greatest teacher alive if you make that good. I'll bet you all the expense of the experiment you can't do it. And I'll pay for the lessons.

LIZA. Oh, you are real good. Thank you, Captain.

HIGGINS (*tempted, looking at her*). It's almost irresistible. She's so deliciously low — so horribly dirty —

LIZA (*protesting extremely*). Ah-ah-ah-ah-ow-ow-oo-oo!!! I ain't dirty: I washed my face and hands afore I come, I did.

PICKERING. You're certainly not going to turn her head with flattery, Higgins.

MRS. PEARCE (*uneasy*). Oh, don't say that, sir. There's more ways than one of turning a girl's head; and nobody can do it better than Mr. Higgins, though he may not always mean it. I do hope, sir, you won't encourage him to do anything foolish.

HIGGINS (*becoming excited as the idea grows on him*). What is life but a series of inspired follies? The difficulty is to find them to do. Never lose a chance. It doesn't come every day. I shall make a duchess of this draggle-tailed guttersnipe.

LIZA (*strongly deprecating this view of her*). Ah-ah-ah-ow-ow-oo!

HIGGINS (*carried away*). Yes, in six months — in three if she has a good ear and a quick tongue — I'll take her anywhere and pass her off as anything. We'll start today! now! this moment! Take her away and clean her, Mrs. Pearce. Monkey Brand, if it won't come off any other way. Is there a good fire in the kitchen?

MRS. PEARCE (*protesting*). Yes, but —

HIGGINS (*storming on*). Take all her clothes off and burn them. Ring up Whiteley or somebody for new ones. Wrap her up in brown paper 'til they come.

LIZA. You're no gentleman, you're not, to talk of such things. I'm a good girl, I am; and I know what the like of you are, I do.

HIGGINS. We want none of your Lisson Grove prudery [1] here, young woman. You've got to learn to behave like a duchess. Take her away, Mrs. Pearce. If she gives you any trouble, wallop her.

LIZA (*springing up and running between* PICKERING *and* MRS. PEARCE *for protection*). No! I'll call the police, I will.

MRS. PEARCE. But I've no place to put her.

HIGGINS. Put her in the dustbin.

LIZA. Ah-ah-ah-ow-ow-oo!

[1] *prudery* (prōōd'ĕr·ĭ): excessive modesty in speech, behavior, or dress.

PICKERING. Oh come, Higgins! Be reasonable.

MRS. PEARCE (*resolutely*). You *must* be reasonable, Mr. Higgins. Really you must. You can't walk over everybody like this.

[HIGGINS, *thus scolded, subsides. The hurricane is succeeded by a zephyr of amiable surprise.*]

HIGGINS (*with professional exquisiteness of modulation*). *I* walk over everybody! My dear Mrs. Pearce, my dear Pickering, I never had the slightest intention of walking over anyone. All I propose is that we should be kind to this poor girl. We must help her to prepare and fit herself for her new station in life. If I did not express myself clearly it was because I did not wish to hurt her delicacy, or yours.

[LIZA, *reassured, steals back to her chair.*]

MRS. PEARCE (*to* PICKERING). Well, did you ever hear anything like that, sir?

PICKERING (*laughing heartily*). Never, Mrs. Pearce. Never.

HIGGINS (*patiently*). What's the matter?

MRS. PEARCE. Well, the matter is, sir, that you can't take a girl up like that as if you were picking up a pebble on the beach.

HIGGINS. Why not?

MRS. PEARCE. Why not! But you don't know anything about her. What about her parents? She may be married.

LIZA. Garn!

HIGGINS. There! As the girl very properly says, Garn! Married indeed! Don't you know that a woman of that class looks a worn-out drudge of fifty a year after she's married?

LIZA. Who'd marry me?

HIGGINS (*suddenly resorting to the most thrillingly beautiful low tones in his best elocutionary* [1] *style*). By

[1] *elocutionary* (ĕl′ō·kū′shŭn·ẽr·ĭ): pertaining to the art of public speaking.

George, Eliza, the streets will be strewn with the bodies of men shooting themselves for your sake before I've done with you.

MRS. PEARCE. Nonsense, sir. You mustn't talk like that to her.

LIZA (*rising and squaring herself determinedly*). I'm going away. He's off his chump, he is. I don't want no balmies teaching me.

HIGGINS (*wounded in his tenderest point by her insensibility to his elocution*). Oh, indeed! I'm mad, am I? Very well, Mrs. Pearce, you needn't order the new clothes for her. Throw her out.

LIZA (*whimpering*). Nah-ow. You got no right to touch me.

MRS. PEARCE. You see now what comes of being saucy. (*Indicating the door*) This way, please.

LIZA (*almost in tears*). I didn't want no clothes. I wouldn't have taken them. (*She throws away the handkerchief.*) I can buy my own clothes.

HIGGINS (*deftly retrieving the handkerchief and intercepting her on her reluctant way to the door*). You're an ungrateful wicked girl. This is my return for offering to take you out of the gutter and dress you beautifully and make a lady of you.

MRS. PEARCE. Stop, Mr. Higgins. I won't allow it. It's you that are wicked. Go home to your parents, girl; and tell them to take better care of you.

LIZA. I ain't got no parents. They told me I was big enough to earn my own living and turned me out.

MRS. PEARCE. Where's your mother?

LIZA. I ain't got no mother. Her that turned me out was my sixth stepmother. But I done without them. And I'm a good girl, I am.

HIGGINS. Very well, then, what on earth is all this fuss about? The girl doesn't belong to anybody — is no use to anybody but me. (*He goes to* MRS. PEARCE *and begins coaxing.*) You can adopt her, Mrs. Pearce. I'm sure a daughter would be a great amusement to you. Now don't make any more fuss. Take her downstairs, and —

MRS. PEARCE. But what's to become of her? Is she to be paid anything? Do be sensible, sir.

HIGGINS. Oh, pay her whatever is necessary. Put it down in the housekeeping book. (*Impatiently*) What on earth will she want with money? She'll have her food and her clothes. She'll only drink if you give her money.

LIZA (*turning on him*). Oh you *are* a brute. It's a lie! Nobody ever saw the sign of liquor on me. (*She goes back to her chair and plants herself there defiantly.*)

PICKERING (*in good-humored remonstrance*). Does it occur to you, Higgins, that the girl has some feelings?

HIGGINS (*looking critically at her*). Oh no, I don't think so. Not any feelings that we need bother about. (*Cheerily*) Have you, Eliza?

LIZA. I got my feelings same as anyone else.

HIGGINS (*to* PICKERING, *reflectively*). You see the difficulty?

PICKERING. Eh? What difficulty?

HIGGINS. To get her to talk grammar. The mere pronunciation is easy enough.

LIZA. I don't want to talk grammar. I want to talk like a lady.

MRS. PEARCE. Will you please keep to the point, Mr. Higgins? I want to know on what terms the girl is to be here. Is she to have any wages? And what is to become of her when you've finished your teaching? You must look ahead a little.

HIGGINS (*impatiently*). What's to become of her if I leave her in the gutter? Tell me that, Mrs. Pearce.

MRS. PEARCE. That's her own business, not yours, Mr. Higgins.

HIGGINS. Well, when I've done with her, we can throw her back into the gutter; and then it will be her own business again; so that's all right.

LIZA. Oh, you've no feeling heart in you: you don't care for nothing but yourself. (*She rises and takes the floor resolutely.*) Here! I've had enough of this. I'm going (*making for the door*). You ought to be ashamed of yourself, you ought.

HIGGINS (*snatching a chocolate cream from the piano, his eyes suddenly beginning to twinkle with mischief*). Have some chocolates, Eliza.

LIZA (*halting, tempted*). How do I know what might be in them? I've heard of girls being drugged by the like of you.

[HIGGINS *whips out his penknife; cuts a chocolate in two; puts one half into his mouth and bolts it; and offers her the other half.*]

HIGGINS. Pledge of good faith, Eliza. I eat one half; you eat the other. (LIZA *opens her mouth to retort; he pops the half chocolate into it.*) You shall have boxes of them, barrels of them, every day. You shall live on them. Eh?

LIZA (*who has disposed of the chocolate after being nearly choked by it*). I wouldn't have ate it, only I'm too lady-like to take it out of my mouth.

HIGGINS. Listen, Eliza. I think you said you came in a taxi.

LIZA. Well, what if I did? I've as good a right to take a taxi as anyone else.

HIGGINS. You have, Eliza; and in future you shall have as many taxis as you want. You shall go up and down and round the town in a taxi every day. Think of that, Eliza.

MRS. PEARCE. Mr. Higgins, you're tempting the girl. It's not right. She should think of the future.

HIGGINS. At her age! Nonsense! Time enough to think of the future when you haven't any future to think of. No, Eliza. Do as this lady does: think of other people's futures; but never think of your own. Think of chocolates, and taxis, and gold, and diamonds.

LIZA. No, I don't want no gold and no diamonds. I'm a good girl, I am. (*She sits down again, with an attempt at dignity.*)

HIGGINS. You shall remain so, Eliza,

under the care of Mrs. Pearce. And you shall marry an officer in the Guards, with a beautiful moustache: the son of a marquis, who will disinherit him for marrying you, but will relent when he sees your beauty and goodness —

PICKERING. Excuse me, Higgins; but I really must interfere. Mrs. Pearce is quite right. If this girl is to put herself in your hands for six months for an experiment in teaching, she must understand thoroughly what she's doing.

HIGGINS. How can she? She's incapable of understanding anything. Besides, do any of us understand what we are doing? If we did, would we ever do it?

PICKERING. Very clever, Higgins; but not sound sense. (*To* ELIZA) Miss Doolittle —

LIZA (*overwhelmed*). Ah-ah-ow-oo!

HIGGINS. There! That's all you'll get out of Eliza. Ah-ah-ow-oo! No use explaining. As a military man you ought to know that. Give her her orders; that's what she wants. Eliza, you are to live here for the next six months, learning how to speak beautifully, like a lady in a florist's shop. If you're good and do whatever you're told, you shall sleep in a proper bedroom, and have lots to eat, and money to buy chocolates and take rides in taxis. If you're naughty and idle you will sleep in the back kitchen among the black beetles, and be walloped by Mrs. Pearce with a broomstick. At the end of six months you shall go to Buckingham Palace in a carriage, beautifully dressed. If the king finds out you're not a lady, you will be taken by the police to the Tower of London, where your head will be cut off as a warning to other presumptuous flower girls. If you are not found out, you shall have a present of seven-and-sixpence to start life with as a lady in a shop. If you refuse this offer you will be a most ungrateful and wicked girl; and the angels will weep for you. (*To* PICKERING) Now are you satisfied, Pickering? (*To* MRS. PEARCE) Can I put it more plainly and fairly, Mrs. Pearce?

MRS. PEARCE (*patiently*). I think you'd better let me speak to the girl properly in private. I don't know that I can take charge of her or consent to the arrangement at all. Of course I know you don't mean her any harm; but when you get what you call interested in people's accents, you never think or care what may happen to them or you. Come with me, Eliza.

HIGGINS. That's all right. Thank you, Mrs. Pearce. Bundle her off to the bathroom.

LIZA (*rising reluctantly and suspiciously*). You're a great bully, you are. I won't stay here if I don't like. I won't let nobody wallop me. I never asked to go to Bucknam Palace, I didn't. I was never in trouble with the police, not me. I'm a good girl —

MRS. PEARCE. Don't answer back, girl. You don't understand the gentleman. Come with me. (*She leads the way to the door, and holds it open for* ELIZA.)

LIZA (*as she goes out*). Well, what I say is right. I won't go near the King, not if I'm going to have my head cut off. If I'd known what I was letting myself in for, I wouldn't have come here. I always been a good girl; and I never offered to say a word to him; and I don't owe him nothing; and I don't care; and I won't be put upon; and I have my feeling the same as anyone else —

[MRS. PEARCE *shuts the door; and* ELIZA'S *plaints* [1] *are no longer audible.* PICKERING *comes from the hearth to the chair and sits astride it with his arms on the back.*]

PICKERING. Excuse the straight question, Higgins. Are you a man of good character where women are concerned?

HIGGINS (*moodily*). Have you ever met a man of good character where women are concerned?

PICKERING. Yes, very frequently.

HIGGINS (*dogmatically, lifting himself on his hands to the level of the piano,*

[1] *plaints:* complaints.

and sitting on it with a bounce). Well, I haven't. I find that the moment I let a woman make friends with me, she becomes jealous, exacting, suspicious, and a damned nuisance. I find that the moment I let myself make friends with a woman, I become selfish and tyrannical. Women upset everything. When you let them into your life, you find that the woman is driving at one thing and you're driving at another.

PICKERING. At what, for example?

HIGGINS (*coming off the piano restlessly*). Oh, Lord knows! I suppose the woman wants to live her own life, and the man wants to live his; and each tries to drag the other on to the wrong track. One wants to go north and the other south; and the result is that both have to go east, though they both hate the east wind. (*He sits down on the bench at the keyboard.*) So here I am, a confirmed old bachelor, and likely to remain so.

PICKERING (*rising and standing over him gravely*). Come, Higgins! You know what I mean. If I'm to be in this business I shall feel responsible for that girl. I hope it's understood that no advantage is to be taken of her position.

HIGGINS. What! That thing! Sacred, I assure you. (*Rising to explain*) You see, she'll be a pupil; and teaching would be impossible unless pupils were sacred. I've taught scores of American millionairesses how to speak English — the best-looking women in the world. I'm seasoned. They might as well be blocks of wood. I might as well be a block of wood. It's —

[MRS. PEARCE *opens the door. She has* ELIZA'S *hat in her hand.* PICKERING *retires to the easy chair at the hearth and sits down.*]

HIGGINS (*eagerly*). Well, Mrs. Pearce, is it all right?

MRS. PEARCE (*at the door*). I just wish to trouble you with a word, if I may, Mr. Higgins.

HIGGINS. Yes, certainly. Come in. (*She comes forward.*) Don't burn that,

Mrs. Pearce. I'll keep it as a curiosity. (*He takes the hat.*)

MRS. PEARCE. Handle it carefully, sir, *please*. I had to promise her not to burn it; but I had better put it in the oven for a while.

HIGGINS (*putting it down hastily on the piano*). Oh! thank you. Well, what have you to say to me?

PICKERING. Am I in the way?

MRS. PEARCE. Not at all, sir. Mr. Higgins, will you please be very particular what you say before the girl?

HIGGINS (*sternly*). Of course. I'm always particular about what I say. Why do you say this to me?

MRS. PEARCE (*unmoved*). No, sir, you're not at all particular when you've mislaid anything or when you get a little impatient. Now it doesn't matter before me. I'm used to it. But you really must not swear before the girl.

HIGGINS (*indignantly*). *I* swear! (*Most emphatically*) I never swear. I detest the habit. What the devil do you mean?

MRS. PEARCE (*stolidly*). That's what I mean, sir. You swear a great deal too much. I don't mind your damning and blasting, and *what* the devil and *where* the devil and *who* the devil —

HIGGINS. Mrs. Pearce, this language from your lips! Really!

MRS. PEARCE (*not to be put off*). — but there is a certain word I must ask you not to use. The girl has just used it herself because the bath was too hot. It begins with the same letter as bath. She knows no better: she learnt it at her mother's knee. But she must not hear it from your lips.

HIGGINS (*loftily*). I cannot charge myself with having ever uttered it, Mrs. Pearce. (*She looks at him steadfastly. He adds, hiding an uneasy conscience with a judicial air*) Except perhaps in a moment of extreme and justifiable excitement.

MRS. PEARCE. Only this morning, sir, you applied it to your boots, to the butter, and to the brown bread.

HIGGINS. Oh, that! Mere alliteration,

Mrs. Pearce, natural to a poet.

MRS. PEARCE. Well, sir, whatever you choose to call it, I beg you not to let the girl hear you repeat it.

HIGGINS. Oh, very well, very well. Is that all?

MRS. PEARCE. No, sir. We shall have to be very particular with this girl as to personal cleanliness.

HIGGINS. Certainly. Quite right. Most important.

MRS. PEARCE. I mean not to be slovenly about her dress or untidy in leaving things about.

HIGGINS (*going to her solemnly*). Just so. I intended to call your attention to that. (*He passes on to* PICKERING, *who is enjoying the conversation immensely*). It is these little things that matter, Pickering. Take care of the pence and the pounds will take care of themselves is as true of personal habits as of money. (*He comes to anchor on the hearthrug, with the air of a man in an unassailable position.*)

MRS. PEARCE. Yes, sir. Then might I ask you not to come down to breakfast in your dressing-gown, or at any rate not to use it as a napkin to the extent you do, sir. And if you would be so good as not to eat everything off the same plate, and to remember not to put the porridge saucepan out of your hand on the clean tablecloth, it would be a better example to the girl. You know you nearly choked yourself with a fish-bone in the jam only last week.

HIGGINS (*routed from the hearthrug and drifting back to the piano*). I may do these things sometimes in absence of mind; but surely I don't do them habitually. (*Angrily*) By the way, my dressing-gown smells most damnably of benzine.

MRS. PEARCE. No doubt it does, Mr. Higgins. But if you *will* wipe your fingers —

HIGGINS (*yelling*). Oh very well, very well! I'll wipe them in my hair in future.

MRS. PEARCE. I hope you're not offended, Mr. Higgins.

HIGGINS (*shocked at finding himself thought capable of an unamiable sentiment*). Not at all, not at all. You're quite right, Mrs. Pearce. I shall be particularly careful before the girl. Is that all?

MRS. PEARCE. No, sir. Might she use some of those Japanese dresses you brought from abroad? I really can't put her back into her old things.

HIGGINS. Certainly. Anything you like. Is *that* all?

MRS. PEARCE. Thank you, sir. That's all. (*She goes out.*)

HIGGINS. You know, Pickering, that woman has the most extraordinary ideas about me. Here I am, a shy, diffident sort of man. I've never been able to feel really grown-up and tremendous, like other chaps. And yet she's firmly persuaded that I'm an arbitrary overbearing bossing kind of person. I can't account for it.

[MRS. PEARCE *returns.*]

MRS. PEARCE. If you please, sir, the trouble's beginning already. There's a dustman [1] downstairs, Alfred Doolittle, wants to see you. He says you have his daughter here.

PICKERING (*rising*). Phew! I say! (*He retreats to the hearthrug.*)

HIGGINS (*promptly*). Send the blackguard [2] up.

MRS. PEARCE. Oh, very well, sir. (*She goes out.*)

PICKERING. He may not be a blackguard, Higgins.

HIGGINS. Nonsense. Of course he's a blackguard.

PICKERING. Whether he is or not, I'm afraid we shall have some trouble with him.

HIGGINS (*confidently*). Oh, no. I think not. If there's any trouble he shall have it with me, not I with him. And we are sure to get something interesting out of him.

[1] *dustman:* a garbage collector. [2] *blackguard* (blăg′ärd): a scoundrel.

PICKERING. About the girl?

HIGGINS. No. I mean his dialect.

PICKERING. Oh!

MRS. PEARCE (*at the door*). Doolittle, sir. (*She admits* DOOLITTLE *and retires.*)

[ALFRED DOOLITTLE *is an elderly but vigorous dustman, clad in the costume of his profession, including a hat with a back brim covering his neck and shoulders. He has well-marked and rather interesting features, and seems equally free from fear and conscience. He has a remarkably expressive voice, the result of a habit of giving vent to his feelings without reserve. His present pose is that of wounded honor and stern resolution.*]

DOOLITTLE (*at the door, uncertain which of the two gentlemen is his man*). Professor Higgins?

HIGGINS. Here. Good morning. Sit down.

DOOLITTLE. Morning, Governor. (*He sits down magisterially.*) I come about a very serious matter, Governor.

HIGGINS (*to* PICKERING). Brought up in Hounslow. Mother Welsh, I should think. (DOOLITTLE *opens his mouth, amazed.* HIGGINS *continues*) What do you want, Doolittle?

DOOLITTLE (*menacingly*). I want my daughter, that's what I want. See?

HIGGINS. Of course you do. You're her father, aren't you? You don't suppose anyone else wants her, do you? I'm glad to see you have some spark of family feeling left. She's upstairs. Take her away at once.

DOOLITTLE (*rising, fearfully taken aback.*) What!

HIGGINS. Take her away. Do you suppose I'm going to keep your daughter for you?

DOOLITTLE (*remonstrating*). Now, now, look here, Governor. Is this reasonable? Is it fairity to take advantage of a man like this? The girl belongs to me. You got her. Where do I come in? (*He sits down again.*)

HIGGINS. Your daughter had the audacity to come to my house and ask me to teach her how to speak properly so that she could get a place in a flower shop. This gentleman and my housekeeper have been here all the time. (*Bullying him*) How dare you come here and attempt to blackmail me? You sent her here on purpose.

DOOLITTLE (*protesting*). No, Governor.

HIGGINS. You must have. How else could you possibly know that she is here?

DOOLITTLE. Don't take a man up like that, Governor.

HIGGINS. The police shall take you up. This is a plant — a plot to extort money by threats. I shall telephone for the police. (*He goes resolutely to the telephone and opens the directory.*)

DOOLITTLE. Have I asked you for a brass farthing? I leave it to the gentleman here. Have I said a word about money?

HIGGINS (*throwing the book aside and marching down on* DOOLITTLE *with a poser.*) What else did you come for?

DOOLITTLE (*sweetly*). Well, what would a man come for? Be human, Governor.

HIGGINS (*disarmed*). Alfred! Did you put her up to it?

DOOLITTLE. So help me, Governor, I never did. I take my Bible oath I ain't seen the girl these two months past.

HIGGINS. Then how did you know she was here?

DOOLITTLE (*"most musical, most melancholy"*). I'll tell you, Governor, if you'll only let me get a word in. I'm willing to tell you. I'm wanting to tell you. I'm waiting to tell you.

HIGGINS. Pickering, this chap has a certain natural gift of rhetoric. Observe the rhythm of his native woodnotes wild. "I'm willing to tell you; I'm wanting to tell you; I'm waiting to tell you." Sentimental rhetoric! That's the Welsh strain in him. It also accounts for his mendacity and dishonesty.

PICKERING. Oh, *please,* Higgins. I'm west country myself. (*To* DOOLITTLE) How did you know the girl was here if you didn't send her?

DOOLITTLE. It was like this, Governor. The girl took a boy in the taxi to give him a jaunt. Son of her landlady, he is. He hung about on the chance of her giving him another ride home. Well, she sent him back for her luggage when she heard you was willing for her to stop here. I met the boy at the corner of Long Acre and Endell Street.

HIGGINS. Public house. Yes?

DOOLITTLE. The poor man's club, Governor. Why shouldn't I?

PICKERING. Do let him tell his story, Higgins.

DOOLITTLE. He told me what was up. And I ask you, what was my feelings and my duty as a father? I says to the boy, "You bring me the luggage," I says —

PICKERING. Why didn't you go for it yourself?

DOOLITTLE. Landlady wouldn't have trusted me with it, Governor. She's that kind of woman, you know. I had to give the boy a penny afore he trusted me with it, the little swine. I brought it to her just to oblige you like, and make myself agreeable. That's all.

HIGGINS. How much luggage?

DOOLITTLE. Musical instrument, Governor. A few pictures, a trifle of jewelry, and a bird cage. She said she didn't want no clothes. What was I to think from that, Governor? I ask you as a parent what was I to think?

HIGGINS. So you came to rescue her from worse than death, eh?

DOOLITTLE (*appreciatively: relieved at being so well understood*). Just so, Governor. That's right.

PICKERING. But why did you bring her luggage if you intended to take her away?

DOOLITTLE. Have I said a word about taking her away? Have I now?

HIGGINS (*determinedly.*) You're go-

ing to take her away, double quick. (*He crosses to the hearth and rings the bell.*)

DOOLITTLE (*rising*). No, Governor. Don't say that. I'm not the man to stand in my girl's light. Here's a career opening for her, as you might say; and —

[MRS. PEARCE *opens the door and awaits orders.*]

HIGGINS. Mrs. Pearce, this is Eliza's father. He has come to take her away. Give her to him. (*He goes back to the piano, with an air of washing his hands of the whole affair.*)

DOOLITTLE. No. This is a misunderstanding. Listen here —

MRS. PEARCE. He can't take her away, Mr. Higgins. How can he? You told me to burn her clothes.

DOOLITTLE. That's right. I can't carry the girl through the streets like a blooming monkey, can I? I put it to you.

HIGGINS. You have put it to me that you want your daughter. Take your daughter. If she has no clothes, go out and buy her some.

DOOLITTLE (*desperate*). Where's the clothes she come in? Did I burn them or did your missus here?

MRS. PEARCE. I am the housekeeper, if you please. I have sent for some clothes for your girl. When they come you can take her away. You can wait in the kitchen. This way, please.

[DOOLITTLE, *much troubled, accompanies her to the door; then hesitates; finally turns confidentially to* HIGGINS.]

DOOLITTLE. Listen here, Governor. You and me is men of the world, ain't we?

HIGGINS. Oh! Men of the world, are we? You'd better go, Mrs. Pearce.

MRS. PEARCE. I think so, indeed, sir. (*She goes, with dignity.*)

PICKERING. The floor is yours, Mr. Doolittle.

DOOLITTLE (*to* PICKERING). I thank you, Governor. (*To* HIGGINS, *who takes refuge on the piano bench, a little over-*

*whelmed by the proximity of his visitor;
for* DOOLITTLE *has a professional flavor
of dust about him*) Well, the truth is,
I've taken a sort of fancy to you, Governor; and if you want the girl, I'm not
so set on having her back home again
but what I might be open to an arrangement. Regarded in the light of a young
woman, she's a fine handsome girl. As
a daughter she's not worth her keep; and
so I tell you straight. All I ask is my
rights as a father; and you're the last
man alive to expect me to let her go for
nothing; for I can see you're one of the
straight sort, Governor. Well, what's a
five-pound note to you? And what's
Eliza to me? (*He returns to his chair
and sits down judicially.*)

PICKERING. I think you ought to know,
Doolittle, that Mr. Higgins' intentions
are entirely honorable.

DOOLITTLE. Course they are, Governor. If I thought they wasn't, I'd ask
fifty.

HIGGINS (*revolted*). Do you mean to
say, you callous rascal, that you would
sell your daughter for £ 50?

DOOLITTLE. Not in a general way I
wouldn't; but to oblige a gentleman like
you I'd do a good deal, I do assure you.

PICKERING. Have you no morals,
man?

DOOLITTLE (*unabashed*). Can't afford
them, Governor. Neither could you if
you was as poor as me. Not that I mean
any harm, you know. But if Liza is going
to have a bit out of this, why not me
too?

HIGGINS (*troubled*). I don't know
what to do, Pickering. There can be no
question that as a matter of morals it's a
positive crime to give this chap a farthing. And yet I feel a sort of rough
justice in his claim.

DOOLITTLE. That's it, Governor.
That's all I say. A father's heart, as it
were.

PICKERING. Well, I know the feeling;
but really it seems hardly right —

DOOLITTLE. Don't say that, Governor.
Don't look at it that way. What am I,

Governors both? I ask you, what am I?
I'm one of the undeserving poor, that's
what I am. Think of what that means
to a man. It means that he's up agen
middle class morality all the time. If
there's anything going, and I put in for
a bit of it, it's always the same story:
"You're undeserving; so you can't have
it." But my needs is as great as the most
deserving widow's that ever got money
out of six different charities in one week
for the death of the same husband. I
don't need less than a deserving man;
I need more. I don't eat less hearty than
him; and I drink a lot more. I want a
bit of amusement, cause I'm a thinking
man. I want cheerfulness and a song and
a band when I feel low. Well, they
charge me just the same for everything
as they charge the deserving. What is
middle class morality? Just an excuse for
never giving me anything. Therefore, I
ask you, as two gentlemen, not to play
that game on me. I'm playing straight
with you. I ain't pretending to be deserving. I'm undeserving; and I mean to
go on being undeserving. I like it; and
that's the truth. Will you take advantage
of a man's nature to do him out of the
price of his own daughter what he's
brought up and fed and clothed by the
sweat of his brow until she's growed big
enough to be interesting to you two gentlemen? Is five pounds unreasonable? I
put it to you; and I leave it to you.

HIGGINS (*rising, and going over to*
PICKERING). Pickering, if we were to
take this man in hand for three months,
he could choose between a seat in the
Cabinet and a popular pulpit in Wales.

PICKERING. What do you say to that,
Doolittle?

DOOLITTLE. Not me, Governor, thank
you kindly. I've heard all the preachers
and all the prime ministers — for I'm
a thinking man and game for politics or
religion or social reform same as all the
other amusements — and I tell you it's
a dog's life any way you look at it. Undeserving poverty is my line. Taking
one station in society with another, it's

— it's — well, it's the only one that has any ginger in it, to my taste.

HIGGINS. I suppose we must give him a fiver.

PICKERING. He'll make a bad use of it, I'm afraid.

DOOLITTLE. Not me, Governor, so help me I won't. Don't you be afraid that I'll save it and spare it and live idle on it. There won't be a penny of it left by Monday. I'll have to go to work same as if I'd never had it. It won't pauperize me, you bet. Just one good spree for myself and the missus, giving pleasure to ourselves and employment to others, and satisfaction to you to think it's not been throwed away. You couldn't spend it better.

HIGGINS (*taking out his pocket book and coming between* DOOLITTLE *and the piano*). This is irresistible. Let's give him ten. (*He offers two notes to the dustman.*)

DOOLITTLE. No, Governor. She wouldn't have the heart to spend ten; and perhaps I shouldn't neither. Ten pounds is a lot of money. It makes a man feel prudent like; and then good-by to happiness. You give me what I ask you, Governor. Not a penny more, and not a penny less.

PICKERING. Why don't you marry that missus of yours? I rather draw the line at encouraging that sort of immorality.

DOOLITTLE. Tell her so, Governor: tell her so. I'm willing. It's me that suffers by it. I've no hold on her. I got to be agreeable to her. I got to give her presents. I got to buy her clothes something sinful. I'm a slave to that woman, Governor, just because I'm not her lawful husband. And she knows it too. Catch her marrying me! Take my advice, Governor: marry Eliza while she's young and don't know no better. If you don't you'll be sorry for it after. If you do, *she'll* be sorry for it after; but better her than you, because you're a man, and she's only a woman and don't know how to be happy anyhow.

HIGGINS. Pickering, if we listen to this man another minute, we shall have no convictions left. (*To* DOOLITTLE) Five pounds I think you said.

DOOLITTLE. Thank you kindly, Governor.

HIGGINS. You're sure you won't take ten?

DOOLITTLE. Not now. Another time, Governor.

HIGGINS (*handing him a five-pound note*). Here you are.

DOOLITTLE. Thank you, Governor. Good morning. (*He hurries to the door, anxious to get away with his booty. When he opens it he is confronted with a dainty and exquisitely clean young Japanese lady in a simple blue cotton kimono printed cunningly with small white jasmine blossoms.* MRS. PEARCE *is with her. He gets out of her way deferentially* [1] *and apologizes.*) Beg pardon, miss.

THE JAPANESE LADY. Garn! Don't you know your own daughter?

DOOLITTLE	exclaiming	Bly me! it's Eliza!
HIGGINS	simul-	What's that!
PICKERING	taneously	This!
		By Jove!

LIZA. Don't I look silly?

HIGGINS. Silly?

MRS. PEARCE (*at the door*). Now, Mr. Higgins, please don't say anything to make the girl conceited about herself.

HIGGINS (*conscientiously*). Oh! Quite right, Mrs. Pearce. (*To* ELIZA) Yes, damned silly.

MRS. PEARCE. Please, sir.

HIGGINS (*correcting himself*). I mean extremely silly.

LIZA. I should look all right with my hat on. (*She takes up her hat; puts it on; and walks across the room to the fireplace with a fashionable air.*)

HIGGINS. A new fashion, by George! And it ought to look horrible!

DOOLITTLE (*with fatherly pride*). Well, I never thought she'd clean up as good looking as that, Governor. She's

---

[1] *deferentially* (dĕf'ẽr·ĕn'shăl·lĭ): respectfully.

a credit to me, ain't she?

LIZA. I tell you, it's easy to clean up here. Hot and cold water on tap, just as much as you like, there is. Woolly towels, there is; and a towel horse so hot, it burns your fingers. Soft brushes to scrub yourself, and a wooden bowl of soap smelling like primroses. Now I know why ladies is so clean. Washing's a treat for them. Wish they saw what it is for the like of me!

HIGGINS. I'm glad the bathroom met with your approval.

LIZA. It didn't. Not all of it, and I don't care who hears me say it. Mrs. Pearce knows.

HIGGINS. What was wrong, Mrs. Pearce?

MRS. PEARCE (*blandly*). Oh, nothing, sir. It doesn't matter.

LIZA. I had a good mind to break it. I didn't know which way to look. But I hung a towel over it, I did.

HIGGINS. Over what?

MRS. PEARCE. Over the looking glass, sir.

HIGGINS. Doolittle, you have brought your daughter up too strictly.

DOOLITTLE. Me! I never brought her up at all, except to give her a lick of a strap now and again. Don't put it on me, Governor. She ain't accustomed to it, you see. That's all. But she'll soon pick up your free-and-easy ways.

LIZA. I'm a good girl, I am; and I won't pick up no free-and-easy ways.

HIGGINS. Eliza, if you say again that you're a good girl, your father shall take you home.

LIZA. Not him. You don't know my father. All he come here for was to touch you for some money to get drunk on.

DOOLITTLE. Well, what else would I want money for? To put into the plate in church, I suppose. (*She puts out her tongue at him. He is so incensed by this that* PICKERING *presently finds it necessary to step between them.*) Don't you give me none of your lip; and don't let me hear you giving this gentleman any

of it neither, or you'll hear from me about it. See?

HIGGINS. Have you any further advice to give her before you go, Doolittle? Your blessing, for instance.

DOOLITTLE. No, Governor. I ain't such a mug as to put up my children to all I know myself. Hard enough to hold them in without that. If you want Eliza's mind improved, Governor, you do it yourself with a strap. So long, gentlemen. (*He turns to go.*)

HIGGINS (*impressively*). Stop. You'll come regularly to see your daughter. It's your duty, you know. My brother is a clergyman, and he could help you in your talks with her.

DOOLITTLE (*evasively*). Certainly. I'll come, Governor. Not just this week, because I have a job at a distance. But later on you may depend on me. Afternoon, gentlemen. Afternoon, ma'am. (*He takes off his hat to* MRS. PEARCE, *who disdains the salutation and goes out. He winks at* HIGGINS, *thinking him probably a fellow-sufferer from* MRS. PEARCE'S *difficult disposition, and follows her.*)

LIZA. Don't you believe the old liar. He'd as soon you set a bulldog on him as a clergyman. You won't see him again in a hurry.

HIGGINS. I don't want to, Eliza. Do you?

LIZA. Not me. I don't want never to see him again, I don't. He's a disgrace to me, he is, collecting dust, instead of working at his trade.

PICKERING. What is his trade, Eliza?

LIZA. Taking money out of other people's pockets into his own. His proper trade's a navvy; [1] and he works at it sometimes too — for exercise — and earns good money at it. Ain't you going to call me Miss Doolittle any more?

PICKERING. I beg your pardon, Miss Doolittle. It was a slip of the tongue.

LIZA. Oh, I don't mind; only it sounded so genteel. I *should* just like to take a taxi to the corner of Tottenham Court

---

[1] *navvy* (năv′ĭ): an unskilled or common laborer.

Road and get out there and tell it to wait for me, just to put the girls in their place a bit. I wouldn't speak to them, you know.

PICKERING. Better wait 'til we get you something really fashionable.

HIGGINS. Besides, you shouldn't cut your old friends now that you have risen in the world. That's what we call snobbery.

LIZA. You don't call the like of them my friends now, I should hope. They've took it out of me often enough with their ridicule when they had the chance; and now I mean to get a bit of my own back. But if I'm to have fashionable clothes, I'll wait. I should like to have some. Mrs. Pearce says you're going to give me some to wear in bed at night different to what I wear in the daytime; but it do seem a waste of money when you could get something to show. Besides, I never could fancy changing into cold things on a winter night.

MRS. PEARCE (*coming back*). Now, Eliza. The new things have come for you to try on.

LIZA. Ah-ow-oo-oooh! (*She rushes out.*)

MRS. PEARCE (*following her.*) Oh, don't rush about like that, girl. (*She shuts the door behind her.*)

HIGGINS. Pickering, we have taken on a stiff job.

PICKERING (*with conviction*). Higgins, we have.

UNDERSTANDING THE CHARACTERS

1. What reason does Eliza give for wanting lessons in speaking? How had she figured the amount she would pay for the instruction? Why does she want Higgins to know that she came in a taxi?

2. Why is Higgins willing to take her? What does Pickering promise to do? How does each man regard Eliza? Find passages that show the differences in their personalities.

3. How does Mrs. Pearce react to Eliza? On what points are Pickering and Mrs. Pearce in agreement? Does their point of view or Higgins' seem more natural to you? What does Higgins mean when he says, "Take care of the pence and the pounds will take care of themselves"?

4. Why does Alfred Doolittle come to see Higgins? How does he feel toward his daughter? What do you learn about Eliza from this visit? Is Doolittle a happy person? Why does he accept five pounds instead of the ten pounds that is offered?

5. Why is Eliza always saying, "I'm a good girl, I am"? Does she have any other virtue to which she can point at this time? Are there any indications that she may have potentialities for growth or change?

ACT III

It is MRS. HIGGINS' *at-home day. Nobody has yet arrived. Her drawing room, in a flat on Chelsea Embankment,*[1] *has three windows looking on the river; and the ceiling is not so lofty as it would be in an older house of the same pretension. The windows are open, giving access to a balcony with flowers in pots. If you stand with your face to the windows, you have the fireplace on your left and the door in the right-hand wall close to the corner nearest the windows.*

MRS. HIGGINS *was brought up on Morris and Burne-Jones;*[2] *and her room, which is very unlike her son's room in Wimpole Street, is not crowded with furniture and little tables and knickknacks. In the middle of the room there is a big ottoman; and this, with the carpet, the Morris wallpapers, and the Morris chintz window curtains and brocade covers of the ottoman and its cushions,*

[1] *Chelsea* (chĕl'sĭ) *Embankment:* a metropolitan borough on the north bank of the Thames.

[2] *Morris and Burne-Jones:* two members of a flourishing company that undertook church decoration, carving, stained glass, metalwork, paper-hangings, chintzes, and carpets.

supply all the ornament, and are much too handsome to be hidden by odds and ends of useless things. A few good oil paintings from the exhibitions in the Grosvenor Gallery thirty years ago (the Burne-Jones, not the Whistler side of them) are on the walls. The only landscape is a Cecil Lawson on the scale of a Rubens. There is a portrait of MRS. HIGGINS *as she was when she defied fashion in her youth in one of the beautiful Rossettian [1] costumes which, when caricatured by people who did not understand, led to the absurdities of popular estheticism in the eighteen-seventies.*

In the corner diagonally opposite the door MRS. HIGGINS, *now over sixty and long past taking the trouble to dress out of the fashion, sits writing at an elegantly simple writing table with a bell button within reach of her hand. There is a Chippendale [2] chair further back in the room between her and the window nearest her side. At the other side of the room, further forward, is an Elizabethan chair roughly carved in the taste of Inigo Jones.[3] On the same side a piano in a decorated case. The corner between the fireplace and the window is occupied by a divan cushioned in Morris chintz.*

It is between four and five in the afternoon.

The door is opened violently; and HIGGINS *enters with his hat on.*

MRS. HIGGINS (*dismayed*). Henry (*scolding him*)! What are you doing here today? It is my at-home day. You promised not to come. (*As he bends to kiss her, she takes his hat off and presents it to him.*)

HIGGINS. Oh bother! (*He throws the hat down on the table.*)

MRS HIGGINS. Go home at once.

HIGGINS (*kissing her*). I know, Mother. I came on purpose.

MRS. HIGGINS. But you mustn't. I'm

serious, Henry. You offend all my friends. They stop coming whenever they meet you.

HIGGINS. Nonsense! I know I have no small talk, but people don't mind. (*He sits on the settee.*)

MRS. HIGGINS. Oh! don't they? Small talk indeed! What about your large talk? Really, dear, you mustn't stay.

HIGGINS. I must. I've a job for you. A phonetic job.

MRS. HIGGINS. No use, dear. I'm sorry, but I can't get round your vowels; and though I like to get pretty postcards in your patent shorthand, I always have to read the copies in ordinary writing you so thoughtfully send me.

HIGGINS. Well, this isn't a phonetic job.

MRS. HIGGINS. You said it was.

HIGGINS. Not your part of it. I've picked up a girl.

MRS. HIGGINS. Does that mean that some girl has picked you up?

HIGGINS. Not at all. I don't mean a love affair.

MRS. HIGGINS. What a pity!

HIGGINS. Why?

MRS. HIGGINS. Well, you never fall in love with anyone under forty-five. When will you discover that there are some rather nice-looking young women about?

HIGGINS. Oh, I can't be bothered with young women. My idea of a lovable woman is something as like you as possible. I shall never get into the way of seriously liking young women. Some habits lie too deep to be changed. (*Rising abruptly and walking about, jingling his money and his keys in his trouser pockets*) Besides, they're all idiots.

MRS. HIGGINS. Do you know what you would do if you really loved me, Henry?

HIGGINS. Oh bother! What? Marry, I suppose?

MRS. HIGGINS. No. Stop fidgeting and take your hands out of your pockets. (*With a gesture of despair, he obeys and sits down again.*) That's a good boy. Now tell me about the girl.

HIGGINS. She's coming to see you.

---

[1] *Rossettian:* in the simple, flowing style of dress found in Dante Gabriel Rossetti's paintings. [2] *Chippendale:* a famous eighteenth-century cabinet maker. [3] *Inigo Jones:* a seventeenth-century architect and designer.

MRS. HIGGINS. I don't remember asking her.

HIGGINS. You didn't. *I* asked her. If you'd known her you wouldn't have asked her.

MRS. HIGGINS. Indeed! Why?

HIGGINS. Well, it's like this. She's a common flower girl. I picked her off the curbstone.

MRS. HIGGINS. And invited her to my at-home!

HIGGINS (*rising and coming to her to coax her*). Oh, that'll be all right. I've taught her to speak properly, and she has strict orders as to her behavior. She's to keep to two subjects: the weather and everybody's health — Fine day and How do you do, you know — and not to let herself go on things in general. That will be safe.

MRS. HIGGINS. Safe! To talk about our health! About our insides! Perhaps about our outsides! How could you be so silly, Henry?

HIGGINS (*impatiently*). Well, she must talk about something. (*He controls himself and sits down again.*) Oh, she'll be all right: don't you fuss. Pickering is in it with me. I've a sort of bet on that I'll pass her off as a duchess in six months. I started on her some months ago; and she's getting on like a house on fire. I shall win my bet. She has a quick ear, and she's been easier to teach than my middle-class pupils because she's had to learn a complete new language. She talks English almost as you talk French.

MRS. HIGGINS. That's satisfactory, at all events.

HIGGINS. Well, it is and it isn't.

MRS. HIGGINS. What does that mean?

HIGGINS. You see, I've got her pronunciation all right; but you have to consider not only *how* a girl pronounces, but *what* she pronounces; and that's where —

[*They are interrupted by the* PARLOR MAID, *announcing guests.*]

THE PARLOR MAID. Mrs. and Miss Eynsford Hill. (*She withdraws.*)

HIGGINS. Oh Lord! (*He rises; snatches his hat from the table; and makes for the door; but before he reaches it his mother introduces him.*)

[MRS. *and* MISS EYNSFORD HILL *are the mother and daughter who sheltered from the rain in Covent Garden. The mother is well-bred, quiet, and has the habitual anxiety of straitened means. The daughter has acquired a gay air of being very much at home in society: the bravado of genteel poverty.*]

MRS EYNSFORD HILL (*to* MRS. HIGGINS). How do you do? (*They shake hands.*)

MISS EYNSFORD HILL. How d'you do? (*She shakes.*)

MRS. HIGGINS (*introducing*). My son Henry.

MRS. EYNSFORD HILL. Your celebrated son! I have so longed to meet you, Professor Higgins.

HIGGINS (*glumly, making no movement in her direction*). Delighted. (*He backs against the piano and bows brusquely.*)

MISS EYNSFORD HILL (*going to him with confident familiarity*). How do you do?

HIGGINS (*staring at her*). I've seen you before somewhere. I haven't the ghost of a notion where; but I've heard your voice. (*Drearily*) It doesn't matter. You'd better sit down.

MRS. HIGGINS. I'm sorry to say that my celebrated son has no manners. You mustn't mind him.

MISS EYNSFORD HILL (*gaily*). I don't. (*She sits in the Elizabethan chair.*)

MRS. EYNSFORD HILL (*a little bewildered*). Not at all. (*She sits on the ottoman between her daughter and* MRS. HIGGINS, *who has turned her chair away from the writing table.*)

HIGGINS. Oh, have I been rude? I didn't mean to be.

[*He goes to the central window, through which, with his back to the company, he contemplates the river and the flowers in Battersea Park on the opposite bank as if they were a frozen desert.*]

[*The* PARLOR MAID *returns, ushering in* PICKERING.]

THE PARLOR MAID. Colonel Pickering. (*She withdraws.*)

PICKERING. How do you do, Mrs. Higgins?

MRS. HIGGINS. So glad you've come. Do you know Mrs. Eynsford Hill — Miss Eynsford Hill? (*Exchange of bows. The* COLONEL *brings the Chippendale chair a little forward between* MRS. HILL *and* MRS. HIGGINS, *and sits down.*)

PICKERING. Has Henry told you what we've come for?

HIGGINS (*over his shoulder*). We were interrupted, damn it!

MRS. HIGGINS. Oh Henry, Henry, really!

MRS. EYNSFORD HILL (*half rising*). Are we in the way?

MRS. HIGGINS (*rising and making her sit down again*). No, no. You couldn't have come more fortunately. We want you to meet a friend of ours.

HIGGINS (*turning hopefully*). Yes, by George! We want two or three people. You'll do as well as anybody else.

[*The* PARLOR MAID *returns, ushering* FREDDY.]

THE PARLOR MAID. Mr. Eynsford Hill.

HIGGINS (*almost audibly, past endurance*). God of Heaven! another of them.

FREDDY (*shaking hands with* MRS. HIGGINS). Ahdedo?

MRS. HIGGINS. Very good of you to come. (*Introducing*) Colonel Pickering.

FREDDY (*bowing*). Ahdedo?

MRS. HIGGINS. I don't think you know my son, Professor Higgins.

FREDDY (*going to* HIGGINS). Ahdedo?

HIGGINS (*looking at him much as if he were a pickpocket*). I'll take my oath I've met *you* before somewhere. Where was it?

FREDDY. I don't think so.

HIGGINS (*resignedly*). It doesn't matter, anyhow. Sit down.

[*He shakes* FREDDY'S *hand, and almost slings him on to the ottoman with his face to the windows; then comes round to the other side of it.*]

HIGGINS. Well, here we are, anyhow! (*He sits down on the ottoman next to* MRS. EYNSFORD HILL, *on her left.*) And now, what the devil are we going to talk about until Eliza comes?

MRS. HIGGINS. Henry! You are the life and soul of the Royal Society soirées; [1] but really you're rather trying on more commonplace occasions.

HIGGINS. Am I? Very sorry. (*Beaming suddenly*) I suppose I am, you know. (*Uproariously*) Ha, ha!

MISS EYNSFORD HILL (*who considers* HIGGINS *quite eligible matrimonially*). I sympathize. *I* haven't any small talk. If people would only be frank and say what they really think!

HIGGINS (*relapsing into gloom*). Lord forbid!

MRS. EYNSFORD HILL (*taking up her daughter's cue*). But why?

HIGGINS. What they think they ought to think is bad enough, Lord knows; but what they really think would break up the whole show. Do you suppose it would be really agreeable if I were to come out now with what *I* really think?

MISS EYNSFORD HILL (*gaily*). Is it so very cynical?

HIGGINS. Cynical! Who the dickens said it was cynical? I mean it wouldn't be decent.

MRS. EYNSFORD HILL (*seriously*). Oh! I'm sure you don't mean that Mr. Higgins.

HIGGINS. You see, we're all savages, more or less. We're supposed to be civilized and cultured — to know all about poetry and philosophy and art and science, and so on; but how many of us know even the meanings of these names? (*To* MISS HILL) What do *you* know of

---

[1] *soirées* (swä·rāz'): evening parties.

poetry? (*To* MRS. HILL) What do *you* know of science? (*Indicating* FREDDY) What does *he* know of art or science or anything else? What the devil do you imagine I know of philosophy?

MRS. HIGGINS (*warningly*). Or of manners, Henry?

THE PARLOR MAID (*opening the door*). Miss Doolittle. (*She withdraws.*)

HIGGINS (*rising hastily and running to* MRS. HIGGINS). Here she is, Mother. (*He stands on tiptoe and makes signs over his mother's head to* ELIZA *to indicate to her which lady is her hostess.*)

[ELIZA, *who is exquisitely dressed, produces an impression of such remarkable distinction and beauty as she enters that they all rise, quite fluttered. Guided by* HIGGINS' *signals, she comes to* MRS. HIGGINS *with studied grace.*]

LIZA (*speaking with pedantic correctness of pronunciation and great beauty of tone*). How do you do, Mrs. Higgins? (*She gasps slightly in making sure of the H in* HIGGINS, *but is quite successful.*) Mr. Higgins told me I might come.

MRS. HIGGINS (*cordially*). Quite right. I'm very glad indeed to see you.

PICKERING. How do you do, Miss Doolittle?

LIZA (*shaking hands with him*). Colonel Pickering, is it not?

MRS. EYNSFORD HILL. I feel sure we have met before, Miss Doolittle. I remember your eyes.

LIZA. How do you do? (*She sits down on the ottoman gracefully in the place just left vacant by* HIGGINS.)

MRS. EYNSFORD HILL (*introducing*). My daughter Clara.

LIZA. How do you do?

CLARA (*impulsively*). How do you do? (*She sits down on the ottoman beside* ELIZA, *devouring her with her eyes.*)

FREDDY (*coming to their side of the ottoman*). I've certainly had the pleasure.

MRS. EYNSFORD HILL (*introducing*). My son Freddy.

LIZA. How do you do?

[FREDDY *bows and sits down in the Elizabethan chair, infatuated.*]

HIGGINS (*suddenly*). By George, yes! It all comes back to me! (*They stare at him.*) Covent Garden! (*Lamentably*) What a damned thing!

MRS. HIGGINS. Henry, please! (*He is about to sit on the edge of the table*) Don't sit on my writing table; you'll break it.

HIGGINS (*sulkily*). Sorry.

[*He goes to the divan, stumbling into the fender and over the fire irons on his way; extricating himself with muttered imprecations* [1] *and finishing his disastrous journey by throwing himself so impatiently on the divan that he almost breaks it.* MRS. HIGGINS *looks at him, but controls herself and says nothing.*]

[*A long and painful pause ensues.*]

MRS. HIGGINS (*at last, conversationally*). Will it rain, do you think?

LIZA. The shallow depression in the west of these islands is likely to move slowly in an easterly direction. There are no indications of any great change in the barometrical situation.

FREDDY. Ha! ha! how awfully funny!

LIZA. What is wrong with that, young man? I bet I got it right.

FREDDY. Killing!

MRS. EYNSFORD HILL. I'm sure I hope it won't turn cold. There's so much influenza about. It runs right through our whole family regularly every spring.

LIZA (*darkly*). My aunt died of influenza, so they said.

MRS. EYNSFORD HILL (*clicks her tongue sympathetically*)!!!

LIZA (*in the same tragic tone*). But it's my belief they done the old woman in.

MRS. HIGGINS (*puzzled*). Done her in?

LIZA. Y-e-e-es, Lord love you! Why should *she* die of influenza? She come

[1] *imprecations* (ĭm'prĕ·kā'shŭns): curses.

through diphtheria right enough the year before. I saw her with my own eyes. Fairly blue with it, she was. They all thought she was dead; but my father he kept ladling gin down her throat 'til she came to so sudden that she bit the bowl off the spoon.

MRS. EYNSFORD HILL (*startled*). Dear me!

LIZA (*piling up the indictment* [1]). What call would a woman with that strength in her have to die of influenza? What become of her new straw hat that should have come to me? Somebody pinched it; and what I say is, them as pinched it done her in.

MRS. EYNSFORD HILL. What does doing her in mean?

HIGGINS (*hastily*). Oh, that's the new small talk. To do a person in means to kill them.

MRS. EYNSFORD HILL (*to* ELIZA, *horrified*). You surely don't believe that your aunt was killed?

LIZA. Do I not! Them she lived with would have killed her for a hatpin, let alone a hat.

MRS. EYNSFORD HILL. But it can't have been right for your father to pour spirits down her throat like that. It might have killed her.

LIZA. Not her. Gin was mother's milk to her. Besides, he'd poured so much down his own throat that he knew the good of it.

MRS. EYNSFORD HILL. Do you mean that he drank?

LIZA. Drank! My word! Something chronic.

MRS. EYNSFORD HILL. How dreadful for you!

LIZA. Not a bit. It never did him no harm what I could see. But then he did not keep it up regular. (*Cheerfully*) On the burst, as you might say, from time to time. And always more agreeable when he had a drop in. When he was out of work, my mother used to give him fourpence and tell him to go out and

---

[1] *indictment* (ĭn·dīt'mĕnt): a statement charging someone with an offense.

not come back until he'd drunk himself cheerful and loving-like. There's lots of women has to make their husbands drunk to make them fit to live with. (*Now quite at her ease*) You see, it's like this. If a man has a bit of a conscience, it always takes him when he's sober; and then it makes him low-spirited. A drop of booze just takes that off and makes him happy. (*To* FREDDY, *who is in convulsions of suppressed laughter*) Here! what are you sniggering at?

FREDDY. The new small talk. You do it so awfully well.

LIZA. If I was doing it proper, what was you laughing at? (*To* HIGGINS) Have I said anything I oughtn't?

MRS. HIGGINS (*interposing*). Not at all, Miss Doolittle.

LIZA. Well, that's a mercy, anyhow. (*Expansively*) What I always say is —

HIGGINS (*rising and looking at his watch*). Ahem!

LIZA (*looking round at him; taking the hint; and rising*). Well, I must go. (*They all rise.* FREDDY *goes to the door.*) So pleased to have met you. Good-by. (*She shakes hands with* MRS. HIGGINS.)

MRS. HIGGINS. Good-by.

LIZA. Good-by, Colonel Pickering.

PICKERING. Good-by, Miss Doolittle. (*They shake hands.*)

LIZA (*nodding to the others*). Good-by, all.

FREDDY (*opening the door for her*). Are you walking across the Park, Miss Doolittle? If so —

LIZA. Walk! Not bloody likely. (*Sensation.*) I am going in a taxi. (*She goes out.*)

[PICKERING *gasps and sits down.* FREDDY *goes out on the balcony to catch another glimpse of* ELIZA.]

MRS. EYNSFORD HILL (*suffering from shock*). Well, I really can't get used to the new ways.

CLARA (*throwing herself discontentedly into the Elizabethan chair*). Oh, it's all right, Mamma, quite right. People will think we never go anywhere or see anybody if you are so old-fashioned.

MRS. EYNSFORD HILL. I daresay I am very old-fashioned, but I do hope you won't begin using that expression, Clara. I have got accustomed to hear you talking about men as rotters, and calling everything filthy and beastly, though I do think it horrible and unladylike. But this last is really too much. Don't you think so, Colonel Pickering?

PICKERING. Don't ask me. I've been away in India for several years, and manners have changed so much that I sometimes don't know whether I'm at a respectable dinner table or in a ship's forecastle.

CLARA. It's all a matter of habit. There's no right or wrong in it. Nobody means anything by it. And it's so quaint, and gives such a smart emphasis to things that are not in themselves very witty. I find the new small talk delightful and quite innocent.

MRS. EYNSFORD HILL (*rising*). Well, after that, I think it's time for us to go.

[PICKERING *and* HIGGINS *rise.*]

CLARA (*rising*). Oh, yes! We have three at-homes to go to still. Good-by, Mrs. Higgins. Good-by, Colonel Pickering. Good-by, Professor Higgins.

HIGGINS (*coming grimly at her from the divan, and accompanying her to the door*). Good-by. Be sure you try that small talk at the three at-homes. Don't be nervous about it. Pitch it in strong.

CLARA (*all smiles*). I will. Good-by. Such nonsense, all this early Victorian prudery!

HIGGINS (*tempting her.*) Such damned nonsense!

CLARA. Such bloody nonsense!

MRS. EYNSFORD HILL (*convulsively*). Clara!

CLARA. Ha! ha! (*She goes out radiant, conscious of being thoroughly up to date, and is heard descending the stairs in a stream of silvery laughter.*)

FREDDY (*to the heavens at large*). Well, I ask you — (*He gives it up, and comes to* MRS. HIGGINS.) Good-by.

MRS. HIGGINS (*shaking hands*). Good-by. Would you like to meet Miss Doolittle again?

FREDDY (*eagerly*). Yes, I should, most awfully.

MRS. HIGGINS. Well, you know my days.

FREDDY. Yes. Thanks awfully. Good-by. (*He goes out.*)

MRS. EYNSFORD HILL. Good-by, Mr. Higgins.

HIGGINS. Good-by. Good-by.

MRS. EYNSFORD HILL (*to* PICKERING). It's no use. I shall never be able to bring myself to use that word.

PICKERING. Don't. It's not compulsory, you know. You'll get on quite well without it.

MRS. EYNSFORD HILL. Only, Clara is so down on me if I am not positively reeking with the latest slang. Good-by.

PICKERING. Good-by. (*They shake hands.*)

MRS. EYNSFORD HILL (*to* MRS. HIGGINS). You mustn't mind Clara. (PICKERING, *catching from her lowered tone that this is not meant for him to hear, discreetly joins* HIGGINS *at the window*). We're so poor! And she gets so few parties, poor child! She doesn't quite know. (MRS. HIGGINS, *seeing that her eyes are moist, takes her hand sympathetically and goes with her to the door.*) But the boy is nice. Don't you think so?

MRS. HIGGINS. Oh, quite nice. I shall always be delighted to see him.

MRS. EYNSFORD HILL. Thank you, dear. Good-by. (*She goes out.*)

HIGGINS (*eagerly*). Well? Is Eliza presentable? (*He swoops on his mother and drags her to the ottoman, where she sits down in Eliza's place with her son on her left.*)

[PICKERING *returns to his chair on her right.*]

MRS. HIGGINS. You silly boy, of course she's not presentable. She's a triumph of your art and of her dressmaker's; but if you suppose for a moment that she doesn't give herself away in every sentence she utters, you must be perfectly cracked about her.

PICKERING. But don't you think something might be done? I mean something to eliminate the sanguinary [1] element from her conversation.

MRS. HIGGINS. Not as long as she is in Henry's hands.

HIGGINS (*aggrieved*). Do you mean that *my* language is improper?

MRS. HIGGINS. No, dearest, it would be quite proper — say on a canal barge; but it would not be proper for her at a garden party.

HIGGINS (*deeply injured*). Well I must say —

PICKERING (*interrupting him*). Come, Higgins. You must learn to know yourself. I haven't heard such language as yours since we used to review the volunteers in Hyde Park twenty years ago.

HIGGINS (*sulkily*). Oh, well, if *you* say so, I suppose I don't always talk like a bishop.

MRS. HIGGINS (*quieting Henry with a touch*). Colonel Pickering, will you tell me what is the exact state of things in Wimpole Street?

PICKERING (*cheerfully, as if this completely changed the subject*). Well, I have come to live there with Henry. We work together at my Indian Dialects, and we think it more convenient —

MRS. HIGGINS. Quite so. I know all about that: it's an excellent arrangement. But where does this girl live?

HIGGINS. With us, of course. Where *should* she live?

MRS. HIGGINS. But on what terms? Is she a servant? If not, what is she?

PICKERING (*slowly*). I think I know what you mean, Mrs. Higgins.

HIGGINS. Well, dash me if *I* do! I've had to work at the girl every day for months to get her to her present pitch. Besides, she's useful. She knows where my things are, and remembers my appointments and so forth.

MRS. HIGGINS. How does your housekeeper get on with her?

HIGGINS. Mrs. Pearce? Oh, she's jolly glad to get so much taken off her hands; for before Eliza came, *she* used to have to find things, and remind me of my appointments. But she's got some silly bee in her bonnet about Eliza. She keeps saying "You don't think, sir." doesn't she, Pick?

PICKERING. Yes, that's the formula. "You don't think, sir." That's the end of every conversation about Eliza.

HIGGINS. As if I ever stop thinking about the girl and her confounded vowels and consonants. I'm worn out, thinking about her, and watching her lips and her teeth and her tongue, not to mention her soul, which is the quaintest of the lot.

MRS. HIGGINS. You certainly are a pretty pair of babies, playing with your live doll.

HIGGINS. Playing! The hardest job I ever tackled — Make no mistake about that, Mother. But you have no idea how frightfully interesting it is to take a human being and change her into a quite different human being by creating a new speech for her. It's filling up the deepest gulf that separates class from class and soul from soul.

PICKERING (*drawing his chair closer to* MRS. HIGGINS *and bending over to her eagerly*). Yes, it's enormously interesting. I assure you, Mrs. Higgins, we take Eliza very seriously. Every week — every day almost — there is some new change. (*Closer again*) We keep records of every stage — dozens of gramophone disks and photographs —

HIGGINS (*assailing her at the other ear*). Yes, by George! It's the most absorbing experiment I ever tackled. She regularly fills our lives up, doesn't she, Pick?

PICKERING. We're always talking Eliza.

HIGGINS. Teaching Eliza.

PICKERING. Dressing Eliza.

---

[1] *sanguinary* (săng'gwĭ·nĕr'ĭ): bloody; a reference to Eliza's use of the slang term "bloody" in her conversation.

MRS. HIGGINS. What!

HIGGINS. Inventing new Elizas.

[speaking together]

HIGGINS.	PICKERING.
You know, she has the most extraordinary quickness of ear: just like a parrot. I've tried her with every possible sort of sound that a human being can make — Continental dialects, African dialects, Hottentot clicks, things it took me years to get hold of; and she picks them up like a shot, right away, as if she had been at it all her life.	I assure you, my dear Mrs. Higgins, that girl is a genius. She can play the piano quite beautifully. We have taken her to classical concerts and to music halls; and it's all the same to her: she plays everything she hears right off when she comes home, whether it's Beethoven and Brahms or Lehar and Lionel Monckton; though six months ago, she'd never as much as touched a piano —

MRS. HIGGINS (*putting her fingers in her ears, as they are by this time shouting one another down with an intolerable noise*). Sh-sh-sh — sh! (*They stop.*)

PICKERING. I beg your pardon. (*He draws his chair back apologetically.*)

HIGGINS. Sorry. When Pickering starts shouting nobody can get a word in edgeways.

MRS. HIGGINS. Be quiet, Henry. Colonel Pickering, don't you realize that when Eliza walked into Wimpole Street, something walked in with her?

PICKERING. Her father did. But Henry soon got rid of him.

MRS. HIGGINS. It would have been more to the point if her mother had. But as her mother didn't something else did.

PICKERING. But what?

MRS. HIGGINS (*unconsciously dating herself by the word*). A problem.

PICKERING. Oh, I see. The problem of

how to pass her off as a lady.

HIGGINS. I'll solve that problem. I've half solved it already.

MRS. HIGGINS. No, you two infinitely stupid male creatures! The problem of what is to be done with her afterwards.

HIGGINS. I don't see anything in that. She can go her own way, with all the advantages I have given her.

MRS. HIGGINS. The advantages of that poor woman who was here just now! The manners and habits that disqualify a fine lady from earning her own living without giving her a fine lady's income! Is that what you mean?

PICKERING (*indulgently, being rather bored*). Oh, that will be all right, Mrs. Higgins. (*He rises to go.*)

HIGGINS (*rising also*). We'll find her some light employment.

PICKERING. She's happy enough. Don't you worry about her. Good-by. (*He shakes hands as if he were consoling a frightened child, and makes for the door.*)

HIGGINS. Anyhow, there's no good bothering now. The thing's done. Good-by, Mother. (*He kisses her, and follows* PICKERING.)

PICKERING (*turning for a final consolation*). There are plenty of openings. We'll do what's right. Good-by.

HIGGINS (*to* PICKERING *as they go out together*). Let's take her to the Shakespeare exhibition at Earl's Court.

PICKERING. Yes, let's. Her remarks will be delicious.

HIGGINS. She'll mimic all the people for us when we get home.

PICKERING. Ripping. (*Both are heard laughing as they go downstairs.*)

MRS. HIGGINS (*rises with an impatient bounce, and returns to her work at the writing table. She sweeps a litter of disarranged papers out of her way; snatches a sheet of paper from her stationery case; and tries resolutely to write. At the third line she gives it up; flings down her pen; grips the table angrily and exclaims*). Oh, men! men!! men!!!

PROGRESS AND A PROBLEM

1. How much time has elapsed since the beginning of the experiment? Why does Higgins choose his mother's "at-home" for Eliza's introduction to society? How would you describe the relationship between Higgins and his mother?

2. Point out the differences that you note between Mrs. Higgins and Mrs. Eynsford Hill. Describe the kind of life that Mrs. Eynsford Hill and her children live.

3. How much has Higgins accomplished in his education of Eliza? Compare Eliza now with the girl she was in Acts I and II. How is she received by Mrs. Higgins' guests? Do they recognize her? Does Eliza recognize them?

4. What is Mrs. Higgins' reaction to her son's experiment? How does she regard Eliza? In this act, do you detect a suggestion of a problem that may prove to be important later on? What is it?

ACT IV

The Wimpole Street laboratory. Midnight. Nobody in the room. The clock on the mantelpiece strikes twelve. The fire is not alight; it is a summer night.

Presently HIGGINS *and* PICKERING *are heard on the stairs.*

HIGGINS (*calling down to* PICKERING). I say, Pick. Lock up, will you? I shan't be going out again.

PICKERING. Right. Can Mrs. Pearce go to bed? We don't want anything more, do we?

HIGGINS. Lord, no!

[ELIZA *opens the door and is seen on the lighted landing in opera cloak, brilliant evening dress, and diamonds, with fan, flowers, and all accessories. She comes to the hearth, and switches*

*on the electric lights there. She is
tired; her pallor contrasts strongly
with her dark eyes and hair; and her
expression is almost tragic. She takes
off her cloak; puts her fan and flowers
on the piano; and sits down on the
bench, brooding and silent.* HIGGINS,
*in evening dress, with overcoat and
hat, comes in, carrying a smoking
jacket which he has picked up downstairs. He takes off the hat and overcoat; throws them carelessly on the
newspaper stand; disposes of his coat
in the same way; puts on the smoking
jacket; and throws himself wearily into the easy chair at the hearth.* PICK-
ERING, *similarly attired, comes in. He
also takes off his hat and overcoat,
and is about to throw them on* HIG-
GINS' *when he hesitates.*]

PICKERING. I say, Mrs. Pearce will
row if we leave these things lying about
in the drawing room.

HIGGINS. Oh, chuck them over the
bannisters into the hall. She'll find them
there in the morning and put them away
all right. She'll think we were drunk.

PICKERING. We are, slightly. Are there
any letters?

HIGGINS. I didn't look. (PICKERING
*takes the overcoats and hats and goes
downstairs.* HIGGINS *begins half singing
half yawning an air from* La Fanciulla
del Golden West.[1] *Suddenly he stops
and exclaims*) I wonder where the devil
my slippers are!

[ELIZA *looks at him darkly; then rises
suddenly and leaves the room.* HIGGINS
yawns again, and resumes his song.
PICKERING *returns, with the contents
of the letter box in his hand.*]

PICKERING. Only circulars, and this
coroneted billet-doux [2] for you. (*He
throws the circulars into the fender, and
posts himself on the hearthrug, with his*

[1] *La Fanciulla del Golden West: The Girl of
the Golden West,* an opera by Puccini. [2] *billet-
doux* (bĭl′å·dōō′): a love letter.

back to the grate.)

HIGGINS (*glancing at the billet-doux*).
Moneylender. (*He throws the letter
after the circulars.*)

[ELIZA *returns with a pair of large down-
at-heel slippers. She places them on
the carpet before* HIGGINS, *and sits as
before without a word.*]

HIGGINS (*yawning again*). Oh Lord!
What an evening! What a crew! What a
silly tomfoolery! (*He raises his shoe to
unlace it, and catches sight of the slippers. He stops unlacing and looks at
them as if they had appeared there of
their own accord.*) Oh! they're there,
are they?

PICKERING (*stretching himself*). Well,
I feel a bit tired. It's been a long day.
The garden party, a dinner party, and
the opera! Rather too much of a good
thing. But you've won your bet, Higgins.
Eliza did the trick, and something to
spare, eh?

HIGGINS (*fervently*). Thank God it's
over!

[ELIZA *flinches violently; but they take
no notice of her; and she recovers
herself and sits stonily as before.*]

PICKERING. Were you nervous at the
garden party? *I* was. Eliza didn't seem
a bit nervous.

HIGGINS. Oh, *she* wasn't nervous. I
knew she'd be all right. No, it's the
strain of putting the job through all
these months that has told on me. It was
interesting enough at first, while we
were at the phonetics; but after that I
got deadly sick of it. If I hadn't backed
myself to do it I should have chucked
the whole thing up two months ago. It
was a silly notion. The whole thing has
been a bore.

PICKERING. Oh come! The garden
party was frightfully exciting. My heart
began beating like anything.

HIGGINS. Yes, for the first three minutes. But when I saw we were going to
win hands down, I felt like a bear in a
cage, hanging about doing nothing. The

dinner was worse: sitting gorging there for over an hour, with nobody but a damned fool of a fashionable woman to talk to! I tell you, Pickering, never again for me. No more artificial duchesses. The whole thing has been simple purgatory.

PICKERING. You've never been broken in properly to the social routine. (*Strolling over to the piano*) I rather enjoy dipping into it occasionally myself. It makes me feel young again. Anyhow, it was a great success: an immense success. I was quite frightened once or twice because Eliza was doing it so well. You see, lots of the real people can't do it at all: they're such fools that they think style comes by nature to people in their position, and so they never learn. There's always something professional about doing a thing superlatively well.

HIGGINS. Yes, that's what drives me mad. The silly people don't know their own silly business. (*Rising*) However, it's over and done with; and now I can go to bed at last without dreading tomorrow.

[ELIZA's *beauty becomes murderous.*]

PICKERING. I think I shall turn in too. Still, it's been a great occasion: a triumph for you. Good night. (*He goes.*)
HIGGINS (*following him*). Good night. (*Over his shoulder, at the door*) Put out the lights, Eliza; and tell Mrs. Pearce not to make coffee for me in the morning. I'll take tea. (*He goes out.*)

[ELIZA *tries to control herself and feel indifferent as she rises and walks across to the hearth to switch off the lights. By the time she gets there she is on the point of screaming. She sits down in* HIGGINS' *chair and holds on hard to the arms. Finally she gives way and flings herself furiously on the floor, raging.*]

HIGGINS (*in despairing wrath outside*). What the devil have I done with my slippers? (*He appears at the door*).
LIZA (*snatching up the slippers, and hurling them at him one after the other with all her force*). There are your slippers. And there. Take your slippers, and may you never have a day's luck with them!

HIGGINS (*astounded*). What on earth —! (*He comes to her.*) What's the matter? Get up. (*He pulls her up.*) Anything wrong?

LIZA (*breathless*). Nothing wrong — with *you.* I've won your bet for you, haven't I. That's enough for you. *I* don't matter, I suppose.

HIGGINS. *You* won my bet! You! Presumptuous insect! *I* won it. What did you throw those slippers at me for?

LIZA. Because I wanted to smash your face. I'd like to kill you, you selfish brute. Why didn't you leave me where you picked me out of — in the gutter? You thank God it's all over, and that now you can throw me back again there, do you? (*She crisps her fingers frantically.*)

HIGGINS (*looking at her in cool wonder*). The creature is nervous, after all.

LIZA (*gives a suffocated scream of fury, and instinctively darts her nails at his face*)!!

HIGGINS (*catching her wrists*). Ah! would you? Claws in, you cat. How dare you show your temper to me? Sit down and be quiet. (*He throws her roughly into the easy chair.*)

LIZA (*crushed by superior strength and weight*). What's to become of me? What's to become of me?

HIGGINS. How the devil do I know what's to become of you? What does it matter what becomes of you?

LIZA. You don't care. I know you don't care. You wouldn't care if I was dead. I'm nothing to you — not so much as them slippers.

HIGGINS (*thundering*). *Those* slippers.

LIZA (*with bitter submission*). Those slippers. I didn't think it made any difference now.

[*A pause.* ELIZA *hopeless and crushed.* HIGGINS *a little uneasy.*]

HIGGINS (*in his loftiest manner*). Why have you begun going on like this? May I ask whether you complain of your treatment here?

LIZA. No.

HIGGINS. Has anybody behaved badly to you? Colonel Pickering? Mrs. Pearce? Any of the servants?

LIZA. No.

HIGGINS. I presume you don't pretend that *I* have treated you badly?

LIZA. No.

HIGGINS. I am glad to hear it. (*He moderates his tone.*) Perhaps you're tired after the strain of the day. Will you have a glass of champagne? (*He moves toward the door.*)

LIZA. No. (*Recollecting her manners.*) Thank you.

HIGGINS (*good-humored again*). This has been coming on you for some days. I suppose it was natural for you to be anxious about the garden party. But that's all over now. (*He pats her kindly on the shoulder. She writhes.*) There's nothing more to worry about.

LIZA. No. Nothing more for *you* to worry about. (*She suddenly rises and gets away from him by going to the piano bench, where she sits and hides her face.*) Oh God! I wish I was dead.

HIGGINS (*staring after her in sincere surprise*). Why? In heaven's name, why? (*Reasonably, going to her*) Listen to me, Eliza. All this irritation is purely subjective.

LIZA. I don't understand. I'm too ignorant.

HIGGINS. It's only imagination. Low spirits and nothing else. Nobody's hurting you. Nothing's wrong. You go to bed like a good girl and sleep it off. Have a little cry and say your prayers. That will make you comfortable.

LIZA. I heard your prayers. "Thank God it's all over!"

HIGGINS (*impatiently*). Well, *don't* you thank God it's all over? Now you are free and can do what you like.

LIZA (*pulling herself together in desperation*). What am I fit for? What have you left me fit for? Where am I to go? What am I to do? What's to become of me?

HIGGINS (*enlightened, but not at all impressed*). Oh *that's* what's worrying you, is it? (*He thrusts his hands into his pockets, and walks about in his usual manner, rattling the contents of his pockets, as if condescending to a trivial subject out of pure kindness.*) I shouldn't bother about it if I were you. I should imagine you won't have much difficulty in settling yourself somewhere or other, though I hadn't quite realized that you were going away. (*She looks quickly at him. He does not look at her, but examines the dessert stand on the piano and decides that he will eat an apple.*) You might marry, you know. (*He bites a large piece out of the apple and munches it noisily.*) You see, Eliza, all men are not confirmed old bachelors like me and the Colonel. Most men are the marrying sort (poor devils!); and you're not bad looking. It's quite a pleasure to look at you sometimes — not now, of course, because you're crying and looking as ugly as the very devil; but when you're all right and quite yourself, you're what I should call attractive. That is, to the people in the marrying line, you understand. You go to bed and have a good nice rest; and then get up and look at yourself in the glass; and you won't feel so cheap.

[ELIZA *again looks at him, speechless, and does not stir. The look is quite lost on him. He eats his apple with a dreamy expression of happiness, as it is quite a good one.*]

HIGGINS (*a genial afterthought occurring to him*). I daresay my mother could find some chap or other who would do very well.

LIZA. We were above that at the corner of Tottenham Court Road.

HIGGINS (*waking up*). What do you mean?

LIZA. I sold flowers. I didn't sell myself. Now you've made a lady of me I'm not fit to sell anything else. I wish you'd left me where you found me.

HIGGINS (*slinging the core of the apple decisively into the grate*). Tosh, Eliza. Don't you insult human relations by dragging all this cant about buying and selling into it. You needn't marry the fellow if you don't like him.

LIZA. What else am I to do?

HIGGINS. Oh, lots of things. What about your old idea of a florist's shop? Pickering could set you up in one. He's lots of money. (*Chuckling*) He'll have to pay for all those togs you have been wearing today; and that, with the hire of the jewelry, will make a big hole in two hundred pounds. Why, six months ago you would have thought it the millennium to have a flower shop of your own. Come! you'll be all right. I must clear off to bed. I'm devilish sleepy. By the way, I came down for something. I forget what it was.

LIZA. Your slippers.

HIGGINS. Oh, yes, of course. You shied them at me. (*He picks them up, and is going out when she rises and speaks to him.*)

LIZA. Before you go, sir —

HIGGINS (*dropping the slippers in his surprise at her calling him Sir*). Eh?

LIZA. Do my clothes belong to me or to Colonel Pickering?

HIGGINS (*coming back into the room as if her question were the very climax of unreason*). What the devil use would they be to Pickering?

LIZA. He might want them for the next girl you pick up to experiment on.

HIGGINS (*shocked and hurt*). Is *that* the way you feel toward us?

LIZA. I don't want to hear anything more about that. All I want to know is whether anything belongs to me. My own clothes were burnt.

HIGGINS. But what does it matter? Why need you start bothering about that in the middle of the night?

LIZA. I want to know what I may take away with me. I don't want to be accused of stealing.

HIGGINS (*now deeply wounded*). Stealing! You shouldn't have said that, Eliza. That shows a want of feeling.

LIZA. I'm sorry. I'm only a common ignorant girl; and in my station I have to be careful. There can't be any feelings between the like of you and the like of me. Please will you tell me what belongs to me and what doesn't?

HIGGINS (*very sulky*). You may take the whole damned houseful if you like. Except the jewels. They're hired. Will that satisfy you? (*He turns on his heel and is about to go in extreme dudgeon.[1]*)

LIZA (*drinking in his emotion like nectar, and nagging him to provoke a further supply*). Stop, please. (*She takes off her jewels.*) Will you take these to your room and keep them safe? I don't want to run the risk of their being missing.

HIGGINS (*furious*). Hand them over. (*She puts them into his hands.*) If these belonged to me instead of to the jeweler, I'd ram them down your ungrateful throat. (*He perfunctorily thrusts them into his pockets, unconsciously decorating himself with the protruding ends of the chains.*)

LIZA (*taking a ring off*). This ring isn't the jeweler's. It's the one you bought me in Brighton. I don't want it now. (HIGGINS *dashes the ring violently into the fireplace, and turns on her so threateningly that she crouches over the piano with her hands over her face, and exclaims*) Don't you hit me.

HIGGINS. Hit you! You infamous creature, how dare you accuse me of such a thing? It is you who have hit me. You have wounded me to the heart.

LIZA (*thrilling with hidden joy*). I'm glad. I've got a little of my own back, anyhow.

HIGGINS (*with dignity, in his finest professional style*). You have caused me to lose my temper — a thing that has

---

[1] *dudgeon* (dŭj'ŭn): angered feeling.

hardly ever happened to me before. I prefer to say nothing more tonight. I am going to bed.

LIZA (*pertly*). You'd better leave a note for Mrs. Pearce about the coffee, for she won't be told by me.

HIGGINS (*formally*). Damn Mrs. Pearce; and damn the coffee; and damn you; and damn my own folly in having lavished hard-earned knowledge and the treasure of my regard and intimacy on a heartless guttersnipe. (*He goes out with impressive decorum, and spoils it by slamming the door savagely.*)

[ELIZA *smiles for the first time; expresses her feelings by a wild pantomime in which an imitation of* HIGGINS' *exit is confused with her own triumph; and finally goes down on her knees on the hearthrug to look for the ring.*]

A CRISIS

1. The experiment is finished and Higgins has won his bet. How does he react to his success? What do Higgins and Pickering have to say about the conventional social routine? Do you think that Shaw means this as a criticism of society?

2. Eliza has been silent and brooding, but finally her "beauty becomes murderous." Why? How does Higgins first react to her outburst? What is really bothering her? When had this problem been suggested before? Is Higgins being honest in his response to Eliza? What effect does his response have on Eliza? What adjectives would you use to describe Higgins in this scene?

3. At this point, what do you think Eliza's feelings for Higgins are? Can you justify what she says and what she does? Why do you think Eliza is smiling at the end of the scene?

ACT V

MRS. HIGGINS' *drawing room. She is at her writing table as before. The* PARLOR MAID *comes in.*

THE PARLOR MAID (*at the door*). Mr. Henry, ma'am, is downstairs with Colonel Pickering.

MRS. HIGGINS. Well, show them up.

THE PARLOR MAID. They're using the telephone, ma'am. Telephoning to the police, I think.

MRS. HIGGINS. What!

THE PARLOR MAID (*coming further in and lowering her voice*). Mr. Henry is in a state, ma'am. I thought I'd better tell you.

MRS. HIGGINS. If you had told me that Mr. Henry was not in a state it would have been more surprising. Tell them to come up when they've finished with the police. I suppose he's lost something.

THE PARLOR MAID. Yes, ma'am (*going*).

MRS. HIGGINS. Go upstairs and tell Miss Doolittle that Mr. Henry and the Colonel are here. Ask her not to come down till I send for her.

THE PARLOR MAID. Yes, ma'am.

[HIGGINS *bursts in. He is, as the* PARLOR MAID *has said, in a state.*]

HIGGINS. Look here, Mother! Here's a confounded thing!

MRS. HIGGINS. Yes, dear. Good morning. (*He checks his impatience and kisses her, while the* PARLOR MAID *goes out.*) What is it?

HIGGINS. Eliza's bolted.

MRS. HIGGINS (*calmly continuing her writing*). You must have frightened her.

HIGGINS. Frightened her! Nonsense! She was left last night, as usual, to turn out the lights and all that; and instead of going to bed, she changed her clothes and went right off. Her bed wasn't slept in. She came in a cab for her things before seven this morning, and that fool Mrs. Pearce let her have them without telling me a word about it. What am I to do?

MRS. HIGGINS. Do without, I'm afraid, Henry. The girl has a perfect right to leave if she chooses.

HIGGINS (*wandering distractedly across the room*). But I can't find anything. I don't know what appointments I've got. I'm — (PICKERING *comes in.* MRS. HIGGINS *puts down her pen and turns away from the writing table.*)

PICKERING (*shaking hands*). Good morning, Mrs. Higgins. Has Henry told you? (*He sits down on the ottoman*).

HIGGINS. What does that fool of an inspector say? Have you offered a reward?

MRS. HIGGINS (*rising in indignant amazement*). You don't mean to say you have set the police after Eliza.

HIGGINS. Of course. What are the police for? What else could we do? (*He sits in the Elizabethan chair.*)

PICKERING. The inspector made a lot of difficulties. I really think he suspected us of some improper purpose.

MRS. HIGGINS. Well, of course he did. What right have you to go to the police and give the girl's name as if she were a thief, or a lost umbrella, or something? Really! (*She sits down again, deeply vexed.*)

HIGGINS. But we want to find her.

PICKERING. We can't let her go like this, you know, Mrs. Higgins. What were we to do?

MRS. HIGGINS. You have no more sense, either of you, than two children. Why —

[*The* PARLOR MAID *comes in and breaks off the conversation.*]

THE PARLOR MAID. Mr. Henry, a gentleman wants to see you very particular. He's been sent on from Wimpole Street.

HIGGINS. Oh, bother! I can't see anyone now. Who is it?

THE PARLOR MAID. A Mr. Doolittle, sir.

PICKERING. Doolittle! Do you mean the dustman?

THE PARLOR MAID. Dustman! Oh no, sir. A gentleman.

HIGGINS (*springing up excitedly*). By George, Pick, it's some relative of hers that she's gone to. Somebody we know nothing about. (*To the* PARLOR MAID) Send him up, quick.

THE PARLOR MAID. Yes, sir. (*She goes.*)

HIGGINS (*eagerly, going to his mother*). Genteel relatives! Now we shall hear something. (*He sits down in the Chippendale chair.*)

MRS. HIGGINS. Do you know any of her people?

PICKERING. Only her father. The fellow we told you about.

THE PARLOR MAID (*announcing*). Mr. Doolittle. (*She withdraws.*)

[DOOLITTLE *enters. He is brilliantly dressed in a new fashionable frock coat, with white waistcoat and gray trousers. A flower in his buttonhole, a dazzling silk hat, and patent leather shoes complete the effect. He is too concerned with the business he has come on to notice* MRS. HIGGINS. *He walks straight to* HIGGINS, *and accosts him with vehement [1] reproach.*]

DOOLITTLE (*indicating his own person*). See here! Do you see this? *You* done this.

HIGGINS. Done what, man?

DOOLITTLE. This, I tell you. Look at it. Look at this hat. Look at this coat.

PICKERING. Has Eliza been buying you clothes?

DOOLITTLE. Eliza! Not she. Not half. Why would she buy me clothes?

MRS. HIGGINS. Good morning, Mr. Doolittle. Won't you sit down?

DOOLITTLE (*taken aback as he becomes conscious that he has forgotten his hostess*). Asking your pardon, ma'am. (*He approaches her and shakes her proffered hand.*) Thank you. (*He sits down on the ottoman, on* PICKERING'S *right.*) I am that full of what has

---

[1] *vehement* (vē'ĕ·mĕnt): furious.

happened to me that I can't think of anything else.

HIGGINS. What the dickens *has* happened to you?

DOOLITTLE. I shouldn't mind if it had only *happened* to me. Anything might happen to anybody and nobody to blame but Providence, as you might say. But this is something that you done to me. Yes, you, Henry Higgins.

HIGGINS. Have you found Eliza? That's the point.

DOOLITTLE. Have you lost her?

HIGGINS. Yes.

DOOLITTLE. You have all the luck, you have. I ain't found her; but she'll find me quick enough now after what you done to me.

MRS. HIGGINS. But what has my son done to you, Mr. Doolittle?

DOOLITTLE. Done to me! Ruined me. Destroyed my happiness. Tied me up and delivered me into the hands of middle class morality.

HIGGINS (*rising intolerantly and standing over* DOOLITTLE). You're raving. You're drunk. You're mad. I gave you five pounds. After that I had two conversations with you, at half-a-crown an hour. I've never seen you since.

DOOLITTLE. Oh! Drunk! am I? Mad! am I? Tell me this. Did you or did you not write a letter to an old blighter in America that was giving five millions to found Moral Reform Societies all over the world, and that wanted you to invent a universal language for him?

HIGGINS. What! Ezra D. Wannafeller! He's dead. (*He sits down again carelessly.*)

DOOLITTLE. Yes, he's dead; and I'm done for. Now did you or did you not write a letter to him to say that the most original moralist at present in England, to the best of your knowledge, was Alfred Doolittle, a common dustman.

HIGGINS. Oh, after your last visit I remember making some silly joke of the kind.

DOOLITTLE. Ah! you may well call it a silly joke. It put the lid on me right

enough. Just give him the chance he wanted to show that Americans is not like us: that they recognize and respect merit in every class of life, however humble. Them words is in his blooming will, in which, Henry Higgins, thanks to your silly joking, he leaves me a share in his Pre-digested Cheese Trust worth three thousand a year on condition that I lecture for his Wannafeller Moral Reform World League as often as they ask me up to six times a year.

HIGGINS. The devil he does! Whew! (*Brightening suddenly*) What a lark!

PICKERING. A safe thing for you, Doolittle. They won't ask you twice.

DOOLITTLE. It ain't the lecturing I mind. I'll lecture them blue in the face, I will, and not turn a hair. It's making a gentleman of me that I object to. Who asked him to make a gentleman of me? I was happy. I was free. I touched pretty nigh everybody for money when I wanted it, same as I touched you, Henry Higgins. Now I am worrited; tied neck and heels; and everybody touches me for money. It's a fine thing for you, says my solicitor. Is it? says I. You mean it's a good thing for you, I say. When I was a poor man and had a solicitor once when they found a pram in the dust cart, he got me off, and got shut of me and got me shut of him as quick as he could. Same with the doctors: used to shove me out of the hospital before I could hardly stand on my legs, and nothing to pay. Now they finds out that I'm not a healthy man and can't live unless they looks after me twice a day. In the house I'm not let do a hand's turn for myself: somebody else must do it and touch me for it. A year ago I hadn't a relative in the world except two or three that wouldn't speak to me. Now I've fifty, and not a decent week's wages among the lot of them. I have to live for others and not for myself. That's middle class morality. *You* talk of losing Eliza. Don't you be anxious: I bet she's on my doorstep by this. She that could support herself easy by selling flowers if I wasn't respectable. And the next one to touch me will be you, Henry Higgins. I'll have to learn to speak middle class language from you, instead of speaking proper English. That's where you'll come in; and I daresay that's what you done it for.

MRS. HIGGINS. But, my dear Mr. Doolittle, you need not suffer all this if you are really in earnest. Nobody can force you to accept this bequest. You can repudiate it. Isn't that so, Colonel Pickering?

PICKERING. I believe so.

DOOLITTLE (*softening his manner in deference to her sex*). That's the tragedy of it, ma'am. It's easy to say chuck it; but I haven't the nerve. Which of us has? We're all intimidated. Intimidated, ma'am: that's what we are. What is there for me if I chuck it but the workhouse in my old age? I have to dye my hair already to keep my job as a dustman. If I was one of the deserving poor, and had put by a bit, I could chuck it; but then why should I, acause the deserving poor might as well be millionaires for all the happiness they ever has. They don't know what happiness is. But I, as one of the undeserving poor, have nothing between me and the pauper's uniform but this here blasted three thousand a year that shoves me into the middle class. (Excuse the expression, ma'am: you'd use it yourself if you had my provocation.) They've got you every way you turn: it's a choice between the Skilly of the workhouse and the Char Bydis [1] of the middle class; and I haven't the nerve for the workhouse. Intimidated! that's what I am. Broke. Bought up. Happier men than me will call for my dust and touch me for their tip; and I'll look on helpless,

and envy them. And that's what your son has brought me to. (*He is overcome by emotion.*)

MRS. HIGGINS. Well, I'm very glad you're not going to do anything foolish, Mr. Doolittle. For this solves the problem of Eliza's future. You can provide for her now.

DOOLITTLE (*with melancholy resignation*). Yes, ma'am: I'm expected to provide for everyone now, out of three thousand a year.

HIGGINS (*jumping up*). Nonsense! He can't provide for her. He shan't provide for her. She doesn't belong to him. I paid him five pounds for her. Doolittle, either you're an honest man or a rogue.

DOOLITTLE (*tolerantly*). A little of both, Henry. Like the rest of us, a little of both.

HIGGINS. Well, you took that money for the girl; and you have no right to take her as well.

MRS. HIGGINS. Henry, don't be absurd. If you want to know where Eliza is, she is upstairs.

HIGGINS (*amazed*). Upstairs!!! Then I shall jolly soon fetch her downstairs. (*He makes resolutely for the door.*)

MRS. HIGGINS (*rising and following him*). Be quiet, Henry. Sit down.

HIGGINS. I —

MRS. HIGGINS. Sit down, dear; and listen to me.

HIGGINS. Oh very well, very well, very well. (*He throws himself ungraciously on the ottoman, with his face toward the windows.*) But I think you might have told us this half an hour ago.

MRS. HIGGINS. Eliza came to me this morning. She passed the night partly walking about in a rage, partly trying to throw herself into the river and being afraid to, and partly in the Carlton Hotel. She told me of the brutal way you two treated her.

HIGGINS (*bounding up again*). What!

PICKERING (*rising also*). My dear Mrs. Higgins, she's been telling you stories. We didn't treat her brutally. We hardly said a word to her; and we parted

---

[1] *Skilly . . . Char Bydis:* Doolittle's distortion of Scylla (sĭl′á) and Charybdis (ká·rĭb′dĭs), a dangerous rock and whirlpool on either side of a narrow strait between Sicily and Italy. The ancient Greeks personified them as two monsters, and they have come to symbolize two dangers between which it is almost impossible to steer a safe course.

on particularly good terms. (*Turning on* HIGGINS) Higgins, did you bully her after I went to bed?

HIGGINS. Just the other way about. She threw my slippers in my face. She behaved in the most outrageous way. I never gave her the slightest provocation. The slippers came bang into my face the moment I entered the room — before I had uttered a word. And used perfectly awful language.

PICKERING (*astonished*). But why? What did we do to her?

MRS. HIGGINS. I think I know pretty well what you did. The girl is naturally rather affectionate, I think. Isn't she, Mr. Doolittle?

DOOLITTLE. Very tender-hearted, ma'am. Takes after me.

MRS. HIGGINS. Just so. She had become attached to you both. She worked very hard for you, Henry! I don't think you quite realize what anything in the nature of brain work means to a girl like that. Well, it seems that when the great day of trial came, and she did this wonderful thing for you without making a single mistake, you two sat there and never said a word to her, but talked together of how glad you were that it was all over and how you had been bored with the whole thing. And then you were surprised because she threw your slippers at you! *I* should have thrown the fire irons at you.

HIGGINS. We said nothing except that we were tired and wanted to go to bed. Did we, Pick?

PICKERING (*shrugging his shoulders*). That was all.

MRS. HIGGINS (*ironically*). Quite sure?

PICKERING. Absolutely. Really, that was all.

MRS. HIGGINS. You didn't thank her, or pet her, or admire her, or tell her how splendid she'd been?

HIGGINS (*impatiently*). But she knew all about that. We didn't make speeches to her, if that's what you mean.

PICKERING (*conscience-stricken*). Per-haps we were a little inconsiderate. Is she very angry?

MRS. HIGGINS (*returning to her place at the writing table*). Well, I'm afraid she won't go back to Wimpole Street, especially now that Mr. Doolittle is able to keep up the position you have thrust on her; but she says she is quite willing to meet you on friendly terms and to let bygones be bygones.

HIGGINS (*furious*). Is she, by George? Ho!

MRS. HIGGINS. If you promise to behave yourself, Henry, I'll ask her to come down. If not, go home; for you have taken up quite enough of my time.

HIGGINS. Oh, all right. Very well. Pick, you behave yourself. Let us put on our best Sunday manners for this creature that we picked out of the mud. (*He flings himself sulkily into the Eizabethan chair.*)

DOOLITTLE (*remonstrating*). Now, now, Henry Higgins! have some consideration for my feelings as a middle class man.

MRS. HIGGINS. Remember your promise, Henry. (*She presses the bell-button on the writing table.*) Mr. Doolittle, will you be so good as to step out on the balcony for a moment? I don't want Eliza to have the shock of your news until she has made it up with these two gentlemen. Would you mind?

DOOLITTLE. As you wish, lady. Anything to help Henry to keep her off my hands. (*He disappears through the window.*)

[*The* PARLOR MAID *answers the bell.* PICKERING *sits down in* DOOLITTLE'S *place.*]

MRS. HIGGINS. Ask Miss Doolittle to come down, please.

THE PARLOR MAID. Yes, ma'am. (*She goes out.*)

MRS. HIGGINS. Now, Henry, be good.

HIGGINS. I am behaving myself perfectly.

PICKERING. He is doing his best, Mrs. Higgins.

[*A pause.* HIGGINS *throws back his head; stretches out his legs; and begins to whistle.*]

MRS. HIGGINS. Henry, dearest, you don't look at all nice in that attitude.

HIGGINS (*pulling himself together*). I was not trying to look nice, Mother.

MRS. HIGGINS. It doesn't matter, dear. I only wanted to make you speak.

HIGGINS. Why?

MRS. HIGGINS. Because you can't speak and whistle at the same time.

[HIGGINS *groans. Another very trying pause.*]

HIGGINS (*springing up, out of patience*). Where the devil is that girl? Are we to wait here all day?

[ELIZA *enters, sunny, self-possessed, and giving a staggeringly convincing exhibition of ease of manner. She carries a little workbasket, and is very much at home.* PICKERING *is too much taken aback to rise.*]

LIZA. How do you do, Professor Higgins? Are you quite well?

HIGGINS (*choking*). Am I — (*He can say no more*).

LIZA. But of course you are. You are never ill. So glad to see you again, Colonel Pickering. (*He rises hastily; and they shake hands.*) Quite chilly this morning, isn't it? (*She sits down on his left. He sits beside her.*)

HIGGINS. Don't you dare try this game on me. I taught it to you, and it doesn't take me in. Get up and come home, and don't be a fool.

[ELIZA *takes a piece of needlework from her basket, and begins to stitch at it, without taking the least notice of this outburst.*]

MRS. HIGGINS. Very nicely put, indeed, Henry. No woman could resist such an invitation.

HIGGINS. You let her alone, Mother. Let her speak for herself. You will jolly soon see whether she has an idea that

I haven't put into her head or a word that I haven't put into her mouth. I tell you I have created this thing out of the squashed cabbage leaves of Covent Garden, and now she pretends to play the fine lady with me.

MRS. HIGGINS (*placidly*). Yes, dear; but you'll sit down, won't you?

[HIGGINS *sits down again, savagely.*]

LIZA (*to* PICKERING, *taking no apparent notice of* HIGGINS, *and working away deftly*). Will *you* drop me altogether now that the experiment is over, Colonel Pickering?

PICKERING. Oh, don't. You mustn't think of it as an experiment. It shocks me, somehow.

LIZA. Oh, I'm only a squashed cabbage leaf —

PICKERING (*impulsively*). No.

LIZA (*continuing quietly*). — but I owe so much to you that I should be very unhappy if you forgot me.

PICKERING. It's very kind of you to say so, Miss Doolittle.

LIZA. It's not because you paid for my dresses. I know you are generous to everybody with money. But it was from you that I learned really nice manners, and that is what makes one a lady, isn't it? You see it was so very difficult for me with the example of Professor Higgins always before me. I was brought up to be just like him, unable to control myself, and using bad language on the slightest provocation. And I should never have known that ladies and gentlemen didn't behave like that if you hadn't been there.

HIGGINS. Well!!

PICKERING. Oh, that's only his way, you know. He doesn't mean it.

LIZA. Oh, I didn't mean it either when I was a flower girl. It was only my way. But you see I did it, and that's what makes the difference after all.

PICKERING. No doubt. Still, he taught you to speak; and I couldn't have done that, you know.

LIZA (*trivially*). Of course. That is

his profession.

HIGGINS. Damnation!

LIZA (*continuing*). It was just like learning to dance in the fashionable way. There was nothing more than that in it. But do you know what began my real education?

PICKERING. What?

LIZA (*stopping her work for a moment*). Your calling me Miss Doolittle that day when I first came to Wimpole Street. That was the beginning of self-respect for me. (*She resumes her stitching.*) And there were a hundred little things you never noticed, because they came naturally to you. Things about standing up and taking off your hat and opening doors —

PICKERING. Oh, that was nothing.

LIZA. Yes, things that showed you thought and felt about me as if I were something better than a scullery maid; though of course I know you would have been just the same to a scullery maid if she had been let into the drawing room. *You* never took off your boots in the dining room when I was there.

PICKERING. You mustn't mind that. Higgins takes off his boots all over the place.

LIZA. I know. I am not blaming him. It is his way, isn't it? But it made *such* a difference to me that you didn't do it. You see, really and truly, apart from the things anyone can pick up (the dressing and the proper way of speaking, and so on), the difference between a lady and a flower girl is not how she behaves, but how she's treated. I shall always be a flower girl to Professor Higgins, because he always treats me as a flower girl, and always will; but I know I can be a lady to you, because you always treat me as a lady, and always will.

MRS. HIGGINS. Please don't grind your teeth, Henry.

PICKERING. Well, this is really very nice of you, Miss Doolittle.

LIZA. I should like you to call me Eliza, now, if you would.

PICKERING. Thank you. Eliza, of course.

LIZA. And I should like Professor Higgins to call me Miss Doolittle.

HIGGINS. I'll see you damned first.

MRS. HIGGINS. Henry! Henry!

PICKERING (*laughing*). Why don't you slang back at him? Don't stand it. It would do him a lot of good.

LIZA. I can't. I could have done it once; but now I can't go back to it. Last night, when I was wandering about, a girl spoke to me; and I tried to get back into the old way with her, but it was no use. You told me, you know, that when a child is brought to a foreign country, it picks up the language in a few weeks and forgets its own. Well, I am a child in your country. I have forgotten my own language and can speak nothing but yours. That's the real break-off with the corner of Tottenham Court Road. Leaving Wimpole Street finishes it.

PICKERING (*much alarmed*). Oh! but you're coming back to Wimpole Street, aren't you? You'll forgive Higgins?

HIGGINS (*rising*). Forgive! Will she, by George! Let her go. Let her find out how she can get on without us. She will relapse into the gutter in three weeks without me at her elbow.

[DOOLITTLE *appears at the center window. With a look of dignified reproach at* HIGGINS, *he comes slowly and silently to his daughter, who, with her back to the window, is unconscious of his approach.*]

PICKERING. He's incorrigible, Eliza. You won't relapse, will you?

LIZA. No, not now. Never again. I have learnt my lesson. I don't believe I could utter one of the old sounds if I tried. (DOOLITTLE *touches her on her left shoulder. She drops her work, losing her self-possession utterly at the spectacle of her father's splendor*) A-a-a-a-a-ah-ow-ooh!

HIGGINS (*with a crow of triumph*). Aha! Just so. A-a-a-a-ahowooh! A-a-a-a-ahowooh! A-a-a-a-ahowooh! Victory!

Victory! (*He throws himself on the divan, folding his arms, and spraddling arrogantly.*)

DOOLITTLE. Can you blame the girl? Don't look at me like that, Eliza. It ain't my fault. I've come into some money.

LIZA. You must have touched a millionaire this time, Dad.

DOOLITTLE. I have. But I'm dressed something special today. I'm going to St. George's, Hanover Square. Your stepmother is going to marry me.

LIZA (*angrily*). You're going to let yourself down to marry that low common woman!

PICKERING (*quietly*). He ought to, Eliza. (*To* DOOLITTLE) Why has she changed her mind?

DOOLITTLE (*sadly*). Intimidated, Governor. Intimidated. Middle class morality claims its victim. Won't you put on your hat, Liza, and come and see me turned off?

LIZA. If the Colonel says I must, I — I'll (*almost sobbing*) I'll demean [1] myself. And get insulted for my pains, like enough.

DOOLITTLE. Don't be afraid. She never comes to words with anyone now, poor woman! Respectability has broke all the spirit out of her.

PICKERING (*squeezing* ELIZA's *elbow gently*). Be kind to them, Eliza. Make the best of it.

LIZA (*forcing a little smile for him through her vexation*). Oh well, just to show there's no ill feeling. I'll be back in a moment. (*She goes out.*)

DOOLITTLE (*sitting down beside* PICKERING). I feel uncommon nervous about the ceremony, Colonel. I wish you'd come and see me through it.

PICKERING. But you've been through it before, man. You were married to Eliza's mother.

DOOLITTLE. Who told you that, Colonel?

PICKERING. Well, nobody told me. But I concluded — naturally —

DOOLITTLE. No, that ain't the natural way, Colonel. It's only the middle class way. My way was always the undeserving way. But don't say nothing to Eliza. She don't know. I always had a delicacy about telling her.

PICKERING. Quite right. We'll leave it so, if you don't mind.

DOOLITTLE. And you'll come to the church, Colonel, and put me through straight?

PICKERING. With pleasure. As far as a bachelor can.

MRS. HIGGINS. May I come, Mr. Doolittle? I should be very sorry to miss your wedding.

DOOLITTLE. I should indeed be honored by your condescension, ma'am; and my poor old woman would take it as a tremendous compliment. She's been very low, thinking of the happy days that are no more.

MRS. HIGGINS (*rising*). I'll order the carriage and get ready. (*The men rise, except* HIGGINS.) I shan't be more than fifteen minutes. (*As she goes to the door* ELIZA *comes in, hatted and buttoning her gloves.*) I'm going to the church to see your father married, Eliza. You had better come in the brougham [2] with me. Colonel Pickering can go on with the bridegroom.

[MRS. HIGGINS *goes out.* ELIZA *comes to the middle of the room between the center window and the ottoman.* PICKERING *joins her.*]

DOOLITTLE. Bridegroom! What a word! It makes a man realize his position, somehow. (*He takes up his hat and goes toward the door.*)

PICKERING. Before I go, Eliza, do forgive him and come back to us.

LIZA. I don't think Papa would allow me. Would you, Dad?

DOOLITTLE (*sad but magnanimous*). They played you off very cunning, Eliza, them two sportsmen. If it had been only one of them, you could have nailed him.

---

[1] *demean* (dĕ·mēn′): lower, degrade.

[2] *brougham* (brōōm): a light, closed carriage.

But you see, there was two; and one of them chaperoned the other, as you might say. (*To* PICKERING) It was artful of you, Colonel; but I bear no malice. I should have done the same myself. I been the victim of one woman after another all my life; and I don't grudge you two getting the better of Eliza. I shan't interfere. It's time for us to go, Colonel. So long, Henry. See you in St. George's, Eliza. (*He goes out*).

PICKERING (*coaxing*). Do stay with us, Eliza. (*He follows* DOOLITTLE.)

[ELIZA *goes out on the balcony to avoid being alone with* HIGGINS. *He rises and joins her there. She immediately comes back into the room and makes for the door; but he goes along the balcony quickly and gets his back to the door before she reaches it.*]

HIGGINS. Well, Eliza, you've had a bit of your own back, as you call it. Have you had enough? And are you going to be reasonable? Or do you want any more?

LIZA. You want me back only to pick up your slippers and put up with your tempers and fetch and carry for you.

HIGGINS. I haven't said I wanted you back at all.

LIZA. Oh, indeed. Then what are we talking about?

HIGGINS. About you, not about me. If you come back I shall treat you just as I have always treated you. I can't change my nature, and I don't intend to change my manners. My manners are exactly the same as Colonel Pickering's.

LIZA. That's not true. He treats a flower girl as if she was a duchess.

HIGGINS And I treat a duchess as if she was a flower girl.

LIZA. I see. (*She turns away composedly, and sits on the ottoman, facing the window.*) The same to everybody.

HIGGINS. Just so.

LIZA. Like father.

HIGGINS. (*grinning, a little taken down*). Without accepting the comparison at all points, Eliza, it's quite true that your father is not a snob, and that he will be quite at home in any station of life to which his eccentric destiny may call him. (*Seriously*) The great secret, Eliza, is not having bad manners or good manners or any other particular sort of manners, but having the same manner for all human souls. In short, behaving as if you were in Heaven, where there are no third class carriages, and one soul is as good as another.

LIZA. Amen. You are a born preacher.

HIGGINS (*irritated*). The question is not whether I treat you rudely, but whether you ever heard me treat anyone else better.

LIZA (*with sudden sincerity*). I don't care how you treat me. I don't mind your swearing at me. I don't mind a black eye: I've had one before this. But (*standing up and facing him*) I won't be passed over.

HIGGINS. Then get out of my way, for I won't stop for you. You talk about me as if I were a motor bus.

LIZA. So you are a motor bus. All bounce and go, and no consideration for anyone. But I can do without you; don't think I can't.

HIGGINS. I know you can. I told you you could.

LIZA (*wounded, getting away from him to the other side of the ottoman with her face to the hearth*). I know you did, you brute. You wanted to get rid of me.

HIGGINS. Liar.

LIZA. Thank you. (*She sits down with dignity.*)

HIGGINS. You never asked yourself, I suppose, whether *I* could do without *you*.

LIZA (*earnestly*). Don't you try to get round me. You'll *have* to do without me.

HIGGINS (*arrogant*). I can do without anybody. I have my own soul, my own spark of divine fire. But (*with sudden humility*) I shall miss you, Eliza. (*He sits down near her on the ottoman.*) I have learned something from your idiotic notions. I confess that humbly and gratefully. And I have grown accustomed to your voice and appearance. I like them, rather.

LIZA. Well, you have both of them on your gramophone and in your book of photographs. When you feel lonely without me, you can turn the machine on. It's got no feelings to hurt.

HIGGINS. I can't turn your soul on. Leave me those feelings, and you can take away the voice and the face. They are not you.

LIZA. Oh, you *are* a devil. You can twist the heart in a girl as easy as some could twist her arms to hurt her. Mrs. Pearce warned me. Time and again she has wanted to leave you, and you always got round her at the last minute. And you don't care a bit for her. And you don't care a bit for me.

HIGGINS. I care for life, for humanity; and you are a part of it that has come my way and been built into my house. What more can you or anyone ask?

LIZA. I won't care for anybody that doesn't care for me.

HIGGINS. Commercial principles, Eliza. Like (*reproducing her Covent Garden pronunciation with professional exactness*) s'yollin voylets [selling violets], isn't it?

LIZA. Don't sneer at me. It's mean to sneer at me.

HIGGINS. I have never sneered in my life. Sneering doesn't become either the human face or the human soul. I am expressing my righteous contempt for commercialism. I don't and won't trade in affection. You call me a brute because you couldn't buy a claim on me by fetching my slippers and finding my spectacles. You were a fool! I think a woman fetching a man's slippers is a disgusting sight. Did I ever fetch *your* slippers? I think a good deal more of you for throwing them in my face. No use slaving for me and then saying you want to be cared for. Who cares for a slave? If you come back, come back for the sake of good fellowship; for you'll get nothing

else. You've had a thousand times as much out of me as I have out of you; and if you dare to set up your little dog's tricks of fetching and carrying slippers against my creation of a Duchess, Eliza, I'll slam the door in your silly face.

LIZA. What did you do it for if you didn't care for me?

HIGGINS (*heartily*). Why, because it was my job.

LIZA. You never thought of the trouble it would make for me.

HIGGINS. Would the world ever have been made if its maker had been afraid of making trouble? Making life means making trouble. There's only one way of escaping trouble, and that's killing things. Cowards, you notice, are always shrieking to have troublesome people killed.

LIZA. I'm no preacher; I don't notice things like that. I notice that you don't notice me.

HIGGINS (*jumping up and walking about intolerantly*). Eliza! You're an idiot. I waste the treasures of my Miltonic mind by spreading them before you. Once for all, understand that I go my way and do my work without caring twopence what happens to either of us. I am not intimidated, like your father and your stepmother. So you can come back or go to the devil — whichever you please.

LIZA. What am I to come back for?

HIGGINS (*bouncing up on his knees on the ottoman and leaning over it to her*). For the fun of it. That's why I took you on.

LIZA (*with averted face*). And you may throw me out tomorrow if I don't do everything you want me to?

HIGGINS. Yes, and you may walk out tomorrow if I don't do everything *you* want me to.

LIZA. And live with my stepmother?

HIGGINS. Yes, or sell flowers.

LIZA. Oh! if I only *could* go back to my flower basket! I should be independent of both you and father and all the world! Why did you take my independence from me? Why did I give it up? I'm a slave now, for all my fine clothes.

HIGGINS. Not a bit. I'll adopt you as my daughter and settle money on you if you like. Or would you rather marry Pickering?

LIZA (*looking fiercely round at him*). I wouldn't marry *you* if you asked me; and you're nearer my age than what he is.

HIGGINS (*gently*). Than he is; not "than what he is."

LIZA (*losing her temper and rising*). I'll talk as I like. You're not my teacher now.

HIGGINS (*reflectively*). I don't suppose Pickering would, though. He's as confirmed an old bachelor as I am.

LIZA. That's not what I want, and don't you think it. I've always had chaps enough wanting me that way. Freddy Hill writes to me twice and three times a day, sheets and sheets.

HIGGINS (*disagreeably surprised*). Damn his impudence! (*He recoils and finds himself sitting on his heels.*)

LIZA. He has a right to if he likes, poor lad. And he does love me.

HIGGINS (*getting off the ottoman*). You have no right to encourage him.

LIZA. Every girl has a right to be loved.

HIGGINS. What! By fools like that?

LIZA. Freddy's not a fool. And if he's weak and poor and wants me, maybe he'd make me happier than my betters that bully me and don't want me.

HIGGINS. Can he *make* anything of you? That's the point.

LIZA. Perhaps I could make something of him. But I never thought of us making anything of one another; and you never think of anything else. I only want to be natural.

HIGGINS. In short, you want me to be as infatuated about you as Freddy? Is that it?

LIZA. No I don't. That's not the sort of feeling I want from you. And don't you be too sure of yourself or of me. I could have been a bad girl if I'd liked.

I've seen more of some things than you, for all your learning. Girls like me can drag gentlemen down to make love to them easy enough. And they wish each other dead the next minute.

HIGGINS. Of course they do. Then what in thunder are we quarreling about?

LIZA (*much troubled*). I want a little kindness. I know I'm a common ignorant girl, and you a book-learned gentleman; but I'm not dirt under your feet. What I done (*correcting herself*) what I did was not for the dresses and the taxis. I did it because we were pleasant together and I come — came — to care for you; not to want you to make love to me, and not forgetting the difference between us, but more friendly like.

HIGGINS. Well, of course. That's just how I feel. And how Pickering feels. Eliza, you're a fool.

LIZA. That's not a proper answer to give me. (*She sinks on the chair at the writing table in tears.*)

HIGGINS. It's all you'll get until you stop being a common idiot. If you're going to be a lady, you'll have to give up feeling neglected if the men you know don't spend half their time sniveling over you and the other half giving you black eyes. If you can't stand the coldness of my sort of life, and the strain of it, go back to the gutter. Work till you are more a brute than a human being; and then cuddle and squabble and drink till you fall asleep. Oh, it's a fine life, the life of the gutter. It's real; it's warm; it's violent. You can feel it through the thickest skin; you can taste it and smell it without any training or any work. Not like Science and Literature and Classical Music and Philosophy and Art. You find me cold, unfeeling, selfish, don't you? Very well. Be off with you to the sort of people you like. Marry some sentimental hog or other with lots of money, and a thick pair of lips to kiss you with and a thick pair of boots to kick you with. If you can't appreciate what you've got, you'd better get what you can appreciate.

LIZA (*desperate*). Oh, you *are* a cruel tyrant. I can't talk to you. You turn everything against me; I'm always in the wrong. But you know very well all the time that you're nothing but a bully. You know I can't go back to the gutter, as you call it, and that I have no real friends in the world but you and the Colonel. You know well I couldn't bear to live with a low common man after you two; and it's wicked and cruel of you to insult me by pretending I could. You think I must go back to Wimpole Street because I have nowhere else to go but father's. But don't you be too sure that you have me under your feet to be trampled on and talked down. I'll marry Freddy, I will, as soon as he's able to support me.

HIGGINS (*sitting down beside her*). Rubbish! You shall marry an ambassador. You shall marry the Governor-General of India or the Lord-Lieutenant of Ireland, or somebody who wants a deputy-queen. I'm not going to have my masterpiece thrown away on Freddy.

LIZA. You think I like you to say that. But I haven't forgot what you said a minute ago, and I won't be coaxed round as if I was a baby or a puppy. If I can't have kindness, I'll have independence.

HIGGINS. Independence? That's middle class blasphemy. We are all dependent on one another, every soul of us on earth.

LIZA (*rising determinedly*). I'll let you see whether I'm dependent on you. If you can preach, I can teach. I'll go and be a teacher.

HIGGINS. What'll you teach, in heaven's name?

LIZA. What you taught me. I'll teach phonetics.

HIGGINS. Ha! ha! ha!

LIZA. I'll offer myself as an assistant to Professor Nepean.

HIGGINS (*rising in a fury*). What! That impostor! That humbug! That toadying ignoramus! Teach him *my* methods! *My* discoveries! You take one step in his direction and I'll wring your neck. (*He lays hands on her.*) Do you hear?

LIZA (*defiantly nonresistant*). Wring away. What do I care? I knew you'd strike me some day. (*He lets her go, stamping with rage at having forgotten himself, and recoils so hastily that he stumbles back into his seat on the ottoman*). Aha! Now I know how to deal with you. What a fool I was not to think of it before! You can't take away the knowledge you gave me. You said I had a finer ear than you. And I can be civil and kind to people, which is more than you can. Aha! That's done you, Henry Higgins, it has. Now I don't care *that* (*snapping her fingers*) for your bullying and your big talk. I'll advertise it in the papers that your duchess is only a flower girl that you taught, and that she'll teach anybody to be a duchess just the same in six months for a thousand guineas. Oh, when I think of myself crawling under your feet and being trampled on and called names, when all the time I had only to lift up my finger to be as good as you, I could just kick myself.

HIGGINS (*wondering at her*). You impudent hussy, you! But it's better than sniveling; better than fetching slippers and finding spectacles, isn't it? (*Rising*) By George, Eliza, I said I'd make a woman of you; and I have. I like you like this.

LIZA. Yes, you turn round and make up to me now that I'm not afraid of you, and can do without you.

HIGGINS. Of course I do, you little fool. Five minutes ago you were like a millstone round my neck. Now you're a tower of strength, a consort battleship. You and I and Pickering will be three old bachelors together instead of only two men and a silly girl.

[MRS. HIGGINS *returns, dressed for the wedding.* ELIZA *instantly becomes cool and elegant.*]

MRS. HIGGINS. The carriage is waiting,

Eliza. Are you ready?

LIZA. Quite. Is the Professor coming?

MRS. HIGGINS. Certainly not. He can't behave himself in church. He makes remarks out loud all the time on the clergyman's pronunciation.

LIZA. Then I shall not see you again, Professor. Good-by. (*She goes to the door.*)

MRS. HIGGINS (*coming to* HIGGINS). Good-by, dear.

HIGGINS. Good-by, Mother. (*He is about to kiss her, when he recollects something.*) Oh, by the way, Eliza, order a ham and a Stilton cheese, will you? And buy me a pair of reindeer gloves, number eights, and a tie to match that new suit of mine, at Eale & Binman's. You can choose the color. (*His cheerful, careless, vigorous voice shows that he is incorrigible.*)

LIZA (*disdainfully*). Buy them yourself. (*She sweeps out.*)

MRS. HIGGINS. I'm afraid you've spoiled that girl, Henry. But never mind, dear. I'll buy you the tie and gloves.

HIGGINS (*sunnily*). Oh, don't bother. She'll buy 'em all right enough. Goodby.

[*They kiss.* MRS. HIGGINS *runs out.* HIGGINS, *left alone, rattles his cash in his pocket; chuckles; and disports himself in a highly self-satisfied manner.*]

AN END AND A BEGINNING

1. Why do you think Eliza goes to Mrs. Higgins? What is Higgins' reaction to Eliza's disappearance?

2. Several months have passed since Alfred Doolittle followed his daughter to Henry Higgins' home. What has happened to him during this interval? How is Higgins responsible for what has happened? Through the character of Doolittle, what is Shaw saying about society?

3. How would you describe Eliza's meeting with Higgins and Pickering? Who is on the defensive? What are Eliza's feelings toward Pickering? Higgins? her father? Find the lines which best illustrate Eliza's feelings. Compare Eliza now with the Eliza in

each preceding act. Do you note any changes in Higgins in this final scene?

4. Higgins offers to adopt Eliza as his daughter and settle money on her; what other suggestions does he make? How does she react to each? What do you think Higgins' true feeling for Eliza is?

5. How is the situation at the end of the play the beginning of a new life for Eliza? Shaw ends the play without resolving the dilemma he has posed. What do you think will happen? If you are interested, read Shaw's prose sequel (in *Selected Plays of Bernard Shaw*, Dodd, Mead) in which he tells whom Eliza married, and why.

UNDERSTANDING SHAW'S SATIRE

The humor of George Bernard Shaw always has a touch of satire — a sharp social lash that he uses with superb skill. Satire, a device for exposing and discrediting vice or folly, was used by ancient Roman poets, and it has been developed into an effective and amusing literary art.

Satirists have moved from private animosity, or bitterness toward individuals, to elements in public life with which we all are concerned. All types of literature may be vehicles for satire. The spirit behind satirical writing, while it is always critical, ranges from lighthearted fun to angry denunciation.

1. *Pygmalion* is a satire on the false values of society. What classes is Shaw satirizing? What social standards does he criticize? According to Shaw, what is the most important thing each group or class does not have?

2. Make a list of the different aspects of society that Shaw satirizes in this play. How many of them do you think are justifiably ridiculed? In which instances do you disagree with Shaw's point of view?

3. Review the play, noticing what types of people are represented. For what purposes does Shaw use each of the following characters: Eliza, Higgins, Pickering, Mrs. Higgins, Mrs. Eynsford Hill, Clara, Freddy, Alfred Doolittle, Mrs. Pearce? To what extent are these characters individuals or representatives of types of people? What kind of people did Shaw admire? What kind did he dislike? Give definite evidence in support of your answers.

OTHER PLAYS BY SHAW

Pygmalion, currently perhaps Shaw's best-known comedy, is but one of the many provocative and entertaining plays written by George Bernard Shaw. On the facing page are pictured scenes from three other memorable Shaw plays: *Caesar and Cleopatra* (top left), with Clare Bloom as Cleopatra; *The Devil's Disciple* (top right), with Maurice Evans as Richard Dudgeon; and *Arms and the Man* (bottom), as staged by the Hunter College Theater Workshop. Each of these plays makes excellent reading. Among other

Shaw favorites are *Major Barbara, Saint Joan, Back to Methuselah, Heartbreak House, Candida, The Doctor's Dilemma,* and *The Apple Cart.*

Shaw, who questioned many of the institutions and social conventions of his day, delighted in writing "problem plays" in which, using his characters as spokesmen for his own ideas, he put conventional beliefs to the test. He also took great pleasure in shocking his audiences. Discarding the accepted rules of the Victorian theater, Shaw wrote as and about what he pleased, letting the stage serve as a forum for his penetrating and often startling views on a wide variety of subjects.

Culver

GBS AS DRAMATIST

Thanks to the stupendous success of *My Fair Lady,* which, squarely based on *Pygmalion,* is one of the most popular musicals ever written, Henry Higgins and Liza Doolittle and her father are easily the most widely known of all the characters that Shaw created. *Pygmalion* is a delightful comedy, typical of its author in many ways. From this play we can learn a good deal about its author and his work.

Pygmalion can be considered one of Shaw's later plays, for he was fifty-six when it was first produced in 1912. One

of his reasons for writing it was to provide a fine acting part — that of Liza Doolittle — for Mrs. Patrick Campbell, one of his favorite actresses and a close friend. Mrs. Campbell was a beautiful woman with a thrilling voice and a fiery temperament, and, though no longer a a young girl by 1912, she made a sensational hit as Liza.

Although I did not see the original production of the play, I well remember the excitement about Liza's "Not bloody likely." To understand this excitement you must imagine some much stronger word — much more shocking to American ears than "bloody" — being spoken on the stage for the first time. Being by this time an old hand in the theater, Shaw of course had carefully calculated the effect this particular word would produce.

SHAW'S LITERARY BEGINNINGS

Shaw did not begin his career by writing plays. First he wrote several novels. Very queer novels they are too, full of ideas, like everything he ever wrote, but not really satisfying as fiction. Then he was for some time a music critic — he had a good knowledge of music and was particularly fond of the operas of Mozart. After this he turned to the theater and wrote dramatic criticism for many of Britain's leading

NBC

NBC

Hunter College Theater Workshop

newspapers and magazines.

Shaw's dramatic criticism, which he published later in volume form, is among the best ever written. In the 1890's, when Shaw was a critic, the London theater appealed chiefly to fashionable audiences, and most of the plays it produced were thin, light comedies about fashionable people, broad farces, and sentimental-romantic costume plays. For nearly all of these, Shaw had sharp contempt. He complained, wittily rather than bitterly, that the English theater was almost entirely lacking in ideas and offered little or nothing to an intelligent playgoer.

But whether it has ideas or not, the theater is still the theater. To capture and maintain the interest of the audience, it depends upon dramatic situations and effects. Although Shaw might have despised nearly all the plays he had to review, he learned a great deal from them about how to achieve dramatic effects. He learned how to take an audience by surprise, how to compel it to applaud or burst into a shout of laughter. Most of Shaw's effects are anything but subtle — he was never afraid of downright clowning — but no audiences can resist them. Indeed, they are mostly foolproof old devices.

One of the most obvious of them, which never fails if properly contrived, is the unexpected entrance of a character dressed in a surprising way. Two very effective examples of this dramatic device are the entrance of Liza, fashionably dressed, in Act III, and a similar entrance by her father, no longer a dustman, in Act V. These are typical of Shaw's broadly theatrical method, based on his knowledge of audiences, which in a comedy need to be visually as well as intellectually amused. But of course there is a lot more in Shaw than this, for he is also essentially a dramatist of ideas and debate. To understand how he came to be such a dramatist, we must take another look at his life.

Shaw was born in Dublin, a charming but untidy city. His father was a wholesale merchant on the Dublin Corn Exchange; his mother, who finally left her husband to earn her living in London, was a gifted musician. A proud and sensitive youth, Shaw reacted violently against his early surroundings, with their Bohemian sloppiness, drink, and easy emotionalism. After this reaction he became not only a good deal of a puritan in his style of living but also a lover of order, authority, and discipline — anything that compelled people to lead sensible and decent lives.

After settling in London and becoming active with the Fabians, a newly founded political society, Shaw learned through his work with them to speak fluently and wittily in public, and for years he seized every opportunity to address any kind of audience and to engage in public debate with any opponent. All this public speaking and debating, all these audiences, were later of immense service to him in the theater.

SHAVIAN DRAMATIC COMEDY

Shaw's special achievement in the theater was to create a type of comedy all his own. The basis of it, in spite of those broadly dramatic effects we have already noted, was debate. Shaw's characters are always arguing about ideas and indeed only stop when some touch of drama, some piece of broad clowning, takes hold of the scene just when the audience might be bored. He was fascinated by opera, and as he wrote his plays he thought of them as operas of talk — first, perhaps, a duet, then a trio, then a quartet — only instead of singing, the characters eloquently express their various points of view and are busy arguing.

Here I must point out that although Shaw is a master comic dramatist, perhaps the greatest since Molière, he has been a very bad influence on younger dramatists, who have produced all too many boring and unsuccessful plays just because they were trying to copy his methods. For the Shaw comedy of debate demands a Shaw to write it. Nobody else has his particular touch or is able to create his special atmosphere.

There are good reasons why this is so. To begin with, Shaw had a lot of strongly held opinions on all manner of subjects. Then, as we have seen, he had enjoyed years of experience in public debating about these opinions. Very eloquent and witty speeches came naturally to him. In addition, as we have also seen, he had learned all the tricks, in and out of the theater, to keep audiences amused. Finally, he was never deeply emotionally involved with most of his opinions, and his natural good humor gave his plays a sunny atmosphere very valuable to comedy.

All this indicates how Shaw could make an effective comedy out of themes that would defeat any other dramatist. He does just this in *Pygmalion,* which is a kind of Cinderella story created out of an unusual combination of elements: his keen interest in phonetics and language, his opinion of the English class structure of society, and his insight into various modes of life — that of the working class, the idly fashionable, the ultra-respectable middle class, and the new classless kind of life led by enthusiastic research scientists, represented here by Higgins. Nobody else but Shaw could have combined these peculiar and seemingly unpromising elements into a brilliant comedy.

SHAVIAN CHARACTERS

People who do not enjoy Shaw always tell us that he cannot really create character, as a dramatist ought to be able to do, that all his characters talk alike, as if they were all Shaw himself. But this is simply not true. Although Shaw does not have the astounding range of a supreme master of the drama like Shakespeare, he is able to create convincing and amusing characters quite different from himself. In *Pygmalion,* for instance, there may be a good deal of Shaw himself in Higgins, but Doolittle and Pickering are very different from Shaw, and Doolittle especially is a wonderfully effective comic character. His women are more limited in range, it is true, for the tolerant, amused, wise type of woman, represented here by Higgins' mother, appears in play after play. As for Liza herself, although a brilliant actress could dazzle us into accepting her, she is not altogether convincing.

In a long afterword to *Pygmalion,* Shaw explains at length that Liza and Higgins remained close friends but that she married Freddy, who finally assisted her in running a flower shop. Here, in my view, Shaw deliberately refused to behave like more conventional dramatists, and he did so really to his own disadvantage. For it is obvious in Act V that Liza is in love with Higgins. Shaw's determination that nothing shall come of it, in the usual theatrical style of "the happy ending," does not belong to him as a creative dramatist but stems from his more superficial role as an anti-romantic, unconventional, paradoxical thinker. Liza's protest against being regarded not as a person but as the mere subject of an experiment — a protest many of us are ready to echo and applaud in these later days of ceaseless scientific experiments — is real enough, but the depth of feeling behind her protest is not truly represented in the play's final action. Cinderella should marry the prince, even if he is crazy about phonetics and twenty years older than she.

Nevertheless, in *Pygmalion* we have merely one helping — of fun, character, argument, insight, wisdom — from the huge feast that this great Irishman, the finest master of comedy in the modern age, has left us. It enchants us in the theater, where Shaw, like a true dramatist, belongs, and it keeps us amused and happy as readers. We should take advantage of this wonderful gift and be grateful.

J. B. P.

George Joseph from the CBS production

The Old Lady Shows Her Medals

JAMES M. BARRIE 1860–1937

No English writer has given more widespread delight to all ages and nations than the creator of *Peter Pan*, James M. Barrie. With Mary Martin as Peter Pan, this perennial favorite has been produced on Broadway and televised in color. While he excelled as a dramatist, Barrie is also known as a story writer and a novelist.

J. M. Barrie began life in a little Lowland village, referred to on the map as Kirriemuir, but known as Thrums to Barrie fans. After receiving his master's degree from the University of Edinburgh when he was twenty-two, Barrie left Scotland for England. When far away from his village and homesick, he recorded the amusing situations and racy speech of his old neighbors in *A Window in Thrums*. But fame shied away from him, and he said later that for three years he kept body and soul together with coffee and penny buns. Thrums won him rewards in the end, however. Many short stories and three novels based on village life brought him enthusiastic readers.

When his best-known novel, *The Little Minister*, was made into a successful play, Barrie turned to the stage. With a fertile imagination, he was able to toss off play after play. Among his most popular comedies are *Quality Street, The Admirable Crichton*, and *What Every Woman Knows*.

In 1913 Barrie was knighted by King George V for his marked contribution to British life and letters. His own University of Edinburgh presented him with a degree of Doctor of Letters in 1922 and made him Chancellor in 1930.

The following short play, set in London during the days of World War I, is typical of Barrie in many ways. It shows Scottish characters, in whose portrayal Barrie excelled. It blends humor and pathos, as do most of his plays. It contains the storylike and lengthy stage directions — in which playwright talks to reader — which are a trademark of Barrie plays. It shows Barrie's sympathetic portrayal of people in the humblest ranks of society and illustrates the comment made about him that "his magic touch has ennobled and endeared the common things of life."

"The Old Lady Shows Her Medals" by James Matthew Barrie, published by Charles Scribner's Sons. Reprinted by permission of the publishers.

Characters

MRS. DOWEY

MRS. TWYMLEY

MRS. HAGGERTY

MRS. MICKLEHAM

THE REVEREND MR. WILLINGS

PRIVATE K. DOWEY

Three nice old ladies and a criminal, who is even nicer, are discussing the war over a cup of tea. The criminal, who is the hostess, calls it a dish of tea, which shows that she comes from Caledonia;[1] but that is not her crime.

They are all London charwomen,[2] but three of them, including the hostess, are what are called professionally "charwomen and" or simply "ands." An "and" is also a caretaker when required; her name is entered as such in ink in a registry book, financial transactions take place across a counter between her and the registrar, and altogether she is of a very different social status from one who, like MRS. HAGGERTY, is a charwoman but nothing else. MRS. HAGGERTY, though present, is not at the party by invitation; having seen MRS. DOWEY buying the winkles,[3] she followed her downstairs — and so has shuffled into the play and sat down in it against our wish. We would remove her by force, or at least print her name in small letters, were it not that she takes offense very readily and says that nobody respects her. So, as you have slipped in, you can sit there, MRS. HAGGERTY; but keep quiet.

There is nothing doing at present in the caretaking way for MRS. DOWEY, our hostess; but this does not damp[4] her, caretaking being only to such as she an extra financially and a halo socially. If

---

[1] *Caledonia* (kăl'ĕ·dōn'yà): Scotland. [2] *charwomen:* cleaning women. [3] *winkles:* small shellfish. [4] *damp:* as used here, discourage.

she had the honor of being served with an income-tax paper she would probably fill in one of the nasty little compartments with the words "Trade — charring. Profession (if any) — caretaking." This home of hers (from which, to look after your house, she makes, occasionally, temporary departures in great style, escorting a barrow) is in one of those what-care-I streets that you discover only when you have lost your way; on discovering them your duty is to report them to the authorities who immediately add them to the map of London. That is why we are now reporting Friday Street. We shall call it, in the rough sketch drawn for tomorrow's press, "Street in which the criminal resided"; and you will find MRS. DOWEY'S home therein marked with an X.

Her abode really consists of one room, but she maintains that there are two; so, rather than argue, let us say that there are two. The other one has no window, and she could not swish her old skirts in it without knocking something over; its grandest display is of tin pans and crockery on top of a dresser which has a lid to it; you have but to whip off the utensils and raise the lid, and, behold, a bath with hot and cold. MRS. DOWEY is very proud of this possession, and when she shows it off, as she does perhaps too frequently, she first signs to you with closed fist (funny old thing that she is) to approach softly. She then tiptoes to the dresser and pops off the lid, as if to take the bath unawares. Then she sucks her lips, and is modest if you have the grace to do the exclamations.

In the real room is a bed, though that is putting the matter too briefly. The fair way to begin, if you love MRS. DOWEY, is to say to her that it is a pity she has no bed. If she is in her best form she will chuckle, and agree that the want of a bed tries her sore; she will keep you on the hooks, so to speak, as long as she can; and then, with that mouselike movement again, she will suddenly spring the bed on you. You thought it was a wardrobe, but she brings it down from the wall, and lo, a bed. There is nothing else in her abode (which we now see to contain four rooms — kitchen, pantry, bedroom, and bathroom) that is absolutely a surprise; but it is full of "bits," every one of which has been paid ready money for and gloated over and tended until it has become part of its owner. Genuine Doweys, the dealers might call them, though there is probably nothing in the place except the bed that would fetch half-a-crown.

Her home is in the basement, so that the view is restricted to the lower half of persons passing overhead beyond the area stairs. Here at the window MRS. DOWEY *sometimes sits of a summer evening gazing, not sentimentally at a flowerpot which contains one poor bulb, nor yearningly at some tiny speck of sky, but with unholy relish at holes in stockings, and the like, which are revealed to her from her point of vantage. You, gentle reader, may flaunt by, thinking that your finery awes the street; but* MRS. DOWEY *can tell (and does) that your soles are in need of neat repair.*

Also, lower parts being as expressive as the face to those whose view is thus limited, she could swear to scores of the passers-by in a court of law.

These four lively old codgers are having a good time at the tea table, and wit is flowing free. As you can see by their everyday garments, and by their pails and mops (which are having a little tea party by themselves in the corner), it is not a gathering by invitations stretching away into yesterday. It is a purely informal affair, so much more attractive — don't you think? — than banquets elaborately prearranged. You know how they come about, especially in wartime. Very likely MRS. DOWEY *met* MRS. TWYMLEY *and* MRS. MICKLEHAM *quite casually in the street, and meant to do no more than pass the time of day; then, naturally enough, the word cam-*

ouflage [1] *was mentioned and they got heated, but in the end* MRS. TWYMLEY *apologized; then, in the odd way in which one thing leads to another, the winkleman appeared, and* MRS. DOWEY *remembered that she had that pot of jam and that* MRS. MICKLEHAM *had stood treat last time; and soon they were all three descending the area stairs, followed cringingly by the* HAGGERTY WOMAN.

They have been extremely merry, and never were four hard-worked old ladies who deserved it better. All a woman can do in wartime they do daily and cheerfully, just as their menfolk are doing it at the Front; and now, with the mops and pails laid aside, they sprawl gracefully at ease. There is no intention on their part to consider peace terms until a decisive victory has been gained in the field (Sarah Ann Dowey), until the Kaiser is put to the rightabout (Emma Mickleham) and singing very small (Amelia Twymley).

At this tea party the lady who is to play the part of MRS. DOWEY *is sure to want to suggest that our heroine has a secret sorrow; namely, the crime. But you should see us knocking that idea out of her head!* MRS. DOWEY *knows she is a criminal, but, unlike the actress, she does not know that she is about to be found out; and she is, to put it bluntly in her own Scotch way, the merriest of the whole clamjamfry. She presses more tea on her guests, but they wave her away from them in the pretty manner of ladies who know that they have already had more than enough.*

MRS. DOWEY. Just one more winkle, Mrs. Mickleham?

[*Indeed there is only one more. But* MRS. MICKLEHAM *indicates politely that if she took this one it would have to swim for it. The* HAGGERTY WOMAN

---

[1] *camouflage* (kăm′ōō·fläzh): in the old ladies' time, a new and exciting word. It refers to various ways of disguising military equipment or installations.

takes it long afterward when she thinks, erroneously, that no one is looking. MRS. TWYMLEY *is sulking. Evidently someone has contradicted her. Probably the* HAGGERTY WOMAN.]

MRS. TWYMLEY. I say it is so.

THE HAGGERTY WOMAN. I say it may be so.

MRS. TWYMLEY. I suppose I ought to know: me that has a son a prisoner in Germany. (*She has so obviously scored that all good feeling seems to call upon her to end here. But she continues, rather shabbily.*) Being the only lady present that has that proud misfortune.

[*The others are stung.*]

MRS. DOWEY. My son is fighting in France.

MRS. MICKLEHAM. Mine is wounded in two places.

THE HAGGERTY WOMAN. Mine is at Salonaiky.[1]

[*The absurd pronunciation of this un-educated person moves the others to mirth.*]

MRS. DOWEY. You'll excuse us, Mrs. Haggerty, but the correct pronunciation is Salonikky.

THE HAGGERTY WOMAN (*to cover her confusion*). I don't think. (*She feels that even this does not prove her case.*) And I speak as one that has War Savings Certificates.

MRS. TWYMLEY. We all have them.

[*The* HAGGERTY WOMAN *whimpers, and the other guests regard her with un-feeling disdain.*]

MRS. DOWEY (*to restore cheerful-ness*). Oh, it's a terrible war.

ALL (*brightening*). It is. You may say so.

MRS. DOWEY (*encouraged*). What I say is, the men is splendid; but I'm

none so easy about the staff. That's your weak point, Mrs. Mickleham.

MRS. MICKLEHAM (*on the defense, but determined to reveal nothing that might be of use to the enemy*). You may take it from me, the staff's all right.

MRS. DOWEY. And very relieved I am to hear you say it.

[*It is here that the* HAGGERTY WOMAN *has the remaining winkle.*]

MRS. MICKLEHAM. You don't under-stand properly about trench warfare. If I had a map —

MRS. DOWEY (*wetting her finger to draw lines on the table*). That's the river Sommy.[2] Now, if we had barrages here —

MRS. TWYMLEY. Very soon you would be enfilided.[3] Where's your sup-ports, my lady?

[MRS. DOWEY *is damped.*]

MRS. MICKLEHAM. What none of you grasps is that this is a artillery war —

THE HAGGERTY WOMAN (*strength-ened by the winkle*). I say that the word is Salonaiky.

[*The others purse their lips.*]

MRS. TWYMLEY (*with terrible mean-ing*). We'll change the subject. Have you seen this week's *Fashion Chat?* (*She has evidently seen and devoured it herself, and even licked up the crumbs.*) The gabardine with accordion pleats has quite gone out.

MRS. DOWEY (*her old face sparkling*). My sakes! You tell me?

MRS. TWYMLEY (*with the touch of haughtiness that comes of great topics*). The plain smock has come in again, with silk lacing, giving that charming chic effect.

MRS. DOWEY. Oho!

---

[1] *Salonaiky:* her mispronunciation of Salonika (săl'ô·nē'kȧ), Greece, where a great naval battle took place in World War I.

[2] *Sommy:* her mispronunciation of the French river Somme (sôm), a scene of many conflicts in World War I. [3] *enfilided:* her mispronunciation of enfiladed (ĕn'fĭ·lād'ĕd), a military term meaning "raked by gunfire."

MRS. MICKLEHAM. I must say I was always partial to the straight line (*thoughtfully regarding the want of line in* MRS. TWYMLEY'S *person*) though trying to them as is of too friendly a figure.

[*It is here that the* HAGGERTY WOMAN'S *fingers close unostentatiously upon a piece of sugar.*]

MRS. TWYMLEY (*sailing into the empyrean* [1]). Lady Dolly Kanister was seen conversing across the railings in a dainty *de jou.* [2]

MRS. DOWEY. Fine would I have liked to see her.

MRS. TWYMLEY. She is equally popular as maid, wife, and munition worker. Her two children is inset. [3] Lady Pops Babington was married in a tight tulle.

MRS. MICKLEHAM. What was her going-away dress?

MRS. TWYMLEY. A champagny cream velvet with dreamy corsage. She's married to Colonel the Honorable Chingford — "Snubs," they called him at Eton.

THE HAGGERTY WOMAN (*having disposed of the sugar*). Very likely he'll be sent to Salonaiky.

MRS. MICKLEHAM. Wherever he is sent, she'll have the same tremors as the rest of us. She'll be as keen to get the letters wrote with pencils as you or me.

MRS. TWYMLEY. Them pencil letters!

MRS. DOWEY (*in her sweet Scotch voice, timidly, afraid she may be going too far*). And women in enemy lands gets those pencil letters and then stop getting them, the same as ourselves. Let's occasionally think of that.

[*She has gone too far. Chairs are pushed back.*]

THE HAGGERTY WOMAN. I ask you!

MRS. MICKLEHAM. That's hardly language, Mrs. Dowey.

MRS. DOWEY (*scared*). Kindly excuse. I swear to death I'm none of your pacifists.

MRS. MICKLEHAM. Freely granted.

MRS. TWYMLEY. I've heard of females that have no male relations, and so they have no man-party at the wars. I've heard of them, but I don't mix with them.

MRS. MICKLEHAM. What can the likes of us have to say to them? It's not their war.

MRS. DOWEY (*wistfully*). They are to be pitied.

MRS. MICKLEHAM. But the place for them, Mrs. Dowey, is within doors with the blinds down.

MRS. DOWEY (*hurriedly*). That's the place for them.

MRS. MICKLEHAM. I saw one of them today buying a flag. I thought it was very impudent of her.

MRS. DOWEY (*meekly*). So it was.

MRS. MICKLEHAM (*trying to look modest with indifferent success*). I had a letter from my son, Percy, yesterday.

MRS. TWYMLEY. Alfred sent me his photo.

THE HAGGERTY WOMAN. Letters from Salonaiky is less common.

[*Three bosoms heave, but not, alas,* MRS. DOWEY'S. *Nevertheless she doggedly knits her lips.*]

MRS. DOWEY (*the criminal*). Kenneth writes to me every week. (*There are exclamations. The dauntless old thing holds aloft a packet of letters.*) Look at this. All his.

[*The* HAGGERTY WOMAN *whimpers.*]

MRS. TWYMLEY. Alfred has little time for writing, being a bombardier.

MRS. DOWEY (*relentlessly*). Do your letters begin "Dear mother"?

MRS. TWYMLEY. Generally.

MRS. MICKLEHAM. Invariable.

THE HAGGERTY WOMAN. Every time.

MRS. DOWEY (*delivering the knock-*

[1] *empyrean* (ĕm'pĭ·rē'ǎn): the highest part of heaven. [2] *de jou* (dĕ zhōō): a dress "for play" (French). [3] *inset:* Pictures of Lady Kanister's two children were apparently inserted into the larger picture of her.

out blow). Kenneth's begin "Dearest mother."

[*No one can think of the right reply.*]

MRS. TWYMLEY (*doing her best*). A short man, I should say, judging by yourself. (*She ought to have left it alone.*)

MRS. DOWEY. Six feet two — and a half.

[*The gloom deepens.*]

MRS. MICKLEHAM (*against her better judgment*). A kilty, did you tell me?

MRS. DOWEY. Most certainly. He's in the famous Black Watch.

THE HAGGERTY WOMAN (*producing her handkerchief*). The Surrey Rifles is the famousest.

MRS. MICKLEHAM. There you and the King disagrees, Mrs. Haggerty. His choice is the Buffs, same as my Percy's.

MRS. TWYMLEY (*magnanimously*). Give me the R.H.A.[1] and you can keep all the rest.

MRS. DOWEY. I'm sure I have nothing to say against the Surreys and the R.H.A. and Buffs; but they are just breeches regiments, I understand.

THE HAGGERTY WOMAN. We can't all be kilties.

MRS. DOWEY (*crushingly*). That's very true.

MRS. TWYMLEY (*it is foolish of her, but she can't help saying it*). Has your Kenneth great hairy legs?

MRS. DOWEY. Tremendous.

[*The wicked woman, but let us also say "Poor Sarah Ann Dowey." For, at this moment, enter Nemesis.[2] In other words, the less important part of a clergyman appears upon the stair.*]

MRS. MICKLEHAM. It's the reverent gent!

MRS. DOWEY (*little knowing what he*

[1] *Black Watch, Surrey Rifles, Buffs*, and *R.H.A.*: well-known British army regiments.
[2] *Nemesis* (nĕm′ĕ·sĭs): avenging fate (Greek mythology).

is bringing her). I see he has had his boots heeled.

[*It may be said of* MR. WILLINGS *that his happy smile always walks in front of him. This smile makes music of his life; it means that once again he has been chosen, in his opinion, as the central figure in romance. No one can well have led a more drab existence, but he will never know it; he will always think of himself, humbly though elatedly, as the chosen of the gods. Of him must it have been originally written that adventures are for the adventurous. He meets them at every street corner. For instance, he assists an old lady off a bus and asks her if he can be of any further help. She tells him that she wants to know the way to Maddox the butcher's. Then comes the kind, triumphant smile; it always comes first, followed by its explanation, "I was there yesterday!" This is the merest sample of the adventures that keep* MR. WILLINGS *up to the mark.*

[*Since the war broke out, his zest for life has become almost terrible. He can scarcely lift a newspaper and read of a hero without remembering that he knows someone of the same name. The Soldiers' Rest he is connected with was once a china emporium, and — mark my words — he had bought his tea service at it. Such is life when you are in the thick of it. Sometimes he feels that he is part of a gigantic spy drama. In the course of his extraordinary comings and goings he meets with Great Personages, of course, and is the confidential recipient of secret news. Before imparting the news he does not, as you might expect, first smile expansively; on the contrary, there comes over his face an awful solemnity, which, however, means the same thing. When divulging the names of the personages, he first looks around to make sure that no suspicious character is about, and then, lowering his voice, tells you, "I had that from Mr. Farthing himself — he is the secretary of the Bethnal Green Branch —H'sh . . ."*

[*There is a commotion about finding a worthy chair for "the reverent," and there is also some furtive pulling down of sleeves; but he stands surveying the ladies through his triumphant smile. This amazing man knows that he is about to score again.*]

MR. WILLINGS (*waving aside the chairs*). I thank you. But not at all. Friends, I have news.

MRS. MICKLEHAM. News?

THE HAGGERTY WOMAN. From the Front?

MRS. TWYMLEY. My Alfred, sir?

[*They are all grown suddenly anxious — all except the hostess, who knows that there can never be any news from the Front for her.*]

MR. WILLINGS. I tell you at once that all is well. The news is for Mrs. Dowey.

MRS. DOWEY (*she stares*). News for me?

MR. WILLINGS. Your son, Mrs. Dowey — he has got five days' leave.

[*She shakes her head slightly, or perhaps it only trembles a little on its stem.*]

Now, now, good news doesn't kill.

MRS. TWYMLEY. We're glad, Mrs. Dowey.

MRS. DOWEY. You're sure?

MR. WILLINGS. Quite sure. He has arrived.

MRS. DOWEY. He is in London?

MR. WILLINGS. He is. I have spoken to him.

MRS. MICKLEHAM. You lucky woman.

[*They might see that she is not looking lucky, but experience has told them how differently these things take people.*]

MR. WILLINGS (*marveling more and more as he unfolds his tale*). Ladies, it is quite a romance. I was in the . . .

(*He looks around cautiously, but he knows that they are all to be trusted.*) . . . in the Church Army quarters in Central Street, trying to get on the track of one or two of our missing men. Suddenly my eyes — I can't account for it — but suddenly my eyes alighted on a Highlander seated rather drearily on a bench, with his kit at his feet.

THE HAGGERTY WOMAN. A big man?

MR. WILLINGS. A great brawny fellow.

[*The* HAGGERTY WOMAN *groans.*]

"My friend," I said at once, "welcome back to Blighty."[1] I make a point of calling it Blighty. "I wonder," I said, "if there is anything I can do for you?" He shook his head "What regiment?" I asked (*Here* MR. WILLINGS *very properly lowers his voice to a whisper.*) "Black Watch, 5th Battalion," he said. "Name?" I asked. "Dowey," he said.

MRS. MICKLEHAM. I declare. I do declare.

MR. WILLINGS (*showing how the thing was done, with the help of a chair*). I put my hand on his shoulder as it might be thus. "Kenneth Dowey," I said, "I know your mother."

MRS. DOWEY (*wetting her lips*). What did he say to that?

MR. WILLINGS. He was incredulous. Indeed, he seemed to think I was balmy. But I offered to bring him straight to you. I told him how much you had talked to me about him.

MRS. DOWEY. Bring him here!

MRS. MICKLEHAM. I wonder he needed to be brought.

MR. WILLINGS. He had just arrived, and was bewildered by the great city. He listened to me in the taciturn Scotch way, and then he gave a curious laugh.

MRS. TWYMLEY. Laugh?

MR. WILLINGS (*whose wild life has brought him into contact with the strangest people*). The Scotch, Mrs. Twymley, express their emotions differently from

[1] *Blighty* (blĭ′tĭ): British slang for home, much used by soldiers.

us. With them tears signify a rollicking mood, while merriment denotes that they are plunged in gloom. When I had finished he said at once, "Let us go and see the old lady."

MRS. DOWEY (*backing, which is the first movement she has made since he began his tale*). Is he — coming?

MR. WILLINGS (*gloriously*). He has come. He is up there. I told him I thought I had better break the joyful news to you.

[*Three women rush to the window.* MRS. DOWEY *looks at her pantry door, but perhaps she remembers that it does not lock on the inside. She stands rigid, though her face has gone very gray.*]

MRS. DOWEY. Kindly get them to go away.

MR. WILLINGS. Ladies, I think this happy occasion scarcely requires you. (*He is not the man to ask of woman a sacrifice that he is not prepared to make himself.*) I also am going instantly.

[*They all survey* MRS. DOWEY, *and understand — or think they understand.*]

MRS. TWYMLEY (*pail and mop in hand*). I would thank none for their company if my Alfred was at the door.

MRS. MICKLEHAM (*similarly burdened*). The same from me. Shall I send him down, Mrs. Dowey?

[*The old lady does not hear her. She is listening, terrified, for a step on the stairs.*]

Look at the poor, joyous thing, sir. She has his letters in her hand.

[*The three women go.* MR. WILLINGS *puts a kind hand on* MRS. DOWEY'S *shoulder. He thinks he so thoroughly understands the situation.*]

MR. WILLINGS. A good son, Mrs. Dowey, to have written to you so often.

[*Our old criminal quakes, but she grips*

the letters more tightly. PRIVATE DOWEY *descends.*]

Dowey, my friend, there she is, waiting for you, with your letters in her hand.

DOWEY (*grimly*). That's great.

[MR. WILLINGS *ascends the stair without one backward glance, like the good gentleman he is; and the* DOWEYS *are left together with nearly the whole room between them. He is a great rough chunk of Scotland, howked out of her not so much neatly as liberally; and in his Black Watch uniform, all caked with mud, his kit and nearly all his worldly possessions on his back, he is an apparition scarcely less fearsome (but so much less ragged) than those ancestors of his who trotted with Prince Charlie [1] to Derby. He stands silent, scowling at the old lady, daring her to raise her head; and she would like very much to do it, for she longs to have a first glimpse of her son. When he does speak, it is to jeer at her.*]

DOWEY. Do you recognize your loving son, missis?

[*"Oh, the fine Scotch tang of him," she thinks.*]

MRS. DOWEY (*trembling*). I'm pleased you wrote so often. (*"Oh, but he's raised," [2] she thinks.*)

[*He strides toward her, and seizes the letters roughly.*]

DOWEY. Let's see them.

[*There is a string round the package and he unties it, and examines the letters at his leisure with much curiosity. The envelopes are in order, all addressed in pencil to* MRS. DOWEY, *with the proud words "Opened by Censor" on them. But the letter paper inside contains not a word of writing.*]

[1] *Prince Charlie:* the Young Pretender to the British throne in the eighteenth century.
[2] *raised:* annoyed.

DOWEY. Nothing but blank paper! Is this your writing in pencil on the envelope? (*She nods, and he gives the matter further consideration.*) The covey [1] told me you were a charwoman. So I suppose you picked the envelopes out of wastepaper baskets, or such like, and then changed the addresses?

[*She nods again; still she dare not look up, but she is admiring his legs. When, however, he would cast the letters into the fire, she flames up with sudden spirit. She clutches them.*]

MRS. DOWEY. Don't burn them letters, mister.

DOWEY. They're not real letters.

MRS. DOWEY. They're all I have.

DOWEY (*returning to irony*). I thought you had a son?

MRS. DOWEY. I never had a man nor a son nor anything. I just call myself Missis to give me a standing.

DOWEY. Well, it's past my seeing through.

[*He turns to look for some explanation from the walls. She gets a peep at him at last. Oh, what a grandly set-up man! Oh, the stride of him. Oh, the noble rage of him. Oh, Samson had been like this before that woman took him in hand.[2]*]

DOWEY (*whirling round on her*). What made you do it?

MRS. DOWEY. It was everybody's war, mister, except mine. (*She beats her arms.*) I wanted it to be my war too.

DOWEY. You'll need to be plainer. And yet I'm d——d if I care to hear you, you lying old trickster.

[*The words are merely what were to be expected, and so are endurable; but he has moved toward the door.*]

MRS. DOWEY. You're not going already, mister?

DOWEY. Yes, I just came to give you an ugly piece of my mind.

MRS. DOWEY (*holding out her arms longingly*). You haven't gave it to me yet.

DOWEY. You have a cheek!

MRS. DOWEY (*giving further proof of it*). You wouldn't drink some tea?

DOWEY. Me! I tell you I came here for the one purpose of blazing away at you.

[*It is such a roaring negative that it blows her into a chair. But she is up again in a moment, is this spirited old lady.*]

MRS. DOWEY. You could drink the tea while you was blazing away. There's winkles.

DOWEY. Is there? (*He turns interestedly toward the table, but his proud Scots character checks him — which is just as well, for what she should have said was that there had been winkles.*) Not me. You're just a common rogue. (*He seats himself far from the table.*) Now, then, out with it. Sit down! (*She sits meekly; there is nothing she would not do for him.*) As you char, I suppose you are on your feet all day.

MRS. DOWEY. I'm more on my knees.

DOWEY. That's where you should be to me.

MRS. DOWEY. Oh, mister. I'm willing.

DOWEY. Stop it. Go on, you accomplished liar.

MRS. DOWEY. It's true that my name is Dowey.

DOWEY. It's enough to make me change mine.

MRS. DOWEY. I've been charring and charring and charring as far back as I mind. I've been in London this twenty years.

DOWEY. We'll skip your early days. I have an appointment.

MRS. DOWEY. And then when I was old the war broke out.

DOWEY. How could it affect you?

MRS. DOWEY. Oh, mister, that's the thing. It didn't affect me. It affected

---

[1] *covey* (kŭv'ĭ): slang for *fellow.* [2] *Samson . . . in hand:* In the Bible, Samson was betrayed to his enemies by Delilah, who sheared his hair — the source of his strength — while he slept.

everybody but me. The neighbors looked down on me. Even the posters, on the walls, of the woman saying "Go, my boy," leered at me. I sometimes cried by myself in the dark. You won't have a cup of tea?

DOWEY. No.

MRS. DOWEY. Suddenlike the idea came to me to pretend I had a son.

DOWEY. You depraved old limmer! [1] But what in the name of Old Nick made you choose me out of the whole British Army?

MRS. DOWEY (*giggling*). Maybe, mister, it was because I like you best.

DOWEY. Now, now, woman.

MRS. DOWEY. I read one day in the papers, "In which he was assisted by Private K. Dowey, 5th Battalion, Black Watch."

DOWEY (*flattered*). Did you, now! Well, I expect that's the only time I was ever in the papers.

MRS. DOWEY (*trying it on again*). I didn't choose you for that alone. I read a history of the Black Watch first, to make sure it was the best regiment in the world.

DOWEY. Anybody could have told you that. (*He is moving about now in better humor, and meeting the loaf in his stride, he cuts a slice from it. He is hardly aware of this, but MRS. DOWEY knows.*) I like the Scotch voice of you, woman. It drumbles on like a hill burn.[2]

MRS. DOWEY. Prosen Water runs by where I was born. Maybe it teached me to speak, mister.

DOWEY. Canny, woman, canny.

MRS. DOWEY. I read about the Black Watch's ghostly piper that plays proudly when the men of the Black Watch do well, and prouder when they fall.

DOWEY. There's some foolish story of that kind. (*He has another careless slice off the loaf.*) But you couldn't have been living here at that time or they would have guessed. I suppose you flitted? [3]

MRS. DOWEY. Yes, it cost me eleven and sixpence.

DOWEY. How did you guess the *K* in my name stood for Kenneth?

MRS. DOWEY. Does it?

DOWEY. Umpha.

MRS. DOWEY. An angel whispered it to me in my sleep.

DOWEY. Well, that's the only angel in the whole black business. (*He chuckles.*) You little thought I would turn up! (*Wheeling suddenly on her*) Or did you?

MRS. DOWEY. I was beginning to weary for a sight of you, Kenneth.

DOWEY. What word was that?

MRS. DOWEY. Mister.

[*He helps himself to butter, and she holds out the jam pot to him; but he haughtily rejects it. Do you think she gives in now? Not a bit of it. He returns to sarcasm.*]

DOWEY. I hope you're pleased with me now you see me.

MRS. DOWEY. I'm very pleased. Does your folk live in Scotland?

DOWEY. Glasgow.

MRS. DOWEY. Both living?

DOWEY. Ay.

MRS. DOWEY. Is your mother terrible proud of you?

DOWEY. Naturally.

MRS. DOWEY. You'll be going to them?

DOWEY. After I've had a skite [4] in London first.

MRS. DOWEY (*sniffing*). So she is in London.

DOWEY. Who?

MRS. DOWEY. Your young lady.

DOWEY. Are you jealyous?

MRS. DOWEY. Not me.

DOWEY. You needna be. She's a young thing.

MRS. DOWEY. You surprises me. A beauty, no doubt?

DOWEY. You may be sure. (*He tries the jam.*) She's a titled person. She is

---

[1] *limmer:* Scotch for rascal. [2] *burn:* Scotch for brook. [3] *flitted:* moved.

[4] *skite:* a good time, or "fling."

equally popular as maid, wife, and munition worker.

[MRS. DOWEY *remembers Lady Dolly
Kanister, so familiar to readers of
fashionable gossip, and a very leery
expression indeed comes into her
face.*]

MRS. DOWEY. Tell me more about
her, man.
DOWEY. She has sent me a lot of
things, especially cakes, and a worsted
waistcoat, with a loving message on the
enclosed card.

[*The old lady is now in a quiver of excitement. She loses control of her
arms, which jump excitedly this way
and that.*]

MRS. DOWEY. You'll try one of my
cakes, mister?
DOWEY. Not me.
MRS. DOWEY. They're of my own
making.
DOWEY. No, I thank you.

[*But with a funny little run she is in the
pantry and back again. She pushes a
cake before him, at sight of which he
gapes.*]

MRS. DOWEY. What's the matter? Tell
me, oh, tell me, mister!
DOWEY. That's exactly the kind of
cake that her ladyship sends me.

[MRS. DOWEY *is now a very glorious old
character indeed.*]

MRS. DOWEY. Is the waistcoat right,
mister? I hope the Black Watch colors
pleased you.
DOWEY. What-at! Was it you?
MRS. DOWEY. I daredna give my own
name, you see, and I was always reading hers in the papers.

[*The badgered man looms over her, terrible for the last time.*]

DOWEY. Woman, is there no getting
rid of you!
MRS. DOWEY. Are you angry?

[*He sits down with a groan.*]

DOWEY. Oh, hell! Give me some tea.

[*She rushes about preparing a meal for
him, every bit of her wanting to cry
out to every other bit, "Oh, glory,
glory, glory!" For a moment she hovers behind his chair. "Kenneth!" she
murmurs. "What?" he asks, no longer aware that she is taking a liberty.
"Nothing," she says. "Just Kenneth," and is off gleefully for the tea
caddy. But when his tea is poured
out, and he has drunk a saucerful, the
instinct of self-preservation returns to
him between two bites.*]

DOWEY. Don't you be thinking, missis,
for one minute that you have got me.
MRS. DOWEY. No, no.

[*On that understanding he unbends.*]

DOWEY. I have a theater tonight, fol-
lowed by a randy-dandy.[1]
MRS. DOWEY. Oho! Kenneth, this is a
queer first meeting!
DOWEY. It is, woman — oh, it is —
(*guardedly*) — and it's also a last meet-
ing.
MRS. DOWEY. Yes, yes.
DOWEY. So here's to you — you old
mop and pail. *Ave atque vale.*
MRS. DOWEY. What's that?
DOWEY. That means Hail and Fare-
well.
MRS. DOWEY. Are you a scholar?
DOWEY. Being Scotch, there's almost
nothing I don't know.
MRS. DOWEY. What was you to trade?
DOWEY. Carter, glazier, orraman,[2]
any rough jobs.
MRS. DOWEY. You're a proper man to
look at.
DOWEY. I'm generally admired.
MRS. DOWEY. She's an enviable wom-
an.
DOWEY. Who?
MRS. DOWEY. Your mother.
DOWEY. Eh? Oh, that was just pro-

[1] *randy-dandy:* a noisy frolic. [2] *orraman:* one
who does odd jobs.

tecting myself from you. I have neither father nor mother nor wife nor grandmama. (*Bitterly*) This party never even knew who his proud parents were.

MRS. DOWEY. Is that — (*gleaming*) — is that true?

DOWEY. It's gospel.

MRS. DOWEY. Heaven be praised!

DOWEY. Eh? None of that! I was a fool to tell you. But don't think you can take advantage of it. Pass the cake.

MRS. DOWEY. I daresay it's true we'll never meet again, Kenneth, but — but if we do, I wonder where it will be?

DOWEY. Not in this world.

MRS. DOWEY. There's no telling — (*leering ingratiatingly*) — it might be at Berlin.

DOWEY. Tod, if I ever get to Berlin, I believe I'll find you there waiting for me!

MRS. DOWEY. With a cup of tea for you in my hand.

DOWEY. Yes, and (*heartily*) very good tea too.

[*He has partaken heavily; he is now in high good humor.*]

MRS. DOWEY. Kenneth, we could come back by Paris!

DOWEY. All the ladies likes to go to Paris.

MRS. DOWEY. Oh, Kenneth, Kenneth, if just once before I die I could be fitted for a Paris gown with dreamy corsage!

DOWEY. You're all alike, old covey. We have a song about it. (*He sings*):

Mrs. Gill is very ill,
    Nothing can improve her
But to see the Tuileries [1]
And waddle through the Louvre. [2]

[*No song ever had a greater success. MRS. DOWEY is doubled up with mirth. When she comes to — when they both come to, for they are a pair of them — she cries:*]

MRS. DOWEY. You must learn me that (*and off she goes in song also*):
    Mrs. Dowey's very ill,
        Nothing can improve her.

DOWEY. Stop!

But dressed up in a Paris gown
    To waddle through the Louvre.

[*They fling back their heads. She points at him; he points at her.*]

MRS. DOWEY (*ecstatically*). Hairy legs!

[*A mad remark, which brings him to his senses; he remembers who and what she is.*]

DOWEY. Mind your manners! (*Rising*) Well, thank you for my tea. I must be stepping.

[*Poor* MRS. DOWEY, *he is putting on his kit.*]

MRS. DOWEY. Where are you living?

DOWEY. (*He sighs.*) That's the question. But there's a place called The Hut, where some of the 2nd Battalion are. They'll take me in. Beggars — (*bitterly*) — can't be choosers.

MRS. DOWEY. Beggars?

DOWEY. I've never been here before. If you knew (*a shadow comes over him*) what it is to be in such a place without a friend. I was crazy with glee, when I got my leave, at the thought of seeing London at last; but after wandering its streets for four hours, I would almost have been glad to be back in the trenches.

[*"If you knew," he has said, but indeed the old lady knows.*]

MRS. DOWEY. That's my quandorum [3] too, Kenneth.

[*He nods sympathetically.*]

DOWEY. I'm sorry for you, you poor old body (*shouldering his kit*) but I see

---

[1] *Tuileries* (twē′lẽr·ĭz): famous royal palace in Paris. [2] *Louvre* (loo′vr′): famous art gallery connected with the Tuileries.

[3] *quandorum:* Mrs. Dowey's way of saying *quandary,* or *predicament.*

no way out for either of us.

MRS. DOWEY (*cooing*). Do you not?

DOWEY. Are you at it again!

[*She knows that it must be now or never. She has left her biggest guns for the end. In her excitement she is rising up and down on her toes.*]

MRS. DOWEY. Kenneth, I've heard that the thing a man on leave longs for more than anything else is a bed with sheets, and a bath.

DOWEY. You never heard anything truer.

MRS. DOWEY. Go into that pantry, Kenneth Dowey, and lift the dresser top, and tell me what you see.

[*He goes. There is an awful stillness. He returns, impressed.*]

DOWEY. It's a kind of a bath!

MRS. DOWEY. You could do yourself there pretty, half at a time.

DOWEY. Me?

MRS. DOWEY. There's a woman through the wall that would be very willing to give me a shakedown till your leave is up.

DOWEY. (*He snorts.*) Oh, is there!

[*She has not got him yet, but there is still one more gun.*]

MRS. DOWEY. Kenneth, look!

[*With these simple words she lets down the bed. She says no more; an effect like this would be spoiled by language. Fortunately he is not made of stone. He thrills.*]

DOWEY. Gosh! That's the dodge we need in the trenches.

MRS. DOWEY. That's your bed, Kenneth.

DOWEY. Mine? (*He grins at her.*) You queer old divert.[1] What can make you so keen to be burdened by a lump like me?

MRS. DOWEY. He! he! he! he!

---

[1] *divert* (dĭ'vŭrt): slang for an odd or different person.

DOWEY. I tell you, I'm the commonest kind of man.

MRS. DOWEY. I'm just the commonest kind of old wifie myself.

DOWEY. I've been a kick-about all my life, and I'm no great shakes at the war.

MRS. DOWEY. Yes, you are. How many Germans have you killed?

DOWEY. Just two for certain, and there was no glory in it. It was just because they wanted my shirt.

MRS. DOWEY. Your shirt?

DOWEY. Well, they said it was their shirt.

MRS. DOWEY. Have you took prisoners?

DOWEY. I once took half a dozen, but that was a poor affair too.

MRS. DOWEY. How could one man take half a dozen?

DOWEY. Just in the usual way. I surrounded them.

MRS. DOWEY. Kenneth, you're just my ideal.

DOWEY. You're easily pleased. (*He turns again to the bed.*) Let's see how the thing works. (*He kneads the mattress with his fist, and the result is so satisfactory that he puts down his kit.*) Old lady, if you really want me, I'll bide.

MRS. DOWEY. Oh oh! oh! oh!

[*Her joy is so demonstrative that he has to drop a word of warning.*]

DOWEY. But, mind you, I don't accept you as a relation. For your personal glory you can go on pretending to the neighbors, but the best I can say for you is that you're on your probation. I'm a cautious character, and we must see how you'll turn out.

MRS. DOWEY. Yes, Kenneth.

DOWEY. And now, I think, for that bath. My theater begins at six-thirty. A cove I met on a bus is going with me.

MRS. DOWEY. (*She is a little alarmed.*) You're sure you'll come back?

DOWEY. Yes, yes. (*Handsomely*) I leave my kit in pledge.

MRS. DOWEY. You won't liquor up

too freely, Kenneth?

DOWEY. You're the first (*chuckling*) to care whether I do or not. (*Nothing she has said has pleased the lonely man so much as this.*) I promise. Tod, I'm beginning to look forward to being wakened in the morning by hearing you cry, "Get up, you lazy swine." I've kind of envied men that had womenfolk with the right to say that.

[*He is passing to the bathroom when a diverting notion strikes him.*]

MRS. DOWEY. What is it, Kenneth?

DOWEY. The theater. It would be showier if I took a lady.

[MRS. DOWEY *feels a thumping at her breast.*]

MRS. DOWEY. Kenneth, tell me this instant what you mean. Don't keep me on the dumps.

[*He turns her around.*]

DOWEY. No, it couldn't be done.

MRS. DOWEY. Was it me you were thinking of?

DOWEY. Just for the moment (*regretfully*) but you have no style.

[*She catches hold of him by the sleeve.*]

MRS. DOWEY. Not in this, of course. But, oh, Kenneth, if you saw me in my merino![1] It's laced up the back in the very latest.

DOWEY. Hum (*doubtfully*) but let's see it.

[*It is produced from a drawer, to which the old lady runs with almost indecent haste. The connoisseur examines it critically.*]

DOWEY. Looks none so bad. Have you a bit of chiffon for the neck? It's not bombs nor Kaisers nor Tipperary that men in the trenches think of; it's chiffon.

MRS. DOWEY. I swear I have, Kenneth. And I have a bangle,[2] and a muff, and gloves.

DOWEY. Ay, ay. (*He considers.*) Do you think you could give your face less of a homely look?

MRS. DOWEY. I'm sure I could.

DOWEY. Then you can have a try. But, mind you, I promise nothing. All will depend on the effect.

[*He goes into the pantry, and the old lady is left alone. Not alone, for she is ringed round by entrancing hopes and dreadful fears. They beam on her and jeer at her; they pull her this way and that. With difficulty she breaks through them and rushes to her pail, hot water, soap, and a looking glass.*
[*Our last glimpse of her for this evening shows her staring — not discontentedly — at her soft old face, licking her palm, and pressing it to her hair. Her eyes are sparkling.*]

[*One evening a few days later* MRS. TWYMLEY *and* MRS. MICKLEHAM *are in* MRS. DOWEY'S *house, awaiting that lady's return from some fashionable dissipation. They have undoubtedly been discussing the war, for the first words we catch are:*]

MRS. MICKLEHAM. I tell you flat, Amelia, I bows no knee to junkerdom.[3]

MRS. TWYMLEY. Sitting here by the fire, you and me, as one to another, what do you think will happen after the war? Are we to go back to being as we were?

MRS. MICKLEHAM. Speaking for myself, Amelia, not me. The war has wakened me up to a understanding of my own importance that is really astonishing.

MRS. TWYMLEY. Same here. Instead of being the poor worms the like of you and me thought we was, we turns out to be visible departments of a great and haughty empire.

[*They are well under way, and with a little luck we might now hear their*

---

[1] *merino:* a fine, soft wool fabric. [2] *bangle:* bracelet.

[3] *junkerdom:* the junkers, Prussian nobility; here means Germany's might.

*views on various passing problems of
the day, such as the neglect of science in our public schools. But in
comes the* HAGGERTY WOMAN, *and
spoils everything. She is attired, like
them, in her best; but the effect of her
is that her clothes have gone out for
a walk, leaving her at home.*]

MRS. MICKLEHAM (*with deep distaste*). Here's that submarine again.

[*The* HAGGERTY WOMAN *cringes to them,
but gets no encouragement.*]

THE HAGGERTY WOMAN. It's a terrible
war.
MRS. TWYMLEY. Is that so?
THE HAGGERTY WOMAN. I wonder
what will happen when it ends?
MRS. MICKLEHAM. I have no idea.

[*The intruder produces her handkerchief, but does not use it. After all,
she is in her best.*]

THE HAGGERTY WOMAN. Are they not
back yet?

[*Perfect ladies must reply to a direct
question.*]

MRS. MICKLEHAM. No. (*Icily*) We
have been waiting this half-hour. They
are at the theater again.
THE HAGGERTY WOMAN. You tell me!
I just popped in with an insignificant
present for him, as his leave is up.
MRS. TWYMLEY. The same errand
brought us.
THE HAGGERTY WOMAN. My present
is cigarettes.

[*They have no intention of telling her
what their presents are, but the secret
leaps from them.*]

MRS. MICKLEHAM. So is mine.
MRS. TWYMLEY. Mine too.

[*Triumph of the* HAGGERTY WOMAN. *But
it is short-lived.*]

MRS. MICKLEHAM. Mine has gold tips.
MRS. TWYMLEY. So has mine.
THE HAGGERTY WOMAN (*need not say*

*a word. You have only to look at her to
know that her cigarettes are not gold-
tipped. She tries to brazen it out, which
is so often a mistake*). What care I?
Mine is Exquisytos.

[*No wonder they titter.*]

MRS. MICKLEHAM. Excuse us, Mrs.
Haggerty — if that's your name — but
the word is Exquiseetos.
THE HAGGERTY WOMAN. Much
obliged! (*Weeps.*)
MRS. MICKLEHAM. I think I heard a
taxi.
MRS. TWYMLEY. It will be her third
this week.

[*They peer through the blind. They are
so excited that rank is forgotten.*]

THE HAGGERTY WOMAN. What is she
in?
MRS. MICKLEHAM. A new astrakhan [1]
jacket he gave her, with Venus sleeves.
THE HAGGERTY WOMAN. Has she sold
her gabardine coat?
MRS. MICKLEHAM. Not her! She has
them both at the theater, warm night
though it is. She's wearing the astrakhan
— and carrying the garbardine, flung
carelesslike over her arm.
THE HAGGERTY WOMAN. I saw her
strutting about with him yesterday, looking as if she thought the two of them
made a procession.
MRS. TWYMLEY. Hsh! (*Peeping*)
Strike me dead — if she's not coming
mincing down the stair, hooked on his
arm!

[*Indeed it is thus that* MRS. DOWEY *enters. Perhaps she had seen shadows
lurking on the blind, and at once
hooked on to* KENNETH *to impress the
visitors. She is quite capable of it.*]

[*Now we see what Kenneth saw that
afternoon five days ago when he
emerged from the bathroom and
found the old trembler awaiting his*

---

[1] *astrakhan:* the fur of Persian lambs which
is used in jackets and coats.

inspection. Here are the muff and the gloves and the chiffon, and such a kind old bonnet that it makes you laugh at once. I don't know how to describe it; but it is trimmed with a kiss, as bonnets should be when the wearer is old and frail. We must take the merino for granted until she steps out of the astrakhan. She is dressed up to the nines; there is no doubt about it. Yes, but is her face less homely? Above all, has she style? The answer is in a stout affirmative. Ask Kenneth. He knows. Many a time he has had to go behind a door to roar hilariously at the old lady. He has thought of her as a lark to tell his mates about by and by; but for some reason that he cannot fathom, he knows now that he will never do that.]

MRS. DOWEY *(affecting surprise).* Kenneth, we have visitors!

DOWEY. Your servant, ladies.

[He is no longer mud-caked and dour. A very smart figure is this Private Dowey; and he winks engagingly at the visitors, like one who knows that for jolly company you cannot easily beat charwomen. The pleasantries that he and they have exchanged this week! The sauce he has given them. The wit of MRS. MICKLEHAM'S *retorts. The badinage* [1] *of* MRS. TWYMLEY. *The neat giggles of the* HAGGERTY WOMAN. *There has been nothing like it since you took the countess in to dinner.]*

MRS. TWYMLEY. We should apologize. We're not meaning to stay.

MRS. DOWEY. You are very welcome. Just wait *(the ostentation of this!)* till I get out of my astrakhan — and my muff — and my gloves — and *(It is the bonnet's turn now)* my Excelsior.

[At last we see her in the merino — a triumph.]

MRS. MICKLEHAM. You've given her

a glory time, Mr. Dowey.

DOWEY. It's her that has given it to me, missis.

MRS. DOWEY. Hey! hey! hey! hey! He just pampers me. *(Waggling her fists)* The Lord forgive us, but, this being the last night, we had a sit-down supper at a restaurant! *(Vehemently)* I swear by God that we had champagny wine. *(There is a dead stillness, and she knows very well what it means; she has even prepared for it.)* And to them as doubts my word — here's the cork. *(She places the cork, in its lovely gold drapery, upon the table.)*

MRS. MICKLEHAM. I'm sure!

MRS. TWYMLEY. I would thank you, Mrs. Dowey, not to say a word against my Alfred.

MRS. DOWEY. Me!

DOWEY. Come, come, ladies! *(In the masterful way that is so hard for women to resist)* If you say another word, I'll kiss the lot of you.

[There is a moment of pleased confusion.]

MRS. MICKLEHAM. Really, them sodgers!

THE HAGGERTY WOMAN. The kilties is the worst!

MRS. TWYMLEY *(heartily).* I'm sure we don't grudge you your treats, Mrs. Dowey; and sorry we are that this is the end.

DOWEY. Yes, it's the end. *(With a troubled look at his old lady)* I must be off in ten minutes.

[The little soul is too gallant to break down in company. She hurries into the pantry and shuts the door.]

MRS. MICKLEHAM. Poor thing! But we must run, for you'll be having some last words to say to her.

DOWEY. I kept her out long on purpose so as to have less time to say them in. *(He more than half wishes that he could make a bolt to a public house.* [2]*)*

---

[1] *badinage:* playful banter or joking.

[2] *public house:* a tavern or bar.

MRS. TWYMLEY. It's the best way. (*In the important affairs of life there is not much that anyone can teach a char-woman.*) Just a mere nothing — to wish you well, Mr. Dowey.

[*All three present him with the ciga-rettes.*]

MRS. MICKLEHAM. A scraping, as one might say.

THE HAGGERTY WOMAN (*enigmatical-ly [1]*). The heart is warm, though it may not be gold-tipped.

DOWEY. You bricks!

THE LADIES. Good luck, cocky.

DOWEY. The same to you. And if you see a sodger man up there in a kilt, he is one that is going back with me. Tell him not to come down, but — but to give me till the last minute, and then to whistle.

[*It is quite a grave man who is left alone, thinking what to do next. He tries a horse laugh, but that proves of no help. He says "Hell!" to himself, but it is equally ineffective. Then he opens the pantry door and calls.*]

DOWEY. Old lady.

[*She comes timidly to the door, her hand up as if to ward off a blow.*]

MRS. DOWEY. Is it time?

[*An encouraging voice answers her.*]

DOWEY. No, no, not yet. I've left word for Dixon to whistle when go I must.

MRS. DOWEY. All is ended.

DOWEY. Now, then, you promised to be gay. We were to help one another.

MRS. DOWEY. Yes, Kenneth.

DOWEY. It's bad for me, but it's worse for you.

MRS. DOWEY. The men have medals to win, you see.

DOWEY. The women have their med-als, too. (*He knows she likes him to order her about, so he tries it again.*) Come here. No, I'll come to you. (*He stands gaping at her wonderingly. He*

[1] *enigmatically:* in a puzzling, or obscure, way.

has no power of words, nor does he quite know what he would like to say.*) God!

MRS. DOWEY. What is it, Kenneth?

DOWEY. You're a woman.

MRS. DOWEY. I had near forgot it.

[*He wishes he was at the station with Dixon. Dixon is sure to have a bottle in his pocket. They will be roaring a song presently. But in the meantime — there is that son business. Bleth-ers,[2] the whole thing, of course — or mostly blethers. But it's the way to please her.*]

DOWEY. Have you noticed you have never called me son?

MRS. DOWEY. Have I noticed it! I was feared, Kenneth. You said I was on pro-bation.

DOWEY. And so you were. Well, the probation's ended. (*He laughs uncom-fortably.*) The like of me! But if you want me you can have me.

MRS. DOWEY. Kenneth, will I do?

DOWEY (*artfully gay*). Woman, don't be so forward. Wait till I have proposed.

MRS. DOWEY. Propose for a mother?

DOWEY. What for no? (*In the grand style*) Mrs. Dowey, you queer carl,[3] you spunky tiddy, have I your permission to ask you the most important question a neglected orphan can ask of an old lady?

[*She bubbles with mirth. Who could help it, the man has such a way with him!*]

MRS. DOWEY. None of your sauce, Kenneth.

DOWEY. For a long time, Mrs. Dowey, you cannot have been unaware of my sonnish feelings for you.

MRS. DOWEY. Wait till I get my mop to you —

DOWEY. And if you're not willing to be my mother, I swear I'll never ask another. (*The old divert pulls him down to her and strokes his hair.*) Was I a well-behaved infant, Mother?

[2] *Blethers:* nonsense. [3] *carl:* fellow or person.

MRS. DOWEY. Not you, sonny — you were a rampaging rogue.

DOWEY. Was I slow in learning to walk?

MRS. DOWEY. The quickest in our street. He! he! he! (*She starts up.*) Was that the whistle?

DOWEY. No, no. See here. In taking me over you have, in a manner of speaking, joined the Black Watch.

MRS. DOWEY. I like to think that, Kenneth.

DOWEY. Then you must behave so that the ghost piper can be proud of you. 'Tion! (*She stands bravely at attention.*) That's the style. Now listen. I've sent in your name as being my nearest of kin, and your allowance will be coming to you weekly in the usual way.

MRS. DOWEY. Hey! hey! hey! Is it wicked, Kenneth?

DOWEY. I'll take the responsibility for it in both worlds. You see, I want you to be safeguarded in case anything hap —

MRS. DOWEY. Kenneth!

DOWEY. 'Tion! Have no fear. I'll come back, covered with mud and medals. Mind you have that cup of tea waiting for me.

[*He is listening for the whistle. He pulls her onto his knee.*]

MRS. DOWEY. Hey! hey! hey! hey!

DOWEY. What fun we'll have writing to one another! Real letters this time!

MRS. DOWEY. Yes.

DOWEY. It would be a good plan if you began the first letter as soon as I've gone.

MRS. DOWEY. I will.

DOWEY. I hope Lady Dolly will go on sending me cakes.

MRS. DOWEY. You may be sure.

[*He ties his scarf round her neck.*]

DOWEY. You must have been a bonny thing when you were young.

MRS. DOWEY. Away with you!

DOWEY. That scarf sets you fine.

MRS. DOWEY. Blue was always my color.

[*The whistle sounds.*]

DOWEY. Old lady, you are what Blighty means to me now.

[*She hides in the pantry again. She is out of sight of us, but she does something that makes* PRIVATE DOWEY *take off his bonnet. Then he shoulders his equipment and departs. That is he laughing coarsely with Dixon.*]

We have one last glimpse of the old lady — a month or two after Kenneth's death in action. It would be rosemary to us to see her in her black dress, of which she is very proud; but let us rather peep at her in the familiar garments that make a third to her mop and pail. It is early morning, and she is having a look at her medals before setting off on the daily round. They are in a drawer with the scarf covering them, and on the scarf a piece of lavender. First the black frock, which she carries in her arms like a baby. Then her War Savings Certificates, Kenneth's bonnet, a thin packet of real letters, and the famous champagne cork. She kisses the letters, but she does not blub over them. She strokes the dress, and waggles her head over the certificates and presses the bonnet to her cheeks, and rubs the tinsel of the cork carefully with her apron. She is a tremulous old 'un; yet she exults, for she owns all these things and also the penny flag on her breast. She puts them away in the drawer, the scarf over them, the lavender on the scarf. Her air of triumph well becomes her. She lifts the pail and the mop, and slouches off gamely to the day's toil.

INTERPRETER OF CHARACTER

1. How do Barrie's stage directions differ from the usual stage directions? How do they affect your interest in the play? How do they affect your understanding of the characters? How would they help actors? How might they hinder them?

2. Point out bits of humor in the opening conversation among the charwomen, especially their discussion of fashions. What apparently unimportant details of this discussion later prove to have bearing on the plot? When do you first realize the nature of Mrs. Dowey's "crime"?

3. Show how each character in the play is made different in personality even though the part is very minor. What do you learn about British "class society" from this play?

4. Trace the steps in Kenneth's change of attitude. Is it made convincing? What are the most telling points in winning him over?

5. Study Mrs. Dowey's character carefully. What leads her to commit her "crime"? How would you characterize her feelings at the end of the play as she looks over her "medals"? In what way does she deserve them?

REPORTING AND DRAMATIZATION

1. In a panel or general discussion examine the contrast between the mother-son relationship in *Pygmalion* and *The Old Lady Shows Her Medals*.

2. Act all or certain chosen parts of *The Old Lady Shows Her Medals*. Discuss how you would handle on the stage the short last scene for which there is no dialogue. How would you indicate the lapse of time? the fact that Kenneth has been killed? Would you try to supply any speech whatever for this scene? Why or why not?

READING LIST FOR MODERN DRAMA

Barrie, Sir James M., *Representative Plays*
A good selection of Barrie's best.

Coward, Noel, *Plays*
Social satires by the dramatist considered the best of his generation in England.

Eliot, T. S., *The Confidential Clerk*
A provocative play in blank verse about a financier whose aspirations are thwarted.

——, *The Elder Statesman*
A drama in verse about a distinguished man who has to face the follies of his youth.

Fry, Christopher, *The Dark Is Light Enough*
The value of human life and the error in using violence to redress wrong are the main themes of this three-act verse play.

——, *The Lady's Not for Burning*
A woman is accused of witchcraft in medieval England.

Galsworthy, John, *Selected Plays*
Successful plays of an outstanding playwright.

Maugham, W. Somerset, *Quartet*
Four Maugham short stories with their accompanying screenplays by R. C. Sheriff.

O'Casey, Sean, *Selected Plays*
Among these eight plays which the author wants to survive him are *The Shadow of a Gunman, Juno and the Paycock,* and *The Plough and the Stars*.

Osborne, John, and Anthony Creighton, *Epitaph for George Dillon*
Osborne's first play has a sympathetic character as its hero.

Priestley, J. B., *Wonderful World of the Theater*
An attractive, illustrated history of the theater.

Rattigan, Terence, *The Winslow Boy*
A dramatic study of the effects of a long court trial on a middle-class family.

Shaw, George Bernard, *Plays*
Witty dramas promoting the rule of the goddess Reason.

Synge, John, *Complete Plays*
A collection of intense plays by a playwright who celebrated his native land, Ireland, in lyric beauty.

Wilde, Oscar, *Plays*
Sophisticated comedies of manners by a wit.

FOR LISTENING

The first half of Act II of Shaw's *Pygmalion* has been recorded and is available on *Many Voices 6B*.

TWENTIETH–CENTURY FRONTIS–PIECE: Pictured on page 602 are flags of the Commonwealth nations; a copy of the London *Times;* the traditional but still indispensable umbrella and tea; an I-bar (used in construction of buildings); a styrofoam model of a salt molecule; test tubes and decanter; an example of modern British sculpture and architecture.

THE GROWTH OF
THE ENGLISH LANGUAGE

The Twentieth Century

You who have spent your entire lives in the twentieth century have probably accepted our language as you hear and see it, without much thought as to how it grew and became what it is now. The chapters running through this book have, we hope, given you a new outlook on language — an understanding that it is not a static thing, but a living, changing organism just as a human body is. Just what English will be one or two hundred years from now we cannot say, but we are quite sure that our present-day language will still be understandable, even if it is dubbed quaint or archaic. Not only the sound of the language but its terminology will differ. Every new advance in technology, science, and even in international relations will add new terms to the vocabulary, probably at the rate of about one thousand words per year. Meanwhile, older terms may well fade out of the language.

The first half of the twentieth century has brought some interesting developments. During the decade of peace before there was such a thing as a world war, there was a miniature war over Simplified Spelling. The movement was started toward the end of the nineteenth century by a group of people who deplored the unphonetic spelling of English and thought that the time had come for drastic action. In 1906, President Theodore Roosevelt directed the Government Printing Office to use three hundred simplified forms. This edict brought on a minor crisis. Protesting letters flooded the White House and storms of disapproval shook the editorial columns of newspapers and magazines. The President retracted his or-

der. Though the Simplified Spelling Board continued to issue new lists from time to time, it never regained the prestige it had lost. Such an experience shows the impossibility of performing a major operation on language. It must change slowly by natural forces which neither man nor reason can completely control.

George Bernard Shaw continued to make caustic thrusts at our illogical language. In the Preface to *Pygmalion* he says: "The English have no respect for their language, and will not teach their children to speak it. They spell it so abominably that no man can teach himself what it sounds like. It is impossible for an Englishman to open his mouth without making some other Englishman hate or despise him. German and Spanish are accessible to foreigners; English is not accessible even to the Englishman. The reformer England needs today is an energetic phonetic enthusiast. That is why I have made such a one the hero of a popular play."

Yet Shaw, who left a good deal of his personal fortune to the cause of simplified spelling, was actually misguided. English is undoubtedly one of the two or three worst spelled languages on earth. But so rapid are the changes occurring at present in English pronunciation that even if we spent the billions of dollars needed to change over to simplified spelling, we would be obliged to make major changes in another seventy-five years or so.

Many Americans think that the British tend to pronounce words even less according to the spelling than we do. The fact is that Americans prefer accentual patterns different from those of British

English. We give value to every syllable of *dictionary* and *millinery,* while the British slur the unaccented syllables until the words sound like *diction'ry* and *millin'ry.* This disparity between spelling and pronunciation is especially true of place names. Some of the most striking examples are Harwich (Hăr'idge), Greenwich (Grĕn'ich), Leicester (Lĕs'ter), Cirencester (Sis'eter), and Featherstonehaugh (Feest''nhay). We also have to watch out for family names, for Beauchamp is pronounced Bee'cham, and Cholmondeley is Chŭm'ly. Sometimes the difference between British and American pronunciation is merely a matter of accent, as when the Englishman says *munici'pal* and *labor'atory.*

English spelling deviates from American spelling in such words as: *storey* (of a house), *pyjama, kerb, tyre* (of a wheel), *gaol* (jail).

Americans abroad encounter different names for many ordinary objects. The Englishman's car wears a bonnet instead of a hood. He takes a tram instead of a streetcar; drives a lorry instead of a truck. He goes to the cinema instead of the movies. He enjoys a spot of tea in the afternoon. At dinner he uses a serviette instead of a napkin. When his wife wants a spool of thread, she asks for a reel of cotton. But misunderstandings because of terminology are decreasing as the interchange between the two countries increases.

World events have given us hundreds of new words. What first appeared as servicemen's slang has often proved useful enough to be accepted in good standing. The new world of the air has produced an entire vocabulary unknown a hundred years ago. Interest in medicine and psychiatry has introduced many new scientific terms. The inventions of the last fifty years have required new terms to describe them. Who can measure the possible effect of broadcasting on unifying speech? Already the British Broadcasting Corporation has appointed a board of six men to endeavor to arrive at a set standard of speech. (The background of these six men is rather surprising — there is one Scot, two Welshmen, one Irishman, and one American by birth, leaving only one who is thoroughly English.) It is possible that movies, radio, and television may have an effect on speech similar to that of printing on spelling.

On the whole, the style of expression of the twentieth century has been much less formal and ornate than that of the nineteenth century. Simplified spelling may have failed, but simplified style has succeeded. Credit for this may be given to the influence of journalism, certain authors like Hemingway who have a large following, and the increased tempo of life which can no longer tolerate verbosity and complicated structure. There has been great reaction against the teaching of formal grammar; some schools do not teach it at all. Those who do have eliminated many of the terms and constructions that were derived from Latin and have made English grammar follow more closely the natural form of the language.

What about English as a world language? It is now the mother tongue of two continents, North America and Australia, besides other widely scattered parts of the British Commonwealth. It is the chief secondary language of most of Western Europe, India, Japan, the Pacific Islands, and some parts of China. Its lack of complicated inflections and involved grammar make it a fairly easy language to learn, even though the discrepancies between spelling and pronunciation are a stumbling block to foreigners.

Thus we see that the English language, which started as a mere rivulet, has grown into a mighty river. What its social and cultural future may be we can only guess, but we can ourselves participate in its linguistic future as sensitive users of English words.

GLOSSARY

The definitions supplied in this glossary apply to each word as it is used in the textbook. These definitions are numbered in order of their appearance in the text. With very few exceptions, words that are footnoted in the text are not included in the glossary.

A

abasement (*a*·bās'mĕnt). Loss of dignity.

abate (*a*·bāt'). To lessen in amount or strength; to subside.

abhor (ăb·hôr'). To detest; to hate. *Adj.*, **abhorrent** (ăb·hôr'ĕnt); **abhorrèd**. *Poetic*.

abject (ăb'jĕkt). Cast down; lowly.

ablution (ăb·lū'shŭn). A washing or cleansing.

abomination (*a*·bŏm'ĭ·nā'shŭn). A feeling of disgust or hatred.

abyss (*a*·bĭs'). Something deep, vast, bottomless. *Adj.*, **abysmal**.

accession (ăk·sĕsh'ŭn). 1. Coming to the throne. 2. Addition.

accost (*a*·kŏst'). To speak to first with aggressiveness.

acme (ăk'mē). The highest point.

acquiesce (ăk'wĭ·ĕs'). To agree to.

actuate (ăk'tū·āt). To arouse.

admonish (ăd·mŏn'ĭsh). To reprove gently; to advise. *Noun*, **admonition** (ăd'mŏ·nĭsh'ŭn).

aeon (ē'ŏn). An immeasurably long period of time.

affability (ăf'*a*·bĭl'ĭ·tĭ). Graciousness.

affronted (*a*·frŭnt'ĕd). Insulted; offended.

agate (ăg'ĭt). A striped, multicolored semiprecious stone.

aggrieve (*a*·grēv'). Distress; offend.

ague (ā'gū). A disease characterized by chills and fever.

alacrity (*a*·lăk'rĭ·tĭ). Readiness.

alchemy (ăl'kĕ·mĭ). Medieval chemistry; the power to change something ordinary into something valuable.

alienate (āl'yĕn·āt'). To withdraw; to turn away.

allay (*a*·lā'). 1. To make quiet, to suppress. 2. To lessen the strength of.

allusion (*a*·lū'zhŭn). Indirect reference; hint.

amends (*a*·mĕndz'). Payment for mistakes.

amiable (ā'mĭ·*a*·b'l). Good-natured; friendly. *Noun*, **amiability** (ā'mĭ·*a*·bĭl'ĭ·tĭ).

amulet (ăm'ū·lĕt). A good-luck charm.

analogy (*a*·năl'ō·jĭ). A degree of similarity between different things.

analytical (ăn'*a*·lĭt'ĭ·kăl). Able to separate a subject into its parts and to describe each part critically.

animosity (ăn'ĭ·mŏs'ĭ·tĭ). Hostility; ill will.

annihilation (*a*·nī'ĭ·lā'shŭn). Total destruction.

annuity (*a*·nū'·ĭ·tĭ). A yearly allowance.

antagonist (ăn·tăg'ō·nĭst). Opponent, adversary.

anthropomorphic (ăn'thrō·pō·môr'fĭc). Representing God in human form.

apathy (ăp'*a*·thĭ). Indifference; lack of emotion or excitement.

aperture (ăp'ēr·tŭr). An opening.

apostate (*a*·pŏs'tāt). One who has forsaken a faith in which he once believed.

apostolical (ăp'ŏs·tŏl'ĭ·kăl). Pertaining to, or derived directly from, the Apostles.

apothecary (*a*·pŏth'ē·kĕr'ĭ). One who prepares and sells drugs.

apparition (ăp'*a*·rĭsh'ŭn). A phantom or specter.

appellation (ăp'ĕ·lā'shŭn). A name or designation.

apprehensive (ăp'rē·hĕn'sĭv). Fearful.

apprise (*a*·prīz'). To inform; to warn.

apropos (ăp'rō·pō'). As suggested by; with respect to.

arbitrary (är'bĭ·trĕr'ĭ). Unreasonably ruled by one's own wishes.

arduous (är'dū·ŭs). Laborious.

argosy (är'gō·sĭ). A large ship or fleet of ships, usually laden with riches.

aridity (*a*·rĭd'ĭ·tĭ). Dryness; lack of variety.

arraign (*a*·rān'). To bring into court to answer charges.

arrogant (ăr'ō·gănt). Haughty.

articulate (är·tĭk'ū·lāt). *Verb*, to speak words distinctly. *Adj.*, (är·tĭk'ū·lát).

artifice (är'tĭ·fĭs). A clever trick. **artificer** (är·tĭf'ĭ·sĕr). One who makes or devises. **The Great Artificer.** The Creator; God.

ascendancy (*a*·sĕn'dăn·sĭ). Control; domination.

ascetic (*a*·sĕt'ĭk). A person who leads a life of self-denial.

asperity (ăs·pĕr'ĭ·tĭ). Harshness.

aspire (ăs·pīr'). To desire to attain a noble goal; to have ambition. *Noun*, **aspiration** (ăs'pĭ·rā'shŭn).

assail (*a*·sāl'). To attack, often with harsh words. *Adj.*, **assailable**.

assignation (ăs'ĭg·nā'shŭn). An appointment for a meeting.

assuage (*a*·swāj'). To soothe; to lessen the pain of.

astrology (ăs·trŏl'ō·jĭ). The practice which claims to predict events by the positions of the stars and their influence on human affairs.

attribute (*a*·trĭb'ūt). *Verb*, to consider that something belongs to someone else. *Noun*, (ăt'rĭ·bût). A quality or characteristic.

audacity (ô·dăs'ĭ·tĭ). Boldness. *Adj.*, **audacious** (ô·dā'shŭs).

augment (ôg·mĕnt'). To increase.

augur (ô'gēr). To foretell. *Noun*, a prophet. **augury** (ô'gŭ·rĭ). An omen.

avarice (ăv'*a*·rĭs). Greed for profits or gain. *Adj.*, **avaricious** (ăv'*a*·rĭsh'·ŭs).

aver (*a*·vûr'). To declare positively.

averse (*a*·vûrs'). Having a dislike; opposed.

āpe, châotic, bâre, ăt, *a*ttend, ärt, flăsk, *a*top; ēke, mẹrely, ĕlect, ĕcho, prudẹnt, doër; ĭtem, ĭnn, rarĭty; ōde, ŏpaque, fôr, dŏt, lôft, cŏnfide; sōon, tŏŏk; sour, toil; tūbe, ūnique, tûrn, sŭp, ŭntil.

bar; church; dog; ardụous; fat; go; hear; jail; key; lame; meat; not; ring; pay; ran; see; shell; ten; there, thick; pastụre; vast; wind; yes; zoo, zh = z in azure.

B

baleful (bāl'fŏŏl). Deadly in influence.
bane (bān). A curse; something that destroys or ruins.
bannister (băn'ĭs·tĕr). A row of upright supports topped by a railing, along a staircase.
barrow (băr'ō). 1. A hill or mound, often an ancient burial ground. 2. A wheelbarrow.
battlement (băt'''l·mĕnt). A wall at the top of a fortified building or tower, with openings for shooting through.
beleaguered (bĕ·lē'gĕrd). Surrounded; besieged.
belligerent (bĕ·lĭj'ĕr·ĕnt). Warlike; quarrelsome.
beneficent (bĕ·nĕf'ĭ·sĕnt). Doing good; kind.
benevolent (bĕ·nĕv'ō·lĕnt). Generous; kind
benign (bĕ·nīn'). Kind; gentle. *Noun,* **benignity** (bĕ·nĭg'nĭ·tĭ).
benison (bĕn'ĭ·z'n). Blessing.
bereavement (bĕ·rēv'mĕnt). Desolation caused by the death of a relative or friend. *Adj.,* **bereaved** (bĕ·rēvd').
beseech (bĕ·sēch'). To beg eagerly for; to implore.
betel (bē't'l). The nut of a climbing pepper vine, often chewed by natives of the Far East.
blanch (blànch). To whiten; to turn pale.
bland (blănd). Gentle; smooth.
blaspheme (blăs·fēm'). To speak with irreverence about God or sacred things. *Noun,* **blasphemy** (blăs'fĕ·mĭ).
blatant (blā'tănt). 1. Offensively obtrusive. 2. Noisy; clamorous.
bode (bōd). To prophesy. *Noun,* **bodement** (bōd'mĕnt).
bounteous (boun'tē·ŭs). Generous.
brandish (brăn'dĭsh). To wave threateningly.
brogue (brōg). A pronunciation in a dialect.
bullion (bŏŏl'yŭn). Gold or silver in bars or lumps rather than in coins.
burlesque (bûr·lĕsk'). An imitation which makes fun of a literary or dramatic work.
burnish (bûr'nĭsh). To polish; to make shiny.
buttery (bŭt'ĕr·ĭ). A pantry or storeroom.
buttress (bŭt'rĕs). A projecting structure to support a wall. *Verb,* 1. To support; to prop. 2. To protect.

C

cadence (kā'dĕns). Rhythmic measure.
caldron (kôl'drŭn). A large kettle.
callous (kăl'ŭs). Unfeeling.
calumny (kăl'ŭm·nĭ). Slander.
candor (kăn'dĕr). Frankness. *Adj.,* **candid** (kăn'dĭd).
canker (kăng'kĕr). To become diseased; to corrode; to eat away.
canny (kăn'ĭ). Shrewd; clever.
cant (kànt). 1. Special words or phrases used by a particular group. 2. Insincere talk; hypocrisy.
capitulate (kà·pĭt'û·lāt). To make terms of surrender.
caricature (kăr'ĭ·kà·tûr). *Noun,* a picture or description exaggerating a person's peculiarities or defects. *Verb,* to make a caricature of.

carouse (kà·rouz'). *Verb,* to engage in wild, drunken revelry. *Noun,* a noisy, drunken party.
cassock (kăs'ŭk). A long, close-fitting garment worn by clergymen.
cataract (kăt'à·răkt). A large, rushing waterfall.
catastrophe (kà·tăs'trō·fĕ). A terrible disaster.
catechize (kăt'ĕ·kīz). To question fully, especially on religious doctrine.
catholic (kăth'ō·lĭk). Universal.
caustic (kôs'tĭk). Sharply satirical.
cavalcade (kăv'ăl·kād'). A procession of persons, usually on horseback or in horse-drawn carriages; a parade.
cede (sēd). To give up; to yield.
celestial (sĕ·lĕs'chăl). Heavenly.
censure (sĕn'shĕr). 1. Judgment; opinion. 2. Criticism; blame.
certitude (sûr'tĭ·tūd). Sureness; certainty.
chalice (chăl'ĭs). A goblet. *Adj.,* **chaliced** (chăl'ĭst). Cup-shaped.
chancel (chán'sĕl). The space surrounding the altar in a church.
cherubin (chĕr'û·bĭn), usually **cherubim.** *Pl. of* **cherub.** The second rank of the angels of light.
circumspection (sûr'kŭm·spĕk'shŭn). Discretion; caution.
citadel (sĭt'à·dĕl). A fortress.
cleave (klēv). 1. To be faithful to. 2. To split apart.
cloister (klois'tĕr). *Verb,* to seclude from the world. *Noun,* 1. A monastery or convent. 2. A covered passage beside or around a courtyard.
cockney (kŏk'nĭ). 1. A person brought up in the East End of London. 2. The dialect spoken by such a person.
coextensive (kō'ĕks·tĕn'sĭv). Extending in the same space or time.
cohorts (kō'hôrts). 1. Troops of soldiers. 2. Colleagues or partners.
collate (kŏ·lāt'). To check the order and number of pages in a book.
colloquy (kŏl'ō·kwĭ). A formal conversation.
combustible (kŏm·bŭs'tĭ·b'l). Capable of catching fire and burning.
commiseration (kŏ·mĭz'ĕr·ā'shŭn). Pity.
compassed (kŭm'pàst). Surrounded.
complacent (kŏm·plā'sĕnt). 1. Satisfied. 2. Self-satisfied. *Noun,* **complacence.**
comprehensive (kŏm'prē·hĕn'sĭv). 1. Able to understand many things. 2. Inclusive. *Noun,* **comprehension.**
compunction (kŏm·pŭngk'shŭn). Regret; a sense of guilt.
concert (kŏn·sûrt'). *Verb,* to plan together. *Noun,* **concert** (kŏn'sûrt). A public musical performance by several participants.
conciliate (kŏn·sĭl'ĭ·āt). To gain the good will of; to make friendly.
concourse (kŏn'kōrs). A gathering.
condemnation (kŏn'dĕm·nā'shŭn). The act of declaring someone guilty.
condescend (kŏn·dĕ·sĕnd'). To show courtesy with an air of superiority. *Noun,* **condescension.**
conducive (kŏn·dū'sĭv). Helpful.
conflagration (kŏn'flà·grā'shŭn). A raging fire.
confound (kŏn·found'). 1. To confuse; to bewilder. 2. To destroy.

āpe, châotic, bâre, ăt, ăttend, ärt, flásk, átop; ēke, mẹrely, ĕlect, ĕcho, prudĕnt, doër; ītem, ĭnn, rarĭty; ōde, ŏpaque, fôr, dŏt, lŏft, cŏnfide; sōon, tŏŏk; sour, toil; tūbe, ûnique, tûrn, sŭp, ŭntil.

confute (kŏn·fūt′). To prove something worthless by argument.

conjecture (kŏn·jĕk′tŭr). *Noun*, supposition; theory. *Verb*, to guess; to suppose.

conjure (kŭn′jẽr). 1. To summon or to bring to mind as if by magic. 2. To plot together; to plan in secret. 3. (kŏn·jŏor′). To plead with; to implore. *Noun*, conjurer (kŭn′jẽr·ẽr). A magician.

connivance (kŏ·nīv′ăns). Knowledge of and agreement of wrongdoing.

connive (kŏ·nīv′). 1. To pretend ignorance. 2. To co-operate secretly.

connoisseur (kŏn′ĭ·sûr′). One competent to pass critical judgment.

consecration (kŏn′sĕ·krā′shŭn). 1. Setting apart for a holy use. 2. Dedication; devotion.

consequential (kŏn′sĕ·kwĕn′shăl). Self-important.

consummate (kŏn·sŭm′ĭt). Perfect; in the highest degree.

contemn (kŏn·tĕm′). To scorn; to despise.

contention (kŏn·tĕn′shŭn). A dispute; a quarrel. *Adj.*, contentious.

contrivance (kŏn·trīv′ăns). An invention; a mechanical device.

conventionalize (kŏn·vĕn′shŭn·ăl·īz). To represent in a typical manner.

conversant (kŏn′vẽr·sănt). Familiar; well-versed.

conviviality (kŏn·vĭv′ĭ·ăl′ĭ·tĭ). Gaiety, festivity.

copious (kō′pĭ·ŭs). Rich; full.

coppice (kŏp′ĭs) or cops or copse (kŏps). A thicket or grove of small trees.

coquette (kŏ·kĕt′). A flirt.

corroborate (kŏ·rŏb′ō·rāt). To confirm.

cosmopolitanism (kŏz′mō·pŏl′ĭ·tăn·ĭz′m). Attitude of being at home anywhere in the world.

countenance (koun′tĕ·năns). *Verb*, 1. To be in keeping with. 2. To favor. *Noun*, 1. Face. 2. The expression on one's face.

covert (kŭv′ẽrt). A shelter; a protection.

covet (kŭv′ĕt). To long for something belonging to another. *Noun*, covetousness.

cow (kou). To frighten.

credulity (krĕ·dū′lĭ·tĭ). Readiness to believe without evidence. *Adj.*, credulous (krĕd′ū·lŭs).

culminate (kŭl′mĭ·nāt). To reach a climax.

cumbersome (kŭm′bẽr·sŭm) or cumbrous (kŭm′-brŭs). Heavy; burdensome.

cunning (kŭn′ĭng). *Noun*, 1. Skill; ability. 2. Craftiness. *Adj.*, 1. Skillfully wrought. 2. Clever. 3. Crafty; sly.

cupola (kū′pō·là). A rounded roof.

cursory (kûr′sō·rĭ). Hurried; superficial.

curtail (kûr·tāl′). To reduce; to cut short.

cynic (sĭn′ĭk). One who doubts the goodness or unselfishness of human nature. *Adj.*, cynical (sĭn′ĭ·kăl).

D

dappled (dăp′l′d). 1. Flecked with clouds. 2. Spotted.

darkling (därk′lĭng). In the dark.

dauntless (dônt′lĕs). Bold; fearless.

dearth (dûrth). Scarcity; insufficient supply.

debauch (dĕ·bôch′). To overindulge in eating and drinking. *Noun*, debauchery.

debonair (dĕb′ō·nâr′). Courteous; graceful; gay.

decorum (dĕ·kō′rŭm). Dignity; formal behavior. *Adj.*, decorous.

decussate (dĕ·kŭs′āt). To crisscross.

deference (dĕf′ẽr·ĕns). Honor; respect. *Adj.*, deferential (dĕf′ẽr·ĕn′shăl).

defile (dĕ·fīl′). 1. A line of march. 2. A long narrow passage or gorge.

deft (dĕft). Skillful; nimble.

degenerate (dĕ·jĕn′ẽr·āt). To become substandard; to deteriorate.

deign (dān). To think fit.

delude (dĕ·lud′). To mislead.

demeanor (dĕ·mēn′ẽr). Behavior.

deprecate (dĕp′rĕ·kāt). To disapprove of. *Noun*, deprecation (dĕp′rĕ·kā′shŭn). *Adj.*, deprecatory (dĕp′rĕ·kà·tō′rĭ).

depreciate (dĕ·prē′shĭ·āt). To belittle.

deputation (dĕp′ū·tā′shŭn). A group of people representing others; a delegation.

derelict (dĕr′ĕ·lĭkt). Abandoned.

deride (dĕ·rīd′). To ridicule; to mock. *Noun*, derision (dĕ·rĭzh′ŭn).

descry (dĕ·skrī′). To catch sight of.

desist (dĕ·zĭst′). To discontinue; to stop.

despondency (dĕ·spŏn′dĕn·sĭ). Depression; dejection.

despot (dĕs′pŏt). A tyrant. *Adj.*, despotic (dĕs·pŏt′ĭk).

desultory (dĕs′ŭl·tō′rĭ). Rambling.

detraction (dĕ·trăk′shŭn). Slander; act of belittling a person's reputation.

dexterity (dĕks·tĕr′ĭ·tĭ). Skill in using the hands.

diabolical (dī′à·bŏl′ĭ·kăl). Devilish; fiendish.

diametrically (dī′à·mĕt′rĭ·kăl·ĭ). As opposite as possible, like the two ends of a diameter.

diffidence (dĭf′ĭ·dĕns). Shyness; lack of self-confidence. *Adj.*, diffident.

diminutive (dĭ·mĭn′ū·tĭv). Tiny.

dire (dīr). 1. Dreadful, terrible. 2. Extreme.

disapprobation (dĭs′ăp·rō·bā′shŭn). Disapproval.

disarm (dĭs·ärm′). To make friendly; to make harmless.

discern (dĭ·zûrn′). To detect; to perceive with one of the senses or with the intellect. *Adj.*, discernible.

disconcerting (dĭs′kŏn·sûrt′ĭng). Embarrassing; upsetting.

discourse (dĭs·kōrs′). 1. To talk; to converse. 2. To give forth. *Noun*, 1. Conversation. 2. *Poetic.* A long commentary in speech or writing.

dispatch (dĭs·păch′). 1. To put to death. 2. To hasten. 3. To finish quickly.

disreputability (dĭs·rĕp′ū·tà·bĭl′ĭ·tĭ). A low or dishonorable act or state.

dissipate (dĭs′ĭ·pāt). To make vanish; to disperse. *Noun*, dissipation (dĭs′ĭ·pā′shŭn). 1. Act of dissipating. 2. Idle, wasteful diversion.

dissolute (dĭs′ō·lūt). Wild; morally loose.

distaff (dĭs′tăf). A stick on which the wool or flax is wound in spinning.

distempered (dĭs·tĕm′pẽrd). 1. Afflicted with the plague. 2. Ill-humored.

divers (dī′vẽrz). Several.

divert (dī·vûrt′). *Verb*, 1. To amuse; to entertain. 2. To turn to a different purpose. *Noun*, (dī′vûrt). Slang. An odd or different person.

---

bar; church; dog; ardŭous; fat; go; hear; jail; key; lame; meat; nŏt; ring; pay; ran; see; shell; ten; there, thick; pastŭre; vast; wind; yes; zoo, zh = z in azure.

divine (dĭ'·vīn'). To see; to perceive. *Noun*, divination (dĭv'ĭ·nā'shŭn).

divulge (dĭ·vŭlj'). To reveal; to make public.

dogmatist (dŏg'mȧ·tĭst). One who states his beliefs positively, as if they were facts. *Adj.*, dogmatic (dŏg·măt'ĭk).

draught (drȧft). A drink.

dynasty (dī'nȧs·tĭ). A line or succession of rulers belonging to the same family.

E

ecclesiastical (ĕ·klē'zĭ·ăs'tĭ·kȧl). Pertaining to the church.

ecstasy (ĕk'stȧ·sĭ). Overwhelming joy or exultation. *Adj.*, ecstatic (ĕk·stăt'ĭk).

edifying (ĕd'ĭ·fī·ĭng). Morally instructive or beneficial.

efface (ĕ·fās'). To erase.

effectual (ĕ·fĕk'·tû·ȧl). Producing the desired result.

effeminacy (ĕ·fĕm'ĭ·nȧ·sĭ). Womanly gentleness and tenderness.

efficacy (ĕf'ĭ·kȧ·sĭ). Power to produce an effect.

effigy (ĕf'ĭ·jĭ). A pictured likeness.

egoistical (ē'gṓ·ĭs'tĭ·kȧl). Excessively self-centered.

eloquent (ĕl'ṓ·kwĕnt). Vividly and forcefully expressed. *Noun*, eloquence (ĕl'ṓ·kwĕns).

elucidation (ĕ·lū'sĭ·dā'shŭn). Explanation.

emanate (ĕm'ȧ·nāt). To flow out or spring from.

embolden (ĕm·bōl'dĕn) or embold. To make bold or brave; to encourage.

emporium (ĕm·pō'rĭ·ŭm). A department store.

encumber (ĕn·kŭm'bēr). To weigh down.

engender (ĕn·jĕn'dēr). To cause to develop.

enigma (ė·nĭg'mȧ). A riddle. *Adv.*, enigmatically (ē'nĭg·măt'ĭ·kȧl·ĭ).

enjoin (ĕn·join'). To command.

enmity (ĕn'mĭ·tĭ). Hatred.

ensconce (ĕn·skŏns'). To settle comfortably.

entrails (ĕn'trȧlz). Internal parts; insides.

equivocate (ė·kwĭv'ṓ·kāt). To lie. *Noun*, equivocation.

esplanade (ĕs'plȧ·nād'). An open, level space used as a public walk or drive.

espouse (ĕs·pouz'). To become a follower of.

essence (ĕs'ĕns). 1. A heavenly being or substance. 2. The real character of a thing. 3. Perfume.

estheticism (ĕs·thĕt'ĭ·sĭz'm). Devotion to principles of beauty and good taste.

ethereal (ė·thēr'ė·ȧl). 1. Heavenly; belonging to the misty upper regions of space. 2. Light; airy.

ethics (ĕth'ĭks). Moral principles. *Adj.*, ethical (ĕth'ĭ·kȧl).

evince (ė·vĭns'). To display; to show.

exaltation (ĕg'zŏl·tā'shŭn). The feeling of extreme personal well-being; elation.

execration (ĕk'sė·krā'shŭn). A curse.

exemplary (ĕg·zĕm'plȧ·rĭ). Worthy of imitation.

exhort (ĕg·zôrt). To encourage; to inspire. *Noun*, exhortation (ĕg'zôr·tā'shŭn).

exigency (ĕk'sĭ·jĕn·sĭ). Immediate necessity.

exotic (ĕks·ŏt'ĭk). Something foreign; belonging to another part of the world.

expend (ĕks·pĕnd'). To use up.

expiate (ĕks'pĭ·āt). To atone.

extemporize (ĕks·tĕm'pṓ·rīz). To do offhand; to improvise.

extort (ĕks·tôrt). To get by force or threats.

extricate (ĕks'trĭ·kāt). To set loose; to disentangle.

exult (ĕg·zŭlt'). To rejoice triumphantly. *Noun*, exultation (ĕk'sŭl·tā'shŭn).

F

facetious (fȧ·sē'shŭs). Purposely taking a light attitude toward a serious matter.

facilitate (fȧ·sĭl'ĭ·tāt). To make less difficult. *Noun*, facility.

fain (fān). Glad; willing.

fealty (fē'ȧl·tĭ). Fidelity, as to a lord.

fetter (fĕt'ēr). Something that restrains; a bond; a shackle. *Verb*, to restrain; to shackle.

filial (fĭl'ĭ·ȧl). Befitting a son or daughter in relation to a parent.

fillip (fĭl'ĭp). Something that stimulates.

finical (fĭn'ĭ·kȧl). Fussy; too particular.

flag (flăg). To lag.

flagon (flăg'ŭn). A vessel for liquors, with a handle and a spout and often a lid.

flaunt (flônt). To show off; to parade conspicuously.

fop (fŏp). A silly, vain, overly fashionable man.

forbear (fôr·bâr'). 1. To refrain; to keep from. 2. To be patient; to endure.

forte (fôrt). One's special talent; that in which one excels.

fossil (fŏs'ĭl). Bones or impressions of prehistoric animals, found in soil or rock.

frieze (frēz). 1. An ornamental band around a wall. 2. A coarse, shaggy woolen cloth.

frugal (frōō'gȧl). Thrifty; not wasteful.

furbish (fûr'bĭsh). To brighten by scouring or rubbing.

furtive (fûr'tĭv). Secret; stealthy.

G

gall (gôl). *Noun*, bitterness. *Verb*, to irritate; to vex.

gambit (găm'bĭt). In chess, an opening move in which a chessman is sacrificed to gain a later advantage.

garish (gâr'ĭsh). Gaudy; glaring.

garner (gär'nēr). A storehouse for grain. *Verb*, to gather; to store.

garrulous (găr'û·lŭs). Talkative.

gauntlet (gônt'lĕt). A glove.

genii (jē'nĭ·ī). Supernatural spirits having strong influence over nature.

genteel (jĕn·tēl'). 1. Well-bred; polite. 2. Elegant.

gentry (jĕn'trĭ). 1. Wellborn people. 2. The upper middle class.

genuflect (jĕn'û·flĕkt). To bend the knee, as in worship.

gibbet (jĭb'ĕt). Gallows from which criminals were hung in chains.

gossamer or gossamere (gŏs'ȧ·mēr). A cobweb floating in air. *Figuratively*, a delicate, imaginative production of the mind.

āpe, chȧotic, bâre, ăt, ȧttend, ärt, flȧsk, ȧtop; ēke, mẽrely, ĕlect, ĕcho, prudĕnt, doër; ītem, ĭnn, rarĭty; ōde, ŏpaque, fôr, dŏt, lŏft, cŏnfide; sōōn, tŏŏk; sour, toil; tūbe, ûnique, tûrn, sŭp, ŭntil.

gregarious (grḗ·gâr′ĭ·ŭs). Sociable.

gross (grōs). 1. Thick. 2. Vulgar.

guerdon (gûr′dŭn). Reward.

guile (gīl). Treachery; craftiness.

gumption (gŭmp′shŭn). Common sense.

gyration (jĭ·rā′shŭn). A whirling or rotating motion.

H

halbert (hăl′bẽrt). A long-handled weapon with a metal head.

hallucination (hă·lū′sĭ·nā′shŭn). A belief that one sees an object not actually present.

harangue (há·răng′). *Noun,* a long speech, usually loud and ranting. *Verb,* harangue.

harbinger (här′bĭn·jẽr). A messenger; a forerunner.

hazard (hăz′ẽrd). 1. To risk. 2. To offer.

herald (hĕr′ăld). *Verb,* to usher in; to announce. *Noun,* an official who took part in public ceremonies, carried messages, read proclamations, etc.

heretic (hĕr′ĕ·tĭk). One who rejects an established doctrine.

hermitage (hûr′mĭ·tĭj). A secluded retreat.

hierarchy (hī′ẽr·är′kĭ). A body of church officials having different ranks.

homage (hŏm′ĭj). 1. Service to a superior, especially a ruler, in return for protection. 2. Loyalty. 3. Reverence; respect.

hoodwink (hŏŏd′wĭngk). To mislead; to deceive.

horologist (hŏ·rŏl′ō·jĭst). A skilled clock-maker.

horoscope (hŏr′ō·skōp). A diagram of the twelve houses of heaven used in foretelling a person's future or determining his character.

I

ignominy (ĭg′nō·mĭn·ĭ). Disgrace. *Adj.,* ignominious (ĭg′nō·mĭm′ĭ·ŭs). Disgraceful.

imminent (ĭm′ĭ·nẽnt). Threatening to occur at any moment. *Noun,* imminence.

immunity (ĭ·mū′nĭ·tĭ). Freedom from any charge or punishment.

immure (ĭ·mūr′). To enclose within walls; to confine.

immutable (ĭ·mū′tá·b'l). Unchangeable.

impalpable (ĭm·păl′pá·b'l). Too delicate to be easily seen or felt.

impeccable (ĭm·pĕk′á·b'l). Faultless.

impecunious (ĭm′pê·kū′nĭ·ŭs). Habitually without money.

impede (ĭm·pēd′). To hinder. *Noun,* impediment (ĭm·pĕd′ĭ·mẽnt). A restraint; an obstacle.

impenetrable (ĭm·pĕn′ê·trá·b'l). Unable to be penetrated; unfathomable.

imperceptible (ĭm′pẽr·sĕp′tĭ·b'l). Not evident to the senses or mind; very slight.

imperturbable (ĭm′pẽr·tûr′bá·b'l). Serene; not capable of being disturbed.

impious (ĭm′pĭ·ŭs). Lacking respect; ungodly.

implacable (ĭm·plā′ká·b'l). Relentless; not to be appeased or pacified.

importunate (ĭm·pôr′tū·nĭt). Urgent; insistent.

impotence (ĭm′pō·tẽns). Inability to bring about a result.

impresario (ĭm′prȧ·sä′rĭ·ō). One who sponsors, produces, or manages a concert, theatrical show, opera, or the like.

impromptu (ĭm·prŏmp′tū). Unrehearsed; suddenly or hastily done.

impunity (ĭm·pū′nĭ·tĭ). Freedom from punishment.

incantation (ĭn′kăn·tā′shŭn). Magic words, sung or recited.

incongruous (ĭn·kŏng′grŏŏ·ŭs). Not suitable; inappropriate.

incorrigible (ĭn·kŏr′ĭ·jĭ·b'l). Uncontrollable; bad beyond correction; unchangeable.

incredulous (ĭn·krĕd′ů·lŭs). Doubting; unbelieving.

incumbent (ĭn·kŭm′bĕnt). One who holds an office or position. *Adj.,* lying down.

indefatigable (ĭn′dē·făt′ĭ·gȧ·b'l). Tireless.

indictment (ĭn·dīt′mẽnt). A statement charging someone with an offense; an accusation.

indiscretion (ĭn′dĭs·krĕsh′ŭn). An unwise or incautious act.

indolent (ĭn′dō·lẽnt). Lazy.

indulgence (ĭn·dŭl′jẽns). Tolerance; patient humoring. *Adj.,* indulgent.

inexorable (ĭn·ĕk′sō·rȧ·b'l). Unyielding; not to be persuaded.

infallible (ĭn·făl′ĭ·b'l). Certain; unfailing. *Adv.,* infallibly.

ingenious (ĭn·jēn′yŭs). Clever, shrewd; possessing ingenuity.

ingenuous (ĭn·jĕn′ů·ŭs). Naïve; innocent.

ingratiating (ĭn·grā′shĭ·āt′ĭng). Bringing or working oneself into another's good graces or favor.

inimical (ĭn·ĭm′ĭ·kăl). Having a harmful effect; unfriendly.

insinuate (ĭn·sĭn′ů·āt). To suggest or hint indirectly.

insipid (ĭn·sĭp′ĭd). Dull; uninteresting.

integrity (ĭn·tĕg′rĭ·tĭ). Honesty.

interloper (ĭn′tẽr·lōp′ẽr). Intruder.

interpose (ĭn′tẽr·pōz′). 1. To place between. 2. To inject a remark into a conversation between or among others.

interstice (ĭn·tûr′stĭs). A space between two objects.

inure (ĭn·ūr′). To accustom to hard conditions; to harden.

irrelevance (ĭr·rĕl′ê·vȧns). Inappropriateness to the subject. *Adj.,* irrelevant.

irrevocable (ĭ·rĕv′ō·kȧ·b'l). Incapable of being brought back or changed.

iteration (ĭt′ẽr·ā′shŭn). Repetition.

itinerant (ĭ·tĭn′ẽr·ȧnt). Wandering or traveling about.

J

jocund (jŏk′ŭnd). Cheerful; merry; lively.

joust (jŭst, joust, jŏŏst). *Verb,* to fight on horseback in single combat. *Noun,* a tournament.

jovial (jō′vĭ·ăl). Merry; good-natured. *Noun,* joviality (jō′vĭ·ăl′ĭ·tĭ). Hilarity.

judicial (jŏŏ·dĭsh′ăl). 1. Impartial. 2. Critical.

judicious (jŏŏ·dĭsh′ŭs). Wise.

jurisprudence (jŏŏr′ĭs·prŏŏ′dẽns). The science of law.

---

bar; church; dog; ardŭous; fat; go; hear; jail; key; lame; meat; not; ring; pay; ran; see; shell; ten; there, thick; pastŭre; vast; wind; yes; zoo, zh = z in azure.

K

knell (nĕl). The sound of a bell tolled for a death or funeral. *Verb*, to toll a bell.

L

labyrinth (lăb′ĭ·rĭnth). A maze of complicated paths.

lagoon (lá·gōōn′). A shallow pool, usually connected with the sea.

lamentation (lăm′ĕn·tā′shŭn). Weeping; wailing; an expression of sorrow.

languor (lăng′gẽr). Dullness; sluggishness. *Adj.*, **languid** (lăng′gwĭd).

laureate (lô′rē·ất). A distinguished person; one worthy of honor.

lavish (lăv′ĭsh). To give generously.

libretto (lĭ·brĕt′ō). The text or words of an opera or other long musical composition. **librettist** (lĭ·brĕt′ĭst). The writer of a libretto.

license (lī′sĕns). 1. Formal permission. 2. Excessive liberty.

liege (lēj). Overlord.

lighter (līt′ẽr). A large boat used to carry goods about a harbor.

limbo (lĭm′bō). A place of confinement, neglect, or oblivion.

litigation (lĭt′ĭ·gā′shŭn). A lawsuit.

livid (lĭv′ĭd). Ashen; the color of bruised flesh.

lorry (lŏr′ĭ). A large, low truck.

luminous (lū′mĭ·nŭs). Shining.

lute (lūt). A stringed instrument with a long neck and a pear-shaped body.

M

magisterial (măj′ĭs·tẽr′ĭ·ăl). Commanding; pompous; having the manner of a magistrate, an important public official.

magnanimous (măg·năn′ĭ·mŭs). Generous; noble; honorable.

malevolence (má·lĕv′ô·lĕns). Ill will.

malicious (má·lĭsh′ŭs). Filled with hatred or ill will.

malignity (má·lĭg′nĭ·tĭ). Bad influence; evil.

mandate (măn′dāt). A command; an official order.

manifest (măn′ĭ·fĕst). *Verb*, to display; to make evident. *Adj.*, apparent; evident. *Noun*, **manifestation** (măn′ĭ·fĕs·tā′shŭn). A display; a disclosure.

marquetry (mär′kĕ·trĭ). Inlaid wood.

martyrdom (mär′tẽr·dŭm). Extreme suffering or death for the sake of a religious belief or a cause.

mead (mēd). 1. An alcoholic drink made of fermented honey. 2. *Poetic*. A meadow.

memoir (mĕm′wär). An account of one's own life or experiences.

mendacity (mĕn·dăs′ĭ·tĭ). Lying.

metaphor (mĕt′á·fẽr). A figure of speech in which the name of one object is applied to a different object to suggest similarity.

mettle (mĕt′′l). Temperament involving vigorous spirit, fortitude, and courage. *Adj.*, **mettled, mettlesome**.

mezzotint (mĕd′zô·tĭnt). An engraving on copper or steel.

millennium (mĭ·lĕn′ĭ·ŭm). The period of greatest happiness and prosperity.

minion (mĭn′yŭn). A favorite.

mobile (mō′bĭl). Easily moved; expressive.

modulation (mŏd′ů·lā′shŭn). Variation or inflection of tone.

moire (mwär). Watered pattern on silk and other textiles or on paper.

molest (mō·lĕst′). To annoy; to interfere with. *Noun*, **molestation** (mō′lĕs·tā′shŭn).

mortify (môr′tĭ·fī). To embarrass; to shame.

motley (mŏt′lĭ). 1. A multicolored costume worn by a jester. 2. Varied because of many different elements.

mountebank (moun′tê·băngk). 1. A boastful pretender. 2. One who sells quack medicines.

multiplicity (mŭl′tĭ·plĭs′ĭ·tĭ). A great number.

multitudinous (mŭl′tĭ·tū′dĭ·nŭs). Very numerous.

munificence (mû·nĭf′ĭ·sĕns). Lavish generosity.

myriad (mĭr′ĭ·ăd). A very great number.

mystic (mĭs′tĭk). Mysterious; magical.

N

nave (nāv). 1. *Rare*. The navel. 2. The hub of a wheel. 3. The central part of a church, between the aisles.

nether (nĕth′ẽr). Lower.

newt (nūt). A small, lizardlike animal.

niggard (nĭg′ẽrd). A stingy person. **niggardliness**.

noisome (noi′sŭm). Disgusting; offensive.

novice (nŏv′ĭs). 1. One who has just entered a religious order. 2. A beginner in any field.

O

obdurate (ŏb′dů·rất; *poetic*, ŏb·dū′rất). Hardhearted; unyielding.

oblivion (ŏb·lĭv′ĭ·ŭn). 1. State of being completely forgotten. 2. Complete unawareness; forgetfulness. *Adj.*, **oblivious** (ŏb·lĭv′ĭ·ŭs).

obsequious (ŏb·sē′kwĭ·ŭs). Fawning; servile.

obsolete (ŏb′sô·lēt). No longer used.

offal (ŏf′ăl). Refuse; rubbish.

ominous (ŏm′ĭ·nŭs). Foreshadowing evil.

oracle (ŏr′á·k'l). A priest or priestess who reveals the future or other hidden knowledge.

orangery (ôr′ĕnj·rĭ). A greenhouse for raising oranges.

oratorio (ŏr′á·tō′rĭ·ō). A dramatic text, usually on a Biblical theme, set to music with instrumental accompaniment and performed without scenery, costumes, or action.

orgy (ôr′jĭ). Excessive indulgence in some activity.

ostensible (ŏs·tĕn′sĭ·b'l). Apparent.

ostentation (ŏs′tĕn·tā′shŭn). Proud show.

ottoman (ŏt′ô·măn). A stuffed footstool or couch.

P

pagoda (pá·gō′dá). An Oriental tower or temple of many stories, built in the form of a pyramid and richly ornamented.

palatable (păl′ĭt·á·b'l). Pleasing to the taste.

āpe, chãotic, bâre, ăt, ắttend, ärt, flȧsk, átop; ēke, mẹrely, ĕlect, ĕcho, prudĕnt, doẽr; ītem, ĭnn; rarĭty; ōde, ŏpaque, fôr, dŏt, lôft, cŏnfide; sōōn, tŏŏk; sour, toil; tūbe, ūnique, tûrn, sŭp, ŭntil.

palisade (păl'ĭ·sād'). A fence of stakes erected for protection.

pall (pôl). To cover or shroud, especially with darkness or gloom; to cloak. *Noun*, a heavy, dark covering.

pallor (păl'ēr). Paleness. *Adj.*, **pallid** (păl'ĭd). Pale.

palpitate (păl'pĭ·tāt'). To flutter; to quiver; to beat abnormally and rapidly. *Noun*, **palpitation** (păl'pĭ·tā'shŭn).

paradox (păr'á·dŏks). A statement that seems absurd or contradictory but is really true.

paragon (păr'á·gŏn). A model; a type of perfection.

paroxysm (păr'ŏk·sĭz'm). A sharp attack of pain; a spasm.

pastoral (păs'tō·răl). Pertaining to rural life or the life of shepherds.

pathos (pā'thŏs). The quality or power that awakens feelings of pity and sympathetic sadness.

patriarchal (pā'trĭ·är'kăl). Like a father or head of a family or tribe.

pavilion (pá·vĭl'yŭn). A tent; a canopy.

pedant (pĕd'ănt). One who shows off his knowledge. *Adj.*, **pedantic** (pê·dăn'tĭk). Overly precise.

peer (pēr). 1. A person of the same rank; an equal. 2. A British nobleman. **peerage** (pēr'ĭj). The rank or dignity of a peer. **peeress** (pēr'ĕs). The wife of a nobleman, or a woman who is herself of noble rank. *Adj.*, **peerless** (pēr'lĕs). Without equal.

penance (pĕn'ăns). An act to show sorrow or repentance for a sin.

penitence (pĕn'ĭ·tĕns). Sorrowful regret for sins or faults.

pensioner (pĕn'shŭn·ēr). A person who receives a regular amount of money from a government for past services.

penury (pĕn'û·rĭ). Extreme poverty.

perambulate (pēr·ăm'bû·lāt). To walk through, often in order to inspect.

perdition (pēr·dĭsh'ŭn). Ruin; damnation.

peremptory (pēr·ĕmp'tō·rĭ). Masterful; positive.

perennial (pēr·ĕn'ĭ·ăl). Enduring; living on through the years.

perfunctory (pēr·fŭngk'tō·rĭ). Indifferent; mechanical.

perilous (pĕr'ĭ·lŭs). Dangerous, risky.

pernicious (pēr·nĭsh'ŭs). Injurious; deadly.

pertinacious (pûr'tĭ·nā'shŭs). Stubborn; persistent.

perturbation (pûr'tēr·bā'shŭn). Distress; agitation.

peruke (pê·rook'). A wig, especially the kind worn by gentlemen in the seventeenth and eighteenth centuries; a periwig.

peruse (pê·rooz'). To read thoroughly, with care.

pestilent (pĕs'tĭ·lĕnt). Troublesome; endangering peace, health, morals, society. *Noun*, **pestilence** (pĕs'tĭ·lĕns).

petulance (pĕt'û·lăns). Peevishness; fretfulness.

phonetics (fô·nĕt'ĭks). The science of speech sounds as elements of language. *Adj.*, **phonetic**.

piety (pī'ĕ·tĭ). Religious devotion; reverence.

pillory (pĭl'ô·rĭ). An instrument for public punishment, consisting of a wooden frame with holes for securing the head and hands.

piquancy (pē'kăn·sĭ). A delightful, charming quality.

pirouette (pĭr'oo·ĕt'). To whirl rapidly on the toes or on one foot.

plaintive (plān'tĭv). Sorrowful; mournful.

plausible (plô'zĭ·b'l). 1. Seemingly worthy of approval. 2. Apparently true.

poach (pōch). To hunt or fish illegally on another's property. *Noun*, **poacher**.

poignant (poin'yánt). Touching; keenly felt.

popish (pōp'ĭsh). Roman Catholic (a scornful, uncomplimentary term).

precarious (prê·kâr'ĭ·ŭs). Uncertain; risky; hazardous.

precedence (prê·sēd'ĕns). Going before others in order, rank, etc.

precedent (prĕs'ê·dĕnt). A past act or statement that serves as a model for the future.

precept (prē'sĕpt). An order or direction to be used as a guide for conduct or action.

precocious (prê·kō'shŭs). Showing exceptionally advanced mental development.

predestined (prê·dĕs'tĭnd). Fated; destined or determined beforehand.

preferment (prê·fûr'mĕnt). Advancement; promotion.

prelude (prĕl'ūd). A short piece of music serving as the introduction to a longer composition.

premonition (prē'mô·nĭsh'ŭn). A foreboding; a warning in advance.

presumptuous (prê·zŭmp'tû·ŭs). Bold; overbearing; taking liberties.

preternatural (prē'tēr·năt'û·răl). Extraordinary; strange and unexplainable.

probity (prō'bĭ·tĭ). Virtue; uprightness.

prodigious (prô·dĭj'ŭs). Extraordinary; marvelous.

prodigy (prŏd'ĭ·jĭ). 1. A remarkable act. 2. An unusually gifted person, especially a child.

prolific (prô·lĭf'ĭk). Producing abundant results; fertile.

promontory (prŏm'ŭn·tō·rĭ). An elevated piece of land or rock extending into a body of water.

propitiate (prô·pĭsh'ĭ·āt). To win over; to make favorable.

prosaic (prô·zā'ĭk). Dull; unimaginative.

prostrate (prŏs'trāt). To humble oneself by lying face down on the ground. *Adj.*, 1. Lying face down on the ground. 2. Helpless; drained of vitality.

protract (prô·trăkt'). To prolong; to lengthen.

provocation (prŏv'ô·kā'shŭn). Cause of irritation or anger.

prowess (prou'ĕs; –ĭs). Bravery; courage; skill.

proximity (prŏks·ĭm'ĭ·tĭ). Being very near to; closeness.

prudent (proo'dĕnt). Wise; sensible; cautious; discreet.

pugnacious (pŭg·nā'shŭs). Ready to fight; belligerent; quarrelsome.

pungent (pŭn'jĕnt). Sharp to the taste, smell, or touch.

---

bar; **ch**urch; **d**og; ard**ŭ**ous; fat; **g**o; **h**ear; jail; key; lame; meat; **n**ot; ring; pay; ran; see; **sh**ell; ten; **th**ere, **th**ick; past**ū**re; vast; wind; yes; zoo, **zh** = z in azure.

Q

quadrant (kwŏd'rănt). A nautical instrument for measuring height.

qualm (kwäm). A sudden fear or attack of illness.

quarto (kwôr'tō). A book size, about 9½ × 12 inches, smaller than a folio.

quench (kwĕnch). 1. To suppress; to calm. 2. To put out; to extinguish. 3. To relieve, as thirst.

querulous (kwĕr'ū·lŭs). Fretful; peevish.

R

rabble (răb''l), **rabblement**. A mob.

rancor (răng'kẽr). Bitter ill will; deep hatred.

ravenous (răv'ĕn·ŭs). Extremely hungry; eager for food.

recantation (rē'kăn·tā'shŭn). A formal public withdrawal of a previous opinion or statement.

recluse (rē·kloōs'). A person who lives alone and secluded from the world.

recompense (rĕk'ŏm·pĕns). Pay; compensation.

redress (rē·drĕs'). To correct; to right a wrong. *Noun*, reform; correction.

refectory (rē·fĕk'tō·rĭ). A dining hall in a monastery. **refectory table.** A long, narrow, wooden dining table.

regicide (rĕj'ĭ·sīd). One who kills a king.

reiterate (rē·ĭt'ẽr·āt). To repeat; to say or do again and again.

rejoinder (rē·join'dẽr). Answer; reply.

relegate (rĕl'ē·gāt). To remove to a less desirable situation; to put out of sight or mind.

relic (rĕl'ĭk). A revered memento of the past.

relinquish (rē·lĭng'kwĭsh). To give up; to abandon.

remonstrate (rē·mŏn'strāt). To protest. *Noun*, **remonstrance** (rē·mŏn'străns).

Renaissance (rĕn'ē·zäns'). The revival of interest in the classics during the fourteenth to sixteenth centuries.

renunciation (rē·nŭn'sĭ·ā'shŭn). The act of giving up or renouncing.

repartee (rĕp'ẽr·tē'). A conversation marked by clever, witty replies.

repentance (rē·pĕn'tăns). Remorse for sins and wrongdoing, with desire to correct one's ways.

replica (rĕp'lĭ·kà). A reproduction; a close copy.

reprobate (rĕp'rō·bāt). A rogue; a scoundrel.

reprobation (rĕp'rō·bā'shŭn). Condemnation; severe disapproval.

repudiate (rē·pū'dĭ·āt). 1. To disown; to refuse to listen to or recognize. 2. To reject.

repugnance (rē·pŭg'năns). Extreme disgust.

resolute (rĕz'ō·lūt). Determined; steadfast.

respite (rĕs'pĭt). Relief; a short rest period.

retrograde (rĕt'rō·grād). Moving backward.

reverberate (rē·vûr'bẽr·āt). To resound; to echo. *Adj.*, **reverberant** (rē·vûr'bẽr·ănt).

ribaldry (rĭb'ăld·rĭ). Coarse, vulgar joking.

roseate (rō'zē·āt). Rose-colored; hence, happy, optimistic.

rotund (rō·tŭnd'). Rounded.

rudiment (roō'dĭ·mĕnt). A basic principle; a first step.

ruminate (roō'mĭ·nāt). To muse; to ponder.

S

sacrilegious (săk'rĭ·lē'jŭs). Guilty of sin against something sacred.

saffron (săf'rŭn). A deep yellow color.

sagacious (sà·gā'shŭs). Shrewd; watchful. *Noun*, **sagacity** (sà·găs'ĭ·tĭ).

salient (sā'lĭ·ĕnt). Noticeable; outstanding.

salver (săl'vẽr). A tray.

sanction (săngk'shŭn). Formal approval.

sanctity (săngk'tĭ·tĭ). Holiness; sacredness.

satiate (sā'shĭ·āt). Satisfied. *Noun*, **satiety** (sà·tī'ĕ·tĭ). State of being overfed.

scission (sĭzh'ŭn). A split; a separation or division.

scruple (skroō'p'l). A feeling of hesitation or doubt as to what is right.

scrupulous (skroō'pū·lŭs). Careful; exact regarding details.

scrutinize (skroō'tĭ·nīz). To examine critically, to look at closely.

scurrilous (skûr'ĭ·lŭs). Coarsely, indecently abusive. *Noun*, **scurrility** (skŭ·rĭl'ĭ·tĭ).

sedentary (sĕd'ĕn·tĕr'ĭ). Accustomed to sitting for long periods of time and taking little exercise.

senility (sē·nĭl'ĭ·tĭ). The physical and mental weakness of old age.

sensuous (sĕn'shoō·ŭs). Appealing pleasurably to the senses.

sepulcher (sĕp'ŭl·kẽr). A tomb; a burial vault. *Verb*, to entomb.

sequestered (sē·kwĕs'tẽrd). Retired; secluded.

sinister (sĭn'ĭs·tẽr). Threatening; indicative of lurking evil.

sinuous (sĭn'ū·ŭs). Winding.

sloth (slōth). Laziness, indolence.

solicitous (sō·lĭs'ĭ·tŭs). Eager; anxious. *Noun*, **solicitude** (sō·lĭs'ĭ·tūd). 1. Anxiety. 2. Attentive care.

somnolence (sŏm'nō·lĕns). Drowsiness.

sonorous (sō·nō'rŭs). Resounding; impressively loud.

sophistry (sŏf'ĭs·trĭ). Clever and subtle, but deceptive, reasoning.

sordid (sôr'dĭd). Filthy; base.

spasmodic (spăz·mŏd'ĭk). 1. Excitable; emotional. 2. With sudden, brief spurts of energy. *Adj.*, **spasmodically**.

specious (spē'shŭs). Apparently true and just, but actually false.

staid (stād). Sober; sedate.

stanchless (stänch'lĕs) or **staunchless** (stônch'lĕs). Not to be stopped or prevented.

stipulate (stĭp'ū·lāt). To promise something as part of an agreement.

stratagem (străt'à·jĕm). A trick designed to deceive; deception.

subaltern (sŭ·bôl'tẽrn). An officer below the rank of captain.

subtile (sŭb'tĭl). Penetrating; wily, subtle.

summarily (sŭm'à·rĭ·lĭ). Instantly and without formality.

sunder (sŭn'dẽr). To separate.

sundry (sŭn'drĭ). Various; several.

supine (sū·pīn'). 1. Lying face upward. 2. Inactive; passive.

supposition (sŭp'ô·zĭsh'ŭn). A theory; something that is supposed.

surfeit (sûr'fĭt). To overfeed; to give too much.

surplice (sûr'plĭs). An outer garment of white linen with wide sleeves, worn by clergymen.

susceptible (sŭ·sĕp'tĭ·b'l). Easily influenced.

T

taciturn (tăs'ĭ·tûrn). Silent; not inclined to talk. *Noun,* **taciturnity** (tăs'ĭ·tûr'nĭ·tĭ).

tawdry (tô'drĭ). Showy; not in good taste.

tendril (tĕn'drĭl). A slender, leafless, climbing part of a plant that attaches itself to something and supports the plant.

tenterhooks (tĕn'tẽr·hōŏks'). (Used with on.) In suspense; under a strain.

thrall (thrôl). A slave.

timorous (tĭm'ẽr·ŭs). Timid; afraid of danger.

tinct (tĭngkt). Delicately colored or flavored. *Noun,* **tincture** (tĭnk'tûr). 1. A touch; a small amount. 2. A stain. *Verb,* to stain.

tippet (tĭp'ĕt). A scarf or scarflike garment of cloth or fur.

titillate (tĭt'ĭ·lāt). To tickle; to give pleasurable excitement.

toady (tōd'ĭ). To fawn upon or flatter; to cater to.

traipse (trāps). To wander about.

transfigure (trăns·fĭg'ûr). To transform; to change in appearance; to cause to shine.

transgress (trăns·grĕs'). To break a law or to sin. *Noun,* **transgression** (trăns·grĕsh'ŭn).

transient (trăn'shĭnt), or **transitory** (trăn'sĭ·tō'rĭ). Fleeting.

travesty (trăv'ĕs·tĭ). A mockery; a ridiculous imitation.

trepidation (trĕp'ĭ·dā'shŭn). Nervous fear.

truckle (trŭk''l). To submit obediently to.

truculent (trŭk' û·lĕnt). Fierce.

tumult (tū'mŭlt). Agitation; violence. *Adj.,* **tumultuous** (tû·mŭl'tû̇·ŭs). Stormy.

turbid (tûr'bĭd). Clouded; muddled.

turbulence (tûr'bû·lĕns). Restlessness; violence. *Adj.,* **turbulent.**

U

unabashed (ŭn'á·băsht'). Not embarrassed.

unassailable (ŭn'á·sāl'á·b'l). Not capable of being attacked.

undaunted (ŭn·dôn'tĕd). Undiscouraged, not dismayed; fearless; resolute.

undeviating (ŭn·dē'vĭ·āt'ĭng). Not changing or turning aside from a set course.

undivulged (ŭn'dĭ·vŭljd). Not revealed; secret.

unduly (ŭn·dū'lĭ). Excessively.

unicorn (ū'nĭ·kôrn). A mythical animal resembling a horse, with a long horn projecting from its forehead.

unimpeachable (ŭn'ĭm·pēch'á·b'l). Blameless; unquestionable.

unostentatious (ŭn'ŏs·tĕn·tā'shŭs). Without show; quiet.

unprecedented (ŭn·prĕs'ĕ·dĕn'tĕd). Unusual; never known or seen before.

unprepossessing (ŭn'prē·pŏ·zĕs'ĭng). Unattractive.

unsanctified (ŭn·săngk'tĭ·fīd). Unholy.

unsavory (ŭn·sā'vẽr·ĭ). Offensive; having a bad reputation.

unseemly (ŭn·sēm'lĭ). Indecent, improper.

upbraid (ŭp·brād'). To rebuke.

usurp (û·zûrp'). To seize and hold by force and without right. *Noun,* **usurper** (û·zûr'pẽr).

V

vassal (văs'ăl). 1. In the feudal system, one who gives his allegiance to an overlord in return for protection. 2. A lover devoted to his lady-love.

vaunt (vônt). *Verb,* to brag; to boast. *Noun,* a proud show; a boast.

vehement (vē'ĕ·mĕnt). Furious.

velocity (vḗ·lŏs'ĭ·tĭ). Speed; rapidity; swiftness of motion.

venerable (vĕn'ẽr·á·b'l). Commanding respect, usually because of age or dignified position.

verdure (vûr'dûr). Greenness. *Adj.,* **verdurous** (vûr'dûr·ŭs), **verdant** (vûr'dănt).

verity (vĕr'ĭ·tĭ). That which is true.

vernacular (vẽr·năk'û·lẽr). Native or commonly spoken language.

vernal (vûr'năl). Occurring in or belonging to spring.

vestige (vĕs'tĭj). A trace.

vestry (vĕs'trĭ). A room in a church in which the vestments, or robes of the clergy, are kept along with the sacred vessels used in services.

vilify (vĭl'ĭ·fī). To defame; to slander.

vindicate (vĭn'dĭ·kāt). To justify; to clear of suspicion.

visionary (vĭzh'ŭn·ĕr'ĭ). Imaginary.

vivacity (vī·văs'ĭ·tĭ). Liveliness, sprightliness.

vociferation (vô·sĭf'ẽr·ā'shŭn). Loud speaking or shouting.

volatile (vŏl'á·tĭl). Lively; lighthearted.

voluble (vŏl'û·b'l). 1. Turning; rotating. 2. Speaking fluently. *Noun,* **volubility** (vŏl'û·bĭl'ĭ·tĭ). Talkativeness.

voluptuous (vô·lŭp'tû·ŭs). Sensuous; delighting the senses. *Noun,* **voluptuousness.**

vouch (vouch). To assure of; to bear witness to.

W

wanton (wŏn'tŭn). Gay; lighthearted; luxuriant. *Verb,* to play; to act freely.

warrant (wŏr'ănt). 1. To justify. 2. To guarantee. *Noun,* an authorization; a guarantee.

wassail (wŏs''l). 1. Festive drinking. 2. An intoxicating drink.

wattles (wŏt''lz). Twigs and easily bent rods woven together and used for walls, fences, etc., or to support straw thatch in a roof.

wax (wăks). To grow; to increase.

whetstone (hwĕt'stōn'). A stone for sharpening edged tools.

whist (hwĭst). An old card game for four players, the forerunner of bridge.

winsome (wĭn'sŭm). Cheerful; gay; pleasurable.

withal (wĭth·ôl'). 1. Besides; moreover. 2. With. 3. Because of this. 4. On the other hand; still.

writhe (rīth). To twist violently.

---

bar; church; dog; arduous; fat; go; hear; jail; key; lame; meat; not; ring; pay; ran; see; shell; ten; there, thick; pasture; vast; wind; yes; zoo, zh = z in azure.

British Money

Throughout this book references are made to various denominations of British money. This section will help you to understand the British money system and to compare the relative values of British and American money.

Although there have been many units of exchange through the years, the beginnings of the modern British system go back to A.D. 775 when Offa, king of Mercia, issued silver pennies; 240 of these pennies weighed a pound. Shortly after the Norman Conquest of 1066, something very close to the modern system was already established, though Latin names were used: the pound was called the *libra* (from which the symbol £ comes); this was worth 20 shillings (called *solidi*, symbol s.); and the shilling was worth 12 pence (called *denarii*, symbol d.). Sums of money can be expressed in writing in either of two ways. Five pounds, six shillings, and sixpence, for example, may be written £5.6s.6d. or £5/6/6.

Through the nineteenth century until 1914, the pound was worth about $4.86. Its value fluctuated through the changing conditions of the next decades. In 1939 its value was fixed at $4.03, and in 1949 the pound was devalued to its present $2.80. The table below gives approximate values of British money in 1912, when *Pygmalion* was written, and today.

You will come across other names for units of money: a *sovereign* is a gold coin worth a pound; a *guinea*, for which there is no coin now, is worth 21 shillings; a *florin* is a silver coin worth 2 shillings. A small denomination, now seldom used, is the *halfpenny* (pronounced hā' penny). The *farthing*, which was worth a quarter of a penny, and the *groat*, which was worth fourpence, are now obsolete denominations.

Some slang terms for money are: *quid* — pound; *tanner* — sixpence; *bob* — shilling; *copper* — penny.

1912		Today
$4.86	1 pound (20 shillings)	$2.80
.60	half a crown (2½ shillings)	.35
.24	shilling (12 pence)	.14
.12	sixpence	.07
.02	1 penny	.01

ACKNOWLEDGMENTS

For permission to use the articles in the frontispieces described on the following pages, we thank: page 45, (1) Trinity College, Dublin, (2) Up Helly Aa Committee of Lerwick, (3) Norwegian Travel Office, (4) Metropolitan Museum of Art, gift of J. Pierpont Morgan; page 209, (1) New York Public Library, Print Room, (3) Scalamandré Museum of Textiles, (5) Dunhill Collection; page 269, (1) Metropolitan Museum of Art, Rogers Fund, 1932, (3) D. E. Smith Collection, Columbia University Library; page 362, (1) Bodleian Library, Oxford; page 477, (1) British Travel.

PICTURE ACKNOWLEDGMENTS: p. 1, Photography for Industry; p. 13, (lower left) Frank Monaco. All others from Photo Researchers, Inc.; p. 16, Magnum; p. 33, Photo Researchers, Inc.; p. 64, Viscount Bridgeman/ Frank Monaco; p. 85, New York Public Library, Print Room; p. 128, Robert Fuhring (This and all other photographs for *Macbeth* are from the National Broadcasting Company's television production, sponsored by Hallmark Cards, Inc.); p. 207, Victoria and Albert Museum/Frank Monaco; p. 245, Giraudon; p. 247, The Huntington Library; p. 261, British Museum; p. 319, New York Public Library, Print Room; p. 331 (top), Mansell Collection; p. 343, Frank Monaco; p. 357, Library of Congress, Rosenwald Collection; p. 392, Frank Monaco; p. 437, National Gallery of Art, Mellon Collection; p. 457, British Museum; p. 511, Whitworth Art Gallery, University of Manchester; p. 518, British Museum; p. 543, Philadelphia Library, Elkins Collection; p. 549, Victoria and Albert Museum; p. 586, Susan McCartney; p. 649, Bateson Mason; p. 689, British Travel; p. 721, Irish Tourist Bureau; p. 736, Sylvia A. Hurwitz; p. 758, Friedman-Abeles.

Special Indexes

READING SKILL STUDY AIDS appear, as listed here according to subject, on the following pages. The names in parentheses indicate the authors of the selections after which each Study Aid appears.

GENERAL INDEX